Mergent's

DIVIDEND

ACHIEVERS

Summer 2008

Mergent's
DIVIDEND
ACHIEVERS

Mergent, Inc.

JONATHAN WORRALL
Publisher
THOMAS WECERA
Associate Publisher
JOHN PEDERNALES
*Executive Managing Director
Equity Research*
MOHAMED HANIF
Director of Equity Research Data
ANDREW J. KALINSKI
Editor
JENNIFER WEIDLICH
Associate Editor

Index Department

SHIRLEY J. PETERSEN
Vice President
KEVIN B. HECKERT
Manager, Equity Research
WILLIAM H. ROGERS
Manager, Equity Analysis

Production

CHARLOT VOLNY
WAYNE ARNOLD
BRIAN COX

John Wiley & Sons, Inc.

SUE LEWIS
Publisher
JOAN O'NEIL
Publisher
ISABELLE COHEN-DEANGELIS
Executive Editor
MARGARET ZIOMKOWSKI
Production Manager
RICHARD REICHERTER
Production Editor

MERGENT'S DIVIDEND ACHIEVERS (ISSN 1547-8335; electronic ISSN 1548-2839) is published quarterly by Mergent, Inc. and Wiley Subscription Services, Inc., a Wiley Company, 111 River Street, Hoboken, NJ 07030-5774.

SUBSCRIPTION PRICE: Print only: $199.00 in U.S., Canada, and Mexico and $223.00 outside of North America for individuals, and $220.00 in U.S., $260.00 in Canada and Mexico, and $294.00 outside North America for institutions, agencies, and libraries. Prices subject to change. Payment must be made in U.S. dollars drawn on a U.S. bank. Claims for undelivered copies will be accepted only after the following issue has been received. Please enclose a copy of the mailing label. Missing copies will be supplied when losses have been sustained in transit and where reserve stock permits. Please allow four weeks for processing a change of address. Address subscription inquiries to Subscription Manager, Jossey-Bass, a Wiley Company, 989 Market Street, San Francisco, CA 94103-1741; Tel.: (888) 378-2537, (415) 433-1767 (International); E-mail: jbsubs@jbp.com.

POSTMASTER: Send address changes to *Mergent's Dividend Achievers*, Jossey-Bass, 989 Market Street, San Francisco, CA 94103-1741.

ADVERTISING SALES: Inquiries concerning advertising should be forwarded to the Advertising Sales Manager, c/o John Wiley & Sons, Inc., 111 River Street, Hoboken, NJ 07030-5774; (201) 748-8832. Advertising Sales, European Contact: Jackie Sibley, c/o John Wiley & Sons, Ltd., The Atrium, Southern Gate, Chichester, West Sussex, PO19 8SQ, England; Tel.: 44 1243 770 351; Fax: 44 1243 770 432; E-mail: adsales@wiley.co.uk.

www.wiley.com/go/mergent

TABLE OF CONTENTS

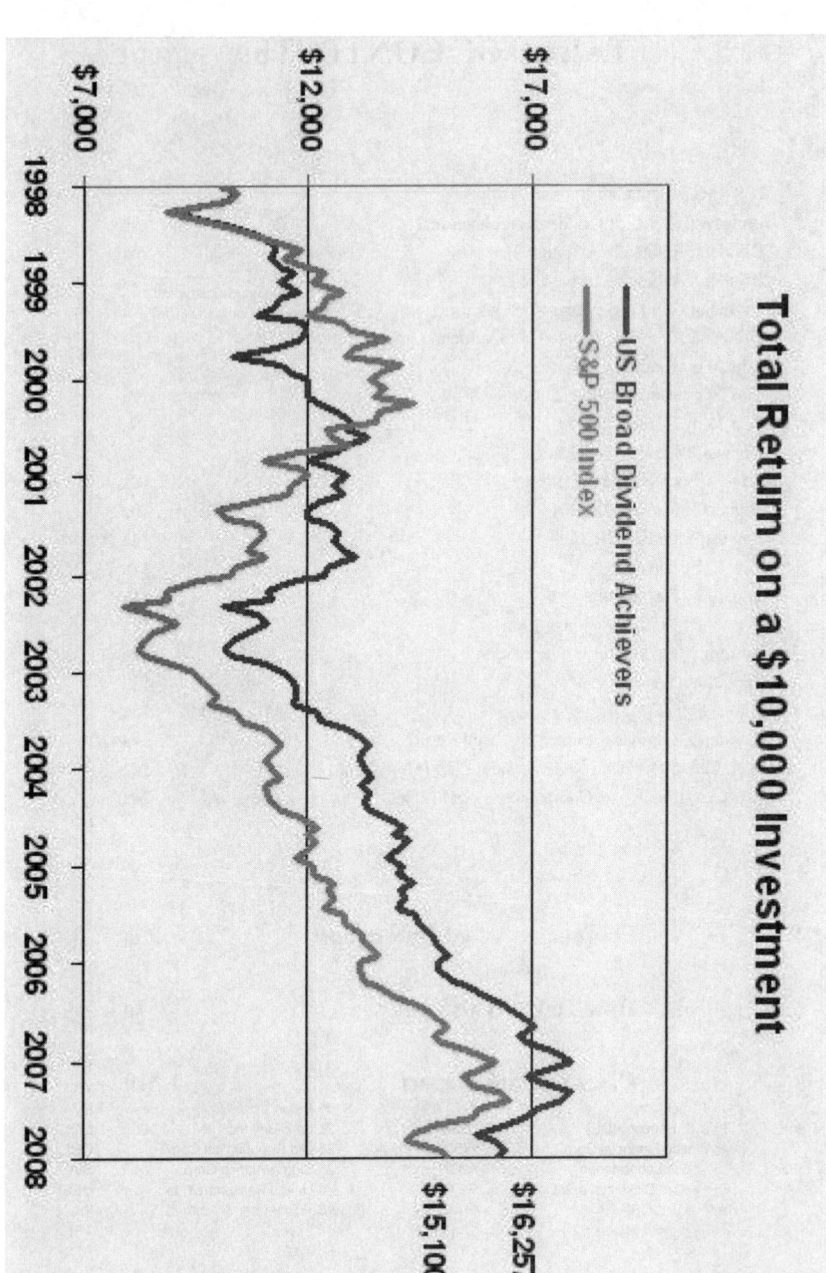

Total Return on a $10,000 Investment

— US Broad Dividend Achievers
— S&P 500 Index

$16,257
$15,100

1998 1999 2000 2001 2002 2003 2004 2005 2006 2007 2008

$7,000 $12,000 $17,000

Longest Records of Dividend Achievement

These Dividend Achievers boast 25 or more years of consecutive dividend increases.

Rank	Years	Company	Ticker
1	54	American States Water Co.	AWR
	54	Diebold, Inc.	DBD
	54	Procter & Gamble Co.	PG
4	52	Dover Corp	DOV
5	52	Northwest Natural Gas Co.	NWN
6	51	Emerson Electric Co.	EMR
	51	Genuine Parts Co.	GPC
	51	Parker Hannifin Corp.	PH
9	49	3M Co	MMM
	49	Integrys Energy Group Inc	TEG
	49	Masco Corp.	MAS
12	47	Cincinnati Financial Corp.	CINF
13	46	Lowe's Companies Inc	LOW
14	45	Coca-Cola Co (The)	KO
	45	Colgate-Palmolive Co.	CL
	45	Illinois Tool Works, Inc.	ITW
	45	Johnson & Johnson	JNJ
18	44	Tootsie Roll Industries Inc	TR
19	43	ABM Industries, Inc.	ABM
	43	Chubb Corp.	CB
21	42	Altria Group Inc	MO
	42	Peoples Bancorp, Inc.	PEBO
23	41	Hormel Foods Corp.	HRL
24	40	Cal. Water Service Group	CWT
	40	Federal Realty Invest. Trust	FRT
	40	Fuller (H.B.) Company	FUL
	40	Lilly (Eli) & Co.	LLY
	40	Pfizer Inc	PFE
	40	SJW Corp.	SJW
	40	Stanley Works (The)	SWK
	40	Stepan Co.	SCL
32	39	Commerce Bancshares	CBSH
33	38	Lancaster Colony Corp.	LANC
	38	Wash. RE Investment Trust	WRE
35	37	Associated Banc-Corp.	ASBC
	37	Hill-Rom Holdings, Inc	HRC
	37	Mine Safety Appliances Co	MSA
	37	Susquehanna Bancshares,	SUSQ
	37	Universal Corp.	UVV
40	36	Bard (C.R.), Inc.	BCR
	36	BB&T Corp.	BBT
	36	Black Hills Corporation	BKH
	36	Gannett Co Inc	GCI
	36	Grainger (W.W.) Inc.	GWW
	36	Leggett & Platt, Inc.	LEG
	36	National Fuel Gas Co. (NJ)	NFG
	36	PepsiCo Inc.	PEP
	36	PPG Industries, Inc.	PPG
	36	Target Corp	TGT
	36	U.S. Bancorp (DE)	USB
	36	Wesco Financial Corp.	WSC
52	35	Abbott Laboratories	ABT
	35	Becton, Dickinson and Co.	BDX
	35	F.N.B. CORP PA	FNB
	35	Fifth Third Bancorp	FITB
	35	Gorman-Rupp Co.	GRC
	35	Marshall & Ilsley Corp.	MI
	35	Nucor Corp.	NUE
	35	Supervalue Inc.	SVU
	35	Tennant Co.	TNC
	35	VF Corp.	VFC
62	34	CenturyTel, Inc.	CTL
	34	Fulton Financial Corp.	FULT
	34	McGraw-Hill Cos., Inc.	MHP
	34	RPM International Inc	RPM
	34	Trustmark Corp.	TRMK
67	33	Anheuser-Busch Cos.,	BUD
	33	Archer Daniels Midland	ADM
	33	Consolidated Edison Inc.	ED
	33	Hershey Company (The)	HSY
	33	Kimberly-Clark Corp.	KMB
72	32	Automatic Data Proc. Inc.	ADP
	32	Avery Dennison Corp.	AVY
	32	Chemical Financial Corp.	CHFC
	32	General Electric Co	GE
	32	Johnson Controls Inc	JCI
	32	MGE Energy Inc	MGEE
	32	Otter Tail Corp.	OTTR
	32	Vectren Corp.	VVC
	32	Walgreen Co.	WAG
	32	Wal-Mart Stores, Inc.	WMT
82	31	Carlisle Companies Inc.	CSL
	31	Clorox Co.	CLX
	31	Family Dollar Stores, Inc.	FDO
	31	Helmerich & Payne Inc.	HP
	31	McDonald's Corp	MCD
	31	Myers Industries Inc.	MYE
	31	Pentair, Inc.	PNR
	31	RLI Corp.	RLI
	31	Synovus Financial Corp.	SNV
	31	Sysco Corp.	SYY
	31	WGL Holdings, Inc.	WGL
93	30	Bank of America Corp.	BAC
	30	Bank of Hawaii Corp	BOH
	30	Medtronic, Inc.	MDT
	30	Rohm & Haas Co.	ROH
	30	Teleflex Incorporated	TFX
98	29	National Penn Bancsh.	NPBC
	29	Valspar Corp.	VAL
100	28	KeyCorp (New)	KEY
	28	Piedmont Natural Gas	PNY
	28	Questar Corp.	STR
	28	Sherwin-Williams Co.	SHW
104	27	Clarcor Inc.	CLC
	27	M & T Bank Corp	MTB
	27	Nordson Corp.	NDSN
	27	State Street Corp.	STT
	27	Wrigley (William) Jr. Co.	WWY
109	26	Eaton Vance Corp	EV
	26	La-Z-Boy Inc.	LZB
	26	Old Republic Intl Corp.	ORI
	26	Sigma-Aldrich Corp.	SIAL
	26	United Bankshares, Inc	UBSI
	26	Wilmington Trust Corp.	WL
115	25	AFLAC Inc.	AFL
	25	Air Products & Chem.	APD
	25	Cintas Corporation	CTAS
	25	Energen Corp.	EGN
	25	Exxon Mobil Corp.	XOM
	25	FirstMerit Corp	FMER

Dividend Achievers Arrivals

The following companies are classified as new Dividend Achievers as they have recorded at least ten consecutive years of dividend increases and satisfied the liquidity requirement.Jan1, 2008 thru May 30, 2008

Alexandria Real Estate Equities, Inc.

American Capital Strategies Ltd.

Bank of the Ozarks, Inc.

Block (H & R), Inc.

Cato Corp.

Corporate Office Properties Trust

Developers Diversified Realty Corp.

Energy East Corp.

Horton (D.R.) Inc.

Nationwide Financial Services Inc.

Northwest Natural Gas Co.

Owens & Minor, Inc.

Robinson (C.H.) Worldwide, Inc.

Royal Bancshares of Pennsylvania, Inc

Security Bank Corp

Shenandoah Telecommunications Co.

Stepan Co.

Suffolk Bancorp

Tompkins Financial Corp

Total System Services, Inc.

Univest Corp. of Penn.(Souderton)

Dividend Achievers Departures

The following former Dividend Achievers have not increased their regular cash dividends in 2008.

Alabama National BanCorporation (DE)

Applebee's International, Inc

Briggs & Stratton Corp.

Chittenden Corp. (Burlington, Vt.)

Colonial Properties Trust (AL)

First Commonwealth Financial Corp. (Indiana, PA)

First Indiana Corp

Freddie Mac

Haverty Furniture Cos., Inc.

Healthcare Realty Trust, Inc.

Omega Financial Corp

Pacific Capital Bancorp

People's United Financial Inc

Progressive Corp. (OH)

SLM Corp.

Sterling Bancorp (N.Y.)

Sterling Financial Corp. (PA)

Sun Communities, Inc.

Superior Industries International, Inc.

The following former Dividend Achievers have been acquired or are in the process of being acquired Since January 1, 2008.

Alabama National Bancorporation

Alfa Corp.

Commerce Bancorp. Inc.

Midland Co.

The following companies did not meet volume/liquidity requirements.

American River Bankshares

Arrow Financial Corp.

Artesian Resources Corp.

Bank of Granite Corp.

BOE Financial Services of Virginia Inc

Bowl America Inc.

C & F Financial Corp.

Center Bancorp, Inc.

Central Virginia Bankshares, Inc.

Centrue Financial Corp (New)

Citizens & Northern Corp

CNB Financial Corp. (Clearfield, PA)

Codorus Valley Bancorp, Inc.

Comm Bancorp, Inc. (PA)

Connecticut Water Service, Inc.

Elmira Savings Bank (NY)

Farmer Bros. Co.

FFD Financial Corp

Fidelity Bancorp, Inc. (PA)

First Defiance Financial Corp.

First Federal Bancshares of Arkansas, Inc.

First National Lincoln Corp. (Damariscotta, ME)

First of Long Island Corp.

First South Bancorp Inc (VA)

First United Corporation (MD)

Firstbank Corp. (MI)

Florida Public Utilities Co.

Greater Community Bancorp.

Harleysville Savings Financial Corp

HF Financial Corp.

Jeffersonville Bancorp

LSB Financial Corp.

MASSBANK Corp.

MBT Financial Corp.

MFB Corp

Middlesex Water Co.

National Bankshares Inc. (VA)

National Security Group, Inc

NB & T Financial Group Inc

North Central Bancshares, Inc.

Northrim BanCorp Inc

Ohio Valley Banc Corp.

Penns Woods Bancorp, Inc. (PA)

Peoples Financial Corp. (Biloxi, MS)

Princeton National Bancorp, Inc.

Quixote Corp.

River Valley Bancorp

Savannah Bancorp, Inc.

Smithtown Bancorp, Inc.

Summit Financial Group Inc

UMH Properties Inc

Union Bankshares, Inc. (Morrisville, VT)

United Bancorp, Inc. (Martins Ferry, OH)

United Security Bancshares (CA)

Weyco Group, Inc

WGNB Corp.

York Water Co

Dividend Achievers Name Changes

Old Name	*New Name*
Health Care Property Investors, Inc.	HCP, Inc.
People's Bank	People's United Financial, Inc.
United Dominion Realty Trust, Inc.	UDR Inc.
WPS Resources Corp.	Intergy Energy Group, Inc.

Top 20 by 10 Year Compounded Annual Dividend Growth Rate (CAGR)

*Companies are listed by the 10-year average annual compound growth of their dividends.
Also shown are the total number of years of consecutive annual dividend growth.*

Rank	Company	CAGR	Years of Increases
1	Robinson (C.H.) Worldwide, Inc.	10	47.27
2	Bank of the Ozarks, Inc.	10	42.45
3	Horton (D.R.) Inc.	10	39.15
4	Expeditors Intl of Washington, Inc.	13	36.47
5	American Capital Strategies Ltd.	10	33.30
6	Harley-Davidson Inc	14	31.70
7	Home Depot Inc	20	30.40
8	Linear Technology Corp.	15	29.33
9	Paychex Inc	19	28.99
10	Citigroup Inc	21	26.87
11	Harte-Hanks, Inc. (United States)	12	26.51
12	Lehman Brothers Holdings Inc	11	25.89
13	Eaton Vance Corp	26	25.53
14	Lowe's Companies Inc	46	25.19
15	Cardinal Health, Inc.	11	25.18
16	Total System Services, Inc.	10	25.03
17	McDonald's Corp	31	24.99
18	Stryker Corp.	15	24.29
19	Legg Mason, Inc.	24	23.86
20	Nationwide Financial Services Inc.	10	23.74

Top 20 by Return on Equity

Based on latest available year-end information. Ratios determined using net income.

Rank	Company	R.O.E.	Rank	Company	R.O.E.
1	HERSHEY CO	91.3	11	CEDAR FAIR L P	40.0
2	POLARIS INDUST	70.9	12	GEN GROWTH PROP	36.7
3	COLGATE-PALMOLIV	68.8	13	CATERPILLAR	35.6
4	ALTRIA GROUP	65.2	14	HARLEY-DAVIDSON	35.5
5	AVON PRODUCTS	64.6	15	INTL BUS MACH	35.2
6	ANHEUSER-BUSCH	61.1	16	HOLLY CORP	34.2
7	MCGRAW-HILL	55.4	17	TJX	33.1
8	NORDSTROM	49.7	18	SHERWIN-WILLIAMS	31.9
9	PAYCHEX	46.4	19	PEPSICO	31.8
10	TANGER FACTORY	43.9	20	EXXON MOBIL	31.7

Top 20 by Return on Assets

Based on latest available year-end information. Ratios determined using net income.

Rank	Company	R.O.A	Rank	Company	R.O.A
1	LINEAR TECH	26.2	11	3M COMPANY	16.1
2	EATON VANCE	22.0	12	ALTRIA GROUP	16.0
3	MERIDIAN BIOSCI	20.5	13	HARLEY-DAVIDSON	15.7
4	SEI INVESTMENTS	20.0	14	BARD C R	15.4
5	T ROWE PRICE	20.0	15	COLGATE-PALMOLIV	15.1
6	RAVEN INDUSTRIES	19.1	16	MCGRAW-HILL	15.0
7	CH ROBINSON	17.5	17	NUCOR	14.1
8	TOTAL SYST SERV	17.5	18	MEDTRONIC	14.1
9	FRANKLIN RES	17.3	19	LILLY ELI	14.0
10	EXXON MOBIL	16.2	20	POLARIS INDUST	13.8

Top 20 by Current Dividend Yields

Based on latest available Prices

Rank	Company	R.O.A	Rank	Company	R.O.A
1	AMER CAP STRAT	12.9	11	TALBOTS	7.2
2	FIFTH THIRD BANC	9.4	12	COMERICA	7.1
3	LEXINGTON CORP P	8.5	13	BUCKEYE PARTNERS	7.1
4	CBL + ASSOC	8.3	14	LIBERTY PPTY TR	7.0
5	CEDAR FAIR L P	8.3	15	DEVELOPERS RLTY	7.0
6	TEPPCO PARTNERS	8.0	16	UNIV HEALTH RLTY	6.8
7	KEYCORP	7.7	17	REALTY INCOME	6.7
8	DUKE REALTY	7.5	18	NATL RETAIL PROP	6.6
9	BANK OF AMERICA	7.5	19	KINDER MORGAN EN	6.6
10	INDEPENDNT BK MI	7.3	20	PFIZER	6.6

Highest Price/Earnings Ratios

Based on latest available year-end information. Ratios determined using net income.
Based on closing prices as of May 31, 2008

Rank	Company	P/E Ratio	Rank	Company	P/E Ratio
1	FOREST CITY ENT	66.7	11	CHURCH + DWIGHT	35.6
2	ALBEMARLE	44.5	12	TENNANT	35.2
3	ROPER INDS	43.4	13	SHENANDOAH TELE	34.9
4	ESSEX PROPERTY	39.8	14	ALEXANDRIA RE EQ	34.8
5	MERIDIAN BIOSCI	39.6	15	WILEY JOHN	33.8
6	WESCO FINL	38.7	16	CH ROBINSON	33.2
7	OLD REPUBLIC	37.6	17	BADGER METER	33.0
8	EXPEDITORS INTL	37.4	18	WRIGLEY WM	32.7
9	HELMERICH PAYNE	36.9	19	SJW CORP	31.7
10	WEST PHARMACEUT	36.5	20	AMER STATES WATR	30.7

Lowest Price/Earnings Ratios

Based on latest available year-end information. Ratios determined using net income.
Based on closing prices as of May 31, 2008

Rank	Company	P/E Ratio	Rank	Company	P/E Ratio
1	BANKATLANTIC	2.0	11	LA-Z-BOY	4.9
2	CORUS BANKSHARES	2.4	12	MEDIA GENERAL	5.0
3	WASH MUTUAL	2.6	13	CITIGROUP	5.0
4	SOUTH FINL GROUP	2.9	14	D R HORTON	5.1
5	INDEPENDNT BK MI	3.0	15	AMER INTL GROUP	5.5
6	AMBAC FINL GROUP	3.1	16	WEST COAST BANCP	5.8
7	COLONIAL BANCGRP	3.4	17	IRWIN FINANCIAL	5.9
8	MBIA	4.1	18	LEHMAN BROS HLDG	6.0
9	NATL CITY CORP	4.5	19	MARSHALL + ILSLE	6.6
10	PROVIDENT BANKSH	4.8	20	ROYAL BANCSHS PA	6.8

Highest Price/Book Ratios

Based on latest available year-end information. Ratios determined using net income.
Based on closing prices as of May 31, 2008

Rank	Company	P/B Ratio	Rank	Company	P/B Ratio
1	EATON VANCE	26.0	11	ALTRIA GROUP	9.7
2	AVON PRODUCTS	18.7	12	MERIDIAN BIOSCI	9.7
3	COLGATE-PALMOLIV	17.1	13	MCGRAW-HILL	8.2
4	BLOCK H + R	15.1	14	EXPEDITORS INTL	7.5
5	HERSHEY CO	14.9	15	WRIGLEY WM	7.5
6	PITNEY-BOWES	13.7	16	TANGER FACTORY	7.5
7	ANHEUSER-BUSCH	12.4	17	CEDAR FAIR L P	7.1
8	PAYCHEX	10.3	18	BADGER METER	7.1
9	POLARIS INDUST	10.2	19	PEPSICO	6.3
10	CH ROBINSON	9.9	20	NORDSTROM	6.1

Lowest Price/Book Ratios

Based on latest available year-end information. Ratios determined using net income.
Based on closing prices as of May 31, 2008

Rank	Company	P/B Ratio	Rank	Company	P/B Ratio
1	BANKATLANTIC	0.23	11	INDEPENDNT BK MI	0.58
2	NATL CITY CORP	0.28	12	PROVIDENT BANKSH	0.59
3	IRWIN FINANCIAL	0.29	13	BANNER CORP	0.66
4	SOUTH FINL GROUP	0.29	14	AMBAC FINL GROUP	0.70
5	WASH MUTUAL	0.36	15	GANNETT	0.72
6	MEDIA GENERAL	0.39	16	LA-Z-BOY	0.72
7	CORUS BANKSHARES	0.40	17	WEBSTER FINL CRP	0.78
8	SECURITY BANK	0.41	18	OLD REPUBLIC	0.79
9	COLONIAL BANCGRP	0.44	19	NACCO INDUST	0.79
10	FIRST STATE BNCP	0.49	20	MBIA	0.80

Top 20 by Revenues

Based on latest available year-end information (in million's US$)

Rank	Company	Revenues	Rank	Company	Revenues
1	EXXON MOBIL	$404,552	11	HOME DEPOT	$77,349
2	WAL-MART STORES	$378,799	12	PROCTER + GAMBLE	$76,476
3	CHEVRON	$220,904	13	ALTRIA GROUP	$73,801
4	GEN ELECTRIC	$172,738	14	TARGET CORP	$63,367
5	CITIGROUP	$159,229	15	JOHNSON JOHNSON	$61,095
6	BANK OF AMERICA	$119,190	16	LEHMAN BROS HLDG	$59,003
7	AT+T INC	$118,928	17	UNITED TECH	$54,759
8	AMER INTL GROUP	$110,064	18	WALGREEN	$53,762
9	INTL BUS MACH	$98,785	19	WELLS FARGO + CO	$53,593
10	CARDINAL HEALTH	$86,852	20	PFIZER	$48,418

Top 20 by Net Income

Based on latest available year-end information (in million's US$)

Rank	Company	Net Income	Rank	Company	Net Income
1	EXXON MOBIL	$40,610	11	PFIZER	$8,144
2	GEN ELECTRIC	$22,208	12	WELLS FARGO + CO	$8,057
3	CHEVRON	$18,688	13	AMER INTL GROUP	$6,200
4	BANK OF AMERICA	$14,982	14	COCA-COLA	$5,981
5	WAL-MART STORES	$12,731	15	PEPSICO	$5,658
6	AT+T INC	$11,951	16	ALLSTATE	$4,636
7	JOHNSON JOHNSON	$10,576	17	HOME DEPOT	$4,395
8	INTL BUS MACH	$10,418	18	U S BANCORP	$4,324
9	PROCTER + GAMBLE	$10,340	19	UNITED TECH	$4,224
10	ALTRIA GROUP	$9,786	20	LEHMAN BROS HLDG	$4,192

Top 20 by Market Capitalization

Based on latest available year-end information (in million's US$)
Based on closing prices as of May 31, 2008

Rank	Company	Current Value	Rank	Company	Current Value
1	EXXON MOBIL	$468,981	11	PFIZER	$130,974
2	GEN ELECTRIC	$306,199	12	CITIGROUP	$114,918
3	AT+T INC	$237,046	13	PEPSICO	$108,331
4	WAL-MART STORES	$228,333	14	WELLS FARGO + CO	$91,053
5	CHEVRON	$205,082	15	AMER INTL GROUP	$89,716
6	PROCTER + GAMBLE	$201,651	16	ABBOTT LABS	$86,965
7	JOHNSON JOHNSON	$188,087	17	UNITED TECH	$69,136
8	INTL BUS MACH	$177,772	18	MCDONALDS	$67,239
9	BANK OF AMERICA	$151,440	19	U S BANCORP	$57,771
10	COCA-COLA	$133,004	20	MEDTRONIC	$56,902

Bottom 20 by Market Capitalization

Based on latest available year-end information (in million's US$)
Based on closing prices as of May 31, 2008

Rank	Company	Current Value	Rank	Company	Current Value
1	BANKATLANTIC	$99	11	PEOPLES BANCORP	$246
2	IRWIN FINANCIAL	$122	12	SOUTHWEST BCP OK	$246
3	ROYAL BANCSHS PA	$127	13	SOUTHWEST WATER	$252
4	SECURITY BANK	$128	14	OLD SECOND BANCP	$260
5	HORIZON FINL	$130	15	FIRST BANCORP-NC	$277
6	INDEPENDNT BK MI	$137	16	COURIER CORP	$289
7	FIRST STATE BNCP	$156	17	BANNER CORP	$291
8	WEST COAST BANCP	$182	18	FIRST FINL HLDGS	$293
9	SEACOAST BNKG FL	$205	19	ANCHOR BANC WIS	$299
10	LSI INDUSTRIES	$230	20	MAINSOURCE FINL	$312

Top 20 by Total Assets

Based on latest available year-end information (in million's US$)

Rank	Company	Total Assets	Rank	Company	Total Assets
1	CITIGROUP	$2,187,631	11	U S BANCORP	$237,615
2	BANK OF AMERICA	$1,715,746	12	LINCOLN NATL	$191,435
3	AMER INTL GROUP	$1,060,505	13	SUNTRUST BANKS	$179,574
4	GEN ELECTRIC	$795,337	14	WAL-MART STORES	$163,514
5	LEHMAN BROS HLDG	$691,063	15	ALLSTATE	$156,408
6	WELLS FARGO + CO	$575,442	16	NATL CITY CORP	$150,374
7	HARTFORD FINL	$360,361	17	CHEVRON	$148,786
8	WASH MUTUAL	$327,913	18	STATE STREET	$142,543
9	AT+T INC	$275,644	19	PROCTER + GAMBLE	$138,014
10	EXXON MOBIL	$242,082	20	BB+T CORP	$132,618

About Total Return

Total return represents one of the best measures of how well an investor of a given stock has fared as it reflects both dividend income and price appreciation. Mergent calculates total return for each Dividend Achievers company on the basis that cash dividends were reinvested on the ex-dividend date of each dividend payment. The following table demonstrates the effect of compounding as well as each stock's performance and the level of dividends paid. Total returns have been adjusted for splits, stock dividends and spin-offs. In the case of a spin-off, shares in the spun-off company were assumed to be converted to cash and reinvested in the original company's stock.

How to read the rankings: On the following pages, the Dividend Achievers companies are listed alphabetically with their respective total returns and rankings over trailing one, three and five year periods ending May 31, 2008. For example, an investor who purchased shares of Abbott Laboratories on May 31, 2007, and sold them on May 31, 2008 would have realized a total return of 2.46% on their original investment. Following each company's one-year total return are its three-year and five-year annualized total returns and their respective rankings for each period. The three-year annualized total return is based on an investment made on May 31, 2005, and the five-year annualized total return represents an investment made on May 31, 2003. Thus an investment made in Abbott Laboratories on May 31, 2005, would have generated an annualized total return of 7.98% during the three year period ended May 31, 2008. If an investor had bought shares in Abbott Laboratories on May 31, 2003, and sold them on May 31, 2008, their annualized total return would have been 8.81%.

Ranking the Dividend Achievers by Total Return

Based on the 1, 3, and 5 year periods ending May 30, 2008

Ticker	Name	Tot Ret. 1 Year	Rank 1 Year	Tot Ret. 3 Year	Rank 3 Year	Tot Ret. 5 Year	Rank 5 Year
SRCE	1ST SOURCE CORP	-14.26%	196	5.69%	147	9.25%	147
MMM	3M CO	-9.68%	169	2.79%	175	6.44%	192
ABT	ABBOTT LABS	2.46%	100	7.98%	122	8.81%	152
ABM	ABM INDS INC	-24.37%	243	6.95%	133	10.54%	134
AFL	AFLAC INC	28.90%	18	18.89%	44	16.70%	79
APD	AIR PRODS & CHEMS INC	32.95%	15	21.54%	37	20.90%	48
ALB	ALBEMARLE CORP	10.64%	59	34.50%	6	29.12%	17
ARE	ALEXANDRIA REAL ESTATE EQ INC	2.35%	103	18.30%	48	22.97%	36
ALL	ALLSTATE CORP	-14.56%	198	-1.79%	226	9.95%	138
MO	ALTRIA GROUP INC	9.62%	63	18.63%	45	24.76%	28
ABK	AMBAC FINL GROUP INC	-96.44%	319	-64.43%	319	-45.23%	319
ACAS	AMERICAN CAPITAL STRATEGIES	-27.11%	254	5.35%	149	13.13%	106
AIG	AMERICAN INTL GROUP INC	-49.69%	298	-12.52%	289	-8.31%	298
AWR	AMERICAN STS WTR CO	-3.86%	135	9.28%	109	9.01%	150
ABCW	ANCHOR BANCORP WIS INC	-49.31%	297	-18.12%	296	-7.22%	296
BUD	ANHEUSER BUSCH COS INC	10.63%	60	9.77%	104	4.09%	218
ATR	APTARGROUP INC	20.63%	31	23.18%	31	22.19%	40
WTR	AQUA AMERICA INC	-23.44%	240	-3.83%	246	6.13%	196
ADM	ARCHER DANIELS MIDLAND CO	14.73%	41	27.58%	18	28.92%	18
ASBC	ASSOCIATED BANC CORP	-13.51%	191	-2.89%	235	5.55%	202
AF	ASTORIA FINL CORP	-6.68%	156	-1.19%	221	9.76%	140
T	AT&T INC	0.20%	116	24.89%	26	14.74%	87
ATO	ATMOS ENERGY CORP	-11.31%	176	3.46%	165	6.85%	184
ADP	AUTOMATIC DATA PROCESSING INC	-11.33%	177	4.83%	158	8.23%	164
AVY	AVERY DENNISON CORP	-18.67%	214	1.93%	186	1.18%	258
AVP	AVON PRODS INC	3.83%	91	1.60%	192	7.07%	181
BMI	BADGER METER INC	93.10%	1	39.29%	5	49.07%	2
BANF	BANCFIRST CORP	2.37%	102	4.95%	155	11.51%	125
BXS	BANCORPSOUTH INC	-2.07%	127	5.35%	150	4.78%	210
BOH	BANK HAWAII CORP	4.38%	88	6.72%	138	12.35%	115
BAC	BANK OF AMERICA CORPORATION	-29.94%	265	-5.48%	261	2.65%	238
OZRK	BANK OF THE OZARKS INC	-13.59%	192	-7.00%	267	8.01%	168
BBX	BANKATLANTIC BANCORP	-81.21%	316	-53.18%	318	-26.52%	315
BANR	BANNER CORP	-48.17%	294	-9.91%	281	-0.62%	277
BCR	BARD C R INC	8.77%	65	10.94%	89	22.04%	41
BBT	BB&T CORP	-21.18%	226	-3.52%	239	2.43%	243
BEC	BECKMAN COULTER INC	7.12%	75	0.70%	200	12.36%	114
BDX	BECTON DICKINSON & CO	12.22%	50	15.23%	63	17.62%	70
BMS	BEMIS INC	-18.43%	213	2.03%	185	5.77%	201
BKH	BLACK HILLS CORP	-10.90%	174	2.31%	180	7.19%	180
HRB	BLOCK H & R INC	1.35%	107	0.17%	210	4.86%	209
BRC	BRADY CORP	6.00%	81	9.92%	102	20.81%	50
BRO	BROWN & BROWN INC	-24.41%	244	-3.54%	240	2.75%	237
BFB	BROWN FORMAN CORP	12.19%	51	10.83%	91	16.38%	80
BPL	BUCKEYE PARTNERS L P	-2.13%	128	9.28%	110	11.97%	118
CHRW	C H ROBINSON WORLDWIDE INC	20.89%	30	32.94%	10	29.79%	13
CWT	CALIFORNIA WTR SVC GROUP	1.02%	108	3.42%	168	8.85%	151
CCBG	CAPITAL CITY BK GROUP INC	-8.57%	161	-3.93%	248	2.14%	245
CAH	CARDINAL HEALTH INC	-21.35%	228	-0.24%	212	0.01%	269
CSL	CARLISLE COS INC	-23.14%	238	0.18%	209	9.78%	139
CAT	CATERPILLAR INC DEL	7.20%	74	22.83%	33	28.30%	20
CTR	CATO CORP NEW	-25.11%	248	-3.75%	244	6.72%	185
CBL	CBL & ASSOC PPTYS INC	-31.11%	267	-8.78%	275	9.52%	142
FUN	CEDAR FAIR L P	-13.96%	195	-2.72%	233	3.29%	232
CTL	CENTURYTEL INC	-28.00%	261	3.26%	170	1.69%	251
CHFC	CHEMICAL FINL CORP	-6.07%	150	-5.05%	258	-0.46%	275

Ticker	Name	Tot Ret. 1 Year	Rank 1 Year	Tot Ret. 3 Year	Rank 3 Year	Tot Ret. 5 Year	Rank 5 Year
CVX	CHEVRON CORP NEW	25.06%	22	26.32%	22	26.74%	26
CB	CHUBB CORP	0.26%	114	10.78%	92	13.33%	101
CHD	CHURCH & DWIGHT INC	14.55%	42	17.08%	55	22.68%	37
CINF	CINCINNATI FINL CORP	-20.14%	223	-0.85%	216	3.79%	225
CTAS	CINTAS CORP	-21.94%	233	-8.93%	276	-3.55%	288
C	CITIGROUP INC	-57.82%	304	-19.14%	298	-8.26%	297
CYN	CITY NATL CORP	-35.49%	274	-9.71%	280	3.89%	222
CLC	CLARCOR INC	31.05%	17	16.65%	58	20.17%	54
CLX	CLOROX CO DEL	-12.62%	185	1.44%	194	7.33%	176
KO	COCA-COLA CO	10.73%	57	11.56%	88	7.26%	177
CL	COLGATE PALMOLIVE CO	13.30%	44	16.58%	59	6.63%	187
CNB	COLONIAL BANCGROUP INC	-74.62%	313	-32.77%	307	-11.77%	303
CMA	COMERICA INC	-37.50%	277	-8.65%	274	-0.14%	273
CBSH	COMMERCE BANCSHARES INC	-0.31%	118	3.42%	167	8.74%	154
CGI	COMMERCE GROUP INC MASS	10.71%	58	10.58%	94	17.87%	67
CBU	COMMUNITY BK SYS INC	22.11%	28	4.92%	156	8.16%	166
CTBI	COMMUNITY TR BANCORP INC	-6.38%	155	4.47%	159	8.01%	167
ED	CONSOLIDATED EDISON INC	-10.83%	173	1.82%	189	4.45%	215
OFC	CORPORATE OFFICE PPTYS TR	-12.73%	186	14.25%	70	23.34%	34
CORS	CORUS BANKSHARES INC	-63.77%	307	-34.94%	309	-9.53%	302
CRRC	COURIER CORP	-40.05%	282	-10.88%	285	3.01%	235
CFR	CULLEN FROST BANKERS INC	8.35%	69	10.69%	93	13.25%	104
CVBF	CVB FINL CORP	-4.30%	136	-5.12%	259	1.25%	256
DHI	D R HORTON INC	-43.55%	288	-26.59%	305	1.22%	257
DHR	DANAHER CORP DEL	6.53%	78	12.50%	79	18.65%	63
XRAY	DENTSPLY INTL INC NEW	12.62%	47	12.95%	75	17.26%	74
DDR	DEVELOPERS DIVERSIFIED RLTY	-31.80%	270	0.18%	208	12.52%	113
DBD	DIEBOLD INC	-18.14%	211	-5.52%	262	1.72%	250
DCI	DONALDSON INC	42.35%	5	18.30%	49	20.76%	51
DOV	DOVER CORP	9.88%	61	14.40%	69	14.07%	94
DRE	DUKE REALTY CORP	-31.29%	268	0.67%	201	4.55%	213
EGP	EASTGROUP PPTY INC	1.76%	105	9.90%	103	17.42%	73
EV	EATON VANCE CORP	-1.65%	125	22.18%	35	24.87%	27
ECL	ECOLAB INC	5.01%	85	12.70%	76	11.96%	119
EMR	EMERSON ELEC CO	22.75%	26	23.27%	30	20.19%	53
EGN	ENERGEN CORP	28.17%	19	33.29%	9	37.35%	5
EAS	ENERGY EAST CORP	9.85%	62	1.40%	195	8.42%	163
ERIE	ERIE INDTY CO	-5.18%	140	2.47%	178	7.65%	171
ESS	ESSEX PPTY TR INC	-2.84%	130	18.09%	50	20.49%	52
EXPD	EXPEDITORS INTL WASH INC	8.54%	67	23.37%	29	22.52%	38
XOM	EXXON MOBIL CORP	8.54%	66	18.60%	46	21.98%	42
FDO	FAMILY DLR STORES INC	-35.13%	273	-4.23%	251	-8.80%	299
FRT	FEDERAL REALTY INVT TR	-6.25%	154	17.32%	53	24.32%	30
FITB	FIFTH THIRD BANCORP	-53.11%	302	-20.41%	300	-17.02%	308
FBNC	FIRST BANCORP N C	-10.58%	171	-3.69%	242	2.77%	236
BUSE	FIRST BUSEY CORP	-5.44%	144	2.50%	177	5.99%	199
FCTR	FIRST CHARTER CORP	43.63%	4	15.19%	64	13.25%	103
FCBC	FIRST CMNTY BANCSHARES INC NEV	12.30%	49	7.59%	127	3.99%	220
FFIN	FIRST FINL BANKSHARES	16.73%	37	17.37%	52	17.05%	76
THFF	FIRST FINL CORP IND	17.47%	36	9.63%	105	6.44%	191
FFCH	FIRST FINL HLDGS INC	-20.92%	225	-0.87%	217	0.10%	267
FMBI	FIRST MIDWEST BANCORP DEL	-26.35%	252	-6.06%	263	0.83%	261
FSNM	FIRST ST BANCORPORATION	-63.97%	308	-23.75%	303	-8.93%	301
FMER	FIRSTMERIT CORP	-0.46%	119	-2.59%	231	2.13%	246

Ticker	Name	Tot Ret. 1 Year	Rank 1 Year	Tot Ret. 3 Year	Rank 3 Year	Tot Ret. 5 Year	Rank 5 Year
FFIC	FLUSHING FINL CORP	22.93%	25	8.04%	121	10.02%	137
FNB	FNB CORP PA	-4.53%	138	-1.43%	223	3.60%	227
FCEA	FOREST CITY ENTERPRISES INC	-42.52%	286	8.74%	115	15.55%	83
FPL	FPL GROUP INC	8.46%	68	22.15%	36	19.17%	60
FELE	FRANKLIN ELEC INC	-13.06%	188	2.80%	174	8.61%	156
BEN	FRANKLIN RES INC	-24.98%	247	12.56%	77	23.49%	33
FUL	FULLER H B CO	-7.76%	160	16.68%	57	17.46%	72
FULT	FULTON FINL CORP PA	-13.39%	189	-5.05%	257	0.16%	265
AJG	GALLAGHER ARTHUR J & CO	-8.94%	163	1.77%	190	2.53%	240
GCI	GANNETT INC	-49.09%	295	-25.23%	304	-16.58%	307
GD	GENERAL DYNAMICS CORP	16.55%	38	21.19%	40	24.27%	31
GE	GENERAL ELECTRIC CO	-15.63%	204	-2.72%	234	4.21%	216
GGP	GENERAL GROWTH PPTYS INC	-26.27%	251	6.18%	141	21.06%	46
GPC	GENUINE PARTS CO	-11.46%	178	3.94%	163	9.39%	145
GBCI	GLACIER BANCORP INC NEW	-0.52%	120	12.55%	78	16.83%	77
GRC	GORMAN RUPP CO	64.60%	3	52.58%	2	31.71%	11
GWW	GRAINGER W W INC	5.45%	84	20.76%	42	16.15%	81
HOG	HARLEY DAVIDSON INC	-30.22%	266	-3.68%	241	1.02%	259
HGIC	HARLEYSVILLE GROUP INC	32.57%	16	27.65%	17	12.98%	108
HNBC	HARLEYSVILLE NATL CORP PA	-11.55%	179	-9.58%	277	-3.38%	287
HSC	HARSCO CORP	20.45%	32	31.83%	11	31.60%	12
HHS	HARTE-HANKS INC	-47.52%	292	-21.76%	302	-4.91%	291
HIG	HARTFORD FINL SVCS GROUP INC	-29.30%	263	0.41%	205	10.96%	129
HCC	HCC INS HLDGS INC	-26.35%	253	-1.73%	225	5.78%	200
HCP	HCP INC	11.17%	55	14.49%	68	18.90%	62
HTLF	HEARTLAND FINL USA INC	-1.01%	122	7.49%	130	4.88%	208
HP	HELMERICH & PAYNE INC	85.73%	2	45.37%	4	33.36%	8
JKHY	HENRY JACK & ASSOC INC	-9.02%	164	11.57%	87	10.58%	133
HSY	HERSHEY CO	-23.37%	239	-13.23%	290	4.11%	217
HRH	HILB ROGAL & HOBBS CO	-27.70%	259	-1.96%	228	-1.23%	279
HRC	HILL-ROM HOLDINGS INC	-13.45%	190	5.82%	145	3.85%	224
HNI	HNI CORP	-41.54%	284	-19.90%	299	-1.46%	280
HOC	HOLLY CORP	-38.84%	280	31.52%	12	43.80%	4
HD	HOME DEPOT INC	-27.54%	258	-9.61%	278	-1.87%	284
HME	HOME PROPERTIES INC	-6.20%	153	13.23%	72	13.56%	99
HRZB	HORIZON FINL CORP WASH	-50.64%	299	-10.17%	282	-1.75%	283
HRL	HORMEL FOODS CORP	2.69%	99	10.27%	97	11.82%	121
IBKC	IBERIABANK CORP	6.09%	80	6.29%	140	8.45%	161
ITW	ILLINOIS TOOL WKS INC	3.87%	90	10.21%	98	13.30%	102
IBCP	INDEPENDENT BANK CORP MICH	-63.15%	306	-35.73%	312	-19.65%	310
TEG	INTEGRYS ENERGY GROUP INC	-3.15%	131	2.31%	179	8.56%	157
IBM	INTERNATIONAL BUSINESS MACHS	23.25%	24	21.26%	38	9.23%	148
IFC	IRWIN FINL CORP	-73.28%	312	-40.46%	315	-28.69%	317
JNJ	JOHNSON & JOHNSON	8.31%	70	2.26%	181	6.52%	189
JCI	JOHNSON CTLS INC	-5.59%	147	23.54%	28	21.53%	44
KEY	KEYCORP	-42.04%	285	-12.05%	287	-1.54%	282
KMB	KIMBERLY CLARK CORP	-7.19%	158	2.86%	173	7.59%	173
KIM	KIMCO REALTY CORP	-11.64%	180	15.02%	66	20.94%	47
KMP	KINDER MORGAN ENERGY PARTNERS	12.50%	48	13.98%	71	15.30%	84
LZB	LA Z BOY INC	-43.75%	289	-19.07%	297	-19.42%	309
LANC	LANCASTER COLONY CORP	-23.10%	237	-5.37%	260	0.10%	266
LM	LEGG MASON INC	-46.09%	290	-12.39%	288	5.44%	204
LEG	LEGGETT & PLATT INC	-18.26%	212	-7.44%	269	0.04%	268
LEH	LEHMAN BROS HLDGS INC	-49.23%	296	-6.42%	265	1.40%	255
LXP	LEXINGTON REALTY TRUST	-7.06%	157	-0.96%	218	7.99%	169

Ticker	Name	Tot Ret. 1 Year	Rank 1 Year	Tot Ret. 3 Year	Rank 3 Year	Tot Ret. 5 Year	Rank 5 Year
LRY	LIBERTY PPTY TR	-18.76%	215	0.94%	198	7.63%	172
LLY	LILLY ELI & CO	-14.99%	201	-3.20%	238	-1.54%	281
LNC	LINCOLN NATL CORP IND	-21.86%	232	9.49%	107	12.85%	109
LLTC	LINEAR TECHNOLOGY CORP	4.93%	86	1.27%	196	1.69%	252
LOW	LOWES COS INC	-25.95%	250	-4.96%	256	3.15%	233
LYTS	LSI INDS INC	-27.27%	257	-4.48%	252	5.49%	203
MTB	M & T BK CORP	-19.07%	216	-3.14%	237	1.47%	254
MAC	MACERICH CO	-16.38%	207	8.39%	120	20.82%	49
MSFG	MAINSOURCE FINANCIAL GP INC	1.51%	106	1.83%	188	6.72%	186
MI	MARSHALL & ILSLEY CORP NEW	-35.87%	275	-9.70%	279	2.17%	244
MLM	MARTIN MARIETTA MATLS INC	-24.08%	242	25.47%	24	29.48%	16
MAS	MASCO CORP	-36.08%	276	-13.87%	291	-2.75%	286
MATW	MATTHEWS INTL CORP	8.25%	71	9.36%	108	15.26%	85
MBI	MBIA INC	-89.30%	318	-49.03%	317	-31.32%	318
MKC	MCCORMICK & CO INC	3.07%	97	5.79%	146	9.05%	149
MCD	MCDONALDS CORP	21.26%	29	27.44%	19	28.73%	19
MGRC	MCGRATH RENTCORP	-8.90%	162	8.76%	114	19.24%	59
MHP	MCGRAW HILL COS INC	-39.84%	281	-0.21%	211	7.21%	179
MDU	MDU RES GROUP INC	11.29%	54	22.51%	34	21.15%	45
MEG	MEDIA GEN INC	-56.25%	303	-35.22%	310	-21.96%	311
MDT	MEDTRONIC INC	-3.78%	134	-1.10%	220	1.56%	253
MCY	MERCURY GENL CORP NEW	-5.41%	143	0.96%	197	4.90%	207
MDP	MEREDITH CORP	-46.32%	291	-11.64%	286	-4.53%	290
VIVO	MERIDIAN BIOSCIENCE INC	41.40%	7	56.45%	1	51.98%	1
MGEE	MGE ENERGY INC	5.58%	83	2.59%	176	6.13%	197
MSA	MINE SAFETY APPLIANCES CO	-2.18%	129	-1.69%	224	29.49%	15
MYE	MYERS INDS INC	-43.33%	287	5.02%	154	8.22%	165
NC	NACCO INDS INC	-47.86%	293	-3.82%	245	10.35%	135
NCC	NATIONAL CITY CORP	-82.35%	317	-42.25%	316	-26.62%	316
NFG	NATIONAL FUEL GAS CO N J	36.01%	12	33.30%	8	23.08%	35
NPBC	NATIONAL PENN BANCSHARES INC	0.81%	110	2.22%	182	3.35%	230
NNN	NATIONAL RETAIL PROPERTIES I	-0.28%	117	12.10%	83	13.42%	100
NFS	NATIONWIDE FINL SVCS INC	-15.83%	205	12.36%	81	11.74%	124
NJR	NEW JERSEY RES	-5.78%	149	6.78%	137	10.64%	132
NYT	NEW YORK TIMES CO	-27.11%	255	-14.90%	292	-16.09%	305
NDSN	NORDSON CORP	40.46%	8	34.41%	7	26.97%	25
JWN	NORDSTROM INC	-31.72%	269	5.85%	144	31.80%	10
NTRS	NORTHERN TR CORP	18.63%	35	20.18%	43	16.72%	78
NWN	NORTHWEST NAT GAS CO	-5.46%	145	11.83%	85	14.59%	88
NUE	NUCOR CORP	15.03%	40	46.78%	3	48.61%	3
ONB	OLD NATL BANCORP IND	3.29%	94	0.38%	206	0.01%	270
ORI	OLD REP INTL CORP	-27.78%	260	-4.85%	254	0.00%	271
OSBC	OLD SECOND BANCORP INC ILL	-33.69%	271	-10.47%	283	-0.52%	276
OTTR	OTTER TAIL CORP	18.70%	34	18.04%	51	10.13%	136
OMI	OWENS & MINOR INC NEW	35.72%	13	17.28%	54	19.48%	57
PRK	PARK NATL CORP	-14.43%	197	-7.99%	272	-4.27%	289
PH	PARKER HANNIFIN CORP	26.72%	20	29.73%	13	27.32%	23
PAYX	PAYCHEX INC	-11.72%	182	8.61%	117	4.55%	214
PNR	PENTAIR INC	2.90%	98	-4.01%	250	15.90%	82
PEBO	PEOPLES BANCORP INC	-11.11%	175	-2.66%	232	2.60%	239

Ticker	Name	Tot Ret. 1 Year	Rank 1 Year	Tot Ret. 3 Year	Rank 3 Year	Tot Ret. 5 Year	Rank 5 Year
PEP	PEPSICO INC	2.11%	104	8.78%	113	11.07%	128
PFE	PFIZER INC	-25.66%	249	-7.61%	271	-5.80%	295
PNY	PIEDMONT NAT GAS INC	5.86%	82	7.41%	131	10.85%	130
PNW	PINNACLE WEST CAP CORP	-23.08%	236	-3.95%	249	2.52%	241
PBI	PITNEY BOWES INC	-21.28%	227	-3.72%	243	1.88%	248
PII	POLARIS INDS INC	-10.67%	172	-0.38%	213	12.34%	116
PPG	PPG INDS INC	-14.71%	199	1.77%	191	8.48%	160
PX	PRAXAIR INC	41.91%	6	28.70%	14	27.96%	21
TROW	PRICE T ROWE GROUP INC	14.51%	43	26.60%	20	27.75%	22
PG	PROCTER & GAMBLE CO	6.18%	79	8.43%	119	9.73%	141
PGN	PROGRESS ENERGY INC	-9.94%	170	4.29%	161	3.44%	228
PLD	PROLOGIS	-1.03%	123	18.52%	47	22.50%	39
PL	PROTECTIVE LIFE CORP	-15.01%	202	3.15%	171	10.68%	131
PBKS	PROVIDENT BANKSHARES CORP	-70.03%	310	-30.29%	306	-14.88%	304
STR	QUESTAR CORP	19.98%	33	28.14%	15	33.76%	6
RAVN	RAVEN INDS INC	7.77%	73	15.11%	65	33.49%	7
O	REALTY INCOME CORP	-4.90%	139	5.97%	142	11.75%	123
REG	REGENCY CTRS CORP	-11.71%	181	10.10%	101	19.37%	58
RNST	RENASANT CORP	-1.51%	124	7.51%	129	6.25%	194
RLI	RLI CORP	-9.51%	168	6.93%	134	13.15%	105
ROH	ROHM & HAAS CO	4.67%	87	7.80%	125	13.58%	97
ROP	ROPER INDS INC NEW	11.96%	52	23.63%	27	29.58%	14
ROST	ROSS STORES INC	12.68%	46	10.11%	100	12.53%	112
RBPAA	ROYAL BANCSHARES PA INC	-52.37%	301	-20.77%	301	-8.86%	300
RPM	RPM INTL INC	11.66%	53	15.57%	62	18.61%	64
STBA	S & T BANCORP INC	3.15%	96	0.90%	199	6.37%	193
SYBT	S Y BANCORP INC	3.58%	93	8.50%	118	8.48%	159
SASR	SANDY SPRING BANCORP INC	-14.89%	200	-4.70%	253	-1.15%	278
SBCF	SEACOAST BKG CORP FLA	-51.63%	300	-16.46%	294	-5.04%	293
SBKC	SECURITY BANK CORP	-72.16%	311	-34.65%	308	-16.50%	306
SEIC	SEI INVESTMENTS CO	-21.44%	231	12.11%	82	11.26%	126
SHEN	SHENANDOAH TELECOMMUNICATIONS	0.66%	112	16.86%	56	18.03%	66
SHW	SHERWIN WILLIAMS CO	-15.15%	203	10.28%	95	17.69%	68
SIAL	SIGMA ALDRICH CORP	37.03%	10	26.56%	21	18.91%	61
SFNC	SIMMONS 1ST NATL CORP	10.88%	56	10.13%	99	11.13%	127
SJW	SJW CORP	-1.75%	126	16.07%	60	19.71%	56
AOS	SMITH A O	-6.16%	152	6.81%	136	4.63%	212
SON	SONOCO PRODS CO	-17.47%	210	12.44%	80	12.55%	111
TSFG	SOUTH FINL GROUP INC	-75.76%	314	-39.28%	314	-23.56%	314
OKSB	SOUTHWEST BANCORP INC OKLA	-29.55%	264	-0.58%	214	7.33%	175
SWWC	SOUTHWEST WTR CO	-19.43%	219	2.22%	183	4.04%	219
SSS	SOVRAN SELF STORAGE INC	-12.26%	183	4.87%	157	14.23%	92
SWK	STANLEY WKS	-21.39%	230	5.36%	148	14.37%	89
STFC	STATE AUTO FINL CORP	-9.22%	167	2.06%	184	4.69%	211
STT	STATE STR CORP	6.79%	76	15.98%	61	14.96%	86
SCL	STEPAN CO	37.00%	11	27.88%	16	13.92%	95
SBIB	STERLING BANCSHARES INC	-9.18%	166	5.94%	143	6.89%	183
SYK	STRYKER CORP	-3.68%	133	10.28%	96	14.23%	93
SUBK	SUFFOLK BANCORP	12.87%	45	5.19%	152	3.11%	234
STI	SUNTRUST BKS INC	-38.77%	279	-7.49%	270	0.81%	263
SVU	SUPERVALU INC	-24.96%	246	4.29%	160	14.31%	90
SUSQ	SUSQUEHANNA BANCSHARES INC PA	-6.15%	151	-1.29%	222	0.52%	264
SNV	SYNOVUS FINL CORP	-19.12%	217	-1.02%	219	5.44%	205
SYY	SYSCO CORP	-4.39%	137	-3.88%	247	1.91%	247
TLB	TALBOTS INC	-65.10%	309	-35.55%	311	-22.45%	312
SKT	TANGER FACTORY OUTLET CTRS INC	-5.26%	141	21.19%	39	24.64%	29

Ticker	Name	Tot Ret. 1 Year	Rank 1 Year	Tot Ret. 3 Year	Rank 3 Year	Tot Ret. 5 Year	Rank 5 Year
TGT	TARGET CORP	-13.66%	193	0.00659	202	0.0867	155
TCO	TAUBMAN CTRS INC	0.75%	111	22.97%	32	27.25%	24
TCB	TCF FINL CORP	-38.69%	278	-10.50%	284	-0.23%	274
TFX	TELEFLEX INC	-24.61%	245	3.82%	164	8.51%	158
TNC	TENNANT CO	9.54%	64	25.57%	23	17.14%	75
TPP	TEPPCO PARTNERS L P	-13.00%	187	1.92%	187	7.88%	170
TJX	TJX COS INC NEW	16.06%	39	13.09%	74	13.10%	107
TMP	TOMPKINS FINANCIAL CORPORATION	25.38%	21	9.58%	106	8.79%	153
TR	TOOTSIE ROLL INDS INC	-5.29%	142	-2.34%	230	0.97%	260
TSS	TOTAL SYS SVCS INC	-16.49%	208	5.20%	151	6.61%	188
TRH	TRANSATLANTIC HLDGS INC	-9.15%	165	5.09%	153	3.93%	221
TRMK	TRUSTMARK CORP	-22.89%	235	-8.35%	273	-2.42%	285
UDR	UDR INC	-13.84%	194	7.54%	128	13.58%	98
UGI	UGI CORP NEW	-3.65%	132	3.45%	166	12.77%	110
UMBF	UMB FINL CORP	37.17%	9	25.13%	25	21.86%	43
UBSI	UNITED BANKSHARES INC WEST VA	-12.59%	184	-2.18%	229	1.83%	249
UTX	UNITED TECHNOLOGIES CORP	2.45%	101	11.85%	84	17.68%	69
UVV	UNIVERSAL CORP VA	-19.50%	220	7.73%	126	7.23%	178
UFPI	UNIVERSAL FST PRODS INC	-29.16%	262	-4.93%	255	12.17%	117
UHT	UNIVERSAL HEALTH RLTY INCM TR	3.80%	92	3.37%	169	11.96%	120
UVSP	UNIVEST CORP PA	8.06%	72	-0.74%	215	4.93%	206
USB	US BANCORP DEL	0.94%	109	9.02%	112	11.78%	122
VFC	V F CORP	-16.96%	209	13.20%	73	17.60%	71
VLY	VALLEY NATL BANCORP	-21.39%	229	-1.84%	227	-0.13%	272
VAL	VALSPAR CORP	-20.11%	222	0.26%	207	2.46%	242
VVC	VECTREN CORP	6.66%	77	7.35%	132	8.42%	162
VNO	VORNADO RLTY TR	-16.35%	206	11.66%	86	23.59%	32
VMC	VULCAN MATLS CO	-34.14%	272	10.85%	90	18.40%	65
WMT	WAL MART STORES INC	23.56%	23	8.68%	116	3.30%	231
WAG	WALGREEN CO	-19.40%	218	-6.69%	266	3.86%	223
WFSL	WASHINGTON FED INC	-7.53%	159	2.90%	172	6.49%	190
WM	WASHINGTON MUT INC	-78.46%	315	-36.91%	313	-22.65%	313
WRE	WASHINGTON REAL ESTATE INVT	-5.61%	148	7.80%	124	9.49%	144
WASH	WASHINGTON TR BANCORP	0.24%	115	-2.91%	236	3.39%	229
WBS	WEBSTER FINL CORP CONN	-40.17%	283	-15.63%	293	-4.98%	292
WRI	WEINGARTEN RLTY INVS	-21.98%	234	1.55%	193	9.51%	143
WFC	WELLS FARGO & CO NEW	-20.54%	224	0.41%	204	6.20%	195
WSBC	WESBANCO INC	-27.18%	256	-6.12%	264	0.82%	262
WSC	WESCO FINL CORP	-0.79%	121	6.33%	139	7.45%	174
WCBO	WEST COAST BANCORP ORE NEW	-61.45%	305	-17.38%	295	-5.42%	294
WST	WEST PHARMACEUTICAL SVSC INC	-5.56%	146	21.08%	41	32.70%	9
WABC	WESTAMERICA BANCORPORATION	22.12%	27	4.17%	162	6.94%	182
WGL	WGL HLDGS INC	3.18%	95	6.83%	135	9.35%	146
WTNY	WHITNEY HLDG CORP	-23.49%	241	-7.15%	268	3.62%	226
JWA	WILEY JOHN & SONS INC	4.09%	89	7.91%	123	14.28%	91
WL	WILMINGTON TRUST CORP	-19.89%	221	0.48%	203	5.99%	198
WWW	WOLVERINE WORLD WIDE INC	0.29%	113	9.06%	111	20.01%	55
WWY	WRIGLEY WM JR CO	34.26%	14	14.90%	67	13.59%	96
WWY	WRIGLEY WM JR CO	13.59%	43	3.01%	174	7.40%	222

Web Site And Dividend Reinvestment Plan Information

Company	Ticker	Web Site	DRIP
1st Source Corp.	SRCE	www.1stsource.com	No
3M Co.	MMM	www.3m.com	Yes
Abbott Laboratories	ABT	www.abbott.com	Yes
ABM Industries, Inc.	ABM	www.abm.com	No
AFLAC Inc.	AFL	www.aflac.com	Yes
Air Products & Chemicals, Inc.	APD	www.airproducts.com	Yes
Albemarle Corp.	ALB	www.albemarle.com	Yes
Alexandria Real Estate Equities	ARE	www.labspace.com	Yes
Allstate Corp.	ALL	www.allstate.com	Yes
Altria Group Inc.	MO	www.altria.com	Yes
Ambac Financial Group, Inc.	ABK	www.ambac.com	No
American Capital Strategies Ltd	ACAS	www.american-capital.com	No
American International Group Inc.	AIG	www.aig.com	No
American States Water Co.	AWR	www.aswater.com	Yes
Anchor BanCorp Wisconsin, Inc.	ABCW	www.anchorbank.com	No
Anheuser-Busch Cos., Inc.	BUD	www.anheuser-busch.com	Yes
AptarGroup Inc.	ATR	www.aptargroup.com	No
Aqua America Inc.	WTR	www.suburbanwater.com	Yes
Archer Daniels Midland Co.	ADM	www.admworld.com	Yes
Associated Banc-Corp.	ASBC	www.associatedbank.com	Yes
Astoria Financial Corp.	AF	www.astoriafederal.com	No
AT&T Inc.	T	www.sbc.com	Yes
Atmos Energy Corp.	ATO	www.atmosenergy.com	Yes
Automatic Data Processing Inc.	ADP	www.adp.com	No
Avery Dennison Corp.	AVY	www.averydennison.com	Yes
Avon Products, Inc.	AVP	www.avon.com	Yes
Badger Meter, Inc.	BMI	www.badgermeter.com	Yes
BancFirst Corp.	BANF	www.bancfirst.com	No
BancorpSouth Inc.	BXS	www.bancorpsouth.com	Yes
Bank of the Ozarks, Inc	OZRK	www.bankozarks.com	Yes
Bank of America Corp.	BAC	www.bankofamerica.com	Yes
Bank of Hawaii Corp.	BOH	www.boh.com	Yes
BankAtlantic Bancorp, Inc.	BBX	www.bankatlanticbancorp.com	No
Banner Corp.	BANR	www.bannerbank.com	No
Bard (C.R.), Inc.	BCR	www.crbard.com	Yes
BB&T Corp.	BBT	www.bbandt.com	Yes
Beckman Coulter, Inc.	BEC	www.beckmancoulter.com	Yes
Becton, Dickinson and Co.	BDX	www.bd.com	Yes
Bemis Co Inc.	BMS	www.bemis.com	Yes
Black Hills Corporation	BKH	www.blackhillscorp.com	Yes
Block (H&R), Inc.	HRB	www.hrblock.com	Yes
Brady Corp.	BRC	www.bradycorp.com	Yes
Brown & Brown, Inc.	BRO	www.bbinsurance.com	No
Brown-Forman Corp.	BF B	www.brown-forman.com	No
Buckeye Partners, L.P.	BPL	www.buckeye.com	No
California Water Service Group	CWT	www.calwatergroup.com	Yes
Capital City Bank Group, Inc.	CCBG	www.mycapitalcitybank.com	No
Cardinal Health, Inc.	CAH	www.cardinalhealth.com	No
Carlisle Companies Inc.	CSL	www.carlisle.com	Yes

Company	Ticker	Web Site	DRIP
Caterpillar Inc.	CAT	www.CAT.com	Yes
Cato Corp.	CTR	www.catofashions.com	Yes
CBL & Associates Properties, Inc.	CBL	www.cblproperties.com	Yes
Cedar Fair, L.P.	FUN	www.cedarfair.com	Yes
CenturyTel, Inc.	CTL	www.centurytel.com	Yes
Chemical Financial Corp.	CHFC	www.chemicalbankmi.com	Yes
Chevron Corporation	CVX	www.chevrontexaco.com	Yes
Chubb Corp.	CB	www.chubb.com	Yes
Church & Dwight Co., Inc.	CHD	www.churchdwight.com	Yes
Cincinnati Financial Corp.	CINF	www.cinfin.com	Yes
Cintas Corporation	CTAS	www.cintas.com	No
Citigroup Inc.	C	www.citigroup.com	Yes
City National Corp.	CYN	www.cnb.com	No
Clarcor Inc.	CLC	www.clarcor.com	Yes
Clorox Co.	CLX	www.thecloroxcompany.com	Yes
Coca-Cola Co.	KO	www.coca-cola.com	Yes
Colgate-Palmolive Co.	CL	www.colgate.com	Yes
Colonial BancGroup Inc.	CNB	www.colonialbank.com	Yes
Comerica, Inc.	CMA	www.comerica.com	Yes
Commerce Bancorp, Inc.	CBH	www.commerceonline.com	Yes
Commerce Bancshares, Inc.	CBSH	www.commercebank.com	Yes
Commerce Group Inc.	CGI	www.commerceinsurance.com	No
Community Bank System, Inc.	CBU	www.communitybankna.com	Yes
Community Trust Bancorp, Inc.	CTBI	www.ctbi.com	No
Consolidated Edison Inc.	ED	www.conedison.com	Yes
Corporate Office Prop. Trust	OFC	www.copt.com	Yes
Corus Bankshares, Inc.	CORS	www.corusbank.com	No
Courier Corp.	CRRC	www.courier.com	No
Cullen/Frost Bankers, Inc.	CFR	www.frostbank.com	No
CVB Financial Corp.	CVBF	www.cbbank.com	No
Danaher Corp.	DHR	www.danaher.com	No
DENTSPLY International, Inc.	XRAY	www.dentsply.com	No
Developers Diversified Realty	DDR	www.ddr.com	No
Diebold, Inc.	DBD	www.diebold.com	Yes
Donaldson Co. Inc.	DCI	www.donaldson.com	Yes
Dover Corp.	DOV	www.dovercorporation.com	Yes
Duke Realty Corp.	DRE	www.dukerealty.com	Yes
EastGroup Properties, Inc.	EGP	www.eastgroup.net	Yes
Eaton Vance Corp.	EV	www.eatonvance.com	No
Ecolab, Inc.	ECL	www.ecolab.com	Yes
Emerson Electric Co.	EMR	www.gotoemerson.com	Yes
Energen Corp.	EGN	www.energen.com	Yes
Energy East Corp.	EAS	www.energyeast.com	Yes
Erie Indemnity Co.	ERIE	www.erieinsurance.com	No
Essex Property Trust, Inc.	ESS	www.expresspropertytrust.com	Yes
Expeditors Int'l of Washington, Inc.	EXPD	www.expeditors.com	No
Exxon Mobil Corp.	XOM	www.exxonmobil.com	Yes
Family Dollar Stores, Inc.	FDO	www.familydollar.com	No
Federal Realty Investment Trust	FRT	www.federalrealty.com	Yes
Fifth Third Bancorp	FITB	www.53.com	Yes
First Bancorp	FBNC	wwwfirstbancorp.com	Yes
First Busey Corp.	BUSE	www.busey.com	No
First Charter Corp.	FCTR	www.firstcharter.com	Yes
First Community Bancshares, Inc.	FCBC	www.fcbinc.com	No
First Financial Corp.	THFF	www.first-online.com	No

Company	Ticker	Web Site	DRIP
First Financial Holdings, Inc.	FFCH	www.firstfinancialholdings.com	Yes
First Financial Bankshares	FFIN	www.ffin.com	No
First Midwest Bancorp, Inc.	FMBI	www.firstmidwest.com	Yes
First State Bancorporation	FSNM	www.fsbnm.com	Yes
FirstMerit Corp.	FMER	www.firstmerit.com	Yes
Flushing Financial Corp.	FFIC	www.flushingsavings.com	No
F.N.B. Corp.	FNB	www.fnbcorporation.com	Yes
Forest City Enterprises, Inc.	FCE A	www.fceinc.com	Yes
FPL Group, Inc.	FPL	www.fplgroup.com	Yes
Franklin Electric Co., Inc.	FELE	www.franklin-electric.com	No
Franklin Resources, Inc.	BEN	www.frk.com	Yes
Fuller (H.B.) Company	FUL	www.hbfuller.com	Yes
Fulton Financial Corp.	FULT	www.fult.com	Yes
Gallagher (Arthur J.) & Co.	AJG	www.ajg.com	No
Gannett Co Inc.	GCI	www.gannett.com	Yes
General Dynamics Corp.	GD	www.generaldynamics.com	No
General Electric Co.	GE	www.ge.com	Yes
General Growth Properties, Inc.	GGP	www.generalgrowth.com	Yes
Genuine Parts Co.	GPC	www.genpt.com	Yes
Glacier Bancorp, Inc.	GBCI	www.glacierbancorp.com	Yes
Gorman-Rupp Co.	GRC	www.gormanrupp.com	Yes
Grainger (W.W.) Inc.	GWW	www.grainger.com	No
Harley-Davidson Inc.	HOG	www.harley-davidson.com	Yes
Harleysville Group, Inc.	HGIC	www.harleysvillegroup.com	Yes
Harleysville National Corp.	HNBC	www.hncbank.com	Yes
Harsco Corp.	HSC	www.harsco.com	Yes
Harte-Hanks, Inc.	HHS	www.harte-hanks.com	No
Hartford Financial Services Group Inc.	HIG	www.thehartford.com	Yes
HCC Insurance Holdings, Inc.	HCC	www.hcch.com	No
HCP Inc.	HCP	www.hcpi.com	Yes
Heartland Financial USA, Inc.	HTLF	www.htlf.com	No
Helmerich & Payne Inc.	HP	www.hpinc.com	No
Henry (Jack) & Associates	JKHY	www.jackhenry.com	Yes
Hershey Company	HSY	www.hersheys.com	Yes
Hilb Rogal & Hobbs Co	HRH	www.hrh.com	No
Hill-Rom Holdings, Inc	HRC	www.hillenbrand.com	Yes
HNI Corp.	HNI	www.honi.com	No
Holly Corp.	HOC	www.hollycorp.com	No
Home Depot Inc.	HD	www.homedepot.com	Yes
Home Properties Inc.	HME	www.homeproperties.com	Yes
Horizon Financial Corp.	HRZB	www.horizonbank.com	Yes
Hormel Foods Corp.	HRL	www.hormel.com	Yes
Horton (D.R.) Inc.	DHI	www.drhorton.com	Yes
IBERIABANK Corp	IBKC	www.iberiabank.com	Yes
Illinois Tool Works, Inc.	ITW	www.itw.com	Yes
Independent Bank Corporation	IBCP	www.ibcp.com	Yes
Integrys Energy Group Inc.	TEG	www.wpsr.com	Yes
International Business Machines Corp.	IBM	www.ibm.com	Yes
Investors Financial Services Corp.	IFIN	www.investorsbnk.com	Yes
Irwin Financial Corp.	IFC	www.irwinfinancial.com	Yes
Johnson & Johnson	JNJ	www.jnj.com	Yes
Johnson Controls Inc.	JCI	www.johnsoncontrols.com	Yes
KeyCorp	KEY	www.key.com	Yes
Kimberly-Clark Corp.	KMB	www.kimberly-clark.com	Yes

Company	Ticker	Web Site	DRIP
Kimco Realty Corp.	KIM	www.kimcorealty.com	Yes
Kinder Morgan Energy Partners	KMP	www.kindermorgan.com	No
Lancaster Colony Corp.	LANC	www.lancastercolony.com	Yes
La-Z-Boy Inc.	LZB	www.la-z-boy.com	Yes
Legg Mason, Inc.	LM	www.leggmason.com	No
Leggett & Platt, Inc.	LEG	www.leggett.com	No
Lehman Brothers Holdings Inc	LEH	www.lehman.com	Yes
Lexington Corporate Properties Trust	LXP	www.lxp.com	No
Liberty Property Trust	LRY	www.libertyproperty.com	Yes
Lilly (Eli) & Co.	LLY	www.lilly.com	Yes
Lincoln National Corp.	LNC	www.lfg.com	Yes
Linear Technology Corp.	LLTC	www.linear.com	No
Lowe's Companies Inc.	LOW	www.lowes.com	Yes
LSI Industries Inc.	LYTS	www.lsi-industries.com	Yes
M & T Bank Corp	MTB	www.mandtbank.com	Yes
Macerich Co.	MAC	www.macerich.com	Yes
MainSource Financial Group Inc.	MSFG	www.mainsourcefinancial.com	Yes
Marshall & Ilsley Corp.	MI	www.micorp.com	Yes
Martin Marietta Materials, Inc.	MLM	www.martinmarietta.com	No
Masco Corp.	MAS	www.masco.com	Yes
Matthews International Corp	MATW	www.matw.com	No
MBIA Inc.	MBI	www.mbia.com	No
McCormick & Co., Inc.	MKC	www.mccormick.com	No
McDonald's Corp.	MCD	www.mcdonalds.com	Yes
McGrath RentCorp	MGRC	www.mgrc.com	No
McGraw-Hill Cos., Inc.	MHP	www.mcgraw-hill.com	Yes
MDU Resources Group Inc.	MDU	www.mdu.com	Yes
Media General, Inc.	MEG	www.mediageneral.com	Yes
Medtronic, Inc.	MDT	www.medtronic.com	Yes
Mercury General Corp.	MCY	www.mercuryinsurance.com	No
Meredith Corp.	MDP	www.meredith.com	No
Meridian Bioscience Inc	VIVO	www.meridianbioscience.com	Yes
MGE Energy Inc.	MGEE	www.mgeenergy.com	Yes
Mine Safety Appliances Co.	MSA	www.msanet.com	No
Myers Industries Inc.	MYE	www.myersind.com	Yes
NACCO Industries Inc.	NC	www.naccoind.com	No
National City Corp.	NCC	www.nationalcity.com	Yes
National Fuel Gas Co.	NFG	www.nationalfuelgas.com	Yes
National Penn Bancshares Inc.	NPBC	www.nationalpennbancshares.com	Yes
National Retail Properties Inc.	NNN	www.nnnreit.com	Yes
Nationwide Financial Services	NFS	www.nationwidefinancial.com	Yes
New Jersey Resources Corp.	NJR	www.njliving.com	Yes
New York Times Co.	NYT	www.nytco.com	Yes
Nordson Corp.	NDSN	www.nordson.com	Yes
Nordstrom, Inc.	JWN	www.nordstrom.com	No
Northern Trust Corp.	NTRS	www.northerntrust.com	No
Northwest Natural Gas	NWN	www.nwnatural.com	No
Nucor Corp.	NUE	www.nucor.com	Yes
Old National Bancorp	ONB	www.oldnational.com	Yes
Old Republic International Corp.	ORI	www.oldrepublic.com	Yes
Old Second Bancorp., Inc.	OSBC	www.o2bancorp.com	No
Otter Tail Corp.	OTTR	www.ottertail.com	Yes
Owens & Minor, Inc.	OMI	www.owens-minor.com	Yes
Park National Corp.	PRK	www.parknationalcorp.com	Yes

Company	Ticker	Web Site	DRIP
Parker Hannifin Corp.	PH	www.phstock.com	Yes
Paychex Inc.	PAYX	www.paychex.com	Yes
Pentair, Inc.	PNR	www.pentair.com	Yes
Peoples Bancorp, Inc.	PEBO	www.peoplesbancorp.com	No
PepsiCo Inc.	PEP	www.pepsico.com	Yes
Pfizer Inc.	PFE	www.pfizer.com	Yes
Piedmont Natural Gas Co., Inc.	PNY	www.piedmontng.com	Yes
Pinnacle West Capital Corp.	PNW	www.pinnaclewest.com	Yes
Pitney Bowes Inc.	PBI	www.pb.com	Yes
Polaris Industries Inc.	PII	www.polarisindustries.com	Yes
PPG Industries, Inc.	PPG	www.ppg.com	Yes
Praxair, Inc.	PX	www.praxair.com	Yes
Procter & Gamble Co.	PG	www.pg.com	Yes
Progress Energy Inc.	PGN	www.progress-energy.com	Yes
ProLogis	PLD	www.prologis.com	Yes
Protective Life Corp.	PL	www.protective.com	Yes
Provident Bankshares Corp	PBKS	www.provbank.com	Yes
Questar Corp.	STR	www.questar.com	Yes
Raven Industries, Inc.	RAVN	www.ravenind.com	Yes
Realty Income Corp.	O	www.realtyincome.com	No
Regency Centers Corp.	REG	www.regencycenters.com	Yes
Renasant Corp.	RNST	www.thepeoplesbankandtrust.com	No
RLI Corp.	RLI	www.rlicorp.com	Yes
Robinson (C.H.) Worldwide, Inc.	CHRW	www.chrobinson.com	Yes
Rohm & Haas Co.	ROH	www.rohmhaas.com	Yes
Roper Industries, Inc.	ROP	www.roperind.com	No
Ross Stores, Inc.	ROST	www.rossstores.com	No
Royal Bancsh. Of Pennsylvania	RBPAA	www.royalbankpa.com	No
RPM International Inc.	RPM	www.rpminc.com	Yes
S & T Bancorp, Inc.	STBA	www.stbank.com	Yes
S.Y. Bancorp, Inc.	SYBT	www.syb.com	Yes
Sandy Spring Bancorp	SASR	www.ssnb.com	Yes
Seacoast Banking Corp.	SBCF	www.seacoastbanking.net	No
Security Bank Corp.	SBKC	www.securitybank.com	Yes
SEI Investments Co.	SEIC	www.seic.com	No
ServiceMaster Co.	SVM	www. servicemaster.com	Yes
Shenandoah Telecomm. Co.	SHEN	www.shentel.com	Yes
Sherwin-Williams Co.	SHW	www.sherwin.com	Yes
Sigma-Aldrich Corp.	SIAL	www.sigma-aldrich.com	No
Simmons First National Corp.	SFNC	www.simmonsfirst.com	No
SJW Corp.	SJW	www.sjwater.com	No
Sky Financial Group, Inc.	SKYF	www.skyfi.com	Yes
Smith (A.O.) Corp	AOS	www.aosmith.com	Yes
Sonoco Products Co.	SON	www.sonoco.com	Yes
South Financial Group Inc.	TSFG	www.thesouthgroup.com	Yes
Southwest Bancorp, Inc.	OKSB	www.oksb.com	No
Southwest Water Co.	SWWC	www.swwc.com	Yes
Sovran Self Storage, Inc.	SSS	www.sovranss.com	Yes
Stanley Works	SWK	www.stanleyworks.com	Yes
State Auto Financial Corp.	STFC	www.STFC.com	Yes
State Street Corp.	STT	www.statestreet.com	Yes
Stepan Co.	SCL	www.stepan.com	No
Sterling Bancshares, Inc.	SBIB	www.banksterling.com	No
Stryker Corp.	SYK	www.stryker.com	No
Suffolk Bancorp.	SUBK	www.scnb.com	No

Company	Ticker	Web Site	DRIP
SunTrust Banks, Inc.	STI	www.suntrust.com	Yes
Supervalu Inc.	SVU	www.supervalu.com	Yes
Susquehanna Bancshares, Inc.	SUSQ	www.susquehanna.net	Yes
Synovus Financial Corp.	SNV	www.synovus.com	Yes
Sysco Corp.	SYY	www.sysco.com	Yes
T Rowe Price Group Inc.	TROW	www.troweprice.com	No
Talbots, Inc.	TLB	www.talbots.com	No
Tanger Factory Outlet Centers, Inc.	SKT	www.tangeroutlet.com	Yes
Target Corp.	TGT	www.target.com	Yes
Taubman Centers, Inc.	TCO	www.taubman.com	Yes
TCF Financial Corp.	TCB	www.tcfexpress.com	Yes
Teleflex Incorporated	TFX	www.teleflex.com	Yes
Tennant Co.	TNC	www.tennantco.com	Yes
TEPPCO Partners, L.P.	TPP	www.teppco.com	No
TJX Companies, Inc.	TJX	www.tjx.com	No
Tompkins Financial Corp.	TMP	www.tompkinstrustco.com	No
Tootsie Roll Industries Inc.	TR	www.tootsie.com	No
Total System Services, Inc.	TSS	www.tsys.com	No
Transatlantic Holdings, Inc.	TRH	www.transre.com	No
Trustmark Corp.	TRMK	www.trustmark.com	Yes
UDR Inc	UDR	www.udrt.com	Yes
UGI Corp.	UGI	www.ugicorp.com	Yes
UMB Financial Corp.	UMBF	www.umb.com	Yes
United Bankshares, Inc.	UBSI	www.ubsi-wv.com	Yes
United Technologies Corp.	UTX	www.utc.com	Yes
Universal Corp.	UVV	www.universalcorp.com	Yes
Universal Forest Products Inc.	UFPI	www.ufpi.com	No
Universal Health Realty Income Trust	UHT	www.uhrit.com	Yes
Univest Corp. of Pennsylvania	UVSP	www.univest.net	Yes
U.S. Bancorp	USB	www.usbank.com	No
Valley National Bancorp	VLY	www.valleynationalbank.com	Yes
Valspar Corp.	VAL	www.valspar.com	Yes
Vectren Corp.	VVC	www.vectren.com	Yes
VF Corp.	VFC	www.vfc.com	Yes
Vornado Realty Trust	VNO	www.vno.com	Yes
Vulcan Materials Co.	VMC	www.vulcanmaterials.com	Yes
Walgreen Co.	WAG	www.walgreens.com	Yes
Wal-Mart Stores, Inc.	WMT	www.wal-mart.com	Yes
Washington Federal Inc.	WFSL	www.washingtonfederal.com	No
Washington Mutual Inc.	WM	www.wamu.com	Yes
Washington Real Estate Invest Trust	WRE	www.writ.com	Yes
Washington Trust Bancorp, Inc.	WASH	www.washtrust.com	Yes
Webster Financial Corp.	WBS	www.websteronline.com	Yes
Weingarten Realty Investors	WRI	www.weingarten.com	Yes
Wells Fargo & Co.	WFC	www.wellsfargo.com	Yes
Wesbanco, Inc.	WSBC	www.wesbanco.com	Yes
Wesco Financial Corp.	WSC	www.wescofinancial.com	No
West Coast Bancorp	WCBO	www.wcb.com	Yes
West Pharmaceutical Services, Inc.	WST	www.westpharma.com	Yes
WestAmerica Bancorporation	WABC	www.westamerica.com	Yes
WGL Holdings, Inc.	WGL	www.wglholdings.com	Yes
Whitney Holding Corp.	WTNY	www.whitneybank.com	Yes
Wiley (John) & Sons Inc.	JW A	www.wiley.com	No
Wilmington Trust Corp.	WL	www.wilmingtontrust.com	Yes
Wolverine World Wide, Inc.	WWW	www.wolverineworldwide.com	No
Wrigley (William) Jr. Co.	WWY	www.wrigley.com	Yes

SIC Classification of Companies By Industry Sector

Mining

Helmerich & Payne Inc.
Questar Corp.
Vulcan Materials Co.

Finance, Insurance & Real Estate

1st Source Corp.
AFLAC Inc.
Alabama National BanCorporation
Alexandria Real Estate Equities, Inc.
Allstate Corp.
Altria Group Inc.
Ambac Financial Group, Inc.
American Capital Strategies Ltd
American International Group Inc.
Anchor BanCorp Wisconsin, Inc.
Associated Banc-Corp.
Astoria Financial Corp.
BancFirst Corp.
BancorpSouth Inc.
Bank of America Corp.
Bank of Hawaii Corp.
BankAtlantic Bancorp, Inc.
Bank of the Ozarks, Inc.
Banner Corp.
BB&T Corp.
Block (H&R)
Brown & Brown, Inc.
Capital City Bank Group, Inc.
Chemical Financial Corp.
Chittenden Corp.
Chubb Corp.
Cincinnati Financial Corp.
Citigroup Inc.
City National Corp.
Colonial BancGroup Inc.
Colonial Properties Trust
Comerica, Inc.
Commerce Bancorp, Inc.
Commerce Bancshares, Inc.
Commerce Group Inc.
Community Bank System, Inc.
Community Trust Bancorp, Inc.
Corporate Office Properties
Corus Bankshares, Inc.
Cullen/Frost Bankers, Inc.
CVB Financial Corp.
Developers Diversified Realty Corp.
Duke Realty Corp.
EastGroup Properties, Inc.
Eaton Vance Corp.
Erie Indemnity Co.
Essex Property Trust, Inc.
F.N.B. Corp.
Federal Realty Investment Trust
Fifth Third Bancorp
First Bancorp
First Busey Corp.
First Charter Corp.

Transportation, Communications, & Utilities

American States Water Co.
AT&T Inc.
Atmos Energy Corp.
Black Hills Corporation
Buckeye Partners, L.P.
California Water Service Group
CBL & Associates Properties, Inc.
CenturyTel, Inc.
Consolidated Edison, Inc.
Energen Corp.
Energy East Corp.
Expeditors International of Washington, Inc.
FPL Group, Inc.
Integrys Energy Group Inc.
Kinder Morgan Energy Partners
MDU Resources Group Inc.
MGE Energy Inc.
National Fuel Gas Co.
New Jersey Resources Corp
Northwest Natural Gas Co.
Otter Tail Corp.
Piedmont Natural Gas Co., Inc.
Pinnacle West Capital Corp.
Progress Energy Inc.
Robinson (C.H.) Worldwide, Inc.
Shenandoah Telecommunications Co.
SJW Corp.
Southwest Water Co.
TEPPCO Partners, L.P.
UGI Corp.
Vectren Corp.
WGL Holdings, Inc.

Services

ABM Industries, Inc.
Automatic Data Processing Inc.
Cedar Fair, L.P.
Harte-Hanks, Inc.
Henry (Jack) & Association
McGrath RentCorp
Paychex Inc.

Retail Trade

Applebee's International, Inc.
Cato Corp.
Family Dollar Stores, Inc.
Home Depot Inc.
Lowe's Companies Inc.
McDonald's Corp.
Nordstrom, Inc.
Owens & Minor, Inc.
Ross Stores, Inc.
Sherwin-Williams Co.
Target Corp.
TJX Companies, Inc.
Tootsie Roll Industries Inc.
Walgreen Co.
Wal-Mart Stores, Inc.

First Commonwealth Financial Corp.
First Community Bancshares, Inc.
First Financial Bankshares
First Financial Corp.
First Financial Holdings, Inc.
First Indiana Corp.
First Midwest Bancorp, Inc.
First State Bancorporation
FirstMerit Corp.
Flushing Financial Corp.
Forest City Enterprises, Inc.
Franklin Resources, Inc.
Freddie Mac
Fulton Financial Corp.
Gallagher (Arthur J.) & Co.
General Growth Properties, Inc.
Glacier Bancorp, Inc.
Harleysville Group, Inc.
Harleysville National Corp.
Hartford Financial Services Group Inc.
HCC Insurance Holdings, Inc.
HCP, Inc.
Healthcare Realty Trust, Inc.
Heartland Financial USA, Inc.
Hilb Rogal & Hobbs Co.
Home Properties Inc.
Horizon Financial Corp.
Horton (D.R.) Inc.
IBERIABANK Corp.
Independent Bank Corporation
Irwin Financial Corp.
KeyCorp
Kimco Realty Corp.
Legg Mason, Inc.
Lehman Brothers Holdings Inc.
Lexington Corporate Properties Trust
Liberty Property Trust
Lincoln National Corp.
M & T Bank Corp
Macerich Co.
MainSource Financial Group Inc.
Marshall & Ilsley Corp.
MBIA Inc.
Mercury General Corp.
National City Corp.
National Penn Bancshares Inc.
National Retail Properties Inc.
Nationwide Financial Services Inc.
Northern Trust Corp.
Old National Bancorp.
Old Republic International Corp.
Old Second Bancorp., Inc.
Omega Financial Corp.
Pacific Capital Bancorp
Park National Corp.
Peoples Bancorp, Inc.

Wholesale Trade
Cardinal Health, Inc.
Carlisle Companies Inc.
Genuine Parts Co.
Grainger (W.W.) Inc.
Haverty Furniture Cos., Inc.
Martin Marietta Materials, Inc.
Supervalu Inc.
Sysco Corp.
Talbots, Inc.

Manufacturing
3M Co.
Abbott Laboratories
Air Products & Chemicals, Inc.
Albemarle Corp.
Anheuser-Busch Cos., Inc.
AptarGroup Inc.
Archer Daniels Midland Co.
Avery Dennison Corp.
Avon Products, Inc.
Badger Meter, Inc.
Bard (C.R.), Inc.
Beckman Coulter, Inc.
Becton, Dickinson and Co.
Bemis Co Inc.
Brady Corp.
Briggs & Stratton Corp.
Brown-Forman Corp.
Caterpillar Inc.
Chevron Corporation
Church & Dwight Co., Inc.
Cintas Corporation
Clarcor Inc.
Clorox Co.
Coca-Cola Co.
Colgate-Palmolive Co.
Courier Corp.
Danaher Corp.
DENTSPLY International, Inc.
Diebold, Inc.
Donaldson Co. Inc.
Dover Corp.
Ecolab, Inc.
Emerson Electric Co.
Exxon Mobil Corp.
Franklin Electric Co., Inc.
Fuller (H.B.) Company
Gannett Co Inc.
General Dynamics Corp.
General Electric Co.
Gorman-Rupp Co.
Harley-Davidson Inc
Harsco Corp.
Hershey Company
Hill-Rom Holdings, Inc

Progressive Corp.
ProLogis
Protective Life Corp.
Provident Bankshares Corp
Realty Income Corp.
Regency Centers Corp.
Renasant Corp.
RLI Corp.
Royal Bacshares of Pennsylvania
S & T Bancorp, Inc.
S.Y. Bancorp, Inc.
Sandy Spring Bancorp
Seacoast Banking Corp.
Security Bank Corp.
SEI Investments Co.
Simmons First National Corp.
Sky Financial Group, Inc.
South Financial Group Inc
Southwest Bancorp, Inc.
Sovran Self Storage, Inc.
State Auto Financial Corp.
State Street Corp.
Sterling Bancorp
Sterling Bancshares, Inc.
Sterling Financial Corp.
Suffolk Bancorp.
Sun Communities, Inc.
SunTrust Banks, Inc.
Susquehanna Bancshares, Inc.
Synovus Financial Corp.
T Rowe Price Group Inc.
Tanger Factory Outlet Centers, Inc.
Taubman Centers, Inc.
TCF Financial Corp.
Tompkins Financial Services
Transatlantic Holdings, Inc.
Trustmark Corp.
U.S. Bancorp
UDR Inc.
UMB Financial Corp.
United Bankshares, Inc.
Universal Health Realty Income Trust
Univest Corp. of Pennsylvania
Valley National Bancorp
Vornado Realty Trust
Washington Federal Inc.
Washington Mutual Inc.
Washington Real Estate Investment Trust
Washington Trust Bancorp, Inc.
Webster Financial Corp.
Weingarten Realty Investors
Wells Fargo & Co.
Wesbanco, Inc.
Wesco Financial Corp.
West Coast Bancorp
WestAmerica Bancorporation
Whitney Holding Corp.
Wilmington Trust Corp.

HNI Corp.
Holly Corp.
Hormel Foods Corp.
Illinois Tool Works, Inc.
International Business Machines Corp.
Johnson & Johnson
Johnson Controls Inc.
Kimberly-Clark Corp.
Lancaster Colony Corp.
La-Z-Boy Inc.
Leggett & Platt, Inc.
Lilly (Eli) & Co.
Linear Technology Corp.
LSI Industries Inc.
Masco Corp.
Matthews International Corp
McCormick & Co., Inc.
McGraw-Hill Cos., Inc.
Media General, Inc.
Medtronic, Inc.
Meredith Corp.
Meridian Bioscience Inc.
Mine Safety Appliances Co
Myers Industries Inc.
NACCO Industries Inc.
New York Times Co.
Nordson Corp.
Nucor Corp.
Parker Hannifin Corp.
Pentair, Inc.
PepsiCo Inc.
Pfizer Inc.
Pitney Bowes Inc.
Polaris Industries Inc.
PPG Industries, Inc.
Praxair, Inc.
Procter & Gamble Co.
Raven Industries, Inc.
Rohm & Haas Co.
Roper Industries, Inc.
RPM International Inc.
Sigma-Aldrich Corp.
Smith (A.O.) Corp.
Sonoco Products Co.
Stanley Works
Stryker Corp.
Superior Industries International, Inc.
Teleflex Incorporated
Tennant Co.
Total System Services, Inc.
United Technologies Corp.
Universal Corp.
Universal Forest Products Inc.
Valspar Corp.
VF Corp.
West Pharmaceutical Services, Inc.
Wiley (John) & Sons Inc.
Wolverine World Wide, Inc.
Wrigley (William) Jr. Co.

Frequently Asked Questions

Topics Questions:

- How does a dividend-paying company become a Dividend Achiever?
- What percentage of dividend-paying companies classified as Dividend Achievers?
- How many economic sectors and industries are represented by Dividend Achievers?
- What distinguishes Dividend Achievers from other U.S. listed companies?
- How often is the Dividend Achievers Index reconstituted?
- How are corporate actions handled?

Q: How does a dividend-paying company become a Dividend Achiever?

A: A publicly-traded company that has increased its dividends for the last ten or more consecutive years will be classified as a Dividend Achiever. Depending on the industry, companies must also meet certain capitalization requirements in order to be considered a Dividend Achiever.

Q: What percentage of dividend-paying companies classified as Dividend Achievers?

A: Just 10.0% of 3,300-plus North American-listed, dividend-paying common stocks are classified as Dividend Achievers.

Q: How many industry sectors and industries are represented by Dividend Achievers?

A: Dividend Achievers represent 13 industry sectors and more than 50 industries.

Q: What distinguishes Dividend Achievers from other U.S. listed companies?

A: Dividend Achievers have demonstrated the ability to consistently increase dividend payments over a substantial period of time, through volatile markets and challenging political climates.

Q: Does Mergent Inc. offer a Dividend Achiever Index?

A: Mergent currently offers an Index that tracks the daily performance of Dividend Achiever constituents. The inception date of the index was January 17, 2003. The real time price appreciation values are published by the American Stock Exchange under the Symbol "DAA".

Q: How often is the index reconstituted?

A: The Dividend Index is reconstituted annually.

Q: How are corporate actions handled?

A: If an Index constituent is acquired and is no longer actively traded, the company will cease classification as a Dividend Achiever. If an Index constituent spins off a portion of its business or merges with another company, it will be handled on a case by case basis.

HOW TO USE THIS BOOK

MERGENT'S Dividend Achievers is a compact, easy-to-use reference that provides basic financial and business information on companies that have increased their cash dividend payments for at least ten consecutive years, adjusting for splits. The presentation of background information plus current and historical data provides the answers to four basic questions for each company:

1. What does the company do?
   (See G.)
2. How has it done in the past?
   (See B, J.)
3. How is it doing now?
   (See C, D, H.)
4. How will it fare in the future?
   (See I.)

A. CAPSULE STOCK INFORMATION shows where the stock is traded and its symbol, a recent price and price/earnings ratio, plus the yield afforded by the indicated dividend based on a recent price. The indicated dividend is the current annualized dividend based on the most recent regular cash payment. Also shown is the 52-week range of the Company's stock price.

B. LONG-TERM PRICE CHART illustrates the pattern of monthly stock price movements, fully adjusted for stock dividends and splits. The chart points out the degree of volatility in the price movement of the company's stock and what its long-term trend has been. It also shows how it has performed long-term relative to an initial investment in the S&P 500 Index equal to the price of the company's stock at the beginning of the period shown in the price chart. It indicates areas of price support and resistance, plus other technical points to be considered by the investor. The bars at the base of the long-term price chart indicate the monthly trading volume. Monthly trading volume offers the individual an opportunity to recognize at what periods stock accumulation occurs and what percent of a company's outstanding shares are traded.

PRICE SCORES – Above each company's price/volume chart are its *Mergent's Price Scores*. These are basic measures of the stock's performance. Each stock is measured against the New York Stock Exchange Composite Index.

A score of 100 indicates that the stock did as well as the New York Stock Exchange Composite Index during the time period. A score of less than 100 means that the stock did not do as well; a score of more than 100 means that the stock outperformed the NYSE Composite Index. All stock prices are adjusted for splits and stock dividends. The time periods measured for each company conclude with the date of the recent price shown in the top line of each company's profile.

The *7 YEAR PRICE SCORE* mirrors the common stock's price growth over the previous seven years. The higher the price score, the better the relative performance. It is based on the ratio of the latest 12-month average price to the current seven-year average. This ratio is then indexed against the same ratio for the market as a whole (the New York Stock Exchange Composite Index), which is taken as 100.

The *12 MONTH PRICE SCORE* is a similar measurement but for a shorter period of time. It is based on the ratio of the latest two-month average price to the current 12-month average. As was done for the Long-Term Price Score, this ratio is also indexed to the same ratio for the market as a whole.

C. INTERIM EARNINGS (Per Share) – Figures are reported before effect of extraordinary items, discontinued operations and cumulative effects of accounting changes. Each figure is for the quarterly period indicated. These figures are essentially as reported by the company, although all figures are adjusted for all stock dividends and splits.

D. INTERIM DIVIDENDS (Per Share) – The cash dividends are the actual dollar amounts declared by the company. No adjustments have been made for stock dividends and splits. **Ex-Dividend Date**: a stockholder must purchase the stock prior to this date in order to be entitled to the dividend. The **Record Date** indicates the date on which the shareholder had to have been a holder of record in order to qualify for the dividend. The **Payable Date** indicates the date the company paid or intends to pay the dividend. The cash amount shown in the first column is followed by a letter (example "Q" for quarterly) to indicate the frequency of the dividend. A notation of "Dividend payment suspended" indicates that dividend payments have been suspended within the most recent ten years.

ILLUSTRATIVE INC.

Exchange	Symbol	Price	52Wk Range	Yield	P/E
NYS	Ill	$46.28 (5/31/2008)	50.72-42.63	2.85	13.30

*7 Year Price Score 114.48 *NYSE Composite Index=100 *12 Month Price Score 95.35

Interim Earnings (Per Share)

Qtr.	Mar	Jun	Sep	Dec
2005	(2.21)	0.19	0.17	0.15
2006	0.22	0.22	0.23	0.24
2007	0.20	0.13	0.21	0.18
2008	0.30	-------	-------	-------

Interim Dividends (Per Share)

Amt	Decl	Ex	Rec	Pay
0.325Q	8/17/2007	9/15/2007	9/17/2007	10/18/2007
0.33Q	11/9/2007	12/16/2007	12/20/2007	1/20/2007
0.33Q	3/15/2008	3/23/2008	3/28/2008	4/20/2008
0.33Q	5/3/2008	6/16/2008	6/20/2008	7/20/2008

Indicated Div: $1.32 (Div. Reinv. Plan)

Valuation Analysis

Forecast P/E	15.29 (5/31/2008)	
Market Cap	$905.8 Million	Book Value 535.8 Million
Price/Book	1.69	Price/Sales 1.03

Dividend Achiever Status

Rank	242	10 Year Growth Rate 6.39%
Total Years of Dividend Growth		28

TRADING VOLUME (thousand shares)

Business Summary: Rubber Products (MIC: 11.6 SIC: 011 NAIC: 26211)
Illustrative manufactures precured tread rubber, equipment and supplies for retreading tires. At February 29, 2008, Co. and its licensees have 900 franchisees worldwide. The majority of Co.'s franchisees are independent operators of full service tire distributorships. Co. sells and maintains new and retread tires to principally commercial and industrial customers through its wholly-owned subsidiary, Tires-R-Always Systems. Also, Co. provides quick-service truck lubrication and tire service through its subsidiary, Stupendous Jacks Lube, through 30 on-highway locations.

Recent Developments: For the quarter ended May 31, 2008, net income increased 48.3% to $5,962,000 from net income of $4,019 thousand in the year-earlier quarter. Revenues were $189,041 thousand, up 7.8% from $175,291 thousand the year before. Operating income was $8,675 thousand versus an income of $5,932 thousand in the prior-year quarter, an increase of 46.2%. Total direct expense was $123,294 thousand versus $112,803 thousand in the prior-year quarter, an increase of 9.3%. Total indirect expense was $57,072 thousand versus $56,556 thousand in the prior-year quarter, an increase of 0.9%.

Prospects: Results reflect strength in the North American trucking industry, offset in part by global high raw material and transportation costs, which are pressuring margins in its traditional business. On the positive side, Co. believes continued strength in the trucking industry in its major markets will work to its benefit as it continues delivering an expanded array of valued-added vehicle services, which complement its traditional business. At the same time, Co. recognizes that continued increases in raw material and transportation costs will be a concern throughout 2008.

Financial Data

(US$ in Thousands)	3 Mos	12/31/2007	12/31/2006	12/31/2005	12/31/2004	12/31/2003	12/31/2002	12/31/2001
Earnings Per Share	3.48	3.39	3.11	0.14	2.12	2.90	2.40	2.63
Cash Flow Per Share	4.20	4.92	4.08	6.65	5.66	4.78	5.18	3.85
Tang Book Value Per Share	25.74	25.55	24.61	21.97	21.22	20.03	18.62	17.84
Dividends Per Share	1.310	1.305	1.285	1.265	1.230	1.190	1.150	1.110
Dividend Payout %	37.64	38.50	41.32	903.57	58.02	41.03	47.92	42.21
Income Statement								
Total Revenue	189,041	867,953	828,186	911,953	982,209	1,013,426	1,027,878	1,079,498
EBITDA	15,157	109,191	113,482	110,708	120,036	158,572	155,581	161,695
Depn & Amortn	6,482	27,182	27,179	32,333	46,155	50,465	53,764	51,410
Income Before Taxes	10,032	84,902	83,900	71,518	66,505	99,375	92,090	99,513
Income Taxes	4,193	17,648	23,700	21,465	22,673	39,042	39,760	40,194
Net Income	5,962	66,880	60,200	2,793	43,832	60,333	52,330	59,319
Average Shares	19,707	19,707	19,369	19,888	20,686	20,778	21,764	22,559
Balance Sheet								
Current Assets	476,100	486,255	466,286	416,082	450,174	427,179	428,118	439,124
Total Assets	722,731	730,727	660,529	617,827	718,572	714,549	722,421	755,729
Current Liabilities	146,412	158,558	148,193	147,862	186,075	132,735	154,053	174,909
Long-Term Obligations	31,025	17,143	22,857	28,571	94,286	100,000	100,000	100,000
Total Liabilities	186,889	198,440	183,452	193,234	229,576	240,392	268,346	288,432
Stockholders' Equity	535,842	532,287	477,077	424,593	488,996	474,157	454,075	467,297
Shares Outstanding	19,572	19,451	19,268	19,151	20,641	20,561	20,770	21,955
Statistical Record								
Return on Assets %	9.90	9.59	9.42	0.42	6.12	8.37	7.08	7.17
Return on Equity %	13.53	13.22	13.35	0.61	9.10	12.96	11.36	12.75
EBITDA Margin %	8.02	12.58	13.70	12.14	12.22	15.65	15.14	14.98
Net Margin %	3.15	7.71	7.27	0.31	4.46	5.95	5.09	5.50
Asset Turnover	1.27	1.24	1.30	1.36	1.37	1.41	1.39	1.30
Current Ratio	3.25	3.07	3.15	2.81	2.42	3.22	2.78	2.51
Debt to Equity	0.06	0.03	0.05	0.07	0.19	0.21	0.22	0.21
Price Range	51.05-38.98	51.05-38.98	42.30-28.67	41.16-26.47	46.19-25.34	42.63-22.38	41.25-23.63	59.50-28.38
P/E Ratio	14.67-11.20	15.06-11.50	13.60-9.22	294.00-189.07	21.79-11.95	14.70-7.72	17.19-9.84	22.62-10.79
Average Yield %	2.84	2.86	3.58	3.63	3.99	4.10	3.62	2.52

Address: Owen Lars Highway, Muscatine, IA R2D2 - C3PO	**Officers:** Leia Organa - Chmn., Pres., C.E.O. Wicket W. Warrick - V.P., C.F.O., Sec.	**Investor Contact:** 563-260-0001 **No of Institutions:** 106
Telephone: 520-260-0000 **Web Site:** www.illustrative.com	**Transfer Agents:** EquiServe Trust Company, N.A.	**Shares:** 5,793,709 **% Held:** 63.55

HOW TO USE THIS BOOK

Indicated Dividend This is the annualized amount (fully adjusted for splits) of the latest regular cash dividend. Companies with Dividend Reinvestment Plans are indicated here.

E. VALUATION ANALYSIS is a tool for evaluating a company's stock. Included are: Forecast Price/Earnings, Market Capitalization, Book Value, Price/Book and Price/Sales.

F. DIVIDEND ACHIEVER STATUS – Presents the total consecutive years of dividend increases.

G. BUSINESS SUMMARY explains what a company does in terms of the products or services it sells, its markets, and the position the company occupies in its industry. For a quick reference, included are the Company's Standard Industrial Classification (SIC), North American Industry Classification (NAIC) and Mergent's Industry Classification (MIC).

H. RECENT DEVELOPMENTS – This section captures what has happened in the most recent quarter for which results are available. It provides analysis of recently released sales and earnings figures, including special charges and credits, and may also include results by sector, expense trends and ratios, and other current information.

I. PROSPECTS – This section focuses on what is anticipated for the immediate future, as well as the outlook for the next few years, based on analysis by Mergent.

J. FINANCIAL DATA (fully adjusted for stock dividends and splits) is provided for at least the past seven fiscal years preceded by the most recent three-, six- and nine-month results if available.

Fiscal Years are the annual financial reporting periods as determined by each company. Annual prices and dividends are displayed based on the Company's fiscal year.

Per Share Data:

The Earnings Per Share figure is based on a trailing 12-month period. Earnings per share, and all per share figures, are adjusted for subsequent stock dividends and splits. Earnings per share reported after 12/15/97 are presented on a diluted basis, as described by Financial Accounting Standards Board Statement 128. Prior to that date, earnings per share are presented on a primary basis.

Cash Flow Per Share represents the annualized cash flow from operating activities (or for quarters, TTM cash flow from operating activities) divided by the average shares outstanding.

Tangible Book Value Per Share is calculated as stockholders equity (the value of common shares, paid-in capital and retained earnings) minus preferred stock and intangibles such as goodwill, patents and excess acquisition costs, divided by shares outstanding. It demonstrates the underlying cash value of each common share if the company were to be liquidated as of that date.

Dividends Per Share is the total of cash payments made per share to shareholders for the trailing 12-month period.

Dividend Payout % is the proportion of earnings available for common stock that is paid to common shareholders in the form of cash dividends. It is significant because it indicates what percentage of earnings is being reinvested in the business for internal growth.

EDITOR'S NOTE: TTM net income is net income for the last 365 days (normally four reported quarters) ended on the quarterly balance sheet date. Where that last 365 days does not exactly equate to the last four reported quarters the net income for any included partial quarter is adjusted on a pro-rata basis.

INCOME STATEMENT, BALANCE SHEET AND STATISTICAL RECORD

Includes pertinent earnings and balance sheet information essential to analyzing a corporation's performance. The comparisons provide the necessary historical perspective to intelligently review the various operating and financial trends. Generic definitions follow.

Income Statement:

Total Revenues consists of all revenues from operations.

EBITDA represents earnings before, interest, taxes, depreciation and amortization, and special items.

Depreciation and Amortization includes all non-cash charges such as depletion and amortization as well as depreciation.

Income Before Taxes is the remaining income *after* deducting all costs, expenses, property charges, interest etc. but *before* deducting income taxes.

HOW TO USE THIS BOOK

Income Taxes includes the amount charged against earnings to provide for current and deferred income taxes.

Net Income consists of all revenues less all expenses (operating and non-operating), and is presented before preference and common dividends.

Average Shares Outstanding is the weighted average number of shares including common equivalent shares outstanding during the year, as reported by the corporation and fully adjusted for all stock dividends and splits. The use of *average shares* minimizes the distortion in *earnings per share* which could result from issuance of a large amount of stock or the company's purchase of a large amount of its own stock during the year.

Balance Sheet:

Current Assets includes the short-term assets expected to be realized or consumed within one year. Normally includes cash and cash equivalents, short term investments, receivables, prepayments and inventories.

Total Assets represents all of the assets of the company, including tangible and intangible, and current and non-current.

Current Liabilities are all of the obligations of the company normally expected to be paid within one year. Includes bank overdrafts, short-term debt, payables and accruals.

Long-Term Obligations are the total long-term debts (due beyond one year) reported by the company, including bonds, capital lease obligations, notes, mortgages, debentures, etc.

Total Liabilities represents all liabilities of the company, whether current or non-current.

Stockholders' Equity is the sum of all capital stock accounts – paid in capital (including additional premium), retained earnings, and all other capital balances.

Shares Outstanding is the number of shares outstanding as of the date of the company's quarterly/annual report, exclusive of treasury stock and adjusted for subsequent stock dividends and splits.

Statistical Record:

Return on Assets % represents the ratio of annualized net income (or for Mos, TTM net income) to average total assets. This ratio represents how effectively assets are being used to produce a profit.

Return on Equity % is the ratio of annualized net income (or for Mos, TTM net income) to average stockholders' equity, expressed as a percentage. This ratio illustrates how effectively the investment of the stockholders is being utilized to earn a profit.

EBITDA Margin % represents earnings before interest, taxes, depreciation and amortization as a percentage of total revenue.

Net Margin % is net income expressed as a percentage of total revenues.

Asset Turnover is annualized total revenue (or for Mos, TTM total revenue) divided by average total assets. A measure of efficiency of the use of assets.

Current Ratio represents current assets divided by current liabilities. The higher the figure the better the company is able to meet its current liabilities out of its current assets. A key measure of liquidity for industrial companies.

Debt to Equity is the ratio of long-term obligations to stockholders' equity.

Price Ranges are based on each Company's fiscal year. Where actual stock sales did not take place, a range of lowest bid and highest asked prices is shown.

Price/Earnings Ratio is shown as a range. The figures are calculated by dividing the stock's highest price for the year and its lowest price by the year's earnings per share. Growth stocks tend to command higher P/Es than cyclical stocks.

Average Yield % is the ratio of annual dividends to the real average of the prices over the fiscal year.

EDITOR'S NOTE: In order to preserve the historical relationships between prices, earnings and dividends, figures are not restated to reflect subsequent events. Figures are presented in U.S. dollars unless otherwise indicated.

K. ADDITIONAL INFORMATION on each stock includes the officers of the company, investor relations contact, address, telephone number, web site and transfer agents.

L. INSTITUTIONAL HOLDINGS indicates the number of investment companies, insurance companies, mutual funds, bank trust and college endowment funds holding the stock and the total number of shares held as last reported.

HOW TO USE THIS BOOK

OTHER DEFINITIONS

Factors Pertaining Especially to Utilities

Net Property, Plant & Equip is the cost of property, plant and equipment, less its accumulated depreciation.

PPE Turnover represents annualized total revenue (or for Mos, TTM total revenue) divided by average net property, plant and equipment.

Factors Pertaining Especially to Banks

Interest Income is all interest income, including income from loans and leases, securities and deposits.

Interest Expense is all interest expense, including from loans and leases, securities and deposits.

Net Interest Income is interest income less interest expense. This figure is presented before provision for losses.

Provision for Losses represents the amount charged against earnings to increase the provision made for losses on loans and leases.

Non-Interest Income is any income that is not interest-related. Such income could include trading revenue and gains on the sale of assets.

Non-Interest Expense is all expenses that are not interest-related, including employment costs, office costs, marketing costs, etc.

Net Loans & Leases includes all loans and leases net of provisions for losses. May include commercial, agricultural, real estate, consumer and foreign loans.

Total Deposits are all time and demand deposits entrusted to a bank.

Net Interest Margin % is net interest income before provisions expressed as a percentage of total interest income. A key measure of bank profitability.

Efficiency Ratio % is non-interest expense expressed as a percentage of total revenue.

Loans to Deposits are net loans and leases divided by total deposits. A key measure of bank liquidity.

Factors Pertaining Especially to Insurance Companies

Premium Income is the amount of insurance premiums received from policyholders. This is the primary revenue source for insurance companies.

Benefits and Claims represents the payments made to policyholders under the terms of insurance contracts.

Loss Ratio % is benefits and claims expressed as a percentage of premium income. A key ratio of insurance company profitability.

Factors Pertaining Especially to Real Estate Investment Trusts

Property Income is income from property rental and other associated activities.

Non-Property Income includes interest income and other income not from property activities.

HOW TO USE THIS BOOK

ABBREVIATIONS AND SYMBOLS

A..Annual
ASE................American Stock Exchange
()..Deficit
(Div. Reinv. Plan)..Dividend Rein. Plan offered
E...Extra
M......................................Monthly
N/A............................Not Applicable
N.M......................Not Meaningful
NYS...............New York Stock Exchange
OTC................Over-The-Counter Market
Q...............................Quarterly
S.................................Semi-Annual
Sp............................Special Dividend
U........................Frequency Unknown

ABBOTT LABORATORIES

Exchange	Symbol	Price	52Wk Range	Yield	P/E
NYS	ABT	$55.96 (5/29/2008)	60.50-50.03	2.57	22.84

*7 Year Price Score 92.36   *NYSE Composite Index=100   *12 Month Price Score 100.05

TRADING VOLUME (thousand shares)

Interim Earnings (Per Share)

Qtr.	Mar	Jun	Sep	Dec
2005	0.53	0.56	0.44	0.63
2006	0.56	0.40	0.46	(0.31)
2007	0.45	0.63	0.46	0.77
2008	0.60	...	...	...

Interim Dividends (Per Share)

Amt	Decl	Ex	Rec	Pay
0.325Q	09/14/2007	10/11/2007	10/15/2007	11/15/2007
0.325Q	12/14/2007	01/11/2008	01/15/2008	02/15/2008
0.36Q	02/15/2008	04/11/2008	04/15/2008	05/15/2008
0.36Q	06/06/2008	07/11/2008	07/15/2008	08/15/2008

Indicated Div: $1.44 (Div. Reinv. Plan)

Valuation Analysis

Forecast EPS $3.24 (05/17/2008)

Market Cap	$86.4 Billion	Book Value	18.0 Billion
Price/Book	4.80	Price/Sales	3.24

Dividend Achiever Status

10 Year Growth Rate	9.24%
Total Years of Dividend Growth	35

Business Summary: Pharmaceuticals (MIC: SIC: 2834 NAIC: 325412)

Abbott Laboratories is principally engaged in the discovery, development, manufacture and sale of a variety of health care products through four business segments: Pharmaceutical Products, Diagnostic Products, Nutritional Products, and Vascular Products. Co.'s primary products are prescription pharmaceuticals, nutritional products, vascular products and diagnostic testing products. In addition, Co. has a 50.0%-owned joint-venture, TAP Pharmaceutical Products Inc. with Takeda Pharmaceutical Company Ltd. of Japan, through which Co. develops, markets and sells pharmaceutical products such as Lupron®, Lupron Depot® and Prevacid® (lansoprazole), within the U.S., Puerto Rico and Canada.

Recent Developments: For the quarter ended Mar 31 2008, net income increased 34.5% to US$937.9 million from US$697.5 million in the year-earlier quarter. Revenues were US$6.77 billion, up 13.8% from US$5.95 billion the year before. Operating income was US$1.15 billion versus US$947.6 million in the prior-year quarter, an increase of 21.1%. Direct operating expenses rose 14.2% to US$2.96 billion from US$2.59 billion in the comparable period the year before. Indirect operating expenses increased 10.4% to US$2.66 billion from US$2.41 billion in the equivalent prior-year period.

Prospects: Co.'s near-term outlook appears constructive. For instance, on Apr 16 2008, Co. announced an approval from the Japanese Ministry of Health, Labour and Welfare for the use of HUMIRA® (adalimumab) to treat rheumatoid arthritis in patients with inadequate response to conventional therapy. Thus, Co. is targeting earnings for 2008 in the range of $3.20 to $3.25 per share, while earnings for the second quarter of 2008 are projected to range from $0.78 to $0.80 per share, both without specified items. Meanwhile, Co. intends to launch its XIENCE® V drug-eluting stent in the U.S. during the second quarter of 2008, given the product launch in Europe and other international markets in late 2006.

Financial Data

(US$ in Thousands)	3 Mos	12/31/2007	12/31/2006	12/31/2005	12/31/2004	12/31/2003	12/31/2002	12/31/2001
Earnings Per Share	2.45	2.31	1.12	2.16	2.06	1.75	1.78	0.99
Cash Flow Per Share	3.58	3.36	3.44	3.25	2.75	2.40	2.68	2.30
Tang Book Value Per Share	1.40	1.24	N.M.	2.89	2.22	2.90	1.93	1.14
Dividends Per Share	1.300	1.270	1.160	1.085	1.025	0.970	0.915	0.820
Dividend Payout %	52.99	54.98	103.57	50.23	49.76	55.43	51.40	82.83
Income Statement								
Total Revenue	6,765,603	25,914,238	22,476,322	22,337,808	19,680,016	19,680,561	17,684,663	16,285,246
EBITDA	1,705,758	6,673,069	3,839,982	5,763,713	5,563,387	5,154,531	5,055,978	3,285,925
Depn & Amortn	451,854	1,747,031	1,271,265	990,131	1,288,700	1,273,991	1,177,345	1,168,018
Income Before Taxes	1,160,726	4,469,648	2,276,370	4,619,920	4,125,600	3,734,417	3,673,413	1,883,148
Income Taxes	222,859	863,334	559,615	1,247,855	949,764	981,184	879,710	332,758
Net Income	937,867	3,606,314	1,716,755	3,372,065	3,235,851	2,753,233	2,793,703	1,550,390
Average Shares	1,560,567	1,560,057	1,536,724	1,564,103	1,570,611	1,571,869	1,573,293	1,565,963
Balance Sheet								
Current Assets	15,111,740	14,042,733	11,281,883	11,386,028	10,734,485	10,290,415	9,121,772	8,419,189
Total Assets	41,177,572	39,713,924	36,178,172	29,141,203	28,767,494	26,715,342	24,259,102	23,296,423
Current Liabilities	10,770,445	9,103,278	11,951,195	7,415,514	6,825,644	7,639,535	7,002,202	7,926,817
Long-Term Obligations	9,042,858	9,487,789	7,009,664	4,571,504	4,787,934	3,452,329	4,273,973	4,335,493
Total Liabilities	23,198,028	21,935,384	22,123,986	14,725,932	14,441,711	13,643,084	13,594,549	14,236,991
Stockholders' Equity	17,979,544	17,778,540	14,054,186	14,415,271	14,325,783	13,072,258	10,664,553	9,059,432
Shares Outstanding	1,543,296	1,549,910	1,537,243	1,539,234	1,560,023	1,564,517	1,563,068	1,554,530
Statistical Record								
Return on Assets %	9.90	9.50	5.26	11.65	11.63	10.80	11.75	8.04
Return on Equity %	23.75	22.66	12.06	23.47	23.56	23.20	28.33	17.59
EBITDA Margin %	25.21	25.75	17.08	25.80	28.27	26.19	28.59	20.18
Net Margin %	13.86	13.92	7.64	15.10	16.44	13.99	15.80	9.52
Asset Turnover	0.69	0.68	0.69	0.77	0.71	0.77	0.74	0.84
Current Ratio	1.40	1.54	0.94	1.54	1.57	1.35	1.30	1.06
Debt to Equity	0.50	0.53	0.50	0.32	0.33	0.26	0.40	0.48
Price Range	60.50-50.03	59.43-48.97	49.48-39.55	49.99-37.63	46.99-36.81	44.10-32.16	53.97-29.00	53.10-39.34
P/E Ratio	24.69-20.42	25.73-21.20	44.18-35.31	23.14-17.42	22.81-17.87	25.20-18.38	30.32-16.29	53.64-39.74
Average Yield %	2.36	2.33	2.58	2.39	2.47	2.51	2.13	1.75

Address: 100 Abbott Park Road, Abbott Park, IL 60064-6400	**Officers:** Miles D. White - Chairman, Chief Executive Officer Richard W. Ashley - Executive Vice President	**No of Institutions:** 1351
Telephone: 847-937-6100	**Transfer Agents:** Computershare, Providence, RI	**Shares:** 1,202,504,320 % **Held:** 66.97
Web Site: www.abbott.com		

1

ABM INDUSTRIES, INC.

Exchange	Symbol	Price	52Wk Range	Yield	P/E
NYS	ABM	$21.64 (5/29/2008)	30.43-18.82	2.31	24.59

*7 Year Price Score 90.87   *NYSE Composite Index=100   *12 Month Price Score 99.05

Interim Earnings (Per Share)

Qtr.	Jan	Apr	Jul	Oct
2004-05	0.16	0.20	0.72	0.07
2005-06	0.08	0.21	0.35	1.24
2006-07	0.18	0.33	0.23	0.30
2007-08	0.13	0.22	...	...

Interim Dividends (Per Share)

Amt	Decl	Ex	Rec	Pay
0.12Q	09/05/2007	10/09/2007	10/11/2007	11/05/2007
0.125Q	12/11/2007	01/08/2008	01/10/2008	02/04/2008
0.125Q	03/04/2008	04/08/2008	04/10/2008	05/05/2008
0.125Q	06/03/2008	07/01/2008	07/03/2008	08/04/2008

Indicated Div: $0.50

Valuation Analysis

Forecast EPS	$1.25 (05/16/2008)		
Market Cap	$1.1 Billion	Book Value	620.4 Million
Price/Book	1.76	Price/Sales	0.33

Dividend Achiever Status

10 Year Growth Rate	9.15%
Total Years of Dividend Growth	43

TRADING VOLUME (thousand shares)

Business Summary: Miscellaneous Business Services (MIC: SIC: 7349 NAIC: 561790)

ABM Industries and its subsidiaries provide janitorial, parking, security, engineering and lighting services for commercial, industrial, institutional and retail facilities in the U.S. and British Columbia, Canada. Co. conducts business through a number of subsidiaries, which are grouped into five segments based on the nature of its business operations. The operating subsidiaries within each segment generally report to the same senior management. Referred to collectively as the ABM Family of Services, as of Oct 31 2007, the five segments were: Janitorial, Parking, Security, Engineering, and Lighting.

Recent Developments: For the quarter ended Apr 30 2008, net income decreased 33.8% to US$11.1 million from US$16.7 million in the year-earlier quarter. Revenues were US$938.5 million, up 34.5% from US$697.9 million the year before. Operating income was US$23.7 million versus US$25.6 million in the prior-year quarter, a decrease of 7.3%. Direct operating expenses rose 34.6% to US$833.3 million from US$619.3 million in the comparable period the year before. Indirect operating expenses increased 53.9% to US$81.5 million from US$52.9 million in the equivalent prior-year period.

Prospects: For the fiscal year ending Oct 31 2008, Co. continues to anticipate earnings in the range of $1.00 to $1.15 per diluted share. Looking ahead, Co. remains focused on pursuing new business, increasing its operating efficiencies, and integrating the OneSource, Inc. business, which was acquired on Nov 14 2007. Meanwhile, Co. is in the process of relocating its Janitorial headquarters to Houston, emphasizing its other business units in Southern California and relocating its corporate headquarters to New York City. Accordingly, Co. expects to fully implement a new payroll and human resources information system as well as complete the improvement to its accounting systems by the end of 2009.

Financial Data

(US$ in Thousands)	6 Mos	3 Mos	10/31/2007	10/31/2006	10/31/2005	10/31/2004	10/31/2003	10/31/2002
Earnings Per Share	0.88	0.99	1.04	1.88	1.15	0.61	1.81	0.92
Cash Flow Per Share	2.06	1.30	1.10	2.66	0.76	0.69	1.23	2.26
Tang Book Value Per Share	0.24	N.M.	6.58	5.54	4.24	3.95	5.01	4.46
Dividends Per Share	0.490	0.485	0.480	0.440	0.420	0.400	0.380	0.360
Dividend Payout %	55.84	48.99	46.15	23.40	36.52	65.57	20.99	39.13
Income Statement								
Total Revenue	1,861,170	922,636	2,842,811	2,792,668	2,587,761	2,416,223	2,262,476	2,191,957
EBITDA	51,904	21,669	98,552	178,505	83,977	64,029	69,681	84,510
Depn & Amortn	12,839	6,336	18,765	20,764	19,591	17,667	14,829	15,182
Income Before Taxes	30,475	10,601	79,787	157,741	64,386	46,362	54,852	69,328
Income Taxes	13,039	4,237	27,347	64,536	20,832	15,889	18,454	22,600
Net Income	17,436	6,364	52,440	93,205	57,941	30,473	90,458	46,728
Average Shares	51,299	50,911	50,629	49,678	50,367	50,064	50,004	51,015
Balance Sheet								
Current Assets	686,120	680,508	642,890	631,741	521,453	486,088	500,648	437,785
Total Assets	1,622,114	1,628,332	1,120,673	1,016,274	903,710	842,524	795,983	704,939
Current Liabilities	389,347	386,163	289,744	319,285	275,074	254,428	256,691	227,090
Long-Term Obligations	301,500	316,000	...	...	...	...	...	...
Total Liabilities	1,001,693	1,021,860	514,915	475,027	427,784	400,363	351,947	318,269
Stockholders' Equity	620,421	606,472	605,758	541,247	475,926	442,161	444,036	386,670
Shares Outstanding	50,476	50,093	50,019	48,634	49,051	48,707	48,367	48,997
Statistical Record								
Return on Assets %	3.37	3.82	4.91	9.71	6.64	3.71	12.05	6.73
Return on Equity %	7.37	8.65	9.14	18.33	12.62	6.86	21.78	12.50
EBITDA Margin %	2.79	2.35	3.47	6.39	3.25	2.65	3.08	3.86
Net Margin %	0.94	0.69	1.84	3.34	2.24	1.26	4.00	2.13
Asset Turnover	2.51	2.34	2.66	2.91	2.96	2.94	3.01	3.16
Current Ratio	1.76	1.76	2.22	1.98	1.90	1.91	1.95	1.93
Debt to Equity	0.49	0.52	...	...	...	...	...	...
Price Range	30.43-18.82	30.43-18.82	30.43-19.59	21.65-16.22	22.39-17.99	20.87-15.25	16.44-12.72	19.43-13.05
P/E Ratio	34.58-21.39	30.74-19.01	29.26-18.84	11.52-8.63	19.47-15.64	34.21-25.00	9.08-7.03	21.12-14.18
Average Yield %	2.17	2.02	1.96	2.38	2.15	2.20	2.56	2.23

Address: 160 Pacific Avenue, Suite 222, San Francisco, CA 94111 Telephone: 415-733-4000 Web Site: www.abm.com	Officers: Maryellen C. Herringer - Chairman Henrik C. Slipsager - President, Chief Executive Officer Transfer Agents:Mellon Investor Services LLC, Jersey City, NJ	Investor Contact: 415-733-4000 No of Institutions: 165 Shares: 41,467,392 % Held: 76.93

AFLAC INC.

Exchange	Symbol	Price	52Wk Range	Yield	P/E
NYS	AFL	$67.45 (5/29/2008)	68.22-50.70	1.42	19.61

*7 Year Price Score 112.95 *NYSE Composite Index=100 *12 Month Price Score 114.21

TRADING VOLUME (thousand shares)

Interim Earnings (Per Share)

Qtr.	Mar	Jun	Sep	Dec
2005	0.64	0.66	0.90	0.72
2006	0.74	0.81	0.73	0.66
2007	0.84	0.84	0.85	0.78
2008	0.98	...	...	...

Interim Dividends (Per Share)

Amt	Decl	Ex	Rec	Pay
0.205Q	07/24/2007	08/15/2007	08/17/2007	09/04/2007
0.205Q	10/24/2007	11/14/2007	11/16/2007	12/03/2007
0.24Q	01/29/2008	02/15/2008	02/20/2008	03/03/2008
0.24Q	04/23/2008	05/19/2008	05/21/2008	06/02/2008

Indicated Div: $0.96 (Div. Reinv. Plan)

Valuation Analysis

Forecast EPS	$4.03 (05/17/2008)
Market Cap	$32.0 Billion	Book Value	8.1 Billion
Price/Book	3.94	Price/Sales	2.02

Dividend Achiever Status

10 Year Growth Rate	21.81%
Total Years of Dividend Growth	25

Business Summary: Insurance (MIC: SIC: 6321 NAIC: 524114)

AFLAC is a holding company that sells supplemental health and life insurance. At Dec 31 2007, Co.'s insurance operations were conducted via American Family Life Assurance Co. of Columbus, which operated in the U.S. (Aflac U.S.) and as a branch in Japan (Aflac Japan). Co.'s Aflac U.S. sells supplemental and life insurance products, including accident/disability, cancer expense, short-term disability, sickness and hospital indemnity, hospital intensive care, fixed-benefit dental, vision care and long-term care plans.. Co.'s Aflac Japan sells cancer, care, living benefit life, ordinary life insurance and general medical indemnity plans as well as medical/sickness riders and annuities.

Recent Developments: For the quarter ended Mar 31 2008, net income increased 13.9% to US$474.0 million from US$416.0 million in the year-earlier quarter. Revenues were US$4.27 billion, up 13.8% from US$3.75 billion the year before. Net premiums earned were US$3.64 billion versus US$3.16 billion in the prior-year quarter, an increase of 15.2%. Net investment income rose 10.8% to US$627.0 million from US$566.0 million a year ago.

Prospects: Despite the challenging economic conditions, Co.'s near-term outlook appears promising. For full year 2008, Co. now anticipates operating earnings growth in the range of 14.0% to 15.0%, or $3.73 to $3.76 per diluted share, excluding the effects of foreign currency translation. In addition, Co. remains optimistic in generating annual sales growth of 3.0% to 7.0% at its Japan segment, driven by the potential of its two new distribution channels. Further, Co. expects to attain an 8.0% to 12.0% increase in new annualized premium sales from its U.S. segment. Meanwhile, for the second quarter of 2008, Co. foresees operating earnings to be in the range of $1.00 to $1.02 per diluted share.

Financial Data

(US$ in Thousands)	3 Mos	12/31/2007	12/31/2006	12/31/2005	12/31/2004	12/31/2003	12/31/2002	12/31/2001
Earnings Per Share	3.44	3.31	2.95	2.92	2.52	1.52	1.55	1.28
Cash Flow Per Share	9.75	9.54	8.87	8.85	8.82	6.60	5.87	5.43
Tang Book Value Per Share	17.12	18.08	16.93	15.89	15.04	13.03	12.43	10.40
Dividends Per Share	0.855	0.800	0.550	0.440	0.380	0.300	0.230	0.193
Dividend Payout %	24.85	24.17	18.64	15.07	15.08	19.74	14.84	15.04
Income Statement								
Premium Income	3,635,000	12,973,000	12,314,000	11,990,000	11,302,000	9,921,000	8,595,000	8,061,000
Total Revenue	4,267,000	15,393,000	14,616,000	14,363,000	13,281,000	11,447,000	10,257,000	9,598,000
Benefits & Claims	2,538,000	9,285,000	9,016,000	8,890,000	8,482,000	7,529,000	6,589,000	6,303,000
Income Before Taxes	726,000	2,499,000	2,264,000	2,226,000	1,807,000	1,225,000	1,259,000	1,081,000
Income Taxes	252,000	865,000	781,000	743,000	508,000	430,000	438,000	394,000
Net Income	474,000	1,634,000	1,483,000	1,483,000	1,299,000	795,000	821,000	687,000
Average Shares	484,417	493,971	501,827	507,704	516,421	522,138	528,326	537,380
Balance Sheet								
Total Assets	72,269,000	65,805,000	59,805,000	56,361,000	59,326,000	50,964,000	45,058,000	37,860,000
Total Liabilities	64,135,000	57,010,000	51,464,000	48,434,000	51,753,000	44,318,000	38,664,000	32,435,000
Stockholders' Equity	8,134,000	8,795,000	8,341,000	7,927,000	7,573,000	6,646,000	6,394,000	5,425,000
Shares Outstanding	475,091	486,530	492,550	498,894	503,608	509,892	514,439	521,615
Statistical Record								
Return on Assets %	2.53	2.60	2.55	2.56	2.35	1.66	1.98	1.83
Return on Equity %	20.30	19.07	18.23	19.14	18.22	12.19	13.89	13.58
Loss Ratio %	69.82	71.57	73.22	74.15	75.05	75.89	76.66	78.19
Net Margin %	11.11	10.62	10.15	10.33	9.78	6.95	8.00	7.16
Price Range	65.55-47.34	62.90-45.64	49.30-42.46	49.60-35.70	42.23-34.95	36.67-30.08	33.17-23.12	34.83-23.01
P/E Ratio	19.06-13.76	19.00-13.79	16.71-14.39	16.99-12.23	16.76-13.87	24.13-19.79	21.40-14.92	27.21-17.98
Average Yield %	1.50	1.50	1.20	1.03	0.96	0.92	0.78	0.67

Address: 1932 Wynnton Road, Columbus, GA 31999 **Telephone:** 706-323-3431 **Web Site:** www.aflac.com	**Officers:** Daniel P. Amos - Chairman, Chief Executive Officer Kriss Cloninger - President, Chief Financial Officer, Treasurer **Transfer Agents:** AFLAC Incorporated, Columbus, GA	**Investor Contact:** 706-596-3264 **No of Institutions:** 827 **Shares:** 337,046,880 **% Held:** 63.66

3

AIR PRODUCTS & CHEMICALS, INC.

Exchange	Symbol	Price	52Wk Range	Yield	P/E
NYS	APD	$101.17 (5/29/2008)	103.08-77.30	1.74	19.46

*7 Year Price Score 120.26 *NYSE Composite Index=100 *12 Month Price Score 109.64

Interim Earnings (Per Share)

Qtr.	Dec	Mar	Jun	Sep
2004-05	0.72	0.75	0.82	0.79
2005-06	0.80	0.89	0.92	0.57
2006-07	1.03	1.02	1.28	1.31
2007-08	1.19	1.43	...	...

Interim Dividends (Per Share)

Amt	Decl	Ex	Rec	Pay
0.38Q	09/20/2007	09/27/2007	10/01/2007	11/12/2007
0.38Q	11/15/2007	12/28/2007	01/02/2008	02/11/2008
0.44Q	03/20/2008	03/28/2008	04/01/2008	05/12/2008
0.44Q	05/15/2008	06/27/2008	07/01/2008	08/11/2008

Indicated Div: $1.76 (Div. Reinv. Plan)

Valuation Analysis

Forecast EPS $5.04 (05/16/2008)
Market Cap $25.2 Billion Book Value 5.5 Billion
Price/Book 4.57 Price/Sales 2.48

Dividend Achiever Status

10 Year Growth Rate 9.92%
Total Years of Dividend Growth 25

TRADING VOLUME (thousand shares)

Business Summary: Chemicals (MIC: SIC: 2813 NAIC: 325120)

Air Products and Chemicals serves technology, energy, industrial and healthcare customers globally with a portfolio of products and services that include atmospheric gases, process and specialty gases, performance materials, equipment and services. Co. is a supplier of hydrogen and helium to growth markets such as semiconductor materials, refinery hydrogen, natural gas liquefaction, home healthcare and enhanced coatings and adhesives. As of Sep 30 2007, Co. served in over 40 countries internationally and operated through six business segments: Merchant Gases; Tonnage Gases; Electronics and Performance Materials; Equipment and Energy; Healthcare; and Chemicals.

Recent Developments: For the quarter ended Mar 31 2008, income from continuing operations increased 16.7% to US$253.1 million from US$216.8 million in the year-earlier quarter. Net income increased 38.1% to US$314.3 million from US$227.6 million in the year-earlier quarter. Revenues were US$2.61 billion, up 13.4% from US$2.30 billion the year before. Operating income was US$338.2 million versus US$308.6 million in the prior-year quarter, an increase of 9.6%. Direct operating expenses rose 13.6% to US$1.90 billion from US$1.68 billion in the comparable period the year before. Indirect operating expenses increased 15.9% to US$363.3 million from US$313.5 million in the equivalent prior-year period.

Prospects: For the fiscal year ending Sep 30 2008, Co. now anticipates domestic and global manufacturing growth to be about 2.0% and 3.0%, respectively. Thus, Co. is forecasting earnings in fiscal 2008 to be about $5.05 per share, while earnings for the third fiscal quarter of 2008 to range from 1.25 to $1.30 per share. Meanwhile, Co. expects volumes at its Merchant Gases segment to improve, driven by new applications and improved loading, while its Tonnage Gases segment is estimated to benefit from new plants brought on-stream. Lastly, Co. expects results at its Electronics and Performance Materials segment to improve from higher volumes and the benefits of product rationalization initiatives.

Financial Data
(US$ in Thousands)

	6 Mos	3 Mos	09/30/2007	09/30/2006	09/30/2005	09/30/2004	09/30/2003	09/30/2002
Earnings Per Share	5.20	4.80	4.64	3.18	3.08	2.64	1.78	2.36
Cash Flow Per Share	8.15	7.86	6.86	5.96	6.10	4.84	4.72	4.90
Tang Book Value Per Share	15.79	19.04	18.53	17.44	16.03	15.45	12.99	13.33
Dividends Per Share	1.580	1.520	1.480	1.340	1.250	1.040	0.880	0.820
Dividend Payout %	30.41	31.67	31.90	42.14	40.58	39.39	49.44	34.75
Income Statement								
Total Revenue	5,078,900	2,473,600	10,037,800	8,850,400	8,143,500	7,411,400	6,297,300	5,401,200
EBITDA	1,220,000	615,300	2,370,900	1,930,300	1,834,900	1,687,300	1,354,000	1,495,400
Depn & Amortn	442,100	218,000	831,400	761,700	727,000	714,900	665,100	588,600
Income Before Taxes	697,800	356,300	1,376,300	1,049,300	997,700	851,400	565,400	784,500
Income Taxes	177,100	93,200	301,200	271,200	263,300	226,600	147,200	240,800
Net Income	578,000	263,700	1,035,600	723,400	711,700	604,100	397,300	525,400
Average Shares	219,200	222,300	223,200	227,500	231,400	228,900	223,600	222,700
Balance Sheet								
Current Assets	2,991,500	2,863,800	2,858,400	2,612,600	2,414,700	2,416,900	2,067,900	1,909,300
Total Assets	13,228,400	13,014,300	12,659,500	11,180,700	10,408,800	10,040,400	9,431,900	8,495,000
Current Liabilities	2,453,700	2,224,600	2,422,700	2,323,400	1,943,200	1,705,600	1,581,200	1,256,200
Long-Term Obligations	3,646,400	3,415,600	2,976,500	2,280,200	2,052,900	2,113,600	2,168,600	2,041,000
Total Liabilities	7,586,700	7,227,800	6,986,600	6,078,700	5,652,200	5,427,500	5,461,300	4,850,200
Stockholders' Equity	5,524,300	5,603,000	5,495,600	4,924,000	4,575,500	4,444,000	3,782,500	3,460,400
Shares Outstanding	249,455	214,448	215,355	217,250	221,898	227,301	227,265	227,219
Statistical Record								
Return on Assets %	9.18	8.72	8.69	6.70	6.96	6.19	4.43	6.34
Return on Equity %	21.34	19.95	19.88	15.23	15.78	14.65	10.97	16.00
EBITDA Margin %	24.02	24.87	23.62	21.81	22.53	22.77	21.50	27.69
Net Margin %	11.38	10.66	10.32	8.17	8.74	8.15	6.31	9.73
Asset Turnover	0.81	0.82	0.84	0.82	0.80	0.76	0.70	0.65
Current Ratio	1.22	1.29	1.18	1.12	1.24	1.42	1.31	1.52
Debt to Equity	0.66	0.61	0.54	0.46	0.45	0.48	0.57	0.59
Price Range	103.08-73.69	103.08-69.11	97.82-66.69	69.23-53.33	65.14-52.31	55.00-44.50	48.64-37.49	53.05-36.82
P/E Ratio	19.82-14.17	21.48-14.40	21.08-14.37	21.77-16.77	21.15-16.98	20.83-16.86	27.33-21.06	22.48-15.60
Average Yield %	1.78	1.80	1.91	2.14	2.13	2.07	2.04	1.77

Address: 7201 Hamilton Boulevard, Allentown, PA 18195-1501	Officers: John E. McGlade - Chairman, Chief Executive Officer, President Paul E. Huck - Vice President, Chief Financial Officer **Transfer Agents:** American Stock Transfer and Trust Company, New York, NY	No of Institutions: 731
Telephone: 610-481-4911		Shares: 198,461,728 % Held: 81.66
Web Site: www.airproducts.com		

ALBEMARLE CORP.

Exchange	Symbol	Price	52Wk Range	Yield	P/E
NYS	ALB	$44.40 (5/29/2008)	47.76-33.82	1.08	18.27

*7 Year Price Score 143.85 *NYSE Composite Index=100   ***12 Month Price Score 99.63**

Interim Earnings (Per Share)

Qtr.	Mar	Jun	Sep	Dec
2005	0.26	0.34	0.28	0.34
2006	0.35	0.45	0.03	0.65
2007	0.60	0.55	0.61	0.60
2008	0.68	...	...	...

Interim Dividends (Per Share)

Amt	Decl	Ex	Rec	Pay
0.105Q	06/20/2007	09/12/2007	09/15/2007	10/01/2007
0.105Q	10/26/2007	12/12/2007	12/15/2007	01/01/2008
0.12Q	02/27/2008	03/12/2008	03/15/2008	04/01/2008
0.12Q	05/29/2008	06/11/2008	06/15/2008	07/01/2008

Indicated Div: $0.48

Valuation Analysis

Forecast EPS $2.75 (05/17/2008)

Market Cap	$4.1 Billion	Book Value	1.2 Billion
Price/Book	3.25	Price/Sales	1.69

Dividend Achiever Status

10 Year Growth Rate	10.44%
Total Years of Dividend Growth	13

TRADING VOLUME (thousand shares)

Business Summary: Chemicals (MIC: SIC: 2821 NAIC: 325211)

Albemarle is a global producer of engineered specialty chemicals. Co.'s Polymer Additives segment consists of brominated, mineral and phosphorus flame retardants and other polymer additives such as curatives, antioxidants and stabilizers. The Catalysts segment includes refinery catalysts to reduce sulphur and other impurities from petroleum products and for cracking petroleum into higher-value products, such as fuels and petrochemical feedstock; and polyolefin catalysts used as co-catalysts in the production of polyolefins. The Fine Chemicals segment produces performance chemicals; pharmachemicals; agrichemicals; and provides fine chemistry services and intermediates.

Recent Developments: For the quarter ended Mar 31 2008, net income increased 8.9% to US$63.3 million from US$58.1 million in the year-earlier quarter. Revenues were US$668.2 million, up 13.4% from US$589.2 million the year before. Operating income was US$83.8 million versus US$81.6 million in the prior-year quarter, an increase of 2.7%. Direct operating expenses rose 16.6% to US$500.8 million from US$429.4 million in the comparable period the year before. Indirect operating expenses increased 6.9% to US$83.6 million from US$78.2 million in the equivalent prior-year period.

Prospects: Looking ahead, Co. expects growth in its Polymer Additives segment to come from higher demand for electrical and electronic equipment, new construction and stringent fire-safety regulations globally. In addition, Co. foresees profit growth in its Catalysts segment to derive from new product introductions, market expansions, Federal Communications Commission pricing improvements, and developments in its polyolefin catalysts business. Meanwhile, Co. is increasing its presence in China with expansions that should grow flame retardants, antioxidants and fine chemicals in 2008. Lastly, Co. anticipates demand for its products to remain strong for 2008 and 2009, assuming no global recession.

Financial Data
(US$ in Thousands)

	3 Mos	12/31/2007	12/31/2006	12/31/2005	12/31/2004	12/31/2003	12/31/2002	12/31/2001
Earnings Per Share	2.43	2.36	1.47	1.21	0.65	0.85	0.86	0.73
Cash Flow Per Share	2.75	2.55	3.98	1.82	2.30	1.82	1.72	1.57
Tang Book Value Per Share	8.63	8.83	6.59	5.73	3.67	6.29	6.41	6.17
Dividends Per Share	0.435	0.420	0.345	0.310	0.292	0.282	0.270	0.260
Dividend Payout %	17.87	17.80	23.47	25.73	45.35	33.04	31.21	35.37
Income Statement								
Total Revenue	668,177	2,336,187	2,368,506	2,107,499	1,513,737	1,110,237	980,215	916,899
EBITDA	113,202	423,006	290,300	282,844	186,462	177,445	189,486	180,342
Depn & Amortn	26,542	106,855	112,950	117,435	97,268	84,014	80,603	77,610
Income Before Taxes	76,444	277,819	133,386	123,438	71,844	88,055	103,813	97,196
Income Taxes	16,626	55,078	2,192	27,593	17,005	13,890	29,068	29,029
Net Income	63,261	229,690	142,969	114,867	54,839	71,945	74,745	68,167
Average Shares	93,688	97,216	97,136	95,496	85,054	84,292	86,274	93,048
Balance Sheet								
Current Assets	1,143,447	1,053,438	960,854	873,663	747,410	481,369	413,064	383,661
Total Assets	2,975,395	2,830,450	2,530,368	2,547,243	2,442,745	1,387,291	1,192,956	1,129,475
Current Liabilities	408,638	402,917	482,949	421,917	373,746	210,071	165,007	303,837
Long-Term Obligations	861,065	707,311	681,859	775,869	899,584	228,389	180,137	12,353
Total Liabilities	1,726,075	1,552,145	1,502,270	1,616,968	1,731,370	751,070	623,216	536,173
Stockholders' Equity	1,249,320	1,278,305	1,028,098	930,275	711,375	636,221	569,740	593,302
Shares Outstanding	91,446	94,734	94,860	93,499	83,796	82,306	83,384	90,996
Statistical Record								
Return on Assets %	8.39	8.57	5.63	4.60	2.86	5.58	6.44	6.46
Return on Equity %	20.08	19.92	14.60	13.99	8.12	11.93	12.85	11.83
EBITDA Margin %	16.94	18.11	12.26	13.42	12.32	15.98	19.33	19.67
Net Margin %	9.47	9.83	6.04	5.45	3.62	6.48	7.63	7.43
Asset Turnover	0.86	0.87	0.93	0.84	0.79	0.86	0.84	0.87
Current Ratio	2.80	2.61	1.99	2.07	2.00	2.29	2.50	1.26
Debt to Equity	0.69	0.55	0.66	0.83	1.26	0.36	0.32	0.02
Price Range	47.76-33.82	47.76-35.02	36.65-19.41	19.45-16.23	20.16-13.68	15.22-11.14	16.45-11.20	12.53-8.68
P/E Ratio	19.65-13.92	20.24-14.84	24.93-13.21	16.08-13.41	31.02-21.04	17.91-13.11	19.12-13.02	17.16-11.88
Average Yield %	1.07	1.02	1.34	1.70	1.83	2.09	1.92	2.36

Address: 330 South Fourth Street, P.O. Box 1335, Richmond, VA 23219 **Telephone:** 804-788-6000 **Web Site:** www.albemarle.com	**Officers:** Mark C. Rohr - Chairman, President, Chief Executive Officer William M. Gottwald - Vice-Chairman **Transfer Agents:** National City Bank, Cleveland, OH	**Investor Contact:** 804-788-6096 **No of Institutions:** 304 **Shares:** 69,316,896 **% Held:** 68.68

ALEXANDRIA REAL ESTATE EQUITIES, INC.

Exchange	Symbol	Price	52Wk Range	Yield	P/E
NYS	ARE	$105.23 (5/29/2008)	107.04-86.13	2.96	32.99

*7 Year Price Score 109.23 *NYSE Composite Index=100 *12 Month Price Score 108.12

TRADING VOLUME (thousand shares)

Interim Earnings (Per Share)

Qtr.	Mar	Jun	Sep	Dec
2005	0.55	0.58	0.56	0.53
2006	0.56	0.57	0.56	0.57
2007	0.52	0.73	0.68	0.70
2008	1.09	...	...	...

Interim Dividends (Per Share)

Amt	Decl	Ex	Rec	Pay
0.76Q	06/18/2007	06/28/2007	07/02/2007	07/13/2007
0.76Q	09/19/2007	09/27/2007	10/01/2007	10/15/2007
0.78Q	12/13/2007	12/28/2007	01/02/2008	01/15/2008
0.78Q	03/20/2008	03/28/2008	04/01/2008	04/15/2008
		Indicated Div: $3.12		

Valuation Analysis

Forecast EPS	$2.64 (05/17/2008)		
Market Cap	$3.4 Billion	Book Value	1.7 Billion
Price/Book	2.00	Price/Sales	8.10

Dividend Achiever Status

10 Year Growth Rate	18.98%
Total Years of Dividend Growth	10

Business Summary: "Property, Real Estate & Development" (MIC: SIC: 6798 NAIC: 525930)

Alexandria Real Estate Equities is a real estate investment trust. Co. is engaged primarily in the ownership, operation, management, redevelopment, development and acquisition of properties for the life sciences industry. Co.'s properties are designed for lease primarily to institutional, pharmaceutical, biotechnology, medical device, life science product, service, biodefense and translational research entities, as well as governmental agencies. As of Dec 31 2007, Co. had 166 properties (162 properties located in 10 states in the U.S. and four properties located in Canada) with approximately 12.1 million rentable square feet of office/laboratory space.

Recent Developments: For the quarter ended Mar 31 2008, income from continuing operations increased 13.7% to US$22.0 million from US$19.3 million in the year-earlier quarter. Net income increased 73.0% to US$37.7 million from US$21.8 million in the year-earlier quarter. Revenues were US$110.0 million, up 16.0% from US$94.8 million the year before. Revenues from property income rose 17.2% to US$106.7 million from US$91.0 million in the corresponding quarter a year earlier.

Prospects: Co. continues to seek to achieve growth primarily from internal growth through development and redevelopment. For instance, at Mar 31 2008, Co. had 29,660 square feet under redevelopment at its California, San Diego market expected to be in service in 2008, and had two buildings under construction with total rentable square feet of 162,000 at its California market expected to be in service in 2009. In addition, Co. has two buildings under construction with total rentable square feet of 280,000 in China, which is expected to be in service in 2009. Meanwhile, for 2008, Co. expects earnings per diluted share of $3.00 and fund from operation of $5.86 per diluted share.

Financial Data

(US$ in Thousands)	3 Mos	12/31/2007	12/31/2006	12/31/2005	12/31/2004	12/31/2003	12/31/2002	12/31/2001
Earnings Per Share	3.19	2.63	2.25	2.22	2.33	3.10	2.24	1.64
Cash Flow Per Share	5.65	6.25	5.11	5.76	3.50	3.94	3.81	3.78
Tang Book Value Per Share	41.84	43.48	40.14	28.64	22.12	21.34	20.54	17.98
Dividends Per Share	3.080	3.040	2.860	2.720	2.520	2.200	2.000	1.840
Dividend Payout %	96.55	115.59	127.11	122.52	108.15	70.97	89.29	112.20
Income Statement								
Property Income	106,709	390,492	304,969	239,286	179,743	158,490	143,062	124,522
Non-Property Income	3,250	14,868	11,852	4,798	3,541	2,068	1,610	3,268
Total Revenue	109,959	405,360	316,821	244,084	183,284	160,558	144,672	127,790
Depn & Amortn	25,630	95,272	77,680	60,993	44,736	40,744	36,090	31,510
Interest Expense	22,245	88,387	71,371	49,116	28,670	26,416	24,984	29,126
Net Income	37,688	93,724	73,416	63,433	60,195	59,643	40,032	30,277
Average Shares	31,801	30,004	25,524	21,316	19,658	19,247	17,859	16,208
Balance Sheet								
Total Assets	4,685,045	4,642,094	3,617,477	2,362,450	1,872,284	1,272,577	1,159,243	962,146
Long-Term Obligations	2,625,852	2,787,904	2,024,866	1,406,666	1,186,946	709,007	614,878	573,161
Total Liabilities	2,918,474	3,062,768	2,208,348	1,512,535	1,251,811	765,442	673,390	629,508
Stockholders' Equity	1,691,714	1,503,820	1,351,652	829,800	620,473	507,135	485,853	332,638
Shares Outstanding	32,080	31,603	29,012	22,441	19,594	19,264	18,973	16,354
Statistical Record								
Return on Assets %	2.60	2.27	2.46	3.00	3.82	4.91	3.77	3.47
Return on Equity %	7.33	6.56	6.73	8.75	10.65	12.01	9.78	9.29
Net Margin %	34.27	23.12	23.17	25.99	32.84	37.15	27.67	23.69
Price Range	111.54-86.13	113.41-86.13	104.79-82.36	85.70-62.87	74.90-51.65	58.90-39.95	49.34-38.50	41.93-35.54
P/E Ratio	34.97-27.00	43.12-32.75	46.57-36.60	38.60-28.32	32.15-22.17	19.00-12.89	22.03-17.19	25.57-21.67
Average Yield %	3.12	3.03	3.08	3.63	4.05	4.74	4.55	4.79

Address: 135 North Los Robles Avenue, Suite 250, Pasadena, CA 91101 Telephone: 626-578-0777 Web Site: www.labspace.com	Officers: Jerry M. Sudarsky - Chairman James H. Richardson - President **Transfer Agents:** American Stock Transfer & Trust Company	No of Institutions: 234 Shares: 41,012,852 % Held: 122.79

ALLSTATE CORP.

Exchange	Symbol	Price	52Wk Range	Yield	P/E
NYS	ALL	$51.23 (5/29/2008)	62.17-45.72	3.20	8.61

*7 Year Price Score 85.83   *NYSE Composite Index=100   *12 Month Price Score 96.91

TRADING VOLUME (thousand shares)

Interim Earnings (Per Share)

Qtr.	Mar	Jun	Sep	Dec
2005	1.64	1.71	(2.36)	1.56
2006	2.19	1.89	1.83	1.93
2007	2.41	2.30	1.70	1.36
2008	0.62	...	...	...

Interim Dividends (Per Share)

Amt	Decl	Ex	Rec	Pay
0.38Q	07/17/2007	08/29/2007	08/31/2007	10/01/2007
0.38Q	11/13/2007	11/28/2007	11/30/2007	01/02/2008
0.41Q	02/26/2008	03/12/2008	03/14/2008	04/01/2008
0.41Q	05/21/2008	05/28/2008	05/30/2008	07/01/2008

Indicated Div: $1.64 (Div. Reinv. Plan)

Valuation Analysis

Forecast EPS $5.67 (05/17/2008)

Market Cap	$28.4 Billion	Book Value	20.3 Billion
Price/Book	1.40	Price/Sales	0.80

Dividend Achiever Status

10 Year Growth Rate	15.26%
Total Years of Dividend Growth	14

Business Summary: Insurance (MIC: SIC: 6331 NAIC: 524126)

Allstate is a holding company. Co. is engaged in the property-liability insurance, life insurance, retirement and investment product business. Co.'s primary business is the sale of private passenger auto and homeowner's insurance. Co. also sells several other personal property and casualty insurance products, life insurance, annuities, funding agreements, and select commercial property and casualty coverages. Co.'s business is conducted principally through Allstate Insurance Co., Allstate Life Insurance Co. as well as their affiliates, and its products are primarily distributed through exclusive agencies, financial specialists and independent agencies.

Recent Developments: For the quarter ended Mar 31 2008, net income decreased 76.7% to US$348.0 million from US$1.50 billion in the year-earlier quarter. Revenues were US$8.09 billion, down 13.3% from US$9.33 billion the year before. Net premiums earned were US$7.22 billion versus US$7.29 billion in the prior-year quarter, a decrease of 1.0%. Net investment income fell 2.9% to US$1.53 billion from US$1.57 billion a year ago.

Prospects: Co. continues to see growth in its Allstate brand standard auto premiums written due to increases in average premium. However, Co. is seeing a decline in homeowners premiums written due to increases in ceded reinsurance premiums and a decline in policies in force (PIF). Notably, Co. believes that PIF and renewal ratio should continue to be adversely affected by its catastrophe management actions, such as its decision to discontinue providing coverage by Allstate Floridian Insurance Co. and its subsidiaries on several property policies as part of a renewal rights and reinsurance arrangement with Royal Palm Insurance Co. entered into in 2006 and 2007.

Financial Data
(US$ in Millions)

	3 Mos	12/31/2007	12/31/2006	12/31/2005	12/31/2004	12/31/2003	12/31/2002	12/31/2001
Earnings Per Share	5.95	7.77	7.84	2.64	4.54	3.83	1.60	1.60
Cash Flow Per Share	8.97	9.17	7.99	8.47	7.84	8.09	6.26	3.18
Tang Book Value Per Share	35.16	37.35	33.80	29.97	30.74	27.89	23.52	22.35
Dividends Per Share	1.550	1.520	1.400	1.280	1.120	0.930	0.840	0.760
Dividend Payout %	26.03	19.56	17.86	48.48	24.67	24.28	52.50	47.50
Income Statement								
Premium Income	7,216	29,099	29,333	29,088	28,061	26,981	25,654	24,427
Total Revenue	8,087	36,769	35,796	35,383	33,936	32,149	29,579	28,865
Benefits & Claims	5,073	19,256	17,587	22,790	19,461	19,283	19,427	19,203
Income Before Taxes	427	6,653	7,178	2,088	4,586	3,571	1,540	1,285
Income Taxes	79	2,017	2,185	323	1,230	846	65	73
Net Income	348	4,636	4,993	1,765	3,181	2,705	1,134	1,158
Average Shares	561	596	637	667	700	706	709	723
Balance Sheet								
Total Assets	152,210	156,408	157,554	156,072	149,725	134,142	117,426	109,175
Total Liabilities	131,907	134,557	135,708	135,886	127,902	113,577	99,788	91,779
Stockholders' Equity	20,303	21,851	21,846	20,186	21,823	20,565	17,438	17,196
Shares Outstanding	554	563	622	646	683	704	702	712
Statistical Record								
Return on Assets %	2.22	2.95	3.18	1.15	2.24	2.15	1.00	1.08
Return on Equity %	16.23	21.22	23.76	8.40	14.97	14.24	6.55	6.68
Loss Ratio %	70.30	66.17	59.96	78.35	69.35	71.47	75.73	78.61
Net Margin %	4.30	12.61	13.95	4.99	9.37	8.41	3.83	4.01
Price Range	63.47-45.72	65.36-49.22	65.92-50.42	62.33-49.67	51.76-42.71	43.03-30.68	41.32-31.56	45.21-31.02
P/E Ratio	10.67-7.68	8.41-6.33	8.41-6.43	23.61-18.81	11.40-9.41	11.23-8.01	25.82-19.72	28.26-19.39
Average Yield %	2.82	2.61	2.44	2.30	2.39	2.52	2.27	2.01

Address: 2775 Sanders Road, Northbrook, IL 60062-6127 **Telephone:** 800-574-3553 **Web Site:** www.allstate.com	**Officers:** Thomas J. Wilson - Chairman, President, Chief Executive Officer Michele Coleman Mayes - Vice President, General Counsel **Transfer Agents:** Wells Fargo Bank, N.A., Shareowner Services, St. Paul, MN	**Investor Contact:** 800-416-8803 **No of Institutions:** 837 **Shares:** 406,441,024 % **Held:** 66.30

ALTRIA GROUP INC

Exchange	Symbol	Price	52Wk Range	Yield	P/E
NYS	MO	$22.45 (5/29/2008)	24.43-20.00	5.17	5.02

*7 Year Price Score 115.93 *NYSE Composite Index=100* ***12 Month Price Score 99.02**

Interim Earnings (Per Share)

Qtr.	Mar	Jun	Sep	Dec
2005	1.25	1.28	1.38	1.09
2006	1.65	1.29	1.36	1.40
2007	1.30	1.05	1.24	1.03
2008	1.16	...	...	...

Interim Dividends (Per Share)

Amt	Decl	Ex	Rec	Pay
0.75Q	12/12/2007	12/21/2007	12/26/2007	01/10/2008
0.00Q	01/30/2008	03/31/2008	03/19/2008	03/28/2008
0.75Q	02/27/2008	03/17/2008	03/19/2008	04/10/2008
0.29Q	05/28/2008	06/11/2008	06/13/2008	07/10/2008

Indicated Div: $1.16 (Div. Reinv. Plan)

Valuation Analysis

Forecast EPS	$1.67 (05/17/2008)		
Market Cap	$47.3 Billion	Book Value	4.7 Billion
Price/Book	10.06	Price/Sales	0.78

Dividend Achiever Status

10 Year Growth Rate	8.19%
Total Years of Dividend Growth	42

TRADING VOLUME (thousand shares)

Business Summary: Tobacco Products (MIC: SIC: 2111 NAIC: 312221)

Altria Group is a holding company. Co., via its wholly owned subsidiaries, Philip Morris USA Inc., Philip Morris International Inc., and John Middleton, Inc., are engaged in the manufacture and sale of cigarettes and other tobacco products. Philip Morris Capital Corporation, another wholly owned subsidiary of Co., maintains a portfolio of controlled and direct finance leases. At Dec 31 2007, Co. held a 28.6% economic and voting interest in SABMiller Plc., which is engaged in the manufacture and sale of various beer products. As of Dec 31 2007, Co.'s reportable segments were U.S. tobacco; European Union; Eastern Europe, Middle East and Africa; Asia; Latin America; and Financial Services.

Recent Developments: For the quarter ended Mar 31 2008, income from continuing operations decreased 11.8% to US$614.0 million from US$696.0 million in the year-earlier quarter. Net income decreased 10.8% to US$2.45 billion from US$2.75 billion in the year-earlier quarter. Revenues were US$4.41 billion, up 2.8% from US$4.29 billion the year before. Operating income was US$1.21 billion versus US$1.12 billion in the prior-year quarter, an increase of 8.4%. Direct operating expenses rose 4.1% to US$2.69 billion from US$2.59 billion in the comparable period the year before. Indirect operating expenses decreased 13.3% to US$504.0 million from US$581.0 million in the equivalent prior-year period.

Prospects: Co. continues to progress with its manufacturing optimization program. In detail, given the declining U.S. cigarette volume, Co. plans to close its Cabarrus, NC manufacturing facility by end of 2010 and consolidate manufacturing for the U.S. market at its Richmond, VA manufacturing center. Co. expects the program to generate annual pre-tax cost savings of $156.0 million by 2011. Meanwhile, Co. completed the spin-off of its interest in Philip Morris International Inc. on Mar 28 2008. In view of that, Co. has restructured its corporate headquarters functions, and expects these actions to reduce its cost structure, yielding approximately $250.0 million in annual savings, beginning in 2009.

Financial Data

(US$ in Thousands)	3 Mos	12/31/2007	12/31/2006	12/31/2005	12/31/2004	12/31/2003	12/31/2002	12/31/2001
Earnings Per Share	4.47	4.62	5.71	4.99	4.56	4.52	5.21	3.87
Cash Flow Per Share	6.82	4.91	6.51	5.34	5.31	5.33	5.03	4.08
Tang Book Value Per Share	0.75	2.66	N.M.	N.M.	N.M.	N.M.	N.M.	N.M.
Dividends Per Share	2.940	3.050	3.320	3.060	2.820	2.640	2.440	2.220
Dividend Payout %	65.79	66.02	58.14	61.32	61.84	58.41	46.83	57.36
Income Statement								
Total Revenue	4,410,000	73,801,000	101,407,000	97,854,000	89,610,000	81,832,000	80,408,000	89,924,000
EBITDA	1,038,000	14,215,000	19,217,000	18,267,000	16,787,000	17,350,000	20,563,000	18,039,000
Depn & Amortn	59,000	980,000	1,804,000	1,675,000	1,607,000	1,440,000	1,331,000	2,337,000
Income Before Taxes	979,000	13,020,000	16,536,000	15,435,000	14,004,000	14,760,000	18,098,000	14,284,000
Income Taxes	365,000	4,096,000	4,351,000	4,618,000	4,540,000	5,151,000	6,424,000	5,407,000
Net Income	2,454,000	9,786,000	12,022,000	10,435,000	9,416,000	9,204,000	11,102,000	8,560,000
Average Shares	2,122,000	2,116,000	2,105,000	2,090,000	2,063,000	2,038,000	2,129,000	2,210,000
Balance Sheet								
Current Assets	14,487,000	22,890,000	26,152,000	25,781,000	25,901,000	21,382,000	17,441,000	17,275,000
Total Assets	25,847,000	57,211,000	104,270,000	107,949,000	101,648,000	96,175,000	87,540,000	84,968,000
Current Liabilities	11,092,000	18,782,000	25,427,000	26,158,000	23,574,000	21,393,000	19,082,000	20,141,000
Long-Term Obligations	736,000	7,963,000	14,498,000	17,868,000	18,683,000	21,163,000	21,355,000	19,163,000
Total Liabilities	21,139,000	38,657,000	64,651,000	72,242,000	70,934,000	71,098,000	68,062,000	65,348,000
Stockholders' Equity	4,708,000	18,554,000	39,619,000	35,707,000	30,714,000	25,077,000	19,478,000	19,620,000
Shares Outstanding	2,108,901	2,107,676	2,097,080	2,084,264	2,059,527	2,037,263	2,039,259	2,152,503
Statistical Record								
Return on Assets %	26.87	12.12	11.33	9.96	9.49	10.02	12.87	10.44
Return on Equity %	98.51	33.64	31.92	31.42	33.66	41.32	56.79	49.44
EBITDA Margin %	23.54	19.26	18.95	18.67	18.73	21.20	25.57	20.06
Net Margin %	55.65	13.26	11.86	10.66	10.51	11.25	13.81	9.52
Asset Turnover	1.72	0.91	0.96	0.93	0.90	0.89	0.93	1.10
Current Ratio	1.31	1.22	1.03	0.99	1.10	1.00	0.91	0.86
Debt to Equity	0.16	0.43	0.37	0.50	0.61	0.84	1.10	0.98
Price Range	24.43-20.10	24.12-19.03	19.96-15.90	17.90-14.01	14.26-10.40	12.71-6.50	13.36-8.37	12.27-9.29
P/E Ratio	5.47-4.50	5.22-4.12	3.50-2.78	3.59-2.81	3.13-2.28	2.81-1.44	2.56-1.61	3.17-2.40
Average Yield %	13.32	14.28	18.65	19.38	23.32	25.77	22.08	20.29

Address: 120 Park Avenue, New York, NY 10017	Officers: Michael E. Szymanczyk - Chairman, Chief Executive Officer David Beran - Executive Vice President, Chief Financial Officer **Transfer Agents:** Computershare Trust Company, N.A., Providence, RI	**Investor Contact:** 917-663-3460
Telephone: 917-663-4000		**No of Institutions:** 1379
Web Site: www.altria.com		Shares: 1,732,557,696 **% Held:** 71.65

AMBAC FINANCIAL GROUP, INC.

Exchange	Symbol	Price	52Wk Range	Yield	P/E
NYS	ABK	$3.21 (5/29/2008)	89.86-2.94	1.25	N/A

*7 Year Price Score 43.70   *NYSE Composite Index=100   ***12 Month Price Score 12.46**

Interim Earnings (Per Share)

Qtr.	Mar	Jun	Sep	Dec
2005	1.66	1.69	1.61	1.90
2006	2.06	2.22	1.98	1.89
2007	2.02	1.67	(3.53)	(31.81)
2008	(11.69)	...	...	...

Interim Dividends (Per Share)

Amt	Decl	Ex	Rec	Pay
0.21Q	07/25/2007	08/08/2007	08/10/2007	09/05/2007
0.21Q	10/24/2007	11/07/2007	11/12/2007	12/05/2007
0.07Q	01/29/2008	02/07/2008	02/11/2008	03/05/2008
0.01Q	05/06/2008	05/16/2008	05/20/2008	06/04/2008
			Indicated Div: $0.04	

Valuation Analysis

Forecast EPS	$-6.82 (05/16/2008)		
Market Cap	$920.7 Million	Book Value	1.3 Billion
Price/Book	0.72	Price/Sales	N/A

Dividend Achiever Status

10 Year Growth Rate	12.99%
Total Years of Dividend Growth	16

TRADING VOLUME (thousand shares)

Business Summary: Insurance (MIC: SIC: 6351 NAIC: 524130)
Ambac Financial Group is a holding company. Co. has two reportable segments: Financial Guarantee, which provides financial guarantees, including credit derivatives, for public finance, structured finance and other obligations; and Financial Services, which provides investment agreements, funding conduits, interest rate, total return and currency swaps, principally to clients of the financial guarantee business, which includes municipalities and other public entities, health care organizations, investor-owned utilities and asset-backed issuers. As of Dec 31 2007, Co. had total assets of $23.57 billion.

Recent Developments: For the quarter ended Mar 31 2008, net loss amounted to US$1.66 billion versus net income of US$213.3 million in the year-earlier quarter. Revenues were US$1.56 billion, compared with US$461.8 million the year before. Net premiums earned were US$186.9 million versus US$216.0 million in the prior-year quarter, a decrease of 13.5%. Net investment income rose 9.5% to US$124.5 million from US$113.6 million a year ago.

Prospects: Co.'s main subsidiary, Ambac Assurance, has been able to write only a limited amount of new financial guarantee business since late 2007, as a result of rating agency actions due to the ongoing uncertainty in the mortgage market, as well as concerns over Ambac Assurance's financial condition by fixed-income investors. Nevertheless, Co. believes that its capital raise of $1.50 billion in the first quarter of 2008 has reduced the uncertainty around its ratings. Also, in order to accumulate capital, Co. has suspended underwriting certain structured finance business for six months from Mar 6 2008, and discontinued the execution of credit enhancement transactions in credit default swap format.

Financial Data
(US$ in Thousands)

	3 Mos	12/31/2007	12/31/2006	12/31/2005	12/31/2004	12/31/2003	12/31/2002	12/31/2001
Earnings Per Share	(45.38)	(31.56)	8.15	6.87	6.53	5.66	3.97	3.97
Cash Flow Per Share	5.51	9.18	8.47	9.30	8.64	9.42	7.60	6.36
Tang Book Value Per Share	4.48	22.45	58.49	50.85	46.13	39.71	34.20	28.26
Dividends Per Share	0.670	0.780	0.660	0.550	0.470	0.420	0.380	0.340
Dividend Payout %	...	...	8.10	8.01	7.20	7.42	9.57	8.56
Income Statement								
Premium Income	186,866	841,461	811,623	816,020	716,659	620,317	471,534	378,734
Total Revenue	(1,562,639)	(4,214,926)	1,832,104	1,661,707	1,406,708	1,272,208	971,818	724,920
Benefits & Claims	1,042,761	256,109	20,004	149,856	69,600	53,400	26,700	20,000
Income Before Taxes	(2,790,784)	(5,146,916)	1,210,213	1,022,764	976,782	849,589	564,190	568,727
Income Taxes	(1,130,441)	(1,898,759)	334,302	271,754	250,942	221,490	131,596	135,821
Net Income	(1,660,343)	(3,248,157)	875,911	751,010	724,551	618,915	432,594	432,906
Average Shares	142,032	102,929	107,536	109,394	110,898	109,409	109,066	108,948
Balance Sheet								
Total Assets	24,919,262	23,565,011	20,267,813	19,725,140	18,585,258	16,747,314	15,355,538	12,267,695
Total Liabilities	23,633,524	21,285,118	14,083,624	14,352,933	13,560,801	12,492,756	11,730,359	9,284,007
Stockholders' Equity	1,285,738	2,279,893	6,184,189	5,372,207	5,024,457	4,254,558	3,625,179	2,983,688
Shares Outstanding	286,829	101,550	105,730	105,639	108,915	107,144	105,990	105,584
Statistical Record								
Return on Assets %	N.M.	N.M.	4.38	3.92	4.09	3.86	3.13	3.87
Return on Equity %	N.M.	N.M.	15.16	14.45	15.57	15.71	13.09	15.52
Loss Ratio %	558.03	30.44	2.46	18.36	9.71	8.61	5.66	5.28
Net Margin %	...	...	47.81	45.20	51.51	48.65	44.51	59.72
Price Range	96.08-5.41	96.08-21.79	89.78-74.17	82.39-62.20	84.42-64.04	72.19-44.51	69.69-49.90	63.43-45.50
P/E Ratio	...	...	11.02-9.10	11.99-9.05	12.93-9.81	12.75-7.86	17.55-12.57	15.98-11.46
Average Yield %	1.28	1.10	0.81	0.75	0.63	0.68	0.63	0.61

Address: One State Plaza, New York, NY 10004 **Telephone:** 212-668-0340 **Web Site:** www.ambac.com	**Officers:** Michael A. Callen - Chairman, Interim President; Interim Chief Executive Officer Douglas C. Renfield-Miller - Executive Vice President **Transfer Agents:**Citibank Stockholder Services, Providence, RI	**Investor Contact:** 212-208-3333 **No of Institutions:** 456 **Shares:** 270,555,744 **% Held:** 255.50

AMERICAN CAPITAL STRATEGIES LTD.

Exchange	Symbol	Price	52Wk Range	Yield	P/E
NMS	ACAS	$32.16 (5/29/2008)	48.43-28.70	12.81	N/A

*7 Year Price Score 89.91   *NYSE Composite Index=100   *12 Month Price Score 87.06

Interim Earnings (Per Share)

Qtr.	Mar	Jun	Sep	Dec
2005	1.22	0.82	0.90	0.18
2006	1.34	2.16	0.92	(1.28)
2007	0.86	4.68	0.11	(2.14)
2008	(4.16)	...	...	...

Interim Dividends (Per Share)

Amt	Decl	Ex	Rec	Pay
0.92Q	07/31/2007	09/05/2007	09/07/2007	10/01/2007
1.00Q	10/31/2007	12/05/2007	12/07/2007	01/16/2008
1.01Q	02/13/2008	03/05/2008	03/07/2008	04/01/2008
1.03Q	05/06/2008	06/11/2008	06/13/2008	07/01/2008

Indicated Div: $4.12

Valuation Analysis

Forecast EPS $3.02 (05/17/2008)
Market Cap $6.5 Billion   Book Value   5.7 Billion
Price/Book   1.14   Price/Sales   5.11

Dividend Achiever Status

10 Year Growth Rate	33.30%
Total Years of Dividend Growth	10

Business Summary: Finance Intermediaries & Services (MIC: SIC: 6726 NAIC: 525990)
American Capital Strategies is a closed end investment company. Co. invests in senior debt, mezzanine debt and equity in the buyouts of private companies that it sponsors, the buyouts of private companies sponsored by other private equity firms and directly to private and small public companies. Co. also invests in structured finance investments including commercial mortgage backed securities, commercial collateralized loan obligation securities and collateralized debt obligation securities and in alternative asset funds that it manages. Co. also provides advisory, management and other services to its portfolio companies through American Capital Financial Services, Inc.

Recent Developments: For the quarter ended Mar 31 2008, net loss amounted to US$813.0 million versus net income of US$134.0 million in the year-earlier quarter. Revenues were US$292.0 million, up 16.8% from US$250.0 million the year before.

Prospects: For 2008, Co. continues to anticipate alternative assets of $19.00 billion to $26.00 billion, of which $7.00 billion to $14.00 billion will be in external funds managed by its wholly-owned portfolio company, American Capital, LLC. For the second quarter of 2008, Co. is forecasting net operating income in the range of $0.68 to $0.75 per diluted share, while earnings are projected to surpass $1.10 per diluted share. Meanwhile, Co.'s Eastern Region Sponsor Finance business continues to implement its restructuring plans, which include expanding the group in its New York office and the closing of its Philadelphia office, along with the May 6 2008 opening of a second office in the Boston.

Financial Data
(US$ in Thousands)

	3 Mos	12/31/2007	12/31/2006	12/31/2005	12/31/2004	12/31/2003	12/31/2002	12/31/2001
Earnings Per Share	(1.56)	3.36	3.11	3.10	3.63	2.15	0.50	0.58
Cash Flow Per Share	2.04	2.83	3.01	3.04	2.58	2.15	1.84	1.15
Tang Book Value Per Share	28.16	32.88	29.42	24.37	21.11	17.83	15.82	16.84
Dividends Per Share	3.840	3.720	3.330	3.080	2.910	2.790	2.570	2.300
Dividend Payout %	...	110.71	107.07	99.35	80.17	129.77	514.00	396.55
Income Statement								
Total Revenue	292,000	1,240,000	860,000	554,500	336,082	206,280	147,022	104,237
Income Taxes	...	6,000	11,000	12,504	2,130	...	...	...
Net Income	(813,000)	594,000	425,000	313,848	220,101	117,984	20,061	18,605
Average Shares	195,200	176,900	136,800	101,376	77,638	54,996	39,880	32,001
Balance Sheet								
Total Assets	10,219,000	11,732,000	8,609,000	5,449,109	3,491,427	2,041,724	1,318,523	904,184
Total Liabilities	4,500,000	5,291,000	4,267,000	2,551,472	1,619,001	865,809	630,864	263,919
Stockholders' Equity	5,719,000	6,441,000	4,342,000	2,897,637	1,872,426	1,175,915	687,659	640,265
Shares Outstanding	203,100	195,900	147,600	118,913	88,705	65,949	43,469	38,017
Statistical Record								
Return on Assets %	N.M.	5.84	6.05	7.02	7.93	7.02	1.81	2.45
Return on Equity %	N.M.	11.02	11.74	13.16	14.40	12.66	3.02	3.43
Price Range	48.83-28.70	49.79-32.96	46.26-32.56	39.50-31.02	34.70-25.27	29.73-21.59	32.45-16.34	29.86-21.88
P/E Ratio	...	14.82-9.81	14.87-10.47	12.74-10.01	9.56-6.96	13.83-10.04	64.90-32.68	51.48-37.72
Average Yield %	9.55	8.63	8.91	8.67	9.53	10.95	10.14	8.66

Address: 2 Bethesda Metro Center, 14th Floor, Bethesda, MD 20814 **Telephone:** 301-951-6122 **Web Site:** www.american-capital.com	**Officers:** Malon Wilkus - Chairman, President, Chief Executive Officer John R. Erickson - Executive Vice President, Chief Financial Officer **Transfer Agents:** ComputerShare Investor Services, Providence, RI	**No of Institutions:** 448 **Shares:** 101,158,544 **% Held:** 48.14

AMERICAN INTERNATIONAL GROUP INC

Exchange	Symbol	Price	52Wk Range	Yield	P/E
NYS	AIG	$35.34 (5/29/2008)	72.65-34.91	2.49	N/A

*7 Year Price Score 68.43   *NYSE Composite Index=100   *12 Month Price Score 78.44

TRADING VOLUME (thousand shares)

Interim Earnings (Per Share)

Qtr.	Mar	Jun	Sep	Dec
2005	1.40	1.53	0.65	0.17
2006	1.22	1.21	1.61	1.32
2007	1.58	1.64	1.19	(2.01)
2008	(3.09)	...	...	...

Interim Dividends (Per Share)

Amt	Decl	Ex	Rec	Pay
0.20Q	09/05/2007	12/05/2007	12/07/2007	12/21/2007
0.20Q	11/14/2007	03/05/2008	03/07/2008	03/21/2008
0.20Q	03/12/2008	06/04/2008	06/06/2008	06/20/2008
0.22Q	05/08/2008	09/03/2008	09/05/2008	09/19/2008

Indicated Div: $0.88

Valuation Analysis

Forecast EPS	$2.94 (05/17/2008)
Market Cap	$88.2 Billion Book Value 79.7 Billion
Price/Book	1.11 Price/Sales 0.95

Dividend Achiever Status

10 Year Growth Rate	21.90%
Total Years of Dividend Growth	22

Business Summary: Insurance (MIC: SIC: 6331 NAIC: 524126)

American International Group is a holding company which, through its subsidiaries, is engaged in an array of insurance and insurance-related activities in the U.S. and abroad. Co.'s primary activities include both General Insurance and Life Insurance & Retirement Services operations as well as other significant activities including Financial Services and Asset Management. As of Dec 31 2007, Co.'s reportable segments by product or service line were General Insurance, Life Insurance & Retirement Services, Financial Services and Asset Management. As of the date above, Co. provided its products and services in more than 130 countries and jurisdictions.

Recent Developments: For the quarter ended Mar 31 2008, net loss amounted to US$7.81 billion versus net income of US$4.13 billion in the year-earlier quarter. Revenues were US$14.03 billion, down 54.2% from US$30.65 billion the year before. Net premiums earned were US$20.67 billion versus US$19.64 billion in the prior-year quarter, an increase of 5.2%. Net investment income fell 30.5% to US$4.95 billion from US$7.12 billion a year ago.

Prospects: Co.'s near-term outlook appears to be challenging. In detail, Co. expects the downward cycle in the U.S. housing market to continue to affect its United Guaranty Corporation subsidiary's results for the foreseeable future. In addition, Co. is projecting further price decline in its commercial lines during 2008. Thus, Co. intends to identify strategic opportunities across its existing product portfolios and distribution networks while maintaining stringent underwriting discipline. Also, Co. intends to file for rate increases and tightening underwriting guidelines to mitigate the weaker underwriting results in its personal lines market, which is anticipated to continue through 2009.

Financial Data
(US$ in Thousands)

	3 Mos	12/31/2007	12/31/2006	12/31/2005	12/31/2004	12/31/2003	12/31/2002	12/31/2001
Earnings Per Share	(2.29)	2.39	5.36	3.99	3.69	3.53	2.10	2.02
Cash Flow Per Share	13.75	13.61	2.62	9.68	13.62	13.85	7.15	2.94
Tang Book Value Per Share	27.85	34.15	35.77	30.13	27.73	24.39	20.32	19.94
Dividends Per Share	0.765	0.730	0.630	0.550	0.280	0.224	0.178	0.158
Dividend Payout %	...	30.54	11.75	13.78	7.59	6.35	8.48	7.82
Income Statement								
Premium Income	20,672,000	79,302,000	74,083,000	70,209,000	66,593,000	54,613,000	44,589,000	38,608,000
Total Revenue	14,031,000	110,064,000	113,194,000	108,905,000	97,987,000	81,303,000	67,482,000	55,911,000
Benefits & Claims	15,882,000	66,115,000	59,706,000	63,711,000	58,313,000	46,886,000	41,927,000	27,222,000
Income Before Taxes	(11,264,000)	8,943,000	21,687,000	15,213,000	14,950,000	13,908,000	8,142,000	8,139,000
Income Taxes	(3,537,000)	1,455,000	6,537,000	4,258,000	4,620,000	4,264,000	2,328,000	2,339,000
Net Income	(7,805,000)	6,200,000	14,048,000	10,477,000	9,731,000	9,274,000	5,519,000	5,363,000
Average Shares	2,528,000	2,598,000	2,623,000	2,627,000	2,637,000	2,628,000	2,634,000	2,650,000
Balance Sheet								
Total Assets	1,051,086,000	1,060,505,000	979,414,000	853,370,000	798,660,000	678,346,000	561,229,000	492,982,000
Total Liabilities	971,283,000	964,604,000	877,546,000	766,867,000	717,854,000	606,901,000	499,973,000	438,630,000
Stockholders' Equity	79,703,000	95,801,000	101,677,000	86,317,000	80,607,000	71,253,000	59,103,000	52,150,000
Shares Outstanding	2,495,828	2,529,584	2,601,196	2,596,647	2,596,423	2,608,447	2,609,600	2,615,432
Statistical Record								
Return on Assets %	N.M.	0.61	1.53	1.27	1.31	1.50	1.05	1.34
Return on Equity %	N.M.	6.28	14.95	12.55	12.78	14.23	9.92	11.69
Loss Ratio %	76.83	83.37	80.59	90.74	87.57	85.85	94.03	70.51
Net Margin %	(55.63)	5.63	12.41	9.62	9.93	11.41	8.18	9.59
Price Range	72.65-39.80	72.65-51.33	72.81-57.76	73.12-50.35	76.77-54.70	66.28-44.47	79.61-51.10	96.88-67.05
P/E Ratio	...	30.40-21.48	13.58-10.78	18.33-12.62	20.80-14.82	18.78-12.60	37.91-24.33	47.96-33.19
Average Yield %	1.23	1.09	0.96	0.90	0.40	0.39	0.27	0.19

Address: 70 Pine Street, New York, NY 10270	Officers: Robert B. Willumstad - Chairman Jacob A. Frenkel - Vice-Chairman **Transfer Agents:**	Investor Contact: 212-770-6293
Telephone: 212-770-7000	Computershare Trust Co., N.A., Providence, RI	No of Institutions: 1557
Web Site: www.aig.com		Shares: 1,926,677,888 % Held: 67.54

AMERICAN STATES WATER CO.

Exchange	Symbol	Price	52Wk Range	Yield	P/E
NYS	AWR	$33.66 (5/29/2008)	45.45-32.29	2.97	22.29

*7 Year Price Score 98.89   *NYSE Composite Index=100   *12 Month Price Score 96.55

Interim Earnings (Per Share)

Qtr.	Mar	Jun	Sep	Dec
2005	0.22	0.34	0.72	0.28
2006	0.35	0.36	0.32	0.30
2007	0.40	0.42	0.44	0.35
2008	0.30	...	...	...

Interim Dividends (Per Share)

Amt	Decl	Ex	Rec	Pay
0.235Q	07/31/2007	08/08/2007	08/10/2007	09/01/2007
0.25Q	10/31/2007	11/07/2007	11/09/2007	12/01/2007
0.25Q	01/29/2008	02/06/2008	02/08/2008	03/01/2008
0.25Q	04/29/2008	05/08/2008	05/12/2008	06/01/2008

Indicated Div: $1.00 (Div. Reinv. Plan)

Valuation Analysis

Forecast EPS	$1.73 (05/16/2008)		
Market Cap	$580.5 Million	Book Value	303.5 Million
Price/Book	1.91	Price/Sales	1.95

Dividend Achiever Status

10 Year Dividend Growth Rate	1.41%
Total Years of Dividend Growth	54

TRADING VOLUME (thousand shares)

Business Summary: Water Utilities (MIC: SIC: 4941 NAIC: 221310)

American States Water is the parent company of Golden State Water Company (GSWC), American States Utility Services, Inc. (ASUS), and Chaparral City Water Company (CCWC). GSWC is a public utility engaged in the purchase, production and distribution of water in California, which served about 254,546 water customers as of Dec 31 2007. GSWC also distributes electricity in one customer service area, which served around 23,273 electric customers at Dec 31 2007. CCWC is a public utility, which served approximately 13,488 customers in the town of Fountain Hills, AZ and a portion of the City of Scottsdale, AZ, at Dec 31 2007. ASUS provides water and wastewater services on a contract basis.

Recent Developments: For the quarter ended Mar 31 2008, net income decreased 24.1% to US$5.3 million from US$7.0 million in the year-earlier quarter. Revenues were US$68.9 million, down 4.6% from US$72.3 million the year before. Operating income was US$14.5 million versus US$16.9 million in the prior-year quarter, a decrease of 14.2%. Indirect operating expenses decreased 1.7% to US$54.5 million from US$55.4 million in the equivalent prior-year period.

Prospects: Co.'s top-line is being negatively affected by a decline in electric revenues and lower contracted services revenues. Nevertheless, Co. is benefiting from higher water revenues, due to the rate increases approved by the California Public Utilities Commission effective Jan 1 2008 and a favorable supply mix change. Meanwhile, Co. is forecasting construction expenditures for 2008 to be in the range of $55.0 million to $60.0 million. Specifically, Co.'s infrastructure investment plan consists of both infrastructure renewal programs, where it replaces infrastructure as needed as well as major capital investment projects, where it will construct new water treatment and delivery facilities.

Financial Data

(US$ in Thousands)	3 Mos	12/31/2007	12/31/2006	12/31/2005	12/31/2004	12/31/2003	12/31/2002	12/31/2001
Earnings Per Share	1.51	1.61	1.33	1.57	1.18	0.78	1.34	1.33
Cash Flow Per Share	2.78	2.98	3.04	3.25	3.21	3.08	1.70	2.62
Tang Book Value Per Share	16.88	16.88	15.96	15.02	14.30	13.97	14.05	13.23
Dividends Per Share	0.967	0.955	0.910	0.900	0.888	0.884	0.872	0.867
Dividend Payout %	64.26	59.32	68.42	57.32	75.25	113.33	65.07	65.00
Income Statement								
Total Revenue	68,942	301,370	268,629	236,197	228,005	212,669	209,205	197,514
EBITDA	22,369	96,972	83,337	...	...	...	...	...
Depn & Amortn	7,793	28,941	26,272	21,846	20,824	19,792	18,302	17,951
Income Before Taxes	9,559	48,820	38,762	...	...	...	...	...
Income Taxes	4,255	20,790	15,681	21,945	13,390	9,167	12,949	15,379
Net Income	5,304	28,030	23,081	26,766	18,541	11,892	20,339	20,447
Average Shares	17,357	17,177	17,101	16,809	15,663	15,227	15,157	15,256
Balance Sheet								
Net PPE	784,788	776,379	750,601	713,225	664,165	602,298	563,311	539,842
Total Assets	975,385	963,898	936,955	876,777	810,277	757,475	701,650	683,764
Long-Term Obligations	267,174	267,226	267,833	268,405	228,902	229,799	231,089	245,692
Total Liabilities	671,876	661,769	653,221	612,683	558,812	544,988	488,371	482,182
Stockholders' Equity	303,509	302,129	283,734	264,094	251,465	212,487	213,279	201,582
Shares Outstanding	17,245	17,231	17,049	16,797	16,752	15,212	15,180	15,119
Statistical Record								
Return on Assets %	2.73	2.95	2.55	3.17	2.36	1.63	2.94	3.14
Return on Equity %	8.89	9.57	8.43	10.38	7.97	5.59	9.81	10.33
EBITDA Margin %	32.45	32.18	31.02	...	...	...	...	...
Net Margin %	7.69	9.30	8.59	11.33	8.13	5.59	9.72	10.35
PPE Turnover	0.39	0.39	0.37	0.34	0.36	0.36	0.38	0.38
Asset Turnover	0.31	0.32	0.30	0.28	0.29	0.29	0.30	0.30
Debt to Equity	0.88	0.88	0.94	1.02	0.91	1.08	1.08	1.22
Price Range	45.45-32.29	45.45-33.82	42.39-30.78	34.06-24.64	26.78-21.37	28.71-21.80	28.85-21.01	25.32-19.35
P/E Ratio	30.10-21.38	28.23-21.01	31.87-23.14	21.69-15.69	22.69-18.11	36.81-27.95	21.53-15.68	19.04-14.55
Average Yield %	0.66	2.46	2.47	3.12	3.65	3.56	3.54	3.86

Address: 630 East Foothill Boulevard, San Dimas, CA 91773-1212 Telephone: 909-394-3600 Web Site: www.aswater.com	Officers: Lloyd E. Ross - Chairman Floyd E. Wicks - President, Chief Executive Officer Transfer Agents: Mellon Investor Services LLC, Jersey City, NJ	Investor Contact: 909-394-3633 No of Institutions: 161 Shares: 11,434,909 % Held: 56.42

ANCHOR BANCORP WISCONSIN, INC

Exchange	Symbol	Price	52Wk Range	Yield	P/E
NMS	ABCW	$14.16 (5/29/2008)	28.99-14.02	5.08	8.96

*7 Year Price Score 71.27 *NYSE Composite Index=100 *12 Month Price Score 73.11

TRADING VOLUME (thousand shares)

Interim Earnings (Per Share)

Qtr.	Jun	Sep	Dec	Mar
2004-05	0.46	0.46	0.47	0.71
2005-06	0.52	0.48	0.50	0.53
2006-07	0.49	0.44	0.48	0.38
2007-08	0.46	0.44	0.30	...

Interim Dividends (Per Share)

Amt	Decl	Ex	Rec	Pay
0.18Q	07/11/2007	07/30/2007	08/01/2007	08/15/2007
0.18Q	10/19/2007	10/30/2007	11/01/2007	11/15/2007
0.18Q	01/22/2008	01/29/2008	01/31/2008	02/15/2008
0.18Q	04/21/2008	04/28/2008	04/30/2008	05/15/2008

Indicated Div: $0.72

Valuation Analysis

Forecast EPS	$1.51 (05/16/2008)		
Market Cap	$302.1 Million	Book Value	341.1 Million
Price/Book	0.89	Price/Sales	0.88

Dividend Achiever Status

10 Year Growth Rate	16.95%
Total Years of Dividend Growth	14

Business Summary: Other Depository Banking (MIC: SIC: 6036 NAIC: 522120)

Anchor BanCorp Wisconsin is a savings and loan holding company. Through its subsidiary, AnchorBank, fsb, Co. is engaged in the provision of checking, savings, money market accounts, mortgages, home equity and other consumer loans, student loans, credit cards, annuities and related consumer financial services; banking services to businesses, including checking accounts, lines of credit, secured loans and commercial real estate loans; investments services; and credit life and disability insurance. Also, Co. invests in real estate partnerships through its non-banking subsidiary, Investment Directions, Inc. At Mar 31 2007, Co. had total assets of $4.54 billion and deposits of $3.25 billion.

Recent Developments: For the quarter ended Dec 31 2007, net income decreased 39.3% to US$6.3 million from US$10.4 million in the year-earlier quarter. Net interest income decreased 3.7% to US$31.3 million from US$32.5 million in the year-earlier quarter. Provision for loan losses was US$7.8 million versus US$3.4 million in the prior-year quarter, an increase of 130.9%. Non-interest income fell 26.1% to US$11.9 million from US$16.1 million, while non-interest expense declined 15.0% to US$25.1 million.

Prospects: On Jan 3 2008, Co. announced that it has acquired all of the outstanding common stock of S&C Bank (S&C), headquartered in New Richmond, WI, for $106.0 million. This acquisition expands Co.'s presence into Northwestern Wisconsin, bringing its total locations to 76 throughout the state. The acquisition will also add about $438.0 million to Co.'s asset base as well as expand its lending and deposit generating base. Concurrently, Co. also announced that it has reached an agreement with Lake Area Bank, based in Lindstrom, MN, to sell three S&C branches that are located in Minnesota. Co. believes that the sale will allow it to focus on integrating its S&C locations in Wisconsin going forward.

Financial Data

(US$ in Thousands)	9 Mos	6 Mos	3 Mos	03/31/2007	03/31/2006	03/31/2005	03/31/2004	03/31/2003
Earnings Per Share	1.58	1.76	1.76	1.80	2.03	2.10	2.02	2.02
Cash Flow Per Share	1.36	1.59	1.62	1.94	2.13	2.86	3.84	2.41
Tang Book Value Per Share	15.05	14.94	14.60	14.62	13.78	13.03	12.27	11.40
Dividends Per Share	0.700	0.690	0.680	0.670	0.615	0.485	0.430	0.362
Dividend Payout %	44.30	39.20	38.64	37.22	30.30	23.10	21.29	17.95
Income Statement								
Interest Income	221,407	147,370	72,647	280,692	238,550	199,979	190,262	209,605
Interest Expense	127,468	84,769	41,630	152,646	105,846	79,276	79,907	92,856
Net Interest Income	93,939	62,601	31,017	128,046	132,704	120,703	110,355	116,749
Provision for Losses	12,158	4,366	2,271	11,255	3,900	1,579	1,950	1,800
Non-Interest Income	37,488	25,578	14,640	53,999	66,976	134,864	82,076	32,753
Non-Interest Expense	77,327	52,215	26,887	107,473	118,447	162,575	113,641	68,004
Income Before Taxes	42,301	31,876	16,574	63,558	75,610	77,867	76,840	79,698
Income Taxes	16,812	12,716	6,688	24,586	30,927	29,532	29,471	30,135
Net Income	25,489	19,160	9,886	38,972	44,683	48,335	47,369	49,563
Average Shares	20,931	21,000	21,320	21,688	22,026	23,011	23,399	24,592
Balance Sheet								
Net Loans & Leases	3,948,061	3,950,383	3,899,115	3,878,523	3,619,774	3,418,969	3,081,390	2,814,042
Total Assets	4,725,773	4,611,526	4,532,758	4,539,685	4,275,140	4,050,456	3,810,386	3,538,621
Total Deposits	3,145,551	3,178,588	3,248,964	3,248,246	3,040,217	2,873,533	2,602,954	2,574,188
Total Liabilities	4,378,492	4,265,841	4,194,184	4,195,333	3,947,118	3,729,976	3,502,147	3,245,617
Stockholders' Equity	341,084	338,907	331,593	336,866	321,025	310,678	301,548	293,004
Shares Outstanding	21,337	21,342	21,344	21,669	21,854	22,319	22,954	23,942
Statistical Record								
Return on Assets %	0.73	0.83	0.86	0.88	1.07	1.23	1.29	1.41
Return on Equity %	9.95	11.30	11.61	11.85	14.15	15.79	15.89	17.37
Net Interest Margin %	42.33	42.27	42.70	45.62	55.63	60.36	58.00	55.70
Efficiency Ratio %	29.22	29.57	30.80	32.11	38.77	48.55	41.73	28.06
Loans to Deposits	1.26	1.24	1.20	1.19	1.19	1.19	1.18	1.09
Price Range	29.95-21.28	29.95-21.28	30.60-26.19	30.60-26.19	32.78-26.32	29.61-24.00	27.10-21.95	24.25-17.99
P/E Ratio	18.96-13.47	17.02-12.09	17.39-14.88	17.00-14.95	16.15-12.97	14.10-11.43	13.42-10.87	12.00-8.91
Average Yield %	2.62	2.48	2.37	2.31	2.05	1.82	1.74	1.69

Address: 25 West Main Street, Madison, WI 53703 Telephone: 608-252-8700 Web Site: www.anchorbank.com	Officers: Douglas J. Timmerman - Chairman, President, Chief Executive Officer J. Anthony Cattelino - Executive Vice President, Recording Secretary Transfer Agents: American Stock Transfer Company, New York, NY	Investor Contact: 608-252-1810 No of Institutions: 119 Shares: 12,487,928 % Held: 56.10

ANHEUSER-BUSCH COS., INC.

Exchange	Symbol	Price	52Wk Range	Yield	P/E
NYS	BUD	$56.55 (5/29/2008)	56.75-45.68	2.33	19.98

*7 Year Price Score 80.05 *NYSE Composite Index=100 *12 Month Price Score 103.33

Interim Earnings (Per Share)

Qtr.	Mar	Jun	Sep	Dec
2005	0.65	0.78	0.66	0.26
2006	0.64	0.82	0.82	0.25
2007	0.67	0.88	0.95	0.30
2008	0.71	...	...	...

Interim Dividends (Per Share)

Amt	Decl	Ex	Rec	Pay
0.33Q	07/25/2007	08/07/2007	08/09/2007	09/10/2007
0.33Q	10/24/2007	11/07/2007	11/09/2007	12/10/2007
0.33Q	01/10/2008	02/07/2008	02/11/2008	03/10/2008
0.33Q	04/23/2008	05/07/2008	05/09/2008	06/09/2008

Indicated Div: $1.32 (Div. Reinv. Plan)

Valuation Analysis

Forecast EPS $3.02 (05/17/2008)

Market Cap	$40.3 Billion	Book Value	3.1 Billion
Price/Book	12.81	Price/Sales	2.39

Dividend Achiever Status

10 Year Growth Rate	9.60%
Total Years of Dividend Growth	33

TRADING VOLUME (thousand shares)

Business Summary: Food (MIC: SIC: 2082 NAIC: 312120)

Anheuser-Busch Companies is the holding company of Anheuser-Busch, Inc., which is engaged in the beer business. Co.'s beer is primarily sold under brand names including Budweiser, Michelob, Busch, Natural Light, and Natural Ice. As of Dec 31 2007, worldwide sales of Co.'s beer brands aggregated 128.4 million barrels. Additionally, Co. is engaged in the family entertainment industry, primarily through its wholly-owned subsidiary, Busch Entertainment Corporation, which owned nine theme parks as of Dec 31 2006. Also, Co. is engaged in packaging, malt and rice production, international beer, non-beer beverages, real estate development, and transportation services.

Recent Developments: For the quarter ended Mar 31 2008, net income decreased 1.3% to US$510.9 million from US$517.5 million in the year-earlier quarter. Revenues were US$4.10 billion, up 6.2% from US$3.86 billion the year before. Operating income was US$762.8 million versus US$718.0 million in the prior-year quarter, an increase of 6.2%. Direct operating expenses rose 6.3% to US$2.63 billion from US$2.47 billion in the comparable period the year before. Indirect operating expenses increased 6.1% to US$706.3 million from US$665.7 million in the equivalent prior-year period.

Prospects: Looking ahead, Co. remains encouraged with the outlook for its beer sales during the summer selling season as it has implemented U.S. beer price increases while its cost reduction efforts have mitigated the effect of industry-wide cost pressures. Meanwhile, on Mar. 28 2008, Co. announced that it will build a new brewery in the Fengnan District of Tangshan, China, to replace a smaller downtown brewery. Scheduled for completion in late 2009, the new Tangshan brewery will be built on a 160,000 square meter site and cost $49 million (346 million RMB) for the first phase. Further, Co. expects the facility to have an initial production capacity of 3.1 million hectoliters (2.6 million barrels).

Financial Data

(US$ in Thousands)	3 Mos	12/31/2007	12/31/2006	12/31/2005	12/31/2004	12/31/2003	12/31/2002	12/31/2001
Earnings Per Share	2.83	2.79	2.53	2.35	2.77	2.48	2.20	1.89
Cash Flow Per Share	4.49	3.94	3.52	3.51	3.67	3.60	3.19	2.65
Tang Book Value Per Share	2.23	2.22	3.36	2.71	1.88	2.74	3.19	4.15
Dividends Per Share	1.285	1.250	1.130	1.030	0.930	0.830	0.750	0.690
Dividend Payout %	45.40	44.80	44.66	43.83	33.57	33.47	34.09	36.51
Income Statement								
Total Revenue	4,099,200	16,685,700	15,717,100	15,035,700	14,934,200	14,146,700	13,566,400	12,911,500
EBITDA	1,011,200	3,882,000	3,697,500	3,602,700	4,332,400	4,076,900	3,820,600	3,545,300
Depn & Amortn	253,300	996,200	988,700	979,000	932,700	877,200	847,300	834,500
Income Before Taxes	634,800	2,422,700	2,276,900	2,191,500	2,999,400	2,824,300	2,623,600	2,377,600
Income Taxes	249,900	969,800	900,500	850,400	1,163,200	1,093,300	1,041,500	913,200
Net Income	510,900	2,115,300	1,965,200	1,839,200	2,240,300	2,075,900	1,933,800	1,704,500
Average Shares	721,600	757,100	777,000	782,600	808,500	837,000	878,900	901,600
Balance Sheet								
Current Assets	2,259,700	2,024,500	1,829,500	1,758,700	1,818,400	1,630,300	1,504,700	1,550,400
Total Assets	17,551,200	17,155,000	16,377,200	16,555,000	16,173,400	14,689,500	14,119,500	13,862,000
Current Liabilities	2,542,000	2,303,800	2,246,100	1,982,600	1,969,400	1,857,200	1,787,700	1,732,300
Long-Term Obligations	9,281,000	9,140,300	7,653,900	7,972,100	8,278,600	7,285,400	6,603,200	5,983,900
Total Liabilities	14,402,600	14,003,400	12,438,500	13,211,700	13,505,300	11,977,800	11,067,200	9,800,500
Stockholders' Equity	3,148,600	3,151,600	3,938,700	3,343,300	2,668,100	2,711,700	3,052,300	4,061,500
Shares Outstanding	713,074	721,300	766,100	777,700	785,000	813,100	846,600	879,100
Statistical Record								
Return on Assets %	12.18	12.62	11.93	11.24	14.48	14.41	13.82	12.65
Return on Equity %	60.32	59.67	53.97	61.19	83.06	72.03	54.37	41.62
EBITDA Margin %	24.67	23.27	23.53	23.96	29.01	28.82	28.16	27.46
Net Margin %	12.46	12.68	12.50	12.23	15.00	14.67	14.25	13.20
Asset Turnover	0.98	1.00	0.95	0.92	0.97	0.98	0.97	0.96
Current Ratio	0.89	0.88	0.81	0.89	0.92	0.88	0.84	0.89
Debt to Equity	2.95	2.90	1.94	2.38	3.10	2.69	2.16	1.47
Price Range	54.41-45.68	54.41-46.95	49.91-40.42	50.73-40.57	54.29-49.45	53.69-45.92	54.97-44.00	46.51-38.50
P/E Ratio	19.23-16.14	19.50-16.83	19.73-15.98	21.59-17.26	19.60-17.85	21.65-18.52	24.99-20.00	24.61-20.37
Average Yield %	2.55	2.46	2.48	2.25	1.80	1.65	1.49	1.62

Address: One Busch Place, St. Louis, MO 63118	Officers: August A. Busch - President, Chief Executive Officer W. Randolph Baker - Vice President, Chief Financial Officer Transfer Agents: Mellon Investor Services, Jersey City, NJ	No of Institutions: 959
Telephone: 314-577-2000		Shares: 482,410,976 % Held: 61.54
Web Site: www.anheuser-busch.com		

14

APTARGROUP INC.

Exchange	Symbol	Price	52Wk Range	Yield	P/E
NYS	ATR	$45.52 (5/29/2008)	45.52-33.78	1.14	21.78

*7 Year Price Score 124.87 *NYSE Composite Index=100 *12 Month Price Score 113.03

Interim Earnings (Per Share)

Qtr.	Mar	Jun	Sep	Dec
2005	0.30	0.41	0.34	0.34
2006	0.28	0.39	0.40	0.39
2007	0.41	0.52	0.56	0.50
2008	0.52	...	...	...

Interim Dividends (Per Share)

Amt	Decl	Ex	Rec	Pay
0.13Q	07/18/2007	07/27/2007	07/31/2007	08/21/2007
0.13Q	10/17/2007	10/29/2007	10/31/2007	11/21/2007
0.13Q	01/17/2008	01/29/2008	01/31/2008	02/21/2008
0.13Q	04/16/2008	04/28/2008	04/30/2008	05/21/2008

Indicated Div: $0.52

Valuation Analysis

Forecast EPS	$2.29 (05/16/2008)		
Market Cap	$3.1 Billion	Book Value	1.2 Billion
Price/Book	2.51	Price/Sales	1.57

Dividend Achiever Status

10 Year Growth Rate	20.89%
Total Years of Dividend Growth	14

Business Summary: Plastics (MIC: SIC: 3089 NAIC: 326199)

AptarGroup is a global supplier of dispensing systems for the personal care, fragrance/cosmetic, pharmaceutical, household and food/beverage markets. Co. has manufacturing facilities worldwide, including in North America, Europe, Asia and South America. Co. operates through three business segments: the Beauty & Home segment, which sells pumps and aerosol valves and accessories to the personal care, household and food/beverage markets and pumps and decorative components to the fragrance/cosmetic market; the Pharma segment, which supplies pumps and metered dose inhaler valves to the pharmaceutical market; and the Closures segment, which supplies dispensing closures in the U.S. and Europe.

Recent Developments: For the quarter ended Mar 31 2008, net income increased 24.7% to US$36.9 million from US$29.6 million in the year-earlier quarter. Revenues were US$532.3 million, up 18.3% from US$449.8 million the year before. Operating income was US$54.7 million versus US$46.6 million in the prior-year quarter, an increase of 17.3%. Direct operating expenses rose 20.8% to US$362.8 million from US$300.3 million in the comparable period the year before. Indirect operating expenses increased 11.5% to US$114.8 million from US$103.0 million in the equivalent prior-year period.

Prospects: Co.'s near-term outlook appears positive. Notably, while some uncertainty about the near-term performance of the U.S. economy remains, Co. expects demand for its dispensing systems to grow and that sales should increase in the second quarter of 2008 over the prior year. Also, while raw material costs are expected to increase in the second quarter of 2008 compared to the prior year, in particular the cost of plastic resin, Co. intends to continue to mitigate the rising cost by increasing selling prices where possible. As a result, for the second quarter of 2008, Co. estimates diluted earnings per share to be $0.60 to $0.63 per share compared to $0.52 per share in the prior year.

Financial Data

(US$ in Thousands)	3 Mos	12/31/2007	12/31/2006	12/31/2005	12/31/2004	12/31/2003	12/31/2002	12/31/2001
Earnings Per Share	2.09	1.98	1.44	1.39	1.25	1.08	0.91	0.81
Cash Flow Per Share	4.07	3.98	2.83	2.76	2.52	1.93	2.15	1.80
Tang Book Value Per Share	14.42	12.88	10.39	8.71	9.40	8.38	6.06	4.50
Dividends Per Share	0.520	0.500	0.420	0.350	0.220	0.130	0.120	0.110
Dividend Payout %	24.83	25.25	29.27	25.27	17.53	12.04	13.19	13.66
Income Statement								
Total Revenue	532,258	1,892,167	1,601,385	1,380,009	1,296,608	1,114,689	926,691	891,986
EBITDA	86,829	334,035	275,683	250,335	237,427	210,022	179,111	175,689
Depn & Amortn	32,955	123,466	114,606	99,242	94,493	85,851	72,141	73,584
Income Before Taxes	52,716	199,995	148,306	141,953	137,177	117,270	98,358	88,355
Income Taxes	15,815	60,488	45,410	41,919	43,890	37,591	31,711	29,447
Net Income	36,901	141,739	102,896	100,034	93,287	79,679	66,647	58,844
Average Shares	71,072	71,523	71,744	72,354	74,314	73,802	73,246	73,058
Balance Sheet								
Current Assets	1,114,985	1,003,445	762,820	605,291	661,229	602,454	447,196	374,915
Total Assets	2,090,870	1,911,950	1,592,012	1,357,319	1,374,026	1,264,343	1,047,671	915,327
Current Liabilities	622,637	565,189	400,185	320,762	276,861	283,220	162,688	154,151
Long-Term Obligations	147,268	146,711	168,877	144,541	142,581	125,196	219,182	239,387
Total Liabilities	856,179	792,932	645,612	547,931	500,829	481,292	453,204	446,123
Stockholders' Equity	1,234,691	1,119,018	946,400	809,388	873,197	783,051	594,467	469,204
Shares Outstanding	68,012	68,200	69,200	69,800	76,400	75,400	74,400	74,000
Statistical Record								
Return on Assets %	7.88	8.09	6.98	7.32	7.05	6.89	6.79	6.30
Return on Equity %	13.41	13.72	11.72	11.89	11.23	11.57	12.53	12.94
EBITDA Margin %	16.31	17.65	17.22	18.14	18.31	18.84	19.33	19.70
Net Margin %	6.93	7.49	6.43	7.25	7.19	7.15	7.19	6.60
Asset Turnover	1.04	1.08	1.09	1.01	0.98	0.96	0.94	0.96
Current Ratio	1.79	1.78	1.91	1.89	2.39	2.13	2.75	2.43
Debt to Equity	0.12	0.13	0.18	0.18	0.16	0.16	0.37	0.51
Price Range	44.70-33.62	44.70-29.10	30.88-23.65	27.50-23.72	27.22-18.69	19.74-13.26	19.35-12.56	18.45-13.69
P/E Ratio	21.39-16.08	22.58-14.70	21.44-16.42	19.78-17.06	21.77-14.95	18.28-12.27	21.26-13.80	22.78-16.90
Average Yield %	1.37	1.36	1.56	1.38	1.01	0.81	0.74	0.69

Address: 475 West Terra Cotta Avenue, Suite E, Crystal Lake. IL 60014 **Telephone:** 815-477-0424 **Web Site:** www.aptargroup.com	Officers: King W. Harris - Chairman Peter H. Pfeiffer - Vice-Chairman, President, Chief Executive Officer **Transfer Agents:**National City Bank, Cleveland, OH	No of Institutions: 309 **Shares:** 68,587,344 **% Held:** 96.53

AQUA AMERICA INC

Exchange	Symbol	Price	52Wk Range	Yield	P/E
NYS	WTR	$16.94 (5/29/2008)	26.44-16.67	2.95	24.55

*7 Year Price Score 90.02   *NYSE Composite Index=100   *12 Month Price Score 88.21

Interim Earnings (Per Share)

Qtr.	Mar	Jun	Sep	Dec
2005	0.15	0.17	0.22	0.18
2006	0.13	0.17	0.21	0.20
2007	0.13	0.18	0.22	0.18
2008	0.11	...	...	...

Interim Dividends (Per Share)

Amt	Decl	Ex	Rec	Pay
0.125Q	08/07/2007	08/15/2007	08/17/2007	09/01/2007
0.125Q	10/05/2007	11/14/2007	11/16/2007	12/01/2007
0.125Q	02/07/2008	02/13/2008	02/15/2008	03/01/2008
0.125Q	05/01/2008	05/14/2008	05/16/2008	06/01/2008

Indicated Div: $0.50 (Div. Reinv. Plan)

Valuation Analysis

Forecast EPS $0.75 (05/16/2008)

Market Cap	$2.3 Billion	Book Value	980.7 Million
Price/Book	2.31	Price/Sales	3.76

Dividend Achiever Status

10 Year Growth Rate 7.22%

Total Years of Dividend Growth 16

TRADING VOLUME (thousand shares)

Business Summary: Water Utilities (MIC: SIC: 4941 NAIC: 221310)

Aqua America is a holding company. As of Dec 31 2007, Co.'s subsidiaries operated regulated utilities that provided water or wastewater services to about 3.0 million people in Pennsylvania, Ohio, North Carolina, Illinois, Texas, New Jersey, New York, Florida, Indiana, Virginia, Maine, Missouri and South Carolina. Co.'s key subsidiary, Aqua Pennsylvania, Inc., provided water or wastewater services to about one-half of its customers, located in the suburban areas north and west of the City of Philadelphia and in 23 other counties in Pennsylvania. Co. also provides water and wastewater services through operating and maintenance contracts with municipal authorities and other parties.

Recent Developments: For the quarter ended Mar 31 2008, net income decreased 15.0% to US$14.3 million from US$16.9 million in the year-earlier quarter. Revenues were US$139.3 million, up 1.4% from US$137.3 million the year before. Operating income was US$40.2 million versus US$43.7 million in the prior-year quarter, a decrease of 8.1%. Direct operating expenses rose 6.6% to US$64.3 million from US$60.3 million in the comparable period the year before. Indirect operating expenses increased 4.5% to US$34.8 million from US$33.3 million in the equivalent prior-year period.

Prospects: While it believes that the City of Fort Wayne's condemnation of the northern portion of its Fort Wayne, IN system will have a slight effect on its 2008 revenues, Co.'s other operations in Indiana remain unaffected by this event. Meanwhile, Co. expects to see improved revenue growth due to turnaround in the economy and higher customer growth, and as rate relief is awarded. Notably, as of May 6 2008, Co. had 17 rate increase requests pending totaling about $65.0 million in annualized revenues. Further, Co.'s Florida and North Carolina subsidiaries are expected to file rate cases in the 2008 second quarter, which are intended to recover the capital investments previously made in those states.

Financial Data

(US$ in Thousands)	3 Mos	12/31/2007	12/31/2006	12/31/2005	12/31/2004	12/31/2003	12/31/2002	12/31/2001
Earnings Per Share	0.69	0.71	0.70	0.71	0.64	0.59	0.58	0.52
Cash Flow Per Share	1.43	1.46	1.31	1.57	1.39	1.22	1.06	0.90
Tang Book Value Per Share	7.06	7.04	6.79	6.14	5.73	5.34	4.36	4.15
Dividends Per Share	0.490	0.480	0.444	0.399	0.367	0.364	0.323	0.303
Dividend Payout %	71.22	67.61	63.40	56.25	57.65	61.78	55.41	57.99
Income Statement								
Total Revenue	139,283	602,499	533,491	496,779	442,039	367,233	322,028	307,280
EBITDA	63,826	310,474	285,723	265,619	239,674	212,843	193,970	179,114
Depn & Amortn	22,654	88,011	75,041	65,488	58,864	51,463	44,322	40,168
Income Before Taxes	24,042	155,542	152,250	148,069	132,131	116,718	109,252	99,087
Income Taxes	9,721	60,528	60,246	56,913	52,124	45,923	42,046	38,976
Net Income	14,321	95,014	92,004	91,156	80,007	70,795	67,206	60,111
Average Shares	133,970	133,602	131,774	129,206	125,709	118,993	115,385	114,591
Balance Sheet								
Net PPE	2,802,123	2,792,794	2,505,995	2,279,950	2,069,812	1,824,291	1,486,703	1,368,115
Total Assets	3,225,883	3,226,912	2,877,903	2,626,725	2,340,248	2,069,736	1,717,069	1,560,339
Long-Term Obligations	1,213,640	1,215,053	951,660	878,438	784,461	696,666	582,910	516,520
Total Liabilities	2,245,168	2,250,614	1,956,273	1,814,802	1,591,780	1,410,706	1,223,972	1,086,506
Stockholders' Equity	980,715	976,298	921,630	811,923	748,468	659,030	493,097	473,833
Shares Outstanding	133,628	133,400	132,325	128,970	127,179	123,452	113,194	113,977
Statistical Record								
Return on Assets %	2.96	3.11	3.34	3.67	3.62	3.74	4.10	4.04
Return on Equity %	9.66	10.01	10.61	11.68	11.34	12.29	13.90	13.27
EBITDA Margin %	45.82	51.53	53.56	53.47	54.22	57.96	60.23	58.29
Net Margin %	10.28	15.77	17.25	18.35	18.10	19.28	20.87	19.56
PPE Turnover	0.22	0.23	0.22	0.23	0.23	0.22	0.23	0.23
Asset Turnover	0.19	0.20	0.19	0.20	0.20	0.19	0.20	0.21
Debt to Equity	1.24	1.24	1.03	1.08	1.05	1.06	1.18	1.09
Price Range	26.44-18.18	26.44-21.20	29.50-20.61	28.97-17.61	18.44-14.18	16.69-11.83	14.99-9.77	14.54-9.60
P/E Ratio	38.32-26.35	37.24-29.86	42.27-29.44	40.80-24.80	28.82-22.16	28.28-20.04	25.84-16.84	27.96-18.46
Average Yield %	2.23	2.11	1.83	1.77	2.30	2.61	2.54	2.51

Address: 762 W. Lancaster Avenue,	Officers: Nicholas DeBenedictis - Chairman, Chief	No of Institutions: 287
Bryn Mawr, PA 19010-3489	Executive Officer Christopher H. Franklin - Senior	Shares: 67,397,600 % Held: 46.54
Telephone: 610-524-8000	Vice President, Region Officer Transfer Agents:	
Web Site: www.aquaamerica.com	Computershare Trust Company, N.A., Providence, RI	

ARCHER DANIELS MIDLAND CO.

Exchange	Symbol	Price	52Wk Range	Yield	P/E
NYS	ADM	$39.50 (5/29/2008)	48.18-32.09	1.32	10.79

*7 Year Price Score 127.90 *NYSE Composite Index=100 ***12 Month Price Score 114.75**

Interim Earnings (Per Share)

Qtr.	Sep	Dec	Mar	Jun
2004-05	0.41	0.48	0.41	0.30
2005-06	0.29	0.56	0.53	0.62
2006-07	0.61	0.67	0.56	1.47
2007-08	0.68	0.73	0.80	...

Interim Dividends (Per Share)

Amt	Decl	Ex	Rec	Pay
0.115Q	08/01/2007	08/13/2007	08/15/2007	09/05/2007
0.115Q	11/08/2007	11/20/2007	11/23/2007	12/06/2007
0.13Q	02/05/2008	02/14/2008	02/19/2008	03/11/2008
0.13Q	05/01/2008	05/13/2008	05/15/2008	06/05/2008

Indicated Div: $0.52 (Div. Reinv. Plan)

Valuation Analysis

Forecast EPS	$2.99 (05/17/2008)
Market Cap	$25.4 Billion	Book Value	13.2 Billion
Price/Book	1.93	Price/Sales	0.42

Dividend Achiever Status

10 Year Growth Rate	11.23%
Total Years of Dividend Growth	33

TRADING VOLUME (thousand shares)

Business Summary: Food (MIC: SIC: 2075 NAIC: 311225)

Archer Daniels Midland is engaged in procuring, transporting, storing, processing and merchandising agricultural commodities and products. Co. operates three key segments: Oilseeds Processing, which processes oilseeds, such as soybeans, cottonseed, sunflower seeds, peanuts, and flaxseed into vegetable oils and meals; Corn Processing, which produces syrups, starches, dextros and sweeteners used in the food and beverage industry, as well as produces bioproducts such as alcohol and amino acids; and Agricultural Services, which buys, stores, cleans and transports agricultural commodities and resells these commodities as feed ingredients and raw materials for the agricultural processing industry.

Recent Developments: For the quarter ended Mar 31 2008, net income increased 42.4% to US$517.0 million from US$363.0 million in the year-earlier quarter. Revenues were US$18.71 billion, up 64.4% from US$11.38 billion the year before. Direct operating expenses rose 65.0% to US$17.55 billion from US$10.64 billion in the comparable period the year before. Indirect operating expenses increased 28.6% to US$378.0 million from US$294.0 million in the equivalent prior-year period.

Prospects: Co.'s near-term outlook appears to be encouraging as it continues to experience an increase in oilseeds processing sales, driven by higher average selling prices resulting primarily from increases in underlying commodity costs and continuing strong demand. In addition, Co. is seeing an improvement in corn processing sales, due mainly to better demand for sweeteners and starches. Further, Co. is benefiting from the accelerating bioproducts sales, attributable to the escalating ethanol sales volumes and, to a lesser extent, higher average selling prices. Meanwhile, Co.'s merchandising and handling operations continue to capitalize on the volatility in the commodity and freight markets.

Financial Data
(US$ in Thousands)

	9 Mos	6 Mos	3 Mos	06/30/2007	06/30/2006	06/30/2005	06/30/2004	06/30/2003
Earnings Per Share	3.66	3.44	3.38	3.30	2.00	1.59	0.76	0.70
Cash Flow Per Share	(4.40)	(3.62)	(1.53)	0.47	2.11	3.25	0.05	1.67
Tang Book Value Per Share	19.93	18.65	17.89	17.80	14.47	12.47	11.31	10.43
Dividends Per Share	0.475	0.460	0.445	0.430	0.370	0.320	0.270	0.240
Dividend Payout %	12.96	13.37	13.17	13.03	18.50	20.13	35.53	34.29
Income Statement								
Total Revenue	48,032,000	29,324,000	12,828,000	44,018,000	36,596,111	35,943,810	36,151,394	30,708,033
EBITDA	2,964,000	1,892,000	920,000	4,289,000	2,877,144	2,507,607	1,749,860	1,639,670
Depn & Amortn	540,000	360,000	185,000	701,000	656,714	664,652	689,858	648,726
Income Before Taxes	2,086,000	1,331,000	647,000	3,154,000	1,855,250	1,516,375	718,011	630,973
Income Taxes	656,000	418,000	206,000	992,000	543,180	471,990	223,301	179,828
Net Income	1,430,000	913,000	441,000	2,162,000	1,312,070	1,044,385	494,710	451,145
Average Shares	647,000	646,000	647,000	656,000	656,287	656,123	647,698	646,086
Balance Sheet								
Current Assets	25,229,000	22,660,000	19,018,000	15,122,000	11,826,277	9,710,701	10,338,996	8,421,857
Total Assets	36,513,000	33,490,000	29,392,000	25,118,000	21,269,030	18,598,105	19,368,821	17,182,879
Current Liabilities	15,885,000	14,561,000	11,526,000	7,868,000	6,164,767	5,366,864	6,750,237	5,147,472
Long-Term Obligations	6,026,000	5,233,000	4,733,000	4,752,000	4,050,323	3,530,140	3,739,875	3,872,287
Total Liabilities	23,351,000	21,166,000	17,572,000	13,865,000	11,462,150	10,164,633	11,670,605	10,113,682
Stockholders' Equity	13,162,000	12,324,000	11,820,000	11,253,000	9,806,880	8,433,472	7,698,216	7,069,197
Shares Outstanding	643,922	643,576	642,890	614,400	655,685	650,399	650,748	644,855
Statistical Record								
Return on Assets %	7.68	7.63	8.57	9.32	6.58	5.50	2.70	2.77
Return on Equity %	19.93	19.33	19.90	20.53	14.39	12.95	6.68	6.53
EBITDA Margin %	6.17	6.45	7.17	9.74	7.86	6.98	4.84	5.34
Net Margin %	2.98	3.11	3.44	4.91	3.59	2.91	1.37	1.47
Asset Turnover	1.94	1.81	1.85	1.90	1.84	1.89	1.97	1.88
Current Ratio	1.59	1.56	1.65	1.92	1.92	1.81	1.53	1.64
Debt to Equity	0.46	0.42	0.40	0.42	0.41	0.42	0.49	0.55
Price Range	47.09-32.09	47.09-30.70	39.87-30.70	44.00-30.70	45.25-20.56	25.32-15.43	17.59-12.08	14.28-10.54
P/E Ratio	12.87-8.77	13.69-8.92	11.80-9.08	13.33-9.30	22.63-10.28	15.92-9.70	23.14-15.89	20.40-15.06
Average Yield %	1.26	1.31	1.28	1.18	1.27	1.60	1.78	1.98

Address: 4666 Faries Parkway, Box 1470, Decatur, IL 62525	**Officers:** Patricia A. Woertz - Chairman, President, Chief Executive Officer Steven R. Mills - Executive	**Investor Contact:** 217-424-4647
Telephone: 217-424-5200	Vice President, Chief Financial Officer **Transfer**	**No of Institutions:** 762
Web Site: www.admworld.com	**Agents:** Hickory Point Bank & Trust, fsb, Decatur, IL	**Shares:** 488,951,488 **% Held:** 69.13

ASSOCIATED BANC-CORP.

Exchange	Symbol	Price	52Wk Range	Yield	P/E
NMS	ASBC	$27.45 (5/29/2008)	33.31-22.60	4.66	12.65

*7 Year Price Score 77.31   *NYSE Composite Index=100   *12 Month Price Score 99.83

Interim Earnings (Per Share)

Qtr.	Mar	Jun	Sep	Dec
2005	0.59	0.57	0.63	0.64
2006	0.60	0.63	0.58	0.57
2007	0.57	0.59	0.56	0.51
2008	0.52	...	...	...

Interim Dividends (Per Share)

Amt	Decl	Ex	Rec	Pay
0.31Q	07/25/2007	08/03/2007	08/07/2007	08/15/2007
0.31Q	10/24/2007	11/02/2007	11/06/2007	11/15/2007
0.31Q	01/23/2008	02/05/2008	02/07/2008	02/15/2008
0.32Q	04/23/2008	05/05/2008	05/07/2008	05/15/2008

Indicated Div: $1.28 (Div. Reinv. Plan)

Valuation Analysis

Forecast EPS $2.00 (05/17/2008)

Market Cap	$3.5 Billion	Book Value	2.4 Billion
Price/Book	1.47	Price/Sales	2.19

Dividend Achiever Status

10 Year Growth Rate	9.55%
Total Years of Dividend Growth	37

Business Summary: Commercial Banking (MIC: SIC: 6022 NAIC: 522110)

Associated Banc-Corp. is a bank holding company. Through its banking subsidiaries and various nonbanking subsidiaries, Co. provides a range of banking and nonbanking products and services to individuals and businesses in the communities it serves. Co.'s banking and wealth management activities are conducted mainly in Wisconsin, Minnesota, and Illinois, and are primarily delivered through branch facilities in this tri-state area, as well as supplemented through loan production offices, supermarket branches, a customer service call center and 24-hour phone-banking services, an interstate ATM network, and internet banking services. As of Dec 31 2007, Co. had total assets of $21.59 billion.

Recent Developments: For the quarter ended Mar 31 2008, net income decreased 9.4% to US$66.5 million from US$73.4 million in the year-earlier quarter. Net interest income increased 3.8% to US$165.1 million from US$159.0 million in the year-earlier quarter. Provision for loan losses was US$23.0 million versus US$5.1 million in the prior-year quarter, an increase of 352.6%. Non-interest income fell 0.1% to US$82.6 million from US$82.7 million, while non-interest expense advanced 6.4% to US$136.3 million.

Prospects: Co.'s near-term outlook appears to be somewhat uncertain. Co. is experiencing a decline in its net interest margin, attributable mainly to lower contribution from net free funds, largely offset by an increase in interest rate spread. On the other hand, Co. is seeing an improvement in its net interest income, driven by changes in the balances and earning assets and interest-bearing liabilities as well as the effects of changes in the interest rate environment and product pricing. Also, Co.'s recent non-interest income is reflecting higher service charges on deposit accounts as well as an increase in card-based and other non-deposit fees, offset by a decline in trust service fees.

Financial Data
(US$ in Thousands)

	3 Mos	12/31/2007	12/31/2006	12/31/2005	12/31/2004	12/31/2003	12/31/2002	12/31/2001
Earnings Per Share	2.17	2.23	2.38	2.43	2.25	2.05	1.86	1.64
Cash Flow Per Share	0.10	2.29	2.41	2.59	3.37	4.49	2.67	(0.00)
Tang Book Value Per Share	10.67	10.28	9.81	9.78	9.39	9.64	9.14	10.92
Dividends Per Share	1.240	1.220	1.140	1.060	0.977	0.887	0.808	0.739
Dividend Payout %	57.05	54.71	47.90	43.62	43.41	43.32	43.43	45.19
Income Statement								
Interest Income	296,870	1,275,712	1,279,379	1,094,025	767,122	727,364	792,106	880,622
Interest Expense	131,753	631,899	609,830	421,770	214,495	216,602	290,840	458,637
Net Interest Income	165,117	643,813	669,549	672,255	552,627	510,762	501,266	421,985
Provision for Losses	23,002	34,509	19,056	13,019	14,668	46,813	50,699	28,210
Non-Interest Income	82,628	344,781	295,501	291,086	210,247	246,435	220,308	195,603
Non-Interest Expense	136,312	534,891	496,215	480,463	377,869	388,668	374,549	338,369
Income Before Taxes	88,431	419,194	449,779	469,859	370,337	321,716	296,326	251,009
Income Taxes	21,966	133,442	133,134	149,698	112,051	93,059	85,607	71,487
Net Income	66,465	285,752	316,645	320,161	258,286	228,657	210,719	179,522
Average Shares	127,825	128,428	133,132	131,931	115,025	111,760	113,239	109,751
Balance Sheet								
Net Loans & Leases	15,701,333	15,410,123	15,048,803	15,060,770	13,757,089	10,218,524	10,446,520	9,193,367
Total Assets	21,903,753	21,592,083	20,861,384	22,100,082	20,520,136	15,247,894	15,043,275	13,604,374
Total Deposits	13,882,174	13,973,913	14,316,071	13,573,089	12,786,239	9,792,843	9,124,852	8,612,611
Total Liabilities	19,521,335	19,262,378	18,615,891	19,775,104	18,502,717	13,899,467	13,771,092	12,533,958
Stockholders' Equity	2,382,418	2,329,705	2,245,493	2,324,978	2,017,419	1,348,427	1,272,183	1,070,416
Shares Outstanding	127,709	127,324	128,874	135,674	129,770	110,040	111,420	98,003
Statistical Record								
Return on Assets %	1.31	1.35	1.47	1.50	1.44	1.51	1.47	1.34
Return on Equity %	12.04	12.49	13.86	14.75	15.31	17.45	17.99	17.61
Net Interest Margin %	55.62	50.47	52.33	61.45	72.04	70.22	63.28	47.92
Efficiency Ratio %	35.92	33.01	31.51	34.69	38.66	39.91	37.00	31.44
Loans to Deposits	1.13	1.10	1.05	1.11	1.08	1.04	1.14	1.07
Price Range	33.49-22.60	35.43-25.23	35.13-30.27	34.74-29.09	34.85-27.09	28.75-21.43	25.50-18.13	22.37-18.03
P/E Ratio	15.43-10.41	15.89-11.31	14.76-12.72	14.30-11.97	15.49-12.04	14.03-10.46	13.71-9.75	13.64-10.99
Average Yield %	4.27	3.92	3.46	3.28	3.22	3.57	3.57	3.57

Address: 1200 Hansen Road, Green Bay, WI 54304 **Telephone:** 920-431-8015 **Web Site:** www.associatedbank.com	Officers: Paul S. Beideman - Chairman, Chief Executive Officer Lisa B. Binder - President, Chief Operating Officer **Transfer Agents:** National City Bank, Cleveland, OH	Investor Contact: 920-491-7120 **No of Institutions:** 241 **Shares:** 71,627,192 % **Held:** 53.59

ASTORIA FINANCIAL CORP.

Exchange	Symbol	Price	52Wk Range	Yield	P/E
NYS	AF	$23.85 (5/29/2008)	28.87-20.76	4.36	18.35

*7 Year Price Score 81.05   *NYSE Composite Index=100   *12 Month Price Score 100.01

Interim Earnings (Per Share)

Qtr.	Mar	Jun	Sep	Dec
2005	0.57	0.55	0.57	0.57
2006	0.49	0.49	0.43	0.40
2007	0.38	0.37	0.39	0.22
2008	0.32	...	...	...

Interim Dividends (Per Share)

Amt	Decl	Ex	Rec	Pay
0.26Q	07/18/2007	08/13/2007	08/15/2007	09/04/2007
0.26Q	10/17/2007	11/13/2007	11/15/2007	12/03/2007
0.26Q	01/23/2008	02/13/2008	02/15/2008	03/03/2008
0.26Q	04/16/2008	05/13/2008	05/15/2008	06/02/2008
		Indicated Div: $1.04		

Valuation Analysis

Forecast EPS $1.55 (05/16/2008)

Market Cap	$2.3 Billion	Book Value	1.2 Billion
Price/Book	1.86	Price/Sales	1.94

Dividend Achiever Status

10 Year Growth Rate	18.74%
Total Years of Dividend Growth	12

TRADING VOLUME (thousand shares)

Business Summary: Other Depository Banking (MIC: SIC: 6035 NAIC: 522120)

Astoria Financial is the holding company of Astoria Federal Savings and Loan Association and its consolidated subsidiaries (Astoria Federal). Astoria Federal's primary business is the acceptance of retail deposits from the general public, and investing primarily in one-to-four family mortgage loans, multi-family mortgage loans, commercial real estate loans and mortgage-backed securities. Astoria Federal also invests in construction loans and other loans, U.S. government, government agency and government-sponsored enterprise, securities and other investments. As of Dec 31 2007, Co. had total assets of $21.72 billion, and total deposits of $13.05 billion.

Recent Developments: For the quarter ended Mar 31 2008, net income decreased 19.2% to US$28.9 million from US$35.8 million in the year-earlier quarter. Net interest income decreased 7.7% to US$80.8 million from US$87.5 million in the year-earlier quarter. Non-interest income fell 0.7% to US$22.4 million from US$22.6 million, while non-interest expense advanced 1.9% to US$58.2 million.

Prospects: Co.'s near-term outlook appears favorable. Notably, Co. expects loan growth to resume in the second quarter of 2008 due to the 95.0% increase in the mortgage loan pipeline during the first quarter of 2008 to $2.20 billion at Mar 31 2008. In addition, Co. expects the net interest margin to expand in the second quarter of 2008, as it increasingly realize the benefit of the repricing of maturing deposit and borrowing liabilities with existing rates that are above current market rates. Furthermore, Co. anticipates the yield curve to remain positively sloped for the remainder of 2008, which should provide opportunities for earnings growth and an expansion of its net interest margin.

Financial Data

(US$ in Thousands)	3 Mos	12/31/2007	12/31/2006	12/31/2005	12/31/2004	12/31/2003	12/31/2002	12/31/2001
Earnings Per Share	1.30	1.36	1.80	2.26	2.00	1.66	1.90	1.57
Cash Flow Per Share	2.54	2.30	2.29	2.68	2.56	3.13	1.26	1.64
Tang Book Value Per Share	10.77	10.58	10.33	10.94	10.59	10.11	10.58	9.69
Dividends Per Share	1.040	1.040	0.960	0.800	0.667	0.573	0.513	0.407
Dividend Payout %	80.25	76.47	53.33	35.40	33.33	34.54	27.02	25.96
Income Statement								
Interest Income	272,096	1,105,322	1,086,814	1,082,987	1,045,901	1,057,291	1,266,262	1,438,563
Interest Expense	191,310	771,794	696,429	604,207	575,335	677,753	801,838	969,189
Net Interest Income	80,786	333,528	390,385	478,780	470,566	379,538	464,424	469,374
Provision for Losses	4,000	2,500	...	...	...	...	2,307	4,028
Non-Interest Income	22,437	75,790	91,350	102,199	80,084	119,561	107,407	100,974
Non-Interest Expense	58,229	231,273	221,803	228,734	225,011	205,877	198,029	206,518
Income Before Taxes	40,994	175,545	259,932	352,245	325,639	293,222	371,495	345,190
Income Taxes	12,091	50,723	85,035	118,442	106,102	96,376	123,066	120,036
Net Income	28,903	124,822	174,897	233,803	219,537	196,846	248,429	222,860
Average Shares	90,969	92,092	97,280	103,408	109,806	115,942	127,379	138,261
Balance Sheet								
Net Loans & Leases	15,634,012	16,076,068	14,891,749	14,311,134	13,180,521	12,603,866	11,975,815	12,084,976
Total Assets	21,454,178	21,719,368	21,554,519	22,380,271	23,415,869	22,457,665	21,697,829	22,667,706
Total Deposits	13,003,542	13,049,438	13,224,024	12,810,455	12,323,257	11,186,594	11,067,196	10,903,693
Total Liabilities	20,223,711	20,508,024	20,338,765	21,030,044	22,046,105	21,061,134	20,143,831	21,000,120
Stockholders' Equity	1,230,467	1,211,344	1,215,754	1,350,227	1,369,764	1,396,531	1,553,998	1,542,586
Shares Outstanding	95,899	95,728	98,211	104,967	110,304	118,005	127,208	136,150
Statistical Record								
Return on Assets %	0.55	0.58	0.80	1.02	0.95	0.89	1.12	0.99
Return on Equity %	9.61	10.29	13.63	17.19	15.83	13.34	16.05	14.59
Net Interest Margin %	29.69	30.17	35.92	44.21	44.99	35.90	36.68	32.63
Efficiency Ratio %	19.77	19.58	18.83	19.30	19.98	17.49	14.42	13.41
Loans to Deposits	1.20	1.23	1.13	1.12	1.07	1.13	1.08	1.11
Price Range	28.87-20.76	30.29-23.00	31.79-27.32	30.21-24.11	28.04-22.47	25.48-15.49	23.37-14.57	21.00-16.19
P/E Ratio	22.21-15.97	22.27-16.91	17.66-15.18	13.37-10.67	14.02-11.23	15.35-9.33	12.30-7.67	13.38-10.31
Average Yield %	4.07	3.94	3.19	2.96	2.68	2.96	2.60	2.21

Address: One Astoria Federal Plaza, Lake Success, NY 11042-1085 Telephone: 516-327-3000 Web Site: www.astoriafederal.com	Officers: George L. Engelke - Chairman, Chief Executive Officer Gerard C. Keegan - Vice-Chairman, Chief Administrative Officer **Transfer Agents:** Mellon Investor Services LLC, Jersey City, NJ	Investor Contact: 516-327-7877 No of Institutions: 274 Shares: 68,623,376 % Held: 68.85

AT&T INC

Exchange	Symbol	Price	52Wk Range	Yield	P/E
NYS	T	$40.20 (5/29/2008)	42.83-34.36	3.98	19.61

*7 Year Price Score 100.05 *NYSE Composite Index=100 *12 Month Price Score 101.67

Interim Earnings (Per Share)

Qtr.	Mar	Jun	Sep	Dec
2005	0.27	0.30	0.38	0.47
2006	0.37	0.46	0.56	0.50
2007	0.45	0.47	0.50	0.52
2008	0.57	...	...	...

Interim Dividends (Per Share)

Amt	Decl	Ex	Rec	Pay
0.355Q	06/29/2007	07/06/2007	07/10/2007	08/01/2007
0.355Q	09/28/2007	10/05/2007	10/10/2007	11/01/2007
0.40Q	12/11/2007	01/08/2008	01/10/2008	02/01/2008
0.40Q	03/28/2008	04/08/2008	04/10/2008	05/01/2008

Indicated Div: $1.60 (Div. Reinv. Plan)

Valuation Analysis

Forecast EPS $3.12 (05/17/2008)

Market Cap	$238.7 Billion	Book Value	112.3 Billion
Price/Book	2.13	Price/Sales	1.98

Dividend Achiever Status

10 Year Growth Rate	4.83%
Total Years of Dividend Growth	23

Business Summary: Communications (MIC: SIC: 4813 NAIC: 517110)

AT&T is a holding company providing telecommunications services. As of Dec 31 2007, Co. was divided into four reportable segments: wireline, which consisted of three product-based categories: voice, data and other; wireless, which provided a range of nationwide wireless voice communications services in a variety of pricing plans, including postpaid and prepaid service plans; advertising & publishing, which included its directory operations that published Yellow and White Pages directories and sold directory and Internet-based advertising; and other, which included operations from Sterling, its business integration software and services subsidiary, as well as corporate and other operations.

Recent Developments: For the quarter ended Mar 31 2008, net income increased 21.5% to US$3.46 billion from US$2.85 billion in the year-earlier quarter. Revenues were US$30.74 billion, up 6.1% from US$28.97 billion the year before. Operating income was US$5.98 billion versus US$4.66 billion in the prior-year quarter, an increase of 28.2%. Direct operating expenses rose 4.6% to US$11.78 billion from US$11.25 billion in the comparable period the year before. Indirect operating expenses decreased 0.5% to US$12.99 billion from US$13.05 billion in the equivalent prior-year period.

Prospects: Co.'s outlook appears solid, reflecting consolidated revenue growth led by improved results in its wireless and enterprise segments, and further expansion of wireless and consolidated margins. Further, Co. recently announced a $1.60 billion five-year agreement to provide global communications services for Royal Dutch Shell. For 2008, Co. expects growth in the upper-teens for its wireless segment, positive growth in enterprise revenues, improving wholesale revenue trends and stable regional consumer and business trends. Co. also expects incremental 2008 expense savings of more than $2.00 billion from the BellSouth and AT&T Corp. merger integration efforts and prior operational initiatives.

Financial Data

(US$ in Thousands)	3 Mos	12/31/2007	12/31/2006	12/31/2005	12/31/2004	12/31/2003	12/31/2002	12/31/2001
Earnings Per Share	2.05	1.94	1.89	1.42	1.77	2.56	1.69	2.13
Cash Flow Per Share	5.72	5.56	4.02	3.85	3.30	4.07	4.57	4.40
Tang Book Value Per Share	N.M.	N.M.	N.M.	8.29	11.78	11.08	9.51	8.62
Dividends Per Share	1.465	1.420	1.330	1.290	1.250	1.367	1.066	1.023
Dividend Payout %	71.30	73.20	70.37	90.85	70.62	53.42	63.09	48.00
Income Statement								
Total Revenue	30,744,000	118,928,000	63,055,000	43,862,000	40,787,000	40,843,000	43,138,000	45,908,000
EBITDA	11,159,000	43,257,000	22,226,000	14,413,000	15,228,000	17,385,000	19,826,000	21,307,000
Depn & Amortn	4,903,000	21,546,000	9,879,000	7,622,000	7,532,000	7,846,000	8,548,000	9,033,000
Income Before Taxes	5,391,000	18,204,000	10,881,000	5,718,000	7,165,000	8,901,000	10,457,000	11,357,000
Income Taxes	1,930,000	6,253,000	3,525,000	932,000	2,186,000	2,930,000	2,984,000	4,097,000
Net Income	3,461,000	11,951,000	7,356,000	4,786,000	5,887,000	8,505,000	5,653,000	7,242,000
Average Shares	6,032,999	6,169,999	3,902,000	3,379,000	3,322,000	3,329,000	3,348,000	3,396,000
Balance Sheet								
Net PPE	96,238,000	95,890,000	94,596,000	58,727,000	50,046,000	52,128,000	48,490,000	49,827,000
Total Assets	278,199,000	275,644,000	270,634,000	145,632,000	108,844,000	100,166,000	95,057,000	96,322,000
Long-Term Obligations	60,189,000	57,255,000	50,063,000	26,115,000	21,231,000	16,060,000	18,536,000	17,133,000
Total Liabilities	165,941,000	160,277,000	155,094,000	90,942,000	68,340,000	61,918,000	61,858,000	63,831,000
Stockholders' Equity	112,258,000	115,367,000	115,540,000	54,690,000	40,504,000	38,248,000	33,199,000	32,491,000
Shares Outstanding	5,938,999	6,043,544	6,238,745	3,876,884	3,300,912	3,305,236	3,318,000	3,354,216
Statistical Record								
Return on Assets %	4.59	4.38	3.53	3.76	5.62	8.71	5.91	7.43
Return on Equity %	11.08	10.35	8.64	10.06	14.91	23.81	17.21	23.01
EBITDA Margin %	36.30	36.37	35.25	32.86	37.34	42.57	45.96	46.41
Net Margin %	11.26	10.05	11.67	10.91	14.43	20.82	13.10	15.78
PPE Turnover	1.27	1.25	0.82	0.81	0.80	0.81	0.88	0.95
Asset Turnover	0.44	0.44	0.30	0.34	0.39	0.42	0.45	0.47
Debt to Equity	0.54	0.50	0.43	0.48	0.52	0.42	0.56	0.53
Price Range	42.83-34.36	42.83-33.81	35.75-24.45	25.77-22.10	27.59-23.00	31.19-19.34	40.17-20.10	52.38-37.38
P/E Ratio	20.89-16.76	22.08-17.43	18.92-12.94	18.15-15.56	15.59-12.99	12.18-7.55	23.77-11.89	24.59-17.55
Average Yield %	3.72	3.62	4.54	5.38	4.95	5.77	3.48	2.37

Address: 175 E. Houston St., San	Officers: Randall L. Stephenson - Chairman,	Investor Contact: 210-351-3990
Antonio, TX 78205-2233	President, Chief Executive Officer William A. Blase -	No of Institutions: 1549
Telephone: 210-821-4105	Senior Executive Vice President **Transfer Agents:**	**Shares:** 4,030,455,552 % Held: N/A
Web Site: www.att.com	Computershare Trust Company, N.A., Providence, RI	

ATMOS ENERGY CORP.

Exchange	Symbol	Price	52Wk Range	Yield	P/E
NYS	ATO	$27.40 (5/29/2008)	32.48-25.09	4.74	14.97

*7 Year Price Score 83.47   *NYSE Composite Index=100   *12 Month Price Score 100.61

Interim Earnings (Per Share)

Qtr.	Dec	Mar	Jun	Sep
2004-05	0.79	1.11	0.06	(0.22)
2005-06	0.88	1.10	(0.22)	0.07
2006-07	0.10	1.20	(0.15)	(0.08)
2007-08	0.82	1.24	...	...

Interim Dividends (Per Share)

Amt	Decl	Ex	Rec	Pay
0.32Q	08/02/2007	08/23/2007	08/27/2007	09/10/2007
0.325Q	11/07/2007	11/21/2007	11/26/2007	12/10/2007
0.325Q	02/05/2008	02/21/2008	02/25/2008	03/10/2008
0.325Q	04/30/2008	05/22/2008	05/27/2008	06/10/2008

Indicated Div: $1.30 (Div. Reinv. Plan)

Valuation Analysis

Forecast EPS $1.99 (05/16/2008)
Market Cap	$2.5 Billion	Book Value	2.1 Billion
Price/Book	1.16	Price/Sales	0.39

Dividend Achiever Status

10 Year Growth Rate	2.34%
Total Years of Dividend Growth	20

Business Summary: Gas Utilities (MIC: SIC: 4924 NAIC: 486210)

Atmos Energy is engaged primarily in the natural gas utility business as well as other natural gas nonutility businesses. As of Sep 30 2007, Co. distributed natural gas through sales and transportation arrangements to approximately 3.2 million residential, commercial, public authority and industrial customers through its six regulated natural gas distribution divisions, which covered service areas in 12 states. Co.'s primary service areas are located in Colorado, Kansas, Kentucky, Louisiana, Mississippi, Tennessee and Texas. Co.'s nonregulated businesses operate in 22 states and include its natural gas marketing operations as well as its pipeline, storage and other operations.

Recent Developments: For the quarter ended Mar 31 2008, net income increased 4.7% to US$111.5 million from US$106.5 million in the year-earlier quarter. Revenues were US$2.48 billion, up 19.7% from US$2.08 billion the year before. Operating income was US$211.1 million versus US$209.0 million in the prior-year quarter, an increase of 1.0%. Direct operating expenses rose 24.5% to US$2.05 billion from US$1.65 billion in the comparable period the year before. Indirect operating expenses increased 1.6% to US$223.3 million from US$219.7 million in the equivalent prior-year period.

Prospects: Co.'s strategy of combining complementary regulated and non-regulated operations continues to drive results as its net income grew. Hence, Co. expects its earnings contributions to return to a more historical mix, with about 70.0% derived from the regulated businesses and about 30.0% from the non-regulated businesses. For the fiscal year ending Sep 2008, Co. continues to project earnings of $1.95 to $2.05 per diluted share, excluding any material mark-to-market effect and assuming a reduced contribution from the natural gas marketing segment due to less volatility in natural gas prices and the continued execution of the rate strategy in the natural gas distribution segment.

Financial Data
(US$ in Thousands)

	6 Mos	3 Mos	09/30/2007	09/30/2006	09/30/2005	09/30/2004	09/30/2003	09/30/2002
Earnings Per Share	1.83	1.79	1.92	1.82	1.72	1.58	1.54	1.45
Cash Flow Per Share	5.75	4.98	6.29	3.86	4.93	5.00	1.07	7.20
Tang Book Value Per Share	15.40	14.40	13.75	11.13	10.74	14.25	11.35	9.19
Dividends Per Share	1.290	1.285	1.280	1.260	1.240	1.220	1.200	1.180
Dividend Payout %	70.43	71.79	66.67	69.23	72.09	77.22	77.92	81.38
Income Statement								
Total Revenue	4,141,495	1,657,510	5,898,431	6,152,363	4,973,326	2,920,037	2,799,916	950,849
EBITDA	468,396	206,952	606,875	569,464	529,472	301,314	279,225	237,931
Depn & Amortn	97,370	48,536	199,055	185,967	178,796	98,112	89,194	83,921
Income Before Taxes	300,693	121,599	262,584	236,890	218,018	137,765	126,371	94,836
Income Taxes	115,356	47,796	94,092	89,153	82,233	51,538	46,910	35,180
Net Income	185,337	73,803	168,492	147,737	135,785	86,227	71,688	59,656
Average Shares	89,990	89,608	87,745	81,390	79,012	54,416	46,496	41,250
Balance Sheet								
Net PPE	3,948,866	3,888,126	3,836,836	3,629,156	3,374,367	1,722,521	1,515,989	1,300,320
Total Assets	6,420,994	6,399,763	5,896,917	5,719,547	5,653,527	2,869,883	2,518,508	1,980,221
Long-Term Obligations	2,119,696	2,124,915	2,126,315	2,180,362	2,183,104	861,311	863,918	670,463
Total Liabilities	4,295,001	4,367,280	3,931,163	4,071,449	4,051,105	1,736,424	1,660,991	1,406,986
Stockholders' Equity	2,125,993	2,032,483	1,965,754	1,648,098	1,602,422	1,133,459	857,517	573,235
Shares Outstanding	90,143	89,906	89,326	81,739	80,539	62,799	51,475	41,675
Statistical Record								
Return on Assets %	2.65	2.55	2.90	2.60	3.19	3.19	3.19	2.97
Return on Equity %	8.01	8.15	9.32	9.09	9.93	8.64	10.02	10.31
EBITDA Margin %	11.31	12.49	10.29	9.26	10.65	10.32	9.97	25.02
Net Margin %	4.48	4.45	2.86	2.40	2.73	2.95	2.56	6.27
PPE Turnover	1.66	1.58	1.58	1.76	1.95	1.80	1.99	0.72
Asset Turnover	1.01	0.94	1.02	1.08	1.17	1.08	1.24	0.47
Debt to Equity	1.00	1.05	1.08	1.32	1.36	0.76	1.01	1.17
Price Range	33.11-25.09	33.11-26.11	33.11-26.47	29.11-25.79	29.76-24.85	26.86-23.68	25.45-20.70	24.46-18.37
P/E Ratio	18.09-13.71	18.50-14.59	17.24-13.79	15.99-14.17	17.30-14.45	17.00-14.99	16.53-13.44	16.87-12.67
Average Yield %	4.50	4.31	4.16	4.66	4.49	4.87	5.21	5.37

Address: Three Lincoln Centre, Suite 1800, 5430 LBJ Freeway, Dallas, TX 75240 Telephone: 972-934-9227 Web Site: www.atmosenergy.com	Officers: Robert W. Best - Chairman, President, Chief Executive Officer John P. Reddy - Senior Vice President, Chief Financial Officer **Transfer Agents:** American Stock Transfer & Trust Company, New York, NY	No of Institutions: 287 Shares: 61,789,804 % Held: 64.45

AUTOMATIC DATA PROCESSING INC.

Exchange	Symbol	Price	52Wk Range	Yield	P/E
NYS	ADP	$42.98 (5/29/2008)	50.11-37.90	2.70	19.19

*7 Year Price Score 85.37 *NYSE Composite Index=100 *12 Month Price Score 98.90

TRADING VOLUME (thousand shares)

Interim Earnings (Per Share)

Qtr.	Sep	Dec	Mar	Jun
2004-05	0.35	0.42	0.57	0.44
2005-06	0.38	0.45	0.64	1.22
2006-07	0.46	0.54	0.70	0.35
2007-08	0.55	0.55	0.79	...

Interim Dividends (Per Share)

Amt	Decl	Ex	Rec	Pay
0.23Q	08/09/2007	09/12/2007	09/14/2007	10/01/2007
0.29Q	11/13/2007	12/12/2007	12/14/2007	01/01/2008
0.29Q	01/31/2008	03/12/2008	03/14/2008	04/01/2008
0.29Q	04/30/2008	06/11/2008	06/13/2008	07/01/2008

Indicated Div: $1.16

Valuation Analysis

Forecast EPS	$2.18 (05/17/2008)		
Market Cap	$22.3 Billion	Book Value	5.5 Billion
Price/Book	4.05	Price/Sales	2.62

Dividend Achiever Status

10 Year Growth Rate	14.87%
Total Years of Dividend Growth	32

Business Summary: IT & Technology (MIC: SIC: 7374 NAIC: 518210)

Automatic Data Processing is a provider of business outsourcing services and integrated computing applications. Co.'s Employer Services segment provides a range of human resource information, payroll processing, tax and benefits administration products and services, including traditional and Web-based outsourcing applications. Co.'s Professional Employer Organization Services segment provides employment administration outsourcing services through a co-employment relationship. Co.'s Dealer Services segment provides integrated dealer management systems and business applications to automotive, heavy truck, and powersports vehicle retailers in the U.S., Canada, South Africa, Asia and Europe.

Recent Developments: For the quarter ended Mar 31 2008, income from continuing operations increased 12.1% to US$403.6 million from US$360.1 million in the year-earlier quarter. Net income increased 6.4% to US$413.6 million from US$388.9 million in the year-earlier quarter. Revenues were US$2.43 billion, up 11.8% from US$2.17 billion the year before. Direct operating expenses rose 15.9% to US$1.03 billion from US$891.4 million in the comparable period the year before. Indirect operating expenses increased 8.7% to US$190.9 million from US$175.7 million in the equivalent prior-year period.

Prospects: For the fiscal year ending June 30 2008, Co. is projecting annual revenue growth to be in the range of 12.0% to 13.0%, while earnings per diluted share improvement are forecasted to range from 18.0% to 21.0%, excluding the net one-time gain recorded in the first quarter of fiscal 2007. In addition, Co. is targeting revenue growth of approximately 10.0% in its Employer Services segment, while top-line improvement in its Professional Employer Organization (PEO) Services segment is estimated to range from 19.0% to 20.0%. Lastly, Co. is anticipating high single-digit new business sales improvement worldwide for both its Employer Services and PEO Services segments.

Financial Data

(US$ in Thousands)	9 Mos	6 Mos	3 Mos	06/30/2007	06/30/2006	06/30/2005	06/30/2004	06/30/2003
Earnings Per Share	2.24	2.15	2.14	2.04	2.68	1.79	1.56	1.68
Cash Flow Per Share	2.85	2.67	2.66	2.36	3.15	2.46	2.35	2.61
Tang Book Value Per Share	4.67	4.00	3.68	3.93	5.21	4.55	4.23	4.57
Dividends Per Share	1.040	0.980	0.920	0.875	0.710	0.605	0.540	0.475
Dividend Payout %	46.51	45.58	42.99	42.89	26.49	33.80	34.62	28.27
Income Statement								
Total Revenue	6,569,300	4,142,100	1,992,000	7,800,000	8,881,500	8,499,100	7,754,942	7,147,017
EBITDA	1,659,700	962,700	442,700	1,787,800	2,037,900	2,039,900	1,867,276	1,822,307
Depn & Amortn	246,200	167,600	75,800	329,300	364,000	424,400	436,694	274,682
Income Before Taxes	1,457,500	822,100	381,500	1,623,500	1,743,000	1,677,900	1,494,530	1,645,200
Income Taxes	521,800	290,100	141,100	602,300	670,600	622,500	558,960	627,050
Net Income	1,002,200	588,500	297,400	1,138,700	1,554,000	1,055,400	935,570	1,018,150
Average Shares	523,200	530,400	536,200	557,900	580,300	590,000	598,749	605,917
Balance Sheet								
Current Assets	27,820,000	3,091,200	3,078,300	3,364,200	4,760,100	4,441,100	2,761,589	3,675,501
Total Assets	32,775,500	27,545,700	25,703,300	26,648,900	27,490,100	27,615,400	21,120,559	19,833,671
Current Liabilities	25,862,800	1,752,900	1,958,100	1,790,800	2,592,700	2,800,700	1,768,424	1,998,783
Long-Term Obligations	52,500	36,700	43,500	43,500	74,300	75,800	76,200	84,674
Total Liabilities	27,276,700	22,368,100	20,705,400	21,501,000	21,478,500	21,831,600	15,702,889	14,462,198
Stockholders' Equity	5,498,800	5,177,600	4,997,900	5,147,900	6,011,600	5,783,800	5,417,670	5,371,473
Shares Outstanding	518,200	521,400	526,100	535,800	561,400	580,200	587,115	594,839
Statistical Record								
Return on Assets %	3.64	3.96	4.54	4.21	5.64	4.33	4.56	5.34
Return on Equity %	20.80	21.15	21.74	20.41	26.35	18.84	17.30	19.42
EBITDA Margin %	25.26	23.24	22.22	22.92	22.95	24.00	24.08	25.50
Net Margin %	15.26	14.21	14.93	14.60	17.50	12.42	12.06	14.25
Asset Turnover	0.26	0.28	0.33	0.29	0.32	0.35	0.38	0.38
Current Ratio	1.08	1.76	1.57	1.88	1.84	1.59	1.56	1.84
Debt to Equity	0.01	0.01	0.01	0.01	0.01	0.01	0.01	0.02
Price Range	50.11-37.90	50.11-42.33	50.11-41.76	50.11-38.29	43.07-37.38	41.52-34.92	42.07-30.41	40.15-24.48
P/E Ratio	22.37-16.92	23.31-19.69	23.42-19.51	24.56-18.77	16.07-13.95	23.20-19.51	26.97-19.50	23.90-14.57
Average Yield %	2.30	2.12	2.03	1.99	1.76	1.57	1.48	1.45

Address: One ADP Boulevard, Roseland, NJ 07068 Telephone: 973-974-5000 Web Site: www.adp.com	Officers: Henry Taub - Honorary Chairman Gary C. Butler - President, Chief Executive Officer **Transfer Agents:** American Stock Transfer, New York, NY	No of Institutions: 979 Shares: 444,210,400 % Held: 71.27

AVERY DENNISON CORP.

Exchange	Symbol	Price	52Wk Range	Yield	P/E
NYS	AVY	$50.55 (5/29/2008)	68.49-45.66	3.24	17.02

*7 Year Price Score 73.21   ***NYSE Composite Index=100**   ***12 Month Price Score 93.95**

Interim Earnings (Per Share)

Qtr.	Mar	Jun	Sep	Dec
2005	0.57	0.89	0.86	(0.07)
2006	0.69	1.12	0.85	1.01
2007	0.80	0.87	0.59	0.81
2008	0.69	...	...	...

Interim Dividends (Per Share)

Amt	Decl	Ex	Rec	Pay
0.40Q	07/25/2007	08/31/2007	09/05/2007	09/19/2007
0.41Q	10/30/2007	12/03/2007	12/05/2007	12/19/2007
0.41Q	01/24/2008	03/03/2008	03/05/2008	03/19/2008
0.41Q	04/24/2008	06/02/2008	06/04/2008	06/18/2008

Indicated Div: $1.64 (Div. Reinv. Plan)

Valuation Analysis
Forecast EPS $4.01 (05/16/2008)

Market Cap	$5.0 Billion	Book Value	2.1 Billion
Price/Book	2.36	Price/Sales	0.76

Dividend Achiever Status

10 Year Growth Rate	8.38%
Total Years of Dividend Growth	32

TRADING VOLUME (thousand shares)

Business Summary: Paper Products (MIC: SIC: 2672 NAIC: 322222)

Avery Dennison is primarily engaged in the production of pressure-sensitive materials, by which some of these materials are converted into labels and other products through embossing, printing, stamping and die-cutting, and some are sold in unconverted form as base materials, tapes and reflective sheeting. Co. also manufactures and sells a variety of office products and other converted products such as binders, organizing systems, markers, fasteners, business forms as well as tickets, tags and imprinting equipment for retail and apparel manufacturers. As of Dec 29 2007, Co. operated approximately 200 manufacturing and distribution facilities located in over 60 countries.

Recent Developments: For the quarter ended Mar 29 2008, net income decreased 13.5% to US$68.4 million from US$79.1 million in the year-earlier quarter. Revenues were US$1.65 billion, up 18.4% from US$1.39 billion the year before. Direct operating expenses rose 19.1% to US$1.22 billion from US$1.03 billion in the comparable period the year before. Indirect operating expenses increased 32.1% to US$328.0 million from US$248.3 million in the equivalent prior-year period.

Prospects: For the full year of 2008, Co. is projecting low double-digit revenue growth, including the benefit from the June 15 2007 acquisition Paxar Corp. and the Apr 1 2008 acquisition of DM Label Group, as well as favourable foreign currency translation based on current exchange rates. Meanwhile, Co. estimates the total annual cost savings associated with the Paxar integration to range from $115.0 million to $125.0 million, of which an estimated $60.0 million to $70.0 million represent incremental savings during 2008. Lastly, Co. anticipates its ongoing restructuring and business realignment initiatives to yield incremental savings of $25.0 million to $30.0 million, net of transition costs.

Financial Data
(US$ in Thousands)

	3 Mos	12/29/2007	12/30/2006	12/31/2005	01/01/2005	12/27/2003	12/28/2002	12/29/2001
Earnings Per Share	2.97	3.07	3.66	2.25	2.78	2.68	2.59	2.47
Cash Flow Per Share	5.52	5.10	5.13	4.42	5.09	3.38	5.32	3.85
Tang Book Value Per Share	0.54	N.M.	8.84	7.42	6.45	4.53	2.53	4.70
Dividends Per Share	1.620	1.610	1.570	1.530	1.490	1.450	1.350	1.230
Dividend Payout %	54.57	52.44	42.90	68.00	53.60	54.10	52.12	49.80
Income Statement								
Total Revenue	1,645,200	6,307,800	5,575,900	5,473,500	5,340,900	4,762,600	4,206,900	3,803,300
EBITDA	158,300	609,900	623,500	568,300	561,600	514,200	517,600	515,800
Depn & Amortn	67,900	234,600	197,900	201,500	188,200	179,300	152,800	156,000
Income Before Taxes	60,900	375,300	425,600	366,800	373,400	334,900	364,800	359,800
Income Taxes	(7,500)	71,800	73,100	75,000	93,700	92,100	107,600	116,400
Net Income	68,400	303,500	367,200	226,400	279,700	267,900	257,200	243,200
Average Shares	98,600	98,900	100,400	100,500	100,500	100,000	99,400	98,600
Balance Sheet								
Current Assets	2,134,100	2,058,300	1,655,400	1,558,300	1,542,400	1,440,900	1,215,500	982,500
Total Assets	6,404,800	6,244,800	4,293,600	4,203,900	4,399,300	4,105,300	3,652,400	2,819,200
Current Liabilities	2,115,300	2,477,600	1,698,800	1,525,600	1,387,300	1,496,000	1,296,100	951,300
Long-Term Obligations	1,545,100	1,145,000	501,600	723,000	1,007,200	887,700	837,200	626,700
Total Liabilities	4,293,200	4,255,400	2,613,100	2,692,000	2,850,600	2,786,600	2,596,000	1,889,800
Stockholders' Equity	2,111,600	1,989,400	1,680,500	1,511,900	1,548,700	1,318,700	1,056,400	929,400
Shares Outstanding	98,464	98,386	98,313	99,727	100,113	99,569	110,467	109,890
Statistical Record								
Return on Assets %	5.47	5.78	8.67	5.28	6.47	6.93	7.97	8.84
Return on Equity %	15.32	16.59	23.07	14.84	19.19	22.62	25.98	27.75
EBITDA Margin %	9.62	9.67	11.18	10.38	10.52	10.80	12.30	13.56
Net Margin %	4.16	4.81	6.59	4.14	5.24	5.63	6.11	6.39
Asset Turnover	1.23	1.20	1.32	1.28	1.24	1.23	1.30	1.38
Current Ratio	1.01	0.83	0.97	1.02	1.11	0.96	0.94	1.03
Debt to Equity	0.73	0.58	0.30	0.48	0.65	0.67	0.79	0.67
Price Range	68.49-45.66	69.67-49.69	69.11-55.09	62.53-50.30	65.78-54.90	63.51-47.75	69.49-52.86	60.24-44.39
P/E Ratio	23.06-15.37	22.69-16.19	18.88-15.05	27.79-22.36	23.66-19.75	23.70-17.82	26.83-20.41	24.39-17.97
Average Yield %	2.82	2.61	2.58	2.73	2.44	2.64	2.19	2.34

Address: 150 North Orange Grove Boulevard, Pasadena, CA 91103
Telephone: 626-304-2000
Web Site: www.averydennison.com

Officers: Dean A. Scarborough - President, Chief Executive Officer Daniel R. O'Bryant - Executive Vice President, Chief Financial Officer **Transfer Agents:** Computershare Trust Co., N.A., Providence, RI

Investor Contact: 626-304-2204
No of Institutions: 478
Shares: 115,452,280 **% Held:** 86.85

AVON PRODUCTS, INC.

Exchange	Symbol	Price	52Wk Range	Yield	P/E
NYS	AVP	$38.80 (5/29/2008)	41.66-31.97	2.06	29.85

*7 Year Price Score 90.17 *NYSE Composite Index=100 ***12 Month Price Score 106.02**

TRADING VOLUME (thousand shares)

Interim Earnings (Per Share)

Qtr.	Mar	Jun	Sep	Dec
2005	0.36	0.69	0.35	0.41
2006	0.12	0.33	0.19	0.41
2007	0.34	0.26	0.32	0.29
2008	0.43	...	...	...

Interim Dividends (Per Share)

Amt	Decl	Ex	Rec	Pay
0.185Q	08/02/2007	08/15/2007	08/17/2007	09/03/2007
0.185Q	11/02/2007	11/13/2007	11/15/2007	12/03/2007
0.20Q	02/07/2008	02/19/2008	02/21/2008	03/03/2008
0.20Q	05/01/2008	05/13/2008	05/15/2008	06/02/2008

Indicated Div: $0.80 (Div. Reinv. Plan)

Valuation Analysis

Forecast EPS	$2.15 (05/17/2008)		
Market Cap	$16.6 Billion	Book Value	870.9 Million
Price/Book	19.01	Price/Sales	1.62

Dividend Achiever Status

10 Year Growth Rate	8.92%
Total Years of Dividend Growth	17

Business Summary: Chemicals (MIC: SIC: 2844 NAIC: 325620)

Avon Products is a global manufacturer and marketer of beauty and related products. Co. has three product categories: Beauty, which consists of cosmetics, fragrances, skin care and toiletries; Beauty Plus, which consists of fashion jewelry, watches, apparel and accessories; and Beyond Beauty, which consists of home products, gifts and decorative products. Co.'s Health and Wellness products and mark., a global cosmetics brand that focuses on the market for young women, are also included among these three categories. Co. operates in six regions: North America; Latin America; Western Europe, Middle East and Africa; Central and Eastern Europe; Asia Pacific; and China.

Recent Developments: For the quarter ended Mar 31 2008, net income increased 23.1% to US$184.7 million from US$150.0 million in the year-earlier quarter. Revenues were US$2.50 billion, up 14.5% from US$2.19 billion the year before. Operating income was US$296.2 million versus US$237.8 million in the prior-year quarter, an increase of 24.6%. Direct operating expenses rose 11.0% to US$923.7 million from US$832.5 million in the comparable period the year before. Indirect operating expenses increased 15.0% to US$1.28 billion from US$1.12 billion in the equivalent prior-year period.

Prospects: Despite the challenges in North America, Co. believes that revenue growth in 2008 will be in line with its long-term target of mid-single-digit growth. Co. also expects its 2008 operating margin to approach about 14.0%, due to its Product Line Simplification (PLS) program, Strategic Sourcing Initiative (SSI), and savings from its restructuring initiatives. Specifically, Co. expects savings from its restructuring to reach $270.0 million in 2008. Moreover, Co. expects annualized savings of about $430.0 million on full implementation of its restructuring initiatives by 2011 to 2012, and further expects annualized benefits in excess of $200.0 million each from its PLS program and SSI.

Financial Data

(US$ in Thousands)	3 Mos	12/31/2007	12/31/2006	12/31/2005	12/31/2004	12/31/2003	12/31/2002	12/31/2001
Earnings Per Share	1.30	1.21	1.06	1.81	1.77	1.39	1.11	0.90
Cash Flow Per Share	1.66	1.36	1.78	1.92	1.86	1.58	1.20	1.59
Tang Book Value Per Share	1.42	1.66	1.79	1.76	2.02	0.79	...	...
Dividends Per Share	0.755	0.740	0.700	0.660	0.560	0.420	0.400	0.380
Dividend Payout %	58.20	61.16	66.04	36.46	31.64	30.22	36.04	42.46
Income Statement								
Total Revenue	2,501,700	9,938,700	8,763,900	8,149,600	7,747,800	6,876,000	6,228,300	5,994,500
EBITDA	339,500	1,050,500	917,000	1,291,100	1,343,000	1,161,500	1,022,000	846,400
Depn & Amortn	44,000	172,100	159,600	141,200	135,300	133,200	142,900	124,000
Income Before Taxes	278,600	796,100	703,500	1,124,200	1,187,500	993,500	835,600	665,700
Income Taxes	92,400	262,800	223,400	269,700	330,600	318,900	292,300	230,900
Net Income	184,700	530,700	477,600	847,600	846,100	664,800	534,600	430,000
Average Shares	430,370	436,890	449,160	469,470	477,960	483,140	490,940	492,100
Balance Sheet								
Current Assets	3,576,900	3,515,400	3,334,400	2,920,900	2,506,400	2,226,100	2,048,200	1,889,100
Total Assets	5,865,600	5,716,200	5,238,200	4,763,300	4,148,100	3,562,300	3,327,500	3,193,100
Current Liabilities	2,533,200	3,053,400	2,550,100	2,501,600	1,525,500	1,587,700	1,975,500	1,461,000
Long-Term Obligations	1,680,300	1,167,900	1,170,700	766,500	866,300	877,700	767,000	1,236,300
Total Liabilities	4,994,700	5,004,600	4,447,800	3,969,100	3,197,900	3,191,000	3,455,200	3,267,700
Stockholders' Equity	870,900	711,600	790,400	794,200	950,200	371,300	(127,700)	(74,600)
Shares Outstanding	426,759	427,700	441,300	451,480	471,530	470,596	470,515	473,362
Statistical Record								
Return on Assets %	10.14	9.69	9.55	19.02	21.89	19.30	16.40	14.29
Return on Equity %	68.67	70.67	60.28	97.18	127.70	545.81	...	...
EBITDA Margin %	13.57	10.57	10.46	15.84	17.33	16.89	16.41	14.12
Net Margin %	7.38	5.34	5.45	10.40	10.92	9.67	8.58	7.17
Asset Turnover	1.84	1.81	1.75	1.83	2.00	2.00	1.91	1.99
Current Ratio	1.41	1.15	1.31	1.17	1.64	1.40	1.04	1.29
Debt to Equity	1.93	1.64	1.48	0.97	0.91	2.36	...	...
Price Range	41.66-31.97	41.66-31.97	33.88-27.06	45.07-24.71	46.14-30.86	34.67-24.58	28.48-21.86	24.80-18.39
P/E Ratio	32.05-24.59	34.43-26.42	31.96-25.53	24.90-13.65	26.07-17.44	24.95-17.68	25.66-19.69	27.55-20.43
Average Yield %	1.99	1.97	2.30	1.86	1.40	1.38	1.58	1.71

Address: 1345 Avenue of the Americas, New York, NY 10105-0196 Telephone: 212-282-5000 Web Site: www.avoncompany.com	Officers: Andrea Jung - Chairman, Chief Executive Officer Charles W. Cramb - Vice-Chairman, Chief Financial Officer, Chief Strategy Officer **Transfer Agents:**Computershare Trust Company, N.A., Providence, RI	Investor Contact: 212-282-5320 No of Institutions: 585 Shares: 484,766,240 % Held: 91.49

BADGER METER, INC.

Exchange	Symbol	Price	52Wk Range	Yield	P/E
ASE	BMI	$47.87 (5/29/2008)	52.81-25.63	0.75	35.20

*7 Year Price Score 166.85 *NYSE Composite Index=100 *12 Month Price Score 129.27

Interim Earnings (Per Share)

Qtr.	Mar	Jun	Sep	Dec
2005	0.26	0.29	0.27	0.12
2006	0.29	0.28	(0.04)	(0.03)
2007	0.18	0.38	0.39	0.18
2008	0.41	...	...	...

Interim Dividends (Per Share)

Amt	Decl	Ex	Rec	Pay
0.09Q	08/09/2007	08/29/2007	08/31/2007	09/14/2007
0.09Q	11/16/2007	11/28/2007	11/30/2007	12/14/2007
0.09Q	02/15/2008	02/27/2008	02/29/2008	03/14/2008
0.09Q	04/25/2008	05/28/2008	05/30/2008	06/13/2008

Indicated Div: $0.36

Valuation Analysis

Forecast EPS	$1.61 (05/16/2008)		
Market Cap	$698.0 Million	Book Value	98.2 Million
Price/Book	7.11	Price/Sales	2.79

Dividend Achiever Status

10 Year Growth Rate	10.95%
Total Years of Dividend Growth	15

Business Summary: Instruments and Related Products (MIC: SIC: 3824 NAIC: 334514)

Badger Meter is a manufacturer and marketer of products using liquid flow measurement and control technologies. Co.'s utility product category is comprised of residential and commercial water meters that are used by water utilities in North America, mainly the U.S. Co.'s industrial product lines include precision valves, electromagnetic inductive flow meters, impeller flow meters, and turbine and positive displacement industrial flow meters. Co.'s own products include the Orion® drive-by automatic meter reading (AMR) system and Galaxy® fixed network advanced metering infrastructure (AMI) system. Co. also remarkets the Itron® drive-by AMR product under a license and distribution agreement.

Recent Developments: For the quarter ended Mar 31 2008, income from continuing operations increased 143.8% to US$6.0 million from US$2.5 million in the year-earlier quarter. Net income increased 134.1% to US$6.0 million from US$2.6 million in the year-earlier quarter. Revenues were US$68.4 million, up 29.9% from US$52.7 million the year before. Operating income was US$9.9 million versus US$4.3 million in the prior-year quarter, an increase of 131.1%. Direct operating expenses rose 20.6% to US$43.9 million from US$36.4 million in the comparable period the year before. Indirect operating expenses increased 22.3% to US$14.7 million from US$12.0 million in the equivalent prior-year period.

Prospects: Co. continues to strengthen its position in the markets it serves through strategic acquisitions. For instance, on Apr 7 2008, Co. announced that it has acquired the advanced metering infrastructure (AMI) technology used in its Galaxy® fixed base network meter reading system from Miltel Communications Ltd. of Israel for about $25.7 million. The agreement included, among others, the acquisition of the core technology, and the right to manufacture the Galaxy® system and distribute it in certain water and gas utility markets going forward. Meanwhile, construction is progressing on Co.'s new manufacturing plant in Nogales, Mexico, which it expects to be in operation by the end of 2008.

Financial Data
(US$ in Thousands)

	3 Mos	12/31/2007	12/31/2006	12/31/2005	12/31/2004	12/31/2003	12/31/2002	12/31/2001
Earnings Per Share	1.36	1.13	0.52	0.94	0.71	0.57	0.55	0.26
Cash Flow Per Share	1.76	1.99	1.21	1.36	0.42	1.09	0.97	0.68
Tang Book Value Per Share	6.22	5.82	4.54	4.80	4.15	3.55	3.20	3.32
Dividends Per Share	0.350	0.340	0.310	0.290	0.275	0.265	0.255	0.250
Dividend Payout %	25.81	30.09	59.62	30.69	38.73	46.09	46.36	97.09
Income Statement								
Total Revenue	68,420	234,816	229,754	216,654	205,010	183,989	167,317	138,537
EBITDA	11,666	37,083	35,795	30,765	26,832	22,920	21,266	13,192
Depn & Amortn	1,797	6,467	7,007	6,359	7,245	7,832	7,980	6,801
Income Before Taxes	9,617	29,325	27,489	22,798	17,980	13,351	11,437	5,010
Income Taxes	3,597	10,939	10,921	9,545	8,347	5,774	4,166	1,646
Net Income	6,020	16,457	7,548	13,253	9,633	7,577	7,271	3,364
Average Shares	14,750	14,617	14,389	14,022	13,614	13,196	13,216	13,100
Balance Sheet								
Current Assets	86,262	79,934	79,359	72,564	71,382	62,998	55,380	44,364
Total Assets	158,211	150,301	139,383	145,867	142,961	133,851	126,463	98,836
Current Liabilities	43,820	41,209	45,711	39,586	45,247	37,052	48,555	23,782
Long-Term Obligations	2,596	3,129	5,928	15,360	14,819	24,450	13,046	20,498
Total Liabilities	60,032	58,332	67,564	72,451	78,895	78,680	78,368	55,834
Stockholders' Equity	98,179	91,969	71,819	73,416	64,066	55,171	48,095	43,002
Shares Outstanding	14,581	14,518	14,154	13,696	13,444	13,169	12,882	12,718
Statistical Record								
Return on Assets %	13.15	11.36	5.29	9.18	6.94	5.82	6.45	3.41
Return on Equity %	23.03	20.10	10.39	19.28	16.11	14.67	15.96	7.79
EBITDA Margin %	17.05	15.79	15.58	14.20	13.09	12.46	12.71	9.52
Net Margin %	8.80	7.01	3.29	6.12	4.70	4.12	4.35	2.43
Asset Turnover	1.66	1.62	1.61	1.50	1.48	1.41	1.49	1.40
Current Ratio	1.97	1.94	1.74	1.83	1.58	1.70	1.14	1.87
Debt to Equity	0.03	0.03	0.08	0.21	0.23	0.44	0.27	0.48
Price Range	46.51-23.53	46.05-23.53	32.50-19.81	25.52-13.06	15.62-8.59	9.94-6.44	8.47-5.58	8.00-5.00
P/E Ratio	34.20-17.30	40.75-20.82	62.50-38.10	27.14-13.89	21.99-12.09	17.43-11.29	15.41-10.14	30.77-19.23
Average Yield %	1.03	1.09	1.21	1.57	2.50	3.30	3.50	3.85

Address: 4545 W. Brown Deer Road, Milwaukee, WI 53224-9536	**Officers:** Richard A. Meeusen - Chairman, President, Chief Executive Officer Ronald H. Dix - Senior Vice	**Investor Contact:** 414-371-5702	
Telephone: 414-355-0400	President **Transfer Agents:**	**No of Institutions:** 118	
Web Site: www.badgermeter.com	American Stock Transfer, New York, NY	**Shares:** 11,036,985 **% Held:** 59.37	

BANCFIRST CORP. (OKLAHOMA CITY, OKLA)

Exchange	Symbol	Price	52Wk Range	Yield	P/E
NMS	BANF	$43.96 (5/29/2008)	48.61-39.30	1.82	13.20

*7 Year Price Score 100.44 *NYSE Composite Index=100 *12 Month Price Score 104.17

TRADING VOLUME (thousand shares)

Interim Earnings (Per Share)
Qtr.	Mar	Jun	Sep	Dec
2005	0.68	0.70	0.57	0.72
2006	0.68	0.76	0.79	0.84
2007	0.69	0.83	1.06	0.71
2008	0.74	...	...	...

Interim Dividends (Per Share)
Amt	Decl	Ex	Rec	Pay
0.20Q	08/23/2007	09/26/2007	09/30/2007	10/15/2007
0.20Q	11/15/2007	12/27/2007	12/31/2007	01/15/2008
0.20Q	02/28/2008	03/27/2008	03/31/2008	04/15/2008
0.20Q	05/22/2008	06/26/2008	06/30/2008	07/15/2008

Indicated Div: $0.80

Valuation Analysis
Forecast EPS $2.85 (05/16/2008)

Market Cap	$667.5 Million	Book Value 386.2 Million
Price/Book	1.73	Price/Sales 2.21

Dividend Achiever Status
10 Year Growth Rate	13.98%
Total Years of Dividend Growth	14

Business Summary: Commercial Banking (MIC: SIC: 6021 NAIC: 522110)

BancFirst is a financial holding company. Co.'s subsidiary, BancFirst (the Bank), provides retail and commercial banking services that include: commercial, real estate, agricultural and consumer lending; depository and funds transfer services; collections; and retail brokerage services for individual and corporate customers. Co. also owns 100.0% common securities of BFC Capital Trust II, a Delaware Business Trust, 100.0% of Council Oak Partners LLC, an Oklahoma limited liability company engaging in investing activities, and 100.0% of Wilcox & Jones, Inc., an Oklahoma business corporation operating as an independent insurance agency. At Dec 31 2007, Co. had total assets of $3.74 billion.

Recent Developments: For the quarter ended Mar 31 2008, net income increased 4.2% to US$11.6 million from US$11.1 million in the year-earlier quarter. Net interest income decreased 2.7% to US$35.4 million from US$36.4 million in the year-earlier quarter. Provision for loan losses was US$1.8 million versus a credit for loan losses of US$31,000 in the prior-year quarter. Non-interest income rose 24.2% to US$17.2 million from US$13.9 million, while non-interest expense advanced 4.4% to US$32.9 million.

Prospects: Co. is experiencing a decline in its net interest margin driven by the Federal Reserve Bank's reduction in rates. Also, Co.'s provision for loan losses is increasing due primarily to a single large relationship that was downgraded by management. Looking ahead, Co. expects that loan losses would increase as a result of declining home sales, rising commodity prices and a declining dollar resulting in an increase in credit losses at many U.S. banks. Nevertheless, Co. remains optimistic regarding its near-term outlook driven by growth in non-interest incomes attributable to growth in deposit accounts, as well as insurance commissions and premiums.

Financial Data
(US$ in Thousands)	3 Mos	12/31/2007	12/31/2006	12/31/2005	12/31/2004	12/31/2003	12/31/2002	12/31/2001
Earnings Per Share	3.33	3.33	3.07	2.68	2.33	2.00	2.03	1.67
Cash Flow Per Share	4.04	3.97	2.81	3.60	8.57	2.02	2.58	2.14
Tang Book Value Per Share	22.65	21.66	19.57	16.87	15.38	14.26	14.12	12.17
Dividends Per Share	0.780	0.760	0.680	0.600	0.530	0.470	0.400	0.360
Dividend Payout %	23.42	22.82	22.15	22.39	22.80	23.50	19.70	21.56
Income Statement								
Interest Income	53,244	230,749	213,225	171,706	144,765	141,032	157,139	182,643
Interest Expense	17,857	82,463	69,537	40,255	27,519	31,915	47,809	77,711
Net Interest Income	35,387	148,286	143,688	131,451	117,246	109,117	109,330	104,932
Provision for Losses	1,780	3,329	1,790	4,607	2,699	3,722	5,276	1,780
Non-Interest Income	17,241	71,138	58,424	54,284	51,855	48,820	45,212	36,908
Non-Interest Expense	32,928	134,446	124,557	117,165	108,744	105,382	98,380	96,620
Income Before Taxes	17,920	81,649	75,765	63,963	57,658	48,833	50,886	43,440
Income Taxes	6,326	28,556	26,413	21,128	20,482	16,951	17,324	15,479
Net Income	11,594	53,093	49,352	42,835	37,176	31,882	33,562	27,961
Average Shares	15,562	15,944	16,094	16,000	15,991	15,945	16,520	16,742
Balance Sheet								
Net Loans & Leases	2,470,656	2,457,972	2,297,848	2,289,909	2,067,769	1,921,075	1,790,495	1,692,902
Total Assets	3,786,111	3,743,006	3,418,574	3,223,030	3,046,977	2,921,369	2,796,862	2,757,045
Total Deposits	3,302,103	3,288,504	2,974,305	2,804,519	2,657,434	2,585,690	2,428,648	2,401,328
Total Liabilities	3,399,934	3,371,044	3,070,219	2,920,681	2,769,480	2,665,997	2,545,354	2,533,877
Stockholders' Equity	386,177	371,962	348,355	302,349	277,497	255,372	251,508	223,168
Shares Outstanding	15,183	15,217	15,764	15,637	15,681	15,645	16,273	16,520
Statistical Record								
Return on Assets %	1.46	1.48	1.49	1.37	1.24	1.12	1.21	1.05
Return on Equity %	14.40	14.74	15.17	14.77	13.92	12.58	14.14	13.31
Net Interest Margin %	66.46	64.26	67.39	76.56	80.99	77.37	69.58	57.45
Efficiency Ratio %	46.72	44.54	45.85	51.85	55.31	55.51	48.62	44.01
Loans to Deposits	0.75	0.75	0.77	0.82	0.78	0.74	0.74	0.70
Price Range	48.61-39.30	54.02-39.30	55.18-39.76	45.22-31.80	39.79-27.50	29.90-21.43	25.87-17.23	21.63-16.88
P/E Ratio	14.60-11.80	16.22-11.80	17.97-12.95	16.87-11.86	17.08-11.80	14.95-10.71	12.74-8.49	12.95-10.10
Average Yield %	1.77	1.67	1.49	1.52	1.74	1.83	1.83	1.86

Address: 101 North Broadway, Oklahoma City, OK 73102-8401 **Telephone:** 405-270-1086 **Web Site:** www.bancfirst.com	**Officers:** H. E. Rainbolt - Chairman James R. Daniel - Vice-Chairman **Transfer Agents:** BancFirst Trust and Investment Management, Oklahoma City, OK	**Investor Contact:** 405-270-1044 **No of Institutions:** 105 **Shares:** 4,202,833 **% Held:** 26.52

BANCORPSOUTH INC.

Exchange	Symbol	Price	52Wk Range	Yield	P/E
NYS	BXS	$23.92 (5/29/2008)	26.00-20.17	3.68	14.15

*7 Year Price Score 83.64   *NYSE Composite Index=100   ***12 Month Price Score 103.07**

Interim Earnings (Per Share)

Qtr.	Mar	Jun	Sep	Dec
2005	0.40	0.33	0.29	0.45
2006	0.47	0.45	0.38	0.26
2007	0.42	0.43	0.44	0.39
2008	0.43	...	...	...

Interim Dividends (Per Share)

Amt	Decl	Ex	Rec	Pay
0.21Q	07/25/2007	09/12/2007	09/14/2007	10/01/2007
0.21Q	10/10/2007	12/12/2007	12/14/2007	01/02/2008
0.21Q	01/23/2008	03/12/2008	03/14/2008	04/01/2008
0.22Q	04/23/2008	06/11/2008	06/13/2008	07/01/2008

Indicated Div: $0.88 (Div. Reinv. Plan)

Valuation Analysis

Forecast EPS $1.72 (05/16/2008)

Market Cap	$2.0 Billion	Book Value	1.2 Billion
Price/Book	1.61	Price/Sales	1.89

Dividend Achiever Status

10 Year Growth Rate	7.99%
Total Years of Dividend Growth	21

Business Summary: Commercial Banking (MIC: SIC: 6022 NAIC: 522110)

BancorpSouth is a financial holding company. Through its principal bank subsidiary, BancorpSouth Bank (the Bank), Co. conducts a general commercial banking, trust and insurance business through 295 offices in Mississippi, Tennessee, Alabama, Arkansas, Texas, Louisiana, Florida, and Missouri. The Bank operates investment services, credit insurance and insurance agency subsidiaries which engage in investment brokerage services and sales of other insurance products. Additionally, the Bank's trust department provides a variety of services. As of Dec 31 2007, Co. and its subsidiaries had total assets of $13.19 billion and total deposits of $10.06 billion.

Recent Developments: For the quarter ended Mar 31 2008, net income increased 4.7% to US$35.1 million from US$33.6 million in the year-earlier quarter. Net interest income increased 11.6% to US$110.1 million from US$98.7 million in the year-earlier quarter. Provision for loan losses was US$10.8 million versus US$1.4 million in the prior-year quarter, an increase of 697.9%. Non-interest income rose 13.5% to US$66.2 million from US$58.4 million, while non-interest expense advanced 7.4% to US$113.5 million.

Prospects: Co. is seeing increased net interest margin as a result of its asset/ liability management strategies which uses short term borrowings from the Federal Home Loan Bank to fund loan growth, resulting in strong net interest revenue gain. Further, Co. is benefiting from its non-interest product and services as they diversify its total revenue and reduce its interest rate dependency. Co. also continues to bolster its position in existing and contiguous markets through additional de novo branch bank development. Looking ahead, Co. expects the two insurance agencies, acquired in the first quarter of 2008, to boost its position in several attractive growth markets and to provide entry into others.

Financial Data

(US$ in Thousands)	3 Mos	12/31/2007	12/31/2006	12/31/2005	12/31/2004	12/31/2003	12/31/2002	12/31/2001
Earnings Per Share	1.69	1.69	1.57	1.47	1.43	1.68	1.39	1.19
Cash Flow Per Share	0.49	1.39	1.57	2.40	1.39	3.12	2.10	1.15
Tang Book Value Per Share	11.57	11.44	11.16	10.58	10.34	10.38	10.40	9.92
Dividends Per Share	0.840	0.830	0.790	0.760	0.730	0.660	0.610	0.570
Dividend Payout %	49.84	49.11	50.32	51.70	51.05	39.29	43.88	47.90
Income Statement								
Interest Income	190,459	801,242	681,891	559,936	497,629	526,911	590,418	665,835
Interest Expense	80,389	378,343	296,092	204,379	163,837	175,805	218,892	331,093
Net Interest Income	110,070	422,899	385,799	355,557	333,792	351,106	371,526	334,742
Provision for Losses	10,811	22,696	8,577	24,467	17,485	25,130	29,411	22,259
Non-Interest Income	66,231	231,799	206,094	198,812	183,519	190,086	132,239	128,633
Non-Interest Expense	113,470	428,058	393,154	362,102	342,945	322,594	312,398	295,313
Income Before Taxes	52,020	203,944	190,162	167,800	156,881	193,468	161,956	145,803
Income Taxes	16,875	66,001	64,968	52,601	46,261	62,334	49,938	47,340
Net Income	35,145	137,943	125,194	115,199	110,620	131,134	112,018	98,463
Average Shares	82,534	81,845	79,542	78,597	77,378	78,164	80,481	82,979
Balance Sheet								
Net Loans & Leases	9,275,536	9,193,019	7,861,960	7,338,326	6,830,250	6,215,624	6,359,314	6,055,587
Total Assets	13,154,871	13,189,841	12,040,521	11,768,674	10,848,193	10,305,035	10,189,247	9,395,429
Total Deposits	10,086,201	10,064,099	9,710,578	9,607,258	9,059,091	8,599,128	8,548,918	7,856,840
Total Liabilities	11,931,218	11,993,215	11,013,936	10,791,508	9,931,765	9,436,129	9,381,424	8,590,026
Stockholders' Equity	1,223,653	1,196,626	1,026,585	977,166	916,428	868,906	807,823	805,403
Shares Outstanding	82,365	82,299	79,109	79,237	78,037	77,926	77,680	81,225
Statistical Record								
Return on Assets %	1.07	1.09	1.05	1.02	1.04	1.28	1.14	1.07
Return on Equity %	11.84	12.41	12.50	12.17	12.36	15.64	13.89	12.35
Net Interest Margin %	57.79	52.78	56.58	63.50	67.08	66.63	62.93	50.27
Efficiency Ratio %	44.21	41.44	44.27	47.72	50.35	44.99	43.23	37.17
Loans to Deposits	0.92	0.91	0.81	0.76	0.75	0.72	0.74	0.77
Price Range	26.00-20.17	27.51-21.60	28.50-22.08	24.99-20.01	25.22-19.82	24.45-17.72	22.00-16.30	17.00-12.88
P/E Ratio	15.38-11.93	16.28-12.78	18.15-14.06	17.00-13.61	17.64-13.86	14.55-10.55	15.83-11.73	14.29-10.82
Average Yield %	3.51	3.38	3.06	3.42	3.25	3.12	3.11	3.76

Address: One Mississippi Plaza, 201 South Spring Street, Tupelo, MS 38804 **Telephone:** 662-680-2000 **Web Site:** www.bancorpsouth.com	Officers: Aubrey B. Patterson - Chairman, Chief Executive Officer James V. Kelley - President, Chief Operating Officer **Transfer Agents:** Computershare Investor Services LLC, Providence, RI	No of Institutions: 152 Shares: 28,495,636 % Held: 32.57

BANK OF AMERICA CORP.

Exchange	Symbol	Price	52Wk Range	Yield	P/E
NYS	BAC	$34.60 (5/29/2008)	52.71-33.87	7.40	14.60

*7 Year Price Score 82.35 *NYSE Composite Index=100 *12 Month Price Score 86.60

Interim Earnings (Per Share)

Qtr.	Mar	Jun	Sep	Dec
2005	1.14	1.06	1.02	0.82
2006	1.07	1.19	1.18	1.15
2007	1.16	1.28	0.82	0.05
2008	0.23	...	...	...

Interim Dividends (Per Share)

Amt	Decl	Ex	Rec	Pay
0.64Q	07/25/2007	09/05/2007	09/07/2007	09/28/2007
0.64Q	10/24/2007	12/05/2007	12/07/2007	12/28/2007
0.64Q	01/23/2008	03/05/2008	03/07/2008	03/28/2008
0.64Q	04/23/2008	06/04/2008	06/06/2008	06/27/2008

Indicated Div: $2.56 (Div. Reinv. Plan)

Valuation Analysis

Forecast EPS $2.75 (05/17/2008)
Market Cap $154.1 Billion   Book Value   156.3 Billion
Price/Book   0.99   Price/Sales   1.31

Dividend Achiever Status

10 Year Growth Rate   13.36%
Total Years of Dividend Growth   30

Business Summary: Commercial Banking (MIC: SIC: 6021 NAIC: 522110)

Bank of America is a bank holding company and a financial holding company. Through its banking subsidiaries and various nonbanking subsidiaries throughout the U.S. and in selected international markets, Co. provides a range of banking and nonbanking financial services and products through three business segments: Global Consumer and Small Business Banking, Global Corporate and Investment Banking, and Global Wealth and Investment Management. As of Dec 31 2007, Co. operated in 32 states, the District of Columbia and more than 30 foreign countries. At Dec 31 2007, Co. had total assets of $1.72 trillion and total deposits of $805.20 billion.

Recent Developments: For the quarter ended Mar 31 2008, net income decreased 77.0% to US$1.21 billion from US$5.26 billion in the year-earlier quarter. Net interest income increased 20.8% to US$9.99 billion from US$8.27 billion in the year-earlier quarter. Provision for loan losses was US$6.01 billion versus US$1.24 billion in the prior-year quarter, an increase of 386.6%. Non-interest income fell 29.1% to US$7.01 billion from US$9.89 billion, while non-interest expense advanced 1.1% to US$9.20 billion.

Prospects: On Apr 7 2008, Co. announced that it would expand its asset-based lending capabilities to serve smaller middle-market businesses as a result of its acquisition of LaSalle Bank business unit, on Oct 2007. Notably, Co. will form a new division, focusing on asset-based financing from $5.0 million to $25.0 million. This new division enhances its ability to provide secured financing services for businesses and allows Co. to offer its products and services to an expanded client base. Accordingly, Co. anticipates moderate growth in each of these markets. Meanwhile, Co. expects its Jan 11 2008 acquisition of Countrywide Financial Corp. for $4.00 billion, to close early in the third quarter of 2008.

Financial Data

(US$ in Millions)	3 Mos	12/31/2007	12/31/2006	12/31/2005	12/31/2004	12/31/2003	12/31/2002	12/31/2001
Earnings Per Share	2.37	3.30	4.59	4.04	3.69	3.56	2.96	2.09
Cash Flow Per Share	6.02	2.49	3.21	(3.05)	(1.05)	8.18	(3.95)	(4.02)
Tang Book Value Per Share	10.74	11.54	12.18	12.48	11.80	11.38	11.88	10.40
Dividends Per Share	2.480	2.400	2.120	1.900	1.700	1.440	1.220	1.140
Dividend Payout %	104.82	72.73	46.19	47.03	46.07	40.39	41.29	54.55
Income Statement								
Interest Income	21,859	87,304	78,585	58,626	43,227	31,643	32,161	38,293
Interest Expense	11,868	52,871	43,994	27,889	14,430	10,179	11,238	18,003
Net Interest Income	9,991	34,433	34,591	30,737	28,797	21,464	20,923	20,290
Provision for Losses	6,010	8,385	5,010	4,014	2,769	2,839	3,697	4,287
Non-Interest Income	7,012	31,886	37,989	26,438	22,220	17,363	14,201	14,823
Non-Interest Expense	9,195	37,010	35,597	28,681	27,027	20,127	18,436	20,709
Income Before Taxes	1,798	20,924	31,973	24,480	21,221	15,861	12,991	10,117
Income Taxes	588	5,942	10,840	8,015	7,078	5,051	3,742	3,325
Net Income	1,210	14,982	21,133	16,465	14,143	10,810	9,249	6,792
Average Shares	4,461	4,480	4,595	4,069	3,824	3,031	3,131	3,252
Balance Sheet								
Net Loans & Leases	858,979	864,756	697,474	565,746	513,211	365,300	335,904	322,278
Total Assets	1,736,502	1,715,746	1,459,737	1,291,803	1,110,457	736,445	660,458	621,764
Total Deposits	797,069	805,177	693,497	634,670	618,570	414,113	386,458	373,495
Total Liabilities	1,580,193	1,568,943	1,324,465	1,190,270	1,010,812	688,465	610,139	573,244
Stockholders' Equity	156,309	146,803	135,272	101,533	99,645	47,980	50,319	48,520
Shares Outstanding	4,452	4,437	4,458	4,000	4,047	2,883	3,002	3,119
Statistical Record								
Return on Assets %	0.67	0.94	1.54	1.37	1.53	1.55	1.44	1.07
Return on Equity %	7.47	10.62	17.85	16.37	19.11	21.99	18.72	14.13
Net Interest Margin %	45.71	39.44	44.02	52.43	66.62	67.83	65.06	52.99
Efficiency Ratio %	31.85	31.05	30.54	33.72	41.30	41.07	39.77	38.99
Loans to Deposits	1.08	1.07	1.01	0.89	0.83	0.88	0.87	0.86
Price Range	52.71-35.31	54.05-41.10	54.90-43.09	47.08-41.57	47.44-38.96	41.77-32.81	38.45-27.07	32.50-23.38
P/E Ratio	22.24-14.90	16.38-12.45	11.96-9.39	11.65-10.29	12.86-10.56	11.73-9.22	12.99-9.15	15.55-11.18
Average Yield %	5.32	4.84	4.27	4.23	3.99	3.82	3.61	3.98

Address: Bank of America Corporate Center, 100 N. Tryon Street, Charlotte, NC 28255 **Telephone:** 704-386-5681 **Web Site:** www.bankofamerica.com	**Officers:** Kenneth D. Lewis - Chairman, President, Chief Executive Officer Joe L. Price - Chief Financial Officer **Transfer Agents:** Computershare Trust Company, N.A., Providence, RI	**Investor Contact:** 800-521-3984 **No of Institutions:** 1600 **Shares:** 3,018,103,040 **% Held:** 61.04

28

BANK OF HAWAII CORP

Exchange	Symbol	Price	52Wk Range	Yield	P/E
NYS	BOH	$54.58 (5/29/2008)	56.84-43.07	3.22	13.96

*7 Year Price Score 92.99 *NYSE Composite Index=100 ***12 Month Price Score 106.72**

Interim Earnings (Per Share)

Qtr.	Mar	Jun	Sep	Dec
2005	0.83	0.87	0.85	0.86
2006	0.87	0.73	0.93	0.99
2007	0.94	0.95	0.96	0.83
2008	1.18	...	...	...

Interim Dividends (Per Share)

Amt	Decl	Ex	Rec	Pay
0.41Q	07/23/2007	08/29/2007	08/31/2007	09/14/2007
0.44Q	10/22/2007	11/28/2007	11/30/2007	12/14/2007
0.44Q	01/28/2008	02/27/2008	02/29/2008	03/14/2008
0.44Q	04/21/2008	05/28/2008	05/30/2008	06/13/2008

Indicated Div: $1.76 (Div. Reinv. Plan)

Valuation Analysis

Forecast EPS $4.03 (05/17/2008)

Market Cap	$2.6 Billion	Book Value	766.7 Million
Price/Book	3.42	Price/Sales	3.04

Dividend Achiever Status

10 Year Growth Rate	10.33%
Total Years of Dividend Growth	30

TRADING VOLUME (thousand shares)

Business Summary: Commercial Banking (MIC: SIC: 6022 NAIC: 522110)

Bank of Hawaii is the bank holding company for Bank of Hawaii (the Bank). The Bank provides financial services and products mainly in Hawaii and the Pacific Islands. The Bank's subsidiaries include Bank of Hawaii Leasing, Inc., Bankoh Investment Services, Inc., Pacific Century Life Insurance Corporation, Triad Insurance Agency, Inc., Bank of Hawaii Insurance Services, Inc., Pacific Century Insurance Services, Inc., Bankoh Investment Partners, LLC, and Bank of Hawaii International, Inc. The Bank's subsidiaries provide equipment leasing, securities brokerage and investment services, and insurance and insurance agency services. As of Dec 31 2007, Co. had total assets of $10.47 billion.

Recent Developments: For the quarter ended Mar 31 2008, net income increased 20.9% to US$57.2 million from US$47.3 million in the year-earlier quarter. Net interest income increased 4.1% to US$102.2 million from US$98.1 million in the year-earlier quarter. Provision for loan losses was US$14.4 million versus US$2.6 million in the prior-year quarter, an increase of 448.3%. Non-interest income rose 41.3% to US$86.1 million from US$61.0 million, while non-interest expense advanced 13.8% to US$93.4 million.

Prospects: Co. is seeing an increase in its net interest margin as a result of lower funding costs and the effects of a steeper yield curve. Specifically, Co.'s net interest income is benefiting largely from lower funding costs resulting from decreases in rates paid on interest-bearing deposits and rates paid on securities sold under agreements to repurchase. Furthermore, lower yields in Co.'s commercial and industrial loans and home equity loans have been primarily driven by the decline in interest rates. In addition, Co.'s non-interest income is being positively affected by increases in mortgage banking income, service charges on deposit accounts, insurance income, and other non-interest income.

Financial Data
(US$ in Thousands)

	3 Mos	12/31/2007	12/31/2006	12/31/2005	12/31/2004	12/31/2003	12/31/2002	12/31/2001
Earnings Per Share	3.91	3.69	3.52	3.41	3.08	2.21	1.70	1.46
Cash Flow Per Share	5.65	4.77	4.16	4.44	4.87	5.46	9.13	(3.28)
Tang Book Value Per Share	14.68	14.15	11.70	12.49	13.83	13.38	15.09	16.16
Dividends Per Share	1.700	1.670	1.520	1.360	1.230	0.870	0.730	0.720
Dividend Payout %	43.48	45.26	43.18	39.88	39.94	39.37	42.94	49.32
Income Statement								
Interest Income	144,676	601,875	572,672	506,442	455,014	442,521	516,538	828,262
Interest Expense	42,496	206,857	170,059	99,329	64,424	76,579	146,307	368,584
Net Interest Income	102,180	395,018	402,613	407,113	390,590	365,942	370,231	459,678
Provision for Losses	14,427	15,507	10,758	4,588	(10,000)	...	11,616	74,339
Non-Interest Income	86,125	240,487	216,176	209,314	205,094	198,720	199,921	452,619
Non-Interest Expense	93,432	335,407	320,962	327,642	334,440	357,875	370,835	597,616
Income Before Taxes	80,446	284,591	287,069	284,197	271,244	206,787	187,701	239,959
Income Taxes	23,231	100,888	106,710	102,636	97,905	71,592	66,521	122,164
Net Income	57,215	183,703	180,359	181,561	173,339	135,195	121,180	117,795
Average Shares	48,628	49,833	51,178	53,310	56,241	61,085	71,447	80,577
Balance Sheet								
Net Loans & Leases	6,492,435	6,502,204	6,544,111	6,095,361	5,897,776	5,637,306	5,256,269	5,950,248
Total Assets	10,822,801	10,472,942	10,571,815	10,187,038	9,766,191	9,461,647	9,516,418	10,627,797
Total Deposits	8,102,855	7,942,372	8,023,394	7,907,468	7,564,667	7,332,779	6,920,161	6,673,596
Total Liabilities	10,056,054	9,722,687	9,852,395	9,493,686	8,951,357	8,668,515	8,500,659	9,380,785
Stockholders' Equity	766,747	750,255	719,420	693,352	814,834	793,132	1,015,759	1,247,012
Shares Outstanding	47,990	48,589	56,827	51,276	54,960	54,928	63,015	73,218
Statistical Record								
Return on Assets %	1.81	1.75	1.74	1.82	1.80	1.42	1.20	0.96
Return on Equity %	26.13	25.00	25.53	24.08	21.50	14.95	10.71	9.24
Net Interest Margin %	70.63	65.63	70.30	80.39	85.84	82.69	71.68	55.50
Efficiency Ratio %	40.48	39.82	40.69	45.78	50.66	55.81	51.76	46.66
Loans to Deposits	0.80	0.82	0.82	0.77	0.78	0.77	0.76	0.89
Price Range	54.85-43.07	54.85-46.78	54.87-47.33	54.14-44.05	50.95-41.70	42.72-29.43	30.75-23.88	27.88-16.94
P/E Ratio	14.03-11.02	14.86-12.68	15.59-13.45	15.88-12.92	16.54-13.54	19.33-13.32	18.09-14.05	19.10-11.60
Average Yield %	3.34	3.21	2.96	2.76	2.68	2.54	2.62	3.13

Address: 130 Merchant Street, Honolulu, HI 96813 **Telephone:** 808-538-4727 **Web Site:** www.boh.com	**Officers:** Allan R. Landon - Chairman, President, Chief Executive Officer Donna A. Tanoue - Vice-Chairman **Transfer Agents:** Computershare Investor Services, LLC, Canton, MA	**Investor Contact:** 808-537-8430 **No of Institutions:** 244 **Shares:** 34,887,236 **% Held:** 69.34

BANK OF THE OZARKS, INC.

Exchange	Symbol	Price	52Wk Range	Yield	P/E
NMS	OZRK	$24.97 (5/29/2008)	33.50-19.61	1.92	13.21

*7 Year Price Score 88.58   ***NYSE Composite Index=100**   ***12 Month Price Score 94.17**

Price chart with TRADING VOLUME (thousand shares), years 1999–2008

Interim Earnings (Per Share)

Qtr.	Mar	Jun	Sep	Dec
2005	0.44	0.46	0.48	0.50
2006	0.50	0.47	0.48	0.44
2007	0.45	0.48	0.50	0.46
2008	0.46	...	...	...

Interim Dividends (Per Share)

Amt	Decl	Ex	Rec	Pay
0.11Q	07/17/2007	07/25/2007	07/27/2007	08/03/2007
0.12Q	10/16/2007	10/24/2007	10/26/2007	11/02/2007
0.12Q	01/15/2008	01/23/2008	01/25/2008	02/01/2008
0.12Q	04/15/2008	04/23/2008	04/25/2008	05/02/2008
		Indicated Div: $0.48		

Valuation Analysis

Forecast EPS $2.00 (05/16/2008)

Market Cap	$420.1 Million	Book Value	213.0 Million
Price/Book	1.97	Price/Sales	2.09

Dividend Achiever Status

10 Year Growth Rate	42.45%
Total Years of Dividend Growth	10

Business Summary: Commercial Banking (MIC: SIC: 6022 NAIC: 522110)

Bank of the Ozarks is a bank holding company whose primary business is commercial banking conducted through its wholly-owned state chartered bank subsidiary, Bank of the Ozarks. Co.'s market areas include primarily the northern, western and central portions of Arkansas, the metropolitan Dallas, TX area, the Texarkana area (including areas in Texas and Arkansas) and the metropolitan Charlotte, NC area. Co. also owns Ozark Capital Statutory Trust II and Ozark Capital Statutory Trust III, Ozark Capital Statutory Trust IV, and Ozark Capital Statutory Trust V, all business trusts. As of Dec 31 2007, Co. had total assets of $2.71 billion, and total deposits of $2.06 billion.

Recent Developments: For the quarter ended Mar 31 2008, net income increased 3.2% to US$7.8 million from US$7.5 million in the year-earlier quarter. Net interest income increased 19.2% to US$21.8 million from US$18.2 million in the year-earlier quarter. Provision for loan losses was US$3.3 million versus US$1.1 million in the prior-year quarter, an increase of 202.3%. Non-interest income fell 14.0% to US$5.1 million from US$6.0 million, while non-interest expense advanced 6.1% to US$12.9 million.

Prospects: Despite challenging market conditions, Co.'s near-term outlook appears favorable, driven by growth in loans and leases, opportunities to acquire certain tax-exempt investment securities, along with continued improvement in net interest margin. For the full year of 2008, Co. is projecting capital expenditures to range from $20.0 million to $26.0 million, including progress payments on construction projects expected to be completed in 2008 through 2009, furniture and equipment costs as well as acquisition of sites for future development. Meanwhile, Co. expects to open two additional banking offices, including its new corporate headquarters, in Little Rock, AR, by the fourth quarter of 2008.

Financial Data

(US$ in Thousands)	3 Mos	12/31/2007	12/31/2006	12/31/2005	12/31/2004	12/31/2003	12/31/2002	12/31/2001
Earnings Per Share	1.89	1.89	1.89	1.88	1.56	1.24	0.92	0.59
Cash Flow Per Share	2.43	2.54	1.35	2.04	2.27	1.89	1.40	0.32
Tang Book Value Per Share	12.32	11.00	10.06	8.58	6.96	5.67	4.53	3.56
Dividends Per Share	0.450	0.430	0.400	0.370	0.300	0.230	0.155	0.115
Dividend Payout %	23.75	22.75	21.16	19.68	19.23	18.55	16.85	19.57
Income Statement								
Interest Income	44,820	176,970	155,198	112,881	85,231	68,883	60,913	60,119
Interest Expense	23,069	99,352	84,478	44,305	24,608	20,115	19,441	30,414
Net Interest Income	21,751	77,618	70,720	68,576	60,623	48,768	41,472	29,705
Provision for Losses	3,325	6,150	2,450	2,300	3,330	3,865	3,660	3,401
Non-Interest Income	5,125	22,975	23,231	19,252	18,225	17,391	11,641	7,353
Non-Interest Expense	12,881	48,252	46,390	40,080	37,605	31,992	24,915	19,030
Income Before Taxes	10,670	46,191	45,111	45,448	37,913	30,302	24,538	14,627
Income Taxes	2,905	14,445	13,418	13,959	12,030	10,101	8,545	4,081
Net Income	7,765	31,746	31,693	31,489	25,883	20,201	14,406	8,959
Average Shares	16,861	16,834	16,803	16,766	16,635	16,287	15,688	15,262
Balance Sheet								
Net Loans & Leases	1,960,600	1,851,578	1,659,690	1,353,716	1,118,458	895,327	706,959	607,364
Total Assets	3,051,971	2,710,875	2,529,400	2,134,882	1,726,840	1,386,529	1,035,853	871,379
Total Deposits	2,201,009	2,057,061	2,045,092	1,591,643	1,379,930	1,062,064	790,173	677,743
Total Liabilities	2,835,545	2,516,614	2,354,767	1,985,479	1,605,434	1,288,043	945,685	797,512
Stockholders' Equity	212,994	190,829	174,633	149,403	121,406	98,486	72,918	56,617
Shares Outstanding	16,822	16,818	16,746	16,664	16,494	16,232	15,505	15,128
Statistical Record								
Return on Assets %	1.14	1.21	1.36	1.63	1.66	1.67	1.51	1.06
Return on Equity %	16.14	17.37	19.56	23.26	23.48	23.57	22.24	17.07
Net Interest Margin %	48.53	43.86	45.57	60.75	71.13	70.80	68.08	49.41
Efficiency Ratio %	25.79	24.13	26.00	30.33	36.35	37.08	34.34	28.20
Loans to Deposits	0.89	0.90	0.81	0.85	0.81	0.84	0.89	0.90
Price Range	33.50-19.61	33.50-26.19	37.69-30.00	38.42-30.84	36.82-21.74	24.11-11.72	13.18-6.34	6.53-3.16
P/E Ratio	17.72-10.38	17.72-13.86	19.94-15.87	20.44-16.40	23.60-13.94	19.44-9.45	14.32-6.89	11.06-5.35
Average Yield %	1.62	1.46	1.19	1.10	1.12	1.26	1.54	2.38

Address: 12615 Chenal Parkway, Suite 3100, Little Rock, AR 72211 Telephone: 501-978-2265 Web Site: www.bankozarks.com	Officers: George Gleason - Chairman, Chief Executive Officer Mark Ross - Vice-Chairman, President, Chief Operating Officer **Transfer Agents:** Bank of the Ozarks, Little Rock, AR	No of Institutions: 102 Shares: 13,189,890 % Held: 76.49

BANKATLANTIC BANCORP, INC.

Exchange	Symbol	Price	52Wk Range	Yield	P/E
NYS	BBX	$1.84 (5/29/2008)	9.50-1.84	1.09	N/A

*7 Year Price Score 38.41   *NYSE Composite Index=100   *12 Month Price Score 52.82

Interim Earnings (Per Share)

Qtr.	Mar	Jun	Sep	Dec
2005	0.31	0.38	0.26	(0.03)
2006	0.11	0.13	0.04	(0.02)
2007	0.09	0.19	(0.52)	(0.17)
2008	(0.42)	...	...	...

Interim Dividends (Per Share)

Amt	Decl	Ex	Rec	Pay
0.041Q	09/12/2007	10/01/2007	10/03/2007	10/18/2007
0.005Q	12/05/2007	12/31/2007	01/03/2008	01/17/2008
0.005Q	02/15/2008	04/02/2008	04/04/2008	04/18/2008
0.005Q	06/06/2008	07/01/2008	07/03/2008	07/18/2008

Indicated Div: $0.02

Valuation Analysis

Forecast EPS $-0.70 (05/16/2008)
Market Cap $103.2 Million   Book Value   433.9 Million
Price/Book   0.24   Price/Sales   0.20

Dividend Achiever Status

10 Year Growth Rate   7.86%
Total Years of Dividend Growth   11

TRADING VOLUME (thousand shares)

Business Summary: Other Depository Banking (MIC: SIC: 6035 NAIC: 522120)

BankAtlantic Bancorp is a financial services holding company and owns BankAtlantic and its subsidiaries. As of Dec 31 2007, BankAtlantic provided traditional retail banking services and a range of business banking products and related financial services through a network of more than 100 branches or stores in southeast and central Florida and the Tampa Bay area, primarily in the metropolitan areas surrounding the cities of Miami, Ft. Lauderdale, West Palm Beach and Tampa, which are located in the Florida counties of Miami-Dade, Broward, Palm Beach, Hillsborough and Pinellas. At such date, Co. had total assets of about $6.38 billion, and total deposits of about $3.95 billion.

Recent Developments: For the quarter ended Mar 31 2008, loss from continuing operations was US$24.6 million compared with a loss of US$2.2 million in the year-earlier quarter. Net loss amounted to US$23.4 million versus net income of US$5.7 million in the year-earlier quarter. Net interest income decreased 9.6% to US$42.6 million from US$47.1 million in the year-earlier quarter. Provision for loan losses was US$42.9 million versus US$7.5 million in the prior-year quarter, an increase of 474.8%. Non-interest income fell 16.6% to US$30.6 million from US$36.8 million, while non-interest expense declined 11.9% to US$70.0 million.

Prospects: Co.'s results are being hurt by higher provision for loan losses reflecting commercial loan charge-offs concentrated in the commercial residential real estate loan categories and growth in its allowance for home equity loan losses due to continued deterioration in the Florida residential real estate market. Meanwhile, Co. is continuing to explore opportunities to reduce operating expenses and improve future operating efficiencies. In this regard, Co. reduced its workforce in Apr 2008 by about 124 associates, or 6.0%. Co. estimates that the annualized expense savings from the reduction will be about $6.0 million with the realization of these savings to begin in the second quarter of 2008.

Financial Data
(US$ in Thousands)

	3 Mos	12/31/2007	12/31/2006	12/31/2005	12/31/2004	12/31/2003	12/31/2002	12/31/2001
Earnings Per Share	(0.92)	(0.38)	0.25	0.92	1.11	1.08	0.81	0.65
Cash Flow Per Share	0.47	0.70	0.05	0.95	1.12	1.71	0.01	1.92
Tang Book Value Per Share	6.39	6.84	7.33	7.10	6.36	5.48	6.46	6.82
Dividends Per Share	0.128	0.128	0.158	0.146	0.169	0.095	0.120	0.138
Dividend Payout %	...	...	63.20	15.87	15.23	8.80	14.81	21.17
Income Statement								
Interest Income	83,732	371,633	367,177	360,405	260,555	261,849	309,770	325,618
Interest Expense	41,101	192,857	167,057	145,328	87,722	113,217	151,962	187,599
Net Interest Income	42,631	178,776	200,120	215,077	172,833	148,632	157,808	138,019
Provision for Losses	42,888	70,842	8,574	(6,615)	(5,109)	(547)	14,077	16,905
Non-Interest Income	30,639	151,832	142,616	341,099	344,789	281,714	248,318	123,273
Non-Interest Expense	70,033	317,350	300,186	470,111	412,053	368,872	334,480	190,376
Income Before Taxes	(39,651)	(57,584)	33,976	92,680	110,678	62,021	57,569	54,011
Income Taxes	(15,087)	(27,572)	7,097	33,498	39,910	23,424	15,876	22,736
Net Income	(23,443)	(22,200)	15,387	59,182	70,768	67,717	50,335	32,160
Average Shares	56,096	58,161	62,563	63,119	63,056	62,354	64,400	54,313
Balance Sheet								
Net Loans & Leases	4,483,305	4,520,101	4,586,607	4,624,772	4,599,048	3,686,153	3,372,630	2,774,238
Total Assets	6,390,690	6,378,817	6,495,662	6,471,411	6,356,777	4,831,549	5,421,011	4,654,486
Total Deposits	3,995,614	3,953,405	3,867,036	3,752,676	3,457,202	3,058,142	2,920,555	2,276,567
Total Liabilities	5,956,794	5,919,496	5,970,680	5,955,075	5,887,512	4,418,097	4,951,677	4,218,813
Stockholders' Equity	433,896	459,321	524,982	516,336	469,265	413,452	469,334	435,673
Shares Outstanding	56,104	56,072	61,033	60,760	60,090	59,272	58,317	58,079
Statistical Record								
Return on Assets %	N.M.	N.M.	0.24	0.92	1.26	1.32	1.00	0.69
Return on Equity %	N.M.	N.M.	2.96	12.01	15.99	15.34	11.12	9.40
Net Interest Margin %	50.91	48.11	54.50	59.68	66.33	56.76	50.94	42.39
Efficiency Ratio %	61.23	60.62	58.88	67.01	68.07	67.86	59.93	42.41
Loans to Deposits	1.12	1.14	1.19	1.23	1.33	1.21	1.15	1.22
Price Range	11.11-2.97	13.98-2.97	15.96-12.66	19.90-13.36	19.99-13.96	14.34-6.45	9.55-5.59	8.15-2.85
P/E Ratio	...	...	63.84-50.64	21.63-14.52	18.01-12.58	13.28-5.97	11.79-6.90	12.54-4.38
Average Yield %	1.84	1.43	1.12	0.86	0.97	0.99	1.58	2.41

Address: 2100 West Cypress Creek Road, Fort Lauderdale, FL 33309 **Telephone:** 954-940-5000 **Web Site:** www.bankatlanticbancorp.com	**Officers:** Alan B. Levan - Chairman, Chief Executive Officer John E. Abdo - Vice-Chairman **Transfer Agents:** American Stock Transfer & Trust Company, New York, NY	**Investor Contact:** 954-940-5300 **No of Institutions:** 145 **Shares:** 38,472,144 **% Held:** 62.87

BANNER CORP.

Exchange	Symbol	Price	52Wk Range	Yield	P/E
NMS	BANR	$18.81 (5/29/2008)	37.13-18.16	4.25	8.91

*7 Year Price Score 79.99 *NYSE Composite Index=100 ***12 Month Price Score 75.85**

TRADING VOLUME (thousand shares)

Interim Earnings (Per Share)

Qtr.	Mar	Jun	Sep	Dec
2005	0.39	0.42	0.47	(0.25)
2006	0.56	0.77	0.65	0.65
2007	0.62	0.48	0.64	0.76
2008	0.24	...	...	...

Interim Dividends (Per Share)

Amt	Decl	Ex	Rec	Pay
0.19Q	07/26/2007	09/26/2007	09/30/2007	10/10/2007
0.20Q	10/26/2007	12/27/2007	12/31/2007	01/10/2008
0.20Q	01/23/2008	03/27/2008	03/31/2008	04/10/2008
0.20Q	04/23/2008	06/26/2008	06/30/2008	07/10/2008

Indicated Div: $0.80

Valuation Analysis

Forecast EPS	$0.98 (05/16/2008)		
Market Cap	$294.6 Million	Book Value	429.5 Million
Price/Book	0.69	Price/Sales	0.89

Dividend Achiever Status

10 Year Growth Rate	13.47%
Total Years of Dividend Growth	11

Business Summary: Commercial Banking (MIC: SIC: 6022 NAIC: 522110)

Banner is a bank holding company. Co. is primarily engaged in the business of planning, directing and coordinating the business activities of its wholly owned subsidiaries, Banner Bank and Islanders Bank. Co.'s primary business is that of traditional financial institutions, accepting deposits and originating loans in locations surrounding its offices in portions of Washington, Oregon and Idaho. Banner Bank also participates in the secondary market, engaging in mortgage banking operations largely through the origination and sale of one- to four-family residential loans. As of Dec 31 2007, Co. had total assets of $4.50 billion and deposits of $3.62 billion.

Recent Developments: For the quarter ended Mar 31 2008, net income decreased 50.9% to US$3.8 million from US$7.8 million in the year-earlier quarter. Net interest income increased 16.1% to US$37.4 million from US$32.2 million in the year-earlier quarter. Provision for loan losses was US$6.5 million versus US$1.0 million in the prior-year quarter, an increase of 550.0%. Non-interest income rose 29.2% to US$8.2 million from US$6.3 million, while non-interest expense advanced 29.3% to US$33.7 million.

Prospects: Co. anticipates further compression of its net interest margin over the second quarter of 2008, as a result of the Federal Reserve's actions to lower short-term interest rates. Notably, while funding costs are expected to continue declining, the lower prime rate has a more immediate effect on a substantial portion of Co.'s loan portfolio. Meanwhile, Co. plans to open two new offices, one in Bellevue, WA, and one in the Pearl District of Portland, OR, during the second quarter of 2008. Co. believes that its new branches should help improve profitability overtime by providing lower cost core deposits which will allow it to proportionately reduce higher cost borrowings as a source of funds.

Financial Data

(US$ in Thousands)	3 Mos	12/31/2007	12/31/2006	12/31/2005	12/31/2004	12/31/2003	12/31/2002	12/31/2001
Earnings Per Share	2.11	2.49	2.63	1.04	1.65	1.44	0.82	0.64
Cash Flow Per Share	3.02	6.24	3.83	1.78	3.17	3.10	3.79	(1.51)
Tang Book Value Per Share	18.68	18.73	17.72	15.73	15.08	14.49	13.59	13.83
Dividends Per Share	0.780	0.770	0.730	0.690	0.650	0.610	0.600	0.560
Dividend Payout %	36.88	30.92	27.76	66.35	39.39	42.36	73.17	87.50
Income Statement								
Interest Income	71,953	295,309	243,019	190,160	156,230	140,441	144,276	157,666
Interest Expense	34,586	145,690	116,114	81,377	59,915	59,848	65,969	85,944
Net Interest Income	37,367	149,619	126,905	108,783	96,315	80,593	78,307	71,722
Provision for Losses	6,500	5,900	5,500	4,903	5,644	7,300	21,000	13,959
Non-Interest Income	8,184	27,009	20,575	10,544	16,968	19,581	15,877	13,465
Non-Interest Expense	33,708	138,172	105,829	107,361	86,722	77,072	66,225	64,533
Income Before Taxes	5,343	54,813	47,599	16,876	27,925	22,998	12,739	11,592
Income Taxes	1,509	17,890	15,436	4,432	8,585	6,891	3,479	4,142
Net Income	3,834	36,923	32,163	12,444	19,340	16,107	9,260	7,450
Average Shares	15,965	14,838	12,239	11,944	11,735	11,217	11,352	11,600
Balance Sheet								
Net Loans & Leases	3,789,547	3,763,790	2,930,455	2,408,833	2,063,238	1,700,865	1,546,927	1,575,425
Total Assets	4,572,225	4,492,658	3,495,566	3,040,555	2,897,067	2,635,313	2,263,172	2,087,094
Total Deposits	3,693,310	3,620,593	2,794,592	2,323,313	1,925,909	1,670,940	1,497,778	1,295,811
Total Liabilities	4,142,687	4,054,812	3,245,339	2,818,890	2,681,847	2,432,513	2,072,795	1,894,754
Stockholders' Equity	429,538	437,846	250,227	221,665	215,220	202,800	190,377	192,340
Shares Outstanding	15,663	16,025	12,073	11,782	11,856	11,473	11,306	11,634
Statistical Record								
Return on Assets %	0.81	0.92	0.98	0.42	0.70	0.66	0.43	0.37
Return on Equity %	9.24	10.73	13.63	5.70	9.23	8.19	4.84	3.86
Net Interest Margin %	51.93	50.67	52.22	57.21	61.65	57.39	54.28	45.49
Efficiency Ratio %	42.06	42.87	40.15	53.49	50.07	48.16	41.35	37.71
Loans to Deposits	1.03	1.04	1.05	1.04	1.07	1.02	1.03	1.22
Price Range	41.68-20.44	45.06-27.38	46.63-31.05	32.63-24.86	34.25-24.80	25.67-15.27	24.75-15.32	23.10-15.06
P/E Ratio	19.75-9.69	18.10-11.00	17.73-11.81	31.38-23.90	20.76-15.03	17.83-10.60	30.18-18.68	36.09-23.54
Average Yield %	2.50	2.15	1.91	2.43	2.28	3.04	2.96	3.02

Address: 10 S. First Avenue, Walla Walla, WA 99362-0265	Officers: Gary Sirmon - Chairman Jesse G. Foster - Vice-Chairman **Transfer Agents:**	No of Institutions: 112
Telephone: 509-527-3636	Computershare Investor Services, Denver, CO	Shares: 10,488,887 **% Held:** 59.72
Web Site: www.bannerbank.com		

BARD (C.R.), INC.

Exchange	Symbol	Price	52Wk Range	Yield	P/E
NYS	BCR	$92.58 (5/29/2008)	99.66-77.99	0.65	25.50

*7 Year Price Score 121.70 *NYSE Composite Index=100 ***12 Month Price Score 108.77**

TRADING VOLUME (thousand shares)

Interim Earnings (Per Share)

Qtr.	Mar	Jun	Sep	Dec
2005	0.75	0.79	0.83	0.75
2006	0.76	0.76	0.82	0.21
2007	0.95	0.91	0.96	1.01
2008	0.76	...	...	...

Interim Dividends (Per Share)

Amt	Decl	Ex	Rec	Pay
0.15Q	06/13/2007	07/19/2007	07/23/2007	08/03/2007
0.15Q	10/10/2007	10/18/2007	10/22/2007	11/02/2007
0.15Q	12/12/2007	01/16/2008	01/21/2008	02/01/2008
0.15Q	04/16/2008	04/24/2008	04/28/2008	05/09/2008

Indicated Div: $0.60 (Div. Reinv. Plan)

Valuation Analysis

Forecast EPS $4.38 (05/16/2008)

Market Cap	$9.2 Billion	Book Value	1.8 Billion
Price/Book	5.03	Price/Sales	4.08

Dividend Achiever Status

10 Year Growth Rate	5.18%
Total Years of Dividend Growth	36

Business Summary: Health (MIC: SIC: 3841 NAIC: 339112)

C. R. Bard designs, produces, packages, distributes and sells medical, surgical, diagnostic and patient care devices. In general, Co.'s products are intended to be used once and then discarded or implanted either temporarily or permanently. Co. provides four key product group categories: vascular, urology, oncology and surgical specialties. Co. also has a product group of other products. These products are distributed domestically directly to hospitals and other healthcare institutions as well as via hospital/surgical supply and other medical specialty distributors with whom Co. has distribution agreements. Internationally, Co.'s products are distributed either directly or via distributors.

Recent Developments: For the quarter ended Mar 31 2008, income from continuing operations decreased 23.2% to US$78.0 million from US$101.6 million in the year-earlier quarter. Net income decreased 23.2% to US$78.0 million from US$101.6 million in the year-earlier quarter. Revenues were US$584.0 million, up 10.6% from US$528.2 million the year before. Direct operating expenses rose 9.2% to US$225.5 million from US$206.5 million in the comparable period the year before. Indirect operating expenses increased 38.0% to US$257.7 million from US$186.7 million in the equivalent prior-year period.

Prospects: Despite the decline in its bottom-line results, Co. continues to expand its business via strategic acquisitions. For instance, on Mar 10 2008, Co. announced that it has signed an agreement to acquire all the outstanding shares of Specialized Health Products International, Inc. (Specialized Health Products), a manufacturer and marketer of vascular access products, including winged infusion sets, for about $68.0 million. Accordingly, the marketing responsibility for the related products is expected to be assumed by Co.'s Access Systems subsidiary, located in Salt Lake City, UT. This acquisition, which represents a strategic addition to Co.'s port franchise, is anticipated to close in 2008.

Financial Data

(US$ in Thousands)	3 Mos	12/31/2007	12/31/2006	12/31/2005	12/31/2004	12/31/2003	12/31/2002	12/31/2001
Earnings Per Share	3.63	3.84	2.55	3.12	2.82	1.60	1.47	1.38
Cash Flow Per Share	5.09	5.33	3.22	3.83	2.65	2.54	2.62	2.42
Tang Book Value Per Share	10.03	10.73	9.46	9.08	7.26	5.35	4.84	3.97
Dividends Per Share	0.590	0.580	0.540	0.500	0.470	0.450	0.430	0.420
Dividend Payout %	16.25	15.10	21.18	16.03	16.67	28.13	29.25	30.55
Income Statement								
Total Revenue	584,000	2,202,000	1,985,500	1,771,300	1,656,100	1,433,100	1,273,800	1,181,300
EBITDA	121,100	626,400	394,600	494,900	460,500	261,300	245,500	238,700
Depn & Amortn	21,900	79,800	74,900	63,800	54,700	44,700	41,000	40,000
Income Before Taxes	104,800	577,300	347,600	449,600	414,200	223,200	211,000	204,900
Income Taxes	26,800	170,900	75,500	112,500	111,400	54,700	56,000	61,700
Net Income	78,000	406,400	272,100	337,100	302,800	168,500	155,000	143,200
Average Shares	103,300	105,900	106,900	108,000	107,200	105,200	105,600	104,001
Balance Sheet								
Current Assets	1,173,400	1,242,000	1,133,900	1,264,100	1,054,000	875,100	758,000	647,400
Total Assets	2,472,200	2,475,500	2,277,200	2,265,600	2,009,100	1,692,000	1,416,700	1,231,100
Current Liabilities	294,200	281,700	295,900	640,600	390,300	421,900	316,900	234,500
Long-Term Obligations	149,800	149,800	150,600	800	151,400	151,500	152,200	156,400
Total Liabilities	646,700	627,500	579,200	729,500	649,000	646,300	536,300	442,400
Stockholders' Equity	1,825,500	1,848,000	1,698,000	1,536,100	1,360,100	1,045,700	880,400	788,700
Shares Outstanding	99,277	100,191	103,155	104,012	104,672	103,509	103,205	104,767
Statistical Record								
Return on Assets %	15.61	17.10	11.98	15.77	16.32	10.84	11.71	12.34
Return on Equity %	20.83	22.92	16.83	23.28	25.10	17.50	18.57	20.42
EBITDA Margin %	20.74	28.45	19.87	27.94	27.81	18.23	19.27	20.21
Net Margin %	13.36	18.46	13.70	19.03	18.28	11.76	12.17	12.12
Asset Turnover	0.92	0.93	0.87	0.83	0.89	0.92	0.96	1.02
Current Ratio	3.99	4.41	3.83	1.97	2.70	2.07	2.39	2.76
Debt to Equity	0.08	0.08	0.09	N.M.	0.11	0.14	0.17	0.20
Price Range	99.66-77.99	95.05-77.25	85.43-61.00	72.79-61.36	64.58-40.20	40.63-27.41	32.25-23.13	32.26-21.00
P/E Ratio	27.45-21.48	24.75-20.12	33.50-23.92	23.33-19.67	22.90-14.26	25.39-17.13	21.94-15.73	23.37-15.21
Average Yield %	0.68	0.70	0.74	0.75	0.88	1.33	1.57	1.62

Address: 730 Central Avenue, Murray Hill, NJ 07974	Officers: Timothy M. Ring - Chairman, Chief Executive Officer John H. Weiland - President, Chief Operating Officer **Transfer Agents:** Computershare Trust Company, N.A., Canton, MA	Investor Contact: 908-277-8413
Telephone: 908-277-8000		**No of Institutions:** 535
Web Site: www.crbard.com		**Shares:** 100,488,680 **% Held:** 87.87

BB&T CORP.

Exchange	Symbol	Price	52Wk Range	Yield	P/E
NYS	BBT	$32.08 (5/29/2008)	42.76-26.88	5.74	10.22

*7 Year Price Score 73.29 *NYSE Composite Index=100 *12 Month Price Score 95.09

Interim Earnings (Per Share)

Qtr.	Mar	Jun	Sep	Dec
2005	0.71	0.70	0.80	0.78
2006	0.79	0.79	0.77	0.46
2007	0.77	0.83	0.80	0.74
2008	0.78	...	...	...

Interim Dividends (Per Share)

Amt	Decl	Ex	Rec	Pay
0.46Q	06/26/2007	07/11/2007	07/13/2007	08/01/2007
0.46Q	08/21/2007	10/10/2007	10/12/2007	11/01/2007
0.46Q	12/11/2007	01/09/2008	01/11/2008	02/01/2008
0.46Q	02/26/2008	04/10/2008	04/14/2008	05/01/2008
	Indicated Div: $1.84 (Div. Reinv. Plan)			

Valuation Analysis

Forecast EPS $3.00 (05/17/2008)

Market Cap	$17.5 Billion	Book Value	12.8 Billion
Price/Book	1.37	Price/Sales	1.63

Dividend Achiever Status

10 Year Growth Rate	11.74%
Total Years of Dividend Growth	36

Business Summary: Commercial Banking (MIC: SIC: 6021 NAIC: 522110)

BB&T is a financial holding company. Co. conducts its operations primarily through its commercial bank subsidiary, Branch Banking and Trust Company, which provides a range of banking services to individuals and businesses, and provides loans and markets deposits to businesses and consumers. Co.'s operations also consist of several nonbank subsidiaries, which provide financial services products, including automobile lending, equipment financing, full-service securities brokerage, payroll processing, asset management and capital markets services. As of Dec 31 2007, Co. had total assets of $132.62 billion and total deposits of $86.77 billion.

Recent Developments: For the quarter ended Mar 31 2008, net income increased 1.7% to US$428.0 million from US$421.0 million in the year-earlier quarter. Net interest income increased 7.6% to US$1.02 billion from US$945.0 million in the year-earlier quarter. Provision for loan losses was US$223.0 million versus US$71.0 million in the prior-year quarter, an increase of 214.1%. Non-interest income rose 18.3% to US$771.0 million from US$652.0 million, while non-interest expense advanced 6.0% to US$936.0 million.

Prospects: On Apr 23 2008, Co. announced that it has signed an agreement to acquire San Diego-based UnionBanc Insurance Services Inc. an insurance subsidiary of Union Bank of California, N.A. The transaction would expand Co.'s insurance operation in California. Co. expects to complete the transaction by the end of the second quarter of 2008, pending regulatory approval. Accordingly, Co. plans to integrate the UnionBanc Insurance Services offices in San Rafael and Roseville into BB&T-Tanner Insurance in Pleasanton and Stockton. Meanwhile, Co. anticipates that the margin will improve in 2008 and foresees increases in nonperforming assets and charge-offs going forward.

Financial Data
(US$ in Thousands)

	3 Mos	12/31/2007	12/31/2006	12/31/2005	12/31/2004	12/31/2003	12/31/2002	12/31/2001
Earnings Per Share	3.14	3.14	2.81	3.00	2.80	2.07	2.72	2.12
Cash Flow Per Share	0.35	1.92	1.44	3.22	5.49	7.47	1.73	0.21
Tang Book Value Per Share	12.32	11.86	11.04	11.76	11.33	10.92	12.04	13.50
Dividends Per Share	1.800	1.760	1.600	1.460	1.340	1.220	1.100	0.980
Dividend Payout %	57.31	56.05	56.94	48.67	47.86	58.94	40.44	46.23
Income Statement								
Income Before Taxes	629,000	2,570,000	2,473,000	2,466,731	2,322,362	1,617,030	1,790,697	1,360,428
Income Taxes	201,000	836,000	945,000	812,962	763,987	552,127	497,468	386,790
Net Income	428,000	1,734,000	1,528,000	1,653,769	1,558,375	1,064,903	1,303,009	973,638
Average Shares	548,946	551,755	543,890	551,379	556,041	514,082	478,792	459,269
Balance Sheet								
Total Assets	136,417,000	132,618,000	121,351,000	109,169,759	100,508,641	90,466,613	80,216,816	70,869,945
Total Liabilities	123,575,000	119,986,000	109,606,000	98,040,645	89,634,167	80,531,882	72,828,902	64,719,736
Stockholders' Equity	12,842,000	12,632,000	11,745,000	11,129,114	10,874,474	9,934,731	7,387,914	6,150,209
Shares Outstanding	546,799	545,955	541,475	543,102	550,406	541,942	470,452	455,682
Statistical Record								
Return on Assets %	1.35	1.37	1.33	1.58	1.63	1.25	1.72	1.50
Return on Equity %	14.18	14.23	13.36	15.03	14.94	12.29	19.25	17.81
Price Range	42.90-26.88	44.15-30.67	44.63-38.37	43.77-37.08	43.25-33.33	39.66-31.15	39.23-31.26	38.48-31.42
P/E Ratio	13.66-8.56	14.06-9.77	15.88-13.65	14.59-12.36	15.45-11.90	19.16-15.05	14.42-11.49	18.15-14.82
Average Yield %	4.81	4.41	3.81	3.60	3.50	3.46	2.99	2.75

Address: 200 West Second Street, PO Box 1250, Winston-Salem, NC 27102-1250
Telephone: 336-733-2000
Web Site: www.BBT.com

Officers: John A. Allison - Chairman, Chief Executive Officer Christopher L. Henson - Senior Executive Vice President, Chief Financial Officer **Transfer Agents:** BB&T Corporate Trust Services, Wilson, NC

Investor Contact: 336-733-3058
No of Institutions: 564
Shares: 215,567,296 **% Held:** 37.45

BECKMAN COULTER, INC.

Exchange	Symbol	Price	52Wk Range	Yield	P/E
NYS	BEC	$68.89 (5/29/2008)	76.64-61.98	0.99	20.44

*7 Year Price Score 99.03   *NYSE Composite Index=100   *12 Month Price Score 98.81

Interim Earnings (Per Share)

Qtr.	Mar	Jun	Sep	Dec
2005	0.62	0.85	0.56	0.27
2006	0.50	0.70	0.74	0.97
2007	0.59	1.09	0.93	0.69
2008	0.67	...	...	...

Interim Dividends (Per Share)

Amt	Decl	Ex	Rec	Pay
0.16Q	07/26/2007	08/01/2007	08/03/2007	08/17/2007
0.16Q	10/22/2007	11/01/2007	11/05/2007	11/19/2007
0.17Q	02/08/2008	02/20/2008	02/22/2008	03/07/2008
0.17Q	04/25/2008	05/07/2008	05/09/2008	05/23/2008

Indicated Div: $0.68 (Div. Reinv. Plan)

Valuation Analysis

Forecast EPS $3.60 (05/17/2008)

Market Cap	$4.3 Billion	Book Value	1.5 Billion
Price/Book	2.80	Price/Sales	1.51

Dividend Achiever Status

10 Year Growth Rate		7.87%
Total Years of Dividend Growth		16

Business Summary: Instruments and Related Products (MIC: SIC: 3826 NAIC: 334516)

Beckman Coulter is a biomedical testing company engaged in the manufacture of biomedical testing instrument systems, tests and supplies. Co. provides laboratory tools used to conduct basic research into the fundamental processes of human biology, to develop vaccines and drugs to treat disease, to conduct clinical trials and related research activities, and to perform various tasks from patient blood tests to diagnostic testing. Co. has four product areas, which include Chemistry Systems, Immunoassay Systems, Cellular Systems, and Discovery and Automation Systems. At Dec 31 2007, Co. marketed its products in more than 130 countries.

Recent Developments: For the quarter ended Mar 31 2008, net income increased 15.6% to US$42.9 million from US$37.1 million in the year-earlier quarter. Revenues were US$730.5 million, up 19.1% from US$613.6 million the year before. Operating income was US$68.3 million versus US$57.3 million in the prior-year quarter, an increase of 19.2%. Direct operating expenses rose 25.0% to US$395.2 million from US$316.2 million in the comparable period the year before. Indirect operating expenses increased 11.2% to US$267.0 million from US$240.1 million in the equivalent prior-year period.

Prospects: On Apr 30 2008, Co. licensed certain rights to testing for the hepatitis C virus from Siemens Healthcare Diagnostics. As a result, Co. expects to take a charge of $12.0 million in the second quarter of 2008. The acquired rights to this intellectual property is part of Co.'s growth strategy to expand the served market for its 'sample-to-result' molecular diagnostics system, which is expected to launch in 2010, while reducing the cost of care. Meanwhile, assuming stable currency, Co. is projecting full-year 2008 revenue growth in the range of 11.0% to 13.0% and operating income margin of about 12.0% to 12.5%. Also, Co. anticipates earnings of between $3.55 and $3.65 per share for 2008.

Financial Data

(US$ in Thousands)	3 Mos	12/31/2007	12/31/2006	12/31/2005	12/31/2004	12/31/2003	12/31/2002	12/31/2001
Earnings Per Share	3.37	3.30	2.92	2.32	3.21	3.21	2.08	2.16
Cash Flow Per Share	5.95	6.35	5.16	6.74	4.32	3.68	5.12	4.57
Tang Book Value Per Share	6.88	5.05	1.38	4.68	6.19	2.99	N.M.	N.M.
Dividends Per Share	0.650	0.640	0.600	0.560	0.480	0.400	0.350	0.340
Dividend Payout %	19.30	19.39	20.55	24.14	14.95	12.46	16.83	15.74
Income Statement								
Total Revenue	730,500	2,761,300	2,528,500	2,443,800	2,408,300	2,192,500	2,059,400	1,984,000
EBITDA	122,300	530,600	430,700	337,500	416,400	409,900	326,600	378,300
Depn & Amortn	59,200	203,000	181,500	146,200	115,200	106,800	109,800	126,400
Income Before Taxes	56,700	292,700	215,200	165,600	278,200	272,800	178,900	205,000
Income Taxes	13,800	83,000	57,000	15,000	67,300	65,600	43,400	63,500
Net Income	42,900	211,300	186,900	150,600	210,900	207,200	135,500	138,400
Average Shares	64,498	64,066	63,971	64,861	65,773	64,493	65,060	64,011
Balance Sheet								
Current Assets	1,526,200	1,488,100	1,338,100	1,233,600	1,279,600	1,161,200	1,056,200	1,035,600
Total Assets	3,640,500	3,594,300	3,291,700	3,027,600	2,795,000	2,558,200	2,263,600	2,178,000
Current Liabilities	723,600	797,200	711,600	758,500	613,300	578,200	611,600	509,900
Long-Term Obligations	919,900	888,600	952,000	589,100	611,700	625,600	626,600	760,300
Total Liabilities	2,094,300	2,152,600	2,137,400	1,832,800	1,700,700	1,660,500	1,671,500	1,659,800
Stockholders' Equity	1,546,200	1,441,700	1,154,300	1,194,800	1,094,300	897,700	592,100	518,200
Shares Outstanding	62,800	62,500	61,000	62,400	61,600	62,000	61,000	61,200
Statistical Record								
Return on Assets %	6.18	6.14	5.92	5.17	7.86	8.59	6.10	6.60
Return on Equity %	15.59	16.28	15.91	13.16	21.12	27.82	24.41	32.11
EBITDA Margin %	16.74	19.22	17.03	13.81	17.29	18.70	15.86	19.07
Net Margin %	5.87	7.65	7.39	6.16	8.76	9.45	6.58	6.98
Asset Turnover	0.82	0.80	0.80	0.84	0.90	0.91	0.93	0.95
Current Ratio	2.11	1.87	1.88	1.63	2.09	2.01	1.73	2.03
Debt to Equity	0.59	0.62	0.82	0.49	0.56	0.70	1.06	1.47
Price Range	76.64-62.06	76.64-59.04	61.35-49.73	72.02-48.75	67.70-49.99	51.31-28.50	52.47-25.78	47.01-34.50
P/E Ratio	22.74-18.42	23.22-17.89	21.01-17.03	31.04-21.01	21.09-15.57	15.98-8.88	25.23-12.39	21.76-15.97
Average Yield %	0.94	0.94	1.07	0.91	0.84	0.98	0.84	0.83

Address: 4300 N. Harbor Boulevard, P.O. Box 3100, Fullerton, CA 92834-3100 **Telephone:** 714-871-4848 **Web Site:** www.beckmancoulter.com	Officers: Betty Woods - Chairwoman Scott Garrett - President, Chief Executive Officer, Chief Operating Officer **Transfer Agents:** Computershare Trust Company, N.A., Providence, RI	Investor Contact: 714-773-7620 No of Institutions: 375 Shares: 62,940,672 % Held: 84.17

BECTON, DICKINSON AND CO.

Exchange	Symbol	Price	52Wk Range	Yield	P/E
NYS	BDX	$85.64 (5/29/2008)	92.34-73.65	1.33	20.74

*7 Year Price Score 119.13 *NYSE Composite Index=100 *12 Month Price Score 106.30

Interim Earnings (Per Share)

Qtr.	Dec	Mar	Jun	Sep
2004-05	0.75	0.72	0.73	0.58
2005-06	0.85	0.60	0.81	0.68
2006-07	0.56	0.95	0.96	1.02
2007-08	1.07	1.09	...	...

Interim Dividends (Per Share)

Amt	Decl	Ex	Rec	Pay
0.245Q	07/24/2007	09/05/2007	09/07/2007	09/28/2007
0.285Q	11/20/2007	12/10/2007	12/12/2007	01/02/2008
0.285Q	01/29/2008	03/06/2008	03/10/2008	03/31/2008
0.285Q	05/20/2008	06/05/2008	06/09/2008	06/30/2008

Indicated Div: $1.14 (Div. Reinv. Plan)

Valuation Analysis

Forecast EPS	$4.37 (05/17/2008)		
Market Cap	$20.9 Billion	Book Value	4.9 Billion
Price/Book	4.30	Price/Sales	3.11

Dividend Achiever Status

10 Year Growth Rate	14.19%
Total Years of Dividend Growth	35

TRADING VOLUME (thousand shares)

Business Summary: Medical Instruments & Equipment (MIC: SIC: 3841 NAIC: 339112)

Becton, Dickinson and Company manufactures and sells a range of medical supplies, devices, laboratory equipment and diagnostic products used by healthcare institutions, life science researchers, clinical laboratories, industry and the general public. Co.'s operations consist of three business segments: BD Medical, which produces an array of medical devices that are used in a range of healthcare settings; BD Diagnostics, which provides products for the collection and transport of diagnostic specimens and instrumentation for analysis across a range of infectious disease testing; and BD Biosciences, which produces research and clinical tools that facilitate the study of cells.

Recent Developments: For the quarter ended Mar 31 2008, income from continuing operations increased 17.0% to US$275.6 million from US$235.5 million in the year-earlier quarter. Net income increased 13.9% to US$276.2 million from US$242.5 million in the year-earlier quarter. Revenues were US$1.75 billion, up 10.9% from US$1.58 billion the year before. Operating income was US$381.6 million versus US$318.1 million in the prior-year quarter, an increase of 20.0%. Direct operating expenses rose 11.7% to US$853.8 million from US$764.5 million in the comparable period the year before. Indirect operating expenses increased 3.7% to US$511.6 million from US$493.3 million in the equivalent prior-year period.

Prospects: On May 13 2008, Co. announced that it has acquired all of the outstanding stock of Cytopeia, a privately held Washington company based in Seattle that develops and sells flow cytometry cell sorting instruments. The acquisition provides Co. with new technologies and capabilities that should enhance its ability to meet growing customer needs in certain areas, including cell therapy research. Meanwhile, as higher costs of raw materials, manufacturing start-up costs, and asset write-offs in the first half of the fiscal year ending Sep 2008 are anticipated to more than offset expected improvements in its gross profit margin, Co. expects this margin to decrease by 30 to 40 basis points in 2008.

Financial Data

(US$ in Thousands)	6 Mos	3 Mos	09/30/2007	09/30/2006	09/30/2005	09/30/2004	09/30/2003	09/30/2002
Earnings Per Share	4.13	4.00	3.49	2.93	2.77	1.77	2.07	1.79
Cash Flow Per Share	5.75	5.87	5.05	4.36	4.87	4.35	3.56	3.24
Tang Book Value Per Share	14.88	13.58	12.82	11.18	9.36	8.01	6.63	4.95
Dividends Per Share	1.060	1.020	0.980	0.860	0.720	0.600	0.400	0.390
Dividend Payout %	25.67	25.50	28.08	29.35	25.99	33.90	19.32	21.79
Income Statement								
Total Revenue	3,452,692	1,705,767	6,359,708	5,834,827	5,414,681	4,934,745	4,527,940	4,033,069
EBITDA	977,831	478,595	1,597,494	1,342,257	1,300,866	1,035,487	1,003,889	901,204
Depn & Amortn	232,059	115,212	393,350	300,550	276,760	253,012	257,623	239,311
Income Before Taxes	748,868	366,572	1,203,945	1,034,957	1,004,854	752,868	709,706	628,589
Income Taxes	202,337	95,676	347,778	279,366	312,571	170,364	162,650	148,607
Net Income	547,732	271,548	890,033	752,280	722,263	467,402	547,056	479,982
Average Shares	252,788	253,116	254,810	256,554	260,712	263,337	263,635	268,183
Balance Sheet								
Current Assets	3,422,601	3,345,067	3,130,566	3,185,253	2,975,314	2,641,334	2,338,569	1,928,707
Total Assets	7,801,256	7,566,534	7,329,365	6,824,525	6,071,969	5,752,579	5,572,253	5,040,460
Current Liabilities	1,378,907	1,496,806	1,478,809	1,576,329	1,299,375	1,050,082	1,043,374	1,252,453
Long-Term Obligations	959,949	957,627	955,713	956,971	1,060,833	1,171,506	1,184,031	802,967
Total Liabilities	2,942,080	3,042,258	2,967,408	2,988,321	2,788,017	2,684,716	2,675,299	2,552,486
Stockholders' Equity	4,859,176	4,524,276	4,361,957	3,836,204	3,283,952	3,067,863	2,896,954	2,487,974
Shares Outstanding	244,065	244,055	243,837	245,468	247,684	249,334	251,133	255,529
Statistical Record								
Return on Assets %	14.23	14.17	12.58	11.67	12.22	8.23	10.31	9.75
Return on Equity %	23.36	24.10	21.71	21.13	22.74	15.63	20.32	19.93
EBITDA Margin %	28.32	28.06	25.12	23.00	24.02	20.98	22.17	22.35
Net Margin %	15.86	15.92	13.99	12.89	13.34	9.47	12.08	11.90
Asset Turnover	0.91	0.91	0.90	0.90	0.92	0.87	0.85	0.82
Current Ratio	2.48	2.23	2.12	2.02	2.29	2.52	2.24	1.54
Debt to Equity	0.20	0.21	0.22	0.25	0.32	0.38	0.41	0.32
Price Range	92.34-73.65	85.30-69.85	82.61-68.81	70.67-50.07	59.98-49.52	53.25-35.71	40.43-28.40	38.47-25.01
P/E Ratio	22.36-17.83	21.32-17.46	23.67-19.72	24.12-17.09	21.65-17.88	30.08-20.18	19.53-13.72	21.49-13.97
Average Yield %	1.30	1.31	1.31	1.30	1.40	1.30	1.17	1.14

Address: 1 Becton Drive, Franklin Lakes, NJ 07417-1880 **Telephone:** 201-847-6800 **Web Site:** www.bd.com	Officers: Edward J. Ludwig - Chairman, President, Chief Executive Officer John R. Considine - Vice-Chairman, Chief Financial Officer **Transfer Agents:**Computershare Trust Company, N.A., Canton, MA	Investor Contact: 800-284-6845 **No of Institutions:** 767 **Shares:** 222,484,048 % Held: 84.48

BEMIS CO INC

Exchange	Symbol	Price	52Wk Range	Yield	P/E
NYS	BMS	$27.03 (5/29/2008)	34.35-23.26	3.26	15.90

*7 Year Price Score 80.48 *NYSE Composite Index=100* ***12 Month Price Score 97.38**

Interim Earnings (Per Share)

Qtr.	Mar	Jun	Sep	Dec
2005	0.30	0.38	0.41	0.42
2006	0.35	0.46	0.45	0.39
2007	0.45	0.47	0.40	0.42
2008	0.42	...	...	...

Interim Dividends (Per Share)

Amt	Decl	Ex	Rec	Pay
0.21Q	08/02/2007	08/15/2007	08/17/2007	09/04/2007
0.21Q	11/01/2007	11/14/2007	11/16/2007	12/03/2007
0.22Q	01/31/2008	02/13/2008	02/15/2008	03/03/2008
0.22Q	05/01/2008	05/14/2008	05/16/2008	06/02/2008

Indicated Div: $0.88 (Div. Reinv. Plan)

Valuation Analysis

Forecast EPS $1.79 (05/16/2008)

Market Cap	$2.7 Billion	Book Value 1.6 Billion
Price/Book	1.70	Price/Sales 0.73

Dividend Achiever Status

10 Year Growth Rate	7.70%
Total Years of Dividend Growth	24

TRADING VOLUME (thousand shares)

Business Summary: Paper Products (MIC: SIC: 2671 NAIC: 322221)

Bemis Company is a manufacturer of flexible packaging products and pressure sensitive materials, selling to customers mainly in the food industry in the U.S., Canada, South America, Europe, Asia Pacific and Mexico. Through its Flexible Packaging segment, Co. produces a range of food, consumer goods, and industrial packaging. Multilayer flexible polymer film structures and laminates are sold for food, medical and personal care products as well as non-food applications utilizing vacuum or modified atmosphere packaging. Through its Pressure Sensitive Materials segment, Co. produces pressure sensitive adhesive coated paper and film substrates sold into the label, graphic and technical markets.

Recent Developments: For the quarter ended Mar 31 2008, net income decreased 12.3% to US$42.3 million from US$48.3 million in the year-earlier quarter. Revenues were US$947.3 million, up 4.2% from US$909.1 million the year before. Direct operating expenses rose 7.1% to US$784.3 million from US$732.0 million in the comparable period the year before. Indirect operating expenses decreased 3.8% to US$95.8 million from US$99.6 million in the equivalent prior-year period.

Prospects: While the market conditions remain difficult to predict, Co. continues to mitigate the effect of the rising raw material costs, particularly with regard to its specialty resin and chemical inputs, with selling price increases and profit improvement programs that it expects to result in improved performance for the remainder of 2008. In addition, Co. continues to look forward to the introduction of new products in 2008 which will further diversify its business and build momentum once the economy begins to recover. In view of these initiatives, Co. is targeting second quarter 2008 earnings of $0.44 to $0.47 per diluted share and full year earnings of $1.78 to $1.88 per diluted share.

Financial Data

(US$ in Thousands)	3 Mos	12/31/2007	12/31/2006	12/31/2005	12/31/2004	12/31/2003	12/31/2002	12/31/2001
Earnings Per Share	1.70	1.74	1.65	1.51	1.67	1.37	1.54	1.32
Cash Flow Per Share	3.87	3.94	3.33	2.63	2.53	2.93	2.71	3.01
Tang Book Value Per Share	8.41	8.12	7.31	6.29	7.48	5.81	4.11	4.39
Dividends Per Share	0.850	0.840	0.760	0.720	0.640	0.560	0.520	0.500
Dividend Payout %	49.86	48.28	46.06	47.68	38.32	40.88	33.77	37.88
Income Statement								
Total Revenue	947,282	3,649,281	3,639,363	3,473,950	2,834,394	2,635,018	2,369,038	2,293,104
EBITDA	108,971	445,306	439,054	427,928	425,549	367,440	386,246	351,572
Depn & Amortn	41,838	159,452	153,258	151,499	131,882	128,195	119,231	124,147
Income Before Taxes	67,133	285,854	285,796	276,429	293,667	239,245	267,015	227,425
Income Taxes	24,800	104,300	109,500	113,900	113,700	92,100	101,500	87,100
Net Income	42,333	181,554	176,296	162,529	179,967	147,145	165,515	140,325
Average Shares	100,919	104,114	106,767	107,819	107,942	107,733	107,492	106,243
Balance Sheet								
Current Assets	1,208,289	1,136,943	1,093,712	987,810	873,767	751,906	721,655	586,897
Total Assets	3,265,823	3,191,396	3,039,009	2,964,600	2,486,743	2,292,932	2,256,650	1,922,974
Current Liabilities	536,023	534,550	555,455	474,362	375,143	315,586	325,853	238,182
Long-Term Obligations	815,772	775,456	722,211	790,107	533,886	583,399	718,277	595,224
Total Liabilities	1,637,390	1,590,138	1,537,808	1,587,553	1,175,904	1,148,802	1,293,236	1,034,698
Stockholders' Equity	1,587,654	1,562,332	1,472,016	1,349,355	1,307,866	1,138,733	958,974	886,148
Shares Outstanding	99,628	100,518	104,841	105,305	106,947	106,242	105,887	105,739
Statistical Record								
Return on Assets %	5.51	5.83	5.87	5.96	7.51	6.47	7.92	7.36
Return on Equity %	11.42	11.97	12.50	12.23	14.67	14.03	17.94	16.66
EBITDA Margin %	11.50	12.20	12.06	12.32	15.01	13.94	16.30	15.33
Net Margin %	4.47	4.98	4.84	4.68	6.35	5.58	6.99	6.12
Asset Turnover	1.16	1.17	1.21	1.27	1.18	1.16	1.13	1.20
Current Ratio	2.25	2.13	1.97	2.08	2.33	2.38	2.21	2.46
Debt to Equity	0.51	0.50	0.49	0.59	0.41	0.51	0.75	0.67
Price Range	34.65-23.26	36.23-25.85	34.82-28.49	31.36-23.44	29.31-23.48	25.53-19.89	29.04-19.94	26.08-14.41
P/E Ratio	20.38-13.68	20.82-14.86	21.10-17.27	20.77-15.52	17.55-14.06	18.64-14.52	18.85-12.95	19.76-10.91
Average Yield %	2.90	2.67	2.41	2.62	2.42	2.47	2.03	2.50

Address: One Neenah Center, 4th Floor, P.O. Box 669, Neenah, WI 54956-0669 **Telephone:** 920-727-4100 **Web Site:** www.bemis.com	Officers: Jeffrey H. Curler - Chairman Henry J. Theisen - President, Chief Executive Officer **Transfer Agents:** Wells Fargo Bank, N.A., South St. Paul, MN	**Investor Contact:** 920-727-4100 **No of Institutions:** 333 **Shares:** 89,861,872 **% Held:** 77.36

BLACK HILLS CORPORATION

Exchange	Symbol	Price	52Wk Range	Yield	P/E
NYS	BKH	$35.58 (5/29/2008)	44.90-34.77	3.93	16.40

*7 Year Price Score 91.71 *NYSE Composite Index=100 *12 Month Price Score 95.81

Interim Earnings (Per Share)

Qtr.	Mar	Jun	Sep	Dec
2005	0.48	0.45	(0.73)	0.80
2006	0.78	0.35	0.66	0.62
2007	0.91	0.66	0.46	0.62
2008	0.44	...	...	...

Interim Dividends (Per Share)

Amt	Decl	Ex	Rec	Pay
0.34Q	07/26/2007	08/15/2007	08/17/2007	09/01/2007
0.35Q	11/01/2007	11/14/2007	11/16/2007	12/01/2007
0.35Q	01/31/2008	02/13/2008	02/15/2008	03/01/2008
0.35Q	04/28/2008	05/14/2008	05/16/2008	06/01/2008

Indicated Div: $1.40 (Div. Reinv. Plan)

Valuation Analysis

Forecast EPS $2.42 (05/16/2008)

Market Cap	$1.4 Billion	Book Value	965.2 Million
Price/Book	1.42	Price/Sales	1.99

Dividend Achiever Status

10 Year Growth Rate	3.77%
Total Years of Dividend Growth	36

TRADING VOLUME (thousand shares)

Business Summary: Electricity (MIC: SIC: 4911 NAIC: 221121)

Black Hills is an energy company operating in two business groups: utilities, and non-regulated energy. Co.'s utilities group consists of the Electric Utility segment, operating via its Black Hills Power (BHP) subsidiary; and Combination Electric and Gas Utility segment, which operates via its Cheyenne Light (CL) subsidiary. BHP generates, transmits and distributes electricity in South Dakota, Wyoming and Montana, while CL distributes electric and natural gas service in the Cheyenne, WY vicinity. Co. operates its non-regulated energy group via its Black Hills Energy subsidiary, which conducts its business through the oil and gas, power generation, coal mining, and energy marketing segments.

Recent Developments: For the quarter ended Mar 31 2008, income from continuing operations decreased 49.0% to US$16.6 million from US$32.5 million in the year-earlier quarter. Net income decreased 48.3% to US$16.8 million from US$32.5 million in the year-earlier quarter. Revenues were US$179.2 million, down 3.9% from US$186.5 million the year before. Operating income was US$36.6 million versus US$56.0 million in the prior-year quarter, a decrease of 34.7%. Direct operating expenses rose 12.5% to US$80.8 million from US$71.8 million in the comparable period the year before. Indirect operating expenses increased 5.3% to US$61.8 million from US$58.7 million in the equivalent prior-year period.

Prospects: On Apr 30 2008, Co. has entered into a definitive agreement with affiliates of Hastings Funds Management Ltd (Hastings) and IIF BH Investment LLC, to sell seven independent power production (IPP) gas-fired plants with a total capacity of 974 megawatts for $840.0 million cash, subject to certain working capital adjustments. The closing of the IPP sale, pending customary regulatory approvals, is expected to occur late second quarter or early third quarter of 2008. Under the terms of the agreement, Co. has the right to retain ownership of the Fountain Valley 240 megawatt power plant in the event closing conditions for its planned acquisition of the Aquila, Inc. utility assets are not met.

Financial Data

(US$ in Thousands)	3 Mos	12/31/2007	12/31/2006	12/31/2005	12/31/2004	12/31/2003	12/31/2002	12/31/2001
Earnings Per Share	2.17	2.64	2.42	1.00	1.76	1.97	2.26	3.42
Cash Flow Per Share	5.63	6.81	7.83	5.34	4.21	5.59	8.16	6.99
Tang Book Value Per Share	23.56	24.32	22.03	20.49	20.37	19.55	15.42	14.67
Dividends Per Share	1.376	1.370	1.320	1.280	1.240	1.200	...	...
Dividend Payout %	63.34	51.89	54.55	128.00	70.45	60.91	...	...
Income Statement								
Total Revenue	179,211	695,914	656,882	1,391,644	1,121,701	1,250,052	423,919	1,558,558
EBITDA	62,552	279,614	247,386	176,095	222,442	219,209	206,360	234,106
Depn & Amortn	25,644	99,700	94,083	89,306	87,833	80,791	69,738	54,051
Income Before Taxes	25,289	147,373	106,705	40,011	84,525	86,915	96,017	142,807
Income Taxes	8,872	45,641	33,802	18,299	26,704	29,920	29,662	50,544
Net Income	16,791	98,772	81,019	33,420	57,973	61,222	61,452	88,077
Average Shares	38,399	37,414	33,549	33,288	32,912	31,015	27,167	25,771
Balance Sheet								
Net PPE	1,874,262	1,823,534	1,646,367	1,435,398	1,445,732	1,442,422	1,476,263	1,238,224
Total Assets	2,525,067	2,472,866	2,244,676	2,119,960	2,056,163	2,063,225	2,035,169	1,658,767
Long-Term Obligations	561,136	564,372	628,340	670,193	733,581	868,459	618,862	415,798
Total Liabilities	1,554,585	1,503,011	1,454,635	1,381,081	1,320,398	1,353,478	1,500,006	1,143,603
Stockholders' Equity	965,238	969,855	790,041	738,879	735,765	709,747	535,163	515,164
Shares Outstanding	38,395	37,796	33,369	33,155	32,477	32,297	27,102	26,890
Statistical Record								
Return on Assets %	3.44	4.19	3.71	1.60	2.81	2.99	3.33	5.91
Return on Equity %	8.65	11.22	10.60	4.53	8.00	9.84	11.70	22.09
EBITDA Margin %	34.90	40.18	37.66	12.65	19.83	17.54	48.68	15.02
Net Margin %	9.37	14.19	12.33	2.40	5.17	4.90	14.50	5.65
PPE Turnover	0.39	0.40	0.43	0.97	0.77	0.86	0.31	1.53
Asset Turnover	0.29	0.30	0.30	0.67	0.54	0.61	0.23	1.05
Debt to Equity	0.58	0.58	0.80	0.91	1.00	1.22	1.16	0.81
Price Range	44.90-34.93	44.90-35.76	37.93-32.75	43.54-29.42	32.25-26.72	33.35-22.26	36.84-19.15	58.05-26.35
P/E Ratio	20.69-16.10	17.01-13.55	15.67-13.53	43.54-29.42	18.32-15.18	16.93-11.30	16.30-8.47	16.97-7.70
Average Yield %	0.87	3.40	3.79	3.51	4.17	4.08	...	...

Address: 625 Ninth Street, Rapid City, SD 57701	Officers: David R. Emery - Chairman, President, Chief Executive Officer Steven J. Helmers - Senior Vice President, General Counsel **Transfer Agents:** Wells Fargo Shareowner Services, St. Paul, MN	Investor Contact: 605-721-2326
Telephone: 605-721-1700		No of Institutions: 207
Web Site: www.blackhillscorp.com		Shares: 28,805,008 % Held: 72.04

38

BLOCK (H & R), INC.

Exchange	Symbol	Price	52Wk Range	Yield	P/E
NYS	HRB	$23.10 (5/29/2008)	24.37-17.00	2.47	N/A

*7 Year Price Score 70.50   ***NYSE Composite Index=100**   ***12 Month Price Score 110.46**

Interim Earnings (Per Share)

Qtr.	Jul	Oct	Jan	Apr
2004-05	(0.13)	(0.16)	0.28	1.90
2005-06	(0.09)	(0.26)	0.04	1.77
2006-07	(0.41)	(0.49)	(0.18)	(0.25)
2007-08	(0.93)	(1.55)	(0.14)	...

Interim Dividends (Per Share)

Amt	Decl	Ex	Rec	Pay
0.142Q	06/06/2007	09/06/2007	09/10/2007	10/01/2007
0.142Q	11/28/2007	12/10/2007	12/12/2007	01/02/2008
0.142Q	02/26/2008	03/07/2008	03/11/2008	04/01/2008
0.142Q	05/06/2008	06/06/2008	06/10/2008	07/01/2008
		Indicated Div: $0.57		

Valuation Analysis

Forecast EPS $1.30 (05/17/2008)

Market Cap	$7.5 Billion	Book Value	463.9 Million
Price/Book	16.20	Price/Sales	1.83

Dividend Achiever Status

10 Year Growth Rate	10.59%
Total Years of Dividend Growth	10

Business Summary: Personal Services (MIC: SIC: 7291 NAIC: 541213)

Block (H&R) is a financial services company. Co.'s Tax Services segment provides income tax return preparation as well as other services and products related to tax return preparation in the U.S., Canada and Australia. Co.'s Business Services segment is a national accounting, tax and business consulting firm under the RSM McGladrey name. Co.'s Consumer Financial Services segment provides brokerage services, along with investment planning and related financial advice through H&R Block Financial Advisors and full-service banking through H&R Block Bank. Co.'s mortgage operations provide home mortgage services through Option One Mortgage Corporation and H&R Block Mortgage Corporation.

Recent Developments: For the quarter ended Jan 31 2008, income from continuing operations decreased 57.7% to US$9.3 million from US$21.9 million in the year-earlier quarter. Net loss amounted to US$47.4 million versus a net loss of US$60.3 million in the year-earlier quarter. Revenues were US$972.6 million, up 4.4% from US$931.2 million the year before. Operating income was US$2.1 million versus US$31.0 million in the prior-year quarter, a decrease of 93.1%. Direct operating expenses rose 8.5% to US$701.4 million from US$646.3 million in the comparable period the year before. Indirect operating expenses increased 5.9% to US$269.0 million from US$254.0 million in the equivalent prior-year period.

Prospects: Co. is encouraged by its ongoing efforts to refocus its overall business and to tighten efficiency, as demonstrated by the Jan 2008 implementation of a program to reduce its expenses by approximately $110.0 million per year. This program includes Kansas City corporate support staff reduction reflecting Co.'s downsizing due to the exit from its mortgage business. Specifically, Co. expects reduced compensation expense of approximately $50.0 million per year, and Co. is seeking to eliminate about $60.0 million of non-compensation overhead expenses going forward. Separately, Co. continues to expect its retail client growth to be flat or an increase of 2.0% for the fiscal year ending Apr 2008.

Financial Data

(US$ in Thousands)	9 Mos	6 Mos	3 Mos	04/30/2007	04/30/2006	04/30/2005	04/30/2004	04/30/2003
Earnings Per Share	(2.87)	(2.91)	(1.85)	(1.33)	1.47	1.89	1.93	1.58
Cash Flow Per Share	(3.61)	(1.04)	(1.72)	(1.81)	1.78	1.55	2.61	1.92
Tang Book Value Per Share	N.M.	N.M.	N.M.	0.74	1.69	1.65	1.44	1.42
Dividends Per Share	0.555	0.547	0.540	0.530	0.485	0.430	0.390	0.350
Dividend Payout %	...	...	...	...	32.99	22.81	20.21	22.22
Income Statement								
Total Revenue	1,788,644	816,033	381,209	4,021,274	4,872,801	4,420,019	4,205,570	3,779,767
EBITDA	(293,337)	(330,823)	(145,910)	832,933	1,068,155	1,348,140	1,405,913	1,196,005
Depn & Amortn	107,989	75,246	37,075	150,215	191,703	268,058	241,756	208,928
Income Before Taxes	(403,197)	(407,316)	(183,580)	635,798	827,393	1,017,715	1,164,157	987,077
Income Taxes	(166,553)	(161,388)	(73,757)	261,461	336,985	381,858	459,901	407,013
Net Income	(852,209)	(804,851)	(302,580)	(433,653)	490,408	635,857	697,897	580,064
Average Shares	327,202	324,694	323,864	326,154	333,187	337,626	361,604	368,156
Balance Sheet								
Current Assets	8,131,347	3,981,033	2,888,591	3,454,292	2,823,947	3,070,634	2,961,299	2,747,361
Total Assets	11,575,211	7,106,771	6,868,070	7,499,493	5,989,135	5,539,283	5,380,026	4,603,905
Current Liabilities	7,670,603	3,876,151	4,710,987	5,176,352	2,893,436	2,208,920	2,472,043	1,897,196
Long-Term Obligations	2,917,411	2,144,012	519,803	519,807	417,539	923,073	545,811	822,302
Total Liabilities	11,111,279	6,562,491	5,786,708	6,084,994	3,841,336	3,562,912	3,483,017	2,940,196
Stockholders' Equity	463,932	544,280	1,081,362	1,414,499	2,147,799	1,976,371	1,897,009	1,663,709
Shares Outstanding	325,323	324,881	324,546	323,218	328,512	331,240	346,190	359,202
Statistical Record								
Return on Assets %	N.M.	N.M.	N.M.	N.M.	8.51	11.65	13.94	13.13
Return on Equity %	N.M.	N.M.	N.M.	N.M.	23.78	32.83	39.09	38.25
EBITDA Margin %	N.M.	N.M.	N.M.	20.71	21.92	30.50	33.43	31.64
Net Margin %	N.M.	N.M.	N.M.	N.M.	10.06	14.39	16.59	15.35
Asset Turnover	0.39	0.61	0.67	0.60	0.85	0.81	0.84	0.86
Current Ratio	1.06	1.03	0.61	0.67	0.98	1.39	1.20	1.45
Debt to Equity	6.29	3.94	0.48	0.37	0.19	0.47	0.29	0.49
Price Range	24.84-17.00	24.84-18.28	24.84-19.95	24.84-20.05	29.81-20.63	26.65-22.39	30.36-18.50	26.57-15.37
P/E Ratio	...	...	...	...	20.28-14.03	14.10-11.84	15.73-9.59	16.82-9.73
Average Yield %	2.63	2.46	2.40	2.34	1.93	1.77	1.64	1.64

Address: One H&R Block Way, Kansas City, MO 64105	Officers: Richard C. Breeden - Chairman Richard C. Breeden - Chairman **Transfer Agents:**	Investor Contact: 800-869-9220Ext2721
Telephone: 816-854-3000	BNY Mellon Shareowner Services, Jersey City, NJ	No of Institutions: 403
Web Site: www.hrblock.com		Shares: 304,800,864 % Held: 90.32

BRADY CORP.

Exchange	Symbol	Price	52Wk Range	Yield	P/E
NYS	BRC	$38.33 (5/29/2008)	43.78-28.58	1.57	17.11

*7 Year Price Score 103.35 *NYSE Composite Index=100 *12 Month Price Score 100.42

Interim Earnings (Per Share)

Qtr.	Oct	Jan	Apr	Jul
2004-05	0.41	0.41	0.50	0.32
2005-06	0.60	0.43	0.61	0.43
2006-07	0.63	0.36	0.53	0.48
2007-08	0.66	0.48	0.63	...

Interim Dividends (Per Share)

Amt	Decl	Ex	Rec	Pay
0.15Q	09/11/2007	10/05/2007	10/10/2007	10/31/2007
0.15Q	11/16/2007	01/08/2008	01/10/2008	01/31/2008
0.15Q	02/19/2008	04/08/2008	04/10/2008	04/30/2008
0.15Q	05/20/2008	07/08/2008	07/10/2008	07/31/2008

Indicated Div: $0.60 (Div. Reinv. Plan)

Valuation Analysis

Forecast EPS $2.36 (05/16/2008)
Market Cap $2.1 Billion   Book Value   1.0 Billion
Price/Book   2.04   Price/Sales   1.39

Dividend Achiever Status

10 Year Growth Rate   7.76%
Total Years of Dividend Growth   23

TRADING VOLUME (thousand shares)

Business Summary: Consumer Accessories (MIC: SIC: 3993 NAIC: 339950)

Brady manufactures and markets identification products and specialty materials globally. Co.'s major product categories focus on facility identification, safety and complimentary products for the Maintenance, Repair and Operations market as well as wire and people identification products. Product lines provided to original equipment manufacturers includes identification products for product identification, work in process identification, bar code labels and precision die-cut components for mobile telecommunications devices, hard disk drives, medical devices and supplies as well as automotive electronics. As of Jul 31 2007, Co. had 61 manufacturing and distribution facilities worldwide.

Recent Developments: For the quarter ended Apr 30 2008, net income increased 18.5% to US$34.4 million from US$29.0 million in the year-earlier quarter. Revenues were US$381.9 million, up 10.3% from US$346.3 million the year before. Operating income was US$52.6 million versus US$46.3 million in the prior-year quarter, an increase of 13.6%. Direct operating expenses rose 8.6% to US$192.3 million from US$177.2 million in the comparable period the year before. Indirect operating expenses increased 11.5% to US$137.0 million from US$122.8 million in the equivalent prior-year period.

Prospects: Co.'s recent sales growth is being driven by solid performance at its Brady Americas segment and improvements from its Europe operations. Specifically, Co. attributes the higher organic sales at its Brady Americas segment to better results in the education and industrial original equipment manufacturers markets. In this respect, for the fiscal year ending Jul 31 2008, Co. is projecting sales to be in the range of $1.50 billion to $1.52 billion, representing an increase from its previous guidance of $1.43 billion to $1.46 billion. In addition, Co. is forecasting net income in the range of $129.0 million to $135.0 million, while earnings are estimated to range from $2.33 to $2.44 per share.

Financial Data

(US$ in Thousands)	9 Mos	6 Mos	3 Mos	07/31/2007	07/31/2006	07/31/2005	07/31/2004	07/31/2003
Earnings Per Share	2.24	2.15	2.03	2.00	2.07	1.64	1.06	0.46
Cash Flow Per Share	3.85	3.43	2.90	2.52	2.32	2.43	1.79	1.19
Tang Book Value Per Share	1.41	1.13	0.97	0.07	0.45	1.89	1.69	4.47
Dividends Per Share	0.590	0.580	0.570	0.560	0.520	0.440	0.420	0.400
Dividend Payout %	26.28	26.98	28.08	28.00	25.12	26.83	39.44	87.91
Income Statement								
Total Revenue	1,126,167	744,258	380,134	1,362,631	1,018,436	816,447	671,219	554,866
EBITDA	202,353	132,838	72,624	228,718	194,063	150,643	91,748	50,347
Depn & Amortn	45,682	29,669	14,168	53,856	35,144	26,822	20,190	17,771
Income Before Taxes	136,242	89,702	51,736	151,928	144,688	115,418	70,327	32,455
Income Taxes	38,829	26,642	15,366	42,540	40,513	33,471	19,456	11,035
Net Income	97,413	63,060	36,370	109,388	104,175	81,947	50,871	21,420
Average Shares	54,627	55,228	55,121	54,741	50,385	49,859	47,812	46,754
Balance Sheet								
Current Assets	659,629	626,593	629,292	583,413	459,157	302,372	251,923	215,157
Total Assets	1,818,131	1,773,912	1,758,512	1,698,857	1,365,186	850,147	694,330	449,519
Current Liabilities	271,276	253,443	263,945	280,054	218,620	160,812	120,217	91,279
Long-Term Obligations	478,572	478,572	478,573	478,575	350,018	150,026	150,019	568
Total Liabilities	810,365	794,914	805,368	807,845	619,140	352,873	291,015	110,558
Stockholders' Equity	1,007,766	978,998	953,144	891,012	746,046	497,274	403,315	338,961
Shares Outstanding	53,709	54,571	54,386	54,125	53,727	49,245	48,160	46,618
Statistical Record								
Return on Assets %	7.09	7.23	7.01	7.14	9.40	10.61	8.87	4.92
Return on Equity %	13.28	13.25	12.85	13.36	16.76	18.20	13.67	6.46
EBITDA Margin %	17.97	17.85	19.10	16.79	19.06	18.45	13.67	9.07
Net Margin %	8.65	8.47	9.57	8.03	10.23	10.04	7.58	3.86
Asset Turnover	0.85	0.89	0.89	0.89	0.92	1.06	1.17	1.28
Current Ratio	2.43	2.47	2.38	2.08	2.10	1.88	2.10	2.36
Debt to Equity	0.47	0.49	0.50	0.54	0.47	0.30	0.37	N.M.
Price Range	43.78-28.58	43.78-29.44	43.78-30.91	40.52-30.91	41.83-27.01	35.40-21.11	23.10-15.90	17.70-12.89
P/E Ratio	19.54-12.76	20.36-13.69	21.57-15.23	20.26-15.46	20.21-13.05	21.59-12.87	21.79-15.00	38.48-28.02
Average Yield %	1.69	1.64	1.58	1.58	1.58	1.48	1.52	2.53

Address: 6555 West Good Hope Road, Milwaukee, WI 53223 Telephone: 414-358-6600 Web Site: www.bradycorp.com	Officers: Frank M. Jaehnert - President, Chief Executive Officer Michael O. Oliver - Senior Vice President Transfer Agents: Wells Fargo Bank Minnesota, N.A., St. Paul, MN	Investor Contact: 414-438-6940 No of Institutions: 183 Shares: 47,532,320 % Held: 90.17

BROWN & BROWN, INC.

Exchange	Symbol	Price	52Wk Range	Yield	P/E
NYS	BRO	$19.20 (5/29/2008)	28.09-16.66	1.46	14.77

*7 Year Price Score 84.37   *NYSE Composite Index=100   *12 Month Price Score 82.89

Interim Earnings (Per Share)

Qtr.	Mar	Jun	Sep	Dec
2005	0.31	0.27	0.25	0.26
2006	0.36	0.32	0.29	0.26
2007	0.42	0.37	0.33	0.23
2008	0.37	...	...	...

Interim Dividends (Per Share)

Amt	Decl	Ex	Rec	Pay
0.06Q	07/26/2007	08/06/2007	08/08/2007	08/22/2007
0.07Q	10/24/2007	11/05/2007	11/07/2007	11/21/2007
0.07Q	01/23/2008	02/04/2008	02/06/2008	02/20/2008
0.07Q	04/30/2008	05/12/2008	05/14/2008	05/28/2008

Indicated Div: $0.28

Valuation Analysis

Forecast EPS $1.25 (05/16/2008)

Market Cap	$2.7 Billion	Book Value	1.1 Billion
Price/Book	2.37	Price/Sales	2.83

Dividend Achiever Status

10 Year Growth Rate	18.93%
Total Years of Dividend Growth	14

TRADING VOLUME (thousand shares)

Business Summary: Insurance (MIC: SIC: 6411 NAIC: 524210)

Brown & Brown is an insurance agency, wholesale brokerage, insurance programs and service organization. Co. markets and sells to its customers insurance products and services, mainly in the property, casualty and employee benefits areas. Co. is compensated for its services primarily by commissions paid by insurance companies and by fees paid by customers for certain services. Co. has four operating segments: Retail; Wholesale Brokerage; National Programs; and Services. As of Dec 31 2007, Co.'s activities were conducted in about 198 locations in 38 states that included Florida, New York, New Jersey, Texas, California, Georgia, Colorado, Illinois, Pennsylvania, Virginia and Washington.

Recent Developments: For the quarter ended Mar 31 2008, net income decreased 13.3% to US$51.8 million from US$59.7 million in the year-earlier quarter. Revenues were US$256.7 million, down 0.7% from US$258.5 million the year before.

Prospects: Co.'s top- and bottom-line results are being adversely affected by the continued difficult insurance market environment in the U.S., governmental involvement in the Florida insurance marketplace, as well as the negative effect of the economy on the home-building industry. Nevertheless, Co. continues to focus on efforts to expand its core business, primarily through strategic acquisitions. For instance, from Apr 1 2008 through May 7 2008, Co. noted that it has acquired the assets and assumed certain liabilities of five insurance intermediaries and several books of business (customer accounts). The aggregate purchase price of these acquisitions was $37.5 million.

Financial Data (US$ in Thousands)	3 Mos	12/31/2007	12/31/2006	12/31/2005	12/31/2004	12/31/2003	12/31/2002	12/31/2001
Earnings Per Share	1.30	1.35	1.22	1.08	0.93	0.80	0.61	0.42
Cash Flow Per Share	1.36	1.53	1.61	1.55	1.23	1.04	0.69	0.56
Tang Book Value Per Share	N.M.	N.M.	N.M.	N.M.	N.M.	0.20	0.08	N.M.
Dividends Per Share	0.260	0.250	0.210	0.170	0.145	0.121	0.100	0.080
Dividend Payout %	20.06	18.52	17.21	15.74	15.59	15.16	16.39	18.82
Income Statement								
Total Revenue	256,715	959,667	878,004	785,807	646,934	551,040	455,742	365,029
Income Before Taxes	84,584	311,527	280,041	244,130	206,949	176,482	134,664	90,478
Income Taxes	32,824	120,568	107,691	93,579	78,106	66,160	49,271	34,834
Net Income	51,760	190,959	172,350	150,551	128,843	110,322	83,122	53,913
Average Shares	141,327	141,257	141,020	139,776	138,888	137,794	136,086	126,444
Balance Sheet								
Total Assets	1,986,149	1,960,659	1,807,952	1,608,660	1,249,517	865,854	754,349	488,737
Total Liabilities	844,318	863,201	878,607	844,316	625,192	367,819	362,759	313,452
Stockholders' Equity	1,141,831	1,097,458	929,345	764,344	624,325	498,035	391,590	175,285
Shares Outstanding	140,724	140,673	140,016	139,383	138,318	137,122	136,356	126,388
Statistical Record								
Return on Assets %	9.57	10.13	10.09	10.53	12.15	13.62	13.37	14.09
Return on Equity %	17.16	18.84	20.35	21.68	22.90	24.80	29.33	36.28
Price Range	28.47-17.19	28.96-23.10	35.23-27.42	31.24-21.30	23.30-16.04	18.72-13.65	18.07-12.37	15.40-7.72
P/E Ratio	21.90-13.22	21.45-17.11	28.88-22.48	28.93-19.72	25.05-17.25	23.40-17.06	29.61-20.28	36.68-18.39
Average Yield %	1.07	0.95	0.69	0.71	0.72	0.76	0.63	0.71

Address: 220 South Ridgewood Avenue, Daytona Beach, FL 32114 **Telephone:** 368-252-9601 **Web Site:** www.bbinsurance.com	**Officers:** J. Hyatt Brown - Chairman, Chief Executive Officer Jim W. Henderson - Vice-Chairman, Chief Operating Officer **Transfer Agents:** American Stock Transfer & Trust Company, New York, NY	**No of Institutions:** 264 **Shares:** 97,594,408 **% Held:** 66.45

BROWN-FORMAN CORP.

Exchange	Symbol	Price	52Wk Range	Yield	P/E
NYS	BF B	$75.19 (5/29/2008)	75.58-62.18	1.81	22.85

*7 Year Price Score 103.05 *NYSE Composite Index=100 *12 Month Price Score 103.57

Interim Earnings (Per Share)

Qtr.	Jul	Oct	Jan	Apr
2004-05	0.42	0.84	0.78	0.47
2005-06	0.10	0.88	0.98	0.64
2006-07	0.76	1.00	0.85	0.54
2007-08	0.77	1.04	0.94	...

Interim Dividends (Per Share)

Amt	Decl	Ex	Rec	Pay
0.302Q	07/26/2007	08/30/2007	09/04/2007	10/01/2007
0.34Q	11/15/2007	12/03/2007	12/05/2007	01/01/2008
0.34Q	01/22/2008	03/03/2008	03/05/2008	04/01/2008
0.34Q	05/22/2008	06/02/2008	06/04/2008	07/01/2008

Indicated Div: $1.36

Valuation Analysis

Forecast EPS $3.46 (05/16/2008)

Market Cap	$9.2 Billion	Book Value	1.7 Billion
Price/Book	5.42	Price/Sales	3.64

Dividend Achiever Status

10 Year Growth Rate	8.40%
Total Years of Dividend Growth	23

TRADING VOLUME (thousand shares)

Business Summary: Food (MIC: SIC: 2084 NAIC: 312130)

Brown-Forman primarily manufactures, bottles, imports, exports and markets a variety of alcoholic beverage brands. Co. also manufactures and markets new and used oak barrels. As of Apr 30 2007, Co.'s primary beverage brands included, but not limited to, Jack Daniel's, Southern Comfort, Finlandia, Gentleman Jack, Amarula, Appleton Estate, Canadian Mist, Bel Arbor, Bonterra, Chambord, Don Eduardo, Fetzer, Bolla and Korbel. In the U.S., Co. sells spirits and wines either via wholesale distributors or directly to state governments in those states that control alcohol sales. Internationally, Co.'s key export markets are the U.K., Germany, Spain, Australia, France, South Africa, Canada and Japan.

Recent Developments: For the quarter ended Jan 31 2008, income from continuing operations increased 3.9% to US$115.9 million from US$111.6 million in the year-earlier quarter. Net income increased 10.4% to US$116.0 million from US$105.1 million in the year-earlier quarter. Revenues were US$672.4 million, up 15.5% from US$582.1 million the year before. Operating income was US$181.6 million versus US$168.8 million in the prior-year quarter, an increase of 7.6%. Direct operating expenses rose 23.1% to US$239.8 million from US$194.8 million in the comparable period the year before. Indirect operating expenses increased 14.9% to US$251.0 million from US$218.5 million in the equivalent prior-year period.

Prospects: Co. is benefiting from the January 2007 acquisition of Casa Herradura brands, favorable foreign exchange volatility, higher global consumer demand for Jack Daniel's Tennessee Whiskey and Finlandia Vodka, better demand for Gentleman Jack in the U.S., as well as continued growth for the Jack Daniel's & Cola ready-to-drink in Australia. However, these positive developments are being partially offset by softness for Southern Comfort and higher raw material costs. Meanwhile, for the fiscal year ending Apr 30 2008, Co. now anticipates earnings to range from $3.42 to $3.50 per diluted share, representing expected growth of 9.0% to 11.0% over its prior fiscal year's earnings of $3.14 per share.

Financial Data

(US$ in Thousands)	9 Mos	6 Mos	3 Mos	04/30/2007	04/30/2006	04/30/2005	04/30/2004	04/30/2003
Earnings Per Share	3.29	3.19	3.15	3.14	2.60	2.52	2.11	1.81
Cash Flow Per Share	3.86	3.62	3.30	2.89	2.83	3.25	2.51	1.80
Tang Book Value Per Share	2.56	2.98	1.96	1.78	8.52	5.69	4.30	2.43
Dividends Per Share	2.901	2.863	2.841	2.818	1.050	0.915	0.800	0.725
Dividend Payout %	88.22	89.65	90.07	89.87	40.45	36.31	37.91	39.94
Income Statement								
Total Revenue	1,975,100	1,302,700	587,100	2,218,000	1,976,000	2,312,000	2,213,000	2,060,000
EBITDA	588,100	393,800	168,200	646,000	607,000	548,000	463,000	433,000
Depn & Amortn	38,400	25,700	12,800	44,000	44,000	58,000	56,000	55,000
Income Before Taxes	517,200	344,700	144,300	586,000	559,000	476,000	388,000	373,000
Income Taxes	176,500	119,900	48,900	186,000	164,000	168,000	130,000	128,000
Net Income	340,700	224,600	95,300	389,000	320,000	308,000	258,000	245,000
Average Shares	123,974	124,534	124,434	124,201	121,986	122,507	121,986	135,126
Balance Sheet								
Current Assets	1,443,900	1,595,200	1,415,400	1,635,000	1,610,000	1,317,000	1,083,000	1,068,000
Total Assets	3,391,600	3,546,300	3,342,200	3,551,000	2,728,000	2,624,000	2,376,000	2,264,000
Current Liabilities	1,007,600	1,123,100	1,075,500	1,347,000	569,000	638,000	369,000	548,000
Long-Term Obligations	417,300	418,200	421,400	422,000	351,000	352,000	630,000	629,000
Total Liabilities	1,697,000	1,796,300	1,735,300	1,978,000	1,165,000	1,314,000	1,291,000	1,424,000
Stockholders' Equity	1,694,600	1,750,000	1,606,900	1,573,000	1,563,000	1,310,000	1,085,000	840,000
Shares Outstanding	122,043	123,427	123,493	123,237	122,465	121,888	121,588	121,134
Statistical Record								
Return on Assets %	11.43	12.24	12.81	12.39	11.96	12.32	11.09	11.45
Return on Equity %	23.37	22.64	24.25	24.81	22.28	25.72	26.73	22.78
EBITDA Margin %	29.78	30.23	28.65	29.13	30.72	23.70	20.92	21.02
Net Margin %	17.25	17.24	16.23	17.54	16.19	13.32	11.66	11.89
Asset Turnover	0.71	0.75	0.76	0.71	0.74	0.92	0.95	0.96
Current Ratio	1.43	1.42	1.32	1.21	2.83	2.06	2.93	1.95
Debt to Equity	0.25	0.24	0.26	0.27	0.22	0.27	0.58	0.75
Price Range	75.58-62.18	75.58-63.54	77.60-63.54	77.60-63.54	81.91-55.10	55.96-43.60	49.95-37.77	40.02-29.66
P/E Ratio	22.97-18.90	23.69-19.92	24.63-20.17	24.71-20.24	31.50-21.19	22.21-17.26	23.67-17.90	22.11-16.38
Average Yield %	4.17	4.16	4.10	4.01	1.62	1.89	1.85	2.04

Address: 850 Dixie Highway, Louisville, KY 40210 **Telephone:** 502-585-1100 **Web Site:** www.brown-forman.com	**Officers:** James S. Welch - Vice-Chairman Paul C. Varga - President, Chief Executive Officer **Transfer Agents:** National City Bank, Cleveland, OH	**No of Institutions:** 76 **Shares:** 7,629,193 **% Held:** 12.09

BUCKEYE PARTNERS, L.P.

Exchange	Symbol	Price	52Wk Range	Yield	P/E
NYS	BPL	$47.72 (5/29/2008)	55.49-44.29	7.12	15.85

*7 Year Price Score 90.51   *NYSE Composite Index=100   *12 Month Price Score 99.14

Interim Earnings (Per Share)

Qtr.	Mar	Jun	Sep	Dec
2005	0.66	0.66	0.65	0.72
2006	0.59	0.61	0.69	0.75
2007	0.77	0.70	0.71	0.85
2008	0.76	...	...	...

Interim Dividends (Per Share)

Amt	Decl	Ex	Rec	Pay
0.813Q	07/26/2007	08/02/2007	08/06/2007	08/31/2007
0.825Q	10/25/2007	11/01/2007	11/05/2007	11/30/2007
0.838Q	01/24/2008	02/01/2008	02/05/2008	02/29/2008
0.85Q	04/29/2008	05/07/2008	05/09/2008	05/30/2008

Indicated Div: $3.40

Valuation Analysis

Forecast EPS $3.28 (05/16/2008)

Market Cap	$2.3 Billion	Book Value	N/A
Price/Book	N/A	Price/Sales	2.98

Dividend Achiever Status

10 Year Growth Rate	6.52%
Total Years of Dividend Growth	12

Business Summary: Oil and Gas (MIC: SIC: 4613 NAIC: 486910)

Buckeye Partners is primarily engaged in the transportation, terminalling and storage of refined petroleum products for key integrated oil companies, large refined products marketing companies and key end-users of petroleum products on a fee basis through facilities owned and operated by Co. Co. also operates pipelines owned by third parties under contracts with integrated oil and chemical companies and performs pipeline construction activities. As of Dec 31 2007, Co.'s facilities included approximately 5,400 miles of 6-inch to 24-inch diameter pipeline, 100 delivery points and 51 active bulk storage and terminal facilities with aggregate capacity of approximately 20.0 million barrels.

Recent Developments: For the quarter ended Mar 31 2008, income from continuing operations increased 9.7% to US$41.4 million from US$37.7 million in the year-earlier quarter. Net income increased 13.5% to US$42.8 million from US$37.7 million in the year-earlier quarter. Revenues were US$380.3 million, up 204.4% from US$124.9 million the year before. Operating income was US$58.1 million versus US$50.3 million in the prior-year quarter, an increase of 15.6%. Direct operating expenses rose to US$236.6 million from US$4.8 million in the comparable period the year before. Indirect operating expenses increased 22.5% to US$85.5 million from US$69.8 million in the equivalent prior-year period.

Prospects: On Apr 15 2008, Co. announced that it has closed its sale of the retail division of its Farm & Home Oil Company LLC subsidiary to a subsidiary of Inergy, L.P. for $42.0 million plus working capital adjustment. As part of the transaction, Co. and Inergy entered into a five-year supply agreement pursuant to which Co. will supply 100.0% of Inergy's liquid products requirements in certain areas of Eastern and Central Pennsylvania. Co. retains the wholesale division of Farm & Home. Separately, Co. is seeing increases in net income and revenue and expects its recent Lodi Gas Storage L.L.C. and Farm & Home acquisitions to continue to contribute to its financial performance in the future.

Financial Data
(US$ in Thousands)

	3 Mos	12/31/2007	12/31/2006	12/31/2005	12/31/2004	12/31/2003	12/31/2002	12/31/2001
Earnings Per Share	3.01	3.03	2.64	2.69	2.75	1.05	2.64	2.55
Cash Flow Per Share	4.53	4.70	3.80	3.84	3.30	3.81	3.43	2.99
Income Statement								
Net Income	42,817	155,356	110,240	99,958	82,962	30,154	71,902	69,402
Average Shares	45,923	42,101	39,202	37,145	30,151	28,748	27,228	27,193
Balance Sheet								
Total Assets	2,830,861	2,133,652	1,995,470	1,816,867	1,534,119	940,046	856,171	807,560
Total Liabilities	1,632,696	1,043,480	1,185,588	1,058,290	928,696	562,634	498,739	454,664
Shares Outstanding	48,366	45,962	39,697	38,162	34,525	28,966	27,182	27,164
Statistical Record								
Return on Assets %	6.59	7.52	5.78	5.97	6.69	3.36	8.64	9.13
Price Range	55.49-44.29	55.49-46.00	46.78-40.71	50.21-41.92	45.65-35.82	45.40-34.20	39.97-30.34	37.90-28.63
P/E Ratio	18.44-14.71	18.31-15.18	17.72-15.42	18.67-15.58	16.60-13.03	43.24-32.57	15.14-11.49	14.86-11.23

Address: 5002 Buckeye Road, Emmaus, PA 18049 **Telephone:** 484-232-4000 **Web Site:** www.buckeye.com	Officers: Eric A. Gustafson - Senior Vice President Stephen C. Muther - Senior Vice President, General Counsel, Secretary **Transfer Agents:** First Chicago Trust Company a Division of Equiserv, Jersey City, NJ	Investor Contact: 800-422-2825 No of Institutions: 205 Shares: 11,321,653 % Held: 24.13

CALIFORNIA WATER SERVICE GROUP (DE)

Exchange	Symbol	Price	52Wk Range	Yield	P/E
NYS	CWT	$36.59 (5/29/2008)	44.39-33.58	3.20	25.41

*7 Year Price Score 91.34 *NYSE Composite Index=100 *12 Month Price Score 102.16

Interim Earnings (Per Share)

Qtr.	Mar	Jun	Sep	Dec
2005	0.03	0.41	0.71	0.31
2006	0.04	0.31	0.68	0.31
2007	0.07	0.37	0.67	0.39
2008	0.01	...	...	...

Interim Dividends (Per Share)

Amt	Decl	Ex	Rec	Pay
0.29Q	08/01/2007	08/02/2007	08/06/2007	08/17/2007
0.29Q	10/25/2007	11/01/2007	11/05/2007	11/16/2007
0.292Q	01/23/2008	01/31/2008	02/04/2008	02/15/2008
0.292Q	05/01/2008	05/02/2008	05/05/2008	05/16/2008
	Indicated Div: $1.17 (Div. Reinv. Plan)			

Valuation Analysis

Forecast EPS	$1.65 (05/16/2008)		
Market Cap	$758.0 Million	Book Value	383.4 Million
Price/Book	1.98	Price/Sales	2.06

Dividend Achiever Status

10 Year Growth Rate	0.95%
Total Years of Dividend Growth	40

TRADING VOLUME (thousand shares)

Business Summary: Water Utilities (MIC: SIC: 4941 NAIC: 221310)

California Water Service Group is a holding company. Through its subsidiaries, Co. is engaged in the production, purchase, storage, treatment, testing, distribution and sale of water for domestic, industrial, public and irrigation uses, and for fire protection. In addition, Co. provides non-regulated water-related services under agreements with municipalities and other private companies including full water system operation, billing and meter reading services. As of Dec 31 2007, Co. provided its services to approximately 463,600 customers in 83 California communities; 15,800 customers in the Tacoma and Olympia areas; 7,500 customers in New Mexico; and 700 customers on the island of Maui.

Recent Developments: For the quarter ended Mar 31 2008, net income decreased 88.3% to US$185,000 from US$1.6 million in the year-earlier quarter. Revenues were US$72.9 million, up 1.9% from US$71.6 million the year before. Operating income was US$4.8 million versus US$5.2 million in the prior-year quarter, a decrease of 7.8%. Direct operating expenses rose 0.3% to US$41.5 million from US$41.4 million in the comparable period the year before. Indirect operating expenses increased 6.6% to US$26.6 million from US$24.9 million in the equivalent prior-year period.

Prospects: Co.'s bottom-line results are being tempered by a decline in the customer usage of water attributable to the unfavorable weather condition, along with a decline in other income. Conversely, Co. is seeing an increase in its operating revenue due to increases in rates and in usage by new customers, offset by decreased usage by existing customers. Meanwhile, Co. expects a decision regarding its 2007 general rate case (GRC) submitted by its California Water Service Company subsidiary, to be issued in the second or third quarter of 2008. Notably, the amount requested in the 2007 GRC is approximately $67.5 million in 2008/2009, $21.9 million in 2009/2010, and $14.8 million in 2010/2011.

Financial Data (US$ in Thousands)	3 Mos	12/31/2007	12/31/2006	12/31/2005	12/31/2004	12/31/2003	12/31/2002	12/31/2001
Earnings Per Share	1.44	1.50	1.34	1.47	1.46	1.21	1.25	0.97
Cash Flow Per Share	2.85	2.42	3.22	4.69	3.13	2.80	2.20	2.54
Tang Book Value Per Share	18.34	18.66	18.31	15.98	15.66	14.44	13.12	12.95
Dividends Per Share	1.163	1.160	1.150	1.140	1.130	1.125	1.120	1.115
Dividend Payout %	80.96	77.33	85.82	77.55	77.40	92.98	89.60	114.95
Income Statement								
Total Revenue	72,921	367,082	334,717	320,728	315,567	277,128	263,151	246,820
Depn & Amortn	9,222	34,236	31,317	28,731	26,114	23,256	21,238	19,226
Income Taxes	...	17,887	15,297	20,006	17,084	12,898	12,568	9,728
Net Income	185	31,159	25,580	27,223	26,026	19,417	19,073	14,965
Average Shares	20,711	20,689	18,925	18,402	17,674	15,893	15,185	15,285
Balance Sheet								
Net PPE	1,022,329	1,010,196	941,475	862,731	800,305	759,498	696,988	624,342
Total Assets	1,187,215	1,184,499	1,165,019	996,945	942,853	873,035	800,582	710,214
Long-Term Obligations	288,495	289,220	291,814	274,142	274,821	272,226	250,365	202,600
Total Liabilities	803,847	795,315	783,242	699,529	651,773	625,036	597,890	510,120
Stockholders' Equity	383,368	389,184	381,777	297,416	291,080	247,999	202,692	200,094
Shares Outstanding	20,716	20,666	20,657	18,390	18,367	16,932	15,182	15,182
Statistical Record								
Return on Assets %	2.53	2.65	2.37	2.81	2.86	2.32	2.52	2.17
Return on Equity %	7.80	8.08	7.53	9.25	9.63	8.62	9.47	7.44
Net Margin %	0.25	8.49	7.64	8.49	8.25	7.01	7.25	6.06
PPE Turnover	0.37	0.38	0.37	0.39	0.40	0.38	0.40	0.41
Asset Turnover	0.31	0.31	0.31	0.33	0.35	0.33	0.35	0.36
Debt to Equity	0.75	0.74	0.76	0.92	0.94	1.10	1.24	1.01
Price Range	44.39-33.58	44.54-34.46	45.36-33.72	41.90-32.12	37.70-26.19	30.97-23.65	26.69-21.60	28.60-23.38
P/E Ratio	30.83-23.32	29.69-22.97	33.85-25.16	28.50-21.85	25.82-17.94	25.60-19.55	21.35-17.28	29.48-24.10
Average Yield %	3.03	2.97	2.94	3.12	3.86	4.22	4.53	4.37

Address: 1720 North First Street, San Jose, CA 95112-4598	Officers: Robert W. Foy - Chairman Peter C. Nelson - President, Chief Executive Officer Transfer Agents:	Investor Contact: 408-367-8200 No of Institutions: 148
Telephone: 408-367-8200 Web Site: www.calwatergroup.com	US Bank Trust, N.A., San Francisco, CA	Shares: 11,773,494 % Held: 50.53

CAPITAL CITY BANK GROUP, INC.

Exchange	Symbol	Price	52Wk Range	Yield	P/E
NMS	CCBG	$27.40 (5/29/2008)	34.28-24.69	2.70	16.12

*7 Year Price Score 79.66 *NYSE Composite Index=100 *12 Month Price Score 94.43

TRADING VOLUME (thousand shares)

Interim Earnings (Per Share)
Qtr.	Mar	Jun	Sep	Dec
2005	0.36	0.44	0.46	0.40
2006	0.40	0.44	0.47	0.48
2007	0.38	0.43	0.41	0.44
2008	0.42	...	...	...

Interim Dividends (Per Share)
Amt	Decl	Ex	Rec	Pay
0.175Q	08/23/2007	08/30/2007	09/04/2007	09/18/2007
0.185Q	11/29/2007	12/04/2007	12/06/2007	12/20/2007
0.185Q	02/21/2008	03/07/2008	03/11/2008	03/25/2008
0.185Q	05/22/2008	06/05/2008	06/09/2008	06/23/2008

Indicated Div: $0.74

Valuation Analysis
Forecast EPS	$1.50 (05/16/2008)		
Market Cap	$470.6 Million	Book Value	297.7 Million
Price/Book	1.58	Price/Sales	2.09

Dividend Achiever Status
10 Year Growth Rate	10.47%
Total Years of Dividend Growth	14

Business Summary: Commercial Banking (MIC: SIC: 6022 NAIC: 522110)

Capital City Bank Group is a financial holding company. Through its bank subsidiaries, Co. provides traditional deposit and credit services, asset management, trust, mortgage banking, merchant services, bank cards, data processing, and securities brokerage services through 70 full service banking locations in Florida, Georgia, and Alabama. Co. also has a two mortgage lending offices located in Florida and one additional Georgia community. Co.'s principal banking services include business banking, commercial real estate lending, residential real estate lending, and retail credit. As of Dec 31 2007, Co. had total assets of $2.62 billion and total deposits of $2.14 billion.

Recent Developments: For the quarter ended Mar 31 2008, net income increased 4.6% to US$7.3 million from US$7.0 million in the year-earlier quarter. Net interest income decreased 6.6% to US$26.5 million from US$28.3 million in the year-earlier quarter. Provision for loan losses was US$4.1 million versus US$1.2 million in the prior-year quarter, an increase of 234.8%. Non-interest income rose 27.5% to US$17.8 million from US$14.0 million, while non-interest expense declined 2.5% to US$29.8 million.

Prospects: Despite experiencing higher earnings, Co. is experiencing lower net interest income attributable to compression in its net interest margin due mainly to higher foregone interest related to nonaccrual loans and the recent influx of higher cost negotiated deposits. Looking ahead, Co. believes that market conditions and competition likely will continue to pressure its net interest margin during the 2008 second quarter. Also, Co. estimates that its income on earning assets will continue to decline in the existing interest rate condition during the second quarter of 2008. On the positive note, Co. expects that its average cost of funds to continue to decline in the 2008 second quarter.

Financial Data
(US$ in Thousands)	3 Mos	12/31/2007	12/31/2006	12/31/2005	12/31/2004	12/31/2003	12/31/2002	12/31/2001
Earnings Per Share	1.70	1.66	1.79	1.66	1.74	1.52	1.39	1.02
Cash Flow Per Share	2.91	2.62	2.49	2.42	2.62	2.29	2.30	2.02
Tang Book Value Per Share	11.68	11.30	11.41	10.48	9.97	10.70	9.55	8.39
Dividends Per Share	0.720	0.710	0.662	0.619	0.584	0.525	0.402	0.381
Dividend Payout %	42.47	42.77	37.01	37.26	33.49	34.53	28.92	37.42
Income Statement								
Interest Income	38,723	165,323	165,893	140,053	101,525	99,487	106,095	118,983
Interest Expense	12,264	53,082	46,757	30,063	15,441	14,839	22,503	48,249
Net Interest Income	26,459	112,241	119,136	109,990	86,084	84,648	83,592	70,734
Provision for Losses	4,142	6,163	1,959	2,507	2,141	3,436	3,297	3,983
Non-Interest Income	17,799	59,300	55,577	49,198	50,553	41,939	37,176	32,037
Non-Interest Expense	29,798	121,992	121,568	109,814	89,226	84,378	81,698	72,804
Income Before Taxes	10,318	43,386	51,186	46,867	45,270	38,773	35,773	25,984
Income Taxes	3,038	13,703	17,921	16,586	15,899	13,580	12,691	9,118
Net Income	7,280	29,683	33,265	30,281	29,371	25,193	23,082	16,866
Average Shares	17,178	17,911	18,609	18,281	16,810	16,563	16,592	16,615
Balance Sheet								
Net Loans & Leases	1,894,181	1,897,784	1,982,504	2,050,084	1,812,788	1,329,203	1,272,726	1,231,255
Total Assets	2,692,512	2,616,327	2,597,910	2,625,462	2,364,013	1,846,502	1,824,771	1,821,423
Total Deposits	2,192,605	2,142,344	2,081,654	2,079,346	1,894,886	1,474,205	1,434,200	1,550,101
Total Liabilities	2,394,839	2,323,652	2,282,140	2,319,686	2,107,213	1,643,693	1,638,240	1,649,640
Stockholders' Equity	297,673	292,675	315,770	305,776	256,800	202,809	186,531	171,783
Shares Outstanding	17,174	17,182	18,518	18,631	17,694	16,545	16,495	16,629
Statistical Record								
Return on Assets %	1.14	1.14	1.27	1.21	1.39	1.37	1.27	1.01
Return on Equity %	9.84	9.76	10.70	10.77	12.75	12.94	12.88	10.56
Net Interest Margin %	68.33	67.89	71.81	78.53	84.79	85.08	78.79	59.45
Efficiency Ratio %	52.72	54.31	54.89	58.03	58.67	59.66	57.02	48.21
Loans to Deposits	0.86	0.89	0.95	0.99	0.96	0.90	0.89	0.79
Price Range	34.28-24.69	34.79-24.69	37.72-29.91	39.30-28.17	36.79-27.59	37.24-21.80	25.27-14.72	16.64-12.59
P/E Ratio	20.16-14.52	20.96-14.87	21.07-16.71	23.67-16.97	21.14-15.86	24.50-14.34	18.18-10.59	16.31-12.51
Average Yield %	2.41	2.27	1.99	1.82	1.81	1.84	2.09	2.55

Address: 217 North Monroe Street, Tallahassee, FL 32301 Telephone: 850-671-0300 Web Site: www.ccbg.com	Officers: William G. Smith - Chairman, President, Chief Executive Officer J. Kimbrough Davis - Executive Vice President, Chief Financial Officer Transfer Agents: American Stock Transfer & Trust Co., New York, NY	Investor Contact: 850-671-0300 No of Institutions: 68 Shares: 4,743,665 % Held: 26.69

CARDINAL HEALTH, INC.

Exchange	Symbol	Price	52Wk Range	Yield	P/E
NYS	CAH	$56.24 (5/29/2008)	72.94-49.80	1.00	11.38

*7 Year Price Score 75.95 *NYSE Composite Index=100 *12 Month Price Score 89.70

Interim Earnings (Per Share)

Qtr.	Sep	Dec	Mar	Jun
2004-05	0.49	0.49	0.84	0.59
2005-06	0.53	0.70	0.34	0.75
2006-07	0.66	1.80	0.05	2.26
2007-08	0.82	0.89	0.99	...

Interim Dividends (Per Share)

Amt	Decl	Ex	Rec	Pay
0.12Q	08/09/2007	09/27/2007	10/01/2007	10/15/2007
0.12Q	11/07/2007	12/27/2007	01/01/2008	01/15/2008
0.12Q	01/31/2008	03/28/2008	04/01/2008	04/15/2008
0.14Q	05/07/2008	06/27/2008	07/01/2008	07/15/2008

Indicated Div: $0.56

Valuation Analysis

Forecast EPS	$3.78 (05/17/2008)		
Market Cap	$20.1 Billion	Book Value	7.4 Billion
Price/Book	2.71	Price/Sales	0.22

Dividend Achiever Status

10 Year Growth Rate	25.18%
Total Years of Dividend Growth	11

Business Summary: Pharmaceuticals (MIC: SIC: 5122 NAIC: 424210)

Cardinal Health is a provider of products and services for the healthcare industry. As of June 30 2007, Co. had four segments: Healthcare Supply Chain Services - Pharmaceutical, which distributes branded and generic pharmaceutical products, over-the-counter healthcare products and consumer products; Healthcare Supply Chain Services - Medical, which distributes branded and private-label medical and laboratory products, as well as Co.'s own line of surgical and respiratory therapy products; Clinical Technologies and Services, which provides products and services to hospitals and other healthcare providers; and Medical Products Manufacturing, which manufactures medical and surgical products.

Recent Developments: For the quarter ended Mar 31 2008, income from continuing operations was US$365.9 million compared with a loss of US$4.9 million in the year-earlier quarter. Net income increased to US$356.0 million from US$19.0 million in the year-earlier quarter. Revenues were US$22.91 billion, up 4.8% from US$21.87 billion the year before. Operating income was US$576.5 million versus a loss of US$9.8 million in the prior-year quarter. Direct operating expenses rose 4.7% to US$21.44 billion from US$20.48 billion in the comparable period the year before. Indirect operating expenses decreased 36.2% to US$891.3 million from US$1.40 billion in the equivalent prior-year period.

Prospects: On May 12 2008, Co. announced it has completed the acquisition of assets of privately held Enturia, Inc., the manufacturer of infection prevention products sold under the ChloraPrep® brand name, for $490.0 million. As a result of this acquisition, the ChloraPrep® product line expands Co.'s infection prevention offerings in its Medical Products and Technologies segment. Subsequently, Co. plans to accelerate sales of ChloraPrep® products to both hospital and alternate-care customers through its U.S. and international sales networks. The acquisition is expected to be $0.01 to $0.02 dilutive to Co.'s earnings in the fiscal year ending June 2008 and accretive in fiscal 2009.

Financial Data

(US$ in Thousands)	9 Mos	6 Mos	3 Mos	06/30/2007	06/30/2006	06/30/2005	06/30/2004	06/30/2003
Earnings Per Share	4.94	4.02	4.93	4.77	2.33	2.41	3.35	3.10
Cash Flow Per Share	3.05	2.69	2.52	3.10	5.08	6.62	6.03	3.13
Tang Book Value Per Share	4.80	3.62	3.44	4.12	8.52	8.20	7.05	12.10
Dividends Per Share	0.480	0.450	0.420	0.390	0.270	0.150	0.120	0.105
Dividend Payout %	9.73	11.19	8.52	8.18	11.59	6.22	3.58	3.39
Income Statement								
Total Revenue	68,165,800	45,256,100	21,973,400	86,852,000	81,363,600	74,910,700	65,053,500	56,737,000
EBITDA	1,746,600	1,108,000	541,800	1,574,400	2,227,700	2,039,000	2,537,600	2,392,400
Depn & Amortn	284,900	191,900	94,900	322,100	392,700	409,700	299,200	265,800
Income Before Taxes	1,461,500	916,100	446,900	1,252,300	1,835,000	1,629,300	2,238,400	2,126,600
Income Taxes	467,200	287,800	143,700	412,600	590,300	582,600	713,700	714,700
Net Income	982,600	626,500	301,800	1,931,100	1,000,100	1,050,100	1,474,500	1,405,800
Average Shares	360,200	364,600	370,200	404,700	428,500	435,700	440,000	453,600
Balance Sheet								
Current Assets	14,907,100	14,721,800	14,333,200	14,544,500	14,776,700	13,442,700	13,057,900	13,249,600
Total Assets	23,603,400	23,466,800	22,998,100	23,153,800	23,374,100	22,059,200	21,369,100	18,521,400
Current Liabilities	11,142,000	11,410,500	11,114,000	11,459,700	11,372,800	10,105,000	9,369,400	7,314,400
Long-Term Obligations	3,450,100	3,396,500	3,347,500	3,457,300	2,599,700	2,319,900	2,834,700	2,471,900
Total Liabilities	16,210,200	16,358,700	15,929,900	15,776,900	14,883,400	13,466,200	13,392,800	10,763,300
Stockholders' Equity	7,393,200	7,108,100	7,068,200	7,376,900	8,490,700	8,593,000	7,976,300	7,758,100
Shares Outstanding	356,700	358,200	362,500	368,100	410,800	426,200	430,900	448,400
Statistical Record								
Return on Assets %	7.83	6.50	8.45	8.30	4.40	4.84	7.37	8.04
Return on Equity %	24.57	19.33	25.34	24.34	11.71	12.68	18.69	19.87
EBITDA Margin %	2.56	2.45	2.47	1.81	2.74	2.72	3.90	4.22
Net Margin %	1.44	1.38	1.37	2.22	1.23	1.40	2.27	2.48
Asset Turnover	3.77	3.76	3.79	3.73	3.58	3.45	3.25	3.25
Current Ratio	1.34	1.29	1.29	1.27	1.30	1.33	1.39	1.81
Debt to Equity	0.47	0.48	0.47	0.47	0.31	0.27	0.36	0.32
Price Range	75.28-49.80	75.28-56.47	75.28-61.83	75.28-61.83	75.34-57.28	70.05-37.65	75.98-54.75	71.16-49.08
P/E Ratio	15.24-10.08	18.73-14.05	15.27-12.54	15.78-12.96	32.33-24.58	29.07-15.62	22.68-16.34	22.95-15.83
Average Yield %	0.74	0.66	0.61	0.57	0.41	0.29	0.19	0.17

Address: 7000 Cardinal Place, Dublin, OH 43017	Officers: R. Kerry Clark - Chairman, Chief Executive Officer Daniel J. Walsh - Executive Vice President,	No of Institutions: 642
Telephone: 614-757-5000	Chief Ethics and Compliance Officer **Transfer**	**Shares:** 339,728,608 **% Held:** 82.52
Web Site: www.cardinalhealth.com	**Agents:**Computershare, Providence, RI	

CARLISLE COMPANIES INC.

Exchange	Symbol	Price	52Wk Range	Yield	P/E
NYS	CSL	$33.13 (5/29/2008)	50.00-28.88	1.75	18.30

*7 Year Price Score 100.47 *NYSE Composite Index=100 *12 Month Price Score 81.39

Interim Earnings (Per Share)

Qtr.	Mar	Jun	Sep	Dec
2005	0.45	0.56	0.32	0.39
2006	0.67	0.90	0.62	1.28
2007	0.59	0.85	1.31	0.69
2008	(1.03)	...	...	...

Interim Dividends (Per Share)

Amt	Decl	Ex	Rec	Pay
0.145Q	08/01/2007	08/15/2007	08/17/2007	09/01/2007
0.145Q	11/07/2007	11/15/2007	11/19/2007	12/01/2007
0.145Q	02/05/2008	02/15/2008	02/20/2008	03/01/2008
0.145Q	05/08/2008	05/14/2008	05/16/2008	06/01/2008
Indicated Div: $0.58 (Div. Reinv. Plan)				

Valuation Analysis

Forecast EPS	$2.92 (05/16/2008)		
Market Cap	$2.0 Billion	Book Value	1.0 Billion
Price/Book	1.93	Price/Sales	0.68

Dividend Achiever Status

10 Year Growth Rate	7.87%
Total Years of Dividend Growth	31

Business Summary: Rubber Products (MIC: SIC: 3069 NAIC: 326211)

Carlisle Companies is a holding company. Co. manufactures and distributes a variety of products across a range of industries, which include roofing, construction, trucking, foodservice, industrial equipment, lawn and garden and aircraft manufacturing. Co. markets its products as a component supplier to original equipment manufacturers, distributors, as well as directly to end-users. As at Dec 31 2007, Co. managed its businesses under three operating groups: Construction Materials, Industrial Components and Diversified Components; and had five reportable segments: Construction Materials, Industrial Components, Specialty Products, Transportation Products, and General Industry.

Recent Developments: For the quarter ended Mar 31 2008, loss from continuing operations was US$61.7 million compared with income of US$33.8 million in the year-earlier quarter. Net loss amounted to US$62.6 million versus net income of US$36.8 million in the year-earlier quarter. Revenues were US$708.3 million, up 12.6% from US$628.9 million the year before. Operating income was US$44.1 million versus US$51.1 million in the prior-year quarter, a decrease of 13.7%. Direct operating expenses rose 14.8% to US$578.9 million from US$504.4 million in the comparable period the year before. Indirect operating expenses increased 16.1% to US$85.3 million from US$73.4 million in the equivalent prior-year period.

Prospects: On Apr 29 2008, Co. announced that it has completed the acquisition of Carlyle Incorporated of Tukwila, WA for a purchase price of $200.0 million. Carlyle is a provider of aerospace and network interconnection systems. The acquisition will strengthen Co.'s Tensolite subsidiary core presence in specialty wire and cable and interconnect applications for the aerospace industry. This deal should also expand Tensolite's global reach and add to its capabilities in other specialty interconnect segments. Meanwhile, on Apr 22 2008, Co. announced its decision to pursue disposition of both its power transmission belt and on-highway brake businesses, in line with its plan to simplify its business.

Financial Data

(US$ in Thousands)	3 Mos	12/31/2007	12/31/2006	12/31/2005	12/31/2004	12/31/2003	12/31/2002	12/31/2001
Earnings Per Share	1.81	3.44	3.46	1.71	1.27	1.44	0.47	0.41
Cash Flow Per Share	3.31	4.20	0.32	3.47	1.79	1.90	3.71	3.68
Tang Book Value Per Share	10.71	11.79	9.98	6.57	6.47	5.19	4.04	3.36
Dividends Per Share	0.570	0.560	0.520	0.480	0.450	0.435	0.425	0.410
Dividend Payout %	31.48	16.28	15.01	28.07	35.43	30.21	90.43	100.00
Income Statement								
Total Revenue	708,266	2,876,383	2,572,510	2,209,610	2,227,614	2,108,164	1,971,280	1,849,477
EBITDA	(60,485)	395,260	335,467	262,687	238,329	206,560	184,645	131,005
Depn & Amortn	18,347	65,874	59,836	53,221	52,639	60,366	56,994	63,960
Income Before Taxes	(83,239)	319,342	255,317	193,558	170,340	131,733	110,500	37,925
Income Taxes	(21,560)	106,321	78,031	60,224	52,026	42,813	38,122	13,084
Net Income	(62,596)	215,637	215,689	106,365	79,612	88,920	28,625	24,841
Average Shares	60,594	62,630	62,236	62,156	62,818	61,726	61,166	60,900
Balance Sheet								
Current Assets	1,083,443	1,023,192	978,241	661,172	652,269	584,381	481,508	553,272
Total Assets	2,029,989	1,988,794	1,877,817	1,563,257	1,501,241	1,436,909	1,315,900	1,397,987
Current Liabilities	392,506	388,187	466,686	372,711	384,022	339,343	324,262	273,779
Long-Term Obligations	418,015	262,809	274,658	282,426	259,554	294,581	293,124	461,744
Total Liabilities	989,244	869,899	935,608	833,018	802,754	804,979	762,823	857,703
Stockholders' Equity	1,040,745	1,118,895	942,209	730,239	698,487	631,930	553,077	540,284
Shares Outstanding	60,509	60,603	61,450	60,714	61,792	61,983	61,195	60,526
Statistical Record								
Return on Assets %	6.04	11.15	12.54	6.94	5.40	6.46	2.11	1.84
Return on Equity %	11.29	20.92	25.79	14.89	11.94	15.01	5.24	4.57
EBITDA Margin %	N.M.	13.74	13.04	11.89	10.70	9.80	9.37	7.08
Net Margin %	N.M.	7.50	8.38	4.81	3.57	4.22	1.45	1.34
Asset Turnover	1.54	1.49	1.50	1.44	1.51	1.53	1.45	1.37
Current Ratio	2.76	2.64	2.10	1.77	1.70	1.72	1.48	2.02
Debt to Equity	0.40	0.23	0.29	0.39	0.37	0.47	0.53	0.85
Price Range	50.00-29.96	50.00-36.80	45.04-33.84	37.31-29.78	33.45-27.36	30.75-19.62	23.45-16.32	21.84-13.20
P/E Ratio	27.62-16.55	14.53-10.70	13.02-9.78	21.82-17.42	26.34-21.54	21.35-13.63	49.90-34.73	53.28-32.20
Average Yield %	1.36	1.28	1.30	1.43	1.49	1.87	2.12	2.33

Address: 13925 Ballantyne Corporate Place, Suite 400, Charlotte, NC 28277	Officers: David A. Roberts - Chairman, President, Chief Executive Officer Carol P. Lowe - Vice	Investor Contact: 704-501-1100
Telephone: 704-501-1100	President, Chief Financial Officer **Transfer Agents:**	**No of Institutions:** 237
Web Site: www.carlisle.com	Computershare Investor Services, LLC, Chicago, IL	**Shares:** 54,290,448 **% Held:** 85.10

CATERPILLAR INC.

Exchange	Symbol	Price	52Wk Range	Yield	P/E
NYS	CAT	$82.78 (5/29/2008)	86.98-62.47	1.74	14.84

*7 Year Price Score 123.73 *NYSE Composite Index=100 *12 Month Price Score 109.81

TRADING VOLUME (thousand shares)

Interim Earnings (Per Share)

Qtr.	Mar	Jun	Sep	Dec
2005	0.81	1.08	0.94	1.20
2006	1.20	1.52	1.14	1.31
2007	1.23	1.24	1.40	1.50
2008	1.45	...	...	...

Interim Dividends (Per Share)

Amt	Decl	Ex	Rec	Pay
0.36Q	06/13/2007	07/18/2007	07/20/2007	08/20/2007
0.36Q	10/10/2007	10/18/2007	10/22/2007	11/20/2007
0.36Q	04/09/2008	04/17/2008	04/21/2008	05/20/2008
0.36Q	12/12/2008	01/17/2008	01/22/2008	02/20/2008

Indicated Div: $1.44 (Div. Reinv. Plan)

Valuation Analysis

Forecast EPS	$6.05 (05/17/2008)
Market Cap	$50.9 Billion	Book Value	9.2 Billion
Price/Book	5.52	Price/Sales	1.09

Dividend Achiever Status

10 Year Growth Rate	11.36%
Total Years of Dividend Growth	14

Business Summary: Industrial Machinery and Equipment (MIC: SIC: 3531 NAIC: 333120)

Caterpillar has three principal lines of business. Co.'s Machinery business designs, produces and sells construction, mining and forestry machinery, and designs, manufactures, remanufactures, maintains and services rail-related products. Co.'s Engines business designs, manufactures and sells engines for its machinery; electric power generation systems; on-highway vehicles and locomotives; marine, petroleum, construction, industrial, agricultural and other applications; and related parts. Co.'s Financial Products business provides financing alternatives, loans and insurance services to customers and dealers for its machinery and engines, gas turbines and other equipment and marine vessels.

Recent Developments: For the quarter ended Mar 31 2008, net income increased 13.0% to US$922.0 million from US$816.0 million in the year-earlier quarter. Revenues were US$11.80 billion, up 17.8% from US$10.02 billion the year before. Operating income was US$1.29 billion versus US$1.14 billion in the prior-year quarter, an increase of 13.4%. Direct operating expenses rose 20.6% to US$8.61 billion from US$7.14 billion in the comparable period the year before. Indirect operating expenses increased 8.9% to US$1.89 billion from US$1.74 billion in the equivalent prior-year period.

Prospects: For 2008, Co. is maintaining its outlook for an increase in sales and revenues of 5.0% to 10.0% and profit per share up 5.0% to 15.0% from 2007 despite further weakening in North America. Specifically, while sales and revenues in North America are now expected to be down 2.0% to up 2.0% compared with flat to up 5.0% in Co.'s prior outlook, robust demand outside North America is expected to offset this weakness. Meanwhile, on Apr 2 2008, Co. announced that it has acquired Lovat Inc., a global manufacturer of tunnel boring machines. Through this acquisition, Co. complements its global business with continued investment in the Lovat product line and in the tunnel boring machine business.

Financial Data

(US$ in Thousands)	3 Mos	12/31/2007	12/31/2006	12/31/2005	12/31/2004	12/31/2003	12/31/2002	12/31/2001
Earnings Per Share	5.58	5.37	5.17	4.04	2.88	1.56	1.15	1.16
Cash Flow Per Share	11.78	12.43	8.80	4.59	(5.81)	2.99	3.44	2.89
Tang Book Value Per Share	11.06	10.33	7.07	9.77	8.31	6.46	5.50	5.74
Dividends Per Share	...	1.380	1.150	0.960	0.800	0.710	0.700	0.695
Dividend Payout %	...	25.70	22.24	23.76	27.83	45.37	60.87	59.91
Income Statement								
Total Revenue	11,796,000	44,958,000	41,517,000	36,339,000	30,251,000	22,763,000	20,152,000	20,450,000
EBITDA	1,877,000	7,038,000	6,737,000	5,638,000	4,334,000	3,070,000	2,613,000	2,623,000
Depn & Amortn	472,000	1,797,000	1,602,000	1,477,000	1,397,000	1,347,000	1,220,000	1,169,000
Income Before Taxes	1,331,000	4,953,000	4,861,000	3,901,000	2,707,000	1,477,000	1,114,000	1,169,000
Income Taxes	420,000	1,485,000	1,405,000	1,120,000	731,000	398,000	312,000	367,000
Net Income	922,000	3,541,000	3,537,000	2,854,000	2,035,000	1,099,000	798,000	805,000
Average Shares	637,900	659,500	683,800	705,800	707,400	702,800	693,800	694,200
Balance Sheet								
Current Assets	26,907,000	25,477,000	23,093,000	22,790,000	20,856,000	16,791,000	14,628,000	13,400,000
Total Assets	58,204,000	56,132,000	50,879,000	47,069,000	43,091,000	36,465,000	32,851,000	30,657,000
Current Liabilities	24,316,000	22,245,000	19,252,000	19,092,000	16,210,000	12,621,000	11,344,000	10,276,000
Long-Term Obligations	17,654,000	17,829,000	17,680,000	15,677,000	15,837,000	14,078,000	11,596,000	11,291,000
Total Liabilities	48,986,000	47,249,000	44,020,000	38,637,000	35,624,000	30,387,000	27,379,000	25,046,000
Stockholders' Equity	9,218,000	8,883,000	6,859,000	8,432,000	7,467,000	6,078,000	5,472,000	5,611,000
Shares Outstanding	614,769	623,986	645,808	670,867	685,873	687,524	688,510	686,752
Statistical Record								
Return on Assets %	6.59	6.62	7.22	6.33	5.10	3.17	2.51	2.72
Return on Equity %	43.54	44.99	46.26	35.90	29.97	19.03	14.40	14.36
EBITDA Margin %	15.91	15.65	16.23	15.52	14.33	13.49	12.97	12.83
Net Margin %	7.82	7.88	8.52	7.85	6.73	4.83	3.96	3.94
Asset Turnover	0.84	0.84	0.85	0.81	0.76	0.66	0.63	0.69
Current Ratio	1.11	1.15	1.20	1.19	1.29	1.33	1.29	1.30
Debt to Equity	1.92	2.01	2.58	1.86	2.12	2.32	2.12	2.01
Price Range	86.98-62.47	86.98-58.17	81.14-57.80	59.64-41.73	49.23-34.61	42.38-21.02	29.90-16.93	28.10-20.05
P/E Ratio	15.59-11.20	16.20-10.83	15.69-11.18	14.76-10.33	17.10-12.09	27.16-13.47	26.00-14.72	24.22-17.28
Average Yield %	...	1.90	1.67	1.89	2.01	2.34	2.91	2.86

Address: 100 NE Adams Street, Peoria, IL. 61629-7310 **Telephone:** 309-675-1000 **Web Site:** www.cat.com	**Officers:** James W. Owens - Chairman, Chief Executive Officer James B. Buda - Vice President, Secretary, General Counsel **Transfer Agents:** BNY Mellon Shareowner Services, Pittsburgh, PA	**Investor Contact:** 309-675-4549 **No of Institutions:** 1085 **Shares:** 508,298,496 **% Held:** 68.42

CATO CORP.

Exchange	Symbol	Price	52Wk Range	Yield	P/E
NYS	CTR	$15.66 (5/29/2008)	25.01-13.49	4.21	15.20

*7 Year Price Score 81.82 *NYSE Composite Index=100 *12 Month Price Score 89.33

Interim Earnings (Per Share)

Qtr.	Apr	Jul	Oct	Jan
2003-04	0.45	0.20	0.03	0.18
2004-05	0.54	0.26	0.06	0.25
2005-06	0.58	0.34	0.13	0.37
2006-07	0.65	0.38	0.18	0.40
2007-08	0.59	0.39	0.09	(0.04)

Interim Dividends (Per Share)

Amt	Decl	Ex	Rec	Pay
0.165Q	08/30/2007	09/06/2007	09/10/2007	09/24/2007
0.165Q	12/07/2007	12/20/2007	12/24/2007	01/07/2008
0.165Q	03/03/2008	03/06/2008	03/10/2008	03/24/2008
0.165Q	05/22/2008	06/05/2008	06/09/2008	06/23/2008

Indicated Div: $0.66

Valuation Analysis

Forecast EPS	$0.87 (05/16/2008)		
Market Cap	$592.8 Million	Book Value	247.4 Million
Price/Book	2.40	Price/Sales	0.70

Dividend Achiever Status

10 Year Growth Rate	19.43%
Total Years of Dividend Growth	10

Business Summary: Retail - Apparel and Accessory Stores (MIC: SIC: 5621 NAIC: 448120)

Cato is engaged as a fashion specialty retailer for fashion and value conscious females. Co.'s stores provide an assortment of on-trend apparel and accessory items in junior/missy, plus sizes and girls sizes seven to 16 and emphasize color, product coordination and selection. Co. has two business segments: the operation of women's fashion specialty stores and a credit card division. As of Feb 2 2008, Co. operated 1,318 under the names Cato, Cato Fashions, Cato Plus, It's Fashion and It's Fashion Metro and are located primarily in strip shopping centers principally in the southeastern U.S.

Recent Developments: For the year ended Feb 2 2008, net income decreased 37.2% to US$32.3 million from US$51.5 million in the prior year. Revenues were US$846.4 million, down 3.4% from US$875.9 million the year before. Direct operating expenses declined 0.1% to US$572.3 million from US$572.7 million in the comparable period the year before. Indirect operating expenses increased 0.6% to US$224.9 million from US$223.5 million in the equivalent prior-year period.

Prospects: For the fiscal year ending Jan 31 2009, Co. is estimating comparable store sales to be down 3.0% to flat. Similarly, Co. is projecting net income to be in the range of $21.0 million to $27.00 million. Specifically, Co.'s net income guidance reflects the effects of closing 32 stores by end of this fiscal year, including the conversion of eight existing It's Fashion stores to the It's Fashion Metro format. In addition, Co. is targeting earnings to be in a range of $0.72 to $0.93 per diluted share, reflecting a decrease of 10.0% to 30.0% from previous fiscal year. Lastly, Co. intends to open 75 new stores, which include 30 new stores of an expanded version of It's Fashion divisions.

Financial Data
(US$ in Thousands)

	02/02/2008	02/03/2007	01/28/2006	01/29/2005	01/31/2004	02/01/2003	02/02/2002	02/03/2001
Earnings Per Share	1.03	1.62	1.41	1.11	0.89	1.18	1.11	1.02
Cash Flow Per Share	2.38	1.85	2.29	2.59	1.90	1.67	1.25	1.16
Tang Book Value Per Share	6.54	8.77	7.69	6.77	6.29	7.05	6.21	5.49
Dividends Per Share	0.645	0.580	0.507	0.457	0.420	0.390	0.353	0.283
Dividend Payout %	62.62	35.80	35.93	41.27	47.37	33.05	31.93	27.78
Income Statement								
Total Revenue	846,437	875,885	836,381	789,604	747,267	748,331	705,658	669,135
EBITDA	71,445	100,572	90,650	75,092	67,976	86,818	77,332	69,660
Depn & Amortn	22,212	20,941	20,275	20,397	18,699	14,979	11,046	9,618
Income Before Taxes	49,233	79,631	70,375	54,695	49,277	71,839	66,286	60,042
Income Taxes	16,914	28,181	25,546	19,854	17,888	26,006	23,200	21,015
Net Income	32,319	51,450	44,829	34,841	31,389	45,833	43,086	39,027
Average Shares	31,513	31,815	31,789	31,478	35,339	38,921	38,832	38,197
Balance Sheet								
Current Assets	293,050	299,513	271,677	266,422	227,400	260,891	223,208	215,489
Total Assets	420,792	432,322	406,636	394,134	351,573	383,410	332,041	310,742
Current Liabilities	148,936	123,049	132,563	132,631	114,492	98,282	83,575	89,765
Long-Term Obligations	...	...	...	16,000	21,500	...	...	...
Total Liabilities	173,422	155,529	166,688	182,959	157,462	113,246	97,343	102,985
Stockholders' Equity	247,370	276,793	239,948	211,175	194,111	270,164	234,698	207,757
Shares Outstanding	37,852	31,552	31,219	31,205	30,870	38,343	37,796	37,872
Statistical Record								
Return on Assets %	7.60	12.07	11.23	9.37	8.56	12.85	13.44	12.87
Return on Equity %	12.37	19.59	19.93	17.24	13.56	18.21	19.53	19.37
EBITDA Margin %	8.44	11.48	10.84	9.51	9.10	11.60	10.96	10.41
Net Margin %	3.82	5.87	5.36	4.41	4.20	6.12	6.11	5.83
Asset Turnover	1.99	2.05	2.09	2.12	2.04	2.10	2.20	2.21
Current Ratio	1.97	2.43	2.05	2.01	1.99	2.65	2.67	2.40
Debt to Equity	...	...	...	0.08	0.11	...	...	...
Price Range	25.01-13.49	26.25-19.80	23.35-17.07	20.07-12.60	16.74-10.95	18.29-9.45	14.50-9.49	11.88-6.25
P/E Ratio	24.28-13.10	16.20-12.22	16.56-12.10	18.08-11.35	18.81-12.31	15.50-8.01	13.06-8.55	11.64-6.13
Average Yield %	3.18	2.54	2.50	3.00	3.08	2.80	2.98	3.54

Address: 8100 Denmark Road, Charlotte, NC 28273-5975 **Telephone:** 704-554-8510 **Web Site:** www.catocorp.com	**Officers:** John P. Derham Cato - Chairman, President, Chief Executive Officer Stuart L. Uselton - Executive Vice President, Chief Administrative Officer **Transfer Agents:** American Stock Transfer, Charlotte, NC	**No of Institutions:** 144 **Shares:** 29,327,754 **% Held:** 92.02

CBL & ASSOCIATES PROPERTIES, INC.

Exchange	Symbol	Price	52Wk Range	Yield	P/E
NYS	CBL	$26.41 (5/29/2008)	41.41-21.87	8.25	36.68

*7 Year Price Score 76.23 *NYSE Composite Index=100 *12 Month Price Score 89.27

TRADING VOLUME (thousand shares)

Interim Earnings (Per Share)

Qtr.	Mar	Jun	Sep	Dec
2005	0.39	0.32	0.92	0.39
2006	0.32	0.32	0.22	0.47
2007	0.26	0.17	0.26	0.20
2008	0.09	...	...	...

Interim Dividends (Per Share)

Amt	Decl	Ex	Rec	Pay
0.505Q	09/07/2007	09/26/2007	09/28/2007	10/15/2007
0.545Q	11/06/2007	12/26/2007	12/28/2007	01/15/2008
0.545Q	02/28/2008	03/27/2008	03/31/2008	04/14/2008
0.545Q	06/02/2008	06/26/2008	06/30/2008	07/15/2008

Indicated Div: $2.18

Valuation Analysis

Forecast EPS	$0.74 (05/16/2008)
Market Cap	$1.8 Billion Book Value 887.8 Million
Price/Book	1.97 Price/Sales 1.64

Dividend Achiever Status

10 Year Growth Rate	8.74%
Total Years of Dividend Growth	12

Business Summary: "Property, Real Estate & Development" (MIC: SIC: 6798 NAIC: 525930)

CBL & Associates Properties is a self-managed, self-administered real estate investment trust that owns, develops, acquires, leases, manages and operates regional malls and open-air and community shopping centers. At Dec 31 2007, Co. owned interests in 84 regional malls/open-air centers, 32 associated centers, 15 community centers and 19 office buildings; interests in four mall expansions, two associated/lifestyle centers, three community/open-air centers, a mixed-use center and an office building that are under construction, as well as options to acquire certain shopping center development sites; and mortgages on 16 properties that are secured by first mortgages or wrap-around mortgages.

Recent Developments: For the quarter ended Mar 31 2008, income from continuing operations decreased 56.2% to US$10.9 million from US$25.0 million in the year-earlier quarter. Net income decreased 53.6% to US$11.6 million from US$25.0 million in the year-earlier quarter. Revenues were US$278.3 million, up 11.8% from US$249.0 million the year before. Revenues from property income rose 11.2% to US$271.3 million from US$244.0 million in the corresponding quarter a year earlier.

Prospects: On May 1 2008, Co. and Forum Development Group, LLC announced the acquisition of about 72 acres in D'Iberville, MS, (Biloxi/Gulf Port) for the development of The Promenade, a 700,000 square foot power center. The project is a joint venture of Co. and Forum, with Co. as the majority partner responsible for development, leasing and management. Construction will begin in May 2008 with an opening scheduled for fall 2009. For 2008, Co. is maintaining guidance for funds from operations of $3.46 to $3.56 per share, assuming same-center net operating income growth of 2.0% coupled with outparcel sales of $0.12 to $0.16, and excluding lease termination fees from both applicable periods.

Financial Data

(US$ in Thousands)	3 Mos	12/31/2007	12/31/2006	12/31/2005	12/31/2004	12/31/2003	12/31/2002	12/31/2001
Earnings Per Share	0.72	0.90	1.33	2.03	1.61	2.00	1.25	1.05
Cash Flow Per Share	7.04	7.20	6.09	6.21	5.49	4.58	4.77	3.33
Tang Book Value Per Share	13.39	13.91	16.58	17.30	16.82	13.81	12.44	10.19
Dividends Per Share	2.100	2.060	1.877	1.766	1.494	1.345	1.160	1.065
Dividend Payout %	292.43	228.89	141.17	87.01	93.07	67.42	93.17	100.95
Income Statement								
Property Income	271,250	1,018,767	978,483	889,227	739,066	653,355	583,236	539,569
Non-Property Income	7,029	21,860	23,658	19,485	20,098	14,176	15,858	4,806
Total Revenue	278,279	1,040,627	1,002,141	908,712	759,164	667,531	599,094	544,375
Depn & Amortn	73,404	149,239	129,169	127,400	97,152	113,170	101,937	89,444
Interest Expense	80,224	287,884	257,067	208,183	177,219	153,373	143,164	154,477
Income Taxes	357	8,390	5,902	...	...	...	...	...
Net Income	11,626	89,147	117,501	162,475	121,111	144,139	84,906	60,908
Average Shares	66,109	65,913	65,269	64,880	64,004	62,386	59,336	51,666
Balance Sheet								
Total Assets	8,028,948	8,105,047	6,518,810	6,352,322	5,204,500	4,264,310	3,795,114	3,372,851
Long-Term Obligations	5,889,620	5,869,318	4,564,535	4,341,055	3,371,679	2,738,102	2,402,079	2,315,955
Total Liabilities	6,252,663	6,264,202	4,874,504	4,661,325	3,583,743	2,899,579	2,553,411	2,419,662
Stockholders' Equity	887,775	920,548	1,084,856	1,081,522	1,054,151	837,300	741,190	522,088
Shares Outstanding	66,306	66,179	65,421	62,512	62,667	60,646	59,594	51,233
Statistical Record								
Return on Assets %	1.03	1.22	1.83	2.81	2.55	3.58	2.37	2.22
Return on Equity %	7.71	8.89	10.85	15.22	12.77	18.26	13.44	12.73
Net Margin %	4.18	8.57	11.72	17.88	15.95	21.59	14.17	11.19
Price Range	47.77-21.87	49.98-23.88	44.03-36.15	46.74-33.84	38.31-23.71	28.69-18.78	20.45-15.75	15.93-12.56
P/E Ratio	66.35-30.38	55.53-26.53	33.11-27.18	23.02-16.67	23.80-14.73	14.35-9.39	16.36-12.60	15.17-11.96
Average Yield %	6.48	5.45	4.60	4.45	5.01	5.80	6.32	7.37

Address: 2030 Hamilton Place Blvd., Suite 500, Chattanooga, TN 37421-6000	Officers: Charles B. Lebovitz - Chairman, Chief Executive Officer John N. Foy - Vice-Chairman, Chief	Investor Contact: 423-855-0001
Telephone: 423-855-0001	Financial Officer, Treasurer Transfer Agents:	No of Institutions: 226
Web Site: www.cblproperties.com	ComputerShare Investor Services, Providence, RI	Shares: 69,042,360 % Held: 100.89

CEDAR FAIR, L.P.

Exchange	Symbol	Price	52Wk Range	Yield	P/E
NYS	FUN	$23.02 (5/29/2008)	29.80-19.73	8.34	230.20

*7 Year Price Score 69.90 *NYSE Composite Index=100 *12 Month Price Score 99.02

TRADING VOLUME (thousand shares)

Interim Earnings (Per Share)

Qtr.	Mar	Jun	Sep	Dec
2005	(0.46)	0.22	3.11	0.04
2006	(0.49)	0.20	2.42	(0.55)
2007	(1.02)	0.10	0.98	(0.16)
2008	(0.81)	...	...	...

Interim Dividends (Per Share)

Amt	Decl	Ex	Rec	Pay
0.475Q	07/23/2007	08/01/2007	08/03/2007	08/15/2007
0.475Q	10/15/2007	11/01/2007	11/05/2007	11/15/2007
0.475Q	01/22/2008	02/01/2008	02/05/2008	02/15/2008
0.48Q	04/24/2008	05/01/2008	05/05/2008	05/15/2008
Indicated Div: $1.92 (Div. Reinv. Plan)				

Valuation Analysis

Forecast EPS	$1.15 (05/16/2008)		
Market Cap	$1.3 Billion	Book Value	N/A
Price/Book	N/A	Price/Sales	1.28

Dividend Achiever Status

10 Year Growth Rate	4.19%
Total Years of Dividend Growth	20

Business Summary: Sporting & Recreational (MIC: SIC: 7996 NAIC: 713110)

Cedar Fair is a publicly traded limited partnership managed by Cedar Fair Management, Inc. As of Dec 31 2007, Co. owned and operated 11 amusement parks, six outdoor water parks, one indoor water park and five hotels. Co.'s amusement parks include: Cedar Point, Sandusky, OH; Kings Island near Cincinnati, OH; Canada's Wonderland near Toronto, Canada; Dorney Park & Wildwater Kingdom, South Whitehall Township, PA; Valleyfair, Shakopee, MN; Michigan's Adventure located near Muskegon, MI; Kings Dominion near Richmond, VA; Carowinds in Charlotte, NC; Worlds of Fun, Kansas City, MO; Knott's Berry Farm, Buena Park, CA; and California's Great America, Santa Clara, CA.

Recent Developments: For the quarter ended Mar 30 2008, net loss amounted to US$43.8 million versus a net loss of US$55.1 million in the year-earlier quarter. Revenues were US$40.4 million, up 34.7% from US$30.0 million the year before. Operating loss was US$56.4 million versus a loss of US$50.9 million in the prior-year quarter. Direct operating expenses rose 23.1% to US$5.4 million from US$4.4 million in the comparable period the year before. Indirect operating expenses increased 19.5% to US$91.4 million from US$76.5 million in the equivalent prior-year period.

Prospects: For 2008, Co. remains committed on its $88.0 million capital expenditure program that features a variety of new shows and attractions across all of its parks, including five roller coasters, three thrill rides and 18 new live shows. Specifically, Co. plans to invest $21.0 million of the capital expenditure program for a roller coaster at its Canada's Wonderland amusement parks. Separately, Co. plans to operate Geauga Lake as a water park beginning in 2008. At the end of the first quarter of 2008, Co. noted that only six of its 18 properties were in operation. Meanwhile, for full-year 2008, Co. expects to generate revenues between $990.0 million and $1.02 billion.

Financial Data
(US$ in Thousands)

	3 Mos	12/31/2007	12/31/2006	12/31/2005	12/31/2004	12/31/2003	12/31/2002	12/31/2001
Earnings Per Share	0.10	(0.08)	1.59	2.93	1.47	1.67	1.39	1.13
Cash Flow Per Share	3.56	3.35	3.08	2.99	2.84	2.67	2.90	2.46
Dividends Per Share	1.900	1.895	1.870	1.830	1.790	1.740	1.650	1.580
Dividend Payout %	1,837.41	...	117.61	62.46	121.77	104.19	118.71	139.82
Income Statement								
Total Revenue	40,402	986,973	831,389	568,707	541,972	509,976	502,851	477,256
EBITDA	(49,606)	285,929	305,561	193,546	172,983	172,569	155,225	141,043
Depn & Amortn	6,183	130,623	90,703	55,765	50,690	44,693	41,682	42,486
Income Before Taxes	(88,590)	9,738	126,564	111,576	97,030	103,806	88,576	74,414
Income Taxes	(44,808)	14,229	39,087	(49,276)	18,715	17,918	17,159	16,520
Net Income	(43,782)	(4,491)	87,477	160,852	78,315	85,888	71,417	57,894
Average Shares	54,330	54,200	54,872	54,950	53,315	51,334	51,263	51,113
Balance Sheet								
Current Assets	112,804	62,748	104,508	40,610	32,960	29,777	29,237	26,868
Total Assets	2,475,263	2,418,668	2,510,921	1,024,794	993,208	819,341	822,257	810,231
Current Liabilities	158,115	122,708	159,258	130,733	121,517	111,694	106,338	96,700
Long-Term Obligations	1,839,166	1,735,461	1,759,713	450,850	442,084	348,647	365,150	373,000
Total Liabilities	2,299,942	2,133,576	2,100,306	590,560	622,725	510,450	516,937	501,981
Shares Outstanding	54,361	54,248	54,092	53,797	53,480	50,673	50,549	50,514
Statistical Record								
Return on Assets %	0.26	N.M.	4.95	15.94	8.62	10.46	8.75	7.35
EBITDA Margin %	N.M.	28.97	36.75	34.03	31.92	33.84	30.87	29.55
Net Margin %	N.M.	N.M.	10.52	28.28	14.45	16.84	14.20	12.13
Asset Turnover	0.39	0.40	0.47	0.56	0.60	0.62	0.62	0.61
Current Ratio	0.71	0.51	0.66	0.31	0.27	0.27	0.27	0.28
Price Range	29.80-19.73	29.89-21.00	29.80-24.15	33.95-26.22	35.71-28.86	31.03-22.74	24.79-20.30	24.98-18.03
P/E Ratio	298.00-197.30	...	18.74-15.19	11.59-8.95	24.29-19.63	18.58-13.62	17.83-14.60	22.11-15.96
Average Yield %	7.54	7.07	6.85	5.97	5.69	6.51	7.10	7.50

Address: One Cedar Point Drive, Sandusky, OH 44870-5259	Officers: Richard L. Kinzel - Chairman, President, Chief Executive Officer Craig J. Freeman - Vice President **Transfer Agents:** American Stock Transfer & Trust Company, New York, NY	Investor Contact: 419-627-2233
Telephone: 419-626-0830		**No of Institutions:** 149
Web Site: www.cedarfair.com		**Shares:** 13,958,646 **% Held:** 22.50

CENTURYTEL, INC.

Exchange	Symbol	Price	52Wk Range	Yield	P/E
NYS	CTL	$35.96 (5/29/2008)	49.52-30.88	0.75	9.29

*7 Year Price Score 91.91   *NYSE Composite Index=100   *12 Month Price Score 84.02

Interim Earnings (Per Share)

Qtr.	Mar	Jun	Sep	Dec
2005	0.59	0.64	0.68	0.58
2006	0.55	1.26	0.65	0.62
2007	0.68	1.00	1.01	1.04
2008	0.83	...	...	...

Interim Dividends (Per Share)

Amt	Decl	Ex	Rec	Pay
0.065Q	08/21/2007	08/30/2007	09/04/2007	09/17/2007
0.065Q	11/14/2007	11/23/2007	11/27/2007	12/10/2007
0.068Q	02/26/2008	03/06/2008	03/10/2008	03/24/2008
0.068Q	05/29/2008	06/09/2008	06/11/2008	06/24/2008

Indicated Div: $0.27 (Div. Reinv. Plan)

Valuation Analysis

Forecast EPS $3.21 (05/17/2008)
Market Cap	$3.8 Billion	Book Value	3.4 Billion
Price/Book	1.12	Price/Sales	1.42

Dividend Achiever Status

10 Year Growth Rate	4.69%
Total Years of Dividend Growth	34

Business Summary: Communications (MIC: SIC: 4813 NAIC: 517110)

CenturyTel is an integrated communications company engaged primarily in providing a variety of communications services, including local and long distance voice, Internet access and broadband services. Co. also provides fiber transport, local exchange carrier, security monitoring, and other communications and business information services. Co. conducts its operations in 25 states located in the continental U.S. As of Dec 31 2007, Co.'s local exchange telephone subsidiaries operated approximately 2.1 million telephone access lines, primarily in rural areas and small to mid-size cities in 24 states, with over 68.0% of these lines located in Missouri, Wisconsin, Alabama, Arkansas and Washington.

Recent Developments: For the quarter ended Mar 31 2008, net income increased 14.0% to US$88.8 million from US$77.9 million in the year-earlier quarter. Revenues were US$648.6 million, up 7.9% from US$600.9 million the year before. Operating income was US$183.5 million versus US$168.1 million in the prior-year quarter, an increase of 9.2%. Direct operating expenses rose 11.4% to US$237.8 million from US$213.5 million in the comparable period the year before. Indirect operating expenses increased 3.7% to US$227.3 million from US$219.2 million in the equivalent prior-year period.

Prospects: For 2008, Co. expects diluted earnings per share to be in the range of $3.05 to $3.20, excluding nonrecurring items, any share repurchases made after Apr 30 2008, and any future mergers, acquisitions, divestitures or other similar business transactions, compared with the previous guidance of $2.90 to $3.00. This guidance is based on several factors including, the first quarter of 2008 results exceeding expectations, along with the expectation that expenses for the remainder of 2008 will be lower than previously anticipated. However, based on its anticipated results for recent sales and retention initiatives, Co. is targeting its access line loss to be between 4.5% and 6.0% for 2008.

Financial Data

(US$ in Thousands)	3 Mos	12/31/2007	12/31/2006	12/31/2005	12/31/2004	12/31/2003	12/31/2002	12/31/2001
Earnings Per Share	3.87	3.72	3.07	2.49	2.41	2.38	5.61	2.41
Cash Flow Per Share	9.40	9.42	7.21	7.37	6.95	7.44	5.62	4.73
Tang Book Value Per Share	N.M.	N.M.	N.M.	0.90	N.M.	N.M.	N.M.	N.M.
Dividends Per Share	0.263	0.260	0.250	0.240	0.230	0.220	0.210	0.200
Dividend Payout %	6.78	6.99	8.14	9.64	9.54	9.24	3.74	8.30
Income Statement								
Total Revenue	648,614	2,656,241	2,447,730	2,479,252	2,407,372	2,380,745	1,971,996	2,117,469
EBITDA	327,594	1,368,103	1,310,612	1,271,502	1,259,327	1,229,351	926,927	1,251,963
Depn & Amortn	135,684	536,255	523,506	531,931	500,904	470,641	411,626	473,384
Income Before Taxes	141,788	618,942	591,149	537,770	547,232	531,959	293,456	553,056
Income Taxes	53,028	200,572	221,122	203,291	210,128	187,252	103,537	210,025
Net Income	88,760	418,370	370,027	334,479	337,244	344,707	801,624	343,031
Average Shares	106,997	113,094	122,229	136,087	142,144	144,700	142,879	142,307
Balance Sheet								
Net PPE	3,033,134	3,108,376	3,109,277	3,304,486	3,341,401	3,455,481	3,531,645	2,999,563
Total Assets	8,118,127	8,184,553	7,441,007	7,762,707	7,796,953	7,895,852	7,770,408	6,318,684
Long-Term Obligations	2,881,310	2,734,357	2,412,852	2,376,070	2,762,019	3,109,302	3,578,132	2,087,500
Total Liabilities	4,718,143	4,775,348	4,250,056	4,145,434	4,387,188	4,417,336	4,682,404	3,981,304
Stockholders' Equity	3,399,984	3,409,205	3,190,951	3,617,273	3,409,765	3,478,516	3,088,004	2,337,380
Shares Outstanding	106,259	108,491	113,253	131,074	132,373	144,364	142,955	141,232
Statistical Record								
Return on Assets %	5.28	5.35	4.87	4.30	4.29	4.40	11.38	5.40
Return on Equity %	13.12	12.68	10.87	9.52	9.77	10.50	29.55	15.70
EBITDA Margin %	50.51	51.51	53.54	51.29	52.31	51.64	47.00	59.13
Net Margin %	13.68	15.75	15.12	13.49	14.01	14.48	40.65	16.20
PPE Turnover	0.89	0.85	0.76	0.75	0.71	0.68	0.60	0.71
Asset Turnover	0.33	0.34	0.32	0.32	0.31	0.30	0.28	0.33
Debt to Equity	0.85	0.80	0.76	0.66	0.81	0.89	1.16	0.89
Price Range	49.52-33.05	49.52-40.30	43.79-32.84	36.28-30.26	35.49-26.33	36.63-25.51	35.20-22.18	39.00-26.18
P/E Ratio	12.80-8.54	13.31-10.83	14.26-10.70	14.57-12.15	14.73-10.93	15.39-10.72	6.27-3.95	16.18-10.86
Average Yield %	0.60	0.57	0.65	0.72	0.74	0.69	0.71	0.64

Address: 100 CenturyTel Drive, Monroe, LA 71203 Telephone: 318-388-9000 Web Site: www.centurytel.com	Officers: Glen F. Post - Chairman, Chief Executive Officer Karen A. Puckett - President, Chief Operating Officer **Transfer Agents:** Computershare Investor Services, L.L.C., Chicago, IL	Investor Contact: 800-833-1188 No of Institutions: 379 Shares: 98,127,264 % Held: 89.75

CHEMICAL FINANCIAL CORP.

Exchange	Symbol	Price	52Wk Range	Yield	P/E
NMS	CHFC	$24.59 (5/29/2008)	28.07-20.40	4.80	14.90

*7 Year Price Score 64.14   *NYSE Composite Index=100   ***12 Month Price Score 100.48**

Interim Earnings (Per Share)

Qtr.	Mar	Jun	Sep	Dec
2005	0.53	0.53	0.54	0.50
2006	0.47	0.49	0.46	0.46
2007	0.36	0.39	0.44	0.41
2008	0.41	...	...	...

Interim Dividends (Per Share)

Amt	Decl	Ex	Rec	Pay
0.285Q	07/17/2007	08/29/2007	08/31/2007	09/21/2007
0.285Q	10/16/2007	11/28/2007	11/30/2007	12/21/2007
0.295Q	01/22/2008	02/27/2008	02/29/2008	03/21/2008
0.295Q	04/22/2008	06/04/2008	06/06/2008	06/20/2008

Indicated Div: $1.18 (Div. Reinv. Plan)

Valuation Analysis

Forecast EPS $1.57 (05/16/2008)

Market Cap	$585.8 Million	Book Value	514.6 Million
Price/Book	1.14	Price/Sales	2.21

Dividend Achiever Status

10 Year Growth Rate	7.53%
Total Years of Dividend Growth	32

Business Summary: Commercial Banking (MIC: SIC: 6022 NAIC: 522110)

Chemical Financial is a financial holding company. Through its subsidiary bank, Chemical Bank, Co. provides various commercial banking services including, deposits, business and personal checking accounts, savings and individual retirement accounts, time deposit instruments, electronically accessed banking products, residential and commercial real estate financing, commercial lending, consumer financing, safe deposit box services, access to insurance products and corporate and personal trust and investment management services. As of Dec 31 2007, Co. had total assets of $3.75 billion, with 129 banking offices and two loan production offices in 31 counties across Michigan's lower Peninsula.

Recent Developments: For the quarter ended Mar 31 2008, net income increased 7.0% to US$9.7 million from US$9.0 million in the year-earlier quarter. Net interest income increased 8.2% to US$34.4 million from US$31.8 million in the year-earlier quarter. Provision for loan losses was US$2.7 million versus US$1.6 million in the prior-year quarter, an increase of 66.2%. Non-interest income fell 4.3% to US$9.6 million from US$10.0 million, while non-interest expense advanced 0.4% to US$26.8 million.

Prospects: Co.'s net interest income is primarily benefiting from lower short-term interest rates reducing interest expense more than interest income. In addition, Co. is seeing an increase in net interest margin primarily due to the decrease in the average cost of interest-bearing liabilities outpacing the decrease in the average yield on interest-earning assets. Looking ahead, Co. remains focused on monitoring its credit quality, while expecting its net interest margin will further increase in 2008 reflecting the Federal Reserve's recent rate cuts. Meanwhile, Co. expects the continued robust competition for core deposits throughout its markets to lessen the growth in core deposits during 2008.

Financial Data
(US$ in Thousands)

	3 Mos	12/31/2007	12/31/2006	12/31/2005	12/31/2004	12/31/2003	12/31/2002	12/31/2001
Earnings Per Share	1.65	1.60	1.88	2.10	2.25	2.24	2.20	1.71
Cash Flow Per Share	2.43	2.40	2.60	2.67	3.22	4.21	3.86	0.10
Tang Book Value Per Share	18.40	18.13	17.28	17.13	16.31	15.25	15.68	13.97
Dividends Per Share	1.150	1.140	1.100	1.060	1.010	0.952	0.871	0.829
Dividend Payout %	69.88	71.25	58.51	50.48	44.87	42.55	39.58	48.37
Income Statement								
Interest Income	53,437	225,894	217,423	199,304	189,250	185,037	211,044	219,250
Interest Expense	19,051	95,805	85,187	57,453	41,616	45,265	65,352	89,182
Net Interest Income	34,386	130,089	132,236	141,851	147,634	139,772	145,692	130,068
Provision for Losses	2,700	11,500	5,200	4,285	3,819	2,834	3,765	2,004
Non-Interest Income	9,580	43,288	40,147	39,220	39,329	39,094	34,534	31,873
Non-Interest Expense	26,844	104,671	97,874	98,463	98,469	91,923	93,526	94,597
Income Before Taxes	14,422	57,206	69,309	78,323	84,675	84,109	82,935	65,340
Income Taxes	4,751	18,197	22,465	25,445	27,993	28,393	27,990	22,617
Net Income	9,671	39,000	46,844	52,878	56,682	55,716	54,945	42,723
Average Shares	23,827	24,371	24,955	25,193	25,217	24,943	24,929	24,876
Balance Sheet								
Net Loans & Leases	2,756,124	2,767,895	2,779,229	2,676,066	2,551,419	2,448,096	2,044,514	2,151,547
Total Assets	3,799,298	3,754,313	3,789,247	3,749,316	3,764,125	3,708,888	3,568,893	3,488,306
Total Deposits	2,952,399	2,875,589	2,898,085	2,819,880	2,863,473	2,967,236	2,847,272	2,789,524
Total Liabilities	3,284,722	3,245,849	3,281,361	3,248,251	3,279,289	3,250,839	3,138,554	3,098,850
Stockholders' Equity	514,576	508,464	507,886	501,065	484,836	458,049	430,339	389,456
Shares Outstanding	23,823	23,814	24,827	25,079	25,169	24,991	24,868	24,821
Statistical Record								
Return on Assets %	1.04	1.03	1.24	1.41	1.51	1.53	1.56	1.56
Return on Equity %	7.66	7.68	9.29	10.73	11.99	12.54	13.40	12.98
Net Interest Margin %	64.35	57.59	60.82	71.17	78.01	75.54	69.03	59.32
Efficiency Ratio %	42.60	38.88	38.00	41.28	43.08	41.01	38.08	37.67
Loans to Deposits	0.93	0.96	0.96	0.95	0.89	0.83	0.72	0.77
Price Range	30.41-20.40	33.47-21.39	33.93-28.73	40.88-28.97	41.11-31.51	36.10-25.27	34.43-24.22	28.79-17.52
P/E Ratio	18.43-12.36	20.92-13.37	18.05-15.28	19.46-13.80	18.27-14.01	16.12-11.28	15.65-11.01	16.84-10.24
Average Yield %	4.56	4.26	3.58	3.22	2.92	3.19	3.15	3.48

Address: 333 East Main Street, Midland, MI 48640-0569	Officers: David B. Ramaker - Chairman, President,	Investor Contact: 989-839-5350
Telephone: 989-839-5350	Chief Executive Officer Lori A. Gwizdala - Executive Vice President, Chief Financial Officer, Treasurer	**No of Institutions:** 100
Web Site: www.chemicalbankmi.com	**Transfer Agents:** Computershare Investor Services LLC, Canton, MA	**Shares:** 13,243,930 % Held: 53.09

CHEVRON CORPORATION

Exchange	Symbol	Price	52Wk Range	Yield	P/E
NYS	CVX	$98.86 (5/29/2008)	103.09-77.51	2.63	10.94

*7 Year Price Score 123.30 *NYSE Composite Index=100 *12 Month Price Score 109.96

TRADING VOLUME (thousand shares)

Interim Earnings (Per Share)

Qtr.	Mar	Jun	Sep	Dec
2005	1.28	1.76	1.64	1.86
2006	1.80	1.97	2.29	1.74
2007	2.18	2.52	1.75	2.32
2008	2.48	...	...	...

Interim Dividends (Per Share)

Amt	Decl	Ex	Rec	Pay
0.58Q	07/25/2007	08/15/2007	08/17/2007	09/10/2007
0.58Q	10/31/2007	11/14/2007	11/16/2007	12/10/2007
0.58Q	01/30/2008	02/13/2008	02/15/2008	03/10/2008
0.65Q	04/30/2008	05/15/2008	05/19/2008	06/10/2008

Indicated Div: $2.60

Valuation Analysis

Forecast EPS	$10.52 (05/17/2008)		
Market Cap	$204.5 Billion	Book Value	79.2 Billion
Price/Book	2.58	Price/Sales	0.86

Dividend Achiever Status

10 Year Growth Rate	7.08%
Total Years of Dividend Growth	20

Business Summary: Oil and Gas (MIC: SIC: 2911 NAIC: 324110)

Chevron is an energy company engaged in petroleum operations, chemicals operations, mining operations of coal and other minerals, power generation and energy services. Co.'s operations consists of exploring for, developing and producing crude oil and natural gas; refining crude oil into finished petroleum products; marketing crude oil, natural gas and the products derived from petroleum; and transporting crude oil, natural gas and petroleum products. In addition, Co. is engaged in the manufacture and marketing of commodity petrochemicals, plastics for industrial uses, and fuel and lubricant oil additives through its chemical operations.

Recent Developments: For the quarter ended Mar 31 2008, net income increased 9.6% to US$5.17 billion from US$4.72 billion in the year-earlier quarter. Revenues were US$65.95 billion, up 36.7% from US$48.23 billion the year before. Direct operating expenses rose 51.2% to US$42.53 billion from US$28.13 billion in the comparable period the year before. Indirect operating expenses increased 10.3% to US$13.71 billion from US$12.44 billion in the equivalent prior-year period.

Prospects: Co.'s near-term outlook appears to be constructive. In detail, Co.'s start-up schedules for 2008 in upstream include deepwater projects at its 68.0%-owned Agbami project in Nigeria and its 75.0%-owned Blind Faith project in the U.S. Gulf of Mexico. Accordingly, Co. is forecasting total maximum oil-equivalent production of 250,000 barrels per day from Agbami within one year of start-up and 70,000 barrels per day at Blind Faith shortly after production begins. In addition, Co. foresees full start-up of new facilities at its 50.0%-owned Tengizchevroil affiliate in Kazakhstan should increase total crude-oil production capacity from 400,000 barrels per day to 540,000 barrels per day.

Financial Data

(US$ in Millions)	3 Mos	12/31/2007	12/31/2006	12/31/2005	12/31/2004	12/31/2003	12/31/2002	12/31/2001
Earnings Per Share	9.04	8.77	7.80	6.54	6.28	3.48	0.54	1.54
Cash Flow Per Share	13.22	11.79	11.13	9.38	6.92	5.80	4.68	5.40
Tang Book Value Per Share	36.06	34.66	29.71	26.00	21.47	16.97	14.79	15.91
Dividends Per Share	2.320	2.260	2.010	1.750	1.530	1.430	1.400	1.325
Dividend Payout %	25.66	25.77	25.77	26.76	24.36	41.09	261.68	85.76
Income Statement								
Total Revenue	65,946	220,904	210,118	198,200	155,300	121,761	99,049	106,245
EBITDA	11,892	40,875	39,482	31,110	25,486	18,154	9,387	15,350
Depn & Amortn	2,215	8,708	7,506	5,913	4,935	5,384	5,231	7,059
Income Before Taxes	9,677	32,167	31,976	25,197	20,551	12,770	4,156	8,291
Income Taxes	4,509	13,479	14,838	11,098	7,517	5,344	3,024	4,360
Net Income	5,168	18,688	17,138	14,099	13,328	7,230	1,132	3,288
Average Shares	2,080	2,132	2,198	2,156	2,122	2,128	2,126	2,125
Balance Sheet								
Current Assets	41,488	39,377	36,304	34,336	28,503	19,426	17,776	18,327
Total Assets	152,847	148,786	132,628	125,833	93,208	81,470	77,359	77,572
Current Liabilities	35,439	33,798	28,409	25,011	18,795	16,111	19,876	20,654
Long-Term Obligations	6,014	6,070	7,679	12,131	10,456	10,894	10,911	8,989
Total Liabilities	73,641	71,698	63,693	63,157	47,978	45,175	45,755	43,614
Stockholders' Equity	79,206	77,088	68,935	62,676	45,230	36,295	31,604	33,958
Shares Outstanding	2,068	2,090	2,165	2,233	2,107	2,138	2,136	2,134
Statistical Record								
Return on Assets %	13.21	13.28	13.26	12.87	15.22	9.10	1.46	5.53
Return on Equity %	25.33	25.60	26.04	26.13	32.61	21.30	3.45	12.20
EBITDA Margin %	18.03	18.50	18.79	15.70	16.41	14.91	9.48	14.45
Net Margin %	7.84	8.46	8.16	7.11	8.58	5.94	1.14	3.09
Asset Turnover	1.65	1.57	1.63	1.81	1.77	1.53	1.28	1.79
Current Ratio	1.17	1.17	1.28	1.37	1.52	1.21	0.89	0.89
Debt to Equity	0.08	0.08	0.11	0.19	0.23	0.30	0.35	0.26
Price Range	94.86-74.83	94.86-66.43	75.97-54.08	65.77-50.51	55.41-42.22	43.20-30.93	45.43-32.95	49.02-39.38
P/E Ratio	10.49-8.28	10.82-7.57	9.74-6.93	10.06-7.72	8.82-6.72	12.41-8.89	84.13-61.02	31.83-25.57
Average Yield %	2.70	2.74	3.19	3.04	3.20	4.04	3.51	2.98

Address: 6001 Bollinger Canyon Road, San Ramon, CA 94583-2324 **Telephone:** 925-842-1000 **Web Site:** www.chevron.com	**Officers:** David J. O'Reilly - Chairman, Chief Executive Officer Peter J. Robertson - Vice-Chairman **Transfer Agents:** Mellon Investor Services LLC, Jersey City, NJ	**Investor Contact:** 925-842-5690 **No of Institutions:** 1592 **Shares:** 1,536,525,440 **% Held:** 25.57

CHUBB CORP.

Exchange	Symbol	Price	52Wk Range	Yield	P/E
NYS	CB	$53.58 (5/29/2008)	55.52-47.36	2.46	7.60

*7 Year Price Score 99.06 ***NYSE Composite Index=100** ***12 Month Price Score 102.77**

Interim Earnings (Per Share)

Qtr.	Mar	Jun	Sep	Dec
2005	1.19	1.23	0.60	1.47
2006	1.58	1.41	1.43	1.55
2007	1.71	1.75	1.87	1.68
2008	1.77	...	...	...

Interim Dividends (Per Share)

Amt	Decl	Ex	Rec	Pay
0.29Q	06/08/2007	06/20/2007	06/22/2007	07/10/2007
0.29Q	09/06/2007	09/19/2007	09/21/2007	10/09/2007
0.29Q	12/13/2007	12/14/2007	12/18/2007	01/15/2008
0.33Q	03/13/2008	03/26/2008	03/28/2008	04/15/2008

Indicated Div: $1.32 (Div. Reinv. Plan)

Valuation Analysis

Forecast EPS $6.10 (05/17/2008)

Market Cap	$19.6 Billion	Book Value	14.3 Billion
Price/Book	1.36	Price/Sales	1.39

Dividend Achiever Status

10 Year Growth Rate	6.99%
Total Years of Dividend Growth	43

Business Summary: Insurance (MIC: SIC: 6331 NAIC: 524126)

Chubb is a holding company with subsidiaries mainly engaged in the property and casualty insurance business, which is divided into three business units: Chubb Commercial Insurance, which provides commercial insurance products, including coverage for multiple peril, casualty, workers' compensation and property and marine; Chubb Specialty Insurance, which offers professional liability products for privately and publicly owned companies, financial institutions, professional firms and healthcare organizations; and Chubb Personal Insurance, which provides products for individuals with fine homes and possessions who require more coverage choices and higher limits than standard insurance policies.

Recent Developments: For the quarter ended Mar 31 2008, net income decreased 6.5% to US$664.0 million from US$710.0 million in the year-earlier quarter. Revenues were US$3.49 billion, down 0.9% from US$3.52 billion the year before. Net premiums earned were US$2.98 billion versus US$2.99 billion in the prior-year quarter, a decrease of 0.3%.

Prospects: Co.'s bottom-line results are being negatively affected by lower realized investments gains. Nevertheless, Co.'s net income is benefiting from substantial underwriting income in its property and casualty insurance business. In addition, Co. is experiencing an increase in net premiums written from its insurance business. However, Co. is seeing fewer opportunities to write new business at acceptable rates, and expects this competitive market environment to continue throughout 2008. Further, Co. expects growth in net premiums written for its surety business primarily due to several large bonds written to slow as the year progresses.

Financial Data

(US$ in Thousands)	3 Mos	12/31/2007	12/31/2006	12/31/2005	12/31/2004	12/31/2003	12/31/2002	12/31/2001
Earnings Per Share	7.05	7.01	5.98	4.47	4.00	2.23	0.65	0.32
Cash Flow Per Share	8.61	8.11	8.10	9.47	10.74	9.39	6.99	2.93
Tang Book Value Per Share	37.98	37.31	32.57	28.56	25.07	21.43	18.67	17.81
Dividends Per Share	1.200	1.160	1.000	0.860	0.780	0.720	0.700	0.680
Dividend Payout %	17.02	16.55	16.72	19.24	19.48	32.29	108.53	215.87
Income Statement								
Premium Income	2,976,000	11,946,000	11,958,000	12,176,000	11,635,700	10,182,500	8,085,300	6,656,400
Total Revenue	3,489,000	14,107,000	14,003,000	14,082,300	13,177,200	11,394,000	9,140,300	7,754,000
Benefits & Claims	1,584,000	6,299,000	6,574,000	7,813,500	7,320,900	6,867,200	6,064,600	5,357,400
Income Before Taxes	929,000	3,937,000	3,525,000	2,447,000	2,068,200	933,600	168,400	(66,000)
Income Taxes	265,000	1,130,000	997,000	621,100	519,800	124,800	(54,500)	(177,500)
Net Income	664,000	2,807,000	2,528,000	1,825,900	1,548,400	808,800	222,900	111,500
Average Shares	375,800	400,300	422,400	408,400	386,400	362,600	345,800	351,600
Balance Sheet								
Total Assets	51,193,000	50,574,000	50,277,000	48,060,700	44,260,300	38,360,600	34,114,400	29,449,000
Total Liabilities	36,846,000	36,129,000	36,414,000	35,653,700	34,133,900	29,838,600	27,255,200	22,923,700
Stockholders' Equity	14,347,000	14,445,000	13,863,000	12,407,000	10,126,400	8,522,000	6,859,200	6,525,300
Shares Outstanding	365,488	374,649	411,276	418,076	385,353	375,926	342,403	340,142
Statistical Record								
Return on Assets %	5.39	5.57	5.14	3.96	3.74	2.23	0.70	0.41
Return on Equity %	19.51	19.83	19.25	16.21	16.56	10.52	3.33	1.65
Loss Ratio %	53.23	52.73	54.98	64.17	62.92	67.44	75.01	80.48
Net Margin %	19.03	19.90	18.05	12.97	11.75	7.10	2.44	1.44
Price Range	55.91-47.36	55.91-47.36	54.65-46.80	49.06-36.67	38.50-32.00	34.62-21.23	39.10-26.10	41.72-29.30
P/E Ratio	7.93-6.72	7.98-6.76	9.14-7.83	10.98-8.20	9.63-8.00	15.52-9.52	60.15-40.15	130.37-91.55
Average Yield %	2.28	2.20	1.99	2.02	2.23	2.42	2.13	1.91

Address: 15 Mountain View Road, P.O. Box 1615, Warren, NJ 07061-1615 **Telephone:** 908-903-2000 **Web Site:** www.chubb.com	**Officers:** John D. Finnegan - Chairman, President, Chief Executive Officer Michael O'Reilly - Vice-Chairman, Chief Financial Officer **Transfer Agents:** Computershare Trust Company, N.A., Providence, RI	**No of Institutions:** 743 **Shares:** 333,245,056 **% Held:** 84.95

CHURCH & DWIGHT CO., INC.

Exchange	Symbol	Price	52Wk Range	Yield	P/E
NYS	CHD	$57.09 (5/29/2008)	57.46-43.25	0.56	21.79

*7 Year Price Score 122.96 *NYSE Composite Index=100 *12 Month Price Score 111.29

TRADING VOLUME (thousand shares)

Interim Earnings (Per Share)

Qtr.	Mar	Jun	Sep	Dec
2005	0.56	0.51	0.51	0.25
2006	0.60	0.54	0.57	0.36
2007	0.66	0.59	0.75	0.46
2008	0.81	...	...	...

Interim Dividends (Per Share)

Amt	Decl	Ex	Rec	Pay
0.08Q	08/02/2007	08/09/2007	08/13/2007	09/03/2007
0.08Q	11/01/2007	11/07/2007	11/12/2007	12/03/2007
0.08Q	02/01/2008	02/07/2008	02/11/2008	03/03/2008
0.08Q	05/02/2008	05/08/2008	05/12/2008	06/02/2008
		Indicated Div: $0.32		

Valuation Analysis

Forecast EPS	$2.80 (05/17/2008)		
Market Cap	$3.8 Billion	Book Value	1.1 Billion
Price/Book	3.35	Price/Sales	1.67

Dividend Achiever Status

10 Year Growth Rate	6.94%
Total Years of Dividend Growth	11

Business Summary: Chemicals (MIC: SIC: 2841 NAIC: 325611)

Church & Dwight produces, manufactures, and markets household, personal care and specialty products. Co.'s Consumer Domestic segment includes household products for deodorizing and cleaning, such as ARM & HAMMER baking soda and cat litter and SCRUB FREE and BRILLO cleaning products; and laundry products, such as XTRA and ARM & HAMMER laundry detergents, OXICLEAN pre-wash laundry additive and XTRA NICE'N FLUFFY fabric softeners. Co.'s Consumer International segment sells several personal care products, some of which use the same brands as its domestic product lines. Co.'s Specialty Products segment produces and sells sodium bicarbonate and animal nutrition and specialty cleaning products.

Recent Developments: For the quarter ended Mar 28 2008, net income increased 24.6% to US$56.2 million from US$45.1 million in the year-earlier quarter. Revenues were US$552.9 million, up 7.5% from US$514.3 million the year before. Operating income was US$92.8 million versus US$82.1 million in the prior-year quarter, an increase of 12.9%. Direct operating expenses rose 4.5% to US$328.8 million from US$314.5 million in the comparable period the year before. Indirect operating expenses increased 11.6% to US$131.3 million from US$117.7 million in the equivalent prior-year period.

Prospects: On Apr 1 2008, Co. signed a definitive agreement to acquire Del Pharmaceuticals, Inc., which makes the Orajel® oral analgesic and other over-the-counter brands, for $380.0 million from Coty Inc. The transaction, which is expected to close in Jul 2008, is part of Co.'s growth strategy of bolstering its businesses by adding brands with gross margins that are accretive to its business. Co. expects the acquisition to have a neutral effect on its 2008 earnings but to be accretive to its 2009 earnings, and anticipates additional cost synergies of over $10.0 million a year by the end of 2009. For 2008, Co. continues to expect earnings per share of $2.77 and gross margin expansion of 100 basis points.

Financial Data
(US$ in Thousands)

	3 Mos	12/31/2007	12/31/2006	12/31/2005	12/31/2004	12/31/2003	12/31/2002	12/31/2001
Earnings Per Share	2.62	2.46	2.07	1.83	1.36	1.28	1.07	0.77
Cash Flow Per Share	4.25	3.78	2.87	2.98	3.14	1.95	1.92	0.71
Tang Book Value Per Share	N.M.	N.M.	N.M.	N.M.	N.M.	0.98	0.92	0.31
Dividends Per Share	0.310	0.300	0.260	0.240	0.227	0.207	0.200	0.193
Dividend Payout %	11.84	12.20	12.56	13.11	16.67	16.15	18.75	25.22
Income Statement								
Total Revenue	552,867	2,220,940	1,945,661	1,736,506	1,462,062	1,056,874	1,047,149	1,080,864
EBITDA	115,119	380,488	318,853	263,230	207,939	171,686	152,956	113,235
Depn & Amortn	15,212	56,671	51,727	44,158	39,093	30,224	27,890	27,843
Income Before Taxes	87,402	264,925	213,098	174,974	127,439	116,935	101,092	73,855
Income Taxes	31,211	95,900	74,171	52,068	38,631	35,974	34,402	26,871
Net Income	56,191	169,025	138,927	122,906	88,808	80,961	66,690	46,984
Average Shares	70,817	70,312	68,946	69,289	68,066	63,298	62,713	61,228
Balance Sheet								
Current Assets	692,789	735,353	556,070	494,438	493,796	289,222	285,436	293,207
Total Assets	2,465,283	2,532,490	2,334,154	1,962,117	1,877,998	1,119,617	988,241	949,085
Current Liabilities	349,394	457,789	444,404	409,710	357,539	232,054	191,167	196,016
Long-Term Obligations	692,982	707,311	792,925	635,261	754,706	331,149	352,488	406,564
Total Liabilities	1,331,955	1,452,225	1,470,317	1,265,239	1,317,968	681,123	640,595	666,782
Stockholders' Equity	1,133,328	1,080,265	863,837	696,878	560,030	438,494	347,646	282,303
Shares Outstanding	66,412	66,243	65,361	64,388	63,188	61,179	59,846	58,714
Statistical Record								
Return on Assets %	7.49	6.95	6.47	6.40	5.91	7.68	6.88	6.69
Return on Equity %	17.58	17.39	17.80	19.56	17.74	20.60	21.17	18.18
EBITDA Margin %	20.82	17.13	16.39	15.16	14.22	16.24	14.61	10.48
Net Margin %	10.16	7.61	7.14	7.08	6.07	7.66	6.37	4.35
Asset Turnover	0.94	0.91	0.91	0.90	0.97	1.00	1.08	1.54
Current Ratio	1.98	1.61	1.25	1.21	1.38	1.25	1.49	1.50
Debt to Equity	0.61	0.65	0.92	0.91	1.35	0.76	1.01	1.44
Price Range	56.93-43.25	56.93-43.25	43.38-32.96	39.04-32.29	33.62-25.78	27.65-18.73	23.93-17.27	18.96-13.21
P/E Ratio	21.73-16.51	23.14-17.58	20.96-15.92	21.33-17.64	24.72-18.96	21.60-14.63	22.36-16.14	24.62-17.15
Average Yield %	0.61	0.61	0.69	0.67	0.78	0.93	0.97	1.18

Address: 469 North Harrison Street, Princeton, NJ 08543-5297	**Officers:** James R. Craigie - Chairman, Chief Executive Officer Matthew Thomas Farrell - Executive Vice President, Chief Financial Officer **Transfer Agents:** Computershare Investor Services LLC, Chicago, IL	**No of Institutions:** 367
Telephone: 609-683-5900		**Shares:** 54,841,812 **% Held:** 79.94
Web Site: www.churchdwight.com		

56

CINCINNATI FINANCIAL CORP.

Exchange	Symbol	Price	52Wk Range	Yield	P/E
NMS	CINF	$35.68 (5/29/2008)	45.89-35.03	4.37	9.99

*7 Year Price Score 77.73 *NYSE Composite Index=100 *12 Month Price Score 94.65

Interim Earnings (Per Share)

Qtr.	Mar	Jun	Sep	Dec
2005	0.81	0.89	0.66	1.03
2006	3.13	0.76	0.66	0.74
2007	1.11	2.02	0.72	1.11
2008	(0.26)	...	...	...

Interim Dividends (Per Share)

Amt	Decl	Ex	Rec	Pay
0.355Q	08/16/2007	09/19/2007	09/21/2007	10/15/2007
0.355Q	11/19/2007	12/19/2007	12/21/2007	01/15/2008
0.39Q	02/01/2008	03/18/2008	03/21/2008	04/15/2008
0.39Q	05/23/2008	06/18/2008	06/20/2008	07/15/2008

Indicated Div: $1.56 (Div. Reinv. Plan)

Valuation Analysis

Forecast EPS $2.85 (05/17/2008)

Market Cap	$5.8 Billion	Book Value	5.4 Billion
Price/Book	1.07	Price/Sales	1.48

Dividend Achiever Status

10 Year Growth Rate	11.21%
Total Years of Dividend Growth	47

Business Summary: Insurance (MIC: SIC: 6331 NAIC: 524126)

Cincinnati Financial is a holding company primarily engaged in the marketing of property casualty insurance. Co. owns 100.0% of four subsidiaries: The Cincinnati Insurance Co., CSU Producer Resources Inc., CFC Investment Company and CinFin Capital Management Co. The Cincinnati Insurance Co. owns 100.0% of Co.'s four insurance subsidiaries: The Cincinnati Casualty Co. and The Cincinnati Indemnity Co. market a range of business, homeowner and auto policies while the Cincinnati Specialty Underwriters Insurance Co. provides excess and surplus lines insurance products, and The Cincinnati Life Insurance Co. markets life insurance policies, disability income policies and annuities.

Recent Developments: For the quarter ended Mar 31 2008, net loss amounted to US$42.0 million versus net income of US$194.0 million in the year-earlier quarter. Revenues were US$704.0 million, down 31.7% from US$1.03 billion the year before. Net premiums earned were US$780.0 million versus US$815.0 million in the prior-year quarter, a decrease of 4.3%. Net investment income rose 2.7% to US$152.0 million from US$148.0 million a year ago.

Prospects: Co. is seeing soft pricing in the property casualty insurance market while pressure on financial stocks in its portfolio reduced its net income and book value. For 2008, Co. expects that its property casualty net written premiums could decrease as much as 5.0% due to competitive pricing. However, Co. is encouraged by its new excess and surplus lines operation and plans to offer commercial property insurance as well as other professional liability and excess capacity by the end of 2008. Also, Co.'s portfolio strategies continue to focus on balancing near-term income generation with long-term book value growth although it expects 2008 investment income growth to be below 2007 level.

Financial Data
(US$ in Thousands)

	3 Mos	12/31/2007	12/31/2006	12/31/2005	12/31/2004	12/31/2003	12/31/2002	12/31/2001
Earnings Per Share	3.57	4.97	5.30	3.40	3.28	2.10	1.32	1.08
Cash Flow Per Share	4.02	4.13	3.55	4.60	4.65	4.61	3.74	3.04
Tang Book Value Per Share	33.43	35.72	39.35	34.98	35.64	35.17	31.34	33.58
Dividends Per Share	1.455	1.420	1.340	1.205	1.035	0.907	0.807	0.762
Dividend Payout %	40.78	28.57	25.28	35.46	31.60	43.29	60.96	70.59
Income Statement								
Premium Income	780,000	3,250,000	3,278,000	3,164,000	3,020,000	2,748,000	2,478,000	2,152,000
Total Revenue	704,000	4,259,000	4,550,000	3,767,000	3,614,000	3,181,000	2,843,000	2,561,000
Benefits & Claims	536,000	1,963,000	2,128,000	1,911,000	1,846,000	1,887,000	1,826,000	1,663,000
Income Before Taxes	(100,000)	1,192,000	1,329,000	823,000	800,000	480,000	279,000	221,000
Income Taxes	(58,000)	337,000	399,000	221,000	216,000	106,000	41,000	28,000
Net Income	(42,000)	855,000	930,000	602,000	584,000	374,000	238,000	193,000
Average Shares	165,105	172,167	175,451	177,116	178,376	178,292	179,920	178,605
Balance Sheet								
Total Assets	15,945,000	16,637,000	17,222,000	16,003,000	16,107,000	15,509,000	14,059,000	13,959,000
Total Liabilities	10,496,000	10,708,000	10,414,000	9,917,000	9,858,000	9,305,000	8,461,000	7,961,000
Stockholders' Equity	5,449,000	5,929,000	6,808,000	6,086,000	6,249,000	6,204,000	5,598,000	5,998,000
Shares Outstanding	163,000	166,000	173,000	174,000	175,350	176,400	178,605	178,605
Statistical Record								
Return on Assets %	3.60	5.05	5.60	3.75	3.68	2.53	1.70	1.42
Return on Equity %	10.12	13.43	14.43	9.76	9.35	6.34	4.10	3.22
Loss Ratio %	68.72	60.40	64.92	60.40	61.13	68.67	73.69	77.28
Net Margin %	(5.97)	20.08	20.44	15.98	16.16	11.76	8.37	7.54
Price Range	47.62-35.10	47.62-36.91	49.07-41.43	45.68-38.62	43.34-36.95	37.91-30.52	42.67-29.65	38.73-32.03
P/E Ratio	13.34-9.83	9.58-7.43	9.26-7.82	13.44-11.36	13.21-11.27	18.05-14.53	32.32-22.46	35.86-29.66
Average Yield %	3.51	3.30	2.94	2.88	2.60	2.60	2.21	2.16

Address: 6200 South Gilmore Road, Fairfield, OH 45014-5141
Telephone: 513-870-2000
Web Site: www.cinfin.com

Officers: John J. Schiff - Chairman, Chief Executive Officer James E. Benoski - Vice-Chairman, President, Chief Operating Officer, Chief Insurance Officer **Transfer Agents:** Cincinnati Financial Corporation, Cincinnati, OH

Investor Contact: 513-870-2639
No of Institutions: 393
Shares: 97,768,680 **% Held:** 55.28

CINTAS CORPORATION

Exchange	Symbol	Price	52Wk Range	Yield	P/E
NMS	CTAS	$29.64 (5/29/2008)	40.90-27.74	1.55	13.92

*7 Year Price Score 63.09 ***NYSE Composite Index=100** ***12 Month Price Score 89.01**

TRADING VOLUME (thousand shares)

Interim Earnings (Per Share)

Qtr.	Aug	Nov	Feb	May
2004-05	0.42	0.43	0.41	0.48
2005-06	0.47	0.46	0.46	0.55
2006-07	0.53	0.51	0.48	0.57
2007-08	0.51	0.53	0.53	...

Interim Dividends (Per Share)

Amt	Decl	Ex	Rec	Pay
0.32A	01/28/2005	02/04/2005	02/08/2005	03/15/2005
0.35A	01/24/2006	02/03/2006	02/07/2006	03/14/2006
0.39A	01/16/2007	02/02/2007	02/06/2007	03/13/2007
0.46A	01/15/2008	02/04/2008	02/06/2008	03/12/2008

Indicated Div: $0.46

Valuation Analysis

Forecast EPS	$2.13 (05/17/2008)
Market Cap	$4.6 Billion Book Value 2.2 Billion
Price/Book	2.10 Price/Sales 1.17

Dividend Achiever Status

10 Year Growth Rate	14.58%
Total Years of Dividend Growth	25

Business Summary: Apparel (MIC: SIC: 2326 NAIC: 315225)

Cintas is engaged in providing highly specialized products and services to businesses of all types throughout the U.S. and Canada. Co. classifies its business into two operating segments, Rentals and Other Services. The Rentals segment reflects the rental and servicing of uniforms and other garments, mats, mops and shop towels. In addition to these rental items, Co. also provide restroom and hygiene products and services within this segment. The Other Services segment consists of the direct sale of uniforms and related items, first aid, safety and fire protection products and services, document management services and branded promotional products.

Recent Developments: For the quarter ended Feb 29 2008, net income increased 6.6% to US$81.8 million from US$76.7 million in the year-earlier quarter. Revenues were US$976.0 million, up 7.8% from US$905.4 million the year before. Direct operating expenses rose 8.7% to US$564.7 million from US$519.6 million in the comparable period the year before. Indirect operating expenses increased 8.3% to US$285.3 million from US$263.4 million in the equivalent prior-year period.

Prospects: For the fiscal year ending May 31 2008, Co. is projecting revenues to be in the range of $3.93 billion to $3.97 billion, while earnings are forecasted to range from $2.12 to $2.16 per diluted share. Going forward, Co. anticipates that the challenging economic conditions, which are negatively affecting its existing customer base and its existing cost structure, will continue in the fourth fiscal quarter of 2008. In addition, Co. believes that this weakness will continue challenge its revenue growth and margins. Nevertheless, Co. foresees that cost management initiatives, technological improvements and ongoing capitalization of its infrastructure will help to mitigate these weaknesses.

Financial Data
(US$ in Thousands)

	9 Mos	6 Mos	3 Mos	05/31/2007	05/31/2006	05/31/2005	05/31/2004	05/31/2003
Earnings Per Share	2.13	2.09	2.07	2.09	1.94	1.74	1.58	1.45
Cash Flow Per Share	3.22	3.15	2.84	2.81	2.75	2.41	2.97	1.94
Tang Book Value Per Share	4.53	4.61	5.08	4.53	4.57	6.16	5.41	4.48
Dividends Per Share	0.460	0.390	0.390	0.390	0.350	0.320	0.290	0.270
Dividend Payout %	21.56	18.66	18.84	18.66	18.04	18.39	18.35	18.62
Income Statement								
Total Revenue	2,928,945	1,952,993	969,128	3,706,900	3,403,608	3,067,283	2,814,059	2,686,585
EBITDA	531,899	357,145	175,509	709,479	682,468	625,168	575,339	538,820
Depn & Amortn	142,447	93,612	46,222	175,926	160,653	148,175	143,259	143,061
Income Before Taxes	389,452	263,533	129,287	533,553	521,815	476,993	432,080	395,759
Income Taxes	143,708	99,617	48,224	199,015	194,637	176,475	159,875	146,506
Net Income	245,744	163,916	81,063	334,538	327,178	300,518	272,205	249,253
Average Shares	153,882	156,813	159,038	160,187	168,545	172,649	172,372	172,037
Balance Sheet								
Current Assets	1,238,818	1,227,663	1,173,902	1,156,736	1,178,008	1,166,544	1,034,243	877,544
Total Assets	3,762,278	3,699,582	3,620,830	3,570,480	3,425,237	3,059,744	2,810,297	2,582,946
Current Liabilities	392,675	363,188	260,911	403,038	411,828	356,481	325,686	304,839
Long-Term Obligations	964,065	947,473	876,522	877,074	794,454	465,291	473,685	534,763
Total Liabilities	1,596,815	1,551,954	1,376,869	1,402,742	1,337,274	955,609	922,328	936,614
Stockholders' Equity	2,165,463	2,147,628	2,243,961	2,167,738	2,087,963	2,104,135	1,887,969	1,646,332
Shares Outstanding	153,683	153,677	158,860	158,676	163,181	170,658	171,377	170,599
Statistical Record								
Return on Assets %	9.22	9.28	9.44	9.56	10.09	10.24	10.07	9.77
Return on Equity %	15.87	15.60	15.40	15.72	15.61	15.06	15.36	16.24
EBITDA Margin %	18.16	18.29	18.11	19.14	20.05	20.38	20.45	20.06
Net Margin %	8.39	8.39	8.36	9.02	9.61	9.80	9.67	9.28
Asset Turnover	1.07	1.07	1.07	1.06	1.05	1.05	1.04	1.05
Current Ratio	3.15	3.38	4.50	2.87	2.86	3.27	3.18	2.88
Debt to Equity	0.45	0.44	0.39	0.40	0.38	0.22	0.25	0.32
Price Range	40.90-28.78	42.81-31.79	43.63-35.37	43.63-34.92	45.32-37.56	47.86-38.21	50.21-34.93	52.21-30.90
P/E Ratio	19.20-13.51	20.48-15.21	21.08-17.09	20.88-16.71	23.36-19.36	27.51-21.96	31.78-22.11	36.01-21.31
Average Yield %	1.28	1.02	0.99	0.99	0.84	0.74	0.68	0.64

Address: 6800 Cintas Boulevard, P.O. Box 625737, Cincinnati, OH 45262-5737 **Telephone:** 513-459-1200 **Web Site:** www.cintas.com	**Officers:** Richard T. Farmer - Chairman Robert J. Kohlhepp - Vice-Chairman **Transfer Agents:** Wells Fargo Bank, South St. Paul, MN	**No of Institutions:** 433 **Shares:** 106,680,808 **% Held:** 64.07

CITIGROUP INC

Exchange	Symbol	Price	52Wk Range	Yield	P/E
NYS	C	$22.04 (5/29/2008)	54.51-18.62	5.81	N/A

*7 Year Price Score 63.57   ***NYSE Composite Index=100**   ***12 Month Score 68.92**

Interim Earnings (Per Share)

Qtr.	Mar	Jun	Sep	Dec
2005	1.04	0.97	1.38	1.36
2006	1.12	1.05	1.10	1.03
2007	1.01	1.24	0.44	(1.97)
2008	(1.02)	...	...	...

Interim Dividends (Per Share)

Amt	Decl	Ex	Rec	Pay
0.54Q	07/16/2007	08/02/2007	08/06/2007	08/24/2007
0.54Q	10/15/2007	11/01/2007	11/05/2007	11/21/2007
0.32Q	01/15/2008	01/31/2008	02/04/2008	02/22/2008
0.32Q	04/21/2008	05/01/2008	05/05/2008	05/23/2008
	Indicated Div: $1.28 (Div. Reinv. Plan)			

Valuation Analysis

Forecast EPS	$0.44 (05/17/2008)		
Market Cap	$115.7 Billion	Book Value	128.2 Billion
Price/Book	0.90	Price/Sales	0.80

Dividend Achiever Status

10 Year Growth Rate	26.87%
Total Years of Dividend Growth	21

Business Summary: Commercial Banking (MIC: SIC: 6021 NAIC: 522110)

Citigroup is a global financial services holding company whose businesses provide a range of financial services to consumer and corporate customers. Co.'s activities are conducted through the Global Consumer Group (U.S. and International)- Credit Cards, Consumer Lending, Retail Distribution, Commercial Business, Consumer Finance and Retail Banking; Citi Markets & Banking - Securities and Banking, and Transaction Services; Global Wealth Management - Smith Barney, Private Bank, and Citigroup Investment Research; Citi Alternative Investments; and Corporate/Other business segments. As of Dec 31 2007, Co. had total assets of $2.19 trillion and total deposits of $826.23 billion.

Recent Developments: For the quarter ended Mar 31 2008, net loss amounted to US$5.11 billion versus net income of US$5.01 billion in the year-earlier quarter. Net interest income increased 27.0% to US$13.47 billion from US$10.61 billion in the year-earlier quarter. Provision for loan losses was US$5.75 billion versus US$2.71 billion in the prior-year quarter, an increase of 112.5%. Non-interest income was US$254.0 million versus US$14.85 billion, while non-interest expense advanced 4.2% to US$16.49 billion.

Prospects: Looking ahead, Co. remains focused on its strategy to divest non-core assets and strategically reallocating capital to the products and regions that will drive increased revenues and enhance its franchise. For instance, on May 2 2008, Co. and State Street Corporation announced that they have entered into a definitive agreement to sell CitiStreet, a joint venture which is owned 50.0% each by Citi and State Street, to ING Group for $900.0 million. Also, on Apr 17 2008, Co. announced that GE Capital has agreed to purchase most of the assets of its North American commercial lending and leasing business, CitiCapital. Both transactions are expected to close by the third quarter of 2008.

Financial Data
(US$ in Thousands)

	3 Mos	12/31/2007	12/31/2006	12/31/2005	12/31/2004	12/31/2003	12/31/2002	12/31/2001
Earnings Per Share	(1.32)	0.72	4.31	4.75	3.26	3.42	2.94	2.72
Cash Flow Per Share	(10.06)	(14.56)	(0.02)	6.28	(0.47)	(2.92)	5.13	5.28
Tang Book Value Per Share	7.86	9.95	14.14	12.76	11.72	10.75	9.70	15.57
Dividends Per Share	1.940	2.160	1.960	1.760	1.600	1.100	0.700	0.600
Dividend Payout %	...	300.00	45.48	37.05	49.08	32.16	23.81	22.06
Income Statement								
Interest Income	29,950,000	124,467,000	96,431,000	76,021,000	66,709,000	57,047,000	58,939,000	66,565,000
Premium Income	983,000	3,534,000	3,202,000	3,132,000	3,993,000	3,749,000	3,410,000	13,460,000
Interest Expense	16,477,000	77,531,000	56,943,000	36,676,000	22,086,000	17,271,000	21,248,000	31,965,000
Benefits & Claims	275,000	935,000	967,000	867,000	3,801,000	3,895,000	3,478,000	11,759,000
Income Before Taxes	(9,023,000)	1,701,000	29,639,000	29,433,000	24,182,000	26,333,000	20,537,000	21,897,000
Income Taxes	(3,891,000)	(2,201,000)	8,101,000	9,078,000	6,909,000	8,195,000	6,998,000	7,526,000
Net Income	(5,111,000)	3,617,000	21,538,000	24,589,000	17,046,000	17,853,000	15,276,000	14,126,000
Average Shares	5,591,099	4,995,299	4,986,099	5,160,399	5,207,399	5,193,599	5,166,199	5,146,999
Balance Sheet								
Total Assets	2,199,848,000	2,187,631,000	1,884,318,000	1,494,037,000	1,484,101,000	1,264,032,000	1,097,190,000	1,051,450,000
Total Liabilities	2,071,629,000	2,074,033,000	1,764,535,000	1,381,500,000	1,374,810,000	1,166,018,000	1,010,472,000	970,203,000
Stockholders' Equity	128,219,000	113,598,000	119,783,000	112,537,000	109,291,000	98,014,000	86,718,000	81,247,000
Shares Outstanding	5,249,832	4,994,581	4,911,993	4,980,223	5,194,642	5,156,949	5,140,681	5,118,688
Statistical Record								
Return on Assets %	N.M.	0.18	1.28	1.65	1.24	1.51	1.42	1.45
Return on Equity %	N.M.	3.10	18.54	22.17	16.40	19.33	18.19	19.16
Net Interest Margin %	44.98	37.71	40.95	51.76	66.89	69.72	63.95	51.98
Loss Ratio %	27.98	26.46	30.20	27.68	95.19	103.89	101.99	87.36
Price Range	55.20-18.62	55.25-29.29	56.41-45.05	49.78-43.05	52.29-42.56	49.00-31.42	48.55-25.21	52.57-33.95
P/E Ratio	...	76.74-40.68	13.09-10.45	10.48-9.06	16.04-13.06	14.33-9.19	16.51-8.57	19.33-12.48
Average Yield %	4.73	4.52	4.01	3.77	3.40	2.63	1.84	1.31

Address: 399 Park Avenue, New York, NY 10043 Telephone: 212-559-1000 Web Site: www.citigroup.com	Officers: Winfried F.W. Bischoff - Chairman, Division Officer William R. Rhodes - Senior Vice-Chairman **Transfer Agents:** Citibank Stockholder Services, Providence, RI	No of Institutions: 1574 Shares: 3,663,790,336 % Held: 65.27

CITY NATIONAL CORP. (BEVERLY HILLS, CA)

Exchange	Symbol	Price	52Wk Range	Yield	P/E
NYS	CYN	$49.45 (5/29/2008)	78.39-44.43	3.88	11.58

*7 Year Price Score 79.82 *NYSE Composite Index=100 *12 Month Price Score 80.17

Interim Earnings (Per Share)

Qtr.	Mar	Jun	Sep	Dec
2005	1.09	1.13	1.17	1.21
2006	1.12	1.16	1.20	1.19
2007	1.15	1.19	1.22	0.96
2008	0.91	...	...	...

Interim Dividends (Per Share)

Amt	Decl	Ex	Rec	Pay
0.46Q	07/25/2007	08/06/2007	08/08/2007	08/22/2007
0.46Q	10/24/2007	11/05/2007	11/07/2007	11/21/2007
0.48Q	01/24/2008	02/04/2008	02/06/2008	02/20/2008
0.48Q	04/23/2008	05/05/2008	05/07/2008	05/21/2008
		Indicated Div: $1.92		

Valuation Analysis

Forecast EPS $3.52 (05/17/2008)

Market Cap	$2.4 Billion	Book Value	1.7 Billion
Price/Book	1.42	Price/Sales	1.99

Dividend Achiever Status

10 Year Growth Rate	15.38%
Total Years of Dividend Growth	13

Business Summary: Commercial Banking (MIC: SIC: 6021 NAIC: 522110)

City National is a bank holding and financial holding company. Co. provides a range of banking, investing and trust services through its wholly-owned banking subsidiary, City National Bank, through 62 offices, including 15 full-service regional centers, in Southern California, the San Francisco Bay area, Nevada and New York City. Co. provides lending, deposit, cash management, international banking, equipment financing, and other products and services. Co. operates via three segments, Commercial and Private Banking, Wealth Management, and Other. As of Dec 31 2007, Co. had consolidated total assets of $15.89 billion, loan balances of $11.63 billion, and total deposits of $11.82 billion.

Recent Developments: For the quarter ended Mar 31 2008, net income decreased 22.2% to US$44.0 million from US$56.5 million in the year-earlier quarter. Net interest income increased 0.6% to US$148.2 million from US$147.3 million in the year-earlier quarter. Non-interest income rose 21.0% to US$79.8 million from US$65.9 million, while non-interest expense advanced 14.9% to US$139.8 million.

Prospects: Due to the ongoing and significant decline of conditions in the residential construction business which have raised the level of nonperforming loans in that sector, Co. expects a somewhat higher provision for credit losses than previously anticipated. Co. also expects the recent decline in short-term interest rates to adversely affect its net interest income while declining values in the equity markets have lowered its expectations for wealth management fee income. Nevertheless, Co. continues to invest in a limited number of longer-term growth initiatives. As a result, Co. has revised its 2008 earnings forecast and now expects net income per share to be 17.0% to 22.0% lower than in 2007.

Financial Data

(US$ in Thousands)	3 Mos	12/31/2007	12/31/2006	12/31/2005	12/31/2004	12/31/2003	12/31/2002	12/31/2001
Earnings Per Share	4.27	4.52	4.66	4.60	4.04	3.72	3.56	2.96
Cash Flow Per Share	3.15	2.75	2.99	5.83	4.23	5.71	3.72	3.06
Tang Book Value Per Share	24.13	23.54	25.13	23.61	21.27	18.65	17.42	14.81
Dividends Per Share	1.860	1.840	1.640	1.440	1.280	0.970	0.780	0.740
Dividend Payout %	43.59	40.71	35.19	31.30	31.68	26.08	21.91	25.00
Income Statement								
Interest Income	207,752	894,101	826,294	718,552	604,325	575,725	609,700	625,248
Interest Expense	59,587	285,829	220,405	106,125	58,437	61,110	94,444	191,094
Net Interest Income	148,165	608,272	605,889	612,427	545,888	514,615	515,256	434,154
Provision for Losses	17,000	20,000	(610)	...	...	29,000	67,000	35,000
Non-Interest Income	79,816	303,202	242,564	208,189	184,265	177,225	146,293	132,384
Non-Interest Expense	139,841	529,245	476,219	438,385	395,410	364,178	332,591	313,395
Income Before Taxes	67,834	353,373	366,886	376,556	329,751	294,623	261,958	218,143
Income Taxes	23,847	130,660	133,363	141,821	123,429	107,946	78,858	71,973
Net Income	43,987	222,713	233,523	234,735	206,322	186,677	183,100	146,170
Average Shares	48,517	49,290	50,063	51,062	51,074	50,198	51,389	49,376
Balance Sheet								
Net Loans & Leases	11,586,587	11,462,115	10,230,663	9,111,619	8,345,619	7,716,756	7,834,968	7,016,344
Total Assets	15,934,032	15,889,290	14,884,381	14,581,860	14,231,513	13,018,242	11,870,392	10,176,316
Total Deposits	11,792,369	11,822,505	12,172,816	12,138,472	11,986,915	10,937,063	9,839,698	8,131,202
Total Liabilities	14,219,505	14,202,007	13,365,041	13,099,501	12,856,616	11,772,942	10,760,433	9,285,739
Stockholders' Equity	1,682,328	1,655,607	1,490,915	1,458,008	1,348,535	1,219,256	1,109,959	890,577
Shares Outstanding	48,375	48,235	47,882	49,713	49,546	49,204	48,983	48,149
Statistical Record								
Return on Assets %	1.34	1.45	1.59	1.63	1.51	1.50	1.66	1.52
Return on Equity %	12.80	14.16	15.84	16.73	16.03	16.03	18.31	17.89
Net Interest Margin %	71.32	68.03	73.33	85.23	90.33	89.39	84.51	69.44
Efficiency Ratio %	48.63	44.20	44.55	47.30	50.14	48.37	43.99	41.37
Loans to Deposits	0.98	0.97	0.84	0.75	0.70	0.71	0.80	0.86
Price Range	78.39-48.57	78.39-59.10	78.00-63.69	75.60-66.88	70.75-57.93	64.00-39.25	56.14-40.40	49.38-33.91
P/E Ratio	18.36-11.37	17.34-13.08	16.74-13.67	16.43-14.54	17.51-14.34	17.20-10.55	15.77-11.35	16.68-11.46
Average Yield %	2.79	2.59	2.33	2.02	2.00	1.96	1.57	1.80

Address: City National Center, 400 North Roxbury Drive, Beverly Hills, CA 90210	Officers: Bram Goldsmith - Chairman Russell D. Goldsmith - President, Chief Executive Officer	Investor Contact: 310-888-6700
Telephone: 310-888-6000	Transfer Agents:Continental Stock Transfer & Trust Co. New York, NY	No of Institutions: 261
Web Site: www.cnb.com		Shares: 36,692,560 % Held: 70.68

CLARCOR INC.

Exchange	Symbol	Price	52Wk Range	Yield	P/E
NYS	CLC	$43.90 (5/29/2008)	43.90-32.47	0.73	24.53

*7 Year Price Score 114.98 *NYSE Composite Index=100 ***12 Month Price Score 110.31**

Interim Earnings (Per Share)

Qtr.	Feb	May	Aug	Nov
2004-05	0.25	0.33	0.40	0.48
2005-06	0.31	0.32	0.44	0.52
2006-07	0.32	0.41	0.53	0.53
2007-08	0.32	...	...	...

Interim Dividends (Per Share)

Amt	Decl	Ex	Rec	Pay
0.072Q	06/26/2007	07/11/2007	07/13/2007	07/27/2007
0.08Q	09/25/2007	10/10/2007	10/12/2007	10/26/2007
0.08Q	12/17/2007	01/09/2008	01/11/2008	01/25/2008
0.08Q	03/31/2008	04/09/2008	04/11/2008	04/25/2008

Indicated Div: $0.32 (Div. Reinv. Plan)

Valuation Analysis

Forecast EPS $1.94 (05/16/2008)

Market Cap	$2.2 Billion	Book Value	608.3 Million
Price/Book	3.64	Price/Sales	2.30

Dividend Achiever Status

10 Year Growth Rate	3.18%
Total Years of Dividend Growth	27

TRADING VOLUME (thousand shares)

Business Summary: Industrial Machinery and Equipment (MIC: SIC: 3714 NAIC: 336399)

Clarcor operates through three principal industry segments: Industrial/Environmental Filtration, Engine/ Mobile Filtration and Packaging. Co.'s Industrial/ Environmental segment manufactures and markets filtration products used in industrial and commercial processes, and in buildings and infrastructures of various types. Co.'s Engine/ Mobile segment sells filtration products used on engines and in mobile equipment applications, construction, industrial, mining and agricultural equipment. Co.'s consumer and industrial packaging products business manufactures a range of different types and sizes of containers and packaging specialties through its wholly-owned subsidiary, J. L. Clark, Inc.

Recent Developments: For the quarter ended Mar 1 2008, net income decreased 1.4% to US$16.1 million from US$16.4 million in the year-earlier period. Revenues were US$250.2 million, up 19.4% from US$209.5 million the year before. Operating income was US$27.7 million versus US$23.6 million in the prior-year quarter, an increase of 17.6%. Direct operating expenses rose 16.9% to US$173.6 million from US$148.6 million in the comparable period the year before. Indirect operating expenses increased 30.5% to US$48.8 million from US$37.4 million in the equivalent prior-year period.

Prospects: For the remainder of fiscal year ending Nov 30 2008, Co. is projecting sales growth and margin improvement, with international sales growth estimated to continue at a rate higher than its domestic growth rate. In addition, Co. believes that ongoing focus on cost reductions and price increases should offset the forecasted cost increases for energy and purchased materials. Also, Co. plans to continue to make capital investments to improve capability, increase manufacturing and distribution capacity, develop new filter media and products as well as implement new enterprise planning systems. Hence, Co. is anticipating earnings for fiscal 2008 to be in the range of $1.85 to $2.05 per share.

Financial Data

(US$ in Thousands)	3 Mos	12/01/2007	12/02/2006	11/30/2005	11/30/2004	11/30/2003	11/30/2002	11/30/2001
Earnings Per Share	1.79	1.78	1.59	1.46	1.24	1.08	0.93	0.84
Cash Flow Per Share	2.76	2.74	1.23	1.73	1.46	1.75	1.71	1.29
Tang Book Value Per Share	5.69	7.68	7.21	6.10	5.48	4.90	3.87	3.20
Dividends Per Share	0.305	0.297	0.275	0.259	0.251	0.246	0.241	0.236
Dividend Payout %	17.01	16.71	17.30	17.72	20.26	22.91	26.08	28.13
Income Statement								
Total Revenue	250,181	921,191	904,347	873,974	787,686	741,358	715,563	666,964
EBITDA	35,358	153,289	149,107	138,717	118,272	107,483	97,583	97,200
Depn & Amortn	7,831	23,389	23,079	21,087	19,151	19,892	20,521	21,850
Income Before Taxes	24,230	130,509	126,941	117,922	99,060	86,059	71,450	65,734
Income Taxes	7,941	39,675	43,795	40,968	34,771	31,371	24,773	23,804
Net Income	16,149	90,659	82,710	76,393	63,997	54,552	46,601	41,893
Average Shares	51,211	50,885	52,176	52,215	51,506	50,745	50,343	49,784
Balance Sheet								
Current Assets	426,663	371,920	380,340	324,933	303,990	257,402	259,746	244,350
Total Assets	959,073	739,135	727,516	675,272	627,797	538,237	546,119	530,617
Current Liabilities	144,503	114,171	118,428	121,470	126,272	111,373	174,255	94,931
Long-Term Obligations	127,418	17,329	15,946	16,009	24,110	16,913	22,648	135,203
Total Liabilities	350,743	183,405	190,007	192,439	199,335	167,845	230,658	256,356
Stockholders' Equity	608,330	555,730	537,509	482,833	428,462	370,392	315,461	274,261
Shares Outstanding	50,491	49,218	51,082	51,594	51,223	50,618	49,837	49,252
Statistical Record								
Return on Assets %	10.67	12.40	11.73	11.73	10.95	10.06	8.66	8.11
Return on Equity %	15.59	16.63	16.12	16.77	15.98	15.91	15.80	16.23
EBITDA Margin %	14.13	16.64	16.49	15.87	15.02	14.50	13.64	14.57
Net Margin %	6.45	9.84	9.15	8.74	8.12	7.36	6.51	6.28
Asset Turnover	1.14	1.26	1.28	1.34	1.35	1.37	1.33	1.29
Current Ratio	2.95	3.26	3.21	2.68	2.41	2.31	1.49	2.57
Debt to Equity	0.21	0.03	0.03	0.03	0.06	0.05	0.07	0.49
Price Range	41.88-30.07	41.88-30.07	36.27-26.97	31.51-24.88	26.26-20.43	22.95-15.53	17.00-12.82	13.80-8.56
P/E Ratio	23.40-16.80	23.53-16.89	22.81-16.96	21.58-17.04	21.18-16.47	21.25-14.37	18.28-13.78	16.43-10.19
Average Yield %	0.86	0.86	0.87	0.94	1.12	1.31	1.61	1.94

Address: 840 Crescent Centre Drive, Suite 600, Franklin, TN 37067 **Telephone:** 615-771-3100 **Web Site:** www.clarcor.com	**Officers:** Norman E. Johnson - Chairman, President, Chief Executive Officer Bruce A. Klein - Vice President, Chief Financial Officer **Transfer Agents:** First Chicago Trust Company of New York, Jersey City, NJ	**No of Institutions:** 205 **Shares:** 47,615,896 **% Held:** 92.36

CLOROX CO.

*7 Year Price Score 89.41   ***NYSE Composite Index=100**   ***12 Month Price Score 94.82**

Interim Earnings (Per Share)

Qtr.	Sep	Dec	Mar	Jun
2004-05	0.57	3.68	0.76	1.09
2005-06	0.71	0.55	0.72	0.92
2006-07	0.73	0.62	0.84	1.07
2007-08	0.76	0.65	0.71	...

Interim Dividends (Per Share)

Amt	Decl	Ex	Rec	Pay
0.40Q	09/19/2007	10/29/2007	10/31/2007	11/15/2007
0.40Q	11/14/2007	01/24/2008	01/28/2008	02/15/2008
0.40Q	02/07/2008	04/23/2008	04/25/2008	05/15/2008
0.46Q	05/14/2008	07/24/2008	07/28/2008	08/15/2008

Indicated Div: $1.84 (Div. Reinv. Plan)

Valuation Analysis

Forecast EPS	$3.23 (05/17/2008)
Market Cap	$7.9 Billion
Book Value	N/A
Price/Book	N/A
Price/Sales	1.55

Dividend Achiever Status

10 Year Growth Rate	8.82%
Total Years of Dividend Growth	31

TRADING VOLUME (thousand shares)

Business Summary: Chemicals (MIC: SIC: 2842 NAIC: 325612)

Clorox manufactures and markets consumer products. Co. has three business segments: Household Group-North America, Specialty Group and International. The products of the Household Group–North America segment include: laundry additives, home-care products, water-filtration systems and filters, professional products for institutional, janitorial, healthcare and food-service markets and auto-care products. The products of the Specialty Group segment include: plastic bags, wraps and containers, cat litter products, food products and charcoal products. The products of the International segment, which are for the Asia-Pacific and Latin America markets, include bleaches, sponges and insecticides.

Recent Developments: For the quarter ended Mar 31 2008, income from continuing operations decreased 22.5% to US$100.0 million from US$129.0 million in the year-earlier quarter. Net income decreased 22.5% to US$100.0 million from US$129.0 million in the year-earlier quarter. Revenues were US$1.35 billion, up 9.0% from US$1.24 billion the year before. Direct operating expenses rose 15.8% to US$815.0 million from US$704.0 million in the comparable period the year before. Indirect operating expenses increased 12.5% to US$387.0 million from US$344.0 million in the equivalent prior-year period.

Prospects: For fiscal year ending June 30 2008, Co. now expects total sales growth of 8.0% to 9.0%, including the anticipated benefit of the bleach business and Burt's Bees acquisitions on Nov 30 2007 as well as the benefit of favorable foreign exchange rates and the unfavorable effect of exiting Co.'s private-label food days business. In addition, Co.'s earnings outlook has been updated to reflect a greater effect from commodity cost inflation and revised estimates for dilution from the Burt's Bees acquisition. Specifically, Co. now anticipates diluted earnings per share in the range of $3.20 to $3.28, including the effect of the Burt's Bees acquisition and announced restructuring-related charges.

Financial Data
(US$ in Thousands)

	9 Mos	6 Mos	3 Mos	06/30/2007	06/30/2006	06/30/2005	06/30/2004	06/30/2003
Earnings Per Share	3.18	3.32	3.29	3.26	2.90	6.11	2.56	2.23
Cash Flow Per Share	5.47	5.51	5.14	4.68	3.47	4.33	4.24	3.68
Tang Book Value Per Share	...	...	...	N.M.	...	...	0.77	N.M.
Dividends Per Share	1.510	1.420	1.310	1.200	1.140	1.100	1.080	0.880
Dividend Payout %	47.51	42.77	39.82	36.81	39.31	18.00	42.19	39.46
Income Statement								
Total Revenue	3,778,000	2,425,000	1,239,000	4,847,000	4,644,000	4,388,000	4,324,000	4,144,000
EBITDA	607,000	400,000	222,000	1,018,000	935,000	964,000	1,028,000	965,000
Depn & Amortn	154,000	98,000	48,000	170,000	165,000	166,000	162,000	138,000
Income Before Taxes	453,000	302,000	174,000	743,000	653,000	729,000	840,000	802,000
Income Taxes	150,000	99,000	63,000	247,000	210,000	214,000	294,000	288,000
Net Income	303,000	203,000	111,000	501,000	444,000	1,096,000	549,000	493,000
Average Shares	140,300	141,026	146,127	153,935	153,001	179,176	214,371	220,692
Balance Sheet								
Current Assets	1,269,000	1,215,000	1,064,000	1,032,000	1,007,000	1,090,000	1,043,000	951,000
Total Assets	4,750,000	4,853,000	3,673,000	3,666,000	3,616,000	3,617,000	3,834,000	3,652,000
Current Liabilities	1,775,000	2,331,000	2,153,000	1,427,000	1,130,000	1,348,000	1,268,000	1,451,000
Long-Term Obligations	2,721,000	2,223,000	1,477,000	1,462,000	1,966,000	2,122,000	475,000	495,000
Total Liabilities	5,222,000	5,407,000	4,310,000	3,495,000	3,772,000	4,170,000	2,294,000	2,437,000
Stockholders' Equity	(472,000)	(554,000)	(637,000)	171,000	(156,000)	(553,000)	1,540,000	1,215,000
Shares Outstanding	137,839	138,856	138,505	151,256	151,298	151,683	212,988	213,676
Statistical Record								
Return on Assets %	11.02	11.70	13.87	13.76	12.28	29.42	14.63	13.54
Return on Equity %	...	...	...	6,680.00	...	222.09	39.75	38.38
EBITDA Margin %	16.07	16.49	17.92	21.00	20.13	21.97	23.77	23.29
Net Margin %	8.02	8.37	8.96	10.34	9.56	24.98	12.70	11.90
Asset Turnover	1.21	1.18	1.37	1.33	1.28	1.18	1.15	1.14
Current Ratio	0.71	0.52	0.49	0.72	0.89	0.81	0.82	0.66
Debt to Equity	...	...	...	8.55	...	...	0.31	0.41
Price Range	68.50-55.61	68.50-57.14	68.50-57.14	68.50-58.35	64.76-53.32	65.27-49.56	53.95-42.00	48.24-32.18
P/E Ratio	21.54-17.49	20.63-17.21	20.82-17.37	21.01-17.90	22.33-18.39	10.68-8.11	21.07-16.41	21.63-14.43
Average Yield %	2.42	2.23	2.05	1.89	1.96	1.93	2.26	2.07

Address: 1221 Broadway, Oakland, CA 94612-1888
Telephone: 510-271-7000
Web Site: www.thecloroxcompany.com

Officers: Donald R. Knauss - Chairman, Chief Executive Officer Lawrence S. Peiros - Executive Vice President **Transfer Agents:** Computershare, Providence, RI

No of Institutions: 571
Shares: 106,893,512 **% Held:** 72.62

COCA-COLA CO (THE)

Exchange	Symbol	Price	52Wk Range	Yield	P/E
NYS	KO	$57.87 (5/29/2008)	65.56-51.14	2.63	21.59

*7 Year Price Score 94.49   *NYSE Composite Index=100   *12 Month Price Score 103.75

Interim Earnings (Per Share)

Qtr.	Mar	Jun	Sep	Dec
2005	0.42	0.72	0.54	0.37
2006	0.47	0.78	0.62	0.29
2007	0.54	0.80	0.71	0.52
2008	0.64	...	...	...

Interim Dividends (Per Share)

Amt	Decl	Ex	Rec	Pay
0.34Q	07/19/2007	09/12/2007	09/15/2007	10/01/2007
0.34Q	10/18/2007	11/28/2007	12/01/2007	12/15/2007
0.38Q	02/21/2008	03/12/2008	03/15/2008	04/01/2008
0.38Q	04/17/2008	06/11/2008	06/15/2008	07/01/2008

Indicated Div: $1.52 (Div. Reinv. Plan)

Valuation Analysis

Forecast EPS $3.07 (05/17/2008)
Market Cap $134.3 Billion   Book Value 23.0 Billion
Price/Book 5.83   Price/Sales 4.45

Dividend Achiever Status

10 Year Growth Rate 9.28%
Total Years of Dividend Growth 45

Business Summary: Food (MIC: SIC: 2086 NAIC: 312111)

Coca-Cola is a global manufacturer, distributor and marketer of nonalcoholic beverage concentrates and syrups. Co. also manufactures, distributes and markets some finished beverages. Co. primarily sells concentrates and syrups, as well as some finished beverages, to bottling and canning operations, distributors, fountain wholesalers and fountain retailers. As of Dec 31 2007, Co. owned or licensed more than 450 brands, including Coca-Cola, Diet Coke, Fanta and Sprite, and a variety of diet and light beverages, waters, juice and juice drinks, teas, coffees, and energy and sports drinks. Additionally, Co. has ownership interests in numerous joint ventures bottling and canning operations.

Recent Developments: For the quarter ended Mar 28 2008, net income increased 18.9% to US$1.50 billion from US$1.26 billion in the year-earlier quarter. Revenues were US$7.38 billion, up 20.9% from US$6.10 billion the year before. Operating income was US$1.87 billion versus US$1.63 billion in the prior-year quarter, an increase of 15.2%. Direct operating expenses rose 22.3% to US$2.62 billion from US$2.15 billion in the comparable period the year before. Indirect operating expenses increased 23.6% to US$2.88 billion from US$2.33 billion in the equivalent prior-year period.

Prospects: For full-year 2008, Co. expects a favorable currency effect on operating income in the mid single-digit range based on existing expectations of market rates for the remainder of 2008 and benefits of hedging coverage in place. Hence, Co. is evaluating whether there might be opportunities to reinvest a portion of the currency benefit in marketing programs and productivity initiatives to drive long-term growth. Separately, as part of its plan to streamline and simplify its operations globally, Co. expects to close its beverage concentrate manufacturing and distribution plant in Drogheda, Ireland in Sep 2008, which is expected to improve operating productivity and capacity utilization.

Financial Data
(US$ in Thousands)

	3 Mos	12/31/2007	12/31/2006	12/31/2005	12/31/2004	12/31/2003	12/31/2002	12/31/2001
Earnings Per Share	2.68	2.57	2.16	2.04	2.00	1.77	1.23	1.60
Cash Flow Per Share	3.16	3.09	2.54	2.69	2.45	2.22	1.91	1.65
Tang Book Value Per Share	4.49	4.11	5.08	5.29	5.02	4.14	3.34	3.53
Dividends Per Share	1.400	1.360	1.240	1.120	1.000	0.880	0.800	0.720
Dividend Payout %	52.32	52.92	57.41	54.90	50.00	49.72	65.04	45.00
Income Statement								
Total Revenue	7,379,000	28,857,000	24,088,000	23,104,000	21,962,000	21,044,000	19,564,000	20,092,000
EBITDA	2,307,000	9,256,000	7,543,000	7,627,000	7,154,000	6,347,000	6,295,000	6,437,000
Depn & Amortn	307,000	1,163,000	938,000	932,000	893,000	850,000	806,000	803,000
Income Before Taxes	1,948,000	7,873,000	6,578,000	6,690,000	6,222,000	5,495,000	5,499,000	5,670,000
Income Taxes	448,000	1,892,000	1,498,000	1,818,000	1,375,000	1,148,000	1,523,000	1,691,000
Net Income	1,500,000	5,981,000	5,080,000	4,872,000	4,847,000	4,347,000	3,050,000	3,969,000
Average Shares	2,351,000	2,331,000	2,350,000	2,393,000	2,429,000	2,462,000	2,483,000	2,487,000
Balance Sheet								
Current Assets	14,888,000	12,105,000	8,441,000	10,250,000	12,094,000	8,396,000	7,352,000	7,171,000
Total Assets	47,004,000	43,269,000	29,963,000	29,427,000	31,327,000	27,342,000	24,501,000	22,417,000
Current Liabilities	15,588,000	13,225,000	8,890,000	9,836,000	10,971,000	7,886,000	7,341,000	8,429,000
Long-Term Obligations	3,259,000	3,277,000	1,314,000	1,154,000	1,157,000	2,517,000	2,701,000	1,219,000
Total Liabilities	23,972,000	21,525,000	13,043,000	13,072,000	15,392,000	13,252,000	12,701,000	11,051,000
Stockholders' Equity	23,032,000	21,744,000	16,920,000	16,355,000	15,935,000	14,090,000	11,800,000	11,366,000
Shares Outstanding	2,320,000	2,318,000	2,318,000	2,369,000	2,409,339	2,441,531	2,470,979	2,486,228
Statistical Record								
Return on Assets %	15.56	16.33	17.11	16.04	16.48	16.77	13.00	18.35
Return on Equity %	30.98	30.94	30.53	30.18	32.20	33.58	26.33	38.38
EBITDA Margin %	31.26	32.08	31.31	33.01	32.57	30.16	32.18	32.04
Net Margin %	20.33	20.73	21.09	21.09	22.07	20.66	15.59	19.75
Asset Turnover	0.75	0.79	0.81	0.76	0.75	0.81	0.83	0.93
Current Ratio	0.96	0.92	0.95	1.04	1.10	1.06	1.00	0.85
Debt to Equity	0.14	0.15	0.08	0.07	0.07	0.18	0.23	0.11
Price Range	65.56-47.91	64.09-45.89	49.00-40.09	45.25-40.31	53.00-38.65	50.75-37.07	57.64-43.47	60.82-42.85
P/E Ratio	24.46-17.88	24.94-17.86	22.69-18.56	22.18-19.76	26.50-19.32	28.67-20.94	46.86-35.34	38.01-26.78
Average Yield %	2.47	2.53	2.83	2.62	2.15	2.00	1.61	1.48

Address: One Coca-Cola Plaza, Atlanta, GA 30313	Officers: E. Neville Isdell - Chairman, Chief Executive Officer Ahmet Muhtar Kent - President, Chief Operating Officer **Transfer Agents:** ComputerShare Investor Services, Providence, RI	Investor Contact: 404-676-5766
Telephone: 404-676-2121		**No of Institutions:** 1451
Web Site: www.coca-cola.com		**Shares:** 1,703,618,560 **% Held:** 65.45

COLGATE-PALMOLIVE CO.

Exchange	Symbol	Price	52Wk Range	Yield	P/E
NYS	CL	$73.50 (5/29/2008)	80.98-64.44	2.18	23.33

*7 Year Price Score 97.09   *NYSE Composite Index=100   ***12 Month Price Score 103.07**

Interim Earnings (Per Share)

Qtr.	Mar	Jun	Sep	Dec
2005	0.53	0.62	0.63	0.65
2006	0.59	0.51	0.63	0.73
2007	0.89	0.76	0.77	0.77
2008	0.86	...	...	...

Interim Dividends (Per Share)

Amt	Decl	Ex	Rec	Pay
0.36Q	07/12/2007	07/19/2007	07/23/2007	08/15/2007
0.36Q	10/04/2007	10/24/2007	10/26/2007	11/15/2007
0.36Q	01/10/2008	01/23/2008	01/25/2008	02/15/2008
0.40Q	02/27/2008	04/22/2008	04/24/2008	05/15/2008

Indicated Div: $1.60 (Div. Reinv. Plan)

Valuation Analysis

Forecast EPS $3.83 (05/17/2008)

Market Cap	$37.3 Billion	Book Value	2.3 Billion
Price/Book	16.57	Price/Sales	2.62

Dividend Achiever Status

10 Year Growth Rate	10.20%
Total Years of Dividend Growth	45

Business Summary: Chemicals (MIC: SIC: 2844 NAIC: 325620)

Colgate-Palmolive manufactures and markets a range of products in two business segments. The products in Oral, Personal and Home Care segment includes toothpaste, oral rinses and toothbrushes, bar and liquid hand soaps, shower gels, shampoos, conditioners, deodorants and antiperspirants, shave products, detergents, fabric conditioners, cleansers and cleaners and bleaches. The products in Pet Nutrition segment includes pet food products manufactured and marketed by Hill's Pet Nutrition. Trademarks include Colgate, Palmolive, Kolynos, Sorriso, Elmex, Mennen, Protex, Softsoap, Irish Spring, Ajax, Axion, Soupline, Suavitel, Tom's of Maine, Hill's Science Diet and Hill's Prescription Diet.

Recent Developments: For the quarter ended Mar 31 2008, net income decreased 4.1% to US$466.5 million from US$486.6 million in the year-earlier quarter. Revenues were US$3.71 billion, up 15.5% from US$3.21 billion the year before. Operating income was US$723.7 million versus US$651.1 million in the prior-year quarter, an increase of 11.2%. Direct operating expenses rose 15.1% to US$1.61 billion from US$1.40 billion in the comparable period the year before. Indirect operating expenses increased 18.5% to US$1.38 billion from US$1.16 billion in the equivalent prior-year period.

Prospects: While market conditions are expected to remain competitive in 2008, Co. believes it is well-positioned for continued growth. Specifically, for 2008, Co. expects gross profit margin, excluding restructuring charges, to be flat to slightly up versus 2007, reflecting higher cost environment balanced by its cost savings efforts. Also, Co. expects strong sales momentum and improved results from its ongoing cost-saving initiatives will enable it to attain double-digit earnings per share growth in 2008. Separately, taking into account of normal lag in the effect of price increases, combined with the effect of its ongoing savings programs, Co. expects gross profit margin to increase in 2009.

Financial Data

(US$ in Thousands)	3 Mos	12/31/2007	12/31/2006	12/31/2005	12/31/2004	12/31/2003	12/31/2002	12/31/2001
Earnings Per Share	3.15	3.20	2.46	2.43	2.33	2.46	2.19	1.89
Cash Flow Per Share	4.48	4.31	3.54	3.43	3.30	3.29	2.97	2.87
Dividends Per Share	1.440	1.400	1.250	1.110	0.960	0.900	0.720	0.675
Dividend Payout %	45.69	43.75	50.81	45.68	41.20	36.59	32.88	35.71
Income Statement								
Total Revenue	3,713,000	13,789,700	12,237,700	11,396,900	10,584,200	9,903,400	9,294,300	9,427,800
EBITDA	812,300	2,987,000	2,489,200	2,544,300	2,449,900	2,481,500	2,309,600	2,171,000
Depn & Amortn	88,600	333,900	328,700	329,300	327,800	315,500	296,500	336,200
Income Before Taxes	690,000	2,496,500	2,001,800	2,079,000	2,002,400	2,041,900	1,870,300	1,668,700
Income Taxes	223,500	759,100	648,400	727,600	675,300	620,600	582,000	522,100
Net Income	466,500	1,737,400	1,353,400	1,351,400	1,327,100	1,421,300	1,288,300	1,146,600
Average Shares	539,500	543,700	550,500	556,500	569,300	578,800	589,100	607,700
Balance Sheet								
Current Assets	4,088,200	3,618,500	3,301,000	2,757,100	2,739,900	2,496,500	2,228,100	2,203,400
Total Assets	10,809,400	10,112,000	9,138,000	8,507,100	8,672,900	7,478,800	7,087,200	6,984,800
Current Liabilities	3,611,200	3,162,700	3,469,100	2,743,000	2,730,700	2,445,400	2,148,700	2,123,500
Long-Term Obligations	3,407,800	3,221,900	2,720,400	2,918,000	3,089,500	2,684,900	3,210,800	2,812,000
Total Liabilities	8,557,200	7,825,800	7,727,100	7,157,000	7,427,500	6,591,700	6,736,900	6,138,400
Stockholders' Equity	2,252,200	2,286,200	1,410,900	1,350,100	1,245,400	887,100	350,300	846,400
Shares Outstanding	507,809	509,034	512,658	516,170	526,625	533,697	536,001	550,722
Statistical Record								
Return on Assets %	16.99	18.05	15.34	15.73	16.39	19.52	18.31	16.11
Return on Equity %	93.34	93.99	98.04	104.13	124.12	229.72	215.31	99.08
EBITDA Margin %	21.88	21.66	20.34	22.32	23.15	25.06	24.85	23.03
Net Margin %	12.56	12.60	11.06	11.86	12.54	14.35	13.86	12.16
Asset Turnover	1.41	1.43	1.39	1.33	1.31	1.36	1.32	1.32
Current Ratio	1.13	1.14	0.95	1.01	1.00	1.02	1.04	1.04
Debt to Equity	1.51	1.41	1.93	2.16	2.48	3.03	9.17	3.32
Price Range	80.98-64.44	80.64-64.44	66.83-53.70	56.39-48.55	58.92-43.06	60.88-49.10	58.73-44.36	62.50-51.00
P/E Ratio	25.71-20.46	25.20-20.14	27.17-21.83	23.21-19.98	25.29-18.48	24.75-19.96	26.82-20.26	33.07-26.98
Average Yield %	2.01	2.02	2.09	2.13	1.82	1.64	1.33	1.19

Address: 300 Park Avenue, New York, NY 10022-7499	Officers: Reuben Mark - Chairman Ian M. Cook - President, Chief Executive Officer **Transfer Agents:** The Bank of New York, New York, NY	Investor Contact: 212-310-3072
Telephone: 212-310-2000		**No of Institutions:** 1085
Web Site: www.colgate.com		**Shares:** 382,574,272 **% Held:** 70.56

64

COLONIAL BANCGROUP INC.

Exchange	Symbol	Price	52Wk Range	Yield	P/E
NYS	CNB	$5.94 (5/29/2008)	25.37-5.79	6.40	5.40

*7 Year Price Score 69.70   *NYSE Composite Index=100   *12 Month Price Score 50.09

Interim Earnings (Per Share)

Qtr.	Mar	Jun	Sep	Dec
2005	0.37	0.38	0.39	0.37
2006	0.42	0.43	0.44	0.43
2007	0.24	0.43	0.45	0.06
2008	0.16	...	...	...

Interim Dividends (Per Share)

Amt	Decl	Ex	Rec	Pay
0.188Q	07/18/2007	07/25/2007	07/27/2007	08/10/2007
0.188Q	10/17/2007	10/24/2007	10/26/2007	11/09/2007
0.19Q	01/16/2008	01/23/2008	01/25/2008	02/08/2008
0.095Q	04/21/2008	04/23/2008	04/25/2008	05/09/2008

Indicated Div: $0.38

Valuation Analysis

Forecast EPS $0.56 (05/17/2008)

Market Cap $939.1 Million   Book Value 2.2 Billion

Price/Book 0.43   Price/Sales 0.53

Dividend Achiever Status

10 Year Growth Rate 9.60%

Total Years of Dividend Growth 12

Business Summary: Commercial Banking (MIC: SIC: 6022 NAIC: 522110)

Colonial BancGroup is a bank holding company. Co. is engaged in providing various products and services that include retail and commercial banking, wealth management services, mortgage banking and insurance through its branch network, private banking offices, automated teller machines and the internet as well as other distribution channels to consumers and businesses. As of Dec 31, 2007, Co. had 338 branches, with 196 branches in Florida, 90 branches in Alabama, 18 branches in Georgia, 18 branches in Texas and 16 branches in Nevada. As of Dec 31 2007, Co. had total assets of approximately US$25.98 billion and total deposits of approximately US$18.54 billion.

Recent Developments: For the quarter ended Mar 31 2008, net income decreased 32.0% to US$24.8 million from US$36.5 million in the year-earlier quarter. Net interest income increased 0.9% to US$181.6 million from US$179.9 million in the year-earlier quarter. Provision for loan losses was US$35.5 million versus US$2.3 million in the prior-year quarter, an increase of. Non-interest income rose 279.4% to US$57.7 million from US$15.2 million, while non-interest expense advanced 18.7% to US$164.0 million.

Prospects: Co.'s results reflect higher net interest income due to improved average earning assets, and higher non-interest income due to increases in retail banking fees, financial planning services, bank-owned life insurance and mortgage banking origination and sales income, other income and net securities gains. However, the results are being more than offset by the difficult credit environment and issues in Co.'s residential real estate construction portfolio, which it expects to persist for the rest of 2008. Nevertheless, Co. noted that, even in these difficult times, opportunities continue to exist, including for deposit growth, which remains a key focus of its funding and liquidity strategy.

Financial Data
(US$ in Thousands)

	3 Mos	12/31/2007	12/31/2006	12/31/2005	12/31/2004	12/31/2003	12/31/2002	12/31/2001
Earnings Per Share	1.10	1.17	1.72	1.52	1.33	1.20	1.16	1.06
Cash Flow Per Share	(9.90)	1.46	(0.74)	(1.26)	(0.33)	1.32	(1.43)	1.13
Tang Book Value Per Share	7.01	7.63	9.05	8.02	7.47	7.06	6.58	6.52
Dividends Per Share	0.752	0.750	0.680	0.610	0.580	0.560	0.520	0.480
Dividend Payout %	68.70	64.10	39.53	40.13	43.61	46.67	44.83	45.28
Income Statement								
Interest Income	383,537	1,556,485	1,455,585	1,162,055	848,017	780,808	783,431	902,167
Interest Expense	201,913	795,111	700,318	452,833	263,501	274,165	322,261	480,238
Net Interest Income	181,624	761,374	755,267	709,222	584,516	506,643	461,170	421,929
Provision for Losses	35,543	106,450	22,142	26,838	26,994	37,378	35,980	39,573
Non-Interest Income	57,747	186,224	189,222	175,976	138,027	127,449	102,332	93,709
Non-Interest Expense	161,231	559,678	519,601	515,255	429,870	369,551	312,779	284,168
Income Before Taxes	34,514	268,486	402,746	343,105	265,679	227,163	214,743	191,897
Income Taxes	9,717	87,561	136,933	114,603	90,331	77,236	73,872	69,181
Net Income	24,797	180,925	265,813	228,502	175,348	149,927	140,025	122,103
Average Shares	157,528	154,391	154,810	150,790	132,315	125,289	120,648	115,881
Balance Sheet								
Net Loans & Leases	18,805,460	17,228,555	16,778,039	15,826,705	13,387,505	11,828,670	11,904,266	10,280,918
Total Assets	27,352,747	25,975,989	22,784,249	21,426,197	18,897,150	16,273,302	15,822,355	13,185,103
Total Deposits	19,271,328	18,544,267	16,091,054	15,483,449	11,646,612	9,768,502	9,319,735	8,322,979
Total Liabilities	24,887,672	23,409,360	20,726,914	19,493,506	17,503,535	15,094,997	14,750,919	12,320,329
Stockholders' Equity	2,172,017	2,273,571	2,057,335	1,932,691	1,393,615	1,178,305	1,071,436	864,774
Shares Outstanding	158,097	157,440	152,852	154,242	133,823	126,974	123,700	115,244
Statistical Record								
Return on Assets %	0.67	0.74	1.20	1.13	0.99	0.93	0.97	0.98
Return on Equity %	7.90	8.36	13.32	13.74	13.60	13.33	14.46	15.06
Net Interest Margin %	47.36	48.92	51.89	61.03	68.93	64.89	58.87	46.77
Efficiency Ratio %	36.54	32.12	31.59	38.51	43.60	40.69	35.31	28.53
Loans to Deposits	0.98	0.93	1.04	1.02	1.15	1.21	1.28	1.24
Price Range	25.37-9.63	26.69-13.27	26.97-23.53	25.74-19.76	22.45-16.52	17.47-10.75	16.11-11.01	14.98-10.75
P/E Ratio	23.06-8.75	22.81-11.34	15.68-13.68	16.93-13.00	16.88-12.42	14.56-8.96	13.89-9.49	14.13-10.14
Average Yield %	3.90	3.34	2.72	2.73	3.06	4.03	3.77	3.66

Address: 100 Colonial Bank Boulevard, Montgomery, AL 36117 **Telephone:** 334-676-5000 **Web Site:** www.colonialbank.com	**Officers:** Robert E. Lowder - Chairman, President, Chief Executive Officer John C. H. Miller - Vice-Chairman **Transfer Agents:** Computershare Investor Services, LLC, Providence, RI	**No of Institutions:** 323 **Shares:** 135,024,320 **% Held:** 62.35

COMERICA, INC.

Exchange	Symbol	Price	52Wk Range	Yield	P/E
NYS	CMA	$37.00 (5/29/2008)	63.72-32.39	7.14	9.37

*7 Year Price Score 66.51 ***NYSE Composite Index=100** ***12 Month Price Score 80.56**

Interim Earnings (Per Share)

Qtr.	Mar	Jun	Sep	Dec
2005	1.16	1.28	1.41	1.26
2006	1.18	1.22	1.23	1.85
2007	1.19	1.25	1.18	0.80
2008	0.73	...	...	...

Interim Dividends (Per Share)

Amt	Decl	Ex	Rec	Pay
0.64Q	07/24/2007	09/12/2007	09/15/2007	10/01/2007
0.64Q	11/13/2007	12/12/2007	12/15/2007	01/01/2008
0.66Q	01/22/2008	03/12/2008	03/15/2008	04/01/2008
0.66Q	05/20/2008	06/11/2008	06/15/2008	07/01/2008

Indicated Div: $2.64 (Div. Reinv. Plan)

Valuation Analysis

Forecast EPS $2.70 (05/17/2008)

Market Cap	$5.6 Billion	Book Value	5.3 Billion
Price/Book	1.06	Price/Sales	1.21

Dividend Achiever Status

10 Year Growth Rate	8.40%
Total Years of Dividend Growth	24

TRADING VOLUME (thousand shares)

Business Summary: Commercial Banking (MIC: SIC: 6021 NAIC: 522110)

Comerica is a financial services company. Co.'s segments include: Business Bank, comprised of the middle market, commercial real estate, national dealer services, international finance, global corporate, leasing, financial services, and technology and life sciences businesses; Retail Bank, which includes small business banking and personal financial services; Wealth & Institutional Management, which provides fiduciary services, private banking, retirement services, investment management and advisory services, investment banking and discount securities brokerage services; and a Finance Division. At Dec 31 2007, Co. had total assets of $62.33 billion, and total deposits of $44.28 billion.

Recent Developments: For the quarter ended Mar 31 2008, income from continuing operations decreased 41.8% to US$110.0 million from US$189.0 million in the year-earlier quarter. Net income decreased 42.6% to US$109.0 million from US$190.0 million in the year-earlier quarter. Net interest income decreased 5.2% to US$476.0 million from US$502.0 million in the year-earlier quarter. Provision for loan losses was US$159.0 million versus US$23.0 million in the prior-year quarter, an increase of 591.3%. Non-interest income rose 16.7% to US$237.0 million from US$203.0 million, while non-interest expense declined 1.0% to US$403.0 million.

Prospects: For full-year 2008, Co. expects mid single-digit average loan growth, excluding Financial Services Division loans, with low single-digit growth in the Midwest market, mid to high single-digit growth in the Western market and low double-digit growth in the Texas market. Co. also anticipates average earning asset growth in excess of average loan growth, with securities averaging about $8.00 billion for the remainder of the year. In addition, Co. estimates low single-digit growth in non-interest income for the full year. Meanwhile, Co. projects 2008 average net credit-related charge offs to be in a range of 75 basis point to 80 basis points of average loans.

Financial Data
(US$ in Thousands)

	3 Mos	12/31/2007	12/31/2006	12/31/2005	12/31/2004	12/31/2003	12/31/2002	12/31/2001
Earnings Per Share	3.95	4.43	5.49	5.11	4.36	3.75	3.40	3.88
Cash Flow Per Share	6.72	6.63	6.09	5.07	5.96	7.55	7.02	5.63
Tang Book Value Per Share	34.93	34.12	32.70	31.11	29.95	29.20	28.30	27.15
Dividends Per Share	2.580	2.560	2.360	2.200	2.080	2.000	1.920	1.760
Dividend Payout %	65.38	57.79	42.99	43.05	47.71	53.33	56.47	45.36
Income Statement								
Interest Income	863,000	3,730,000	3,422,000	2,726,000	2,237,000	2,412,000	2,797,000	3,393,547
Interest Expense	387,000	1,727,000	1,439,000	770,000	427,000	486,000	665,000	1,291,209
Net Interest Income	476,000	2,003,000	1,983,000	1,956,000	1,810,000	1,926,000	2,132,000	2,102,338
Provision for Losses	159,000	212,000	37,000	(47,000)	64,000	377,000	635,000	236,000
Non-Interest Income	237,000	888,000	855,000	942,000	857,000	887,000	900,000	803,332
Non-Interest Expense	403,000	1,691,000	1,674,000	1,666,000	1,493,000	1,483,000	1,515,000	1,559,033
Income Before Taxes	151,000	988,000	1,127,000	1,279,000	1,110,000	953,000	882,000	1,110,637
Income Taxes	41,000	306,000	345,000	418,000	353,000	292,000	281,000	401,059
Net Income	109,000	686,000	893,000	861,000	757,000	661,000	601,000	709,578
Average Shares	151,000	155,000	162,000	169,000	174,000	176,000	177,000	177,665
Balance Sheet								
Net Loans & Leases	51,747,000	50,186,000	46,938,000	42,731,000	40,170,000	39,499,000	41,490,000	40,541,248
Total Assets	67,017,000	62,331,000	58,001,000	53,013,000	51,766,000	52,592,000	53,301,000	50,731,973
Total Deposits	46,819,000	44,278,000	44,927,000	42,431,000	40,936,000	41,463,000	41,775,000	37,570,379
Total Liabilities	61,760,000	57,214,000	52,848,000	47,945,000	46,661,000	47,482,000	48,354,000	45,924,509
Stockholders' Equity	5,257,000	5,117,000	5,153,000	5,068,000	5,105,000	5,110,000	4,947,000	4,807,464
Shares Outstanding	150,501	149,988	157,574	162,900	170,475	175,000	174,775	177,074
Statistical Record								
Return on Assets %	0.97	1.14	1.61	1.64	1.45	1.25	1.16	1.53
Return on Equity %	11.62	13.36	17.47	16.93	14.78	13.15	12.32	16.10
Net Interest Margin %	55.16	53.70	57.95	71.75	80.91	79.85	76.22	61.95
Efficiency Ratio %	36.64	36.62	39.14	45.42	48.25	44.95	40.98	37.15
Loans to Deposits	1.11	1.13	1.04	1.01	0.98	0.95	0.99	1.08
Price Range	63.72-35.06	63.72-40.89	60.07-50.70	63.21-53.46	63.46-51.02	56.31-37.61	65.30-35.53	64.95-44.66
P/E Ratio	16.13-8.88	14.38-9.23	10.94-9.23	12.37-10.46	14.56-11.70	15.02-10.03	19.21-10.45	16.74-11.51
Average Yield %	5.08	4.59	4.16	3.79	3.62	4.33	3.47	3.11

Address: Comerica Tower at Detroit Center, 500 Woodward Avenue, MC 3391, Detroit, MI 48226 **Telephone:** 313-222-9743 **Web Site:** www.comerica.com	**Officers:** Ralph W. Babb - Chairman, President, Chief Executive Officer Joseph J. Buttigieg - Vice-Chairman **Transfer Agents:** Wells Fargo Shareowner Services, St. Paul, MN	**Investor Contact:** 313-222-2840 **No of Institutions:** 448 **Shares:** 119,771,920 **% Held:** 73.92

COMMERCE BANCSHARES, INC.

Exchange	Symbol	Price	52Wk Range	Yield	P/E
NMS	CBSH	$43.89 (5/29/2008)	46.23-39.24	2.28	14.58

*7 Year Price Score 86.48 ***NYSE Composite Index=100** ***12 Month Price Score 100.93**

Interim Earnings (Per Share)

Qtr.	Mar	Jun	Sep	Dec
2005	0.63	0.69	0.81	0.73
2006	0.71	0.74	0.73	0.76
2007	0.70	0.75	0.77	0.60
2008	0.89	...	...	...

Interim Dividends (Per Share)

Amt	Decl	Ex	Rec	Pay
0.238Q	10/26/2007	11/27/2007	11/29/2007	12/13/2007
5%	10/26/2007	11/27/2007	11/29/2007	12/13/2007
0.25Q	02/01/2008	03/06/2008	03/10/2008	03/28/2008
0.25Q	04/16/2008	06/05/2008	06/09/2008	06/27/2008

Indicated Div: $1.00 (Div. Reinv. Plan)

Valuation Analysis

Forecast EPS $3.02 (05/17/2008)

Market Cap	$3.2 Billion	Book Value	1.6 Billion
Price/Book	2.00	Price/Sales	2.37

Dividend Achiever Status

10 Year Growth Rate	11.54%
Total Years of Dividend Growth	39

Business Summary: Commercial Banking (MIC: SIC: 6022 NAIC: 522110)

Commerce Bancshares is a bank holding company. As of Dec 31 2007, Co. owned all of the outstanding capital stock of three national banking associations, which are headquartered in Missouri (the Missouri bank), Kansas (the Kansas bank), and Nebraska (the Nebraska bank). The Nebraska bank is limited in its activities to the issuance of credit cards. The remaining two banking subsidiaries are engaged in general banking business, providing a range of retail, corporate, investment, trust, and asset management products and services to individuals and businesses. As of Dec 31 2007, Co. had total assets of $16.20 billion and total deposits of $12.55 billion.

Recent Developments: For the quarter ended Mar 31 2008, net income increased 24.6% to US$64.2 million from US$51.5 million in the year-earlier quarter. Net interest income increased 6.6% to US$140.1 million from US$131.5 million in the year-earlier quarter. Provision for loan losses was US$20.0 million versus US$8.2 million in the prior-year quarter, an increase of 145.1%. Non-interest income rose 31.0% to US$115.5 million from US$88.2 million, while non-interest expense advanced 3.2% to US$140.8 million.

Prospects: Co.'s near-term outlook appears to be constructive. Specifically, Co. is seeing an increase in net interest income mainly due to lower rates paid on interest bearing deposits and short-term borrowings coupled with higher loan balances, partially offset by lower loan yields. In addition, Co. is experiencing higher non-interest income, mainly the result of double digit growth in bank card, brokerage, and bond trading income, as well as solid growth in trust and corporate cash management fees. Meanwhile, Co. expects to complete the sale of its branch in Independence, KS in May 2008. In this transaction, Co. anticipates to receive approximately $7.3 million in cash.

Financial Data
(US$ in Thousands)

	3 Mos	12/31/2007	12/31/2006	12/31/2005	12/31/2004	12/31/2003	12/31/2002	12/31/2001
Earnings Per Share	3.01	2.82	2.94	2.87	2.68	2.43	2.26	2.04
Cash Flow Per Share	5.28	4.64	6.13	3.83	3.26	3.20	3.02	3.10
Tang Book Value Per Share	19.90	19.22	18.02	17.28	17.42	16.95	15.99	13.93
Dividends Per Share	0.964	0.952	0.889	0.829	0.757	0.611	0.485	0.455
Dividend Payout %	32.07	33.77	30.20	28.93	28.26	25.18	21.42	22.33
Income Statement								
Interest Income	222,553	936,101	832,306	697,566	610,090	617,410	652,553	750,962
Interest Expense	82,446	398,029	319,107	195,864	112,759	115,018	152,588	283,052
Net Interest Income	140,107	538,072	513,199	501,702	497,331	502,392	499,965	467,910
Provision for Losses	20,000	42,732	25,649	28,785	30,351	40,676	34,108	36,423
Non-Interest Income	115,483	379,815	361,621	341,199	326,931	301,667	280,572	277,512
Non-Interest Expense	140,755	574,758	525,425	496,522	482,769	472,144	452,927	439,638
Income Before Taxes	94,835	300,397	323,746	317,594	311,142	291,239	293,502	269,361
Income Taxes	30,668	93,737	103,904	94,347	90,801	84,715	94,004	87,387
Net Income	64,167	206,660	219,842	223,247	220,341	206,524	199,498	181,974
Average Shares	72,397	73,189	74,678	77,793	82,267	85,221	88,111	89,413
Balance Sheet								
Net Loans & Leases	11,119,982	10,707,678	9,828,388	8,770,736	8,172,965	8,007,458	7,745,326	7,508,509
Total Assets	16,767,800	16,204,831	15,230,349	13,885,545	14,250,368	14,287,164	13,308,415	12,902,806
Total Deposits	12,591,065	12,551,552	11,744,854	10,851,813	10,434,309	10,206,208	9,913,311	10,031,966
Total Liabilities	15,189,679	14,677,145	13,788,235	12,547,707	12,823,488	12,836,210	11,892,078	11,630,323
Stockholders' Equity	1,578,121	1,527,686	1,442,114	1,337,838	1,426,880	1,450,954	1,416,337	1,272,483
Shares Outstanding	71,939	71,886	73,536	74,632	79,109	82,615	85,641	87,691
Statistical Record								
Return on Assets %	1.37	1.31	1.51	1.59	1.54	1.50	1.52	1.52
Return on Equity %	14.46	13.92	15.82	16.15	15.27	14.41	14.84	15.06
Net Interest Margin %	62.95	57.48	61.66	71.92	81.52	81.37	76.62	62.31
Efficiency Ratio %	41.64	43.68	44.01	47.80	51.52	51.37	48.54	42.75
Loans to Deposits	0.88	0.85	0.84	0.81	0.78	0.78	0.78	0.75
Price Range	46.23-39.24	48.30-41.42	48.16-43.72	48.34-40.24	43.36-36.25	40.54-27.76	34.69-25.93	30.69-23.62
P/E Ratio	15.36-13.04	17.13-14.69	16.38-14.87	16.84-14.02	16.18-13.53	16.68-11.42	15.35-11.47	15.05-11.58
Average Yield %	2.20	2.12	1.93	1.89	1.92	1.85	1.55	1.69

Address: 1000 Walnut, Kansas City, MO 64141-6248	Officers: David W. Kemper - Chairman, President, Chief Executive Officer Jonathan M. Kemper -	Investor Contact: 800-892-7100
Telephone: 816-234-2000	Vice-Chairman **Transfer Agents:**	**No of Institutions:** 218
Web Site: www.commercebank.com	Computershare Trust Company, N.A., Providence, RI	**Shares:** 37,110,872 **% Held:** 45.90

COMMERCE GROUP INC (MA)

Exchange	Symbol	Price	52Wk Range	Yield	P/E
NYS	CGI	$36.68 (5/29/2008)	36.69-27.40	N/A	16.52

*7 Year Price Score 104.30 *NYSE Composite Index=100 *12 Month Price Score 108.22

Interim Earnings (Per Share)

Qtr.	Mar	Jun	Sep	Dec
2005	0.86	0.93	0.89	0.94
2006	0.98	0.86	0.83	0.87
2007	1.11	0.63	0.88	0.34
2008	0.38	...	...	...

Interim Dividends (Per Share)

Amt	Decl	Ex	Rec	Pay
0.30Q	05/18/2007	05/24/2007	05/29/2007	06/08/2007
0.30Q	08/17/2007	08/23/2007	08/27/2007	09/12/2007
0.30Q	11/16/2007	11/21/2007	11/26/2007	12/10/2007
0.30Q	02/14/2008	02/21/2008	02/25/2008	03/07/2008

Valuation Analysis

Forecast EPS	$2.81 (05/16/2008)		
Market Cap	$2.2 Billion	Book Value	1.3 Billion
Price/Book	1.69	Price/Sales	1.17

Dividend Achiever Status

10 Year Growth Rate	8.83%
Total Years of Dividend Growth	13

Business Summary: Insurance (MIC: SIC: 6331 NAIC: 524126)

Commerce Group provides personal and commercial property and casualty insurance primarily in Massachusetts, and in other states. Co.'s core product lines are personal automobile, homeowners, and commercial automobile insurance. Co. markets its products mainly through its network of independent agents in all states, except California and New York, where it uses agents and brokers. Co. writes insurance through its principal subsidiary, The Commerce Insurance Company. Co. also writes insurance through four other subsidiaries: Citation Insurance Company, Commerce West Insurance Company, American Commerce Insurance Company, and State-Wide Insurance Company.

Recent Developments: For the quarter ended Mar 31 2008, net income decreased 68.9% to US$23.1 million from US$74.4 million in the year-earlier quarter. Revenues were US$444.1 million, down 16.4% from US$531.2 million the year before. Net premiums earned were US$439.4 million versus US$451.9 million in the prior-year quarter, a decrease of 2.8%. Net investment income fell 4.0% to US$38.2 million from US$39.8 million a year ago.

Prospects: On June 4, 2008, MAPFRE S.A. and Co. jointly announced that MAPFRE has completed its acquisition of Co. MAPFRE paid $36.70 in cash per share of Commerce's publicly traded stock, with total consideration of $2.21 billion, as of the date of the closing. Separately, Co.'s recent results reflect a decline in net realized investment gains, resulting from lower transaction net gains and other-than-temporary impairment write-downs in its preferred stock portfolio. Specifically, these other-than-temporary write-downs are due to mark-to-market price declines of Co.'s securities under the recent market environment.

Financial Data

(US$ in Thousands)	3 Mos	12/31/2007	12/31/2006	12/31/2005	12/31/2004	12/31/2003	12/31/2002	12/31/2001
Earnings Per Share	2.22	2.97	3.55	3.61	3.25	2.50	0.71	1.38
Cash Flow Per Share	2.81	3.21	5.08	4.64	4.93	4.06	3.47	1.58
Tang Book Value Per Share	21.65	21.87	22.53	19.39	16.73	14.20	12.27	12.22
Dividends Per Share	1.200	1.200	0.975	0.735	0.655	0.635	0.615	0.595
Dividend Payout %	53.98	40.40	27.46	20.39	20.12	25.45	86.62	43.27
Income Statement								
Premium Income	439,358	1,816,967	1,760,700	1,709,924	1,638,833	1,445,628	1,210,040	1,043,652
Total Revenue	444,137	1,982,447	1,949,469	1,884,381	1,806,571	1,640,822	1,257,119	1,153,838
Benefits & Claims	288,946	1,171,431	1,068,414	1,050,186	1,044,840	1,070,147	909,769	777,543
Income Before Taxes	33,334	267,730	346,420	352,605	304,186	219,305	52,026	115,425
Income Taxes	10,000	75,275	103,994	107,768	89,003	58,068	17,063	23,194
Net Income	23,105	190,903	241,535	243,912	214,431	160,943	46,755	93,094
Average Shares	61,270	64,280	68,012	67,695	65,905	64,509	66,056	67,589
Balance Sheet								
Total Assets	3,931,066	3,914,687	4,110,869	3,927,010	3,610,396	3,164,231	2,382,688	2,140,082
Total Liabilities	2,612,514	2,583,700	2,600,639	2,615,984	2,489,114	2,247,630	1,588,530	1,327,808
Stockholders' Equity	1,304,379	1,316,924	1,503,271	1,305,069	1,116,156	912,211	790,052	812,274
Shares Outstanding	60,255	60,224	66,727	67,306	66,645	64,121	64,232	66,260
Statistical Record								
Return on Assets %	3.43	4.76	6.01	6.47	6.31	5.80	2.07	4.42
Return on Equity %	9.87	13.54	17.20	20.15	21.09	18.91	5.84	11.68
Loss Ratio %	65.77	64.47	60.68	61.42	63.76	74.03	75.19	74.50
Net Margin %	5.20	9.63	12.39	12.94	11.87	9.81	3.72	8.07
Price Range	36.55-27.40	36.55-27.40	32.00-25.86	34.85-26.79	31.06-19.70	20.47-16.15	21.02-14.74	20.02-12.32
P/E Ratio	16.46-12.34	12.31-9.23	9.01-7.29	9.65-7.42	9.56-6.06	8.19-6.46	29.61-20.76	14.51-8.92
Average Yield %	3.55	3.73	3.36	2.43	2.69	3.40	3.31	3.46

Address: 211 Main Street, Webster, MA 01570	**Officers:** Gerald Fels - Chairman, President, Chief Executive Officer James A. Ermilio - Executive Vice President, Secretary, General Counsel **Transfer Agents:** Computershare Trust Company, N.A.	**No of Institutions:** 185
Telephone: 508-943-9000		**Shares:** 28,798,972 **% Held:** 43.16
Web Site: www.commerceinsurance.com		

COMMUNITY BANK SYSTEM, INC.

Exchange	Symbol	Price	52Wk Range	Yield	P/E
NYS	CBU	$24.21 (5/29/2008)	26.19-17.09	3.47	16.47

*7 Year Price Score 80.48   *NYSE Composite Index=100   *12 Month Price Score 119.81

Interim Earnings (Per Share)

Qtr.	Mar	Jun	Sep	Dec
2005	0.43	0.46	0.48	0.28
2006	0.31	0.33	0.36	0.26
2007	0.32	0.34	0.37	0.40
2008	0.36	...	...	...

Interim Dividends (Per Share)

Amt	Decl	Ex	Rec	Pay
0.21Q	08/15/2007	09/12/2007	09/14/2007	10/10/2007
0.21Q	11/29/2007	12/12/2007	12/14/2007	01/10/2008
0.21Q	02/04/2008	03/12/2008	03/14/2008	04/10/2008
0.21Q	05/22/2008	06/12/2008	06/16/2008	07/10/2008

Indicated Div: $0.84 (Div. Reinv. Plan)

Valuation Analysis

Forecast EPS $1.49 (05/16/2008)

Market Cap	$723.7 Million	Book Value	488.7 Million
Price/Book	1.48	Price/Sales	2.30

Dividend Achiever Status

10 Year Growth Rate	8.15%
Total Years of Dividend Growth	16

Business Summary: Commercial Banking (MIC: SIC: 6021 NAIC: 522110)

Community Bank System is a bank holding company. Co. operates a community bank business through its Community Bank, N.A. subsidiary, whose branches are generally located in smaller towns and cities within its geographic market areas of Upstate New York and Northeastern Pennsylvania. In addition, Co. provides administration, consulting and actuarial services to sponsors of employee benefit plans through its Benefit Plans Administrative Services, Inc. subsidiary. As of Dec 31 2007, Co. had total assets of $4.70 billion and total deposits of $3.23 billion.

Recent Developments: For the quarter ended Mar 31 2008, net income increased 12.9% to US$10.9 million from US$9.7 million in the year-earlier quarter. Net interest income increased 6.7% to US$35.6 million from US$33.4 million in the year-earlier quarter. Provision for loan losses was US$780,000 versus US$200,000 in the prior-year quarter, an increase of 290.0%. Non-interest income rose 30.7% to US$17.6 million from US$13.5 million, while non-interest expense advanced 13.1% to US$38.4 million.

Prospects: Co. is seeing growth in its bottom-line result, reflecting higher interest income due to solid loan growth, continued expansion of non-interest income sources, improved net interest margin and favorable asset quality results. Looking ahead, Co. plans to continue to focus on its core operating objective to grow its branch network primarily via acquisition and certain selective de novo expansions. In addition, Co. intends to increase the non-interest income component of total revenues via development of banking-related fee income, growth in existing financial service business units, and the acquisition of additional financial services and banking businesses.

Financial Data
(US$ in Thousands)

	3 Mos	12/31/2007	12/31/2006	12/31/2005	12/31/2004	12/31/2003	12/31/2002	12/31/2001
Earnings Per Share	1.47	1.42	1.26	1.65	1.64	1.50	1.47	0.81
Cash Flow Per Share	1.68	1.69	2.44	2.39	2.85	2.78	2.24	1.92
Tang Book Value Per Share	7.81	7.51	7.17	7.77	7.90	7.37	7.33	4.87
Dividends Per Share	0.830	0.820	0.780	0.740	0.680	0.610	0.560	0.540
Dividend Payout %	56.61	57.75	61.90	44.85	41.46	40.80	38.23	66.67
Income Statement								
Interest Income	63,151	256,237	231,901	219,194	212,795	191,129	204,870	197,850
Interest Expense	27,553	120,263	97,092	75,572	61,752	59,301	77,020	101,195
Net Interest Income	35,598	135,974	134,809	143,622	151,043	131,828	127,850	96,655
Provision for Losses	780	2,004	6,585	8,534	8,750	11,195	12,222	7,097
Non-Interest Income	17,618	53,286	49,276	60,846	44,445	34,981	32,600	29,083
Non-Interest Expense	38,374	142,074	127,203	127,389	119,899	102,461	95,824	89,039
Income Before Taxes	14,062	45,182	50,297	68,545	66,839	53,153	52,404	29,602
Income Taxes	3,164	2,291	11,920	17,740	16,643	12,773	13,887	8,891
Net Income	10,898	42,891	38,377	50,805	50,196	40,380	38,517	19,129
Average Shares	30,036	30,232	30,392	30,838	30,670	30,670	26,334	23,650
Balance Sheet								
Net Loans & Leases	2,801,358	2,784,628	2,665,245	2,379,236	2,326,715	2,099,414	1,780,574	1,708,969
Total Assets	4,658,415	4,697,502	4,497,797	4,152,734	4,393,831	3,855,397	3,434,204	3,210,833
Total Deposits	3,243,382	3,228,464	3,168,299	2,984,768	2,928,978	2,725,488	2,505,356	2,545,970
Total Liabilities	4,169,747	4,218,718	4,036,269	3,695,139	3,919,203	3,450,569	3,109,166	2,942,853
Stockholders' Equity	488,668	478,784	461,528	457,595	474,628	404,828	325,038	267,980
Shares Outstanding	29,892	29,634	30,020	29,956	30,641	28,330	25,957	25,805
Statistical Record								
Return on Assets %	0.96	0.93	0.89	1.19	1.21	1.11	1.16	0.73
Return on Equity %	9.21	9.12	8.35	10.90	11.38	11.07	12.99	9.39
Net Interest Margin %	56.37	53.07	58.13	65.52	70.98	68.97	62.41	48.85
Efficiency Ratio %	47.51	45.90	45.24	45.49	46.61	45.31	40.35	39.24
Loans to Deposits	0.86	0.86	0.84	0.80	0.79	0.77	0.71	0.67
Price Range	26.06-17.09	23.61-17.09	24.85-18.90	28.25-21.42	28.35-19.25	25.13-15.55	17.01-13.07	14.82-12.45
P/E Ratio	17.73-11.63	16.63-12.04	19.72-15.00	17.12-12.98	17.29-11.74	16.75-10.37	11.57-8.89	18.30-15.37
Average Yield %	4.05	4.00	3.57	3.13	2.84	3.07	3.67	3.95

Address: 5790 Widewaters Parkway, DeWitt, NY 13214-1883 **Telephone:** 315-445-2282 **Web Site:** www.communitybankna.com	**Officers:** Mark E. Tryniski - President, Chief Executive Officer George J. Getman - Executive Vice President, General Counsel **Transfer Agents:** American Stock Transfer & Trust Company, New York, NY	**Investor Contact:** 315-445-7300 **No of Institutions:** 144 **Shares:** 19,153,028 % **Held:** 61.40

COMMUNITY TRUST BANCORP, INC.

Exchange	Symbol	Price	52Wk Range	Yield	P/E
NMS	CTBI	$31.47 (5/29/2008)	34.41-25.64	3.69	13.00

*7 Year Price Score 82.21   *NYSE Composite Index=100   *12 Month Price Score 102.65

Interim Earnings (Per Share)

Qtr.	Mar	Jun	Sep	Dec
2005	0.53	0.56	0.60	0.59
2006	0.64	0.65	0.64	0.62
2007	0.52	0.57	0.68	0.61
2008	0.57	...	...	...

Interim Dividends (Per Share)

Amt	Decl	Ex	Rec	Pay
0.27Q	07/24/2007	09/12/2007	09/15/2007	10/01/2007
0.29Q	10/23/2007	12/12/2007	12/15/2007	01/01/2008
0.29Q	01/29/2008	03/13/2008	03/15/2008	04/01/2008
0.29Q	04/22/2008	06/11/2008	06/15/2008	07/01/2008
		Indicated Div: $1.16		

Valuation Analysis

Forecast EPS $2.34 (05/16/2008)

Market Cap	$471.4 Million	Book Value	306.8 Million
Price/Book	1.54	Price/Sales	2.06

Dividend Achiever Status

10 Year Growth Rate	9.17%
Total Years of Dividend Growth	19

TRADING VOLUME (thousand shares)

Business Summary: Commercial Banking (MIC: SIC: 6021 NAIC: 522110)

Community Trust Bancorp is a bank holding company that owns all the capital stock of one commercial bank and one trust company, serving small and mid-sized communities in eastern, northeast, central, and south central Kentucky and southern West Virginia. Through its subsidiaries, Co. engages in a range of commercial and personal banking and trust activities, which include accepting time and demand deposits; making secured and unsecured loans; providing cash management services; issuing letters of credit; and providing funds transfer services. Lending activities include making commercial, construction, mortgage, and personal loans. At Dec 31 2007, Co. had total assets of $2.90 billion.

Recent Developments: For the quarter ended Mar 31 2008, net income increased 6.5% to US$8.5 million from US$8.0 million in the year-earlier quarter. Net interest income increased 1.6% to US$26.3 million from US$25.9 million in the year-earlier quarter. Provision for loan losses was US$2.4 million versus US$470,000 in the prior-year quarter, an increase of 404.0%. Non-interest income rose 2.9% to US$8.7 million from US$8.5 million, while non-interest expense declined 11.1% to US$20.0 million.

Prospects: Going forward, Co. anticipates its nonperforming loans to remain higher than recent level as the normal legal collection time period for real estate secured assets has been slowed due to increased volumes in the industry. In addition, Co. expects to continue experiencing downward pressure on its net interest margin as loans and deposits continue to reprice and new loan yields continue to reflect the recent interest rate environment resulting from the Federal Reserve lowering the interest rates. Also, Co. expects future rate cuts to continue to put pressure on its net interest margin as its loans reprice quicker than its deposits.

Financial Data

(US$ in Thousands)	3 Mos	12/31/2007	12/31/2006	12/31/2005	12/31/2004	12/31/2003	12/31/2002	12/31/2001
Earnings Per Share	2.42	2.38	2.55	2.27	2.05	1.92	1.81	1.45
Cash Flow Per Share	3.57	3.37	3.68	3.06	8.08	15.36	13.15	9.40
Tang Book Value Per Share	16.02	15.36	14.17	12.48	11.64	10.63	9.70	8.36
Dividends Per Share	1.120	1.100	1.050	0.980	0.867	0.746	0.647	0.609
Dividend Payout %	46.21	46.22	41.18	43.17	42.31	38.91	35.74	41.97
Income Statement								
Interest Income	44,680	196,864	189,145	160,162	130,401	128,514	146,550	176,835
Interest Expense	18,372	90,832	81,538	56,957	37,189	43,895	57,293	93,717
Net Interest Income	26,308	106,032	107,607	103,205	93,212	84,619	89,257	83,118
Provision for Losses	2,369	6,540	4,305	8,285	8,648	9,332	10,086	9,185
Non-Interest Income	8,743	36,608	32,719	33,467	33,917	36,372	27,928	23,774
Non-Interest Expense	20,001	83,055	80,407	78,569	74,595	70,735	67,341	64,938
Income Before Taxes	12,681	53,045	55,614	49,818	43,886	40,924	39,758	32,769
Income Taxes	4,136	16,418	16,550	15,406	12,936	12,033	12,158	10,497
Net Income	8,545	36,627	39,064	34,412	30,950	28,891	27,600	22,272
Average Shares	15,116	15,372	15,299	15,139	15,082	15,044	15,255	15,396
Balance Sheet								
Net Loans & Leases	2,224,557	2,202,177	2,141,363	2,077,973	1,875,502	1,711,922	1,613,615	1,687,424
Total Assets	2,904,484	2,902,684	2,969,761	2,849,213	2,709,094	2,474,039	2,487,911	2,503,905
Total Deposits	2,305,567	2,293,164	2,341,167	2,246,551	2,140,418	2,067,615	2,127,716	2,155,772
Total Liabilities	2,597,635	2,601,329	2,687,386	2,595,268	2,472,925	2,252,646	2,278,492	2,312,299
Stockholders' Equity	306,849	301,355	282,375	253,945	236,169	221,393	209,419	191,606
Shares Outstanding	14,979	15,044	15,158	14,997	14,845	14,807	14,941	15,207
Statistical Record								
Return on Assets %	1.23	1.25	1.34	1.24	1.19	1.16	1.11	0.93
Return on Equity %	12.46	12.55	14.57	14.04	13.49	13.41	13.76	11.93
Net Interest Margin %	58.88	53.86	56.89	64.44	71.48	65.84	60.91	47.00
Efficiency Ratio %	37.44	35.57	36.24	40.58	45.40	42.90	38.60	32.37
Loans to Deposits	0.96	0.96	0.91	0.92	0.88	0.83	0.76	0.78
Price Range	37.76-25.64	40.89-26.38	42.50-31.30	34.79-28.00	34.00-25.25	30.27-20.73	24.30-16.46	18.41-11.55
P/E Ratio	15.69-10.60	17.18-11.08	16.67-12.27	15.33-12.33	16.59-12.31	15.77-10.80	13.42-9.09	12.69-7.97
Average Yield %	3.69	3.36	2.94	3.11	3.04	3.15	3.28	3.95

Address: 346 North Mayo Trail, P.O. Box 2947, Pikeville, KY 41502-2947	Officers: Jean R. Hale - Chairman, President, Chief Executive Officer Mark A. Gooch - Executive Vice President, Secretary Transfer Agents: Community Trust Bank, Inc., Pikeville, KY	Investor Contact: 606-432-1414
Telephone: 606-432-1414		No of Institutions: 97
Web Site: www.ctbi.com		Shares: 7,170,026 % Held: 45.91

CONSOLIDATED EDISON, INC.

Exchange	Symbol	Price	52Wk Range	Yield	P/E
NYS	ED	$41.34 (5/29/2008)	50.21-39.45	5.66	11.55

*7 Year Price Score 79.92   *NYSE Composite Index=100   *12 Month Price Score 94.51

Interim Earnings (Per Share)

Qtr.	Mar	Jun	Sep	Dec
2005	0.75	0.47	1.16	0.56
2006	0.74	0.50	0.92	0.79
2007	0.99	0.58	1.15	0.75
2008	1.11	...	...	...

Interim Dividends (Per Share)

Amt	Decl	Ex	Rec	Pay
0.58Q	07/19/2007	08/13/2007	08/15/2007	09/15/2007
0.58Q	10/18/2007	11/09/2007	11/14/2007	12/15/2007
0.585Q	01/24/2008	02/11/2008	02/13/2008	03/15/2008
0.585Q	04/17/2008	05/12/2008	05/14/2008	06/15/2008

Indicated Div: $2.34 (Div. Reinv. Plan)

Valuation Analysis

Forecast EPS	$3.05 (05/17/2008)
Market Cap	$10.3 Billion Book Value 9.5 Billion
Price/Book	1.09 Price/Sales 0.78

Dividend Achiever Status

10 Year Growth Rate	1.00%
Total Years of Dividend Growth	33

TRADING VOLUME (thousand shares)

Business Summary: Electricity (MIC: SIC: 4931 NAIC: 221121)

Consolidated Edison is a holding company. Through its subsidiaries, Co. provides energy-related services. Con Edison of New York provides electric service in all of New York City (except part of Queens) and most of Westchester County, an approximately 660 square mile service area with a population of more than 9.0 million. It also provides gas service in Manhattan, the Bronx and parts of Queens and Westchester, and steam service in parts of Manhattan. Orange and Rockland Utilities, Inc. and its utility subsidiaries provide electric service in southeastern New York and in adjacent areas of northern New Jersey and eastern Pennsylvania, an approximately 1,350 square mile service area.

Recent Developments: For the quarter ended Mar 31 2008, income from continuing operations increased 16.3% to US$300.0 million from US$258.0 million in the year-earlier quarter. Net income increased 18.4% to US$303.0 million from US$256.0 million in the year-earlier quarter. Revenues were US$3.58 billion, up 6.6% from US$3.36 billion the year before. Operating income was US$390.0 million versus US$376.0 million in the prior-year quarter, an increase of 3.7%. Direct operating expenses rose 7.9% to US$2.53 billion from US$2.34 billion in the comparable period the year before. Indirect operating expenses increased 3.3% to US$661.0 million from US$640.0 million in the equivalent prior-year period.

Prospects: On May 1 2008, Co.'s subsidiary, ConEdison Solutions, has acquired Custom Energy Services, LLC, of Overland Park, KS, an energy services company serving a portfolio of clients. Notably, this acquisition further expands Co.'s capacity to deliver energy services in the Midwest region. Meanwhile, for 2008, Co. is projecting earnings per share from ongoing operations to be in the range of $2.95 to $3.15 a share, which considers the effects of the recently approved Con Edison of New York electric rate order. In addition, Co. anticipates spending approximately $2.50 billion in 2008 for capital investments, which mainly will be used for its regulated utilities.

Financial Data

(US$ in Thousands)	3 Mos	12/31/2007	12/31/2006	12/31/2005	12/31/2004	12/31/2003	12/31/2002	12/31/2001
Earnings Per Share	3.58	3.47	2.95	2.94	2.27	2.38	3.02	3.21
Cash Flow Per Share	6.00	5.84	5.43	3.25	5.58	5.97	7.07	6.36
Tang Book Value Per Share	35.52	34.83	32.09	30.68	29.86	29.15	25.40	24.21
Dividends Per Share	2.325	2.320	2.300	2.280	2.280	2.260	2.240	2.220
Dividend Payout %	64.88	66.86	77.97	77.55	99.56	94.12	73.51	68.54
Income Statement								
Total Revenue	3,577,000	13,120,000	12,137,000	11,690,000	9,758,000	9,827,000	8,481,860	9,633,962
Depn & Amortn	165,000	667,000	621,000	584,000	551,000	529,000	494,553	526,235
Income Taxes	163,000	449,000	402,000	355,000	284,000	327,000	388,881	(21,922)
Net Income	303,000	929,000	737,000	719,000	537,000	528,000	646,036	682,242
Average Shares	273,000	267,300	250,300	244,700	236,400	221,800	214,049	212,919
Balance Sheet								
Net PPE	20,285,000	19,914,000	18,445,000	17,112,000	16,106,000	15,225,000	13,329,175	12,248,375
Total Assets	28,665,000	28,343,000	26,699,000	24,850,000	22,560,000	20,966,000	18,820,310	16,996,111
Long-Term Obligations	7,906,000	7,633,000	8,324,000	7,428,000	6,594,000	6,769,000	6,206,917	5,542,305
Total Liabilities	19,188,000	19,011,000	18,441,000	17,285,000	15,254,000	14,288,000	12,677,761	11,070,708
Stockholders' Equity	9,477,000	9,076,000	8,004,000	7,310,000	7,054,000	6,423,000	5,921,079	5,666,268
Shares Outstanding	249,290	248,814	234,245	222,075	219,303	202,629	213,932	212,146
Statistical Record								
Return on Assets %	3.52	3.38	2.86	3.03	2.46	2.65	3.61	4.04
Return on Equity %	10.89	10.88	9.63	10.01	7.95	8.55	11.15	12.25
Net Margin %	8.47	7.08	6.07	6.15	5.50	5.37	7.62	7.08
PPE Turnover	0.68	0.68	0.68	0.70	0.62	0.69	0.66	0.80
Asset Turnover	0.48	0.48	0.47	0.49	0.45	0.49	0.47	0.57
Debt to Equity	0.83	0.84	1.04	1.02	0.93	1.05	1.05	0.98
Price Range	52.63-39.45	52.63-43.65	49.13-41.40	49.24-41.41	45.59-37.26	45.99-37.00	45.10-33.58	42.18-32.38
P/E Ratio	14.70-11.02	15.17-12.58	16.65-14.03	16.75-14.09	20.08-16.41	19.32-15.55	14.93-11.12	13.14-10.09
Average Yield %	4.99	4.84	5.04	5.04	5.35	5.53	5.35	5.72

Address: 4 Irving Place, New York, NY 10003	Officers: Kevin Burke - Chairman, President, Chief Executive Officer Robert N. Hoglund - Senior Vice President, Chief Financial Officer Transfer Agents: The Bank of New York, New York, NY	Investor Contact: 212-460-6611
Telephone: 212-460-4600		No of Institutions: 522
Web Site: www.conedison.com		Shares: 142,828,112 % Held: 49.11

CORPORATE OFFICE PROPERTIES TRUST

Exchange	Symbol	Price	52Wk Range	Yield	P/E
NYS	OFC	$38.46 (5/29/2008)	45.57-26.76	3.54	76.92

*7 Year Price Score 104.35 *NYSE Composite Index=100 *12 Month Price Score 103.24

Interim Earnings (Per Share)

Qtr.	Mar	Jun	Sep	Dec
2005	0.14	0.14	0.18	0.17
2006	0.15	0.13	0.33	0.08
2007	0.03	0.08	0.15	0.12
2008	0.15	...	...	...

Interim Dividends (Per Share)

Amt	Decl	Ex	Rec	Pay
0.34Q	09/20/2007	09/26/2007	09/28/2007	10/16/2007
0.34Q	12/06/2007	12/27/2007	12/31/2007	01/15/2008
0.34Q	02/28/2008	03/27/2008	03/31/2008	04/15/2008
0.34Q	05/22/2008	06/26/2008	06/30/2008	07/15/2008
	Indicated Div: $1.36			

Valuation Analysis

Forecast EPS	$0.76 (05/16/2008)		
Market Cap	$1.8 Billion	Book Value	814.7 Million
Price/Book	2.25	Price/Sales	4.40

Dividend Achiever Status

10 Year Growth Rate	9.77%
Total Years of Dividend Growth	10

Business Summary: "Property, Real Estate & Development" (MIC: SIC: 6798 NAIC: 525930)

Corporate Office Properties Trust is an integrated and self-managed real estate investment trust that focuses on acquiring, developing, owning, managing and leasing suburban office properties in select markets and submarkets. As of Dec 31 2007, Co. owned 228 operating properties in Maryland, Virginia, Colorado, Texas, Pennsylvania and New Jersey containing 17.8 million rentable square feet; 19 office properties under construction or development that totals about 1.8 million square feet upon completion, and one wholly owned office property totaling 74,749 square feet under redevelopment; and partial ownership interests through joint ventures, including land parcels totaling 225 acres.

Recent Developments: For the quarter ended Mar 31 2008, income from continuing operations increased 74.7% to US$9.6 million from US$5.5 million in the year-earlier quarter. Net income increased 105.4% to US$11.4 million from US$5.5 million in the year-earlier quarter. Revenues were US$106.3 million, up 7.3% from US$99.1 million the year before. Revenues from property income rose 9.3% to US$97.3 million from US$89.0 million in the corresponding quarter a year earlier.

Prospects: For full-year 2008, Co. expects earnings per share guidance to be in the range of $0.62 to $0.70 per diluted share. In addition, Co. expects funds from operations (FFO) guidance to be in the range of $2.41 to $2.49 per diluted share, representing FFO growth between 8.0% and 11.0% compared with 2007 actual results. Meanwhile, Co. noted that as of Mar 31 2008, it had construction activities underway on 11 office properties totaling 1.1 million square feet that were 15.6% leased, or considered committed to lease. Accordingly, Co. estimates remaining costs for the construction of these properties will total approximately $107.8 million, which is expected to be incurred through 2010.

Financial Data
(US$ in Thousands)

	3 Mos	12/31/2007	12/31/2006	12/31/2005	12/31/2004	12/31/2003	12/31/2002	12/31/2001
Earnings Per Share	0.50	0.39	0.69	0.63	0.54	0.27	0.56	0.63
Cash Flow Per Share	3.10	2.96	2.73	2.57	2.54	2.54	2.77	2.53
Tang Book Value Per Share	14.77	15.07	13.68	12.31	12.33	13.42	12.22	12.78
Dividends Per Share	1.330	1.300	1.180	1.070	0.980	0.910	0.860	0.820
Dividend Payout %	266.47	333.33	171.01	169.84	181.48	337.04	153.57	130.16
Income Statement								
Property Income	97,280	406,023	353,501	324,268	239,591	203,288	147,995	125,546
Non-Property Income	8,992	4,151	7,902	4,877	3,885	2,875	3,888	3,864
Total Revenue	106,272	410,174	361,403	329,145	243,476	206,163	151,883	129,410
Depn & Amortn	25,686	109,316	81,151	65,369	53,404	38,123	31,185	22,794
Interest Expense	20,329	85,708	74,225	58,895	46,694	41,079	39,067	32,773
Income Taxes	112	569	887	668	795	(124)	(242)	(269)
Net Income	11,395	34,784	49,227	39,031	37,032	30,877	23,301	19,922
Average Shares	47,766	47,630	43,262	38,997	34,982	28,021	24,547	21,623
Balance Sheet								
Total Assets	2,936,744	2,931,853	2,419,601	2,130,376	1,732,026	1,332,076	1,126,471	984,210
Long-Term Obligations	1,845,968	1,825,842	1,498,537	1,348,351	1,022,688	738,698	705,056	573,327
Total Liabilities	1,992,917	1,979,116	1,629,111	1,442,036	1,111,224	801,899	737,088	615,507
Stockholders' Equity	814,702	822,642	674,303	582,513	521,924	450,381	288,497	263,921
Shares Outstanding	47,616	47,366	42,897	39,927	36,842	29,397	23,606	20,648
Statistical Record								
Return on Assets %	1.41	1.30	2.16	2.02	2.41	2.51	2.21	2.24
Return on Equity %	4.91	4.65	7.83	7.07	7.60	8.36	8.44	8.71
Net Margin %	10.72	8.48	13.62	11.86	15.21	14.98	15.34	15.39
Price Range	48.55-26.76	56.00-30.97	51.20-36.24	36.90-25.35	29.35-19.47	22.14-13.59	14.59-11.85	12.50-9.10
P/E Ratio	97.10-53.52	143.59-79.41	74.20-52.52	58.57-40.24	54.35-36.06	82.00-50.33	26.05-21.16	19.84-14.44
Average Yield %	3.45	3.00	2.70	3.50	4.01	5.32	6.44	7.84

Address: 6711 Columbia Gateway Drive, Columbia, MD 21046 **Telephone:** 443-285-5400 **Web Site:** www.copt.com	Officers: Jay H. Shidler - Chairman Clay W. Hamlin - Vice-Chairman **Transfer Agents:** Wells Fargo Bank, N.A., South St. Paul, MN	Investor Contact: 443-285-5450 No of Institutions: 199 Shares: 55,033,012 % Held: 111.23

CORUS BANKSHARES, INC.

Exchange	Symbol	Price	52Wk Range	Yield	P/E
NMS	CORS	$5.71 (5/29/2008)	18.19-5.34	N/A	3.91

*7 Year Price Score 52.12   ***NYSE Composite Index=100**   ***12 Month Price Score 65.89**

Interim Earnings (Per Share)

Qtr.	Mar	Jun	Sep	Dec
2005	0.48	0.54	0.69	0.67
2006	0.75	0.82	0.88	0.83
2007	0.46	0.74	0.61	0.04
2008	0.08	...	...	...

Interim Dividends (Per Share)

Amt	Decl	Ex	Rec	Pay
1.00Q	06/21/2007	07/16/2007	07/18/2007	08/01/2007
0.25Q	08/28/2007	09/24/2007	09/26/2007	10/09/2007
0.25Q	11/13/2007	12/21/2007	12/26/2007	01/09/2008
0.25Q	02/12/2008	03/24/2008	03/26/2008	04/10/2008

Valuation Analysis

Forecast EPS	$0.25 (05/16/2008)		
Market Cap	$314.1 Million	Book Value	771.7 Million
Price/Book	0.41	Price/Sales	0.44

Dividend Achiever Status

10 Year Growth Rate	22.63%
Total Years of Dividend Growth	21

Business Summary: Commercial Banking (MIC: SIC: 6021 NAIC: 522110)

Corus Bankshares is a bank holding company with total assets of $8.93 billion and total deposits of $7.62 billion as of Dec 31 2007. Co., through its wholly-owned banking subsidiary, Corus Bank, N.A. (the Bank), is primarily focused on commercial real estate lending and deposit gathering. The third, and smaller, business of the Bank is servicing the check cashing industry. As of Dec 31 2007, the Bank had 11 branches in the Chicago metropolitan area that provides general banking services such as checking, savings, money market, and time deposit accounts as well as safe deposit boxes and a range of additional services.

Recent Developments: For the quarter ended Mar 31 2008, net income decreased 82.9% to US$4.5 million from US$26.4 million in the year-earlier quarter. Net interest income decreased 37.3% to US$46.9 million from US$74.8 million in the year-earlier quarter. Provision for loan losses was US$36.8 million versus US$5.5 million in the prior-year quarter, an increase of 569.1%. Non-interest income was US$15.1 million versus US$11.4 million, while non-interest expense advanced 12.0% to US$20.0 million.

Prospects: Co. noted that severe disruption in the mortgage, housing and credit markets that has continued into 2008 has led to significant increases in nonaccrual loans, charge-offs and loan loss provisions. For instance, during the first quarter of 2008, Co. recorded a provision for credit losses of $36.8 million, which, after charge-offs, added $18.0 million to its loan loss reserves. The provision was in response to both issues with specific loans as well as declines in the quality of Co.'s portfolio overall. Also, credit concerns resulted in nonaccrual commercial real estate loans increasing to $420.0 million at Mar 31 2008, up from $282.0 million at Dec 31 2007, and $196.0 million one year ago.

Financial Data
(US$ in Thousands)

	3 Mos	12/31/2007	12/31/2006	12/31/2005	12/31/2004	12/31/2003	12/31/2002	12/31/2001
Earnings Per Share	1.46	1.85	3.28	2.38	1.70	1.02	0.86	0.95
Cash Flow Per Share	(1.41)	(1.44)	(0.18)	1.63	1.44	1.00	0.99	0.76
Tang Book Value Per Share	14.03	14.35	14.93	12.27	10.70	9.66	8.46	7.88
Dividends Per Share	2.000	2.000	0.900	0.700	0.625	0.415	0.159	0.154
Dividend Payout %	136.81	108.11	27.44	29.41	36.76	40.69	18.41	16.23
Income Statement								
Interest Income	143,676	718,258	741,227	446,949	222,059	170,239	152,878	188,630
Interest Expense	96,754	430,000	399,326	197,291	70,595	46,812	54,591	80,921
Net Interest Income	46,922	288,258	341,901	249,658	151,464	123,427	98,287	107,709
Provision for Losses	36,800	66,000	7,500	6,000	...	...	...	...
Non-Interest Income	15,114	18,371	19,201	27,949	51,415	16,920	23,079	25,716
Non-Interest Expense	19,951	77,108	65,881	61,322	56,273	52,533	47,472	51,100
Income Before Taxes	5,285	163,521	287,721	210,285	146,606	87,814	73,894	82,325
Income Taxes	777	57,317	98,277	73,056	48,667	29,404	24,580	28,142
Net Income	4,508	106,204	189,444	137,229	97,939	58,410	49,314	54,183
Average Shares	55,829	57,265	57,705	57,710	57,636	57,406	57,180	57,236
Balance Sheet								
Net Loans & Leases	4,469,458	4,338,395	4,096,686	4,484,771	2,760,946	2,397,323	1,705,340	1,434,788
Total Assets	9,072,057	8,926,577	10,057,791	8,458,740	5,017,787	3,643,830	2,617,050	2,659,322
Total Deposits	7,783,786	7,619,682	8,704,675	7,275,346	4,100,152	2,846,402	2,059,773	2,121,456
Total Liabilities	8,300,342	8,137,180	9,213,264	7,768,965	4,418,196	3,097,650	2,135,009	2,208,436
Stockholders' Equity	771,715	789,397	844,527	689,775	599,591	546,180	482,041	450,886
Shares Outstanding	55,012	55,011	56,245	56,245	55,591	56,073	56,476	56,638
Statistical Record								
Return on Assets %	0.89	1.12	2.05	2.04	2.26	1.87	1.87	2.06
Return on Equity %	10.31	13.00	24.69	21.29	17.05	11.36	10.57	12.70
Net Interest Margin %	32.66	40.13	46.13	55.86	68.21	72.50	64.29	57.10
Efficiency Ratio %	12.56	10.47	8.66	12.91	20.58	28.07	26.98	23.84
Loans to Deposits	0.57	0.57	0.47	0.62	0.67	0.84	0.83	0.68
Price Range	19.04-8.99	24.44-8.99	33.47-19.83	32.32-21.65	25.09-15.51	16.05-9.86	13.35-9.74	15.29-10.13
P/E Ratio	13.04-6.16	13.21-4.86	10.20-6.05	13.58-9.09	14.76-9.12	15.73-9.67	15.52-11.33	16.09-10.66
Average Yield %	14.94	12.72	3.48	2.60	3.02	3.32	1.37	1.25

Address: 3959 N. Lincoln Avenue, Chicago, IL 60613-2431 **Telephone:** 773-832-3088 **Web Site:** www.corusbank.com	**Officers:** Joseph C. Glickman - Chairman Robert J. Glickman - President, Chief Executive Officer **Transfer Agents:** Mellon Investor Services, LLC, Ridgefield Park, NJ	**Investor Contact:** 773-832-3088 **No of Institutions:** 195 **Shares:** 37,835,324 **% Held:** 57.38

COURIER CORP.

Exchange	Symbol	Price	52Wk Range	Yield	P/E
NMS	CRRC	$24.00 (5/29/2008)	40.96-22.08	3.33	14.55

*7 Year Price Score 87.64   *NYSE Composite Index=100   *12 Month Price Score 76.04

Interim Earnings (Per Share)

Qtr.	Dec	Mar	Jun	Sep
2004-05	0.33	0.33	0.47	0.64
2005-06	0.36	0.35	0.48	1.06
2006-07	0.32	0.44	0.53	0.74
2007-08	0.11	0.27	...	...

Interim Dividends (Per Share)

Amt	Decl	Ex	Rec	Pay
0.18Q	07/18/2007	08/08/2007	08/10/2007	08/31/2007
0.20Q	11/08/2007	11/15/2007	11/19/2007	11/30/2007
0.20Q	01/16/2008	02/06/2008	02/08/2008	02/29/2008
0.20Q	04/16/2008	05/07/2008	05/09/2008	05/30/2008
		Indicated Div: $0.80		

Valuation Analysis

Forecast EPS	$1.60 (05/16/2008)		
Market Cap	$297.5 Million	Book Value	197.1 Million
Price/Book	1.51	Price/Sales	1.04

Dividend Achiever Status

10 Year Growth Rate	22.31%
Total Years of Dividend Growth	14

Business Summary: Printing (MIC: SIC: 2732 NAIC: 323117)

Courier is engaged in book manufacturing and specialty publishing. Co.'s book manufacturing segment provides services from prepress and production through storage and distribution. Co.'s principal book manufacturing markets are religious, educational and specialty trade books with products including Bibles, educational texts and consumer books. Co.'s specialty publishing segment consists of: Dover Publications, Inc., which, at Sep 29 2007, published over 9,000 titles in more than 30 specialty categories; and Research & Education Association, Inc., which publishes test preparation and study-guide books and software for high school, college and graduate students, as well as professionals.

Recent Developments: For the quarter ended Mar 29 2008, net income decreased 39.7% to US$3.4 million from US$5.6 million in the year-earlier quarter. Revenues were US$67.8 million, down 11.2% from US$76.3 million the year before. Direct operating expenses declined 8.1% to US$48.4 million from US$52.7 million in the comparable period the year before. Indirect operating expenses decreased 5.0% to US$13.9 million from US$14.7 million in the equivalent prior-year period.

Prospects: For the fiscal year ending Sep 29 2008, Co. projects total sales to be in the range of $296.0 million to $301.0 million. Similarly, Co. expects full-year earnings per share to range from $1.70 to $1.80. Also, Co. estimates capital expenditures to be in the range of $17.0 million to $22.0 million, which includes completion of the expansion of printing and binding capacity in the religious book manufacturing operation in Philadelphia and the construction of a 150,000 square foot warehouse to support the expanded capacity at the Kendallville, IN facility. For the remainder of fiscal 2008, Co. expects sales growth of 7.0% to 10.0%, resulting in earnings per share of $1.32 to $1.42.

Financial Data
(US$ in Thousands)

	6 Mos	3 Mos	09/29/2007	09/30/2006	09/24/2005	09/25/2004	09/27/2003	09/28/2002
Earnings Per Share	1.65	1.82	2.03	2.25	1.77	1.67	1.65	1.35
Cash Flow Per Share	2.73	3.03	3.01	3.13	2.89	2.38	2.65	2.51
Tang Book Value Per Share	9.63	9.69	10.70	9.10	9.96	8.45	7.61	6.00
Dividends Per Share	0.760	0.740	0.720	0.480	0.333	0.233	0.200	0.178
Dividend Payout %	45.93	40.58	35.47	21.33	18.83	14.00	12.10	13.16
Income Statement								
Total Revenue	130,650	62,863	294,592	269,051	227,039	211,179	202,002	202,184
EBITDA	18,211	7,699	61,293	53,176	45,508	42,457	39,376	35,278
Depn & Amortn	10,558	5,174	18,856	14,804	11,660	10,929	9,798	10,687
Income Before Taxes	7,653	2,230	40,866	38,190	34,236	31,551	29,526	24,111
Income Taxes	2,854	814	15,121	9,810	12,102	11,011	10,254	7,936
Net Income	4,799	1,416	25,745	28,380	22,134	20,540	20,120	16,175
Average Shares	12,521	12,695	12,689	12,599	12,490	12,331	12,180	11,988
Balance Sheet								
Current Assets	95,810	83,195	92,424	81,863	97,603	86,837	77,673	61,722
Total Assets	270,749	258,839	269,835	247,188	196,965	175,199	151,101	131,658
Current Liabilities	29,572	27,522	36,392	35,690	30,662	29,363	26,813	27,755
Long-Term Obligations	29,746	18,147	17,375	17,222	425	510	593	674
Total Liabilities	73,628	59,289	66,724	64,862	41,031	40,209	35,681	35,739
Stockholders' Equity	197,121	199,550	203,111	182,326	155,934	134,990	115,420	95,919
Shares Outstanding	12,396	12,527	12,612	12,445	12,313	12,046	11,896	11,733
Statistical Record								
Return on Assets %	7.96	9.07	9.99	12.57	11.93	12.62	14.27	12.23
Return on Equity %	10.85	12.06	13.40	16.51	15.26	16.45	19.09	18.41
EBITDA Margin %	13.94	12.25	20.81	19.76	20.04	20.10	19.49	17.45
Net Margin %	3.67	2.25	8.74	10.55	9.75	9.73	9.96	8.00
Asset Turnover	1.08	1.15	1.14	1.19	1.22	1.30	1.43	1.53
Current Ratio	3.24	3.02	2.54	2.29	3.18	2.96	2.90	2.22
Debt to Equity	0.15	0.09	0.09	0.09	N.M.	N.M.	0.01	0.01
Price Range	42.02-23.94	42.02-31.37	42.02-34.17	44.90-32.71	41.96-27.55	30.41-22.63	24.89-15.74	19.78-9.33
P/E Ratio	25.47-14.51	23.09-17.24	20.70-16.83	19.96-14.54	23.71-15.56	18.21-13.55	15.08-9.54	14.65-6.91
Average Yield %	2.17	1.95	1.85	1.27	0.96	0.94	0.95	1.11

Address: 15 Wellman Avenue, North Chelmsford, MA 01863
Telephone: 978-251-6000
Web Site: www.courier.com

Officers: James F. Conway - Chairman, President, Chief Executive Officer Robert P. Story - Executive Vice President, Chief Operating Officer **Transfer Agents:** Equiserve Trust Company, N.A.

No of Institutions: 89
Shares: 9,278,133 **% Held:** 70.10

CULLEN/FROST BANKERS, INC.

Exchange	Symbol	Price	52Wk Range	Yield	P/E
NYS	CFR	$56.01 (5/29/2008)	58.53-45.38	3.00	15.35

*7 Year Price Score 91.04   *NYSE Composite Index=100   *12 Month Price Score 108.45

Interim Earnings (Per Share)

Qtr.	Mar	Jun	Sep	Dec
2005	0.70	0.77	0.79	0.81
2006	0.83	0.86	0.88	0.84
2007	0.78	0.89	0.95	0.93
2008	0.89	...	...	...

Interim Dividends (Per Share)

Amt	Decl	Ex	Rec	Pay
0.40Q	07/26/2007	08/29/2007	08/31/2007	09/14/2007
0.40Q	10/25/2007	11/28/2007	11/30/2007	12/14/2007
0.40Q	01/24/2008	02/27/2008	02/29/2008	03/14/2008
0.42Q	04/24/2008	05/28/2008	05/30/2008	06/13/2008
		Indicated Div: $1.68		

Valuation Analysis

Forecast EPS	$3.62 (05/17/2008)		
Market Cap	$3.3 Billion	Book Value	1.6 Billion
Price/Book	2.09	Price/Sales	3.22

Dividend Achiever Status

10 Year Growth Rate	12.36%
Total Years of Dividend Growth	14

TRADING VOLUME (thousand shares)

Business Summary: Commercial Banking (MIC: SIC: 6021 NAIC: 522110)
Cullen/Frost Bankers is a financial holding company. Co., through its subsidiaries, provides commercial and consumer banking services, as well as trust and investment management, investment banking, insurance brokerage, leasing, asset-based lending, treasury management and item processing services throughout various markets in Texas. Co. serves a range of industries including, among others, energy, manufacturing, services, construction, retail, telecommunications, healthcare, military and transportation. As of Dec 31 2007, Co. had consolidated total assets of $13.49 billion, and total deposits of $10.53 billion.

Recent Developments: For the quarter ended Mar 31 2008, net income increased 11.6% to US$52.8 million from US$47.3 million in the year-earlier quarter. Net interest income increased 1.6% to US$129.9 million from US$127.8 million in the year-earlier quarter. Provision for loan losses was US$4.0 million versus US$2.7 million in the prior-year quarter, an increase of 51.1%. Non-interest income rose 4.7% to US$70.2 million from US$67.1 million, while non-interest expense declined 1.7% to US$120.0 million.

Prospects: Co.'s near-term outlook appears to be positive, reflecting increases in its bottom-line performance. Notably, Co. attributes the growth to primarily the improvement in its non-interest income, an increase in net interest income and a reduction in non-interest expense, partly offset by higher provision for possible loan losses due to higher levels of charge-offs and an increase in classified loans. In particular, Co. is seeing growth in its trust fee income as a result of increases in investment fees, oil and gas trust management fees, as well as securities lending income.

Financial Data
(US$ in Thousands)

	3 Mos	12/31/2007	12/31/2006	12/31/2005	12/31/2004	12/31/2003	12/31/2002	12/31/2001
Earnings Per Share	3.65	3.55	3.42	3.07	2.66	2.48	2.23	1.52
Cash Flow Per Share	5.45	3.41	(0.96)	2.52	2.49	3.93	5.34	1.91
Tang Book Value Per Share	17.38	15.66	13.61	14.65	13.59	12.65	11.40	11.58
Dividends Per Share	1.600	1.540	1.320	1.165	1.035	0.940	0.875	0.840
Dividend Payout %	43.83	43.38	38.60	37.95	38.91	37.90	39.24	55.26
Income Statement								
Interest Income	175,703	768,847	683,959	509,827	393,544	368,946	389,898	460,976
Interest Expense	45,823	250,110	214,796	118,561	62,106	55,188	75,865	144,759
Net Interest Income	129,880	518,737	469,163	391,266	331,438	313,758	314,033	316,217
Provision for Losses	4,005	14,660	14,150	10,250	2,500	10,544	22,546	40,031
Non-Interest Income	70,228	268,231	240,747	230,379	225,110	215,361	200,709	192,891
Non-Interest Expense	120,040	462,446	410,353	367,007	345,030	326,035	312,142	352,606
Income Before Taxes	76,063	309,862	285,407	244,388	209,018	192,540	180,054	116,471
Income Taxes	23,283	97,791	91,816	78,965	67,693	62,039	57,821	38,565
Net Income	52,780	212,071	193,591	165,423	141,325	130,501	116,986	80,916
Average Shares	59,058	59,713	56,642	53,803	53,140	52,658	52,423	53,348
Balance Sheet								
Net Loans & Leases	7,920,399	7,677,023	7,277,299	6,004,730	5,089,181	4,507,245	4,436,329	4,445,727
Total Assets	13,793,929	13,485,014	13,224,189	11,741,437	9,952,787	9,672,114	9,552,318	8,369,584
Total Deposits	10,727,883	10,529,673	10,387,909	9,146,394	8,105,678	8,068,857	7,628,143	7,098,007
Total Liabilities	12,216,730	12,007,926	11,847,306	10,759,201	9,130,392	8,902,110	8,848,528	7,774,665
Stockholders' Equity	1,577,199	1,477,088	1,376,883	982,236	822,395	770,004	703,790	594,919
Shares Outstanding	58,746	58,662	59,839	54,482	51,923	51,776	51,295	51,355
Statistical Record								
Return on Assets %	1.61	1.59	1.55	1.53	1.44	1.36	1.31	1.01
Return on Equity %	14.49	14.86	16.41	18.33	17.70	17.71	18.02	13.86
Net Interest Margin %	73.92	67.47	68.60	76.74	84.22	85.04	80.54	68.60
Efficiency Ratio %	48.81	44.59	44.38	49.58	55.77	55.80	52.85	53.93
Loans to Deposits	0.74	0.73	0.70	0.66	0.63	0.56	0.58	0.63
Price Range	55.81-45.38	56.84-48.10	59.44-52.26	56.05-42.45	49.00-38.90	41.00-29.40	40.04-29.40	41.19-23.84
P/E Ratio	15.29-12.43	16.01-13.55	17.38-15.28	18.26-13.83	18.42-14.62	16.53-11.85	17.96-13.18	27.10-15.68
Average Yield %	3.10	2.94	2.35	2.40	2.35	2.80	2.53	2.54

Address: 100 W. Houston Street, San Antonio, TX 78205 Telephone: 210-220-4011 Web Site: www.frostbank.com	Officers: Richard W. Evans - Chairman, President, Chief Executive Officer Phillip D. Green - Group Executive Vice President, Chief Financial Officer Transfer Agents:Bank of New York	Investor Contact: 210-220-5632 No of Institutions: 272 Shares: 44,187,560 % Held: 72.27

CVB FINANCIAL CORP.

Exchange	Symbol	Price	52Wk Range	Yield	P/E
NMS	CVBF	$10.82 (5/29/2008)	12.71-8.45	3.14	14.82

*7 Year Price Score 72.33   ***NYSE Composite Index=100**   ***12 Month Price Score 102.89**

Interim Earnings (Per Share)

Qtr.	Mar	Jun	Sep	Dec
2005	0.21	0.20	0.22	0.19
2006	0.22	0.23	0.22	0.20
2007	0.18	0.19	0.19	0.16
2008	0.19	...	...	...

Interim Dividends (Per Share)

Amt	Decl	Ex	Rec	Pay
0.085Q	06/20/2007	07/02/2007	07/05/2007	07/20/2007
0.085Q	09/19/2007	10/01/2007	10/03/2007	10/18/2007
0.085Q	12/19/2007	01/02/2008	01/04/2008	01/18/2008
0.085Q	03/21/2008	04/02/2008	04/04/2008	04/18/2008

Indicated Div: $0.34

Valuation Analysis

Forecast EPS $0.80 (05/16/2008)
Market Cap $899.1 Million Book Value 451.8 Million
Price/Book 1.99 Price/Sales 2.43

Dividend Achiever Status

10 Year Growth Rate 19.28%
Total Years of Dividend Growth 17

TRADING VOLUME (thousand shares)

Business Summary: Commercial Banking (MIC: SIC: 6022 NAIC: 522110)

CVB Financial is a bank holding company, with assets of $6.29 billion and deposits of $3.36 billion as of Dec 31 2007. Co.'s Citizens Business Bank (the Bank), operates 44 business financial centers located in the San Bernardino County, Riverside County, Orange County, Los Angeles County, Madera County, Fresno County, Tulare County, and Kern County areas of California as of Dec 31 2007. The Bank provides a full range of banking and trust services for businesses, professionals and individuals located in the service areas of its offices. Co. also provides a range of financial services and trust services through CitizensTrust.

Recent Developments: For the quarter ended Mar 31 2008, net income increased 6.9% to US$16.2 million from US$15.1 million in the year-earlier quarter. Net interest income increased 11.0% to US$44.1 million from US$39.8 million in the year-earlier quarter. Non-interest income rose 3.1% to US$8.1 million from US$7.9 million, while non-interest expense advanced 9.6% to US$28.4 million.

Prospects: Economic conditions in Co.'s California service area are tempering its results. Specifically, Co. has seen a slow down in housing and it is being affected by the resulting slower growth in construction loans and the decrease in deposit balances from escrow companies. Also, the inland empire area has been significantly effected by slowing job growth. Notably, about 22.0% of Co.'s total loan portfolio of $3.40 billion is located in the Inland Empire region of California. The balance of the portfolio is from outside of this region. Co. stated that weaknesses in the local economy could adversely affect it through diminished loan demand and credit quality deterioration.

Financial Data

(US$ in Thousands)	3 Mos	12/31/2007	12/31/2006	12/31/2005	12/31/2004	12/31/2003	12/31/2002	12/31/2001
Earnings Per Share	0.73	0.72	0.85	0.83	0.73	0.63	0.59	0.48
Cash Flow Per Share	0.87	0.85	0.84	1.06	0.91	0.87	0.74	0.49
Tang Book Value Per Share	4.61	4.27	4.13	3.55	3.50	3.13	2.97	2.61
Dividends Per Share	0.340	0.340	0.327	0.240	0.295	0.324	0.233	0.186
Dividend Payout %	46.71	47.22	38.50	29.01	40.60	51.75	39.64	38.94
Income Statement								
Interest Income	83,219	341,277	316,660	248,488	197,702	166,346	154,323	155,877
Interest Expense	39,089	180,135	147,464	77,436	46,517	37,053	40,439	52,806
Net Interest Income	44,130	161,142	169,196	171,052	151,185	129,293	113,884	103,071
Provision for Losses	1,700	4,000	3,000	...	...	...	...	1,750
Non-Interest Income	8,140	31,325	33,258	27,505	27,907	29,989	29,018	22,192
Non-Interest Expense	28,399	105,404	95,824	91,593	89,722	77,794	66,056	60,155
Income Before Taxes	22,171	83,063	103,630	106,964	89,370	81,488	76,846	63,358
Income Taxes	5,987	22,479	31,724	36,346	27,884	28,656	27,101	23,300
Net Income	16,184	60,584	71,906	70,618	61,486	52,832	49,745	40,058
Average Shares	83,522	84,005	84,813	84,912	84,258	84,407	84,280	83,695
Balance Sheet								
Net Loans & Leases	3,357,481	3,462,095	3,042,459	2,640,659	2,117,580	1,738,659	1,424,343	1,167,071
Total Assets	6,374,802	6,293,963	6,094,262	5,422,971	4,511,011	3,854,349	3,123,411	2,514,102
Total Deposits	3,260,668	3,364,349	3,406,808	3,424,046	2,875,039	2,660,510	2,309,964	1,876,959
Total Liabilities	5,923,013	5,869,015	5,704,923	5,080,094	4,193,528	3,567,628	2,863,590	2,293,354
Stockholders' Equity	451,789	424,948	389,339	342,877	317,483	286,721	259,821	220,748
Shares Outstanding	83,095	83,164	84,281	84,073	83,416	82,997	82,304	82,200
Statistical Record								
Return on Assets %	0.99	0.98	1.25	1.42	1.47	1.51	1.76	1.66
Return on Equity %	14.51	14.88	19.64	21.39	20.30	19.33	20.70	19.57
Net Interest Margin %	53.03	47.22	53.43	68.84	76.47	77.73	73.80	66.12
Efficiency Ratio %	31.09	28.29	27.38	33.19	39.77	39.62	36.03	33.78
Loans to Deposits	1.03	1.03	0.89	0.77	0.74	0.65	0.62	0.62
Price Range	12.71-8.45	13.47-9.51	15.60-12.83	15.93-12.36	16.24-11.00	11.71-9.71	11.31-7.28	8.31-4.91
P/E Ratio	17.41-11.58	18.71-13.21	18.35-15.09	19.19-14.90	22.25-15.07	18.58-15.41	19.16-12.34	17.31-10.23
Average Yield %	3.10	2.94	2.32	1.71	2.30	3.02	2.57	2.97

Address: 701 North Haven Avenue, Suite 350, Ontario, CA 91764 **Telephone:** 909-980-4030 **Web Site:** www.cbbank.com	Officers: George A. Borba - Chairman Ronald O. Kruse - Vice-Chairman **Transfer Agents:** U.S. Stock Transfer Corporation, Glendale, CA	No of Institutions: 116 **Shares:** 25,690,964 **% Held:** 29.43

DANAHER CORP.

Business Summary: Instruments and Related Products (MIC: SIC: 3823 NAIC: 334513)

Danaher operates four business segments: Professional Instrumentation, which provides professional and technical customers products and services for use in the performance of their work; Medical Technologies, which provides dentists, doctors, and scientific professionals products and services for use in the performance of their work; Industrial Technologies, which produces products and sub-systems that are usually incorporated by customers and systems integrators into production and packaging lines and by original equipment manufacturers into various end-products and systems; and Tools & Components, which produces mechanics' hand tools for the professional and do-it-yourself markets.

Recent Developments: For the quarter ended Mar 28 2008, income from continuing operations increased 9.9% to US$276.5 million from US$251.6 million in the year-earlier quarter. Net income increased 8.5% to US$276.5 million from US$254.8 million in the year-earlier quarter. Revenues were US$3.03 billion, up 20.1% from US$2.52 billion the year before. Operating income was US$413.2 million versus US$370.1 million in the prior-year quarter, an increase of 11.6%. Direct operating expenses rose 16.6% to US$1.61 billion from US$1.38 billion in the comparable period the year before. Indirect operating expenses increased 30.5% to US$1.00 billion from US$769.8 million in the equivalent prior-year period.

Prospects: Co.'s results reflect growth in its water quality, test and measurement, acute care diagnostics and life sciences businesses, largely offset by slower demand in its original equipment manufacturer and consumer oriented businesses, mainly in the U.S. For the full year of 2008, Co. is anticipating capital investment to exceed $200.0 million, primarily for increasing capacity, replacing equipment, supporting new product development and improving information technology systems. Meanwhile, Co. expects to further improve its operating margins at both existing and newly acquired businesses through the ongoing application of Danaher Business System application in each of its segment's businesses.

Financial Data

(US$ in Thousands)	3 Mos	12/31/2007	12/31/2006	12/31/2005	12/31/2004	12/31/2003	12/31/2002	12/31/2001
Earnings Per Share	4.25	4.19	3.48	2.76	2.30	1.69	0.94	1.00
Cash Flow Per Share	5.21	5.29	5.02	3.90	3.33	2.81	2.36	2.12
Tang Book Value Per Share	N.M.	N.M.	N.M.	N.M.	N.M.	0.99	0.01	N.M.
Dividends Per Share	0.120	0.110	0.080	0.070	0.058	0.050	0.045	0.040
Dividend Payout %	2.82	2.63	2.30	2.54	2.50	2.97	4.79	3.98
Income Statement								
Total Revenue	3,028,874	11,025,917	9,596,404	7,984,704	6,889,301	5,293,876	4,577,232	3,782,444
EBITDA	500,316	2,009,201	1,735,210	1,441,640	1,261,261	979,431	830,687	680,401
Depn & Amortn	87,094	268,492	217,217	176,972	156,128	133,436	129,565	178,390
Income Before Taxes	376,075	1,637,099	1,446,172	1,234,442	1,057,717	797,035	657,468	476,264
Income Taxes	99,570	423,101	324,143	336,642	311,717	260,201	223,327	178,599
Net Income	276,505	1,369,904	1,122,029	897,800	746,000	536,834	290,391	297,665
Average Shares	335,974	329,459	325,251	327,983	327,701	323,140	316,964	303,696
Balance Sheet								
Current Assets	4,155,273	4,049,767	3,394,902	2,945,019	2,918,690	2,942,151	2,387,266	1,874,615
Total Assets	17,853,022	17,471,935	12,864,151	9,163,109	8,493,893	6,890,050	6,029,145	4,820,483
Current Liabilities	2,981,444	2,899,853	2,459,556	2,268,586	2,202,286	1,380,003	1,265,312	1,017,294
Long-Term Obligations	3,204,144	3,395,764	2,422,861	857,771	925,535	1,284,498	1,197,422	1,119,333
Total Liabilities	8,278,427	8,386,247	6,219,491	4,082,759	3,874,211	3,243,341	3,019,546	2,591,897
Stockholders' Equity	9,574,595	9,085,688	6,644,660	5,080,350	4,619,682	3,646,709	3,009,599	2,228,586
Shares Outstanding	318,431	317,984	308,242	305,571	308,920	307,362	305,064	286,628
Statistical Record								
Return on Assets %	9.01	9.03	10.19	10.17	9.67	8.31	5.35	6.73
Return on Equity %	16.78	17.42	19.14	18.51	18.00	16.13	11.09	14.27
EBITDA Margin %	16.52	18.22	18.08	18.06	18.31	18.50	18.15	17.99
Net Margin %	9.13	12.42	11.69	11.24	10.83	10.14	6.34	7.87
Asset Turnover	0.75	0.73	0.87	0.90	0.89	0.82	0.84	0.85
Current Ratio	1.39	1.40	1.38	1.30	1.33	2.13	1.89	1.84
Debt to Equity	0.33	0.37	0.36	0.17	0.20	0.35	0.40	0.50
Price Range	88.62-70.13	88.62-69.88	74.98-54.30	58.07-48.56	58.64-43.99	45.98-30.23	37.66-26.62	33.84-22.77
P/E Ratio	20.85-16.50	21.15-16.68	21.55-15.60	21.04-17.59	25.50-19.13	27.20-17.88	40.07-28.32	33.84-22.77
Average Yield %	0.15	0.14	0.12	0.13	0.12	0.14	0.14	0.14

Address: 2099 Pennsylvania Avenue NW, 12th Floor, Washington, DC 20006-1813 **Telephone:** 202-828-0850 **Web Site:** www.danaher.com	**Officers:** Steven M. Rales - Chairman H. Lawrence Culp - President, Chief Executive Officer **Transfer Agents:** Computershare, Providence, RI	**Investor Contact:** 202-828-0850 **No of Institutions:** 797 **Shares:** 254,454,320 **% Held:** 78.10

DENTSPLY INTERNATIONAL, INC.

Exchange	Symbol	Price	52Wk Range	Yield	P/E
NMS	XRAY	$40.65 (5/29/2008)	46.65-35.32	0.44	23.36

*7 Year Price Score 118.94 *NYSE Composite Index=100 *12 Month Price Score 100.25

Interim Earnings (Per Share)

Qtr.	Mar	Jun	Sep	Dec
2005	0.30	0.35	(0.39)	(0.01)
2006	0.31	0.37	0.31	0.41
2007	0.38	0.42	0.42	0.45
2008	0.45	...	...	...

Interim Dividends (Per Share)

Amt	Decl	Ex	Rec	Pay
0.04Q	07/31/2007	09/25/2007	09/27/2007	10/09/2007
0.045Q	09/18/2007	12/24/2007	12/27/2007	01/08/2008
0.045Q	02/13/2008	03/25/2008	03/27/2008	04/07/2008
0.045Q	05/13/2008	06/25/2008	06/27/2008	07/08/2008

Indicated Div: $0.18

Valuation Analysis

Forecast EPS	$1.88 (05/17/2008)		
Market Cap	$6.0 Billion	Book Value	1.5 Billion
Price/Book	3.98	Price/Sales	2.89

Dividend Achiever Status

10 Year Growth Rate	9.71%
Total Years of Dividend Growth	13

TRADING VOLUME (thousand shares)

Business Summary: Medical Instruments & Equipment (MIC: SIC: 3843 NAIC: 339114)

DENTSPLY International is a worldwide designer, developer, manufacturer and marketer of a range of products for the dental market. As of Dec 31 2007, Co. conducted its business through four operating segments, all of which were primarily engaged in the design, manufacture and distribution of dental products in three key categories: dental consumables, dental laboratory products and specialty dental products. Co. conducts its business in over 120 foreign countries, mainly through its foreign subsidiaries. Co. has market presence in Canada and in Europe, particularly in Germany, Switzerland, France, Italy and the U.K; as well as in Central and South America; South Africa; and the Pacific Rim.

Recent Developments: For the quarter ended Mar 31 2008, net income increased 16.6% to US$68.2 million from US$58.5 million in the year-earlier quarter. Revenues were US$560.8 million, up 18.6% from US$472.9 million the year before. Operating income was US$101.0 million versus US$81.2 million in the prior-year quarter, an increase of 24.4%. Direct operating expenses rose 21.6% to US$275.5 million from US$226.6 million in the comparable period the year before. Indirect operating expenses increased 11.6% to US$184.2 million from US$165.1 million in the equivalent prior-year period.

Prospects: Despite the softer economic conditions in the U.S., Co. is accelerating investment in several areas, such as product expansion through acquisitions and investments in other companies. Co. also remains focused on reducing costs and enhancing capabilities by consolidating operations, improving its service and expanding the use of technology, process improvement initiatives and new marketing strategies. These efforts are expected to improve Co.'s cost structure and offset areas of rising costs such as energy, benefits, and regulatory oversight and compliance. For 2008, Co. has reiterated its internal growth guidance of 5.5% to 6.5% and earnings guidance $1.83 to $1.88 per diluted share.

Financial Data
(US$ in Thousands)

	3 Mos	12/31/2007	12/31/2006	12/31/2005	12/31/2004	12/31/2003	12/31/2002	12/31/2001
Earnings Per Share	1.74	1.68	1.41	0.28	1.54	1.08	0.93	0.77
Cash Flow Per Share	2.50	2.56	1.75	1.46	1.90	1.64	1.11	1.36
Tang Book Value Per Share	1.76	2.07	1.39	1.52	1.18	N.M.	N.M.	N.M.
Dividends Per Share	0.170	0.165	0.145	0.125	0.109	0.099	0.092	0.092
Dividend Payout %	9.80	9.82	10.28	44.64	7.04	9.12	9.95	11.90
Income Statement								
Total Revenue	560,782	2,009,833	1,810,496	1,715,135	1,694,232	1,570,925	1,513,742	1,129,094
EBITDA	112,150	405,779	360,588	130,366	343,080	321,062	292,229	260,035
Depn & Amortn	14,210	50,289	47,434	50,560	49,296	45,661	43,859	54,334
Income Before Taxes	94,898	358,135	314,837	71,038	274,155	251,196	220,985	185,127
Income Taxes	26,718	98,481	91,119	25,625	63,869	81,343	73,033	63,631
Net Income	68,180	259,654	223,718	45,413	253,165	174,183	147,952	121,496
Average Shares	152,983	154,721	158,271	162,016	164,028	161,294	159,988	157,950
Balance Sheet								
Current Assets	1,093,331	982,022	718,191	1,030,043	1,056,409	727,452	541,001	484,243
Total Assets	2,915,065	2,675,569	2,181,350	2,407,329	2,798,145	2,445,587	2,087,033	1,798,151
Current Liabilities	297,040	312,411	311,434	741,234	404,607	337,684	365,745	358,517
Long-Term Obligations	586,811	482,063	367,161	270,104	779,940	790,202	769,823	723,524
Total Liabilities	1,394,760	1,159,167	907,293	1,165,561	1,353,572	1,323,100	1,249,846	1,188,195
Stockholders' Equity	1,519,941	1,516,106	1,273,835	1,241,580	1,443,973	1,122,069	835,928	609,519
Shares Outstanding	148,800	150,822	151,800	157,800	161,200	158,600	156,800	155,800
Statistical Record								
Return on Assets %	10.31	10.69	9.75	1.74	9.63	7.69	7.62	9.12
Return on Equity %	18.80	18.61	17.79	3.38	19.68	17.79	20.47	21.51
EBITDA Margin %	20.00	20.19	19.92	7.60	20.25	20.44	19.31	23.03
Net Margin %	12.16	12.92	12.36	2.65	14.94	11.09	9.77	10.76
Asset Turnover	0.80	0.83	0.79	0.66	0.64	0.69	0.78	0.85
Current Ratio	3.68	3.14	2.31	1.39	2.61	2.15	1.48	1.35
Debt to Equity	0.39	0.32	0.29	0.22	0.54	0.70	0.92	1.19
Price Range	46.65-32.83	46.19-29.79	33.17-26.29	28.98-25.55	28.24-20.98	23.59-16.35	21.45-15.64	16.92-11.27
P/E Ratio	26.81-18.87	27.49-17.73	23.52-18.65	103.52-91.25	18.34-13.63	21.85-15.14	23.06-16.81	21.97-14.64
Average Yield %	0.43	0.44	0.48	0.46	0.44	0.49	0.50	0.65

Address: 221 West Philadelphia Street, York, PA 17405-0872	Officers: Bret W. Wise - Chairman, President, Chief Executive Officer Christopher T. Clark - Executive	Investor Contact: 717-849-4370
Telephone: 717-845-7511	Vice President, Chief Operating Officer **Transfer**	No of Institutions: 525
Web Site: www.dentsply.com	Agents:American Stock Transfer & Trust Company	Shares: 130,194,088 % Held: 81.52

DEVELOPERS DIVERSIFIED REALTY CORP.

Exchange	Symbol	Price	52Wk Range	Yield	P/E
NYS	DDR	$40.27 (5/29/2008)	61.80-32.92	6.85	23.97

*7 Year Price Score 93.34 ***NYSE Composite Index=100** ***12 Month Price Score 94.15**

TRADING VOLUME (thousand shares)

Interim Earnings (Per Share)

Qtr.	Mar	Jun	Sep	Dec
2005	0.84	0.50	0.43	0.32
2006	0.33	0.59	0.45	0.44
2007	0.42	0.89	0.26	0.26
2008	0.28	...	...	...

Interim Dividends (Per Share)

Amt	Decl	Ex	Rec	Pay
0.66Q	08/15/2007	09/20/2007	09/24/2007	10/02/2007
0.66Q	11/19/2007	12/19/2007	12/21/2007	01/08/2008
0.69Q	01/09/2008	03/18/2008	03/21/2008	04/08/2008
0.69Q	05/15/2008	06/18/2008	06/20/2008	07/08/2008

Indicated Div: $2.76

Valuation Analysis

Forecast EPS $1.70 (05/16/2008)

Market Cap	$4.8 Billion	Book Value	2.9 Billion
Price/Book	1.64	Price/Sales	4.98

Dividend Achiever Status

10 Year Growth Rate	7.68%
Total Years of Dividend Growth	14

Business Summary: "Property, Real Estate & Development" (MIC: SIC: 6798 NAIC: 525930)

Developers Diversified Realty is a self-administered and self-managed real estate investment trust primarily engaged in the business of acquiring, developing, redeveloping, owning, leasing as well as managing shopping and business centers. As of Feb 15 2008, Co.'s portfolio consisted of 709 shopping centers and seven business centers, which included 317 properties owned through unconsolidated joint ventures, as well as more than 1,600 acres of undeveloped land, of which approximately 600 acres were owned through joint ventures. These properties consist of shopping centers, enclosed malls and lifestyle centers.

Recent Developments: For the quarter ended Mar 31 2008, income from continuing operations decreased 18.6% to US$41.3 million from US$50.8 million in the year-earlier quarter. Net income decreased 30.6% to US$43.4 million from US$62.5 million in the year-earlier quarter. Revenues were US$241.9 million, up 10.4% from US$219.0 million the year before. Revenues from property income rose 9.8% to US$222.1 million from US$202.3 million in the corresponding quarter a year earlier.

Prospects: Despite experiencing lower earnings, Co. remains encouraged with its portfolio performance and its outlook for the balance of the year. Specifically, while some deceleration in retailer new store growth is expected, Co. believes that many tenants actually view these challenges as an opportunity to gain market share. Also, Co. believes that is well-positioned to benefit from the existing economy environment in which consumers are increasingly price-sensitive and less inclined to buy fully-priced optional items. Meanwhile, Co. expects management fee income to continue to grow as unconsolidated joint ventures acquire additional properties and as assets under development become operational.

Financial Data
(US$ in Thousands)

	3 Mos	12/31/2007	12/31/2006	12/31/2005	12/31/2004	12/31/2003	12/31/2002	12/31/2001
Earnings Per Share	1.68	1.85	1.81	2.08	2.24	2.27	1.16	1.17
Cash Flow Per Share	3.07	3.43	3.10	3.28	3.02	3.21	3.30	3.16
Tang Book Value Per Share	19.53	20.01	16.30	16.96	16.90	12.35	9.63	8.92
Dividends Per Share	2.670	2.640	2.360	2.160	1.940	1.690	1.520	1.480
Dividend Payout %	158.91	142.70	130.39	103.85	86.61	74.45	131.03	126.50
Income Statement								
Property Income	222,122	880,286	773,618	695,017	568,631	446,231	333,569	294,209
Non-Property Income	19,774	64,565	44,480	32,159	30,302	29,866	23,674	28,030
Total Revenue	241,896	944,851	818,098	727,176	598,933	476,097	357,243	322,239
Depn & Amortn	57,139	234,125	201,283	178,134	139,947	101,733	82,200	66,915
Interest Expense	62,214	261,318	221,525	182,279	129,659	89,678	76,831	81,770
Income Taxes	1,045	(14,642)	(2,481)	342	1,469	...	...	...
Net Income	43,424	276,047	253,264	282,643	269,762	240,261	101,970	92,372
Average Shares	119,349	121,497	109,613	109,142	99,024	84,188	64,837	55,834
Balance Sheet								
Total Assets	9,153,743	9,089,816	7,179,753	6,862,977	5,583,547	3,941,151	2,776,852	2,497,207
Long-Term Obligations	5,709,801	5,591,014	4,248,812	3,891,001	2,718,690	2,083,131	1,498,798	1,308,301
Total Liabilities	6,212,099	6,090,991	4,683,570	4,292,696	3,029,228	2,327,081	1,831,291	1,663,193
Stockholders' Equity	2,941,644	2,998,825	2,496,183	2,570,281	2,554,319	1,614,070	945,561	834,014
Shares Outstanding	119,600	119,448	108,986	108,947	108,082	86,433	66,608	59,454
Statistical Record								
Return on Assets %	2.59	3.39	3.61	4.54	5.65	7.15	3.87	3.83
Return on Equity %	7.98	10.05	10.00	11.03	12.91	18.77	11.46	11.42
Net Margin %	17.95	29.22	30.96	38.87	45.04	50.46	28.54	28.67
Price Range	66.25-32.92	71.38-37.69	66.11-47.80	49.08-38.91	45.85-31.47	33.60-21.28	23.47-18.20	19.20-12.94
P/E Ratio	39.43-19.60	38.58-20.37	36.52-26.41	23.60-18.71	20.47-14.05	14.80-9.37	20.23-15.69	16.41-11.06
Average Yield %	5.35	4.68	4.34	4.68	5.17	6.12	7.10	8.86

Address: 3300 Enterprise Parkway, Beachwood, OH 44122 **Telephone:** 216-755-5500 **Web Site:** www.ddrc.com	**Officers:** Scott A. Wolstein - Chairman, Chief Executive Officer Daniel B. Hurwitz - President, Chief Operating Officer **Transfer Agents:** National City Bank, Cleveland, Ohio	**No of Institutions:** 344 **Shares:** 117,433,584 **% Held:** 90.20

DIEBOLD, INC.

Exchange	Symbol	Price	52Wk Range	Yield	P/E
NYS	DBD	$39.30 (5/29/2008)	54.25-23.71	2.54	38.16

*7 Year Price Score 71.11 *NYSE Composite Index=100 *12 Month Price Score 100.90

Interim Earnings (Per Share)

Qtr.	Mar	Jun	Sep	Dec
2004	0.40	0.60	0.67	0.87
2005	0.37	0.45	0.37	0.15
2006	0.18	0.26	0.45	0.41
2007	(0.09)	...	...	...

Interim Dividends (Per Share)

Amt	Decl	Ex	Rec	Pay
0.235Q	08/08/2007	08/22/2007	08/24/2007	09/07/2007
0.235Q	10/18/2007	11/14/2007	11/16/2007	12/07/2007
0.25Q	02/13/2008	02/21/2008	02/25/2008	03/07/2008
0.25Q	04/24/2008	05/07/2008	05/09/2008	05/30/2008

Indicated Div: $1.00 (Div. Reinv. Plan)

Valuation Analysis

Forecast EPS	$1.75 (05/16/2008)		
Market Cap	$2.6 Billion	Book Value	1.1 Billion
Price/Book	2.35	Price/Sales	0.89

Dividend Achiever Status

10 Year Growth Rate	6.52%
Total Years of Dividend Growth	54

Business Summary: Office Equipment Supplies (MIC: SIC: 3578 NAIC: 333313)

Diebold is engaged primarily in the sale, manufacture, installation and service of automated self-service transaction systems, electronic and physical security products, election systems and software. Co. specializes in technology that enables people worldwide to access services when, where and how they may choose. Co.'s segments comprises of three main sales channels: Diebold North America (DNA), Diebold International (DI) and Election Systems (ES) & Other. Co.'s primary customers include banks and financial institutions, as well as public libraries, government agencies, utilities and various retail outlets.

Recent Developments: Co. has concluded its review of the impact on revenue from its change in revenue recognition method for 2006 and 2007 and continues to review other accounting items, with completion expected by June 30 2008. Following the review of the other accounting items, but prior to filing its restated financial statements, Co. intends to provide preliminary financial results for 2007 and the first and second quarters of 2008. Co. stated that while the restated financial statements will address the issues identified in the review, investigations by the SEC and US Department of Justice remain ongoing and there can be no assurance that the results will not impact previously reported financial statements.

Prospects: On Mar 2 2008, United Technologies Corporation (UTX) announced that it has made a proposal to acquire all the outstanding shares of Co. for $40.00 per share in cash. Subsequently, on Mar 3 2008, Co. rejected UTX's unsolicited proposal to acquire it. Separately, for full year 2008, Co. expects revenue growth of 6.0% to 8.0%. Specifically, Co. sees financial self-service revenue growth of 4.0% to 5.0% and security revenue growth of 6.0% to 7.0%. Also, election systems revenue, including Brazil, is anticipated to be in the range of $105.0 million to $115.0 million, while Brazilian lottery systems revenue is anticipated to be in the range of $10.0 million to $13.0 million.

Financial Data
(US$ in Thousands)

	3 Mos	12/31/2006	12/31/2005	12/31/2004	12/31/2003	12/31/2002	12/31/2001	12/31/2000
Earnings Per Share	1.03	1.29	1.36	2.54	2.40	1.37	0.93	1.92
Cash Flow Per Share	2.98	3.76	1.66	3.22	2.90	2.27	2.16	2.04
Tang Book Value Per Share	9.56	9.62	11.11	11.84	11.24	9.32	8.79	8.94
Dividends Per Share	0.880	0.860	0.820	0.740	0.680	0.660	0.640	0.620
Dividend Payout %	85.44	66.67	60.29	29.13	28.33	48.18	68.82	32.29
Income Statement								
Total Revenue	628,444	2,906,232	2,587,049	2,380,910	2,109,673	1,940,163	1,760,297	1,743,608
EBITDA	28,431	230,283	231,001	354,583	330,609	306,526	157,960	257,939
Depn & Amortn	19,165	69,810	76,239	74,983	64,301	61,296	45,453	35,901
Income Before Taxes	(160)	124,449	138,251	268,943	257,023	218,551	99,839	204,357
Income Taxes	5,725	37,902	55,347	84,986	82,247	86,250	32,946	67,438
Net Income	(5,885)	86,547	96,746	183,957	174,776	99,154	66,893	136,919
Average Shares	66,156	66,885	70,966	72,534	72,924	72,297	71,783	71,479
Balance Sheet								
Current Assets	1,454,144	1,595,681	1,427,880	1,234,632	1,105,159	924,888	952,426	804,363
Total Assets	2,406,080	2,514,279	2,353,193	2,135,592	1,900,502	1,625,081	1,651,913	1,585,427
Current Liabilities	614,872	598,736	580,031	728,623	618,653	564,962	658,018	566,792
Long-Term Obligations	544,784	665,481	454,722	...	...	...	20,800	20,800
Total Liabilities	1,305,578	1,422,878	1,200,344	875,077	752,264	684,258	748,803	649,361
Stockholders' Equity	1,100,502	1,091,401	1,152,849	1,260,475	1,148,238	940,823	903,110	936,066
Shares Outstanding	65,722	65,595	68,721	71,592	72,649	72,111	71,356	71,547
Statistical Record								
Return on Assets %	2.76	3.56	4.31	9.09	9.91	6.05	4.13	9.47
Return on Equity %	6.09	7.71	8.02	15.23	16.73	10.75	7.27	15.34
EBITDA Margin %	4.52	7.92	8.93	14.89	15.67	15.80	8.97	14.79
Net Margin %	N.M.	2.98	3.74	7.73	8.28	5.11	3.80	7.85
Asset Turnover	1.18	1.19	1.15	1.18	1.20	1.18	1.09	1.21
Current Ratio	2.36	2.67	2.46	1.69	1.79	1.64	1.45	1.42
Debt to Equity	0.50	0.61	0.39	...	...	...	0.02	0.02
Price Range	48.25-37.48	46.93-37.01	57.58-33.37	56.06-44.85	57.43-33.94	42.41-31.00	41.00-25.96	34.56-21.63
P/E Ratio	46.84-36.39	36.38-28.69	42.34-24.54	22.07-17.66	23.93-14.14	30.96-22.63	44.09-27.91	18.00-11.26
Average Yield %	2.02	2.05	1.74	1.48	1.52	1.76	1.93	2.24

Address: 5995 Mayfair Road, North	Officers: Thomas W. Swidarski - President, Chief	Investor Contact: 330-490-5900
Canton, OH 44720-8077	Executive Officer Sheila M. Rutt - Vice President,	No of Institutions: 351
Telephone: 330-490-4000	Chief Human Resources Officer **Transfer Agents:**	Shares: 62,668,964 % Held: 79.00
Web Site: www.diebold.com	The Bank of New York, New York, NY	

DONALDSON CO. INC.

Exchange	Symbol	Price	52Wk Range	Yield	P/E
NYS	DCI	$50.50 (5/29/2008)	50.50-34.30	0.87	24.75

*7 Year Price Score 111.38 *NYSE Composite Index=100 *12 Month Price Score 109.45

Interim Earnings (Per Share)

Qtr.	Oct	Jan	Apr	Jul
2004-05	0.31	0.31	0.36	0.29
2005-06	0.37	0.32	0.43	0.43
2006-07	0.43	0.38	0.49	0.53
2007-08	0.53	0.42	0.57	...

Interim Dividends (Per Share)

Amt	Decl	Ex	Rec	Pay
0.10Q	07/27/2007	08/15/2007	08/17/2007	09/07/2007
0.10Q	11/16/2007	11/21/2007	11/26/2007	12/07/2007
0.11Q	01/25/2008	02/20/2008	02/22/2008	03/14/2008
0.11Q	05/20/2008	05/28/2008	05/30/2008	06/13/2008

Indicated Div: $0.44

Valuation Analysis

Forecast EPS $2.07 (05/16/2008)

Market Cap	$3.9 Billion	Book Value	729.7 Million
Price/Book	5.39	Price/Sales	1.84

Dividend Achiever Status

10 Year Growth Rate	15.18%
Total Years of Dividend Growth	12

Business Summary: Industrial Machinery and Equipment (MIC: SIC: 3564 NAIC: 333412)

Donaldson is engaged in the manufacture of filtration systems and replacement parts. Co.'s product includes air and liquid filters, exhaust and emission control products for mobile equipment; in-plant air cleaning systems; compressed air purification systems; air intake systems for industrial gas turbines and filters for applications such as computer disk drives and semi-conductor processing. Co.'s products are manufactured at over 35 plants globally and through three of its joint ventures. As of Jul 31 2007, Co. had two reporting segments: Engine Products and Industrial Products, which were engaged in the design, manufacture and sale of systems to filter air and liquid and other products.

Recent Developments: For the quarter ended Apr 30 2008, net income increased 14.5% to US$46.0 million from US$40.1 million in the year-earlier quarter. Revenues were US$587.8 million, up 21.4% from US$484.0 million the year before. Operating income was US$63.5 million versus US$50.2 million in the prior-year quarter, an increase of 26.6%. Direct operating expenses rose 19.5% to US$399.5 million from US$334.2 million in the comparable period the year before. Indirect operating expenses increased 25.2% to US$124.7 million from US$99.6 million in the equivalent prior-year period.

Prospects: For the fiscal year ending Jul 31 2008, Co. now anticipates sales growth in its Engine Products segment to be in the range of 11.0% to 13.0%, while sales at its Industrial Products segment are forecasted to grow by 17.0% to 19.0%. Concurrently, Co. is targeting sales of both its Industrial Filtration and Special Applications Products segments to improve by 15.0% to 20.0%, while sales at its Gas Turbine Products segment are estimated to improve by about 25.0% to 30.0%. In addition, Co. is projecting operating margin of at least 11.0%, while operating income is estimated to increase by 17.0% to 19.0% annually. Thus, Co. now foresees earnings to be in the range of $2.08 to $2.13 per share.

Financial Data

(US$ in Thousands)	9 Mos	6 Mos	3 Mos	07/31/2007	07/31/2006	07/31/2005	07/31/2004	07/31/2003
Earnings Per Share	2.04	1.97	1.93	1.83	1.55	1.27	1.18	1.05
Cash Flow Per Share	2.20	1.80	1.52	1.45	1.89	1.68	1.34	1.69
Tang Book Value Per Share	7.05	6.43	6.51	5.73	5.14	4.77	5.03	3.40
Dividends Per Share	0.400	0.380	0.370	0.360	0.320	0.235	0.205	0.175
Dividend Payout %	19.57	19.29	19.17	19.67	20.65	18.50	17.37	16.59
Income Statement								
Total Revenue	1,625,099	1,037,339	525,576	1,918,828	1,694,327	1,595,733	1,414,980	1,218,252
EBITDA	224,375	144,403	77,707	268,986	243,742	208,431	188,345	174,013
Depn & Amortn	41,850	27,967	14,059	49,566	44,700	44,284	41,555	37,557
Income Before Taxes	169,970	108,120	59,465	204,861	189,167	154,733	141,836	130,567
Income Taxes	46,590	30,727	16,142	54,144	56,860	44,179	35,519	35,253
Net Income	123,380	77,393	43,323	150,717	132,307	110,554	106,317	95,314
Average Shares	80,525	81,702	81,882	82,435	85,139	86,883	90,429	90,469
Balance Sheet								
Current Assets	808,132	752,318	732,037	673,644	561,405	618,822	557,380	454,705
Total Assets	1,513,545	1,427,278	1,393,279	1,319,017	1,124,067	1,111,773	1,001,609	881,997
Current Liabilities	497,896	461,259	443,701	458,944	359,869	354,202	275,524	214,076
Long-Term Obligations	177,362	176,910	149,667	129,004	100,495	103,302	70,856	105,156
Total Liabilities	783,853	749,226	703,134	694,319	577,265	587,157	452,316	434,604
Stockholders' Equity	729,692	678,052	690,145	624,698	546,802	524,616	549,293	447,393
Shares Outstanding	77,938	78,367	79,298	79,142	80,540	83,059	86,281	99,311
Statistical Record								
Return on Assets %	11.81	12.35	12.37	12.34	11.84	10.46	11.26	11.01
Return on Equity %	24.79	26.16	24.81	25.73	24.70	20.59	21.28	22.97
EBITDA Margin %	13.81	13.92	14.79	14.02	14.39	13.06	13.31	14.28
Net Margin %	7.59	7.46	8.24	7.85	7.81	6.93	7.51	7.82
Asset Turnover	1.52	1.57	1.56	1.57	1.52	1.51	1.50	1.41
Current Ratio	1.62	1.63	1.65	1.47	1.56	1.75	2.02	2.12
Debt to Equity	0.24	0.26	0.22	0.21	0.18	0.20	0.13	0.24
Price Range	48.18-34.30	48.18-34.30	42.86-33.87	38.55-32.00	35.93-28.70	33.97-25.24	30.52-23.63	24.41-15.43
P/E Ratio	23.62-16.81	24.46-17.41	22.21-17.55	21.07-17.49	23.18-18.52	26.75-19.87	25.87-20.02	23.25-14.70
Average Yield %	1.00	0.99	1.01	1.01	0.99	0.77	0.74	0.94

Address: 1400 West 94th Street, Minneapolis, MN 55431 **Telephone:** 952-887-3131 **Web Site:** www.donaldson.com	**Officers:** William M. Cook - Chairman, President, Chief Executive Officer Charles J. McMurray - Senior Vice President, Region Officer **Transfer Agents:** Wells Fargo Bank, N.A., South St. Paul, MN	**Investor Contact:** 952-887-3753 **No of Institutions:** 284 **Shares:** 58,990,800 % **Held:** 72.81

DOVER CORP

Exchange	Symbol	Price	52Wk Range	Yield	P/E
NYS	DOV	$53.88 (5/29/2008)	54.44-35.55	1.48	15.89

*7 Year Price Score 90.80 ***NYSE Composite Index=100** ***12 Month Price Score 107.23**

Interim Earnings (Per Share)

Qtr.	Mar	Jun	Sep	Dec
2005	0.48	0.85	0.60	0.57
2006	0.99	0.35	0.82	0.57
2007	0.63	0.84	0.86	0.94
2008	0.76	...	...	...

Interim Dividends (Per Share)

Amt	Decl	Ex	Rec	Pay
0.20Q	08/03/2007	08/29/2007	08/31/2007	09/15/2007
0.20Q	11/08/2007	11/28/2007	11/30/2007	12/15/2007
0.20Q	02/14/2008	02/27/2008	02/29/2008	03/14/2008
0.20Q	05/01/2008	05/28/2008	05/31/2008	06/15/2008

Indicated Div: $0.80 (Div. Reinv. Plan)

Valuation Analysis

Forecast EPS $3.65 (05/17/2008)

Market Cap	$10.2 Billion	Book Value	4.0 Billion
Price/Book	2.56	Price/Sales	1.38

Dividend Achiever Status

10 Year Growth Rate	7.90%
Total Years of Dividend Growth	52

Business Summary: Industrial Machinery and Equipment (MIC: SIC: 3532 NAIC: 333131)

Dover owns and operates a global portfolio of manufacturing companies providing components and equipment, specialty systems and support services for a variety of applications in the industrial products, engineered systems, fluid management and electronic technologies markets. In addition, Co. provides engineering, testing and other services. Co.'s operating companies are based primarily in the U.S. and Europe with manufacturing and other operations throughout the world. As of Dec 31 2007, Co. reported its results in four business segments: Industrial Products, Engineered Systems, Fluid Management and Electronic Technologies, in addition to six core business platforms.

Recent Developments: For the quarter ended Mar 31 2008, income from continuing operations increased 8.8% to US$146.3 million from US$134.5 million in the year-earlier quarter. Net income increased 14.2% to US$147.2 million from US$128.9 million in the year-earlier quarter. Revenues were US$1.86 billion, up 7.9% from US$1.72 billion the year before. Operating income was US$233.2 million versus US$209.2 million in the prior-year quarter, an increase of 11.5%. Direct operating expenses rose 7.0% to US$1.17 billion from US$1.10 billion in the comparable period the year before. Indirect operating expenses increased 8.6% to US$448.5 million from US$413.2 million in the equivalent prior-year period.

Prospects: Looking ahead, Co. anticipates that the combination of organic growth and acquisitions, coupled with its focus on internal improvements will continue to bolster its results. Specifically, on Apr 11 2007, Co. announced the completion of its acquisition of Neptune Chemical Pump Co., a manufacturer of chemical metering pumps, chemical feed systems and peripheral products, for an undisclosed amount. Accordingly, Co. expects the transaction to complement and enhance its existing pump portfolio while providing solid prospects within the Pump Solutions Group. Consequently, Co. has increased its full year 2008 earnings per share growth guidance to 12% from 10%.

Financial Data
(US$ in Thousands)	3 Mos	12/31/2007	12/31/2006	12/31/2005	12/31/2004	12/31/2003	12/31/2002	12/31/2001
Earnings Per Share	3.39	3.26	2.73	2.50	2.02	1.44	(0.60)	1.22
Cash Flow Per Share	5.11	4.48	4.31	3.25	2.93	2.93	1.95	3.35
Tang Book Value Per Share	N.M.	N.M.	N.M.	N.M.	2.16	2.70	2.65	1.97
Dividends Per Share	0.785	0.770	0.710	0.660	0.620	0.570	0.540	0.520
Dividend Payout %	23.15	23.62	26.01	26.40	30.69	39.58	...	42.62
Income Statement								
Total Revenue	1,855,062	7,226,089	6,511,623	6,078,380	5,488,112	4,413,296	4,183,664	4,459,695
EBITDA	296,756	1,221,640	1,101,354	891,513	774,281	585,367	495,523	533,677
Depn & Amortn	66,073	245,028	201,501	175,719	160,845	151,309	161,003	219,963
Income Before Taxes	207,353	887,604	822,869	643,588	552,146	371,892	269,691	238,434
Income Taxes	61,090	234,331	219,541	169,135	143,006	86,676	58,542	71,595
Net Income	147,176	661,080	561,782	510,142	412,755	292,927	(121,261)	248,537
Average Shares	193,257	202,918	205,497	204,177	204,786	203,614	203,346	204,013
Balance Sheet								
Current Assets	2,653,265	2,544,238	2,271,506	1,975,925	2,149,947	1,849,640	1,658,001	1,654,928
Total Assets	8,203,445	8,069,770	7,626,658	6,573,032	5,792,179	5,133,752	4,437,385	4,602,202
Current Liabilities	1,323,694	1,681,192	1,433,980	1,207,454	1,355,976	910,801	696,938	819,171
Long-Term Obligations	1,896,015	1,452,003	1,480,491	1,344,173	753,063	1,003,915	1,030,299	1,033,243
Total Liabilities	4,216,851	4,123,597	3,815,636	3,243,509	2,673,497	2,391,081	2,042,762	2,082,663
Stockholders' Equity	3,986,594	3,946,173	3,811,022	3,329,523	3,118,682	2,742,671	2,394,623	2,519,539
Shares Outstanding	189,373	194,038	204,316	202,850	203,496	202,912	202,402	202,579
Statistical Record								
Return on Assets %	8.44	8.42	7.91	8.25	7.53	6.12	N.M.	5.24
Return on Equity %	17.27	17.04	15.73	15.82	14.05	11.40	N.M.	10.02
EBITDA Margin %	16.00	16.91	16.91	14.67	14.11	13.26	11.84	11.97
Net Margin %	7.93	9.15	8.63	8.39	7.52	6.64	N.M.	5.57
Asset Turnover	0.92	0.92	0.92	0.98	1.00	0.92	0.93	0.94
Current Ratio	2.00	1.51	1.58	1.64	1.59	2.03	2.38	2.02
Debt to Equity	0.48	0.37	0.39	0.40	0.24	0.37	0.43	0.41
Price Range	54.44-35.55	54.44-44.34	51.58-41.49	41.94-34.70	44.02-36.03	40.08-23.35	43.31-23.91	43.32-28.77
P/E Ratio	16.06-10.49	16.70-13.60	18.89-15.20	16.78-13.88	21.79-17.84	27.83-16.22	...	35.51-23.58
Average Yield %	1.67	1.57	1.67	1.69	1.56	1.76	1.63	1.39

Address: 280 Park Avenue, New York, NY 10017-1292	Officers: Thomas L. Reece - Chairman Ronald L. Hoffman - President, Chief Executive Officer	Investor Contact: 212-922-1640
Telephone: 212-922-1640	Transfer Agents: Mellon Investor Services, Ridgefield Park, NJ	No of Institutions: 564
Web Site: www.dovercorporation.com		Shares: 171,381,664 % Held: 82.27

DUKE REALTY CORP.

Exchange	Symbol	Price	52Wk Range	Yield	P/E
NYS	DRE	$25.69 (5/29/2008)	40.12-21.23	7.47	23.57

*7 Year Price Score 71.93 ***NYSE Composite Index=100** ***12 Month Price Score 88.62**

TRADING VOLUME (thousand shares)

Interim Earnings (Per Share)

Qtr.	Mar	Jun	Sep	Dec
2005	0.18	0.28	1.48	0.23
2006	0.08	0.16	0.45	0.37
2007	0.49	0.27	0.39	0.40
2008	0.03	...	...	...

Interim Dividends (Per Share)

Amt	Decl	Ex	Rec	Pay
0.48Q	07/25/2007	08/10/2007	08/14/2007	08/31/2007
0.48Q	10/31/2007	11/09/2007	11/14/2007	11/30/2007
0.48Q	01/30/2008	02/12/2008	02/14/2008	02/29/2008
0.48Q	04/30/2008	05/12/2008	05/14/2008	05/30/2008

Indicated Div: $1.92 (Div. Reinv. Plan)

Valuation Analysis

Forecast EPS $0.66 (05/17/2008)

Market Cap	$3.8 Billion	Book Value	3.0 Billion
Price/Book	1.26	Price/Sales	3.11

Dividend Achiever Status

10 Year Growth Rate		5.63%
Total Years of Dividend Growth		14

Business Summary: "Property, Real Estate & Development" (MIC: SIC: 6798 NAIC: 525930)

Duke Realty is a self-administered and self-managed real estate investment trust company. As of Dec 31 2007, Co.'s 726 rental properties encompassed approximately 121.1 million rentable square feet and were leased by more than 3,400 tenants whose businesses include manufacturing, retailing, wholesale trade, distribution and professional services. In addition, Co. owned or controlled more than 7,700 acres of unencumbered land ready for development. Through its service operations, Co. provides, on a fee basis, leasing, property and asset management, development, construction, build-to-suit, and other tenant-related services.

Recent Developments: For the quarter ended Mar 31 2008, income from continuing operations decreased 44.8% to US$18.5 million from US$33.5 million in the year-earlier quarter. Net income decreased 76.9% to US$19.4 million from US$83.8 million in the year-earlier quarter. Revenues were US$312.8 million, up 14.5% from US$273.2 million the year before. Revenues from property income rose 7.8% to US$217.8 million from US$202.1 million in the corresponding quarter a year earlier.

Prospects: Co.'s pipeline of projects amounts to $1.80 billion, including $614.0 million of developments with an expected stabilized return of 8.8% that it plans to own indefinitely after completion; $1.10 billion of developments with an expected stabilized return of 8.2% that Co. plans to sell within about one year of completion; and a $116.0 million backlog of third-party construction volume with an average overall profit margin of 18.2%. For 2008, Co. remains focused on attaining a stabilized in-service occupancy of 95.0% and leasing its newly developed properties. Thus, Co. is projecting Funds From Operations in the range of $2.60 to $2.90 per share.

Financial Data
(US$ in Thousands)

	3 Mos	12/31/2007	12/31/2006	12/31/2005	12/31/2004	12/31/2003	12/31/2002	12/31/2001
Earnings Per Share	1.09	1.55	1.07	2.17	1.06	1.19	1.19	1.75
Cash Flow Per Share	2.15	2.33	2.04	2.86	2.67	2.72	4.25	3.34
Tang Book Value Per Share	13.20	13.72	12.15	13.33	15.18	15.57	16.11	16.56
Dividends Per Share	1.915	1.910	1.890	2.920	1.850	1.830	1.810	1.760
Dividend Payout %	176.17	123.23	176.64	134.56	174.53	153.78	152.10	100.57
Income Statement								
Property Income	217,802	794,488	780,671	676,634	744,065	706,722	684,311	691,958
Non-Property Income	94,979	375,611	412,762	459,753	421,934	343,074	268,319	341,695
Total Revenue	312,781	1,170,099	1,193,433	1,136,387	1,165,999	1,049,796	952,630	1,033,653
Depn & Amortn	82,520	288,903	262,885	260,324	233,486	199,860	179,346	164,303
Interest Expense	47,534	168,358	179,007	120,369	135,130	129,160	117,073	113,830
Net Income	19,354	279,467	204,147	355,662	188,701	199,232	206,325	282,409
Average Shares	154,596	149,614	149,393	155,877	157,062	151,141	150,839	151,710
Balance Sheet								
Total Assets	7,760,243	7,661,981	7,238,595	5,647,560	5,896,643	5,561,249	5,348,823	5,330,033
Long-Term Obligations	4,262,139	4,316,460	3,961,845	2,600,651	2,518,704	2,335,536	2,106,285	1,814,856
Total Liabilities	4,703,971	4,828,265	4,578,159	3,012,196	2,875,661	2,681,706	2,424,002	2,149,834
Stockholders' Equity	2,979,653	2,750,033	2,503,583	2,452,798	2,825,869	2,666,749	2,616,180	2,785,009
Shares Outstanding	146,670	146,175	133,921	134,697	142,894	136,594	135,007	131,416
Statistical Record								
Return on Assets %	2.85	3.75	3.17	6.16	3.28	3.65	3.86	5.23
Return on Equity %	7.65	10.64	8.24	13.48	6.85	7.54	7.64	10.27
Net Margin %	6.19	23.88	17.11	31.30	16.18	18.98	21.66	27.32
Price Range	44.66-21.23	48.21-24.76	43.95-33.33	34.72-29.40	35.77-28.76	31.75-24.50	28.95-22.42	25.97-22.00
P/E Ratio	40.97-19.48	31.10-15.97	41.07-31.15	16.00-13.55	33.75-27.13	26.68-20.59	24.33-18.84	14.84-12.57
Average Yield %	6.04	5.19	5.09	9.05	5.68	6.53	7.15	7.36

Address: 600 East 96th Street, Suite 100, Indianapolis, IN 46240 **Telephone:** 317-808-6000 **Web Site:** www.dukerealty.com	**Officers:** Dennis D. Oklak - Chairman, President, Chief Executive Officer Robert M. Chapman - Senior Executive Vice President, Chief Operating Officer **Transfer Agents:** American Stock Transfer & Trust Company, New York, NY	**Investor Contact:** 317-808-6005 **No of Institutions:** 372 **Shares:** 113,275,888 **% Held:** 73.70

EASTGROUP PROPERTIES, INC.

Exchange	Symbol	Price	52Wk Range	Yield	P/E
NYS	EGP	$47.65 (5/29/2008)	49.75-39.44	4.37	39.71

*7 Year Price Score 95.05 *NYSE Composite Index=100 *12 Month Price Score 109.38

Interim Earnings (Per Share)

Qtr.	Mar	Jun	Sep	Dec
2005	0.23	0.24	0.23	0.19
2006	0.25	0.22	0.23	0.47
2007	0.25	0.23	0.30	0.36
2008	0.31	...	...	...

Interim Dividends (Per Share)

Amt	Decl	Ex	Rec	Pay
0.50Q	09/06/2007	09/14/2007	09/18/2007	09/28/2007
0.50Q	12/07/2007	12/14/2007	12/18/2007	12/31/2007
0.52Q	03/06/2008	03/18/2008	03/21/2008	03/31/2008
0.52Q	05/29/2008	06/18/2008	06/20/2008	06/30/2008

Indicated Div: $2.08 (Div. Reinv. Plan)

Valuation Analysis

Forecast EPS	$1.16 (05/16/2008)		
Market Cap	$1.1 Billion	Book Value	397.6 Million
Price/Book	2.86	Price/Sales	7.34

Dividend Achiever Status

10 Year Growth Rate	4.11%
Total Years of Dividend Growth	15

Business Summary: "Property, Real Estate & Development" (MIC: SIC: 6798 NAIC: 525930)

EastGroup Properties is a self-administered equity real estate investment trust focused on the development, acquisition and operation of industrial properties in major Sunbelt markets throughout the U.S. with an emphasis in the states of Florida, Texas, Arizona and California, the majority of which are clustered around major transportation features in supply constrained submarkets. Co. focuses on business distribution space for location sensitive tenants primarily in the 5,000 to 50,000 square foot range. As of Dec 31 2007, Co. owned 202 industrial properties and one office building with an additional 5.73 million square feet under development.

Recent Developments: For the quarter ended Mar 31 2008, income from continuing operations increased 23.6% to US$8.1 million from US$6.5 million in the year-earlier quarter. Net income increased 22.8% to US$8.1 million from US$6.6 million in the year-earlier quarter. Revenues were US$40.4 million, up 12.3% from US$36.0 million the year before. Revenues from property income rose 11.9% to US$40.2 million from US$36.0 million in the corresponding quarter a year earlier.

Prospects: For the full year of 2008, Co. is projecting net income to be in the range of $1.07 to $1.17 per share, while Funds From Operations (FFO) are forecasted to range from $3.26 to $3.36 per share. Co.'s expectations for 2008 are based on several factors such as average occupancy of 93.5% to 95.5%, same property net operating income growth of flat to 2.5%, no sales of land or other nondepreciable real estate as well as no gains on sales of securities and no termination fees, net of bad debt, for the remainder of the year. For the second quarter of 2008, Co. is anticipating net income in the range of $0.25 to $0.27 per share, while FFO are estimated to range from $0.77 to $0.79 per share.

Financial Data
(US$ in Thousands)

	3 Mos	12/31/2007	12/31/2006	12/31/2005	12/31/2004	12/31/2003	12/31/2002	12/31/2001
Earnings Per Share	1.20	1.14	1.17	0.89	0.98	0.70	0.84	1.51
Cash Flow Per Share	3.60	3.67	2.98	3.11	2.76	2.84	3.39	3.23
Tang Book Value Per Share	15.00	15.28	16.07	14.77	14.98	16.05	15.40	16.48
Dividends Per Share	2.020	2.000	1.960	1.940	1.920	1.900	1.880	1.800
Dividend Payout %	168.69	175.44	167.52	217.98	195.92	271.43	223.81	119.21
Income Statement								
Property Income	40,245	150,638	133,144	125,548	114,051	107,771	103,048	100,560
Non-Property Income	195	92	469	957	633	670	2,762	4,735
Total Revenue	40,440	150,730	133,613	126,505	114,684	108,441	105,810	105,295
Depn & Amortn	10,192	42,719	37,913	35,443	30,059	32,397	30,818	27,413
Interest Expense	7,373	27,314	24,616	23,444	20,481	19,015	17,387	17,823
Net Income	8,091	29,734	29,234	22,191	23,327	20,445	23,626	34,182
Average Shares	23,829	23,781	22,692	21,892	21,088	18,194	16,237	16,046
Balance Sheet								
Total Assets	1,115,787	1,055,833	911,787	863,538	768,664	729,267	702,341	683,782
Long-Term Obligations	672,292	465,360	417,440	346,961	303,674	285,722	248,343	205,014
Total Liabilities	715,782	651,136	490,842	496,972	414,974	360,518	344,097	311,333
Stockholders' Equity	397,613	402,385	418,797	364,864	351,806	366,945	356,485	370,710
Shares Outstanding	23,839	23,808	23,701	22,030	21,059	20,853	16,104	15,912
Statistical Record								
Return on Assets %	2.99	3.02	3.29	2.72	3.11	2.86	3.41	5.06
Return on Equity %	7.69	7.24	7.46	6.19	6.47	5.65	6.50	9.16
Net Margin %	20.01	19.73	21.88	17.54	20.34	18.85	22.33	32.46
Price Range	51.60-39.44	57.40-39.44	56.09-43.06	46.60-35.64	38.59-28.01	32.90-23.88	26.35-22.40	23.90-20.19
P/E Ratio	43.00-32.87	50.35-34.60	47.94-36.80	52.36-40.04	39.38-28.58	47.00-34.11	31.37-26.67	15.83-13.37
Average Yield %	4.49	4.20	4.06	4.72	5.70	6.93	7.61	8.10

Address: 300 One Jackson Place, 188 East Capitol Street, Jackson, MS 39201 Telephone: 601-354-3555 Web Site: www.eastgroup.net	Officers: Leland R. Speed - Chairman David H. Hoster - President, Chief Executive Officer **Transfer Agents:**Computershare Trust Company, N.A., Providence, RI	No of Institutions: 180 Shares: 21,001,992 % Held: 84.03

EATON VANCE CORP

Exchange	Symbol	Price	52Wk Range	Yield	P/E
NYS	EV	$42.00 (5/29/2008)	50.03-28.33	1.43	23.86

*7 Year Price Score 127.70 *NYSE Composite Index=100   ***12 Month Price Score 94.50**

Interim Earnings (Per Share)

Qtr.	Jan	Apr	Jul	Oct
2004-05	0.27	0.27	0.29	0.30
2005-06	0.28	0.29	0.31	0.29
2006-07	0.02	0.17	0.41	0.46
2007-08	0.46	0.43	...	...

Interim Dividends (Per Share)

Amt	Decl	Ex	Rec	Pay
0.12Q	07/11/2007	07/27/2007	07/31/2007	08/13/2007
0.15Q	10/24/2007	10/29/2007	10/31/2007	11/12/2007
0.15Q	01/09/2008	01/29/2008	01/31/2008	02/11/2008
0.15Q	04/16/2008	04/28/2008	04/30/2008	05/12/2008

Indicated Div: $0.60

Valuation Analysis

Forecast EPS	$1.85 (05/17/2008)		
Market Cap	$4.8 Billion	Book Value	184.2 Million
Price/Book	26.31	Price/Sales	4.25

Dividend Achiever Status

10 Year Growth Rate	25.53%
Total Years of Dividend Growth	26

Business Summary: Wealth Management (MIC: SIC: 6282 NAIC: 523930)

Eaton Vance is primarily engaged in the business of providing investment advisory and distribution services to mutual funds and other investment funds as well as investment management and counseling services to individual high-net-worth investors, family offices and institutional clients. Co.'s income investment products consists of an expanded duration and credit quality range, including both taxable and tax-free investments. Co.'s equity products provide a spectrum of investment objectives, risk profiles, income levels and geographic representation. As of Oct 31 2007, Co.'s total assets were $966.8 million and assets under management amounted to $161.7 billion.

Recent Developments: For the quarter ended Apr 30 2008, net income increased 130.2% to US$53.2 million from US$23.1 million in the year-earlier quarter. Revenues were US$273.4 million, up 5.1% from US$260.2 million the year before. Operating income was US$96.1 million versus US$36.3 million in the prior-year quarter, an increase of 164.9%. Indirect operating expenses decreased 20.8% to US$177.3 million from US$223.9 million in the equivalent prior-year period.

Prospects: Despite the challenges on revenues due to the softness in market price, Co.'s near-term outlook appears to be favorable. In particular, Co. will remain focused on acquiring additional long-term net-leased office, retail, and industrial properties in the U.S. For instance, on Apr 21 2008, Co.'s real estate investment group announced that it has acquired a Miami, FL office building with a total value of approximately $50.0 million on behalf of an investment fund that it manages. In addition, on Apr 7 2008, Co.'s real estate investment group announced that it has acquired a Santa Clara, CA building with a value of approximately $53.0 million, on behalf of investment funds that it manages.

Financial Data
(US$ in Thousands)

	6 Mos	3 Mos	10/31/2007	10/31/2006	10/31/2005	10/31/2004	10/31/2003	10/31/2002
Earnings Per Share	1.76	1.50	1.06	1.17	1.13	1.00	0.76	0.85
Cash Flow Per Share	2.35	2.63	2.14	2.06	0.82	0.87	0.32	0.97
Tang Book Value Per Share	0.40	0.04	0.76	2.89	2.51	2.37	2.06	1.92
Dividends Per Share	0.570	0.510	0.480	0.400	0.340	0.275	0.200	0.149
Dividend Payout %	32.47	34.00	45.28	34.19	30.09	27.64	26.49	17.50
Income Statement								
Total Revenue	563,222	289,796	1,084,100	862,194	753,175	661,813	523,133	522,985
Income Before Taxes	185,384	94,645	238,349	263,002	261,190	221,658	164,858	186,241
Income Taxes	70,932	37,023	93,200	102,245	97,500	79,797	57,700	65,184
Net Income	111,090	57,928	142,811	159,377	159,884	138,943	106,123	121,057
Average Shares	123,271	127,132	135,252	137,004	141,632	139,578	140,750	142,824
Balance Sheet								
Total Assets	845,390	831,390	966,831	668,195	702,544	743,566	658,702	616,619
Total Liabilities	651,996	680,636	729,439	162,165	242,971	226,190	234,734	242,919
Stockholders' Equity	184,237	142,860	229,168	496,485	454,953	449,506	416,277	372,302
Shares Outstanding	115,407	115,648	118,169	126,435	129,552	133,581	136,810	138,514
Statistical Record								
Return on Assets %	31.04	27.61	17.47	23.25	22.11	19.76	16.64	18.74
Return on Equity %	69.47	63.05	39.36	33.50	35.35	32.01	26.91	35.95
Price Range	50.03-28.33	50.03-32.93	50.03-29.87	31.10-24.14	27.30-21.80	21.81-16.46	17.80-11.70	20.36-11.98
P/E Ratio	28.43-16.10	33.35-21.95	47.20-28.18	26.58-20.63	24.16-19.29	21.81-16.46	23.42-15.39	23.95-14.09
Average Yield %	1.43	1.23	1.20	1.47	1.38	1.45	1.30	0.90

Address: The Eaton Vance Building, 255 State Street, Boston, MA 02109 **Telephone:** 617-482-8260 **Web Site:** www.eatonvance.com	**Officers:** Thomas E. Faust - Chairman, President, Chief Executive Officer, Chief Investment Officer Duncan W. Richardson - Executive Vice President, Chief Equity Investment Officer **Transfer Agents:** Computershare Trust Company, Providence, RI	**Investor Contact:** 617-482-8260 **No of Institutions:** 346 **Shares:** 92,400,928 **% Held:** 69.60

ECOLAB, INC.

Exchange	Symbol	Price	52Wk Range	Yield	P/E
NYS	ECL	$44.65 (5/29/2008)	52.30-40.16	1.16	25.37

*7 Year Price Score 109.01 *NYSE Composite Index=100 *12 Month Price Score 102.34

Interim Earnings (Per Share)

Qtr.	Mar	Jun	Sep	Dec
2005	0.29	0.33	0.40	0.21
2006	0.30	0.36	0.43	0.34
2007	0.35	0.44	0.46	0.45
2008	0.41	...	...	...

Interim Dividends (Per Share)

Amt	Decl	Ex	Rec	Pay
0.115Q	08/03/2007	09/14/2007	09/18/2007	10/15/2007
0.13Q	12/06/2007	12/14/2007	12/18/2007	01/15/2008
0.13Q	02/22/2008	03/07/2008	03/11/2008	04/15/2008
0.13Q	05/02/2008	06/13/2008	06/17/2008	07/15/2008

Indicated Div: $0.52 (Div. Reinv. Plan)

Valuation Analysis

Forecast EPS $1.88 (05/16/2008)

Market Cap	$11.0 Billion	Book Value	2.1 Billion
Price/Book	5.36	Price/Sales	1.95

Dividend Achiever Status

10 Year Growth Rate	11.14%
Total Years of Dividend Growth	15

Business Summary: Chemicals (MIC: SIC: 2842 NAIC: 325612)

Ecolab is engaged in developing and marketing products and services for the hospitality, foodservice, healthcare and industrial markets. Co. provides cleaning and sanitizing products and programs, as well as pest elimination, maintenance and repair services primarily to hotels and restaurants, healthcare and educational facilities, quick-service (fast-food and other convenience store) units, grocery stores, commercial and institutional laundries, light industry, dairy plants and farms, food and beverage processors and the vehicle wash industry. Co. has three segments: U.S. Cleaning & Sanitizing, U.S. Other Services and International.

Recent Developments: For the quarter ended Mar 31 2008, net income increased 15.0% to US$102.9 million from US$89.5 million in the year-earlier quarter. Revenues were US$1.46 billion, up 16.2% from US$1.25 billion the year before. Operating income was US$160.5 million versus US$148.4 million in the prior-year quarter, an increase of 8.2%. Direct operating expenses rose 19.9% to US$738.3 million from US$615.7 million in the comparable period the year before. Indirect operating expenses increased 14.1% to US$559.1 million from US$490.1 million in the equivalent prior-year period.

Prospects: Co. is optimistic with its near-term outlook, as it expects continued good sales momentum in the second quarter of 2008, and solid earnings growth more than offsetting the effects of acquisition dilution. Notably, Co. projects sales for domestic and international operations (in fixed currencies) to increase year-over-year in the quarter, with gross margins in a range of 49.0% to 50.0%. Furthermore, Co. expects earnings in the second half of 2008 to show favorable comparisons as expected top line growth and operating income gains from its ongoing businesses, contributions from acquisitions, and benefits from expected permanent tax rate improvement, should result in improved earnings growth.

Financial Data

(US$ in Thousands)	3 Mos	12/31/2007	12/31/2006	12/31/2005	12/31/2004	12/31/2003	12/31/2002	12/31/2001
Earnings Per Share	1.76	1.70	1.43	1.23	1.19	1.06	0.80	0.72
Cash Flow Per Share	3.43	3.23	2.49	2.31	2.26	2.04	1.64	1.43
Tang Book Value Per Share	1.02	1.33	1.67	2.00	1.33	1.14	0.83	0.41
Dividends Per Share	0.490	0.475	0.415	0.362	0.328	0.297	0.275	0.263
Dividend Payout %	27.92	27.94	29.02	29.47	27.52	28.07	34.38	36.21
Income Statement								
Total Revenue	1,457,900	5,469,600	4,895,814	4,534,832	4,184,933	3,761,819	3,403,585	2,354,723
EBITDA	245,400	958,400	872,442	788,632	769,345	716,475	607,606	481,169
Depn & Amortn	84,900	291,100	260,800	246,212	235,223	222,712	211,740	162,990
Income Before Taxes	145,700	616,300	567,224	498,182	488,778	448,418	351,971	289,745
Income Taxes	42,800	189,100	198,609	178,701	178,290	171,070	140,081	117,408
Net Income	102,900	427,200	368,615	319,481	310,488	277,348	209,770	188,170
Average Shares	251,500	251,800	257,144	260,098	261,776	262,737	261,574	259,856
Balance Sheet								
Current Assets	1,891,000	1,717,300	1,853,557	1,421,666	1,279,066	1,150,340	1,015,937	929,583
Total Assets	5,234,300	4,722,800	4,419,365	3,796,628	3,716,174	3,228,918	2,878,429	2,525,000
Current Liabilities	1,604,200	1,518,300	1,502,730	1,119,357	939,547	851,942	866,350	827,952
Long-Term Obligations	864,900	599,900	557,058	519,374	645,445	604,441	539,743	512,280
Total Liabilities	3,174,900	2,787,100	2,739,135	2,147,418	2,153,655	1,933,492	1,778,678	1,644,648
Stockholders' Equity	2,059,400	1,935,700	1,680,230	1,649,210	1,562,519	1,295,426	1,099,751	880,352
Shares Outstanding	247,100	246,825	251,336	254,143	257,541	257,416	259,880	255,800
Statistical Record								
Return on Assets %	9.52	9.35	8.97	8.50	8.92	9.08	7.76	8.88
Return on Equity %	24.01	23.63	22.14	19.89	21.67	23.16	21.19	22.98
EBITDA Margin %	16.83	17.52	17.82	17.39	18.38	19.05	17.85	20.43
Net Margin %	7.06	7.81	7.53	7.05	7.42	7.37	6.16	7.99
Asset Turnover	1.23	1.20	1.19	1.21	1.20	1.23	1.26	1.11
Current Ratio	1.18	1.13	1.23	1.27	1.36	1.35	1.17	1.12
Debt to Equity	0.42	0.31	0.33	0.31	0.41	0.47	0.49	0.58
Price Range	52.30-40.16	52.30-40.16	46.19-33.85	36.76-31.06	35.26-26.22	27.91-23.36	25.07-18.36	21.97-15.48
P/E Ratio	29.72-22.82	30.76-23.62	32.30-23.67	29.89-25.25	29.63-22.03	26.33-22.04	31.34-22.96	30.51-21.51
Average Yield %	1.08	1.07	1.02	1.10	1.08	1.16	1.22	1.33

Address: 370 Wabasha Street North, St. Paul, MN 55102 Telephone: 651-293-2233 Web Site: www.ecolab.com	Officers: Douglas M. Baker - Chairman, President, Chief Executive Officer Steven L. Fritze - Executive Vice President, Chief Financial Officer **Transfer Agents:** Computershare Investor Services, Canton, MA	Investor Contact: 612-293-2809 No of Institutions: 552 Shares: 148,630,448 % Held: 54.51

EMERSON ELECTRIC CO.

Exchange	Symbol	Price	52Wk Range	Yield	P/E
NYS	EMR	$57.52 (5/29/2008)	58.32-45.42	2.09	19.90

*7 Year Price Score 113.65 *NYSE Composite Index=100 ***12 Month Price Score 106.72**

Interim Earnings (Per Share)

Qtr.	Dec	Mar	Jun	Sep
2004-05	0.35	0.41	0.43	0.51
2005-06	0.48	0.53	0.59	0.65
2006-07	0.55	0.61	0.72	0.78
2007-08	0.71	0.69	...	...

Interim Dividends (Per Share)

Amt	Decl	Ex	Rec	Pay
0.263Q	08/07/2007	08/15/2007	08/17/2007	09/10/2007
0.30Q	11/06/2007	11/14/2007	11/16/2007	12/10/2007
0.30Q	02/05/2008	02/13/2008	02/15/2008	03/10/2008
0.30Q	05/06/2008	05/14/2008	05/16/2008	06/10/2008

Indicated Div: $1.20 (Div. Reinv. Plan)

Valuation Analysis

Forecast EPS $3.07 (05/17/2008)
Market Cap $45.0 Billion Book Value 9.5 Billion
Price/Book 4.75 Price/Sales 1.91

Dividend Achiever Status

10 Year Growth Rate 7.01%
Total Years of Dividend Growth 51

Business Summary: Electrical (MIC: SIC: 3823 NAIC: 335312)

Emerson Electric is engaged in the design and supply of product technology and delivery of engineering services in industrial, commercial and consumer markets globally. As of Sep 30 2007, Co. had approximately 265 manufacturing locations worldwide, of which approximately 165 were located outside the U.S., primarily in Europe and to a lesser extent in Asia, Canada and Latin America. Co. is organized into five business segments, based on the nature of the products and services rendered, namely Process Management, Industrial Automation, Network Power, Climate Technologies, and Appliance and Tools.

Recent Developments: For the quarter ended Mar 31 2008, income from continuing operations increased 21.3% to US$598.0 million from US$493.0 million in the year-earlier quarter. Net income increased 10.7% to US$547.0 million from US$494.0 million in the year-earlier quarter. Revenues were US$6.02 billion, up 11.7% from US$5.39 billion the year before. Direct operating expenses rose 9.4% to US$3.78 billion from US$3.46 billion in the comparable period the year before. Indirect operating expenses increased 12.9% to US$1.25 billion from US$1.11 billion in the equivalent prior-year period.

Prospects: Co. has raised its outlook for earnings per share from continuing operations to $3.00 to $3.10 for the fiscal year ending Sep. 2008 as a result of the solid first half results of the fiscal year. Co. also expects its fiscal 2008 underlying sales growth of 5% to 7% and reported sales of $25.00 billion, excluding discontinued operations. Meanwhile, Co. estimates its rationalization expense for the fiscal year to total $85.0 million to $95.0 million. Going forward, in connection with a longer term strategy to divest selective slower-growth businesses, Co. is pursuing the sale of its European appliance motor and pump business and plans to complete the sale over the next term near.

Financial Data
(US$ in Thousands)

	6 Mos	3 Mos	09/30/2007	09/30/2006	09/30/2005	09/30/2004	09/30/2003	09/30/2002
Earnings Per Share	2.89	2.82	2.66	2.24	1.70	1.49	1.29	0.14
Cash Flow Per Share	4.22	3.96	3.80	3.08	2.64	2.64	2.07	2.17
Tang Book Value Per Share	2.55	2.24	2.99	2.66	2.34	2.36	1.80	0.99
Dividends Per Share	1.125	1.087	1.050	0.890	0.830	0.800	0.785	0.775
Dividend Payout %	38.90	38.56	39.47	39.73	48.82	53.69	60.62	534.48
Income Statement								
Total Revenue	11,543,000	5,637,000	22,572,000	20,133,000	17,305,000	15,615,000	13,958,000	13,824,000
EBITDA	2,096,000	998,000	3,923,000	3,438,000	2,858,000	2,561,000	2,179,000	2,339,000
Depn & Amortn	350,000	171,000	588,000	547,000	500,000	499,000	534,000	541,000
Income Before Taxes	1,645,000	778,000	3,107,000	2,684,000	2,149,000	1,852,000	1,414,000	1,565,000
Income Taxes	528,000	256,000	971,000	839,000	727,000	595,000	401,000	505,000
Net Income	1,112,000	565,000	2,136,000	1,845,000	1,422,000	1,257,000	1,089,000	122,000
Average Shares	792,000	796,500	803,900	824,400	837,800	844,400	841,800	841,800
Balance Sheet								
Current Assets	9,438,000	8,994,000	8,065,000	7,330,000	6,837,000	6,416,000	5,500,000	4,961,000
Total Assets	21,450,000	20,854,000	19,680,000	18,672,000	17,227,000	16,361,000	15,194,000	14,545,000
Current Liabilities	6,588,000	6,408,000	5,546,000	5,374,000	4,931,000	4,339,000	3,417,000	4,400,000
Long-Term Obligations	3,338,000	3,197,000	3,372,000	3,128,000	3,128,000	3,136,000	3,733,000	2,990,000
Total Liabilities	11,970,000	11,680,000	10,908,000	10,518,000	9,827,000	9,123,000	8,734,000	8,804,000
Stockholders' Equity	9,480,000	9,174,000	8,772,000	8,154,000	7,400,000	7,238,000	6,460,000	5,741,000
Shares Outstanding	782,377	787,639	788,434	804,693	821,303	838,857	842,308	841,419
Statistical Record								
Return on Assets %	11.24	11.29	11.14	10.28	8.47	7.95	7.32	0.82
Return on Equity %	25.84	25.96	25.24	23.72	19.43	18.30	17.85	2.06
EBITDA Margin %	18.16	17.70	17.38	17.08	16.52	16.40	15.61	16.92
Net Margin %	9.63	10.02	9.46	9.16	8.22	8.05	7.80	0.88
Asset Turnover	1.15	1.16	1.18	1.12	1.03	0.99	0.94	0.93
Current Ratio	1.43	1.40	1.45	1.36	1.39	1.48	1.61	1.13
Debt to Equity	0.35	0.35	0.38	0.38	0.42	0.43	0.58	0.52
Price Range	58.32-41.85	58.32-41.85	53.37-41.10	43.73-33.97	35.94-30.68	34.23-26.32	28.40-21.21	32.76-21.60
P/E Ratio	20.18-14.48	20.68-14.84	20.06-15.45	19.52-15.16	21.14-18.04	22.97-17.67	22.01-16.44	233.96-154.29
Average Yield %	2.24	2.25	2.31	2.24	2.50	2.62	3.11	2.88

Address: 8000 W. Florissant Avenue, St. Louis, MO 63136	**Officers:** David N. Farr - Chairman, President, Chief Executive Officer Walter J. Galvin - Senior Executive Vice President, Chief Financial Officer **Transfer Agents:** Mellon Investor Services LLC, Pittsburgh, PA	**Investor Contact:** 314-553-2197
Telephone: 314-553-2000		**No of Institutions:** 1186
Web Site: www.emerson.com		**Shares:** 658,951,488 **% Held:** 73.61

ENERGEN CORP.

Exchange	Symbol	Price	52Wk Range	Yield	P/E
NYS	EGN	$74.10 (5/29/2008)	75.95-49.10	0.65	16.65

*7 Year Price Score 152.73 *NYSE Composite Index=100 *12 Month Price Score 116.23

TRADING VOLUME (thousand shares)

Interim Earnings (Per Share)

Qtr.	Mar	Jun	Sep	Dec
2005	0.80	0.51	0.26	0.78
2006	1.18	0.67	0.56	1.31
2007	1.44	0.94	0.80	1.10
2008	1.62	...	...	...

Interim Dividends (Per Share)

Amt	Decl	Ex	Rec	Pay
0.115Q	07/25/2007	08/13/2007	08/15/2007	09/04/2007
0.115Q	10/24/2007	11/13/2007	11/15/2007	12/03/2007
0.12Q	01/23/2008	02/13/2008	02/15/2008	03/03/2008
0.12Q	04/23/2008	05/13/2008	05/15/2008	06/02/2008

Indicated Div: $0.48 (Div. Reinv. Plan)

Valuation Analysis

Forecast EPS $4.45 (05/17/2008)

Market Cap	$5.3 Billion	Book Value	1.4 Billion
Price/Book	3.83	Price/Sales	3.63

Dividend Achiever Status

10 Year Growth Rate	4.19%
Total Years of Dividend Growth	25

Business Summary: Gas Utilities (MIC: SIC: 4924 NAIC: 221210)

Energen is an energy holding company engaged mainly in the development, acquisition, exploration and production of oil and gas in the continental U.S. (oil and gas operations) and in the purchase, distribution, and sale of natural gas principally in central and north Alabama (natural gas distribution). Co.'s two principal subsidiaries are Energen Resources Corporation (Energen Resources) and Alabama Gas Corporation (Alagasco). As of Dec 31 2007, Energen Resources' proved oil and gas reserves totaled 1,754 billion cubic feet equivalent. Also, as of Dec 31 2007, Alagasco's service territory is located in central and parts of north Alabama and included 177 cities and communities in 28 counties.

Recent Developments: For the quarter ended Mar 31 2008, income from continuing operations increased 12.3% to US$116.7 million from US$103.9 million in the year-earlier quarter. Net income increased 12.3% to US$116.7 million from US$103.9 million in the year-earlier quarter. Revenues were US$521.6 million, up 5.9% from US$492.7 million the year before. Operating income was US$195.3 million versus US$173.2 million in the prior-year quarter, an increase of 12.8%. Direct operating expenses declined 0.9% to US$247.9 million from US$250.2 million in the comparable period the year before. Indirect operating expenses increased 13.1% to US$78.4 million from US$69.3 million in the equivalent prior-year period.

Prospects: Co.'s bottom-line results are benefiting from higher oil and gas revenues due to increased commodity prices as well as the effect of higher production volumes. Meanwhile, for full-year 2008, Co. is projecting its oil and gas capital spending to total about $330.0 million, including $305.0 million for existing properties. For full-year 2009, Co. expects capital spending to total about $271.0 million, including approximately $260.0 million for existing properties. Separately, Co. is raising its 2008 earnings guidance range by $0.20 to $4.15 to $4.55 per diluted share. Also, Co. is increasing its 2009 earnings guidance range by $0.20 to a new range of $4.65 to $5.05 per diluted share.

Financial Data

(US$ in Thousands)	3 Mos	12/31/2007	12/31/2006	12/31/2005	12/31/2004	12/31/2003	12/31/2002	12/31/2001
Earnings Per Share	4.45	4.28	3.73	2.35	1.75	1.55	1.01	0.06
Cash Flow Per Share	6.35	6.76	6.66	4.59	4.00	3.43	3.18	0.27
Tang Book Value Per Share	19.33	19.47	17.06	12.15	10.98	9.65	8.39	7.59
Dividends Per Share	0.464	0.460	0.440	0.400	0.378	0.365	0.355	0.087
Dividend Payout %	10.42	10.75	11.80	17.02	21.63	23.55	34.98	145.83
Income Statement								
Total Revenue	521,646	1,435,060	1,393,986	1,128,394	937,384	842,221	677,175	146,164
EBITDA	237,403	685,118	619,291	448,896	366,766	334,440	245,575	36,013
Depn & Amortn	42,416	161,377	142,086	131,719	120,960	117,785	110,767	25,184
Income Before Taxes	183,865	476,641	428,553	.270,377	203,063	174,393	91,095	195
Income Taxes	67,177	167,429	155,030	97,491	75,613	64,128	20,509	(3,384)
Net Income	116,688	309,233	273,570	173,012	127,463	110,654	68,639	3,658
Average Shares	72,125	72,180	73,278	73,714	73,117	71,433	67,676	62,554
Balance Sheet								
Net PPE	2,579,651	2,538,243	2,252,414	2,068,011	1,783,059	1,433,451	1,256,803	1,005,679
Total Assets	3,139,291	3,079,653	2,836,887	2,618,226	2,181,739	1,781,432	1,530,891	1,240,356
Long-Term Obligations	562,108	562,365	582,490	683,236	612,891	552,842	512,954	544,133
Total Liabilities	1,756,834	1,700,995	1,634,818	1,725,548	1,378,073	1,082,400	948,081	766,151
Stockholders' Equity	1,382,457	1,378,658	1,202,069	892,678	803,666	699,032	582,810	474,205
Shares Outstanding	71,504	70,816	70,445	73,493	73,165	72,447	69,490	62,497
Statistical Record								
Return on Assets %	10.84	10.45	10.03	7.21	6.41	6.68	4.95	0.24
Return on Equity %	24.43	23.96	26.12	20.40	16.92	17.26	12.99	0.67
EBITDA Margin %	45.51	47.74	44.43	39.78	39.13	39.71	36.26	24.64
Net Margin %	22.37	21.55	19.63	15.33	13.60	13.14	10.14	2.50
PPE Turnover	0.60	0.60	0.65	0.59	0.58	0.63	0.60	0.12
Asset Turnover	0.49	0.49	0.51	0.47	0.47	0.51	0.49	0.10
Debt to Equity	0.41	0.41	0.48	0.77	0.76	0.79	0.88	1.15
Price Range	69.18-49.10	69.18-43.99	47.38-32.77	43.40-27.14	29.90-20.00	20.98-14.12	14.90-10.93	19.86-11.00
P/E Ratio	15.55-11.03	16.16-10.28	12.70-8.79	18.47-11.55	17.09-11.43	13.54-9.11	14.75-10.82	330.92-183.33
Average Yield %	0.20	0.83	1.12	1.16	1.60	2.14	2.76	0.61

Address: 605 Richard Arrington Jr. Blvd. N., Birmingham, AL 35203-2707	Officers: James T. McManus - Chairman, President, Chief Executive Officer, Chief Operating Officer	Investor Contact: 205-326-8421
Telephone: 205-326-2700	Charles W. Porter - Vice President, Chief Financial	No of Institutions: 373
Web Site: www.energen.com	Officer, Treasurer Transfer Agents: BNY Mellon Shareowner Services, New York, NY	Shares: 58,331,024 % Held: 74.72

ENERGY EAST CORP.

Exchange	Symbol	Price	52Wk Range	Yield	P/E
NYS	EAS	$25.01 (5/29/2008)	27.90-22.37	4.96	15.93

*7 Year Price Score 85.49 ***NYSE Composite Index=100** ***12 Month Price Score 94.94**

TRADING VOLUME (thousand shares)

Interim Earnings (Per Share)

Qtr.	Mar	Jun	Sep	Dec
2005	1.05	0.12	0.14	0.43
2006	0.90	0.19	0.14	0.52
2007	0.90	0.12	0.16	0.46
2008	0.83	...	...	...

Interim Dividends (Per Share)

Amt	Decl	Ex	Rec	Pay
0.30Q	07/12/2007	07/19/2007	07/23/2007	08/15/2007
0.31Q	10/11/2007	10/18/2007	10/22/2007	11/15/2007
0.31Q	01/08/2008	01/16/2008	01/21/2008	02/15/2008
0.31Q	04/17/2008	04/24/2008	04/28/2008	05/15/2008

Indicated Div: $1.24

Valuation Analysis

Forecast EPS $1.53 (05/16/2008)

Market Cap	$4.0 Billion	Book Value	3.3 Billion
Price/Book	1.20	Price/Sales	0.77

Dividend Achiever Status

10 Year Growth Rate	5.63%
Total Years of Dividend Growth	10

Business Summary: Electricity (MIC: SIC: 4911 NAIC: 221121)

Energy East is a public utility holding company. Co.'s business consists of regulated electricity transmission and distribution operations in upstate New York and Maine and its regulated natural gas transportation, storage and distribution operations in upstate New York, Connecticut, Maine and Massachusetts. Additionally, Co.'s other businesses include retail energy marketing companies, a non-utility generating company, a Federal Energy Regulatory Commission-regulated liquefied natural gas peaking plant, a natural gas delivery company, a propane air delivery company, telecommunications assets, a district heating and cooling system, and an energy consulting services company.

Recent Developments: For the quarter ended Mar 31 2008, net income decreased 1.0% to US$132.0 million from US$133.3 million in the year-earlier quarter. Revenues were US$1.67 billion, down 2.7% from US$1.71 billion the year before. Operating income was US$268.5 million versus US$279.7 million in the prior-year quarter, a decrease of 4.0%. Direct operating expenses declined 3.0% to US$1.25 billion from US$1.29 billion in the comparable period the year before. Indirect operating expenses increased 1.5% to US$146.7 million from US$144.5 million in the equivalent prior-year period.

Prospects: Co. remains focused on maintaining its energy delivery and services strategy by addressing several initiatives such as investing in transmission and improving its distribution infrastructure capability. Notably, Co. is investing $660.0 million in 2008, principally for the installation of an advanced metering infrastructure in New York and Maine, the transmission mainly in Maine, and a transformer replacement program. Meanwhile, the Connecticut Department of Public Utility Control has recently approved financing commitment for the Milford, CT DFC-ERG® installation project, under which Co. will provide 80.0% of the construction phase financing and will acquire 80.0% of the completed project.

Financial Data

(US$ in Thousands)	3 Mos	12/31/2007	12/31/2006	12/31/2005	12/31/2004	12/31/2003	12/31/2002	12/31/2001
Earnings Per Share	1.57	1.61	1.76	1.74	1.56	1.44	1.44	1.61
Cash Flow Per Share	3.35	3.30	2.58	3.40	2.31	3.31	3.13	1.16
Tang Book Value Per Share	11.20	10.62	9.05	9.12	7.52	7.11	6.53	7.57
Dividends Per Share	1.220	1.210	1.170	1.115	1.055	1.000	0.960	0.920
Dividend Payout %	77.77	75.16	66.48	64.08	67.63	69.44	66.67	57.14
Income Statement								
Total Revenue	1,666,650	5,178,108	5,230,665	5,298,543	4,756,692	4,593,819	4,008,918	3,759,787
EBITDA	358,730	1,028,144	1,142,063	1,098,600	1,132,183	1,032,584	800,656	763,295
Depn & Amortn	84,608	386,850	418,152	382,873	377,181	419,237	255,782	204,281
Income Before Taxes	205,386	365,356	415,087	426,830	489,065	335,074	287,127	341,986
Income Taxes	73,431	114,058	155,255	169,997	251,444	127,687	98,524	154,379
Net Income	131,955	251,298	259,832	256,833	229,337	210,446	188,603	187,607
Average Shares	158,251	155,805	147,717	147,474	146,713	145,730	131,117	116,708
Balance Sheet								
Net PPE	6,197,646	6,158,494	5,948,023	5,783,454	5,662,168	5,778,109	4,801,839	3,626,432
Total Assets	11,894,040	11,878,709	11,562,401	11,487,708	10,796,113	11,306,432	10,269,879	7,269,232
Long-Term Obligations	3,877,536	3,877,029	3,726,709	3,667,065	3,797,685	3,994,096	3,351,959	2,471,278
Total Liabilities	8,570,734	8,647,029	8,673,462	8,590,403	8,118,184	8,643,013	7,348,305	5,099,682
Stockholders' Equity	3,298,719	3,207,093	2,864,347	2,872,674	2,631,258	2,572,324	2,460,612	1,781,177
Shares Outstanding	158,299	158,279	147,907	147,701	147,118	146,262	144,392	116,718
Statistical Record								
Return on Assets %	2.12	2.14	2.25	2.31	2.07	1.95	2.15	2.63
Return on Equity %	7.69	8.28	9.06	9.33	8.79	8.36	8.89	10.73
EBITDA Margin %	21.52	19.86	21.83	20.73	23.80	22.48	19.97	20.30
Net Margin %	7.92	4.85	4.97	4.85	4.82	4.58	4.70	4.99
PPE Turnover	0.84	0.86	0.89	0.93	0.83	0.87	0.95	1.04
Asset Turnover	0.43	0.44	0.45	0.48	0.43	0.43	0.46	0.53
Debt to Equity	1.18	1.21	1.30	1.28	1.44	1.55	1.36	1.39
Price Range	27.90-22.37	27.90-22.37	25.47-22.55	30.06-22.79	27.01-22.15	23.71-17.46	23.10-17.25	21.99-17.23
P/E Ratio	17.77-14.25	17.33-13.89	14.47-12.81	17.28-13.10	17.31-14.20	16.47-12.13	16.04-11.98	13.66-10.70
Average Yield %	4.70	4.72	4.82	4.29	4.33	4.79	4.58	4.68

Address: 52 Farm View Drive, New Gloucester, ME 04260-5116	**Officers:** Wesley W. von Schack - Chairman, President, Chief Executive Officer Robert E. Rude -	**No of Institutions:** 314
Telephone: 800-542-7480	Senior Vice President, Chief Regulatory Officer	**Shares:** 94,320,048 **% Held:** 53.75
Web Site: www.energyeast.com	**Transfer Agents:** Mellon Investor Services LLC	

ERIE INDEMNITY CO.

Exchange	Symbol	Price	52Wk Range	Yield	P/E
NMS	ERIE	$50.83 (5/29/2008)	61.31-48.13	3.46	16.72

*7 Year Price Score 88.26   ***NYSE Composite Index=100**   ***12 Month Price Score 101.30**

TRADING VOLUME (thousand shares)

Interim Earnings (Per Share)

Qtr.	Mar	Jun	Sep	Dec
2005	0.83	1.10	0.76	0.65
2006	0.73	0.86	0.82	0.90
2007	0.88	1.11	0.87	0.56
2008	0.51	...	...	...

Interim Dividends (Per Share)

Amt	Decl	Ex	Rec	Pay
0.40Q	08/01/2007	10/02/2007	10/04/2007	10/19/2007
0.44Q	12/12/2007	01/02/2008	01/04/2008	01/18/2008
0.44Q	02/21/2008	04/02/2008	04/04/2008	04/18/2008
0.44Q	04/21/2008	07/01/2008	07/03/2008	07/18/2008

Indicated Div: $1.76

Valuation Analysis

Forecast EPS $3.18 (05/16/2008)

Market Cap	$2.7 Billion	Book Value	996.0 Million
Price/Book	2.66	Price/Sales	2.42

Dividend Achiever Status

10 Year Growth Rate	15.46%
Total Years of Dividend Growth	12

Business Summary: Insurance (MIC: SIC: 6411 NAIC: 524126)

Erie Indemnity operates primarily as the management services company that provides sales, underwriting and policy issuance services to the policyholders of Erie Insurance Exchange (Exchange). In addition, Co. operates as a property or casualty insurer through its wholly-owned subsidiaries, Erie Insurance Company, Erie Insurance Property and Casualty Company, and Erie Insurance Company of New York. The Exchange and its property/casualty subsidiary, Flagship City Insurance Company, and Co.'s three property/casualty subsidiaries write personal and commercial lines property and casualty coverages and pool their underwriting results.

Recent Developments: For the quarter ended Mar 31 2008, net income decreased 46.8% to US$30.0 million from US$56.4 million in the year-earlier quarter. Revenues were US$271.4 million, down 10.7% from US$303.8 million the year before. Net premiums earned were US$51.9 million versus US$52.0 million in the prior-year quarter, a decrease of 0.1%.

Prospects: For 2008, Co. continues to expect its rate actions that include pricing actions, which has been approved, filed for filing in 2008 to result in a net reduction to direct written premiums of $23.2 million, of which approximately $9.0 million occurred in 2008 first quarter. Further, Co. continues to project rate increases of about 2.0% to 3.0% overall that will affect its 2009 pricing. However, Co. is continuing to grow its Property and Casualty Group premiums, and believes that expanding the size of its agency force will contribute to future growth as new agents build up their book of business with the Property and Casualty Group. Thus, Co. plans to add 140 new agency appointments in 2008.

Financial Data
(US$ in Thousands)

	3 Mos	12/31/2007	12/31/2006	12/31/2005	12/31/2004	12/31/2003	12/31/2002	12/31/2001
Earnings Per Share	3.04	3.43	3.31	3.34	3.21	2.81	2.42	1.71
Cash Flow Per Share	4.21	4.44	4.60	4.83	3.46	3.17	2.64	2.08
Tang Book Value Per Share	19.10	19.71	20.11	20.90	20.11	18.16	15.42	13.55
Dividends Per Share	1.640	1.600	1.440	1.300	0.645	0.975	0.680	0.610
Dividend Payout %	53.99	46.65	43.50	38.92	20.09	34.70	28.10	35.67
Income Statement								
Premium Income	51,926	207,562	213,665	215,824	208,202	191,592	163,958	137,648
Total Revenue	271,359	1,132,291	1,133,982	1,124,950	1,123,144	1,048,788	963,387	799,861
Benefits & Claims	33,760	125,903	139,630	140,385	153,220	152,984	139,225	117,201
Income Before Taxes	44,481	309,168	298,799	339,456	326,347	295,053	255,401	182,876
Income Taxes	14,251	99,137	99,055	111,733	105,140	102,237	84,886	60,615
Net Income	29,977	212,945	204,025	231,104	226,413	199,725	172,126	122,261
Average Shares	58,967	62,096	65,256	69,293	70,492	70,997	71,081	71,342
Balance Sheet								
Total Assets	2,850,956	2,878,623	3,039,361	3,101,261	2,979,744	2,754,607	2,357,676	1,935,566
Total Liabilities	1,854,996	1,827,344	1,877,513	1,822,659	1,712,863	1,590,437	1,370,304	1,070,311
Stockholders' Equity	995,960	1,051,279	1,161,848	1,278,602	1,266,881	1,164,170	987,372	865,255
Shares Outstanding	52,136	53,341	57,778	61,165	62,995	64,092	64,037	63,836
Statistical Record								
Return on Assets %	6.37	7.20	6.65	7.60	7.88	7.81	8.02	6.76
Return on Equity %	17.07	19.24	16.72	18.16	18.58	18.57	18.58	14.87
Loss Ratio %	65.02	60.66	65.35	65.05	73.59	79.85	84.92	85.15
Net Margin %	11.05	18.81	17.99	20.54	20.16	19.04	17.87	15.29
Price Range	61.31-48.13	61.31-50.94	58.19-48.58	54.83-50.15	53.00-41.75	43.24-34.10	45.49-35.90	40.63-26.50
P/E Ratio	20.17-15.83	17.87-14.85	17.58-14.68	16.42-15.01	16.51-13.01	15.39-12.14	18.80-14.83	23.76-15.50
Average Yield %	3.04	2.91	2.76	2.47	1.35	2.49	1.67	1.82

Address: 100 Erie Insurance Place, Erie, PA 16530 Telephone: 814-870-2000 Web Site: www.erieinsurance.com	Officers: John J. Brinling - President, Chief Executive Officer Philip A. Garcia - Executive Vice President, Chief Financial Officer **Transfer Agents:** American Stock Transfer & Trust Company, New York, NY	No of Institutions: 142 Shares: 22,849,528 % Held: 40.20

ESSEX PROPERTY TRUST, INC.

Exchange	Symbol	Price	52Wk Range	Yield	P/E
NYS	ESS	$120.10 (5/29/2008)	127.23-87.58	3.40	34.91

*7 Year Price Score 105.71 *NYSE Composite Index=100 *12 Month Price Score 107.90

TRADING VOLUME (thousand shares)

Interim Earnings (Per Share)

Qtr.	Mar	Jun	Sep	Dec
2005	1.13	1.64	0.35	0.19
2006	0.43	0.95	0.45	0.63
2007	1.46	0.39	0.39	2.03
2008	0.63	...	...	...

Interim Dividends (Per Share)

Amt	Decl	Ex	Rec	Pay
0.93Q	06/07/2007	06/27/2007	06/29/2007	07/16/2007
0.93Q	09/18/2007	09/26/2007	09/28/2007	10/15/2007
0.93Q	12/07/2007	12/26/2007	12/28/2007	01/15/2008
1.02Q	02/27/2008	03/27/2008	03/31/2008	04/15/2008
		Indicated Div: $4.08		

Valuation Analysis

Forecast EPS	$2.10 (05/16/2008)		
Market Cap	$3.0 Billion	Book Value	758.0 Million
Price/Book	3.92	Price/Sales	7.49

Dividend Achiever Status

10 Year Growth Rate	7.54%
Total Years of Dividend Growth	13

Business Summary: "Property, Real Estate & Development" (MIC: SIC: 6798 NAIC: 525930)

Essex Property Trust operates as a self-administered and self-managed real estate investment trust. Co. is engaged primarily in the ownership, operation, management, acquisition, development and redevelopment of real estate. The majority of Co.'s real estate consists of apartment communities. As of Dec 31 2007, Co. owned or held an interest in 134 apartment communities, aggregating 27,489 units, located predominantly along the West Coast. Co.'s other properties included two recreational vehicle parks totaling 338 spaces, six office buildings that Co. primarily occupies and uses as office space, and one manufactured housing community containing 157 pads.

Recent Developments: For the quarter ended Mar 31 2008, income from continuing operations increased 30.8% to US$18.0 million from US$13.8 million in the year-earlier quarter. Net income decreased 52.0% to US$18.0 million from US$37.5 million in the year-earlier quarter. Revenues were US$102.7 million, up 13.2% from US$90.7 million the year before. Revenues from property income rose 13.2% to US$101.5 million from US$89.7 million in the corresponding quarter a year earlier.

Prospects: Co. indicated that it has 16 projects in various stages of development totaling approximately 3,110 units, valued at $958.0 million. Notably, Co. purchased approximately 7.1 acres of land in Apr 2008 in Sunnyvale, CA for the Tasman Place project, which will consist of approximately 284 residential units and 48,300 square feet of retail space spread out over three five-story buildings. The total estimated cost of the development is $139.0 million with construction commencing in Feb 2009. In the meantime, for the full-year 2008, Co. is targeting funds from operations in the range of $5.90 to $6.15 per diluted share along with earnings in the range of $1.85 to $2.10 per diluted share.

Financial Data
(US$ in Thousands)

	3 Mos	12/31/2007	12/31/2006	12/31/2005	12/31/2004	12/31/2003	12/31/2002	12/31/2001
Earnings Per Share	3.44	4.24	2.45	3.32	3.36	1.70	2.82	2.59
Cash Flow Per Share	7.18	7.78	6.93	5.41	5.30	4.81	4.63	5.36
Tang Book Value Per Share	29.62	30.76	25.08	24.14	24.58	24.74	23.41	20.98
Dividends Per Share	3.810	3.720	3.360	3.240	3.160	3.120	3.080	2.800
Dividend Payout %	110.89	87.74	137.14	97.59	94.05	183.53	109.22	108.11
Income Statement								
Property Income	101,477	383,433	343,044	316,340	283,483	222,868	177,265	183,482
Non-Property Income	1,227	5,090	5,030	10,951	...	11,582	22,857	22,152
Total Revenue	102,704	388,523	348,074	327,291	283,483	234,450	200,122	205,634
Depn & Amortn	28,456	103,460	85,779	82,045	74,510	50,417	37,841	36,952
Interest Expense	20,183	80,995	72,898	73,614	63,023	42,751	35,012	39,105
Income Before Taxes	...	42,064	35,862	53,980	...	...	...	...
Income Taxes	...	400	525	2,538	...	...	...	...
Net Income	18,014	115,638	62,748	79,716	79,693	37,947	52,874	48,545
Average Shares	24,877	25,100	23,551	23,388	23,156	21,678	18,725	18,768
Balance Sheet								
Total Assets	3,001,276	2,980,323	2,485,840	2,239,290	2,217,217	1,728,564	1,619,734	1,329,458
Long-Term Obligations	1,685,483	1,657,691	1,411,554	1,354,918	1,316,984	832,229	804,063	638,660
Total Liabilities	1,819,024	1,762,133	1,491,599	1,425,109	1,385,810	895,064	865,890	691,379
Stockholders' Equity	757,975	790,318	612,209	580,967	591,277	589,701	491,314	386,599
Shares Outstanding	24,746	24,876	23,416	23,033	23,033	22,825	20,983	18,428
Statistical Record								
Return on Assets %	3.44	4.23	2.66	3.58	4.03	2.27	3.59	3.72
Return on Equity %	13.81	16.49	10.52	13.60	13.46	7.02	12.05	12.48
Net Margin %	17.54	29.76	18.03	24.36	28.11	16.19	26.42	23.61
Price Range	132.66-87.58	146.40-95.34	133.47-94.42	93.15-69.10	85.11-60.05	66.08-49.50	55.75-45.23	55.94-43.20
P/E Ratio	38.56-25.46	34.53-22.49	54.48-38.54	28.06-20.81	25.33-17.87	38.87-29.12	19.77-16.04	21.60-16.68
Average Yield %	3.38	3.08	2.95	3.92	4.55	5.36	6.11	5.67

Address: 925 East Meadow Drive, Palo Alto, CA 94303	Officers: George M. Marcus - Chairman Keith R. Guericke - Vice-Chairman, President, Chief Executive Officer Transfer Agents:	Investor Contact: 650-849-1600
Telephone: 650-494-3700		No of Institutions: 229
Web Site: www.expresspropertytrust.com	Computershare Investor Services, LLC, Chicago, IL	Shares: 30,868,732 % Held: 115.40

EXPEDITORS INTERNATIONAL OF WASHINGTON, INC.

Exchange	Symbol	Price	52Wk Range	Yield	P/E
NMS	EXPD	$47.06 (5/29/2008)	53.34-38.27	0.68	37.65

*7 Year Price Score 123.91 *NYSE Composite Index=100 *12 Month Price Score 104.98

Interim Earnings (Per Share)

Qtr.	Mar	Jun	Sep	Dec
2005	0.17	0.20	0.25	0.36
2006	0.23	0.25	0.29	0.28
2007	0.27	0.30	0.34	0.31
2008	0.30	...	...	...

Interim Dividends (Per Share)

Amt	Decl	Ex	Rec	Pay
0.11S	11/08/2006	11/29/2006	12/01/2006	12/15/2006
0.14S	05/03/2007	05/30/2007	06/01/2007	06/15/2007
0.14S	11/13/2007	11/29/2007	12/03/2007	12/17/2007
0.16S	05/08/2008	05/29/2008	06/02/2008	06/16/2008

Indicated Div: $0.32

Valuation Analysis

Forecast EPS $1.42 (05/17/2008)

Market Cap	$10.0 Billion	Book Value	1.3 Billion
Price/Book	7.71	Price/Sales	1.85

Dividend Achiever Status

10 Year Growth Rate	36.47%
Total Years of Dividend Growth	13

Business Summary: Misc. Transportation Services (MIC: SIC: 4731 NAIC: 541614)

Expeditors International of Washington is engaged in the business of providing global logistics services. Co. provides its customers with an international network supporting the movement and strategic positioning of goods. Co.'s services include the consolidation or forwarding of air and ocean freight. In each U.S. office, and in many overseas offices, Co. acts as a customs broker. In addition, Co. provides additional services including distribution management, vendor consolidation, cargo insurance, purchase order management and customized logistics information.

Recent Developments: For the quarter ended Mar 31 2008, net income increased 12.1% to US$66.5 million from US$59.3 million in the year-earlier quarter. Revenues were US$1.31 billion, up 16.8% from US$1.12 billion the year before. Operating income was US$105.6 million versus US$94.5 million in the prior-year quarter, an increase of 11.7%. Direct operating expenses rose 18.9% to US$933.0 million from US$784.8 million in the comparable period the year before. Indirect operating expenses increased 12.2% to US$268.8 million from US$239.6 million in the equivalent prior-year period.

Prospects: Co.'s financial performance is being driven by growth in its airfreight net revenues due to an increase in airfreight tonnages that it has handled. In addition, Co.'s customs brokerage and other services net revenues are being positively affected by its focused marketing efforts and continued emphasis on providing enhanced service. Separately, Co. estimates its total capital spending in 2008 to exceed $85.0 million, including $71.0 million for leasehold improvements, warehouse equipment, computer hardware as well as furniture and fixtures. Going forward, Co. believes that increased focus on regulatory compliance will continue to provide prospects to expand its customs brokerage services.

Financial Data
(US$ in Thousands)

	3 Mos	12/31/2007	12/31/2006	12/31/2005	12/31/2004	12/31/2003	12/31/2002	12/31/2001
Earnings Per Share	1.25	1.21	1.06	0.98	0.70	0.56	0.52	0.44
Cash Flow Per Share	1.76	1.47	1.56	1.31	0.90	0.55	0.56	0.80
Tang Book Value Per Share	6.03	5.68	4.95	4.21	3.70	2.98	2.49	2.01
Dividends Per Share	0.280	0.280	0.220	0.150	0.110	0.080	0.060	0.050
Dividend Payout %	22.46	23.14	20.75	15.31	15.60	14.29	11.65	11.30
Income Statement								
Total Revenue	1,307,321	5,235,171	4,625,966	3,901,781	3,317,499	2,624,941	2,296,903	1,652,633
EBITDA	116,610	468,073	414,659	341,362	271,933	217,122	195,544	170,232
Depn & Amortn	9,772	40,786	36,817	32,310	27,978	25,816	23,675	24,618
Income Before Taxes	111,731	449,673	395,664	320,154	249,580	195,642	177,990	154,294
Income Taxes	45,210	179,815	160,661	94,624	88,415	71,142	65,461	57,051
Net Income	66,472	269,154	235,094	218,634	156,126	121,952	112,529	97,243
Average Shares	220,437	221,799	222,223	223,267	221,635	218,003	217,762	219,482
Balance Sheet								
Total Assets	2,183,703	2,069,065	1,822,338	1,566,044	1,364,053	1,040,847	879,948	688,437
Total Liabilities	883,891	825,286	735,888	638,440	549,177	392,122	356,136	273,814
Stockholders' Equity	1,299,812	1,226,571	1,069,935	913,721	807,404	645,501	523,812	414,623
Shares Outstanding	212,995	212,996	213,080	213,227	213,287	210,112	208,441	206,447
Statistical Record								
Return on Assets %	13.71	13.83	13.88	14.92	12.95	12.70	14.35	14.40
Return on Equity %	22.96	23.44	23.70	25.41	21.43	20.86	23.98	25.05
EBITDA Margin %	8.92	8.94	8.96	8.75	8.20	8.27	8.51	10.30
Net Margin %	5.08	5.14	5.08	5.60	4.71	4.65	4.90	5.88
Asset Turnover	2.69	2.69	2.73	2.66	2.75	2.73	2.93	2.45
Price Range	53.34-38.27	53.34-40.91	58.28-33.11	36.26-23.86	28.86-17.88	20.14-14.95	17.14-12.70	16.32-10.81
P/E Ratio	42.67-30.62	44.08-33.81	54.98-31.24	36.99-24.35	41.22-25.54	35.96-26.70	32.95-24.42	37.09-24.57
Average Yield %	0.63	0.63	0.50	0.53	0.48	0.45	0.41	0.37

Address: 1015 Third Avenue, 12th Floor, Seattle, WA 98104	Officers: Peter J. Rose - Chairman, Chief Executive Officer R. Jordan Gates - President, Chief Financial	Investor Contact: 206-674-3427
Telephone: 206-674-3400	Officer, Chief Operating Officer **Transfer Agents:**	No of Institutions: 495
Web Site: www.expeditors.com	Computershare Trust Company, N.A., Canton, MA	Shares: 221,665,040 % Held: 98.99

EXXON MOBIL CORP.

Exchange	Symbol	Price	52Wk Range	Yield	P/E
NYS	XOM	$89.35 (5/29/2008)	95.05-80.67	1.79	11.65

*7 Year Price Score 123.75 *NYSE Composite Index=100 ***12 Month Price Score 105.66**

Interim Earnings (Per Share)

Qtr.	Mar	Jun	Sep	Dec
2005	1.22	1.20	1.58	1.71
2006	1.37	1.72	1.77	1.76
2007	1.62	1.83	1.70	2.13
2008	2.03	...	...	...

Interim Dividends (Per Share)

Amt	Decl	Ex	Rec	Pay
0.35Q	07/25/2007	08/09/2007	08/13/2007	09/10/2007
0.35Q	10/31/2007	11/07/2007	11/09/2007	12/10/2007
0.35Q	01/30/2008	02/07/2008	02/11/2008	03/10/2008
0.40Q	04/30/2008	05/09/2008	05/13/2008	06/10/2008

Indicated Div: $1.60 (Div. Reinv. Plan)

Valuation Analysis

Forecast EPS	$8.60 (05/17/2008)
Market Cap	$472.1 Billion	Book Value	123.1 Billion
Price/Book	3.83	Price/Sales	1.09

Dividend Achiever Status

10 Year Growth Rate	5.36%
Total Years of Dividend Growth	25

TRADING VOLUME (thousand shares)

Business Summary: Oil and Gas (MIC: SIC: 2911 NAIC: 324110)

ExxonMobil, through its affiliates, is primarily engaged in the energy business, involving exploration for, and production of, crude oil and natural gas, manufacture of petroleum products and transportation and sale of crude oil, natural gas and petroleum products. Co. manufactures and markets commodity petrochemicals, including olefins, aromatics, polyethylene and polypropylene plastics and a variety of specialty products. Co. also has interests in electric power generation facilities. Affiliates of Co. conduct research programs in support of these businesses. Co. has several divisions and hundreds of affiliates, many with names that include ExxonMobil, Exxon, Esso or Mobil.

Recent Developments: For the quarter ended Mar 31 2008, net income increased 17.3% to US$10.89 billion from US$9.28 billion in the year-earlier quarter. Revenues were US$116.85 billion, up 34.0% from US$87.22 billion the year before. Direct operating expenses rose 47.6% to US$69.86 billion from US$47.33 billion in the comparable period the year before. Indirect operating expenses increased 12.4% to US$26.80 billion from US$23.83 billion in the equivalent prior-year period.

Prospects: Looking ahead, Co. expects to begin production of its Kizomba C deepwater development from the Saxi and Batuque fields later in 2008, and combined peak production from the Mondo, Saxi and Batuque fields is expected to reach 200,000 barrels of oil per day (gross). Separately, Co. remains committed to complete the development and testing of a natural gas treating technology, Controlled Freeze Zone® (CFZ®) technology. For example, Co. plans to build a commercial demonstration plant near LaBarge, WY in order to advance CFZ® to commercial application. Construction will commence in the summer of 2008 for operational startup in late 2009, and testing is expected to occur over one to two years.

Financial Data

(US$ in Thousands)	3 Mos	12/31/2007	12/31/2006	12/31/2005	12/31/2004	12/31/2003	12/31/2002	12/31/2001
Earnings Per Share	7.67	7.28	6.62	5.71	3.89	3.23	1.68	2.21
Cash Flow Per Share	11.13	9.43	8.34	7.68	6.24	4.30	3.15	3.33
Tang Book Value Per Share	23.31	22.62	19.87	18.13	15.90	13.69	11.13	10.74
Dividends Per Share	1.400	1.370	1.280	1.140	1.060	0.980	0.920	0.910
Dividend Payout %	18.25	18.82	19.34	19.96	27.25	30.34	54.76	41.18
Income Statement								
Total Revenue	116,854,000	404,552,000	377,635,000	370,680,000	298,035,000	246,738,000	204,506,000	213,488,000
EBITDA	23,296,000	83,124,000	79,472,000	70,181,000	51,646,000	41,220,000	26,218,000	32,356,000
Depn & Amortn	3,104,000	12,250,000	11,416,000	10,253,000	9,767,000	9,047,000	8,310,000	7,944,000
Income Before Taxes	20,192,000	70,474,000	67,402,000	59,432,000	41,241,000	31,966,000	17,510,000	24,119,000
Income Taxes	9,302,000	29,864,000	27,902,000	23,302,000	15,911,000	11,006,000	6,499,000	9,014,000
Net Income	10,890,000	40,610,000	39,500,000	36,130,000	25,330,000	21,510,000	11,460,000	15,320,000
Average Shares	5,361,999	5,576,999	5,969,999	6,321,999	6,519,001	6,662,001	6,803,001	6,941,001
Balance Sheet								
Current Assets	97,758,000	85,963,000	75,777,000	73,342,000	60,377,000	45,960,000	38,291,000	35,681,000
Total Assets	258,202,000	242,082,000	219,015,000	208,335,000	195,256,000	174,278,000	152,644,000	143,174,000
Current Liabilities	70,983,000	58,312,000	48,817,000	46,307,000	42,981,000	38,386,000	33,175,000	30,114,000
Long-Term Obligations	7,235,000	7,183,000	6,645,000	6,220,000	5,013,000	4,756,000	6,655,000	7,099,000
Total Liabilities	135,063,000	120,320,000	105,171,000	97,149,000	93,500,000	84,363,000	78,047,000	70,013,000
Stockholders' Equity	123,139,000	121,762,000	113,844,000	111,186,000	101,756,000	89,915,000	74,597,000	73,161,000
Shares Outstanding	5,283,694	5,381,999	5,728,999	6,132,999	6,400,999	6,568,001	6,700,001	6,809,001
Statistical Record								
Return on Assets %	17.49	17.61	18.49	17.90	13.67	13.16	7.75	10.49
Return on Equity %	35.50	34.47	35.11	33.93	26.36	26.15	15.51	21.29
EBITDA Margin %	19.94	20.55	21.04	18.93	17.33	16.71	12.82	15.16
Net Margin %	9.32	10.04	10.46	9.75	8.50	8.72	5.60	7.18
Asset Turnover	1.80	1.75	1.77	1.84	1.61	1.51	1.38	1.46
Current Ratio	1.38	1.47	1.55	1.58	1.40	1.20	1.15	1.18
Debt to Equity	0.06	0.06	0.06	0.06	0.05	0.05	0.09	0.10
Price Range	95.05-76.16	95.05-69.86	78.73-56.65	64.98-49.49	51.97-40.10	41.00-31.82	44.38-30.27	45.77-35.83
P/E Ratio	12.39-9.93	13.06-9.60	11.89-8.56	11.38-8.67	13.36-10.31	12.69-9.85	26.42-18.02	20.71-16.21
Average Yield %	1.62	1.65	1.96	1.96	2.34	2.71	2.44	2.20

Address: 5959 Las Colinas Boulevard, Irving, TX 75039-2298	**Officers:** Rex W. Tillerson - Chairman, Chief Executive Officer Donald D. Humphreys - Senior Vice President, Treasurer **Transfer Agents:** Computershare Trust Company, N.A., Providence, RI	**No of Institutions:** 1784
Telephone: 972-444-1000		**Shares:** 2,977,165,824 **% Held:** 50.75
Web Site: www.exxonmobil.com		

F.N.B. CORP (PA)

Exchange	Symbol	Price	52Wk Range	Yield	P/E
NYS	FNB	$14.79 (5/29/2008)	17.91-13.29	6.49	13.09

*7 Year Price Score 72.53   *NYSE Composite Index=100   *12 Month Price Score 101.53

TRADING VOLUME (thousand shares)

Interim Earnings (Per Share)

Qtr.	Mar	Jun	Sep	Dec
2005	0.28	0.31	0.32	0.08
2006	0.27	0.28	0.29	0.29
2007	0.29	0.29	0.29	0.28
2008	0.27	...	...	...

Interim Dividends (Per Share)

Amt	Decl	Ex	Rec	Pay
0.24Q	08/15/2007	08/29/2007	09/01/2007	09/15/2007
0.24Q	11/14/2007	11/28/2007	12/01/2007	12/15/2007
0.24Q	02/20/2008	02/28/2008	03/03/2008	03/15/2008
0.24Q	05/14/2008	05/28/2008	06/01/2008	06/15/2008

Indicated Div: $0.96 (Div. Reinv. Plan)

Valuation Analysis

Forecast EPS $1.13 (05/16/2008)

Market Cap	$896.5 Million	Book Value	543.6 Million
Price/Book	1.65	Price/Sales	2.00

Dividend Achiever Status

10 Year Growth Rate	6.21%
Total Years of Dividend Growth	35

Business Summary: Commercial Banking (MIC: SIC: 6021 NAIC: 522110)

F.N.B. is a financial holding company. As of Dec 31 2007, Co. had four segments: Community Banking, Wealth Management, Insurance and Consumer Finance. Through its subsidiaries, Co. provides a range of financial services, mainly to consumers and small- to medium-sized businesses in its market areas. As of the date above, Co. had 155 Community Banking offices in Pennsylvania and Ohio and 54 Consumer Finance offices in those states and Tennessee. Through its Community Banking affiliate, Co. had six commercial loan production offices in Pennsylvania and Florida and one mortgage loan production office in Tennessee as of that date. As of Dec 31 2007, Co. had total assets of $6.09 billion.

Recent Developments: For the quarter ended Mar 31 2008, net income decreased 5.1% to US$16.5 million from US$17.4 million in the year-earlier quarter. Net interest income increased 2.2% to US$49.0 million from US$47.9 million in the year-earlier quarter. Provision for loan losses was US$3.6 million versus US$1.8 million in the prior-year quarter, an increase of 94.0%. Non-interest income rose 6.0% to US$22.2 million from US$20.9 million, while non-interest expense advanced 5.9% to US$44.4 million.

Prospects: Co.'s net interest income is being driven by higher average earning assets. In addition, Co. is experiencing an increase in net interest margin, as lower rates paid on interest bearing liabilities are offsetting the lower yields on interest earning assets and lower balances of non-interest bearing demand deposits. Further, Co.'s recent non-interest income growth is due to increases in all major fee businesses except insurance-related fees, along with higher other non-interest income. Meanwhile, Co. is encouraged by the Apr 1 2008 acquisition of Omega Financial Corp. which should expand its presence in the Central and Northeast Pennsylvania markets.

Financial Data
(US$ in Thousands)

	3 Mos	12/31/2007	12/31/2006	12/31/2005	12/31/2004	12/31/2003	12/31/2002	12/31/2001
Earnings Per Share	1.13	1.15	1.14	0.98	1.29	1.25	1.34	1.52
Cash Flow Per Share	1.51	1.66	2.00	1.33	2.23	2.17	1.05	1.36
Tang Book Value Per Share	4.67	4.67	4.49	4.89	4.79	8.73	11.08	13.02
Dividends Per Share	0.955	0.950	0.940	0.925	0.920	0.930	0.810	0.526
Dividend Payout %	84.75	82.61	82.46	94.39	71.32	74.36	60.32	34.52
Income Statement								
Interest Income	88,525	368,890	342,422	297,189	254,448	423,313	426,784	296,693
Interest Expense	39,560	174,053	153,585	108,780	84,390	129,836	145,671	125,667
Net Interest Income	48,965	194,837	188,837	188,409	170,058	293,477	281,113	171,026
Provision for Losses	3,583	12,693	10,412	12,176	16,280	24,339	19,094	12,915
Non-Interest Income	22,168	81,609	79,275	57,947	78,141	130,571	120,873	82,799
Non-Interest Expense	44,363	165,614	160,514	157,075	142,587	315,323	289,444	174,830
Income Before Taxes	23,187	98,139	97,186	77,105	89,332	84,386	93,448	66,080
Income Taxes	6,696	33,912	34,219	21,847	27,537	25,597	30,113	21,508
Net Income	16,491	69,678	67,649	55,258	61,795	58,789	63,335	44,572
Average Shares	60,592	60,629	59,376	56,578	48,012	46,972	47,073	29,311
Balance Sheet								
Net Loans & Leases	4,386,641	4,297,066	4,204,524	3,703,080	3,344,813	5,650,924	5,176,275	3,162,982
Total Assets	6,164,590	6,088,021	6,007,592	5,590,326	5,027,009	8,308,310	7,090,232	4,129,087
Total Deposits	4,436,654	4,397,684	4,372,842	4,011,943	3,598,087	6,159,499	5,426,157	3,292,392
Total Liabilities	5,620,968	5,543,664	5,470,220	5,113,124	4,702,907	7,701,401	6,491,636	3,759,890
Stockholders' Equity	543,622	544,357	537,372	477,202	324,102	606,909	598,596	369,197
Shares Outstanding	60,613	60,554	60,394	57,419	50,058	46,313	46,055	28,346
Statistical Record								
Return on Assets %	1.13	1.15	1.17	1.04	0.92	0.76	1.13	1.11
Return on Equity %	12.68	12.88	13.34	13.79	13.24	9.75	13.09	12.91
Net Interest Margin %	55.31	52.82	55.15	63.40	66.83	69.33	65.87	57.64
Efficiency Ratio %	40.08	36.76	38.06	44.23	42.87	56.93	52.85	46.07
Loans to Deposits	0.99	0.98	0.96	0.92	0.93	0.92	0.95	0.96
Price Range	17.91-13.29	18.46-13.93	18.74-15.32	20.99-16.47	22.77-18.80	18.80-13.58	16.03-12.39	13.52-9.85
P/E Ratio	15.85-11.76	16.05-12.11	16.44-13.44	21.42-16.81	17.65-14.57	15.04-10.87	11.96-9.24	8.89-6.48
Average Yield %	5.98	5.70	5.62	4.95	4.40	5.75	5.62	4.46

Address: 2150 Goodlette Road North, Naples, FL 34102	Officers: Stephen J. Gurgovits - Chairman Robert V. New - President, Chief Executive Officer **Transfer**	Investor Contact: 239-659-9894
Telephone: 239-262-7600	**Agents:** F.N.B. Shareholder Services, Naples, FL	No of Institutions: 150
Web Site: www.fnbcorporation.com		Shares: 30,789,648 % Held: 32.28

FAMILY DOLLAR STORES, INC.

Exchange	Symbol	Price	52Wk Range	Yield	P/E
NYS	FDO	$20.87 (5/29/2008)	35.23-15.85	2.40	14.01

*7 Year Price Score 64.37   *NYSE Composite Index=100   *12 Month Price Score 87.20

Interim Earnings (Per Share)

Qtr.	Nov	Feb	May	Aug
2004-05	0.33	0.48	0.32	0.18
2005-06	0.32	0.35	0.37	0.22
2006-07	0.36	0.60	0.40	0.26
2007-08	0.37	0.45	...	...

Interim Dividends (Per Share)

Amt	Decl	Ex	Rec	Pay
0.115Q	08/29/2007	09/12/2007	09/14/2007	10/15/2007
0.115Q	11/05/2007	12/12/2007	12/14/2007	01/15/2008
0.125Q	01/17/2008	03/12/2008	03/14/2008	04/15/2008
0.125Q	04/25/2008	06/11/2008	06/13/2008	07/15/2008

Indicated Div: $0.50

Valuation Analysis

Forecast EPS	$1.52 (05/16/2008)		
Market Cap	$2.9 Billion	Book Value	1.2 Billion
Price/Book	2.50	Price/Sales	0.43

Dividend Achiever Status

10 Year Growth Rate	11.13%
Total Years of Dividend Growth	31

TRADING VOLUME (thousand shares)

Business Summary: Retail - General (MIC: SIC: 5331 NAIC: 452990)

Family Dollar Stores is engaged in operating a chain of general merchandise retail discount stores, providing primarily low to lower-middle income consumers with a selection of merchandise, including consumables, home products, apparel and accessories, and electronics. As of Sep 1 2007, Co. operated more than 6,400 stores located in 44 states of the U.S. Co.'s store is between 7,500 and 9,500 square feet and generally serves customers who live within five miles of the store. Co.'s stores are located in urban, suburban, small town and rural markets.

Recent Developments: For the quarter ended Mar 1 2008, net income decreased 30.1% to US$63.3 million from US$90.5 million in the year-earlier quarter. Revenues were US$1.83 billion, down 5.9% from US$1.95 billion the year before. Operating income was US$96.5 million versus US$143.3 million in the prior-year quarter, a decrease of 32.7%. Direct operating expenses declined 4.7% to US$1.23 billion from US$1.29 billion in the comparable period the year before. Indirect operating expenses decreased 1.3% to US$502.6 million from US$509.2 million in the equivalent prior-year period.

Prospects: For the fiscal year ending Aug 27 2008, Co. now anticipates earnings in the range of $1.50 to $1.60 per diluted share. In addition, Co. expects to open approximately 200 stores and close approximately 75 stores, while comparable store sales are estimated to be flat or increase slightly. Similarly, Co. foresees capital expenditures of $140.0 million to $150.0 million, mainly for new store openings, existing store expansions, relocations and renovations, distribution center improvements, as well as store technology infrastructure. For the third fiscal quarter of 2008, Co. is projecting earnings of $0.39 to $0.44 per diluted share, while store sales are expected to be flat to up slightly.

Financial Data

(US$ in Thousands)	6 Mos	3 Mos	09/01/2007	08/26/2006	08/27/2005	08/28/2004	08/30/2003	08/31/2002
Earnings Per Share	1.49	1.59	1.62	1.26	1.30	1.53	1.43	1.25
Cash Flow Per Share	3.07	2.91	2.74	2.92	1.80	2.21	1.72	2.34
Tang Book Value Per Share	8.33	8.05	8.19	8.04	8.64	8.13	7.61	6.66
Dividends Per Share	0.460	0.450	0.440	0.400	0.360	0.320	0.280	0.250
Dividend Payout %	30.95	28.24	27.16	31.75	27.69	20.92	19.58	20.00
Income Statement								
Total Revenue	3,515,654	1,683,043	6,834,305	6,394,772	5,824,808	5,281,888	4,750,171	4,162,652
EBITDA	258,392	123,198	532,693	451,942	457,528	512,098	478,040	418,636
Depn & Amortn	76,789	38,058	144,060	134,637	114,733	97,883	88,315	77,015
Income Before Taxes	179,066	82,614	381,896	311,144	342,795	414,215	389,725	341,621
Income Taxes	63,817	30,668	139,042	116,033	125,286	151,530	142,250	124,692
Net Income	115,249	51,946	242,854	195,111	217,509	262,685	247,475	216,929
Average Shares	140,617	141,324	149,599	155,124	167,092	171,624	173,354	174,049
Balance Sheet								
Current Assets	1,467,012	1,502,471	1,537,280	1,418,848	1,354,768	1,225,308	1,156,492	1,055,859
Total Assets	2,537,948	2,605,090	2,624,156	2,523,029	2,409,501	2,167,422	1,985,695	1,754,619
Current Liabilities	1,039,697	1,107,298	1,130,303	986,111	894,611	713,551	595,331	530,780
Long-Term Obligations	250,000	250,000	250,000	250,000	...	...	...	...
Total Liabilities	1,373,877	1,473,824	1,449,515	1,314,636	981,435	807,022	674,726	599,671
Stockholders' Equity	1,164,071	1,131,266	1,174,641	1,208,393	1,428,066	1,360,400	1,310,969	1,154,948
Shares Outstanding	139,695	140,527	143,344	150,210	165,262	167,396	172,208	173,329
Statistical Record								
Return on Assets %	8.19	9.05	9.28	7.93	9.53	12.72	13.27	13.79
Return on Equity %	17.12	19.70	20.05	14.84	15.64	19.78	20.13	20.58
EBITDA Margin %	7.35	7.32	7.79	7.07	7.85	9.70	10.06	10.06
Net Margin %	3.28	3.09	3.55	3.05	3.73	4.97	5.21	5.21
Asset Turnover	2.61	2.62	2.61	2.60	2.55	2.56	2.55	2.65
Current Ratio	1.41	1.36	1.36	1.44	1.51	1.72	1.94	1.99
Debt to Equity	0.21	0.22	0.21	0.21	...	...	...	...
Price Range	35.23-15.85	35.23-21.65	35.23-23.81	27.22-19.67	34.98-20.20	43.61-25.60	40.25-24.16	36.86-24.56
P/E Ratio	23.64-10.64	22.16-13.62	21.75-14.70	21.60-15.61	26.91-15.54	28.50-16.73	28.15-16.90	29.49-19.65
Average Yield %	1.70	1.52	1.45	1.68	1.28	0.92	0.87	0.80

Address: 10401 Old Monroe Road, Matthews, NC 28105 **Telephone:** 704-847-6961 **Web Site:** www.familydollar.com	**Officers:** Howard R. Levine - Chairman, Chief Executive Officer R. James Kelly - President, Chief Operating Officer **Transfer Agents:** Mellon Investor Services LLC, Ridgefield Park, NJ	**No of Institutions:** 347 **Shares:** 157,185,760 **% Held:** 104.67

FEDERAL REALTY INVESTMENT TRUST (MD)

Exchange	Symbol	Price	52Wk Range	Yield	P/E
NYS	FRT	$80.88 (5/29/2008)	95.19-64.48	3.02	22.91

*7 Year Price Score 119.84 *NYSE Composite Index=100 *12 Month Price Score 103.41

Interim Earnings (Per Share)

Qtr.	Mar	Jun	Sep	Dec
2005	0.40	0.41	0.52	0.60
2006	0.53	0.66	0.41	0.32
2007	0.41	0.47	0.41	2.15
2008	0.51	...	...	...

Interim Dividends (Per Share)

Amt	Decl	Ex	Rec	Pay
0.61Q	08/01/2007	09/19/2007	09/21/2007	10/15/2007
0.61Q	10/31/2007	12/28/2007	01/02/2008	01/15/2008
0.61Q	02/12/2008	03/17/2008	03/19/2008	04/15/2008
0.61Q	05/07/2008	06/20/2008	06/24/2008	07/15/2008

Indicated Div: $2.44 (Div. Reinv. Plan)

Valuation Analysis

Forecast EPS $2.15 (05/16/2008)

Market Cap	$4.8 Billion	Book Value	1.1 Billion
Price/Book	4.27	Price/Sales	9.68

Dividend Achiever Status

10 Year Growth Rate	3.29%
Total Years of Dividend Growth	40

TRADING VOLUME (thousand shares)

Business Summary: "Property, Real Estate & Development" (MIC: SIC: 6798 NAIC: 525930)

Federal Realty Investment Trust is an equity Real-Estate-Investment-Trust (REIT) focusing in the ownership, management, development and redevelopment of retail and mixed-use properties. As of Dec 31 2007, Co. owned or had a majority ownership interest in 82 community and neighborhood shopping centers and mixed-used properties, comprising of approximately 18.2 million square feet, located primarily in communities metropolitan markets in the Northeast and Mid-Atlantic regions of U.S., as well as California. In addition, Co. owned, through a joint venture in which it owns a 30.0% interest, seven retail real estate projects totaling approximately 1.0 million square feet as of Dec 31 2007.

Recent Developments: For the quarter ended Mar 31 2008, income from continuing operations increased 37.8% to US$30.0 million from US$21.8 million in the year-earlier quarter. Net income increased 29.6% to US$30.0 million from US$23.1 million in the year-earlier quarter. Revenues were US$127.2 million, up 10.4% from US$115.3 million the year before. Revenues from property income rose 9.8% to US$122.7 million from US$111.8 million in the corresponding quarter a year earlier.

Prospects: For the full year of 2008, Co. continues to anticipate Funds From Operations in the range of $3.89 to $3.94 per diluted share. In addition, Co. is projecting earnings to range from $2.10 to $2.15 per diluted share. Meanwhile, Co. expects income from continuing operations to grow over its previous year's level, driven primarily by increased earnings in its same-center portfolio and from properties under redevelopment as well as higher earnings as it expands through property acquisitions. Lastly, Co. expects earnings to grow from the acquisition of neighborhood and community shopping centers in the East and West regions markets, as well as a reduction in earnings from selective dispositions.

Financial Data

(US$ in Thousands)	3 Mos	12/31/2007	12/31/2006	12/31/2005	12/31/2004	12/31/2003	12/31/2002	12/31/2001
Earnings Per Share	3.53	3.45	1.92	1.94	1.41	1.59	0.85	1.52
Cash Flow Per Share	3.60	3.82	3.45	3.32	3.15	2.58	2.86	2.77
Tang Book Value Per Share	18.76	18.84	14.17	12.10	12.57	11.31	9.40	8.92
Dividends Per Share	2.405	2.370	2.460	2.365	1.990	1.950	1.930	1.900
Dividend Payout %	68.04	68.70	128.13	121.91	141.13	122.64	227.06	125.00
Income Statement								
Property Income	122,721	481,332	445,927	404,960	389,359	352,497	313,678	293,912
Non-Property Income	4,502	4,560	5,095	5,370	4,915	5,379	5,156	6,590
Total Revenue	127,223	485,892	451,022	410,330	394,274	357,876	318,834	300,502
Depn & Amortn	25,400	105,966	97,879	91,503	90,438	74,616	64,529	59,914
Interest Expense	24,353	111,365	102,808	88,566	85,058	75,232	65,054	69,313
Net Income	29,986	195,537	118,712	114,612	84,156	94,497	55,287	68,756
Average Shares	58,811	56,543	53,962	53,050	51,547	48,619	42,882	40,266
Balance Sheet								
Total Assets	2,979,130	2,989,297	2,688,606	2,350,852	2,266,896	2,143,435	1,999,378	1,837,978
Long-Term Obligations	1,636,457	1,427,640	1,587,906	1,073,388	979,006	949,357	1,003,212	935,625
Total Liabilities	1,834,361	1,842,847	1,882,337	1,556,812	1,457,408	1,422,479	1,325,725	1,212,572
Stockholders' Equity	1,112,489	1,114,632	784,078	774,847	790,534	691,374	644,287	592,388
Shares Outstanding	58,780	58,645	55,320	52,890	52,136	49,200	43,535	40,071
Statistical Record								
Return on Assets %	6.84	6.89	4.71	4.96	3.81	4.56	2.88	3.98
Return on Equity %	20.42	20.60	15.23	14.64	11.33	14.15	8.94	12.97
Net Margin %	23.57	40.24	26.32	27.93	21.34	26.40	17.34	22.88
Price Range	95.19-64.48	97.12-73.82	87.15-61.63	65.73-46.50	52.55-34.73	39.80-26.75	28.75-22.93	23.71-18.98
P/E Ratio	26.97-18.27	28.15-21.40	45.39-32.10	33.88-23.97	37.27-24.63	25.03-16.82	33.82-26.98	15.60-12.49
Average Yield %	2.95	2.76	3.40	4.17	4.57	5.81	7.32	9.03

Address: 1626 East Jefferson Street, Rockville, MD 20852-4041	Officers: Donald C. Wood - President, Chief Executive Officer Dawn M. Becker - Executive Vice President, Secretary, General Counsel **Transfer Agents:** American Stock Transfer & Trust Company, New York, NY	No of Institutions: 289
Telephone: 301-998-8100		**Shares:** 74,147,584 **% Held:** 117.58
Web Site: www.federalrealty.com		

FIFTH THIRD BANCORP (CINCINNATI, OH)

Exchange	Symbol	Price	52Wk Range	Yield	P/E
NMS	FITB	$19.22 (5/29/2008)	43.06-18.85	9.16	10.28

*7 Year Price Score 48.07   *NYSE Composite Index=100   *12 Month Price Score 72.11

Interim Earnings (Per Share)

Qtr.	Mar	Jun	Sep	Dec
2005	0.72	0.75	0.71	0.59
2006	0.65	0.69	0.68	0.12
2007	0.65	0.69	0.61	0.04
2008	0.54	...	...	...

Interim Dividends (Per Share)

Amt	Decl	Ex	Rec	Pay
0.42Q	06/19/2007	06/27/2007	06/29/2007	07/19/2007
0.42Q	09/18/2007	09/26/2007	09/28/2007	10/19/2007
0.44Q	12/18/2007	12/27/2007	12/31/2007	01/22/2008
0.44Q	03/18/2008	03/27/2008	03/31/2008	04/22/2008

Indicated Div: $1.76 (Div. Reinv. Plan)

Valuation Analysis

Forecast EPS	$2.05 (05/17/2008)		
Market Cap	$10.2 Billion	Book Value	9.4 Billion
Price/Book	1.09	Price/Sales	1.18

Dividend Achiever Status

10 Year Growth Rate	16.28%
Total Years of Dividend Growth	35

TRADING VOLUME (thousand shares)

Business Summary: Commercial Banking (MIC: SIC: 6022 NAIC: 522110)

Fifth Third Bancorp is a financial holding company. Through its subsidiaries, Co. provides a range of financial products and services to the retail, commercial, financial, governmental, educational and medical sectors, including a variety of checking, savings and money market accounts, as well as credit products such as credit cards, installment loans, mortgage loans and leases. Co. operates through five business segments: Commercial Banking, Branch Banking, Consumer Lending, Investment Advisors, and Fifth Third Processing Solutions. As of Dec 31 2007, Co. had total assets of approximately $110.96 billion and total deposits of approximately $75.45 billion.

Recent Developments: For the quarter ended Mar 31 2008, net income decreased 20.3% to US$286.0 million from US$359.0 million in the year-earlier quarter. Net interest income increased 11.4% to US$820.0 million from US$736.0 million in the year-earlier quarter. Provision for loan losses was US$544.0 million versus US$84.0 million in the prior-year quarter, an increase of 547.6%. Non-interest income rose 42.1% to US$864.0 million from US$608.0 million, while non-interest expense declined 5.0% to US$715.0 million.

Prospects: Looking ahead to full-year 2008, Co. expects net interest income growth in the mid-to-high single digits, non-interest income growth in the low teens, and net interest margin to be 3.30% to 3.40%. Notably, Co.'s outlook for 2008 excludes the effects of its pending acquisition of First Charter Corporation, which is anticipated to close on June 6 2008, as well as its completed acquisition of nine branches from First Horizon National Corporation, which was announced on May 5 2008. Also, Co.'s non-interest income guidance excludes gains from Visa's initial public offering in the first quarter of 2008 and certain non-cash charges in the first quarter of 2008 and the fourth quarter of 2007.

Financial Data
(US$ in Thousands)

	3 Mos	12/31/2007	12/31/2006	12/31/2005	12/31/2004	12/31/2003	12/31/2002	12/31/2001
Earnings Per Share	1.87	1.99	2.13	2.77	2.68	3.03	2.76	1.86
Cash Flow Per Share	1.53	(1.28)	6.29	7.56	6.23	14.19	3.84	1.66
Tang Book Value Per Share	11.55	11.11	12.82	11.91	13.33	12.92	12.65	13.09
Dividends Per Share	1.720	1.700	1.580	1.460	1.310	1.130	0.980	0.830
Dividend Payout %	91.86	85.43	74.18	52.71	48.88	37.29	35.51	44.62
Income Statement								
Interest Income	1,447,000	6,027,000	5,955,000	4,995,000	4,114,000	3,991,000	4,129,000	4,709,000
Interest Expense	627,000	3,018,000	3,082,000	2,030,000	1,102,000	1,086,000	1,429,000	2,276,000
Net Interest Income	820,000	3,009,000	2,873,000	2,965,000	3,012,000	2,905,000	2,700,000	2,433,000
Provision for Losses	544,000	628,000	343,000	330,000	268,000	399,000	246,000	236,000
Non-Interest Income	864,000	2,467,000	2,153,000	2,500,000	2,465,000	2,483,000	2,194,000	1,797,000
Non-Interest Expense	715,000	3,311,000	3,056,000	2,927,000	2,972,000	2,442,000	2,216,000	2,341,000
Income Before Taxes	425,000	1,537,000	1,627,000	2,208,000	2,237,000	2,547,000	2,432,000	1,653,000
Income Taxes	139,000	461,000	443,000	659,000	712,000	805,000	759,000	550,000
Net Income	286,000	1,076,000	1,188,000	1,549,000	1,525,000	1,755,000	1,635,000	1,094,000
Average Shares	530,000	540,000	557,000	558,000	568,000	580,000	592,020	591,316
Balance Sheet								
Net Loans & Leases	82,254,000	83,645,000	74,732,000	70,485,000	59,654,000	53,419,000	48,603,000	43,104,000
Total Assets	111,396,000	110,962,000	100,669,000	105,225,000	94,456,000	91,143,000	80,894,000	71,026,000
Total Deposits	71,401,000	75,445,000	69,380,000	67,434,000	58,226,000	57,095,000	52,208,000	45,854,000
Total Liabilities	102,044,000	101,801,000	90,647,000	95,779,000	85,532,000	82,618,000	71,958,000	62,966,000
Stockholders' Equity	9,352,000	9,161,000	10,022,000	9,446,000	8,924,000	8,525,000	8,475,000	7,639,000
Shares Outstanding	532,106	532,671	556,252	555,623	557,648	566,685	574,355	582,674
Statistical Record								
Return on Assets %	0.95	1.02	1.15	1.55	1.64	2.04	2.15	1.87
Return on Equity %	10.44	11.22	12.20	16.86	17.43	20.65	20.29	17.46
Net Interest Margin %	56.67	49.93	48.25	59.36	73.21	72.79	65.39	51.67
Efficiency Ratio %	30.94	38.98	37.69	39.05	45.17	37.72	35.05	35.98
Loans to Deposits	1.15	1.11	1.08	1.05	1.02	0.94	0.93	0.94
Price Range	43.06-20.82	43.06-25.13	41.44-36.53	48.09-35.23	59.90-45.78	61.81-47.73	69.40-55.86	64.43-47.19
P/E Ratio	23.03-11.13	21.64-12.63	19.46-17.02	17.36-12.72	22.35-17.08	20.40-15.75	25.14-20.24	34.64-25.37
Average Yield %	5.22	4.61	4.06	3.46	2.49	2.03	1.54	1.44

Address: Fifth Third Center, Cincinnati, OH 45263 **Telephone:** 513-579-5300 **Web Site:** www.53.com	**Officers:** George A. Schaefer - Chairman Kevin T. Kabat - President, Chief Executive Officer **Transfer Agents:**Computershare Investor Services LLC, Chicago, IL	**Investor Contact:** 513-534-0983 **No of Institutions:** 548 **Shares:** 420,825,728 **% Held:** 72.01

FIRST BANCORP (NC)

Exchange	Symbol	Price	52Wk Range	Yield	P/E
NMS	FBNC	$17.66 (5/29/2008)	21.15-16.40	4.30	11.39

*7 Year Price Score 74.49 *NYSE Composite Index=100 *12 Month Price Score 102.20

Interim Earnings (Per Share)

Qtr.	Mar	Jun	Sep	Dec
2005	0.33	0.32	(0.05)	0.52
2006	0.35	0.33	0.30	0.36
2007	0.34	0.37	0.40	0.40
2008	0.38	...	...	...

Interim Dividends (Per Share)

Amt	Decl	Ex	Rec	Pay
0.19Q	08/29/2007	09/26/2007	09/30/2007	10/25/2007
0.19Q	11/28/2007	12/27/2007	12/31/2007	01/25/2008
0.19Q	03/03/2008	03/27/2008	03/31/2008	04/25/2008
0.19Q	05/27/2008	06/26/2008	06/30/2008	07/25/2008
			Indicated Div: $0.76	

Valuation Analysis

Forecast EPS	$1.55 (05/16/2008)		
Market Cap	$254.1 Million	Book Value	178.0 Million
Price/Book	1.43	Price/Sales	1.50

Dividend Achiever Status

10 Year Growth Rate	13.08%
Total Years of Dividend Growth	20

TRADING VOLUME (thousand shares)

Business Summary: Commercial Banking (MIC: SIC: 6022 NAIC: 522110)
First Bancorp is a bank holding company. Co. is principally engaged in the ownership and operation of First Bank (the Bank), a state chartered bank As of Dec 31 2007, the Bank operated in a 26-county area centered in Troy, NC. The Bank engages in a range of banking activities, providing such services as checking, savings, and money market accounts; loans for business, agriculture, real estate, personal uses, home improvement and automobiles; credit cards; debit cards; letters of credit; and internet banking. In addition, Co. owns and operates a non-bank subsidiary, Montgomery Data Services, Inc., a data processing company. As of Dec 31 2007, Co. had total assets of $2.32 billion.

Recent Developments: For the quarter ended Mar 31 2008, net income increased 13.2% to US$5.5 million from US$4.9 million in the year-earlier quarter. Net interest income increased 4.8% to US$19.8 million from US$18.9 million in the year-earlier quarter. Provision for loan losses was US$1.5 million versus US$1.1 million in the prior-year quarter, an increase of 36.8%. Non-interest income rose 26.9% to US$5.4 million from US$4.2 million, while non-interest expense advanced 4.5% to US$14.8 million.

Prospects: Co. is seeing solid growth in loans and deposits, resulting in an increase in its net interest income. However, Co. noted a decrease in net interest margin due to the Federal Reserve lowering interest rates since Sep 2007 and expects the cumulative impact of the magnitude of interest rate reduction will amplify and lengthen the negative effect on its net interest margin in 2008 and possibly beyond. Thus, Co. expects its net interest margin will continue to decline until interest rates stabilize. Separately, on Apr 1 2008, Co. announced that it has completed the acquisition of Great Pee Dee Bancorp, Inc.; exchanging 1.15 shares of its stock with each share of Great Pee Dee stock outstanding.

Financial Data

(US$ in Thousands)	3 Mos	12/31/2007	12/31/2006	12/31/2005	12/31/2004	12/31/2003	12/31/2002	12/31/2001
Earnings Per Share	1.55	1.51	1.34	1.12	1.40	1.35	1.23	0.98
Cash Flow Per Share	2.38	2.13	1.75	2.04	1.97	2.95	0.81	0.89
Tang Book Value Per Share	8.83	8.56	7.76	7.48	7.04	6.44	7.22	6.75
Dividends Per Share	0.760	0.760	0.740	0.700	0.657	0.627	0.600	0.587
Dividend Payout %	49.16	50.33	55.22	62.50	46.90	46.31	48.65	59.86
Income Statement								
Interest Income	36,307	148,942	129,207	101,429	81,593	74,667	73,261	76,773
Interest Expense	16,543	69,658	54,671	32,838	20,303	18,907	23,871	35,720
Net Interest Income	19,764	79,284	74,536	68,591	61,290	55,760	49,390	41,053
Provision for Losses	1,533	5,217	4,923	3,040	2,905	2,680	2,545	1,151
Non-Interest Income	5,375	18,473	14,310	15,004	15,864	14,918	11,968	9,655
Non-Interest Expense	14,771	57,580	53,198	47,636	43,717	37,964	32,301	28,634
Income Before Taxes	8,835	34,960	30,725	32,919	30,532	30,034	26,512	20,923
Income Taxes	3,306	13,150	11,423	16,829	10,418	10,617	9,282	7,307
Net Income	5,529	21,810	19,302	16,090	20,114	19,417	17,230	13,616
Average Shares	14,446	14,468	14,435	14,360	14,395	14,351	13,981	13,910
Balance Sheet								
Net Loans & Leases	1,911,863	1,872,971	1,721,449	1,466,895	1,352,336	1,205,326	987,640	880,922
Total Assets	2,380,134	2,317,249	2,136,624	1,801,050	1,638,913	1,475,769	1,218,146	1,144,691
Total Deposits	1,921,443	1,838,277	1,695,679	1,494,577	1,388,768	1,249,364	1,055,957	1,000,281
Total Liabilities	2,202,153	2,143,179	1,973,919	1,645,322	1,490,435	1,333,913	1,094,161	1,027,965
Stockholders' Equity	177,981	174,070	162,705	155,728	148,478	141,856	123,985	116,726
Shares Outstanding	14,387	14,377	14,352	14,229	14,083	14,152	13,682	13,668
Statistical Record								
Return on Assets %	0.98	0.98	0.98	0.94	1.29	1.44	1.46	1.32
Return on Equity %	13.05	12.95	12.12	10.58	13.82	14.61	14.32	11.97
Net Interest Margin %	54.44	53.23	57.69	67.62	75.12	74.68	67.42	53.47
Efficiency Ratio %	35.44	34.39	37.07	40.91	44.86	42.38	37.90	33.13
Loans to Deposits	1.00	1.02	1.02	0.98	0.97	0.96	0.94	0.88
Price Range	21.53-16.40	25.50-16.40	23.44-19.64	27.23-19.39	29.30-18.61	21.37-15.49	18.34-13.72	17.63-10.58
P/E Ratio	13.89-10.58	16.89-10.86	17.49-14.66	24.31-17.31	20.93-13.30	15.83-11.48	14.91-11.15	17.99-10.80
Average Yield %	3.97	3.78	3.47	3.20	2.93	3.48	3.78	4.05

Address: 341 North Main Street, P.O. Box 508, Troy, NC 27371 Telephone: 910-576-6171 Web Site: www.firstbancorp.com	Officers: David L. Burns - Chairman Jerry L. Ocheltree - President, Chief Executive Officer Transfer Agents: Registrar & Transfer Co., Inc., Cranford, NJ	Investor Contact: 800-548-9377 No of Institutions: 71 Shares: 3,175,744 % Held: 18.86

FIRST BUSEY CORP.

Exchange	Symbol	Price	52Wk Range	Yield	P/E
NMS	BUSE	$18.21 (5/29/2008)	23.00-17.62	4.39	17.34

*7 Year Price Score 85.96   *NYSE Composite Index=100   *12 Month Price Score 100.70

Interim Earnings (Per Share)

Qtr.	Mar	Jun	Sep	Dec
2005	0.32	0.31	0.36	0.31
2006	0.32	0.33	0.36	0.35
2007	0.36	0.37	0.36	0.04
2008	0.28	...	...	...

Interim Dividends (Per Share)

Amt	Decl	Ex	Rec	Pay
0.18Q	07/02/2007	07/13/2007	07/17/2007	07/20/2007
0.18Q	10/01/2007	10/19/2007	10/23/2007	10/26/2007
0.20Q	01/02/2008	01/17/2008	01/22/2008	01/25/2008
0.20Q	04/01/2008	04/18/2008	04/22/2008	04/25/2008
		Indicated Div: $0.80		

Valuation Analysis

Forecast EPS	$1.16 (05/16/2008)
Market Cap	$654.8 Million Book Value 522.6 Million
Price/Book	1.25 Price/Sales 2.43

Dividend Achiever Status

10 Year Growth Rate	11.93%
Total Years of Dividend Growth	16

Business Summary: Commercial Banking (MIC: SIC: 6022 NAIC: 522110)

First Busey is a financial holding company. Co. has two wholly owned banking subsidiaries: Busey Bank and Busey Bank, National Association (the Banks). The Banks uses the deposits, as well as other funds to originate commercial, financial, agricultural and real estate loans. The Banks also make investments in securities issued by the U.S. Treasury, agency obligations, as well as mortgage-backed securities. Retail banking includes money transfers, safe deposit services, individual retirement accounts, Keogh and other fiduciary services, automated banking and automated fund transfers. As of Dec 31 2007, Co.'s total assets were $4.19 billion and total deposits were $3.21 billion.

Recent Developments: For the quarter ended Mar 31 2008, net income increased 29.3% to US$10.0 million from US$7.7 million in the year-earlier quarter. Net interest income increased 62.3% to US$31.3 million from US$19.3 million in the year-earlier quarter. Provision for loan losses was US$2.2 million versus US$300,000 in the prior-year quarter, an increase of 616.7%. Non-interest income rose 104.6% to US$14.2 million from US$6.9 million, while non-interest expense advanced 91.1% to US$28.1 million.

Prospects: Co. continues to be challenged by the deterioration in its loan portfolio, primarily in southwest Florida market. Also, despite seeing continuing positive demand for new loans in its existing markets, Co. expects that the present credit issues across the industry could further hurt its financial performance through 2008 and 2009. However, Co. remains focused on positioning it to face the difficult earnings environment and capitalizing on growth opportunities. Notably, Co. continues to identify potential problem loans related to the weakening overall real estate markets and the credit environment, gain further information on existing problem loans, and makes adjustments to the provision.

Financial Data
(US$ in Thousands)

	3 Mos	12/31/2007	12/31/2006	12/31/2005	12/31/2004	12/31/2003	12/31/2002	12/31/2001
Earnings Per Share	1.05	1.13	1.35	1.29	1.09	0.97	0.87	0.77
Cash Flow Per Share	0.93	1.28	1.37	1.46	2.42	2.68	(0.70)	0.11
Tang Book Value Per Share	6.75	6.84	5.93	5.14	5.01	5.64	5.17	4.64
Dividends Per Share	0.740	0.770	0.640	0.560	0.510	0.453	0.400	0.347
Dividend Payout %	70.75	68.14	47.41	43.41	46.79	46.90	45.80	45.22
Income Statement								
Interest Income	58,557	201,903	146,366	116,304	85,919	73,849	76,085	89,985
Interest Expense	27,295	100,405	69,851	45,342	30,041	25,618	30,494	46,435
Net Interest Income	31,262	101,498	76,515	70,962	55,878	48,231	45,591	43,550
Provision for Losses	2,150	14,475	1,300	3,490	2,905	3,058	3,125	2,020
Non-Interest Income	14,184	41,692	28,461	23,537	23,790	24,685	22,537	21,460
Non-Interest Expense	28,093	84,305	60,087	51,115	43,085	39,969	38,926	38,974
Income Before Taxes	15,203	44,410	43,589	39,894	33,678	29,889	26,077	24,016
Income Taxes	5,199	12,933	14,701	12,960	11,224	10,025	8,173	8,363
Net Income	10,004	31,477	28,888	26,934	22,454	19,864	17,904	15,653
Average Shares	36,130	27,924	21,406	20,918	20,511	20,534	20,425	20,432
Balance Sheet								
Net Loans & Leases	3,088,954	3,010,665	1,933,339	1,725,972	1,456,683	1,176,168	1,085,583	964,418
Total Assets	4,251,822	4,192,925	2,509,514	2,263,422	1,964,441	1,522,084	1,435,578	1,300,689
Total Deposits	3,248,308	3,207,198	2,014,839	1,809,399	1,558,822	1,256,595	1,213,605	1,105,999
Total Liabilities	3,729,201	3,663,228	2,324,240	2,093,708	1,825,569	1,396,907	1,320,415	1,194,899
Stockholders' Equity	522,621	529,697	185,274	169,714	138,872	125,177	115,163	105,790
Shares Outstanding	35,957	36,431	21,455	21,504	20,608	20,516	20,352	20,516
Statistical Record								
Return on Assets %	1.00	0.94	1.21	1.27	1.28	1.34	1.31	1.18
Return on Equity %	9.48	8.81	16.28	17.46	16.96	16.53	16.21	15.80
Net Interest Margin %	53.39	50.27	52.28	61.01	65.04	65.31	59.92	48.40
Efficiency Ratio %	38.62	34.61	34.37	36.55	39.27	40.56	39.47	34.97
Loans to Deposits	0.95	0.94	0.96	0.95	0.93	0.94	0.89	0.87
Price Range	23.00-17.62	23.83-18.98	23.87-19.78	21.23-18.06	21.53-17.83	18.81-14.93	15.78-13.04	14.67-11.88
P/E Ratio	21.90-16.78	21.09-16.80	17.68-14.65	16.46-14.00	19.75-16.36	19.40-15.40	18.14-14.99	19.05-15.42
Average Yield %	3.64	3.64	3.00	2.83	2.71	2.70	2.77	2.60

Address: 201 West Main Street, Urbana, IL 61801 **Telephone:** 217-365-4556 **Web Site:** www.busey.com	**Officers:** Douglas C. Mills - Chairman Gregory B. Lykins - Vice-Chairman **Transfer Agents:** First Busey Corporation	**No of Institutions:** 75 **Shares:** 11,669,520 **% Held:** 18.02

FIRST CHARTER CORP.

Exchange	Symbol	Price	52Wk Range	Yield	P/E
NMS	FCTR	$30.48 (5/29/2008)	30.74-17.91	2.56	30.79

*7 Year Price Score 93.80 *NYSE Composite Index=100 *12 Month Price Score 109.52

Interim Earnings (Per Share)

Qtr.	Mar	Jun	Sep	Dec
2005	0.34	0.37	0.39	(0.28)
2006	0.37	0.37	0.41	0.35
2007	0.35	0.26	0.32	0.25
2008	0.16	...	...	...

Interim Dividends (Per Share)

Amt	Decl	Ex	Rec	Pay
0.195Q	06/27/2007	07/10/2007	07/12/2007	07/26/2007
0.195Q	09/26/2007	10/09/2007	10/11/2007	10/25/2007
0.195Q	12/19/2007	01/02/2008	01/04/2008	01/18/2008
0.195Q	03/26/2008	03/31/2008	04/02/2008	04/16/2008

Indicated Div: $0.78 (Div. Reinv. Plan)

Valuation Analysis

Forecast EPS $1.43 (05/16/2008)

Market Cap	$1.1 Billion	Book Value	463.5 Million
Price/Book	2.30	Price/Sales	2.81

Dividend Achiever Status

10 Year Growth Rate	4.24%
Total Years of Dividend Growth	15

Business Summary: Commercial Banking (MIC: SIC: 6021 NAIC: 522110)

First Charter is a bank holding company. Co.'s principal asset is the stock of its banking subsidiary, First Charter Bank, which provides a range of banking products, as well as commercial, consumer, real estate, residential mortgage, and home equity loans. As at Dec 31 2007, Co. operated 60 financial centers, four insurance offices, and 137 automated teller machines throughout North Carolina and Georgia and also operated loan origination offices in Asheville, NC and Reston, VA. Co.'s primary market area is located within North Carolina and is centered primarily around the Charlotte Metro region. As of Dec 31 2007, Co. had total assets of $4.86 billion and total deposits of $3.22 billion.

Recent Developments: For the quarter ended Mar 31 2008, net income decreased 55.1% to US$5.5 million from US$12.4 million in the year-earlier quarter. Net interest income decreased 10.8% to US$32.8 million from US$36.7 million in the year-earlier quarter. Provision for loan losses was US$4.7 million versus US$1.4 million in the prior-year quarter, an increase of 244.6%. Non-interest income rose 4.4% to US$20.4 million from US$19.6 million, while non-interest expense declined 5.7% to US$33.9 million.

Prospects: Co.'s near-term outlook appears challenging, reflecting decreases in net interest income and net interest margin. Furthermore, Co. is experiencing lower earning-asset yields driven by a decline in loan yields. Specifically, Co. is seeing a decline in loan yields primarily as a result of a reduction in the prime lending rate following the recent Federal Reserve's reduction of the federal funds rate. In addition, loan yields are negatively affected by an increase in non accrual loans. Meanwhile, Co. is progressing on its agreement to be acquired by Fifth Third Bancorp, which is anticipated to close on June 6 2008, subject to customary closing conditions.

Financial Data
(US$ in Thousands)

	3 Mos	12/31/2007	12/31/2006	12/31/2005	12/31/2004	12/31/2003	12/31/2002	12/31/2001
Earnings Per Share	0.99	1.18	1.49	0.82	1.40	0.47	1.30	1.12
Cash Flow Per Share	1.16	1.92	3.00	1.26	1.07	(3.61)	1.20	1.43
Tang Book Value Per Share	10.88	11.02	10.37	9.82	9.70	10.08	10.80	10.06
Dividends Per Share	0.780	0.780	0.775	0.760	0.750	0.740	0.730	0.720
Dividend Payout %	78.79	66.10	52.01	92.68	53.57	157.45	56.15	64.29
Income Statement								
Interest Income	68,584	309,892	264,929	224,605	187,303	178,292	196,388	215,276
Interest Expense	35,833	163,006	131,219	99,722	64,293	70,490	83,227	109,912
Net Interest Income	32,751	146,886	133,710	124,883	123,010	107,802	113,161	105,364
Provision for Losses	4,707	19,945	5,290	9,343	8,425	27,518	8,270	4,465
Non-Interest Income	20,418	78,254	67,678	50,213	60,896	64,180	47,631	38,773
Non-Interest Expense	33,863	142,528	124,937	131,222	111,017	127,032	97,772	87,579
Income Before Taxes	14,599	62,667	71,161	34,531	64,464	17,432	54,750	52,093
Income Taxes	9,057	21,363	23,799	9,220	22,022	3,286	14,947	16,768
Net Income	5,542	41,304	47,395	25,311	42,442	14,146	39,803	35,325
Average Shares	35,121	34,988	31,838	30,784	30,277	30,007	30,702	31,660
Balance Sheet								
Net Loans & Leases	3,450,310	3,474,738	3,462,379	2,923,467	2,417,855	2,232,167	2,203,670	1,929,052
Total Assets	4,795,861	4,862,417	4,856,717	4,232,420	4,431,605	4,206,693	3,745,949	3,332,737
Total Deposits	3,219,339	3,221,619	3,248,128	2,799,479	2,609,846	2,427,897	2,322,647	2,162,945
Total Liabilities	4,332,335	4,394,073	4,409,355	3,908,825	4,116,918	3,907,254	3,421,263	3,023,396
Stockholders' Equity	463,526	468,344	447,362	323,595	314,687	299,439	324,686	309,341
Shares Outstanding	35,003	34,978	34,922	30,736	30,054	29,720	30,069	30,742
Statistical Record								
Return on Assets %	0.71	0.85	1.04	0.58	0.98	0.36	1.12	1.13
Return on Equity %	7.49	9.02	12.30	7.93	13.78	4.53	12.56	11.42
Net Interest Margin %	47.75	47.40	50.47	55.60	65.67	60.46	57.62	48.94
Efficiency Ratio %	38.05	36.72	37.56	47.75	44.73	52.39	40.07	34.47
Loans to Deposits	1.07	1.08	1.07	1.04	0.93	0.92	0.95	0.89
Price Range	30.74-17.91	30.74-17.91	25.38-23.09	26.66-20.85	28.11-19.52	21.20-16.69	20.57-15.33	18.75-13.44
P/E Ratio	31.05-18.09	26.05-15.18	17.03-15.50	32.51-25.43	20.08-13.94	45.11-35.51	15.82-11.79	16.74-12.00
Average Yield %	3.21	3.34	3.20	3.23	3.32	3.92	4.11	4.37

Address: 10200 David Taylor Drive, Charlotte, NC 28262 Telephone: 704-688-4300 Web Site: www.firstcharter.com	Officers: James E. Burt - Chairman Michael R. Coltrane - Vice-Chairman **Transfer Agents:** Registrar and Transfer Company, Cranford, NJ	No of Institutions: 119 Shares: 15,419,078 % Held: 42.44

FIRST COMMUNITY BANCSHARES, INC. (NV)

Exchange	Symbol	Price	52Wk Range	Yield	P/E
NMS	FCBC	$34.72 (5/29/2008)	38.71-25.52	3.23	13.62

*7 Year Price Score 81.61   *NYSE Composite Index=100   *12 Month Price Score 106.69

Interim Earnings (Per Share)

Qtr.	Mar	Jun	Sep	Dec
2005	0.53	0.55	0.61	0.64
2006	0.61	0.65	0.64	0.68
2007	0.63	0.66	0.65	0.68
2008	0.57	...	...	...

Interim Dividends (Per Share)

Amt	Decl	Ex	Rec	Pay
0.27Q	08/28/2007	09/12/2007	09/14/2007	09/28/2007
0.27Q	10/24/2007	11/28/2007	11/30/2007	12/14/2007
0.28Q	02/26/2008	03/13/2008	03/17/2008	03/31/2008
0.28Q	05/27/2008	06/12/2008	06/16/2008	06/30/2008

Indicated Div: $1.12

Valuation Analysis

Forecast EPS	$2.40 (05/16/2008)
Market Cap	$382.4 Million Book Value 209.0 Million
Price/Book	1.83 Price/Sales 2.47

Dividend Achiever Status

10 Year Growth Rate	5.37%
Total Years of Dividend Growth	13

TRADING VOLUME (thousand shares)

Business Summary: Commercial Banking (MIC: SIC: 6022 NAIC: 522110)

First Community Bancshares is a one-bank holding company. Co. serves as the holding company for First Community Bank, N.A., which conducts commercial banking operations in the states of Virginia, West Virginia, North Carolina, South Carolina and Tennessee. Co. also owns GreenPoint Insurance Group, Inc., a full-service insurance agency, as well as Investment Planning Consultants, an investment advisory firm. As of Dec 31 2007, Co. conducted its banking operations through 57 locations and four wealth management offices. Also, as of Dec 31 2007, Co. had total consolidated assets of $2.15 billion and total deposits of $1.39 billion.

Recent Developments: For the quarter ended Mar 31 2008, net income decreased 11.4% to US$6.3 million from US$7.1 million in the year-earlier quarter. Net interest income decreased 3.8% to US$16.4 million from US$17.0 million in the year-earlier quarter. Non-interest income rose 75.3% to US$9.1 million from US$5.2 million, while non-interest expense advanced 33.9% to US$16.3 million.

Prospects: Co. is seeing a decline in its net interest income due to decreases in loan balances and in loan yields as a result of the recent declines in the prime rate and the target lending rates for banks. Nevertheless, Co.'s asset quality remains favorable, with a sequential decline in loan delinquencies as a percent of total loans. Also, Co. is seeing an increase in its non-interest income, with increases in service charges on deposit accounts, other service charges, commissions, and fees, insurance commissions as well as other operating income. Meanwhile, Co. intends to open one branch location in Summersville, WV.

Financial Data
(US$ in Thousands)

	3 Mos	12/31/2007	12/31/2006	12/31/2005	12/31/2004	12/31/2003	12/31/2002	12/31/2001
Earnings Per Share	2.55	2.62	2.57	2.32	1.97	2.25	2.25	1.75
Cash Flow Per Share	3.16	2.90	3.13	2.20	3.05	7.28	2.95	(2.02)
Tang Book Value Per Share	12.51	13.28	13.39	11.85	10.84	11.95	11.53	9.75
Dividends Per Share	1.090	1.080	1.040	1.020	1.000	0.973	0.909	0.810
Dividend Payout %	42.70	41.22	40.47	43.97	50.76	43.23	40.32	46.40
Income Statement								
Interest Income	29,547	127,591	120,026	109,508	96,136	93,040	96,204	92,829
Interest Expense	13,187	59,276	48,381	35,880	26,953	28,374	35,008	42,409
Net Interest Income	16,360	68,315	71,645	73,628	69,183	64,666	61,196	50,420
Provision for Losses	323	717	2,706	3,706	2,671	3,419	4,208	5,134
Non-Interest Income	9,141	24,831	21,323	22,305	17,329	21,707	20,049	20,275
Non-Interest Expense	16,283	50,463	49,837	55,591	48,035	47,351	42,269	38,025
Income Before Taxes	8,895	41,966	40,425	36,636	35,806	35,603	34,768	27,536
Income Taxes	2,583	12,334	11,477	10,191	9,786	10,365	10,049	8,402
Net Income	6,312	29,632	28,948	26,303	22,364	25,238	24,719	19,134
Average Shares	11,107	11,292	11,279	11,341	11,337	11,198	10,970	10,979
Balance Sheet								
Net Loans & Leases	1,168,758	1,213,480	1,271,095	1,317,577	1,223,611	1,029,719	979,575	956,076
Total Assets	2,065,113	2,149,838	2,033,698	1,952,483	1,830,822	1,672,727	1,524,363	1,478,235
Total Deposits	1,358,953	1,393,443	1,394,771	1,405,944	1,359,064	1,225,617	1,139,727	1,078,260
Total Liabilities	1,856,135	1,932,740	1,820,968	1,757,982	1,647,589	1,497,692	1,371,901	1,345,194
Stockholders' Equity	208,978	217,098	212,730	194,501	183,233	175,035	152,462	133,041
Shares Outstanding	11,012	11,069	11,245	11,251	11,250	11,242	10,877	10,930
Statistical Record								
Return on Assets %	1.37	1.42	1.45	1.39	1.27	1.58	1.65	1.42
Return on Equity %	13.47	13.79	14.22	13.93	12.45	15.41	17.32	15.08
Net Interest Margin %	55.37	53.54	59.69	67.24	71.96	69.50	63.61	54.31
Efficiency Ratio %	42.09	33.11	35.26	42.17	42.33	41.27	36.36	33.62
Loans to Deposits	0.86	0.87	0.91	0.94	0.90	0.84	0.86	0.89
Price Range	38.77-25.52	42.10-25.52	40.65-29.86	36.08-26.31	37.67-25.00	37.60-25.73	30.60-23.11	28.10-14.26
P/E Ratio	15.20-10.01	16.07-9.74	15.82-11.62	15.55-11.34	19.12-12.69	16.71-11.44	13.60-10.27	16.06-8.15
Average Yield %	3.30	3.15	3.03	3.13	3.13	3.00	3.32	3.77

Address: One Community Place, P.O. Box 989, Bluefield, VA 24605-0989	**Officers:** William P. Stafford - Chairman John M. Mendez - President, Chief Executive Officer **Transfer Agents:** Mellon Investor Services LLC, Jersey City, NJ	**Investor Contact:** 276-326-9000
Telephone: 276-326-9000		**No of Institutions:** 75
Web Site: www.fcbinc.com		**Shares:** 3,573,899 % **Held:** 22.11

FIRST FINANCIAL BANKSHARES, INC.

Exchange	Symbol	Price	52Wk Range	Yield	P/E
NMS	FFIN	$46.40 (5/29/2008)	46.40-35.36	2.93	18.86

*7 Year Price Score 98.80 ***NYSE Composite Index=100** ***12 Month Price Score 113.54**

Interim Earnings (Per Share)

Qtr.	Mar	Jun	Sep	Dec
2005	0.58	0.51	0.52	0.51
2006	0.55	0.55	0.55	0.56
2007	0.55	0.64	0.59	0.61
2008	0.63	...	...	...

Interim Dividends (Per Share)

Amt	Decl	Ex	Rec	Pay
0.32Q	07/24/2007	09/13/2007	09/17/2007	10/01/2007
0.32Q	10/23/2007	12/13/2007	12/17/2007	01/02/2008
0.32Q	01/22/2008	03/12/2008	03/14/2008	04/01/2008
0.34Q	04/22/2008	06/12/2008	06/16/2008	07/01/2008
		Indicated Div: $1.36		

Valuation Analysis

Forecast EPS	$2.54 (05/16/2008)
Market Cap	$957.0 Million	Book Value	351.8 Million
Price/Book	2.72	Price/Sales	4.37

Dividend Achiever Status

10 Year Growth Rate	12.15%
Total Years of Dividend Growth	20

TRADING VOLUME (thousand shares)

Business Summary: Commercial Banking (MIC: SIC: 6022 NAIC: 522110)

First Financial Bankshares is a financial holding company. Through its wholly-owned subsidiary, First Financial Bankshares of Delaware, Inc., Co. owns 10 banks, as well as a trust company, First Financial Trust & Asset Management Company, and a technology operating company, National Association and First Technology Services, Inc., all organized and located in Texas. Through its subsidiary banks, Co. conducts a commercial banking business, with service centers located primarily in North Central and West Texas. Co.'s banks provide loans and banking services to consumers and commercial customers. As of Dec 31 2007, Co. had total assets of $3.07 billion and deposits of $2.55 billion.

Recent Developments: For the quarter ended Mar 31 2008, net income increased 14.8% to US$13.2 million from US$11.5 million in the year-earlier quarter. Net interest income increased 12.3% to US$29.8 million from US$26.6 million in the year-earlier quarter. Provision for loan losses was US$1.1 million versus US$242,076 in the prior-year quarter, an increase of 341.3%. Non-interest income rose 12.7% to US$12.3 million from US$10.9 million, while non-interest expense advanced 8.6% to US$22.7 million.

Prospects: Going forward, Co. believes that ongoing decreases in interest rates will put pressure on its net interest margin as it works to reduce interest rates on deposits to compensate for lower rates on loans and investments. Meanwhile, due to legislative changes and turmoil in the liquidity markets, Co.'s outlook for its student loan sales and premiums business appears uncertain. In addition, Co. noted that, effective Jul 1, 2008, the higher education authority, which has previously purchased Co.'s student loans, will no longer provide premiums for the student loans or enhanced borrower benefits and that it would suspend acquisitions of student loans should it be unable to obtain needed funds.

Financial Data

(US$ in Thousands)	3 Mos	12/31/2007	12/31/2006	12/31/2005	12/31/2004	12/31/2003	12/31/2002	12/31/2001
Earnings Per Share	2.46	2.38	2.21	2.12	1.89	1.71	1.65	1.43
Cash Flow Per Share	2.73	2.64	2.52	1.98	3.30	2.20	2.15	1.96
Tang Book Value Per Share	13.91	13.02	11.29	10.04	10.91	11.01	10.41	9.26
Dividends Per Share	1.280	1.260	1.180	1.095	0.998	0.907	0.810	0.698
Dividend Payout %	51.97	52.94	53.39	51.65	52.65	53.17	49.15	48.89
Income Statement								
Interest Income	41,746	169,369	154,494	123,944	99,973	95,285	104,862	116,473
Interest Expense	11,917	58,557	48,628	28,757	16,077	17,131	24,380	44,834
Net Interest Income	29,830	110,812	105,866	95,187	83,896	78,154	80,482	71,639
Provision for Losses	1,068	2,331	2,061	1,320	1,633	1,178	2,370	1,964
Non-Interest Income	12,312	48,273	44,668	44,180	38,823	34,109	29,552	27,578
Non-Interest Expense	22,662	86,827	83,136	75,649	66,128	61,154	59,082	55,072
Income Before Taxes	18,412	69,926	65,337	62,398	54,958	49,931	48,583	42,182
Income Taxes	5,250	20,437	19,308	18,375	15,787	14,626	14,630	12,827
Net Income	13,162	49,490	46,029	44,023	39,171	35,305	33,953	29,355
Average Shares	20,801	20,800	20,787	20,777	20,700	20,658	20,630	20,554
Balance Sheet								
Net Loans & Leases	1,517,513	1,510,558	1,357,534	1,273,885	1,150,386	975,947	952,821	929,529
Total Assets	3,061,936	3,070,309	2,850,165	2,733,827	2,315,224	2,092,571	1,993,183	1,929,694
Total Deposits	2,504,682	2,546,083	2,384,024	2,366,277	1,994,312	1,796,271	1,711,562	1,685,163
Total Liabilities	2,710,177	2,734,814	2,549,263	2,457,551	2,049,679	1,841,085	1,754,415	1,716,040
Stockholders' Equity	351,759	335,495	300,901	276,276	265,545	251,487	238,768	213,654
Shares Outstanding	20,625	20,766	20,739	20,714	20,630	20,589	20,555	20,504
Statistical Record								
Return on Assets %	1.72	1.67	1.65	1.74	1.77	1.73	1.73	1.59
Return on Equity %	15.47	15.55	15.95	16.25	15.11	14.40	15.01	14.33
Net Interest Margin %	71.45	65.43	68.52	76.80	83.92	82.02	76.75	61.51
Efficiency Ratio %	41.92	39.89	41.74	45.00	47.64	47.26	43.96	38.23
Loans to Deposits	0.61	0.59	0.57	0.54	0.58	0.54	0.56	0.55
Price Range	43.71-35.36	43.71-35.36	42.73-34.28	38.63-29.51	34.46-28.50	32.87-20.47	25.71-17.81	19.75-14.16
P/E Ratio	17.77-14.37	18.37-14.86	19.33-15.51	18.22-13.92	18.23-15.08	19.22-11.97	15.58-10.80	13.81-9.90
Average Yield %	3.25	3.14	3.11	3.23	3.23	3.46	3.73	4.02

Address: 400 Pine Street, Abilene, TX 79601	**Officers:** Kenneth T. Murphy - Chairman F. Scott Dueser - President, Chief Executive Officer **Transfer Agents:**The Bank of New York. New York, NY	**Investor Contact:** 325-627-7167
Telephone: 325-627-7155		**No of Institutions:** 92
Web Site: www.ffin.com		**Shares:** 5,151,797 % Held: 24.26

102

FIRST FINANCIAL CORP. (IN)

Exchange	Symbol	Price	52Wk Range	Yield	P/E
NMS	THFF	$32.89 (5/29/2008)	32.92-23.48	2.68	16.70

*7 Year Price Score 80.47 *NYSE Composite Index=100 *12 Month Price Score 107.80

Interim Earnings (Per Share)

Qtr.	Mar	Jun	Sep	Dec
2005	0.48	0.37	0.47	0.41
2006	0.41	0.48	0.41	0.46
2007	0.48	0.48	0.48	0.49
2008	0.53	...	...	...

Interim Dividends (Per Share)

Amt	Decl	Ex	Rec	Pay
0.43S	11/22/2006	12/13/2006	12/15/2006	01/02/2007
0.43S	05/16/2007	06/13/2007	06/15/2007	07/02/2007
0.44S	11/21/2007	12/12/2007	12/14/2007	01/02/2008
0.44S	05/20/2008	06/12/2008	06/16/2008	07/01/2008

Indicated Div: $0.88

Valuation Analysis

Forecast EPS	$1.98 (05/16/2008)		
Market Cap	$431.0 Million	Book Value	293.2 Million
Price/Book	1.47	Price/Sales	2.54

Dividend Achiever Status

10 Year Growth Rate	9.94%
Total Years of Dividend Growth	19

TRADING VOLUME (thousand shares)

Business Summary: Commercial Banking (MIC: SIC: 6022 NAIC: 522110)

First Financial is a financial holding company that offers a variety of financial services including commercial, mortgage and consumer lending, lease financing, trust account services and depositor services through its subsidiaries: First Financial Bank N.A., The Morris Plan Company, First Financial Reinsurance Company and Forrest Sherer Inc. Co.'s primary source of revenue is derived from loans to customers, primarily middle-income individuals, and investment activities. As of Dec 31 2007, Co. operated 48 branches in west-central Indiana and east-central Illinois. Also, as of Dec 31 2007, Co. had total assets of approximately $2.23 billion and total deposits of $1.53 billion.

Recent Developments: For the quarter ended Mar 31 2008, net income increased 8.2% to US$7.0 million from US$6.4 million in the year-earlier quarter. Net interest income increased 2.7% to US$19.0 million from US$18.5 million in the year-earlier quarter. Provision for loan losses was US$1.9 million versus US$1.7 million in the prior-year quarter, an increase of 13.9%. Non-interest income rose 6.2% to US$8.6 million from US$8.1 million, while non-interest expense advanced 2.3% to US$16.4 million.

Prospects: Co.'s outlook seems mixed. For instance, Co. is seeing a slight decrease in net interest margin primarily driven by a faster decline in the costs of funding than the decline in the income realized on earning assets. Nonetheless, despite the pressure on margins that resulted from the decreased federal funds rate, Co. is encouraged by the increase in its net interest income mainly attributable to the increase in earning assets. In addition, Co. is experiencing an increase in non-interest income, with growth in income from trust activity, deposit fees and insurance commissions. Moreover, Co. is bolstered by the growth in its total assets with increasing deposits, as well as loan growth.

Financial Data (US$ in Thousands)	3 Mos	12/31/2007	12/31/2006	12/31/2005	12/31/2004	12/31/2003	12/31/2002	12/31/2001
Earnings Per Share	1.97	1.94	1.77	1.72	2.07	1.95	2.10	1.78
Cash Flow Per Share	2.65	2.69	3.19	2.90	3.20	3.30	2.55	2.26
Tang Book Value Per Share	21.70	20.76	19.73	19.39	19.07	18.01	16.93	15.10
Dividends Per Share	0.870	0.870	0.850	0.820	0.790	0.700	0.620	0.570
Dividend Payout %	44.06	44.85	48.02	47.67	38.16	35.90	29.52	32.02
Income Statement								
Interest Income	34,287	137,734	130,832	121,647	116,888	122,661	136,262	144,673
Interest Expense	15,331	62,961	57,129	47,469	44,686	48,225	58,086	74,125
Net Interest Income	18,956	74,773	73,703	74,178	72,202	74,436	78,176	70,548
Provision for Losses	1,925	6,580	6,983	11,698	8,292	7,455	9,478	6,615
Non-Interest Income	8,649	31,497	28,826	32,025	35,754	30,819	30,468	21,468
Non-Interest Expense	16,424	64,726	64,656	63,538	63,656	62,461	63,317	53,329
Income Before Taxes	9,256	34,964	30,890	30,967	36,008	35,339	35,849	32,072
Income Taxes	2,306	9,384	7,351	7,913	7,999	8,846	7,209	7,876
Net Income	6,950	25,580	23,539	23,054	28,009	26,493	28,640	24,196
Average Shares	13,123	13,178	13,295	13,433	13,525	13,588	13,652	13,600
Balance Sheet								
Net Loans & Leases	1,410,273	1,427,716	1,376,586	1,379,699	1,443,953	1,408,286	1,411,315	1,330,148
Total Assets	2,298,834	2,231,562	2,175,998	2,136,918	2,183,992	2,223,057	2,169,748	2,041,905
Total Deposits	1,592,650	1,529,721	1,502,682	1,464,918	1,443,121	1,479,347	1,434,654	1,313,656
Total Liabilities	2,005,606	1,949,870	1,904,738	1,867,595	1,915,657	1,967,778	1,927,777	1,824,394
Stockholders' Equity	293,228	281,692	271,260	269,323	268,335	255,279	241,971	217,511
Shares Outstanding	13,103	13,136	13,270	13,373	13,535	13,578	13,618	13,688
Statistical Record								
Return on Assets %	1.16	1.16	1.09	1.07	1.27	1.21	1.36	1.18
Return on Equity %	9.13	9.25	8.71	8.58	10.67	10.66	12.47	11.84
Net Interest Margin %	55.29	54.29	56.33	60.98	61.77	60.68	57.37	48.76
Efficiency Ratio %	38.25	38.25	40.50	41.35	41.70	40.70	37.98	32.10
Loans to Deposits	0.89	0.93	0.92	0.94	1.00	0.95	0.98	1.01
Price Range	32.78-23.48	35.74-23.48	35.92-27.00	35.03-25.39	37.07-27.81	32.25-23.36	26.84-21.35	24.07-15.25
P/E Ratio	16.64-11.92	18.42-12.10	20.29-15.25	20.37-14.76	17.91-13.43	16.54-11.98	12.78-10.17	13.52-8.57
Average Yield %	2.99	2.90	2.76	2.85	2.54	2.56	2.61	2.94

Address: One First Financial Plaza, Terre Haute, IN 47807	Officers: Donald E. Smith - Chairman, President Norman L. Lowery - Vice-Chairman, Chief Executive	Investor Contact: 812-238-6264 No of Institutions: 70
Telephone: 812-238-6000 Web Site: www.first-online.com	Officer Transfer Agents: American Stock Transfer & Trust Company, New York, NY	Shares: 6,205,151 % Held: 46.43

FIRST FINANCIAL HOLDINGS, INC.

Exchange	Symbol	Price	52Wk Range	Yield	P/E
NMS	FFCH	$25.45 (5/29/2008)	35.64-20.21	4.01	13.68

*7 Year Price Score 72.61 *NYSE Composite Index=100 *12 Month Price Score 88.42

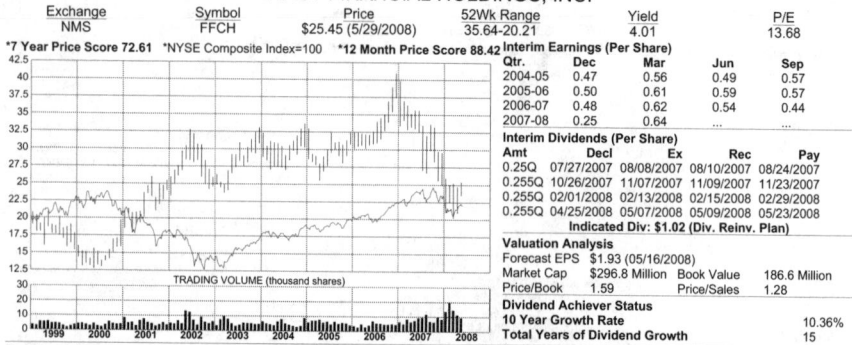

Interim Earnings (Per Share)

Qtr.	Dec	Mar	Jun	Sep
2004-05	0.47	0.56	0.49	0.57
2005-06	0.50	0.61	0.59	0.57
2006-07	0.48	0.62	0.54	0.44
2007-08	0.25	0.64	...	...

Interim Dividends (Per Share)

Amt	Decl	Ex	Rec	Pay
0.25Q	07/27/2007	08/08/2007	08/10/2007	08/24/2007
0.255Q	10/26/2007	11/07/2007	11/09/2007	11/23/2007
0.255Q	02/01/2008	02/13/2008	02/15/2008	02/29/2008
0.255Q	04/25/2008	05/07/2008	05/09/2008	05/23/2008

Indicated Div: $1.02 (Div. Reinv. Plan)

Valuation Analysis

Forecast EPS $1.93 (05/16/2008)

Market Cap	$296.8 Million	Book Value	186.6 Million
Price/Book	1.59	Price/Sales	1.28

Dividend Achiever Status

10 Year Growth Rate	10.36%
Total Years of Dividend Growth	15

TRADING VOLUME (thousand shares)

Business Summary: Other Depository Banking (MIC: SIC: 6035 NAIC: 522120)

First Financial Holdings is a savings and loan holding company. Co. originates construction, consumer, non-residential mortgage and commercial business loans as well as invests in mortgage-backed securities, federal government and agency obligations, money market obligations and certain corporate obligations. Co. also engages in full-service brokerage activities, property, casualty, life and health insurance sales, third party administrative services, trust and fiduciary services, reinsurance of private mortgage insurance, finance activities as well as certain passive investment activities. As of Sep 30 2007, Co. had total assets of $2.71 billion and total deposits of $1.85 billion.

Recent Developments: For the quarter ended Mar 31 2008, net income was unchanged at US$7.5 million versus US$7.5 million in the year-earlier quarter. Net interest income increased 8.2% to US$22.1 million from US$20.5 million in the year-earlier quarter. Provision for loan losses was US$3.6 million versus US$1.1 million in the prior-year quarter, an increase of 233.1%. Non-interest income rose 21.2% to US$17.8 million from US$14.7 million, while non-interest expense advanced 7.8% to US$24.1 million.

Prospects: Co. remains focused on growing its non-interest revenues and improving its operating capability, while working on technology initiatives such as merchant capture systems and document imaging systems to further improve its efficiency. For instance, in Apr 2008, Co.'s First Southeast Insurance Services, Inc. subsidiary acquired the operations of The Somers-Pardue Agency, Inc., a Burlington, NC based independent insurance agency, which will enable strategic partners in Co.'s insurance and financial services businesses, and contribute further diversification of its non-interest revenues. Meanwhile, Co. plans to open two additional in-store sales centers in late fiscal year ending Sep 30 2008.

Financial Data

(US$ in Thousands)	6 Mos	3 Mos	09/30/2007	09/30/2006	09/30/2005	09/30/2004	09/30/2003	09/30/2002
Earnings Per Share	1.86	1.85	2.07	2.27	2.09	1.92	2.07	2.04
Cash Flow Per Share	2.30	2.90	2.13	3.91	3.82	1.26	4.37	0.04
Tang Book Value Per Share	14.08	14.14	14.02	13.40	12.23	11.60	13.02	12.55
Dividends Per Share	1.010	1.005	1.000	0.960	0.920	0.880	0.760	0.680
Dividend Payout %	54.18	54.32	48.31	42.29	44.02	45.83	36.71	33.33
Income Statement								
Interest Income	88,172	44,363	168,044	151,340	130,776	126,593	134,381	154,026
Interest Expense	44,972	23,303	85,214	71,615	54,318	49,991	55,921	71,342
Net Interest Income	43,200	21,060	82,830	79,725	76,458	76,602	78,460	82,684
Provision for Losses	6,814	3,248	4,726	4,695	4,826	5,675	6,235	5,888
Non-Interest Income	31,441	13,640	55,232	54,164	49,245	42,175	40,965	30,959
Non-Interest Expense	50,702	26,640	92,889	86,344	80,052	74,764	70,781	63,944
Income Before Taxes	17,125	4,812	40,447	42,850	40,825	38,338	42,409	43,811
Income Taxes	6,698	1,915	15,375	15,221	14,600	13,784	15,198	15,659
Net Income	10,427	2,897	25,072	27,629	26,225	24,554	27,211	28,152
Average Shares	11,675	11,726	12,089	12,190	12,528	12,818	13,173	13,832
Balance Sheet								
Net Loans & Leases	2,232,058	2,194,972	2,140,769	2,061,129	1,888,389	1,817,585	1,801,932	1,924,828
Total Assets	2,888,504	2,817,707	2,711,370	2,658,128	2,522,405	2,442,313	2,322,882	2,264,674
Total Deposits	1,875,099	1,806,585	1,854,051	1,823,028	1,657,072	1,520,817	1,481,651	1,440,271
Total Liabilities	2,701,878	2,630,411	2,525,655	2,474,363	2,351,276	2,277,126	2,159,876	2,099,026
Stockholders' Equity	186,626	187,296	185,715	183,765	171,129	165,187	163,006	165,648
Shares Outstanding	11,663	11,656	11,635	12,021	12,115	12,303	12,522	13,195
Statistical Record								
Return on Assets %	0.79	0.81	0.93	1.07	1.06	1.03	1.19	1.23
Return on Equity %	11.73	11.79	13.57	15.57	15.60	14.92	16.56	17.46
Net Interest Margin %	50.54	47.47	49.29	52.68	58.46	60.51	58.39	53.68
Efficiency Ratio %	39.05	45.93	41.60	42.02	44.47	44.30	40.37	34.57
Loans to Deposits	1.19	1.21	1.15	1.13	1.14	1.20	1.22	1.34
Price Range	35.66-20.21	39.84-24.94	40.90-26.69	35.05-28.06	33.70-25.55	33.10-27.05	30.96-23.70	32.74-22.04
P/E Ratio	19.17-10.87	21.54-13.48	19.76-12.89	15.44-12.36	16.12-12.22	17.24-14.09	14.96-11.45	16.05-10.80
Average Yield %	3.46	3.11	2.91	3.04	3.10	2.95	2.84	2.51

Address: 34 Broad Street, Charleston, SC 29401	Officers: James C. Murray - Chairman A. Thomas	Investor Contact: 843-529-5933
Telephone: 843-529-5933	Hood - President, Chief Executive Officer **Transfer**	No of Institutions: 80
Web Site: www.firstfinancialholdings.com	Agents:Register & Transfer Company, Cranford, NJ	Shares: 4,596,224 % Held: 37.43

FIRST MIDWEST BANCORP, INC. (NAPERVILLE, IL)

Exchange	Symbol	Price	52Wk Range	Yield	P/E
NMS	FMBI	$26.25 (5/29/2008)	37.62-24.24	4.72	16.83

*7 Year Price Score 75.08 *NYSE Composite Index=100 *12 Month Price Score 86.27

Interim Earnings (Per Share)

Qtr.	Mar	Jun	Sep	Dec
2005	0.55	0.58	0.59	0.50
2006	0.55	0.57	0.62	0.63
2007	0.58	0.59	0.55	(0.09)
2008	0.52	...	...	...

Interim Dividends (Per Share)

Amt	Decl	Ex	Rec	Pay
0.295Q	08/16/2007	09/26/2007	09/28/2007	10/16/2007
0.31Q	11/29/2007	12/19/2007	12/21/2007	01/15/2008
0.31Q	02/25/2008	03/26/2008	03/28/2008	04/15/2008
0.31Q	05/28/2008	06/25/2008	06/27/2008	07/15/2008

Indicated Div: $1.24 (Div. Reinv. Plan)

Valuation Analysis

Forecast EPS	$2.08 (05/17/2008)		
Market Cap	$1.3 Billion	Book Value	737.9 Million
Price/Book	1.73	Price/Sales	2.43

Dividend Achiever Status

10 Year Growth Rate	10.71%
Total Years of Dividend Growth	15

TRADING VOLUME (thousand shares)

Business Summary: Commercial Banking (MIC: SIC: 6021 NAIC: 522110)

First Midwest Bancorp is a bank-holding company. Through its primary bank subsidiary, First Midwest Bank, Co. is engaged in commercial and retail banking, providing various lending, depository, and related financial services such as accepting deposits; commercial and industrial, consumer, and real estate lending; collections; trust and investment management services; cash management services; safe deposit box operations; and other banking services for commercial and industrial, and public or governmental customers. As of Dec 31 2007, Co. had $8.09 billion in total assets, $5.78 billion in total deposits, and 99 banking offices primarily in suburban metropolitan Chicago.

Recent Developments: For the quarter ended Mar 31 2008, net income decreased 13.7% to US$25.0 million from US$29.0 million in the year-earlier quarter. Net interest income decreased 3.1% to US$58.5 million from US$60.4 million in the year-earlier quarter. Provision for loan losses was US$9.1 million versus US$3.0 million in the prior-year quarter, an increase of 206.1%. Non-interest income rose 4.6% to US$30.0 million from US$28.7 million, while non-interest expense advanced 2.5% to US$49.3 million.

Prospects: Co.'s results are being negatively affected by several counterbalancing economic events, including aggressive Federal Reserve actions to lower interest rates and provide liquidity to the stalled financial markets, coupled with the negative trends in the residential development markets. As a result, Co. is mitigating these challenges, which is manifested in higher credit charges, in valuation reserve expansion, in Other Real Estate Owned designations, and in ninety-day past due totals. Nevertheless, Co. is experiencing good progress in commercial sales activity, which is expanding loan balances at a 9.1% rate, driven by growth in commercial real estate and commercial and industrial loans.

Financial Data
(US$ in Thousands)

	3 Mos	12/31/2007	12/31/2006	12/31/2005	12/31/2004	12/31/2003	12/31/2002	12/31/2001
Earnings Per Share	1.56	1.62	2.37	2.21	2.12	1.97	1.86	1.63
Cash Flow Per Share	1.91	2.46	2.32	2.71	3.19	2.67	2.74	1.74
Tang Book Value Per Share	9.28	8.99	9.16	9.87	9.45	9.09	10.07	9.18
Dividends Per Share	1.210	1.195	1.120	1.015	0.900	0.790	0.700	0.650
Dividend Payout %	77.39	73.77	47.26	45.93	42.45	40.10	37.63	39.88
Income Statement								
Interest Income	108,475	476,961	476,409	366,700	315,342	291,067	329,664	385,218
Interest Expense	49,975	236,832	224,550	130,850	86,478	81,313	110,910	180,838
Net Interest Income	58,500	240,129	251,859	235,850	228,864	209,754	218,754	204,380
Provision for Losses	9,060	7,233	10,229	8,930	12,923	10,805	15,410	19,084
Non-Interest Income	30,019	60,253	103,283	74,612	79,381	74,170	66,991	68,866
Non-Interest Expense	49,343	199,137	192,615	165,703	163,338	149,452	148,052	145,356
Income Before Taxes	30,116	94,012	152,298	135,829	131,984	123,667	122,283	108,806
Income Taxes	5,078	13,853	35,052	34,452	32,848	30,889	32,133	26,668
Net Income	25,038	80,159	117,246	101,377	99,136	92,778	90,150	82,138
Average Shares	48,589	49,622	49,469	45,893	46,860	46,982	48,415	50,401
Balance Sheet								
Net Loans & Leases	4,980,985	4,901,872	4,946,574	4,249,798	4,078,560	4,003,378	3,358,917	3,324,561
Total Assets	8,315,368	8,091,518	8,441,654	7,210,151	6,863,381	6,906,658	5,980,533	5,667,919
Total Deposits	5,721,562	5,778,861	6,167,216	5,147,832	4,905,378	4,815,108	4,172,954	4,193,921
Total Liabilities	7,577,441	7,367,543	7,690,512	6,666,083	6,331,343	6,384,118	5,488,580	5,220,652
Stockholders' Equity	737,927	723,975	751,014	544,068	532,038	522,540	491,953	447,267
Shares Outstanding	48,561	48,453	50,025	45,387	46,065	46,581	47,206	48,725
Statistical Record								
Return on Assets %	0.92	0.97	1.50	1.44	1.44	1.44	1.55	1.42
Return on Equity %	10.17	10.87	18.11	18.84	18.75	18.29	19.20	18.38
Net Interest Margin %	53.93	50.35	52.87	64.32	72.58	72.06	66.36	53.06
Efficiency Ratio %	35.63	37.07	33.23	37.55	41.38	40.92	37.33	32.01
Loans to Deposits	0.87	0.85	0.80	0.83	0.83	0.83	0.80	0.79
Price Range	38.11-24.76	39.26-29.89	39.14-32.86	39.16-31.30	38.19-31.38	32.57-25.08	31.85-24.02	29.19-20.95
P/E Ratio	24.43-15.87	24.23-18.45	16.51-13.86	17.72-14.16	18.01-14.80	16.53-12.73	17.12-12.91	17.91-12.85
Average Yield %	3.68	3.39	3.07	2.86	2.62	2.73	2.48	2.64

Address: 300 Park Blvd., Suite 400, P.O. Box 459, Itasca, IL 60143-9768 Telephone: 630-875-7450 Web Site: www.firstmidwest.com	Officers: John M. O'Meara - Chairman, Chief Executive Officer Robert P. O'Meara - Vice-Chairman Transfer Agents:Mellon Investor Services, Ridgefield Park, NJ	Investor Contact: 630-875-7345 No of Institutions: 194 Shares: 39,659,868 % Held: 72.40

1ST SOURCE CORP.

Exchange	Symbol	Price	52Wk Range	Yield	P/E
NMS	SRCE	$22.28 (5/29/2008)	26.46-15.62	2.51	17.27

*7 Year Price Score 75.53   ***NYSE Composite Index=100**   ***12 Month Price Score 102.71**

Interim Earnings (Per Share)

Qtr.	Mar	Jun	Sep	Dec
2005	0.30	0.35	0.41	0.39
2006	0.44	0.45	0.48	0.36
2007	0.37	0.34	0.25	0.32
2008	0.38	...	...	...

Interim Dividends (Per Share)

Amt	Decl	Ex	Rec	Pay
0.14Q	07/19/2007	08/02/2007	08/06/2007	08/15/2007
0.14Q	10/25/2007	11/01/2007	11/05/2007	11/15/2007
0.14Q	01/24/2008	02/01/2008	02/05/2008	02/15/2008
0.14Q	04/24/2008	05/01/2008	05/05/2008	05/15/2008
		Indicated Div: $0.56		

Valuation Analysis

Forecast EPS	N/A		
Market Cap	$543.1 Million	Book Value	440.3 Million
Price/Book	1.23	Price/Sales	1.63

Dividend Achiever Status

10 Year Growth Rate	10.53%
Total Years of Dividend Growth	20

TRADING VOLUME (thousand shares)

Business Summary: Commercial Banking (MIC: SIC: 6022 NAIC: 522110)

1st Source, through its subsidiary, 1st Source Bank and First National Bank, Valparaiso, provides commercial and consumer banking services, trust and investment management services, and insurance to individual and business clients through 83 banking center locations in 17 counties in Indiana and Michigan. Through its 1st Source Bank Specialty Finance Group subsidiary with 24 locations across the U.S., Co. provides financing services for new and used private and cargo aircraft, automobiles and light trucks for leasing and rental agencies, medium and heavy duty trucks, construction equipment, and environmental equipment. As of Dec 31 2007, Co. had total assets of $4.45 billion.

Recent Developments: For the quarter ended Mar 31 2008, net income increased 9.8% to US$9.4 million from US$8.5 million in the year-earlier quarter. Net interest income increased 22.9% to US$32.3 million from US$26.3 million in the year-earlier quarter. Provision for loan losses was US$1.5 million versus a credit for loan losses of US$623,000 in the prior-year quarter. Non-interest income rose 20.3% to US$21.0 million from US$17.5 million, while non-interest expense advanced 19.2% to US$37.9 million.

Prospects: Co.'s bottom-line continues to be negatively affected by an increase in the provision for loan and lease losses and higher non-interest expense. Nevertheless, Co. remains optimistic regarding its near-term outlook. In particular, Co. is experiencing an increase in net interest income, driven primarily by the acquisition of First National Bank, Valparaiso on May 31 2007 and higher average earning assets, partially offset by a decline in yield on average earning assets. In addition, Co. is benefiting from an improvement in non-interest income, due primarily to an acceleration in trust fees, service charges on deposits, mortgage banking income and insurance commissions.

Financial Data (US$ in Thousands)	3 Mos	12/31/2007	12/31/2006	12/31/2005	12/31/2004	12/31/2003	12/31/2002	12/31/2001
Earnings Per Share	1.29	1.28	1.72	1.46	1.08	0.83	0.43	1.65
Cash Flow Per Share	2.63	3.59	3.73	2.17	2.85	8.66	3.59	3.68
Tang Book Value Per Share	13.98	13.82	16.21	15.03	14.16	13.65	13.28	13.26
Dividends Per Share	0.560	0.560	0.535	0.445	0.382	0.336	0.327	0.319
Dividend Payout %	43.54	43.75	31.08	30.43	35.29	40.66	76.60	19.31
Income Statement								
Interest Income	62,124	253,587	208,994	168,532	151,437	162,322	199,503	242,183
Interest Expense	29,827	134,677	102,561	70,104	52,749	59,070	80,817	123,397
Net Interest Income	32,297	118,910	106,433	98,428	98,688	103,252	118,686	118,786
Provision for Losses	1,539	7,534	(2,736)	(5,855)	229	17,361	39,657	28,623
Non-Interest Income	21,027	70,619	76,585	68,533	62,733	80,196	73,117	92,836
Non-Interest Expense	37,901	140,312	126,211	123,439	127,091	138,904	137,735	121,232
Income Before Taxes	13,884	41,683	59,543	49,377	34,101	27,183	11,405	61,767
Income Taxes	4,530	11,144	20,246	15,626	9,136	8,029	1,366	21,059
Net Income	9,354	30,539	39,297	33,751	24,965	19,154	10,039	38,498
Average Shares	24,382	23,810	22,830	23,052	23,083	23,265	23,441	23,287
Balance Sheet								
Net Loans & Leases	3,122,413	3,124,839	2,643,735	2,404,734	2,216,496	2,160,955	2,266,874	2,477,740
Total Assets	4,462,320	4,447,104	3,807,315	3,511,277	3,563,715	3,330,153	3,407,468	3,562,691
Total Deposits	3,505,124	3,469,663	3,048,284	2,745,587	2,807,003	2,487,215	2,712,905	2,882,806
Total Liabilities	4,022,005	4,016,600	3,438,411	3,165,701	3,237,115	3,015,462	3,098,039	3,211,751
Stockholders' Equity	440,315	430,504	368,904	345,576	326,600	314,691	309,429	306,190
Shares Outstanding	24,374	24,376	22,759	22,996	23,062	23,058	23,306	23,094
Statistical Record								
Return on Assets %	0.76	0.74	1.07	0.95	0.72	0.57	0.29	1.14
Return on Equity %	7.67	7.64	11.00	10.04	7.76	6.14	3.26	13.35
Net Interest Margin %	51.99	46.89	50.93	58.40	65.17	63.61	59.49	49.05
Efficiency Ratio %	45.58	43.28	44.19	52.07	59.34	57.28	50.52	36.19
Loans to Deposits	0.89	0.90	0.87	0.88	0.79	0.87	0.84	0.86
Price Range	27.46-15.62	32.36-16.66	33.28-23.33	23.64-17.88	25.39-18.91	20.36-11.55	24.25-9.96	25.45-15.53
P/E Ratio	21.29-12.11	25.28-13.02	19.35-13.56	16.19-12.25	23.51-17.51	24.53-13.91	56.41-23.15	15.43-9.41
Average Yield %	2.59	2.33	1.92	2.12	1.74	2.09	1.82	1.71

Address: 100 North Michigan Street, South Bend, IN 46601 **Telephone:** 574-235-2000 **Web Site:** www.1stsource.com	**Officers:** Christopher J. Murphy - Chairman, President, Chief Executive Officer Wellington D. Jones - Executive Vice President **Transfer Agents:** 1st Source Bank, South Bend, IN	**Investor Contact:** 574-235-2702 **No of Institutions:** 79 **Shares:** 17,360,600 **% Held:** 71.21

FIRST STATE BANCORPORATION

Exchange	Symbol	Price	52Wk Range	Yield	P/E
NMS	FSNM	$7.81 (5/29/2008)	22.50-7.81	4.61	7.23

*7 Year Price Score 70.27 *NYSE Composite Index=100 *12 Month Price Score 68.41

Interim Earnings (Per Share)

Qtr.	Mar	Jun	Sep	Dec
2005	0.28	0.32	0.39	0.38
2006	0.24	0.33	0.37	0.31
2007	0.31	0.35	0.32	0.22
2008	0.19	...	...	...

Interim Dividends (Per Share)

Amt	Decl	Ex	Rec	Pay
0.09Q	07/25/2007	08/06/2007	08/08/2007	09/05/2007
0.09Q	10/26/2007	11/05/2007	11/07/2007	12/05/2007
0.09Q	01/25/2008	02/04/2008	02/06/2008	03/05/2008
0.09Q	04/25/2008	05/05/2008	05/07/2008	06/04/2008

Indicated Div: $0.36

Valuation Analysis

Forecast EPS	$0.85 (05/16/2008)		
Market Cap	$157.1 Million	Book Value	316.1 Million
Price/Book	0.50	Price/Sales	0.62

Dividend Achiever Status

10 Year Growth Rate	17.46%
Total Years of Dividend Growth	13

Business Summary: Commercial Banking (MIC: SIC: 6022 NAIC: 522110)

First State Bancorporation is a New Mexico-based bank holding company. Through its First Community Bank subsidiary, Co. provides a range of financial services to its customers, including checking accounts, short and medium term loans, revolving credit facilities, inventory and accounts receivable financing, equipment financing, residential and commercial construction lending, residential mortgage loans, various savings programs, installment and personal loans, and safe deposit services. As of Dec 31 2007, Co. operated 61 branch offices in New Mexico, Colorado, Utah, and Arizona. As of Dec 31 2007, Co. had total assets of $3.42 billion and total deposits of $2.57 billion.

Recent Developments: For the quarter ended Mar 31 2008, net income decreased 39.4% to US$3.9 million from US$6.5 million in the year-earlier quarter. Net interest income increased 0.9% to US$31.4 million from US$31.1 million in the year-earlier quarter. Provision for loan losses was US$3.9 million versus US$2.0 million in the prior-year quarter, an increase of 90.8%. Non-interest income rose 6.7% to US$6.3 million from US$5.9 million, while non-interest expense advanced 11.6% to US$27.8 million.

Prospects: Looking ahead, Co. expects further reduction in its net interest margin as the Federal Reserve Bank has continued to lower target rates in Apr 30 2008 by 25 basis points. Co. also expects with the combination of the Federal Reserve Bank rate cut in late Mar will unfavorably affect net income going forward. Based solely on its interest rate gap of 12 months or less, Co. anticipates that net income could be further unfavorably affected by additional decreases in interest rates or favorably affected by increases in interest rates. However, Co. expects the effect of these cuts by Federal Reserve Bank will begin to moderate as its deposits continue to reprice from earlier rate cuts.

Financial Data
(US$ in Thousands)

	3 Mos	12/31/2007	12/31/2006	12/31/2005	12/31/2004	12/31/2003	12/31/2002	12/31/2001
Earnings Per Share	1.08	1.20	1.26	1.36	0.99	0.97	0.83	0.81
Cash Flow Per Share	2.46	2.23	2.46	2.04	1.07	2.59	1.12	0.45
Tang Book Value Per Share	8.52	8.23	11.04	7.60	6.60	5.87	5.05	5.93
Dividends Per Share	0.359	0.350	0.320	0.280	0.240	0.215	0.200	0.170
Dividend Payout %	33.36	29.17	25.40	20.59	24.24	22.05	24.10	21.12
Income Statement								
Interest Income	52,969	229,232	181,852	121,957	93,442	83,713	62,448	55,713
Interest Expense	21,564	96,425	67,051	37,712	23,875	22,629	18,384	20,478
Net Interest Income	31,405	132,807	114,801	84,245	69,567	61,084	44,064	35,235
Provision for Losses	3,900	10,267	6,993	3,920	4,500	5,543	2,589	2,386
Non-Interest Income	6,284	25,465	19,472	16,451	14,191	14,521	12,698	9,414
Non-Interest Expense	27,833	109,886	92,008	63,590	55,043	47,242	38,584	29,600
Income Before Taxes	5,956	38,119	35,272	33,186	23,780	22,820	15,589	12,663
Income Taxes	2,031	13,312	12,497	11,788	8,555	7,969	5,631	4,521
Net Income	3,925	24,807	22,775	21,398	15,225	14,851	9,958	8,142
Average Shares	20,157	20,628	18,061	15,689	15,443	15,196	11,995	10,098
Balance Sheet								
Net Loans & Leases	2,575,696	2,509,498	2,018,482	1,508,514	1,362,464	1,217,364	1,005,187	541,515
Total Assets	3,460,038	3,424,203	2,801,572	2,157,571	1,815,510	1,646,739	1,386,870	827,921
Total Deposits	2,580,601	2,574,687	2,120,924	1,510,007	1,401,303	1,195,875	1,079,684	685,022
Total Liabilities	3,143,894	3,113,341	2,496,680	1,997,392	1,671,201	1,514,298	1,269,402	769,577
Stockholders' Equity	316,144	310,862	304,892	160,179	144,309	132,441	117,468	58,345
Shares Outstanding	20,115	20,091	20,777	15,394	15,324	15,209	14,655	9,771
Statistical Record								
Return on Assets %	0.66	0.80	0.92	1.08	0.88	0.98	0.90	1.10
Return on Equity %	7.09	8.06	9.79	14.06	10.97	11.89	11.33	14.85
Net Interest Margin %	59.29	57.94	63.13	69.08	74.45	72.97	70.56	63.24
Efficiency Ratio %	46.97	43.14	45.70	45.94	51.14	48.09	51.35	45.45
Loans to Deposits	1.00	0.97	0.95	1.00	0.97	1.02	0.93	0.79
Price Range	22.75-10.04	25.01-12.09	27.31-22.50	25.79-16.85	19.25-14.51	17.99-10.70	13.90-9.26	10.74-6.63
P/E Ratio	21.06-9.30	20.84-10.08	21.67-17.86	18.96-12.39	19.45-14.66	18.55-11.03	16.75-11.15	13.27-8.18
Average Yield %	0.52	1.77	1.28	1.38	1.49	1.57	1.70	1.98

Address: 7900 Jefferson N.E., Albuquerque, NM 87109 Telephone: 505-241-7500 Web Site: www.fsbnm.com	Officers: Leonard J. Delayo - Chairman Michael R. Stanford - President, Chief Executive Officer Transfer Agents: American Stock Transfer & Trust Company, Brooklyn, New York	Investor Contact: 505-241-7500 No of Institutions: 127 Shares: 17,066,890 % Held: 77.26

FIRSTMERIT CORP

Exchange	Symbol	Price	52Wk Range	Yield	P/E
NMS	FMER	$20.35 (5/29/2008)	22.53-17.12	5.70	13.30

*7 Year Price Score 64.59 *NYSE Composite Index=100 *12 Month Price Score 105.10

Interim Earnings (Per Share)

Qtr.	Mar	Jun	Sep	Dec
2005	0.36	0.43	0.43	0.34
2006	0.37	0.35	0.39	0.07
2007	0.39	0.37	0.38	0.39
2008	0.39	...	...	...

Interim Dividends (Per Share)

Amt	Decl	Ex	Rec	Pay
0.29Q	08/16/2007	08/23/2007	08/27/2007	09/17/2007
0.29Q	11/15/2007	11/21/2007	11/26/2007	12/17/2007
0.29Q	02/21/2008	02/28/2008	03/03/2008	03/17/2008
0.29Q	05/14/2008	05/29/2008	06/02/2008	06/16/2008

Indicated Div: $1.16

Valuation Analysis

Forecast EPS $1.47 (05/16/2008)

Market Cap	$1.9 Billion	Book Value	937.4 Million
Price/Book	2.00	Price/Sales	2.27

Dividend Achiever Status

10 Year Growth Rate	6.64%
Total Years of Dividend Growth	25

Business Summary: Commercial Banking (MIC: SIC: 6021 NAIC: 522110)

FirstMerit is a bank-holding company with total assets of $10.40 billion and total deposits of $7.33 billion as of Dec 31 2007. Through its banking subsidiary, FirstMerit Bank, N.A. (FirstMerit Bank), Co. operates primarily as a line of business banking organization that provides a range of banking, fiduciary, financial, insurance and investment services to corporate, institutional and individual customers throughout northern and central Ohio, as well as western Pennsylvania. As of the date stated above, FirstMerit Bank operated a network of 159 full-service banking offices and 176 automated teller machines.

Recent Developments: For the quarter ended Mar 31 2008, net income was unchanged at US$31.4 million versus US$31.4 million the year-earlier quarter. Net interest income increased 2.8% to US$84.3 million from US$82.0 million in the year-earlier quarter. Provision for loan losses was US$11.5 million versus US$4.2 million in the prior-year quarter, an increase of 173.7%. Non-interest income rose 8.1% to US$52.9 million from US$48.9 million, while non-interest expense declined 0.4% to US$81.2 million.

Prospects: Co.'s outlook appears favorable as it is seeing an increase in net interest income on a fully tax-equivalent basis due to net interest margin expansion and average earning asset growth. Further, the mix shift in Co.'s deposit composition to a higher concentration of core deposits contributed to lower funding costs and provided a partial offset to decreased average earning asset yields. Looking ahead, Co. believes that it is positioned to profitably grow its balance sheet by winning new business and deepening its existing customer relationships. In addition, Co. intends to execute its community banking model with an aggressive sales approach tempered by its improved credit discipline.

Financial Data
(US$ in Thousands)

	3 Mos	12/31/2007	12/31/2006	12/31/2005	12/31/2004	12/31/2003	12/31/2002	12/31/2001
Earnings Per Share	1.53	1.53	1.18	1.56	1.21	1.42	1.81	1.35
Cash Flow Per Share	2.10	2.12	2.05	2.21	2.19	3.63	10.73	5.80
Tang Book Value Per Share	8.65	9.64	8.79	9.48	9.95	9.94	9.68	9.06
Dividends Per Share	1.160	1.160	1.140	1.100	1.060	1.020	0.980	0.930
Dividend Payout %	76.02	75.82	96.61	70.51	87.60	71.83	54.14	68.89
Income Statement								
Income Before Taxes	44,398	173,408	131,322	182,133	139,238	174,596	222,340	183,471
Income Taxes	12,955	50,381	36,376	51,650	36,024	52,939	67,974	60,867
Net Income	31,443	123,027	94,946	130,483	103,214	120,969	154,366	116,305
Average Shares	80,722	80,510	80,351	83,844	84,995	84,929	85,317	86,288
Balance Sheet								
Total Assets	10,516,828	10,400,666	10,252,572	10,161,317	10,122,627	10,473,635	10,688,206	10,193,374
Total Liabilities	9,579,389	9,483,689	9,406,461	9,223,737	9,141,370	9,486,460	9,723,549	9,282,567
Stockholders' Equity	937,439	916,977	846,111	937,580	981,257	987,175	964,657	910,807
Shares Outstanding	92,026	80,482	80,100	83,843	84,190	84,724	84,505	84,991
Statistical Record								
Return on Assets %	1.18	1.19	0.93	1.29	1.00	1.14	1.48	1.14
Return on Equity %	13.63	13.96	10.65	13.60	10.46	12.40	16.46	12.74
Price Range	22.53-17.12	24.57-17.52	26.45-20.94	28.89-24.36	28.74-23.23	27.81-18.16	29.49-18.89	27.94-21.10
P/E Ratio	14.73-11.19	16.06-11.45	22.42-17.75	18.52-15.62	23.75-19.20	19.58-12.79	16.29-10.44	20.70-15.63
Average Yield %	5.75	5.60	4.82	4.13	4.08	4.42	3.87	3.71

Address: 111 Cascade Plaza, 7th Floor, Akron, OH 44308-1103 **Telephone:** 330-996-6300 **Web Site:** www.firstmerit.com	**Officers:** Paul G. Greig - Chairman, President, Chief Executive Officer Robert P. Brecht - Senior Executive Vice President **Transfer Agents:** American Stock Transfer & Trust Co., New York, NY	**Investor Contact:** 330-996-6300 **No of Institutions:** 201 **Shares:** 55,452,668 **% Held:** 59.88

FLUSHING FINANCIAL CORP.

Exchange	Symbol	Price	52Wk Range	Yield	P/E
NMS	FFIC	$20.12 (5/29/2008)	20.12-13.06	2.58	18.13

*7 Year Price Score 82.73 *NYSE Composite Index=100 *12 Month Price Score 115.38

Interim Earnings (Per Share)

Qtr.	Mar	Jun	Sep	Dec
2005	0.33	0.33	0.33	0.32
2006	0.33	0.30	0.27	0.25
2007	0.27	0.24	0.29	0.22
2008	0.36	...	...	...

Interim Dividends (Per Share)

Amt	Decl	Ex	Rec	Pay
0.12Q	08/21/2007	09/05/2007	09/07/2007	09/28/2007
0.12Q	11/21/2007	12/05/2007	12/07/2007	12/28/2007
0.13Q	02/27/2008	03/06/2008	03/10/2008	03/31/2008
0.13Q	05/21/2008	06/05/2008	06/09/2008	06/30/2008

Indicated Div: $0.52

Valuation Analysis

Forecast EPS $1.40 (05/16/2008)

Market Cap	$429.4 Million	Book Value	235.4 Million
Price/Book	1.82	Price/Sales	2.02

Dividend Achiever Status

10 Year Growth Rate		22.10%
Total Years of Dividend Growth		11

TRADING VOLUME (thousand shares)

Business Summary: Other Depository Banking (MIC: SIC: 6035 NAIC: 522120)

Flushing Financial is the holding company for Flushing Savings Bank, a federally chartered stock savings bank. Co.'s principal business is accepting retail deposits from the public and investing those deposits together with funds from operations and borrowings primarily in: originations and purchases of one-to-four family, multi-family residential and commercial real estate mortgage loans; construction loans; Small Business Administration loans and other small business loans; mortgage loan surrogates; and U.S. government securities, corporate fixed-income securities and other marketable securities. As of Dec 31 2007, Co. had total assets of $3.35 billion and deposits of $2.03 billion.

Recent Developments: For the quarter ended Mar 31 2008, net income increased 32.8% to US$7.2 million from US$5.4 million in the year-earlier quarter. Net interest income increased 19.7% to US$20.7 million from US$17.3 million in the year-earlier quarter. Non-interest income rose 8.8% to US$4.0 million from US$3.7 million, while non-interest expense advanced 5.5% to US$13.2 million.

Prospects: Co. is seeing growth in its net interest income due to higher average balance of interest-earning assets, combined with higher net interest spread. Also, Co.'s yield on interest earning assets grew due to an increase in the average balance of the loan portfolio. Going forward, Co. continues to emphasize the origination of higher-yielding multi-family residential, commercial real estate and one-to-four family mixed-use property mortgage loans. In addition, Co. intends to cross sell to its lending and deposit customers by further expanding its product offerings in 2008. Moreover, Co. continues to expand and enhance its strengths in multicultural banking and mixed-use and multi-family lending.

Financial Data
(US$ in Thousands)

	3 Mos	12/31/2007	12/31/2006	12/31/2005	12/31/2004	12/31/2003	12/31/2002	12/31/2001
Earnings Per Share	1.11	1.02	1.14	1.31	1.25	1.22	0.89	0.78
Cash Flow Per Share	1.56	1.30	1.63	1.46	1.68	1.69	1.44	0.83
Tang Book Value Per Share	10.15	10.07	9.48	8.86	8.15	7.41	6.75	6.40
Dividends Per Share	0.490	0.480	0.440	0.400	0.350	0.280	0.240	0.204
Dividend Payout %	44.25	47.06	38.60	30.53	28.00	22.95	26.87	26.21
Income Statement								
Income Before Taxes	11,170	31,115	34,757	38,593	37,045	35,222	26,230	23,798
Income Taxes	4,019	10,930	13,118	15,051	14,396	13,544	9,967	8,869
Net Income	7,151	20,185	21,639	23,542	22,649	21,678	16,263	14,929
Average Shares	19,987	19,861	18,932	18,001	18,092	17,770	18,171	19,156
Balance Sheet								
Total Assets	3,468,753	3,354,519	2,836,521	2,353,208	2,058,044	1,910,751	1,652,958	1,487,529
Total Liabilities	3,233,341	3,120,865	2,618,106	2,176,741	1,897,391	1,763,989	1,521,572	1,354,142
Stockholders' Equity	235,412	233,654	218,415	176,467	160,653	146,762	131,386	133,387
Shares Outstanding	21,343	21,321	21,131	19,465	19,232	19,290	18,897	20,231
Statistical Record								
Return on Assets %	0.68	0.65	0.83	1.07	1.14	1.22	1.04	1.06
Return on Equity %	9.62	8.93	10.96	13.97	14.69	15.59	12.28	11.48
Price Range	18.41-13.06	18.41-14.52	18.58-15.29	20.22-14.40	21.34-16.46	18.83-10.78	13.75-9.96	12.63-7.33
P/E Ratio	16.59-11.77	18.05-14.24	16.30-13.41	15.44-10.99	17.07-13.17	15.43-8.84	15.45-11.19	16.20-9.40
Average Yield %	3.02	2.91	2.59	2.30	1.90	1.99	2.03	2.06

Address: 144-51 Northern Blvd., Flushing, NY 11354 **Telephone:** 718-961-5400 **Web Site:** www.flushingsavings.com	**Officers:** Gerard P. Tully - Chairman John R. Buran - President, Chief Executive Officer **Transfer Agents:** Computershare Trust Company NA, Providence, RI	**No of Institutions:** 87 **Shares:** 17,228,796 **% Held:** 78.17

FOREST CITY ENTERPRISES, INC.

Exchange	Symbol	Price	52Wk Range	Yield	P/E
NYS	FCE A	$40.20 (5/29/2008)	70.98-34.47	0.80	160.80

*7 Year Price Score 113.73 *NYSE Composite Index=100 *12 Month Price Score 80.69

Interim Earnings (Per Share)

Qtr.	Apr	Jul	Oct	Jan
2005-06	0.22	0.20	0.13	0.27
2006-07	0.52	0.07	0.45	0.67
2007-08	(0.17)	0.63	(0.11)	0.13
2008-09	(0.39)	...	...	...

Interim Dividends (Per Share)

Amt	Decl	Ex	Rec	Pay
0.08Q	06/21/2007	08/30/2007	09/04/2007	09/18/2007
0.08Q	09/26/2007	11/29/2007	12/03/2007	12/17/2007
0.08Q	12/14/2007	02/28/2008	03/03/2008	03/17/2008
0.08Q	03/26/2008	05/29/2008	06/02/2008	06/17/2008

Indicated Div: $0.32

Valuation Analysis

Forecast EPS $-0.66 (05/16/2008)

Market Cap	$3.2 Billion	Book Value	929.0 Million
Price/Book	3.41	Price/Sales	2.38

Dividend Achiever Status

10 Year Dividend Rate	22.32%
Total Years of Dividend Growth	13

TRADING VOLUME (thousand shares)

Business Summary: "Property, Real Estate & Development" (MIC: SIC: 6512 NAIC: 236220)

Forest City Enterprises is mainly engaged in the ownership, development, management and acquisition of commercial and residential real estate properties in 27 states and the District of Columbia. The Commercial Group owns, develops, acquires and operates regional malls, specialty/urban retail centers, office and life science buildings, hotels and mixed-use projects. The Residential Group owns, develops, acquires and operates residential rental properties, including upscale and middle-market apartments as well as adaptive re-use developments. The Land Development Group acquires and sells both land and developed lots to residential, commercial and industrial customers.

Recent Developments: For the quarter ended Apr 30 2008, loss from continuing operations was US$40.3 million compared with a loss of US$17.7 million in the year-earlier quarter. Net loss amounted to US$40.3 million versus a net loss of US$17.2 million in the year-earlier quarter. Revenues were US$307.6 million, up 14.6% from US$268.4 million the year before.

Prospects: Co.'s near-term outlook appears to be constructive. In 2008, Co. expects to begin construction of 80 DeKalb, a 365-unit apartment community in Brooklyn. In addition, Co. intends to initiate the construction of Presidio, a 161-unit apartment community in San Francisco, by the end of 2008. Meanwhile, Co. continues to progress with the construction of The Shops at Wiregrass, a 646,000-square-foot open-air lifestyle center in Tampa, as well as White Oak Village, a 792,000-square-foot lifestyle/power center near Richmond. Accordingly, Co. foresees the opening of these two properties by the end of 2008. Lastly, Co. expects to open its Ridge Hill and East River Plaza retail projects by 2009.

Financial Data
(US$ in Thousands)

	3 Mos	01/31/2008	01/31/2007	01/31/2006	01/31/2005	01/31/2004	01/31/2003	01/31/2002
Earnings Per Share	0.25	0.51	1.70	0.81	0.83	0.42	0.48	1.09
Cash Flow Per Share	2.71	2.66	3.05	3.40	3.74	1.49	2.16	0.85
Tang Book Value Per Share	11.79	7.89	10.07	8.78	7.99	7.49	7.11	6.70
Dividends Per Share	0.310	0.300	0.260	0.220	0.290	0.150	0.110	0.088
Dividend Payout %	122.46	58.82	15.29	27.16	34.73	35.71	22.68	8.14
Income Statement								
Property Income	307,646	1,295,620	1,168,835	1,200,775	1,041,851	898,339	791,806	738,508
Non-Property Income	...	...	...	...	...	123,249	135,744	168,062
Total Revenue	307,646	1,295,620	1,168,835	1,200,775	1,041,851	1,021,588	927,550	906,570
Depn & Amortn	69,557	244,208	200,189	189,132	176,416	127,631	115,001	97,842
Interest Expense	83,371	328,887	293,803	273,115	248,328	198,122	177,237	178,580
Income Before Taxes	(49,586)	(3,415)	79,838	114,538	102,476	77,052	81,998	159,957
Income Taxes	(19,579)	3,064	34,412	23,238	37,326	28,799	31,826	63,487
Net Income	(40,269)	52,425	177,251	83,519	85,206	42,669	48,831	103,029
Average Shares	102,613	102,261	104,454	102,603	101,846	101,144	100,357	94,773
Balance Sheet								
Total Assets	10,544,712	10,251,597	8,981,604	7,990,341	7,289,260	5,895,072	5,077,209	4,417,646
Long-Term Obligations	7,759,079	7,408,384	6,321,399	5,930,506	5,480,023	4,162,938	3,451,241	2,959,552
Total Liabilities	9,226,628	8,929,964	7,580,692	6,993,243	6,388,962	5,097,687	4,292,171	3,687,256
Stockholders' Equity	928,976	972,116	1,025,811	894,382	804,525	748,911	705,972	662,513
Shares Outstanding	78,781	102,589	101,882	101,844	100,702	99,972	99,311	98,927
Statistical Record								
Return on Assets %	0.29	0.55	2.09	1.09	1.29	0.78	1.03	2.44
Return on Equity %	2.98	5.25	18.46	9.83	10.94	5.87	7.14	18.41
Net Margin %	(13.09)	4.05	15.16	6.96	8.18	4.18	5.26	11.36
Price Range	72.23-34.47	72.23-35.38	61.58-37.79	40.71-28.98	29.18-25.00	26.00-15.48	20.14-14.50	20.45-13.63
P/E Ratio	288.92-137.88	141.63-69.37	36.22-22.23	50.26-35.78	35.15-30.12	61.90-36.85	41.95-30.21	18.76-12.51
Average Yield %	0.61	0.52	0.52	0.63	1.08	0.74	0.63	0.54

Address: Terminal Tower, 50 Public Square, Suite 1100, Cleveland, OH 44113 **Telephone:** 216-621-6060 **Web Site:** www.forestcity.net	Officers: Albert B. Ratner - Co-Chairman Samuel H. Miller - Co-Chairman, Treasurer **Transfer Agents:** National City Bank, Cleveland, OH	No of Institutions: 1 Shares: N/A % Held: 61.56

FPL GROUP, INC.

Exchange	Symbol	Price	52Wk Range	Yield	P/E
NYS	FPL	$67.40 (5/29/2008)	72.56-54.92	2.64	19.26

*7 Year Price Score 121.72 *NYSE Composite Index=100 *12 Month Price Score 106.35

Interim Earnings (Per Share)

Qtr.	Mar	Jun	Sep	Dec
2005	0.36	0.52	0.87	0.52
2006	0.63	0.60	1.32	0.68
2007	0.38	1.01	1.33	0.55
2008	0.62	...	...	...

Interim Dividends (Per Share)

Amt	Decl	Ex	Rec	Pay
0.41Q	08/03/2007	08/29/2007	08/31/2007	09/17/2007
0.41Q	10/19/2007	11/28/2007	11/30/2007	12/17/2007
0.445Q	02/15/2008	02/27/2008	02/29/2008	03/17/2008
0.445Q	05/23/2008	06/04/2008	06/06/2008	06/16/2008
		Indicated Div: $1.78		

Valuation Analysis

Forecast EPS $3.90 (05/16/2008)

Market Cap	$27.5 Billion	Book Value	10.7 Billion
Price/Book	2.57	Price/Sales	1.77

Dividend Achiever Status

10 Year Growth Rate		5.50%
Total Years of Dividend Growth		12

TRADING VOLUME (thousand shares)

Business Summary: Electricity (MIC: SIC: 4911 NAIC: 221121)

FPL Group is a holding company whose operations are conducted primarily through its wholly-owned subsidiary Florida Power & Light Company (FPL) and its wholly-owned indirect subsidiary FPL Energy, LLC (FPL Energy). FPL, a rate-regulated public utility, supplied electric service to approximately 4.5 million customer accounts throughout most of the east and lower west coasts of Florida, as of Dec 31 2007. FPL Energy invests in independent power projects through both controlled and consolidated entities and non-controlling ownership interests in joint ventures essentially all of which are accounted for under the equity method.

Recent Developments: For the quarter ended Mar 31 2008, net income increased 66.0% to US$249.0 million from US$150.0 million in the year-earlier quarter. Revenues were US$3.43 billion, up 11.7% from US$3.08 billion the year before. Operating income was US$443.0 million versus US$298.0 million in the prior-year quarter, an increase of 48.7%. Direct operating expenses rose 8.2% to US$2.37 billion from US$2.19 billion in the comparable period the year before. Indirect operating expenses increased 5.8% to US$623.0 million from US$589.0 million in the equivalent prior-year period.

Prospects: For the full year of 2008, Co. is forecasting operations and maintenance expenses to increase, reflecting higher nuclear, fossil generation and customer service costs. Meanwhile, Co. is constructing two natural gas-fired combined-cycle units of about 1,220 megawatts (mw) each at its West County Energy Center, which are expected to be in service by mid-2009 and 2010. Co. also plans to build a third natural gas-fired combined-cycle unit of about 1,220 mw at the same site that should be operational in 2011. Lastly, Co. is in the process of adding about 400 mw of baseload capacity at its existing St. Lucie and Turkey Point nuclear units, which is projected to be in service by late 2012.

Financial Data
(US$ in Thousands)

	3 Mos	12/31/2007	12/31/2006	12/31/2005	12/31/2004	12/31/2003	12/31/2002	12/31/2001
Earnings Per Share	3.50	3.27	3.23	2.29	2.46	2.50	1.37	2.31
Cash Flow Per Share	9.23	9.03	6.35	4.07	7.37	6.35	6.76	5.76
Tang Book Value Per Share	26.25	26.35	24.49	21.52	20.24	18.93	17.46	17.09
Dividends Per Share	1.675	1.640	1.500	1.420	1.300	1.200	1.160	1.120
Dividend Payout %	47.87	50.15	46.44	62.01	52.95	48.00	84.98	48.48
Income Statement								
Total Revenue	3,434,000	15,263,000	15,710,000	11,846,000	10,522,000	9,630,000	8,311,000	8,475,000
EBITDA	854,000	3,809,000	3,731,000	3,159,000	2,852,000	2,758,000	2,158,000	2,467,000
Depn & Amortn	391,000	1,479,000	1,421,000	1,496,000	1,246,000	1,118,000	908,000	983,000
Income Before Taxes	279,000	1,680,000	1,678,000	1,157,000	1,154,000	1,261,000	939,000	1,160,000
Income Taxes	30,000	368,000	397,000	272,000	267,000	368,000	244,000	379,000
Net Income	249,000	1,312,000	1,281,000	885,000	887,000	890,000	473,000	781,000
Average Shares	402,000	400,600	396,500	385,700	361,600	356,400	346,600	337,800
Balance Sheet								
Net PPE	29,451,000	28,652,000	24,499,000	22,463,000	21,226,000	20,297,000	14,304,000	11,662,000
Total Assets	41,330,000	40,123,000	35,991,000	33,004,000	28,333,000	26,935,000	19,790,000	17,463,000
Long-Term Obligations	12,304,000	11,280,000	9,591,000	8,039,000	8,027,000	8,723,000	5,790,000	4,858,000
Total Liabilities	30,616,000	29,388,000	26,061,000	24,505,000	20,796,000	19,963,000	13,174,000	11,222,000
Stockholders' Equity	10,714,000	10,735,000	9,930,000	8,499,000	7,537,000	6,972,000	6,616,000	6,241,000
Shares Outstanding	408,119	407,344	405,404	394,854	372,351	368,000	366,000	352,000
Statistical Record								
Return on Assets %	3.66	3.45	3.71	2.89	3.20	3.81	2.54	4.77
Return on Equity %	13.67	12.70	13.90	11.04	12.19	13.10	7.36	12.95
EBITDA Margin %	24.87	24.96	23.75	26.67	27.11	28.64	25.97	29.11
Net Margin %	7.25	8.60	8.15	7.47	8.43	9.24	5.69	9.22
PPE Turnover	0.57	0.57	0.67	0.54	0.51	0.56	0.64	0.78
Asset Turnover	0.41	0.40	0.46	0.39	0.38	0.41	0.45	0.52
Debt to Equity	1.15	1.05	0.97	0.95	1.07	1.25	0.88	0.78
Price Range	72.56-54.92	72.56-53.85	55.10-38.03	47.84-36.03	37.98-30.48	33.91-27.10	32.45-23.15	35.13-25.95
P/E Ratio	20.73-15.69	22.19-16.47	17.06-11.77	20.89-15.73	15.44-12.39	13.57-10.84	23.69-16.90	15.21-11.23
Average Yield %	2.65	2.66	3.41	3.42	3.89	3.88	4.06	3.87

Address: 700 Universe Boulevard, Juno	Officers: Lewis Hay - Chairman, President, Chief	No of Institutions: 837
Beach, FL 33408-0420	Executive Officer James L. Robo - President, Chief	Shares: 300,957,248 % Held: 68.67
Telephone: 561-694-4000	Operating Officer **Transfer Agents:**	
Web Site: www.fplgroup.com	ComputerShare Investor Services, Chicago, IL	

FRANKLIN ELECTRIC CO., INC.

Exchange	Symbol	Price	52Wk Range	Yield	P/E
NMS	FELE	$40.32 (5/29/2008)	51.78-30.92	1.24	29.65

*7 Year Price Score 87.60   *NYSE Composite Index=100   *12 Month Price Score 95.01

Interim Earnings (Per Share)

Qtr.	Mar	Jun	Sep	Dec
2005	0.25	0.59	0.57	0.57
2006	0.42	0.70	0.72	0.60
2007	0.21	0.28	0.50	0.23
2008	0.35	...	...	...

Interim Dividends (Per Share)

Amt	Decl	Ex	Rec	Pay
0.12Q	07/23/2007	07/31/2007	08/02/2007	08/16/2007
0.12Q	10/19/2007	10/30/2007	11/01/2007	11/15/2007
0.12Q	01/25/2008	02/05/2008	02/07/2008	02/21/2008
0.125Q	04/25/2008	05/06/2008	05/08/2008	05/22/2008

Indicated Div: $0.50

Valuation Analysis

Forecast EPS	$2.35 (05/16/2008)		
Market Cap	$922.0 Million	Book Value	382.0 Million
Price/Book	2.41	Price/Sales	1.43

Dividend Achiever Status

10 Year Growth Rate	12.68%
Total Years of Dividend Growth	14

Business Summary: Electrical (MIC: SIC: 3621 NAIC: 335312)

Franklin Electric Company is primarily engaged in the production and marketing of groundwater and fuel pumping systems, submersible pumps and motors, drives, electronic controls and monitoring devices. As of Dec 29 2007, Co. conducted its businesses through two operating segments: Co.'s Water Systems segment designs, manufactures and sells motors, pumps, electronic controls, as well as related parts and equipment mainly for use in submersible water and other fluid system applications. Co.'s Fueling Systems segment designs, manufactures and sells pumps, electronic controls, and related parts and equipment primarily for use in submersible fueling system applications.

Recent Developments: For the quarter ended Mar 31 2008, net income increased 66.4% to US$8.1 million from US$4.9 million in the year-earlier quarter. Revenues were US$176.0 million, up 34.9% from US$130.5 million the year before. Operating income was US$15.1 million versus US$8.2 million in the prior-year quarter, an increase of 82.9%. Direct operating expenses rose 36.0% to US$124.6 million from US$91.6 million in the comparable period the year before. Indirect operating expenses increased 18.6% to US$36.4 million from US$30.7 million in the equivalent prior-year period.

Prospects: Co.'s results are benefiting from higher sales growth within its Water Systems segment in spite of the drop in housing starts in the U.S. Additionally, Co.'s Fueling Systems business is benefiting from stronger demand for vapor recovery systems in California. Meanwhile, for the fiscal year ending Jan 3 2009, Co. is targeting organic sales growth in excess of 12.0% and total sales growth in the range of 25.0%. Overall, Co. believes this growth coupled with spending controls should allow it to attain Fixed Costs improvement, which is fixed manufacturing costs, restructuring costs and selling, general and administrative costs less commissions of about 220 basis points for fiscal year 2008.

Financial Data

(US$ in Thousands)	3 Mos	12/29/2007	12/30/2006	12/31/2005	01/01/2005	01/03/2004	12/28/2002	12/29/2001
Earnings Per Share	1.36	1.22	2.44	1.98	1.65	1.52	1.42	1.20
Cash Flow Per Share	1.13	0.18	2.44	3.35	2.62	2.14	2.69	1.84
Tang Book Value Per Share	6.21	7.43	7.26	9.32	8.03	6.26	5.28	5.10
Dividends Per Share	0.480	0.470	0.430	0.380	0.310	0.275	0.255	0.235
Dividend Payout %	35.37	38.52	17.62	19.19	18.79	18.03	18.02	19.67
Income Statement								
Total Revenue	176,010	602,025	557,948	439,559	404,305	359,502	354,872	322,908
EBITDA	21,439	72,564	108,806	86,830	74,665	66,182	64,672	57,238
Depn & Amortn	6,229	20,300	18,000	14,971	15,143	13,748	12,878	12,660
Income Before Taxes	12,586	44,117	87,433	71,093	59,034	51,327	50,477	43,385
Income Taxes	4,438	15,434	30,671	25,084	20,951	16,847	18,273	16,235
Net Income	8,148	28,683	56,998	46,009	38,083	34,480	32,204	27,150
Average Shares	23,300	23,500	23,300	23,200	23,100	22,626	22,732	22,740
Balance Sheet								
Current Assets	323,954	309,479	217,790	203,020	166,142	128,041	113,009	109,583
Total Assets	718,751	662,237	526,925	379,762	333,473	281,971	258,583	195,643
Current Liabilities	142,777	90,649	93,957	64,022	54,445	45,401	50,247	40,425
Long-Term Obligations	152,202	151,287	51,043	12,324	13,752	14,960	25,946	14,465
Total Liabilities	336,721	283,693	181,094	112,200	99,140	89,033	105,445	72,374
Stockholders' Equity	382,030	378,544	345,831	267,562	234,333	192,938	153,138	123,269
Shares Outstanding	22,866	23,091	23,009	22,485	22,041	21,828	21,648	21,336
Statistical Record								
Return on Assets %	4.96	4.84	12.61	12.94	12.41	12.55	14.22	13.86
Return on Equity %	8.66	7.94	18.64	18.38	17.88	19.60	23.37	22.76
EBITDA Margin %	12.18	12.05	19.50	19.75	18.47	18.41	18.22	17.73
Net Margin %	4.63	4.76	10.22	10.47	9.42	9.59	9.07	8.41
Asset Turnover	1.01	1.02	1.23	1.24	1.32	1.31	1.57	1.65
Current Ratio	2.27	3.41	2.32	3.17	3.05	2.82	2.25	2.71
Debt to Equity	0.40	0.40	0.15	0.05	0.06	0.08	0.17	0.12
Price Range	51.78-30.92	51.78-36.19	62.08-40.47	44.70-34.93	43.30-29.57	32.50-23.14	29.50-19.98	21.02-16.00
P/E Ratio	38.07-22.74	42.44-29.66	25.44-16.59	22.58-17.64	26.24-17.92	21.38-15.22	20.77-14.07	17.52-13.33
Average Yield %	1.16	1.05	0.85	0.94	0.87	0.98	1.08	1.30

Address: 400 East Spring Street,	Officers: R. Scott Trumbull - Chairman, Chief	Investor Contact: 260-824-2900
Bluffton, IN 46714	Executive Officer Peter Christian Maske - Senior Vice	No of Institutions: 142
Telephone: 260-824-2900	President **Transfer Agents:**	Shares: 21,264,584 % Held: 84.58
Web Site: www.franklin-electric.com	LaSalle Bank National Association, Chicago, IL	

FRANKLIN RESOURCES, INC.

Exchange	Symbol	Price	52Wk Range	Yield	P/E
NYS	BEN	$98.87 (5/29/2008)	143.95-87.22	0.81	13.60

*7 Year Price Score 125.62 *NYSE Composite Index=100   *12 Month Price Score 88.19

Interim Earnings (Per Share)

Qtr.	Dec	Mar	Jun	Sep
2004-05	0.92	0.85	1.00	1.28
2005-06	1.21	0.74	1.41	1.49
2006-07	1.67	1.73	1.86	1.77
2007-08	2.12	1.54	...	...

Interim Dividends (Per Share)

Amt	Decl	Ex	Rec	Pay
0.15Q	06/19/2007	06/27/2007	06/29/2007	07/13/2007
0.15Q	09/19/2007	10/02/2007	10/04/2007	10/12/2007
0.20Q	12/14/2007	12/26/2007	12/28/2007	01/11/2008
0.20Q	03/04/2008	03/26/2008	03/28/2008	04/11/2008

Indicated Div: $0.80 (Div. Reinv. Plan)

Valuation Analysis

Forecast EPS $7.07 (05/16/2008)

Market Cap	$23.4 Billion	Book Value	7.0 Billion
Price/Book	3.35	Price/Sales	3.63

TRADING VOLUME (thousand shares)

Dividend Achiever Status

10 Year Growth Rate	13.44%
Total Years of Dividend Growth	18

Business Summary: Wealth Management (MIC: SIC: 6282 NAIC: 523930)

Franklin Resources provides investment management, fund administration, shareholder services, transfer agency, underwriting, distribution, custodial, trustee and other fiduciary services (collectively investment management and related services) to the Franklin, Templeton, Mutual Series, Bissett, Fiduciary Trust and Darby funds, and institutional, high net-worth and other investment accounts and products, collectively called its sponsored investment products. Services to Co.'s sponsored investment products are provided under contracts that set forth the level and nature of the fees to be charged for these services. As of Sep 30 2007, Co. had $645.90 billion in assets under its management.

Recent Developments: For the quarter ended Mar 31 2008, net income decreased 17.0% to US$366.1 million from US$440.9 million in the year-earlier quarter. Revenues were US$1.50 billion, down 0.4% from US$1.51 billion the year before. Operating income was US$519.1 million versus US$499.1 million in the prior-year quarter, an increase of 4.0%. Indirect operating expenses decreased 2.5% to US$984.6 million from US$1.01 billion in the equivalent prior-year period.

Prospects: Co.'s earnings are being hampered by lower net realized gains on sale of investments, lower interest and dividend income, and a decline in the underwriting and distribution margin, partially offset by an increase in fees for providing investment management and fund administration services due to an increase in its simple monthly average assets under management. Going forward, Co. will continue to focus on its core strategies of expanding its assets under management and related operations internationally, seeking positive investment performance, as well as closely monitoring its costs.

Financial Data

(US$ in Thousands)	6 Mos	3 Mos	09/30/2007	09/30/2006	09/30/2005	09/30/2004	09/30/2003	09/30/2002
Earnings Per Share	7.27	7.48	7.03	4.86	4.06	2.80	1.97	1.65
Cash Flow Per Share	5.41	5.49	6.72	5.01	4.35	3.78	2.16	2.82
Tang Book Value Per Share	20.88	20.67	21.49	18.57	14.39	12.23	9.31	8.69
Dividends Per Share	0.700	0.650	0.570	0.510	2.400	0.415	0.295	0.275
Dividend Payout %	9.63	8.69	8.11	10.49	59.11	14.82	14.97	16.67
Income Statement								
Total Revenue	3,189,283	1,685,591	6,205,769	5,050,726	4,310,098	3,438,208	2,624,448	2,518,532
Income Before Taxes	1,228,948	709,480	2,465,301	1,835,566	1,420,855	993,866	700,203	578,275
Income Taxes	344,536	191,164	692,363	567,998	363,224	291,981	197,373	145,552
Net Income	884,412	518,316	1,772,938	1,267,568	1,057,631	706,664	502,830	432,723
Average Shares	238,360	244,147	252,118	261,745	262,561	252,152	254,681	262,054
Balance Sheet								
Total Assets	9,944,722	9,672,751	9,943,250	9,499,859	8,893,927	8,228,135	6,970,749	6,422,738
Total Liabilities	2,914,469	2,621,858	2,569,571	2,719,335	3,133,436	3,045,262	2,660,641	2,155,792
Stockholders' Equity	6,984,109	7,012,891	7,332,275	6,684,728	5,684,384	5,106,784	4,310,108	4,266,946
Shares Outstanding	236,362	239,729	245,469	253,249	252,744	249,680	245,931	258,555
Statistical Record								
Return on Assets %	18.25	19.28	18.24	13.78	12.35	9.27	7.51	6.82
Return on Equity %	25.47	26.39	25.30	20.50	19.60	14.97	11.73	10.50
Price Range	143.95-87.22	143.95-109.29	143.95-103.87	105.79-78.24	84.34-55.76	60.05-43.56	46.80-28.18	44.13-30.97
P/E Ratio	19.80-12.00	19.24-14.61	20.48-14.78	21.77-16.10	20.77-13.73	21.45-15.56	23.76-14.30	26.75-18.77
Average Yield %	0.58	0.51	0.46	0.55	3.38	0.80	0.80	0.73

Address: One Franklin Parkway, San Mateo, CA 94403 Telephone: 650-312-2000 Web Site: www.franklinresources.com	Officers: Charles B. Johnson - Chairman Rupert H. Johnson, Jr. - Vice Chairman Transfer Agents: The Bank of New York, New York, NY	Investor Contact: 800-632-2350 No of Institutions: 676 Shares: 117,664,456 % Held: 45.38

FULLER (H.B.) COMPANY

Exchange	Symbol	Price	52Wk Range	Yield	P/E
NYS	FUL	$25.45 (5/29/2008)	31.35-17.99	1.04	16.85

*7 Year Price Score 112.36 *NYSE Composite Index=100   ***12 Month Price Score 92.82**

TRADING VOLUME (thousand shares)

Interim Earnings (Per Share)

Qtr.	Feb	May	Aug	Nov
2004-05	0.11	0.28	0.27	0.40
2005-06	0.26	0.33	0.40	1.24
2006-07	0.34	0.44	0.46	0.43
2008-09	0.32	...	...	...

Interim Dividends (Per Share)

Amt	Decl	Ex	Rec	Pay
0.065Q	07/12/2007	07/24/2007	07/26/2007	08/09/2007
0.065Q	10/04/2007	10/16/2007	10/18/2007	11/01/2007
0.065Q	01/24/2008	02/05/2008	02/07/2008	02/21/2008
0.066Q	04/03/2008	04/15/2008	04/17/2008	05/01/2008

Indicated Div: $0.26 (Div. Reinv. Plan)

Valuation Analysis

Forecast EPS $1.80 (05/16/2008)

Market Cap	$1.4 Billion	Book Value	765.7 Million
Price/Book	1.82	Price/Sales	1.11

Dividend Achiever Status

10 Year Growth Rate	3.58%
Total Years of Dividend Growth	40

Business Summary: Chemicals (MIC: SIC: 2891 NAIC: 325520)

H.B. Fuller manufactures and markets adhesives and specialty chemical products. Co.'s business is reported in four operating segments: North America, Europe, Latin America and Asia Pacific, with adhesives as the main business component of each of the operating segments. The adhesives business components produce and supply industrial and performance adhesives products for applications in various markets, including assembly, such as woodworking and appliances; converting that includes packaging, corrugated, tape and label, and graphic arts; nonwoven, including disposable diapers, feminine care and adult incontinence products; and footwear.

Recent Developments: For the quarter ended Mar 31 2008, income from continuing operations decreased 2.5% to US$18.2 million from US$18.7 million in the year-earlier quarter. Net income decreased 12.5% to US$18.2 million from US$20.8 million in the year-earlier quarter. Revenues were US$322.6 million, down 3.2% from US$333.4 million the year before. Direct operating expenses declined 1.1% to US$231.1 million from US$233.7 million in the comparable period the year before. Indirect operating expenses decreased 9.2% to US$65.0 million from US$71.6 million in the equivalent prior-year period.

Prospects: For the fiscal year ending Dec 1 2008, Co. continues to anticipate earnings in the range of $1.76 and $1.86 per diluted share. Going forward, Co. intends to make strategic investments, improve its top line results while managing the overall profitability of its operations to attain its near-and-long term objectives. For instance, Co. plans to open a regional technology center in Shanghai, China, which should help drive growth in the Asia Pacific region. Co. believes that the new center will focus on reactive chemistry while promoting product development and localization of initiatives in key market segments. Co. expects the center to be operation before the end of fiscal 2008.

Financial Data

(US$ in Thousands)	3 Mos	12/01/2007	12/02/2006	12/03/2005	11/27/2004	11/29/2003	11/30/2002	12/01/2001
Earnings Per Share	1.51	1.68	2.23	1.05	0.61	0.68	0.49	0.79
Cash Flow Per Share	1.84	2.35	3.20	2.15	2.17	1.06	1.47	1.61
Tang Book Value Per Share	7.71	7.92	6.84	8.33	7.62	7.26	6.30	6.19
Dividends Per Share	0.258	0.256	0.249	0.241	0.229	0.224	0.219	0.214
Dividend Payout %	17.09	15.24	11.15	22.87	37.20	33.15	44.64	27.23
Income Statement								
Total Revenue	322,648	1,400,258	1,472,391	1,512,193	1,409,606	1,287,331	1,256,210	1,274,059
EBITDA	39,479	180,630	144,963	135,651	103,549	104,218	97,203	117,871
Depn & Amortn	11,690	50,358	48,455	55,475	56,030	54,136	57,544	54,401
Income Before Taxes	24,861	136,887	100,031	82,401	48,298	50,808	40,312	63,470
Income Taxes	7,210	37,712	23,682	24,990	14,713	14,307	12,973	19,833
Net Income	18,213	102,173	134,213	61,576	35,603	38,619	28,176	44,439
Average Shares	57,492	60,991	60,065	58,474	57,818	57,389	57,202	56,660
Balance Sheet								
Current Assets	601,648	635,950	669,094	582,434	553,650	448,492	408,874	403,873
Total Assets	1,329,313	1,364,602	1,478,471	1,107,557	1,135,359	1,007,588	961,439	966,173
Current Liabilities	246,745	297,835	342,442	261,858	293,449	200,026	214,846	204,163
Long-Term Obligations	177,000	137,000	224,000	112,001	138,149	161,447	161,763	203,001
Total Liabilities	563,572	565,609	700,679	523,114	582,300	498,250	513,109	532,147
Stockholders' Equity	765,741	798,993	777,792	584,443	553,059	509,338	448,330	434,026
Shares Outstanding	54,640	57,436	59,931	58,369	57,282	56,870	56,724	56,561
Statistical Record								
Return on Assets %	6.72	7.21	10.41	5.40	3.33	3.93	2.93	4.51
Return on Equity %	11.59	13.00	19.76	10.65	6.72	8.09	6.40	10.63
EBITDA Margin %	12.24	12.90	9.85	8.97	7.35	8.10	7.74	9.25
Net Margin %	5.64	7.30	9.12	4.07	2.53	3.00	2.24	3.49
Asset Turnover	0.93	0.99	1.14	1.33	1.32	1.31	1.31	1.29
Current Ratio	2.44	2.14	1.95	2.22	1.89	2.24	1.90	1.98
Debt to Equity	0.23	0.17	0.29	0.19	0.25	0.32	0.36	0.47
Price Range	31.35-17.99	31.35-24.11	27.54-15.65	17.93-12.73	15.10-12.42	14.75-10.00	16.25-12.27	15.48-8.30
P/E Ratio	20.76-11.91	18.66-14.35	12.35-7.02	17.08-12.12	24.75-20.36	21.69-14.71	33.16-25.04	19.59-10.50
Average Yield %	0.99	0.94	1.14	1.60	1.67	1.83	1.53	1.85

<table>
<tr><td>Address: 1200 Willow Lake Boulevard,
St. Paul, MN 55110-5101
Telephone: 651-236-5900
Web Site: www.hbfuller.com</td><td>Officers: Lee R. Mitau - Chairman Michele Volpi -
President, Chief Executive Officer Transfer Agents:
Wells Fargo Shareowner Services, Minnesota, MN</td><td>Investor Contact: 651-236-5150
No of Institutions: 207
Shares: 55,575,880 % Held: 84.12</td></tr>
</table>

FULTON FINANCIAL CORP. (PA)

Exchange	Symbol	Price	52Wk Range	Yield	P/E
NMS	FULT	$12.70 (5/29/2008)	15.49-10.03	4.72	14.43

*7 Year Price Score 69.00   ***NYSE Composite Index=100**   ***12 Month Price Score 99.28**

Interim Earnings (Per Share)

Qtr.	Mar	Jun	Sep	Dec
2005	0.25	0.26	0.26	0.25
2006	0.27	0.27	0.28	0.26
2007	0.24	0.23	0.19	0.22
2008	0.24	...	...	...

Interim Dividends (Per Share)

Amt	Decl	Ex	Rec	Pay
0.15Q	07/17/2007	09/19/2007	09/21/2007	10/15/2007
0.15Q	10/16/2007	12/19/2007	12/21/2007	01/15/2008
0.15Q	01/22/2008	03/18/2008	03/21/2008	04/15/2008
0.15Q	04/22/2008	06/18/2008	06/20/2008	07/15/2008
Indicated Div: $0.60 (Div. Reinv. Plan)				

Valuation Analysis

Forecast EPS	$0.94 (05/16/2008)		
Market Cap	$2.4 Billion	Book Value	1.6 Billion
Price/Book	1.51	Price/Sales	2.25

Dividend Achiever Status

10 Year Growth Rate	9.65%
Total Years of Dividend Growth	34

TRADING VOLUME (thousand shares)

Business Summary: Commercial Banking (MIC: SIC: 6021 NAIC: 522110)

Fulton Financial is a multi-bank financial holding company with 11 wholly owned banking subsidiaries: Fulton Bank, Swineford National Bank, Lafayette Ambassador Bank, FNB Bank N.A., Hagerstown Trust Company, Delaware National Bank, The Bank, The Peoples Bank of Elkton, Skylands Community Bank, Resource Bank and The Columbia Bank, as well as two financial services subsidiaries, Fulton Financial Advisors, N.A., and Fulton Insurance Services Group, Inc. Through its banking subsidiaries, Co. provides a range of retail and commercial banking services across central and eastern Pennsylvania, Delaware, Maryland, New Jersey and Virginia. As of Dec 31 2007, Co. had total assets of $15.92 billion.

Recent Developments: For the quarter ended Mar 31 2008, net income increased 0.9% to US$41.5 million from US$41.1 million in the year-earlier quarter. Net interest income increased 3.4% to US$125.9 million from US$121.8 million in the year-earlier quarter. Provision for loan losses was US$11.2 million versus US$957,000 in the prior-year quarter, an increase of. Non-interest income fell 3.5% to US$37.7 million from US$39.1 million, while non-interest expense declined 4.2% to US$96.7 million.

Prospects: On Apr 18 2008, Co. announced that it has entered into a definitive agreement with U.S. Bank National Association ND, d/b/a Elan Financial Services (Elan), to sell its approximately $85.0 million credit card portfolio to Elan. Consequently, Co. estimates that the transaction will result in a gain in the second quarter of 2008 of about $10.0 million, which is dependent on the balance of the portfolio on the sale date, among other factors. In the meantime, under a separate agreement with Elan, Co. will provide ongoing marketing services on behalf of Elan and will receive a fee for each new account originated and a percentage of the revenue earned on both new accounts and accounts sold.

Financial Data
(US$ in Thousands)

	3 Mos	12/31/2007	12/31/2006	12/31/2005	12/31/2004	12/31/2003	12/31/2002	12/31/2001
Earnings Per Share	0.88	0.88	1.06	1.00	0.97	0.93	0.89	0.76
Cash Flow Per Share	1.66	1.76	1.15	0.89	0.93	1.28	0.64	0.70
Tang Book Value Per Share	4.99	5.30	4.91	5.06	5.17	5.49	5.41	4.94
Dividends Per Share	0.600	0.598	0.581	0.540	0.493	0.452	0.405	0.366
Dividend Payout %	68.38	67.90	54.77	54.00	50.97	48.66	45.43	48.35
Income Statement								
Income Before Taxes	55,699	216,250	265,949	237,435	218,181	197,543	189,416	159,956
Income Taxes	14,203	63,532	80,422	71,361	65,264	59,363	56,468	46,367
Net Income	41,496	152,718	185,527	166,074	152,917	138,180	132,948	113,589
Average Shares	174,209	174,386	174,872	166,260	158,341	148,490	149,491	150,402
Balance Sheet								
Total Assets	16,052,867	15,923,098	14,918,964	12,401,555	11,158,351	9,767,288	8,387,778	7,770,711
Total Liabilities	14,441,147	14,348,178	13,402,654	11,118,584	9,916,061	8,820,352	7,524,036	6,959,257
Stockholders' Equity	1,611,720	1,574,920	1,516,310	1,282,971	1,242,290	946,936	863,742	811,454
Shares Outstanding	192,000	173,500	173,700	164,850	164,981	149,388	146,294	149,405
Statistical Record								
Return on Assets %	0.99	0.99	1.36	1.41	1.46	1.52	1.65	1.58
Return on Equity %	9.74	9.88	13.26	13.15	13.93	15.26	15.87	15.24
Price Range	15.49-10.03	16.69-10.88	17.29-15.46	17.81-15.00	17.90-14.84	15.89-12.20	14.02-11.64	12.61-10.14
P/E Ratio	17.60-11.40	18.97-12.36	16.31-14.58	17.81-15.00	18.45-15.30	17.09-13.12	15.75-13.08	16.59-13.34
Average Yield %	4.48	4.17	3.57	3.26	3.09	3.16	3.15	3.14

Address: One Penn Square, P.O. Box 4887, Lancaster, PA 17604 **Telephone:** 717-291-2411 **Web Site:** www.fult.com	**Officers:** R. Scott Smith - Chairman, President, Chief Operating Officer Beth Ann L. Chivinski - Executive Vice President, Controller **Transfer Agents:** Stock Transfer Department, Lancaster, PA	**Investor Contact:** 717-291-2739 **No of Institutions:** 198 **Shares:** 52,432,568 **% Held:** 28.66

GALLAGHER (ARTHUR J.) & CO.

Exchange	Symbol	Price	52Wk Range	Yield	P/E
NYS	AJG	$25.34 (5/29/2008)	31.08-23.24	5.05	21.84

*7 Year Price Score 70.55 *NYSE Composite Index=100 *12 Month Price Score 96.89

Interim Earnings (Per Share)

Qtr.	Mar	Jun	Sep	Dec
2005	(0.80)	0.54	0.52	0.02
2006	0.17	0.37	0.51	0.25
2007	0.20	0.44	0.54	0.25
2008	(0.07)	...	...	...

Interim Dividends (Per Share)

Amt	Decl	Ex	Rec	Pay
0.31Q	07/19/2007	09/26/2007	09/28/2007	10/15/2007
0.31Q	10/18/2007	12/27/2007	12/31/2007	01/15/2008
0.32Q	01/25/2008	03/27/2008	03/31/2008	04/15/2008
0.32Q	04/24/2008	06/26/2008	06/30/2008	07/15/2008

Indicated Div: $1.28

Valuation Analysis

Forecast EPS $1.50 (05/16/2008)

Market Cap	$2.4 Billion	Book Value	698.6 Million
Price/Book	3.37	Price/Sales	1.46

Dividend Achiever Status

10 Year Growth Rate	14.96%
Total Years of Dividend Growth	23

TRADING VOLUME (thousand shares)

Business Summary: Insurance (MIC: SIC: 6411 NAIC: 524210)

Arthur J. Gallagher & Co. provides insurance brokerage and third-party claims settlement and administration services to entities in the U.S. and abroad. Co. has three operating segments: Brokerage, which primarily comprised of retail and wholesale brokerage operations; Risk Management, which provides contract claim settlement and administration services; and Financial Services, which manages Co.'s interests in tax-advantaged and clean-energy investments as well as its equity ownership. As of Dec 31 2007, Co. operated through a network of more than 200 sales and service offices in the U.S. and 12 countries and correspondent brokers and consultants in more than 100 countries.

Recent Developments: For the quarter ended Mar 31 2008, income from continuing operations decreased 23.5% to US$16.3 million from US$21.3 million in the year-earlier quarter. Net loss amounted to US$6.0 million versus net income of US$19.8 million in the year-earlier quarter. Revenues were US$375.8 million, up 0.2% from US$375.0 million the year before. Net investment income fell 76.5% to US$9.0 million from US$38.3 million a year ago.

Prospects: Co. continues to see softening in the property/casualty pricing environment across all lines, which poses challenges to organic growth and margin expansion. However, Co. continues to work on its headcount reduction and cost savings initiatives. Also, Co. remains focused on acquisitions, with the acquisitions of Specialty Risk, Inc. and Life Insurance Strategies in May and Apr 2008, respectively. Co. believes that acquisitions should allow it to further extend its presence in the retail and wholesale insurance brokerage services industries and grow the volume of general services provided. Co. also projects its Brokerage segment's commission and fee revenues to benefit from acquisitions.

Financial Data
(US$ in Thousands)

	3 Mos	12/31/2007	12/31/2006	12/31/2005	12/31/2004	12/31/2003	12/31/2002	12/31/2001
Earnings Per Share	1.16	1.43	1.31	0.32	1.99	1.57	1.41	1.39
Cash Flow Per Share	2.48	2.63	1.08	2.01	3.02	2.54	1.71	1.54
Tang Book Value Per Share	N.M.	N.M.	3.40	3.67	4.20	4.40	4.44	3.60
Dividends Per Share	1.250	1.240	1.200	1.120	1.000	0.720	0.600	0.520
Dividend Payout %	108.21	86.71	91.60	350.00	50.25	45.86	42.55	37.41
Income Statement								
Total Revenue	375,800	1,623,300	1,534,000	1,483,900	1,480,300	1,263,800	1,101,222	910,043
Income Before Taxes	26,900	200,100	153,100	(2,800)	235,500	193,300	185,342	141,853
Income Taxes	10,600	45,500	24,600	(31,400)	47,000	47,100	55,603	16,597
Net Income	(6,000)	138,800	128,500	30,800	188,500	146,200	129,739	125,256
Average Shares	92,900	97,100	98,400	96,100	94,500	93,300	91,861	90,127
Balance Sheet								
Total Assets	3,340,900	3,556,800	3,420,100	3,389,500	3,237,900	2,901,600	2,463,574	1,471,823
Total Liabilities	2,642,300	2,841,300	2,556,000	2,620,400	2,476,900	2,282,500	1,935,419	1,100,210
Stockholders' Equity	698,600	715,500	864,100	769,100	761,000	619,100	528,155	371,613
Shares Outstanding	92,800	92,000	98,400	95,700	92,100	90,000	88,548	85,111
Statistical Record								
Return on Assets %	3.34	3.98	3.77	0.93	6.12	5.45	6.59	9.89
Return on Equity %	14.37	17.57	15.74	4.03	27.24	25.49	28.84	36.52
Price Range	31.08-23.24	31.08-24.19	31.76-24.56	32.68-26.50	33.96-27.06	32.65-23.45	36.86-22.10	38.30-22.00
P/E Ratio	26.79-20.03	21.73-16.92	24.24-18.75	102.13-82.81	17.07-13.60	20.80-14.94	26.14-15.67	27.55-15.83
Average Yield %	4.60	4.39	4.32	3.87	3.17	2.63	1.94	1.77

Address: Two Pierce Place, Itasca, IL 60143-3141	**Officers:** J. Patrick Gallagher - Chairman, President, Chief Executive Officer Walter D. Bay - Corporate	**No of Institutions:** 264
Telephone: 630-773-3800	Vice-President, Secretary, General Counsel **Transfer**	**Shares:** 81,041,160 % **Held:** 68.12
Web Site: www.ajg.com	**Agents:** ComputerShare Investor Services, Chicago, IL	

GANNETT CO INC

Exchange	Symbol	Price	52Wk Range	Yield	P/E
NYS	GCI	$29.32 (5/29/2008)	59.79-25.86	5.46	6.54

*7 Year Price Score 46.23 *NYSE Composite Index=100 *12 Month Price Score 74.26

Interim Earnings (Per Share)

Qtr.	Mar	Jun	Sep	Dec
2005	1.05	1.37	1.22	1.43
2006	0.99	1.31	1.11	1.50
2007	0.90	1.56	1.01	1.06
2008	0.84	...	...	...

Interim Dividends (Per Share)

Amt	Decl	Ex	Rec	Pay
0.40Q	07/24/2007	09/12/2007	09/14/2007	10/01/2007
0.40Q	10/23/2007	12/12/2007	12/14/2007	01/02/2008
0.40Q	02/27/2008	03/05/2008	03/07/2008	04/01/2008
0.40Q	04/30/2008	06/04/2008	06/06/2008	07/01/2008

Indicated Div: $1.60 (Div. Reinv. Plan)

Valuation Analysis

Forecast EPS $4.05 (05/16/2008)

Market Cap	$6.7 Billion	Book Value	9.1 Billion
Price/Book	0.74	Price/Sales	0.92

Dividend Achiever Status

10 Year Growth Rate	6.18%
Total Years of Dividend Growth	36

TRADING VOLUME (thousand shares)

Business Summary: Media (MIC: SIC: 2711 NAIC: 511110)

Gannett is a news and information company. In the U.S., Co. published 85 daily newspapers and nearly 900 non-daily publications as of Dec 31 2007. Co. also operates Web sites providing news, information and advertising that is customized for the market served and integrated with its publishing operations. Co.'s newspaper publishing operations in the U.K., operating as Newsquest, included locally integrated Web sites, classified business Web sites, 17 paid-for daily newspapers, and almost 300 non-daily publications as of Dec 31 2007. In broadcasting, Co. operated 23 television stations in the U.S. with a market reach of more than 20.0 million households as of Dec 31 2007.

Recent Developments: For the quarter ended Mar 30 2008, income from continuing operations decreased 7.1% to US$191.8 million from US$206.4 million in the year-earlier quarter. Net income decreased 8.9% to US$191.8 million from US$210.6 million in the year-earlier quarter. Revenues were US$1.68 billion, down 8.4% from US$1.83 billion the year before. Operating income was US$327.6 million versus US$381.7 million in the prior-year quarter, a decrease of 14.2%. Direct operating expenses declined 6.8% to US$986.5 million from US$1.06 billion in the comparable period the year before. Indirect operating expenses decreased 7.4% to US$362.7 million from US$391.6 million in the equivalent prior-year period.

Prospects: Co.'s near-term outlook appears mixed. For instance, Co. is experiencing lower revenues within its publishing segment reflecting a softening in economy led by a difficult real estate market condition that continues to have an unfavorable effect on classified categories as well as some retail categories. Further, higher political advertising within Co.'s broadcasting segment is being offset by softer ad demand in other categories and the absence of Super Bowl related ad revenue. Conversely, these factors are being partially offset by growth in politically related advertising revenue and online revenues. Also, Co. is seeing lower expenses driven by its continued focus on cost containment.

Financial Data
(US$ in Thousands)

	3 Mos	12/30/2007	12/31/2006	12/25/2005	12/26/2004	12/28/2003	12/29/2002	12/30/2001
Earnings Per Share	4.48	4.52	4.90	5.05	4.92	4.46	4.31	3.12
Cash Flow Per Share	5.68	5.79	6.16	5.86	6.01	5.50	3.88	4.96
Dividends Per Share	1.510	1.420	1.200	1.120	1.040	0.980	0.940	0.900
Dividend Payout %	33.71	31.42	24.49	22.18	21.14	21.97	21.81	28.85
Income Statement								
Total Revenue	1,676,869	7,439,460	8,033,354	7,598,939	7,381,283	6,711,115	6,422,249	6,344,245
EBITDA	407,829	1,983,406	2,279,475	2,298,734	2,375,506	2,205,909	2,129,883	2,031,552
Depn & Amortn	67,802	285,125	276,770	276,186	244,021	231,532	222,444	443,777
Income Before Taxes	291,478	1,448,877	1,719,482	1,817,855	1,995,386	1,840,313	1,764,528	1,370,597
Income Taxes	99,700	473,300	558,700	606,600	678,200	629,100	604,400	539,400
Net Income	191,778	1,055,612	1,160,782	1,244,654	1,317,186	1,211,213	1,160,128	831,197
Average Shares	229,661	233,740	236,756	246,256	267,590	271,872	269,286	266,833
Balance Sheet								
Current Assets	1,313,946	1,343,255	1,532,019	1,462,071	1,370,695	1,223,261	1,133,079	1,178,198
Total Assets	15,798,160	15,887,727	16,223,804	15,743,396	15,399,251	14,706,239	13,733,014	13,096,101
Current Liabilities	947,317	962,163	1,116,948	1,096,341	1,005,450	961,837	958,625	1,127,737
Long-Term Obligations	3,980,282	4,098,338	5,210,021	5,438,273	4,607,743	3,834,511	4,547,265	5,080,025
Total Liabilities	6,720,575	6,850,289	7,817,230	8,147,658	7,143,888	6,190,819	6,821,219	7,360,179
Stockholders' Equity	9,058,590	9,017,159	8,382,263	7,570,562	8,164,002	8,422,981	6,911,795	5,735,922
Shares Outstanding	228,685	230,202	234,743	238,045	254,344	272,417	267,909	265,797
Statistical Record								
Return on Assets %	6.40	6.59	7.14	8.02	8.77	8.54	8.67	6.39
Return on Equity %	11.83	12.17	14.32	15.86	15.93	15.84	18.40	15.38
EBITDA Margin %	24.32	26.66	28.38	30.25	32.18	32.87	33.16	32.02
Net Margin %	11.44	14.19	14.45	16.38	17.84	18.05	18.06	13.10
Asset Turnover	0.45	0.46	0.49	0.49	0.49	0.47	0.48	0.49
Current Ratio	1.39	1.40	1.37	1.33	1.36	1.27	1.18	1.04
Debt to Equity	0.44	0.45	0.62	0.72	0.56	0.46	0.66	0.89
Price Range	59.79-28.43	63.11-35.30	64.80-51.67	82.41-59.19	91.00-78.99	88.93-67.68	79.87-63.39	71.10-55.55
P/E Ratio	13.35-6.35	13.96-7.81	13.22-10.54	16.32-11.72	18.50-16.05	19.94-15.17	18.53-14.71	22.79-17.80
Average Yield %	3.36	2.76	2.08	1.53	1.22	1.27	1.28	1.40

Address: 7950 Jones Branch Drive, McLean, VA 22107	Officers: Craig A. Dubow - Chairman, President, Chief Executive Officer Gracia C. Martore - Executive	Investor Contact: 703-854-6918
Telephone: 703-854-6000	Vice President, Chief Financial Officer Transfer	No of Institutions: 571
Web Site: www.gannett.com	Agents:Wells Fargo Bank, N.A., St. Paul, MN	Shares: 236,415,168 % Held: 94.64

GENERAL DYNAMICS CORP.

Exchange	Symbol	Price	52Wk Range	Yield	P/E
NYS	GD	$91.85 (5/29/2008)	94.60-74.24	1.52	16.82

*7 Year Price Score 116.91 *NYSE Composite Index=100 *12 Month Price Score 108.05

TRADING VOLUME (thousand shares)

Interim Earnings (Per Share)

Qtr.	Mar	Jun	Sep	Dec
2005	0.83	0.85	0.92	1.00
2006	0.92	1.56	1.08	1.00
2007	1.06	1.26	1.34	1.43
2008	1.42	...	...	...

Interim Dividends (Per Share)

Amt	Decl	Ex	Rec	Pay
0.29Q	08/01/2007	10/03/2007	10/05/2007	11/09/2007
0.29Q	12/05/2007	01/16/2008	01/18/2008	02/08/2008
0.35Q	03/05/2008	04/09/2008	04/11/2008	05/09/2008
0.35Q	06/04/2008	07/01/2008	07/03/2008	08/08/2008

Indicated Div: $1.40

Valuation Analysis

Forecast EPS $5.90 (05/17/2008)

Market Cap	$36.6 Billion	Book Value	11.8 Billion
Price/Book	3.11	Price/Sales	1.31

Dividend Achiever Status

10 Year Growth Rate	10.37%
Total Years of Dividend Growth	16

Business Summary: Shipping (MIC: SIC: 3731 NAIC: 336611)

General Dynamics is engaged in the provision of products and services in business aviation; combat vehicles, weapons systems and munitions; shipbuilding design and construction; and information systems, technologies and services. Co.'s Aerospace group designs, manufactures and services mid-size and large-cabin business-jet aircraft. Co.'s Combat Systems group design, develop, produce and support tracked and wheeled military vehicles, weapons systems and munitions. Co.'s Marine Systems group designs, builds and supports submarines and surface ships. Co.'s Information Systems and Technology group provide technologies, products and services for government and commercial clients.

Recent Developments: For the quarter ended Mar 30 2008, net income increased 31.8% to US$572.0 million from US$434.0 million in the year-earlier quarter. Revenues were US$7.01 billion, up 11.2% from US$6.30 billion the year before. Operating income was US$861.0 million versus US$681.0 million in the prior-year quarter, an increase of 26.4%. Direct operating expenses rose 9.3% to US$6.14 billion from US$5.62 billion in the comparable period the year before.

Prospects: For 2008, Co. expects sales growth in the Aerospace group to be between 13.0% and 15.0%, based on the planned new aircraft delivery schedule. In addition, Co. expects its Aerospace group's 2008 margins to be above 18.0% in the first half of 2008. For the Marine Systems group, Co. expects sales to increase by 2.0% to 3.0% percent over 2007 with operating margins in the mid-8.0% range, based on continued performance improvements tempered by a shift away from the mature production contracts to early-stage design and construction programs. Also, Co. is forecasting modest sales in its Information Systems and Technology group with operating margins to be 10 to 20 basis points lower than 2007.

Financial Data
(US$ in Millions)

	3 Mos	12/31/2007	12/31/2006	12/31/2005	12/31/2004	12/31/2003	12/31/2002	12/31/2001
Earnings Per Share	5.46	5.08	4.56	3.61	3.04	2.52	2.26	2.33
Cash Flow Per Share	7.11	7.23	5.27	5.12	4.50	4.36	2.79	2.74
Tang Book Value Per Share	4.63	4.59	0.25	1.40	N.M.	N.M.	2.81	1.92
Dividends Per Share	1.160	1.100	0.890	0.780	0.700	0.630	0.590	0.550
Dividend Payout %	21.24	21.65	19.52	21.61	22.99	25.00	26.11	23.66
Income Statement								
Total Revenue	7,005	27,240	24,063	21,244	19,178	16,617	13,829	12,163
EBITDA	966	3,685	3,145	2,560	2,259	1,747	1,842	1,751
Depn & Amortn	102	568	517	342	326	277	213	271
Income Before Taxes	845	3,047	2,527	2,100	1,785	1,372	1,584	1,424
Income Taxes	272	967	817	632	582	375	533	481
Net Income	572	2,072	1,856	1,461	1,227	1,004	917	943
Average Shares	403	408	406	404	402	398	405	405
Balance Sheet								
Current Assets	12,190	12,298	9,880	9,173	7,287	6,394	5,098	4,893
Total Assets	25,707	25,733	22,376	19,591	17,544	16,183	11,731	11,069
Current Liabilities	9,056	9,164	7,824	6,907	5,374	5,616	4,582	4,579
Long-Term Obligations	2,117	2,118	2,774	2,781	3,291	3,296	718	724
Total Liabilities	13,930	13,965	12,549	11,446	10,355	10,262	6,532	6,541
Stockholders' Equity	11,777	11,768	9,827	8,145	7,189	5,921	5,199	4,528
Shares Outstanding	398	403	405	400	402	395	401	401
Statistical Record								
Return on Assets %	9.14	8.61	8.85	7.87	7.26	7.19	8.04	9.90
Return on Equity %	20.27	19.19	20.65	19.06	18.67	18.06	18.85	22.59
EBITDA Margin %	13.79	13.53	13.07	12.05	11.78	10.51	13.32	14.40
Net Margin %	8.17	7.61	7.71	6.88	6.40	6.04	6.63	7.75
Asset Turnover	1.16	1.13	1.15	1.14	1.13	1.19	1.21	1.28
Current Ratio	1.35	1.34	1.26	1.33	1.36	1.14	1.11	1.07
Debt to Equity	0.18	0.18	0.28	0.34	0.46	0.56	0.14	0.16
Price Range	94.00-74.24	94.00-73.95	77.69-56.80	60.53-49.38	54.91-43.05	45.20-26.18	55.29-37.28	47.49-30.50
P/E Ratio	17.22-13.60	18.50-14.56	17.04-12.46	16.77-13.68	18.06-14.16	17.93-10.39	24.46-16.50	20.38-13.09
Average Yield %	1.40	1.35	1.33	1.41	1.44	1.72	1.34	1.43

Address: 2941 Fairview Park Drive, Suite 100, Falls Church, VA 22042-4513	Officers: Nicholas D. Chabraja - Chairman, Chief Executive Officer Gerard J. DeMuro - Executive Vice President **Transfer Agents:** Computershare Trust Company N.A., Providence, RI	Investor Contact: 703-876-3195
Telephone: 703-876-3000 Web Site: www.generaldynamics.com		No of Institutions: 844 Shares: 359,648,800 % Held: 78.80

GENERAL ELECTRIC CO

Exchange	Symbol	Price	52Wk Range	Yield	P/E
NYS	GE	$30.64 (5/29/2008)	42.12-30.40	4.05	14.25

*7 Year Price Score 84.30   *NYSE Composite Index=100   *12 Month Price Score 92.57

Interim Earnings (Per Share)

Qtr.	Mar	Jun	Sep	Dec
2005	0.37	0.44	0.44	0.29
2006	0.41	0.47	0.48	0.64
2007	0.44	0.53	0.54	0.66
2008	0.43	...	...	...

Interim Dividends (Per Share)

Amt	Decl	Ex	Rec	Pay
0.28Q	09/07/2007	09/20/2007	09/24/2007	10/25/2007
0.31Q	12/11/2007	12/20/2007	12/24/2007	01/25/2008
0.31Q	02/08/2008	02/21/2008	02/25/2008	04/25/2008
0.31Q	06/06/2008	06/19/2008	06/23/2008	07/25/2008

Indicated Div: $1.24 (Div. Reinv. Plan)

Valuation Analysis

Forecast EPS	$2.21 (05/17/2008)		
Market Cap	$305.4 Billion	Book Value	116.0 Billion
Price/Book	2.63	Price/Sales	1.74

Dividend Achiever Status

10 Year Growth Rate	12.44%
Total Years of Dividend Growth	32

Business Summary: Electrical (MIC: SIC: 3699 NAIC: 335999)

General Electric is a technology, media, and financial services corporation. With products and services ranging from aircraft engines, power generation, water processing, and security technology to medical imaging, business and consumer financing, media content and industrial products, Co. serves customers in more than 100 countries and employs more than 300,000 people worldwide. As of Dec 31 2007, Co. conducted its businesses through six operating segments which are: Infrastructure, Commercial Finance, GE Money, Healthcare, NBC Universal and Industrial.

Recent Developments: For the quarter ended Mar 31 2008, income from continuing operations decreased 11.5% to US$4.36 billion from US$4.93 billion in the year-earlier quarter. Net income decreased 5.8% to US$4.30 billion from US$4.57 billion in the year-earlier quarter. Revenues were US$42.27 billion, up 7.8% from US$39.20 billion the year before. Direct operating expenses rose 14.9% to US$26.69 billion from US$23.22 billion in the comparable period the year before. Indirect operating expenses increased 6.6% to US$10.24 billion from US$9.60 billion in the equivalent prior-year period.

Prospects: For 2008, Co. is projecting earnings per share to be about $2.20 to $2.30 from continuing operations for growth of 0.0% to 5.0%. Meanwhile, for the second quarter of 2008, Co. is anticipating earnings per share in the range of $0.53 to $0.55. Separately, on Apr 17 2008, Co. announced an acquisition most of CitiCapital, Citigroup's North American commercial lending and leasing business. Financial terms were not disclosed and the acquisition is expected to close by third quarter 2008. Through this transaction, Co. will acquire seven CitiCapital equipment finance business lines and the deal will add approximately $13.40 billion in assets to Co.'s Commercial Finance business subsequently.

Financial Data
(US$ in Millions)

	3 Mos	12/31/2007	12/31/2006	12/31/2005	12/31/2004	12/31/2003	12/31/2002	12/31/2001
Earnings Per Share	2.15	2.17	2.00	1.54	1.59	1.49	1.41	1.37
Cash Flow Per Share	4.78	4.51	2.96	3.56	3.50	3.02	2.96	3.24
Tang Book Value Per Share	1.70	1.83	2.52	2.64	2.55	2.40	1.76	2.33
Dividends Per Share	1.180	1.150	1.030	0.910	0.820	0.770	0.730	0.660
Dividend Payout %	54.78	53.00	51.50	59.09	51.57	51.68	51.77	48.18
Income Statement								
Total Revenue	42,273	172,738	163,391	149,702	152,363	134,187	131,698	125,913
EBITDA	7,872	36,876	33,778	30,667	31,722	26,860	24,889	26,790
Depn & Amortn	2,682	10,278	9,158	8,538	11,616	6,956	5,998	7,089
Income Before Taxes	5,190	26,598	24,620	22,129	20,106	19,904	18,891	19,701
Income Taxes	829	4,130	3,954	3,854	3,513	4,315	3,758	5,573
Net Income	4,304	22,208	20,829	16,353	16,593	15,002	14,118	13,684
Average Shares	10,006	10,218	10,394	10,611	10,445	10,075	10,028	10,052
Balance Sheet								
Current Assets	96,918	50,903	39,630	34,336	39,339	32,148	28,838	27,237
Total Assets	833,890	795,337	697,239	673,342	750,330	647,483	575,244	495,023
Current Liabilities	253,921	246,113	220,514	204,927	206,280	176,530	181,827	198,904
Long-Term Obligations	346,680	319,015	260,804	212,281	213,161	170,004	140,632	79,806
Total Liabilities	709,656	671,774	577,347	555,934	623,663	562,523	506,065	434,984
Stockholders' Equity	116,000	115,559	112,314	109,354	110,284	79,180	63,706	54,824
Shares Outstanding	9,967	9,987	10,277	10,484	10,586	10,063	9,969	9,926
Statistical Record								
Return on Assets %	2.83	2.98	3.04	2.30	2.37	2.45	2.64	2.94
Return on Equity %	19.02	19.49	18.79	14.89	17.47	21.00	23.82	25.99
EBITDA Margin %	18.62	21.35	20.67	20.49	20.82	20.02	18.90	21.28
Net Margin %	10.18	12.86	12.75	10.92	10.89	11.18	10.72	10.87
Asset Turnover	0.23	0.23	0.24	0.21	0.22	0.22	0.25	0.27
Current Ratio	0.38	0.21	0.18	0.17	0.19	0.18	0.16	0.14
Debt to Equity	2.99	2.76	2.32	1.94	1.93	2.15	2.21	1.46
Price Range	42.12-31.70	42.12-34.09	38.15-32.11	37.18-32.68	37.48-29.18	32.11-22.17	41.55-22.00	53.40-30.37
P/E Ratio	19.59-14.74	19.41-15.71	19.07-16.06	24.14-21.22	23.57-18.35	21.55-14.88	29.47-15.60	38.98-22.17
Average Yield %	3.14	3.04	3.00	2.58	2.49	2.75	2.34	1.52

Address: 3135 Easton Turnpike, Fairfield, CT 06828-0001	Officers: Jeffrey R. Immelt - Chairman, Chief Executive Officer Keith S. Sherin - Vice-Chairman,	Investor Contact: 203-373-2816
Telephone: 203-373-2211	Senior Vice President, Chief Financial Officer	No of Institutions: 1916
Web Site: www.ge.com	Transfer Agents:The Bank of New York, New York, NY	Shares: 6,616,559,104 % Held: 58.15

GENERAL GROWTH PROPERTIES, INC. (DE)

Exchange	Symbol	Price	52Wk Range	Yield	P/E
NYS	GGP	$41.92 (5/29/2008)	59.15-31.65	4.77	161.23

*7 Year Price Score 104.82 *NYSE Composite Index=100 *12 Month Price Score 92.08

Interim Earnings (Per Share)

Qtr.	Mar	Jun	Sep	Dec
2005	0.06	0.01	(0.03)	0.28
2006	0.10	(0.11)	(0.03)	0.29
2007	0.94	0.03	(0.04)	0.24
2008	0.03	...	...	...

Interim Dividends (Per Share)

Amt	Decl	Ex	Rec	Pay
0.45Q	07/05/2007	07/13/2007	07/17/2007	07/31/2007
0.50Q	10/04/2007	10/15/2007	10/17/2007	10/31/2007
0.50Q	01/07/2008	01/15/2008	01/17/2008	01/31/2008
0.50Q	04/04/2008	04/14/2008	04/16/2008	04/30/2008
Indicated Div: $2.00 (Div. Reinv. Plan)				

Valuation Analysis

Forecast EPS	$0.73 (05/16/2008)		
Market Cap	$11.1 Billion	Book Value	2.0 Billion
Price/Book	5.60	Price/Sales	3.31

Dividend Achiever Status

10 Year Growth Rate	12.04%
Total Years of Dividend Growth	14

Business Summary: "Property, Real Estate & Development" (MIC: SIC: 6798 NAIC: 525930)

General Growth Properties is a self-administered and self-managed real estate investment trust. Co. has two segments: Retail and Other, which includes the operation, development and management of retail and other rental property, mainly shopping centers; and Master Planned Communities, which includes the development and sale of land, mainly in community development projects in and around Columbia, MD; Summerlin, NV; and Houston, TX. As of Dec 31 2007, Co. had ownership interest in or management responsibility for over 200 regional shopping malls in 45 states. Also, Co. owned non-controlling interests in international joint ventures in Brazil, Turkey and Costa Rica.

Recent Developments: For the quarter ended Mar 31 2008, net income decreased 96.3% to US$8.6 million from US$230.2 million in the year-earlier quarter. Revenues were US$830.3 million, up 13.9% from US$728.8 million the year before. Revenues from property income rose 15.5% to US$779.2 million from US$674.9 million in the corresponding quarter a year earlier.

Prospects: Co. is seeing an increase in revenue due to higher effective rents and leased area across its portfolio at its Retail and Other segment. However, Co. noted that the pace of land sales for standard residential and commercial lots continues to be slow in its Master Planned Community segment, which is expected to continue for the balance of 2008. For 2008, Co.'s core funds from operations (FFO) guidance, which excludes real estate property net operating income from its Master Planned Communities segment and the provision for income taxes, is $3.52 to $3.58 per share, compared to core FFO of about $2.97 per share for 2007. Notably, core FFO for 2007 excludes certain earnings charges.

Financial Data (US$ in Thousands)	3 Mos	12/31/2007	12/31/2006	12/31/2005	12/31/2004	12/31/2003	12/31/2002	12/31/2001
Earnings Per Share	0.26	1.18	0.24	0.32	1.21	1.22	0.98	0.43
Cash Flow Per Share	3.08	2.90	3.38	3.54	3.41	2.88	2.47	1.31
Tang Book Value Per Share	4.74	4.39	5.34	6.32	9.13	7.69	6.39	6.37
Dividends Per Share	1.900	1.850	1.680	1.490	1.260	1.020	0.890	0.747
Dividend Payout %	731.70	156.78	700.00	465.63	104.13	83.61	90.51	175.00
Income Statement								
Total Revenue	830,322	3,261,801	3,256,283	3,073,416	1,802,845	1,270,728	980,466	803,709
Depn & Amortn	168,836	614,928	670,091	640,901	377,056	240,234	185,124	152,878
Income Taxes	9,392	(294,160)	98,984	50,646	2,383	...	...	...
Net Income	8,558	287,954	59,273	75,553	267,852	263,411	209,258	92,310
Average Shares	244,918	244,538	242,054	238,469	220,829	215,079	212,553	158,721
Balance Sheet								
Total Assets	29,519,446	28,814,319	25,241,445	25,307,019	25,718,625	9,582,897	7,280,822	5,646,807
Long-Term Obligations	24,365,831	24,282,139	20,521,967	20,418,875	20,310,947	6,649,490	4,592,311	3,398,207
Total Liabilities	26,980,217	26,884,779	23,046,785	22,737,865	22,621,032	7,008,664	4,900,850	3,570,562
Stockholders' Equity	1,984,454	1,456,696	1,664,079	1,932,918	2,143,150	1,670,409	1,196,525	1,183,386
Shares Outstanding	264,951	243,898	242,066	239,196	234,724	217,293	187,191	185,771
Statistical Record								
Return on Assets %	0.24	1.07	0.23	0.30	1.51	3.12	3.24	1.69
Return on Equity %	3.48	18.45	3.30	3.71	14.01	18.38	17.59	8.70
Net Margin %	1.03	8.83	1.82	2.46	14.86	20.73	21.34	11.49
Price Range	65.72-31.65	67.00-40.55	55.70-42.36	47.86-31.64	36.63-25.51	27.89-16.09	17.33-12.91	13.39-11.00
P/E Ratio	252.77-121.73	56.78-34.36	232.08-176.50	149.56-98.88	30.27-21.08	22.86-13.19	17.69-13.17	31.15-25.58
Average Yield %	3.89	3.36	3.50	3.70	4.07	4.78	5.71	6.10

Address: 110 North Wacker Drive, Chicago, IL 60606 Telephone: 312-960-5000 Web Site: www.generalgrowth.com	Officers: John Bucksbaum - Chairman, Chief Executive Officer Robert Michaels - President, Chief Operating Officer **Transfer Agents:** Mellon Investor Services, LLC, Jersey City, NJ	No of Institutions: 449 Shares: 263,486,192 % Held: 103.86

GENUINE PARTS CO.

*7 Year Price Score 90.99 ***NYSE Composite Index=100** ***12 Month Price Score 94.94**

Interim Earnings (Per Share)

Qtr.	Mar	Jun	Sep	Dec
2005	0.61	0.63	0.63	0.63
2006	0.66	0.70	0.71	0.70
2007	0.71	0.76	0.76	0.75
2008	0.75	...	...	...

Interim Dividends (Per Share)

Amt	Decl	Ex	Rec	Pay
0.365Q	08/20/2007	09/05/2007	09/07/2007	10/01/2007
0.365Q	11/19/2007	12/05/2007	12/07/2007	01/02/2008
0.39Q	02/19/2008	03/05/2008	03/07/2008	04/01/2008
0.39Q	04/21/2008	06/04/2008	06/06/2008	07/01/2008

Indicated Div: $1.56 (Div. Reinv. Plan)

Valuation Analysis

Forecast EPS $3.15 (05/16/2008)
Market Cap	$7.2 Billion	Book Value	2.7 Billion
Price/Book	2.71	Price/Sales	0.66

Dividend Achiever Status

10 Year Growth Rate	4.27%
Total Years of Dividend Growth	51

Business Summary: Retail - Automotive (MIC: SIC: 5013 NAIC: 423120)

Genuine Parts is a service organization that distributes automotive replacement parts, industrial replacement parts, office products and electrical/electronic materials. Co.'s Automotive Parts Group distributes automotive replacement parts and accessory items. The Industrial Parts Group distributes industrial replacement parts and related supplies in the U.S. and Canada. The Office Products Group is engaged in the wholesale distribution of office and other business related products that are used in the daily operation of businesses, schools, offices and institutions. The Electrical/Electronic Materials Group distributes materials to electrical and electronic manufacturers in North America.

Recent Developments: For the quarter ended Mar 31 2008, net income increased 1.6% to US$123.5 million from US$121.6 million in the year-earlier quarter. Revenues were US$2.74 billion, up 3.4% from US$2.65 billion the year before. Direct operating expenses rose 3.3% to US$1.92 billion from US$1.86 billion in the comparable period the year before. Indirect operating expenses increased 5.7% to US$627.8 million from US$593.8 million in the equivalent prior-year period.

Prospects: Co.'s near-term outlook appears constructive, reflecting growth in its Industrial Group, Automotive Parts Group and Electrical Group, despite a decrease in sales in its Office Products Group. Nevertheless, Co. expects results in its Office Products Group to improve during the remainder of 2008 due to the initiatives in place. In addition, Co. expects sales and product initiatives in the Automotive Parts Group to continue to provide further growth opportunities. For full-year 2008, Co. continues to expect total revenue to be up 3.0% to 6.0%, with the second half being stronger. On the earnings side, Co. expects earnings per share of $3.12 to $3.22 per share, which will be up 5.0% to 8.0%.

Financial Data

(US$ in Thousands)	3 Mos	12/31/2007	12/31/2006	12/31/2005	12/31/2004	12/31/2003	12/31/2002	12/31/2001
Earnings Per Share	3.01	2.98	2.76	2.50	2.25	1.91	(0.16)	1.71
Cash Flow Per Share	3.51	3.79	2.53	2.53	3.17	2.31	1.56	1.93
Tang Book Value Per Share	15.60	15.86	14.59	15.21	14.21	12.95	11.88	10.97
Dividends Per Share	1.485	1.460	1.350	1.250	1.200	1.180	1.160	1.140
Dividend Payout %	49.31	48.99	48.91	50.00	53.33	61.78	...	66.67
Income Statement								
Total Revenue	2,739,473	10,843,195	10,457,942	9,783,050	9,097,267	8,449,300	8,258,927	8,220,668
EBITDA	214,365	935,774	875,915	774,593	698,126	640,756	675,887	581,806
Depn & Amortn	22,684	87,702	73,423	65,529	62,207	69,013	70,151	85,793
Income Before Taxes	191,681	816,745	770,916	709,064	635,919	571,743	605,736	496,013
Income Taxes	68,138	310,406	295,511	271,630	240,367	218,101	238,236	198,866
Net Income	123,543	506,339	475,405	437,434	395,552	334,101	(27,590)	297,147
Average Shares	165,706	170,135	172,486	175,007	175,660	174,480	175,104	173,633
Balance Sheet								
Current Assets	4,025,733	4,053,012	3,835,127	3,806,882	3,633,484	3,417,626	3,335,775	3,146,212
Total Assets	4,755,418	4,774,069	4,496,984	4,771,538	4,455,247	4,116,497	4,019,843	4,206,646
Current Liabilities	1,569,452	1,547,976	1,198,768	1,249,104	1,132,715	1,016,931	1,069,718	919,181
Long-Term Obligations	250,000	263,707	512,248	500,000	500,000	625,108	674,796	835,580
Total Liabilities	2,085,744	2,057,353	1,946,993	2,077,581	1,910,870	1,804,214	1,889,834	1,861,523
Stockholders' Equity	2,669,674	2,716,716	2,549,991	2,693,957	2,544,377	2,312,283	2,130,009	2,345,123
Shares Outstanding	163,817	166,065	170,530	173,032	174,964	174,045	174,380	173,473
Statistical Record								
Return on Assets %	10.81	10.92	10.26	9.48	9.20	8.21	N.M.	7.12
Return on Equity %	19.21	19.23	18.13	16.70	16.24	15.04	N.M.	12.90
EBITDA Margin %	7.83	8.63	8.38	7.92	7.67	7.58	8.18	7.08
Net Margin %	4.51	4.67	4.55	4.47	4.35	3.95	N.M.	3.61
Asset Turnover	2.32	2.34	2.26	2.12	2.12	2.08	2.01	1.97
Current Ratio	2.57	2.62	3.20	3.05	3.21	3.36	3.12	3.42
Debt to Equity	0.09	0.10	0.20	0.19	0.20	0.27	0.32	0.36
Price Range	51.43-39.15	51.43-46.30	48.02-40.26	46.50-40.98	44.06-32.13	33.66-27.43	38.08-27.64	37.44-24.26
P/E Ratio	17.09-13.01	17.26-15.54	17.40-14.59	18.60-16.39	19.58-14.28	17.62-14.36	...	21.89-14.19
Average Yield %	3.13	2.98	3.09	2.87	3.20	3.74	3.48	3.78

Address: 2999 Circle 75 Parkway, Atlanta, GA 30339 Telephone: 770-953-1700 Web Site: www.genpt.com	Officers: Thomas C. Gallagher - Chairman, President, Chief Executive Officer Jerry W. Nix - Vice-Chairman, Executive Vice President, Chief Financial Officer Transfer Agents: Computershare, Providence, RI	Investor Contact: 770-953-1700 No of Institutions: 459 Shares: 135,958,016 % Held: 73.46

GLACIER BANCORP, INC.

Exchange	Symbol	Price	52Wk Range	Yield	P/E
NMS	GBCI	$20.91 (5/29/2008)	23.84-15.54	2.49	16.08

*7 Year Price Score 59.33   ***NYSE Composite Index=100**   ***12 Month Price Score 103.31**

Interim Earnings (Per Share)

Qtr.	Mar	Jun	Sep	Dec
2005	0.25	0.27	0.28	0.29
2006	0.28	0.30	0.31	0.32
2007	0.30	0.31	0.33	0.34
2008	0.32	...	...	...

Interim Dividends (Per Share)

Amt	Decl	Ex	Rec	Pay
0.12Q	06/27/2007	07/06/2007	07/10/2007	07/19/2007
0.13Q	09/26/2007	10/04/2007	10/09/2007	10/18/2007
0.13Q	12/27/2007	01/04/2008	01/08/2008	01/17/2008
0.13Q	03/26/2008	04/04/2008	04/08/2008	04/17/2008

Indicated Div: $0.52 (Div. Reinv. Plan)

Valuation Analysis

Forecast EPS $1.31 (05/16/2008)
Market Cap $1.1 Billion Book Value 542.9 Million
Price/Book 2.08 Price/Sales 3.02

Dividend Achiever Status

10 Year Growth Rate 14.01%
Total Years of Dividend Growth 16

Business Summary: Commercial Banking (MIC: SIC: 6022 NAIC: 522110)

Glacier Bancorp is a multi-bank holding company that provides a range of banking services to individual and corporate customers in Montana, Idaho, Wyoming, Utah and Washington through its subsidiary banks. Co. is engaged in providing a range of banking products and services which include transaction and savings deposits, commercial, consumer, and real estate loans, mortgage origination services, and retail brokerage services. Co. serves individuals, small to medium-sized businesses, community organizations and public entities. As of Dec 31 2007, Co. had total assets of $4.82 billion and total deposits of $3.18 billion.

Recent Developments: For the quarter ended Mar 31 2008, net income increased 8.1% to US$17.4 million from US$16.1 million in the year-earlier quarter. Net interest income increased 12.9% to US$48.6 million from US$43.1 million in the year-earlier quarter. Provision for loan losses was US$2.5 million versus US$1.2 million in the prior-year quarter, an increase of 109.2%. Non-interest income rose 3.6% to US$16.3 million from US$15.7 million, while non-interest expense advanced 7.3% to US$35.6 million.

Prospects: Co.'s total interest income is being driven by the increase in commercial loan volume. At the same time, Co. is seeing higher provision for credit losses, attributable primarily to growth in the commercial real estate loan portfolio, increased reserves for certain commercial real estate loans in the high growth areas of Western Montana and Idaho, most notably the Coeur d'Alene, Sandpoint and Boise markets, and the increase in non-performing assets. Separately, Co. believes that a softening of economic conditions combined with declines in the values of real estate that collateralize most of its loan and lease portfolios may adversely affect its operations going forward.

Financial Data
(US$ in Thousands)

	3 Mos	12/31/2007	12/31/2006	12/31/2005	12/31/2004	12/31/2003	12/31/2002	12/31/2001
Earnings Per Share	1.30	1.28	1.21	1.09	0.95	0.83	0.72	0.52
Cash Flow Per Share	1.66	1.66	1.36	1.64	1.52	2.11	0.38	(0.69)
Tang Book Value Per Share	7.22	6.98	5.96	5.10	4.95	4.30	3.86	3.11
Dividends Per Share	0.500	0.490	0.433	0.387	0.356	0.306	0.248	0.233
Dividend Payout %	38.56	38.28	35.81	35.37	37.32	36.97	34.43	44.78
Income Statement								
Income Before Taxes	26,778	103,690	92,388	77,684	65,630	56,161	48,826	33,715
Income Taxes	9,379	35,087	31,257	25,311	21,014	18,153	16,424	12,026
Net Income	17,399	68,603	61,131	52,373	44,616	38,008	32,402	21,689
Average Shares	54,034	53,748	50,497	47,839	46,716	45,985	44,974	41,613
Balance Sheet								
Total Assets	4,834,872	4,817,330	4,467,739	3,706,344	3,010,737	2,739,633	2,281,344	2,085,747
Total Liabilities	4,291,924	4,288,754	4,011,596	3,373,105	2,740,553	2,501,794	2,069,095	1,908,764
Stockholders' Equity	542,948	528,576	456,143	333,239	270,184	237,839	212,249	176,983
Shares Outstanding	53,950	53,646	52,302	48,258	46,030	45,381	44,564	43,504
Statistical Record								
Return on Assets %	1.50	1.48	1.50	1.56	1.55	1.51	1.48	1.38
Return on Equity %	13.73	13.93	15.49	17.36	17.52	16.89	16.65	15.77
Price Range	24.61-15.54	25.28-17.63	37.24-24.30	34.04-23.35	35.44-25.95	32.98-23.56	24.75-19.12	21.00-12.56
P/E Ratio	18.93-11.95	19.75-13.77	30.78-20.08	31.23-21.42	37.31-27.32	39.73-28.39	34.38-26.56	40.38-24.16
Average Yield %	2.46	2.25	1.38	1.31	1.17	1.13	1.14	1.38

Address: 49 Commons Loop, Kalispell, MT 59901-2679 Telephone: 406-756-4200 Web Site: www.glacierbancorp.com	Officers: Everit A. Sliter - Chairman Michael J. Blodnick - President, Chief Executive Officer Transfer Agents:Stock Transfer & Trust Company	No of Institutions: 155 Shares: 40,911,072 % Held: 73.77

GORMAN-RUPP CO.

Exchange	Symbol	Price	52Wk Range	Yield	P/E
ASE	GRC	$45.08 (5/29/2008)	45.08-22.95	0.89	31.97

*7 Year Price Score 135.12 *NYSE Composite Index=100 *12 Month Price Score 128.50

Interim Earnings (Per Share)

Qtr.	Mar	Jun	Sep	Dec
2005	0.12	0.26	0.20	0.08
2006	0.34	0.42	0.50	(0.10)
2007	0.38	0.49	0.41	0.09
2008	0.43	...	...	...

Interim Dividends (Per Share)

Amt	Decl	Ex	Rec	Pay
5-for-4	10/25/2007	12/11/2007	11/15/2007	12/10/2007
0.10Q	10/25/2007	11/13/2007	11/15/2007	12/10/2007
0.10Q	01/24/2008	02/13/2008	02/15/2008	03/10/2008
0.10Q	04/24/2008	05/13/2008	05/15/2008	06/10/2008
	Indicated Div: $0.40			

Valuation Analysis

Forecast EPS $1.71 (05/16/2008)

Market Cap	$753.0 Million	Book Value	154.6 Million
Price/Book	4.87	Price/Sales	2.42

Dividend Achiever Status

10 Year Growth Rate	3.07%
Total Years of Dividend Growth	35

Business Summary: Industrial Machinery and Equipment (MIC: SIC: 3561 NAIC: 333911)

Gorman-Rupp designs, manufactures and sells pumps and related equipment for use in water, wastewater, construction, industrial, petroleum, original equipment, agriculture, fire protection, heating, ventilating and air conditioning, military and other liquid-handling applications. The types of pumps Co. produces include self priming, standard and magnetic drive centrifugal, axial and mixed flow, rotary gear, diaphragm, bellows and oscillating. Co.'s larger pumps are sold mainly for use in the construction, industrial, sewage and waste handling fields; boosting low residential water pressure; pumping refined petroleum products; agricultural purposes; and for firefighting and flood control.

Recent Developments: For the quarter ended Mar 31 2008, net income increased 40.5% to US$7.2 million from US$5.1 million in the year-earlier quarter. Revenues were US$81.4 million, up 9.4% from US$74.5 million the year before. Operating income was US$10.3 million versus US$7.6 million in the prior-year quarter, an increase of 35.7%. Direct operating expenses rose 5.5% to US$61.6 million from US$58.4 million in the comparable period the year before. Indirect operating expenses increased 12.5% to US$9.5 million from US$8.4 million in the equivalent prior-year period.

Prospects: Co.'s near-term outlook appears favorable, reflecting increases in net sales and net income driven by growth in international sales and higher sales of fire protection pumps and fabricated components. Co. is also pursuing its expansion into the areas of water and wastewater handling and infrastructure renewal and expansion, and has approved the second phase of consolidation and expansion plans for its Mansfield, OH, facilities to accommodate increasing sales growth. Co. expects the consolidation and expansion of the facilities to result in increased capacity and anticipates construction of the second phase of the project to begin during 2008, with completion projected by the end of 2009.

Financial Data

(US$ in Thousands)	3 Mos	12/31/2007	12/31/2006	12/31/2005	12/31/2004	12/31/2003	12/31/2002	12/31/2001
Earnings Per Share	1.41	1.37	1.14	0.65	0.56	0.59	0.54	0.87
Cash Flow Per Share	1.78	2.09	1.12	0.18	0.87	0.84	1.28	1.57
Tang Book Value Per Share	9.25	8.37	7.23	7.17	6.87	6.55	6.25	6.47
Dividends Per Share	0.392	0.388	0.368	0.358	0.353	0.348	0.333	0.328
Dividend Payout %	27.80	28.32	32.17	54.90	63.45	59.13	61.90	37.65
Income Statement								
Total Revenue	81,434	305,562	270,910	231,249	203,554	195,826	194,075	203,813
EBITDA	12,823	42,980	34,414	23,946	21,531	21,517	21,238	30,163
Depn & Amortn	1,935	7,597	6,688	6,808	7,179	7,117	7,035	7,128
Income Before Taxes	10,888	35,383	27,726	17,138	14,352	14,400	14,203	23,035
Income Taxes	3,736	12,524	8,654	6,235	5,075	4,613	5,267	8,450
Net Income	7,152	22,859	19,072	10,903	9,277	9,787	8,936	14,585
Average Shares	16,703	16,701	16,697	16,694	16,688	16,683	16,677	16,710
Balance Sheet								
Current Assets	139,165	135,288	120,118	110,501	96,645	94,262	83,859	89,119
Total Assets	216,241	211,534	187,540	179,541	165,344	160,939	152,846	148,113
Current Liabilities	32,901	33,481	27,646	28,219	21,112	21,908	19,282	18,103
Long-Term Obligations	...	...	...	...	...	...	291	...
Total Liabilities	61,069	62,094	59,398	52,493	43,446	44,477	41,390	40,203
Stockholders' Equity	154,581	149,440	128,142	127,048	121,898	116,462	111,456	107,910
Shares Outstanding	16,703	16,703	16,699	16,696	16,691	16,686	16,680	16,674
Statistical Record								
Return on Assets %	12.21	11.46	10.39	6.32	5.67	6.24	5.94	9.92
Return on Equity %	17.37	16.47	14.95	8.76	7.76	8.59	8.15	14.03
EBITDA Margin %	15.75	14.07	12.70	10.36	10.58	10.99	10.94	14.80
Net Margin %	8.78	7.48	7.04	4.71	4.56	5.00	4.60	7.16
Asset Turnover	1.53	1.53	1.48	1.34	1.24	1.25	1.29	1.39
Current Ratio	4.23	4.04	4.34	3.92	4.58	4.30	4.35	4.92
Price Range	36.50-22.95	36.50-21.68	30.68-13.82	17.50-12.25	15.69-12.00	13.81-9.52	16.13-10.50	13.90-8.96
P/E Ratio	25.89-16.28	26.64-15.82	26.91-12.13	26.93-18.85	28.01-21.43	23.41-16.14	29.87-19.45	15.98-10.30
Average Yield %	1.32	1.41	2.02	2.52	2.60	2.97	2.53	2.91

Address: 305 Bowman St., Mansfield, OH 44903-1689 **Telephone:** 419-755-1011 **Web Site:** www.gormanrupp.com	**Officers:** James C. Gorman - Chairman Jeffrey S. Gorman - President, Chief Executive Officer **Transfer Agents:**National City Bank, Cleveland, Ohio	**Investor Contact:** 419-755-1294 **No of Institutions:** 96 **Shares:** 9,486,199 **% Held:** 56.44

GRAINGER (W.W.) INC.

Exchange	Symbol	Price	52Wk Range	Yield	P/E
NYS	GWW	$91.16 (5/29/2008)	98.45-71.60	1.76	17.56

*7 Year Price Score 108.30 *NYSE Composite Index=100 ***12 Month Price Score 102.77**

Interim Earnings (Per Share)

Qtr.	Mar	Jun	Sep	Dec
2005	0.79	0.89	0.97	1.13
2006	0.93	1.02	1.16	1.13
2007	1.17	1.21	1.29	1.27
2008	1.43	...	...	...

Interim Dividends (Per Share)

Amt	Decl	Ex	Rec	Pay
0.35Q	07/25/2007	08/09/2007	08/13/2007	09/01/2007
0.35Q	10/31/2007	11/07/2007	11/12/2007	12/01/2007
0.35Q	01/30/2008	02/07/2008	02/11/2008	03/01/2008
0.40Q	04/30/2008	05/08/2008	05/12/2008	06/01/2008
		Indicated Div: $1.60		

Valuation Analysis

Forecast EPS $5.87 (05/17/2008)

Market Cap	$7.0 Billion	Book Value	2.0 Billion
Price/Book	3.50	Price/Sales	1.07

Dividend Achiever Status

10 Year Growth Rate	9.72%
Total Years of Dividend Growth	36

TRADING VOLUME (thousand shares)

Business Summary: Engineering Services (MIC: SIC: 5063 NAIC: 423610)

W.W. Grainger is a supplier of facilities maintenance and other related products. Co. has three operating segments: Grainger Branch-based, which provides customers with products for facility maintenance and other product needs through logistics networks which are configured for product availability; Acklands - Grainger Branch-based, which distributes tools, fasteners, safety supplies, instruments, welding and shop equipment, and many other items; and Lab Safety Supply, Inc., which is a direct marketer of safety and other industrial products to U.S. and Canadian businesses through the distribution of multiple catalogs and other marketing materials distributed to targeted markets.

Recent Developments: For the quarter ended Mar 31 2008, net income increased 12.2% to US$114.2 million from US$101.8 million in the year-earlier quarter. Revenues were US$1.66 billion, up 7.4% from US$1.55 billion the year before. Operating income was US$185.8 million versus US$162.6 million in the prior-year quarter, an increase of 14.3%. Direct operating expenses rose 7.3% to US$981.1 million from US$914.6 million in the comparable period the year before. Indirect operating expenses increased 5.2% to US$494.1 million from US$469.5 million in the equivalent prior-year period.

Prospects: For full-year 2008, Co. has raised its forecasted earnings per share range to $5.80 to $6.10 compared with its previously announced range of $5.65 to $6.00. In addition, Co. expects operating margin expansion going forward to come from a combination of gross margin improvement and operating expense leverage. For its Grainger branch-based business, Co. plans to open nine new branches in 2008 and expects some short-term losses. Further, Co. expects to essentially complete phases 5 and 6 of its market expansion program of its Grainger branch-based business in the U.S. by mid-year of 2008 and expects to see continued incremental sales growth from the program for another five years.

Financial Data
(US$ in Thousands)

	3 Mos	12/31/2007	12/31/2006	12/31/2005	12/31/2004	12/31/2003	12/31/2002	12/31/2001
Earnings Per Share	5.19	4.94	4.24	3.78	3.13	2.46	2.24	1.84
Cash Flow Per Share	5.12	5.69	4.97	4.83	4.49	4.34	3.30	5.48
Tang Book Value Per Share	23.03	23.47	23.40	23.48	20.44	18.20	16.59	15.09
Dividends Per Share	1.400	1.340	1.110	0.920	0.785	0.735	0.715	0.695
Dividend Payout %	26.99	27.13	26.18	24.34	25.08	29.88	31.92	37.77
Income Statement								
Total Revenue	1,661,046	6,418,014	5,883,654	5,526,636	5,049,785	4,667,014	4,643,898	4,754,317
EBITDA	218,685	804,709	702,021	630,437	541,407	474,011	492,915	408,336
Depn & Amortn	31,556	131,999	118,568	108,782	98,256	90,253	93,488	103,209
Income Before Taxes	186,500	681,861	603,023	532,674	445,139	381,090	397,837	297,280
Income Taxes	72,262	261,741	219,624	186,350	158,216	154,119	162,349	122,750
Net Income	114,238	420,120	383,399	346,324	286,923	226,971	211,567	174,530
Average Shares	80,131	85,044	90,523	91,588	91,673	92,394	94,303	94,727
Balance Sheet								
Current Assets	1,854,521	1,800,817	1,862,086	1,997,868	1,754,713	1,633,413	1,484,947	1,392,611
Total Assets	3,155,833	3,094,028	3,046,088	3,107,921	2,809,573	2,624,678	2,437,448	2,331,246
Current Liabilities	993,509	826,403	706,323	726,964	662,434	706,640	586,266	553,811
Long-Term Obligations	4,895	4,895	4,895	4,895	...	4,895	119,693	118,219
Total Liabilities	1,165,606	995,920	868,473	818,945	741,603	779,543	769,750	728,057
Stockholders' Equity	1,990,227	2,098,108	2,177,615	2,288,976	2,067,970	1,845,135	1,667,698	1,603,189
Shares Outstanding	76,507	79,459	84,067	89,715	90,597	91,020	91,568	93,344
Statistical Record								
Return on Assets %	13.85	13.68	12.46	11.71	10.53	8.97	8.87	7.29
Return on Equity %	20.53	19.65	17.17	15.90	14.62	12.92	12.94	11.11
EBITDA Margin %	13.17	12.54	11.93	11.41	10.72	10.16	10.61	8.59
Net Margin %	6.88	6.55	6.52	6.27	5.68	4.86	4.56	3.67
Asset Turnover	2.09	2.09	1.91	1.87	1.85	1.84	1.95	1.98
Current Ratio	1.87	2.18	2.64	2.75	2.65	2.31	2.53	2.51
Debt to Equity	N.M.	N.M.	N.M.	N.M.	...	N.M.	0.07	0.07
Price Range	98.45-71.60	98.45-69.34	79.73-60.62	71.97-52.29	66.62-45.17	53.11-41.93	59.27-39.82	48.52-30.23
P/E Ratio	18.97-13.80	19.93-14.04	18.80-14.30	19.04-13.83	21.28-14.43	21.59-17.04	26.46-17.78	26.37-16.43
Average Yield %	1.64	1.57	1.56	1.48	1.46	1.56	1.42	1.72

Address: 100 Grainger Parkway, Lake Forest, IL 60045-5201	Officers: Richard L. Keyser - Chairman P. Ogden Loux - Vice-Chairman **Transfer Agents:**	Investor Contact: 847-535-1000
Telephone: 847-535-1000	BankBoston, N.A. c/o EquiServe, Boston, MA	**No of Institutions:** 486
Web Site: www.grainger.com		**Shares:** 59,118,648 **% Held:** 70.84

HARLEY-DAVIDSON INC

Exchange	Symbol	Price	52Wk Range	Yield	P/E
NYS	HOG	$40.52 (5/29/2008)	62.81-34.68	3.26	10.66

*7 Year Price Score 69.86   *NYSE Composite Index=100   *12 Month Price Score 83.56

Interim Earnings (Per Share)

Qtr.	Mar	Jun	Sep	Dec
2005	0.77	0.84	0.96	0.84
2006	0.86	0.91	1.20	0.97
2007	0.74	1.14	1.07	0.79
2008	0.79	...	...	...

Interim Dividends (Per Share)

Amt	Decl	Ex	Rec	Pay
0.30Q	09/13/2007	09/27/2007	10/01/2007	10/11/2007
0.30Q	12/11/2007	12/19/2007	12/21/2007	12/28/2007
0.30Q	02/13/2008	03/03/2008	03/05/2008	03/18/2008
0.33Q	04/26/2008	06/03/2008	06/05/2008	06/20/2008

Indicated Div: $1.32 (Div. Reinv. Plan)

Valuation Analysis

Forecast EPS	$3.06 (05/17/2008)		
Market Cap	$9.6 Billion	Book Value	2.4 Billion
Price/Book	3.94	Price/Sales	1.53

Dividend Achiever Status

10 Year Growth Rate	31.70%
Total Years of Dividend Growth	14

TRADING VOLUME (thousand shares)

Business Summary: Automotive (MIC: SIC: 3751 NAIC: 336991)

Harley-Davidson operates in two business segments: Motorcycles and Financial Services. Co.'s Motorcycles segment consists primarily of the group of companies doing business as Harley-Davidson Motor Company and Buell Motorcycle Company, which designs, manufactures and sells primarily heavyweight (engine displacement of 651+cc) touring, custom, standard and sport motorcycles and a range of related products, such as motorcycle parts and accessories and general merchandise. Meanwhile, Co.'s Financial Services segment consists of Harley-Davidson Financial Services, which provides wholesale and retail financing and insurance programs primarily to Harley-Davidson® and Buell dealers and customers.

Recent Developments: For the quarter ended Mar 30 2008, net income decreased 2.5% to US$187.6 million from US$192.3 million in the year-earlier quarter. Revenues were US$1.40 billion, up 8.7% from US$1.29 billion the year before. Operating income was US$291.1 million versus US$289.2 million in the prior-year quarter, an increase of 0.6%. Direct operating expenses rose 10.2% to US$888.6 million from US$806.1 million in the comparable period the year before. Indirect operating expenses increased 14.1% to US$220.0 million from US$192.7 million in the equivalent prior-year period.

Prospects: For 2008, in view of the continued challenging U.S. retail trends and economy, Co. remains committed to shipping fewer Harley-Davidson® motorcycles to its worldwide dealer network. In detail, Co. plans to ship 23,000 to 27,000 fewer Harley-Davidson® motorcycles in 2008 than it shipped in 2007, resulting in total planned 2008 shipments between 303,500 and 307,500 units. This shipment reduction will be attained through temporary plant shutdowns and adjustments to daily production rates. In light of these actions, for 2008, Co. expects diluted earnings per share to decrease by 15.0% to 20.0% from 2007, resulting in expected annual diluted earnings per share of $3.00 to $3.18.

Financial Data

(US$ in Thousands)	3 Mos	12/31/2007	12/31/2006	12/31/2005	12/31/2004	12/31/2003	12/31/2002	12/31/2001
Earnings Per Share	3.80	3.74	3.93	3.41	3.00	2.50	1.90	1.43
Cash Flow Per Share	1.82	3.20	2.88	3.43	3.28	3.10	2.58	2.50
Tang Book Value Per Share	10.01	9.70	10.45	11.05	10.73	9.63	7.21	5.64
Dividends Per Share	1.150	1.060	0.810	0.625	0.405	0.195	0.135	0.115
Dividend Payout %	30.28	28.34	20.61	18.33	13.50	7.80	7.11	8.04
Income Statement								
Total Revenue	1,399,602	6,143,044	6,185,577	5,673,832	5,320,452	4,903,733	4,302,470	3,544,959
EBITDA	342,817	1,629,733	1,810,672	1,670,667	1,570,497	1,339,865	1,045,064	809,038
Depn & Amortn	49,722	204,172	213,769	205,705	214,112	196,918	175,778	153,061
Income Before Taxes	293,095	1,447,819	1,624,240	1,487,759	1,379,486	1,166,035	885,827	673,455
Income Taxes	105,514	513,976	581,087	528,155	489,720	405,107	305,610	235,709
Net Income	187,581	933,843	1,043,153	959,604	889,766	760,928	580,217	437,746
Average Shares	237,250	249,882	265,273	281,035	296,852	304,470	305,158	306,248
Balance Sheet								
Current Assets	3,586,787	3,467,314	3,550,633	3,145,237	3,266,272	2,729,127	2,066,586	1,665,264
Total Assets	5,864,399	5,656,606	5,532,150	5,255,209	5,483,293	4,923,088	3,861,217	3,118,495
Current Liabilities	2,036,050	1,905,079	1,595,677	873,112	1,172,696	955,773	990,052	716,110
Long-Term Obligations	980,000	980,000	870,000	1,000,000	800,000	670,000	380,000	380,000
Total Liabilities	3,432,974	3,281,115	2,775,413	2,171,604	2,264,822	1,965,396	1,628,302	1,362,212
Stockholders' Equity	2,431,425	2,375,491	2,756,737	3,083,605	3,218,471	2,957,692	2,232,915	1,756,283
Shares Outstanding	236,555	238,485	258,052	274,001	294,310	301,510	302,662	302,789
Statistical Record								
Return on Assets %	16.47	16.69	19.34	17.87	17.05	17.32	16.63	15.76
Return on Equity %	35.36	36.39	35.72	30.45	28.73	29.32	29.09	27.69
EBITDA Margin %	24.49	26.53	29.28	29.45	29.52	27.32	24.29	22.82
Net Margin %	13.40	15.20	16.86	16.91	16.72	15.52	13.49	12.35
Asset Turnover	1.11	1.10	1.15	1.06	1.02	1.12	1.23	1.28
Current Ratio	1.76	1.82	2.23	3.60	2.79	2.86	2.09	2.33
Debt to Equity	0.40	0.41	0.32	0.32	0.25	0.23	0.17	0.22
Price Range	65.55-34.68	73.85-44.96	75.50-47.96	62.18-44.40	62.97-46.00	52.45-35.95	57.00-42.83	55.66-35.19
P/E Ratio	17.25-9.13	19.75-12.02	19.21-12.20	18.23-13.02	20.99-15.33	20.98-14.38	30.00-22.54	38.92-24.61
Average Yield %	2.25	1.83	1.41	1.18	0.71	0.44	0.27	0.25

Address: 3700 West Juneau Avenue, P.O. Box 653, Milwaukee, WI 53201-0653 **Telephone:** 414-342-4680 **Web Site:** www.harley-davidson.com	**Officers:** Jeffrey L. Bleustein - Chairman James L. Ziemer - President, Chief Executive Officer **Transfer Agents:** Computershare Investor Services, LLC, Chicago, IL	**No of Institutions:** 612 **Shares:** 219,976,208 **% Held:** 80.28

HARLEYSVILLE GROUP, INC. (PA)

Exchange	Symbol	Price	52Wk Range	Yield	P/E
NMS	HGIC	$39.49 (5/29/2008)	39.49-28.01	2.53	12.15

*7 Year Price Score 99.00 ***NYSE Composite Index=100** ***12 Month Price Score 112.42**

Interim Earnings (Per Share)

Qtr.	Mar	Jun	Sep	Dec
2005	0.39	0.48	0.54	0.60
2006	0.70	1.43	0.69	0.71
2007	0.71	0.82	0.83	0.82
2008	0.79	...	...	...

Interim Dividends (Per Share)

Amt	Decl	Ex	Rec	Pay
0.19Q	06/05/2007	06/13/2007	06/15/2007	06/29/2007
0.25Q	08/01/2007	09/12/2007	09/14/2007	09/28/2007
0.25Q	10/31/2007	12/12/2007	12/14/2007	12/31/2007
0.25Q	02/21/2008	03/12/2008	03/14/2008	03/31/2008

Indicated Div: $1.00 (Div. Reinv. Plan)

Valuation Analysis

Forecast EPS $3.35 (05/16/2008)

Market Cap	$1.2 Billion	Book Value	763.4 Million
Price/Book	1.55	Price/Sales	1.20

Dividend Achiever Status

10 Year Growth Rate	7.18%
Total Years of Dividend Growth	21

TRADING VOLUME (thousand shares)

Business Summary: Insurance (MIC: SIC: 6331 NAIC: 524126)

Harleysville Group underwrites property and casualty insurance in both the personal and commercial lines of insurance. As an underwriter of property and casualty insurance, Co. has three segments which consisted of the personal lines of insurance, the commercial lines of insurance and the investment function. Co.'s personal lines of insurance include both auto and homeowners, while its commercial lines include auto, commercial multi-peril and workers compensation. Co.'s business is marketed primarily in the eastern and midwestern U.S. through independent agents. As of Dec 31 2007, these insurance coverages were marketed through approximately 1,500 insurance agencies.

Recent Developments: For the quarter ended Mar 31 2008, net income increased 5.4% to US$24.1 million from US$22.9 million in the year-earlier quarter. Revenues were US$261.9 million, up 10.5% from US$236.9 million the year before. Net premiums earned were US$229.4 million versus US$205.4 million in the prior-year quarter, an increase of 11.7%. Net investment income rose 3.4% to US$29.0 million from US$28.0 million a year ago.

Prospects: Co.'s near-term outlook appears to be favorable. In detail, Co. is seeing higher premiums earned, mainly due to an increase in premiums earned for commercial lines and personal lines premiums earned. Specifically, the increase in premiums earned for commercial lines is driven by a slight increase in direct premiums earned, while the increase in premiums earned for personal lines is fueled by an increase in homeowners business due to higher average premiums. In addition, Co. is experiencing an increase in investment income, primarily due to a higher level of invested assets, partially offset by a lower investment yield on fixed income securities.

Financial Data
(US$ in Thousands)

	3 Mos	12/31/2007	12/31/2006	12/31/2005	12/31/2004	12/31/2003	12/31/2002	12/31/2001
Earnings Per Share	3.25	3.19	3.52	2.01	1.55	(1.59)	1.53	1.46
Cash Flow Per Share	7.55	5.55	5.35	5.44	3.84	4.49	3.81	1.56
Tang Book Value Per Share	25.55	25.03	22.49	20.07	19.47	19.16	21.13	20.05
Dividends Per Share	0.940	0.880	0.730	0.690	0.680	0.670	0.630	0.580
Dividend Payout %	28.91	27.59	20.74	34.33	43.87	...	41.18	39.73
Income Statement								
Total Revenue	261,855	962,012	999,171	948,340	953,392	924,965	847,736	827,751
Income Before Taxes	33,846	142,995	156,368	78,921	55,637	(89,450)	56,482	51,800
Income Taxes	9,704	42,941	46,241	17,490	8,759	(41,821)	10,227	8,307
Net Income	24,142	100,054	111,069	61,431	46,878	(47,629)	46,255	43,493
Average Shares	30,447	31,354	31,525	30,585	30,154	29,985	30,295	29,818
Balance Sheet								
Total Assets	3,277,311	3,072,445	2,990,984	2,905,266	2,718,063	2,680,389	2,311,524	2,045,290
Total Liabilities	2,513,934	2,313,604	2,278,822	2,290,883	2,130,139	2,107,642	1,679,412	1,454,992
Stockholders' Equity	763,377	758,841	712,162	614,383	587,924	572,747	632,112	590,298
Shares Outstanding	29,879	30,322	31,662	30,610	30,191	29,900	29,917	29,444
Statistical Record								
Return on Assets %	3.20	3.30	3.77	2.18	1.73	N.M.	2.12	2.14
Return on Equity %	13.47	13.60	16.75	10.22	8.06	N.M.	7.57	7.52
Net Margin %	9.22	10.40	11.12	6.48	4.92	(5.15)	5.46	5.25
Price Range	37.55-28.01	37.55-28.01	38.64-26.11	27.80-18.90	24.96-17.84	27.50-18.99	31.44-19.90	30.00-20.40
P/E Ratio	11.55-8.62	11.77-8.78	10.98-7.42	13.83-9.40	16.10-11.51	...	20.55-13.01	20.55-13.97
Average Yield %	2.84	2.70	2.32	3.08	3.37	2.86	2.43	2.28

Address: 355 Maple Avenue, Harleysville, PA 19438-2297
Telephone: 215-256-5000
Web Site: www.harleysvillegroup.com

Officers: Michael L. Browne - President, Chief Executive Officer Mark R. Cummins - Executive Vice President, Chief Investment Officer, Treasurer, Affiliate Officer **Transfer Agents:** Mellon Investor Services, South Hackensack, NJ

Investor Contact: 215-256-5151
No of Institutions: 139
Shares: 13,397,682 **% Held:** 41.30

HARLEYSVILLE NATIONAL CORP.

Exchange	Symbol	Price	52Wk Range	Yield	P/E
NMS	HNBC	$13.66 (5/29/2008)	18.58-12.50	5.86	14.85

*7 Year Price Score 61.74 *NYSE Composite Index=100 *12 Month Price Score 97.10

Interim Earnings (Per Share)

Qtr.	Mar	Jun	Sep	Dec
2005	0.31	0.33	0.34	0.33
2006	0.30	0.31	0.27	0.45
2007	0.21	0.24	0.25	0.20
2008	0.23	...	...	...

Interim Dividends (Per Share)

Amt	Decl	Ex	Rec	Pay
0.20Q	08/09/2007	08/28/2007	08/30/2007	09/14/2007
0.20Q	11/08/2007	11/28/2007	11/30/2007	12/14/2007
0.20Q	02/14/2008	02/27/2008	02/29/2008	03/14/2008
0.20Q	05/08/2008	05/28/2008	05/30/2008	06/16/2008

Indicated Div: $0.80 (Div. Reinv. Plan)

Valuation Analysis

Forecast EPS	N/A		
Market Cap	$428.3 Million	Book Value	343.3 Million
Price/Book	1.25	Price/Sales	1.75

Dividend Achiever Status

10 Year Growth Rate	11.79%
Total Years of Dividend Growth	21

Business Summary: Commercial Banking (MIC: SIC: 6021 NAIC: 522110)

Harleysville National is the bank holding company for Harleysville National Bank and Trust Company. Co., through its subsidiary, provides a range of banking services including loans and deposits, investment management and trust and investment advisory services to individual and corporate customers located in eastern Pennsylvania. Co. also engages in the full-service commercial banking and trust business. As of Dec 31 2007, Co. had 55 branch offices located in Montgomery, Bucks, Chester, Berks, Carbon, Lehigh, Monroe, and Northampton counties, PA. At Dec 31 2007, Co. had total assets of $3.90 billion and total deposits of $2.99 billion.

Recent Developments: For the quarter ended Mar 31 2008, net income increased 19.1% to US$7.3 million from US$6.1 million in the year-earlier quarter. Net interest income increased 22.0% to US$24.2 million from US$19.8 million in the year-earlier quarter. Provision for loan losses was US$2.0 million versus US$2.4 million in the prior-year quarter, a decrease of 19.2%. Non-interest income rose 18.4% to US$10.8 million from US$9.1 million, while non-interest expense advanced 26.3% to US$23.7 million.

Prospects: On May 21 2008, Co. and Willow Financial Bancorp, Inc. (Willow) reached a definitive agreement for Willow to be acquired by Co. in a total transaction value at about $162.0 million. The acquisition provides Co. with the opportunity to enhance its investment consulting, estate and business planning, and compensation planning practices. In addition, the acquisition provides cross-sell opportunities for Co.'s Millennium Wealth Management and private banking business to Willow's customers base. Also, Co. expects the acquisition to be accretive to its earnings in 2009. The transaction is subject to regulatory and shareholder approval and is expected to close in the fourth quarter of 2008.

Financial Data

(US$ in Thousands)	3 Mos	12/31/2007	12/31/2006	12/31/2005	12/31/2004	12/31/2003	12/31/2002	12/31/2001
Earnings Per Share	0.92	0.90	1.34	1.31	1.31	1.24	1.15	1.01
Cash Flow Per Share	0.92	1.15	1.21	1.24	1.74	1.72	1.17	1.54
Tang Book Value Per Share	6.98	6.86	8.41	8.25	8.07	8.23	7.49	6.77
Dividends Per Share	0.800	0.800	0.752	0.718	0.649	0.565	0.487	0.428
Dividend Payout %	87.21	88.89	56.15	54.62	49.67	45.42	42.23	42.21
Income Statement								
Income Before Taxes	9,361	33,867	53,491	51,231	51,133	43,930	41,876	36,994
Income Taxes	2,057	7,272	14,076	12,403	12,566	8,597	8,949	8,174
Net Income	7,304	26,595	39,415	38,828	38,567	35,333	32,927	28,820
Average Shares	31,522	29,459	29,353	29,490	29,465	28,505	28,507	28,505
Balance Sheet								
Total Assets	3,894,019	3,903,001	3,249,828	3,117,359	3,024,515	2,510,939	2,490,864	2,208,971
Total Liabilities	3,550,737	3,563,691	2,955,077	2,844,127	2,753,983	2,283,886	2,284,658	2,019,622
Stockholders' Equity	343,282	339,310	294,751	273,232	270,532	227,053	206,206	189,349
Shares Outstanding	31,354	31,332	28,964	28,807	28,970	27,603	27,534	27,779
Statistical Record								
Return on Assets %	0.77	0.74	1.24	1.26	1.39	1.41	1.40	1.39
Return on Equity %	8.66	8.39	13.88	14.28	15.46	16.31	16.65	15.88
Price Range	18.58-12.50	20.25-13.15	24.90-18.06	24.13-17.83	26.93-19.26	28.05-16.81	18.59-14.53	17.07-11.27
P/E Ratio	20.20-13.59	22.50-14.61	18.59-13.48	18.42-13.61	20.55-14.71	22.62-13.56	16.17-12.64	16.90-11.16
Average Yield %	5.14	4.80	3.76	3.48	2.81	2.78	2.95	3.10

Address: 483 Main Street, P.O. Box 195, Harleysville, PA 19438 Telephone: 215-256-8851 Web Site: www.hncbank.com	Officers: Walter E. Daller - Chairman Paul D. Geraghty - President, Chief Executive Officer Transfer Agents:American Stock Transfer & Trust Company, New York, NY	Investor Contact: 888-462-2100 No of Institutions: 99 Shares: 7,964,780 % Held: 25.65

HARSCO CORP.

Exchange	Symbol	Price	52Wk Range	Yield	P/E
NYS	HSC	$62.64 (5/29/2008)	65.75-48.25	1.25	17.30

*7 Year Price Score 145.69 *NYSE Composite Index=100 ***12 Month Price Score 109.22**

Interim Earnings (Per Share)

Qtr.	Mar	Jun	Sep	Dec
2005	0.28	0.50	0.47	0.61
2006	0.41	0.64	0.66	0.62
2007	0.56	0.98	0.91	1.07
2008	0.67	...	...	...

Interim Dividends (Per Share)

Amt	Decl	Ex	Rec	Pay
0.177Q	09/25/2007	10/11/2007	10/15/2007	11/15/2007
0.00Q	...	10/09/2007	...	...
0.195Q	11/13/2007	01/11/2008	01/15/2008	02/15/2008
0.195Q	02/27/2008	04/11/2008	04/15/2008	05/15/2008

Indicated Div: $0.78

Valuation Analysis

Forecast EPS $3.55 (05/16/2008)

Market Cap	$5.3 Billion	Book Value	1.7 Billion
Price/Book	3.16	Price/Sales	1.38

Dividend Achiever Status

10 Year Growth Rate	5.91%
Total Years of Dividend Growth	13

Business Summary: Metal Products (MIC: SIC: 3441 NAIC: 332312)

Harsco is a provider of industrial services and engineered products. As of Dec 31 2007, Co.'s operations were divided into two reportable segments: Access Services and Mill Services, plus an All Other category labeled Minerals & Rail Services and Products. The Access Services segment provides rental scaffolding, shoring, forming and other access applications to the global construction services industry. The Mill Services segment is a global provider of on-site, outsourced mill services to the global steel and metals industries. The All Other category includes the Excell Minerals, Reed Minerals, Harsco Track Technologies, IKG Industries, Patterson-Kelley and Air-X-Changers Divisions.

Recent Developments: For the quarter ended Mar 31 2008, income from continuing operations increased 25.2% to US$56.9 million from US$45.4 million in the year-earlier quarter. Net income increased 19.7% to US$57.0 million from US$47.7 million in the year-earlier quarter. Revenues were US$987.8 million, up 17.6% from US$840.0 million the year before. Operating income was US$99.4 million versus US$86.6 million in the prior-year quarter, an increase of 14.8%. Direct operating expenses rose 16.8% to US$731.0 million from US$625.6 million in the comparable period the year before. Indirect operating expenses increased 23.1% to US$157.4 million from US$127.8 million in the equivalent prior-year period.

Prospects: For 2008, based on several factors including its continuing robust end markets and international expansion opportunities, Co. has raised its guidance for diluted earnings per share from continuing operations to $3.45 to $3.55 from previous range of $3.40 to $3.50, reflecting a 16.0% improvement over $3.01 in 2007, using the mid-point of the new range. Meanwhile, Co. continues to expand its presence in the Middle East, Eastern Europe, and Latin America. For example, Co. acquired Romania-based Baviera S.R.L., a distributor of formwork and scaffolding products in Mar 2008, and Sovereign Access Services Limited, a U.K-based provider of mastclimber work platform rental equipment in Apr 2008.

Financial Data

(US$ in Thousands)	3 Mos	12/31/2007	12/31/2006	12/31/2005	12/31/2004	12/31/2003	12/31/2002	12/31/2001
Earnings Per Share	3.62	3.53	2.33	1.86	1.46	1.13	1.11	0.90
Cash Flow Per Share	5.46	5.60	4.88	3.79	3.28	3.23	3.14	3.02
Tang Book Value Per Share	8.81	7.78	5.30	4.25	5.81	4.52	3.30	4.16
Dividends Per Share	0.728	0.710	0.650	0.600	0.550	0.525	0.500	0.480
Dividend Payout %	20.10	20.11	27.96	32.26	37.80	46.67	45.25	53.63
Income Statement								
Total Revenue	987,790	3,688,160	3,423,293	2,766,210	2,502,059	2,118,516	1,976,732	2,108,474
EBITDA	184,077	765,267	611,643	467,087	394,348	343,148	331,995	338,294
Depn & Amortn	84,292	306,413	252,982	198,065	184,371	168,935	155,661	176,531
Income Before Taxes	83,579	382,439	301,892	230,269	171,239	135,902	136,699	113,795
Income Taxes	24,188	117,598	97,523	64,771	49,034	41,708	42,240	36,982
Net Income	57,039	299,492	196,398	156,657	121,211	92,217	90,106	71,725
Average Shares	84,851	84,724	84,430	84,160	83,196	81,946	81,360	80,132
Balance Sheet								
Current Assets	1,469,177	1,345,337	1,231,622	1,101,023	924,924	764,351	702,402	716,067
Total Assets	4,137,848	3,905,430	3,326,423	2,975,804	2,389,756	2,138,035	1,999,297	2,090,766
Current Liabilities	1,013,315	873,970	910,775	748,403	578,397	495,075	473,850	474,674
Long-Term Obligations	1,007,350	1,012,087	864,817	905,859	594,747	584,425	605,613	720,197
Total Liabilities	2,469,882	2,339,311	2,180,059	1,981,910	1,475,566	1,361,047	1,354,757	1,404,593
Stockholders' Equity	1,667,966	1,566,119	1,146,364	993,894	914,190	776,988	644,540	686,173
Shares Outstanding	84,261	84,459	84,037	83,566	82,862	81,732	81,078	79,969
Statistical Record								
Return on Assets %	7.84	8.28	6.23	5.84	5.34	4.46	4.41	3.36
Return on Equity %	21.49	22.08	18.35	16.42	14.30	12.97	13.54	10.55
EBITDA Margin %	18.64	20.75	17.87	16.89	15.76	16.20	16.80	16.04
Net Margin %	5.77	8.12	5.74	5.66	4.84	4.35	4.56	3.40
Asset Turnover	0.97	1.02	1.09	1.03	1.10	1.02	0.97	0.99
Current Ratio	1.45	1.54	1.35	1.47	1.60	1.54	1.48	1.51
Debt to Equity	0.60	0.65	0.75	0.91	0.65	0.75	0.94	1.05
Price Range	65.75-44.72	65.75-37.21	44.01-34.28	34.70-24.97	28.00-20.18	22.14-13.87	22.00-12.43	17.95-11.91
P/E Ratio	18.16-12.35	18.63-10.54	18.89-14.71	18.66-13.42	19.18-13.83	19.59-12.27	19.82-11.20	19.95-13.23
Average Yield %	1.32	1.37	1.65	2.02	2.38	2.96	2.98	3.29

Address: 350 Poplar Church Road, Camp Hill, PA 17001-8888	**Officers:** Geoffrey D. H. Butler - President, Division Officer Salvatore D. Fazzolari - Chief Executive Officer **Transfer Agents:** Mellon Investor Services LLC, South Hackensack, NJ	**Investor Contact:** 717-975-5677 **No of Institutions:** 372 **Shares:** 59,990,592 **% Held:** 69.22
Telephone: 717-763-7064		
Web Site: www.harsco.com		

HARTE-HANKS, INC.

Exchange	Symbol	Price	52Wk Range	Yield	P/E
NYS	HHS	$13.65 (5/29/2008)	26.83-12.87	2.20	11.28

*7 Year Price Score 64.53 *NYSE Composite Index=100 *12 Month Price Score 74.69

Interim Earnings (Per Share)

Qtr.	Mar	Jun	Sep	Dec
2005	0.29	0.34	0.34	0.38
2006	0.29	0.37	0.35	0.39
2007	0.27	0.31	0.30	0.39
2008	0.21	...	...	...

Interim Dividends (Per Share)

Amt	Decl	Ex	Rec	Pay
0.07Q	08/28/2007	09/04/2007	09/06/2007	09/14/2007
0.07Q	11/15/2007	11/29/2007	12/03/2007	12/14/2007
0.075Q	01/29/2008	02/27/2008	02/29/2008	03/14/2008
0.075Q	05/13/2008	05/28/2008	05/30/2008	06/13/2008
		Indicated Div: $0.30		

Valuation Analysis

Forecast EPS	$1.19 (05/16/2008)		
Market Cap	$862.2 Million	Book Value	343.5 Million
Price/Book	2.51	Price/Sales	0.75

Dividend Achiever Status

10 Year Growth Rate	26.51%
Total Years of Dividend Growth	12

Business Summary: "Advertising, Marketing & PR" (MIC: SIC: 7331 NAIC: 541860)

Harte-Hanks is a direct and targeted marketing company that provides direct marketing services and shopper advertising to local, regional, national and international consumer and business-to-business marketers. Co.'s direct marketing services are targeted to specific industries or markets with services and software products tailored to each industry or market. Co.'s Shoppers unit owns, operates and distributes shopper publications, which are weekly advertising publications delivered free to households and businesses in a particular geographic area. As of Dec 31 2007, Co. published 1,077 individual shopper editions each week distributed to zones with circulation of about 12,000 each.

Recent Developments: For the quarter ended Mar 31 2008, net income decreased 33.2% to US$13.6 million from US$20.3 million in the year-earlier quarter. Revenues were US$268.5 million, down 5.1% from US$283.0 million the year before. Operating income was US$25.8 million versus US$36.1 million in the prior-year quarter, a decrease of 28.5%. Direct operating expenses declined 3.6% to US$96.4 million from US$100.0 million in the comparable period the year before. Indirect operating expenses decreased 0.4% to US$146.3 million from US$146.9 million in the equivalent prior-year period.

Prospects: Co. continues to see steady sales growth in its Direct Marketing segment while its Shoppers segment continues to decline due to adverse economic conditions. Nevertheless, Co. believes that its Shoppers segment will recover as the California and Florida economies show signs of stability going forward. Meanwhile, on Apr 15, 2008, Co. announced its expansion of the Harte-Hanks Ci Technology Database® (CiTDB) into the Asia-Pacific region. The CiTDB in China lists significant technology buying initiatives and profiles of key decision makers of business locations in China. Accordingly, Co. anticipates 10,000 completed profiles by Jul 2008, and expects further expansion based on market demand.

Financial Data

(US$ in Thousands)	3 Mos	12/31/2007	12/31/2006	12/31/2005	12/31/2004	12/31/2003	12/31/2002	12/31/2001
Earnings Per Share	1.21	1.26	1.39	1.34	1.11	0.97	0.96	0.82
Cash Flow Per Share	2.08	1.97	1.85	1.74	1.77	1.40	1.53	1.61
Tang Book Value Per Share	N.M.	N.M.	N.M.	0.51	1.31	1.32	1.03	1.22
Dividends Per Share	0.285	0.280	0.240	0.200	0.160	0.120	0.098	0.080
Dividend Payout %	23.62	22.22	17.27	14.93	14.41	12.37	10.24	9.76
Income Statement								
Total Revenue	268,509	1,162,886	1,184,688	1,134,993	1,030,461	944,576	908,777	917,928
EBITDA	34,196	200,294	219,382	219,584	192,416	174,625	181,012	183,936
Depn & Amortn	9,053	36,704	34,032	31,345	28,769	30,033	32,728	48,920
Income Before Taxes	21,491	151,137	179,248	186,479	162,968	143,905	147,350	132,438
Income Taxes	7,905	58,497	67,456	72,021	65,400	56,543	56,605	52,754
Net Income	13,586	92,640	111,792	114,458	97,568	87,362	90,745	79,684
Average Shares	66,137	73,703	80,646	85,406	87,806	89,982	94,872	97,174
Balance Sheet								
Current Assets	244,373	265,680	279,975	253,704	250,497	217,297	198,612	202,807
Total Assets	938,828	951,926	969,285	889,663	828,353	759,130	736,732	771,049
Current Liabilities	165,483	180,108	171,236	175,347	182,192	134,072	121,761	121,774
Long-Term Obligations	321,250	259,125	205,000	62,000	...	5,000	16,300	48,312
Total Liabilities	595,338	543,414	475,809	328,317	256,554	203,532	204,199	218,683
Stockholders' Equity	343,490	408,512	493,476	561,346	571,799	555,598	532,533	552,366
Shares Outstanding	63,164	67,936	75,214	81,488	84,981	87,492	90,204	93,212
Statistical Record								
Return on Assets %	9.03	9.64	12.03	13.32	12.26	11.68	12.04	10.10
Return on Equity %	20.65	20.54	21.20	20.20	17.26	16.06	16.73	14.44
EBITDA Margin %	12.74	17.22	18.52	19.35	18.67	18.49	19.92	20.04
Net Margin %	5.06	7.97	9.44	10.08	9.47	9.25	9.99	8.68
Asset Turnover	1.21	1.21	1.27	1.32	1.29	1.26	1.21	1.16
Current Ratio	1.48	1.48	1.64	1.45	1.37	1.62	1.63	1.67
Debt to Equity	0.94	0.63	0.42	0.11	...	0.01	0.03	0.09
Price Range	27.56-13.38	28.65-15.65	30.00-23.00	30.98-25.24	26.87-21.50	22.13-17.33	22.30-16.18	18.78-13.73
P/E Ratio	22.78-11.06	22.74-12.42	21.58-16.55	23.12-18.84	24.21-19.37	22.81-17.87	23.23-16.85	22.90-16.74
Average Yield %	1.37	1.18	0.90	0.73	0.67	0.63	0.50	0.51

Address: 200 Concord Plaza Drive, San Antonio, TX 78216	**Officers:** Larry Franklin - Chairman Houston H. Harte - Vice-Chairman **Transfer Agents:**	**Investor Contact:** 210-829-9140
Telephone: 210-829-9000	Computershare Trust Company, N.A.	**No of Institutions:** 186
Web Site: www.harte-hanks.com		**Shares:** 47,353,476 **% Held:** 60.36

HARTFORD FINANCIAL SERVICES GROUP INC.

Exchange	Symbol	Price	52Wk Range	Yield	P/E
NYS	HIG	$71.49 (5/29/2008)	103.17-66.05	2.97	10.26

*7 Year Price Score 94.37   *NYSE Composite Index=100   *12 Month Price Score 87.55

Interim Earnings (Per Share)

Qtr.	Mar	Jun	Sep	Dec
2005	2.21	1.98	1.76	1.50
2006	2.34	1.52	2.39	2.44
2007	2.71	1.96	2.68	1.89
2008	0.46	...	...	...

Interim Dividends (Per Share)

Amt	Decl	Ex	Rec	Pay
0.50Q	07/19/2007	08/30/2007	09/04/2007	10/01/2007
0.53Q	10/18/2007	11/29/2007	12/03/2007	01/02/2008
0.53Q	02/21/2008	02/28/2008	03/03/2008	04/01/2008
0.53Q	05/21/2008	05/29/2008	06/02/2008	07/01/2008

Indicated Div: $2.12

Valuation Analysis

Forecast EPS	$9.40 (05/17/2008)		
Market Cap	$22.5 Billion	Book Value	17.8 Billion
Price/Book	1.26	Price/Sales	1.09

Dividend Achiever Status

10 Year Growth Rate	9.60%
Total Years of Dividend Growth	11

TRADING VOLUME (thousand shares)

Business Summary: Insurance (MIC: SIC: 6411 NAIC: 524210)

Hartford Financial Services is an insurance and financial services company. Co. has two major operations. Through its Life operations, Co. provides retail and institutional investment products, life insurance for wealth protection, accumulation and transfer needs, group benefits products, as well as fixed and variable annuity products. Through its Property & Casualty operations, Co. provides workers' compensation, property, automobile, liability, umbrella, specialty casualty, marine, livestock and fidelity and surety coverage, professional liability coverage, homeowners and home-based business coverage, and insurance-related services. At Dec 31 2007, Co. had total assets of $360.36 billion.

Recent Developments: For the quarter ended Mar 31 2008, net income decreased 83.4% to US$145.0 million from US$876.0 million in the year-earlier quarter. Revenues were US$1.54 billion, down 77.2% from US$6.76 billion the year before. Net premiums earned were US$3.84 billion versus US$3.83 billion in the prior-year quarter, an increase of 0.3%. Net investment loss was US$2.39 billion versus a net investment income of US$1.48 billion a year ago.

Prospects: For 2008, Co. expects its core earnings per diluted share estimate of $9.20 to $9.50 compared with prior estimate of $9.80 to $10.20, based on several assumptions, including the expectation that the U.S. equity markets will produce an annualized return of 9.0%, an anticipated pre-tax underwriting loss of $160.0 million from other operations in its Property & Casualty operations, and the effect of lower expected pre-tax net investment income on fixed income securities for the last nine months of 2008, which reduced expected core earnings by $80.0 million from prior guidance. Meanwhile, Co. expects written premium for Property & Casualty to be 1% lower to 2% higher in 2008 than in 2007.

Financial Data
(US$ in Millions)

	3 Mos	12/31/2007	12/31/2006	12/31/2005	12/31/2004	12/31/2003	12/31/2002	12/31/2001
Earnings Per Share	6.97	9.24	8.69	7.44	7.12	(0.33)	3.97	2.10
Cash Flow Per Share	16.68	18.94	18.26	12.52	8.99	14.30	10.62	9.69
Tang Book Value Per Share	51.02	55.69	53.07	45.03	42.55	35.00	35.31	29.81
Dividends Per Share	2.060	2.030	1.700	1.170	1.130	1.090	1.050	1.010
Dividend Payout %	29.56	21.97	19.56	15.73	15.87	...	26.45	48.10
Income Statement								
Premium Income	3,843	15,619	15,023	14,359	13,566	11,891	10,301	9,409
Total Revenue	1,544	25,916	26,500	27,083	22,693	18,733	15,907	15,147
Income Before Taxes	91	4,005	3,602	2,985	2,523	(550)	1,068	354
Income Taxes	(54)	1,056	857	711	385	(459)	68	(195)
Net Income	145	2,949	2,745	2,274	2,115	(91)	1,000	507
Average Shares	315	319	315	305	297	272	251	241
Balance Sheet								
Total Assets	344,168	360,361	326,710	285,557	259,735	225,853	182,043	181,238
Total Liabilities	326,332	341,157	307,834	270,232	245,497	214,214	171,309	172,225
Stockholders' Equity	17,836	19,204	18,876	15,325	14,238	11,639	10,734	9,013
Shares Outstanding	314	313	323	302	294	283	255	245
Statistical Record								
Return on Assets %	0.65	0.86	0.90	0.83	0.87	N.M.	0.55	0.29
Return on Equity %	12.05	15.49	16.05	15.38	16.30	N.M.	10.13	6.15
Net Margin %	9.39	11.38	10.36	8.40	9.32	(0.49)	6.29	3.35
Price Range	106.02-66.05	106.02-85.44	93.61-79.24	89.00-65.51	69.31-53.29	59.03-32.30	69.97-37.38	70.46-50.10
P/E Ratio	15.21-9.48	11.47-9.25	10.77-9.12	11.96-8.81	9.73-7.48	...	17.62-9.42	33.55-23.86
Average Yield %	2.28	2.13	1.99	1.55	1.77	2.26	1.87	1.63

Address: One Hartford Plaza, Hartford, CT 06115-1900	Officers: Ramani Ayer - Chairman, Chief Executive Officer Thomas M. Marra - President, Chief Operating Officer **Transfer Agents:**	No of Institutions: 788
Telephone: 860-547-5000		**Shares:** 298,090,016 **% Held:** 88.97
Web Site: www.thehartford.com	The Bank of New York, New York, NY	

HCC INSURANCE HOLDINGS, INC.

Exchange	Symbol	Price	52Wk Range	Yield	P/E
NYS	HCC	$24.05 (5/29/2008)	34.24-21.77	1.83	7.45

*7 Year Price Score 91.20 *NYSE Composite Index=100   ***12 Month Price Score 88.36**

Interim Earnings (Per Share)

Qtr.	Mar	Jun	Sep	Dec
2005	0.54	0.59	0.07	0.59
2006	0.67	0.76	0.80	0.69
2007	0.83	0.86	0.84	0.84
2008	0.70	...	...	...

Interim Dividends (Per Share)

Amt	Decl	Ex	Rec	Pay
0.10Q	05/25/2007	06/28/2007	07/02/2007	07/16/2007
0.11Q	09/20/2007	09/27/2007	10/01/2007	10/15/2007
0.11Q	12/20/2007	12/28/2007	01/02/2008	01/14/2008
0.11Q	03/17/2008	03/28/2008	04/01/2008	04/14/2008

Indicated Div: $0.44

Valuation Analysis

Forecast EPS $3.14 (05/16/2008)

Market Cap	$2.8 Billion	Book Value	2.5 Billion
Price/Book	1.10	Price/Sales	1.18

Dividend Achiever Status

10 Year Growth Rate	18.78%
Total Years of Dividend Growth	11

Business Summary: Insurance (MIC: SIC: 6331 NAIC: 524126)

HCC Insurance Holdings provides property and casualty, surety, and group life, accident and health insurance coverages and related agency and reinsurance brokerage services to commercial customers and individuals. Co. operates primarily in the U.S., the U.K., Spain, Bermuda, Belgium and Ireland. Co. underwrites both on a direct basis, where it insures a risk in exchange for a premium, and on a reinsurance basis, where it insures all or a portion of another insurance company's risk in exchange for all or a portion of the premium. Co. markets its products both directly to customers and through a network of independent and affiliated brokers, producers, agents and third party administrators.

Recent Developments: For the quarter ended Mar 31 2008, net income decreased 16.1% to US$81.1 million from US$96.7 million in the year-earlier quarter. Revenues were US$567.4 million, down 5.0% from US$597.2 million the year before. Net premiums earned were US$493.5 million versus US$497.6 million in the prior-year quarter, a decrease of 0.8%. Net investment income fell 3.7% to US$47.6 million from US$49.5 million a year ago.

Prospects: Co.'s recent results are being unfavorably affected by a decrease in gross written premium due to the effect of competition and the resulting softening of rates in several of its markets. In addition, Co.'s net investment income is declining due to lower income from its alternative investments, primarily fund-of-fund hedge fund investments. Nevertheless, Co. is seeing an increase in revenue from its agency segment due to its Jan 2008 acquisition of MultiNational Underwriters, LLC. Meanwhile, Co. expects other operating income for 2008 of approximately $3.3 million per quarter, excluding the effect of any trading portfolio activity or sales of strategic investments.

Financial Data
(US$ in Thousands)

	3 Mos	12/31/2007	12/31/2006	12/31/2005	12/31/2004	12/31/2003	12/31/2002	12/31/2001
Earnings Per Share	3.23	3.38	2.93	1.79	1.65	1.49	1.12	0.34
Cash Flow Per Share	5.47	6.44	5.87	5.92	6.86	5.56	1.88	1.21
Tang Book Value Per Share	14.79	14.46	11.64	10.48	8.62	6.88	5.85	4.72
Dividends Per Share	0.430	0.420	0.375	0.282	0.213	0.187	0.170	0.163
Dividend Payout %	13.31	12.43	12.80	15.74	12.96	12.56	15.18	48.04
Income Statement								
Total Revenue	567,388	2,388,373	2,075,295	1,644,342	1,283,154	941,964	669,382	505,461
Income Before Taxes	118,931	585,870	509,834	278,747	240,753	166,734	163,179	60,383
Income Taxes	37,830	190,441	167,549	85,647	81,732	59,857	57,351	30,186
Net Income	81,101	395,429	342,285	195,860	163,025	143,561	105,828	30,197
Average Shares	116,372	116,997	116,736	109,437	98,826	96,574	94,404	89,428
Balance Sheet								
Total Assets	8,218,418	8,074,645	7,630,132	7,026,066	5,933,437	4,864,296	3,704,151	3,219,120
Total Liabilities	5,696,224	5,634,280	5,587,329	5,332,370	4,609,772	3,817,376	2,821,244	2,455,667
Stockholders' Equity	2,522,194	2,440,365	2,042,803	1,693,696	1,323,665	1,046,920	882,907	763,453
Shares Outstanding	115,298	115,069	111,731	110,803	102,057	95,946	93,537	92,157
Statistical Record								
Return on Assets %	4.78	5.04	4.67	3.02	3.01	3.35	3.06	1.01
Return on Equity %	16.27	17.64	18.32	12.98	13.72	14.88	12.86	4.67
Net Margin %	14.29	16.56	16.49	11.91	12.71	15.24	15.81	5.97
Price Range	34.24-21.77	34.24-26.57	35.09-28.58	32.86-21.34	23.04-18.63	21.29-14.99	19.15-13.19	19.34-13.67
P/E Ratio	10.60-6.74	10.13-7.86	11.98-9.75	18.36-11.92	13.96-11.29	14.29-10.06	17.10-11.77	56.88-40.20
Average Yield %	1.47	1.37	1.18	1.07	1.01	0.99	1.01	0.96

Address: 13403 Northwest Freeway, Houston, TX 77040-6094 **Telephone:** 713-690-7300 **Web Site:** www.hcc.com	**Officers:** J. Robert Dickerson - Chairman John N. Molbeck - President, Chief Operating Officer **Transfer Agents:** American Stock Transfer & Trust Company, New York, NY	**No of Institutions:** 352 **Shares:** 122,745,272 **% Held:** 100.39

HCP, INC.

Exchange	Symbol	Price	52Wk Range	Yield	P/E
NYS	HCP	$34.59 (5/29/2008)	38.35-25.76	5.26	15.44

*7 Year Price Score 95.24 *NYSE Composite Index=100 *12 Month Price Score 114.71

Interim Earnings (Per Share)

Qtr.	Mar	Jun	Sep	Dec
2005	0.28	0.28	0.29	0.26
2006	0.38	0.26	0.52	1.49
2007	0.68	0.32	1.53	0.18
2008	0.21	...	...	...

Interim Dividends (Per Share)

Amt	Decl	Ex	Rec	Pay
0.445Q	07/26/2007	08/02/2007	08/06/2007	08/21/2007
0.445Q	10/25/2007	11/01/2007	11/05/2007	11/19/2007
0.455Q	01/28/2008	02/05/2008	02/07/2008	02/21/2008
0.455Q	04/24/2008	05/01/2008	05/05/2008	05/19/2008

Indicated Div: $1.82 (Div. Reinv. Plan)

Valuation Analysis

Forecast EPS $0.81 (05/17/2008)

Market Cap	$7.5 Billion	Book Value	4.0 Billion
Price/Book	1.87	Price/Sales	7.58

Dividend Achiever Status

10 Year Growth Rate		3.77%
Total Years of Dividend Growth		22

TRADING VOLUME (thousand shares)

Business Summary: "Property, Real Estate & Development" (MIC: SIC: 6798 NAIC: 525930)

HCP is a self-administered real estate investment trust, which together with its consolidated subsidiaries, invests primarily in real estate serving the healthcare industry in the U.S. Co. acquires healthcare facilities and leases them to healthcare providers and provides mortgage financing secured by healthcare facilities. Co.'s portfolio includes investments in: senior housing that consists of independent living facilities, assisted living facilities and continuing care retirement communities; medical office buildings; hospitals; skilled nursing facilities; and other healthcare facilities, including laboratory and office buildings.

Recent Developments: For the quarter ended Mar 31 2008, income from continuing operations increased 37.1% to US$33.2 million from US$24.2 million in the year-earlier quarter. Net income decreased 65.3% to US$50.4 million from US$145.3 million in the year-earlier quarter. Revenues were US$252.2 million, up 18.0% from US$213.6 million the year before. Revenues from property income rose 49.8% to US$22.4 million from US$15.0 million in the corresponding quarter a year earlier.

Prospects: Co.'s improved top-line performance is attributable to higher senior housing rental and related revenues due to the effect of its business acquisitions made during 2007 and 2008 as well as rent escalations and resets. In addition, Co. is experiencing an increase in its life science rental and related revenues primarily due to its Aug 1 2007 acquisitions of Slough Estates USA Inc. Meanwhile, for the full-year 2008, Co. expects net income applicable to common shares to range between $1.91 and $2.41 per diluted common share and funds from operations applicable to common shares to range between $2.21 and $2.29 per diluted common share.

Financial Data (US$ in Thousands)	3 Mos	12/31/2007	12/31/2006	12/31/2005	12/31/2004	12/31/2003	12/31/2002	12/31/2001
Earnings Per Share	2.24	2.71	2.66	1.12	1.11	0.97	0.96	0.89
Cash Flow Per Share	2.29	2.18	2.25	2.09	2.06	2.06	1.94	1.86
Tang Book Value Per Share	14.20	14.50	12.74	7.90	8.49	8.82	8.46	8.62
Dividends Per Share	1.790	1.780	1.700	1.680	1.670	1.660	1.630	1.550
Dividend Payout %	80.04	65.68	63.91	150.00	150.45	171.13	168.91	174.16
Income Statement								
Property Income	22,449	905,076	...	...	388,631	348,649	331,737	310,602
Non-Property Income	229,728	77,433	619,087	477,276	40,053	51,534	27,839	21,858
Total Revenue	252,177	982,509	619,087	477,276	428,684	400,183	359,576	332,460
Depn & Amortn	80,187	295,536	167,805	109,235	99,342	87,551	82,259	84,098
Interest Expense	96,370	357,024	213,304	107,201	89,136	90,749	77,952	78,489
Net Income	50,412	589,015	417,547	173,057	169,040	158,585	137,380	121,166
Average Shares	217,663	209,254	149,226	135,560	133,362	126,130	116,294	107,950
Balance Sheet								
Total Assets	12,500,064	12,521,772	10,012,749	3,597,265	3,102,634	3,035,957	2,748,417	2,431,153
Long-Term Obligations	7,570,940	7,510,907	6,202,015	1,956,946	1,486,206	1,407,284	1,333,848	1,057,752
Total Liabilities	8,158,679	8,078,792	6,556,948	2,048,215	1,561,411	1,595,340	1,467,528	1,184,429
Stockholders' Equity	4,027,647	4,103,709	3,294,036	1,399,766	1,419,442	1,440,617	1,280,889	1,246,724
Shares Outstanding	217,816	216,818	198,599	136,193	133,658	131,039	118,939	112,773
Statistical Record								
Return on Assets %	4.51	5.23	6.14	5.17	5.49	5.48	5.30	5.02
Return on Equity %	12.90	15.92	17.79	12.28	11.79	11.65	10.87	10.13
Net Margin %	19.99	59.95	67.45	36.26	39.43	39.63	38.21	36.45
Price Range	37.03-25.76	41.88-25.76	36.88-25.37	28.68-23.45	29.09-21.68	25.63-16.68	22.43-18.11	19.51-14.78
P/E Ratio	16.53-11.50	15.45-9.51	13.86-9.54	25.61-20.94	26.21-19.53	26.42-17.19	23.36-18.86	21.92-16.61
Average Yield %	5.68	5.33	5.85	6.43	6.43	8.01	8.00	8.87

Address: 3760 Kilroy Airport Way, Suite 300, Long Beach, CA 90806 Telephone: 562-733-5100 Web Site: www.hcpi.com	Officers: James F. Flaherty - Chairman, President, Chief Executive Officer Mark A. Wallace - Executive Vice President, Chief Financial Officer, Treasurer Transfer Agents:The Bank of New York, New York, NY	Investor Contact: 949-221-0600 No of Institutions: 435 Shares: 192,385,232 % Held: N/A

HEARTLAND FINANCIAL USA, INC. (DUBUQUE, IA)

Exchange	Symbol	Price	52Wk Range	Yield	P/E
NMS	HTLF	$23.40 (5/29/2008)	25.30-16.78	1.71	14.90

*7 Year Price Score 86.26 *NYSE Composite Index=100 ***12 Month Price Score 107.49**

Interim Earnings (Per Share)

Qtr.	Mar	Jun	Sep	Dec
2005	0.32	0.32	0.38	0.35
2006	0.27	0.37	0.41	0.45
2007	0.34	0.37	0.42	0.40
2008	0.38	...	...	...

Interim Dividends (Per Share)

Amt	Decl	Ex	Rec	Pay
0.09Q	07/17/2007	08/30/2007	08/31/2007	09/14/2007
0.10Q	10/16/2007	11/28/2007	11/30/2007	12/14/2007
0.10Q	01/24/2008	02/27/2008	02/29/2008	03/14/2008
0.10Q	04/22/2008	05/28/2008	05/30/2008	06/13/2008
			Indicated Div: $0.40	

Valuation Analysis

Forecast EPS $1.45 (05/16/2008)

Market Cap	$381.7 Million	Book Value	235.9 Million
Price/Book	1.62	Price/Sales	1.55

Dividend Achiever Status

10 Year Growth Rate	7.88%
Total Years of Dividend Growth	12

TRADING VOLUME (thousand shares)

Business Summary: Commercial Banking (MIC: SIC: 6022 NAIC: 522110)

Heartland Financial USA is a multi-bank holding company with nine bank subsidiaries in Iowa, Illinois, Wisconsin, New Mexico, Arizona, Montana and Colorado. At Dec 31 2007, Co. operated 59 banking locations. Co.'s subsidiaries provide deposit products such as checking and other demand deposit accounts, savings accounts, money market accounts, and certificates of deposit; loans including commercial and industrial, agricultural, real estate mortgage, consumer, and home equity; as well as other products and services such as automated teller machines, on-line banking, safe deposit boxes and trust services. As of Dec 31 2007, Co. had total assets of $3.26 billion and deposits of $2.38 billion.

Recent Developments: For the quarter ended Mar 31 2008, income from continuing operations increased 11.0% to US$6.3 million from US$5.6 million in the year-earlier quarter. Net income increased 8.6% to US$6.3 million from US$5.8 million in the year-earlier quarter. Net interest income increased 3.1% to US$27.7 million from US$26.9 million in the year-earlier quarter. Provision for loan losses was US$1.8 million versus US$1.9 million in the prior-year quarter, a decrease of 8.6%. Non-interest income rose 11.3% to US$8.5 million from US$7.6 million, while non-interest expense advanced 5.6% to US$25.8 million.

Prospects: Co. remains focused on non- interest income, and to supplement the revenue growth from its Wealth Management Group and Investment Services unit, it is evaluating the pricing of its service line to assure a fair return that is in line with its costs. Further, Co. will work toward improving its earning asset and funding mix for the remainder of 2008 through targeted organic growth strategies, which it believes will result in additional net interest income. Meanwhile, Co.'s 2008 expansion plan anticipates a slower pace, with the addition of only two or three new locations and the enhancement of its existing locations, which it believes will provide a significant opportunity for earnings growth.

Financial Data

(US$ in Thousands)	3 Mos	12/31/2007	12/31/2006	12/31/2005	12/31/2004	12/31/2003	12/31/2002	12/31/2001
Earnings Per Share	1.57	1.54	1.50	1.36	1.26	1.16	1.27	0.79
Cash Flow Per Share	2.18	2.07	1.82	2.13	2.51	2.68	3.33	1.20
Tang Book Value Per Share	11.48	11.08	9.71	8.74	7.92	7.63	6.98	6.07
Dividends Per Share	0.380	0.370	0.360	0.330	0.320	0.273	0.267	0.247
Dividend Payout %	24.27	24.03	24.00	24.26	25.40	23.56	20.94	31.36
Income Statement								
Interest Income	51,297	215,231	192,539	154,002	121,394	99,517	100,012	110,088
Interest Expense	23,559	105,891	86,210	61,135	44,264	38,327	42,332	60,193
Net Interest Income	27,738	109,340	106,329	92,867	77,130	61,190	57,680	49,895
Provision for Losses	1,761	10,073	3,886	6,564	4,846	4,183	3,553	4,283
Non-Interest Income	8,474	31,961	29,087	41,585	37,841	36,541	32,757	30,334
Non-Interest Expense	25,764	97,857	94,521	95,012	81,936	67,692	62,771	58,818
Income Before Taxes	8,687	33,371	37,009	32,876	28,189	25,856	24,113	17,128
Income Taxes	2,420	9,409	11,989	10,150	7,937	8,137	7,523	5,714
Net Income	6,267	25,633	25,102	22,726	20,252	17,719	18,867	11,414
Average Shares	16,466	16,597	16,735	16,702	16,085	15,258	14,784	14,557
Balance Sheet								
Net Loans & Leases	2,249,190	2,259,853	2,168,245	1,966,020	1,780,142	1,329,737	1,159,145	1,090,545
Total Assets	3,300,480	3,264,126	3,058,242	2,818,332	2,629,055	2,018,366	1,785,979	1,644,064
Total Deposits	2,420,939	2,376,299	2,311,657	2,118,178	1,983,846	1,492,488	1,337,985	1,205,159
Total Liabilities	3,064,627	3,033,526	2,848,531	2,630,520	2,453,273	1,877,443	1,661,938	1,536,974
Stockholders' Equity	235,853	230,600	209,711	187,812	175,782	140,923	124,041	107,090
Shares Outstanding	16,312	16,427	16,572	16,390	16,441	15,163	14,769	14,519
Statistical Record								
Return on Assets %	0.81	0.81	0.85	0.83	0.87	0.93	1.10	0.73
Return on Equity %	11.64	11.64	12.63	12.50	12.75	13.37	16.33	11.23
Net Interest Margin %	54.07	50.80	55.22	60.30	63.54	61.49	57.67	45.32
Efficiency Ratio %	43.10	39.59	42.65	48.58	51.46	49.75	47.28	41.89
Loans to Deposits	0.93	0.95	0.94	0.93	0.90	0.89	0.87	0.90
Price Range	27.20-16.78	28.80-17.04	31.08-20.11	21.74-18.37	22.07-16.75	21.53-11.50	11.80-8.60	9.42-7.01
P/E Ratio	17.32-10.69	18.70-11.06	20.72-13.41	15.99-13.51	17.52-13.29	18.56-9.91	9.29-6.77	11.92-8.87
Average Yield %	1.80	1.60	1.44	1.65	1.72	1.53	2.75	2.81

Address: 1398 Central Avenue, Dubuque, IA 52004	Officers: Lynn B. Fuller - Chairman, President, Chief Executive Officer Thomas L. Flynn - Vice-Chairman	Investor Contact: 563-589-1994
Telephone: 563-589-2100	Transfer Agents:Heartland Financial USA, Inc.	No of Institutions: 50
Web Site: www.htlf.com		Shares: 2,340,782 % Held: 13.99

HELMERICH & PAYNE, INC.

Exchange	Symbol	Price	52Wk Range	Yield	P/E
NYS	HP	$60.77 (5/29/2008)	62.25-29.07	0.33	14.61

*7 Year Price Score 139.41 *NYSE Composite Index=100 *12 Month Price Score 141.21

Interim Earnings (Per Share)

Qtr.	Dec	Mar	Jun	Sep
2004-05	0.39	0.22	0.28	0.34
2005-06	0.48	0.61	0.75	0.93
2006-07	1.06	1.02	1.09	1.10
2007-08	1.02	0.96	...	...

Interim Dividends (Per Share)

Amt	Decl	Ex	Rec	Pay
0.045Q	09/06/2007	11/13/2007	11/15/2007	12/03/2007
0.045Q	...	02/13/2008	02/15/2008	03/03/2008
0.045Q	...	05/13/2008	05/15/2008	06/02/2008
0.05Q	...	08/13/2008	08/15/2008	09/02/2008
		Indicated Div: $0.20		

Valuation Analysis

Forecast EPS	$4.06 (05/16/2008)		
Market Cap	$6.5 Billion	Book Value	2.0 Billion
Price/Book	3.23	Price/Sales	3.62

Dividend Achiever Status

10 Year Growth Rate	3.31%
Total Years of Dividend Growth	31

Business Summary: Oil and Gas (MIC: SIC: 1381 NAIC: 213111)

Helmerich & Payne is a holding company. Co. is engaged in contract drilling of oil and gas wells for others. Co.'s contract drilling business is composed of three segments: U.S. land drilling conducted primarily in Oklahoma, California, Texas, Wyoming, Colorado, Louisiana, Mississippi, Alabama, Arkansas, New Mexico, and North Dakota; U.S. offshore platform drilling in the Gulf of Mexico, California, Trinidad and Equatorial Guinea; and international drilling in which Co. operates in Venezuela, Ecuador, Colombia, Argentina, Bolivia, Tunisia, and Chile. Co. is also engaged in the ownership, development, and operation of commercial real estate, and these operations are conducted in Tulsa, OK.

Recent Developments: For the quarter ended Mar 31 2008, net income decreased 4.5% to US$102.1 million from US$106.9 million in the year-earlier quarter. Revenues were US$473.6 million, up 27.1% from US$372.5 million the year before. Operating income was US$155.7 million versus US$164.3 million in the prior-year quarter, a decrease of 5.2%. Indirect operating expenses increased 52.7% to US$318.0 million from US$208.3 million in the equivalent prior-year period.

Prospects: Co.'s offshore and international business has declined while its U.S. land segment continues to attain solid growth. However, demand for Co.'s FlexRigs® land drilling rigs continues to be favorable. For instance, on May 1 2008, Co. announced three additional long-term contracts with three exploration and production companies to operate three FlexRigs in the U.S. Meanwhile, Co. expects its four idle rigs in Ecuador to return to work in the third quarter of fiscal 2008 while it transfers two rigs from Ecuador to Colombia with work expected to begin in the third quarter of fiscal 2008. Accordingly, Co. expects FlexRigs to represent about 70.0% of its global land fleet by the end of 2008.

Financial Data
(US$ in Thousands)

	6 Mos	3 Mos	09/30/2007	09/30/2006	09/30/2005	09/30/2004	09/30/2003	09/30/2002
Earnings Per Share	4.16	4.23	4.27	2.77	1.23	0.04	0.17	0.63
Cash Flow Per Share	5.55	5.16	5.43	2.83	2.08	1.34	0.96	1.52
Tang Book Value Per Share	18.81	18.47	17.54	13.30	10.39	9.06	9.15	8.95
Dividends Per Share	0.180	0.180	0.180	0.169	0.165	0.161	0.160	0.153
Dividend Payout %	4.33	4.26	4.22	6.09	13.47	358.33	91.43	24.21
Income Statement								
Total Revenue	930,307	456,663	1,629,658	1,224,813	800,726	620,928	515,284	510,928
EBITDA	427,664	213,246	846,521	549,208	321,599	102,435	116,635	153,789
Depn & Amortn	95,856	43,984	146,042	101,583	96,300	94,435	82,693	62,569
Income Before Taxes	322,204	164,431	690,353	440,981	212,657	8,000	33,942	91,220
Income Taxes	118,930	60,146	250,984	154,391	87,463	4,365	14,649	40,573
Net Income	209,884	107,830	449,261	293,858	127,606	4,359	17,873	63,517
Average Shares	106,090	105,615	105,128	106,091	104,066	101,666	101,192	100,690
Balance Sheet								
Current Assets	543,985	541,282	498,964	428,691	499,797	245,886	197,531	178,751
Total Assets	3,156,118	3,058,789	2,885,369	2,134,712	1,663,350	1,406,844	1,415,835	1,227,313
Current Liabilities	210,996	231,199	226,612	264,548	89,481	59,903	88,618	72,899
Long-Term Obligations	480,000	485,000	445,000	175,000	200,000	200,000	200,000	100,000
Total Liabilities	1,142,038	1,144,770	1,069,853	752,820	584,112	492,734	498,584	332,143
Stockholders' Equity	2,014,080	1,914,019	1,815,516	1,381,892	1,079,238	914,110	917,251	895,170
Shares Outstanding	107,055	103,605	103,484	103,869	103,869	100,890	100,280	100,021
Statistical Record								
Return on Assets %	15.61	16.74	17.90	15.47	8.31	0.31	1.35	4.90
Return on Equity %	24.57	26.47	28.10	23.88	12.80	0.47	1.97	6.61
EBITDA Margin %	45.97	46.70	51.94	44.84	40.16	16.50	22.64	30.10
Net Margin %	22.56	23.61	27.57	23.99	15.94	0.70	3.47	12.43
Asset Turnover	0.64	0.64	0.65	0.64	0.52	0.44	0.39	0.39
Current Ratio	2.58	2.34	2.20	1.62	5.59	4.10	2.23	2.45
Debt to Equity	0.24	0.25	0.25	0.13	0.19	0.22	0.22	0.11
Price Range	47.42-29.07	40.28-23.06	36.43-21.75	39.95-22.02	30.56-13.83	15.31-11.89	16.17-11.79	15.71-9.20
P/E Ratio	11.40-6.99	9.52-5.45	8.53-5.09	14.42-7.95	24.85-11.24	382.63-297.13	95.12-69.32	24.93-14.60
Average Yield %	0.51	0.57	0.61	0.56	0.80	1.20	1.17	1.24

Address: 1437 South Boulder Avenue, Suite 1400, Tulsa, OK 74119-3623 Telephone: 918-742-5531 Web Site: www.hpinc.com	Officers: W. H. Helmerich - Chairman Hans Helmerich - President, Chief Executive Officer Transfer Agents:Computershare Trust Company, N.A.	Investor Contact: 918-742-5531 No of Institutions: 415 Shares: 92,313,680 % Held: 83.56

HERSHEY COMPANY (THE)

Exchange	Symbol	Price	52Wk Range	Yield	P/E
NYS	HSY	$40.23 (5/29/2008)	53.04-34.04	2.96	50.29

*7 Year Price Score 72.80 *NYSE Composite Index=100 *12 Month Price Score 92.25

Interim Earnings (Per Share)

Qtr.	Mar	Jun	Sep	Dec
2005	0.47	0.39	0.48	0.65
2006	0.50	0.41	0.77	0.66
2007	0.40	0.01	0.27	0.24
2008	0.28	...	...	...

Interim Dividends (Per Share)

Amt	Decl	Ex	Rec	Pay
0.297Q	08/07/2007	08/22/2007	08/24/2007	09/14/2007
0.297Q	10/02/2007	11/19/2007	11/21/2007	12/14/2007
0.297Q	02/13/2008	02/21/2008	02/25/2008	03/14/2008
0.297Q	04/21/2008	05/21/2008	05/23/2008	06/13/2008

Indicated Div: $1.19 (Div. Reinv. Plan)

Valuation Analysis

Forecast EPS	$1.84 (05/17/2008)		
Market Cap	$9.1 Billion	Book Value	591.2 Million
Price/Book	15.45	Price/Sales	1.84

Dividend Achiever Status

10 Year Growth Rate	10.45%
Total Years of Dividend Growth	33

Business Summary: Food (MIC: SIC: 2064 NAIC: 311340)

Hershey is a North American manufacturer of chocolate and sugar confectionery products. Co.'s product groups include confectionery and snack products; gum and mint refreshment products; and food and beverage enhancers such as baking ingredients, peanut butter, toppings and beverages. Co. also provides a range of products specifically developed to address the nutritional interests of health-conscious consumers. Co.'s five operating segments comprise geographic regions including the U.S., Canada, Mexico, Brazil and other international locations, such as Japan, Korea, the Philippines, India and China. Co. markets its confectionery products in approximately 50 countries worldwide.

Recent Developments: For the quarter ended Mar 30 2008, net income decreased 32.3% to US$63.2 million from US$93.5 million in the year-earlier quarter. Revenues were US$1.16 billion, up 0.6% from US$1.15 billion the year before. Operating income was US$122.4 million versus US$170.1 million in the prior-year quarter, a decrease of 28.0%. Direct operating expenses rose 6.1% to US$783.9 million from US$739.1 million in the comparable period the year before. Indirect operating expenses increased 4.1% to US$254.0 million from US$244.0 million in the equivalent prior-year period.

Prospects: For the rest of 2008, Co. expects the launch of new products, increased levels of brand support, consumer investment, retail coverage and merchandising to result in sequential improvement in net sales. Co. is also encouraged by the development of its international investments and will continue to invest in key international markets, notably China and India. However, Co. expects that business realignment and impairment charges related to its global supply chain transformation program and the restructuring of its business in Brazil will reduce its earnings in 2008. Thus, Co. estimates earnings per share of $1.43 to $1.53 but continues to project total net sales growth of 3.0% to 4.0% for 2008.

Financial Data

(US$ in Thousands)	3 Mos	12/31/2007	12/31/2006	12/31/2005	12/31/2004	12/31/2003	12/31/2002	12/31/2001
Earnings Per Share	0.80	0.93	2.34	1.99	2.30	1.73	1.47	0.75
Cash Flow Per Share	3.24	3.40	3.07	1.89	3.13	2.26	2.29	2.59
Tang Book Value Per Share	N.M.	N.M.	0.18	1.63	2.03	3.29	3.55	2.16
Dividends Per Share	1.163	1.135	1.030	0.930	0.835	0.723	0.630	0.583
Dividend Payout %	144.52	122.04	44.02	46.73	36.30	41.76	42.86	77.67
Income Statement								
Total Revenue	1,160,342	4,946,716	4,944,230	4,835,974	4,429,248	4,172,551	4,120,317	4,557,241
EBITDA	190,715	769,752	1,192,469	1,078,943	1,091,842	976,923	876,195	603,128
Depn & Amortn	68,297	310,925	199,911	218,032	189,665	180,567	177,908	190,494
Income Before Taxes	98,032	340,242	876,502	772,926	835,644	732,827	637,565	343,541
Income Taxes	34,787	126,088	317,441	279,682	244,765	267,875	233,987	136,385
Net Income	63,245	214,154	559,061	493,244	590,879	457,584	403,578	207,156
Average Shares	228,926	231,449	239,071	248,292	256,827	264,532	275,429	275,392
Balance Sheet								
Current Assets	1,262,603	1,426,574	1,417,812	1,408,940	1,182,441	1,131,569	1,263,618	1,167,541
Total Assets	4,067,017	4,247,113	4,157,565	4,295,236	3,797,531	3,582,540	3,480,551	3,247,430
Current Liabilities	1,200,990	1,618,770	1,453,538	1,518,223	1,285,382	585,810	546,846	606,444
Long-Term Obligations	1,528,691	1,279,965	1,248,128	942,755	690,602	968,499	851,800	876,972
Total Liabilities	3,431,891	3,623,593	3,474,142	3,274,160	2,708,229	2,302,674	2,108,848	2,100,226
Stockholders' Equity	591,191	592,922	683,423	1,021,076	1,089,302	1,279,866	1,371,703	1,147,204
Shares Outstanding	227,021	227,049	230,263	240,524	246,587	259,059	268,440	332,145
Statistical Record								
Return on Assets %	4.58	5.10	13.23	12.19	15.97	12.96	12.00	6.19
Return on Equity %	30.52	33.56	65.60	46.74	49.74	34.51	32.04	17.84
EBITDA Margin %	16.44	15.56	24.12	22.31	24.65	23.41	21.27	13.23
Net Margin %	5.45	4.33	11.31	10.20	13.34	10.97	9.79	4.55
Asset Turnover	1.23	1.18	1.17	1.20	1.20	1.18	1.22	1.36
Current Ratio	1.05	0.88	0.98	0.93	0.92	1.93	2.31	1.93
Debt to Equity	2.59	2.16	1.83	0.92	0.63	0.76	0.62	0.76
Price Range	56.22-34.04	56.22-38.25	57.00-49.34	66.65-53.14	56.58-37.42	39.26-30.65	39.74-28.68	34.66-28.50
P/E Ratio	70.28-42.55	60.45-41.13	24.36-21.09	33.49-26.70	24.60-16.27	22.69-17.72	27.04-19.51	46.21-38.00
Average Yield %	2.60	2.34	1.94	1.55	1.82	2.05	1.86	1.85

Address: 100 Crystal A Drive, Hershey, PA 17033	**Officers:** Kenneth L. Wolfe - Chairman David J. West - President, Chief Executive Officer **Transfer Agents:** Mellon Investor Services, LLC, Ridgefield Park, NJ	**Investor Contact:** 800-539-0291
Telephone: 717-534-4200		**No of Institutions:** 518
Web Site: www.hersheys.com		**Shares:** 118,822,008 **% Held:** 68.38

HILB ROGAL & HOBBS CO

Exchange	Symbol	Price	52Wk Range	Yield	P/E
NYS	HRH	$31.15 (5/29/2008)	47.08-28.16	1.80	16.93

*7 Year Price Score 82.88   *NYSE Composite Index=100   *12 Month Price Score 79.17

Interim Earnings (Per Share)

Qtr.	Mar	Jun	Sep	Dec
2005	0.76	0.44	(0.19)	0.54
2006	0.71	0.57	0.53	0.58
2007	0.69	0.60	0.53	0.30
2008	0.42	...	...	...

Interim Dividends (Per Share)

Amt	Decl	Ex	Rec	Pay
0.13Q	07/17/2007	09/12/2007	09/14/2007	09/28/2007
0.13Q	11/13/2007	12/12/2007	12/14/2007	12/31/2007
0.13Q	02/12/2008	03/12/2008	03/14/2008	03/31/2008
0.14Q	05/06/2008	06/11/2008	06/13/2008	06/30/2008
		Indicated Div: $0.56		

Valuation Analysis
Forecast EPS $2.00 (05/16/2008)

Market Cap	$1.1 Billion	Book Value	680.2 Million
Price/Book	1.67	Price/Sales	1.41

Dividend Achiever Status

10 Year Dividend Rate	5.10%
Total Years of Dividend Growth	21

Business Summary: Insurance (MIC: SIC: 6411 NAIC: 524210)

Hilb Rogal & Hobbs is a holding company. Through its subsidiaries, Co. is engaged as an insurance and risk management intermediary between its clients and insurance companies that underwrite client risks. Co. is engaged in assisting clients in managing their risks in areas such as property and casualty, executive and employee benefits and other areas of specialized exposure. Co. also provides advises to its clients on risk management and employee benefits, as well as claims management and loss control consulting services. Co.'s client base ranges from personal to national accounts and is primarily comprised of middle-market and major commercial and industrial accounts.

Recent Developments: For the quarter ended Mar 31 2008, net income decreased 38.5% to US$15.5 million from US$25.2 million in the year-earlier quarter. Revenues were US$206.8 million, up 4.4% from US$198.2 million the year before.

Prospects: Co.'s bottom-line results are being hampered by continued declines in property and casualty premium rates, coupled with lower contingent commissions mainly due to its Domestic Retail segment shift from contingent to supplemental commissions for certain carriers. However, Co. is experiencing growth in revenues, reflecting an increase in core commissions and fees resulting from acquisitions, new business and amounts recorded under supplemental commission agreements with certain underwriters. Going forward, Co. remains focused on its growth strategies, which include managing costs through process improvements and performance accountability, and deploying its capital through acquisitions.

Financial Data
(US$ in Thousands)

	3 Mos	12/31/2007	12/31/2006	12/31/2005	12/31/2004	12/31/2003	12/31/2002	12/31/2001
Earnings Per Share	1.84	2.11	2.39	1.55	2.23	2.06	2.01	1.07
Cash Flow Per Share	3.22	3.13	3.49	2.80	3.19	3.19	2.51	2.27
Dividends Per Share	0.520	0.510	0.475	0.450	0.407	0.367	0.357	0.347
Dividend Payout %	28.21	24.17	19.87	29.03	18.27	17.84	17.79	32.48
Income Statement								
Total Revenue	206,829	799,664	710,845	673,885	619,603	563,647	452,726	330,267
Income Before Taxes	25,431	130,990	141,412	92,907	137,977	124,901	103,257	56,730
Income Taxes	9,908	52,865	54,381	36,707	56,563	49,947	42,082	24,381
Net Income	15,523	78,125	87,031	56,200	81,414	74,954	65,119	32,349
Average Shares	36,756	37,060	36,369	36,314	36,493	36,304	29,240	27,411
Balance Sheet								
Total Assets	1,763,405	1,817,426	1,438,147	1,329,767	1,277,999	1,049,227	833,024	499,301
Total Liabilities	1,083,240	1,134,223	834,778	783,510	770,843	614,960	522,376	356,500
Stockholders' Equity	680,165	683,203	603,369	546,257	507,156	434,267	310,648	142,801
Shares Outstanding	36,391	36,749	36,312	35,955	35,886	35,446	33,484	28,310
Statistical Record								
Return on Assets %	4.13	4.80	6.29	4.31	6.98	7.96	9.78	7.59
Return on Equity %	10.36	12.14	15.14	10.67	17.25	20.12	28.72	28.00
Price Range	50.75-29.76	50.75-40.23	44.83-36.22	39.55-32.10	38.75-31.49	43.85-28.34	45.40-27.75	31.08-16.97
P/E Ratio	27.58-16.17	24.05-19.07	18.76-15.15	25.52-20.71	17.38-14.12	21.29-13.76	22.59-13.81	29.05-15.86
Average Yield %	1.25	1.15	1.18	1.26	1.16	1.12	0.93	1.56

Address: 4951 Lake Brook Drive, Suite 500, Glen Allen, VA 23060-9272 **Telephone:** 804-747-6500 **Web Site:** www.hrh.com	**Officers:** Martin L. Vaughan - Chairman, Chief Executive Officer F. Michael Crowley - President **Transfer Agents:** Mellon Investor Services LLC, Jersey City, NJ	**Investor Contact:** 804-747-6500 **No of Institutions:** 193 **Shares:** 38,814,680 **% Held:** 103.18

HILL-ROM HOLDINGS, INC.

Exchange	Symbol	Price	52Wk Range	Yield	P/E
NYS	HRC	$31.04 (5/29/2008)	36.22-24.38	1.32	12.57

*7 Year Price Score 78.30 ***NYSE Composite Index=100** ***12 Month Price Score 93.19**

Interim Earnings (Per Share)

Qtr.	Dec	Mar	Jun	Sep
2004-05	0.70	0.87	0.61	(3.70)
2005-06	0.79	0.89	0.83	1.09
2006-07	0.84	0.89	0.57	0.77
2007-08	0.72	0.42	...	...

Interim Dividends (Per Share)

Amt	Decl	Ex	Rec	Pay
0.285Q	12/06/2007	12/13/2007	12/17/2007	12/31/2007
0.285Q	02/07/2008	03/13/2008	03/17/2008	03/31/2008
0.00Q	03/17/2008	04/01/2008	03/24/2008	03/31/2008
0.102Q	05/28/2008	06/12/2008	06/16/2008	06/30/2008

Indicated Div: $0.41

Valuation Analysis

Forecast EPS $1.27 (05/17/2008)

Market Cap	$1.9 Billion	Book Value	1.1 Billion
Price/Book	1.84	Price/Sales	1.02

Dividend Achiever Status

10 Year Growth Rate	5.62%
Total Years of Dividend Growth	37

Business Summary: Hospitals & Health Care (MIC: SIC: 5047 NAIC: 423450)

Hill-Rom Holdings is a manufacturer and provider of medical technologies and related services for the health care industry, including patient support systems, non-invasive therapeutic products for a variety of acute and chronic medical conditions, medical equipment rentals, and information technology solutions. Co.'s product and service offerings are used by health care providers in hospitals, extended care facilities and home care settings.

Recent Developments: For the quarter ended Mar 31 2008, income from continuing operations decreased 40.1% to US$9.4 million from US$15.7 million in the year-earlier quarter. Net income decreased 51.9% to US$26.4 million from US$54.9 million in the year-earlier quarter. Revenues were US$375.2 million, up 12.0% from US$335.0 million the year before. Operating income was US$20.4 million versus US$30.0 million in the prior-year quarter, a decrease of 32.0%. Direct operating expenses rose 13.7% to US$207.9 million from US$182.8 million in the comparable period the year before. Indirect operating expenses increased 20.2% to US$146.9 million from US$122.2 million in the equivalent prior-year period.

Prospects: For the second half of 2008, Co. is targeting revenue growth rate to be mid-to-high single digits, gross profit to increase 10.0% to 20.0%, and operating income as adjusted to increase in excess of gross profit as Co. experiences better operating expense control, assuming . These projections assume that Co. continues to focus on its robust pipeline of capital spending projects in North America. For fiscal year ending Sep 2008, Co. has increased its consolidated revenue guidance range to US$1.46 billion to $1.49 billion from $1.43 billion to $1.48 billion and earnings per fully diluted share from continuing operations is expected to decrease to $1.05 to $1.18 from $1.11 to $1.30.

Financial Data

(US$ in Thousands)	6 Mos	3 Mos	09/30/2007	09/30/2006	09/30/2005	09/30/2004	09/30/2003	09/30/2002
Earnings Per Share	2.47	2.95	3.07	3.59	(1.52)	1.75	2.22	(0.16)
Cash Flow Per Share	5.65	4.89	4.62	0.47	3.88	5.58	6.06	6.31
Tang Book Value Per Share	7.92	11.68	11.19	9.12	6.00	8.81	15.79	12.72
Dividends Per Share	1.140	1.140	1.138	1.130	1.120	1.080	1.000	0.977
Dividend Payout %	46.08	38.64	37.05	31.48	...	61.71	45.05	...
Income Statement								
Total Revenue	716,600	504,300	2,023,700	1,962,900	1,938,100	1,829,000	2,042,000	1,757,000
EBITDA	106,800	104,000	421,000	469,100	(97,500)	387,000	374,000	43,000
Depn & Amortn	59,200	29,000	107,300	108,800	...	64,000	73,000	64,000
Income Before Taxes	37,500	69,400	291,500	339,000	(115,900)	308,000	282,000	(35,000)
Income Taxes	15,700	24,600	100,900	117,500	(19,600)	120,000	100,000	(25,000)
Net Income	71,200	44,800	190,600	221,200	(94,100)	110,000	138,000	(10,000)
Average Shares	62,566	62,403	62,115	61,576	61,774	62,725	62,184	62,921
Balance Sheet								
Current Assets	733,600	941,700	894,400	763,900	890,500	739,000	708,000	958,000
Total Assets	1,636,900	2,165,000	2,117,000	1,952,200	2,229,200	1,992,000	5,412,000	5,442,000
Current Liabilities	326,000	331,900	339,600	325,200	669,000	313,000	367,000	551,000
Long-Term Obligations	126,600	351,500	348,600	347,000	350,700	360,000	155,000	322,000
Total Liabilities	584,000	858,400	839,200	820,500	1,265,200	896,000	4,253,000	4,443,000
Stockholders' Equity	1,052,900	1,306,600	1,277,800	1,131,700	964,000	1,096,000	1,159,000	999,000
Shares Outstanding	62,262	62,230	61,991	61,415	61,263	61,953	61,814	61,702
Statistical Record								
Return on Assets %	8.42	8.81	9.37	10.58	N.M.	2.96	2.54	N.M.
Return on Equity %	13.62	14.82	15.82	21.11	N.M.	9.73	12.79	N.M.
EBITDA Margin %	14.90	20.62	20.80	23.90	N.M.	21.16	18.32	2.45
Net Margin %	9.94	8.88	9.42	11.27	N.M.	6.01	6.76	N.M.
Asset Turnover	1.03	0.98	0.99	0.94	0.92	0.49	0.38	0.40
Current Ratio	2.25	2.84	2.63	2.35	1.33	2.36	1.93	1.74
Debt to Equity	0.12	0.27	0.27	0.31	0.36	0.33	0.13	0.32
Price Range	36.29-25.70	36.29-28.01	36.29-29.34	31.18-24.19	30.59-25.07	37.75-26.75	30.99-25.22	35.48-26.21
P/E Ratio	14.69-10.40	12.30-9.50	11.82-9.56	8.68-6.74	...	21.57-15.29	13.96-11.36	...
Average Yield %	3.67	3.58	3.51	4.15	3.96	3.34	3.63	3.19

Address: 1069 State Route 46 East, Batesville, IN 47006-8835 **Telephone:** 812-934-7000 **Web Site:** www.hillenbrand.com	**Officers:** Rolf A. Classon - Chairman Joanne C. Smith - Vice-Chairman **Transfer Agents:** ComputerShare Investor Services, Chicago, IL	**Investor Contact:** 812-934-8400 **No of Institutions:** 244 **Shares:** 45,095,636 **% Held:** 64.84

HNI CORP

Exchange	Symbol	Price	52Wk Range	Yield	P/E
NYS	HNI	$24.44 (5/29/2008)	45.25-21.31	3.52	10.91

*7 Year Price Score 70.13 *NYSE Composite Index=100 *12 Month Price Score 70.16

TRADING VOLUME (thousand shares)

Interim Earnings (Per Share)

Qtr.	Mar	Jun	Sep	Dec
2005	0.47	0.63	0.73	0.67
2006	0.55	0.56	0.72	0.63
2007	0.43	0.57	0.76	0.82
2008	0.09	...	...	...

Interim Dividends (Per Share)

Amt	Decl	Ex	Rec	Pay
0.195Q	08/07/2007	08/15/2007	08/17/2007	08/31/2007
0.195Q	11/09/2007	11/15/2007	11/19/2007	11/30/2007
0.215Q	02/13/2008	02/20/2008	02/22/2008	02/29/2008
0.215Q	05/06/2008	05/14/2008	05/16/2008	05/30/2008

Indicated Div: $0.86

Valuation Analysis

Forecast EPS $1.57 (05/16/2008)

Market Cap	$1.1 Billion	Book Value	441.3 Million
Price/Book	2.46	Price/Sales	0.43

Dividend Achiever Status

10 Year Growth Rate	10.79%
Total Years of Dividend Growth	19

Business Summary: Furniture and Fixtures (MIC: SIC: 2522 NAIC: 337214)

HNI is engaged in providing office furniture and hearth products. Co. designs, manufactures, and markets a range of office furniture in four basic categories: storage; seating; office systems; and desks and related products. Co.'s office furniture product offering is sold to dealers, wholesalers, retail superstores, end-user customers, and federal, state, and local governments. Co.'s office furniture products are sold under its HON®, Allsteel®, Maxon®, Gunlocke®, Paoli®, Whitehall®, basyx®, and Lamex® brands, as well as private labels. Co.'s hearth products includes gas, electric, and wood burning fireplaces, inserts, stoves, facings, and accessories.

Recent Developments: For the quarter ended Mar 29 2008, income from continuing operations decreased 80.7% to US$4.0 million from US$20.7 million in the year-earlier quarter. Net income decreased 80.8% to US$4.0 million from US$20.7 million in the year-earlier quarter. Revenues were US$563.4 million, down 7.5% from US$609.2 million the year before. Operating income was US$10.7 million versus US$36.0 million in the prior-year quarter, a decrease of 70.4%. Direct operating expenses declined 5.8% to US$379.3 million from US$402.5 million in the comparable period the year before. Indirect operating expenses increased 1.6% to US$173.4 million from US$170.7 million in the equivalent prior-year period.

Prospects: Looking ahead, Co. expects continuous challenging economic conditions and foresees ongoing weakness in the supplies-driven channel of its office furniture business. In response, Co. intends to continue its investment in growth opportunities and position for the market recovery by improving its selling capabilities and launching of several new products. Further, Co. plans to address the market softness as well as rising fuel and material costs by focusing on its structural cost and streamlining its businesses. Meanwhile, Co. is encouraged by the Mar 29 2008 acquisition of HBF from Furniture Brands International, Inc. for about $75.0 million, which should be accretive to its earnings.

Financial Data

(US$ in Thousands)	3 Mos	12/29/2007	12/30/2006	12/31/2005	01/01/2005	01/03/2004	12/28/2002	12/29/2001
Earnings Per Share	2.24	2.57	2.45	2.50	1.97	1.68	1.55	1.26
Cash Flow Per Share	5.68	6.25	3.20	3.69	3.41	2.39	3.45	3.87
Tang Book Value Per Share	2.80	4.51	5.10	6.78	8.04	8.89	7.79	6.45
Dividends Per Share	0.800	0.780	0.720	0.620	0.560	0.520	0.500	0.480
Dividend Payout %	35.64	30.35	29.39	24.80	28.43	30.95	32.26	38.10
Income Statement								
Total Revenue	563,383	2,570,472	2,679,803	2,450,572	2,093,447	1,755,728	1,692,622	1,792,438
EBITDA	27,686	261,831	275,919	281,060	253,636	227,358	215,762	217,123
Depn & Amortn	17,021	68,173	69,503	65,514	75,224	77,397	73,072	94,031
Income Before Taxes	7,251	176,726	193,232	214,709	178,869	150,931	140,554	116,261
Income Taxes	3,180	57,141	63,670	77,295	65,287	52,826	49,194	41,854
Net Income	3,977	120,378	123,375	137,420	113,582	98,105	91,360	74,407
Average Shares	44,705	46,925	50,374	55,033	57,577	58,545	59,040	59,087
Balance Sheet								
Current Assets	451,493	489,072	504,174	486,598	374,579	462,122	405,054	319,657
Total Assets	1,233,224	1,206,976	1,226,359	1,140,271	1,021,657	1,021,826	1,020,552	961,891
Current Liabilities	346,227	384,461	358,542	358,174	266,250	245,816	298,680	230,443
Long-Term Obligations	286,966	281,091	285,974	103,869	3,645	4,126	9,837	80,830
Total Liabilities	791,947	748,068	730,440	546,327	352,494	311,937	373,659	369,211
Stockholders' Equity	441,277	458,908	495,919	593,944	669,163	709,889	646,893	592,680
Shares Outstanding	44,439	44,834	47,905	51,848	55,303	58,238	58,373	58,672
Statistical Record								
Return on Assets %	8.64	9.92	10.45	12.75	11.15	9.45	9.24	7.52
Return on Equity %	21.89	25.28	22.70	21.82	16.52	14.23	14.78	12.80
EBITDA Margin %	4.91	10.19	10.30	11.47	12.12	12.95	12.75	12.11
Net Margin %	0.71	4.68	4.60	5.61	5.43	5.59	5.40	4.15
Asset Turnover	2.10	2.12	2.27	2.27	2.05	1.69	1.71	1.81
Current Ratio	1.30	1.27	1.41	1.36	1.41	1.88	1.36	1.39
Debt to Equity	0.65	0.61	0.58	0.17	0.01	0.01	0.02	0.14
Price Range	47.81-27.67	51.61-34.87	61.55-38.81	61.53-38.89	45.71-35.40	43.87-24.67	30.64-23.37	28.82-19.96
P/E Ratio	21.34-12.35	20.08-13.57	25.12-15.84	24.61-15.56	23.20-17.97	26.11-14.68	19.77-15.08	22.87-15.84
Average Yield %	2.10	1.85	1.47	1.22	1.39	1.57	1.83	1.95

Address: 408 East Second Street, Muscatine, IA 52761-0071
Telephone: 563-264-7400
Web Site: www.hnicorp.com

Officers: Stanley A. Askren - Chairman, President, Chief Executive Officer, Interim Chief Financial Officer David C. Burdakin - Executive Vice President
Transfer Agents: Computershare Investor Services, LLC, Chicago, IL

Investor Contact: 563-272-7400
No of Institutions: 204
Shares: 36,081,552 **% Held:** 76.16

HOLLY CORP.

Exchange	Symbol	Price	52Wk Range	Yield	P/E
NYS	HOC	$42.35 (5/29/2008)	79.87-39.00	1.42	8.61

*7 Year Price Score 178.22 *NYSE Composite Index=100   *12 Month Price Score 80.02

Interim Earnings (Per Share)

Qtr.	Mar	Jun	Sep	Dec
2005	0.20	0.81	0.98	0.65
2006	0.78	1.60	1.37	0.85
2007	1.20	2.84	1.04	0.90
2008	0.17	...	...	...

Interim Dividends (Per Share)

Amt	Decl	Ex	Rec	Pay
0.12Q	09/10/2007	09/19/2007	09/21/2007	10/02/2007
0.12Q	12/12/2007	12/19/2007	12/21/2007	01/03/2008
0.15Q	02/25/2008	03/17/2008	03/19/2008	04/02/2008
0.15Q	06/02/2008	06/13/2008	06/17/2008	07/02/2008
		Indicated Div: $0.60		

Valuation Analysis

Forecast EPS $3.32 (05/17/2008)

Market Cap	$2.1 Billion	Book Value	500.0 Million
Price/Book	4.29	Price/Sales	0.40

Dividend Achiever Status

10 Year Growth Rate	20.06%
Total Years of Dividend Growth	14

Business Summary: Oil and Gas (MIC: SIC: 2911 NAIC: 324110)

Holly is an independent petroleum refiner producing light products such as gasoline, diesel fuel and jet fuel. Co.'s operations are organized into one business division, the refining business, which includes the Navajo Refinery in Artesia, NM; the Woods Cross Refinery, located just north of Salt Lake City, UT; and Holly Asphalt Company, which manufactures and markets asphalt products from various terminals in Arizona, New Mexico, Texas and northern Mexico. As of Dec 31 2007, Co. owned 900 miles of crude gathering pipelines, 67 crude oil trucks and 67 trailers as well as over 600,000 barrels of related tankage, and a 45.0% interest in Holly Energy Partners, L.P.

Recent Developments: For the quarter ended Mar 31 2008, income from continuing operations decreased 100.0% to nil from US$67.5 million in the year-earlier quarter. Net income decreased 87.2% to US$8.6 million from US$67.5 million in the year-earlier quarter. Revenues were US$1.48 billion, up 59.8% from US$925.9 million the year before. Operating income was US$9.6 million versus US$96.6 million in the prior-year quarter, a decrease of 90.1%. Direct operating expenses rose 84.0% to US$1.38 billion from US$751.7 million in the comparable period the year before. Indirect operating expenses increased 12.1% to US$87.0 million from US$77.6 million in the equivalent prior-year period.

Prospects: For full year 2008, Co. now anticipates capital expenditures to be approximately $37.5 million. These investments consist of $21.0 million for refining improvement projects for its Navajo Refinery, $7.7 million for projects at its Woods Cross Refinery, $1.6 million for marketing-related projects, $2.0 million for asphalt plant projects and $5.2 million for other miscellaneous projects. Meanwhile, Co. will be installing a new 15,000 barrels per day hydrocracker and a new 28.0 million standard cubic feet per day hydrogen plant at a budgeted cost of approximately $125.0 million, which should increase liquid volume recovery and improve the refinery's capacity to process outside feedstocks.

Financial Data

(US$ in Thousands)	3 Mos	12/31/2007	12/31/2006	12/31/2005	12/31/2004	12/31/2003	12/31/2002	07/31/2002
Earnings Per Share	4.92	5.98	4.58	2.65	1.30	0.72	0.09	0.50
Cash Flow Per Share	8.47	7.71	4.30	4.07	2.63	1.14	(0.10)	0.68
Tang Book Value Per Share	9.86	11.29	8.43	6.42	5.43	4.33	3.68	3.67
Dividends Per Share	0.510	0.460	0.290	0.190	0.145	0.110	0.108	0.102
Dividend Payout %	10.37	7.69	6.33	7.17	11.11	15.28	126.47	20.40
Income Statement								
Total Revenue	1,479,984	4,791,742	4,023,217	3,212,745	2,246,373	1,403,244	448,637	888,906
EBITDA	25,090	528,897	415,090	310,430	178,102	112,312	20,842	80,020
Depn & Amortn	13,309	43,456	40,270	43,817	40,481	36,275	11,726	27,699
Income Before Taxes	13,344	499,444	383,501	268,413	138,469	74,359	8,517	50,896
Income Taxes	4,695	165,316	136,603	101,424	54,590	28,306	3,114	18,867
Net Income	8,649	334,128	266,566	167,658	83,879	46,053	5,403	32,029
Average Shares	51,515	55,850	58,210	63,244	64,340	64,064	63,608	63,884
Balance Sheet								
Current Assets	1,213,757	1,034,621	806,852	775,929	572,906	336,406	254,347	278,844
Total Assets	2,276,722	1,663,945	1,237,869	1,142,900	982,713	708,892	515,793	502,306
Current Liabilities	958,498	818,080	559,393	577,367	424,264	364,667	241,902	218,971
Long-Term Obligations	341,416	...	...	...	25,000	8,571	17,143	25,714
Total Liabilities	1,378,673	893,725	607,370	608,523	485,247	425,808	287,299	273,750
Stockholders' Equity	500,033	593,794	466,094	377,351	339,916	268,609	228,494	228,556
Shares Outstanding	50,709	52,616	55,316	58,752	62,589	62,056	62,071	62,245
Statistical Record								
Return on Assets %	15.52	23.03	22.39	15.78	9.89	7.52	0.76	6.45
Return on Equity %	54.74	63.05	63.21	46.75	27.49	18.53	1.77	14.89
EBITDA Margin %	1.70	11.04	10.32	9.66	7.93	8.00	4.65	9.00
Net Margin %	0.58	6.97	6.63	5.22	3.73	3.28	1.20	3.60
Asset Turnover	3.03	3.30	3.38	3.02	2.65	2.29	0.63	1.79
Current Ratio	1.27	1.26	1.44	1.34	1.35	0.92	1.05	1.27
Debt to Equity	0.68	...	...	...	0.07	0.03	0.08	0.11
Price Range	79.87-39.00	79.87-45.65	55.68-28.38	32.35-12.69	14.22-6.80	7.50-5.00	5.75-3.75	5.29-3.67
P/E Ratio	16.23-7.93	13.36-7.63	12.16-6.20	12.21-4.79	10.93-5.23	10.41-6.94	63.83-41.67	10.57-7.33
Average Yield %	0.86	0.75	0.68	0.83	1.48	1.72	2.36	2.27

Address: 100 Crescent Court, Suite 1600, Dallas, TX 75201-6915 **Telephone:** 214-871-3555 **Web Site:** www.hollycorp.com	**Officers:** Matthew P. Clifton - Chairman, Chief Executive Officer Stephen J. McDonnell - Assistant Chairman, Senior Vice President, Chief Financial Officer **Transfer Agents:** American Stock Transfer & Trust Company, NewYork, NY	**No of Institutions:** 310 **Shares:** 39,638,840 **% Held:** 74.60

HOME DEPOT INC

Exchange	Symbol	Price	52Wk Range	Yield	P/E
NYS	HD	$27.71 (5/29/2008)	40.94-24.71	3.25	13.86

*7 Year Price Score 66.07   *NYSE Composite Index=100   *12 Month Price Score 93.05

Interim Earnings (Per Share)

Qtr.	Apr	Jul	Oct	Jan
2005-06	0.57	0.82	0.72	0.61
2006-07	0.70	0.90	0.73	0.47
2007-08	0.53	0.81	0.60	0.43
2008-09	0.21	...	...	...

Interim Dividends (Per Share)

Amt	Decl	Ex	Rec	Pay
0.225Q	08/16/2007	08/28/2007	08/30/2007	09/13/2007
0.225Q	11/15/2007	11/27/2007	11/29/2007	12/13/2007
0.225Q	02/28/2008	03/11/2008	03/13/2008	03/27/2008
0.225Q	05/22/2008	06/03/2008	06/05/2008	06/19/2008

Indicated Div: $0.90 (Div. Reinv. Plan)

Valuation Analysis

Forecast EPS $1.78 (05/17/2008)

Market Cap	$47.1 Billion	Book Value	17.7 Billion
Price/Book	2.66	Price/Sales	0.63

Dividend Achiever Status

10 Year Growth Rate	30.40%
Total Years of Dividend Growth	20

Business Summary: Retail - Hardware (MIC: SIC: 5211 NAIC: 444110)

The Home Depot is a home improvement retailer that provides an array of building materials, home improvement and lawn and garden products and related services. Co. also operates EXPO Design Center (EXPO) stores, which provides products and services related to design and renovation projects. As of Feb 3 2008, Co. operated a total of 2,234 stores, which included 1,950 The Home Depot stores, 34 EXPO stores, five Yardbirds stores and two The Home Depot Design Center stores in the U.S., which include the territories of Puerto Rico, the Virgin Islands and Guam, as well as 165 The Home Depot stores in Canada, 66 The Home Depot stores in Mexico and 12 The Home Depot stores in China.

Recent Developments: For the quarter ended May 4 2008, income from continuing operations decreased 62.4% to US$356.0 million from US$947.0 million in the year-earlier quarter. Net income decreased 66.0% to US$356.0 million from US$1.05 billion in the year-earlier quarter. Revenues were US$17.91 billion, down 3.4% from US$18.55 billion the year before. Operating income was US$728.0 million versus US$1.67 billion in the prior-year quarter, a decrease of 56.5%. Direct operating expenses declined 3.6% to US$11.84 billion from US$12.28 billion in the comparable period the year before. Indirect operating expenses increased 16.4% to US$5.34 billion from US$4.59 billion in the equivalent prior-year period.

Prospects: For fiscal 2008 ending Jan 28 2009, Co. continues to expect the opening of 55 new stores, including 36 new stores in the U.S. Accordingly, Co. is projecting a charge of approximately $400.0 million related to capitalized development costs and ongoing requirement associated with its future store locations. Excluding the effects of this charge, Co. now anticipates earnings for fiscal 2008 to decline by 19.0% to 24.0%. Lastly, Co. is forecasting capital expenditures of about $2.30 billion, including investments in maintenance, merchandising resets and other initiatives. Meanwhile, for the fiscal year ending January 2010, Co. intends to grow square footage by approximately 1.5% annually.

Financial Data

(US$ in Thousands)	3 Mos	02/03/2008	01/28/2007	01/29/2006	01/30/2005	02/01/2004	02/02/2003	02/03/2002
Earnings Per Share	2.00	2.37	2.79	2.72	2.26	1.88	1.56	1.29
Cash Flow Per Share	3.19	3.05	3.74	3.04	3.14	2.87	2.06	2.51
Tang Book Value Per Share	9.71	9.77	9.50	11.12	10.42	9.56	8.39	7.53
Dividends Per Share	0.900	0.900	0.675	0.400	0.325	0.260	0.210	0.170
Dividend Payout %	45.08	37.97	24.19	14.71	14.38	13.83	13.46	13.18
Income Statement								
Total Revenue	17,907,000	77,349,000	90,837,000	81,511,000	73,094,000	64,816,000	58,247,000	53,553,000
EBITDA	1,202,000	9,148,000	11,559,000	10,942,000	9,245,000	7,922,000	6,733,000	5,696,000
Depn & Amortn	474,000	1,906,000	1,886,000	1,579,000	1,319,000	1,076,000	903,000	764,000
Income Before Taxes	564,000	6,620,000	9,308,000	9,282,000	7,912,000	6,843,000	5,872,000	4,957,000
Income Taxes	208,000	2,410,000	3,547,000	3,444,000	2,911,000	2,539,000	2,208,000	1,913,000
Net Income	356,000	4,395,000	5,761,000	5,838,000	5,001,000	4,304,000	3,664,000	3,044,000
Average Shares	1,683,000	1,856,000	2,062,000	2,147,000	2,216,000	2,289,000	2,344,000	2,353,000
Balance Sheet								
Current Assets	16,340,000	14,674,000	18,000,000	15,346,000	14,190,000	13,328,000	11,917,000	10,361,000
Total Assets	45,596,000	44,324,000	52,263,000	44,482,000	38,907,000	34,437,000	30,011,000	26,394,000
Current Liabilities	14,119,000	12,706,000	12,931,000	12,901,000	10,529,000	9,554,000	8,035,000	6,501,000
Long-Term Obligations	11,339,000	11,383,000	11,643,000	2,672,000	2,148,000	856,000	1,321,000	1,250,000
Total Liabilities	27,890,000	26,610,000	27,233,000	17,573,000	14,749,000	12,030,000	10,209,000	8,312,000
Stockholders' Equity	17,706,000	17,714,000	25,030,000	26,909,000	24,158,000	22,407,000	19,802,000	18,082,000
Shares Outstanding	1,698,000	1,690,000	1,970,000	2,124,000	2,185,000	2,257,000	2,293,000	2,345,888
Statistical Record								
Return on Assets %	7.08	8.95	11.94	14.04	13.67	13.39	13.03	12.54
Return on Equity %	16.60	20.23	22.24	22.93	21.54	20.45	19.40	18.10
EBITDA Margin %	6.71	11.83	12.72	13.42	12.65	12.22	11.56	10.64
Net Margin %	1.99	5.68	6.34	7.16	6.84	6.64	6.29	5.68
Asset Turnover	1.48	1.58	1.88	1.96	2.00	2.02	2.07	2.21
Current Ratio	1.16	1.15	1.39	1.19	1.35	1.40	1.48	1.59
Debt to Equity	0.64	0.64	0.47	0.10	0.09	0.04	0.07	0.07
Price Range	40.94-24.71	41.76-24.71	43.81-33.13	43.95-35.09	43.79-32.88	37.52-20.70	52.07-20.53	53.45-32.80
P/E Ratio	20.47-12.36	17.62-10.43	15.70-11.87	16.16-12.90	19.38-14.55	19.96-11.01	33.38-13.16	41.43-25.43
Average Yield %	2.80	2.57	1.77	1.00	0.86	0.83	0.60	0.37

Address: 2455 Paces Ferry Road N.W., Atlanta, GA 30339-4024
Telephone: 770-433-8211
Web Site: www.homedepot.com

Officers: Francis S. Blake - Chairman, Chief Executive Officer Carol B. Tome - Executive Vice President, Chief Financial Officer **Transfer Agents:** Computershare Trust Company, N.A., Providence, RI

No of Institutions: 1181
Shares: 1,238,214,272 **% Held:** 68.50

HOME PROPERTIES INC

Exchange	Symbol	Price	52Wk Range	Yield	P/E
NYS	HME	$51.46 (5/29/2008)	57.63-40.35	5.13	21.62

*7 Year Price Score 90.17   *NYSE Composite Index=100   *12 Month Price Score 106.26

Interim Earnings (Per Share)

Qtr.	Mar	Jun	Sep	Dec
2005	(0.06)	0.25	0.47	1.67
2006	0.13	0.33	0.30	2.38
2007	0.15	0.26	0.84	0.48
2008	0.80	...	...	...

Interim Dividends (Per Share)

Amt	Decl	Ex	Rec	Pay
0.65Q	08/02/2007	08/09/2007	08/13/2007	08/24/2007
0.66Q	11/05/2007	11/14/2007	11/16/2007	11/27/2007
0.66Q	02/11/2008	02/20/2008	02/22/2008	02/29/2008
0.66Q	05/01/2008	05/12/2008	05/14/2008	05/23/2008

Indicated Div: $2.64

Valuation Analysis

Forecast EPS	$1.40 (05/16/2008)		
Market Cap	$1.6 Billion	Book Value	632.5 Million
Price/Book	2.57	Price/Sales	3.19

Dividend Achiever Status

10 Year Growth Rate	4.14%
Total Years of Dividend Growth	13

TRADING VOLUME (thousand shares)

Business Summary: "Property, Real Estate & Development" (MIC: SIC: 6798 NAIC: 525930)

Home Properties is a self-administered and self-managed real estate investment trust that owns, operates, acquires, develops and rehabilitates apartment communities. Co.'s properties are regionally focused in select Northeast, Mid-Atlantic, and Southeast Florida markets of the U.S. Co. conducts its business through Home Properties, L.P. in which Co. held a 70.8% partnership interest as of Dec 31 2007. Co., as of Dec 31 2007, operated 125 communities with 38,646 apartment units. Of these, 37,496 units in 123 communities are owned outright, 868 units in one community are managed and partially owned by Co. as general partner, and 282 units in one community are managed for other owners.

Recent Developments: For the quarter ended Mar 31 2008, income from continuing operations decreased 19.9% to US$5.9 million from US$7.4 million in the year-earlier quarter. Net income increased 215.6% to US$26.1 million from US$8.3 million in the year-earlier quarter. Revenues were US$129.5 million, up 5.2% from US$123.1 million the year before. Revenues from property income rose 6.7% to US$129.2 million from US$121.1 million in the corresponding quarter a year earlier.

Prospects: For full-year 2008, Co. is reconfirming the $3.39 midpoint of its earnings guidance while tightening the range to $3.33 to $3.45 per share from $3.31 to $3.47 per share. Co. noted that the new range will produce 2008 funds from operations per share growth of 4.0% to 7.7% compared to 2007 results. Co. also anticipates acquisition of communities of $100.0 million in 2008. Meanwhile, on Mar 4 2008, Co. has acquired a 1.4 acre development parcel located in Silver Spring, MD for $15.9 million. Co. is proceeding with the approval of a final site plan, developed by the prior owner, which includes the construction of up to 314 apartment units and approximately 5,300 square feet of retail space.

Financial Data
(US$ in Thousands)

	3 Mos	12/31/2007	12/31/2006	12/31/2005	12/31/2004	12/31/2003	12/31/2002	12/31/2001
Earnings Per Share	2.38	1.73	3.15	2.33	1.18	1.03	0.96	2.11
Cash Flow Per Share	5.06	4.91	4.98	4.16	4.82	4.99	5.51	6.71
Tang Book Value Per Share	20.04	20.49	21.01	19.14	19.48	20.53	20.67	21.10
Dividends Per Share	2.620	2.610	2.570	2.530	2.490	2.450	2.410	2.310
Dividend Payout %	110.22	150.87	81.59	108.58	211.02	237.86	251.04	109.48
Income Statement								
Total Revenue	129,538	505,188	453,992	443,801	458,330	434,504	395,562	367,523
Depn & Amortn	29,369	112,584	101,695	100,115	95,228	79,279	68,799	65,521
Net Income	26,099	61,544	110,485	81,512	47,022	41,798	44,939	64,506
Average Shares	32,589	33,794	33,337	32,328	33,314	29,575	26,335	22,227
Balance Sheet								
Total Assets	3,197,797	3,216,423	3,240,418	2,977,870	2,816,796	2,513,317	2,456,266	2,063,789
Long-Term Obligations	2,161,697	1,989,289	1,924,313	1,850,483	1,702,722	1,380,696	1,335,807	992,858
Total Liabilities	2,292,845	2,269,301	2,202,259	1,997,789	1,785,599	1,441,510	1,396,963	1,052,606
Stockholders' Equity	632,516	668,061	755,617	656,812	720,422	741,263	726,242	620,596
Shares Outstanding	31,564	32,600	33,103	31,184	32,625	31,966	27,027	24,010
Statistical Record								
Return on Assets %	2.46	1.91	3.55	2.81	1.76	1.68	1.99	3.28
Return on Equity %	11.92	8.65	15.64	11.84	6.42	5.70	6.67	10.84
Net Margin %	20.15	12.18	24.34	18.37	10.26	9.62	11.36	17.55
Price Range	58.15-40.35	64.65-41.53	63.52-41.70	46.27-36.05	43.92-36.85	40.92-31.19	37.94-28.90	33.14-26.13
P/E Ratio	24.43-16.95	37.37-24.01	20.17-13.24	19.86-15.47	37.22-31.23	39.73-30.28	39.52-30.10	15.71-12.38
Average Yield %	5.24	4.91	4.76	6.17	6.23	6.76	7.16	7.81

Address: 850 Clinton Square, Rochester, NY 14604 **Telephone:** 585-546-4900 **Web Site:** www.homeproperties.com	**Officers:** Norman P. Leenhouts - Co-Chairman Nelson B. Leenhouts - Co-Chairman **Transfer Agents:** Mellon Investor Services, LLC, Jersey City, NJ	**Investor Contact:** 716-546-4900 **No of Institutions:** 191 **Shares:** 35,354,372 **% Held:** 104.29

HORIZON FINANCIAL CORP.

Exchange	Symbol	Price	52Wk Range	Yield	P/E
NMS	HRZB	$10.87 (5/29/2008)	23.75-10.55	4.97	6.84

*7 Year Price Score 87.78 *NYSE Composite Index=100 *12 Month Price Score 74.15

Interim Earnings (Per Share)
Qtr.	Jun	Sep	Dec	Mar
2004-05	0.25	0.26	0.25	0.26
2005-06	0.30	0.30	0.32	0.34
2006-07	0.37	0.37	0.39	0.39
2007-08	0.41	0.40	0.39	...

Interim Dividends (Per Share)
Amt	Decl	Ex	Rec	Pay
0.13Q	06/27/2007	07/06/2007	07/10/2007	08/01/2007
0.13Q	09/26/2007	10/09/2007	10/11/2007	11/02/2007
0.135Q	12/19/2007	01/04/2008	01/08/2008	02/01/2008
0.135Q	03/26/2008	04/03/2008	04/07/2008	05/02/2008

Indicated Div: $0.54

Valuation Analysis
Forecast EPS $1.25 (05/17/2008)

Market Cap	$130.4 Million	Book Value	127.9 Million
Price/Book	1.02	Price/Sales	1.22

Dividend Achiever Status
10 Year Growth Rate	9.09%
Total Years of Dividend Growth	11

TRADING VOLUME (thousand shares)

Business Summary: Commercial Banking (MIC: SIC: 6022 NAIC: 522190)

Horizon Financial is a bank holding company. Co., through its subsidiary, Horizon Bank provides an array of commercial and mortgage lending services to borrowers and a range of customer services to depositors through 18 full-service office facilities, four commercial loan centers and four real estate loan centers, located in Whatcom, Skagit, Snohomish and Pierce counties of Washington State. The Bank originates both fixed rate and adjustable rate mortgages secured by residential, business, and commercial real estate. As of Mar 31 2007, Co. had total assets of $1.27 billion and total deposits of $975.3 million.

Recent Developments: For the quarter ended Dec 31 2007, net income decreased 3.5% to US$4.7 million from US$4.9 million in the year-earlier quarter. Net interest income increased 2.8% to US$13.8 million from US$13.4 million in the year-earlier quarter. Provision for loan losses was US$900,000 versus US$450,000 in the prior-year quarter, an increase of 100.0%. Non-interest income rose 6.8% to US$1.5 million from US$1.4 million, while non-interest expense advanced 5.2% to US$7.4 million.

Prospects: Co.'s results are benefiting from employment and population growth, driven by aerospace, software, export trade and services. In addition, Co. is experiencing an increase in its non-interest income primarily from growth in service fees associated with its increased deposit base, coupled by higher residential mortgage originations, which also contributed to its portfolio growth. Nevertheless, Co. remains cautious with its outlook in the residential development within its region due to the slowing of home sales and downward pressure on home prices. Accordingly, Co. remains diligent in monitoring its construction and development portfolios for signs of credit weakness.

Financial Data
(US$ in Thousands)	9 Mos	6 Mos	3 Mos	03/31/2007	03/31/2006	03/31/2005	03/31/2004	03/31/2003
Earnings Per Share	1.59	1.59	1.56	1.53	1.25	1.01	0.96	0.90
Cash Flow Per Share	1.67	1.28	1.50	1.56	1.42	0.60	1.24	0.62
Tang Book Value Per Share	10.66	10.56	10.31	10.11	9.16	8.53	8.40	8.06
Dividends Per Share	0.510	0.505	0.495	0.486	0.448	0.416	0.384	0.345
Dividend Payout %	32.08	31.76	31.73	31.76	35.90	41.27	40.00	38.48
Income Statement								
Interest Income	76,700	50,791	24,898	92,600	69,388	52,182	48,980	50,229
Interest Expense	35,516	23,407	11,457	40,133	24,896	16,144	15,509	19,461
Net Interest Income	41,184	27,384	13,441	52,467	44,492	36,038	33,470	30,768
Provision for Losses	2,100	1,200	400	1,850	2,575	1,700	1,915	2,740
Non-Interest Income	4,830	3,315	1,703	5,838	6,423	6,517	7,882	7,408
Non-Interest Expense	22,129	14,707	7,255	27,861	25,782	22,423	20,238	17,346
Income Before Taxes	21,785	14,792	7,489	28,594	22,558	18,432	19,199	18,090
Income Taxes	7,144	4,863	2,473	9,566	6,903	5,369	6,332	5,950
Net Income	14,641	9,929	5,016	19,028	15,655	13,063	12,866	12,140
Average Shares	12,157	12,256	12,339	12,409	12,542	12,952	13,357	13,581
Balance Sheet								
Net Loans & Leases	1,193,199	1,147,984	1,087,788	1,059,363	923,761	809,049	659,560	585,107
Total Assets	1,391,315	1,346,131	1,303,541	1,270,327	1,116,728	997,570	858,876	819,872
Total Deposits	1,009,940	997,555	987,704	975,295	834,299	746,849	670,259	646,722
Total Liabilities	1,263,377	1,218,066	1,177,906	1,146,472	1,003,405	890,546	749,569	713,628
Stockholders' Equity	127,938	128,065	125,635	123,855	113,323	107,024	109,307	106,244
Shares Outstanding	11,998	12,123	12,186	12,254	12,372	12,547	13,006	13,187
Statistical Record								
Return on Assets %	1.48	1.53	1.56	1.59	1.48	1.41	1.53	1.53
Return on Equity %	15.70	16.04	16.22	16.05	14.21	12.08	11.91	11.74
Net Interest Margin %	53.26	53.85	53.98	56.66	64.12	69.06	68.34	61.26
Efficiency Ratio %	27.06	27.09	27.27	28.30	34.01	38.20	35.59	30.10
Loans to Deposits	1.18	1.15	1.10	1.09	1.11	1.08	0.98	0.90
Price Range	25.00-15.13	25.62-18.47	25.62-19.51	25.62-17.28	20.93-14.30	17.57-13.41	15.50-11.72	12.35-7.92
P/E Ratio	15.72-9.52	16.11-11.62	16.42-12.51	16.75-11.29	16.74-11.44	17.39-13.28	16.15-12.21	13.72-8.80
Average Yield %	2.43	2.24	2.14	2.16	2.57	2.69	2.78	3.49

Address: 1500 Cornwall Avenue, Bellingham, WA 98225 **Telephone:** 360-733-3050 **Web Site:** www.horizonbank.com	Officers: V. Lawrence Evans - Chairman Richard P. Jacobson - President, Chief Executive Officer **Transfer Agents:** American Stock Transfer & Trust Company, New York, NY	Investor Contact: 360-733-3050 No of Institutions: 68 Shares: 3,933,055 % Held: 31.71

HORMEL FOODS CORP.

Exchange	Symbol	Price	52Wk Range	Yield	P/E
NYS	HRL	$38.26 (5/29/2008)	42.47-31.76	1.93	16.28

*7 Year Price Score 97.74 *NYSE Composite Index=100 *12 Month Price Score 108.40

Interim Earnings (Per Share)

Qtr.	Jan	Apr	Jul	Oct
2004-05	0.46	0.40	0.37	0.59
2005-06	0.50	0.48	0.43	0.64
2006-07	0.54	0.49	0.41	0.73
2007-08	0.64	0.56	...	...

Interim Dividends (Per Share)

Amt	Decl	Ex	Rec	Pay
0.15Q	10/02/2007	10/17/2007	10/20/2007	11/15/2007
0.185Q	11/20/2007	01/16/2008	01/19/2008	02/15/2008
0.185Q	04/01/2008	04/16/2008	04/19/2008	05/15/2008
0.185Q	05/20/2008	07/16/2008	07/19/2008	08/15/2008

Indicated Div: $0.74 (Div. Reinv. Plan)

Valuation Analysis

Forecast EPS $2.38 (05/16/2008)

Market Cap	$5.2 Billion	Book Value	2.0 Billion
Price/Book	2.56	Price/Sales	0.81

Dividend Achiever Status

10 Year Growth Rate	6.83%
Total Years of Dividend Growth	41

Business Summary: Food (MIC: SIC: 2011 NAIC: 311611)

Hormel Foods is engaged in the production of a range of meat and food products and the marketing of those products throughout the U.S. and internationally. Although pork and turkey remain the major raw materials for its products, Co. has emphasized for several years the manufacture and distribution of branded, consumer packaged items rather than the commodity fresh meat business. As of Oct 28 2007, Co. operated in five segments: grocery products, refrigerated foods, Jennie-O Turkey store, Specialty foods and all other. Co.'s meat products are sold fresh, frozen, cured, smoked, cooked, and canned.

Recent Developments: For the quarter ended Apr 27 2008, net income increased 14.1% to US$77.6 million from US$68.0 million in the year-earlier quarter. Revenues were US$1.59 billion, up 5.9% from US$1.50 billion the year before. Operating income was US$124.6 million versus US$112.9 million in the prior-year quarter, an increase of 10.3%. Direct operating expenses rose 5.1% to US$1.22 billion from US$1.16 billion in the comparable period the year before. Indirect operating expenses increased 8.2% to US$252.1 million from US$233.0 million in the equivalent prior-year period.

Prospects: Co. continues to experience volatility in protein input costs. Looking ahead, Co. is projecting further pressure from the increasing grain and energy costs, amidst its recent strong operating results. Nevertheless, Co. remains optimistic regarding its near-term outlook, driven by the introduction of Chi-Chi's sauces with improved packaging and advertising. In this respect, Co. continues to anticipate earnings for the fiscal year ending Oct 31 2008 to be in the range of $2.30 to $2.40 per share. Meanwhile, Co. intends to continue to pursue additional pricing initiatives and operational efficiencies throughout the remainder of fiscal 2008 to mitigate the additional corn and hog input costs.

Financial Data

(US$ in Thousands)	6 Mos	3 Mos	10/28/2007	10/29/2006	10/30/2005	10/30/2004	10/25/2003	10/26/2002
Earnings Per Share	2.35	2.28	2.17	2.05	1.82	1.65	1.33	1.35
Cash Flow Per Share	2.68	3.19	2.46	2.38	3.11	2.09	1.83	2.36
Tang Book Value Per Share	9.36	8.94	8.30	8.04	6.77	6.43	5.36	5.41
Dividends Per Share	0.670	0.635	0.600	0.560	0.520	0.450	0.420	0.390
Dividend Payout %	28.57	27.90	27.65	27.32	28.57	27.27	31.58	28.89
Income Statement								
Total Revenue	3,215,249	1,621,165	6,193,032	5,745,481	5,413,997	4,779,875	4,200,328	3,910,314
EBITDA	337,808	179,091	636,402	589,021	557,234	486,452	413,861	409,631
Depn & Amortn	63,971	33,060	138,858	132,842	124,604	94,745	92,666	84,236
Income Before Taxes	260,688	139,311	469,837	430,543	404,886	364,565	289,331	293,970
Income Taxes	94,946	51,130	167,945	144,404	151,427	132,902	103,552	104,648
Net Income	165,742	88,181	301,892	286,139	253,459	231,663	185,779	189,322
Average Shares	137,620	137,666	139,151	139,561	139,577	140,179	139,710	140,292
Balance Sheet								
Current Assets	1,300,968	1,279,357	1,231,725	1,141,671	1,041,084	1,029,403	823,974	962,170
Total Assets	3,471,148	3,431,258	3,393,650	3,060,306	2,822,406	2,533,968	2,393,121	2,220,196
Current Liabilities	553,115	582,578	664,777	585,014	583,172	464,366	441,990	410,111
Long-Term Obligations	350,000	350,000	350,005	350,054	350,430	361,510	395,273	409,648
Total Liabilities	1,442,362	1,462,407	1,508,867	1,257,394	1,247,830	1,134,720	1,140,386	1,104,941
Stockholders' Equity	2,028,786	1,968,851	1,884,783	1,802,912	1,574,576	1,399,248	1,252,735	1,115,255
Shares Outstanding	135,764	135,677	135,677	137,339	137,843	137,875	138,596	138,411
Statistical Record								
Return on Assets %	9.88	9.69	9.38	9.75	9.46	9.25	8.08	8.66
Return on Equity %	16.47	16.39	16.42	16.99	17.05	17.19	15.73	17.98
EBITDA Margin %	10.51	11.05	10.28	10.25	10.29	10.18	9.85	10.48
Net Margin %	5.15	5.44	4.87	4.98	4.68	4.85	4.42	4.84
Asset Turnover	1.95	1.94	1.92	1.96	2.02	1.91	1.83	1.79
Current Ratio	2.35	2.20	1.85	1.95	1.79	2.22	1.86	2.35
Debt to Equity	0.17	0.18	0.19	0.19	0.22	0.26	0.32	0.37
Price Range	42.47-31.76	41.70-31.76	39.49-31.76	38.02-31.70	33.08-27.58	31.63-23.80	24.98-20.18	28.03-20.50
P/E Ratio	18.07-13.51	18.29-13.93	18.20-14.64	18.55-15.46	18.18-15.15	19.17-14.42	18.78-15.17	20.76-15.19
Average Yield %	1.76	1.71	1.62	1.61	1.69	1.60	1.85	1.58

Address: 1 Hormel Place, Austin, MN 55912-3680	Officers: Jeffrey M. Ettinger - Chairman, President, Chief Executive Officer Jody H. Feragen - Senior Vice President, Chief Financial Officer Transfer Agents: Wells Fargo Bank, N.A., South St. Paul, MN	Investor Contact: 507-437-5007
Telephone: 507-437-5611		No of Institutions: 296
Web Site: www.hormel.com		Shares: 45,109,560 % Held: 30.84

Exchange	Symbol	Price	52Wk Range	Yield	P/E
NYS	DHI	$12.63 (5/29/2008)	23.37-10.27	2.38	N/A

*7 Year Price Score 58.87 ***NYSE Composite Index=100** ***12 Month Price Score 103.19**

Interim Earnings (Per Share)

Qtr.	Dec	Mar	Jun	Sep
2004-05	0.76	0.92	1.17	1.77
2005-06	0.98	1.11	0.93	0.88
2006-07	0.35	0.16	(2.62)	(0.16)
2007-08	(0.41)	(4.14)	...	...

Interim Dividends (Per Share)

Amt	Decl	Ex	Rec	Pay
0.15Q	08/02/2007	08/15/2007	08/17/2007	08/27/2007
0.15Q	10/24/2007	11/01/2007	11/05/2007	11/16/2007
0.15Q	02/01/2008	02/08/2008	02/12/2008	02/20/2008
0.075Q	05/06/2008	05/15/2008	05/19/2008	05/29/2008
		Indicated Div: $0.30		

Valuation Analysis

Forecast EPS $-1.50 (05/16/2008)

Market Cap	$4.0 Billion	Book Value	4.1 Billion
Price/Book	0.98	Price/Sales	0.44

Dividend Achiever Status

10 Year Growth Rate	39.15%
Total Years of Dividend Growth	10

Business Summary: Building & General Construction (MIC: SIC: 1531 NAIC: 236117)

D.R. Horton is a national homebuilder. Co. constructs and sells single-family homes, designed principally for first-time and move-up homebuyers, through its operating divisions in 27 states and 83 metropolitan markets of the United States, primarily under the name of D.R. Horton, America's Builder. Co.'s homebuilding operations generate most of their revenues from the sale of completed homes, with a lesser amount from the sale of land and lots. Co. also builds attached homes, such as town homes, duplexes, triplexes and condominiums. Co.'s financial services segment generates revenues from originating and selling mortgages and collecting fees for title insurance agency and closing services.

Recent Developments: For the quarter ended Mar 31 2008, net loss amounted to US$1.31 billion versus net income of US$51.7 million in the year-earlier quarter. Revenues were US$1.66 billion, down 37.6% from US$2.66 billion the year before. Direct operating expenses rose 2.6% to US$2.30 billion from US$2.24 billion in the comparable period the year before. Indirect operating expenses decreased 27.3% to US$240.5 million from US$330.6 million in the equivalent prior-year period.

Prospects: Co. is cautious of its outlook for the fiscal year ending Sep 2008 as it expects housing market conditions remain challenging and may deteriorate further in the form of declining net sales orders and sales order backlog. Thus, Co. expects to close fewer homes than in fiscal 2007 and is continuing to reduce its land and lot inventory from existing levels through sales of excess lots and land parcels, as well as controlling its inventory of homes under construction and limiting its developmental spending for the rest of fiscal 2008. Co. also continues to offer incentives and price reductions to grow sales volumes as necessary and modifies its product offerings to provide more affordable homes.

Financial Data

(US$ in Thousands)	6 Mos	3 Mos	09/30/2007	09/30/2006	09/30/2005	09/30/2004	09/30/2003	09/30/2002
Earnings Per Share	(7.30)	(3.03)	(2.27)	3.90	4.62	3.09	2.06	1.44
Cash Flow Per Share	6.00	5.14	4.32	(3.81)	(1.99)	(1.36)	1.43	(0.34)
Tang Book Value Per Share	12.59	16.89	17.44	18.75	15.28	11.02	8.08	5.78
Dividends Per Share	0.600	0.600	0.600	0.440	0.308	0.215	0.135	0.097
Dividend Payout %	...	...	...	11.28	6.66	6.96	6.57	6.72
Income Statement								
Total Revenue	3,403,000	1,742,600	11,296,500	15,051,300	13,863,700	10,840,800	8,728,100	6,738,831
EBITDA	(1,054,900)	(186,400)	(856,600)	2,085,900	2,452,500	1,644,300	1,061,461	693,657
Depn & Amortn	32,600	16,500	71,000	61,700	57,100	55,500	45,861	40,645
Income Before Taxes	(1,087,500)	(202,900)	(951,200)	1,987,100	2,378,600	1,582,900	1,008,162	647,507
Income Taxes	347,000	(74,100)	(238,700)	753,800	908,100	607,800	382,207	242,815
Net Income	(1,434,500)	(128,800)	(712,500)	1,233,300	1,470,500	975,100	625,955	404,692
Average Shares	315,400	315,000	314,100	316,200	318,100	315,210	305,250	282,569
Balance Sheet								
Current Assets	7,626,300	8,715,400	9,613,100	12,179,000	9,636,600	7,085,400	5,665,200	4,447,413
Total Assets	8,955,200	10,401,000	11,556,300	14,820,700	12,514,800	8,985,200	7,279,377	6,017,527
Current Liabilities	290,400	358,600	954,000	2,174,000	2,070,200	946,600	397,978	391,355
Long-Term Obligations	3,744,800	3,724,200	3,989,000	4,886,900	3,660,100	3,006,500	2,565,145	2,486,976
Total Liabilities	4,848,100	4,948,800	5,901,000	8,262,700	6,951,200	4,858,100	4,112,216	3,726,719
Stockholders' Equity	4,072,800	5,414,100	5,586,900	6,452,900	5,360,400	3,960,700	3,031,260	2,269,863
Shares Outstanding	315,847	314,976	314,914	313,246	312,938	306,861	303,466	292,277
Statistical Record								
Return on Assets %	N.M.	N.M.	N.M.	9.02	13.68	11.96	9.42	8.37
Return on Equity %	N.M.	N.M.	N.M.	20.88	31.55	27.82	23.62	22.99
EBITDA Margin %	N.M.	N.M.	N.M.	13.86	17.69	15.17	12.16	10.29
Net Margin %	N.M.	N.M.	N.M.	8.19	10.61	8.99	7.17	6.01
Asset Turnover	0.81	0.85	0.86	1.10	1.29	1.33	1.31	1.39
Current Ratio	26.26	24.30	10.08	5.60	4.65	7.49	14.23	11.36
Debt to Equity	0.92	0.69	0.71	0.76	0.68	0.76	0.85	1.10
Price Range	23.75-10.27	30.86-10.41	30.86-12.81	41.39-20.00	42.11-20.71	26.79-16.35	16.43-8.03	14.37-6.79
P/E Ratio	...	...	...	10.61-5.13	9.11-4.48	8.67-5.29	7.98-3.90	9.98-4.72
Average Yield %	3.65	3.11	2.49	1.47	0.97	0.98	1.16	0.88

Address: 301 Commerce Street, Suite 500, Fort Worth, TX 76102	Officers: Donald R. Horton - Chairman Donald J. Tomnitz - Vice-Chairman, President, Chief Executive Officer Transfer Agents:	Investor Contact: 817-390-8200
Telephone: 817-390-8200		No of Institutions: 387
Web Site: www.drhorton.com	American Stock Transfer & Trust Co., New York, NY	Shares: 311,600,896 % Held: 88.53

IBERIABANK CORP

Exchange	Symbol	Price	52Wk Range	Yield	P/E
NMS	IBKC	$52.89 (5/29/2008)	54.19-40.02	2.57	14.90

*7 Year Price Score 84.44 *NYSE Composite Index=100 *12 Month Price Score 103.62

TRADING VOLUME (thousand shares)

Interim Earnings (Per Share)

Qtr.	Mar	Jun	Sep	Dec
2005	0.75	0.82	(0.15)	0.80
2006	0.81	0.89	0.99	0.87
2007	0.76	0.78	0.94	0.79
2008	1.05	...	...	...

Interim Dividends (Per Share)

Amt	Decl	Ex	Rec	Pay
0.34Q	06/27/2007	06/29/2007	06/29/2007	07/20/2007
0.34Q	09/19/2007	09/26/2007	09/28/2007	10/19/2007
0.34Q	12/17/2007	12/27/2007	12/31/2007	01/25/2008
0.34Q	03/18/2008	03/27/2008	03/31/2008	04/25/2008
		Indicated Div: $1.36		

Valuation Analysis

Forecast EPS	$3.52 (05/16/2008)		
Market Cap	$680.7 Million	Book Value	511.7 Million
Price/Book	1.33	Price/Sales	1.89

Dividend Achiever Status

10 Year Growth Rate	14.94%
Total Years of Dividend Growth	12

Business Summary: Commercial Banking (MIC: SIC: 6022 NAIC: 522110)

IBERIABANK is the bank holding company for IBERIABANK (the Bank), a Louisiana banking corporation. As of Dec 31 2007, The Bank operated 150 combined offices, including 81 bank branch offices in Louisiana, Arkansas and Tennessee, 30 title insurance offices in Arkansas and Louisiana, and mortgage representatives in 39 locations in eight states. Co. offers commercial and retail banking products and services through IBERIABANK and Pulaski Bank; operates mortgage production offices through Pulaski Mortgage Company, and offers a line of title insurance and closing services. As of Dec 31 2007, Co. had total assets of $4.92 billion and total deposits of $3.48 billion.

Recent Developments: For the quarter ended Mar 31 2008, net income increased 45.9% to US$13.4 million from US$9.2 million in the year-earlier quarter. Net interest income increased 19.4% to US$32.8 million from US$27.5 million in the year-earlier quarter. Provision for loan losses was US$2.7 million versus US$211,000 in the prior-year quarter, an increase of. Non-interest income rose 85.6% to US$26.3 million from US$14.2 million, while non-interest expense advanced 26.5% to US$36.8 million.

Prospects: On May 9 2008, Co. announced that its subsidiary, Pulaski Bank and Trust Company, has entered into a Purchase and Assumption Agreement with the Federal Deposit Insurance Corp. (FDIC), as receiver of ANB Financial, N.A., which has $2.10 billion in assets as of Jan 31 2008. In association with this transaction, Pulaski paid a deposit premium to the FDIC equal to 1.011% of the insured deposits assumed. Co. will assume about $213.0 million in insured deposits, and purchase about $2.0 million of loans secured by deposits as well as $46.0 millin of investment securities. Upon completion of the transaction, Co. will have 89 bank branch offices, 32 title insurance offices and 39 mortgage locations.

Financial Data (US$ in Thousands)	3 Mos	12/31/2007	12/31/2006	12/31/2005	12/31/2004	12/31/2003	12/31/2002	12/31/2001
Earnings Per Share	3.55	3.27	3.57	2.24	3.01	2.74	2.42	1.89
Cash Flow Per Share	4.58	6.03	2.53	4.57	3.97	4.79	5.19	0.24
Tang Book Value Per Share	21.36	20.89	22.05	17.85	18.06	16.15	14.59	13.20
Dividends Per Share	1.360	1.340	1.220	1.004	0.848	0.720	0.608	0.560
Dividend Payout %	38.29	40.98	34.17	44.82	28.19	26.32	25.17	29.66
Income Statement								
Income Before Taxes	19,621	57,560	49,648	29,432	38,907	33,768	27,231	22,737
Income Taxes	6,266	16,250	13,953	7,432	11,568	10,216	8,778	8,229
Net Income	13,355	41,310	35,695	22,000	27,339	23,552	18,453	14,508
Average Shares	12,737	12,641	9,993	9,812	9,092	8,606	7,649	7,678
Balance Sheet								
Total Assets	5,132,292	4,916,958	3,203,046	2,852,592	2,448,602	2,115,811	1,570,588	1,426,825
Total Liabilities	4,620,634	4,418,899	2,883,495	2,589,023	2,228,440	1,920,642	1,430,990	1,292,408
Stockholders' Equity	511,658	498,059	319,551	263,569	220,162	195,169	139,598	134,417
Shares Outstanding	12,870	12,774	10,286	9,548	8,605	8,398	7,141	7,485
Statistical Record								
Return on Assets %	0.93	1.02	1.18	0.83	1.19	1.28	1.23	1.03
Return on Equity %	9.23	10.11	12.24	9.10	13.13	14.07	13.47	11.10
Price Range	55.90-40.02	59.11-40.81	65.00-51.69	56.20-44.26	53.68-42.93	48.16-30.45	32.80-21.88	24.10-16.20
P/E Ratio	15.75-11.27	18.08-12.48	18.21-14.48	25.09-19.76	17.83-14.26	17.58-11.11	13.55-9.04	12.75-8.57
Average Yield %	2.79	2.61	2.11	2.00	1.80	1.89	2.09	2.63

Address: 200 West Congress Street, Lafayette, LA 70501 Telephone: 337-521-4012 Web Site: www.iberiabank.com	Officers: William H. Fenstermaker - Chairman E. Stewart Shea - Vice-Chairman Transfer Agents: Registrar & Transfer Company, Cranford, NJ	No of Institutions: 115 Shares: 9,064,296 % Held: 67.56

ILLINOIS TOOL WORKS, INC.

Exchange	Symbol	Price	52Wk Range	Yield	P/E
NYS	ITW	$53.70 (5/30/2008)	60.00-46.27	2.09	N/A

*7 Year Price Score 98.72   *NYSE Composite Index=100   *12 Month Price Score 100.05

Interim Earnings (Per Share)

Qtr.	Mar	Jun	Sep	Dec
2005	0.53	0.65	0.71	0.71
2006	0.65	0.81	0.78	0.77
2007	0.71	0.90	0.89	0.86
2008	0.57	...	...	...

Interim Dividends (Per Share)

Amt	Decl	Ex	Rec	Pay
0.28Q	08/03/2007	09/26/2007	09/30/2007	10/15/2007
0.28Q	10/25/2007	12/27/2007	12/31/2007	01/14/2008
0.28Q	02/08/2008	03/27/2008	03/31/2008	04/14/2008
0.28Q	05/02/2008	06/26/2008	06/30/2008	07/14/2008
	Indicated Div: $1.12 (Div. Reinv. Plan)			

Valuation Analysis

Forecast EPS $3.65 (05/17/2008)

Market Cap	$28.1 Billion	Book Value	9.2 Billion
Price/Book	3.04	Price/Sales	N/A

Dividend Achiever Status

10 Year Growth Rate	15.52%
Total Years of Dividend Growth	45

TRADING VOLUME (thousand shares)

Business Summary: Industrial Machinery and Equipment (MIC: SIC: 3566 NAIC: 333612)

Illinois Tool Works is a manufacturer of industrial products and equipment. Co. has eight business segments: Industrial Packaging that produces steel, plastic and paper products; Power Systems & Electronics that produces equipment and consumables related with power conversion; Transportation that produces components for transportation-related applications; Construction Products that produces tools for construction applications; Food Equipment that produces commercial food equipment; Decorative Surfaces that produces decorative surfacing materials; Polymers & Fluids that produces adhesives and sealants; and All Other, which produces products such as plastic packaging and metal fasteners.

Recent Developments: For the quarter ended Mar 31 2008, income from continuing operations decreased 21.7% to US$301.4 million from US$385.0 million in the year-earlier quarter. Net income decreased 24.6% to US$303.6 million from US$402.4 million in the year-earlier quarter. Revenues were US$4.14 billion, up 11.4% from US$3.72 billion the year before. Operating income was US$520.0 million versus US$568.5 million in the prior-year quarter, a decrease of 8.5%. Direct operating expenses rose 11.8% to US$2.70 billion from US$2.41 billion in the comparable period the year before. Indirect operating expenses increased 25.3% to US$921.5 million from US$735.2 million in the equivalent prior-year period.

Prospects: For the full year of 2008, Co. is forecasting income from continuing operations to be in the range of $3.35 to $3.49 per diluted share, assuming total company revenue growth of 8.0% to 12.0%. For the second quarter of 2008, Co. is targeting income from continuing operations in the range of $0.94 to $1.00 per diluted share, assuming total company growth of 9.0% to 12.0%. Separately, on May 8 2008, Co. announced that it has signed an agreement to acquire Enodis plc for a total transaction value of approximately $2.10 billion. Co. believes that this transaction, which is expected to close in August 2008, should further expand its existing product portfolio in its food equipment businesses.

Financial Data

(US$ in Thousands)	3 Mos	12/31/2007	12/31/2006	12/31/2005	12/31/2004	12/31/2003	12/31/2002	12/31/2001
Earnings Per Share	3.22	3.36	3.01	2.60	2.19	1.66	1.16	1.31
Cash Flow Per Share	...	4.50	3.65	3.23	2.53	2.23	2.10	2.22
Tang Book Value Per Share	6.52	6.92	6.94	6.89	7.59	8.22	6.56	5.41
Dividends Per Share	1.050	0.980	0.750	0.610	0.520	0.470	0.450	0.420
Dividend Payout %	32.61	29.17	24.92	23.46	23.69	28.31	38.96	31.94
Income Statement								
Total Revenue	4,139,414	16,170,611	14,055,049	12,921,792	11,731,425	10,035,623	9,467,740	9,292,791
EBITDA	631,575	3,184,401	2,943,859	2,623,780	2,396,308	1,922,705	1,790,193	1,669,032
Depn & Amortn	133,012	521,494	443,906	383,074	353,283	302,090	305,752	386,308
Income Before Taxes	461,075	2,580,972	2,445,246	2,181,569	1,999,405	1,576,114	1,433,560	1,230,849
Income Taxes	159,700	754,900	727,500	686,700	659,800	535,900	501,750	428,400
Net Income	303,621	1,869,862	1,717,746	1,494,869	1,338,694	1,023,680	712,592	805,659
Average Shares	529,725	556,030	569,892	575,434	609,702	617,500	616,090	612,612
Balance Sheet								
Current Assets	6,428,717	6,165,655	5,206,405	4,111,605	4,322,198	4,783,202	3,878,809	3,163,244
Total Assets	15,984,943	15,525,862	13,880,439	11,445,643	11,351,934	11,193,321	10,623,101	9,822,349
Current Liabilities	3,923,200	2,960,285	2,636,584	2,000,731	1,850,971	1,488,903	1,567,162	1,518,158
Long-Term Obligations	1,435,464	1,888,839	955,610	958,321	921,098	920,360	1,460,381	1,267,141
Total Liabilities	6,736,971	6,174,537	4,862,931	3,898,748	3,724,324	3,319,035	3,974,030	3,781,611
Stockholders' Equity	9,247,972	9,351,325	9,017,508	7,546,895	7,627,610	7,874,286	6,649,071	6,040,738
Shares Outstanding	522,781	530,096	558,749	561,627	584,456	617,272	613,165	609,852
Statistical Record								
Return on Assets %	1.90	12.72	13.57	13.11	11.84	9.38	6.97	8.29
Return on Equity %	3.28	20.36	20.74	19.70	17.22	14.10	11.23	14.08
EBITDA Margin %	15.26	19.69	20.95	20.31	20.43	19.16	18.91	17.96
Net Margin %	7.33	11.56	12.22	11.57	11.41	10.20	7.53	8.67
Asset Turnover	...	1.10	1.11	1.13	1.04	0.92	0.93	0.96
Current Ratio	1.64	2.08	1.97	2.06	2.34	3.21	2.48	2.08
Debt to Equity	0.16	0.20	0.11	0.13	0.12	0.12	0.22	0.21
Price Range	60.00-46.27	60.00-45.89	53.29-42.00	47.15-39.43	47.99-36.71	42.08-27.57	38.69-27.86	35.60-24.57
P/E Ratio	18.63-14.37	17.86-13.66	17.70-13.95	18.13-15.17	21.92-16.76	25.35-16.61	33.35-24.02	27.18-18.76
Average Yield %	1.96	1.82	1.61	1.42	1.18	1.39	1.33	1.34

Address: 3600 West Lake Avenue, Glenview, IL 60026-1215 Telephone: 847-724-7500 Web Site: www.itw.com	Officers: David B. Speer - Chairman, Chief Executive Officer Thomas J. Hansen - Vice-Chairman **Transfer Agents:** Computershare Investor Services LLC, Chicago, IL	Investor Contact: 847-657-4104 No of Institutions: 854 Shares: 512,081,120 % Held: 78.80

INDEPENDENT BANK CORPORATION (IONIA, MI)

Exchange	Symbol	Price	52Wk Range	Yield	P/E
NMS	IBCP	$5.57 (5/29/2008)	17.51-5.57	7.90	20.63

*7 Year Price Score 42.60   ***NYSE Composite Index=100**   ***12 Month Price Score 74.56**

Interim Earnings (Per Share)

Qtr.	Mar	Jun	Sep	Dec
2005	0.47	0.51	0.50	0.49
2006	0.53	0.46	0.43	0.02
2007	0.18	0.00	0.16	0.10
2008	0.01	...	...	...

Interim Dividends (Per Share)

Amt	Decl	Ex	Rec	Pay
0.21Q	05/25/2007	07/02/2007	07/05/2007	07/31/2007
0.21Q	08/03/2007	10/03/2007	10/05/2007	10/31/2007
0.21Q	11/21/2007	01/02/2008	01/04/2008	01/31/2008
0.11Q	03/19/2008	04/02/2008	04/04/2008	04/30/2008

Indicated Div: $0.44 (Div. Reinv. Plan)

Valuation Analysis

Forecast EPS $0.42 (05/16/2008)

Market Cap	$128.2 Million	Book Value	238.5 Million
Price/Book	0.54	Price/Sales	0.48

Dividend Achiever Status

10 Year Growth Rate	15.34%
Total Years of Dividend Growth	19

Business Summary: Commercial Banking (MIC: SIC: 6022 NAIC: 522110)

Independent Bank is a bank holding company. Co.'s commercial banking activities include providing checking and savings accounts, commercial lending, direct and indirect consumer financing, mortgage lending, insurance premium and automobile warranty financing and safe deposit box services. Co. also provides title insurance services through a separate subsidiary and provides investment and insurance services through a third party agreement with PrimeVest Financial Services, Inc. As of Dec 31 2007, Co. served its markets through its main office and a total of 106 branches, three drive-thru facilities and nine loan production offices. At such date, Co. had total assets of $3.28 billion.

Recent Developments: For the quarter ended Mar 31 2008, income from continuing operations decreased 91.2% to US$341,000 from US$3.9 million in the year-earlier quarter. Net income decreased 92.0% to US$341,000 from US$4.2 million in the year-earlier quarter. Net interest income increased 2.5% to US$30.4 million from US$29.6 million in the year-earlier quarter. Provision for loan losses was US$11.3 million versus US$8.1 million in the prior-year quarter, an increase of 39.0%. Non-interest income fell 11.0% to US$9.5 million from US$10.7 million, while non-interest expense advanced 8.2% to US$30.3 million.

Prospects: Looking ahead, Co. remains committed to its core strategies for attaining long-term growth in earnings per share including, earning asset growth, diversification of revenues within the financial services industry, effective capital management, as well as improved risk management. Nevertheless, Co. continues to expect that its level of other real estate and repossessed assets will continue to rise during 2008 and will likely remain at elevated levels for the foreseeable future. As a result, Co. expects a high level of non-performing assets to adversely affect its tax equivalent net interest income.

Financial Data
(US$ in Thousands)

	3 Mos	12/31/2007	12/31/2006	12/31/2005	12/31/2004	12/31/2003	12/31/2002	12/31/2001
Earnings Per Share	0.27	0.45	1.43	1.97	1.67	1.70	1.30	1.05
Cash Flow Per Share	0.66	0.78	0.98	2.07	2.85	6.46	(0.66)	(0.91)
Tang Book Value Per Share	6.17	7.00	8.82	7.86	6.99	6.40	6.39	5.82
Dividends Per Share	0.840	0.830	0.762	0.680	0.444	0.653	0.377	0.314
Dividend Payout %	311.11	184.44	53.28	34.48	26.63	38.50	28.93	30.00
Income Statement								
Income Before Taxes	(1,690)	8,852	45,487	65,119	52,354	51,319	40,863	33,721
Income Taxes	(2,031)	(1,103)	11,662	18,207	13,796	13,727	11,396	9,288
Net Income	341	10,357	33,203	46,912	38,558	37,592	29,467	24,398
Average Shares	22,768	22,830	23,272	23,797	23,042	22,115	22,619	23,345
Balance Sheet								
Total Assets	3,247,411	3,276,082	3,429,898	3,355,848	3,094,027	2,358,557	2,057,562	1,888,457
Total Liabilities	3,008,871	3,035,580	3,171,731	3,107,589	2,863,735	2,196,341	1,919,515	1,756,554
Stockholders' Equity	238,540	240,502	258,167	248,259	230,292	162,216	138,047	131,903
Shares Outstanding	23,015	22,647	22,864	23,090	23,367	21,574	21,613	22,662
Statistical Record								
Return on Assets %	0.20	0.31	0.98	1.45	1.41	1.70	1.49	1.33
Return on Equity %	2.63	4.15	13.11	19.61	19.59	25.04	21.83	18.75
Price Range	20.01-7.63	25.29-8.86	27.39-23.11	28.56-24.46	27.76-21.64	27.66-16.09	18.43-13.63	15.18-9.29
P/E Ratio	74.11-28.26	56.20-19.69	19.15-16.16	14.50-12.42	16.62-12.96	16.27-9.46	14.18-10.48	14.46-8.84
Average Yield %	6.67	5.33	3.04	2.53	1.82	3.05	2.32	2.58

Address: 230 West Main Street, P.O. Box 491, Ionia, MI 48846 **Telephone:** 616-527-9450 **Web Site:** www.ibcp.com	**Officers:** Charles C. Van Loan - Chairman William B. Kessel - President, Chief Executive Officer **Transfer Agents:** American Stock Transfer & Trust Company, New York, NY	**Investor Contact:** 616-527-9450 **No of Institutions:** 121 **Shares:** 12,135,785 **% Held:** 51.30

INTEGRYS ENERGY GROUP INC

Exchange	Symbol	Price	52Wk Range	Yield	P/E
NYS	TEG	$51.42 (5/29/2008)	55.90-44.76	5.21	15.87

*7 Year Price Score 83.60 ***NYSE Composite Index=100** ***12 Month Price Score 99.64**

Interim Earnings (Per Share)

Qtr.	Mar	Jun	Sep	Dec
2005	1.73	0.62	1.25	0.47
2006	1.48	0.83	0.91	0.47
2007	2.41	(0.22)	0.56	1.13
2008	1.77	...	...	...

Interim Dividends (Per Share)

Amt	Decl	Ex	Rec	Pay
0.66Q	07/16/2007	08/29/2007	08/31/2007	09/20/2007
0.66Q	10/24/2007	11/28/2007	11/30/2007	12/20/2007
0.67Q	02/18/2008	02/27/2008	02/29/2008	03/20/2008
0.67Q	04/15/2008	05/28/2008	05/30/2008	06/20/2008

Indicated Div: $2.68

Valuation Analysis
Forecast EPS $3.80 (05/16/2008)

Market Cap	$3.9 Billion	Book Value	3.4 Billion
Price/Book	1.16	Price/Sales	0.34

Dividend Achiever Status
10 Year Growth Rate	2.93%
Total Years of Dividend Growth	49

Business Summary: Electricity (MIC: SIC: 4931 NAIC: 221121)

Integrys Energy Group is a holding company with regulated utility operations operating through six subsidiaries, Wisconsin Public Service Corporation, The Peoples Gas Light and Coke Company, North Shore Gas Company, Upper Peninsula Power Company, Michigan Gas Utilities Corporation and Minnesota Energy Resources Corporation; nonregulated energy operations through its Integrys Energy Services subsidiary; and a 34.5% equity ownership interest in American Transmission Company LLC, an electric transmission company operating in Wisconsin, Michigan, Minnesota and Illinois. At Dec 31 2007, Co. served 485,000 regulated electric utility customers and 1,674,000 regulated natural gas utility customers.

Recent Developments: For the quarter ended Mar 31 2008, income from continuing operations increased 16.6% to US$136.6 million from US$117.2 million in the year-earlier quarter. Net income decreased 2.6% to US$136.6 million from US$140.2 million in the year-earlier quarter. Revenues were US$3.99 billion, up 45.2% from US$2.75 billion the year before. Operating income was US$234.7 million versus US$183.1 million in the prior-year quarter, an increase of 28.2%. Direct operating expenses rose 47.0% to US$3.68 billion from US$2.50 billion in the comparable period the year before. Indirect operating expenses increased 25.8% to US$77.1 million from US$61.3 million in the equivalent prior-year period.

Prospects: Co.'s long-term diluted earnings per share growth rate target remains at 6.0% to 8.0% on an average annualized basis. Notably, Co. anticipates 2008 earnings of $3.37 to $3.82 per diluted share, excluding the effect of mark-to-market volatility. Separately, on Apr 22 2008, Co. announced that it has agreed to purchase a 99-megawatt wind generation facility to be constructed in Howard County, IA, with closing of the sale to occur in the third quarter of 2008. The construction is scheduled to begin late in 2008 or early in 2009. The wind farm should be operational late in Dec 2009, in order to meet Co.'s target of generating 10.0% of its retail electrical sales with renewable power by 2015.

Financial Data

(US$ in Thousands)	3 Mos	12/31/2007	12/31/2006	12/31/2005	12/31/2004	12/31/2003	12/31/2002	12/31/2001
Earnings Per Share	3.24	3.50	3.67	4.07	3.72	2.85	3.42	2.74
Cash Flow Per Share	5.37	3.33	1.72	1.63	6.48	1.89	6.12	5.07
Tang Book Value Per Share	31.05	29.97	28.35	32.76	29.30	27.39	24.43	22.73
Dividends Per Share	2.650	2.563	2.280	2.240	2.200	2.160	2.120	2.080
Dividend Payout %	81.73	73.23	62.13	55.04	59.14	75.79	61.99	75.91
Income Statement								
Total Revenue	3,989,200	10,292,400	6,890,700	6,962,700	4,890,600	4,321,300	2,674,900	2,675,500
EBITDA	309,100	452,600	313,800	271,500	230,900	186,700	246,000	141,300
Depn & Amortn	56,300	21,000	18,000	62,700	44,700	42,400	50,600	...
Income Before Taxes	214,900	267,100	196,600	208,800	186,200	144,300	137,300	85,500
Income Taxes	78,300	86,000	45,000	46,700	30,000	33,700	24,800	4,800
Net Income	136,600	254,400	158,900	160,500	142,800	97,800	112,500	80,700
Average Shares	76,800	71,800	42,400	38,700	37,600	33,200	31,700	28,300
Balance Sheet								
Net PPE	4,470,800	4,463,800	2,534,800	2,049,400	2,002,600	1,828,700	1,610,200	1,463,600
Total Assets	12,378,900	11,234,400	6,861,700	5,455,200	4,445,600	4,292,300	3,207,900	2,870,000
Long-Term Obligations	2,263,400	2,265,100	1,287,200	867,100	865,700	871,900	824,400	727,800
Total Liabilities	9,009,400	7,947,500	5,277,000	4,115,100	3,302,700	3,238,000	2,324,000	2,053,000
Stockholders' Equity	3,369,500	3,286,900	1,584,700	1,355,300	1,142,900	1,054,300	833,900	767,000
Shares Outstanding	76,340	76,330	43,375	39,807	37,259	36,621	32,040	31,496
Statistical Record								
Return on Assets %	2.15	2.81	2.58	3.24	3.26	2.61	3.70	2.84
Return on Equity %	7.58	10.44	10.81	12.85	12.96	10.36	14.05	11.86
EBITDA Margin %	7.75	4.40	4.55	3.90	4.72	4.32	9.20	5.28
Net Margin %	3.42	2.47	2.31	2.31	2.92	2.26	4.21	3.02
PPE Turnover	2.63	2.94	3.01	3.44	2.55	2.51	1.74	2.01
Asset Turnover	0.99	1.14	1.12	1.41	1.12	1.15	0.88	0.94
Debt to Equity	0.67	0.69	0.81	0.64	0.76	0.83	0.99	0.95
Price Range	60.21-44.76	60.21-49.06	57.43-47.63	59.40-47.84	50.32-43.52	46.77-37.12	42.45-31.52	36.55-31.82
P/E Ratio	18.58-13.81	17.20-14.02	15.65-12.98	14.59-11.75	13.53-11.70	16.41-13.02	12.41-9.22	13.34-11.61
Average Yield %	5.13	4.82	4.43	4.10	4.68	5.27	5.55	6.08

Address: 130 East Randolph Drive, Chicago, IL 60601	Officers: Larry L. Weyers - President, Chief Executive Officer Thomas P. Meinz - Executive Vice	Investor Contact: 920-433-1857 No of Institutions: 358
Telephone: 312-228-5400 Web Site: www.integrysgroup.com	President Transfer Agents: American Stock Transfer & Trust Company, New York, NY	Shares: 38,841,240 % Held: N/A

148

INTERNATIONAL BUSINESS MACHINES CORP.

Exchange	Symbol	Price	52Wk Range	Yield	P/E
NYS	IBM	$129.71 (5/29/2008)	129.71-97.59	1.54	17.02

*7 Year Price Score 94.58   *NYSE Composite Index=100   *12 Month Price Score 111.67

Interim Earnings (Per Share)

Qtr.	Mar	Jun	Sep	Dec
2005	0.84	1.12	0.94	1.97
2006	1.08	1.30	1.45	2.30
2007	1.21	1.55	1.68	2.76
2008	1.65	...	...	...

Interim Dividends (Per Share)

Amt	Decl	Ex	Rec	Pay
0.40Q	07/31/2007	08/08/2007	08/10/2007	09/10/2007
0.40Q	10/30/2007	11/07/2007	11/09/2007	12/10/2007
0.40Q	01/29/2008	02/06/2008	02/08/2008	03/10/2008
0.50Q	04/29/2008	05/07/2008	05/09/2008	06/10/2008
		Indicated Div: $2.00		

Valuation Analysis

Forecast EPS $8.52 (05/17/2008)

Market Cap	$178.2 Billion	Book Value	28.7 Billion
Price/Book	6.20	Price/Sales	1.76

Dividend Achiever Status

10 Year Growth Rate	14.49%
Total Years of Dividend Growth	12

TRADING VOLUME (thousand shares)

Business Summary: IT & Technology (MIC: SIC: 3571 NAIC: 334111)

International Business Machines is a worldwide information technology company which primarily provides a variety of business products and services through the utilization of information technology. Co.'s primary operations comprise a Global Technology Services segment, which primarily reflects Internet Technology infrastructure services and business process services; a Global Business Services segment, which primarily reflects professional services and application outsourcing services; a Software segment, which consists primarily of middleware and operating systems software; a Systems and Technology that provides business applications; and a Global Financing segment.

Recent Developments: For the quarter ended Mar 31 2008, income from continuing operations increased 25.8% to US$2.32 billion from US$1.84 billion in the year-earlier quarter. Net income increased 25.8% to US$2.32 billion from US$1.84 billion in the year-earlier quarter. Revenues were US$24.50 billion, up 11.2% from US$22.03 billion the year before. Direct operating expenses rose 8.9% to US$14.34 billion from US$13.16 billion in the comparable period the year before. Indirect operating expenses increased 8.1% to US$6.91 billion from US$6.39 billion in the equivalent prior-year period.

Prospects: Going forward, Co. will continue to pursue acquisitions to expand its capabilities. For instance, on Apr 3 2008, Co. announced the acquisition of Telelogic AB for a total transaction value of approximately $845.0 million. Specifically, Co. believes that this transaction complements both its acquisition strategy and capital allocation structure, and should contribute towards its objective for earnings-per-share growth through 2010. Separately, on Apr 29 2008, Co. announced the acquisition of InfoDyne Corporation, a privately held software company based in Park Ridge, IL. Co. believes that this transaction should expand its existing software products for the financial markets industry.

Financial Data

(US$ in Thousands)	3 Mos	12/31/2007	12/31/2006	12/31/2005	12/31/2004	12/31/2003	12/31/2002	12/31/2001
Earnings Per Share	7.62	7.18	6.11	4.87	4.93	4.32	2.06	4.35
Cash Flow Per Share	12.47	11.31	9.81	9.32	9.17	8.46	8.10	8.23
Tang Book Value Per Share	5.08	8.72	8.93	13.97	11.86	11.54	10.03	12.40
Dividends Per Share	1.600	1.500	1.100	0.780	0.700	0.630	0.590	0.550
Dividend Payout %	20.99	20.89	18.00	16.02	14.20	14.58	28.64	12.64
Income Statement								
Total Revenue	24,502,000	98,786,000	91,424,000	91,134,000	96,293,000	89,131,000	81,186,000	85,866,000
EBITDA	4,589,000	19,736,000	18,042,000	17,327,000	16,902,000	15,568,000	12,048,000	16,011,000
Depn & Amortn	1,347,000	5,201,000	4,983,000	5,188,000	4,915,000	4,701,000	4,379,000	4,820,000
Income Before Taxes	3,198,000	14,489,000	13,317,000	12,226,000	12,028,000	10,874,000	7,524,000	10,953,000
Income Taxes	879,000	4,071,000	3,901,000	4,232,000	3,580,000	3,261,000	2,190,000	3,230,000
Net Income	2,319,000	10,418,000	9,492,000	7,934,000	8,430,000	7,583,000	3,579,000	7,723,000
Average Shares	1,404,322	1,450,570	1,553,535	1,627,632	1,708,872	1,756,090	1,730,941	1,771,230
Balance Sheet								
Current Assets	48,425,000	53,177,000	44,660,000	45,661,000	46,970,000	44,998,000	41,652,000	42,461,000
Total Assets	121,823,000	120,431,000	103,234,000	105,748,000	109,183,000	104,457,000	96,484,000	88,313,000
Current Liabilities	47,048,000	44,310,000	40,091,000	35,152,000	39,798,000	37,900,000	34,550,000	35,119,000
Long-Term Obligations	19,951,000	23,039,000	13,780,000	15,425,000	14,828,000	16,986,000	19,986,000	15,963,000
Total Liabilities	93,095,000	91,962,000	74,728,000	72,650,000	79,436,000	76,593,000	73,702,000	64,699,000
Stockholders' Equity	28,728,000	28,470,000	28,506,000	33,098,000	29,747,000	27,864,000	22,782,000	23,614,000
Shares Outstanding	1,373,478	1,385,234	1,506,482	1,573,979	1,645,592	1,694,508	1,722,366	1,723,193
Statistical Record								
Return on Assets %	9.73	9.32	9.08	7.38	7.87	7.55	3.87	8.74
Return on Equity %	38.44	36.57	30.82	25.25	29.19	29.95	15.43	34.92
EBITDA Margin %	18.73	19.98	19.73	19.01	17.55	17.47	14.84	18.65
Net Margin %	9.46	10.55	10.38	8.71	8.75	8.51	4.41	8.99
Asset Turnover	0.90	0.88	0.87	0.85	0.90	0.89	0.88	0.97
Current Ratio	1.03	1.20	1.11	1.30	1.18	1.19	1.21	1.21
Debt to Equity	0.69	0.81	0.48	0.47	0.50	0.61	0.88	0.68
Price Range	119.60-94.29	119.60-90.90	97.20-73.57	98.58-72.01	100.19-82.21	93.98-75.18	125.60-55.07	123.89-84.81
P/E Ratio	15.70-12.37	16.66-12.66	15.91-12.04	20.24-14.79	20.32-16.68	21.75-17.40	60.97-26.73	28.48-19.50
Average Yield %	1.47	1.42	1.32	0.93	0.77	0.74	0.70	0.51

Address: One New Orchard Road, Armonk, NY 10504 **Telephone:** 914-499-1900 **Web Site:** www.ibm.com	Officers: Samuel J. Palmisano - Chairman, President, Chief Executive Officer Nicholas M. Donofrio - Executive Vice President **Transfer Agents:** Computershare Trust Company, N.A., Providence, RI	Investor Contact: 888-421-8860 **No of Institutions:** 1578 **Shares:** 989,138,176 % **Held:** 62.18

IRWIN FINANCIAL CORP. (COLUMBUS, IN)

Exchange	Symbol	Price	52Wk Range	Yield	P/E
NYS	IFC	$4.31 (5/29/2008)	16.17-4.27	N/A	N/A

*7 Year Price Score 36.53 ***NYSE Composite Index=100** ***12 Month Price Score 57.84**

TRADING VOLUME (thousand shares)

Interim Earnings (Per Share)

Qtr.	Mar	Jun	Sep	Dec
2005	0.13	(0.04)	0.61	0.22
2006	(0.07)	0.09	(0.14)	0.17
2007	(0.36)	(0.03)	(0.64)	(0.91)
2008	(0.77)	...	...	...

Interim Dividends (Per Share)

Amt	Decl	Ex	Rec	Pay
0.12Q	02/15/2007	03/14/2007	03/16/2007	03/30/2007
0.12Q	05/10/2007	06/13/2007	06/15/2007	06/29/2007
0.12Q	08/31/2007	09/12/2007	09/14/2007	09/28/2007
0.12Q	10/23/2007	12/12/2007	12/14/2007	12/28/2007

Valuation Analysis

Forecast EPS $-1.45 (05/16/2008)

Market Cap	$126.1 Million	Book Value	436.0 Million
Price/Book	0.29	Price/Sales	0.24

Dividend Achiever Status

10 Year Growth Rate	13.11%
Total Years of Dividend Growth	18

Business Summary: Commercial Banking (MIC: SIC: 6022 NAIC: 522110)

Irwin Financial is a bank holding company which is engaged primarily in the extension of credit to consumers and small businesses as well as providing the ongoing servicing of those customer accounts. Through its subsidiaries, Co. operates three primary lines of business: commercial banking through Irwin Union Bank & Trust Company and Irwin Union Bank, F.S.B.; commercial finance through Irwin Commercial Finance Corporation; as well as home equity lending through Irwin Home Equity Corporation. Also, Co. is engaged in conducting part of its finance line of business in Canadian markets. As of Dec 31 2007, Co. had $6.17 billion in assets and $3.33 billion in deposits.

Recent Developments: For the quarter ended Mar 31 2008, loss from continuing operations was US$22.2 million compared with a loss of US$6.1 million in the year-earlier quarter. Net loss amounted to US$22.2 million versus a net loss of US$10.1 million in the year-earlier quarter. Net interest income decreased 2.6% to US$64.4 million from US$66.1 million in the year-earlier quarter. Provision for loan losses was US$44.5 million versus US$23.2 million in the prior-year quarter, an increase of 91.8%. Non-interest income was US$4.5 million versus US$814,000, while non-interest expense declined 0.6% to US$52.0 million.

Prospects: Co. is refocusing on its core banking services to small business customers. Thus, Co. has suspended originations in its home equity segment of loans for its own portfolio, including second mortgages. Co. noted that the home equity segment is now focused on government-insured and conforming, conventional first mortgage loans that can be sold into the secondary markets. Co. has also engaged Stifel, Nicolaus & Company, Incorporated and Milestone Advisors, LLC to explore alternatives to achieve its strategic refocusing objectives and resolve its home equity loan exposure. Co. stated that these steps could include but are not limited to sales of loans, a spin off of assets, or a recapitalization.

Financial Data

(US$ in Thousands)	3 Mos	12/31/2007	12/31/2006	12/31/2005	12/31/2004	12/31/2003	12/31/2002	12/31/2001
Earnings Per Share	(2.35)	(1.94)	0.05	0.66	2.32	2.45	1.89	2.00
Cash Flow Per Share	14.20	14.64	34.94	(8.81)	0.55	21.38	(24.11)	(12.84)
Tang Book Value Per Share	13.75	15.22	17.35	17.90	17.67	15.36	12.98	10.84
Dividends Per Share	0.360	0.480	0.440	0.400	0.320	0.280	0.270	0.260
Dividend Payout %	...	...	880.00	60.61	13.79	11.43	14.29	13.00
Income Statement								
Interest Income	120,090	513,029	482,128	422,258	344,303	370,984	311,442	268,233
Interest Expense	55,655	250,636	224,689	156,368	92,225	99,099	97,795	121,084
Net Interest Income	64,435	262,393	257,439	265,890	252,078	271,885	213,647	147,149
Provision for Losses	44,520	134,988	35,101	26,852	14,195	47,583	43,996	17,505
Non-Interest Income	(4,456)	27,384	44,621	120,486	287,050	329,299	257,433	271,391
Non-Interest Expense	51,954	199,767	210,688	331,555	407,235	435,199	340,853	327,420
Income Before Taxes	(36,495)	(44,978)	56,271	27,969	117,698	118,402	86,231	73,615
Income Taxes	(14,329)	(20,848)	18,870	8,982	47,794	45,585	33,398	28,624
Net Income	(22,166)	(54,673)	1,727	18,987	69,904	72,817	53,328	45,516
Average Shares	29,249	29,353	29,690	28,841	31,278	30,850	29,675	24,173
Balance Sheet								
Net Loans & Leases	5,427,687	5,557,509	5,401,235	5,732,599	4,296,708	3,980,664	4,079,189	2,619,221
Total Assets	6,057,067	6,166,105	6,237,958	6,646,524	5,239,341	4,988,359	4,884,722	3,439,795
Total Deposits	3,398,992	3,325,488	3,551,516	3,898,993	3,395,263	2,899,662	2,694,344	2,309,018
Total Liabilities	5,621,061	5,706,805	5,707,456	6,134,190	4,736,697	4,556,099	4,523,311	3,207,472
Stockholders' Equity	436,006	459,300	530,502	512,334	502,644	432,260	360,555	232,323
Shares Outstanding	29,259	29,226	29,736	28,618	28,452	28,134	27,771	21,305
Statistical Record								
Return on Assets %	N.M.	N.M.	0.03	0.32	1.36	1.48	1.28	1.55
Return on Equity %	N.M.	N.M.	0.33	3.74	14.91	18.37	17.99	21.56
Net Interest Margin %	53.66	51.15	53.40	62.97	73.21	73.29	68.60	54.86
Efficiency Ratio %	44.93	36.97	40.00	61.09	64.50	62.15	59.92	60.68
Loans to Deposits	1.60	1.67	1.52	1.47	1.27	1.37	1.51	1.13
Price Range	18.47-4.56	22.94-7.35	22.94-18.01	28.39-19.72	35.95-23.20	31.99-16.10	20.36-13.90	27.50-14.51
P/E Ratio	...	...	458.80-360.20	43.02-29.88	15.50-10.00	13.06-6.57	10.77-7.35	13.75-7.25
Average Yield %	3.22	3.32	2.17	1.81	1.18	1.20	1.58	1.22

Address: 500 Washington Street, Columbus, IN 47201	Officers: William I. Miller - Chairman, President, Chief Executive Officer Gregory F. Ehlinger - Senior Vice President, Chief Financial Officer **Transfer Agents:** National City Bank	Investor Contact: 812-376-1909
Telephone: 812-376-1909		No of Institutions: 109
Web Site: www.irwinfinancial.com		Shares: 12,695,208 % Held: 41.12

JACK HENRY & ASSOCIATES, INC.

Exchange	Symbol	Price	52Wk Range	Yield	P/E
NMS	JKHY	$23.52 (5/29/2008)	29.22-22.33	1.28	19.60

*7 Year Price Score 97.14 ***NYSE Composite Index=100** ***12 Month Price Score 101.23**

Interim Earnings (Per Share)

Qtr.	Sep	Dec	Mar	Jun
2004-05	0.18	0.19	0.21	0.23
2005-06	0.21	0.23	0.25	0.27
2006-07	0.23	0.30	0.29	0.32
2007-08	0.26	0.32	0.30	...

Interim Dividends (Per Share)

Amt	Decl	Ex	Rec	Pay
0.065Q	08/27/2007	09/05/2007	09/07/2007	09/21/2007
0.065Q	10/31/2007	11/09/2007	11/14/2007	12/04/2007
0.075Q	02/04/2008	02/14/2008	02/19/2008	03/06/2008
0.075Q	05/12/2008	05/15/2008	05/19/2008	05/29/2008

Indicated Div: $0.30 (Div. Reinv. Plan)

Valuation Analysis

Forecast EPS	$1.20 (05/16/2008)		
Market Cap	$2.1 Billion	Book Value	608.8 Million
Price/Book	3.38	Price/Sales	2.80

Dividend Achiever Status

10 Year Growth Rate	16.89%
Total Years of Dividend Growth	16

Business Summary: IT & Technology (MIC: SIC: 7373 NAIC: 541512)

Jack Henry & Associates provides integrated computer systems for in-house as well as outsourced data processing to commercial banks, credit unions and other financial institutions. Co. also performs data conversion and software implementation services for its systems and provide continuing customer support services after the systems are implemented. For customers who prefer not to make an up-front capital investment in software and hardware, Co. provides its products and services on an outsourced basis through its eight data centers and 23 item-processing centers located throughout the U.S., as of June 30 2007. Co. has three marketed brands: Jack Henry Banking, Symitar and ProfitStars.

Recent Developments: For the quarter ended Mar 31 2008, net income increased 0.9% to US$26.6 million from US$26.4 million in the year-earlier quarter. Revenues were US$187.9 million, up 11.3% from US$168.9 million the year before. Operating income was US$42.3 million versus US$40.8 million in the prior-year quarter, an increase of 3.6%. Direct operating expenses rose 14.1% to US$111.0 million from US$97.2 million in the comparable period the year before. Indirect operating expenses increased 12.3% to US$34.7 million from US$30.9 million in the equivalent prior-year period.

Prospects: Co.'s outlook appears favorable, reflecting continued steady gains in revenue. In detail, Co.'s improved top-line performance is being positively driven by strong support and services revenue as well as higher license revenue primarily attributable to strong sales of Episys®, its core processing system aimed at larger credit unions. Also, Co. is benefiting from stronger sales of Yellow Hammer® BSA, its new compliance and risk mitigation application. Notably, both of these products continue to be the primary drivers of Co.'s license revenue growth during fiscal 2008. Furthermore, Co. noted that it had backlog of $249,000 at Mar 31 2008 compared with $221,200 at the same period in 2007.

Financial Data

(US$ in Thousands)	9 Mos	6 Mos	3 Mos	06/30/2007	06/30/2006	06/30/2005	06/30/2004	06/30/2003
Earnings Per Share	1.20	1.19	1.17	1.14	0.96	0.81	0.68	0.55
Cash Flow Per Share	2.05	1.92	2.04	1.93	1.85	1.19	1.26	1.13
Tang Book Value Per Share	2.03	2.28	2.51	2.53	2.76	2.45	3.06	2.78
Dividends Per Share	0.270	0.260	0.250	0.240	0.200	0.170	0.150	0.140
Dividend Payout %	22.57	21.85	21.37	21.05	20.83	20.99	22.06	25.45
Income Statement								
Total Revenue	555,458	367,552	175,326	668,062	592,205	535,863	467,415	404,627
EBITDA	170,154	111,780	50,208	209,508	183,131	157,980	132,346	107,465
Depn & Amortn	46,245	30,122	14,405	50,954	43,774	38,911	33,540	30,194
Income Before Taxes	125,094	83,159	37,069	160,203	140,068	119,843	99,705	77,791
Income Taxes	45,792	30,469	13,530	55,522	50,145	44,342	37,390	28,394
Net Income	79,302	52,690	23,539	104,681	89,923	75,501	62,315	49,397
Average Shares	88,907	90,922	90,833	92,032	93,787	92,998	91,859	89,270
Balance Sheet								
Current Assets	215,963	208,610	237,669	350,385	306,410	260,293	259,058	217,262
Total Assets	915,595	907,805	901,852	999,340	906,067	814,153	653,644	548,575
Current Liabilities	223,459	204,162	210,189	330,477	263,492	246,583	173,240	146,780
Total Liabilities	306,820	277,602	285,246	400,975	330,855	296,999	210,696	183,352
Stockholders' Equity	608,775	630,203	616,606	598,365	575,212	517,154	442,918	365,223
Shares Outstanding	87,400	89,134	89,399	89,102	91,189	91,497	90,204	88,156
Statistical Record								
Return on Assets %	12.35	12.45	12.40	10.99	10.45	10.29	10.34	9.55
Return on Equity %	18.00	17.89	17.92	17.84	16.46	15.73	15.38	13.99
EBITDA Margin %	30.63	30.41	28.64	31.36	30.92	29.48	28.31	26.56
Net Margin %	14.28	14.34	13.43	15.67	15.18	14.09	13.33	12.21
Asset Turnover	0.84	0.83	0.80	0.70	0.69	0.73	0.78	0.78
Current Ratio	0.97	1.02	1.13	1.06	1.16	1.06	1.50	1.48
Price Range	29.22-22.77	29.22-20.97	27.35-20.97	26.52-17.63	23.67-17.29	21.76-17.15	21.97-16.53	17.79-8.31
P/E Ratio	24.35-18.98	24.55-17.62	23.38-17.92	23.26-15.46	24.66-18.01	26.86-21.17	32.31-24.31	32.35-15.11
Average Yield %	1.06	1.04	1.05	1.08	1.00	0.89	0.79	1.07

Address: 663 Highway 60, P.O. Box 807, Monett, MO 65708 **Telephone:** 417-235-6652 **Web Site:** www.jackhenry.com	Officers: Michael E. Henry - Chairman John W. Henry - Vice-Chairman **Transfer Agents:** Boston Equiserve, Boston, MA	Investor Contact: 417-235-6652 No of Institutions: 263 **Shares:** 77,744,176 % Held: 82.69

JOHNSON CONTROLS INC

Exchange	Symbol	Price	52Wk Range	Yield	P/E
NYS	JCI	$33.84 (5/29/2008)	44.42-31.05	1.54	14.71

*7 Year Price Score 130.97 *NYSE Composite Index=100 *12 Month Price Score 95.71

Interim Earnings (Per Share)

Qtr.	Dec	Mar	Jun	Sep
2004-05	0.29	0.35	0.44	0.49
2005-06	0.28	0.28	0.57	0.61
2006-07	0.27	0.38	0.66	0.77
2007-08	0.39	0.48	...	...

Interim Dividends (Per Share)

Amt	Decl	Ex	Rec	Pay
0.11Q	07/25/2007	09/12/2007	09/14/2007	10/02/2007
0.13Q	11/14/2007	12/12/2007	12/14/2007	01/03/2008
0.13Q	01/23/2008	03/12/2008	03/14/2008	04/02/2008
0.13Q	05/20/2008	06/11/2008	06/13/2008	07/03/2008

Indicated Div: $0.52 (Div. Reinv. Plan)

Valuation Analysis

Forecast EPS $2.46 (05/16/2008)

Market Cap	$20.1 Billion	Book Value	9.6 Billion
Price/Book	2.09	Price/Sales	0.55

Dividend Achiever Status

10 Year Growth Rate	11.87%
Total Years of Dividend Growth	32

Business Summary: Automotive (MIC: SIC: 2531 NAIC: 336360)

Johnson Controls operates in three primary businesses. The Building Efficiency business is engaged in designing, producing, marketing and installing Heating, Ventilation, & Air Conditioning (HVAC) equipment and building control systems that monitor, automate and integrate critical building operating equipment and conditions. The Automotive Experience is engaged in providing seating, instrument panel, overhead, floor console and door systems. The Power Solutions business services both automotive original equipment manufacturers and the general vehicle battery aftermarket by providing improved battery technology, coupled with systems engineering, marketing and enhanced services.

Recent Developments: For the quarter ended Mar 31 2008, income from continuing operations increased 10.3% to US$289.0 million from US$262.0 million in the year-earlier quarter. Net income increased 26.8% to US$289.0 million from US$228.0 million in the year-earlier quarter. Revenues were US$9.41 billion, up 10.8% from US$8.49 billion the year before. Direct operating expenses rose 10.9% to US$8.10 billion from US$7.30 billion in the comparable period the year before. Indirect operating expenses increased 3.1% to US$888.0 million from US$861.0 million in the equivalent prior-year period.

Prospects: For third fiscal quarter ending June 2008, Co. is expecting diluted earnings per share from continuing operations to increase 12.0% to 15.0%, to $0.74 to $0.76, excluding the potential effect on vehicle production from a prolonged labor strike of a supplier to a North American automotive customer. Meanwhile, for the full fiscal year ending Sept 30 2008, Co. continues to project an increase in diluted earnings per share from continuing operations of approximately 18.0% to a range of $2.45 to $2.50 from $2.10 per diluted share in 2007. Further, Co. is raising its revenue forecast for 2008 and expects sales to grow 13.0% to $39.00 billion, versus its previous guidance of $38.00 billion.

Financial Data
(US$ in Thousands)

	6 Mos	3 Mos	09/30/2007	09/30/2006	09/30/2005	09/30/2004	09/30/2003	09/30/2002
Earnings Per Share	2.30	2.20	2.09	1.74	1.56	1.41	1.20	1.06
Cash Flow Per Share	3.00	3.27	3.24	2.43	1.61	2.64	1.43	1.86
Tang Book Value Per Share	4.05	3.44	3.37	1.10	3.52	1.94	1.27	0.75
Dividends Per Share	0.480	0.460	0.440	0.373	0.333	0.300	0.240	0.220
Dividend Payout %	20.91	20.88	21.05	21.41	21.37	21.23	20.00	20.79
Income Statement								
Total Revenue	18,890,000	9,484,000	34,624,000	32,235,000	27,479,400	26,553,400	22,646,000	20,103,400
EBITDA	1,212,000	496,000	2,339,000	2,091,000	1,747,200	1,922,300	1,718,800	1,632,800
Depn & Amortn	385,000	191,000	732,000	705,000	636,300	613,400	557,800	516,400
Income Before Taxes	692,000	305,000	1,607,000	1,138,000	1,003,400	1,212,100	1,057,500	1,006,000
Income Taxes	145,000	64,000	300,000	63,000	205,100	315,700	327,800	347,600
Net Income	524,000	235,000	1,252,000	1,028,000	909,400	817,500	682,900	600,500
Average Shares	600,700	602,900	599,200	589,800	582,900	577,800	567,600	564,600
Balance Sheet								
Current Assets	10,609,000	10,229,000	10,872,000	9,264,000	7,138,800	6,376,800	5,620,300	4,946,200
Total Assets	24,619,000	23,803,000	24,105,000	21,921,000	16,144,400	15,090,800	13,127,300	11,165,300
Current Liabilities	9,513,000	9,252,000	9,920,000	8,146,000	6,841,400	6,601,600	5,584,100	4,806,200
Long-Term Obligations	3,301,000	3,249,000	3,255,000	4,166,000	1,577,500	1,630,600	1,776,600	1,826,600
Total Liabilities	15,024,000	14,733,000	15,198,000	14,566,000	10,086,300	9,884,500	8,866,000	7,665,600
Stockholders' Equity	9,595,000	9,070,000	8,907,000	7,355,000	6,058,100	5,206,300	4,261,300	3,499,700
Shares Outstanding	593,417	593,770	593,766	587,321	578,612	570,962	540,932	533,280
Statistical Record								
Return on Assets %	5.87	5.76	5.44	5.40	5.82	5.78	5.62	5.70
Return on Equity %	15.87	15.92	15.40	15.33	16.15	17.22	17.60	18.52
EBITDA Margin %	6.42	5.23	6.76	6.49	6.36	7.24	7.59	8.12
Net Margin %	2.77	2.48	3.62	3.19	3.31	3.08	3.02	2.99
Asset Turnover	1.56	1.56	1.50	1.69	1.76	1.88	1.86	1.91
Current Ratio	1.12	1.11	1.10	1.14	1.04	0.97	1.01	1.03
Debt to Equity	0.34	0.36	0.37	0.57	0.26	0.31	0.42	0.52
Price Range	44.42-31.05	44.42-28.25	42.12-23.98	30.00-20.09	21.28-17.64	20.30-15.77	16.78-11.75	15.51-10.92
P/E Ratio	19.31-13.50	20.19-12.84	20.15-11.47	17.24-11.55	13.64-11.31	14.40-11.18	13.98-9.79	14.63-10.30
Average Yield %	1.31	1.28	1.33	1.51	1.71	1.62	1.71	1.61

Address: 5757 North Green Bay Avenue, P.O. Box 591, Milwaukee, WI 53201	Officers: Keith E. Wandell - President, Chief Operating Officer Stephen A. Roell - Chief Executive Officer **Transfer Agents:**	Investor Contact: 414-524-2363
Telephone: 414-524-1200	Wells Fargo Bank Minnesota, N.A., St. Paul, MN	**No of Institutions:** 702 **Shares:** 537,788,096 **% Held:** 74.98
Web Site: www.johnsoncontrols.com		

JOHNSON & JOHNSON

Exchange	Symbol	Price	52Wk Range	Yield	P/E
NYS	JNJ	$66.42 (5/29/2008)	68.40-59.77	2.77	16.52

*7 Year Price Score 83.82 ***NYSE Composite Index=100** ***12 Month Price Score 105.64**

Interim Earnings (Per Share)

Qtr.	Mar	Jun	Sep	Dec
2005	0.97	0.89	0.87	0.73
2006	1.10	0.95	0.94	0.74
2007	0.88	1.05	0.88	0.82
2008	1.26	...	...	...

Interim Dividends (Per Share)

Amt	Decl	Ex	Rec	Pay
0.415Q	07/16/2007	08/24/2007	08/28/2007	09/11/2007
0.415Q	10/18/2007	11/23/2007	11/27/2007	12/11/2007
0.415Q	01/02/2008	02/22/2008	02/26/2008	03/11/2008
0.46Q	04/24/2008	05/22/2008	05/27/2008	06/10/2008

Indicated Div: $1.84 (Div. Reinv. Plan)

Valuation Analysis

Forecast EPS $4.45 (05/16/2008)

Market Cap	$187.1 Billion	Book Value	45.6 Billion
Price/Book	4.10	Price/Sales	3.00

Dividend Achiever Status

10 Year Growth Rate	14.32%
Total Years of Dividend Growth	45

TRADING VOLUME (thousand shares)

Business Summary: Health (MIC: SIC: 2834 NAIC: 325412)

Johnson & Johnson is engaged in the research and development, manufacture and sale of a range of products in the health care field. As of Dec 31 2007, Co. operated through three segments. Co.'s Consumer segment includes a range of products used in the baby and child care, skin care, oral and wound care and women's health care fields, as well as nutritional and over-the-counter pharmaceutical products. Co.'s Pharmaceutical segment includes a range of products used in therapeutics areas. Co.'s Medical Devices and Diagnostics segment includes a range of products used primarily in the professional fields by physicians, nurses, therapists, hospitals, diagnostic laboratories and clinics.

Recent Developments: For the quarter ended Mar 30 2008, net income increased 39.8% to US$3.60 billion from US$2.57 billion in the year-earlier quarter. Revenues were US$16.19 billion, up 7.7% from US$15.04 billion the year before. Direct operating expenses rose 5.2% to US$4.61 billion from US$4.39 billion in the comparable period the year before. Indirect operating expenses decreased 2.4% to US$6.83 billion from US$7.00 billion in the equivalent prior-year period.

Prospects: Co.'s near-term outlook appears constructive. In detail, Co. will continue to focus on its restructuring initiatives implemented in 2007 to offset the anticipated negative effects associated with generic competition in its Pharmaceutical segment and challenges in the drug-eluting stent market. Hence, Co.'s Pharmaceuticals segment plans to reduce its cost by consolidating certain operations, while continuing to invest in recently launched products and its late-stage pipeline of new products. In addition, Co. is accelerating steps to streamline certain aspects of its enterprise functions, such as human resources, finance and information technology to support growth across the business.

Financial Data

(US$ in Millions)	3 Mos	12/30/2007	12/31/2006	01/01/2006	01/02/2005	12/28/2003	12/29/2002	12/30/2001
Earnings Per Share	4.02	3.63	3.73	3.46	2.84	2.40	2.16	1.84
Cash Flow Per Share	5.19	5.30	4.87	4.00	3.69	3.58	2.73	2.93
Tang Book Value Per Share	5.75	5.12	3.67	8.64	6.72	5.17	4.53	4.97
Dividends Per Share	1.660	1.620	1.455	1.275	1.095	0.925	0.795	0.700
Dividend Payout %	41.30	44.63	39.01	36.85	38.56	38.54	36.81	38.04
Income Statement								
Total Revenue	16,194	61,095	53,324	50,514	47,348	41,862	36,298	33,004
EBITDA	5,413	15,871	16,015	15,244	14,933	12,192	10,900	9,200
Depn & Amortn	666	2,744	2,194	2,021	2,103	1,854	1,705	1,605
Income Before Taxes	4,747	13,283	14,587	13,656	12,838	10,308	9,291	7,898
Income Taxes	1,149	2,707	3,534	3,245	4,329	3,111	2,694	2,230
Net Income	3,598	10,576	11,053	10,411	8,509	7,197	6,597	5,668
Average Shares	2,867	2,911	2,962	3,013	3,004	3,009	3,055	3,100
Balance Sheet								
Current Assets	33,818	29,945	22,975	31,394	27,320	22,995	19,266	18,473
Total Assets	85,995	80,954	70,556	58,025	53,317	48,263	40,556	38,488
Current Liabilities	22,071	19,837	19,161	12,635	13,927	13,448	11,449	8,044
Long-Term Obligations	7,166	7,074	2,014	2,017	2,565	2,955	2,022	2,217
Total Liabilities	40,370	37,635	31,238	20,154	21,504	21,394	17,859	14,255
Stockholders' Equity	45,625	43,319	39,318	37,871	31,813	26,869	22,697	24,233
Shares Outstanding	2,818	2,841	2,894	2,975	2,972	2,969	2,969	3,048
Statistical Record								
Return on Assets %	14.62	14.00	17.24	18.75	16.48	16.25	16.74	16.28
Return on Equity %	26.87	25.67	28.72	29.96	28.53	29.12	28.19	26.41
EBITDA Margin %	33.43	25.98	30.03	30.18	31.54	29.12	30.03	27.88
Net Margin %	22.22	17.31	20.73	20.61	17.97	17.19	18.17	17.17
Asset Turnover	0.78	0.81	0.83	0.91	0.92	0.95	0.92	0.95
Current Ratio	1.53	1.51	1.20	2.48	1.96	1.71	1.68	2.30
Debt to Equity	0.16	0.16	0.05	0.05	0.08	0.11	0.09	0.09
Price Range	68.40-59.77	68.40-59.77	69.10-56.80	69.40-60.04	63.76-49.50	58.67-48.73	65.49-41.85	60.97-41.63
P/E Ratio	17.01-14.87	18.84-16.47	18.53-15.23	20.06-17.35	22.45-17.43	24.45-20.30	30.32-19.38	33.14-22.62
Average Yield %	2.60	2.53	2.34	1.97	1.96	1.76	1.38	1.35

Address: One Johnson & Johnson Plaza, New Brunswick, NJ 08933 **Telephone:** 732-524-0400 **Web Site:** www.jnj.com	**Officers:** William C. Weldon - Chairman, Chief Executive Officer Christine A. Poon - Vice-Chairman **Transfer Agents:** Computershare Trust Company, Canton, MA	**Investor Contact:** 735-524-2455 **No of Institutions:** 1822 **Shares:** 1,980,574,336 **% Held:** 63.73

KEYCORP

Exchange	Symbol	Price	52Wk Range	Yield	P/E
NYS	KEY	$20.00 (5/29/2008)	36.78-19.66	7.50	10.10

*7 Year Price Score 71.97 ***NYSE Composite Index=100** ***12 Month Price Score 84.43**

Interim Earnings (Per Share)

Qtr.	Mar	Jun	Sep	Dec
2005	0.64	0.70	0.67	0.72
2006	0.70	0.75	0.76	0.36
2007	0.87	0.84	0.54	0.07
2008	0.54	...	...	...

Interim Dividends (Per Share)

Amt	Decl	Ex	Rec	Pay
0.365Q	07/20/2007	08/24/2007	08/28/2007	09/14/2007
0.365Q	11/15/2007	11/23/2007	11/27/2007	12/14/2007
0.375Q	12/20/2007	02/29/2008	03/04/2008	03/14/2008
0.375Q	05/15/2008	05/22/2008	05/27/2008	06/13/2008

Indicated Div: $1.50 (Div. Reinv. Plan)

Valuation Analysis

Forecast EPS	$1.95 (05/17/2008)
Market Cap	$8.0 Billion Book Value 8.6 Billion
Price/Book	0.93 Price/Sales 1.04

Dividend Achiever Status

10 Year Growth Rate	5.68%
Total Years of Dividend Growth	28

TRADING VOLUME (thousand shares)

Business Summary: Commercial Banking (MIC: SIC: 6021 NAIC: 522110)

KeyCorp is a bank holding company. Through its subsidiaries, Co. provides retail and commercial banking, commercial leasing, investment management, consumer finance, and investment banking products and services to individual, corporate and institutional clients through two major business groups: Community Banking and National Banking. Also, Co.'s bank and trust company subsidiaries provide personal and corporate trust services, personal financial services, access to mutual funds, cash management services, investment banking and capital markets products, and international banking services. At Dec 31 2007, Co. had total assets of around $100.00 billion and total deposits of $63.10 billion.

Recent Developments: For the quarter ended Mar 31 2008, income from continuing operations decreased 39.1% to US$218.0 million from US$358.0 million in the year-earlier quarter. Net income decreased 37.7% to US$218.0 million from US$350.0 million in the year-earlier quarter. Net interest income increased 5.0% to US$713.0 million from US$679.0 million in the year-earlier quarter. Provision for loan losses was US$187.0 million versus US$44.0 million in the prior-year quarter, an increase of 325.0%. Non-interest income fell 19.3% to US$528.0 million from US$654.0 million, while non-interest expense declined 6.6% to US$732.0 million.

Prospects: For the rest of 2008, Co. expects net interest margin to be about 3.3% as it benefits from a modestly liability-sensitive interest rate risk position and new loans with better interest rate spreads. Meanwhile, for full year 2008, Co. foresees loans to increase in the low- to mid-single digit percentage range, excluding acquired balances. In addition, Co. is targeting a low single digit percentage improvement in core deposits, while net loan charge-offs are estimated to range from 0.65% to 0.9% of average loans. However, Co. is anticipating a low single digit percentage rise in expenses, excluding the 2007 charges for its liability to Visa and for losses on lending-related commitments.

Financial Data
(US$ in Thousands)

	3 Mos	12/31/2007	12/31/2006	12/31/2005	12/31/2004	12/31/2003	12/31/2002	12/31/2001
Earnings Per Share	1.98	2.32	2.57	2.73	2.30	2.12	2.27	0.31
Cash Flow Per Share	1.06	(0.50)	2.48	5.30	3.95	2.97	3.43	3.99
Tang Book Value Per Share	17.07	16.39	15.99	15.05	13.91	13.88	13.35	11.85
Dividends Per Share	1.470	1.460	1.380	1.300	1.240	1.220	1.200	1.180
Dividend Payout %	74.21	62.93	53.70	47.62	53.91	57.55	52.86	380.65
Income Statement								
Income Before Taxes	322,000	1,221,000	1,643,000	1,588,000	1,388,000	1,242,000	1,312,000	259,000
Income Taxes	104,000	280,000	450,000	459,000	434,000	339,000	336,000	102,000
Net Income	218,000	919,000	1,055,000	1,129,000	954,000	903,000	976,000	132,000
Average Shares	399,769	395,823	410,222	414,014	415,430	426,157	430,703	429,573
Balance Sheet								
Total Assets	101,492,000	99,983,000	92,337,000	93,126,000	90,739,000	84,487,000	85,202,000	80,938,000
Total Liabilities	92,900,000	92,237,000	84,634,000	85,528,000	83,622,000	77,518,000	78,367,000	74,783,000
Stockholders' Equity	8,592,000	7,746,000	7,703,000	7,598,000	7,117,000	6,969,000	6,835,000	6,155,000
Shares Outstanding	400,070	388,792	399,153	406,623	407,569	416,494	423,943	424,005
Statistical Record								
Return on Assets %	0.80	0.96	1.14	1.23	1.09	1.06	1.17	0.16
Return on Equity %	9.60	11.90	13.79	15.34	13.51	13.08	15.03	2.07
Price Range	38.58-20.50	39.79-21.91	38.60-33.13	34.83-30.81	34.46-28.43	29.32-22.52	29.00-21.30	28.44-20.75
P/E Ratio	19.48-10.35	17.15-9.44	15.02-12.89	12.76-11.29	14.98-12.36	13.83-10.62	12.78-9.38	91.73-66.94
Average Yield %	4.86	4.32	3.78	3.94	3.97	4.71	4.66	4.75

Address: 127 Public Square, Cleveland, OH 44114-1306 **Telephone:** 216-689-6300 **Web Site:** www.key.com	**Officers:** Henry L. Meyer - Chairman, President, Chief Executive Officer Beth E. Mooney - Vice-Chairman **Transfer Agents:** ComputerShare Investor Services, Providence, RI	**No of Institutions:** 514 **Shares:** 246,724,992 **% Held:** 58.52

KIMBERLY-CLARK CORP.

Exchange	Symbol	Price	52Wk Range	Yield	P/E
NYS	KMB	$64.22 (5/29/2008)	71.98-62.35	3.61	15.55

*7 Year Price Score 85.81 *NYSE Composite Index=100 *12 Month Price Score 97.47

Interim Earnings (Per Share)

Qtr.	Mar	Jun	Sep	Dec
2005	0.93	0.88	0.68	0.79
2006	0.60	0.82	0.79	1.04
2007	0.98	1.00	1.04	1.06
2008	1.04	...	...	...

Interim Dividends (Per Share)

Amt	Decl	Ex	Rec	Pay
0.53Q	08/01/2007	09/05/2007	09/07/2007	10/02/2007
0.53Q	11/14/2007	12/05/2007	12/07/2007	01/03/2008
0.58Q	02/21/2008	03/05/2008	03/07/2008	04/02/2008
0.58Q	04/17/2008	06/04/2008	06/06/2008	07/02/2008

Indicated Div: $2.32 (Div. Reinv. Plan)

Valuation Analysis

Forecast EPS $4.52 (05/17/2008)

Market Cap	$26.9 Billion	Book Value	5.6 Billion
Price/Book	4.83	Price/Sales	1.44

Dividend Achiever Status

10 Year Growth Rate	8.15%
Total Years of Dividend Growth	33

TRADING VOLUME (thousand shares)

Business Summary: Paper Products (MIC: SIC: 2679 NAIC: 322299)

Kimberly-Clark is engaged in the manufacturing and marketing of a range of health and hygiene products around the world. Most of these products are made from natural or synthetic fibers using technologies in fibers, nonwovens and absorbency. Co. operates through the following four global business segments: Personal Care; Consumer Tissue; K-C Professional & Other; as well as Health Care. Co.'s products are sold under brands such as Huggies, Pull-Ups, Little Swimmers, GoodNites, Kotex, Lightdays, Depend, Poise, Kleenex, Scott, Cottonelle, Viva, Andrex, Scottex, Hakle, Page, Kimberly-Clark, WypAll, Kimtech, Kleenguard, Kimcare, Ballard as well as other brand names.

Recent Developments: For the quarter ended Mar 31 2008, net income decreased 2.5% to US$440.9 million from US$452.0 million in the year-earlier quarter. Revenues were US$4.81 billion, up 9.7% from US$4.39 billion the year before. Operating income was US$664.1 million versus US$616.1 million in the prior-year quarter, an increase of 7.8%. Direct operating expenses rose 10.7% to US$3.36 billion from US$3.03 billion in the comparable period the year before. Indirect operating expenses increased 7.5% to US$791.6 million from US$736.2 million in the equivalent prior-year period.

Prospects: Looking ahead, Co. expects favorable currency effects, at existing rates of exchange, to benefit sales comparisons. However, Co. anticipates inflation to continue to put pressure on its margins, mainly in light of recent increases in fiber and oil costs. However, Co. expects to generate strong bottom-line improvement for 2008, as it focuses on improving revenue realization and reducing costs. Notably, Co. estimates net workforce reduction of about 10.0%, or about 6,000 employees by the end of 2008. In the meantime, Co. plans to continue to support its growth and further strengthen its competitive position with higher levels of spending for strategic marketing and customer development.

Financial Data

(US$ in Thousands)	3 Mos	12/31/2007	12/31/2006	12/31/2005	12/31/2004	12/31/2003	12/31/2002	12/31/2001
Earnings Per Share	4.13	4.09	3.25	3.28	3.61	3.33	3.22	3.02
Cash Flow Per Share	5.57	5.50	5.63	4.88	5.49	5.15	4.69	4.26
Tang Book Value Per Share	6.11	5.42	7.10	6.22	8.13	8.21	6.65	7.10
Dividends Per Share	2.170	2.120	1.960	1.800	1.600	1.360	1.200	1.120
Dividend Payout %	52.55	51.83	60.31	54.88	44.32	40.84	37.27	37.09
Income Statement								
Total Revenue	4,812,700	18,266,000	16,746,900	15,902,600	15,083,200	14,348,000	13,566,300	14,524,400
EBITDA	863,600	3,356,000	2,968,800	2,976,100	3,148,300	3,065,700	3,182,400	3,077,800
Depn & Amortn	199,500	806,500	932,800	844,500	800,300	758,800	718,600	739,600
Income Before Taxes	597,700	2,317,500	1,844,900	1,968,900	2,203,400	2,157,000	2,297,400	2,164,400
Income Taxes	164,600	536,500	469,200	438,400	483,900	514,200	666,600	645,700
Net Income	440,900	1,822,900	1,499,500	1,568,300	1,800,200	1,694,200	1,674,600	1,609,900
Average Shares	423,000	445,600	461,600	477,400	499,200	508,600	520,000	533,200
Balance Sheet								
Current Assets	6,253,100	6,096,600	5,269,700	4,783,100	4,961,900	4,438,100	4,273,900	3,922,200
Total Assets	18,912,400	18,439,700	17,067,000	16,303,200	17,018,000	16,779,900	15,585,800	15,007,600
Current Liabilities	5,040,100	4,928,600	5,015,800	4,642,900	4,537,200	3,918,700	4,038,300	4,168,300
Long-Term Obligations	4,442,600	4,393,900	2,276,000	2,594,700	2,298,000	2,733,700	2,844,000	2,424,000
Total Liabilities	13,344,200	12,211,400	10,176,200	9,987,600	9,665,600	9,445,700	9,382,000	8,822,300
Stockholders' Equity	5,568,200	5,223,700	6,097,400	5,558,200	6,629,500	6,766,300	5,650,300	5,646,900
Shares Outstanding	418,434	420,921	455,619	461,489	482,903	501,589	510,800	521,000
Statistical Record								
Return on Assets %	10.01	10.27	8.99	9.41	10.62	10.47	10.95	10.92
Return on Equity %	30.31	32.20	25.73	25.74	26.80	27.29	29.65	28.21
EBITDA Margin %	17.94	18.37	17.73	18.71	20.87	21.37	23.46	21.19
Net Margin %	9.16	9.98	8.95	9.86	11.94	11.81	12.34	11.08
Asset Turnover	1.03	1.03	1.00	0.95	0.89	0.89	0.89	0.99
Current Ratio	1.24	1.24	1.05	1.03	1.09	1.13	1.06	0.94
Debt to Equity	0.80	0.84	0.37	0.47	0.35	0.40	0.50	0.43
Price Range	71.98-62.99	71.98-65.76	68.13-57.07	68.15-55.97	66.98-55.52	58.10-42.66	65.34-45.28	70.58-51.36
P/E Ratio	17.43-15.25	17.60-16.08	20.96-17.56	20.78-17.06	18.56-15.38	17.45-12.81	20.29-14.06	23.37-17.01
Average Yield %	3.17	3.06	3.17	2.88	2.56	2.76	2.08	1.86

Address: 351 Phelps Drive, Irving, TX 75038	**Officers:** Thomas J. Falk - Chairman, President, Chief Executive Officer Mark A. Buthman - Senior Vice President, Chief Financial Officer **Transfer Agents:** ComputerShare Investor Services, Providence, RI	**Investor Contact:** 972-281-1478
Telephone: 972-281-1200		**No of Institutions:** 939
Web Site: www.kimberly-clark.com		**Shares:** 372,217,760 **% Held:** 77.78

KIMCO REALTY CORP.

Exchange	Symbol	Price	52Wk Range	Yield	P/E
NYS	KIM	$40.05 (5/29/2008)	47.63-30.47	4.00	28.81

*7 Year Price Score 107.73 *NYSE Composite Index=100 *12 Month Price Score 104.60

Interim Earnings (Per Share)

Qtr.	Mar	Jun	Sep	Dec
2005	0.36	0.35	0.36	0.45
2006	0.40	0.43	0.36	0.51
2007	0.59	0.49	0.29	0.28
2008	0.34	...	...	...

Interim Dividends (Per Share)

Amt	Decl	Ex	Rec	Pay
0.36Q	06/15/2007	07/02/2007	07/05/2007	07/16/2007
0.40Q	07/24/2007	10/01/2007	10/03/2007	10/15/2007
0.40Q	12/17/2007	12/28/2007	01/02/2008	01/15/2008
0.40Q	03/17/2008	04/02/2008	04/04/2008	04/15/2008

Indicated Div: $1.60 (Div. Reinv. Plan)

Valuation Analysis

Forecast EPS	$1.48 (05/16/2008)		
Market Cap	$10.1 Billion	Book Value	3.9 Billion
Price/Book	2.62	Price/Sales	14.24

Dividend Achiever Status

10 Year Growth Rate	9.95%
Total Years of Dividend Growth	15

Business Summary: "Property, Real Estate & Development" (MIC: SIC: 6798 NAIC: 525930)

Kimco Realty, its subsidiaries, affiliates and related real estate joint ventures are engaged principally in the operation of neighborhood and community shopping centers which are anchored generally by discount department stores, supermarkets or drugstores. In addition, Co. provides property management services for shopping centers owned by affiliated entities, various real estate joint ventures and unaffiliated third parties. As of Dec 31 2007, Co. had interests in 1,973 properties, totaling approximately 183.0 million square feet of gross leasable area located in 45 states, Canada, Mexico, Puerto Rico and Chile.

Recent Developments: For the quarter ended Mar 31 2008, income from continuing operations decreased 6.2% to US$94.7 million from US$100.9 million in the year-earlier quarter. Net income decreased 36.0% to US$98.5 million from US$153.8 million in the year-earlier quarter. Revenues were US$190.5 million, up 20.7% from US$157.8 million the year before.

Prospects: For 2008, Co. is projecting Funds From Operations to be in the range of $2.70 to $2.78 per diluted share and growth in same-store net operating income is expected to range from 3.5% to 4.0%. Meanwhile, Co. noted that as of Mar 31 2008, it had in progress a total of 61 ground-up development projects including 28 merchant building projects, nine U.S. ground-up development projects, and 24 ground-up development projects located throughout Mexico. Hence, for 2008, Co. expects capital commitment for development projects to be approximately $200.0 million to $250.0 million, while capital commitment for redevelopment projects is expected to be approximately $90.0 million to $110.0 million.

Financial Data
(US$ in Thousands)

	3 Mos	12/31/2007	12/31/2006	12/31/2005	12/31/2004	12/31/2003	12/31/2002	12/31/2001
Earnings Per Share	1.39	1.65	1.70	1.52	1.25	1.31	1.08	1.08
Cash Flow Per Share	2.46	2.64	1.90	1.81	1.63	1.44	1.34	1.49
Tang Book Value Per Share	15.31	15.40	13.42	10.46	9.94	9.65	9.11	9.14
Dividends Per Share	1.520	1.520	1.380	1.270	1.160	1.095	1.050	0.980
Dividend Payout %	108.99	92.12	81.18	83.55	92.43	83.59	97.22	90.74
Income Statement								
Total Revenue	190,538	681,553	593,880	522,545	516,967	479,664	450,829	468,616
Depn & Amortn	49,253	191,270	144,767	108,042	102,872	89,068	76,674	74,209
Income Before Taxes	50,235	78,034	164,199	185,917	226,397	200,889	261,474	255,914
Income Taxes	9,410	(44,490)	4,387	430	3,919	1,516	12,904	19,376
Net Income	98,467	442,830	428,259	363,628	297,137	307,879	245,668	236,538
Average Shares	255,916	257,058	244,615	230,868	227,144	217,540	211,938	202,326
Balance Sheet								
Total Assets	9,431,593	9,097,816	7,869,280	5,534,636	4,749,597	4,603,925	3,756,878	3,384,779
Long-Term Obligations	4,539,070	1,084,650	838,898	543,791	509,697	468,698	274,732	292,829
Total Liabilities	5,087,344	4,755,083	4,077,079	3,024,578	2,406,306	2,368,162	1,755,610	1,486,320
Stockholders' Equity	3,880,507	3,894,574	3,366,959	2,387,214	2,236,400	2,135,846	1,907,328	1,890,084
Shares Outstanding	253,396	252,803	250,870	228,059	224,852	221,247	209,203	206,705
Statistical Record								
Return on Assets %	4.43	5.22	6.39	7.07	6.34	7.36	6.88	7.22
Return on Equity %	10.54	12.20	14.89	15.73	13.55	15.23	12.94	13.16
Net Margin %	51.68	64.97	72.11	69.59	57.48	64.19	54.49	50.48
Price Range	49.55-30.47	53.41-35.30	46.88-32.73	33.25-26.20	29.47-20.27	22.93-15.25	16.81-14.01	17.00-13.63
P/E Ratio	35.65-21.92	32.37-21.39	27.58-19.25	21.88-17.23	23.58-16.22	17.50-11.64	15.56-12.97	15.74-12.62
Average Yield %	3.77	3.47	3.51	4.33	4.75	5.70	6.68	6.43

Address: 3333 New Hyde Park Road, Suite 100, New Hyde Park, NY 11042 Telephone: 516-869-9000 Web Site: www.kimcorealty.com	Officers: Milton Cooper - Chairman, Chief Executive Officer Michael J. Flynn - Vice-Chairman, President, Chief Operating Officer Transfer Agents: The Bank of New York, New York, NY	Investor Contact: 516-869-7288 No of Institutions: 419 Shares: 226,272,624 % Held: 80.65

KINDER MORGAN ENERGY PARTNERS, L.P.

Exchange	Symbol	Price	52Wk Range	Yield	P/E
NYS	KMP	$58.43 (5/29/2008)	60.54-48.60	6.57	33.39

*7 Year Price Score 94.72 ***NYSE Composite Index=100** ***12 Month Price Score 110.08**

TRADING VOLUME (thousand shares)

Interim Earnings (Per Share)

Qtr.	Mar	Jun	Sep	Dec
2005	0.54	0.50	0.57	(0.03)
2006	0.53	0.53	0.40	0.59
2007	0.33	0.36	0.24	0.52
2008	0.63	...	...	...

Interim Dividends (Per Share)

Amt	Decl	Ex	Rec	Pay
0.85Q	07/18/2007	07/27/2007	07/31/2007	08/14/2007
0.88Q	10/17/2007	10/29/2007	10/31/2007	11/14/2007
0.92Q	01/16/2008	01/29/2008	01/31/2008	02/14/2008
0.96Q	04/16/2008	04/28/2008	04/30/2008	05/15/2008

Indicated Div: $3.84

Valuation Analysis

Forecast EPS	$2.25 (05/17/2008)
Market Cap	$15.0 Billion Book Value N/A
Price/Book	N/A Price/Sales 1.53

Dividend Achiever Status

10 Year Growth Rate	15.32%
Total Years of Dividend Growth	11

Business Summary: Gas Utilities (MIC: SIC: 4922 NAIC: 486210)

Kinder Morgan Energy Partners is a pipeline transportation and energy storage company. As of Dec 31 2007, Co. owned an interest or operated over 25,000 miles of pipelines and approximately 165 terminals; its pipelines transported natural gas, gasoline, crude oil, carbon dioxide and other products, and its terminals store petroleum products and chemicals and handle bulk materials like coal and petroleum coke . Co. is also a provider of carbon dioxide (CO2) for oil recovery projects in North America. Co. operates through five segments: Products Pipelines, Natural Gas Pipelines, CO2, Terminals, and Trans Mountain.

Recent Developments: For the quarter ended Mar 31 2008, income from continuing operations was US$346.2 million compared with a loss of US$156.6 million in the year-earlier quarter. Net income amounted to US$346.7 million versus a net loss of US$149.5 million in the year-earlier quarter. Revenues were US$2.72 billion, up 25.3% from US$2.17 billion the year before. Operating income was US$419.4 million versus a loss of US$75.5 million in the prior-year quarter. Direct operating expenses rose 23.3% to US$2.02 billion from US$1.64 billion in the comparable period the year before. Indirect operating expenses decreased 53.7% to US$282.4 million from US$610.5 million in the equivalent prior-year period.

Prospects: Co.'s near-term outlook appears constructive, reflecting higher customer demand for energy products, including crude oil, natural gas and carbon dioxide; higher crude oil and natural gas liquids prices, and contributions from capital expansion and improvement projects completed since the end of the first quarter of 2007. For instance, Co. is progressing towards completing its $426.0 million CALNEV expansion pipeline system from Colton, CA, to Las Vegas, NV. Upon completion, capacity on the pipeline will rise to about 200,000 barrels per day (bpd) and could be further increased to over 300,000 bpd by installing extra pump stations. The expansion is expected to be completed in April 2011.

Financial Data

(US$ in Thousands)	3 Mos	12/31/2007	12/31/2006	12/31/2005	12/31/2004	12/31/2003	12/31/2002	12/31/2001
Earnings Per Share	1.75	(0.09)	2.04	1.58	2.22	2.00	1.96	1.56
Cash Flow Per Share	6.89	7.35	5.60	6.08	5.85	4.15	5.06	3.78
Dividends Per Share	3.601	3.480	3.260	3.130	2.810	2.575	2.360	2.075
Dividend Payout %	206.22	...	159.80	198.10	126.58	128.75	120.41	133.01
Income Statement								
Total Revenue	2,720,300	9,217,700	8,954,583	9,787,128	7,932,861	6,624,322	4,237,057	2,946,676
EBITDA	614,100	1,431,600	1,742,079	1,451,020	1,338,387	1,116,467	977,736	781,261
Depn & Amortn	159,500	552,800	419,389	355,471	294,201	224,607	177,616	151,088
Income Before Taxes	357,900	487,400	991,191	836,688	851,304	710,503	623,660	458,716
Income Taxes	11,700	71,000	19,048	24,461	19,726	16,631	15,283	16,373
Net Income	346,700	590,300	972,143	812,227	831,578	697,337	608,377	442,343
Average Shares	251,000	236,900	224,914	212,429	197,038	185,494	172,186	154,110
Balance Sheet								
Net PPE	12,041,700	11,591,300	9,445,471	8,864,584	8,168,680	7,091,558	6,244,242	5,082,612
Total Assets	16,277,000	15,177,800	12,246,394	11,923,462	10,552,942	9,139,182	8,353,576	6,732,666
Long-Term Obligations	7,365,900	6,608,100	4,426,962	5,319,356	4,852,563	4,438,142	3,826,489	2,231,574
Total Liabilities	11,682,000	10,742,100	8,224,741	8,309,722	6,656,422	5,628,255	4,937,647	3,573,632
Shares Outstanding	256,054	247,966	230,431	220,237	207,008	189,039	180,910	165,804
Statistical Record								
Return on Assets %	7.57	4.30	8.04	7.23	8.42	7.97	8.07	7.79
EBITDA Margin %	22.57	15.53	19.45	14.83	16.87	16.85	23.08	26.51
Net Margin %	12.74	6.40	10.86	8.30	10.48	10.53	14.36	15.01
PPE Turnover	0.90	0.88	0.98	1.15	1.04	0.99	0.75	0.70
Asset Turnover	0.68	0.67	0.74	0.87	0.80	0.76	0.56	0.52
Price Range	59.35-48.60	56.96-47.46	50.88-43.15	54.18-42.95	49.27-38.33	49.69-34.25	38.65-28.00	39.05-26.13
P/E Ratio	33.91-27.77	...	24.94-21.15	34.29-27.18	22.19-17.27	24.84-17.13	19.72-14.29	25.03-16.75
Average Yield %	1.79	6.65	7.02	6.38	6.33	6.43	7.09	6.08

Address: 500 Dallas Street, Suite 1000, Houston, TX 77002	**Officers:** C. Park Sharper - President Joseph Listengart - V.P., Sec., Gen. Couns. **Transfer Agents:**	**Investor Contact:** 713-369-9490	
Telephone: 713-369-9000	Computershare Trust Company, N.A., Providence, RI	**No of Institutions:** 437	
Web Site: www.kindermorgan.com		**Shares:** 50,342,248 **% Held:** 27.90	

157

LA-Z-BOY INC.

Exchange	Symbol	Price	52Wk Range	Yield	P/E
NYS	LZB	$6.40 (5/29/2008)	12.30-5.46	2.50	N/A

*7 Year Price Score 39.07 *NYSE Composite Index=100 *12 Month Price Score 84.93

Interim Earnings (Per Share)

Qtr.	Jul	Oct	Jan	Apr
2004-05	(0.07)	0.17	0.21	0.40
2005-06	0.06	(0.12)	0.20	(0.20)
2006-07	0.04	0.04	(0.15)	0.15
2007-08	(0.17)	(0.19)	0.18	...

Interim Dividends (Per Share)

Amt	Decl	Ex	Rec	Pay
0.12Q	08/15/2007	08/27/2007	08/29/2007	09/10/2007
0.12Q	11/13/2007	11/21/2007	11/26/2007	12/10/2007
0.04Q	02/19/2008	02/27/2008	02/29/2008	03/10/2008
0.04Q	04/29/2008	05/23/2008	05/28/2008	06/10/2008

Indicated Div: $0.16 (Div. Reinv. Plan)

Valuation Analysis

Forecast EPS	$-0.02 (05/16/2008)		
Market Cap	$329.1 Million	Book Value	455.6 Million
Price/Book	0.72	Price/Sales	0.22

Dividend Achiever Status

10 Year Growth Rate	5.54%
Total Years of Dividend Growth	26

Business Summary: Chemicals (MIC: SIC: 2511 NAIC: 337121)

La-Z-Boy is a manufacturer of reclining-chair and upholstered furniture. Co. also manufactures and imports casegoods (wood) furniture products from outside the U.S. for resale in North America. As of Apr 28 2007, Co. operated within three segments: the Upholstery Group, the Casegoods Group, and the Retail Group. The operating units in the Upholstery Group are Bauhaus, England, La-Z-Boy, U.K., and La-Z-Boy while the operating units in the Casegoods Group are American Drew, Hammary, Kincaid, and Lea. The Retail Group consists of 70 company-owned La-Z-Boy Furniture Galleries® stores located in nine markets ranging from the Midwest to the East Coast of the U.S. and southeastern Florida.

Recent Developments: For the quarter ended Jan 26 2008, income from continuing operations increased 31.4% to US$9.1 million from US$6.9 million in the year-earlier quarter. Net income amounted to US$9.5 million versus a net loss of US$7.8 million in the year-earlier quarter. Revenues were US$373.1 million, down 7.8% from US$404.8 million the year before. Operating income was US$3.1 million versus US$9.5 million in the prior-year quarter, a decrease of 67.4%. Direct operating expenses declined 9.2% to US$264.4 million from US$291.3 million in the comparable period the year before. Indirect operating expenses increased 1.4% to US$105.5 million from US$104.1 million in the equivalent prior-year period.

Prospects: Co. anticipates the furniture industry will continue to be affected by the overall macroeconomic environment. Accordingly, Co. expects its sales to be down 4.0% to 8.0%, coupled with earnings per share of $0.06 to $0.14 for the second half of fiscal 2008, excluding the $6.0 million make-whole provision related to its credit refinancing, restructuring charges, income from anti-dumping monies, or any further effect from discontinued operations. Meanwhile, Co. plans to open four New Generation format La-Z-Boy Furniture Galleries® stores, of which one will be a new store and three will be store remodels or relocations, and will close one in the quarter ending Apr 2008.

Financial Data

(US$ in Thousands)	9 Mos	6 Mos	3 Mos	04/28/2007	04/29/2006	04/30/2005	04/24/2004	04/26/2003
Earnings Per Share	(0.03)	(0.36)	(0.13)	0.08	(0.06)	0.71	(0.11)	0.63
Cash Flow Per Share	1.33	1.08	0.36	0.65	1.74	0.87	2.49	2.19
Tang Book Value Per Share	7.72	7.69	7.87	8.18	8.39	8.17	8.19	8.36
Dividends Per Share	0.480	0.480	0.480	0.480	0.440	0.440	0.400	0.400
Dividend Payout %	...	...	...	600.00	...	61.97	...	63.49
Income Statement								
Total Revenue	1,082,911	709,830	344,396	1,617,302	1,916,777	2,048,381	1,998,876	2,111,830
EBITDA	17,445	(3,899)	(5,268)	64,327	50,207	92,150	62,653	196,202
Depn & Amortn	18,506	12,313	6,220	27,204	29,234	28,329	29,112	30,695
Income Before Taxes	(7,426)	(20,429)	(13,585)	29,858	9,433	53,379	22,288	154,997
Income Taxes	(4,359)	(8,235)	(5,043)	10,090	12,474	20,284	19,760	58,899
Net Income	(9,117)	(18,628)	(8,694)	4,139	(3,041)	37,185	(5,796)	36,316
Average Shares	51,590	51,410	51,380	51,606	51,801	52,138	53,679	57,435
Balance Sheet								
Current Assets	501,481	483,996	492,893	540,798	584,559	638,365	653,674	679,494
Total Assets	838,778	825,917	835,395	878,691	971,174	1,026,357	1,047,496	1,123,066
Current Liabilities	170,809	197,341	191,875	228,210	228,410	228,724	283,321	214,587
Long-Term Obligations	146,415	110,774	111,238	111,714	173,368	213,549	181,807	222,371
Total Liabilities	383,165	371,673	366,488	393,343	460,829	499,071	525,168	513,127
Stockholders' Equity	455,613	454,244	468,907	485,348	510,345	527,286	522,328	609,939
Shares Outstanding	51,417	51,416	51,379	51,377	51,782	52,225	52,031	55,027
Statistical Record								
Return on Assets %	N.M.	N.M.	N.M.	0.45	N.M.	3.53	N.M.	3.19
Return on Equity %	N.M.	N.M.	N.M.	0.83	N.M.	6.97	N.M.	5.50
EBITDA Margin %	1.61	N.M.	N.M.	3.98	2.62	4.50	3.13	9.29
Net Margin %	N.M.	N.M.	N.M.	0.26	N.M.	1.82	N.M.	1.72
Asset Turnover	1.73	1.73	1.82	1.75	1.92	1.94	1.85	1.85
Current Ratio	2.94	2.45	2.57	2.37	2.56	2.79	2.31	3.17
Debt to Equity	0.32	0.24	0.24	0.23	0.34	0.40	0.35	0.36
Price Range	14.89-5.46	14.89-6.94	15.46-10.29	16.37-11.30	17.04-10.67	21.31-11.84	24.12-18.90	30.20-16.45
P/E Ratio	...	...	...	204.63-141.25	...	30.01-16.68	...	47.94-26.11
Average Yield %	4.67	4.18	3.78	3.60	3.11	2.82	1.86	1.73

Address: 1284 North Telegraph Road, Monroe, MI 48162-3390	**Officers:** James W. Johnston - Chairman Kurt L. Darrow - President, Chief Executive Officer **Transfer Agents:** American Stock Transfer & Trust Company, New York, NY	**Investor Contact:** 734-241-4414	
Telephone: 734-242-1444		**No of Institutions:** 144	
Web Site: www.lazboy.com		**Shares:** 49,575,000 **% Held:** 95.30	

LANCASTER COLONY CORP.

Exchange	Symbol	Price	52Wk Range	Yield	P/E
NMS	LANC	$32.87 (5/29/2008)	44.43-32.06	3.41	41.61

*7 Year Price Score 75.21 *NYSE Composite Index=100 *12 Month Price Score 97.23

Interim Earnings (Per Share)

Qtr.	Sep	Dec	Mar	Jun
2004-05	0.52	1.08	0.46	0.60
2005-06	0.53	0.89	0.35	0.70
2006-07	0.43	0.56	0.43	(0.57)
2007-08	0.51	0.54	0.30	...

Interim Dividends (Per Share)

Amt	Decl	Ex	Rec	Pay
0.27Q	08/22/2007	09/06/2007	09/10/2007	09/28/2007
0.28Q	11/19/2007	12/06/2007	12/10/2007	12/28/2007
0.28Q	02/27/2008	03/06/2008	03/10/2008	03/31/2008
0.28Q	05/28/2008	06/06/2008	06/10/2008	06/30/2008

Indicated Div: $1.12 (Div. Reinv. Plan)

Valuation Analysis

Forecast EPS $1.83 (05/16/2008)

Market Cap	$947.3 Million	Book Value	383.7 Million
Price/Book	2.47	Price/Sales	0.89

Dividend Achiever Status

10 Year Growth Rate	7.96%
Total Years of Dividend Growth	38

Business Summary: Food (MIC: SIC: 2038 NAIC: 311412)

Lancaster Colony is a manufacturer and marketer of consumer products including specialty foods for the retail and foodservice markets; glassware and candles for the retail, floral, industrial and foodservice markets; and automotive accessories. Co. operates in three business segments - Specialty Foods which manufactures and sells salad dressings and sauces, fruit glazes, vegetable dips, fruit dips, frozen hearth-baked breads, and dry egg noodles, frozen noodles and pastas, croutons and caviar; Glassware and Candles which includes candles, candle accessories and glass products; and Automotive which manufactures and sells running boards, tube steps, toolboxes and other accessories.

Recent Developments: For the quarter ended Mar 31 2008, income from continuing operations decreased 35.4% to US$8.8 million from US$13.6 million in the year-earlier quarter. Net income decreased 36.1% to US$8.6 million from US$13.5 million in the year-earlier quarter. Revenues were US$270.3 million, up 1.7% from US$265.7 million the year before. Operating income was US$13.6 million versus US$21.2 million in the prior-year quarter, a decrease of 35.9%. Direct operating expenses rose 6.4% to US$234.0 million from US$220.0 million in the comparable period the year before. Indirect operating expenses decreased 7.6% to US$22.6 million from US$24.5 million in the equivalent prior-year period.

Prospects: Co.'s improved sales performance reflects growth in sales in its Specialty Foods segment along with an increase in sales in its Automotive segment, partially offset by lower sales within its Glassware and Candles segment. Meanwhile, Co. is also experiencing a decline in its gross margins as a result of higher food commodity costs. While Co. anticipates that the gross margins of its Specialty Foods business to continue to be unfavorably affected by these higher costs, it believes that retail pricing actions, both the one taken during the third fiscal quarter ended Mar 2008 and another it plans to implement after the fiscal year ends, should mitigate the effect of these escalating costs.

Financial Data

(US$ in Thousands)	9 Mos	6 Mos	3 Mos	06/30/2007	06/30/2006	06/30/2005	06/30/2004	06/30/2003
Earnings Per Share	0.79	0.91	0.93	0.85	2.48	2.67	2.24	3.11
Cash Flow Per Share	3.28	3.47	2.82	2.82	2.90	3.35	3.34	4.31
Tang Book Value Per Share	9.78	10.43	10.77	11.11	12.74	14.71	14.16	13.20
Dividends Per Share	1.100	1.090	1.080	1.070	3.030	0.980	0.890	0.780
Dividend Payout %	139.90	119.78	116.13	125.88	122.18	36.70	39.73	25.08
Income Statement								
Total Revenue	861,458	591,182	285,570	1,091,162	1,175,260	1,131,466	1,096,953	1,106,800
EBITDA	87,690	66,535	33,067	130,919	161,142	181,283	159,731	212,470
Depn & Amortn	22,276	15,027	7,810	28,766	32,341	33,262	31,267	31,669
Income Before Taxes	62,869	49,584	24,299	102,003	128,801	148,021	128,464	180,801
Income Taxes	22,516	18,016	8,729	37,322	45,847	54,933	48,462	68,255
Net Income	40,194	31,568	15,570	45,684	82,954	93,088	80,002	112,546
Average Shares	29,128	29,860	30,420	31,603	33,502	34,925	35,778	36,243
Balance Sheet								
Current Assets	263,529	254,225	307,792	278,911	338,783	474,405	451,005	414,385
Total Assets	566,913	562,620	627,926	598,497	628,021	731,278	712,887	667,716
Current Liabilities	88,775	87,922	185,538	141,790	103,500	103,846	92,731	84,923
Long-Term Obligations	77,500	47,600	...	...	...	...	...	...
Total Liabilities	183,241	152,955	200,543	154,188	133,600	143,552	126,102	120,051
Stockholders' Equity	383,672	409,665	427,383	444,309	494,421	587,726	586,785	547,665
Shares Outstanding	28,818	29,508	30,175	30,748	32,245	34,235	35,472	35,770
Statistical Record								
Return on Assets %	6.97	7.80	7.57	7.45	12.21	12.89	11.56	17.50
Return on Equity %	9.49	10.23	10.41	9.73	15.33	15.85	14.07	21.46
EBITDA Margin %	10.18	11.25	11.58	12.00	13.71	16.02	14.56	19.20
Net Margin %	4.67	5.34	5.45	4.19	7.06	8.23	7.29	10.17
Asset Turnover	1.83	1.86	1.75	1.78	1.73	1.57	1.58	1.72
Current Ratio	2.97	2.89	1.66	1.97	3.27	4.57	4.86	4.88
Debt to Equity	0.20	0.12	...	...	...	...	...	...
Price Range	45.03-34.02	45.49-35.90	47.32-35.90	47.32-37.62	45.75-37.05	44.63-38.26	46.11-38.20	46.74-32.68
P/E Ratio	57.00-43.06	49.99-39.45	50.88-38.60	55.67-44.26	18.45-14.94	16.72-14.33	20.58-17.05	15.03-10.51
Average Yield %	2.76	2.63	2.53	2.49	7.39	2.32	2.15	2.00

Address: 37 West Broad Street, Columbus, OH 43215 **Telephone:** 614-224-7141 **Web Site:** www.lancastercolony.com	**Officers:** John B. Gerlach - Chairman, President, Chief Executive Officer John L. Boylan - Vice President, Chief Financial Officer, Treasurer **Transfer Agents:** American Stock Transfer and Trust Company, New York, NY	**No of Institutions:** 157 **Shares:** 16,826,630 **% Held:** 52.13

LEGG MASON, INC.

Exchange	Symbol	Price	52Wk Range	Yield	P/E
NYS	LM	$54.13 (5/29/2008)	102.05-52.72	1.77	29.26

*7 Year Price Score 87.29   *NYSE Composite Index=100   *12 Month Price Score 78.77

Interim Earnings (Per Share)

Qtr.	Jun	Sep	Dec	Mar
2003-04	0.55	0.62	0.71	0.81
2004-05	0.76	0.81	0.98	0.98
2005-06	0.93	0.99	5.80	0.85
2006-07	1.08	1.00	1.21	1.19
2007-08	1.32	1.23	1.07	(1.76)

Interim Dividends (Per Share)

Amt	Decl	Ex	Rec	Pay
0.24Q	07/19/2007	09/25/2007	09/27/2007	10/15/2007
0.24Q	10/16/2007	12/03/2007	12/05/2007	12/31/2007
0.24Q	01/29/2008	03/04/2008	03/06/2008	04/07/2008
0.24Q	04/29/2008	06/06/2008	06/10/2008	07/07/2008

Indicated Div: $0.96

Valuation Analysis

Forecast EPS $4.25 (05/17/2008)
Market Cap $7.5 Billion   Book Value   6.6 Billion
Price/Book   1.13   Price/Sales   1.62

Dividend Achiever Status

10 Year Growth Rate   23.86%
Total Years of Dividend Growth   24

TRADING VOLUME (thousand shares)

Business Summary: Finance Intermediaries & Services (MIC: SIC: 6211 NAIC: 523120)

Legg Mason is a global asset management company. Acting through its subsidiaries, Co. provides investment management and related services to institutional and individual clients, company-sponsored mutual funds as well as other pooled investment vehicles. Co. provides these products and services directly and through various financial intermediaries. As of Mar 31 2008, Co. conducted its businesses through three operating divisions: Managed Investments, Institutional, and Wealth Management. Within each of its divisions, Co. provides its services through a number of asset managers, each of which is an individual business that markets its products and services under their own brand name.

Recent Developments: For the year ended Mar 31 2008, income from continuing operations decreased 58.6% to US$267.6 million from US$646.2 million a year earlier. Net income decreased 58.6% to US$267.6 million from US$646.8 million in the prior year. Revenues were US$4.63 billion, up 6.7% from US$4.34 billion the year before. Operating income was US$1.05 billion versus US$1.03 billion in the prior year, an increase of 2.1%. Indirect operating expenses increased 8.1% to US$3.58 billion from US$3.32 billion in the equivalent prior-year period.

Prospects: Co.'s near-term outlook appears to be challenging, due to the continuous volatility of the U.S. and global economies, attributable to disruptions in the credit markets, driven by the subprime mortgage crisis, a weaker U.S. dollar, major write-downs related to the credit crisis within the financial sector, and increased oil prices. Nevertheless, Co.'s investment managers will continue to expand its business into new markets and launch new products while focusing on its core asset management business, as exhibited by the April 1 2008 divestiture of its Private Portfolio Group to Citigroup Global Markets Inc. for proceeds of approximately $181.0 million and after-tax gain of $3.0 million.

Financial Data

(US$ in Thousands)	03/31/2008	03/31/2007	03/31/2006	03/31/2005	03/31/2004	03/31/2003	03/31/2002	03/31/2001
Earnings Per Share	1.86	4.48	8.80	3.53	2.71	1.85	1.49	1.53
Cash Flow Per Share	6.77	6.42	4.52	3.98	1.88	3.09	0.88	2.34
Tang Book Value Per Share	N.M.	N.M.	N.M.	7.91	6.50	3.32	1.52	8.26
Dividends Per Share	0.960	0.810	0.690	0.550	0.373	0.287	0.260	0.233
Dividend Payout %	51.61	18.08	7.84	15.58	13.79	15.47	17.41	15.22
Income Statement								
Total Revenue	4,634,086	4,343,675	2,645,212	2,489,552	2,004,267	1,615,382	1,578,612	1,536,253
Income Before Taxes	443,871	1,043,854	715,462	658,707	472,309	308,321	253,249	265,820
Income Taxes	175,995	397,612	275,595	250,276	181,701	117,412	100,313	109,590
Net Income	267,610	646,818	1,144,168	408,431	297,764	190,909	152,936	156,230
Average Shares	143,976	144,386	130,279	117,074	110,769	103,140	102,393	101,874
Balance Sheet								
Total Assets	11,830,352	9,604,488	9,302,490	8,219,472	7,262,981	6,067,450	5,939,614	4,687,626
Total Liabilities	5,209,849	3,062,998	3,452,374	5,926,326	5,703,371	4,819,493	4,855,066	3,759,906
Stockholders' Equity	6,620,503	6,541,490	5,850,116	2,293,146	1,559,610	1,247,957	1,084,548	927,720
Shares Outstanding	138,556	131,776	129,709	106,683	99,823	97,241	96,665	94,274
Statistical Record								
Return on Assets %	2.49	6.84	13.06	5.28	4.46	3.18	2.88	3.30
Return on Equity %	4.06	10.44	28.10	21.20	21.15	16.37	15.20	18.60
Price Range	105.87-52.72	126.10-82.30	136.40-70.20	84.12-48.97	63.22-32.49	37.98-25.44	37.87-23.83	39.96-23.96
P/E Ratio	56.92-28.34	28.15-18.37	15.50-7.98	23.83-13.87	23.33-11.99	20.53-13.75	25.41-16.00	26.12-15.66
Average Yield %	1.15	0.82	0.64	0.86	0.75	0.89	0.82	0.70

Address: 100 Light Street, Baltimore, MD 21202	Officers: Mark R. Fetting - President, Chief Executive Officer Peter L. Bain - Senior Executive Vice President Transfer Agents:	No of Institutions: 594
Telephone: 410-539-0000		Shares: 117,548,392 % Held: 83.57
Web Site: www.leggmason.com	American Stock Transfer & Trust Company, New York, NY	

LEGGETT & PLATT, INC.

Exchange	Symbol	Price	52Wk Range	Yield	P/E
NYS	LEG	$19.34 (5/29/2008)	24.61-14.30	5.17	N/A

*7 Year Price Score 63.46   *NYSE Composite Index=100   ***12 Month Price Score 90.47**

Interim Earnings (Per Share)

Qtr.	Mar	Jun	Sep	Dec
2005	0.37	0.41	0.28	0.24
2006	0.33	0.45	0.45	0.38
2007	0.41	0.33	0.37	(1.17)
2008	0.25	...	...	...

Interim Dividends (Per Share)

Amt	Decl	Ex	Rec	Pay
0.18Q	08/09/2007	09/12/2007	09/14/2007	10/15/2007
0.25Q	11/13/2007	12/12/2007	12/14/2007	01/15/2008
0.25Q	02/21/2008	03/12/2008	03/14/2008	04/15/2008
0.25Q	05/08/2008	06/11/2008	06/13/2008	07/15/2008

Indicated Div: $1.00

Valuation Analysis

Forecast EPS $1.07 (05/16/2008)

Market Cap	$3.2 Billion	Book Value	2.1 Billion
Price/Book	1.54	Price/Sales	0.81

Dividend Achiever Status

10 Year Growth Rate	10.41%
Total Years of Dividend Growth	36

TRADING VOLUME (thousand shares)

Business Summary: Furniture and Fixtures (MIC: SIC: 2519 NAIC: 337121)

Leggett & Platt is engaged in designing and producing a range of components and products that are used in homes, offices, retail stores and automobiles. Co.'s products include manufactured components for residential furniture and bedding, adjustable beds, carpet underlay, retail store fixtures and point-of-purchase displays, office furniture, drawn steel wire, automotive seat support and lumbar systems, and machinery for wire forming, sewing, and quilting. As of Dec 31 2007, Co.'s operations were organized into 22 business units, which are divided into 10 groups under four segments: Residential Furnishings; Commercial Fixturing & Components; Industrial Materials; and Specialized Product.

Recent Developments: For the quarter ended Mar 31 2008, income from continuing operations decreased 30.5% to US$39.2 million from US$56.4 million in the year-earlier quarter. Net income decreased 42.7% to US$43.4 million from US$75.7 million in the year-earlier quarter. Revenues were US$998.3 million, down 4.7% from US$1.05 billion the year before. Operating income was US$69.1 million versus US$91.8 million in the prior-year quarter, a decrease of 24.7%. Direct operating expenses declined 3.5% to US$821.2 million from US$851.1 million in the comparable period the year before. Indirect operating expenses increased 3.2% to US$108.0 million from US$104.7 million in the equivalent prior-year period.

Prospects: For full-year 2008, Co. continues to target sales from continuing operations of about $4.20 billion, or about 2.0% lower than in 2007. This decline reflects the estimated reduction by the end of 2008 of about $100.0 million of revenue with lower profit margins in its Store Fixtures business, minimal acquisition revenue, and essentially flat sales from its business operations other than Store Fixtures. Also, Co. expects its earnings per share from continuing operations for 2008 to be in the range of $1.00 to $1.30, including about $0.05 per share in restructuring-related costs, but excludes potential earnings from discontinued operations, nor possible gains or losses from divestitures.

Financial Data

(US$ in Thousands)	3 Mos	12/31/2007	12/31/2006	12/31/2005	12/31/2004	12/31/2003	12/31/2002	12/31/2001
Earnings Per Share	(0.22)	(0.06)	1.61	1.30	1.45	1.05	1.17	0.94
Cash Flow Per Share	2.99	3.42	2.57	2.33	1.75	2.01	2.29	2.68
Tang Book Value Per Share	5.60	5.74	5.72	5.55	6.37	5.62	5.36	4.81
Dividends Per Share	0.860	0.780	0.670	0.630	0.580	0.540	0.500	0.480
Dividend Payout %	...	...	41.61	48.46	40.00	51.43	42.74	51.06
Income Statement								
Total Revenue	998,300	4,306,400	5,505,400	5,299,300	5,085,500	4,388,200	4,271,800	4,113,800
EBITDA	104,100	357,700	657,400	567,300	638,900	530,700	575,400	587,700
Depn & Amortn	35,000	180,200	175,400	171,100	177,200	175,400	174,800	236,500
Income Before Taxes	58,100	128,400	434,800	356,200	422,600	315,100	363,500	297,300
Income Taxes	18,900	77,400	134,500	104,900	137,200	109,200	130,400	109,700
Net Income	43,400	(11,200)	300,300	251,300	285,400	205,900	233,100	187,600
Average Shares	173,200	179,827	186,832	193,574	196,875	196,953	199,795	200,434
Balance Sheet								
Current Assets	1,870,600	1,834,400	1,894,100	1,763,300	2,064,800	1,819,400	1,488,000	1,421,900
Total Assets	4,103,000	4,072,500	4,265,300	4,052,600	4,197,200	3,889,700	3,501,100	3,412,900
Current Liabilities	772,500	799,600	691,200	738,000	959,600	625,900	598,000	457,000
Long-Term Obligations	1,095,800	1,000,600	1,060,000	921,600	779,400	1,012,200	808,600	977,600
Total Liabilities	2,015,800	1,939,800	1,914,200	1,803,600	1,884,100	1,775,700	1,524,200	1,546,300
Stockholders' Equity	2,087,200	2,132,700	2,351,100	2,249,000	2,313,100	2,114,000	1,976,900	1,866,600
Shares Outstanding	166,329	168,725	178,000	182,576	190,886	192,102	194,498	196,298
Statistical Record								
Return on Assets %	N.M.	N.M.	7.22	6.09	7.04	5.57	6.74	5.53
Return on Equity %	N.M.	N.M.	13.06	11.02	12.86	10.07	12.13	10.25
EBITDA Margin %	10.43	8.31	11.94	10.71	12.56	12.09	13.47	14.29
Net Margin %	4.35	N.M.	5.45	4.74	5.61	4.69	5.46	4.56
Asset Turnover	0.94	1.03	1.32	1.28	1.25	1.19	1.24	1.21
Current Ratio	2.42	2.29	2.74	2.39	2.15	2.91	2.49	3.11
Debt to Equity	0.53	0.47	0.45	0.41	0.34	0.48	0.41	0.52
Price Range	24.62-14.88	24.62-17.27	26.96-22.39	29.44-18.55	30.56-21.35	23.57-17.40	27.16-18.90	24.23-17.00
P/E Ratio	...	...	16.75-13.91	22.65-14.27	21.08-14.72	22.45-16.57	23.21-16.15	25.78-18.09
Average Yield %	4.30	3.59	2.76	2.47	2.25	2.58	2.13	2.26

Address: No. 1 Leggett Road, Carthage, MO 64836	Officers: Felix E. Wright - Chairman David S. Haffner - President, Chief Executive Officer **Transfer**	Investor Contact: 417-358-8131
Telephone: 417-358-8131	**Agents:** UMB Bank, N.A., Kansas City , MO	**No of Institutions:** 332
Web Site: www.leggett.com		**Shares:** 169,973,472 **% Held:** 85.03

LEHMAN BROTHERS HOLDINGS INC

Exchange	Symbol	Price	52Wk Range	Yield	P/E
NYS	LEH	$37.37 (5/29/2008)	81.30-31.75	1.82	6.14

*7 Year Price Score 93.65 ***NYSE Composite Index=100** ***12 Month Price Score 75.73**

Interim Earnings (Per Share)

Qtr.	Feb	May	Aug	Nov
2004-05	1.46	1.13	1.47	1.38
2005-06	1.83	1.69	1.57	1.72
2006-07	1.96	2.21	1.54	1.55
2007-08	0.81	...	...	...

Interim Dividends (Per Share)

Amt	Decl	Ex	Rec	Pay
0.15Q	08/01/2007	08/13/2007	08/15/2007	08/24/2007
0.15Q	10/30/2007	11/13/2007	11/15/2007	11/23/2007
0.17Q	01/29/2008	02/13/2008	02/15/2008	02/22/2008
0.17Q	05/01/2008	05/13/2008	05/15/2008	05/23/2008
			Indicated Div: $0.68	

Valuation Analysis

Forecast EPS $4.53 (05/16/2008)
Market Cap $20.6 Billion   Book Value 24.8 Billion
Price/Book 0.83   Price/Sales 0.36

Dividend Achiever Status

10 Year Growth Rate ... 25.89%
Total Years of Dividend Growth ... 11

Business Summary: Finance Intermediaries & Services (MIC: SIC: 6211 NAIC: 523110)

Lehman Brothers Holdings serves the financial needs of corporations, governments and municipalities, institutional clients and high-net-worth individuals worldwide. Co. provides an array of equities and fixed income sales, trading and research, investment banking, asset management, private investment management and private equity. Co. is a member of all principal securities and commodities exchanges in the U.S., as well as NASD, Inc., and holds memberships or associate memberships on several principal international securities and commodities exchanges, including the London, Tokyo, Hong Kong, Frankfurt, Paris, Milan and Australian. At Nov 30 2007, Co. had total assets of $691.06 billion.

Recent Developments: For the quarter ended Feb 29 2008, net income decreased 57.3% to US$489.0 million from US$1.15 billion in the year-earlier quarter. Revenues were US$12.37 billion, down 10.3% from US$13.80 billion the year before. Direct operating expenses rose 1.3% to US$8.86 billion from US$8.75 billion in the comparable period the year before. Indirect operating expenses decreased 15.1% to US$2.84 billion from US$3.35 billion in the equivalent prior-year period.

Prospects: Looking ahead, Co. foresees global economic growth to be lower versus the levels in the fiscal quarter ended Feb 29 2008. Specifically, Co. anticipates mergers and acquisitions volumes for the fiscal year ending Nov 30 2008 to decline over its volumes in the prior fiscal year. Also, Co. expects the investment banking activities for the rest of 2008 to be modest. Further, Co. believes that the tighter bank and credit conditions, lower forecasted global growth and a stronger Euro will slow growth in Eurozone countries and U.K. during 2008. Nevertheless, Co. expects debt origination in 2008 to be driven by demand for industrial non-frequent paper and continued financial sector issuance.

Financial Data
(US$ in Millions)

	3 Mos	11/30/2007	11/30/2006	11/30/2005	11/30/2004	11/30/2003	11/30/2002	11/30/2001
Earnings Per Share	6.09	7.26	6.81	5.43	3.95	3.17	1.74	2.19
Cash Flow Per Share	(76.26)	(84.34)	(66.99)	(13.46)	(19.80)	5.18	49.83	13.74
Tang Book Value Per Share	32.15	32.47	27.62	22.92	18.77	16.06	17.37	15.98
Dividends Per Share	0.620	0.600	0.480	0.400	0.320	0.240	0.180	0.140
Dividend Payout %	10.19	8.26	7.05	7.36	8.10	7.56	10.37	6.39
Income Statement								
Interest Income	9,635	41,693	30,284	19,043	11,032	9,942	11,728	16,470
Interest Expense	8,863	39,746	29,126	17,790	9,674	8,640	10,626	15,656
Net Interest Income	772	1,947	1,158	1,253	1,358	1,302	1,102	814
Non-Interest Income	2,735	17,310	16,425	13,377	10,218	7,345	5,053	5,922
Non-Interest Expense	2,844	13,244	11,678	9,801	8,058	6,111	4,676	4,988
Income Before Taxes	663	...	...	...	...	...	...	...
Income Taxes	174	1,821	1,945	1,569	1,125	765	368	437
Net Income	489	4,192	4,007	3,260	2,369	1,699	975	1,255
Average Shares	572	568	578	587	581	519	522	530
Balance Sheet								
Total Assets	786,035	691,063	503,545	410,063	357,168	312,061	260,336	247,816
Total Deposits	28,829	29,363	21,412	...	...	...	...	...
Total Liabilities	761,203	668,573	484,354	393,269	342,248	297,577	250,684	238,647
Stockholders' Equity	24,832	22,490	19,191	16,794	14,920	13,174	8,942	8,459
Shares Outstanding	551	531	533	542	548	533	462	475
Statistical Record								
Return on Assets %	0.52	0.70	0.88	0.85	0.71	0.59	0.38	0.53
Return on Equity %	15.71	20.11	22.27	20.56	16.82	15.36	11.21	15.46
Net Interest Margin %	8.01	4.67	3.82	6.58	12.31	13.10	9.40	4.94
Efficiency Ratio %	22.99	22.45	25.00	30.23	37.92	35.35	27.86	22.28
Price Range	81.30-50.99	85.80-51.57	78.55-59.42	66.42-41.63	44.75-33.83	37.90-25.18	34.76-21.30	42.86-23.32
P/E Ratio	13.35-8.37	11.82-7.10	11.53-8.73	12.23-7.67	11.33-8.56	11.96-7.94	19.98-12.24	19.57-10.65
Average Yield %	0.95	0.85	0.69	0.80	0.82	0.75	0.60	0.41

Address: 745 Seventh Avenue, New York, NY 10019	**Officers:** Richard S. Fuld - Chairman, Chief Executive Officer Joseph M. Gregory - President, Chief	**Investor Contact:** 212-526-0858
Telephone: 212-526-7000	Operating Officer **Transfer Agents:**	**No of Institutions:** 738
Web Site: www.lehman.com	The Bank of New York	**Shares:** 430,653,248 **% Held:** 76.35

LEXINGTON REALTY TRUST

Exchange	Symbol	Price	52Wk Range	Yield	P/E
NYS	LXP	$15.73 (5/29/2008)	21.54-13.04	8.39	18.51

*7 Year Price Score 71.00 ***NYSE Composite Index=100** ***12 Month Score 86.74**

Interim Earnings (Per Share)

Qtr.	Mar	Jun	Sep	Dec
2005	0.11	0.22	0.08	(0.08)
2006	0.04	0.41	(0.42)	(0.20)
2007	(0.05)	0.34	0.12	0.38
2008	0.01	...	...	...

Interim Dividends (Per Share)

Amt	Decl	Ex	Rec	Pay
0.375Q	09/17/2007	09/26/2007	09/28/2007	10/15/2007
0.375Q	12/17/2007	12/27/2007	12/31/2007	01/15/2008
2.10Q	12/24/2007	12/27/2007	12/31/2007	01/15/2008
0.33Q	02/21/2008	03/27/2008	03/31/2008	04/15/2008

Indicated Div: $1.32

Valuation Analysis

Forecast EPS	$-0.66 (05/17/2008)		
Market Cap	$947.5 Million	Book Value	901.8 Million
Price/Book	1.05	Price/Sales	2.08

Dividend Achiever Status

10 Year Growth Rate	2.54%
Total Years of Dividend Growth	13

TRADING VOLUME (thousand shares)

Business Summary: "Property, Real Estate & Development" (MIC: SIC: 6798 NAIC: 525930)

Lexington Realty Trust is a self-managed and self-administered real estate investment trust that acquires, owns, and manages a portfolio of net leased office and industrial properties. In addition, Co. acquires and hold investments in loan assets and debt securities related to real estate, which are primarily acquired through a 50.0% owned co-investment program. As of Dec 31 2007, Co. had ownership interests in approximately 280 consolidated real estate assets, located in 42 states and the Netherlands and containing an aggregate of approximately 45.5 million net rentable square feet of space, approximately 95.6% of which is subject to a lease.

Recent Developments: For the quarter ended Mar 31 2008, income from continuing operations was US$8.1 million compared with a loss of US$2.1 million in the year-earlier quarter. Net income increased 252.7% to US$7.8 million from US$2.2 million in the year-earlier quarter. Revenues were US$107.6 million, up 33.2% from US$80.8 million the year before. Revenues from property income rose 30.3% to US$97.2 million from US$74.6 million in the corresponding quarter a year earlier.

Prospects: Co. expects the payment for the Apr 2008 100 Light Street lease termination of $27.1 million, the transfer of the fee interest in the land, the write-off of $18.4 million in an above-market lease intangible and the post-lease termination operation of the property to increase its funds from operations (FFO) for the second quarter of 2008 by $0.22 per common share/unit. However, Co. estimates that this transaction will reduce its FFO by $0.03 per common share/unit in the second half of 2008. For 2008, Co. reaffirmed its FFO guidance range of $1.56 to $1.64 per diluted share/unit, excluding the effect of the 100 Light Street lease termination transaction and other non-recurring items.

Financial Data
(US$ in Thousands)

	3 Mos	12/31/2007	12/31/2006	12/31/2005	12/31/2004	12/31/2003	12/31/2002	12/31/2001
Earnings Per Share	0.85	0.77	(0.17)	0.33	0.80	0.88	1.09	0.77
Cash Flow Per Share	4.28	4.43	2.07	2.26	1.95	2.11	2.15	2.28
Tang Book Value Per Share	1.08	0.75	6.19	10.27	12.03	12.02	11.09	9.89
Dividends Per Share	3.555	3.600	2.058	1.440	1.400	1.340	1.320	1.270
Dividend Payout %	420.08	467.53	...	436.36	175.00	152.27	121.10	164.94
Income Statement								
Total Revenue	107,588	431,747	207,391	197,132	151,225	120,520	100,619	82,862
Depn & Amortn	56,301	253,535	84,734	73,034	41,710	29,572	23,375	19,952
Income Before Taxes	(10,785)	(74,392)	(3,476)	13,933	41,860	34,812	...	...
Income Taxes	1,344	3,374	(238)	(150)	1,181	...	...	...
Net Income	7,812	76,851	7,753	32,695	44,807	33,649	30,595	18,062
Average Shares	59,837	64,910	52,163	49,902	52,048	39,493	32,602	19,862
Balance Sheet								
Total Assets	4,607,568	5,265,163	4,624,857	2,160,232	1,697,086	1,207,411	902,471	822,153
Long-Term Obligations	2,128,167	2,312,422	2,123,174	1,139,971	765,144	455,940	460,517	445,771
Total Liabilities	3,705,812	3,560,229	2,599,672	1,207,550	793,037	564,534	508,840	469,403
Stockholders' Equity	901,756	939,071	1,122,444	891,310	847,290	579,848	332,976	266,713
Shares Outstanding	60,236	61,064	69,051	52,155	48,621	40,682	30,030	24,507
Statistical Record								
Return on Assets %	1.77	1.55	0.23	1.70	3.08	3.19	3.55	2.42
Return on Equity %	7.87	7.46	0.77	3.76	6.26	7.37	10.20	8.18
Net Margin %	7.26	17.80	3.74	16.59	29.63	27.92	30.41	21.80
Price Range	21.65-13.04	22.22-14.52	22.78-19.63	25.19-20.37	23.23-17.30	20.85-15.63	16.75-14.25	15.56-11.94
P/E Ratio	25.47-15.34	28.86-18.86	...	76.33-61.73	29.04-21.63	23.69-17.76	15.37-13.07	20.21-15.50
Average Yield %	19.07	17.77	9.72	6.39	6.70	7.41	8.40	9.13

Address: One Penn Plaza, Suite 4015, New York, NY 10119-4015	Officers: E. Robert Roskind - Chairman Richard J. Rouse - Vice-Chairman, Chief Investment Officer	No of Institutions: 205
Telephone: 212-692-7200	Transfer Agents: Mellon Investor Services LLC, Jersey City, NJ	Shares: 58,692,440 % Held: 87.37
Web Site: www.lxp.com		

LIBERTY PROPERTY TRUST

Exchange	Symbol	Price	52Wk Range	Yield	P/E
NYS	LRY	$36.09 (5/29/2008)	47.84-25.85	6.93	21.36

*7 Year Price Score 71.98 *NYSE Composite Index=100 *12 Month Price Score 101.25

TRADING VOLUME (thousand shares)

Interim Earnings (Per Share)

Qtr.	Mar	Jun	Sep	Dec
2005	0.52	0.51	0.58	1.21
2006	1.01	0.76	0.52	0.67
2007	0.43	0.57	0.41	0.39
2008	0.33	...	...	...

Interim Dividends (Per Share)

Amt	Decl	Ex	Rec	Pay
0.62Q	06/19/2007	06/27/2007	07/01/2007	07/15/2007
0.625Q	09/17/2007	09/27/2007	10/01/2007	10/15/2007
0.625Q	12/18/2007	12/27/2007	01/01/2008	01/15/2008
0.625Q	03/17/2008	03/28/2008	04/01/2008	04/15/2008

Indicated Div: $2.50

Valuation Analysis

Forecast EPS $1.33 (05/17/2008)

Market Cap	$3.3 Billion	Book Value	1.8 Billion
Price/Book	1.83	Price/Sales	4.55

Dividend Achiever Status

10 Year Growth Rate	4.18%
Total Years of Dividend Growth	13

Business Summary: "Property, Real Estate & Development" (MIC: SIC: 6798 NAIC: 525930)

Liberty Property Trust is a self-administered and self-managed real estate investment trust. Co. provides leasing, property management, development, acquisition and other tenant-related services for its industrial and office properties. Co.'s industrial properties consist of a range of warehouse, distribution, service, assembly, light manufacturing and research and development facilities, including both single-tenant and multi-tenant facilities. Co.'s office properties are multi-story and single-story office buildings located in suburban mixed-use developments or office parks. At Dec 31 2007, Co. owned and operated 353 industrial and 296 office properties totaling 62.1 million square feet.

Recent Developments: For the quarter ended Mar 31 2008, income from continuing operations decreased 15.6% to US$29.4 million from US$34.8 million in the year-earlier quarter. Net income decreased 24.5% to US$30.0 million from US$39.7 million in the year-earlier quarter. Revenues were US$193.5 million, up 17.4% from US$164.8 million the year before.

Prospects: Despite the present sluggish credit markets and increasing economic slowdown, Co.'s outlook seems constructive as it continues to pursue development opportunities. Notably, as of Mar 31 2008, Co. projected total investment of its wholly owned properties under development of $450.8 million and expects to bring into service $200.0 million to $300.0 million of total investment in operating real estate from its development pipeline. For 2008, Co. expects straight line rents on renewal and replacement leases of 0.0% to 2.0% greater than rents on expiring leases, and projects that average occupancy for its properties in operation will not raise or decline by more than 1.0% in 2008 versus 2007.

Financial Data
(US$ in Thousands)

	3 Mos	12/31/2007	12/31/2006	12/31/2005	12/31/2004	12/31/2003	12/31/2002	12/31/2001
Earnings Per Share	1.69	1.80	2.95	2.82	1.88	2.05	2.02	2.15
Cash Flow Per Share	3.40	4.22	3.86	4.14	3.45	3.32	3.93	4.27
Tang Book Value Per Share	19.76	20.52	20.59	19.34	18.63	18.61	17.69	17.68
Dividends Per Share	2.495	2.490	2.470	2.450	2.430	2.410	2.380	2.320
Dividend Payout %	147.31	138.33	83.73	86.88	129.26	117.56	117.82	107.91
Income Statement								
Total Revenue	193,488	698,747	666,719	680,730	655,355	625,032	606,029	587,165
Depn & Amortn	44,777	167,802	156,210	155,480	141,015	127,115	114,870	106,642
Income Before Taxes	35,246	147,613	155,336	163,368	168,413	171,051	...	...
Income Taxes	484	(709)	288	14,827	1,820	2,326	...	...
Net Income	29,961	164,831	266,574	249,351	161,443	163,610	161,665	166,537
Average Shares	91,943	91,803	90,492	88,376	86,024	79,868	76,272	73,580
Balance Sheet								
Total Assets	5,207,170	5,638,749	4,910,911	4,497,529	4,162,827	3,834,008	3,627,061	3,552,825
Long-Term Obligations	2,656,085	3,021,129	2,387,938	2,249,178	2,133,171	1,885,866	1,866,187	1,753,131
Total Liabilities	3,012,185	3,429,107	2,741,580	2,535,214	2,358,702	2,081,444	2,067,033	1,935,009
Stockholders' Equity	1,823,998	1,837,021	1,871,604	1,709,182	1,596,259	1,544,897	1,351,589	1,423,422
Shares Outstanding	92,289	91,567	90,913	88,356	85,675	83,012	76,425	73,661
Statistical Record								
Return on Assets %	3.01	3.12	5.67	5.76	4.03	4.39	4.50	4.79
Return on Equity %	8.34	8.89	14.89	15.09	10.25	11.30	11.65	12.14
Net Margin %	15.48	23.59	39.98	36.63	24.63	26.18	26.68	28.36
Price Range	50.24-25.85	53.91-28.16	52.35-41.32	45.80-38.19	45.47-35.05	38.90-29.31	35.17-27.60	31.10-25.75
P/E Ratio	29.73-15.30	29.95-15.64	17.75-14.01	16.24-13.54	24.19-18.64	18.98-14.30	17.41-13.66	14.47-11.98
Average Yield %	6.62	5.81	5.35	5.87	6.04	7.10	7.60	8.15

Address: 500 Chesterfield Parkway, Malvern, PA 19355 **Telephone:** 610-648-1700 **Web Site:** www.libertyproperty.com	**Officers:** William P. Hankowsky - Chairman, President, Chief Executive Officer George J. Alburger - Executive Vice President, Chief Financial Officer, Treasurer **Transfer Agents:** Wells Fargo Shareholder Services, St. Paul, MN	**Investor Contact:** 610-648-1704 **No of Institutions:** 294 **Shares:** 100,917,448 **% Held:** 98.77

LILLY (ELI) & CO.

Exchange	Symbol	Price	52Wk Range	Yield	P/E
NYS	LLY	$48.60 (5/29/2008)	59.47-47.55	3.87	15.19

*7 Year Price Score 67.71 *NYSE Composite Index=100 *12 Month Price Score 94.97

Interim Earnings (Per Share)

Qtr.	Mar	Jun	Sep	Dec
2005	0.68	(0.23)	0.73	0.64
2006	0.77	0.76	0.80	0.12
2007	0.47	0.61	0.85	0.78
2008	0.97	...	...	...

Interim Dividends (Per Share)

Amt	Decl	Ex	Rec	Pay
0.425Q	06/21/2007	08/13/2007	08/15/2007	09/10/2007
0.425Q	10/15/2007	11/13/2007	11/15/2007	12/10/2007
0.47Q	12/17/2007	02/13/2008	02/15/2008	03/10/2008
0.47Q	04/21/2008	05/13/2008	05/15/2008	06/10/2008

Indicated Div: $1.88 (Div. Reinv. Plan)

Valuation Analysis

Forecast EPS $3.94 (05/17/2008)

Market Cap	$55.3 Billion	Book Value	14.9 Billion
Price/Book	3.71	Price/Sales	2.88

Dividend Achiever Status

10 Year Growth Rate	8.67%
Total Years of Dividend Growth	40

Business Summary: Pharmaceuticals (MIC: SIC: 2834 NAIC: 325412)

Eli Lilly is engaged primarily in the discovery, development, manufacture, and sale of pharmaceutical products. Co.'s principal products are: Neurosciences products, which includes Zyprexa®, Strattera®, Prozac®, Cymbalta® and Symbyax®; Endocrinology products, including Humalog®, Humalog Mix 75/25®, and Humalog Mix 50/50®, Humulin®, Actos®, Byetta®, Evista®, Humatrope®, and Forteo®; Oncology products, including Gemzar® and Alimta®; Cardiovascular products, including Cialis®, ReoPro® and Xigris®; and other pharmaceutical products, including Vancocin® and Ceclor® . Co. also has an animal health segment.

Recent Developments: For the quarter ended Mar 31 2008, net income increased 109.2% to US$1.06 billion from US$508.7 million in the year-earlier quarter. Revenues were US$4.81 billion, up 13.8% from US$4.23 billion the year before. Direct operating expenses rose 20.5% to US$1.11 billion from US$922.5 million in the comparable period the year before. Indirect operating expenses increased 1.4% to US$2.66 billion from US$2.62 billion in the equivalent prior-year period.

Prospects: On Apr 16 2008, Co. announced a streamlining of a portion of its manufacturing operations in Indianapolis. In detail, Co. is offering a voluntary exit program, which should reduce its Indianapolis employment by up to 500 people mainly in manufacturing but with a small portion in selected areas of research and development. These actions, which affect sites that manufacture active pharmaceutical ingredients for the insulin products Humalog® and Humulin® as well as for the osteoporosis medicine Forteo®, will align manufacturing capacity and engineering support services with the needs of the business. Meanwhile, Co. expects its 2008 earnings to be in the range of $3.90 to $4.05 per share.

Financial Data
(US$ in Thousands)

	3 Mos	12/31/2007	12/31/2006	12/31/2005	12/31/2004	12/31/2003	12/31/2002	12/31/2001
Earnings Per Share	3.20	2.71	2.45	1.81	1.66	2.37	2.50	2.55
Cash Flow Per Share	5.45	4.73	3.66	1.76	2.64	3.39	1.92	3.40
Tang Book Value Per Share	11.02	9.88	9.70	9.55	9.65	8.69	7.37	6.32
Dividends Per Share	1.745	1.700	1.600	1.520	1.420	1.340	1.240	1.120
Dividend Payout %	54.48	62.73	65.31	83.98	85.54	56.54	49.60	43.92
Income Statement								
Total Revenue	4,807,600	18,633,500	15,691,000	14,645,300	13,857,900	12,582,500	11,077,500	11,542,500
EBITDA	1,337,300	4,937,700	4,219,800	3,443,900	3,539,400	3,810,200	3,950,700	4,007,000
Depn & Amortn	277,500	1,047,900	801,800	726,400	597,500	548,500	493,000	454,900
Income Before Taxes	1,056,300	3,876,800	3,418,000	2,717,500	2,941,900	3,261,700	3,457,700	3,552,100
Income Taxes	(8,000)	923,800	755,300	715,900	1,131,800	700,900	749,800	742,700
Net Income	1,064,300	2,953,000	2,662,700	1,979,600	1,810,100	2,560,800	2,707,900	2,780,000
Average Shares	1,094,100	1,090,750	1,087,490	1,092,150	1,088,936	1,082,230	1,085,088	1,090,793
Balance Sheet								
Current Assets	12,494,200	12,256,900	9,694,400	10,795,800	12,835,800	8,758,700	7,804,100	6,938,900
Total Assets	27,220,200	26,787,800	21,955,400	24,580,800	24,867,000	21,678,100	19,042,000	16,434,100
Current Liabilities	4,164,300	5,268,300	5,085,600	5,716,300	7,593,700	5,550,600	5,063,500	5,203,000
Long-Term Obligations	4,648,300	4,593,500	3,494,400	5,763,500	4,491,900	4,687,800	4,358,200	3,132,100
Total Liabilities	12,310,000	13,123,400	10,974,700	13,788,900	13,947,100	11,913,300	10,768,400	9,330,100
Stockholders' Equity	14,910,200	13,664,400	10,980,700	10,791,900	10,919,900	9,764,800	8,273,600	7,104,000
Shares Outstanding	1,136,974	1,134,313	1,131,668	1,130,137	1,131,942	1,123,725	1,122,443	1,123,348
Statistical Record								
Return on Assets %	13.74	12.12	11.44	8.01	7.76	12.58	15.27	17.86
Return on Equity %	26.48	23.96	24.46	18.24	17.45	28.39	35.22	42.28
EBITDA Margin %	27.82	26.50	26.89	23.52	25.54	30.28	35.66	34.72
Net Margin %	22.14	15.85	16.97	13.52	13.06	20.35	24.45	24.08
Asset Turnover	0.75	0.76	0.67	0.59	0.59	0.62	0.62	0.74
Current Ratio	3.00	2.33	1.91	1.89	1.69	1.58	1.54	1.33
Debt to Equity	0.31	0.34	0.32	0.53	0.41	0.48	0.53	0.44
Price Range	60.56-47.81	60.56-49.09	58.86-50.41	60.44-49.76	76.26-50.44	73.89-53.70	80.69-48.15	91.50-72.59
P/E Ratio	18.93-14.94	22.35-18.11	24.02-20.58	33.39-27.49	45.94-30.39	31.18-22.66	32.28-19.26	35.88-28.47
Average Yield %	3.17	3.06	2.90	2.76	2.15	2.11	1.91	1.40

Address: Lilly Corporate Center, Indianapolis, IN 46285	Officers: Sidney Taurel - Chairman John C. Lechleiter - President, Chief Executive Officer Transfer Agents:	Investor Contact: 317-276-2506
Telephone: 317-276-2000	Wells Fargo Shareowner Services, St. Paul, MN	No of Institutions: 1002
Web Site: www.lilly.com		Shares: 995,549,376 % Held: 75.38

LINCOLN NATIONAL CORP. (ID)

Exchange	Symbol	Price	52Wk Range	Yield	P/E
NYS	LNC	$55.55 (5/29/2008)	73.07-46.59	2.99	13.58

*7 Year Price Score 93.12   *NYSE Composite Index=100   *12 Month Price Score 92.88

Interim Earnings (Per Share)

Qtr.	Mar	Jun	Sep	Dec
2005	1.01	1.13	1.30	1.28
2006	1.24	1.23	1.29	1.37
2007	1.42	1.37	1.21	0.43
2008	1.10	...	...	...

Interim Dividends (Per Share)

Amt	Decl	Ex	Rec	Pay
0.395Q	08/03/2007	10/05/2007	10/10/2007	11/01/2007
0.415Q	11/06/2007	01/08/2008	01/10/2008	02/01/2008
0.415Q	02/08/2008	04/07/2008	04/09/2008	05/01/2008
0.415Q	05/08/2008	07/08/2008	07/10/2008	08/01/2008

Indicated Div: $1.66 (Div. Reinv. Plan)

Valuation Analysis

Forecast EPS	$5.50 (05/17/2008)
Market Cap	$14.4 Billion Book Value 11.1 Billion
Price/Book	1.30 Price/Sales 1.38

Dividend Achiever Status

10 Year Growth Rate	4.89%
Total Years of Dividend Growth	24

Business Summary: Insurance (MIC: SIC: 6311 NAIC: 524113)

Lincoln National is a holding company, which operates multiple insurance and investment management businesses through subsidiary companies. Co. sells a range of wealth protection, accumulation and retirement income products and services. These products include institutional and/or retail fixed and indexed annuities, variable annuities, universal life insurance, variable universal life insurance, term life insurance, mutual funds and managed accounts. At Dec 31 2007, Co. provided products and services in four operating businesses: Individual Markets, Employer Markets, Investment Management and Lincoln UK.

Recent Developments: For the quarter ended Mar 31 2008, income from continuing operations decreased 24.5% to US$293.0 million from US$388.0 million in the year-earlier quarter. Net income decreased 27.0% to US$289.0 million from US$396.0 million in the year-earlier quarter. Revenues were US$2.52 billion, down 4.0% from US$2.63 billion the year earlier. Net premiums earned were US$509.0 million versus US$459.0 million in the prior-year quarter, an increase of 10.9%. Net investment income fell 11.2% to US$968.0 million from US$1.09 billion a year ago.

Prospects: For the rest of 2008, Co. anticipates a continuation of volatility in the equity and credit markets as well as competitive pressures in the life insurance and annuity marketplace in a prevailing low interest rate environment, compounded by a continued decline in the economy or recession. Nevertheless, Co. will continue to invest in expanding its distribution in each of its core Individual Markets, Investment Management and Employer Markets businesses. Going forward, Co. expects sales at its Individual Life business to increase throughout 2008 due to product improvements and seasonality trends and projects Investment Management income from operations in the low to mid $50.0 million range.

Financial Data
(US$ in Thousands)

	3 Mos	12/31/2007	12/31/2006	12/31/2005	12/31/2004	12/31/2003	12/31/2002	12/31/2001
Earnings Per Share	4.09	4.43	5.13	4.72	3.95	2.85	0.49	3.05
Cash Flow Per Share	6.03	7.23	12.08	5.62	6.29	5.89	2.68	6.64
Tang Book Value Per Share	26.84	28.66	27.92	23.89	22.26	18.77	15.62	14.11
Dividends Per Share	1.600	1.580	1.520	1.460	1.400	1.340	1.280	1.220
Dividend Payout %	39.07	35.67	29.63	30.93	35.44	47.02	261.22	40.00
Income Statement								
Total Revenue	2,524,000	10,594,000	9,063,000	5,487,938	5,371,274	5,283,881	4,635,462	6,380,638
Income Before Taxes	418,000	1,874,000	1,811,000	1,074,644	1,035,658	1,047,563	1,624	764,139
Income Taxes	125,000	553,000	495,000	243,589	304,147	280,408	(89,966)	158,362
Net Income	289,000	1,215,000	1,316,000	831,055	707,009	511,936	91,590	590,211
Average Shares	262,764	273,905	256,169	176,144	179,017	179,441	185,596	193,303
Balance Sheet								
Total Assets	185,349,000	191,435,000	178,494,000	124,787,566	116,219,265	106,744,868	93,133,422	98,001,304
Total Liabilities	174,263,000	179,717,000	166,293,000	118,403,177	110,043,676	100,933,243	87,837,155	92,737,820
Stockholders' Equity	11,086,000	11,718,000	12,201,000	6,384,389	6,175,589	5,811,625	5,296,267	5,263,484
Shares Outstanding	259,206	264,233	275,752	174,820	173,557	178,212	177,307	186,943
Statistical Record								
Return on Assets %	0.60	0.66	0.87	0.69	0.63	0.51	0.10	0.60
Return on Equity %	9.55	10.16	14.16	13.23	11.76	9.22	1.73	11.55
Net Margin %	11.45	11.47	14.52	15.14	13.16	9.69	1.98	9.25
Price Range	74.46-46.59	74.46-56.16	66.46-52.20	53.89-41.95	49.95-40.17	41.32-25.17	53.50-25.17	52.55-39.10
P/E Ratio	18.21-11.39	16.81-12.68	12.96-10.18	11.42-8.89	12.65-10.17	14.50-8.83	109.18-51.37	17.23-12.82
Average Yield %	2.57	2.39	2.59	3.04	3.08	3.87	3.13	2.63

Address: Centre Square, West Tower, 1500 Market Street, 39th Floor, Philadelphia, PA 19102-2112 **Telephone:** 215-448-1400 **Web Site:** www.lfg.com	**Officers:** Dennis R. Glass - President, Chief Executive Officer Charles C. Cornelio - Senior Vice President, Chief Information Officer **Transfer Agents:** Mellon Investor Services LLC, South Hackensack, NJ	**Investor Contact:** 215-448-1422 **No of Institutions:** 701 **Shares:** 201,463,568 **% Held:** 68.52

LINEAR TECHNOLOGY CORP.

Exchange	Symbol	Price	52Wk Range	Yield	P/E
NMS	LLTC	$36.40 (5/29/2008)	38.22-26.54	2.31	22.61

*7 Year Price Score 71.18   *NYSE Composite Index=100   *12 Month Price Score 107.45

Interim Earnings (Per Share)

Qtr.	Sep	Dec	Mar	Jun
2004-05	0.33	0.33	0.39	0.34
2005-06	0.31	0.33	0.35	0.37
2006-07	0.37	0.34	0.32	0.36
2007-08	0.40	0.41	0.44	...

Interim Dividends (Per Share)

Amt	Decl	Ex	Rec	Pay
0.18Q	07/24/2007	08/08/2007	08/10/2007	08/22/2007
0.18Q	10/16/2007	11/14/2007	11/16/2007	11/28/2007
0.21Q	01/15/2008	02/13/2008	02/15/2008	02/27/2008
0.21Q	04/15/2008	05/14/2008	05/16/2008	05/28/2008
			Indicated Div: $0.84	

Valuation Analysis

Forecast EPS	$1.70 (05/17/2008)		
Market Cap	$8.0 Billion	Book Value	N/A
Price/Book	N/A	Price/Sales	7.07

Dividend Achiever Status

10 Year Growth Rate	29.33%
Total Years of Dividend Growth	15

Business Summary: IT & Technology (MIC: SIC: 3674 NAIC: 334413)

Linear Technology designs, manufactures and markets a range of standard linear integrated circuits. Applications for Co.'s products include telecommunications, cellular telephones, networking products, notebook computers, computer peripherals, video/multimedia, industrial instrumentation, security monitoring devices, high-end consumer products, complex medical devices, automotive electronics, factory automation, process control, and military and space systems. Co.'s principal product categories are: Amplifiers, High Speed Amplifiers, Voltage regulators, Voltage References, Interface, Data Converters, Radio Frequency Circuits, DC/DC uModule Power Systems and Other.

Recent Developments: For the quarter ended Mar 30 2008, net income increased 0.7% to US$99.2 million from US$98.6 million in the year-earlier quarter. Revenues were US$297.9 million, up 16.8% from US$255.0 million the year before. Operating income was US$145.9 million versus US$120.3 million in the prior-year quarter, an increase of 21.3%. Direct operating expenses rose 18.4% to US$66.9 million from US$56.5 million in the comparable period the year before. Indirect operating expenses increased 8.8% to US$85.0 million from US$78.2 million in the equivalent prior-year period.

Prospects: Co.'s recent improved top-line performance is attributable primarily to the selling of more units into the industrial and communication end-markets, partially offset by a reduction in its consumer end-market sales. Looking ahead, given the concerns about challenging economic environment particularly within the U.S., Co. presently estimates that its revenues and income before taxes for the fiscal quarter ending June 2008 will grow 1.0% to 5.0% sequentially from the Mar 2008 quarter. Meanwhile, Co. noted that it had backlog of released and firm orders of approximately $112.2 million at July 1 2007 as compared with $93.7 million at July 2 2006.

Financial Data
(US$ in Thousands)

	9 Mos	6 Mos	3 Mos	07/01/2007	07/02/2006	07/03/2005	06/27/2004	06/29/2003
Earnings Per Share	1.61	1.49	1.42	1.39	1.37	1.38	1.02	0.74
Cash Flow Per Share	2.44	2.21	2.20	1.65	1.68	1.58	1.47	0.91
Tang Book Value Per Share	...	...	...	...	6.94	6.55	5.87	5.80
Dividends Per Share	0.750	0.720	0.690	0.660	0.500	0.360	0.280	0.210
Dividend Payout %	46.48	48.20	48.45	47.48	36.50	26.09	27.45	28.38
Income Statement								
Total Revenue	868,073	570,208	281,488	1,083,078	1,092,977	1,049,694	807,281	606,573
EBITDA	460,260	302,779	149,457	575,035	613,222	638,466	485,475	340,414
Depn & Amortn	36,352	24,761	12,591	50,717	49,272	48,837	48,745	45,903
Income Before Taxes	401,563	262,774	128,838	569,924	616,808	619,964	462,213	333,226
Income Taxes	117,099	77,544	37,363	158,249	188,128	185,990	134,042	96,635
Net Income	284,464	185,230	91,475	411,675	428,680	433,974	328,171	236,591
Average Shares	224,489	227,119	229,230	296,616	313,285	315,067	321,456	321,375
Balance Sheet								
Current Assets	1,161,432	1,060,846	979,696	861,104	2,077,136	2,007,309	1,832,095	1,776,000
Total Assets	1,503,657	1,409,780	1,334,471	1,218,857	2,390,895	2,286,234	2,087,703	2,056,879
Current Liabilities	157,560	148,415	152,328	179,869	236,826	207,739	202,614	162,029
Long-Term Obligations	1,700,000	1,700,000	1,700,000	1,700,000	...	...	...	...
Total Liabilities	1,991,229	1,974,142	1,970,400	1,926,822	286,397	279,200	277,098	241,950
Stockholders' Equity	(487,572)	(564,362)	(635,929)	(707,965)	2,104,498	2,007,034	1,810,605	1,814,929
Shares Outstanding	221,138	223,977	223,200	229,655	303,092	306,587	308,548	312,706
Statistical Record								
Return on Assets %	19.54	20.11	21.00	22.87	18.38	19.52	15.88	11.73
Return on Equity %	45.14	49.12	53.23	59.12	20.91	22.37	18.15	13.19
EBITDA Margin %	53.02	53.10	53.10	53.09	56.11	60.82	60.14	56.12
Net Margin %	32.77	32.48	32.50	38.01	39.22	41.34	40.65	39.00
Asset Turnover	0.58	0.58	0.58	0.60	0.47	0.47	0.39	0.30
Current Ratio	7.37	7.15	6.43	4.79	8.77	9.66	9.04	10.96
Price Range	38.74-26.54	38.74-29.65	38.74-29.87	38.74-29.87	41.54-32.90	40.31-34.42	44.95-32.38	36.77-19.61
P/E Ratio	24.06-16.48	26.00-19.90	27.28-21.04	27.87-21.49	30.32-24.01	29.21-24.94	44.07-31.75	49.69-26.50
Average Yield %	2.26	2.12	2.04	2.00	1.37	0.96	0.71	0.71

Address: 1630 McCarthy Boulevard, Milpitas, CA 95035 **Telephone:** 408-432-1900 **Web Site:** www.linear.com	**Officers:** Robert H. Swanson - Executive Chairman Lothar Maier - Chief Executive Officer **Transfer Agents:** Computershare Trust Company N.A., Providence, RI	**Investor Contact:** 408-432-1900 **No of Institutions:** 464 **Shares:** 302,569,152 **% Held:** 77.99

LOWE'S COMPANIES INC

Exchange	Symbol	Price	52Wk Range	Yield	P/E
NYS	LOW	$24.39 (5/29/2008)	32.99-20.31	1.39	13.55

*7 Year Price Score 77.62   *NYSE Composite Index=100   *12 Month Price Score 96.36

Interim Earnings (Per Share)

Qtr.	Apr	Jul	Oct	Jan
2005-06	0.37	0.53	0.41	0.44
2006-07	0.53	0.60	0.46	0.40
2007-08	0.48	0.67	0.43	0.28
2008-09	0.41	...	...	...

Interim Dividends (Per Share)

Amt	Decl	Ex	Rec	Pay
0.08Q	08/20/2007	10/17/2007	10/19/2007	11/02/2007
0.08Q	11/19/2007	01/16/2008	01/18/2008	02/01/2008
0.08Q	03/24/2008	04/16/2008	04/18/2008	05/02/2008
0.08SQ	05/30/2008	07/16/2008	07/18/2008	08/01/2008

Indicated Div: $0.34 (Div. Reinv. Plan)

Valuation Analysis

Forecast EPS $1.55 (05/17/2008)

Market Cap	$35.7 Billion	Book Value	16.6 Billion
Price/Book	2.15	Price/Sales	0.74

Dividend Achiever Status

10 Year Growth Rate	25.19%
Total Years of Dividend Growth	46

Business Summary: Retail - Furniture & Home Furnishings (MIC: SIC: 5211 NAIC: 444110)

Lowe's Companies is engaged in retailing home improvement products, with focus on retail do-it-yourself (DIY) customers, do-it-for-me (DIFM) customers who utilize its installation services, and Commercial Business Customers. Co. provides a range of products and services for home decorating, maintenance, repair, remodeling, and property maintenance. In additions, Co. also carries certain brands for categories like lighting, flooring, home style and organization, tools and others. These band names are Premier® Kobalt®, Portfolio®, Harbor Breeze®, Reliabilt®, Perfect Flame® Top-Choice® Lumber and Utilitech® As of Feb 1 2008, Co. operated 1,534 stores throughout the U.S. and Canada.

Recent Developments: For the quarter ended May 2 2008, net income decreased 17.9% to US$607.0 million from US$739.0 million in the year-earlier quarter. Revenues were US$12.01 billion, down 1.3% from US$12.17 billion the year before. Direct operating expenses declined 0.9% to US$7.84 billion from US$7.91 billion in the comparable period the year before. Indirect operating expenses increased 3.2% to US$3.12 billion from US$3.02 billion in the equivalent prior-year period.

Prospects: For the fiscal year ending Jan 30 2009, Co. intends to open about 120 stores, reflecting square footage growth of 7.0% to 8.0%, while total sales are forecasted to grow by 1.0%. In addition, Co. projects comparable store sales to decline by 6.0% to 7.0%, while store opening costs are estimated to be about $106.0 million. Thus, Co. is targeting earnings of $1.45 to $1.55 per diluted share. For the fiscal quarter ended Aug 1 2008, Co. plans to open about 23 new stores, reflecting square footage growth of 11.0%, while total sales are expected to grow by 1.0%. Lastly, Co. is anticipating comparable store sales to decrease by 6.0% to 8.0% and earnings of $0.54 to $0.59 per diluted share.

Financial Data

(US$ in Thousands)	3 Mos	02/01/2008	02/02/2007	02/03/2006	01/28/2005	01/30/2004	01/31/2003	02/01/2002
Earnings Per Share	1.80	1.86	1.99	1.73	1.36	1.17	0.93	0.65
Cash Flow Per Share	3.28	2.94	2.94	2.43	1.96	1.94	1.74	1.05
Tang Book Value Per Share	11.37	11.04	10.31	9.14	7.45	6.55	5.31	4.30
Dividends Per Share	0.320	0.290	0.180	0.110	0.075	0.055	0.043	0.039
Dividend Payout %	17.82	15.59	9.05	6.36	5.55	4.70	4.59	5.96
Income Statement								
Total Revenue	12,009,000	48,283,000	46,927,000	43,243,000	36,464,000	30,838,000	26,491,000	22,111,108
EBITDA	1,452,000	5,975,000	6,235,000	5,557,000	4,456,000	3,779,000	3,004,000	2,158,353
Depn & Amortn	404,000	1,464,000	1,237,000	1,051,000	920,000	781,000	645,000	534,102
Income Before Taxes	972,000	4,511,000	4,998,000	4,506,000	3,536,000	2,998,000	2,359,000	1,624,251
Income Taxes	365,000	1,702,000	1,893,000	1,735,000	1,360,000	1,136,000	888,000	600,989
Net Income	607,000	2,809,000	3,105,000	2,771,000	2,176,000	1,877,000	1,471,000	1,023,262
Average Shares	1,480,000	1,510,000	1,566,000	1,606,000	1,616,000	1,612,000	1,600,000	1,589,194
Balance Sheet								
Current Assets	10,158,000	8,686,000	8,314,000	7,831,000	6,974,000	6,687,000	5,568,000	4,920,392
Total Assets	32,654,000	30,869,000	27,767,000	24,682,000	21,209,000	19,042,000	16,109,000	13,736,219
Current Liabilities	8,973,000	7,751,000	6,539,000	5,832,000	5,719,000	4,368,000	3,578,000	3,016,830
Long-Term Obligations	5,576,000	5,576,000	4,325,000	3,499,000	3,060,000	3,678,000	3,736,000	3,734,011
Total Liabilities	16,035,000	14,771,000	12,042,000	10,343,000	9,674,000	8,733,000	7,807,000	7,061,777
Stockholders' Equity	16,619,000	16,098,000	15,725,000	14,339,000	11,535,000	10,309,000	8,302,000	6,674,442
Shares Outstanding	1,462,000	1,458,000	1,524,500	1,568,200	1,547,600	1,574,600	1,563,800	1,551,428
Statistical Record								
Return on Assets %	8.58	9.61	11.87	11.88	10.84	10.71	9.88	8.17
Return on Equity %	16.60	17.70	20.71	21.07	19.98	20.23	19.70	16.86
EBITDA Margin %	12.09	12.37	13.29	12.85	12.22	12.25	11.34	9.76
Net Margin %	5.05	5.82	6.62	6.41	5.97	6.09	5.55	4.63
Asset Turnover	1.54	1.65	1.79	1.85	1.82	1.76	1.78	1.77
Current Ratio	1.13	1.12	1.27	1.34	1.22	1.53	1.56	1.63
Debt to Equity	0.34	0.35	0.28	0.24	0.27	0.36	0.45	0.56
Price Range	32.99-20.31	34.93-20.31	34.65-26.37	34.70-25.75	30.13-23.25	30.02-17.00	24.05-16.75	23.75-12.50
P/E Ratio	18.33-11.28	18.78-10.92	17.41-13.25	20.06-14.88	22.15-17.09	25.66-14.53	25.86-18.01	36.54-19.23
Average Yield %	1.20	1.01	0.59	0.36	0.28	0.23	0.20	0.22

Address: 1000 Lowe's Boulevard, Mooresville, NC 28117 Telephone: 704-758-1000 Web Site: www.lowes.com	Officers: Robert A. Niblock - Chairman, Chief Executive Officer Larry D. Stone - President, Chief Operating Officer Transfer Agents: Computershare Trust Company, N.A., Providence, RI	No of Institutions: 949 Shares: 1,554,029,824 % Held: 80.56

LSI INDUSTRIES INC.

Exchange	Symbol	Price	52Wk Range	Yield	P/E
NMS	LYTS	$10.66 (5/29/2008)	22.91-10.34	5.63	11.71

*7 Year Price Score 94.00   *NYSE Composite Index=100   *12 Month Price Score 72.31

TRADING VOLUME (thousand shares)

Interim Earnings (Per Share)

Qtr.	Sep	Dec	Mar	Jun
2004-05	0.17	0.24	0.12	0.20
2005-06	0.18	0.19	0.12	0.22
2006-07	0.25	0.23	0.15	0.32
2007-08	0.32	0.22	0.05	...

Interim Dividends (Per Share)

Amt	Decl	Ex	Rec	Pay
0.05Q	08/23/2007	08/30/2007	09/04/2007	09/11/2007
0.15Q	10/26/2007	11/02/2007	11/06/2007	11/13/2007
0.15Q	01/24/2008	02/01/2008	02/05/2008	02/12/2008
0.15Q	04/23/2008	05/02/2008	05/06/2008	05/13/2008

Indicated Div: $0.60

Valuation Analysis

Forecast EPS	$0.65 (05/16/2008)		
Market Cap	$230.1 Million	Book Value	177.9 Million
Price/Book	1.29	Price/Sales	0.69

Dividend Achiever Status

10 Year Growth Rate	16.90%
Total Years of Dividend Growth	14

Business Summary: Electrical (MIC: SIC: 3648 NAIC: 335129)

LSI Industries is a provider of corporate visual image services through the combination of screen and digital graphics capabilities, various indoor and outdoor lighting products, and related services. Co. is also a provider of graphics and lighting products and services on a stand-alone basis. Co. provides corporate visual image services to the petroleum/convenience store industry, providing its services to national retailers and multi-site retailers, including quick service and casual restaurants, video rental and eyewear chains, retail chain stores and automobile dealerships located primarily in the U.S. At June 30 2007, Co. operated three segments: Lighting, Graphics and Technology.

Recent Developments: For the quarter ended Mar 31 2008, net income decreased 69.8% to US$997,000 from US$3.3 million in the year-earlier quarter. Revenues were US$64.8 million, down 14.0% from US$75.3 million the year before. Operating income was US$1.5 million versus US$5.1 million in the prior-year quarter, a decrease of 70.2%. Direct operating expenses declined 14.2% to US$48.8 million from US$56.8 million in the comparable period the year before. Indirect operating expenses increased 8.3% to US$14.5 million from US$13.4 million in the equivalent prior-year period.

Prospects: For the fiscal year ending June 30 2008, Co. has reduced its earnings guidance from a range of $0.75 to $0.81 per diluted share to a range of $0.65 to $0.69 per diluted share, reflecting a decrease of 27.4% to 31.6% over its fiscal 2007 earnings. Co. has also lowered its net sales guidance from a range of $322.0 million to $332.0 million to a range of $305.0 million to $317.0 million for the year. Notwithstanding these guidance reductions, Co. continues to invest in the development of new products, particularly solid-state light-emitting diode based products, and it is in the early stages of formulating plans to access selected international markets with these products going forward.

Financial Data

(US$ in Thousands)	9 Mos	6 Mos	3 Mos	06/30/2007	06/30/2006	06/30/2005	06/30/2004	06/30/2003
Earnings Per Share	0.91	1.01	1.02	0.95	0.71	0.73	0.43	(0.54)
Cash Flow Per Share	1.10	2.26	2.30	1.71	1.07	1.39	0.61	0.67
Tang Book Value Per Share	5.48	5.53	5.41	5.34	4.73	5.87	5.41	5.20
Dividends Per Share	0.610	0.590	0.570	0.510	0.560	0.344	0.264	0.192
Dividend Payout %	67.29	58.42	55.88	53.68	78.87	47.12	61.40	...
Income Statement								
Total Revenue	238,843	174,063	90,001	337,453	280,470	282,440	241,405	213,133
EBITDA	26,605	22,906	12,948	41,552	28,288	30,000	19,959	17,068
Depn & Amortn	6,644	4,471	2,222	9,002	6,773	6,974	5,925	5,702
Income Before Taxes	20,224	18,647	10,858	31,727	21,987	22,873	13,797	11,247
Income Taxes	7,451	6,871	3,905	10,938	7,544	8,237	5,107	3,454
Net Income	12,773	11,776	6,953	20,789	14,443	14,636	8,690	(10,748)
Average Shares	21,908	22,063	22,005	21,924	20,429	20,087	20,038	19,922
Balance Sheet								
Current Assets	101,775	109,251	119,658	123,358	107,088	98,804	97,123	83,505
Total Assets	208,616	217,565	228,357	233,612	224,401	172,637	174,732	162,776
Current Liabilities	25,307	32,719	45,893	54,961	40,301	31,615	32,399	23,872
Long-Term Obligations	...	...	2,174	...	16,571	...	11,554	13,999
Total Liabilities	30,725	38,040	51,146	57,551	59,416	34,597	45,869	37,871
Stockholders' Equity	177,891	179,525	177,211	176,061	164,985	138,040	128,863	124,905
Shares Outstanding	21,587	21,560	21,531	21,493	21,462	19,869	19,733	19,702
Statistical Record								
Return on Assets %	9.10	9.76	9.53	9.08	7.28	8.43	5.14	N.M.
Return on Equity %	11.25	12.59	12.89	12.19	9.53	10.97	6.83	N.M.
EBITDA Margin %	11.14	13.16	14.39	12.31	10.09	10.62	8.27	8.01
Net Margin %	5.35	6.77	7.73	6.16	5.15	5.18	3.60	N.M.
Asset Turnover	1.54	1.52	1.46	1.47	1.41	1.63	1.43	1.21
Current Ratio	4.02	3.34	2.61	2.24	2.66	3.13	3.00	3.50
Debt to Equity	...	...	0.01	...	0.10	...	0.09	0.11
Price Range	22.91-11.37	22.91-14.74	21.04-14.74	20.07-13.09	19.02-12.08	14.26-8.49	14.37-8.73	14.79-6.94
P/E Ratio	25.18-12.49	22.68-14.59	20.63-14.45	21.13-13.78	26.79-17.01	19.53-11.63	33.42-20.30	...
Average Yield %	3.59	3.27	3.27	3.04	3.49	3.11	2.28	2.18

Address: 10000 Alliance Road, Cincinnati, OH 45242 **Telephone:** 513-793-3200 **Web Site:** www.lsi-industries.com	**Officers:** Robert J. Ready - Chairman, President, Chief Executive Officer James P. Sferra - Executive Vice President, Secretary **Transfer Agents:** Computershare Investor Services, LLC, Chicago, IL	**Investor Contact:** 513-793-3200 **No of Institutions:** 138 **Shares:** 18,155,308 **% Held:** 79.95

M & T BANK CORP

Exchange	Symbol	Price	52Wk Range	Yield	P/E
NYS	MTB	$87.58 (5/29/2008)	112.69-71.59	3.20	14.15

*7 Year Price Score 76.79 *NYSE Composite Index=100 *12 Month Price Score 96.79

Interim Earnings (Per Share)

Qtr.	Mar	Jun	Sep	Dec
2005	1.62	1.69	1.64	1.78
2006	1.77	1.87	1.85	1.88
2007	1.57	1.95	1.83	0.61
2008	1.82	...	...	...

Interim Dividends (Per Share)

Amt	Decl	Ex	Rec	Pay
0.70Q	07/18/2007	08/30/2007	09/04/2007	09/28/2007
0.70Q	11/20/2007	12/13/2007	12/17/2007	12/31/2007
0.70Q	02/20/2008	02/27/2008	02/29/2008	03/31/2008
0.70Q	04/15/2008	05/29/2008	06/02/2008	06/30/2008

Indicated Div: $2.80 (Div. Reinv. Plan)

Valuation Analysis

Forecast EPS $6.85 (05/17/2008)

Market Cap	$9.6 Billion	Book Value	6.5 Billion
Price/Book	1.49	Price/Sales	2.11

Dividend Achiever Status

10 Year Growth Rate	23.31%
Total Years of Dividend Growth	27

Business Summary: Commercial Banking (MIC: SIC: 6022 NAIC: 522110)

M&T Bank is a bank holding company. Through its M&T Bank and M&T Bank, National Association subsidiaries, Co. is engaged in providing individuals, corporations and other businesses, as well as institutions with commercial and retail banking services, including loans and deposits, trust, mortgage banking, asset management, insurance and other financial services. As of Dec 31 2007, M&T Bank had 704 banking offices located throughout New York State, Pennsylvania, Maryland, Delaware, New Jersey, Virginia, West Virginia and the District of Columbia, plus a branch in George Town, Cayman Islands. As of Dec 31, 2007, Co. had total assets of $64.88 billion and total deposits of $41.27 billion.

Recent Developments: For the quarter ended Mar 31 2008, net income increased 14.9% to US$202.2 million from US$176.0 million in the year-earlier quarter. Net interest income increased 6.3% to US$478.9 million from US$450.4 million in the year-earlier quarter. Provision for loan losses was US$60.0 million versus US$27.0 million in the prior-year quarter, an increase of 122.2%. Non-interest income rose 32.2% to US$312.7 million from US$236.5 million, while non-interest expense advanced 6.7% to US$425.7 million.

Prospects: Despite the negative effect of the turbulence in the U.S. residential real estate market, Co. continues to expand its business through strategic investments. For instance, in Feb 2008, Co. invested $300.0 million in Bayview Lending Group LLC (BLG), a privately-held commercial mortgage lender that focuses on originating, securitizing and servicing small balance commercial real estate loans. While BLG's results for the second quarter of 2008 are expected to be hurt by severance and certain lease terminations, Co. believes BLG has adequate liquidity and an appropriately-sized business plan to preserve the franchise through the existing period of reduced liquidity in the securitization market.

Financial Data
(US$ in Thousands)

	3 Mos	12/31/2007	12/31/2006	12/31/2005	12/31/2004	12/31/2003	12/31/2002	12/31/2001
Earnings Per Share	6.19	5.95	7.37	6.73	6.00	4.95	5.07	3.82
Cash Flow Per Share	11.40	12.34	4.86	2.62	6.14	10.94	6.90	1.61
Tang Book Value Per Share	27.86	27.68	28.33	25.56	23.08	21.42	21.36	17.84
Dividends Per Share	2.700	2.600	2.250	1.750	1.600	1.200	1.050	1.000
Dividend Payout %	43.63	43.70	30.53	26.00	26.67	24.24	20.71	26.18
Income Statement								
Income Before Taxes	305,809	963,537	1,231,642	1,170,919	1,066,523	850,670	716,484	583,896
Income Taxes	103,613	309,278	392,453	388,736	344,002	276,728	231,392	205,821
Net Income	202,196	654,259	839,189	782,183	722,521	573,942	485,092	378,075
Average Shares	110,967	110,012	113,918	116,232	120,406	115,932	95,663	99,024
Balance Sheet								
Total Assets	66,085,573	64,875,639	57,064,905	55,146,406	52,938,721	49,826,081	33,174,525	31,450,196
Total Liabilities	59,597,611	58,390,383	50,783,810	49,270,020	47,209,107	44,108,871	29,992,702	28,510,745
Stockholders' Equity	6,487,962	6,485,256	6,281,095	5,876,386	5,729,614	5,717,210	3,181,823	2,939,451
Shares Outstanding	110,030	109,852	110,216	112,059	115,227	120,106	92,028	93,683
Statistical Record								
Return on Assets %	1.09	1.07	1.50	1.45	1.40	1.38	1.50	1.25
Return on Equity %	10.64	10.25	13.81	13.48	12.59	12.90	15.85	13.41
Price Range	113.62-71.59	124.74-79.31	124.21-106.45	112.28-96.93	108.01-83.37	98.55-75.69	89.94-68.00	81.23-61.09
P/E Ratio	18.36-11.57	20.96-13.33	16.85-14.44	16.68-14.40	18.00-13.90	19.91-15.29	17.74-13.41	21.26-15.99
Average Yield %	2.76	2.43	1.92	1.67	1.69	1.39	1.30	1.39

Address: One M&T Plaza, Buffalo, NY 14203 Telephone: 716-842-5445 Web Site: www.mtb.com	Officers: Robert G. Wilmers - Chairman, Chief Executive Officer Robert E. Sadler - Vice-Chairman Transfer Agents:Registrar and Transfer Company, Cranford, NJ	No of Institutions: 396 Shares: 83,477,736 % Held: 72.99

MACERICH CO. (THE)

Exchange	Symbol	Price	52Wk Range	Yield	P/E
NYS	MAC	$71.70 (5/29/2008)	92.66-58.91	4.46	31.59

*7 Year Price Score 107.50 *NYSE Composite Index=100   *12 Month Price Score 97.41

Interim Earnings (Per Share)

Qtr.	Mar	Jun	Sep	Dec
2005	0.30	0.11	0.07	0.39
2006	0.11	0.36	0.66	2.06
2007	0.04	0.19	0.24	0.54
2008	1.30	...	...	...

Interim Dividends (Per Share)

Amt	Decl	Ex	Rec	Pay
0.71Q	07/30/2007	08/17/2007	08/21/2007	09/07/2007
0.80Q	10/26/2007	11/13/2007	11/15/2007	12/07/2007
0.80Q	02/09/2008	02/20/2008	02/22/2008	03/07/2008
0.80Q	05/02/2008	05/15/2008	05/19/2008	06/09/2008

Indicated Div: $3.20

Valuation Analysis

Forecast EPS $5.85 (05/17/2008)

Market Cap	$5.2 Billion	Book Value	1.3 Billion
Price/Book	3.87	Price/Sales	5.82

Dividend Achiever Status

10 Year Growth Rate	5.11%
Total Years of Dividend Growth	13

Business Summary: "Property, Real Estate & Development" (MIC: SIC: 6798 NAIC: 525930)

Macerich is a self-administered and self-managed real estate investment trust engaged in the acquisition, ownership, development, redevelopment, management and leasing of regional and community shopping centers located throughout the U.S. As of Dec 31 2007, Co. is the sole general partner of, and owns a majority of the ownership interests in, The Macerich Partnership, L.P., a Delaware limited partnership. Additionally, as of such date, The Macerich Partnership owned or had an ownership interest in 74 regional shopping centers and 20 community shopping centers aggregating approximately 80.7 million square feet of gross leasable area.

Recent Developments: For the quarter ended Mar 31 2008, net income increased to US$98.1 million from US$6.1 million in the year-earlier quarter. Revenues were US$210.9 million, up 9.4% from US$192.8 million the year before. Revenues from property income rose 9.8% to US$194.9 million from US$177.5 million in the corresponding quarter a year earlier.

Prospects: For the full year of 2008, Co. is projecting Funds From Operation to be in the range of $5.00 to $5.15 per share. Meanwhile, Co. is progressing towards the expansion of The Oaks, a 1.1 million square-foot super regional mall in Thousand Oaks, CA. Accordingly, Co. is forecasting a multi-phased opening beginning with a 138,000-square-foot Nordstrom Department Store during the fall of 2008. In addition, Co. is redeveloping Santa Monica Place into an open-air shopping and dining destination. Co. anticipates re-opening of that center in fall 2009. Further, Co. is making progress towards the construction of a new wing at Scottsdale Fashion Square and anticipates the opening in fall 2009.

Financial Data
(US$ in Thousands)

	3 Mos	12/31/2007	12/31/2006	12/31/2005	12/31/2004	12/31/2003	12/31/2002	12/31/2001
Earnings Per Share	2.27	1.00	3.19	0.88	1.40	2.09	1.62	1.72
Cash Flow Per Share	4.21	4.54	2.99	3.97	3.31	4.88	5.52	4.16
Tang Book Value Per Share	16.14	17.29	20.54	11.92	14.30	15.34	15.49	10.27
Dividends Per Share	3.020	2.930	2.750	2.630	2.480	2.320	2.220	2.140
Dividend Payout %	133.16	293.00	86.21	298.86	177.14	111.00	137.04	124.42
Income Statement								
Property Income	194,924	861,603	799,727	743,104	528,099	468,255	366,883	323,038
Non-Property Income	16,020	34,765	29,929	24,281	19,169	17,749	12,041	11,535
Total Revenue	210,944	896,368	829,656	767,385	547,268	486,004	378,924	334,573
Depn & Amortn	47,954	245,556	234,442	207,025	145,573	106,794	77,767	66,016
Interest Expense	70,827	263,726	274,667	249,910	146,252	132,512	122,934	109,646
Income Taxes	301	(470)	33	(2,031)	...	...	...	...
Net Income	98,082	96,540	252,358	71,686	91,633	128,034	81,382	77,723
Average Shares	88,290	84,760	88,058	73,573	73,099	75,198	50,066	44,963
Balance Sheet								
Total Assets	7,838,193	8,121,134	7,562,163	7,178,944	4,637,096	4,145,593	3,662,080	2,294,502
Long-Term Obligations	5,767,698	5,762,958	4,993,879	5,424,730	3,230,120	2,682,599	2,291,908	1,523,660
Total Liabilities	6,126,538	6,156,060	5,298,454	5,732,806	3,403,314	2,855,559	2,395,449	1,584,226
Stockholders' Equity	1,344,537	1,312,634	1,542,305	827,108	913,533	953,485	797,798	348,954
Shares Outstanding	72,530	72,311	71,567	59,941	58,785	57,902	51,490	33,981
Statistical Record								
Return on Assets %	2.44	1.23	3.42	1.21	2.08	3.28	2.73	3.36
Return on Equity %	13.58	6.76	21.30	8.24	9.79	14.62	14.19	21.86
Net Margin %	46.50	10.77	30.42	9.34	16.74	26.34	21.48	23.23
Price Range	97.69-58.91	103.32-70.63	87.00-67.90	71.19-53.28	64.66-39.75	44.50-28.82	31.48-26.30	26.60-18.75
P/E Ratio	43.04-25.95	103.32-70.63	27.27-21.29	80.90-60.55	46.19-28.39	21.29-13.79	19.43-16.23	15.47-10.90
Average Yield %	3.80	3.40	3.71	4.21	4.86	6.46	7.59	9.26

Address: 401 Wilshire Boulevard, Suite 700, Santa Monica, CA 90401
Telephone: 310-394-6000
Web Site: www.macerich.com

Officers: Mace Siegel - Chairman Dana K. Anderson - Vice-Chairman **Transfer Agents:** Computershare Trust Company, N.A., Providence, RI

No of Institutions: 275
Shares: 83,514,696 **% Held:** 107.72

MAINSOURCE FINANCIAL GROUP INC

Exchange	Symbol	Price	52Wk Range	Yield	P/E
NMS	MSFG	$17.31 (5/29/2008)	19.01-12.15	3.35	14.19

*7 Year Price Score 77.95 *NYSE Composite Index=100 *12 Month Price Score 100.36

Interim Earnings (Per Share)

Qtr.	Mar	Jun	Sep	Dec
2005	0.31	0.35	0.32	0.25
2006	0.33	0.33	0.31	0.32
2007	0.29	0.32	0.30	0.26
2008	0.34	...	...	...

Interim Dividends (Per Share)

Amt	Decl	Ex	Rec	Pay
0.14Q	08/20/2007	08/30/2007	09/04/2007	09/14/2007
0.14Q	11/20/2007	11/30/2007	12/04/2007	12/14/2007
0.14Q	02/25/2008	03/06/2008	03/10/2008	03/17/2008
0.145Q	05/19/2008	06/04/2008	06/06/2008	06/16/2008

Indicated Div: $0.58

Valuation Analysis

Forecast EPS	$1.37 (05/16/2008)		
Market Cap	$321.4 Million	Book Value	273.8 Million
Price/Book	1.17	Price/Sales	1.83

Dividend Achiever Status

10 Year Growth Rate	8.25%
Total Years of Dividend Growth	19

Business Summary: Commercial Banking (MIC: SIC: 6022 NAIC: 522110)

MainSource Financial Group is a financial holding company. Through its banking subsidiaries, Co. provides a range of financial services, including: accepting time and transaction deposits; making consumer, commercial, agribusiness and real estate mortgage loans; renting safe deposit facilities; providing general agency personal and business insurance services; and providing personal and corporate trust services. Co. also provides services incidental to the business of banking through its non-bank affiliates. As of Dec 31 2007, Co. had total assets of about $2.54 billion, and operated 79 branch banking offices in Indiana, Illinois, and Ohio as well as eight insurance offices in Indiana.

Recent Developments: For the quarter ended Mar 31 2008, net income increased 15.4% to US$6.3 million from US$5.4 million in the year-earlier quarter. Net interest income increased 5.7% to US$19.7 million from US$18.6 million in the year-earlier quarter. Provision for loan losses was US$2.2 million versus US$696,000 in the prior-year quarter, an increase of 215.5%. Non-interest income rose 28.8% to US$7.8 million from US$6.1 million, while non-interest expense advanced 5.6% to US$17.8 million.

Prospects: Co.'s bottom-line results are benefiting primarily from an increase in net interest income mainly attributable to a higher level of earning assets, as well as an increase in non-interest income as a result of increases in mortgage banking income, service charges on deposit accounts, and security gains. In addition, Co. noted an increase in net interest margin primarily due to the rate cuts that occurred during the fourth quarter of 2007 and the first quarter of 2008 as its cost of funds decreased at a faster rate than the yield on earning assets. Looking ahead, Co. continues to emphasize on generating strong loan growth to increase averages in both its earning assets and loan portfolio.

Financial Data
(US$ in Thousands)

	3 Mos	12/31/2007	12/31/2006	12/31/2005	12/31/2004	12/31/2003	12/31/2002	12/31/2001
Earnings Per Share	1.22	1.17	1.29	1.23	1.41	1.37	1.25	0.99
Cash Flow Per Share	0.78	1.17	1.41	2.67	2.26	3.57	2.56	(0.10)
Tang Book Value Per Share	7.49	8.11	6.53	7.10	6.61	6.04	6.92	6.05
Dividends Per Share	0.560	0.555	0.529	0.495	0.454	0.415	0.378	0.347
Dividend Payout %	46.03	47.44	40.97	40.31	32.18	30.23	30.38	35.07
Income Statement								
Income Before Taxes	7,511	28,758	29,846	21,364	23,066	21,902	20,824	16,807
Income Taxes	1,260	6,888	7,605	5,172	6,273	6,597	6,813	5,630
Net Income	6,251	21,870	22,241	16,192	16,793	15,305	14,011	11,177
Average Shares	18,572	18,700	17,188	13,191	11,940	11,161	11,255	11,277
Balance Sheet								
Total Assets	2,528,343	2,536,437	2,429,773	1,645,605	1,549,379	1,442,729	1,251,760	1,178,392
Total Liabilities	2,254,586	2,272,335	2,176,526	1,484,536	1,426,059	1,337,305	1,151,989	1,068,095
Stockholders' Equity	273,757	264,102	253,247	161,069	123,320	105,424	99,771	87,872
Shares Outstanding	18,570	15,870	17,859	14,146	11,534	10,598	10,699	10,750
Statistical Record								
Return on Assets %	0.92	0.88	1.09	1.01	1.12	1.14	1.15	0.93
Return on Equity %	8.55	8.45	10.74	11.39	14.64	14.92	14.93	13.48
Price Range	19.01-12.15	19.01-14.36	18.52-15.30	22.82-16.33	25.21-15.69	19.20-12.96	14.37-9.38	10.15-7.70
P/E Ratio	15.58-9.96	16.25-12.27	14.36-11.86	18.55-13.28	17.88-11.13	14.02-9.46	11.49-7.50	10.25-7.78
Average Yield %	3.46	3.31	3.13	2.68	2.31	2.79	3.03	3.99

Address: 201 North Broadway, P.O. Box 87, Greensburg, IN 47240 **Telephone:** 812-663-0157 **Web Site:** www.mainsourcefinancial.com	**Officers:** Robert E. Hoptry - Chairman, Interim President, Chief Executive Officer James M. Anderson - Senior Vice President, Chief Financial Officer, Secretary **Transfer Agents:** Registrar and Transfer Company, Cranford, NJ	No of Institutions: 72 **Shares:** 6,580,572 **% Held:** 34.31

MARSHALL & ILSLEY CORP (NEW)

Exchange	Symbol	Price	52Wk Range	Yield	P/E
NYS	MI	$23.36 (5/29/2008)	34.50-21.61	5.48	5.77

*7 Year Price Score N/A   ***NYSE Composite Index=100**   ***12 Month Price Score N/A**

Interim Earnings (Per Share)

Qtr.	Mar	Jun	Sep	Dec
2007	0.83	0.83	0.83	1.83
2008	0.56	...	...	...

Interim Dividends (Per Share)

Amt	Decl	Ex	Rec	Pay
0.31Q	10/18/2007	11/28/2007	11/30/2007	12/14/2007
0.31Q	02/21/2008	02/28/2008	03/03/2008	03/14/2008
0.32Q	04/22/2008	05/28/2008	05/30/2008	06/13/2008

Indicated Div: $1.28

Valuation Analysis

Forecast EPS	$1.91 (05/17/2008)		
Market Cap	$6.1 Billion	Book Value	7.0 Billion
Price/Book	0.87	Price/Sales	N/A

TRADING VOLUME (thousand shares)

Dividend Achiever Status

10 Year Growth Rate	11.82%
Total Years of Dividend Growth	35

Business Summary: Commercial Banking (MIC: SIC: 6021 NAIC: 522110)

Marshall & Ilsley is a bank holding company with total assets of $59.85 billion and deposits of $35.19 billion at Dec 31 2007. Co.'s key activities consist of banking and wealth management services. Banking services, lending and accepting deposits from commercial banking and community banking customers are provided via Co.'s key bank, M&I Marshall & Ilsley Bank (M&I Bank), Southwest Bank, which is headquartered in St. Louis, MO, M&I Bank FSB, a federal savings bank subsidiary of Co. in Las Vegas, and an asset-based lending subsidiary based in Minneapolis, MN. Co.'s wealth management services include trust, brokerage and insurance services, and investment management and advisory services.

Recent Developments: For the quarter ended Mar 31 2008, income from continuing operations decreased 13.4% to US$146.2 million from US$168.8 million in the year-earlier quarter. Net income decreased 32.5% to US$146.2 million from US$216.8 million in the year-earlier quarter. Net interest income increased 9.1% to US$430.4 million from US$394.5 million in the year-earlier quarter. Provision for loan losses was US$146.3 million versus US$17.1 million in the prior-year quarter, an increase of 753.3%. Non-interest income rose 35.8% to US$211.2 million from US$155.6 million, while non-interest expense advanced 12.4% to US$315.8 million.

Prospects: For the remainder of 2008, Co. is forecasting continuous net interest margin compression due to the ongoing pricing competition for loan products, increased funding costs and the elevated levels of nonperforming loans. In addition, Co. foresees challenging market conditions for the residential real estate markets. Nevertheless, Co. anticipates that commercial and industrial loan growth as well as commercial real estate loan growth will show mid single-digit growth rates over its previous year's level. Further, Co. expects wealth management revenue, which is somewhat dependent on market volatility, to show high single-digit to low double-digit growth rates versus its prior year's level.

Financial Data

(US$ in Thousands)	3 Mos	12/31/2007	12/31/2006	12/31/2005
Earnings Per Share	4.05	4.34	3.17	2.99
Cash Flow Per Share	...	3.66	3.39	...
Tang Book Value Per Share	18.25	19.83	17.92	...
Dividends Per Share	1.24	1.20	1.050	0.930
Dividend Payout %	30.62	27.65	33.12	31.10
Income Statement				
Total Revenue	1,090,243	4,398,231	3,835,920	2,862,651
EBITDA	185,454	774,248	1,016,200	913,865
Depn & Amortn	5,945	63,668	61,051	49,082
Income Before Taxes	179,509	710,580	955,149	864,783
Income Taxes	33,300	213,641	307,435	278,124
Net Income	146,209	1,150,936	807,838	706,190
Average Shares	262,269	265,480	254,584	236,031
Balance Sheet				
Current Assets	1,861,575	1,955,428	1,491,086	...
Total Assets	63,398,348	59,848,596	56,230,257	...
Current Liabilities	46,368,305	43,667,736	41,051,507	...
Long-Term Obligations	9,075,921	8,207,406	8,026,155	...
Total Liabilities	56,424,192	52,815,867	50,078,886	...
Stockholders' Equity	6,974,156	7,032,729	6,151,371	...
Shares Outstanding	259,117	263,486	255,469	...
Statistical Record				
Return on Assets %	...	1.98	...	...
Return on Equity %	...	17.46	...	...
EBITDA Margin %	17.01	17.60	26.49	31.92
Net Margin %	13.41	26.17	21.06	24.67
Asset Turnover	...	0.08	...	...
Current Ratio	0.04	0.04	0.04	...
Debt to Equity	1.30	1.17	1.30	...
Price Range	34.50-21.71	34.50-26.36	...	...
P/E Ratio	8.52-5.36	7.95-6.07	...	...
Average Yield %	4.41	3.94	...	...

Address: 770 North Water Street, Milwaukee, WI 53202 **Telephone:** 414-765-7801 **Web Site:** www.micorp.com	Officers: Dennis J. Kuester - Chairman Mark F. Furlong - President, Chief Executive Officer **Transfer Agents:**Continental Stock Transfer & Trust Company, New York, NY	No of Institutions: N/A Shares: N/A % Held: N/A

MARTIN MARIETTA MATERIALS, INC.

Exchange	Symbol	Price	52Wk Range	Yield	P/E
NYS	MLM	$117.39 (5/29/2008)	168.77-95.67	1.18	20.07

*7 Year Price Score 142.65 *NYSE Composite Index=100   *12 Month Price Score 90.62

Interim Earnings (Per Share)

Qtr.	Mar	Jun	Sep	Dec
2005	0.15	1.30	1.62	1.02
2006	0.66	1.63	1.65	1.36
2007	0.73	1.92	2.12	1.33
2008	0.50	...	...	...

Interim Dividends (Per Share)

Amt	Decl	Ex	Rec	Pay
0.345Q	08/15/2007	08/29/2007	08/31/2007	09/28/2007
0.345Q	11/09/2007	11/28/2007	11/30/2007	12/31/2007
0.345Q	01/31/2008	02/27/2008	02/29/2008	03/31/2008
0.345Q	05/29/2008	05/30/2008	06/03/2008	06/30/2008

Indicated Div: $1.38

Valuation Analysis

Forecast EPS $6.27 (05/16/2008)

Market Cap	$4.9 Billion	Book Value	955.2 Million
Price/Book	5.08	Price/Sales	2.21

Dividend Achiever Status

10 Year Growth Rate	9.96%
Total Years of Dividend Growth	13

Business Summary: Earth & Rock Mining (MIC: SIC: 1481 NAIC: 213115)

Martin Marietta Materials is a producer of aggregates for the construction industry, including infrastructure, commercial, agricultural, and residential. As of Dec 31 2007, Co.'s aggregates, asphalt products, and ready mixed concrete are sold and shipped from a network of approximately 287 quarries, underground mines, distribution facilities, and plants in 28 states, Canada, and the Bahamas. Co. operates through four reportable business segments: the Mideast Group, Southeast Group, and West Group, comprising the Aggregates business, and the Specialty Products segment, which manufactures and markets magnesia-based chemical products, dolomitic lime, and structural composite products.

Recent Developments: For the quarter ended Mar 31 2008, income from continuing operations decreased 35.7% to US$21.2 million from US$32.9 million in the year-earlier quarter. Net income decreased 36.8% to US$20.9 million from US$33.0 million in the year-earlier quarter. Revenues were US$453.9 million, down 1.2% from US$459.7 million the year before. Operating income was US$42.9 million versus US$58.2 million in the prior-year quarter, a decrease of 26.2%. Direct operating expenses rose 3.6% to US$378.7 million from US$365.5 million in the comparable period the year before. Indirect operating expenses decreased 10.3% to US$32.3 million from US$36.0 million in the equivalent prior-year period.

Prospects: For the full year of 2008, Co. now anticipates heritage aggregates price increases in the 6.0% to 8.0% range, while heritage aggregates volumes are forecasted to range from down 3.0% to up 1.0%, both excluding acquisitions. Thus, Co. is projecting earnings of $6.25 to $7.00 per diluted share. Separately, on Apr 14 2008, Co. announced the acquisition of six quarry locations in Georgia and Tennessee from Vulcan Materials Co. for about $192.0 million. Co. believes that this transaction should expend its presence in the Georgia and Tennessee areas, particularly south and west of Atlanta. Hence, Co. foresees aggregates production in Georgia and Tennessee will increase by about 30.0% annually.

Financial Data

(US$ in Thousands)	3 Mos	12/31/2007	12/31/2006	12/31/2005	12/31/2004	12/31/2003	12/31/2002	12/31/2001
Earnings Per Share	5.85	6.06	5.29	4.08	2.66	1.91	1.77	2.19
Cash Flow Per Share	10.18	9.27	7.44	6.83	5.53	5.67	4.18	5.28
Tang Book Value Per Share	8.82	8.35	14.99	12.81	11.99	10.83	9.70	8.55
Dividends Per Share	1.310	1.240	1.010	0.860	0.760	0.690	0.580	0.560
Dividend Payout %	22.40	20.46	19.09	21.08	28.57	36.13	32.77	25.57
Income Statement								
Total Revenue	453,934	2,207,141	2,206,401	2,004,243	1,759,613	1,711,453	1,692,437	1,718,050
EBITDA	82,729	589,811	532,232	448,895	359,849	324,324	326,994	359,866
Depn & Amortn	38,922	150,338	141,429	138,251	132,173	139,606	138,696	154,635
Income Before Taxes	27,969	378,580	350,444	268,047	184,722	142,131	144,270	158,439
Income Taxes	6,813	116,073	106,640	72,534	56,543	41,047	46,455	53,077
Net Income	20,864	262,749	245,422	192,666	129,163	93,623	86,305	105,362
Average Shares	41,924	43,347	46,367	47,279	48,534	49,136	48,858	48,066
Balance Sheet								
Current Assets	620,880	626,010	592,354	602,041	624,253	621,519	526,149	496,232
Total Assets	2,760,108	2,683,805	2,506,421	2,433,316	2,355,852	2,330,093	2,258,530	2,224,580
Current Liabilities	544,508	506,616	315,072	200,122	203,813	220,164	197,827	192,037
Long-Term Obligations	855,655	848,186	579,308	709,159	713,661	717,073	733,471	797,385
Total Liabilities	1,804,921	1,737,814	1,252,449	1,259,631	1,202,425	1,200,246	1,175,520	1,202,368
Stockholders' Equity	955,187	945,991	1,253,972	1,173,685	1,153,427	1,129,847	1,083,010	1,022,212
Shares Outstanding	41,326	43,318	44,851	45,727	47,306	48,670	48,847	48,559
Statistical Record								
Return on Assets %	9.39	10.12	9.94	8.05	5.50	4.08	3.85	5.18
Return on Equity %	25.53	23.89	20.22	16.56	11.28	8.46	8.20	11.18
EBITDA Margin %	18.22	26.72	24.12	22.40	20.45	18.95	19.32	20.95
Net Margin %	4.60	11.90	11.12	9.61	7.34	5.47	5.10	6.13
Asset Turnover	0.82	0.85	0.89	0.84	0.75	0.75	0.76	0.85
Current Ratio	1.14	1.24	1.88	3.01	3.06	2.82	2.66	2.58
Debt to Equity	0.90	0.90	0.46	0.60	0.62	0.63	0.68	0.78
Price Range	168.77-95.67	168.77-99.93	112.37-76.39	79.93-50.01	53.66-41.66	47.78-26.15	48.12-27.45	51.27-36.00
P/E Ratio	28.85-16.35	27.85-16.49	21.24-14.44	19.59-12.26	20.17-15.66	25.02-13.69	27.19-15.51	23.41-16.44
Average Yield %	0.99	0.92	1.11	1.32	1.66	1.97	1.56	1.27

Address: 2710 Wycliff Road, Raleigh, NC 27607-3033

Telephone: 919-781-4550

Web Site: www.martinmarietta.com

Officers: Stephen P. Zelnak - Chairman, Chief Executive Officer, Division Officer C. Howard Nye - President, Chief Operating Officer **Transfer Agents:** American Stock Transfer & Trust Company, New York, NY

No of Institutions: 301

Shares: 50,712,776 **% Held:** 117.29

174

MASCO CORP.

Exchange	Symbol	Price	52Wk Range	Yield	P/E
NYS	MAS	$18.58 (5/29/2008)	30.21-17.70	4.95	27.73

*7 Year Price Score 65.73 *NYSE Composite Index=100 *12 Month Price Score 85.00

Interim Earnings (Per Share)

Qtr.	Mar	Jun	Sep	Dec
2005	0.52	0.64	0.61	0.42
2006	0.50	0.54	0.64	(0.46)
2007	0.37	0.51	0.56	(0.40)
2008	0.01	...	...	...

Interim Dividends (Per Share)

Amt	Decl	Ex	Rec	Pay
0.23Q	06/22/2007	07/03/2007	07/06/2007	08/06/2007
0.23Q	09/14/2007	10/03/2007	10/05/2007	11/05/2007
0.23Q	12/05/2007	01/02/2008	01/04/2008	02/04/2008
0.23Q	03/28/2008	04/09/2008	04/11/2008	05/12/2008

Indicated Div: $0.92 (Div. Reinv. Plan)

Valuation Analysis

Forecast EPS	$0.64 (05/16/2008)		
Market Cap	$6.6 Billion	Book Value	4.0 Billion
Price/Book	1.65	Price/Sales	0.58

Dividend Achiever Status

10 Year Growth Rate	8.43%
Total Years of Dividend Growth	49

Business Summary: Wood Products (MIC: SIC: 2434 NAIC: 337110)

Masco is engaged in the manufacture, distribution, and installation of home improvement and building products, with an emphasis on brand name consumer products and services. These products and services are sold to the home improvement and new home construction markets through mass merchandisers, hardware stores, home centers, builders, distributors and other outlets for consumers and contractors. As of Dec 31 2007, Co. operated through three business segments: Cabinets and Related Products; Plumbing Products; Installation and Other Services; Decorative Architectural Products; and Other Specialty Products.

Recent Developments: For the quarter ended Mar 31 2008, income from continuing operations decreased 82.5% to US$24.0 million from US$137.0 million in the year-earlier quarter. Net income decreased 98.6% to US$2.0 million from US$143.0 million in the year-earlier quarter. Revenues were US$2.45 billion, down 12.7% from US$2.80 billion the year before. Operating income was US$160.0 million versus US$252.0 million in the prior-year quarter, a decrease of 36.5%. Direct operating expenses declined 12.0% to US$1.82 billion from US$2.07 billion in the comparable period the year before. Indirect operating expenses decreased 3.3% to US$468.0 million from US$484.0 million in the equivalent prior-year period.

Prospects: Given the ongoing difficult business conditions in some of its markets, Co. believes that consumer spending for home improvement products and demand for certain of its International products will be weaker than expected. Accordingly, Co. continues to estimate that its 2008 housing starts will decline an additional 25.0% to 33.0% to between 900,000 and 1.0 million units. Thus for 2008, Co. now projects percentage sales decline of low-double digits to mid-teens versus 2007, and has lowered its earnings target to $0.50 to $0.65 per share. Separately, on Apr 30 2008, Co. announced the sale of its European-based The Heating Group for about $155.0 million to an affiliate of Vaessen Industries.

Financial Data

(US$ in Thousands)	3 Mos	12/31/2007	12/31/2006	12/31/2005	12/31/2004	12/31/2003	12/31/2002	12/31/2001
Earnings Per Share	0.67	1.03	1.22	2.19	1.96	1.64	1.15	0.42
Cash Flow Per Share	3.01	3.44	3.07	3.26	3.26	2.97	2.53	2.10
Tang Book Value Per Share	N.M.	N.M.	0.54	0.88	1.54	1.35	1.31	1.30
Dividends Per Share	0.920	0.910	0.860	0.780	0.660	0.580	0.545	0.525
Dividend Payout %	136.42	88.35	70.49	35.62	33.67	35.37	47.39	125.00
Income Statement								
Total Revenue	2,446,000	11,770,000	12,778,000	12,642,000	12,074,000	10,936,000	9,419,400	8,358,000
EBITDA	132,000	1,266,000	1,378,000	1,882,000	1,958,000	1,702,000	1,462,440	773,860
Depn & Amortn	...	241,000	240,000	230,000	229,000	232,000	200,600	269,500
Income Before Taxes	76,000	770,000	900,000	1,412,000	1,518,000	1,216,000	1,031,000	300,700
Income Taxes	40,000	336,000	412,000	518,000	569,000	463,000	348,900	102,200
Net Income	2,000	386,000	488,000	940,000	893,000	806,000	589,700	198,500
Average Shares	356,000	373,000	400,000	430,000	456,000	491,000	514,100	474,900
Balance Sheet								
Current Assets	3,788,000	3,808,000	5,115,000	5,123,000	4,402,000	3,804,000	3,949,770	2,626,920
Total Assets	10,889,000	10,907,000	12,325,000	12,559,000	12,541,000	12,149,000	12,050,430	9,183,330
Current Liabilities	1,863,000	1,908,000	3,389,000	2,894,000	2,147,000	2,099,000	1,932,450	1,236,560
Long-Term Obligations	3,996,000	3,966,000	3,533,000	3,915,000	4,187,000	3,848,000	4,316,470	3,627,630
Total Liabilities	6,897,000	6,882,000	7,854,000	7,711,000	7,118,000	6,693,000	6,756,590	5,063,500
Stockholders' Equity	3,992,000	4,025,000	4,471,000	4,848,000	5,423,000	5,456,000	5,293,840	4,119,830
Shares Outstanding	354,500	358,900	383,890	419,040	446,720	458,380	488,890	459,050
Statistical Record								
Return on Assets %	2.15	3.32	3.92	7.49	7.21	6.66	5.55	2.35
Return on Equity %	5.89	9.09	10.47	18.30	16.37	15.00	12.53	5.26
EBITDA Margin %	5.40	10.76	10.78	14.89	16.22	15.56	15.53	9.26
Net Margin %	0.08	3.28	3.82	7.44	7.40	7.37	6.26	2.37
Asset Turnover	1.00	1.01	1.03	1.01	0.98	0.90	0.89	0.99
Current Ratio	2.03	2.00	1.51	1.77	2.05	1.81	2.04	2.12
Debt to Equity	1.00	0.99	0.79	0.80	0.77	0.71	0.82	0.88
Price Range	30.71-18.22	33.93-20.94	33.20-26.00	38.03-27.37	36.80-26.02	28.31-16.82	29.08-17.68	26.49-18.00
P/E Ratio	45.84-27.19	32.94-20.33	27.21-21.31	17.37-12.50	18.78-13.28	17.26-10.26	25.29-15.37	63.07-42.86
Average Yield %	3.76	3.38	2.93	2.43	2.13	2.50	2.24	2.24

Address: 21001 Van Born Road, Taylor, MI 48180	**Officers:** Richard A. Manoogian - Executive Chairman Timothy Wadhams - President, Chief Executive Officer **Transfer Agents:** The Bank of New York, New York, NY	**Investor Contact:** 313-274-7400
Telephone: 313-274-7400		**No of Institutions:** 462
Web Site: www.masco.com		**Shares:** 410,997,088 **% Held:** 100.38

MATTHEWS INTERNATIONAL CORP

Exchange	Symbol	Price	52Wk Range	Yield	P/E
NMS	MATW	$47.52 (5/29/2008)	51.44-37.61	0.51	21.31

*7 Year Price Score 106.20 ***NYSE Composite Index=100** ***12 Month Price Score 111.20**

Interim Earnings (Per Share)

Qtr.	Dec	Mar	Jun	Sep
2004-05	0.39	0.47	0.50	0.48
2005-06	0.40	0.52	0.55	0.59
2006-07	0.44	0.58	0.38	0.64
2007-08	0.56	0.65	...	...

Interim Dividends (Per Share)

Amt	Decl	Ex	Rec	Pay
0.055Q	07/19/2007	07/27/2007	07/31/2007	08/14/2007
0.06Q	10/18/2007	10/29/2007	10/31/2007	11/14/2007
0.06Q	01/24/2008	01/31/2008	02/04/2008	02/18/2008
0.06Q	04/24/2008	05/01/2008	05/05/2008	05/19/2008

Indicated Div: $0.24

Valuation Analysis

Forecast EPS $2.48 (05/16/2008)

Market Cap	$1.5 Billion	Book Value	467.8 Million
Price/Book	3.17	Price/Sales	1.98

Dividend Achiever Status

10 Year Growth Rate	10.72%
Total Years of Dividend Growth	13

Business Summary: Metal Works (MIC: SIC: 3364 NAIC: 331522)

Matthews International is a designer, manufacturer and marketer principally of memorialization products and brand products and services. Memorialization products consist primarily of bronze memorials and other memorialization products, caskets and cremation equipment for the cemetery and funeral home industries. Brand products and services include graphics imaging products and services, marking products, as well as merchandising products and services. Co.'s products and operations are comprised of six business segments: Bronze, Casket, Cremation, Graphics Imaging, Marking Products and Merchandising Solutions.

Recent Developments: For the quarter ended Mar 31 2008, net income increased 9.6% to US$20.3 million from US$18.5 million in the year-earlier quarter. Revenues were US$197.8 million, down 2.5% from US$203.0 million the year before. Operating income was US$34.4 million versus US$31.6 million in the prior-year quarter, an increase of 8.7%. Direct operating expenses declined 8.7% to US$117.6 million from US$128.8 million in the comparable period the year before. Indirect operating expenses increased 7.7% to US$45.8 million from US$42.6 million in the equivalent prior-year period.

Prospects: For fiscal 2008 ending Sep 2008, Co. anticipates the cost of raw materials, particularly bronze ingot and steel will continue to affect its Casket segment. In response, Co. will continue its efforts to integrate and manage direct distribution operations. Separately, on May 8 2008, Co. announced the completed purchase of 78.0% interest in Saueressig GmbH & Co. KG, a European provider of pre-press services and gravure printing forms with manufacturing operations in Germany, Poland, England and Jordan, for $120.0 million. The purchase expands Co.'s products and services in the graphics imaging market. Accordingly, Co. expects earnings to range between $2.48 and $2.54 per share for fiscal 2008.

Financial Data (US$ in Thousands)	6 Mos	3 Mos	09/30/2007	09/30/2006	09/30/2005	09/30/2004	09/30/2003	09/30/2002
Earnings Per Share	2.23	2.16	2.04	2.06	1.84	1.72	1.39	1.10
Cash Flow Per Share	3.34	3.08	2.36	2.07	2.29	2.58	1.85	1.80
Tang Book Value Per Share	2.90	2.25	1.84	1.56	0.85	2.81	2.75	0.74
Dividends Per Share	0.230	0.225	0.220	0.200	0.180	0.160	0.110	0.105
Dividend Payout %	10.33	10.42	10.78	9.71	9.78	9.30	7.91	9.55
Income Statement								
Total Revenue	380,175	182,348	749,352	715,891	639,822	508,801	458,865	428,086
EBITDA	71,524	32,026	132,363	133,866	118,789	109,459	91,078	80,484
Depn & Amortn	10,250	5,043	20,528	21,463	19,893	15,628	14,872	13,856
Income Before Taxes	57,240	24,839	103,716	105,408	95,930	91,833	73,354	62,457
Income Taxes	19,526	7,408	38,990	38,964	36,106	35,638	28,461	24,225
Net Income	37,714	17,431	64,726	66,444	59,824	56,195	44,893	35,006
Average Shares	31,202	31,151	31,679	32,251	32,525	32,688	32,314	31,795
Balance Sheet								
Current Assets	287,504	268,809	266,514	242,843	232,133	202,478	166,054	156,020
Total Assets	803,309	775,450	771,069	716,090	662,067	530,542	436,741	422,601
Current Liabilities	133,131	120,393	123,456	137,209	145,577	111,572	76,323	87,186
Long-Term Obligations	124,888	137,070	142,273	120,289	118,952	54,389	57,023	96,487
Total Liabilities	335,512	335,589	344,291	323,665	327,706	218,292	180,513	241,226
Stockholders' Equity	467,797	439,861	426,778	392,425	334,361	312,250	256,228	181,375
Shares Outstanding	31,186	31,094	31,057	31,634	32,026	32,410	32,162	31,167
Statistical Record								
Return on Assets %	9.01	9.03	8.70	9.64	10.03	11.59	10.45	9.84
Return on Equity %	15.68	16.04	15.80	18.28	18.50	19.72	20.52	21.54
EBITDA Margin %	18.81	17.56	17.66	18.70	18.57	21.51	19.85	18.80
Net Margin %	9.92	9.56	8.64	9.28	9.35	11.04	9.78	8.18
Asset Turnover	0.97	1.00	1.01	1.04	1.07	1.05	1.07	1.20
Current Ratio	2.16	2.23	2.16	1.77	1.59	1.81	2.18	1.79
Debt to Equity	0.27	0.31	0.33	0.31	0.36	0.17	0.22	0.53
Price Range	50.75-37.61	49.44-37.61	46.76-35.66	40.23-31.87	41.57-31.64	36.08-26.33	28.46-21.71	28.67-21.23
P/E Ratio	22.76-16.87	22.89-17.41	22.92-17.48	19.53-15.47	22.59-17.20	20.98-15.31	20.47-15.62	26.06-19.30
Average Yield %	0.52	0.53	0.53	0.55	0.50	0.51	0.46	0.43

Address: Two Northshore Center, Pittsburgh, PA 15212-5851 **Telephone:** 412-442-8200 **Web Site:** www.matw.com	Officers: William J. Stallkamp - Chairman Joseph C. Bartolacci - President, Chief Executive Officer, Chief Operating Officer **Transfer Agents:** Computershare Investor Services LLC, Chicago Illinois	**Investor Contact:** 412-442-8200 **No of Institutions:** 187 **Shares:** 27,258,872 **% Held:** 82.28

MBIA INC.

Exchange	Symbol	Price	52Wk Range	Yield	P/E
NYS	MBI	$7.37 (5/29/2008)	67.78-7.05	N/A	N/A

*7 Year Price Score 50.95 *NYSE Composite Index=100 ***12 Month Price Score 30.63**

TRADING VOLUME (thousand shares)

Interim Earnings (Per Share)

Qtr.	Mar	Jun	Sep	Dec
2005	1.43	1.37	1.04	1.34
2006	1.46	1.62	1.59	1.32
2007	1.46	1.61	(0.30)	(18.01)
2008	(13.03)	...	...	...

Interim Dividends (Per Share)

Amt	Decl	Ex	Rec	Pay
0.34Q	02/27/2007	03/21/2007	03/23/2007	04/16/2007
0.34Q	06/07/2007	06/20/2007	06/22/2007	07/16/2007
0.34Q	09/06/2007	09/19/2007	09/21/2007	10/15/2007
0.34Q	12/06/2007	12/19/2007	12/21/2007	01/15/2008

Valuation Analysis

Forecast EPS	$-0.70 (05/17/2008)		
Market Cap	$1.7 Billion	Book Value	2.1 Billion
Price/Book	0.85	Price/Sales	N/A

Dividend Achiever Status

10 Year Growth Rate	10.06%
Total Years of Dividend Growth	20

Business Summary: Insurance (MIC: SIC: 6351 NAIC: 524130)

MBIA provides financial guarantee insurance and other credit protection, as well as investment management services to public finance and structured finance issuers and investors and capital market participants on a global basis. Co.'s financial guarantee insurance provides an unconditional and irrevocable guarantee of the payment of the principal of, and interest or other amounts owing on, insured obligations when due or, in the event that Co. has the right, at its discretion, to accelerate insured obligations upon default or otherwise, upon such acceleration by Co. In addition, Co. conducts its business through its subsidiaries, MBIA Insurance Corporation and MBIA Asset Management, LLC.

Recent Developments: For the quarter ended Mar 31 2008, net loss amounted to US$2.41 billion versus net income of US$198.6 million in the year-earlier quarter. Revenues were US$2.96 billion, compared with US$729.9 million the year before. Net premiums earned were US$155.3 million versus US$186.2 million in the prior-year quarter, a decrease of 16.6%. Net investment income rose 0.8% to US$514.9 million from US$510.9 million a year ago.

Prospects: Co. noted that during the first quarter of 2008, several monoline financial guarantee insurers were downgraded by one or more of the major rating agencies, while others have maintained their triple-A insurance financial strength ratings. Also, a new triple-A financial guarantee insurer began competing in the municipal finance market. Accordingly, Co. stated that these recent ratings actions have adversely affected its ability to attract new financial guarantee business and compete with those competitors that did not experience negative ratings actions. Subsequently, on June 5 2008, Standard & Poor's Ratings Services (S&P) downgraded Co.'s insurance financial strength rating from AAA to AA.

Financial Data
(US$ in Thousands)

	3 Mos	12/31/2007	12/31/2006	12/31/2005	12/31/2004	12/31/2003	12/31/2002	12/31/2001
Earnings Per Share	(29.75)	(15.17)	5.99	5.18	5.63	5.61	3.92	3.82
Cash Flow Per Share	6.14	8.07	5.00	5.83	6.34	6.82	5.95	4.87
Tang Book Value Per Share	8.36	28.53	52.84	48.95	46.63	42.88	37.32	31.56
Dividends Per Share	1.020	1.360	1.240	1.120	0.960	0.800	0.680	0.600
Dividend Payout %	...	...	20.70	21.62	17.05	14.26	17.35	15.71
Income Statement								
Premium Income	155,315	824,017	835,593	842,742	822,467	732,997	588,509	523,870
Total Revenue	(2,956,120)	(282,554)	2,712,256	2,300,507	2,000,902	1,688,881	1,217,358	1,135,785
Benefits & Claims	287,608	900,345	80,889	84,274	81,880	72,888	61,688	56,651
Income Before Taxes	(3,699,837)	(3,065,692)	1,133,263	1,015,948	1,129,913	1,148,640	792,581	790,984
Income Taxes	(1,293,105)	(1,143,744)	320,080	303,869	317,185	335,055	205,763	207,826
Net Income	(2,406,732)	(1,921,948)	819,288	710,986	815,304	813,585	579,087	570,091
Average Shares	184,708	126,670	136,694	137,220	144,799	144,980	147,574	149,282
Balance Sheet								
Total Assets	49,686,725	47,415,074	39,763,030	34,561,394	33,027,410	30,267,734	18,852,101	16,199,685
Total Liabilities	47,626,551	43,759,269	32,558,776	27,969,750	26,448,339	24,008,719	13,358,750	11,417,047
Stockholders' Equity	2,060,174	3,655,805	7,204,254	6,591,644	6,579,071	6,259,015	5,493,351	4,782,638
Shares Outstanding	236,857	125,372	134,835	133,047	139,391	143,875	144,773	148,434
Statistical Record								
Return on Assets %	N.M.	N.M.	2.20	2.10	2.57	3.31	3.30	3.79
Return on Equity %	N.M.	N.M.	11.88	10.80	12.67	13.85	11.27	12.66
Loss Ratio %	185.18	109.26	9.68	10.00	9.96	9.94	10.48	10.81
Net Margin %	...	...	30.21	30.91	40.75	48.17	47.57	50.19
Price Range	71.54-8.55	73.02-18.63	73.31-56.50	63.83-50.50	67.13-53.67	60.08-34.64	59.65-35.32	57.25-39.21
P/E Ratio	...	...	12.24-9.43	12.32-9.75	11.92-9.53	10.71-6.17	15.22-9.01	14.99-10.26
Average Yield %	2.25	2.31	2.03	1.92	1.61	1.61	1.37	1.18

Address: 113 King Street, Armonk, NY 10504	Officers: Joseph W. Brown - Chairman, President, Chief Executive Officer Ram D. Wertheim - Vice President, Secretary, General Counsel **Transfer Agents:** Wells Fargo Shareowner Services, St. Paul, MN	Investor Contact: 914-765-3190
Telephone: 914-273-4545		No of Institutions: 464
Web Site: www.mbia.com		Shares: 226,938,816 % Held: 80.16

MCCORMICK & CO., INC.

Exchange	Symbol	Price	52Wk Range	Yield	P/E
NYS	MKC	$37.54 (5/29/2008)	38.99-33.55	2.34	20.97

*7 Year Price Score 90.61 *NYSE Composite Index=100 *12 Month Price Score 104.84

Interim Earnings (Per Share)

Qtr.	Feb	May	Aug	Nov
2004-05	0.26	0.31	0.35	0.65
2005-06	0.11	0.46	0.32	0.62
2006-07	0.33	0.31	0.43	0.66
2007-08	0.39	...	...	...

Interim Dividends (Per Share)

Amt	Decl	Ex	Rec	Pay
0.20Q	06/26/2007	07/03/2007	07/06/2007	07/20/2007
0.20Q	09/26/2007	10/03/2007	10/05/2007	10/19/2007
0.22Q	11/27/2007	12/26/2007	12/28/2007	01/18/2008
0.22Q	04/02/2008	04/10/2008	04/14/2008	04/25/2008

Indicated Div: $0.88

Valuation Analysis

Forecast EPS $2.12 (05/16/2008)

Market Cap	$4.8 Billion	Book Value	1.2 Billion
Price/Book	4.17	Price/Sales	1.62

Dividend Achiever Status

10 Year Growth Rate	10.31%
Total Years of Dividend Growth	21

Business Summary: Food (MIC: SIC: 2099 NAIC: 311942)

McCormick is specialty food company engaged in the manufacture, marketing and distribution of flavor products, such as spices, herbs, seasoning and flavorings, as well as other specialty food products to the food industry. Co.'s Consumer segment sells spices, herbs, extracts, seasoning blends, sauces, marinades and specialty foods to the consumer food market under a variety of brands, including McCormick, Zatarain's, Simply Asia and Thai Kitchens, Ducros, Vahine and Silvo, Club House and Schwartz. Co.'s Industrial segment sells seasoning blends, natural spices and herbs, wet flavors, coating systems and compound flavors to food manufacturers and the food service industry.

Recent Developments: For the quarter ended Feb 29 2008, net income increased 16.3% to US$51.4 million from US$44.2 million in the year-earlier quarter. Revenues were US$724.0 million, up 10.9% from US$652.6 million the year before. Operating income was US$77.4 million versus US$66.4 million in the prior-year quarter, an increase of 16.6%. Direct operating expenses rose 12.9% to US$438.2 million from US$388.3 million in the comparable period the year before. Indirect operating expenses increased 5.2% to US$208.4 million from US$198.0 million in the equivalent prior-year period.

Prospects: For the fiscal year ending Nov 30 2008, Co. now anticipates sales growth in the range of 5.0% to 7.0%, excluding sales related to the pending acquisition of the Lawry's business. In addition, Co. is forecasting earnings to range from $1.97 to $2.01 per share, reflecting an increase of 8.0% to 10.0% over its previous fiscal year's level. Separately, on Feb 20 2008, Co. announced the acquisition of Billy Bee Honey Products Ltd. for approximately $75.0 million. Co. believes that this transaction should complement its savory products in Canada while strengthening its sweet products in Europe and the Asia/Pacific region. Co. expects this acquisition to be immediately accretive to its earnings.

Financial Data
(US$ in Thousands)

	3 Mos	11/30/2007	11/30/2006	11/30/2005	11/30/2004	11/30/2003	11/30/2002	11/30/2001
Earnings Per Share	1.79	1.73	1.50	1.56	1.52	1.48	1.26	1.04
Cash Flow Per Share	2.53	1.74	2.36	2.52	2.54	1.40	1.60	1.48
Tang Book Value Per Share	N.M.	N.M.	N.M.	N.M.	0.45	0.28	0.62	N.M.
Dividends Per Share	0.820	0.800	0.720	0.640	0.560	0.460	0.420	0.400
Dividend Payout %	45.90	46.24	48.00	41.03	36.84	31.08	33.33	38.28
Income Statement								
Total Revenue	723,950	2,916,200	2,716,400	2,592,000	2,526,200	2,269,600	2,320,000	2,218,500
EBITDA	103,138	445,600	363,500	418,500	406,800	373,900	345,200	315,700
Depn & Amortn	22,449	82,600	86,800	74,600	72,000	65,300	66,800	73,000
Income Before Taxes	65,932	302,400	223,000	295,700	293,800	270,000	234,800	190,400
Income Taxes	19,873	92,200	64,700	96,700	89,000	83,400	74,300	62,900
Net Income	51,423	230,100	202,200	214,900	214,500	210,800	179,800	146,600
Average Shares	131,067	132,700	135,000	138,100	141,300	142,600	142,300	140,200
Balance Sheet								
Current Assets	951,344	983,100	899,400	800,200	864,000	762,100	724,600	635,800
Total Assets	2,858,276	2,787,500	2,568,000	2,272,700	2,369,600	2,148,200	1,930,800	1,772,000
Current Liabilities	737,726	861,300	780,500	699,000	772,700	712,700	673,400	713,700
Long-Term Obligations	676,665	573,500	569,600	463,900	465,000	448,600	453,900	454,100
Total Liabilities	1,693,778	1,692,500	1,631,100	1,443,600	1,448,900	1,370,800	1,338,500	1,308,900
Stockholders' Equity	1,155,372	1,085,100	933,300	799,900	889,700	755,200	592,300	463,100
Shares Outstanding	128,280	127,800	116,900	132,600	135,500	137,200	140,000	138,400
Statistical Record								
Return on Assets %	8.74	8.59	8.35	9.26	9.47	10.34	9.71	8.54
Return on Equity %	22.10	22.80	23.33	25.44	26.01	31.29	34.07	35.65
EBITDA Margin %	14.25	15.28	13.38	16.15	16.10	16.47	14.88	14.23
Net Margin %	7.10	7.89	7.44	8.29	8.49	9.29	7.75	6.61
Asset Turnover	1.10	1.09	1.12	1.12	1.12	1.11	1.25	1.29
Current Ratio	1.29	1.14	1.15	1.14	1.12	1.07	1.08	0.89
Debt to Equity	0.59	0.53	0.61	0.58	0.52	0.59	0.77	0.98
Price Range	39.18-33.55	39.58-34.16	38.92-29.82	39.06-29.24	37.41-28.84	30.21-22.10	26.93-20.36	23.00-17.13
P/E Ratio	21.89-18.74	22.88-19.75	25.95-19.88	25.04-18.74	24.61-18.97	20.41-14.93	21.37-16.16	22.11-16.47
Average Yield %	2.24	2.15	2.21	1.86	1.68	1.79	1.78	1.95

Address: 18 Loveton Circle, Sparks, MD 21152-6000	**Officers:** Robert J. Lawless - Chairman Alan D. Wilson - President, Chief Executive Officer **Transfer Agents:** Wells Fargo Bank, N.A., South St. Paul, MN	**Investor Contact:** 410-771-7244
Telephone: 410-771-7301		**No of Institutions:** 426
Web Site: www.mccormick.com		**Shares:** 99,073,472 **% Held:** 71.18

MCDONALD'S CORP

Exchange	Symbol	Price	52Wk Range	Yield	P/E
NYS	MCD	$59.48 (5/29/2008)	63.13-47.56	2.52	27.41

*7 Year Price Score 129.01 *NYSE Composite Index=100* ***12 Month Price Score 108.89**

TRADING VOLUME (thousand shares)

Interim Earnings (Per Share)

Qtr.	Mar	Jun	Sep	Dec
2005	0.56	0.42	0.58	0.48
2006	0.49	0.67	0.68	1.00
2007	0.62	(0.60)	0.89	1.06
2008	0.81	...	...	...

Interim Dividends (Per Share)

Amt	Decl	Ex	Rec	Pay
1.00Q	09/27/2006	11/13/2006	11/15/2006	12/01/2006
1.50Q	09/12/2007	11/13/2007	11/15/2007	12/03/2007
0.375Q	01/24/2008	02/28/2008	03/03/2008	03/17/2008
0.375Q	05/21/2008	06/05/2008	06/09/2008	06/23/2008
	Indicated Div: $1.50 (Div. Reinv. Plan)			

Valuation Analysis

Forecast EPS	$3.36 (05/17/2008)		
Market Cap	$67.4 Billion	Book Value	14.4 Billion
Price/Book	4.68	Price/Sales	2.90

Dividend Achiever Status

10 Year Growth Rate	24.99%
Total Years of Dividend Growth	31

Business Summary: Food (MIC: SIC: 5812 NAIC: 722211)

McDonald's primarily franchises and operates McDonald's restaurants. Co.'s business is operated in distinct geographic segments: U.S.; Europe; Asia/Pacific, Middle East and Africa; and Other Countries and Corporate that includes operations in Latin America and Canada. In addition, Co. has a minority ownership interest in U.K.-based Pret A Manger. As of Dec 31 2007, Co. had 31,377 McDonald's restaurants in 118 countries, with 20,505 operated by franchisees that include 2,781 which are operated by developmental licensees, 3,966 that are operated by affiliates as well as 6,906 that are Company-operated.

Recent Developments: For the quarter ended Mar 31 2008, income from continuing operations increased 23.4% to US$946.1 million from US$766.5 million in the year-earlier quarter. Net income increased 24.1% to US$946.1 million from US$762.4 million in the year-earlier quarter. Revenues were US$5.61 billion, up 6.1% from US$5.29 billion the year before. Operating income was US$1.46 billion versus US$1.18 billion in the prior-year quarter, an increase of 23.8%. Direct operating expenses rose 1.4% to US$3.34 billion from US$3.29 billion in the comparable period the year before. Indirect operating expenses decreased 0.7% to US$812.4 million from US$818.1 million in the equivalent prior-year period.

Prospects: Co. is seeing comparable sales growth across all geographic segments primarily due to its customer-centered Plan to Win strategy. For 2008, Co. expects net restaurant additions to add slightly more than 1.0% to Systemwide sales growth (in constant currencies), primarily due to the 503 net traditional restaurants added in 2007, and expects net additions of about 600 restaurants in 2008. Co. also expects to optimize its restaurant ownership mix by refranchising 1,000 to 1,500 Co.-operated restaurants over the next three or more years, primarily in its major markets, and by continuing its developmental license strategy. However, Co. expects interest income to decrease about 30.0% over 2007.

Financial Data

(US$ in Thousands)	3 Mos	12/31/2007	12/31/2006	12/31/2005	12/31/2004	12/31/2003	12/31/2002	12/31/2001
Earnings Per Share	2.17	1.98	2.83	2.04	1.79	1.15	0.70	1.25
Cash Flow Per Share	4.73	4.10	3.52	3.44	3.09	2.57	2.27	2.08
Tang Book Value Per Share	10.62	11.14	11.01	10.45	9.74	8.18	6.88	6.30
Dividends Per Share	1.875	1.500	1.000	0.670	0.550	0.400	0.235	0.225
Dividend Payout %	86.54	75.76	35.34	32.84	30.73	34.78	33.57	18.00
Income Statement								
Total Revenue	5,614,800	22,786,600	21,586,400	20,460,200	19,064,700	17,140,500	15,405,700	14,870,000
EBITDA	1,796,400	5,196,300	5,818,300	5,307,200	4,761,800	3,882,600	3,087,000	3,868,400
Depn & Amortn	304,700	1,214,100	1,249,900	1,249,500	1,201,000	1,148,200	1,050,800	1,086,300
Income Before Taxes	1,363,200	3,572,100	4,166,400	3,701,600	3,202,400	2,346,400	1,662,100	2,329,700
Income Taxes	417,100	1,237,100	1,293,400	1,099,400	923,900	838,200	670,000	693,100
Net Income	946,100	2,395,100	3,544,200	2,602,200	2,278,500	1,471,400	893,500	1,636,600
Average Shares	1,165,300	1,211,800	1,251,700	1,274,200	1,273,700	1,276,500	1,281,500	1,309,300
Balance Sheet								
Current Assets	4,325,600	3,581,900	3,625,300	5,849,700	2,857,800	1,885,400	1,715,400	1,819,300
Total Assets	30,922,000	29,391,700	29,023,800	29,988,800	27,837,500	25,525,100	23,970,500	22,534,500
Current Liabilities	3,683,300	4,498,500	3,008,100	4,036,300	3,520,500	2,485,800	2,422,300	2,248,300
Long-Term Obligations	10,443,600	7,310,000	8,416,500	8,937,400	8,357,300	9,342,500	9,703,600	8,555,500
Total Liabilities	16,507,800	14,111,900	13,565,500	14,842,700	13,636,000	13,543,200	13,689,600	13,046,100
Stockholders' Equity	14,414,200	15,279,800	15,458,300	15,146,100	14,201,500	11,981,900	10,280,900	9,488,400
Shares Outstanding	1,133,500	1,165,300	1,203,700	1,263,200	1,269,900	1,261,900	1,268,200	1,280,700
Statistical Record								
Return on Assets %	8.57	8.20	12.01	9.00	8.52	5.95	3.84	7.40
Return on Equity %	17.14	15.58	23.16	17.73	17.36	13.22	9.04	17.51
EBITDA Margin %	31.99	22.80	26.95	25.94	24.98	22.65	20.04	26.01
Net Margin %	16.85	10.51	16.42	12.72	11.95	8.58	5.80	11.01
Asset Turnover	0.77	0.78	0.73	0.71	0.71	0.69	0.66	0.67
Current Ratio	1.17	0.80	1.21	1.45	0.81	0.76	0.71	0.81
Debt to Equity	0.72	0.48	0.54	0.59	0.59	0.78	0.94	0.90
Price Range	63.13-44.82	63.13-42.91	44.36-31.94	35.50-27.70	32.66-24.64	26.56-12.38	30.65-15.48	34.69-25.00
P/E Ratio	29.09-20.65	31.88-21.67	15.67-11.29	17.40-13.58	18.25-13.77	23.10-10.77	43.79-22.11	27.75-20.00
Average Yield %	3.50	2.94	2.72	2.10	1.98	1.98	0.97	0.79

Address: McDonald's Plaza, Oak Brook, IL 60523	**Officers:** James A. Skinner - Vice-Chairman, Chief Executive Officer Ralph Alvarez - President, Chief Operating Officer **Transfer Agents:** Computershare Trust Company, N.A., Canton, MA	**Investor Contact:** 630-623-7428
Telephone: 630-623-3000		**No of Institutions:** 1189
Web Site: www.mcdonalds.com		**Shares:** 956,159,424 **% Held:** 74.96

MCGRATH RENTCORP

Exchange	Symbol	Price	52Wk Range	Yield	P/E
NMS	MGRC	$27.73 (5/29/2008)	35.88-18.80	2.88	16.03

*7 Year Price Score 105.77 *NYSE Composite Index=100 ***12 Month Price Score 93.16**

Interim Earnings (Per Share)

Qtr.	Mar	Jun	Sep	Dec
2005	0.29	0.38	0.48	0.47
2006	0.31	0.34	0.50	0.47
2007	0.37	0.36	0.46	0.48
2008	0.43	...	...	...

Interim Dividends (Per Share)

Amt	Decl	Ex	Rec	Pay
0.18Q	10/05/2007	10/11/2007	10/15/2007	10/31/2007
0.18Q	12/06/2007	01/11/2008	01/15/2008	01/31/2008
0.20Q	02/21/2008	04/14/2008	04/16/2008	04/30/2008
0.20Q	06/04/2008	07/14/2008	07/16/2008	07/31/2008

Indicated Div: $0.80

Valuation Analysis

Forecast EPS	$1.80 (05/16/2008)		
Market Cap	$655.4 Million	Book Value	229.0 Million
Price/Book	2.86	Price/Sales	2.31

Dividend Achiever Status

10 Year Growth Rate	16.27%
Total Years of Dividend Growth	17

TRADING VOLUME (thousand shares)

Business Summary: General Construction Supplies & Services (MIC: SIC: 7359 NAIC: 532490)

McGrath RentCorp is a rental company with two rental products; relocatable modular buildings and electronic test equipment. Co. operates through three business segments: Mobile Modular Management Corporation (MMMC), its modular building rental division; TRS-RenTelco, its electronic test equipment division; and Enviroplex, Inc., its subsidiary classroom manufacturing business selling modular buildings used primarily as classrooms in California. MMMC rents and sells modular buildings and accessories to customers in California, Texas, Florida, North Carolina and Georgia, while TRS-RenTelco rents and sells electronic test equipment nationally and internationally.

Recent Developments: For the quarter ended Mar 31 2008, net income increased 10.0% to US$10.3 million from US$9.3 million in the year-earlier quarter. Revenues were US$65.4 million, up 7.7% from US$60.8 million the year before. Operating income was US$19.4 million versus US$17.9 million in the prior-year quarter, an increase of 8.3%. Direct operating expenses rose 4.1% to US$32.5 million from US$31.2 million in the comparable period the year before. Indirect operating expenses increased 16.3% to US$13.5 million from US$11.6 million in the equivalent prior-year period.

Prospects: Co.'s operating results are being positively affected by the continued growth of its modulars and electronics rental businesses. Notably, gross profits at both Co.'s Mobile Modular and TRS-RenTelco segments increased due to higher rental revenue level, as well as lower direct costs of rental operations to maintain and process rental equipment. Looking forward to full-year 2008, Co. has reconfirmed its earnings guidance range of $1.72 to $1.82 per diluted share. Meanwhile, Co. continues to consider expansion opportunities domestically and internationally for its rental businesses.

Financial Data

(US$ in Thousands)	3 Mos	12/31/2007	12/31/2006	12/31/2005	12/31/2004	12/31/2003	12/31/2002	12/31/2001
Earnings Per Share	1.73	1.67	1.63	1.61	1.21	0.93	0.50	1.07
Cash Flow Per Share	4.33	3.76	3.97	3.32	2.55	1.98	2.10	2.41
Tang Book Value Per Share	9.69	9.93	9.20	7.99	6.80	5.94	5.57	5.33
Dividends Per Share	0.720	0.700	0.620	0.530	0.430	0.390	0.340	0.310
Dividend Payout %	41.71	41.92	38.04	32.92	35.54	42.16	68.00	28.97
Income Statement								
Total Revenue	65,415	280,409	267,066	272,180	202,520	130,971	145,086	159,394
EBITDA	33,400	134,532	123,788	120,053	88,577	55,400	43,107	81,677
Depn & Amortn	14,050	54,002	47,461	46,433	34,501	14,692	17,872	29,632
Income Before Taxes	16,883	69,811	65,567	65,730	48,888	38,040	21,253	44,967
Income Taxes	6,618	27,337	24,209	24,649	18,843	15,178	8,459	17,807
Net Income	10,265	42,410	41,078	40,819	29,997	22,692	12,633	26,678
Average Shares	24,094	25,443	25,231	25,331	24,804	24,518	25,238	24,990
Balance Sheet								
Current Assets	60,711	72,151	60,183	63,978	54,035	32,203	33,253	36,900
Total Assets	643,189	642,236	585,542	542,438	474,280	323,858	313,134	354,884
Current Liabilities	267,244	55,642	55,509	51,690	39,460	28,695	29,889	30,745
Long-Term Obligations	...	197,729	165,557	163,232	151,888	47,266	55,523	104,140
Total Liabilities	414,178	398,205	354,750	343,969	307,392	179,880	174,115	223,249
Stockholders' Equity	229,011	244,031	230,792	198,469	166,888	143,978	139,019	131,595
Shares Outstanding	23,635	24,578	25,090	24,832	24,543	24,244	24,980	24,670
Statistical Record								
Return on Assets %	6.97	6.91	7.28	8.03	7.50	7.12	3.78	7.49
Return on Equity %	18.51	17.86	19.14	22.34	19.25	16.04	9.34	22.18
EBITDA Margin %	51.06	47.98	46.35	44.11	43.74	42.30	29.71	51.24
Net Margin %	15.69	15.12	15.38	15.00	14.81	17.33	8.71	16.74
Asset Turnover	0.46	0.46	0.47	0.54	0.51	0.41	0.43	0.45
Current Ratio	0.23	1.30	1.08	1.24	1.37	1.12	1.11	1.20
Debt to Equity	...	0.81	0.72	0.82	0.91	0.33	0.40	0.79
Price Range	35.88-18.80	35.88-23.66	33.05-21.53	29.69-20.65	22.75-13.63	14.88-10.90	18.82-9.40	18.77-9.06
P/E Ratio	20.74-10.87	21.49-14.17	20.28-13.21	18.44-12.82	18.80-11.26	16.00-11.73	37.64-18.80	17.54-8.47
Average Yield %	2.49	2.28	2.22	2.16	2.51	3.01	2.65	2.60

Address: 5700 Las Positas Road, Livermore, CA 94551-7800	Officers: Robert P. McGrath - Chairman Dennis C. Kakures - President, Chief Executive Officer	Investor Contact: 206-652-9704
Telephone: 925-606-9200	Transfer Agents: U.S. Stock Transfer, Glendale, CA	No of Institutions: 124
Web Site: www.mgrc.com		Shares: 23,302,280 % Held: 88.72

MCGRAW-HILL COS., INC. (THE)

Exchange	Symbol	Price	52Wk Range	Yield	P/E
NYS	MHP	$41.39 (5/29/2008)	71.96-35.20	2.13	14.73

*7 Year Price Score 88.34   *NYSE Composite Index=100   ***12 Month Price Score 85.29**

Interim Earnings (Per Share)

Qtr.	Mar	Jun	Sep	Dec
2005	0.20	0.51	1.00	0.50
2006	0.20	0.60	1.06	0.56
2007	0.40	0.79	1.34	0.44
2008	0.25	...	...	...

Interim Dividends (Per Share)

Amt	Decl	Ex	Rec	Pay
0.205Q	07/25/2007	08/24/2007	08/28/2007	09/12/2007
0.205Q	10/24/2007	11/26/2007	11/28/2007	12/12/2007
0.22Q	01/30/2008	02/25/2008	02/27/2008	03/12/2008
0.22Q	04/30/2008	05/23/2008	05/28/2008	06/11/2008

Indicated Div: $0.88 (Div. Reinv. Plan)

Valuation Analysis

Forecast EPS $2.81 (05/16/2008)

Market Cap	$13.3 Billion	Book Value	1.5 Billion
Price/Book	8.75	Price/Sales	1.99

Dividend Achiever Status

10 Year Growth Rate	8.58%
Total Years of Dividend Growth	34

Business Summary: Non-Media Publishing (MIC: SIC: 2731 NAIC: 511130)

McGraw-Hill Companies is a global information services provider serving the financial services, education and business information markets with information products and services. Co.'s other markets also include energy, construction, aerospace and defense, and marketing information services. Co. operates through three business segments: Education; Financial Services; and Information and Media. Co. serves its customers through a range of distribution channels including printed books, magazines and newsletters; online via Internet Web sites and digital platforms; through wireless and traditional on-air broadcasting; and through a variety of conferences and trade shows.

Recent Developments: For the quarter ended Mar 31 2008, net income decreased 43.6% to US$81.1 million from US$143.8 million in the year-earlier quarter. Revenues were US$1.22 billion, down 6.1% from US$1.30 billion the year before. Operating income was US$147.6 million versus US$232.2 million in the prior-year quarter, a decrease of 36.4%. Direct operating expenses declined 0.6% to US$501.4 million from US$504.4 million in the comparable period the year before. Indirect operating expenses increased 1.6% to US$568.9 million from US$559.9 million in the equivalent prior-year period.

Prospects: For 2008, Co. expects earnings per share of $2.65 to $2.75 based on existing trends in financial markets. Notably, Co. expects revenue at its Financial Services segment to decrease 7.0% to 9.0% and operating margin to decline 500 to 600 basis points, but projects revenue growth of 6.0% to 8.0% at its Education and Information & Media segments as well as improved operating profit and operating margin in its Education and Information & Media segments, respectively. Separately, on May 20 2008, Co. announced the restructuring of several businesses in its Financial Services and Education segments through workforce reduction to streamline its operations, lower costs and boost its growth prospects.

Financial Data
(US$ in Thousands)

	3 Mos	12/31/2007	12/31/2006	12/31/2005	12/31/2004	12/31/2003	12/31/2002	12/31/2001
Earnings Per Share	2.81	2.94	2.40	2.21	1.96	1.79	1.48	0.96
Cash Flow Per Share	4.60	5.11	4.23	4.16	2.79	3.63	2.96	2.76
Tang Book Value Per Share	N.M.	N.M.	1.00	2.04	2.72	2.24	0.94	0.09
Dividends Per Share	0.835	0.820	0.726	0.660	0.600	0.540	0.510	0.490
Dividend Payout %	29.70	27.89	30.25	29.86	30.61	30.17	34.46	51.04
Income Statement								
Total Revenue	1,217,871	6,772,281	6,255,138	6,003,642	5,250,538	4,827,857	4,787,668	4,645,535
EBITDA	217,516	1,824,102	1,580,041	1,516,149	1,299,428	1,255,066	1,055,960	850,485
Depn & Amortn	69,909	160,989	161,587	150,985	124,738	117,692	128,378	180,357
Income Before Taxes	129,777	1,622,532	1,404,823	1,359,962	1,168,905	1,130,277	905,065	615,058
Income Taxes	48,667	608,973	522,592	515,656	412,495	442,466	328,305	238,027
Net Income	81,110	1,013,559	882,231	844,306	755,943	687,650	576,760	377,031
Average Shares	323,400	344,785	366,878	382,570	385,824	384,010	389,146	391,746
Balance Sheet								
Current Assets	2,204,083	2,333,035	2,257,938	2,590,939	2,447,830	2,256,152	1,674,307	1,812,947
Total Assets	6,266,851	6,357,336	6,042,890	6,395,808	5,862,989	5,394,068	5,032,182	5,161,191
Current Liabilities	2,666,424	2,656,860	2,468,016	2,224,826	1,968,662	1,993,734	1,775,291	1,876,393
Long-Term Obligations	1,197,472	1,197,425	314	339	513	389	458,923	833,571
Total Liabilities	4,746,265	4,750,686	3,363,272	3,282,660	2,878,476	2,837,017	2,866,360	3,307,306
Stockholders' Equity	1,520,586	1,606,650	2,679,618	3,113,148	2,984,513	2,557,051	2,165,822	1,853,885
Shares Outstanding	321,300	322,367	353,958	372,698	379,626	380,792	383,665	386,436
Statistical Record								
Return on Assets %	15.61	16.35	14.19	13.77	13.39	13.19	11.32	7.47
Return on Equity %	54.22	47.29	30.46	27.69	27.20	29.12	28.70	20.86
EBITDA Margin %	17.86	26.93	25.26	25.25	24.75	26.00	22.06	18.31
Net Margin %	6.66	14.97	14.10	14.06	14.40	14.24	12.05	8.12
Asset Turnover	1.10	1.09	1.01	0.98	0.93	0.93	0.94	0.92
Current Ratio	0.83	0.88	0.91	1.16	1.24	1.13	0.94	0.97
Debt to Equity	0.79	0.75	N.M.	N.M.	N.M.	N.M.	0.21	0.45
Price Range	71.96-35.20	71.96-43.81	69.10-47.06	53.52-40.56	45.93-34.75	34.96-26.25	34.45-25.57	35.23-24.65
P/E Ratio	25.61-12.53	24.48-14.90	28.79-19.61	24.22-18.35	23.43-17.73	19.53-14.66	23.27-17.28	36.69-25.68
Average Yield %	1.58	1.38	1.28	1.42	1.53	1.76	1.63	1.62

Address: 1221 Avenue Of The Americas, New York, NY 10020-1095	Officers: Harold McGraw - Chairman, President, Chief Executive Officer Robert J. Bahash - Executive	No of Institutions: 740
Telephone: 212-512-2000	Vice President, Chief Financial Officer **Transfer**	**Shares:** 269,850,528 **% Held:** 76.85
Web Site: www.mcgraw-hill.com	**Agents:**The Bank of New York, New York, NY	

MDU RESOURCES GROUP INC.

Exchange	Symbol	Price	52Wk Range	Yield	P/E
NYS	MDU	$32.86 (5/29/2008)	32.86-24.35	1.77	13.20

*7 Year Price Score 112.26 *NYSE Composite Index=100 *12 Month Price Score 107.82

Interim Earnings (Per Share)

Qtr.	Mar	Jun	Sep	Dec
2005	0.19	0.45	0.48	0.40
2006	0.29	0.39	0.60	0.45
2007	0.25	0.49	1.10	0.52
2008	0.39	...	...	...

Interim Dividends (Per Share)

Amt	Decl	Ex	Rec	Pay
0.145Q	08/16/2007	09/11/2007	09/13/2007	10/01/2007
0.145Q	11/15/2007	12/11/2007	12/13/2007	01/01/2008
0.145Q	02/14/2008	03/11/2008	03/13/2008	04/01/2008
0.145Q	05/15/2008	06/10/2008	06/12/2008	07/01/2008

Indicated Div: $0.58 (Div. Reinv. Plan)

Valuation Analysis
Forecast EPS $2.05 (05/17/2008)
Market Cap $6.0 Billion   Book Value 2.5 Billion
Price/Book 2.36   Price/Sales 1.31

Dividend Achiever Status
10 Year Growth Rate 5.18%
Total Years of Dividend Growth 17

TRADING VOLUME (thousand shares)

Business Summary: Earth & Rock Mining (MIC: SIC: 1429 NAIC: 212319)

MDU Resources Group is a diversified natural resource company. Through its Montana-Dakota Utilities Co. subsidiary, Co. generates, transmits and distributes electricity as well as distributes natural gas in Montana, North Dakota, South Dakota and Wyoming. Co.'s Great Plains Natural Gas Co. subsidiary distributes natural gas in western Minnesota and southeastern North Dakota. Co.'s Cascade Natural Gas Corp. indirect subsidiary distributes natural gas in Washington and Oregon. Through its Centennial Energy Holdings, Inc. subsidiary, Co. owns WBI Holdings Inc., Knife River Corp., MDU Construction Services Group, Inc., Centennial Energy Resources LLC and Centennial Holdings Capital LLC.

Recent Developments: For the quarter ended Mar 31 2008, income from continuing operations increased 71.6% to US$71.1 million from US$41.4 million in the year-earlier quarter. Net income increased 52.3% to US$71.1 million from US$46.7 million in the year-earlier quarter. Revenues were US$1.12 billion, up 42.5% from US$787.5 million the year before. Operating income was US$127.6 million versus US$79.0 million in the prior-year quarter, an increase of 61.5%. Direct operating expenses rose 40.6% to US$852.6 million from US$606.5 million in the comparable period the year before. Indirect operating expenses increased 38.9% to US$141.8 million from US$102.1 million in the equivalent prior-year period.

Prospects: Going forward, Co. remains focused on expanding its operations through strategic acquisitions. For instance, on May 9 2008, Co. acquired Yarbrough's Dirt Pit, Inc., a supplier and ready-mix concrete producer near Sour Lake, TX. Subsequently, on May 19 2008, Co. acquired Amador Transit Mix, Inc., a ready-mix concrete producer in Sutter Creek, CA. Co. anticipates the two acquisitions to be accretive to 2008 earnings per share. Thus, Co. has increased its 2008 earnings guidance to a range of $1.85 to $2.10, up from previous guidance of $1.65 to $1.90 per share. Meanwhile, Co. is accelerating its drilling plans and now expects to participate in about 50 to 60 wells in 2008 in the Bakken.

Financial Data
(US$ in Thousands)

	3 Mos	12/31/2007	12/31/2006	12/31/2005	12/31/2004	12/31/2003	12/31/2002	12/31/2001
Earnings Per Share	2.49	2.36	1.74	1.53	1.17	1.03	0.92	1.02
Cash Flow Per Share	3.28	3.10	3.66	2.71	2.47	2.50	2.05	2.30
Tang Book Value Per Share	11.33	11.31	10.49	9.04	8.14	6.13	5.50	7.07
Dividends Per Share	0.570	0.560	0.523	0.493	0.467	0.440	0.418	0.400
Dividend Payout %	22.85	23.73	30.08	32.31	39.77	42.58	45.41	39.30
Income Statement								
Total Revenue	1,121,907	4,247,896	4,070,684	3,455,414	2,719,257	2,352,189	2,031,537	2,223,632
EBITDA	218,193	886,979	826,843	704,269	567,248	522,616	437,650	440,006
Depn & Amortn	87,231	301,932	271,583	228,657	208,770	188,337	157,961	139,917
Income Before Taxes	112,306	512,810	483,165	420,862	301,041	281,485	234,674	254,190
Income Taxes	41,255	190,024	165,248	145,779	93,974	98,572	86,230	98,341
Net Income	71,051	432,120	315,757	275,083	207,067	175,324	148,444	155,849
Average Shares	183,130	182,902	181,392	179,490	176,116	168,690	160,294	152,705
Balance Sheet								
Net PPE	3,959,985	3,659,555	2,993,351	3,049,893	2,572,705	2,222,293	1,924,886	1,809,318
Total Assets	5,830,817	5,592,434	4,903,474	4,423,562	3,733,521	3,380,592	2,937,249	2,623,071
Long-Term Obligations	1,269,963	1,146,781	1,170,548	1,104,752	873,441	939,450	819,558	783,709
Total Liabilities	3,289,475	3,061,115	2,738,561	2,531,940	2,052,508	1,929,956	1,638,504	1,498,400
Stockholders' Equity	2,541,342	2,531,319	2,164,913	1,891,622	1,681,013	1,450,636	1,298,745	1,124,771
Shares Outstanding	182,797	182,407	181,018	179,856	177,341	170,036	166,595	156,998
Statistical Record								
Return on Assets %	8.51	8.23	6.77	6.74	5.81	5.55	5.34	6.31
Return on Equity %	19.25	18.40	15.57	15.40	13.19	12.75	12.25	15.42
EBITDA Margin %	19.45	20.88	20.31	20.38	20.86	22.22	21.54	19.79
Net Margin %	6.33	10.17	7.76	7.96	7.61	7.45	7.31	7.01
PPE Turnover	1.30	1.28	1.35	1.23	1.13	1.13	1.09	1.30
Asset Turnover	0.85	0.81	0.87	0.85	0.76	0.74	0.73	0.90
Debt to Equity	0.50	0.45	0.54	0.58	0.52	0.65	0.63	0.70
Price Range	31.27-24.35	31.27-24.80	26.90-21.99	24.47-17.07	18.31-14.71	16.17-11.13	14.82-8.31	17.88-10.13
P/E Ratio	12.56-9.78	13.25-10.51	15.46-12.64	15.99-11.15	15.65-12.57	15.70-10.80	16.11-9.03	17.53-9.93
Average Yield %	2.06	2.02	2.18	2.48	2.86	3.15	3.55	2.96

Address: 1200 West Century Avenue, Bismarck, ND 58506-5650	Officers: Harry J. Pearce - Chairman Terry D. Hildestad - President, Chief Executive Officer	Investor Contact: 800-437-8000x1020
Telephone: 701-530-1000	Transfer Agents:Wells Fargo Bank, N.A., St. Paul, MN	No of Institutions: 353
Web Site: www.mdu.com		Shares: 99,765,952 % Held: 50.75

MEDIA GENERAL, INC.

Exchange	Symbol	Price	52Wk Range	Yield	P/E
NYS	MEG	$15.36 (5/29/2008)	37.67-13.40	5.99	N/A

*7 Year Price Score 36.47   *NYSE Composite Index=100   *12 Month Price Score 65.31

Interim Earnings (Per Share)

Qtr.	Mar	Jun	Sep	Dec
2005	(13.25)	1.61	0.41	1.04
2006	0.28	0.85	0.87	1.33
2007	(0.27)	0.22	0.11	0.42
2008	(0.91)	...	...	...

Interim Dividends (Per Share)

Amt	Decl	Ex	Rec	Pay
0.23Q	07/26/2007	08/29/2007	08/31/2007	09/15/2007
0.23Q	09/27/2007	11/28/2007	11/30/2007	12/15/2007
0.23Q	01/31/2008	02/27/2008	02/29/2008	03/15/2008
0.23Q	04/24/2008	05/28/2008	05/30/2008	06/15/2008
			Indicated Div: $0.92	

Valuation Analysis

Forecast EPS	$0.76 (05/16/2008)		
Market Cap	$351.1 Million	Book Value	881.7 Million
Price/Book	0.40	Price/Sales	0.39

Dividend Achiever Status

10 Year Growth Rate	5.67%
Total Years of Dividend Growth	13

TRADING VOLUME (thousand shares)

Business Summary: Media (MIC: SIC: 2711 NAIC: 511110)

Media General is a publicly owned communications company with interests in newspapers, television stations and interactive media. Co. operates in three segments: Publishing, which includes daily and Sunday newspaper operations in Virginia, North Carolina, South Carolina, Alabama, and Florida; Broadcast, which operates network-affiliated television stations in the U.S.; and Interactive Media, which operates in conjunction with its Publishing and Broadcast Divisions to provide online news, information and entertainment to its customers. As of Dec 30 2007, Co. owned 25 daily newspapers, over 150 other publications and 23 television stations, as well as operated more than 75 online enterprises.

Recent Developments: For the quarter ended Mar 30 2008, loss from continuing operations was US$9.8 million compared with a loss of US$6.6 million in the year-earlier quarter. Net loss amounted to US$20.3 million versus a net loss of US$6.5 million in the year-earlier quarter. Revenues were US$194.5 million, down 10.9% from US$218.3 million the year before. Operating loss was US$4.3 million versus an income of US$6.6 million in the prior-year quarter. Direct operating expenses declined 6.9% to US$98.0 million from US$105.3 million in the comparable period the year before. Indirect operating expenses decreased 5.2% to US$100.8 million from US$106.3 million in the equivalent prior-year period.

Prospects: On Mar 31 2008, Co. along with its two other equal partners in SP Newsprint Company, Cox Enterprises, Inc. and The McClatchy Company, completed the sale of SP Newsprint to White Birch Paper Company. Co. received proceeds of approximately $58.0 million from the transaction and will use the funds to reduce debt. Meanwhile, Co. expects its Interactive Media Division to achieve profitability by the end of 2008 through the combination of strong advergaming revenues and profits generated from Co.'s Mar 2008 acquisition of DealTaker.com, an online shopping portal, which is expected to be accretive to earnings in 2008.

Financial Data

(US$ in Thousands)	3 Mos	12/30/2007	12/31/2006	12/25/2005	12/26/2004	12/28/2003	12/29/2002	12/30/2001
Earnings Per Share	(0.16)	0.47	3.32	(10.18)	3.38	2.50	(3.14)	0.79
Cash Flow Per Share	7.03	5.79	6.59	4.34	5.94	5.34	7.54	5.49
Dividends Per Share	0.920	0.920	0.880	0.840	0.800	0.760	0.720	0.680
Dividend Payout %	...	195.74	26.51	...	23.67	30.40	...	86.08
Income Statement								
Total Revenue	194,464	932,181	983,189	917,937	900,420	837,423	836,800	807,176
EBITDA	14,549	151,981	225,033	225,147	219,003	187,074	201,519	198,925
Depn & Amortn	18,709	78,450	72,633	62,596	60,643	58,804	65,495	113,732
Income Before Taxes	(16,449)	13,954	103,895	133,143	127,278	93,846	88,150	30,946
Income Taxes	(6,637)	3,622	38,493	50,732	47,093	34,800	34,731	13,022
Net Income	(20,255)	10,687	79,042	(243,042)	80,185	58,685	(72,917)	18,204
Average Shares	22,112	22,827	23,784	23,884	23,729	23,408	23,236	22,956
Balance Sheet								
Current Assets	274,827	273,726	202,748	184,373	170,847	162,621	160,552	163,038
Total Assets	2,420,370	2,471,066	2,505,228	1,975,354	2,368,812	2,386,755	2,347,011	2,534,059
Current Liabilities	139,451	137,316	131,520	111,914	126,871	114,403	111,501	100,497
Long-Term Obligations	874,566	897,572	916,320	485,304	533,280	627,289	642,937	777,662
Total Liabilities	1,538,629	1,558,059	1,567,868	1,059,528	1,185,043	1,279,294	1,287,757	1,370,391
Stockholders' Equity	881,741	913,007	937,360	915,826	1,183,769	1,107,461	1,059,254	1,163,668
Shares Outstanding	22,859	22,611	24,112	24,046	23,786	23,545	23,208	22,976
Statistical Record								
Return on Assets %	N.M.	0.43	3.47	N.M.	3.38	2.49	N.M.	0.72
Return on Equity %	N.M.	1.16	8.39	N.M.	7.02	5.43	N.M.	1.56
EBITDA Margin %	7.48	16.30	22.89	24.53	24.32	22.34	24.08	24.64
Net Margin %	N.M.	1.15	8.04	N.M.	8.91	7.01	N.M.	2.26
Asset Turnover	0.37	0.38	0.43	0.42	0.42	0.35	0.34	0.32
Current Ratio	1.97	1.99	1.54	1.65	1.35	1.42	1.44	1.62
Debt to Equity	0.99	0.98	0.98	0.53	0.45	0.57	0.61	0.67
Price Range	39.34-14.01	43.93-20.69	51.42-34.50	68.80-49.16	72.40-53.97	67.88-47.53	69.49-47.38	53.50-34.09
P/E Ratio	...	93.47-44.02	15.49-10.39	...	21.42-15.97	27.15-19.01	...	67.72-43.15
Average Yield %	3.36	2.80	2.13	1.38	1.27	1.31	1.26	1.45

Address: 333 East Franklin Street, Richmond, VA 23219	Officers: J. Stewart Bryan - Chairman Marshall N. Morton - President, Chief Executive Officer **Transfer**	Investor Contact: 804-649-6000
Telephone: 804-649-6000	**Agents:** American Stock Transfer & Trust Company,	No of Institutions: 141
Web Site: www.mediageneral.com	New York, NY	Shares: 25,877,352 % Held: 102.85

MEDTRONIC, INC.

Exchange	Symbol	Price	52Wk Range	Yield	P/E
NYS	MDT	$50.70 (5/29/2008)	57.86-45.25	0.99	26.00

*7 Year Price Score 79.57   *NYSE Composite Index=100   *12 Month Price Score 99.46

Interim Earnings (Per Share)

Qtr.	Jul	Oct	Jan	Apr
2004-05	0.43	0.44	0.45	0.16
2005-06	0.26	0.67	0.55	0.61
2006-07	0.51	0.59	0.61	0.70
2007-08	0.59	0.58	0.07	...

Interim Dividends (Per Share)

Amt	Decl	Ex	Rec	Pay
0.125Q	06/22/2007	07/03/2007	07/06/2007	07/27/2007
0.125Q	08/23/2007	10/03/2007	10/05/2007	10/26/2007
0.125Q	10/19/2007	01/02/2008	01/04/2008	01/25/2008
0.125Q	02/21/2008	04/02/2008	04/04/2008	04/25/2008

Indicated Div: $0.50 (Div. Reinv. Plan)

Valuation Analysis

Forecast EPS $2.55 (05/17/2008)
Market Cap $56.9 Billion   Book Value   11.0 Billion
Price/Book   5.19   Price/Sales   4.39

Dividend Achiever Status

10 Year Growth Rate   16.45%
Total Years of Dividend Growth   30

Business Summary: Medical Instruments & Equipment (MIC: SIC: 3845 NAIC: 334510)

Medtronic is a provider of enhanced products and therapies for use by medical professionals to address the healthcare needs of their patients. Co.'s primary products include those for cardiac rhythm disorders, cardiovascular disease, neurological disorders, spinal conditions and musculoskeletal trauma, urological and digestive disorders, diabetes, and ear, nose, and throat conditions. As of Apr 27 2007, Co. operated in eight operating segments that manufacture and sell device-based medical therapies: Cardiac Rhythm Disease Management, Spinal and Navigation, Vascular, Neurological, Diabetes, Cardiac Surgery, Ear, Nose, and Throat, as well as Physio-Control.

Recent Developments: For the quarter ended Jan 25 2008, net income decreased 89.2% to US$77.0 million from US$710.0 million in the year-earlier quarter. Revenues were US$3.41 billion, up 11.7% from US$3.05 billion the year before. Direct operating expenses rose 12.3% to US$870.0 million from US$775.0 million in the comparable period the year before. Indirect operating expenses increased 72.1% to US$2.29 billion from US$1.33 billion in the equivalent prior-year period.

Prospects: Going forward, Co. expects to benefit from the introduction of new products and the launch of existing products in new markets. For instance, Co. expects FDA approval and U.S. launch of its Talent AAA Stent Graft System in the first half of calendar year 2008, and of its Talent Thoracic device in the second half of the year. At the same time, Co. expects its ongoing restructuring plans, which are designed to, among others, drive manufacturing capabilities in its CardioVascular business and downsize its Physio-Control business, to be substantially completed by the end of Apr 2008. These actions should produce annual savings of about $125.0 million, driven by reduced compensation expense.

Financial Data

(US$ in Thousands)	9 Mos	6 Mos	3 Mos	04/27/2007	04/28/2006	04/29/2005	04/30/2004	04/25/2003
Earnings Per Share	1.95	2.49	2.50	2.41	2.09	1.48	1.60	1.30
Cash Flow Per Share	3.40	3.08	2.91	2.60	1.84	2.34	2.31	1.71
Tang Book Value Per Share	1.05	5.09	4.76	4.56	2.98	4.26	3.18	2.21
Dividends Per Share	0.485	0.470	0.455	0.440	0.385	0.335	0.290	0.250
Dividend Payout %	24.91	18.90	18.23	18.26	18.42	22.64	18.13	19.23
Income Statement								
Total Revenue	9,655,000	6,250,000	3,127,000	12,299,000	11,292,000	10,054,600	9,087,200	7,665,200
EBITDA	2,224,000	1,918,000	984,000	3,944,000	3,617,500	2,961,700	3,236,700	2,756,600
Depn & Amortn	457,000	276,000	149,000	583,000	543,600	463,300	442,600	408,100
Income Before Taxes	1,881,000	1,747,000	879,000	3,515,000	3,161,300	2,543,500	2,796,900	2,341,300
Income Taxes	463,000	406,000	204,000	713,000	614,600	739,600	837,600	741,500
Net Income	1,418,000	1,341,000	675,000	2,802,000	2,546,700	1,803,900	1,959,300	1,599,800
Average Shares	1,135,000	1,147,700	1,153,100	1,161,800	1,217,300	1,220,800	1,225,200	1,227,900
Balance Sheet								
Current Assets	6,681,000	10,541,000	7,668,000	7,918,000	10,376,600	7,421,500	5,312,700	4,605,500
Total Assets	21,412,000	20,586,000	19,660,000	19,512,000	19,664,800	16,617,400	14,110,800	12,320,800
Current Liabilities	3,536,000	2,651,000	2,040,000	2,563,000	4,405,800	3,380,000	4,240,600	1,813,300
Long-Term Obligations	5,656,000	5,494,000	5,576,000	5,578,000	5,486,300	1,973,200	1,100	1,980,300
Total Liabilities	10,446,000	9,111,000	8,517,000	8,535,000	10,282,300	6,167,900	5,033,800	4,414,400
Stockholders' Equity	10,966,000	11,475,000	11,143,000	10,977,000	9,382,500	10,449,500	9,077,000	7,906,400
Shares Outstanding	1,123,027	1,130,658	1,134,122	1,143,407	1,155,237	1,210,186	1,209,459	1,218,128
Statistical Record								
Return on Assets %	10.92	14.54	14.48	14.34	14.08	11.77	14.59	13.81
Return on Equity %	20.39	26.39	27.42	27.60	25.75	18.53	22.70	22.38
EBITDA Margin %	23.03	30.69	31.47	32.07	32.04	29.46	35.62	35.96
Net Margin %	14.69	21.46	21.59	22.78	22.55	17.94	21.56	20.87
Asset Turnover	0.63	0.64	0.63	0.63	0.62	0.66	0.68	0.66
Current Ratio	1.89	3.98	3.76	3.09	2.36	2.20	1.25	2.54
Debt to Equity	0.52	0.48	0.50	0.51	0.58	0.19	N.M.	0.25
Price Range	57.86-45.25	57.86-47.00	54.58-42.47	54.58-42.47	59.54-49.05	54.92-46.40	52.65-43.36	48.95-33.74
P/E Ratio	29.67-23.21	23.24-18.88	21.83-16.99	22.65-17.62	28.49-23.47	37.11-31.35	32.91-27.10	37.65-25.95
Average Yield %	0.94	0.90	0.90	0.88	0.71	0.66	0.60	0.57

Address: 710 Medtronic Parkway, Minneapolis, MN 55432-5604 **Telephone:** 763-514-4000 **Web Site:** www.medtronic.com	**Officers:** Arthur D. Collins - Chairman William A. Hawkins - President, Chief Executive Officer **Transfer Agents:** Wells Fargo Bank, N.A., South St. Paul, MN	**Investor Contact:** 763-505-2692 **No of Institutions:** 1250 **Shares:** 1,016,508,864 **% Held:** 75.26

MERCURY GENERAL CORP.

Exchange	Symbol	Price	52Wk Range	Yield	P/E
NYS	MCY	$51.05 (5/29/2008)	57.32-42.35	4.54	16.16

*7 Year Price Score 79.35   *NYSE Composite Index=100   *12 Month Price Score 98.88

Interim Earnings (Per Share)

Qtr.	Mar	Jun	Sep	Dec
2005	1.10	1.35	1.33	0.85
2006	1.07	0.69	1.25	0.91
2007	1.10	1.27	1.15	0.82
2008	(0.07)	...	...	...

Interim Dividends (Per Share)

Amt	Decl	Ex	Rec	Pay
0.52Q	08/06/2007	09/12/2007	09/14/2007	09/27/2007
0.52Q	11/05/2007	12/12/2007	12/14/2007	12/27/2007
0.58Q	02/11/2008	03/13/2008	03/17/2008	03/27/2008
0.58Q	05/05/2008	06/11/2008	06/13/2008	06/26/2008

Indicated Div: $2.32

Valuation Analysis

Forecast EPS	$3.95 (05/16/2008)		
Market Cap	$2.8 Billion	Book Value	1.8 Billion
Price/Book	1.53	Price/Sales	0.92

Dividend Achiever Status

10 Year Growth Rate	13.62%
Total Years of Dividend Growth	21

Business Summary: Insurance (MIC: SIC: 6331 NAIC: 524126)

Mercury General and its subsidiaries are engaged primarily in writing automobile insurance in a number of states, principally California. Co. provides a range of coverage to automobile policyholders, including bodily injury liability, underinsured and uninsured motorist, personal injury protection, property damage liability, comprehensive, collision, and other hazards. Co. also provides homeowners, mechanical breakdown, commercial and dwelling fire, and commercial property insurance. As of Dec 31 2007, Co. sold its policies through more than 4,500 independent agents and brokers, of which approximately 1,000 are located in each of California and Florida.

Recent Developments: For the quarter ended Mar 31 2008, net loss amounted to US$4.0 million versus net income of US$60.5 million in the year-earlier quarter. Revenues were US$669.4 million, down 16.1% from US$798.2 million the year before. Net premiums earned were US$720.9 million versus US$755.8 million in the prior-year quarter, a decrease of 4.6%. Net investment income fell 6.8% to US$39.3 million from US$42.1 million a year ago.

Prospects: Co.'s near-term outlook appears to be somewhat challenging in light of the recent soft market conditions. To be specific, Co. is experiencing a decline in premiums earned primarily attributable to the decrease in the number of policies written, which are reflecting lower net premiums written in both its California and non-California operations. Correspondingly, Co.'s operating income are being adversely affected by the decrease in its premiums earned, which led to a higher combined ratio as well as a decrease in after-tax investment income which resulted from lower overall investment yields earned on new purchases that were made primarily throughout 2007.

Financial Data
(US$ in Thousands)

	3 Mos	12/31/2007	12/31/2006	12/31/2005	12/31/2004	12/31/2003	12/31/2002	12/31/2001
Earnings Per Share	3.16	4.34	3.92	4.63	5.24	3.38	1.21	1.94
Cash Flow Per Share	3.61	3.95	6.62	8.98	8.58	8.17	6.31	3.68
Tang Book Value Per Share	33.37	34.02	31.54	29.44	26.77	23.07	20.21	19.71
Dividends Per Share	2.140	2.080	1.920	1.720	1.480	1.320	1.200	1.060
Dividend Payout %	67.81	47.93	48.98	37.15	28.24	39.05	99.17	54.64
Income Statement								
Total Revenue	669,372	3,178,750	3,168,743	2,991,913	2,668,157	2,265,517	1,786,271	1,506,980
Income Before Taxes	(19,067)	315,036	312,409	352,639	407,843	245,801	60,668	124,809
Income Taxes	(15,106)	77,204	97,592	99,380	121,635	61,480	(5,437)	19,470
Net Income	(3,961)	237,832	214,817	253,259	286,208	184,321	66,105	105,339
Average Shares	54,750	54,829	54,786	54,717	54,633	54,547	54,502	54,382
Balance Sheet								
Total Assets	4,344,058	4,414,496	4,301,062	4,041,551	3,609,743	3,119,766	2,645,296	2,316,540
Total Liabilities	2,517,885	2,552,498	2,576,932	2,433,714	2,150,195	1,864,263	1,546,510	1,246,829
Stockholders' Equity	1,826,173	1,861,998	1,724,130	1,607,837	1,459,548	1,255,503	1,098,786	1,069,711
Shares Outstanding	54,729	54,729	54,669	54,605	54,514	54,424	54,361	54,276
Statistical Record								
Return on Assets %	3.96	5.46	5.15	6.62	8.48	6.39	2.66	4.72
Return on Equity %	9.61	13.26	12.89	16.51	21.03	15.66	6.10	10.02
Net Margin %	(0.59)	7.48	6.78	8.46	10.73	8.14	3.70	6.99
Price Range	57.57-42.35	57.57-49.17	59.52-49.02	60.45-51.62	59.98-46.44	48.58-34.30	50.63-37.37	43.85-32.21
P/E Ratio	18.22-13.40	13.26-11.33	15.18-12.51	13.06-11.15	11.45-8.86	14.37-10.15	41.84-30.88	22.60-16.60
Average Yield %	4.15	3.90	3.54	3.04	2.90	3.07	2.74	2.83

Address: 4484 Wilshire Boulevard, Los Angeles, CA 90010 Telephone: 323-937-1060 Web Site: www.mercuryinsurance.com	Officers: George Joseph - Chairman Gabriel Tirador - President, Chief Executive Officer Transfer Agents: The Bank of New York, New York, NY	No of Institutions: 251 Shares: 27,020,582 % Held: 46.45

MEREDITH CORP.

Exchange	Symbol	Price	52Wk Range	Yield	P/E
NYS	MDP	$33.07 (5/29/2008)	63.25-31.85	2.60	9.61

*7 Year Price Score 82.66   *NYSE Composite Index=100   *12 Month Price Score 70.03

Interim Earnings (Per Share)

Qtr.	Sep	Dec	Mar	Jun
2004-05	0.50	0.54	0.69	0.83
2005-06	0.52	0.58	0.80	0.96
2006-07	0.62	0.72	0.92	1.05
2007-08	0.68	0.75	0.97	...

Interim Dividends (Per Share)

Amt	Decl	Ex	Rec	Pay
0.185Q	08/08/2007	08/29/2007	08/31/2007	09/14/2007
0.185Q	11/07/2007	11/28/2007	11/30/2007	12/14/2007
0.215Q	02/04/2008	02/27/2008	02/29/2008	03/14/2008
0.215Q	05/14/2008	05/28/2008	05/30/2008	06/13/2008

Indicated Div: $0.86

Valuation Analysis

Forecast EPS $3.19 (05/16/2008)

Market Cap	$1.5 Billion	Book Value	816.2 Million
Price/Book	1.87	Price/Sales	0.96

Dividend Achiever Status

10 Year Growth Rate	11.03%
Total Years of Dividend Growth	14

Business Summary: Media (MIC: SIC: 2721 NAIC: 511120)

Meredith is engaged in the business of magazine and book publishing, television broadcasting, integrated marketing, and interactive media. As of June 30 2007, Co. conducted its businesses through two operating segments: Publishing and Broadcasting. The publishing segment focuses on the home and family market. In addition, Co. is a publisher of magazines serving women. The publishing segment also includes book publishing; integrated marketing; a consumer database; an Internet presence; brand licensing activities; and other related operations. The broadcasting segment includes 13 network-affiliated television stations located across the U.S. and one AM radio station.

Recent Developments: For the quarter ended Mar 31 2008, income from continuing operations decreased 12.7% to US$46.4 million from US$53.2 million in the year-earlier quarter. Net income increased 1.7% to US$46.1 million from US$45.3 million in the year-earlier quarter. Revenues were US$401.0 million, down 0.2% from US$401.8 million the year before. Operating income was US$78.3 million versus US$78.2 million in the prior-year quarter, an increase of 0.2%. Indirect operating expenses decreased 0.3% to US$322.7 million from US$323.6 million in the equivalent prior-year period.

Prospects: Co. is seeing lower magazine circulation revenues, reflecting declines in both subscription and newsstand revenues. Specifically, the decrease in subscription revenues is due to strategic initiatives taken to improve long-term subscription contribution including Co.'s ongoing initiative to move the readers of Family Circle, Parents, and Fitness to its direct-to-publisher circulation model, while the decrease in newsstand revenues is mainly due to a reduction in the number of special interest publications. For the full fiscal year ending June 30 2008, Co. is projecting earnings per share to be in the range of $3.15 to $3.20, compared with fiscal 2007 earnings per share of $3.31.

Financial Data

(US$ in Thousands)	9 Mos	6 Mos	3 Mos	06/30/2007	06/30/2006	06/30/2005	06/30/2004	06/30/2003
Earnings Per Share	3.44	3.40	3.37	3.31	2.86	2.52	2.14	0.10
Cash Flow Per Share	5.27	5.50	5.04	4.38	3.93	3.43	3.40	3.47
Dividends Per Share	0.770	0.740	0.715	0.690	0.600	0.520	0.430	0.370
Dividend Payout %	22.39	21.76	21.22	20.85	20.98	20.63	20.09	370.00
Income Statement								
Total Revenue	1,201,338	800,318	404,494	1,615,985	1,597,564	1,221,289	1,161,652	1,080,104
EBITDA	260,595	163,781	79,884	362,027	340,563	293,941	269,428	244,554
Depn & Amortn	56,517	38,052	19,368	73,778	73,972	65,887	66,314	68,786
Income Before Taxes	187,692	114,480	54,705	262,653	237,364	209,052	180,613	148,559
Income Taxes	72,595	45,799	21,335	93,823	92,572	80,903	69,897	57,491
Net Income	115,513	69,429	33,370	162,346	144,792	129,042	110,716	5,319
Average Shares	47,420	48,325	48,828	49,108	50,610	51,220	51,689	51,093
Balance Sheet								
Current Assets	467,822	453,385	466,869	452,640	431,520	304,495	314,014	268,429
Total Assets	2,123,882	2,105,880	2,086,129	2,089,951	2,040,675	1,491,308	1,465,927	1,436,721
Current Liabilities	558,103	564,527	529,757	487,029	463,946	439,080	370,961	297,199
Long-Term Obligations	320,000	295,000	325,000	375,000	515,000	125,000	225,000	375,000
Total Liabilities	1,307,640	1,284,065	1,273,628	1,256,750	1,342,571	839,481	877,197	935,956
Stockholders' Equity	816,242	821,815	812,501	833,201	698,104	651,827	588,730	500,765
Shares Outstanding	46,267	47,139	47,445	48,232	48,191	49,296	50,484	50,149
Statistical Record								
Return on Assets %	7.87	7.94	7.96	7.86	8.20	8.73	7.61	0.37
Return on Equity %	20.90	21.28	21.81	21.20	21.45	20.80	20.27	1.05
EBITDA Margin %	21.69	20.46	19.75	22.40	21.32	24.07	23.19	22.64
Net Margin %	9.62	8.68	8.25	10.05	9.06	10.57	9.53	0.49
Asset Turnover	0.76	0.77	0.78	0.78	0.90	0.83	0.80	0.75
Current Ratio	0.84	0.80	0.88	0.93	0.93	0.69	0.85	0.90
Debt to Equity	0.39	0.36	0.40	0.45	0.74	0.19	0.38	0.75
Price Range	63.25-37.35	63.25-50.49	63.25-49.50	63.25-46.18	56.48-47.65	55.13-44.81	55.75-44.00	47.58-34.09
P/E Ratio	18.39-10.86	18.60-14.85	18.77-14.69	19.11-13.95	19.75-16.66	21.88-17.78	26.05-20.56	475.80-340.90
Average Yield %	1.40	1.27	1.25	1.26	1.17	1.04	0.87	0.89

Address: 1716 Locust Street, Des Moines, IA 50309-3023 **Telephone:** 515-284-3000 **Web Site:** www.meredith.com	**Officers:** William T. Kerr - Chairman Stephen M. Lacy - President, Chief Executive Officer, Principal Accounting Officer, Principal Financial Officer, Acting Vice President **Transfer Agents:** Wells Fargo Bank, N.A., South St. Paul, MN	**Investor Contact:** 800-284-4236 **No of Institutions:** 311 **Shares:** 36,732,052 **% Held:** 90.33

MERIDIAN BIOSCIENCE INC.

Exchange	Symbol	Price	52Wk Range	Yield	P/E
NMS	VIVO	$28.98 (5/29/2008)	35.90-21.12	1.93	39.16

*7 Year Price Score 204.15 *NYSE Composite Index=100 ***12 Month Price Score 105.75**

TRADING VOLUME (thousand shares)

Interim Earnings (Per Share)

Qtr.	Dec	Mar	Jun	Sep
2004-05	0.06	0.09	0.09	0.10
2005-06	0.10	0.12	0.12	0.11
2006-07	0.14	0.15	0.22	0.16
2007-08	0.18	0.18	...	...

Interim Dividends (Per Share)

Amt	Decl	Ex	Rec	Pay
0.11Q	07/19/2007	07/26/2007	07/30/2007	08/06/2007
0.11Q	11/14/2007	11/21/2007	11/26/2007	12/03/2007
0.14Q	01/22/2008	01/29/2008	01/31/2008	02/07/2008
0.14Q	04/17/2008	04/24/2008	04/28/2008	05/05/2008

Indicated Div: $0.56 (Div. Reinv. Plan)

Valuation Analysis

Forecast EPS $0.73 (05/16/2008)

Market Cap	$1.2 Billion	Book Value	121.8 Million
Price/Book	9.55	Price/Sales	8.81

Dividend Achiever Status

10 Year Growth Rate	17.46%
Total Years of Dividend Growth	15

Business Summary: Biotechnology (MIC: SIC: 2835 NAIC: 325413)

Meridian Bioscience is a life science company engaged in the development, manufacture, sale and distribution of diagnostic test kits, primarily for certain respiratory, gastrointestinal, viral and parasitic infectious diseases; the manufacture and distribution of bulk antigens, antibodies, and reagents used by researchers and other diagnostic manufacturers; and the contract manufacture of proteins and other biologicals for use by biopharmaceutical and biotechnology companies engaged in research for new drugs and vaccines. As of Sep 30 2007, Co. conducted its operations in three operating segments: U.S. Diagnostics, European Diagnostics, and Life Science.

Recent Developments: For the quarter ended Mar 31 2008, net income increased 23.9% to US$7.3 million from US$5.9 million in the year-earlier quarter. Revenues were US$36.2 million, up 12.9% from US$32.1 million the year before. Operating income was US$10.7 million versus US$8.8 million in the prior-year quarter, an increase of 21.3%. Direct operating expenses rose 14.2% to US$15.1 million from US$13.3 million in the comparable period the year before. Indirect operating expenses increased 3.9% to US$10.4 million from US$10.0 million in the equivalent prior-year period.

Prospects: On May 13 2008, Co. executed a letter of intent to acquire a line of infectious disease recombinant proteins and cardiac antigens from Vybion, Inc. The assets to be acquired include a portfolio of recombinant viral proteins and cardiac antigens, customer lists, supply agreements, patent and technology rights, equipment, and on-hand inventory. This acquisition should add key capabilities and revenues to Co.'s life science business. Completion of the transaction is subject to execution of a definitive purchase agreement and other customary conditions, and is expected to be completed in the next 30 to 60 days. Meanwhile, for fiscal 2008, Co. expects earnings per share of $0.72 to $0.75.

Financial Data
(US$ in Thousands)

	6 Mos	3 Mos	09/30/2007	09/30/2006	09/30/2005	09/30/2004	09/30/2003	09/30/2002
Earnings Per Share	0.74	0.71	0.66	0.45	0.35	0.27	0.21	0.15
Cash Flow Per Share	0.77	0.77	0.67	0.57	0.52	0.38	0.37	0.35
Tang Book Value Per Share	2.57	2.45	2.35	1.89	1.59	0.54	0.37	0.26
Dividends Per Share	0.467	0.433	0.400	0.283	0.204	0.173	0.151	0.122
Dividend Payout %	63.27	61.32	60.61	62.50	58.97	65.00	72.34	80.88
Income Statement								
Total Revenue	70,096	33,847	122,963	108,413	92,965	79,606	65,864	59,104
EBITDA	23,322	11,818	39,474	32,335	24,483	18,540	17,047	13,898
Depn & Amortn	1,418	705	4,396	5,277	4,160	3,819	3,780	3,719
Income Before Taxes	22,755	11,568	36,682	28,053	19,596	13,195	11,591	8,243
Income Taxes	8,000	4,112	9,961	9,728	7,031	4,010	4,573	3,212
Net Income	14,755	7,456	26,721	18,325	12,565	9,185	7,018	5,031
Average Shares	41,038	40,967	40,738	40,164	36,156	34,332	33,637	33,210
Balance Sheet								
Current Assets	94,465	96,432	93,745	81,169	70,160	36,111	33,161	30,375
Total Assets	140,712	135,011	132,698	120,955	110,569	69,322	66,420	65,095
Current Liabilities	16,410	15,624	17,067	20,617	19,791	16,650	15,330	15,249
Long-Term Obligations	...	...	...	1,803	2,684	17,093	21,505	23,626
Total Liabilities	18,942	18,235	19,750	26,178	26,801	36,390	38,936	40,714
Stockholders' Equity	121,770	116,776	112,948	94,777	83,768	32,932	27,484	24,381
Shares Outstanding	40,125	39,969	39,847	39,235	38,891	33,666	33,120	32,906
Statistical Record								
Return on Assets %	22.82	22.24	21.07	15.83	13.97	13.50	10.67	7.68
Return on Equity %	26.63	26.59	25.73	20.53	21.53	30.32	27.06	21.26
EBITDA Margin %	33.27	34.92	32.10	29.83	26.34	23.29	25.88	23.51
Net Margin %	21.05	22.03	21.73	16.90	13.52	11.54	10.66	8.51
Asset Turnover	1.01	1.00	0.97	0.94	1.03	1.17	1.00	0.90
Current Ratio	5.76	6.17	5.49	3.94	3.55	2.17	2.16	1.99
Debt to Equity	...	...	...	0.02	0.03	0.52	0.78	0.97
Price Range	35.34-18.61	34.09-16.43	30.67-14.03	18.37-12.03	13.80-5.80	5.92-4.34	4.92-2.49	3.36-2.02
P/E Ratio	47.76-25.14	48.01-23.15	46.47-21.25	40.81-26.81	39.43-16.57	21.93-16.07	23.41-11.88	22.37-13.45
Average Yield %	1.72	1.82	1.99	1.86	2.47	3.56	4.08	4.40

Address: 3471 River Hills Drive, Cincinnati, OH 45244	Officers: William J. Motto - Founder, Executive Chairman John A. Kraeutler - Chief Executive Officer	Investor Contact: 513-271-3700
Telephone: 513-271-3700	Transfer Agents:Computershare Investor Services LLC, Providence, RI	No of Institutions: 212
Web Site: www.meridianbioscience.com		Shares: 33,315,748 % Held: 78.92

MGE ENERGY INC

Exchange	Symbol	Price	52Wk Range	Yield	P/E
NMS	MGEE	$33.94 (5/29/2008)	36.96-29.48	4.18	14.76

*7 Year Price Score 82.55 *NYSE Composite Index=100 *12 Month Price Score 105.75

Interim Earnings (Per Share)

Qtr.	Mar	Jun	Sep	Dec
2005	0.40	0.31	0.48	0.42
2006	0.56	0.34	0.62	0.53
2007	0.59	0.47	0.71	0.50
2008	0.63	...	...	...

Interim Dividends (Per Share)

Amt	Decl	Ex	Rec	Pay
0.355Q	08/17/2007	08/29/2007	09/01/2007	09/15/2007
0.355Q	11/16/2007	11/28/2007	12/01/2007	12/15/2007
0.355Q	02/15/2008	02/27/2008	03/01/2008	03/15/2008
0.355Q	05/20/2008	05/28/2008	06/01/2008	06/15/2008

Indicated Div: $1.42 (Div. Reinv. Plan)

Valuation Analysis

Forecast EPS N/A

Market Cap	$749.5 Million	Book Value	436.7 Million
Price/Book	1.72	Price/Sales	1.34

Dividend Achiever Status

10 Year Growth Rate	0.90%
Total Years of Dividend Growth	32

Business Summary: Electricity (MIC: SIC: 4931 NAIC: 221121)

MGE Energy is a holding company. Co.'s Electric Utility operations generate, purchase and distribute natural gas through its Madison Gas and Electric Co. subsidiary (MGE). Co.'s Gas Utility operations purchase and distribute natural gas through MGE. Co.'s Nonregulated Energy operations construct, own, and lease new electric generating capacity through its MGE Power, MGE Power Elm Road and MGE Power West Campus subsidiaries. Co.'s Transmission Investments operations invest in companies that provide electric transmission services. Co.'s Others operations invest in companies and property through its MGE Construct, MAGAEL and Central Wisconsin Development Corporation subsidiaries.

Recent Developments: For the quarter ended Mar 31 2008, net income increased 12.5% to US$13.8 million from US$12.3 million in the year-earlier quarter. Revenues were US$190.0 million, up 13.2% from US$167.9 million in the prior-year quarter, an increase of 12.4%. Direct operating expenses rose 13.3% to US$161.3 million from US$142.3 million in the comparable period the year before. Indirect operating expenses increased 12.1% to US$4.4 million from US$3.9 million in the equivalent prior-year period.

Prospects: Co. is seeing an increase in earnings primarily due to increased earnings from the gas utility supported by higher retail therm sales. In addition, Co.'s revenues benefited from the recovery of costs related to its construction activities at its Elm Road coal power project and the Top of Iowa III wind project. Looking ahead, Co.'s primary focus is to provide its customers with reliable power at competitive prices. Hence, Co. plans to meet this challenge by building more efficient generation projects and continuing its efforts to control operational costs. For instance, Co. placed the Top of Iowa III wind-powered electric generating facility in service during the first quarter of 2008.

Financial Data

(US$ in Thousands)	3 Mos	12/31/2007	12/31/2006	12/31/2005	12/31/2004	12/31/2003	12/31/2002	12/31/2001
Earnings Per Share	2.30	2.27	2.06	1.57	1.77	1.71	1.69	1.62
Cash Flow Per Share	3.95	3.56	4.91	2.44	3.25	3.83	3.28	4.44
Tang Book Value Per Share	19.78	19.49	17.89	16.81	16.59	14.34	12.94	12.67
Dividends Per Share	1.413	1.407	1.387	1.373	1.360	1.348	1.338	1.328
Dividend Payout %	61.32	61.97	67.31	87.47	76.84	78.85	79.19	81.99
Income Statement								
Total Revenue	189,996	537,594	507,546	513,370	424,881	401,547	347,096	333,711
EBITDA	34,332	122,068	114,828	94,718	90,861	85,145	89,307	...
Depn & Amortn	9,448	32,332	31,505	29,308	24,931	22,828	28,842	36,459
Income Before Taxes	21,451	76,680	68,322	51,962	54,496	50,541	47,920	...
Income Taxes	7,614	27,855	25,899	19,871	20,656	19,901	18,727	2,105
Net Income	13,837	48,825	42,423	32,091	33,840	30,640	29,193	27,245
Average Shares	21,989	21,520	20,564	20,436	19,119	17,894	17,311	16,819
Balance Sheet								
Net PPE	861,710	843,988	728,423	667,657	607,398	537,511	460,328	401,249
Total Assets	1,109,371	1,111,587	982,232	916,907	827,371	721,687	628,895	541,451
Long-Term Obligations	232,361	232,346	237,284	222,312	202,257	202,204	192,149	157,600
Total Liabilities	672,635	683,861	606,884	573,024	489,174	458,617	401,525	325,159
Stockholders' Equity	436,736	427,726	375,348	343,883	338,197	263,070	227,370	216,292
Shares Outstanding	22,084	21,950	20,975	20,451	20,389	18,343	17,574	17,071
Statistical Record								
Return on Assets %	4.81	4.66	4.47	3.68	4.36	4.54	4.99	4.90
Return on Equity %	12.22	12.16	11.80	9.41	11.23	12.49	13.16	13.08
EBITDA Margin %	18.07	22.71	22.62	18.45	21.39	21.20	25.73	...
Net Margin %	7.28	9.08	8.36	6.25	7.96	7.63	8.41	8.16
PPE Turnover	0.70	0.68	0.73	0.81	0.74	0.80	0.81	0.79
Asset Turnover	0.54	0.51	0.53	0.59	0.55	0.59	0.59	0.60
Debt to Equity	0.53	0.54	0.63	0.65	0.60	0.77	0.85	0.73
Price Range	37.00-29.48	37.00-29.48	36.97-29.28	38.63-31.18	36.30-28.57	34.45-25.27	29.84-25.01	27.80-21.06
P/E Ratio	16.09-12.82	16.30-12.99	17.95-14.21	24.61-19.86	20.51-16.14	20.15-14.78	17.66-14.80	17.16-13.00
Average Yield %	4.19	4.12	4.25	3.90	4.28	4.50	4.97	5.53

Address: 133 South Blair Street, Madison, WI 53703 Telephone: 608-252-7000 Web Site: www.mgeenergy.com	Officers: Gary J. Wolter - Chairman, President, Chief Executive Officer Terry A. Hanson - Vice President, Chief Financial Officer, Secretary **Transfer Agents:** Continental Stock Transfer & Trust Co., New York, NY	No of Institutions: 113 Shares: 9,124,354 % Held: 37.62

MINE SAFETY APPLIANCES CO

Exchange	Symbol	Price	52Wk Range	Yield	P/E
NYS	MSA	$40.52 (5/29/2008)	56.00-35.74	2.37	21.90

*7 Year Price Score 114.13 *NYSE Composite Index=100 *12 Month Price Score 90.00

TRADING VOLUME (thousand shares)

Interim Earnings (Per Share)

Qtr.	Mar	Jun	Sep	Dec
2005	0.57	0.52	0.46	0.65
2006	0.42	0.43	0.34	0.53
2007	0.44	0.48	0.46	0.48
2008	0.44	...	...	...

Interim Dividends (Per Share)

Amt	Decl	Ex	Rec	Pay
0.22Q	08/02/2007	08/15/2007	08/17/2007	09/10/2007
0.22Q	11/06/2007	11/14/2007	11/16/2007	12/10/2007
0.22Q	01/15/2008	02/13/2008	02/15/2008	03/10/2008
0.24Q	05/13/2008	05/21/2008	05/23/2008	06/10/2008

Indicated Div: $0.96

Valuation Analysis

Forecast EPS $2.11 (05/16/2008)

Market Cap	$1.4 Billion	Book Value	483.0 Million
Price/Book	3.00	Price/Sales	1.38

Dividend Achiever Status

10 Year Growth Rate	19.81%
Total Years of Dividend Growth	37

Business Summary: Medical Instruments & Equipment (MIC: SIC: 3842 NAIC: 339112)

Mine Safety Appliances is engaged in the global development, manufacture and supply of enhanced products that protect people's health and safety. Co.'s line of safety products is used by workers around the world in the fire service, homeland security, construction and other industries, as well as the military. Co.'s product offering includes self-contained breathing apparatus, gas masks, gas detection instruments, head protection, respirators and thermal imaging devices. Co. also provides an offering of consumer and contractor safety products through retail channels. As of Dec 31 2007, Co. operated through three geographic segments: North America, Europe, and International.

Recent Developments: For the quarter ended Mar 31 2008, net income decreased 0.3% to US$16.0 million from US$16.1 million in the year-earlier quarter. Revenues were US$267.3 million, up 18.1% from US$226.3 million the year before. Direct operating expenses rose 17.0% to US$160.0 million from US$136.8 million in the comparable period the year before. Indirect operating expenses increased 24.9% to US$81.1 million from US$65.0 million in the equivalent prior-year period.

Prospects: Co.'s top-line results are benefiting from higher sales of self-contained breathing apparatus, an increase in shipments of advanced combat helmets to the U.S. military and CG634 helmets to the Canadian Forces, as well as growth in sales of head protection to the North American construction and industrial markets. However, Co.'s research and development expense is increasing, mainly due to its continued focus on developing new products. In addition, Co. is seeing higher capital spending, which includes costs associated with the construction of its new facility in Suzhou, China, as well as building improvement projects in Brazil and Australia.

Financial Data

(US$ in Thousands)	3 Mos	12/31/2007	12/31/2006	12/31/2005	12/31/2004	12/31/2003	12/31/2002	12/31/2001
Earnings Per Share	1.85	1.86	1.73	2.19	1.86	1.75	0.95	0.87
Cash Flow Per Share	0.51	1.16	1.73	2.35	1.45	1.10	1.35	0.86
Tang Book Value Per Share	10.99	10.40	9.85	8.84	8.69	7.03	6.62	5.96
Dividends Per Share	0.880	0.840	0.680	0.520	0.370	1.717	0.217	0.180
Dividend Payout %	47.45	45.16	39.31	23.74	19.89	98.10	22.81	20.69
Income Statement								
Total Revenue	267,260	1,007,648	919,098	911,970	857,513	698,197	566,697	545,666
EBITDA	32,897	130,551	114,787	148,141	139,364	96,967	69,608	79,357
Depn & Amortn	6,769	24,363	22,147	24,345	25,496	23,208	21,525	26,471
Income Before Taxes	26,128	106,188	92,640	123,796	113,868	73,759	48,083	52,886
Income Taxes	10,101	38,600	28,722	42,013	42,821	24,835	16,870	21,255
Net Income	16,027	67,588	63,918	81,783	71,047	65,267	35,077	31,631
Average Shares	36,021	36,240	36,928	37,301	38,130	37,264	36,885	36,237
Balance Sheet								
Current Assets	524,191	497,050	416,859	377,226	397,660	323,242	282,944	217,686
Total Assets	1,062,851	1,016,306	898,620	725,357	734,110	643,885	579,765	520,698
Current Liabilities	228,479	209,189	127,435	130,859	127,067	114,715	99,700	82,500
Long-Term Obligations	103,611	103,726	112,541	45,834	54,463	59,915	64,350	67,381
Total Liabilities	579,075	554,775	460,767	342,960	356,499	336,027	290,703	267,194
Stockholders' Equity	483,018	461,531	437,853	382,397	377,611	307,858	289,062	253,504
Shares Outstanding	35,723	35,661	36,015	36,545	37,341	36,927	36,621	36,302
Statistical Record								
Return on Assets %	6.77	7.06	7.87	11.21	10.28	10.67	6.37	6.26
Return on Equity %	14.59	15.03	15.59	21.52	20.67	21.87	12.93	13.18
EBITDA Margin %	12.31	12.96	12.49	16.24	16.25	13.89	12.28	14.54
Net Margin %	6.00	6.71	6.95	8.97	8.29	9.35	6.19	5.80
Asset Turnover	1.05	1.05	1.13	1.25	1.24	1.14	1.03	1.08
Current Ratio	2.29	2.38	3.27	2.88	3.13	2.82	2.84	2.64
Debt to Equity	0.21	0.22	0.26	0.12	0.14	0.19	0.22	0.27
Price Range	56.00-38.87	56.00-37.39	43.50-34.45	51.00-34.45	51.57-23.42	28.21-10.23	16.83-9.17	16.98-7.58
P/E Ratio	30.27-21.01	30.11-20.10	25.14-19.91	23.29-15.73	27.73-12.59	16.12-5.85	17.72-9.65	19.52-8.72
Average Yield %	1.93	1.88	1.76	1.23	1.06	10.91	1.70	1.69

Address: 121 Gamma Drive, RIDC Industrial Park, O'Hara Township, Pittsburgh, PA 15238 **Telephone:** 412-967-3000 **Web Site:** www.msanet.com	**Officers:** William M. Lambert - President, Chief Executive Officer Roberto Canizares M. - Executive Vice President **Transfer Agents:** Wells Fargo Shareowner Services, South St.Paul, MN	**No of Institutions:** 175 **Shares:** 29,247,080 **% Held:** 72.62

MYERS INDUSTRIES INC.

Exchange	Symbol	Price	52Wk Range	Yield	P/E
NYS	MYE	$11.97 (5/29/2008)	22.28-10.18	2.01	13.01

*7 Year Price Score 101.29 ***NYSE Composite Index=100** ***12 Month Price Score 73.79**

Interim Earnings (Per Share)

Qtr.	Mar	Jun	Sep	Dec
2005	0.22	0.15	0.14	0.25
2006	0.31	(2.85)	0.17	0.40
2007	0.93	0.07	0.04	0.51
2008	0.30	...	...	...

Interim Dividends (Per Share)

Amt	Decl	Ex	Rec	Pay
0.06Q	12/10/2007	12/18/2007	12/20/2007	01/02/2008
0.28Q	12/10/2007	12/18/2007	12/20/2007	01/02/2008
0.06Q	02/27/2008	03/06/2008	03/10/2008	04/04/2008
0.06Q	04/24/2008	06/03/2008	06/05/2008	07/03/2008

Indicated Div: $0.24 (Div. Reinv. Plan)

Valuation Analysis

Forecast EPS $1.14 (05/16/2008)

Market Cap	$421.2 Million	Book Value	326.2 Million
Price/Book	1.29	Price/Sales	0.46

Dividend Achiever Status

10 Year Growth Rate	7.51%
Total Years of Dividend Growth	31

TRADING VOLUME (thousand shares)

Business Summary: Plastics (MIC: SIC: 3089 NAIC: 326199)

Myers Industries manufactures polymer products for industrial, agricultural, automotive, commercial, and consumer markets. Principal products include reusable plastic containers, plastic horticultural pots, trays, and flower planters. Other principal product lines include plastic storage and organization containers, plastic and rubber original equipment manufacturer parts, rubber tire repair products, and custom plastic and rubber products. Co. is also a wholesale distributor of tools, equipment, and supplies for the tire, wheel, and undervehicle service industry. Co.'s distribution products range from tire balancers and alignment systems to valve caps and other consumable service supplies.

Recent Developments: For the quarter ended Mar 31 2008, net income decreased 68.1% to US$10.4 million from US$32.5 million in the year-earlier quarter. Revenues were US$249.3 million, up 1.2% from US$246.5 million the year before. Operating income was US$16.8 million versus US$27.0 million in the prior-year quarter, a decrease of 37.8%. Direct operating expenses rose 9.7% to US$189.4 million from US$172.7 million in the comparable period the year before. Indirect operating expenses decreased 7.7% to US$43.2 million from US$46.8 million in the equivalent prior-year period.

Prospects: Despite an increase in sales, Co. is seeing its profitability being adversely affected by weakening economic conditions and raw material inflation. Notably, economic softness resulted in lower volumes, while prices for raw materials such as high-density polyethylene and polypropylene resins, increased. Accordingly, in the near-term, Co. intends to continue to focus on managing the recovery of raw material costs and implementing measures to increase benefits from cost saving programs to mitigate the effects of economic conditions. In addition, Co. remains focused on selling price adjustments, expense controls and continuous productivity initiatives.

Financial Data

(US$ in Thousands)	3 Mos	12/31/2007	12/31/2006	12/31/2005	12/31/2004	12/31/2003	12/31/2002	12/31/2001
Earnings Per Share	0.92	1.55	(1.97)	0.76	0.76	0.49	0.73	0.47
Cash Flow Per Share	2.30	2.76	2.33	1.94	1.37	1.54	1.99	2.35
Tang Book Value Per Share	3.57	3.34	3.21	1.83	1.73	2.05	1.48	0.82
Dividends Per Share	0.505	0.498	0.205	0.200	0.191	0.182	0.178	0.167
Dividend Payout %	54.94	32.10	...	26.32	25.12	37.04	24.50	35.80
Income Statement								
Total Revenue	249,346	918,793	779,984	903,679	803,070	661,092	607,991	607,950
EBITDA	26,856	110,278	89,135	91,988	91,226	71,276	87,884	89,844
Depn & Amortn	10,095	37,727	28,213	35,997	39,175	36,555	35,714	43,905
Income Before Taxes	13,760	57,051	45,074	40,407	38,729	24,647	40,361	27,240
Income Taxes	5,112	20,103	16,364	13,851	13,019	8,321	16,401	12,049
Net Income	10,380	54,736	(69,024)	26,556	25,710	16,326	23,960	15,191
Average Shares	35,202	35,249	35,044	34,724	33,846	33,138	32,969	32,727
Balance Sheet								
Current Assets	292,396	277,809	307,523	284,328	284,072	207,933	201,140	196,619
Total Assets	709,604	697,552	661,983	760,007	785,603	621,627	602,482	582,166
Current Liabilities	134,464	158,475	134,727	141,242	136,252	94,175	117,369	104,899
Long-Term Obligations	195,260	167,254	198,275	249,524	275,252	211,003	212,223	247,145
Total Liabilities	383,406	380,282	381,325	420,606	439,599	327,102	346,793	364,640
Stockholders' Equity	326,198	317,270	280,659	339,401	346,004	294,524	255,690	217,526
Shares Outstanding	35,191	35,180	35,067	34,806	34,645	33,201	33,078	32,790
Statistical Record								
Return on Assets %	4.52	8.05	N.M.	3.44	3.64	2.67	4.05	2.52
Return on Equity %	10.38	18.31	N.M.	7.75	8.01	5.93	10.13	7.04
EBITDA Margin %	10.77	12.00	11.43	10.18	11.36	10.78	14.45	14.78
Net Margin %	4.16	5.96	N.M.	2.94	3.20	2.47	3.94	2.50
Asset Turnover	1.27	1.35	1.10	1.17	1.14	1.08	1.03	1.01
Current Ratio	2.17	1.75	2.28	2.01	2.08	2.21	1.71	1.87
Debt to Equity	0.60	0.53	0.71	0.74	0.80	0.72	0.83	1.14
Price Range	22.55-10.18	22.55-13.57	18.62-14.24	14.70-9.36	13.50-10.06	12.05-8.00	13.16-8.51	10.41-7.60
P/E Ratio	24.51-11.07	14.55-8.75	...	19.34-12.32	17.76-13.24	24.60-16.33	18.03-11.66	22.16-16.18
Average Yield %	2.72	2.51	1.26	1.59	1.67	1.87	1.66	1.81

Address: 1293 South Main Street, Akron, OH 44301	Officers: Stephen E. Myers - Chairman John C. Orr - President, Chief Executive Officer **Transfer Agents:** National City Bank, Cleveland, OH	Investor Contact: 330-253-5592
Telephone: 330-253-5592		No of Institutions: 164
Web Site: www.myersind.com		**Shares:** 25,296,244 **% Held:** 69.81

NACCO INDUSTRIES INC.

Exchange	Symbol	Price	52Wk Range	Yield	P/E
NYS	NC	$85.96 (5/29/2008)	170.00-69.96	2.40	8.33

*7 Year Price Score 87.04   *NYSE Composite Index=100   ***12 Month Price Score 83.82**

TRADING VOLUME (thousand shares)

Interim Earnings (Per Share)

Qtr.	Mar	Jun	Sep	Dec
2005	0.63	1.37	1.65	3.94
2006	1.54	0.57	2.28	8.50
2007	0.80	1.20	2.55	6.25
2008	0.33	...	...	...

Interim Dividends (Per Share)

Amt	Decl	Ex	Rec	Pay
0.50Q	08/08/2007	08/29/2007	08/31/2007	09/14/2007
0.50Q	11/07/2007	11/28/2007	11/30/2007	12/14/2007
0.50Q	02/13/2008	02/27/2008	02/29/2008	03/14/2008
0.515Q	05/14/2008	05/29/2008	06/02/2008	06/16/2008

Indicated Div: $2.06

Valuation Analysis
Forecast EPS $6.33 (05/01/2008)
Market Cap $711.9 Million   Book Value 897.6 Million
Price/Book 0.79   Price/Sales 0.19

Dividend Achiever Status
10 Year Growth Rate 9.87%
Total Years of Dividend Growth 24

Business Summary: Industrial Machinery and Equipment (MIC: SIC: 3537 NAIC: 333924)

NACCO Industries is a holding company with three principal businesses. Co.'s NACCO Materials Handling Group designs, engineers, manufactures, sells, services and leases a line of lift trucks and replacement parts marketed worldwide under the Hyster® and Yale® brand names. Co.'s NACCO Housewares Group consists of Hamilton Beach Brands, Inc., a designer, marketer and distributor of small electric household appliances, as well as commercial products for restaurants, bars and hotels; and The Kitchen Collection, Inc., a retailer of kitchenware and gourmet foods. Co.'s North American Coal Corporation subsidiary mines and markets lignite coal primarily as fuel for power generation.

Recent Developments: For the quarter ended Mar 31 2008, net income decreased 59.1% to US$2.7 million from US$6.6 million in the year-earlier quarter. Revenues were US$865.0 million, up 7.6% from US$803.9 million the year before. Operating income was US$11.6 million versus US$15.0 million in the prior-year quarter, a decrease of 22.7%. Direct operating expenses rose 9.6% to US$737.4 million from US$672.9 million in the comparable period the year before. Indirect operating expenses were unchanged at US$116.0 million versus the equivalent prior-year period.

Prospects: The economic condition continues to be uncertain the consumer markets in which Co.'s Hamilton Beach and Kitchen Collection subsidiaries participate and the capital goods markets in the U.S. in which its NACCO Materials Handling Group (NMHG) participates. Hence, key improvement programs continue to be implemented at NMHG. However, these programs will incur significant costs in 2008, mainly in the first half of 2008. Also, product price recoveries are expected to cover rising costs, which should lead to a challenging 2008 second quarter for NMHG. In the meantime, Co. also expects that its North American Coal subsidiary to continue to experience difficult operating environments in 2008.

Financial Data

(US$ in Thousands)	3 Mos	12/31/2007	12/31/2006	12/31/2005	12/31/2004	12/31/2003	12/31/2002	12/31/2001
Earnings Per Share	10.32	10.80	12.89	7.60	5.83	6.44	5.17	(4.40)
Cash Flow Per Share	7.84	9.88	21.07	9.15	15.33	15.03	18.20	16.61
Tang Book Value Per Share	46.26	45.86	34.12	23.49	21.01	14.67	5.73	1.98
Dividends Per Share	2.000	1.980	1.905	1.847	1.675	1.260	0.970	0.930
Dividend Payout %	19.39	18.33	14.78	24.31	28.73	19.57	18.76	...
Income Statement								
Total Revenue	865,000	3,602,700	3,349,000	3,157,400	2,782,600	2,472,600	2,285,000	2,637,900
EBITDA	27,200	203,800	227,200	185,300	167,300	184,400	182,800	128,000
Depn & Amortn	15,900	62,800	64,900	67,000	67,600	68,400	70,200	116,500
Income Before Taxes	3,400	112,300	120,500	70,800	52,300	65,000	59,700	(45,400)
Income Taxes	700	23,100	27,800	13,100	5,300	15,800	11,300	(9,900)
Net Income	2,700	89,300	106,200	62,500	47,900	52,800	42,400	(36,000)
Average Shares	8,282	8,272	8,242	8,226	8,214	8,204	8,198	8,190
Balance Sheet								
Current Assets	1,428,700	1,434,800	1,153,800	1,073,700	996,800	812,900	739,500	770,000
Total Assets	2,427,500	2,428,200	2,156,300	2,094,000	2,038,600	1,839,800	1,780,800	2,161,900
Current Liabilities	874,100	856,500	751,000	704,700	672,000	589,800	545,500	874,300
Long-Term Obligations	419,100	439,500	359,900	406,200	407,400	363,200	416,100	519,400
Total Liabilities	1,529,900	1,536,100	1,363,200	1,390,700	1,350,600	1,202,800	1,221,400	1,632,600
Stockholders' Equity	897,600	892,100	793,100	703,300	688,000	637,000	559,400	529,300
Shares Outstanding	8,281	8,268	8,237	8,226	8,214	8,206	8,201	8,195
Statistical Record								
Return on Assets %	3.78	3.90	5.00	3.02	2.46	2.92	2.15	N.M.
Return on Equity %	10.10	10.60	14.19	8.98	7.21	8.83	7.79	N.M.
EBITDA Margin %	3.14	5.66	6.78	5.87	6.01	7.46	8.00	4.85
Net Margin %	0.31	2.48	3.17	1.98	1.72	2.14	1.86	N.M.
Asset Turnover	1.62	1.57	1.58	1.53	1.43	1.37	1.16	1.21
Current Ratio	1.63	1.68	1.54	1.52	1.48	1.38	1.36	0.88
Debt to Equity	0.47	0.49	0.45	0.58	0.59	0.57	0.74	0.98
Price Range	174.03-69.96	174.03-90.57	170.70-119.85	122.44-94.95	111.70-77.15	93.77-37.99	75.25-36.65	81.47-42.63
P/E Ratio	16.86-6.78	16.11-8.39	13.24-9.30	16.11-12.49	19.16-13.23	14.56-5.90	14.56-7.09	...
Average Yield %	1.68	1.51	1.35	1.70	1.86	2.01	1.79	1.47

Address: 5875 Landerbrook Drive, Mayfield Heights, OH 44124-4017 **Telephone:** 440-449-9600 **Web Site:** www.naccoind.com	**Officers:** Alfred M. Rankin - Chairman, President, Chief Executive Officer Charles A. Bittenbender - Vice President, Secretary, General Counsel **Transfer Agents:** National City Bank, Cleveland, OH	**No of Institutions:** 112 **Shares:** 4,697,855 **% Held:** 69.32

NATIONAL CITY CORP

Exchange	Symbol	Price	52Wk Range	Yield	P/E
NYS	NCC	$5.68 (5/29/2008)	34.96-5.58	0.70	N/A

*7 Year Price Score 49.74   *NYSE Composite Index=100   *12 Month Price Score 35.51

Interim Earnings (Per Share)

Qtr.	Mar	Jun	Sep	Dec
2005	0.74	0.97	0.74	0.64
2006	0.74	0.77	0.86	1.36
2007	0.50	0.60	(0.03)	(0.56)
2008	(0.27)	...	...	...

Interim Dividends (Per Share)

Amt	Decl	Ex	Rec	Pay
0.41Q	07/02/2007	07/11/2007	07/13/2007	08/01/2007
0.41Q	10/01/2007	10/09/2007	10/11/2007	11/01/2007
0.21Q	01/02/2008	01/10/2008	01/14/2008	02/01/2008
0.01Q	04/21/2008	04/29/2008	05/01/2008	05/16/2008

Indicated Div: $0.04 (Div. Reinv. Plan)

Valuation Analysis

Forecast EPS $-0.33 (05/17/2008)

Market Cap	$3.6 Billion	Book Value	13.2 Billion
Price/Book	0.27	Price/Sales	0.30

Dividend Achiever Status

10 Year Growth Rate	6.72%
Total Years of Dividend Growth	15

TRADING VOLUME (thousand shares)

Business Summary: Commercial Banking (MIC: SIC: 6021 NAIC: 522110)

National City is a financial holding company. Co. operates through its banking network in Ohio, Florida, Illinois, Indiana, Kentucky, Michigan, Missouri, Pennsylvania and Wisconsin, and also conducts selected lending and other financial services businesses on a nationwide basis. Co.'s primary businesses include commercial and retail banking, mortgage financing and servicing, consumer finance, and asset management. Co.'s businesses are organized by product and service offerings as well as the distribution channels. As of Dec 31 2007, Co. had total assets of $150.37 billion, and total deposits of $97.56 billion.

Recent Developments: For the quarter ended Mar 31 2008, net loss amounted to US$171.0 million versus net income of US$319.0 million in the year-earlier quarter. Net interest income decreased 4.4% to US$1.06 billion from US$1.11 billion in the year-earlier quarter. Provision for loan losses was US$1.39 billion versus US$122.0 million in the prior-year quarter, an increase of. Non-interest income rose 83.3% to US$1.14 billion from US$621.0 million, while non-interest expense declined 12.5% to US$1.01 billion.

Prospects: Co.'s operating results have been hampered by the deterioration in credit quality of residential real estate loans. Notably, economic conditions and the housing market continued to worsen, resulting in higher nonperforming assets and net charge-offs, specifically within residential construction, nonprime mortgage, and broker-sourced mortgage and home equity portfolios. Co. expects the weakness in the housing markets to adversely affect the credit quality of the residential real estate portfolio through 2008 and into 2009. Also, Co. is seeing a decline in its net interest margin, reflecting lower asset yields, driven by decreases in the Federal Funds rate, while deposit costs declined less.

Financial Data
(US$ in Thousands)

	3 Mos	12/31/2007	12/31/2006	12/31/2005	12/31/2004	12/31/2003	12/31/2002	12/31/2001
Earnings Per Share	(0.27)	0.51	3.72	3.09	4.31	3.43	2.59	2.27
Cash Flow Per Share	(0.21)	(1.22)	10.17	10.20	7.78	20.92	(10.25)	(19.67)
Tang Book Value Per Share	8.67	8.05	13.42	11.41	12.03	11.33	10.70	12.15
Dividends Per Share	1.420	1.600	1.520	1.440	1.340	1.250	1.200	1.160
Dividend Payout %	...	313.73	40.86	46.60	31.09	36.44	46.33	51.10
Income Statement								
Income Before Taxes	(206,000)	370,677	3,422,636	2,961,163	4,077,940	3,237,466	2,405,826	2,166,501
Income Taxes	(35,000)	56,702	1,122,800	975,934	1,298,006	1,120,402	812,228	778,393
Net Income	(171,000)	313,975	2,299,836	1,985,229	2,779,934	2,117,064	1,593,598	1,388,108
Average Shares	633,433	612,236	617,671	641,600	645,510	616,410	616,174	611,936
Balance Sheet								
Total Assets	155,038,000	150,374,028	140,190,842	142,397,114	139,280,377	113,933,460	118,258,415	105,816,700
Total Liabilities	141,815,000	136,966,200	125,609,839	129,784,243	126,476,848	104,604,789	109,950,403	98,435,477
Stockholders' Equity	13,223,000	13,407,828	14,581,003	12,612,871	12,803,529	9,328,671	8,308,012	7,381,223
Shares Outstanding	634,117	633,945	632,381	615,047	646,749	605,996	611,491	607,354
Statistical Record								
Return on Assets %	N.M.	0.22	1.63	1.41	2.19	1.82	1.42	1.43
Return on Equity %	N.M.	2.24	16.91	15.62	25.05	24.01	20.31	19.62
Price Range	37.90-7.52	38.49-16.13	37.75-33.36	37.75-31.01	39.44-32.36	34.58-26.75	33.69-24.68	32.51-24.50
P/E Ratio	...	75.47-31.63	10.15-8.97	12.22-10.04	9.15-7.51	10.08-7.80	13.01-9.53	14.32-10.79
Average Yield %	5.64	5.23	4.23	4.15	3.71	4.03	4.06	4.06

Address: 1900 East Ninth Street, Cleveland, OH 44114-3484
Telephone: 216-222-2000
Web Site: www.nationalcity.com

Officers: Peter E. Raskind - Chairman, President, Chief Executive Officer Jeffrey D. Kelly - Vice-Chairman, Chief Financial Officer **Transfer Agents:** National City Bank, Corporate Trust Operations, Cleveland, OH

Investor Contact: 800-622-4204
No of Institutions: 608
Shares: 503,746,784 **% Held:** 78.65

NATIONAL FUEL GAS CO. (NJ)

Exchange	Symbol	Price	52Wk Range	Yield	P/E
NYS	NFG	$60.56 (5/29/2008)	61.93-39.55	2.05	14.02

*7 Year Price Score 118.10 *NYSE Composite Index=100 *12 Month Price Score 116.13

Interim Earnings (Per Share)

Qtr.	Dec	Mar	Jun	Sep
2004-05	0.60	0.83	0.23	0.58
2005-06	0.67	1.82	0.00	0.03
2006-07	0.64	0.92	0.55	1.85
2007-08	0.82	1.11	...	...

Interim Dividends (Per Share)

Amt	Decl	Ex	Rec	Pay
0.31Q	06/07/2007	06/27/2007	06/29/2007	07/16/2007
0.31Q	09/20/2007	09/26/2007	09/28/2007	10/15/2007
0.31Q	12/06/2007	12/27/2007	12/31/2007	01/15/2008
0.31Q	02/21/2008	03/27/2008	03/31/2008	04/15/2008

Indicated Div: $1.24 (Div. Reinv. Plan)

Valuation Analysis

Forecast EPS $3.00 (05/16/2008)

Market Cap	$4.9 Billion	Book Value	1.6 Billion
Price/Book	3.04	Price/Sales	2.28

Dividend Achiever Status

10 Year Growth Rate		3.62%
Total Years of Dividend Growth		36

Business Summary: Gas Utilities (MIC: SIC: 4924 NAIC: 221210)

National Fuel Gas is a holding company consisting of five business segments. The Utility segment operations are carried out by National Fuel Gas Distribution Corporation; the Pipeline and Storage segment operations are carried out by National Fuel Gas Supply Corporation; the Exploration and Production segment operations are carried out by Seneca Resources Corporation; the Energy Marketing segment operations are carried out by National Fuel Resources, Inc.; while The Timber segment operations are carried out by Highland Forest Resources, Inc. As of Sep 30 2007, Co. had U.S. and Canadian reserves of 47,586 thousand barrels of oil and 205,389 million cubic feet equivalent of natural gas.

Recent Developments: For the quarter ended Mar 31 2008, income from continuing operations increased 25.9% to US$95.0 million from US$75.5 million in the year-earlier quarter. Net income increased 21.1% to US$95.0 million from US$78.4 million in the year-earlier quarter. Revenues were US$885.9 million, up 11.0% from US$798.1 million the year before. Operating income was US$170.0 million versus US$142.4 million in the prior-year quarter, an increase of 19.4%. Direct operating expenses rose 9.2% to US$652.0 million from US$597.3 million in the comparable period the year before. Indirect operating expenses increased 9.3% to US$63.8 million from US$58.4 million in the equivalent prior-year period.

Prospects: For the fiscal year ending Sep 30, 2008, Co. is projecting consolidated earnings in the range of $2.90 to $3.00 an increase from previous guidance of $2.60 to $2.80 per share. Co. believes that this increase is a result of the higher than forecasted crude oil prices realized by its Seneca during Mar 31 2008, combined with the certainty of pricing on planned commodity sales in both its Pipeline and Storage and its Exploration and Production segments, which are now hedged. Meanwhile, Co. continues to explore opportunities to expand its capabilities to transport gas to the East Coast, as exhibited by the construction of the Empire Connector, which is expected to be in-service by Nov 2008.

Financial Data

(US$ in Thousands)	6 Mos	3 Mos	09/30/2007	09/30/2006	09/30/2005	09/30/2004	09/30/2003	09/30/2002
Earnings Per Share	4.32	4.14	3.96	1.61	2.23	2.01	2.20	1.46
Cash Flow Per Share	5.10	5.10	4.74	5.61	3.80	5.40	4.04	4.33
Tang Book Value Per Share	19.55	19.74	19.12	16.87	14.01	14.49	13.29	12.44
Dividends Per Share	1.240	1.230	1.220	1.180	1.140	1.100	1.060	1.025
Dividend Payout %	28.68	29.71	30.81	73.29	51.12	54.73	48.18	70.21
Income Statement								
Total Revenue	1,454,121	568,268	2,039,566	2,311,659	1,923,549	2,031,393	2,035,471	1,464,496
EBITDA	389,202	173,659	577,216	462,098	515,454	541,384	617,064	...
Depn & Amortn	86,533	44,121	170,803	179,615	193,144	189,538	195,226	180,668
Income Before Taxes	272,352	115,618	333,488	214,177	246,493	261,256	316,782	...
Income Taxes	106,744	45,014	131,813	76,086	92,978	92,737	128,161	...
Net Income	165,608	70,604	337,455	138,091	189,488	166,586	178,944	117,682
Average Shares	85,385	85,819	85,301	86,028	85,029	82,900	81,357	80,534
Balance Sheet								
Net PPE	2,943,265	2,909,120	2,878,405	2,877,726	2,839,300	3,006,764	2,999,087	2,844,745
Total Assets	4,163,075	4,031,423	3,888,412	3,734,331	3,722,652	3,711,798	3,727,915	3,401,309
Long-Term Obligations	899,000	799,000	799,000	1,095,675	1,119,012	1,133,317	1,147,779	1,145,341
Total Liabilities	2,534,411	2,340,436	2,258,293	2,290,769	2,493,069	2,458,097	2,590,525	2,394,451
Stockholders' Equity	1,628,664	1,690,987	1,630,119	1,443,562	1,229,583	1,253,701	1,137,390	1,006,858
Shares Outstanding	81,636	83,946	83,461	83,402	84,356	82,990	81,438	80,264
Statistical Record								
Return on Assets %	9.10	9.03	8.85	3.70	5.10	4.47	5.02	3.44
Return on Equity %	23.58	22.48	21.96	10.33	15.26	13.90	16.69	11.71
EBITDA Margin %	26.77	30.56	28.30	19.99	26.80	26.65	30.32	...
Net Margin %	11.39	12.42	16.55	5.97	9.85	8.20	8.79	8.04
PPE Turnover	0.74	0.72	0.71	0.81	0.66	0.67	0.70	0.52
Asset Turnover	0.53	0.54	0.54	0.62	0.52	0.54	0.57	0.43
Debt to Equity	0.55	0.47	0.49	0.76	0.91	0.90	1.01	1.14
Price Range	49.75-39.55	49.75-37.26	47.76-35.59	38.78-29.53	34.50-26.61	28.33-21.86	27.17-18.33	25.37-15.97
P/E Ratio	11.52-9.16	12.02-9.00	12.06-8.99	24.09-18.34	15.47-11.93	14.09-10.88	12.35-8.33	17.38-10.94
Average Yield %	2.71	2.75	2.89	3.49	3.98	4.41	4.73	4.54

Address: 6363 Main Street, Williamsville, NY 14221	Officers: Philip C. Ackerman - Chairman David F. Smith - President, Chief Executive Officer, Chief Operating Officer Transfer Agents:	Investor Contact: 716-857-6987 No of Institutions: 342
Telephone: 716-857-7000 Web Site: www.nationalfuelgas.com	The Bank of New York, New York, NY	Shares: 48,336,888 % Held: 55.05

NATIONAL PENN BANCSHARES INC (BOYERTOWN, PENN.)

Exchange	Symbol	Price	52Wk Range	Yield	P/E
NMS	NPBC	$17.24 (5/29/2008)	19.11-13.71	3.94	12.96

*7 Year Price Score 74.74 ***NYSE Composite Index=100** ***12 Month Price Score 108.48**

Interim Earnings (Per Share)

Qtr.	Mar	Jun	Sep	Dec
2005	0.30	0.32	(0.28)	0.35
2006	0.31	0.32	0.33	0.33
2007	0.31	0.32	0.34	0.34
2008	0.33	...	...	...

Interim Dividends (Per Share)

Amt	Decl	Ex	Rec	Pay
3%	08/22/2007	09/05/2007	09/07/2007	09/28/2007
0.17Q	10/24/2007	10/31/2007	11/03/2007	11/17/2007
0.17Q	01/18/2008	01/28/2008	01/30/2008	02/15/2008
0.17Q	04/23/2008	04/30/2008	05/03/2008	05/17/2008

Indicated Div: $0.68 (Div. Reinv. Plan)

Valuation Analysis

Forecast EPS $1.32 (05/16/2008)

Market Cap	$1.4 Billion	Book Value	1.0 Billion
Price/Book	1.31	Price/Sales	3.08

Dividend Achiever Status

10 Year Growth Rate	8.14%
Total Years of Dividend Growth	29

Business Summary: Commercial Banking (MIC: SIC: 6021 NAIC: 522110)

National Penn Bancshares is a bank holding company. Co. provides a range of financial services, principally through its national bank subsidiary, National Penn Bank (the Bank) community bank, including its KNBT Division. In addition, Co. conducts business through Christiana Bank & Trust Company, a Delaware chartered bank. As of Dec 31 2007, the Bank operated 75 community banking offices throughout nine counties in southeastern Pennsylvania, six community offices in Centre County, PA, and one community office in Cecil County, MD. At Dec 31 2007, the Bank had total assets of $5.82 billion and total deposits of $3.95 billion.

Recent Developments: For the quarter ended Mar 31 2008, net income increased 39.5% to US$21.6 million from US$15.5 million in the year-earlier quarter. Net interest income increased 48.7% to US$56.4 million from US$37.9 million in the year-earlier quarter. Provision for loan losses was US$3.4 million versus US$1.1 million in the prior-year quarter, an increase of 217.2%. Non-interest income rose 45.0% to US$24.2 million from US$16.7 million, while non-interest expense advanced 44.9% to US$48.9 million.

Prospects: Going forward, Co. remains focused on improving its earnings despite the compression of its net interest margin due to the current and anticipated interest rate levels. In this respect, Co. intends to increase its net interest income primarily through higher volumes, including volume from consolidations and acquisitions. For instance, Co. is progressing towards the integration of Christiana Bank & Trust Company and KNBT Bancorp, Inc., acquired in Jan 4 2008 and Feb 1 2008, respectively. Meanwhile, Co. will continue its efforts to increase non-interest income, primarily through revenues from insurance and wealth management activities, while stringently managing its costs at the same time.

Financial Data
(US$ in Thousands)

	3 Mos	12/31/2007	12/31/2006	12/31/2005	12/31/2004	12/31/2003	12/31/2002	12/31/2001
Earnings Per Share	1.33	1.31	1.29	1.28	1.09	1.07	0.99	0.89
Cash Flow Per Share	0.78	1.06	1.55	1.47	1.57	2.00	1.68	1.28
Tang Book Value Per Share	5.77	5.83	5.25	5.23	4.88	5.13	6.17	5.37
Dividends Per Share	0.665	0.658	0.629	0.608	0.585	0.541	0.487	0.452
Dividend Payout %	50.14	50.22	48.73	47.43	53.89	50.40	49.28	50.94
Income Statement								
Income Before Taxes	28,301	82,613	84,354	79,362	62,765	43,430	45,580	40,764
Income Taxes	6,708	17,380	20,245	19,607	14,851	8,697	9,346	8,030
Net Income	21,593	65,233	64,109	59,755	47,914	43,354	36,234	32,734
Average Shares	65,900	49,908	49,739	46,730	44,227	40,465	36,638	36,958
Balance Sheet								
Total Assets	9,108,114	5,824,421	5,452,288	4,600,609	4,478,793	3,512,574	2,858,262	2,727,482
Total Liabilities	8,062,077	5,260,474	4,909,419	4,155,721	4,050,668	3,194,761	2,635,902	2,531,800
Stockholders' Equity	1,046,037	563,947	542,869	444,888	428,125	317,813	222,360	195,682
Shares Outstanding	79,410	49,068	49,379	46,023	45,648	40,255	36,028	36,417
Statistical Record								
Return on Assets %	0.97	1.16	1.28	1.32	1.20	1.36	1.30	1.25
Return on Equity %	8.92	11.79	12.98	13.69	12.81	16.05	17.34	17.55
Price Range	19.11-13.71	20.01-14.11	21.47-17.32	20.89-16.91	22.34-16.53	20.63-13.35	15.69-12.04	13.28-10.03
P/E Ratio	14.37-10.31	15.27-10.77	16.65-13.42	16.32-13.21	20.50-15.16	19.28-12.48	15.85-12.16	14.92-11.27
Average Yield %	4.02	3.85	3.29	3.22	3.09	3.21	3.46	3.83

Address: Philadelphia and Reading Avenues, Boyertown, PA 19512 **Telephone:** 610-367-6001 **Web Site:** www.nationalpennbancshares.com	**Officers:** Wayne R. Weidner - Chairman Glenn E. Moyer - President, Chief Executive Officer **Transfer Agents:** Mellon Investor Services, L.L.C., Ridgefield Park, NJ	**Investor Contact:** 610-369-6291 **No of Institutions:** 165 **Shares:** 30,504,416 **% Held:** 37.13

NATIONAL RETAIL PROPERTIES INC

Exchange	Symbol	Price	52Wk Range	Yield	P/E
NYS	NNN	$22.91 (5/29/2008)	26.11-19.93	6.55	10.23

*7 Year Price Score 94.20 ***NYSE Composite Index=100** ***12 Month Price Score 101.78**

Interim Earnings (Per Share)

Qtr.	Mar	Jun	Sep	Dec
2005	0.47	0.51	0.28	0.30
2006	0.39	1.37	0.35	0.93
2007	0.41	0.70	0.68	0.44
2008	0.43	...	...	...

Interim Dividends (Per Share)

Amt	Decl	Ex	Rec	Pay
0.355Q	07/13/2007	07/27/2007	07/31/2007	08/15/2007
0.355Q	10/15/2007	10/29/2007	10/31/2007	11/15/2007
0.355Q	01/15/2008	01/29/2008	01/31/2008	02/15/2008
0.375Q	04/15/2008	04/28/2008	04/30/2008	05/15/2008

Indicated Div: $1.50

Valuation Analysis

Forecast EPS $1.65 (05/16/2008)
Market Cap $1.7 Billion   Book Value   1.4 Billion
Price/Book   1.18   Price/Sales   8.33

Dividend Achiever Status

10 Year Growth Rate   1.55%
Total Years of Dividend Growth   18

TRADING VOLUME (thousand shares)

Business Summary: "Property, Real Estate & Development" (MIC: SIC: 6798 NAIC: 525930)

National Retail Properties is a real estate investment trust that operates through two primary business segments: investment assets, including real estate assets and mortgages and notes receivable (including structured finance investments) and commercial mortgage residual interests; as well as inventory real estate assets. Co. acquires, owns, invests in, manages and develops properties that are leased primarily to retail tenants under long-term net leases (Investment Properties). As of Dec 31 2007, Co. owned 908 Investment Properties, with an aggregate gross leasable area of approximately 10.6 million square feet, located in 44 states.

Recent Developments: For the quarter ended Mar 31 2008, income from continuing operations increased 23.6% to US$23.1 million from US$18.7 million in the year-earlier quarter. Net income increased 23.8% to US$33.1 million from US$26.7 million in the year-earlier quarter. Revenues were US$55.2 million, up 36.5% from US$40.5 million the year before. Revenues from property income rose 39.6% to US$52.6 million from US$37.7 million in the corresponding quarter a year earlier.

Prospects: Co.'s operating results are benefiting from growth in rental income, due to its continued acquisition of properties. Looking ahead, Co. believes that any significant increase in its rental income will continue to come primarily from additional property acquisitions. Meanwhile, Co. has increased its 2008 funds from operations guidance to a range of $1.97 to $2.02 per share, which represents a 5.0% to 8.0% increase over its 2007 results. Notably, this guidance equates to earnings before any gains or losses from the sale of investment properties of $1.54 to $1.59 per share plus $0.43 per share of expected real estate related depreciation and amortization.

Financial Data
(US$ in Thousands)

	3 Mos	12/31/2007	12/31/2006	12/31/2005	12/31/2004	12/31/2003	12/31/2002	12/31/2001
Earnings Per Share	2.24	2.26	3.05	1.56	1.15	1.13	1.09	0.91
Cash Flow Per Share	1.85	1.96	0.32	0.58	1.45	1.26	1.45	1.21
Tang Book Value Per Share	18.19	18.13	16.05	13.76	13.20	13.22	12.49	12.68
Dividends Per Share	1.420	1.400	1.320	1.300	1.290	1.280	1.270	1.260
Dividend Payout %	63.33	61.95	43.28	83.33	112.17	113.27	116.51	138.46
Income Statement								
Total Revenue	55,221	186,411	150,788	145,177	129,309	102,658	93,827	80,526
Depn & Amortn	10,229	32,831	24,316	22,129	17,064	13,119	11,315	8,803
Income Before Taxes	19,358	76,374	52,299	50,014	44,589	...	...	...
Income Taxes	(2,652)	(8,537)	(11,143)	(2,776)	(2,542)	...	...	...
Net Income	33,053	157,110	182,505	89,400	64,934	53,473	48,058	28,963
Average Shares	72,447	66,407	58,079	54,640	51,742	43,896	40,588	31,717
Balance Sheet								
Total Assets	2,662,760	2,539,605	1,916,785	1,733,416	1,300,048	1,208,310	954,108	1,006,628
Long-Term Obligations	1,052,064	930,270	748,737	698,745	506,341	437,338	345,689	327,933
Total Liabilities	1,236,724	1,129,986	819,182	900,390	541,022	477,556	404,967	441,988
Stockholders' Equity	1,420,795	1,407,285	1,096,505	828,087	756,998	730,754	549,141	564,640
Shares Outstanding	73,031	72,527	59,823	55,130	52,077	50,001	40,403	40,599
Statistical Record								
Return on Assets %	7.01	7.05	10.00	5.89	5.16	4.95	4.90	3.28
Return on Equity %	12.47	12.55	18.97	11.28	8.71	8.36	8.63	6.04
Net Margin %	59.86	84.28	121.03	61.58	50.22	52.09	51.22	35.97
Price Range	26.11-19.93	26.11-20.77	23.97-18.90	21.53-18.16	21.20-15.49	18.30-14.37	16.34-13.00	14.25-10.25
P/E Ratio	11.66-8.90	11.55-9.19	7.86-6.20	13.80-11.64	18.43-13.47	16.19-12.72	14.99-11.93	15.66-11.26
Average Yield %	6.11	5.88	6.10	6.61	7.06	7.70	8.50	9.97

Address: 450 South Orange Avenue, Suite 900, Orlando, FL 32801 **Telephone:** 407-265-7348 **Web Site:** www.nnnreit.com	**Officers:** Craig Macnab - Chairman, Chief Executive Officer Julian E. Whitehurst - President, Chief Operating Officer **Transfer Agents:** American Stock Transfer & Trust Company, New York, NY	**No of Institutions:** 239 **Shares:** 67,752,144 **% Held:** N/A

NATIONWIDE FINANCIAL SERVICES INC.

Exchange	Symbol	Price	52Wk Range	Yield	P/E
NYS	NFS	$51.00 (5/29/2008)	64.59-37.93	2.27	15.69

*7 Year Price Score 95.77 ***NYSE Composite Index=100** ***12 Month Price Score 101.62**

Interim Earnings (Per Share)

Qtr.	Mar	Jun	Sep	Dec
2005	1.05	0.92	1.08	0.85
2006	0.93	1.72	1.06	1.03
2007	1.38	1.37	1.03	0.55
2008	0.32	...	...	...

Interim Dividends (Per Share)

Amt	Decl	Ex	Rec	Pay
0.26Q	08/01/2007	09/27/2007	10/01/2007	10/15/2007
0.26Q	12/05/2007	12/28/2007	01/02/2008	01/14/2008
0.29Q	02/20/2008	03/28/2008	04/01/2008	04/14/2008
0.29Q	05/07/2008	06/27/2008	07/01/2008	07/14/2008

Indicated Div: $1.16

Valuation Analysis

Forecast EPS	$4.55 (05/17/2008)		
Market Cap	$7.0 Billion	Book Value	5.0 Billion
Price/Book	1.40	Price/Sales	1.65

Dividend Achiever Status

10 Year Growth Rate	23.74%
Total Years of Dividend Growth	10

Business Summary: Insurance (MIC: SIC: 6311 NAIC: 524113)

Nationwide Financial Services is the holding company for Nationwide Life Insurance and other companies that comprise the domestic life insurance and retirement savings operations of the Nationwide group of companies. This group includes Nationwide Financial Network, which refers to Nationwide Life Insurance Company of America and its subsidiaries, including the affiliated distribution network. Co. develops and sells a range of products including individual annuities, private and public group retirement plans, other investment products sold to institutions, life insurance and advisory services. In addition, Co. provides a range of banking products and services through Nationwide Bank.

Recent Developments: For the quarter ended Mar 31 2008, income from continuing operations decreased 74.2% to US$43.6 million from US$168.8 million in the year-earlier quarter. Net income decreased 78.6% to US$44.5 million from US$208.3 million in the year-earlier quarter. Revenues were US$916.3 million, down 21.0% from US$1.16 billion the year before. Net premiums earned were US$109.1 million versus US$110.4 million in the prior-year quarter, a decrease of 1.2%. Net investment income fell 11.9% to US$519.5 million from US$589.8 million a year ago.

Prospects: For 2008, at its Individual Investments segment, Co. expects sales of variable annuities to grow 7.0% to 12.0%, while expecting sales of fixed annuities to remain flat. At its Retirement Plans segment, Co. expects private sector sales to show 0.0% to 4.0% growth, and expects public sector sales to grow 4.0% to 6.0%. Also, at its Individual Protection segment, Co. expects first year individual VUL sales to grow 7.0% to 10.0%, first year corporate-owned life insurance sales to be $150.0 million to $175.0 million, and first year fixed life sales to grow 40.0% to 50.0%. Meanwhile, Co. remains focused on developing new products and deepening relationships with key distribution partners.

Financial Data
(US$ in Thousands)

	3 Mos	12/31/2007	12/31/2006	12/31/2005	12/31/2004	12/31/2003	12/31/2002	12/31/2001
Earnings Per Share	3.25	4.37	4.74	3.90	3.28	2.61	1.09	3.20
Cash Flow Per Share	7.21	15.62	16.28	12.78	13.68	9.19	11.19	9.75
Tang Book Value Per Share	34.13	36.27	35.47	32.40	31.37	29.07	26.25	26.73
Dividends Per Share	1.070	1.040	0.920	0.760	0.720	0.520	0.510	0.480
Dividend Payout %	32.87	23.80	19.41	19.49	21.95	19.92	46.79	15.00
Income Statement								
Total Revenue	916,300	4,528,900	4,415,500	4,339,900	4,180,200	3,935,400	3,287,800	3,179,000
Income Before Taxes	32,800	800,400	778,900	755,800	674,600	517,800	133,500	562,700
Income Taxes	(10,800)	190,700	65,100	132,600	169,200	119,400	(7,300)	142,800
Net Income	44,500	626,800	713,800	598,700	502,000	397,800	144,200	412,800
Average Shares	138,300	143,500	150,700	153,600	152,900	152,300	132,600	129,200
Balance Sheet								
Total Assets	112,612,600	119,207,100	119,411,600	116,159,900	116,950,600	111,027,300	95,560,300	91,960,900
Total Liabilities	107,608,700	113,882,500	113,873,300	110,809,500	111,735,500	106,151,900	90,817,000	88,217,600
Stockholders' Equity	5,003,900	5,324,600	5,538,300	5,350,400	5,215,100	4,875,400	4,443,300	3,443,300
Shares Outstanding	137,800	138,500	146,000	152,500	152,500	151,900	151,800	128,800
Statistical Record								
Return on Assets %	0.40	0.53	0.61	0.51	0.44	0.39	0.15	0.45
Return on Equity %	8.60	11.54	13.11	11.33	9.92	8.54	3.66	12.82
Net Margin %	4.86	13.84	16.17	13.80	12.01	10.11	4.39	12.99
Price Range	64.59-37.93	64.59-42.12	54.32-42.19	44.00-33.85	39.00-32.33	34.50-21.70	45.35-22.10	47.19-33.74
P/E Ratio	19.87-11.67	14.78-9.64	11.46-8.90	11.28-8.68	11.89-9.86	13.22-8.31	41.61-20.28	14.75-10.54
Average Yield %	2.06	1.91	1.99	1.97	2.00	1.74	1.43	1.17

Address: One Nationwide Plaza, Columbus, OH 43215	Officers: Arden L. Shisler - Chairman Mark R. Thresher - President, Chief Operating Officer, Parent	No of Institutions: 257
Telephone: 614-249-7111	Company Officer **Transfer Agents:**	Shares: 28,592,056 % Held: 17.80
Web Site: www.nationwidefinancial.com	Mellon Investor Services, South Hackensack, NJ	

NEW JERSEY RESOURCES CORP

Exchange	Symbol	Price	52Wk Range	Yield	P/E
NYS	NJR	$33.88 (5/29/2008)	36.78-29.81	3.31	N/A

*7 Year Price Score 92.90 ***NYSE Composite Index=100** ***12 Month Price Score 102.52**

Interim Earnings (Per Share)

Qtr.	Dec	Mar	Jun	Sep
2004-05	0.71	1.23	0.05	(0.17)
2005-06	0.82	1.43	(0.09)	(0.28)
2006-07	0.67	1.91	(0.12)	(0.91)
2007-08	0.72	0.30	...	...

Interim Dividends (Per Share)

Amt	Decl	Ex	Rec	Pay
0.267Q	11/15/2007	12/12/2007	12/15/2007	01/02/2008
3-for-2	01/23/2008	03/04/2008	02/08/2008	03/03/2008
0.28Q	01/23/2008	03/12/2008	03/14/2008	04/01/2008
0.28Q	05/16/2008	06/11/2008	06/13/2008	07/01/2008
		Indicated Div: $1.12		

Valuation Analysis

Forecast EPS $2.17 (05/16/2008)

Market Cap	$1.4 Billion	Book Value	670.9 Million
Price/Book	2.11	Price/Sales	0.44

Dividend Achiever Status

10 Year Growth Rate			3.61%
Total Years of Dividend Growth			12

Business Summary: Gas Utilities (MIC: SIC: 4924 NAIC: 221210)

New Jersey Resources is an energy services holding company providing retail and wholesale energy services to customers in New Jersey, in states from the Gulf Coast to New England, and Canada. As of Sep 30 2007, Co. conducted its businesses through three operating segments. The Natural Gas Distribution segment consists of regulated energy and off-system, capacity and storage management operations. The Energy Services segment consists of unregulated wholesale energy operations. The Retail and Other segment consists of appliance repair, sales and installation services, natural gas and related investments, commercial real estate development and other corporate activities.

Recent Developments: For the quarter ended Mar 31 2008, net income increased 57.5% to US$12.5 million from US$8.0 million in the year-earlier quarter. Revenues were US$1.18 billion, up 14.4% from US$1.03 billion the year before. Operating income was US$20.3 million versus US$16.3 million in the prior-year quarter, an increase of 25.0%. Direct operating expenses rose 15.2% to US$1.10 billion from US$955.4 million in the comparable period the year before. Indirect operating expenses decreased 1.2% to US$56.7 million from US$57.4 million in the equivalent prior-year period.

Prospects: Co.'s outlook appears constructive. Notably, Co. continues to add new customers at its Natural Gas Distribution segment, with the addition of 3,125 new customers during the six months ended Mar 2008, which are expected to contribute about $1.7 million to utility gross margin annually. Co. expects to achieve a new customer growth rate of approximately 1.6% in the fiscal year ending Sep 2008. Meanwhile, at its Retail and Other segment, Co. continues to work towards the development of Steckman Ridge natural gas storage facility under joint development with a partner in western Pennsylvania, which is expected to contribute to earnings beginning in the fiscal year ending Sep 2010.

Financial Data

(US$ in Thousands)	6 Mos	3 Mos	09/30/2007	09/30/2006	09/30/2005	09/30/2004	09/30/2003	09/30/2002
Earnings Per Share	(0.01)	1.60	1.55	1.87	1.81	1.70	1.87	1.39
Cash Flow Per Share	1.18	2.48	2.92	(0.55)	5.00	(1.18)	2.27	1.24
Tang Book Value Per Share	16.03	16.03	15.50	14.24	10.36	11.17	10.26	8.95
Dividends Per Share	1.053	1.027	1.013	0.960	0.907	0.867	0.827	0.800
Dividend Payout %	...	64.17	65.24	51.43	50.18	50.98	44.29	57.42
Income Statement								
Total Revenue	1,988,683	811,138	3,021,765	3,299,608	3,148,262	2,533,607	2,544,379	1,830,754
EBITDA	97,010	65,543	168,080	189,264	180,954	167,164	158,241	145,061
Depn & Amortn	19,070	9,478	36,534	35,054	35,227	34,250	36,375	35,737
Income Before Taxes	63,438	48,255	103,931	128,541	125,253	117,519	107,874	92,768
Income Taxes	21,888	18,494	40,312	50,022	48,913	45,945	42,462	35,924
Net Income	42,720	30,185	65,281	78,519	76,340	71,574	65,412	56,844
Average Shares	42,099	41,928	42,112	42,121	42,181	42,079	41,298	40,752
Balance Sheet								
Net PPE	990,419	978,707	970,871	934,939	905,130	880,389	852,604	756,397
Total Assets	2,367,642	2,367,755	2,230,745	2,398,928	2,209,828	1,855,600	1,570,979	1,319,304
Long-Term Obligations	357,712	359,165	383,184	332,332	317,204	315,887	257,899	370,628
Total Liabilities	1,696,729	1,698,786	1,585,948	1,777,266	1,771,776	1,387,683	1,152,038	957,851
Stockholders' Equity	670,913	668,969	644,797	621,662	438,052	467,917	418,941	361,453
Shares Outstanding	41,852	41,723	41,611	43,647	42,274	41,871	40,849	40,375
Statistical Record								
Return on Assets %	N.M.	2.76	2.82	3.41	3.76	4.17	4.53	4.53
Return on Equity %	N.M.	10.25	10.31	14.82	16.85	16.10	16.76	15.93
EBITDA Margin %	4.88	8.08	5.56	5.74	5.75	6.60	6.22	7.92
Net Margin %	2.15	3.72	2.16	2.38	2.42	2.82	2.57	3.10
PPE Turnover	3.34	3.22	3.17	3.59	3.53	2.92	3.16	2.44
Asset Turnover	1.41	1.26	1.31	1.43	1.55	1.47	1.76	1.46
Debt to Equity	0.53	0.54	0.59	0.53	0.72	0.68	0.62	1.03
Price Range	37.00-29.81	37.00-30.83	37.00-30.83	34.01-27.69	32.67-27.07	28.20-24.03	24.83-20.03	21.93-17.01
P/E Ratio	...	23.13-19.27	23.87-19.89	18.19-14.81	18.05-14.95	16.59-14.13	13.28-10.71	15.78-12.24
Average Yield %	3.17	3.08	3.01	3.19	3.06	3.34	3.70	3.90

Address: 1415 Wyckoff Road, P.O. Box 1468, Wall, NJ 07719	Officers: Laurence M. Downes - Chairman, President, Chief Executive Officer Glenn C. Lockwood - Senior Vice President, Chief Financial Officer **Transfer**	Investor Contact: 732-938-1229
Telephone: 732-938-1480	**Agents:** ComputerShare Investor Services, Providence, RI	No of Institutions: 199
Web Site: www.njliving.com		Shares: 27,913,382 % Held: 63.09

NEW YORK TIMES CO.

Exchange	Symbol	Price	52Wk Range	Yield	P/E
NYS	NYT	$17.53 (5/29/2008)	26.55-14.48	5.25	13.70

*7 Year Price Score 43.50   *NYSE Composite Index=100   *12 Month Price Score 99.04

Interim Earnings (Per Share)

Qtr.	Mar	Jun	Sep	Dec
2005	0.76	0.42	0.16	0.45
2006	0.24	0.42	0.10	(4.52)
2007	0.17	0.82	0.09	0.37
2008	0.00	...	...	...

Interim Dividends (Per Share)

Amt	Decl	Ex	Rec	Pay
0.23Q	06/21/2007	08/30/2007	09/04/2007	09/12/2007
0.23Q	11/15/2007	11/29/2007	12/03/2007	12/12/2007
0.23Q	02/21/2008	02/28/2008	03/03/2008	03/12/2008
0.23Q	04/22/2008	05/29/2008	06/02/2008	06/11/2008
		Indicated Div: $0.92		

Valuation Analysis

Forecast EPS $1.01 (05/16/2008)
Market Cap	$2.5 Billion	Book Value	949.9 Million
Price/Book	2.65	Price/Sales	0.80

Dividend Achiever Status

10 Year Growth Rate	10.46%
Total Years of Dividend Growth	12

Business Summary: Media (MIC: SIC: 2711 NAIC: 511110)

New York Times is a media company that includes newspapers, Internet businesses, a radio station, investments in paper mills and other investments. Co.'s operates through two segments, the News Media Group and the About Group. The News Media Group includes The New York Times, NYTimes.com, the International Herald Tribune, IHT.com, its New York City radio station, WQXR-FM, and The Boston Globe, Boston.com, the Worcester Telegram & Gazette, in Worcester, MA, as well as 14 daily newspapers in Alabama, California, Florida, Louisiana, North Carolina and South Carolina. The About Group is an online source that provides users with information and advice on various topics.

Recent Developments: For the quarter ended Mar 30 2008, income from continuing operations decreased 98.7% to US$265,000 from US$20.1 million in the year-earlier quarter. Net loss amounted to US$335,000 versus net income of US$23.9 million in the year-earlier quarter. Revenues were US$747.9 million, down 4.9% from US$786.0 million the year before. Operating income was US$6.2 million versus US$54.5 million in the prior-year quarter, a decrease of 88.6%. Direct operating expenses declined 1.3% to US$340.6 million from US$345.0 million in the comparable period the year before. Indirect operating expenses increased 3.8% to US$401.1 million from US$386.5 million in the equivalent prior-year period.

Prospects: Co. remains focused on diligently managing its business for the long term, and will continue introducing new products in print and online while managing costs. Meanwhile, Co. expects to attain a reduction in costs from its year-end 2007 cost base of a total of about $230.0 million in 2008 and 2009, excluding the effects of inflation, buyout costs and one-time costs. Co. expects about $130.0 million of these savings in the fiscal year ending Dec 28 2008. In addition, Co. is raising its fiscal 2008 income from joint ventures guidance to $16.0 million to $20.0 million from $12.0 million to $16.0 million as it expects better operating results at the paper mills at which it has an interest in.

Financial Data
(US$ in Thousands)

	3 Mos	12/30/2007	12/31/2006	12/25/2005	12/26/2004	12/28/2003	12/29/2002	12/30/2001
Earnings Per Share	1.28	1.45	(3.76)	1.78	1.96	1.98	1.94	2.78
Cash Flow Per Share	0.77	0.77	2.87	2.03	3.02	3.11	1.81	3.01
Tang Book Value Per Share	0.89	1.16	0.25	N.M.	N.M.	N.M.	N.M.	N.M.
Dividends Per Share	0.920	0.865	0.690	0.650	0.610	0.570	0.530	0.490
Dividend Payout %	71.77	59.66	...	36.52	31.12	28.79	27.32	17.63
Income Statement								
Total Revenue	747,855	3,195,077	3,289,903	3,372,775	3,303,642	3,227,200	3,079,007	3,015,958
EBITDA	46,353	414,372	(331,418)	634,274	706,953	737,108	690,169	581,061
Depn & Amortn	41,931	189,561	169,853	143,769	146,788	147,747	153,347	194,008
Income Before Taxes	(7,323)	184,969	(551,922)	446,104	476,645	499,847	491,387	339,854
Income Taxes	(7,692)	76,137	16,608	180,242	183,499	197,762	191,640	137,632
Net Income	(335)	208,704	(543,443)	259,753	292,557	302,655	299,747	444,672
Average Shares	144,006	144,158	144,579	145,877	149,357	152,840	154,805	160,081
Balance Sheet								
Current Assets	611,564	664,445	1,185,043	657,746	613,893	603,311	563,056	559,890
Total Assets	3,383,620	3,473,092	3,855,928	4,533,037	3,949,857	3,804,739	3,633,842	3,438,684
Current Liabilities	943,365	975,736	1,297,994	1,066,522	1,119,749	760,364	735,736	860,876
Long-Term Obligations	678,838	678,699	795,030	898,300	471,474	725,725	728,789	598,703
Total Liabilities	2,426,581	2,488,985	3,030,119	2,827,813	2,414,695	2,321,086	2,364,535	2,289,031
Stockholders' Equity	949,873	978,200	819,842	1,516,248	1,400,542	1,392,242	1,269,307	1,149,653
Shares Outstanding	143,775	143,727	143,859	145,215	146,105	149,878	152,216	151,456
Statistical Record								
Return on Assets %	5.14	5.71	N.M.	6.14	7.57	8.16	8.50	12.66
Return on Equity %	21.13	23.28	N.M.	17.86	21.01	22.81	24.85	36.69
EBITDA Margin %	6.20	12.97	N.M.	18.81	21.40	22.84	22.42	19.27
Net Margin %	N.M.	6.53	N.M.	7.70	8.86	9.38	9.74	14.74
Asset Turnover	0.88	0.87	0.77	0.80	0.85	0.87	0.87	0.86
Current Ratio	0.65	0.68	0.91	0.62	0.55	0.79	0.77	0.65
Debt to Equity	0.71	0.69	0.97	0.59	0.34	0.52	0.57	0.52
Price Range	26.55-14.48	26.55-16.45	28.90-21.58	40.80-26.36	49.13-38.72	48.84-42.87	52.79-39.98	47.60-37.42
P/E Ratio	20.74-11.31	18.31-11.34	...	22.92-14.81	25.07-19.76	24.67-21.65	27.21-20.61	17.12-13.46
Average Yield %	4.42	3.86	2.81	1.98	1.40	1.25	1.13	1.15

Address: 620 Eighth Avenue, New York, NY 10018 **Telephone:** 212-556-1234 **Web Site:** www.nytco.com	Officers: Arthur Sulzberger - Chairman Michael Golden - Vice-Chairman **Transfer Agents:** BNY Mellon Shareowner Services, Pittsburgh, PA	**Investor Contact:** 212-556-1981 **No of Institutions:** 341 **Shares:** 147,109,152 **% Held:** 89.71

NORDSON CORP.

Exchange	Symbol	Price	52Wk Range	Yield	P/E
NMS	NDSN	$71.47 (5/29/2008)	72.16-44.64	1.02	22.62

*7 Year Price Score 110.13 *NYSE Composite Index=100 *12 Month Price Score 118.13

Interim Earnings (Per Share)

Qtr.	Jan	Apr	Jul	Oct
2004-05	0.39	0.47	0.50	0.78
2005-06	0.47	0.64	0.72	0.81
2006-07	0.46	0.61	0.72	0.86
2007-08	0.62	0.97	...	...

Interim Dividends (Per Share)

Amt	Decl	Ex	Rec	Pay
0.175Q	08/21/2007	08/30/2007	09/04/2007	09/18/2007
0.183Q	12/12/2007	12/19/2007	12/21/2007	01/04/2008
0.183Q	02/19/2008	02/29/2008	03/04/2008	03/18/2008
0.183Q	05/20/2008	05/30/2008	06/03/2008	06/17/2008
		Indicated Div: $0.73 (Div. Reinv. Plan)		

Valuation Analysis

Forecast EPS	$3.35 (05/16/2008)		
Market Cap	$2.4 Billion	Book Value	589.9 Million
Price/Book	4.08	Price/Sales	2.22

Dividend Achiever Status

10 Year Growth Rate	5.76%
Total Years of Dividend Growth	27

Business Summary: Industrial Machinery and Equipment (MIC: SIC: 3569 NAIC: 333999)

Nordson is engaged in the business of manufacturing equipment used for precision dispensing, testing and inspection, surface preparation and curing. Co.'s Adhesive Dispensing Systems segment provides its dispensing technology to a range of markets for applications that reduce material consumption, increase line efficiency as well as enhance product brand and appearance. Co.'s Advanced Technology Systems segment integrates its product technologies found in progressive stages of a customer's production process. Co.'s Industrial Coating and Automotive Systems segment provides equipment used primarily for applying coatings, paint, finishes, sealants and other materials.

Recent Developments: For the quarter ended Apr 30 2008, net income increased 57.5% to US$33.0 million from US$21.0 million in the year-earlier quarter. Revenues were US$294.1 million, up 21.9% from US$241.3 million the year before. Operating income was US$54.2 million versus US$34.4 million in the prior-year quarter, an increase of 57.7%. Direct operating expenses rose 17.2% to US$128.2 million from US$109.4 million in the comparable period the year before. Indirect operating expenses increased 14.5% to US$111.7 million from US$97.5 million in the equivalent prior-year period.

Prospects: For the fiscal quarter ending Jul 31 2008, Co. is projecting sales growth in the 13.0% to 17.0% range over its previous fiscal year's level, with sales volume forecasted to grow 8.0% to 12.0%, and the remainder deriving from favorable currency effects. In addition, Co. is targeting earnings in the range of $0.91 to $1.01 per diluted share. The midpoint of Co.'s earnings guidance represents a 33.0% increase over its earnings of $0.72 per diluted share in the prior fiscal year. Meanwhile, on June 3 2008, Co. announced that it has acquired the remaining 51.0% stake in its Nordson Sang San Ltd. joint venture in order to expand its service capability in the potential Asia Pacific Markets.

Financial Data
(US$ in Thousands)

	6 Mos	3 Mos	10/31/2007	10/31/2006	10/30/2005	10/31/2004	11/02/2003	11/03/2002
Earnings Per Share	3.16	2.81	2.65	2.65	2.14	1.73	1.04	0.66
Cash Flow Per Share	4.19	3.55	3.70	3.59	3.34	3.09	2.60	3.84
Tang Book Value Per Share	N.M.	N.M.	N.M.	2.69	N.M.	1.50	N.M.	N.M.
Dividends Per Share	0.715	0.708	0.700	0.670	0.645	0.625	0.605	0.570
Dividend Payout %	22.61	25.18	26.42	25.28	30.14	36.13	58.17	86.36
Income Statement								
Total Revenue	538,805	244,689	993,649	892,221	839,162	793,544	667,347	647,756
EBITDA	109,090	45,818	185,197	171,761	150,784	136,136	99,780	84,144
Depn & Amortn	15,547	7,733	27,933	23,310	25,683	26,876	29,240	29,487
Income Before Taxes	83,700	32,482	135,722	136,434	111,276	93,828	52,477	32,944
Income Taxes	29,312	11,143	45,030	38,767	32,938	30,494	17,317	10,872
Net Income	54,388	21,339	90,692	90,598	78,338	63,334	35,160	22,072
Average Shares	34,111	34,189	34,182	34,180	36,527	36,546	33,899	33,690
Balance Sheet								
Current Assets	426,539	417,174	409,924	347,304	311,716	363,111	277,370	274,573
Total Assets	1,225,348	1,214,094	1,211,840	822,890	788,526	839,387	766,806	764,472
Current Liabilities	404,736	486,170	509,914	241,325	250,074	195,749	211,662	252,647
Long-Term Obligations	72,840	22,840	29,878	52,201	106,351	152,479	176,725	174,895
Total Liabilities	635,440	664,938	680,723	392,362	457,614	436,054	466,697	495,582
Stockholders' Equity	589,908	549,156	531,117	430,528	330,912	403,333	300,109	268,890
Shares Outstanding	33,687	33,646	33,710	33,411	32,911	36,278	34,035	33,613
Statistical Record								
Return on Assets %	9.21	8.55	8.91	11.21	9.65	7.91	4.60	2.67
Return on Equity %	20.32	19.30	18.86	23.73	21.40	18.06	12.39	8.15
EBITDA Margin %	20.25	18.72	18.64	19.25	17.97	17.16	14.95	12.99
Net Margin %	10.09	8.72	9.13	10.15	9.34	7.98	5.27	3.41
Asset Turnover	0.92	0.92	0.98	1.10	1.03	0.99	0.87	0.78
Current Ratio	1.05	0.86	0.80	1.44	1.25	1.85	1.31	1.09
Debt to Equity	0.12	0.04	0.06	0.12	0.32	0.38	0.59	0.65
Price Range	60.90-44.64	60.90-44.57	57.14-43.71	57.17-37.17	40.46-29.96	43.74-28.23	28.11-20.72	33.32-21.45
P/E Ratio	19.27-14.13	21.67-15.86	21.56-16.49	21.57-14.03	18.91-14.00	25.28-16.32	27.03-19.92	50.48-32.50
Average Yield %	1.40	1.41	1.42	1.48	1.80	1.72	2.42	2.17

Address: 28601 Clemens Road,	Officers: Edward P. Campbell - Chairman, President,	Investor Contact: 440-414-5344
Westlake, OH 44145-4551	Chief Executive Officer John J. Keane - Senior Vice	No of Institutions: 192
Telephone: 440-892-1580	President Transfer Agents:	Shares: 25,387,992 % Held: 72.59
Web Site: www.nordson.com	National City Bank, Cleveland, OH	

NORDSTROM, INC.

Exchange	Symbol	Price	52Wk Range	Yield	P/E
NYS	JWN	$35.71 (5/29/2008)	53.54-29.04	1.79	12.31

*7 Year Price Score 120.67 *NYSE Composite Index=100   *12 Month Price Score 89.78

Interim Earnings (Per Share)

Qtr.	Apr	Jul	Oct	Jan
2003-04	0.10	0.24	0.17	0.38
2004-05	0.24	0.38	0.27	0.50
2005-06	0.38	0.53	0.39	0.68
2006-07	0.48	0.67	0.52	0.88
2007-08	0.60	0.71	0.68	0.90

Interim Dividends (Per Share)

Amt	Decl	Ex	Rec	Pay
0.135Q	08/21/2007	08/29/2007	08/31/2007	09/14/2007
0.135Q	11/19/2007	11/28/2007	11/30/2007	12/14/2007
0.16Q	02/20/2008	02/27/2008	02/29/2008	03/14/2008
0.16Q	05/20/2008	05/28/2008	05/30/2008	06/16/2008
		Indicated Div: $0.64		

Valuation Analysis

Forecast EPS	$2.74 (05/17/2008)		
Market Cap	$7.9 Billion	Book Value	1.1 Billion
Price/Book	7.08	Price/Sales	0.89

Dividend Achiever Status

10 Year Growth Rate	15.08%
Total Years of Dividend Growth	11

Business Summary: Retail - Apparel and Accessory Stores (MIC: SIC: 5651 NAIC: 448140)

Nordstrom is a fashion specialty retailer of clothing, shoes and accessories for men, women and children. Co. provides several brand name and private label merchandise through multiple retail channels, including 103 Full-Line Nordstrom stores, 50 discount Nordstrom Rack stores, two Jeffrey boutiques, two Last Chance clearance stores, its catalogs and through its online store. Co.'s stores are located throughout the U.S., in addition to 37 Fa®nnable boutiques located in France, Portugal, and Belgium. Through its wholly owned federal savings bank, Nordstrom fsb, Co. also provides a private label card, two co-branded Nordstrom VISA credit cards and a debit card for Nordstrom purchases.

Recent Developments: For the year ended Feb 2 2008, net income increased 5.5% to US$715.0 million from US$678.0 million in the prior year. Revenues were US$8.83 billion, up 3.1% from US$8.56 billion the year before. Direct operating expenses rose 3.2% to US$5.53 billion from US$5.35 billion in the comparable period the year before. Indirect operating expenses were unchanged at US$2.06 billion versus the equivalent prior-year period.

Prospects: For the fiscal year ending Jan 31 2009, Co. is targeting a flat to a 2.0% decrease in same-store sales and earnings of $2.75 to $2.90 per diluted share, while gross profit is projected to decline by 30 to 60 basis points. In addition, Co. intends to open six additional full-line stores and three Rack stores, which is expected to increase retail square footage by approximately 6.0%. For the fiscal quarter ended May 2008, Co. is anticipating a 3.0% to 5.0% decrease in same-store sales, while earnings are estimated to range from $0.49 to $0.54 per diluted share. Meanwhile, for the first half of fiscal year ending Jan 30 2010, Co. plans to open three new full-line stores and two Rack stores.

Financial Data

(US$ in Thousands)	02/02/2008	02/03/2007	01/28/2006	01/29/2005	01/31/2004	01/31/2003	01/31/2002	01/31/2001
Earnings Per Share	2.88	2.55	1.98	1.39	0.88	0.33	0.47	0.39
Cash Flow Per Share	0.66	4.31	2.86	2.18	2.10	1.03	1.54	0.68
Tang Book Value Per Share	4.81	7.90	7.26	6.09	5.40	4.55	4.37	4.06
Dividends Per Share	0.540	0.420	0.320	0.240	0.205	0.190	0.180	0.175
Dividend Payout %	18.75	16.47	16.16	17.33	23.30	57.58	38.71	44.87
Income Statement								
Total Revenue	8,828,000	8,560,698	7,722,860	7,131,388	6,491,673	5,975,076	5,634,130	5,528,537
EBITDA	1,480,000	1,396,638	1,173,503	958,100	712,064	489,297	488,707	421,666
Depn & Amortn	233,000	248,227	242,978	233,391	222,971	211,752	209,181	191,950
Income Before Taxes	1,173,000	1,105,653	885,225	647,281	398,141	195,624	204,488	167,018
Income Taxes	458,000	427,654	333,886	253,831	155,300	92,041	79,800	65,100
Net Income	715,000	677,999	551,339	393,450	242,841	90,224	124,688	101,918
Average Shares	249,000	265,712	277,776	284,534	275,478	271,448	268,678	262,226
Balance Sheet								
Current Assets	3,361,000	2,742,193	2,874,157	2,572,444	2,455,430	2,072,618	2,054,598	1,812,982
Total Assets	5,600,000	4,821,578	4,921,349	4,605,390	4,465,688	4,096,376	4,048,779	3,608,503
Current Liabilities	1,635,000	1,433,143	1,623,312	1,341,152	1,049,549	870,091	947,738	950,568
Long-Term Obligations	2,236,000	623,652	627,776	929,010	1,227,410	1,341,826	1,351,044	1,099,710
Total Liabilities	4,485,000	2,653,057	2,828,668	2,816,396	2,831,679	2,724,319	2,734,291	2,378,935
Stockholders' Equity	1,115,000	2,168,521	2,092,681	1,788,994	1,634,009	1,372,057	1,314,488	1,229,568
Shares Outstanding	221,000	257,313	269,549	271,330	276,753	270,888	268,937	267,595
Statistical Record								
Return on Assets %	13.76	13.69	11.61	8.70	5.67	2.22	3.26	3.05
Return on Equity %	43.67	31.31	28.49	23.05	16.16	6.72	9.80	8.42
EBITDA Margin %	16.76	16.31	15.20	13.43	10.97	8.19	8.67	7.63
Net Margin %	8.10	7.92	7.14	5.52	3.74	1.51	2.21	1.84
Asset Turnover	1.70	1.73	1.63	1.58	1.52	1.47	1.47	1.65
Current Ratio	2.06	1.91	1.77	1.92	2.34	2.38	2.17	1.91
Debt to Equity	2.01	0.29	0.30	0.52	0.75	0.98	1.03	0.89
Price Range	59.66-29.04	56.94-32.36	42.28-24.13	24.38-17.72	20.18-7.93	13.19-7.75	12.65-7.05	16.88-7.16
P/E Ratio	20.72-10.08	22.33-12.69	21.35-12.18	17.54-12.75	22.93-9.01	39.95-23.47	26.91-15.00	43.27-18.35
Average Yield %	1.16	1.01	0.98	1.16	1.71	1.77	1.94	1.66

Address: 1617 Sixth Avenue, Suite 500, Seattle, WA 98101-1742 **Telephone:** 206-628-2111 **Web Site:** www.nordstrom.com	**Officers:** Blake W. Nordstrom - President Paul F. Favaro - Executive Vice President **Transfer Agents:** Mellon Investor Services LLC, South Hackensack, NJ	**No of Institutions:** 526 **Shares:** 175,390,416 **% Held:** 74.97

NORTHERN TRUST CORP.

Exchange	Symbol	Price	52Wk Range	Yield	P/E
NMS	NTRS	$76.29 (5/29/2008)	80.99-59.35	1.47	18.61

*7 Year Price Score 104.23 *NYSE Composite Index=100 *12 Month Price Score 107.07

Interim Earnings (Per Share)

Qtr.	Mar	Jun	Sep	Dec
2005	0.63	0.68	0.67	0.67
2006	0.74	0.76	0.74	0.77
2007	0.84	0.92	0.93	0.55
2008	1.71	...	...	...

Interim Dividends (Per Share)

Amt	Decl	Ex	Rec	Pay
0.25Q	07/17/2007	09/06/2007	09/10/2007	10/01/2007
0.28Q	10/16/2007	12/06/2007	12/10/2007	01/02/2008
0.28Q	02/19/2008	03/06/2008	03/10/2008	04/01/2008
0.28Q	04/15/2008	06/06/2008	06/10/2008	07/01/2008
		Indicated Div: $1.12		

Valuation Analysis

Forecast EPS $4.05 (05/17/2008)

Market Cap	$16.8 Billion	Book Value	4.8 Billion
Price/Book	3.53	Price/Sales	2.95

Dividend Achiever Status

10 Year Growth Rate	10.76%
Total Years of Dividend Growth	22

Business Summary: Commercial Banking (MIC: SIC: 6022 NAIC: 522110)

Northern Trust is a financial holding company that provides investment management, asset and fund administration, fiduciary, and banking products and services for corporations, institutions, and affluent individuals. Co. conducts business through U.S. and non-U.S. subsidiaries, including its primary bank subsidiary, The Northern Trust Co. Co. has two business units: Corporate and Institutional Services; and Personal Financial Services. As of Dec 31 2007, Co. had a network of 85 offices in 18 U.S. states and international offices in 15 locations in North America, Europe, and the Asia-Pacific region; and had consolidated total assets of $67.61 billion and total deposits of $51.21 billion.

Recent Developments: For the quarter ended Mar 31 2008, net income increased 106.3% to US$385.2 million from US$186.7 million in the year-earlier quarter. Net interest income increased 27.5% to US$253.5 million from US$198.8 million in the year-earlier quarter. Non-interest income rose 44.4% to US$879.9 million from US$609.4 million, while non-interest expense advanced 1.8% to US$535.3 million.

Prospects: Notwithstanding the difficult economic environment, Co.'s outlook appears encouraging as it is seeing solid operating earnings primarily driven by growth in trust, investment and other servicing fees that reflects strong new business, and higher foreign exchange trading income due to continued strong client volumes and higher currency volatility. In addition, Co. is experiencing net interest income growth reflecting higher levels of average earning assets, as well as an increase in the net interest margin attributable to a widening of the spread between interest rates on short term investments and on overnight funding sources, including the effect of Federal Reserve Bank rate reductions.

Financial Data
(US$ in Thousands)

	3 Mos	12/31/2007	12/31/2006	12/31/2005	12/31/2004	12/31/2003	12/31/2002	12/31/2001
Earnings Per Share	4.10	3.24	3.00	2.64	2.27	1.80	1.97	2.11
Cash Flow Per Share	4.71	4.01	1.78	2.68	2.97	2.32	3.17	3.28
Tang Book Value Per Share	19.69	18.51	18.03	16.51	15.04	13.88	13.04	11.97
Dividends Per Share	1.060	1.030	0.940	0.860	0.780	0.700	0.680	0.635
Dividend Payout %	25.85	31.79	31.33	32.58	34.36	38.89	34.52	30.09
Income Statement								
Income Before Taxes	578,100	1,060,800	1,024,200	887,800	754,500	631,100	669,000	731,900
Income Taxes	192,900	333,900	358,800	303,400	249,700	207,800	221,900	244,400
Net Income	385,200	726,900	665,400	584,400	505,600	404,800	447,100	487,500
Average Shares	224,820	224,315	221,784	221,557	223,135	224,067	225,834	228,971
Balance Sheet								
Total Assets	77,480,300	67,611,200	60,712,200	53,413,800	45,276,700	41,450,200	39,478,200	39,664,500
Total Liabilities	72,721,900	63,102,100	56,768,300	49,813,000	41,981,100	38,394,900	36,478,400	36,891,000
Stockholders' Equity	4,758,400	4,509,100	3,943,900	3,600,800	3,295,600	3,055,300	2,999,800	2,773,500
Shares Outstanding	220,135	220,608	218,700	218,128	219,067	220,118	220,800	221,647
Statistical Record								
Return on Assets %	1.35	1.13	1.17	1.18	1.16	1.00	1.13	1.29
Return on Equity %	20.98	17.20	17.64	16.95	15.88	13.37	15.49	18.62
Price Range	80.99-59.35	80.99-56.82	61.29-49.42	54.83-41.60	50.76-38.87	48.02-28.27	62.02-30.74	81.30-45.25
P/E Ratio	19.75-14.48	25.00-17.54	20.43-16.47	20.77-15.76	22.36-17.12	26.68-15.71	31.48-15.60	38.53-21.45
Average Yield %	1.56	1.57	1.68	1.80	1.76	1.77	1.47	1.02

Address: 50 South La Salle Street, Chicago, IL 60603 **Telephone:** 312-630-6000 **Web Site:** www.northerntrust.com	**Officers:** William A. Osborn - Chairman Frederick H. Waddell - President, Chief Executive Officer **Transfer Agents:** Wells Fargo Shareowner Services, St. Paul, MN	**Investor Contact:** 312-444-7811 **No of Institutions:** 643 **Shares:** 169,661,376 **% Held:** 72.86

NORTHWEST NATURAL GAS CO.

Exchange	Symbol	Price	52Wk Range	Yield	P/E
NYS	NWN	$45.77 (5/29/2008)	50.50-41.38	3.28	17.47

*7 Year Price Score 103.84 *NYSE Composite Index=100   *12 Month Price Score 99.64

Interim Earnings (Per Share)

Qtr.	Mar	Jun	Sep	Dec
2005	1.43	0.04	(0.31)	0.94
2006	1.48	0.07	(0.35)	1.09
2007	1.76	0.10	(0.22)	1.11
2008	1.63	...	...	...

Interim Dividends (Per Share)

Amt	Decl	Ex	Rec	Pay
0.355Q	07/02/2007	07/27/2007	07/31/2007	08/15/2007
0.375Q	10/03/2007	10/29/2007	10/31/2007	11/15/2007
0.375Q	01/03/2008	01/29/2008	01/31/2008	02/15/2008
0.375Q	04/04/2008	04/28/2008	04/30/2008	05/15/2008
		Indicated Div: $1.50		

Valuation Analysis

Forecast EPS $2.62 (05/16/2008)
Market Cap $1.2 Billion   Book Value 629.3 Million
Price/Book 1.92   Price/Sales 1.18

Dividend Achiever Status

10 Year Growth Rate 1.80%
Total Years of Dividend Growth 52

Business Summary: Gas Utilities (MIC: SIC: 4924 NAIC: 221210)

Northwest Natural Gas is principally engaged in the distribution of natural gas in Oregon and southwest Washington. Co.'s Local Gas Distribution segment involves in purchasing gas from producers, transporting the gas over interstate pipelines from the supply basins to service territory, and reselling the gas to customers. The Gas Storage segment offers underground natural gas storage services to large intrastate and interstate customers. Also, Co. has other investments, including assets in NNG Financial Corp., a Boeing 737-300 aircraft under lease to Continental Airlines but held for sale as of Dec 31 2007, and investments in development projects such as Gill Ranch and Palomar Pipeline.

Recent Developments: For the quarter ended Mar 31 2008, net income decreased 10.2% to US$43.2 million from US$48.1 million in the year-earlier quarter. Revenues were US$387.7 million, down 1.6% from US$394.1 million the year before. Operating income was US$78.1 million versus US$85.6 million in the prior-year quarter, a decrease of 8.7%. Direct operating expenses declined 0.1% to US$283.7 million from US$283.9 million in the comparable period the year before. Indirect operating expenses increased 5.0% to US$25.8 million from US$24.6 million in the equivalent prior-year period.

Prospects: Going forward, while Co. expects to continue with a customer growth rate above the national average for local gas distribution companies due to the growing market in the Pacific Northwest, Co. expects to experience a slowdown in new construction through 2008. Accordingly, Co. anticipates that its annual growth rate could decline further in 2008. Meanwhile, Co. continues to target long-term earnings per share growth of at least 5.0%, and is reaffirming its earnings per share guidance for 2008 of $2.48 to $2.63, assuming several factors including continued customer growth, benefits from cost reduction initiatives, and no additional gains or losses from its gas commodity sharing mechanism.

Financial Data

(US$ in Thousands)	3 Mos	12/31/2007	12/31/2006	12/31/2005	12/31/2004	12/31/2003	12/31/2002	12/31/2001
Earnings Per Share	2.62	2.76	2.29	2.11	1.86	1.76	1.62	1.88
Cash Flow Per Share	5.78	6.85	5.39	2.87	3.98	4.15	4.87	2.84
Tang Book Value Per Share	23.82	22.52	21.97	21.28	20.64	19.52	18.88	18.56
Dividends Per Share	1.460	1.440	1.390	1.320	1.300	1.270	1.260	1.245
Dividend Payout %	55.75	52.17	60.70	62.56	69.89	72.16	77.78	66.22
Income Statement								
Total Revenue	387,694	1,033,193	1,013,172	910,486	707,604	611,256	641,376	650,252
EBITDA	96,172	224,174	203,331	189,797	170,225	158,671	153,458	161,185
Depn & Amortn	17,705	68,343	64,435	61,645	57,371	54,249	52,090	49,640
Income Before Taxes	68,869	118,557	99,649	90,869	77,103	69,323	67,236	77,740
Income Taxes	33,833	44,060	36,234	32,720	26,531	23,340	23,444	27,553
Net Income	43,168	74,497	63,415	58,149	50,572	45,983	43,792	50,187
Average Shares	26,560	26,995	27,657	27,621	27,283	26,061	25,814	25,612
Balance Sheet								
Net PPE	1,504,361	1,495,873	1,425,141	1,373,423	1,318,405	1,205,913	995,595	964,976
Total Assets	1,988,289	2,014,183	1,956,856	2,042,031	1,732,195	1,591,332	1,342,791	1,435,022
Long-Term Obligations	512,000	512,000	517,000	521,500	484,027	500,319	445,945	378,377
Total Liabilities	1,359,024	1,419,432	1,357,311	1,455,100	1,163,678	1,085,016	859,688	966,861
Stockholders' Equity	629,265	594,751	599,545	586,931	568,517	506,316	483,103	468,161
Shares Outstanding	26,415	26,407	27,283	27,579	27,546	25,938	25,586	25,228
Statistical Record								
Return on Assets %	3.60	3.75	3.17	3.08	3.03	3.13	3.15	3.70
Return on Equity %	11.04	12.48	10.69	10.07	9.38	9.29	9.21	10.90
EBITDA Margin %	24.81	21.70	20.07	20.85	24.06	25.96	23.93	24.79
Net Margin %	11.13	7.21	6.26	6.39	7.15	7.52	6.83	7.72
PPE Turnover	0.70	0.71	0.72	0.68	0.56	0.56	0.65	0.68
Asset Turnover	0.53	0.52	0.51	0.48	0.42	0.42	0.46	0.48
Debt to Equity	0.81	0.86	0.86	0.89	0.85	0.99	0.92	0.81
Price Range	52.62-41.38	52.62-40.21	43.00-33.27	39.50-32.61	33.90-27.92	31.22-24.13	30.45-24.00	26.56-21.75
P/E Ratio	20.08-15.79	19.07-14.57	18.78-14.53	18.72-15.45	18.23-15.01	17.74-13.71	18.80-14.81	14.13-11.57
Average Yield %	3.11	3.12	3.74	3.67	4.19	4.58	4.52	5.14

Address: 220 N.W. Second Avenue, Portland, OR 97209
Telephone: 503-226-4211
Web Site: www.nwnatural.com

Officers: Russell F. Tromley - Chairman Gregg S. Kantor - President, Chief Operating Officer **Transfer Agents:** American Stock Transfer & Trust Company, New York, NY

Investor Contact: 503-226-4211
No of Institutions: 210
Shares: 17,620,984 **% Held:** 62.32

NUCOR CORP.

Exchange	Symbol	Price	52Wk Range	Yield	P/E
NYS	NUE	$72.90 (5/29/2008)	82.07-45.86	1.76	14.27

*7 Year Price Score 152.16 *NYSE Composite Index=100 *12 Month Price Score 124.78

Interim Earnings (Per Share)

Qtr.	Mar	Jun	Sep	Dec
2005	1.10	1.01	0.93	1.09
2006	1.21	1.45	1.68	1.35
2007	1.26	1.14	1.29	1.26
2008	1.41	...	...	...

Interim Dividends (Per Share)

Amt	Decl	Ex	Rec	Pay
0.32Q	02/20/2008	03/26/2008	03/28/2008	05/09/2008
0.20Q	02/20/2008	03/26/2008	03/28/2008	05/09/2008
0.20Q	06/03/2008	06/26/2008	06/30/2008	08/11/2008
0.32Q	06/03/2008	06/26/2008	06/30/2008	08/11/2008

Indicated Div: $1.28 (Div. Reinv. Plan)

Valuation Analysis

Forecast EPS	$6.65 (05/17/2008)
Market Cap	$21.0 Billion	Book Value	5.4 Billion
Price/Book	3.88	Price/Sales	1.18

Dividend Achiever Status

10 Year Growth Rate	16.30%
Total Years of Dividend Growth	35

TRADING VOLUME (thousand shares)

Business Summary: Metal Works (MIC: SIC: 3312 NAIC: 331111)

Nucor produces and sells steel and steel products via its steel mills and steel products segments. Co.'s steel mills segment produces hot-rolled steel (angles, rounds, flats, channels, sheet, beams, pilings, blooms, beam blanks and plate) and cold-rolled steel, while its steel products segment produces steel joists and joist girders, steel deck, cold finish steel, steel fasteners, metal building systems, light gauge steel framing, steel grating and expanded metal, and wire and wire mesh. Co. sells hot- and cold-rolled steel to steel service centers, fabricators and manufacturers, as well as steel joists/ joist girders and steel deck to general contractors and fabricators in the U.S.

Recent Developments: For the quarter ended Mar 29 2008, net income increased 7.5% to US$409.8 million from US$381.0 million in the year-earlier quarter. Revenues were US$4.97 billion, up 32.0% from US$3.77 billion the year before. Direct operating expenses rose 36.1% to US$4.07 billion from US$2.99 billion in the comparable period the year before. Indirect operating expenses increased 49.1% to US$279.8 million from US$187.6 million in the equivalent prior-year period.

Prospects: For the second quarter of 2008, Co. expects earnings of $1.55 to $1.60 per diluted share. Notably, Co. expects its sheet, plate, beam and bar businesses to benefit from solid global demand for steel, and expects favorable conditions in its downstream businesses, particularly for rebar fabrication, cold finish bars, steel grating, and wire rod and mesh products. Meanwhile, on May 13 2008, Co. announced an agreement to acquire 50.0% of Duferdofin-Nucor S.r.l., a joint venture being created with Duferco S.A. for the production of beams in Italy and the distribution of beams in Europe and North Africa, for about $658.0 million. Co. expects the transaction to close in the third quarter of 2008.

Financial Data
(US$ in Thousands)

	3 Mos	12/31/2007	12/31/2006	12/31/2005	12/31/2004	12/31/2003	12/31/2002	12/31/2001
Earnings Per Share	5.11	4.94	5.68	4.13	3.51	0.20	0.52	0.36
Cash Flow Per Share	7.09	6.54	7.34	6.80	3.24	1.58	1.59	1.59
Tang Book Value Per Share	9.82	13.18	16.04	13.80	10.83	7.45	7.43	7.08
Dividends Per Share	2.350	2.440	2.150	0.925	0.235	0.200	0.190	0.170
Dividend Payout %	45.95	49.39	37.85	22.40	6.70	100.00	36.71	46.90
Income Statement								
Total Revenue	4,974,269	16,592,976	14,751,270	12,700,999	11,376,828	6,265,823	4,801,777	4,139,249
EBITDA	745,920	2,686,340	3,020,389	2,395,623	2,136,933	455,616	551,440	469,449
Depn & Amortn	123,073	427,556	363,936	375,054	383,305	364,112	307,101	289,063
Income Before Taxes	622,847	2,253,315	2,693,818	2,016,368	1,731,276	66,877	230,053	173,861
Income Taxes	213,093	781,368	936,137	706,084	609,791	4,096	67,973	60,900
Net Income	409,754	1,471,947	1,757,681	1,310,284	1,121,485	62,781	162,080	112,961
Average Shares	290,201	297,788	309,381	317,130	319,508	313,666	312,998	311,132
Balance Sheet								
Current Assets	4,874,642	5,073,249	4,675,036	4,071,553	3,174,948	1,620,560	1,424,139	1,373,666
Total Assets	11,340,521	9,826,122	7,884,989	7,138,787	6,133,207	4,492,353	4,381,001	3,759,348
Current Liabilities	2,369,645	1,582,036	1,450,028	1,255,699	1,065,790	629,595	591,536	484,159
Long-Term Obligations	2,491,600	2,250,300	922,300	922,300	923,550	903,550	878,550	460,450
Total Liabilities	5,914,827	4,713,205	3,059,000	2,858,999	2,677,222	2,150,275	2,058,012	1,557,888
Stockholders' Equity	5,425,694	5,112,917	4,825,989	4,279,788	3,455,985	2,342,078	2,322,989	2,201,460
Shares Outstanding	288,559	287,993	300,949	310,220	319,024	314,360	312,720	310,831
Statistical Record								
Return on Assets %	15.18	16.62	23.40	19.75	21.05	1.42	3.98	3.02
Return on Equity %	28.50	29.62	38.61	33.88	38.58	2.69	7.16	5.21
EBITDA Margin %	15.00	16.19	20.48	18.86	18.78	7.27	11.48	11.34
Net Margin %	8.24	8.87	11.92	10.32	9.86	1.00	3.38	2.73
Asset Turnover	1.80	1.87	1.96	1.91	2.14	1.41	1.18	1.11
Current Ratio	2.06	3.21	3.22	3.24	2.98	2.57	2.41	2.84
Debt to Equity	0.46	0.44	0.19	0.22	0.27	0.39	0.38	0.21
Price Range	74.45-45.86	69.25-45.86	65.84-34.23	34.62-22.81	27.54-13.34	14.48-8.99	17.29-9.47	14.00-8.63
P/E Ratio	14.57-8.97	14.02-9.28	11.59-6.03	8.38-5.52	7.85-3.80	72.38-44.97	33.25-18.22	38.89-23.96
Average Yield %	3.91	4.07	4.3	3.26	1.24	1.71	1.41	1.48

Address: 1915 Rexford Road, Charlotte, NC 28211	Officers: Daniel R. DiMicco - Chairman, President, Chief Executive Officer Terry S. Lisenby - Executive Vice President, Chief Financial Officer, Treasurer	No of Institutions: 675
Telephone: 704-366-7000	Transfer Agents: American Stock Transfer & Trust Company, New York, NY	Shares: 246,437,760 % Held: 76.40
Web Site: www.nucor.com		

OLD NATIONAL BANCORP (EVANSVILLE, IN)

Exchange	Symbol	Price	52Wk Range	Yield	P/E
NYS	ONB	$17.42 (5/29/2008)	19.26-13.26	5.28	13.72

*7 Year Price Score 61.86   *NYSE Composite Index=100   *12 Month Price Score 108.90

Interim Earnings (Per Share)

Qtr.	Mar	Jun	Sep	Dec
2005	0.27	0.33	0.11	0.22
2006	0.31	0.30	0.32	0.27
2007	0.16	0.30	0.34	0.34
2008	0.29	...	...	...

Interim Dividends (Per Share)

Amt	Decl	Ex	Rec	Pay
0.22Q	07/30/2007	08/30/2007	09/04/2007	09/18/2007
0.22Q	10/30/2007	11/29/2007	12/03/2007	12/17/2007
0.23Q	12/18/2007	02/28/2008	03/03/2008	03/17/2008
0.23Q	04/24/2008	05/29/2008	06/02/2008	06/16/2008

Indicated Div: $0.92 (Div. Reinv. Plan)

Valuation Analysis

Forecast EPS $1.17 (05/16/2008)

Market Cap	$1.2 Billion	Book Value	675.4 Million
Price/Book	1.71	Price/Sales	1.88

Dividend Achiever Status

10 Year Growth Rate	7.80%
Total Years of Dividend Growth	24

TRADING VOLUME (thousand shares)

Business Summary: Commercial Banking (MIC: SIC: 6021 NAIC: 522110)

Old National Bancorp, with total assets of $7.85 billion and deposits of $5.66 billion as of Dec 31 2007, is a financial holding company headquartered in Evansville, IN. Co., through its wholly owned banking subsidiary, provides a range of services, including commercial and consumer loan and depository services, investment and brokerage services, lease financing and other traditional banking services. Through its non-bank affiliates, Co. provides services to supplement the banking business including fiduciary and wealth management services, insurance and other financial services. As of Dec 31 2007, Co. operated 115 banking financial centers primarily in Indiana, Illinois, and Kentucky.

Recent Developments: For the quarter ended Mar 31 2008, net income increased 79.2% to US$19.3 million from US$10.8 million in the year-earlier quarter. Net interest income increased 15.4% to US$59.8 million from US$51.8 million in the year-earlier quarter. Provision for loan losses was US$21.9 million versus US$2.4 million in the prior-year quarter, an increase of 795.9%. Non-interest income rose 34.9% to US$46.9 million from US$34.8 million, while non-interest expense declined 2.9% to US$70.9 million.

Prospects: Looking into the foreseeable future, Co. expects conditions in the overall residential real estate and credit markets to remain uncertain. In addition, Co. anticipates that the current weakening of underlying loan collateral could result in further deterioration in the performance of its asset-backed securities. Nonetheless, Co. remains optimistic about its prospects as it continues to focus on improving its credit quality, as well as implementing strategic initiatives to improve its operating platform such as strengthening its credit profile and cost reduction efforts. In the meantime, Co. is reaffirming its earnings outlook for full-year 2008 of approximately $1.13 to $1.19 per share.

Financial Data

(US$ in Thousands)	3 Mos	12/31/2007	12/31/2006	12/31/2005	12/31/2004	12/31/2003	12/31/2002	12/31/2001
Earnings Per Share	1.27	1.14	1.20	0.93	0.97	1.00	1.67	1.29
Cash Flow Per Share	1.34	1.13	1.81	1.35	1.27	2.91	0.99	1.48
Tang Book Value Per Share	7.33	6.98	7.64	7.59	7.48	7.58	8.40	9.03
Dividends Per Share	0.890	0.880	0.840	0.760	0.724	0.689	0.622	0.559
Dividend Payout %	70.26	77.19	70.00	81.72	74.62	68.93	37.27	43.46
Income Statement								
Interest Income	104,134	461,368	451,713	425,239	417,198	469,748	547,383	629,707
Interest Expense	44,344	242,177	238,996	206,087	166,391	197,741	257,954	338,408
Net Interest Income	59,790	219,191	212,717	219,152	250,807	272,007	289,429	291,299
Provision for Losses	21,905	4,118	7,000	23,100	22,400	85,000	33,500	28,700
Non-Interest Income	46,876	155,138	153,791	159,898	182,163	192,149	154,497	112,967
Non-Interest Expense	70,936	277,998	264,561	262,107	335,927	299,716	257,845	254,812
Income Before Taxes	13,825	92,213	94,947	93,843	74,643	79,440	152,581	120,754
Income Taxes	(5,515)	17,323	15,574	15,254	7,072	9,027	34,649	27,710
Net Income	19,340	74,890	79,373	63,764	67,571	70,413	117,932	93,044
Average Shares	65,754	65,750	66,261	68,256	70,024	70,173	70,673	72,037
Balance Sheet								
Net Loans & Leases	4,618,727	4,642,893	4,648,847	4,858,784	4,901,577	5,481,884	5,681,893	6,058,613
Total Assets	7,723,466	7,846,126	8,149,515	8,492,022	8,898,304	9,353,896	9,612,556	9,080,473
Total Deposits	5,346,485	5,663,383	6,321,494	6,465,636	6,414,263	6,493,092	6,439,280	6,616,440
Total Liabilities	7,048,073	7,193,245	7,507,146	7,842,124	8,195,096	8,638,406	8,871,846	8,441,238
Stockholders' Equity	675,393	652,881	642,369	649,898	703,208	715,490	740,710	639,235
Shares Outstanding	66,202	66,205	66,503	67,649	69,287	69,903	70,401	70,816
Statistical Record								
Return on Assets %	1.04	0.94	0.95	0.73	0.74	0.74	1.26	1.04
Return on Equity %	12.65	11.56	12.28	9.42	9.50	9.67	17.09	14.70
Net Interest Margin %	57.42	47.51	47.09	51.54	60.12	57.90	52.88	46.26
Efficiency Ratio %	46.97	45.09	43.69	44.79	56.05	45.28	36.74	34.31
Loans to Deposits	0.86	0.82	0.74	0.75	0.76	0.84	0.88	0.92
Price Range	19.26-13.26	19.42-14.03	21.90-18.27	24.63-18.71	25.41-20.02	21.73-19.22	22.89-19.70	23.51-16.92
P/E Ratio	15.17-10.44	17.04-12.31	18.25-15.23	26.48-20.12	26.20-20.64	21.73-19.22	13.71-11.80	18.22-13.12
Average Yield %	5.45	5.19	4.24	3.56	3.19	3.35	2.93	2.71

Address: 1 Main Street, Evansville, IN 47708	Officers: Larry E. Dunigan - Chairman Robert G. Jones - President, Chief Executive Officer **Transfer Agents:** Old National Bancorp, Evansville, IN	Investor Contact: 812-464-1366
Telephone: 812-464-1294		No of Institutions: 162
Web Site: www.oldnational.com		Shares: 36,044,200 % Held: 49.58

OLD REPUBLIC INTERNATIONAL CORP.

Exchange	Symbol	Price	52Wk Range	Yield	P/E
NYS	ORI	$15.00 (5/29/2008)	22.17-12.31	4.53	24.59

*7 Year Price Score 69.20 *NYSE Composite Index=100 *12 Month Price Score 91.44

Interim Earnings (Per Share)

Qtr.	Mar	Jun	Sep	Dec
2005	0.50	0.74	0.52	0.61
2006	0.51	0.54	0.50	0.44
2007	0.46	0.49	0.12	0.09
2008	(0.08)	...	...	...

Interim Dividends (Per Share)

Amt	Decl	Ex	Rec	Pay
0.16Q	08/23/2007	08/31/2007	09/05/2007	09/14/2007
0.16Q	12/06/2007	12/03/2007	12/05/2007	12/14/2007
0.16Q	02/21/2008	03/03/2008	03/05/2008	03/14/2008
0.17Q	05/23/2008	06/03/2008	06/05/2008	06/13/2008

Indicated Div: $0.68 (Div. Reinv. Plan)

Valuation Analysis

Forecast EPS	$-0.10 (05/16/2008)		
Market Cap	$3.5 Billion	Book Value	4.4 Billion
Price/Book	0.79	Price/Sales	0.85

Dividend Achiever Status

10 Year Growth Rate	13.49%
Total Years of Dividend Growth	26

TRADING VOLUME (thousand shares)

Business Summary: Insurance (MIC: SIC: 6351 NAIC: 524126)

Old Republic International is a Chicago-based insurance holding company. As of Dec 31 2007, Co. operates through three major segments. Co.'s General Insurance Group segment is a commercial lines insurance business with a focus on liability insurance coverages. Co.'s Mortgage Guaranty Group insures only first mortgage loans, primarily on residential properties incorporating one-to-four family dwelling units. Co.'s title insurance business consists primarily of the issuance of policies to real estate purchasers and investors based upon searches of the public records, which contain information concerning interests in real property.

Recent Developments: For the quarter ended Mar 31 2008, net loss amounted to US$19.0 million versus net income of US$107.7 million in the year-earlier quarter. Revenues were US$951.5 million, down 2.3% from US$973.5 million the year before. Net premiums earned were US$804.1 million versus US$814.2 million in the prior-year quarter, a decrease of 1.2%. Net investment income rose 4.0% to US$95.2 million from US$91.5 million a year ago.

Prospects: Co.'s result is reflecting ongoing difficulties in its housing-related mortgage guaranty and title insurance lines. Notably, Co.'s mortgage guaranty segment is being hurt by a continued rise in claim costs, driven by higher mortgage loan delinquencies and claim severity, while the ongoing downturn in the housing and related mortgage lending sectors of the U.S. economy has led to further reductions of premiums and fees revenues for its title insurance segment. However, Co. believes that the solid financial position of its general insurance business should provide necessary earnings support and capital management capability for the resumption of positive operating trends in 2010 and beyond.

Financial Data
(US$ in Thousands)

	3 Mos	12/31/2007	12/31/2006	12/31/2005	12/31/2004	12/31/2003	12/31/2002	12/31/2001
Earnings Per Share	0.61	1.17	1.99	2.37	1.89	2.01	1.72	1.54
Cash Flow Per Share	3.74	3.73	4.35	3.83	3.62	3.33	2.97	2.36
Tang Book Value Per Share	18.99	19.71	18.91	17.53	16.68	15.41	13.60	12.15
Dividends Per Share	0.640	0.630	0.590	1.312	0.402	0.891	0.336	0.315
Dividend Payout %	104.13	53.85	29.65	55.36	21.31	44.36	19.50	20.49
Income Statement								
Total Revenue	951,600	4,091,000	3,794,200	3,805,900	3,491,600	3,285,800	2,756,400	2,373,400
Income Before Taxes	(39,600)	...	...	...	...	...	...	...
Income Taxes	(20,500)	105,900	215,200	195,900	215,900	219,900	167,700	159,700
Net Income	(19,000)	272,400	464,800	551,400	435,000	459,800	392,900	346,900
Average Shares	230,495	232,912	233,034	232,108	230,759	229,128	227,904	225,614
Balance Sheet								
Total Assets	13,249,700	13,290,600	12,612,200	11,543,200	10,570,800	9,712,300	8,715,400	7,920,200
Total Liabilities	8,873,000	8,749,000	8,243,000	7,519,100	6,705,100	6,158,600	5,559,500	5,136,100
Stockholders' Equity	4,376,700	4,541,600	4,369,200	4,024,000	3,865,600	3,553,600	3,155,800	2,783,700
Shares Outstanding	230,512	230,472	231,047	229,575	231,786	230,589	232,108	229,066
Statistical Record								
Return on Assets %	1.11	2.10	3.85	4.99	4.28	4.99	4.72	4.56
Return on Equity %	3.26	6.11	11.08	13.98	11.69	13.71	13.23	13.29
Net Margin %	(2.00)	6.66	12.25	14.49	12.46	13.99	14.25	14.62
Price Range	22.38-12.31	23.51-13.73	23.50-20.20	22.44-17.85	21.75-17.10	20.63-13.22	18.52-13.48	16.03-12.08
P/E Ratio	36.69-20.18	20.09-11.74	11.81-10.15	9.47-7.53	11.51-9.05	10.26-6.58	10.77-7.84	10.41-7.84
Average Yield %	3.62	3.19	2.71	6.55	2.09	5.17	2.06	2.16

Address: 307 North Michigan Avenue, Chicago, IL 60601 **Telephone:** 312-346-8100 **Web Site:** www.oldrepublic.com	Officers: Aldo C. Zucaro - Chairman, Chief Executive Officer James A. Kellogg - President, Chief Operating Officer **Transfer Agents:** EquiServe Trust Company, N.A.	No of Institutions: 324 **Shares:** 207,094,336 **% Held:** 83.12

OLD SECOND BANCORP., INC. (AURORA, ILL.)

Exchange	Symbol	Price	52Wk Range	Yield	P/E
NMS	OSBC	$19.15 (5/29/2008)	30.92-19.15	3.13	10.19

*7 Year Price Score 84.90 *NYSE Composite Index=100 *12 Month Price Score 90.13

Interim Earnings (Per Share)

Qtr.	Mar	Jun	Sep	Dec
2005	0.46	0.48	0.52	0.57
2006	0.45	0.46	0.37	0.47
2007	0.43	0.45	0.49	0.52
2008	0.42	...	...	...

Interim Dividends (Per Share)

Amt	Decl	Ex	Rec	Pay
0.15Q	06/19/2007	06/27/2007	06/29/2007	07/09/2007
0.15Q	09/18/2007	09/26/2007	09/28/2007	10/08/2007
0.15Q	12/18/2007	12/26/2007	12/28/2007	01/08/2008
0.15Q	03/18/2008	03/26/2008	03/28/2008	04/08/2008

Indicated Div: $0.60

Valuation Analysis

Forecast EPS $1.95 (05/16/2008)

Market Cap	$263.1 Million	Book Value	198.8 Million
Price/Book	1.32	Price/Sales	1.37

Dividend Achiever Status

10 Year Growth Rate	14.48%
Total Years of Dividend Growth	13

Business Summary: Commercial Banking (MIC: SIC: 6022 NAIC: 522110)

Old Second Bancorp is a bank holding company. Through its subsidiaries, Co. provides financial services through its 29 banking locations and one commercial loan production office located in Kane, Kendall, DeKalb, DuPage, LaSalle and Will counties in Illinois. Co.'s services include demand, money market, savings, time deposit, individual retirement, and Keogh deposit accounts; commercial, industrial, consumer, and real estate lending, including installment loans, student loans, farm loans, lines of credit, and overdraft checking; safe deposit operations; wealth management services and trust services. At Dec 31 2007, Co. had total assets of $2.66 billion and total deposits of $2.11 billion.

Recent Developments: For the quarter ended Mar 31 2008, net income decreased 3.2% to US$5.6 million from US$5.7 million in the year-earlier quarter. Net interest income increased 21.0% to US$19.9 million from US$16.5 million in the year-earlier quarter. Non-interest income rose 11.1% to US$8.9 million from US$8.0 million, while non-interest expense advanced 21.6% to US$20.2 million.

Prospects: Co. is experiencing an increase in net interest income primarily attributable to the increase in average earning assets, as well as earnings contribution from its Feb 2008 acquisition of HeritageBanc, Inc. (Heritage). Looking ahead, with the systems conversions of Heritage completed in Mar 2008, Co. expects to begin to realize the economic benefits of the transaction in the second quarter of 2008. Also, Co. expects to realize cost savings and revenue enhancements by applying its relationship focused banking strategies, including offering the new client base wealth management services, as well as expanded mortgage, treasury and retail services.

Financial Data

(US$ in Thousands)	3 Mos	12/31/2007	12/31/2006	12/31/2005	12/31/2004	12/31/2003	12/31/2002	12/31/2001
Earnings Per Share	1.88	1.89	1.75	2.03	1.94	1.55	1.35	1.11
Cash Flow Per Share	2.39	1.11	2.81	0.77	0.75	4.48	0.88	(0.03)
Tang Book Value Per Share	9.38	11.96	11.70	10.91	9.84	8.50	8.75	7.94
Dividends Per Share	0.600	0.590	0.550	0.510	0.460	0.400	0.375	0.281
Dividend Payout %	32.00	31.22	31.43	25.12	23.71	25.72	27.88	25.25
Income Statement								
Interest Income	40,792	155,741	142,029	120,223	97,398	87,844	85,491	84,791
Interest Expense	20,852	87,143	70,830	46,224	29,039	25,468	28,009	35,290
Net Interest Income	19,940	68,598	71,199	73,999	68,359	62,376	57,482	49,501
Provision for Losses	900	1,188	1,244	353	(2,900)	3,251	3,805	3,840
Non-Interest Income	8,860	31,855	28,707	28,149	25,914	29,227	25,276	22,301
Non-Interest Expense	20,161	66,473	65,136	60,500	57,608	54,175	48,056	41,476
Income Before Taxes	7,739	32,792	33,526	41,295	39,565	34,177	30,897	26,486
Income Taxes	2,175	8,820	9,870	13,612	13,278	12,069	10,751	9,263
Net Income	5,564	23,972	23,656	27,683	26,287	22,108	20,146	17,223
Average Shares	13,216	12,655	13,526	13,661	13,535	14,198	14,859	15,442
Balance Sheet								
Net Loans & Leases	2,170,218	1,890,952	1,762,097	1,700,450	1,510,178	1,315,993	1,094,756	927,401
Total Assets	3,000,645	2,658,576	2,459,140	2,367,830	2,102,266	1,838,844	1,608,087	1,333,348
Total Deposits	2,419,610	2,113,618	2,062,693	1,935,278	1,798,849	1,524,634	1,390,661	1,090,816
Total Liabilities	2,801,874	2,508,687	2,300,585	2,215,568	1,967,278	1,721,850	1,475,011	1,208,402
Stockholders' Equity	198,771	149,889	158,555	152,262	134,988	116,994	133,076	124,946
Shares Outstanding	13,740	12,149	13,127	13,520	13,424	13,387	14,786	15,215
Statistical Record								
Return on Assets %	0.87	0.94	0.98	1.24	1.33	1.28	1.37	1.39
Return on Equity %	13.14	15.54	15.22	19.27	20.81	17.68	15.62	14.48
Net Interest Margin %	48.88	44.05	50.13	61.55	70.19	71.01	67.24	58.38
Efficiency Ratio %	40.60	35.43	38.15	40.78	46.72	46.28	43.38	38.73
Loans to Deposits	0.90	0.89	0.85	0.88	0.84	0.86	0.79	0.85
Price Range	30.92-24.25	30.92-25.81	33.20-29.06	34.81-28.01	34.73-23.11	25.96-18.25	21.27-14.40	15.00-8.77
P/E Ratio	16.45-12.90	16.36-13.66	18.97-16.61	17.15-13.80	17.90-11.91	16.75-11.77	15.76-10.67	13.51-7.90
Average Yield %	2.13	2.06	1.79	1.66	1.70	1.90	2.14	2.35

Address: 37 South River Street, Aurora, IL 60507-4172	Officers: William B. Skoglund - Chairman, President, Chief Executive Officer J. Douglas Cheatham - Executive Vice President, Chief Financial Officer, Chief Accounting Officer, Assistant Secretary	Investor Contact: 708-892-0202
Telephone: 630-892-0202		No of Institutions: 92
Web Site: www.oldsecond.com		Shares: 5,159,518 % Held: 41.19
	Transfer Agents:Old Second Bancorp, Inc., Aurora, IL	

OTTER TAIL CORP.

Exchange	Symbol	Price	52Wk Range	Yield	P/E
NMS	OTTR	$37.73 (5/29/2008)	39.15-29.42	3.15	22.19

*7 Year Price Score 91.56   *NYSE Composite Index=100   *12 Month Price Score 109.88

TRADING VOLUME (thousand shares)

Interim Earnings (Per Share)

Qtr.	Mar	Jun	Sep	Dec
2005	0.33	0.76	0.59	0.43
2006	0.50	0.38	0.45	0.38
2007	0.34	0.53	0.44	0.47
2008	0.27	...	...	...

Interim Dividends (Per Share)

Amt	Decl	Ex	Rec	Pay
0.292Q	08/06/2007	08/13/2007	08/15/2007	09/10/2007
0.292Q	11/01/2007	11/13/2007	11/15/2007	12/10/2007
0.297Q	02/05/2008	02/13/2008	02/15/2008	03/10/2008
0.297Q	04/14/2008	05/13/2008	05/15/2008	06/10/2008

Indicated Div: $1.19 (Div. Reinv. Plan)

Valuation Analysis

Forecast EPS	$1.85 (05/16/2008)		
Market Cap	$1.1 Billion	Book Value	522.6 Million
Price/Book	2.16	Price/Sales	0.91

Dividend Achiever Status

10 Year Growth Rate	2.32%
Total Years of Dividend Growth	32

Business Summary: Electricity (MIC: SIC: 4911 NAIC: 221121)

Otter Tail operates through six business segments. Co.'s Electric segment produces, transmits, distributes and sells electric energy; its Plastics segment produces polyvinyl chloride and polyethylene pipe; its manufacturing activities include the production of waterfront equipment; and metal parts stamping and fabrication; its Health Services segment sells diagnostic medical equipment, patient monitoring equipment and related supplies; its Food Ingredient Processing segment consists of Idaho Pacific Holdings, Inc., which operates potato dehydration plants; and its other businesses consists of businesses in other industries such as the fiber optic, wastewater and transportation industries.

Recent Developments: For the quarter ended Mar 31 2008, net income decreased 20.9% to US$8.2 million from US$10.4 million in the year-earlier quarter. Revenues were US$300.2 million, down 0.3% from US$301.1 million the year before. Operating income was US$17.1 million versus US$20.8 million in the prior-year quarter, a decrease of 17.7%. Direct operating expenses rose 0.3% to US$265.6 million from US$264.7 million in the comparable period the year before. Indirect operating expenses increased 12.3% to US$17.5 million from US$15.6 million in the equivalent prior-year period.

Prospects: Co. has revised its 2008 diluted earnings per share guidance to a range of $1.75 to $2.00, from its initial range of $1.85 to $2.10, given the uncertainty of economic conditions for the balance of the year. Notably, Co. expects growth in its manufacturing segment to be offset by the softening economy and the effects on its ShoreMaster subsidiary. Co. also expects its plastics segment to be affected by the sluggish housing and construction markets. Nonetheless, Co. expects increased levels of net income from the electric segment, due to an increase in revenues from a pending rate case in Minnesota and rate riders for wind energy and transmission investments in North Dakota and Minnesota.

Financial Data
(US$ in Thousands)

	3 Mos	12/31/2007	12/31/2006	12/31/2005	12/31/2004	12/31/2003	12/31/2002	12/31/2001
Earnings Per Share	1.70	1.78	1.70	2.11	1.58	1.51	1.79	1.68
Cash Flow Per Share	3.60	2.86	2.73	3.28	2.29	3.00	3.05	3.15
Tang Book Value Per Share	13.47	13.50	12.62	11.74	10.95	9.88	9.51	9.31
Dividends Per Share	1.175	1.170	1.150	1.120	1.100	1.080	1.060	1.040
Dividend Payout %	68.95	65.73	67.65	53.08	69.62	71.52	59.22	61.90
Income Statement								
Total Revenue	300,237	1,238,887	1,104,954	1,046,408	882,324	753,239	710,116	654,132
EBITDA	32,972	155,616	147,340	145,838	119,600	118,414	126,652	121,777
Depn & Amortn	14,913	52,830	49,983	46,458	44,344	45,962	42,613	42,100
Income Before Taxes	11,348	81,929	77,856	80,822	56,984	54,586	66,189	63,686
Income Taxes	5,742	27,968	27,106	27,967	17,004	14,930	20,061	20,083
Net Income	8,230	53,961	51,112	62,551	42,195	39,656	46,128	43,603
Average Shares	30,061	29,970	29,664	29,348	26,207	25,826	25,397	24,832
Balance Sheet								
Net PPE	875,345	854,024	718,609	697,091	682,098	633,325	587,886	542,977
Total Assets	1,458,893	1,454,754	1,258,650	1,181,496	1,134,148	986,423	878,736	782,541
Long-Term Obligations	342,490	342,694	255,436	258,260	261,810	265,193	258,229	227,360
Total Liabilities	936,264	916,607	752,380	701,566	689,438	637,036	549,771	487,733
Stockholders' Equity	522,629	538,147	506,270	479,930	444,710	349,387	328,965	294,808
Shares Outstanding	29,920	29,849	29,521	29,401	28,976	25,723	25,592	24,653
Statistical Record								
Return on Assets %	3.74	3.98	4.19	5.40	3.97	4.25	5.55	5.80
Return on Equity %	10.13	10.33	10.37	13.53	10.60	11.69	14.79	14.84
EBITDA Margin %	10.98	12.56	13.33	13.94	13.56	15.72	17.84	18.62
Net Margin %	2.74	4.36	4.63	5.98	4.78	5.26	6.50	6.67
PPE Turnover	1.54	1.58	1.56	1.52	1.34	1.23	1.26	1.24
Asset Turnover	0.90	0.91	0.91	0.90	0.83	0.81	0.85	0.87
Debt to Equity	0.66	0.64	0.50	0.54	0.59	0.76	.0.78	0.77
Price Range	37.92-29.42	37.92-29.42	31.87-25.95	31.75-24.13	27.36-23.85	28.50-24.00	34.12-23.80	30.69-23.88
P/E Ratio	22.31-17.31	21.30-16.53	18.75-15.26	15.05-11.44	17.32-15.09	18.87-15.89	19.06-13.30	18.27-14.21
Average Yield %	3.45	3.45	3.93	4.09	4.24	4.02	3.70	3.76

Address: 215 South Cascade Street, P.O. Box 496, Fergus Falls, MN 56538-0496 Telephone: 866-410-8780 Web Site: www.ottertail.com	Officers: John C. Macfarlane - Chairman John D. Erickson - President, Chief Executive Officer Transfer Agents:Wells Fargo Bank, Minnesota, N.A., St. Paul, MN	No of Institutions: 123 Shares: 15,152,985 % Held: 46.55

OWENS & MINOR, INC.

Exchange	Symbol	Price	52Wk Range	Yield	P/E
NYS	OMI	$47.49 (5/29/2008)	47.49-33.60	1.68	22.40

*7 Year Price Score 116.19 *NYSE Composite Index=100 *12 Month Price Score 112.48

Interim Earnings (Per Share)

Qtr.	Mar	Jun	Sep	Dec
2005	0.40	0.40	0.42	0.39
2006	0.41	0.26	0.36	0.17
2007	0.27	0.45	0.52	0.56
2008	0.59	...	...	...

Interim Dividends (Per Share)

Amt	Decl	Ex	Rec	Pay
0.17Q	07/19/2007	09/12/2007	09/14/2007	09/28/2007
0.17Q	10/18/2007	12/12/2007	12/14/2007	12/31/2007
0.20Q	02/04/2008	03/12/2008	03/14/2008	03/31/2008
0.20Q	04/24/2008	06/11/2008	06/13/2008	06/30/2008
	Indicated Div: $0.80			

Valuation Analysis

Forecast EPS	$2.31 (05/17/2008)		
Market Cap	$2.0 Billion	Book Value	635.4 Million
Price/Book	3.07	Price/Sales	0.28

Dividend Achiever Status

10 Year Growth Rate	17.55%
Total Years of Dividend Growth	10

Business Summary: Specialist Equipment Supplies (MIC: SIC: 5047 NAIC: 423450)

Owens & Minor is a distributor of medical and surgical supplies to the acute-care market, a healthcare supply chain management company and a national direct-to-consumer supplier of testing and monitoring supplies for diabetics. As of Dec 31 2007, Co. distributed 180,000 finished medical and surgical products produced by over 1,200 suppliers to about 4,100 healthcare provider customers from 45 distribution centers. Most of Co.'s sales consist of consumable goods such as disposable gloves, dressings, endoscopic products, intravenous products, needles and syringes, sterile procedure trays, surgical products and gowns, urological products and wound closure products.

Recent Developments: For the quarter ended Mar 31 2008, net income increased 123.8% to US$24.2 million from US$10.8 million in the year-earlier quarter. Revenues were US$1.75 billion, up 3.9% from US$1.69 billion the year before. Operating income was US$43.2 million versus US$24.8 million in the prior-year quarter, an increase of 74.3%. Direct operating expenses rose 3.6% to US$1.57 billion from US$1.51 billion in the comparable period the year before. Indirect operating expenses decreased 4.0% to US$143.9 million from US$149.9 million in the equivalent prior-year period.

Prospects: Co.'s near-term business outlook appears to be favorable, reflecting increases in its top- and bottom-line performance. At the same time, Co. is experiencing growth in its gross margins, driven primarily by the improved gross margin from the McKesson Medical-Surgical, Inc., business, which it acquired in Sep 2006. Meanwhile, given the results for the quarter ending Mar 2008, Co. is expecting its annual revenue growth in the range of 5% to 7% for the year ending Dec 31 2008. Consequently, Co. believes that this expected revenue growth, coupled with its management capability, will result in earnings in a range of $2.20 to $2.30 per diluted share for the year.

Financial Data

(US$ in Thousands)	3 Mos	12/31/2007	12/31/2006	12/31/2005	12/31/2004	12/31/2003	12/31/2002	12/31/2001
Earnings Per Share	2.12	1.79	1.20	1.61	1.53	1.42	1.27	0.68
Cash Flow Per Share	8.15	5.46	(1.85)	3.43	1.50	2.70	(0.42)	0.05
Tang Book Value Per Share	8.12	7.59	5.84	6.29	6.57	5.45	2.15	1.12
Dividends Per Share	0.710	0.680	0.600	0.520	0.440	0.350	0.310	0.273
Dividend Payout %	33.57	37.99	50.00	32.30	28.76	24.65	24.41	40.07
Income Statement								
Total Revenue	1,752,717	6,800,466	5,533,736	4,822,414	4,525,105	4,244,067	3,959,781	3,814,994
EBITDA	52,657	168,913	111,153	128,932	124,752	112,475	94,123	87,046
Depn & Amortn	9,458	25,700	19,800	11,500	14,884	15,718	15,926	22,469
Income Before Taxes	39,685	120,230	78,080	105,574	97,610	87,799	78,197	64,577
Income Taxes	15,477	47,520	29,328	41,154	37,110	34,158	30,980	34,474
Net Income	24,208	72,710	48,752	64,420	60,500	53,641	47,267	23,035
Average Shares	41,216	40,656	40,467	40,056	39,668	39,333	40,698	40,387
Balance Sheet								
Current Assets	1,109,013	1,089,857	1,266,770	894,552	864,476	781,375	729,753	679,452
Total Assets	1,536,857	1,515,080	1,685,750	1,239,850	1,131,833	1,045,748	1,009,477	953,853
Current Liabilities	640,537	568,464	670,503	488,868	430,531	395,632	344,730	367,674
Long-Term Obligations	211,962	283,845	433,133	204,418	207,476	209,499	240,185	203,449
Total Liabilities	901,503	900,721	1,138,296	727,852	671,577	635,393	612,890	585,610
Stockholders' Equity	635,354	614,359	547,454	511,998	460,256	410,355	271,437	236,243
Shares Outstanding	41,074	40,874	40,257	39,890	39,519	38,979	34,113	33,885
Statistical Record								
Return on Assets %	5.34	4.54	3.33	5.43	5.54	5.22	4.81	2.53
Return on Equity %	14.44	12.52	9.20	13.25	13.86	15.74	18.62	10.26
EBITDA Margin %	3.00	2.48	2.01	2.67	2.76	2.65	2.38	2.28
Net Margin %	1.38	1.07	0.88	1.34	1.34	1.26	1.19	0.60
Asset Turnover	4.26	4.25	3.78	4.07	4.14	4.13	4.03	4.19
Current Ratio	1.73	1.92	1.89	1.83	2.01	1.98	2.12	1.85
Debt to Equity	0.33	0.46	0.79	0.40	0.45	0.51	0.88	0.86
Price Range	45.28-33.60	43.77-30.40	34.72-27.96	33.28-26.35	29.34-21.91	26.80-15.86	20.86-13.40	20.96-14.35
P/E Ratio	21.36-15.85	24.45-16.98	28.93-23.30	20.67-16.37	19.18-14.32	18.87-11.17	16.43-10.55	30.82-21.10
Average Yield %	1.82	1.84	1.93	1.79	1.74	1.70	1.79	1.52

Address: 4800 Cox Road, Glen Allen, VA 23060 **Telephone:** 804-747-9794 **Web Site:** www.owens-minor.com	**Officers:** G. Gilmer Minor - Chairman Craig R. Smith - President, Chief Executive Officer **Transfer Agents:** The Bank of New York, New York, NY	**Investor Contact:** 804-747-9794 **No of Institutions:** 250 **Shares:** 42,684,908 **% Held:** 98.62

PARK NATIONAL CORP. (NEWARK, OH)

Exchange	Symbol	Price	52Wk Range	Yield	P/E
ASE	PRK	$71.15 (5/29/2008)	93.45-56.80	5.28	40.89

*7 Year Price Score 59.99   *NYSE Composite Index=100   *12 Month Price Score 96.64

Interim Earnings (Per Share)

Qtr.	Mar	Jun	Sep	Dec
2005	1.61	1.72	1.69	1.61
2006	1.69	1.70	1.71	1.63
2007	1.49	1.62	1.50	(3.01)
2008	1.65	...	...	...

Interim Dividends (Per Share)

Amt	Decl	Ex	Rec	Pay
0.93Q	07/16/2007	08/17/2007	08/21/2007	09/07/2007
0.94Q	11/19/2007	12/17/2007	12/19/2007	01/03/2008
0.94Q	01/16/2008	02/21/2008	02/25/2008	03/10/2008
0.94Q	04/21/2008	05/23/2008	05/28/2008	06/10/2008

Indicated Div: $3.76 (Div. Reinv. Plan)

Valuation Analysis

Forecast EPS $5.04 (05/16/2008)
Market Cap $993.6 Million   Book Value 591.2 Million
Price/Book 1.68   Price/Sales 2.04

Dividend Achiever Status

10 Year Growth Rate 9.87%
Total Years of Dividend Growth 20

Business Summary: Commercial Banking (MIC: SIC: 6021 NAIC: 522110)

Park National is a financial holding company. Through its subsidiary banks, Co. is engaged in the commercial banking and trust business, primarily conducted in small and medium population Ohio communities. Co.'s subsidiaries are engaged in the acceptance of deposits for demand, savings and time accounts; commercial, industrial, consumer and real estate lending, including installment loans, credit cards, home equity lines of credit and commercial and auto leasing; trust services; cash management; safe deposit operations; electronic funds transfers; Internet banking; and other banking-related services. At Dec 31 2007, Co. had total assets of $6.50 billion and total deposits of $4.44 billion.

Recent Developments: For the quarter ended Mar 31 2008, net income increased 9.1% to US$23.0 million from US$21.1 million in the year-earlier quarter. Net interest income increased 12.0% to US$61.5 million from US$54.9 million in the year-earlier quarter. Provision for loan losses was US$7.4 million versus US$2.2 million in the prior-year quarter, an increase of 235.3%. Non-interest income rose 32.0% to US$21.3 million from US$16.2 million, while non-interest expense advanced 10.1% to US$43.3 million.

Prospects: For 2008, Co. now expects net interest income of $247.0 million to $250.0 million. In addition, Co. expects tax equivalent net interest margin to be approximately 4.15% and average interest earning assets to be approximately $6.02 billion. Co. also expects the yield on loans to continue to decrease in 2008 with modest deposit growth of 1.0% to 2.0%. Separately, as part of its effort to improve efficiency, Co. is working at consolidating its eight Ohio-based banks onto one common operating system whereby several of its Ohio-based banks will be consolidated into The Park National Bank during the second half of 2008. This process is expected to be completed in the second quarter of 2009.

Financial Data
(US$ in Thousands)	3 Mos	12/31/2007	12/31/2006	12/31/2005	12/31/2004	12/31/2003	12/31/2002	12/31/2001
Earnings Per Share	1.74	1.60	6.74	6.64	6.32	5.97	5.86	5.31
Cash Flow Per Share	6.50	5.85	6.12	5.68	6.03	6.86	10.94	6.67
Tang Book Value Per Share	32.05	30.45	34.63	34.72	39.28	37.57	35.17	32.00
Dividends Per Share	3.740	3.730	3.690	3.620	3.414	3.210	2.962	2.752
Dividend Payout %	214.67	233.13	54.75	54.52	54.02	53.75	50.57	51.79
Income Statement								
Income Before Taxes	32,161	52,677	133,077	135,424	129,249	123,189	121,175	110,916
Income Taxes	9,183	32,739	41,218	43,079	40,210	38,829	37,883	35,893
Net Income	22,978	22,707	94,091	95,238	91,507	86,878	85,579	78,362
Average Shares	13,964	14,217	13,966	14,348	14,486	14,551	14,605	14,753
Balance Sheet								
Total Assets	6,781,365	6,501,102	5,470,876	5,436,048	5,412,584	5,034,956	4,446,625	4,569,515
Total Liabilities	6,190,186	5,921,090	4,900,437	4,877,618	4,850,023	4,491,915	3,937,333	4,101,169
Stockholders' Equity	591,179	580,012	570,439	558,430	562,561	543,041	509,292	468,346
Shares Outstanding	13,964	13,964	13,921	14,092	14,320	14,455	14,481	14,637
Statistical Record								
Return on Assets %	0.37	0.38	1.73	1.76	1.75	1.83	3.77	2.01
Return on Equity %	3.89	3.95	16.67	16.99	16.51	16.51	34.73	19.89
Price Range	95.50-56.80	101.25-64.50	117.21-92.36	135.50-99.04	141.25-105.33	114.29-88.86	97.24-80.01	97.62-71.52
P/E Ratio	54.89-32.64	63.28-40.31	17.39-13.70	20.41-14.92	22.35-16.67	19.14-14.88	16.59-13.65	18.38-13.47
Average Yield %	4.72	4.29	3.64	3.27	2.92	3.11	3.28	3.24

Address: 50 North Third Street, Newark, OH 43055
Telephone: 740-349-8451
Web Site: www.parknationalcorp.com

Officers: C. Daniel DeLawder - Chairman, Chief Executive Officer Harry O. Egger - Vice-Chairman
Transfer Agents: First-Knox National Bank, Mount Vernon, OH

Investor Contact: 740-349-8451
No of Institutions: 113
Shares: 5,131,908 **% Held:** 35.23

PARKER HANNIFIN CORP.

Exchange	Symbol	Price	52Wk Range	Yield	P/E
NYS	PH	$83.46 (5/29/2008)	86.15-60.32	1.01	15.87

*7 Year Price Score 126.72 *NYSE Composite Index=100 *12 Month Price Score 112.97

Interim Earnings (Per Share)

Qtr.	Sep	Dec	Mar	Jun
2004-05	0.74	0.94	0.77	0.89
2005-06	0.95	0.71	0.97	1.07
2006-07	1.17	1.09	1.19	1.23
2007-08	1.33	1.23	1.49	...

Interim Dividends (Per Share)

Amt	Decl	Ex	Rec	Pay
50%	08/16/2007	10/02/2007	09/17/2007	10/01/2007
0.21Q	10/24/2007	11/13/2007	11/15/2007	11/30/2007
0.21Q	01/25/2008	02/19/2008	02/21/2008	03/07/2008
0.21Q	04/17/2008	05/13/2008	05/15/2008	06/06/2008

Indicated Div: $0.84 (Div. Reinv. Plan)

Valuation Analysis

Forecast EPS $5.55 (05/17/2008)

Market Cap	$14.0 Billion	Book Value	5.1 Billion
Price/Book	2.73	Price/Sales	1.20

Dividend Achiever Status

10 Year Growth Rate	7.33%
Total Years of Dividend Growth	51

Business Summary: Metal Products (MIC: SIC: 3491 NAIC: 332911)

Parker-Hannifin is engaged as a manufacturer of motion control products, including fluid power systems, electromechanical controls and related components. Co. is also a producer of fluid purification, fluid and fuel control, process instrumentation, air conditioning, refrigeration, electromagnetic shielding as well as thermal management products and systems. Co.'s motion control technology is used in the products of its three key business segments: Industrial; Aerospace; and Climate & Industrial Controls. The products are sold as original and replacement equipment, and are marketed through direct-sales employees, independent distributors, sales representatives and builder/dealers.

Recent Developments: For the quarter ended Mar 31 2008, net income increased 22.0% to US$255.4 million from US$209.3 million in the year-earlier quarter. Revenues were US$3.18 billion, up 14.4% from US$2.78 billion the year before. Direct operating expenses rose 13.1% to US$2.45 billion from US$2.16 billion in the comparable period the year before. Indirect operating expenses increased 12.5% to US$347.0 million from US$308.6 million in the equivalent prior-year period.

Prospects: For the fiscal year ending June 2008, Co. raises its diluted earnings per share guidance to $5.40 to $5.60 from prior guidance of $5.15 to $5.40. Meanwhile, on Apr 30 2008, Co. acquired the residual stake in its joint venture, Parker Seal de Mexico, which provides Co. with greater access to Mexican sealing markets. Separately, on Apr 7 2008, Co. stated that it has acquired Vansco Electronics, a designer and manufacturer of electronic controls, displays and terminals, communication and operator interfaces, and sensors, which allows Co. to integrate motion control systems for mobile equipment. The purchase is expected to be accretive to Co.'s earnings in the first full-year of operations.

Financial Data

(US$ in Thousands)	9 Mos	6 Mos	3 Mos	06/30/2007	06/30/2006	06/30/2005	06/30/2004	06/30/2003
Earnings Per Share	5.26	4.97	4.84	4.67	3.71	3.35	1.94	1.12
Cash Flow Per Share	7.61	6.67	6.53	5.47	5.34	4.89	3.74	3.19
Tang Book Value Per Share	10.38	8.78	9.61	10.69	9.75	9.23	9.38	7.63
Dividends Per Share	0.803	0.767	0.730	0.693	0.613	0.520	0.507	0.493
Dividend Payout %	15.26	15.42	15.09	14.84	16.52	15.54	26.12	44.05
Income Statement								
Total Revenue	8,798,853	5,616,316	2,787,256	10,718,059	9,385,888	8,215,095	7,106,907	6,410,610
EBITDA	1,277,363	817,495	416,339	1,537,262	1,256,692	1,088,202	820,249	638,121
Depn & Amortn	231,680	155,146	76,176	294,566	280,971	264,699	252,785	259,178
Income Before Taxes	971,706	613,912	317,742	1,159,282	899,958	756,473	494,068	297,382
Income Taxes	274,805	172,452	88,145	329,236	261,682	208,500	148,285	101,110
Net Income	696,901	441,460	229,597	830,046	673,167	604,692	345,783	196,272
Average Shares	170,892	171,993	173,221	177,494	181,326	180,673	178,509	175,341
Balance Sheet								
Current Assets	3,872,174	3,621,580	3,524,424	3,386,175	3,138,978	2,785,872	2,536,933	2,396,807
Total Assets	9,609,177	9,217,506	8,692,993	8,441,413	8,173,432	6,898,961	6,256,904	5,985,633
Current Liabilities	2,487,286	2,496,498	2,244,939	1,925,245	1,681,105	1,335,927	1,259,741	1,423,727
Long-Term Obligations	1,189,736	1,151,469	1,117,677	1,089,916	1,059,461	938,424	953,804	966,332
Total Liabilities	4,490,184	4,440,270	4,146,865	3,729,748	3,932,229	3,558,814	3,274,450	3,464,722
Stockholders' Equity	5,118,993	4,777,236	4,546,128	4,711,665	4,241,203	3,340,147	2,982,454	2,520,911
Shares Outstanding	167,731	168,499	168,222	174,238	180,472	179,540	179,225	177,247
Statistical Record								
Return on Assets %	9.95	9.82	9.98	9.99	8.93	9.19	5.63	3.34
Return on Equity %	18.92	19.09	19.26	18.54	17.76	19.13	12.53	7.69
EBITDA Margin %	14.52	14.56	14.94	14.34	13.39	13.25	11.54	9.95
Net Margin %	7.92	7.86	8.24	7.74	7.17	7.36	4.87	3.06
Asset Turnover	1.27	1.28	1.29	1.29	1.25	1.25	1.16	1.09
Current Ratio	1.56	1.45	1.57	1.76	1.87	2.09	2.01	1.68
Debt to Equity	0.23	0.24	0.25	0.23	0.25	0.28	0.32	0.38
Price Range	86.15-57.61	86.15-50.79	76.80-50.79	68.39-46.50	57.34-40.53	51.87-35.71	40.61-27.81	32.53-23.10
P/E Ratio	16.38-10.95	17.33-10.22	15.87-10.49	14.65-9.96	15.46-10.93	15.48-10.66	20.93-14.33	29.05-20.63
Average Yield %	1.17	1.15	1.21	1.25	1.28	1.22	1.43	1.77

Address: 6035 Parkland Boulevard, Cleveland, OH 44124-4141 **Telephone:** 216-896-3000 **Web Site:** www.parker.com	Officers: Donald E. Washkewicz - Chairman, President, Chief Executive Officer Timothy K. Pistell - Executive Vice President, Chief Financial Officer **Transfer Agents:** National City Bank, Cleveland, OH	**Investor Contact:** 216-896-2240 **No of Institutions:** 561 **Shares:** 151,183,728 **% Held:** 83.16

PAYCHEX INC

Exchange	Symbol	Price	52Wk Range	Yield	P/E
NMS	PAYX	$35.01 (5/29/2008)	46.31-30.48	3.43	23.19

*7 Year Price Score 84.29   *NYSE Composite Index=100   *12 Month Price Score 96.05

Interim Earnings (Per Share)
Qtr.	Aug	Nov	Feb	May
2004-05	0.23	0.23	0.24	0.27
2005-06	0.30	0.30	0.30	0.32
2006-07	0.35	0.35	0.33	0.32
2007-08	0.40	0.40	0.39	...

Interim Dividends (Per Share)
Amt	Decl	Ex	Rec	Pay
0.30Q	07/12/2007	07/30/2007	08/01/2007	08/15/2007
0.30Q	10/03/2007	10/30/2007	11/01/2007	11/15/2007
0.30Q	01/11/2008	01/30/2008	02/01/2008	02/15/2008
0.30Q	04/10/2008	04/29/2008	05/01/2008	05/15/2008

Indicated Div: $1.20 (Div. Reinv. Plan)

Valuation Analysis
Forecast EPS	$1.57 (05/17/2008)		
Market Cap	$12.6 Billion	Book Value	1.2 Billion
Price/Book	10.95	Price/Sales	6.22

Dividend Achiever Status
10 Year Growth Rate	28.99%
Total Years of Dividend Growth	19

Business Summary: Accounting & Management Consulting Services (MIC: SIC: 8721 NAIC: 541214)

Paychex is a provider of payroll and integrated human resource and employee benefits outsourcing services for small- to medium-sized businesses in the U.S. Co.'s services and products include: payroll processing; payroll tax administration services; employee payment services; regulatory compliance services; human resource outsourcing services; retirement services administration; workers' compensation insurance services; health and benefits services; employee benefits administration; time and attendance services; and other human resource services and products. As of May 31 2007, Co. serviced approximately 561,000 clients through more than 100 offices nationwide.

Recent Developments: For the quarter ended Feb 29 2008, net income increased 12.5% to US$142.5 million from US$126.6 million in the year-earlier quarter. Revenues were US$532.2 million, up 9.7% from US$485.3 million the year before. Operating income was US$210.4 million versus US$173.0 million in the prior-year quarter, an increase of 21.6%. Indirect operating expenses increased 3.0% to US$321.8 million from US$312.3 million in the equivalent prior-year period.

Prospects: For the fiscal year ending May 31 2008, Co. is revising its expectations to reflect the existing Federal Funds rate and economic conditions. Specifically, Co. now anticipates total revenue growth in the range of 9.0% to 11.0% and is projecting total service revenue to improve by 10.0% to 12.0%. Similarly, Co. foresees payroll service revenue to grow by about 8.0% to 9.0%, while human resource services revenue is estimated to grow by 19.0% to 22.0%. However, Co. anticipates interest on funds held for clients to be down 5.0% to relatively flat and is forecasting corporate investment income to decline by 35.0% to 40.0%. Lastly, Co. is targeting net income to improve by about 11.0% to 13.0%.

Financial Data
(US$ in Thousands)	9 Mos	6 Mos	3 Mos	05/31/2007	05/31/2006	05/31/2005	05/31/2004	05/31/2003
Earnings Per Share	1.51	1.45	1.40	1.35	1.22	0.97	0.80	0.78
Cash Flow Per Share	1.91	1.92	1.80	1.66	1.50	1.24	1.03	0.99
Tang Book Value Per Share	1.78	2.04	3.04	3.87	3.12	2.40	1.88	1.55
Dividends Per Share	1.110	1.020	0.930	0.790	0.610	0.510	0.470	0.440
Dividend Payout %	73.68	70.34	66.43	58.52	50.00	52.58	58.75	56.41
Income Statement								
Total Revenue	1,547,095	1,014,923	507,130	1,886,964	1,674,596	1,445,143	1,294,347	1,099,079
EBITDA	711,860	477,804	241,790	798,534	743,985	625,630	516,106	465,596
Depn & Amortn	58,060	38,000	18,965	96,988	94,414	91,855	82,791	64,555
Income Before Taxes	653,800	439,804	222,825	743,269	674,766	546,166	449,784	431,544
Income Taxes	213,139	141,617	71,750	227,822	209,852	177,317	146,834	138,092
Net Income	440,661	298,187	151,075	515,447	464,914	368,849	302,950	293,452
Average Shares	361,770	371,404	382,255	382,802	381,351	379,763	379,524	378,083
Balance Sheet								
Current Assets	5,048,274	4,229,604	4,259,861	4,861,319	4,444,301	3,689,070	3,280,447	3,032,642
Total Assets	5,872,015	5,026,355	5,557,937	6,246,519	5,549,302	4,379,116	3,950,203	3,690,783
Current Liabilities	4,647,850	3,711,740	3,845,490	4,237,470	3,838,372	2,941,824	2,721,903	2,587,525
Total Liabilities	4,720,024	3,781,944	3,913,815	4,294,271	3,894,459	2,993,441	2,750,230	2,613,412
Stockholders' Equity	1,151,991	1,244,411	1,644,122	1,952,248	1,654,843	1,385,675	1,199,973	1,077,371
Shares Outstanding	360,358	363,673	374,716	382,151	380,303	378,629	377,968	376,698
Statistical Record								
Return on Assets %	9.63	10.02	9.31	8.74	9.37	8.86	7.91	8.83
Return on Equity %	36.69	35.54	31.36	28.58	30.58	28.53	26.53	29.33
EBITDA Margin %	46.01	47.08	47.68	42.32	44.43	43.29	39.87	42.36
Net Margin %	28.48	29.38	29.79	27.32	27.76	25.52	23.41	26.70
Asset Turnover	0.35	0.36	0.34	0.32	0.34	0.35	0.34	0.33
Current Ratio	1.09	1.14	1.11	1.15	1.16	1.25	1.21	1.17
Price Range	46.31-31.46	46.31-36.25	46.31-34.92	42.38-33.19	43.18-28.88	38.84-28.88	40.14-28.52	35.00-20.55
P/E Ratio	30.67-20.83	31.94-25.00	33.08-24.94	31.39-24.59	35.39-23.67	40.04-29.77	50.17-35.65	44.87-26.35
Average Yield %	2.82	2.51	2.34	2.06	1.63	1.60	1.33	1.61

Address: 911 Panorama Trail South, Rochester, NY 14625-2396	Officers: B. Thomas Golisano - Chairman Jonathan J.	Investor Contact: 585-383-3406
Telephone: 585-385-6666	Judge - President, Chief Executive Officer **Transfer**	**No of Institutions:** 627
Web Site: www.paychex.com	**Agents:** American Stock Transfer & Trust Co., Brooklyn, NY	**Shares:** 313,134,048 **% Held:** 68.52

PENTAIR, INC.

Exchange	Symbol	Price	52Wk Range	Yield	P/E
NYS	PNR	$37.39 (5/29/2008)	39.21-27.78	1.82	17.55

*7 Year Price Score 92.60 *NYSE Composite Index=100 ***12 Month Price Score 105.49**

TRADING VOLUME (thousand shares)

Interim Earnings (Per Share)
Qtr.	Mar	Jun	Sep	Dec
2005	0.42	0.63	0.46	0.29
2006	0.41	0.67	0.34	0.39
2007	0.42	0.62	0.58	0.48
2008	0.45	...	...	...

Interim Dividends (Per Share)
Amt	Decl	Ex	Rec	Pay
0.15Q	07/13/2007	07/25/2007	07/27/2007	08/10/2007
0.15Q	10/12/2007	10/24/2007	10/26/2007	11/09/2007
0.17Q	01/14/2008	01/23/2008	01/25/2008	02/08/2008
0.17Q	04/11/2008	04/23/2008	04/25/2008	05/09/2008

Indicated Div: $0.68 (Div. Reinv. Plan)

Valuation Analysis
Forecast EPS $2.35 (05/16/2008)

Market Cap	$3.7 Billion	Book Value	2.0 Billion
Price/Book	1.88	Price/Sales	1.08

Dividend Achiever Status
10 Year Growth Rate	8.31%
Total Years of Dividend Growth	31

Business Summary: Industrial Machinery and Equipment (MIC: SIC: 3553 NAIC: 333210)

Pentair is an industrial manufacturing company comprised of two operating segments: Water and Technical Products. Co.'s Water Group is engaged in providing products and systems used in the movement, storage, and treatment of water. Co.'s Technical Products Group is engaged in designing and manufacturing standard, modified and custom enclosures that house and protect sensitive electronics and electrical components; thermal management products; and accessories. As of Dec 31 2007, Co.'s primary brand names for its Technical Products Group are: Hoffman®, Schroff®, Pentair Electronic Packaging®, Taunus®, McLean®, Electronic Solutions®, Birtcher®, Calmark® and Aspen Motion®.

Recent Developments: For the quarter ended Mar 29 2008, income from continuing operations increased 23.5% to US$52.6 million from US$42.6 million in the year-earlier quarter. Net income increased 4.8% to US$44.3 million from US$42.3 million in the year-earlier quarter. Revenues were US$840.4 million, up 6.0% from US$792.8 million the year before. Operating income was US$96.8 million versus US$81.5 million in the prior-year quarter, an increase of 18.8%. Direct operating expenses rose 5.8% to US$589.1 million from US$556.9 million in the comparable period the year before. Indirect expenses increased 0.1% to US$154.5 million from US$154.4 million in the equivalent prior-year period.

Prospects: For 2008, Co. has raised its guidance and now anticipates growth in its earnings from continuing operations between 10% and 14% to $2.30 to $2.40 per share from prior guidance of $2.25 to $2.40 per share, as it expects continued favorable performance in its international and Technical Products businesses. This guidance is based on several assumptions including, modest organic growth in the low single digits, such as some price and product mix improvements, which bring its 2008 revenues to $3.50 billion, and its expectation that its manufacturing productivity initiatives, mainly its materials sourcing programs, will improve through its lean enterprise initiatives and higher unit volumes.

Financial Data
(US$ in Thousands)	3 Mos	12/31/2007	12/31/2006	12/31/2005	12/31/2004	12/31/2003	12/31/2002	12/31/2001
Earnings Per Share	2.13	2.10	1.81	1.80	1.68	1.42	1.30	0.34
Cash Flow Per Share	3.34	3.46	2.32	2.46	2.65	2.69	2.75	2.37
Dividends Per Share	0.620	0.600	0.560	0.522	0.430	0.410	0.370	0.350
Dividend Payout %	29.04	28.57	30.94	29.03	25.60	28.87	28.35	104.48
Income Statement								
Total Revenue	840,404	3,398,698	3,154,469	2,946,579	2,278,129	2,724,365	2,580,783	2,615,944
EBITDA	117,518	458,429	382,446	401,067	308,151	325,197	300,694	259,125
Depn & Amortn	21,616	84,549	75,096	72,560	60,909	65,643	64,702	104,349
Income Before Taxes	79,814	303,643	255,469	283,518	210,032	218,618	192,447	93,288
Income Taxes	27,170	93,154	71,702	98,469	73,000	74,330	62,545	35,772
Net Income	44,290	210,927	183,731	185,049	171,225	141,352	129,902	32,869
Average Shares	99,558	100,205	101,371	102,618	101,706	99,620	99,488	98,594
Balance Sheet								
Current Assets	1,192,568	1,038,021	957,628	895,024	825,137	829,451	810,808	835,603
Total Assets	4,170,388	4,000,614	3,364,979	3,253,755	3,120,575	2,780,677	2,514,450	2,372,198
Current Liabilities	575,227	560,906	521,282	524,670	526,879	497,451	476,200	428,433
Long-Term Obligations	1,119,105	1,042,223	721,873	748,477	724,148	732,862	673,911	714,977
Total Liabilities	2,196,168	2,089,743	1,694,980	1,698,145	1,672,781	1,519,199	1,408,726	1,357,196
Stockholders' Equity	1,974,220	1,910,871	1,669,999	1,555,610	1,447,794	1,261,478	1,105,724	1,015,002
Shares Outstanding	99,090	99,221	99,777	101,202	100,967	99,005	98,444	98,221
Statistical Record								
Return on Assets %	5.40	5.73	5.55	5.81	5.79	5.34	5.32	1.31
Return on Equity %	11.60	11.78	11.39	12.32	12.61	11.94	12.25	3.25
EBITDA Margin %	13.98	13.49	12.12	13.61	13.53	11.94	11.65	9.91
Net Margin %	5.27	6.21	5.82	6.28	7.52	5.19	5.03	1.26
Asset Turnover	0.87	0.92	0.95	0.92	0.77	1.03	1.06	1.04
Current Ratio	2.07	1.85	1.84	1.71	1.57	1.67	1.70	1.95
Debt to Equity	0.57	0.55	0.43	0.48	0.50	0.58	0.61	0.70
Price Range	39.21-27.78	39.21-29.50	41.69-26.13	46.03-30.80	44.03-22.52	23.29-16.40	24.81-14.67	19.64-11.25
P/E Ratio	18.41-13.04	18.67-14.05	23.03-14.44	25.57-17.11	26.21-13.40	16.40-11.55	19.08-11.28	57.76-33.09
Average Yield %	1.81	1.77	1.65	1.32	1.35	2.09	1.85	2.19

Address: 5500 Wayzata Boulevard, Suite 800, Golden Valley, MN 55416-1261 **Telephone:** 763-545-1730 **Web Site:** www.pentair.com	**Officers:** Randall J. Hogan - Chairman, Chief Executive Officer Michael V. Schrock - President, Chief Operating Officer **Transfer Agents:** Wells Fargo Bank, N.A	**Investor Contact:** 651-639-5278 **No of Institutions:** 303 **Shares:** 88,564,888 **% Held:** 82.58

PEOPLES BANCORP, INC. (MARIETTA, OH)

Exchange	Symbol	Price	52Wk Range	Yield	P/E
NMS	PEBO	$24.55 (5/29/2008)	28.00-20.69	3.75	13.95

*7 Year Price Score 74.79 ***NYSE Composite Index=100** ***12 Month Price Score 99.92**

TRADING VOLUME (thousand shares)

Interim Earnings (Per Share)

Qtr.	Mar	Jun	Sep	Dec
2005	0.44	0.50	0.50	0.50
2006	0.56	0.52	0.50	0.44
2007	0.53	0.51	0.49	0.22
2008	0.55	...	...	...

Interim Dividends (Per Share)

Amt	Decl	Ex	Rec	Pay
0.22Q	08/09/2007	09/13/2007	09/17/2007	10/01/2007
0.22Q	11/08/2007	12/13/2007	12/17/2007	01/02/2008
0.22Q	02/14/2008	03/13/2008	03/17/2008	04/01/2008
0.23Q	05/08/2008	06/12/2008	06/16/2008	07/01/2008

Indicated Div: $0.92

Valuation Analysis

Forecast EPS	$2.02 (05/16/2008)		
Market Cap	$252.8 Million	Book Value	207.4 Million
Price/Book	1.22	Price/Sales	1.84

Dividend Achiever Status

10 Year Growth Rate	10.79%
Total Years of Dividend Growth	42

Business Summary: Commercial Banking (MIC: SIC: 6021 NAIC: 522110)

Peoples Bancorp is a finance holding company. Through its main operating subsidiary, Co. provides a range of financial products and services to its customers, including interest-bearing and non-interest-bearing demand deposit accounts, savings and money market accounts, certificates of deposit, commercial, consumer, and real estate mortgage loans, credit and debit cards, corporate and personal trust services, and safe deposit rental facilities. Co. also provides a range of life, health, property and casualty insurance products and provides custom-tailored applications for asset management needs. As of Dec 31 2007, Co. had total assets of $1.89 billion and total deposits of $1.19 billion.

Recent Developments: For the quarter ended Mar 31 2008, net income was unchanged at US$5.6 million versus US$5.6 million the year-earlier quarter. Net interest income increased 5.7% to US$14.3 million from US$13.5 million in the year-earlier quarter. Provision for loan losses was US$1.4 million versus US$623,000 in the prior-year quarter, an increase of 130.7%. Non-interest income rose 4.9% to US$8.5 million from US$8.1 million, while non-interest expense advanced 3.0% to US$13.7 million.

Prospects: Despite further deterioration of economic conditions, Co. remains focused on earnings quality and conservative growth in 2008. However, Co.'s ongoing focus on loan quality, coupled with the possibility of additional payoffs, is expected to restrain loan growth in the near-term. Further, Co. believes it will experience even more competitive loan and deposit pricing, and an increase in demand from customers to refinance existing loans to lower rates, due to the magnitude of the interest rate cuts and the expectation of further reductions in the near term. Co. also expects non-interest expenses to increase 3.0% to 5.0%, partly due to expenses related to the new office in Huntington, WV.

Financial Data
(US$ in Thousands)

	3 Mos	12/31/2007	12/31/2006	12/31/2005	12/31/2004	12/31/2003	12/31/2002	12/31/2001
Earnings Per Share	1.76	1.74	2.01	1.94	1.71	1.52	2.19	1.47
Cash Flow Per Share	3.33	2.95	2.92	3.06	3.11	2.71	3.03	2.73
Tang Book Value Per Share	13.58	13.09	12.05	10.82	10.00	11.52	11.85	11.43
Dividends Per Share	0.880	0.880	0.830	0.780	0.720	0.645	0.601	0.488
Dividend Payout %	49.88	50.57	41.29	40.21	42.11	42.45	27.43	33.15
Income Statement								
Interest Income	27,299	113,419	108,794	95,775	87,030	91,655	82,968	86,107
Interest Expense	13,013	59,498	55,577	43,469	35,160	38,050	32,970	42,974
Net Interest Income	14,286	53,921	53,217	52,306	51,870	53,605	49,998	43,133
Provision for Losses	1,437	3,959	3,622	2,028	2,546	3,601	4,067	2,659
Non-Interest Income	8,527	25,364	31,125	29,167	22,208	17,538	15,236	10,650
Non-Interest Expense	13,742	51,452	51,297	51,342	47,198	45,903	35,967	33,412
Income Before Taxes	7,634	23,874	29,423	28,103	24,334	21,639	25,200	17,712
Income Taxes	1,986	5,560	7,865	7,604	6,059	5,385	6,858	5,377
Net Income	5,648	18,314	21,558	20,499	18,275	16,254	18,752	12,335
Average Shares	10,345	10,529	10,723	10,581	10,710	10,660	8,557	8,403
Balance Sheet								
Net Loans & Leases	1,100,599	1,107,217	1,118,926	1,058,259	1,008,910	903,270	837,805	760,499
Total Assets	1,891,438	1,885,553	1,875,255	1,855,277	1,809,086	1,736,104	1,394,361	1,193,966
Total Deposits	1,248,991	1,186,377	1,233,529	1,089,286	1,069,421	1,028,530	955,877	814,368
Total Liabilities	1,684,017	1,682,717	1,678,086	1,672,200	1,633,668	1,565,224	1,218,088	1,071,056
Stockholders' Equity	207,421	202,836	197,169	183,077	175,418	170,880	147,183	93,854
Shares Outstanding	10,295	10,296	10,651	10,518	10,435	10,603	9,829	8,213
Statistical Record								
Return on Assets %	0.97	0.97	1.16	1.12	1.03	1.04	1.45	1.06
Return on Equity %	9.00	9.16	11.34	11.44	10.53	10.22	15.56	13.93
Net Interest Margin %	52.33	47.54	48.92	54.61	59.60	58.49	60.26	50.09
Efficiency Ratio %	38.36	37.07	36.66	41.09	43.21	42.04	36.62	34.53
Loans to Deposits	0.88	0.93	0.91	0.97	0.94	0.88	0.88	0.93
Price Range	28.00-20.69	30.30-21.68	31.45-27.28	30.50-24.99	32.12-23.47	30.10-19.68	29.56-15.84	20.09-12.59
P/E Ratio	15.91-11.76	17.41-12.46	15.65-13.57	15.72-12.88	18.78-13.73	19.80-12.95	13.50-7.23	13.66-8.57
Average Yield %	3.51	3.35	2.82	2.83	2.66	2.57	2.56	3.21

Address: 138 Putnam Street, P.O. Box 738, Marietta, OH 45750-0738 Telephone: 740-373-3155 Web Site: www.peoplesbancorp.com	Officers: Joseph H. Wesel - Chairman Paul T. Theisen - Vice-Chairman Transfer Agents: Shareowner Services, St. Paul, MN	Investor Contact: 740-374-6136 No of Institutions: 83 Shares: 5,526,250 % Held: 52.20

PEPSICO INC.

Exchange	Symbol	Price	52Wk Range	Yield	P/E
NYS	PEP	$68.83 (5/29/2008)	79.57-64.65	2.47	19.78

*7 Year Price Score 99.84   *NYSE Composite Index=100   *12 Month Price Score 99.96

Interim Earnings (Per Share)

Qtr.	Mar	Jun	Aug	Dec
2005	0.53	0.70	0.51	0.65
2006	0.60	0.80	0.88	1.06
2007	0.65	0.94	1.06	0.77
2008	0.70	...	...	...

Interim Dividends (Per Share)

Amt	Decl	Ex	Rec	Pay
0.375Q	07/19/2007	09/05/2007	09/07/2007	09/28/2007
0.375Q	11/16/2007	12/05/2007	12/07/2007	01/02/2008
0.375Q	02/01/2008	03/05/2008	03/07/2008	03/31/2008
0.425Q	05/07/2008	06/04/2008	06/06/2008	06/30/2008

Indicated Div: $1.70 (Div. Reinv. Plan)

Valuation Analysis

Forecast EPS $3.74 (05/17/2008)

Market Cap	$109.4 Billion	Book Value	16.8 Billion
Price/Book	6.51	Price/Sales	2.70

Dividend Achiever Status

10 Year Growth Rate	10.89%
Total Years of Dividend Growth	36

Business Summary: Food (MIC: SIC: 2086 NAIC: 312111)

PepsiCo is engaged in manufacturing, marketing and selling a range of salty, sweet and grain-based snacks as well as carbonated and non-carbonated beverages and foods. Co. is organized into four divisions: Frito-Lay North America (FLNA); PepsiCo Beverages North America (PBNA); PepsiCo International (PI); and Quaker Foods North America (QFNA). FLNA branded snacks include Lay's potato chips, Doritos tortilla chips and Rold Gold pretzels. PBNA's brands include Pepsi, Mountain Dew, Gatorade, Tropicana Pure Premium, and Dole. PI's brands include Lay's, Walkers, Cheetos, Doritos, Ruffles, Gamesa and Sabritas. QFNA's brands include Quaker oatmeal, Rice-A-Roni and Near East side dishes.

Recent Developments: For the quarter ended Mar 22 2008, net income increased 4.7% to US$1.15 billion from US$1.10 billion in the year-earlier quarter. Revenues were US$8.33 billion, up 13.4% from US$7.35 billion the year before. Operating income was US$1.55 billion versus US$1.42 billion in the prior-year quarter, an increase of 9.4%. Direct operating expenses rose 16.7% to US$3.83 billion from US$3.29 billion in the comparable period the year before. Indirect operating expenses increased 11.3% to US$2.95 billion from US$2.65 billion in the equivalent prior-year period.

Prospects: For full-year 2008, Co. expects 3.0% to 5.0% volume growth, high-single-digit net revenue growth and earnings per share of at least $3.72. Meanwhile, on May 6 2008, The Pepsi Bottling Group, Inc. and Co. announced that, through their PR Beverages Limited joint venture in Russia, they have completed their acquisition of Sobol-Aqua JSC, a beverage manufacturing company based in Novosibirsk, Russia. Separately, on Apr 30 2008, Co. announced the acquisition of V Water, a vitamin water brand in the U.K. This acquisition reflects Co.'s strategy to transforming its portfolio of products and extending its range of healthier beverages, and should provide Co. with significant opportunities.

Financial Data
(US$ in Thousands)

	3 Mos	12/29/2007	12/30/2006	12/31/2005	12/25/2004	12/27/2003	12/28/2002	12/29/2001
Earnings Per Share	3.48	3.41	3.34	2.39	2.44	2.05	1.85	1.47
Cash Flow Per Share	4.27	4.29	3.70	3.45	2.99	2.53	2.65	2.39
Tang Book Value Per Share	6.01	6.30	5.50	5.20	4.84	3.82	4.93	2.17
Dividends Per Share	1.500	1.425	1.160	1.010	0.850	0.630	0.595	0.575
Dividend Payout %	43.10	41.79	34.73	42.26	34.84	30.73	32.16	39.12
Income Statement								
Total Revenue	8,333,000	39,474,000	35,137,000	32,562,000	29,261,000	26,971,000	25,112,000	26,935,000
EBITDA	1,926,000	9,092,000	8,399,000	7,732,000	6,848,000	6,269,000	6,077,000	5,189,000
Depn & Amortn	303,000	1,362,000	1,344,000	1,253,000	1,209,000	1,165,000	1,067,000	1,008,000
Income Before Taxes	1,566,000	7,631,000	6,989,000	6,382,000	5,546,000	4,992,000	4,868,000	4,029,000
Income Taxes	418,000	1,973,000	1,347,000	2,304,000	1,372,000	1,424,000	1,555,000	1,367,000
Net Income	1,148,000	5,658,000	5,642,000	4,078,000	4,212,000	3,568,000	3,313,000	2,662,000
Average Shares	1,632,000	1,658,000	1,687,000	1,706,000	1,729,000	1,739,000	1,789,000	1,807,000
Balance Sheet								
Current Assets	11,065,000	10,151,000	9,130,000	10,454,000	8,639,000	6,930,000	6,413,000	5,853,000
Total Assets	35,699,000	34,628,000	29,930,000	31,727,000	27,987,000	25,327,000	23,474,000	21,695,000
Current Liabilities	8,587,000	7,753,000	6,860,000	9,406,000	6,752,000	6,415,000	6,052,000	4,998,000
Long-Term Obligations	4,884,000	4,203,000	2,550,000	2,313,000	2,397,000	1,702,000	2,187,000	2,651,000
Total Liabilities	18,985,000	17,394,000	14,562,000	17,476,000	14,464,000	13,453,000	14,183,000	13,021,000
Stockholders' Equity	16,806,000	17,325,000	15,447,000	14,320,000	13,572,000	11,896,000	9,298,000	8,648,000
Shares Outstanding	1,590,000	1,605,000	1,638,000	1,656,000	1,679,000	1,705,000	1,722,000	1,756,000
Statistical Record								
Return on Assets %	17.47	17.58	18.35	13.44	15.84	14.66	14.71	13.34
Return on Equity %	35.51	34.62	38.01	28.77	33.17	33.76	37.02	33.58
EBITDA Margin %	23.11	23.03	23.90	23.75	23.40	23.24	24.20	19.26
Net Margin %	13.78	14.33	16.06	12.52	14.39	13.23	13.19	9.88
Asset Turnover	1.24	1.23	1.14	1.07	1.10	1.11	1.11	1.35
Current Ratio	1.29	1.31	1.33	1.11	1.28	1.08	1.06	1.17
Debt to Equity	0.29	0.24	0.17	0.16	0.18	0.14	0.24	0.31
Price Range	79.57-62.89	78.69-62.16	65.91-56.77	59.90-51.57	55.55-45.39	48.71-37.30	53.12-35.50	50.28-41.26
P/E Ratio	22.86-18.07	23.08-18.23	19.73-17.00	25.06-21.58	22.77-18.60	23.76-18.20	28.71-19.19	34.20-28.07
Average Yield %	2.11	2.09	1.90	1.82	1.66	1.43	1.29	1.25

Address: 700 Anderson Hill Road, Purchase, NY 10577-1444	**Officers:** Indra K. Nooyi - Chairman, President, Chief Executive Officer Michael D. White - Vice-Chairman	**Investor Contact:** 914-253-3035
Telephone: 914-253-2000	**Transfer Agents:** The Bank of New York	**No of Institutions:** 1555
Web Site: www.pepsico.com		**Shares:** 1,260,148,608 **% Held:** 66.57

PFIZER INC

Exchange	Symbol	Price	52Wk Range	Yield	P/E
NYS	PFE	$19.40 (5/29/2008)	27.68-19.30	6.60	17.64

*7 Year Price Score 60.29   *NYSE Composite Index=100   *12 Month Price Score 89.19

Interim Earnings (Per Share)

Qtr.	Mar	Jun	Sep	Dec
2005	0.04	0.47	0.22	0.37
2006	0.56	0.33	0.46	1.31
2007	0.48	0.18	0.11	0.39
2008	0.41	...	...	...

Interim Dividends (Per Share)

Amt	Decl	Ex	Rec	Pay
0.29Q	06/28/2007	08/08/2007	08/10/2007	09/05/2007
0.29Q	10/25/2007	11/07/2007	11/09/2007	12/04/2007
0.32Q	12/17/2007	02/06/2008	02/08/2008	03/04/2008
0.32Q	04/24/2008	05/07/2008	05/09/2008	06/03/2008

Indicated Div: $1.28 (Div. Reinv. Plan)

Valuation Analysis

Forecast EPS $2.35 (05/17/2008)

Market Cap	$131.2 Billion	Book Value	67.4 Billion
Price/Book	1.95	Price/Sales	2.74

Dividend Achiever Status

10 Year Growth Rate	17.74%
Total Years of Dividend Growth	40

TRADING VOLUME (thousand shares)

Business Summary: Pharmaceuticals (MIC: SIC: 2834 NAIC: 325412)

Pfizer discovers, develops, produces and markets prescription medicines for humans and animals. Co. has two segments: Pharmaceutical, which develops and produces products that treat cardiovascular and metabolic diseases, central nervous system disorders, arthritis and pain, infectious and respiratory diseases, urology, oncology, ophthalmology, and endocrine disorders; and Animal Health, which discovers, develops and sells products for the prevention and treatment of diseases in livestock and companion animals. Co. also operates several other businesses, such as the manufacture of gelatin capsules, contract manufacturing and bulk pharmaceutical chemicals.

Recent Developments: For the quarter ended Mar 30 2008, income from continuing operations decreased 17.0% to US$2.79 billion from US$3.36 billion in the year-earlier quarter. Net income decreased 17.9% to US$2.78 billion from US$3.39 billion in the year-earlier quarter. Revenues were US$11.85 billion, down 5.0% from US$12.47 billion the year before. Direct operating expenses rose 5.2% to US$1.99 billion from US$1.89 billion in the comparable period the year before. Indirect operating expenses decreased 4.3% to US$6.64 billion from US$6.94 billion in the equivalent prior-year period.

Prospects: For 2008, Co. forecasts revenues of $47.00 billion to $49.00 billion and reported diluted earnings per common share of $1.73 to $1.88. Separately, on Apr 23 2008, Co. announced an agreement to acquire animal health product lines from Schering-Plough Corporation for sale in the European Economic Area in the several categories, including swine escherichia coli vaccines, equine influenza and tetanus vaccines, ruminant neonatal and clostridia vaccines, rabies vaccines, and parasiticides and anti-inflammatories. Meanwhile, in Apr 2008, Co. completed a tender offer and acquired 85.0% of the outstanding shares of Encysive Pharmaceuticals Inc., a biopharmaceutical company, for $200.0 million.

Financial Data

(US$ in Thousands)	3 Mos	12/31/2007	12/31/2006	12/31/2005	12/31/2004	12/31/2003	12/31/2002	12/31/2001
Earnings Per Share	1.10	1.17	2.66	1.09	1.49	0.54	1.46	1.22
Cash Flow Per Share	2.28	1.93	2.43	2.00	2.16	1.63	1.60	1.49
Tang Book Value Per Share	3.83	3.41	3.65	1.89	1.48	0.85	3.04	2.64
Dividends Per Share	1.190	1.160	0.960	0.760	0.680	0.600	0.520	0.440
Dividend Payout %	108.65	99.15	36.09	69.72	45.64	111.11	35.62	36.07
Income Statement								
Total Revenue	11,848,000	48,418,000	48,371,000	51,298,000	52,516,000	45,188,000	32,373,000	32,259,000
EBITDA	5,044,000	13,379,000	17,884,000	16,841,000	19,101,000	7,265,000	12,701,000	11,124,000
Depn & Amortn	1,487,000	5,200,000	5,293,000	5,576,000	5,093,000	4,078,000	1,036,000	1,068,000
Income Before Taxes	3,557,000	9,278,000	13,028,000	11,534,000	14,007,000	3,263,000	11,796,000	10,329,000
Income Taxes	763,000	1,023,000	1,992,000	3,424,000	2,665,000	1,621,000	2,609,000	2,561,000
Net Income	2,784,000	8,144,000	19,337,000	8,085,000	11,361,000	3,910,000	9,126,000	7,788,000
Average Shares	6,762,001	6,939,001	7,274,001	7,411,001	7,614,001	7,286,001	6,240,999	6,360,999
Balance Sheet								
Current Assets	51,011,000	46,849,000	46,949,000	41,896,000	39,694,000	29,741,000	24,781,000	18,450,000
Total Assets	118,550,000	115,268,000	114,837,000	117,565,000	123,684,000	116,775,000	46,356,000	39,153,000
Current Liabilities	21,682,000	21,835,000	21,389,000	28,448,000	26,458,000	23,657,000	18,555,000	13,640,000
Long-Term Obligations	8,143,000	7,314,000	5,546,000	6,347,000	7,279,000	5,755,000	3,140,000	2,609,000
Total Liabilities	50,990,000	50,144,000	43,479,000	51,938,000	55,406,000	51,398,000	26,406,000	20,860,000
Stockholders' Equity	67,417,000	65,010,000	71,358,000	65,627,000	68,278,000	65,377,000	19,950,000	18,293,000
Shares Outstanding	6,765,198	6,761,001	7,124,001	7,361,001	7,473,001	7,629,001	6,161,999	6,276,999
Statistical Record								
Return on Assets %	6.61	7.08	16.64	6.70	9.42	4.79	21.35	21.44
Return on Equity %	10.83	11.94	28.23	12.08	16.95	9.16	47.73	45.32
EBITDA Margin %	42.57	27.63	36.97	32.83	36.37	16.08	39.23	34.48
Net Margin %	23.50	16.82	39.98	15.76	21.63	8.65	28.19	24.14
Asset Turnover	0.42	0.42	0.42	0.43	0.44	0.55	0.76	0.89
Current Ratio	2.35	2.15	2.20	1.47	1.50	1.26	1.34	1.35
Debt to Equity	0.12	0.11	0.08	0.10	0.11	0.09	0.16	0.14
Price Range	27.68-20.50	27.68-22.30	28.47-22.41	28.90-20.60	38.85-24.29	36.18-28.56	42.15-25.92	46.13-35.67
P/E Ratio	25.16-18.64	23.66-19.06	10.70-8.42	26.51-18.90	26.07-16.30	67.00-52.89	28.87-17.75	37.81-29.24
Average Yield %	4.88	4.59	3.74	2.97	2.06	1.88	1.49	1.06

Address: 235 East 42nd Street, New York, NY 10017-5755 Telephone: 212-573-2323 Web Site: www.pfizer.com	Officers: Jeffrey B. Kindler - Chairman, Chief Executive Officer Frank A. D'Amelio - Senior Vice President, Chief Financial Officer **Transfer Agents:** EquiServe Trust Company, N.A., Jersey City, NJ	No of Institutions: 1640 Shares: 5,081,996,800 % Held: 68.66

PIEDMONT NATURAL GAS CO., INC.

Exchange	Symbol	Price	52Wk Range	Yield	P/E
NYS	PNY	$27.11 (5/29/2008)	27.76-23.19	3.84	17.49

*7 Year Price Score 90.83 *NYSE Composite Index=100 *12 Month Price Score 106.46

Interim Earnings (Per Share)

Qtr.	Jan	Apr	Jul	Oct
2004-05	0.93	0.52	(0.06)	(0.06)
2005-06	0.94	0.57	(0.16)	(0.08)
2006-07	0.94	0.69	(0.12)	(0.11)
2007-08	1.12	0.00	...	...

Interim Dividends (Per Share)

Amt	Decl	Ex	Rec	Pay
0.25Q	09/10/2007	09/20/2007	09/24/2007	10/15/2007
0.25Q	12/13/2007	12/20/2007	12/24/2007	01/15/2008
0.26Q	03/06/2008	03/20/2008	03/25/2008	04/15/2008
0.26Q	06/06/2008	06/23/2008	06/25/2008	07/15/2008

Indicated Div: $1.04 (Div. Reinv. Plan)

Valuation Analysis

Forecast EPS $1.51 (05/16/2008)
Market Cap $2.0 Billion   Book Value 951.1 Million
Price/Book 2.09   Price/Sales 1.04

Dividend Achiever Status

10 Year Growth Rate   5.09%
Total Years of Dividend Growth   28

Business Summary: Gas Utilities (MIC: SIC: 4924 NAIC: 221210)

Piedmont Natural Gas Company is an energy services company primarily engaged in the distribution of natural gas to over 1.0 million residential, commercial and industrial customers in portions of North Carolina, South Carolina and Tennessee, including 62,000 customers served by municipalities who are Co.'s wholesale customers. Co. is also engaged in investing in joint venture, and energy-related businesses, including unregulated retail natural gas marketing, interstate natural gas storage and intrastate natural gas transportation. As of Oct 31 2007, Co. operated through two business segments, regulated utility and non-utility activities, both of which were conducted in the U.S.

Recent Developments: For the quarter ended Apr 30 2008, net income decreased 4.9% to US$48.6 million from US$51.1 million in the year-earlier quarter. Revenues were US$634.2 million, up 19.3% from US$531.6 million the year before. Operating income was US$51.8 million versus US$50.6 million in the prior-year quarter, an increase of 2.4%. Direct operating expenses rose 27.2% to US$472.9 million from US$371.9 million in the comparable period the year before. Indirect operating expenses increased 0.3% to US$109.5 million from US$109.1 million in the equivalent prior-year period.

Prospects: On June 9 2008, Co. announced plans to design, construct, own and operate a new Liquefied Natural Gas peak storage facility in North Carolina, which is forecasted to be in service in time for the 2012 - 2013 winter heating season. Co. believes that this project should provide the additional capacity in addressing the demand of its customer base in California, while expanding its presence in Robeson County. Accordingly, Co. will focus its project development activities on survey work and evaluation of potential sites during the next two to three months. Separately, for the fiscal year ending Oct 31 2008, Co. is projecting earnings to be in the range of $1.45 to $1.55 per diluted share.

Financial Data
(US$ in Thousands)

	6 Mos	3 Mos	10/31/2007	10/31/2006	10/31/2005	10/31/2004	10/31/2003	10/31/2002
Earnings Per Share	1.55	1.58	1.40	1.28	1.32	1.27	1.11	0.94
Cash Flow Per Share	...	2.89	3.14	1.37	2.39	2.07	1.49	1.66
Tang Book Value Per Share	...	11.88	11.18	11.07	10.91	10.52	8.61	8.91
Dividends Per Share	1.010	1.000	0.990	0.950	0.905	0.853	0.823	0.792
Dividend Payout %	65.11	63.29	70.71	74.22	68.56	67.13	74.10	83.86
Income Statement								
Total Revenue	...	788,470	1,711,292	1,924,628	1,761,091	1,529,739	1,220,822	832,028
Depn & Amortn	...	22,614	92,921	93,577	91,136	86,786	63,611	57,837
Income Taxes	...	54,587	66,494	63,498	63,408	63,147	48,617	39,794
Net Income	...	82,268	104,387	97,189	101,270	95,188	74,362	62,217
Average Shares	...	73,563	74,472	76,156	76,992	74,797	67,006	65,874
Balance Sheet								
Net PPE	...	2,159,896	2,142,544	2,076,464	1,939,806	1,850,796	1,813,414	1,159,601
Total Assets	...	3,079,438	2,820,318	2,733,939	2,602,490	2,335,877	2,296,406	1,445,088
Long-Term Obligations	...	824,773	824,887	825,000	625,000	660,000	460,000	462,000
Total Liabilities	...	2,158,313	1,941,944	1,851,014	1,718,298	1,480,979	1,666,211	855,492
Stockholders' Equity	...	921,125	878,374	882,925	884,192	854,898	630,195	589,596
Shares Outstanding	...	73,395	74,208	75,464	76,698	76,670	67,310	66,180
Statistical Record								
Return on Assets %	...	3.88	3.76	3.64	4.10	4.10	3.97	4.38
Return on Equity %	...	12.65	11.85	11.00	11.65	12.78	12.19	10.82
Net Margin %	...	10.43	6.10	5.05	5.75	6.22	6.09	7.48
PPE Turnover	...	0.86	0.81	0.96	0.93	0.83	0.82	0.73
Asset Turnover	...	0.61	0.62	0.72	0.71	0.66	0.65	0.59
Debt to Equity	...	0.90	0.94	0.93	0.71	0.77	0.73	0.78
Price Range	27.76-23.19	27.76-23.19	28.28-23.19	27.27-22.09	25.47-21.93	22.84-19.30	20.38-16.45	18.98-14.18
P/E Ratio	17.91-14.96	17.57-14.68	20.20-16.56	21.30-17.26	19.30-16.61	17.98-15.20	18.36-14.82	20.19-15.09
Average Yield %	...	3.86	3.78	3.86	3.83	4.06	4.44	4.56

Address: 4720 Piedmont Row Drive, Charlotte, NC 28210	Officers: Thomas E. Skains - Chairman, President, Chief Executive Officer David J. Dzuricky - Senior Vice President, Chief Financial Officer **Transfer Agents:** American Stock Transfer & Trust Company, New York, NY	Investor Contact: 704-731-4226
Telephone: 704-364-3120 **Web Site:** www.piedmontng.com		**No of Institutions:** 235 **Shares:** 42,116,368 **% Held:** 50.22

PINNACLE WEST CAPITAL CORP.

Exchange	Symbol	Price	52Wk Range	Yield	P/E
NYS	PNW	$33.96 (5/29/2008)	46.43-33.30	6.18	12.00

*7 Year Price Score 74.75   *NYSE Composite Index=100   ***12 Month Price Score 90.89**

Interim Earnings (Per Share)

Qtr.	Mar	Jun	Sep	Dec
2005	0.27	0.28	1.05	0.20
2006	0.13	1.13	1.84	0.17
2007	0.16	0.78	2.07	0.03
2008	(0.04)	...	...	...

Interim Dividends (Per Share)

Amt	Decl	Ex	Rec	Pay
0.525Q	07/18/2007	07/30/2007	08/01/2007	09/04/2007
0.525Q	10/18/2007	10/30/2007	11/01/2007	12/03/2007
0.525Q	01/23/2008	01/30/2008	02/01/2008	03/03/2008
0.525Q	04/22/2008	04/29/2008	05/01/2008	06/02/2008
Indicated Div: $2.10 (Div. Reinv. Plan)				

Valuation Analysis
Forecast EPS $2.42 (05/17/2008)
Market Cap	$3.4 Billion	Book Value	3.5 Billion
Price/Book	0.96	Price/Sales	0.96

Dividend Achiever Status
10 Year Growth Rate	6.44%
Total Years of Dividend Growth	14

Business Summary: Electricity (MIC: SIC: 4911 NAIC: 221121)

Pinnacle West Capital is a holding company that operates in two segments: regulated electricity and real estate. Co. owns all of the outstanding equity securities of Arizona Public Service Co. (APS), its key subsidiary. APS, a vertically-integrated electric utility, provides retail or wholesale electric service to most of the state of Arizona, with the major exceptions of about one-half of the Phoenix and Tucson metropolitan areas as well as Mohave County in northwestern Arizona. Co.'s other principal subsidiary include SunCor Development Co., while its other first-tier subsidiaries are APS Energy Services Co., Inc., El Dorado Investment Co. and Pinnacle West Marketing & Trading Co., LLC.

Recent Developments: For the quarter ended Mar 31 2008, loss from continuing operations was US$4.7 million compared with income of US$16.5 million in the year-earlier quarter. Net loss amounted to US$4.5 million versus net income of US$16.5 million in the year-earlier quarter. Revenues were US$736.7 million, up 6.0% from US$695.0 million the year before. Operating income was US$38.8 million versus US$68.2 million in the prior-year quarter, a decrease of 43.1%. Direct operating expenses rose 14.0% to US$563.2 million from US$494.2 million in the comparable period the year before. Indirect operating expenses increased 1.6% to US$134.7 million from US$132.6 million in the equivalent prior-year period.

Prospects: Going forward, Co. now anticipates customer growth decline, averaging about 1.0% to 2.0% per year for 2008 through 2010 due mainly to factors reflecting the economic conditions both nationally and in Arizona. In addition, Co. foresees that total retail electricity sales in kilowatt-hours will grow 1.0% to 2.0% on average per year for 2008 through 2010, excluding the effects of weather variations. Further, Co. estimates retail sales growth in 2008 to be below average due to the potential effects on customer usage from the economic conditions. Lastly, Co. currently expects minimal net income contributions from its SunCor subsidiary's in 2008, reflecting the weak real estate market.

Financial Data

(US$ in Thousands)	3 Mos	12/31/2007	12/31/2006	12/31/2005	12/31/2004	12/31/2003	12/31/2002	12/31/2001
Earnings Per Share	2.83	3.05	3.27	1.82	2.66	2.63	1.76	3.68
Cash Flow Per Share	6.84	6.56	3.96	7.57	9.19	9.88	10.26	6.74
Tang Book Value Per Share	35.22	35.15	34.48	34.58	32.14	31.00	18.99	29.46
Dividends Per Share	2.100	2.100	2.025	1.925	1.825	1.725	1.625	1.525
Dividend Payout %	74.17	68.85	61.93	105.77	68.61	65.59	92.33	41.44
Income Statement								
Total Revenue	736,738	3,523,620	3,401,748	2,987,965	2,899,725	2,817,852	2,637,279	4,551,373
EBITDA	196,746	1,010,302	1,002,979	878,140	962,819	955,630	953,567	1,125,127
Depn & Amortn	155,127	403,896	386,760	381,000	431,551	463,000	456,071	456,265
Income Before Taxes	(5,225)	449,700	473,561	350,055	364,075	336,136	353,253	540,902
Income Taxes	(557)	150,920	156,418	126,892	128,857	105,560	138,100	213,535
Net Income	(4,473)	307,143	327,255	176,267	243,195	240,579	149,408	312,166
Average Shares	100,521	100,835	100,010	96,590	91,532	91,405	84,964	84,930
Balance Sheet								
Net PPE	8,543,126	8,436,389	7,881,928	7,577,083	7,535,487	7,480,090	6,479,398	5,907,315
Total Assets	11,197,577	11,243,712	11,455,943	11,322,645	9,896,747	9,536,378	8,425,806	7,981,748
Long-Term Obligations	3,114,579	3,127,125	3,232,633	2,608,455	2,584,985	2,897,725	2,881,695	2,673,078
Total Liabilities	7,653,376	7,712,101	8,009,827	7,897,681	6,946,551	6,706,599	5,739,653	5,482,425
Stockholders' Equity	3,544,201	3,531,611	3,446,116	3,424,964	2,950,196	2,829,779	1,732,900	2,499,323
Shares Outstanding	100,633	100,485	99,958	99,057	91,793	91,287	91,255	84,824
Statistical Record								
Return on Assets %	2.57	2.71	2.87	1.66	2.50	2.68	1.82	4.13
Return on Equity %	8.16	8.80	9.53	5.53	8.39	10.55	7.06	12.79
EBITDA Margin %	26.71	28.67	29.48	29.39	33.20	33.91	36.16	24.72
Net Margin %	(0.61)	8.72	9.62	5.90	8.39	8.54	5.67	6.86
PPE Turnover	0.43	0.43	0.44	0.40	0.39	0.40	0.43	0.82
Asset Turnover	0.32	0.31	0.30	0.28	0.30	0.31	0.32	0.60
Debt to Equity	0.88	0.89	0.94	0.76	0.88	1.02	1.66	1.07
Price Range	50.52-34.61	51.60-37.10	50.92-38.70	46.39-39.85	45.41-36.85	40.24-29.07	46.16-22.49	50.37-38.10
P/E Ratio	17.85-12.23	16.92-12.16	15.57-11.83	25.49-21.90	17.07-13.85	15.30-11.05	26.23-12.78	13.69-10.35
Average Yield %	5.05	4.75	4.68	4.46	4.48	4.90	4.46	3.45

Address: 400 North Fifth Street, P.O. Box 53999, Phoenix, AZ 85072-3999
Telephone: 602-250-1000
Web Site: www.pinnaclewest.com

Officers: William J. Post - Chairman, Chief Executive Officer Donald E. Brandt - President, Chief Financial Officer, Chief Operating Officer **Transfer Agents:** Pinnacle West Capital Corporation, Phoenix, AZ

Investor Contact: 602-250-5668
No of Institutions: 356
Shares: 89,483,264 **% Held:** 85.22

PITNEY BOWES INC

Exchange	Symbol	Price	52Wk Range	Yield	P/E
NYS	PBI	$36.30 (5/29/2008)	48.30-34.06	3.86	23.27

*7 Year Price Score 76.04 *NYSE Composite Index=100 *12 Month Price Score 92.05

Interim Earnings (Per Share)

Qtr.	Mar	Jun	Sep	Dec
2005	0.64	0.60	0.62	0.41
2006	0.67	(1.59)	0.66	0.71
2007	0.65	0.68	0.58	(0.25)
2008	0.56	...	...	...

Interim Dividends (Per Share)

Amt	Decl	Ex	Rec	Pay
0.33Q	07/09/2007	08/15/2007	08/17/2007	09/12/2007
0.33Q	11/12/2007	11/20/2007	11/23/2007	12/12/2007
0.35Q	11/15/2007	02/13/2008	02/18/2008	03/12/2008
0.35Q	04/14/2008	05/14/2008	05/16/2008	06/12/2008

Indicated Div: $1.40 (Div. Reinv. Plan)

Valuation Analysis

Forecast EPS $2.83 (05/16/2008)
Market Cap $7.6 Billion   Book Value   553.6 Million
Price/Book   13.76   Price/Sales   1.21

Dividend Achiever Status

10 Year Growth Rate   5.14%
Total Years of Dividend Growth   24

Business Summary: Office Equipment Supplies (MIC: SIC: 3579 NAIC: 423420)

Pitney Bowes provides equipment, supplies, software and services for end-to-end mailstream applications that allow its customers to optimize the flow of physical and electronic mail, documents and packages across their operations. At Dec 31 2007, Co. operated in two business groups; Mailstream Solutions, which included its U.S. mailing, international mailing, production mail and software segments; and Mailstream Services, which included its management services, marketing services, and mail services segments. Co.'s products and services are marketed via a network of direct sales offices in the U.S. and through its subsidiaries and independent distributors and dealers worldwide.

Recent Developments: For the quarter ended Mar 31 2008, income from continuing operations decreased 16.1% to US$122.9 million from US$146.6 million in the year-earlier quarter. Net income decreased 17.7% to US$119.1 million from US$144.8 million in the year-earlier quarter. Revenues were US$1.57 billion, up 11.3% from US$1.41 billion the year before. Direct operating expenses rose 13.8% to US$748.3 million from US$657.5 million in the comparable period the year before. Indirect operating expenses increased 18.4% to US$622.4 million from US$525.7 million in the equivalent prior-year period.

Prospects: For 2008, Co. expects a continued change in its revenue mix, with less revenue coming from larger system sales and a larger portion of revenue from diversified revenue streams related to fully featured smaller systems. In addition, Co. expects a higher percentage of revenue growth from its Software and Mail Services segments, and anticipates further cost savings from its completed acquisitions. Accordingly, Co. has reaffirmed its revenue growth guidance of 6.0% to 9.0% for the year. Co. is also expecting earnings per diluted share from continuing operations of $2.47 to $2.75. At the same time, Co. remains committed to its target to realize $150.0 million in pre-tax annual benefits in 2009.

Financial Data

(US$ in Thousands)	3 Mos	12/31/2007	12/31/2006	12/31/2005	12/31/2004	12/31/2003	12/31/2002	12/31/2001
Earnings Per Share	1.56	1.66	0.47	2.27	2.05	2.11	1.97	1.97
Cash Flow Per Share	5.13	4.85	(1.29)	2.36	4.08	3.64	2.10	4.22
Tang Book Value Per Share	N.M.	N.M.	N.M.	N.M.	N.M.	N.M.	0.10	1.05
Dividends Per Share	1.340	1.320	1.280	1.240	1.220	1.200	1.180	1.160
Dividend Payout %	85.76	79.52	272.34	54.63	59.51	56.87	59.90	58.88
Income Statement								
Total Revenue	1,573,957	6,129,795	5,730,018	5,492,183	4,957,440	4,576,853	4,409,758	4,122,474
EBITDA	300,807	1,285,723	1,490,344	1,407,345	1,174,944	1,174,840	1,062,849	1,268,006
Depn & Amortn	97,527	383,141	363,258	331,963	306,750	288,808	264,250	317,449
Income Before Taxes	203,280	660,711	914,490	867,124	699,448	721,091	619,445	766,384
Income Taxes	75,547	280,222	335,004	340,546	218,922	226,244	181,739	252,064
Net Income	119,103	366,781	105,347	526,578	480,526	498,117	475,750	488,343
Average Shares	213,282	221,219	225,443	231,771	234,133	236,165	241,483	247,615
Balance Sheet								
Current Assets	3,379,322	3,319,613	2,918,670	2,742,315	2,693,086	2,513,175	2,552,625	2,556,608
Total Assets	9,629,536	9,549,943	8,480,420	10,621,382	9,820,580	8,891,388	8,732,314	8,318,471
Current Liabilities	3,451,198	3,556,439	2,746,833	2,910,897	3,294,477	2,646,969	3,350,309	3,083,042
Long-Term Obligations	4,047,013	3,802,075	3,847,617	3,849,623	2,798,894	2,840,943	2,316,844	2,419,150
Total Liabilities	8,691,751	8,522,475	7,397,066	9,009,441	8,220,499	7,494,026	7,568,987	7,117,116
Stockholders' Equity	553,634	643,303	699,189	1,301,941	1,290,081	1,087,362	853,327	891,355
Shares Outstanding	209,795	214,514	220,613	226,707	230,318	232,288	235,373	242,028
Statistical Record								
Return on Assets %	3.75	4.07	1.10	5.15	5.12	5.65	5.58	6.02
Return on Equity %	55.64	54.64	10.53	40.63	40.31	51.33	54.54	44.88
EBITDA Margin %	19.11	20.97	26.01	25.62	23.70	25.67	24.10	30.76
Net Margin %	7.57	5.98	1.84	9.59	9.69	10.88	10.79	11.85
Asset Turnover	0.69	0.68	0.60	0.54	0.53	0.52	0.52	0.51
Current Ratio	0.98	0.93	1.06	0.94	0.82	0.95	0.76	0.83
Debt to Equity	7.31	5.91	5.50	2.96	2.17	2.61	2.72	2.71
Price Range	48.66-34.06	48.66-36.94	47.68-40.34	47.30-40.49	46.88-39.23	42.44-29.90	43.92-28.80	43.33-31.78
P/E Ratio	31.19-21.83	29.31-22.25	101.45-85.83	20.84-17.84	22.87-19.14	20.11-14.17	22.29-14.62	21.99-16.13
Average Yield %	3.15	2.92	2.94	2.84	2.83	3.26	3.11	3.09

Address: 1 Elmcroft Road, Stamford, CT 06926-0700	Officers: Michael J. Critelli - Executive Chairman	No of Institutions: 549
Telephone: 203-356-5000	Murray D. Martin - President, Chief Executive Officer	Shares: 198,531,472 % Held: 83.81
Web Site: www.pb.com	Transfer Agents:EquiServe Trust Company, N.A.	

218

POLARIS INDUSTRIES INC.

Exchange	Symbol	Price	52Wk Range	Yield	P/E
NYS	PII	$47.58 (5/29/2008)	57.74-36.45	3.19	14.55

*7 Year Price Score 84.10   ***NYSE Composite Index=100**   ***12 Month Price Score 98.20**

TRADING VOLUME (thousand shares)

Interim Earnings (Per Share)

Qtr.	Mar	Jun	Sep	Dec
2005	0.42	0.68	1.16	1.02
2006	0.27	0.48	1.03	0.82
2007	0.34	0.62	1.06	1.05
2008	0.55	...	...	...

Interim Dividends (Per Share)

Amt	Decl	Ex	Rec	Pay
0.34Q	07/26/2007	07/30/2007	08/01/2007	08/15/2007
0.34Q	10/25/2007	10/30/2007	11/01/2007	11/15/2007
0.38Q	01/24/2008	01/30/2008	02/01/2008	02/15/2008
0.38Q	04/25/2008	04/29/2008	05/01/2008	05/15/2008

Indicated Div: $1.52

Valuation Analysis

Forecast EPS	$3.41 (05/16/2008)		
Market Cap	$1.6 Billion	Book Value	145.0 Million
Price/Book	10.85	Price/Sales	0.85

Dividend Achiever Status

10 Year Growth Rate	15.57%
Total Years of Dividend Growth	12

Business Summary: Automotive (MIC: SIC: 3799 NAIC: 336999)

Polaris Industries designs and manufactures all-terrain vehicles (ATVs), snowmobiles and motorcycles, and markets them, together with replacement parts, garments and accessories, through dealers and distributors in the U.S., Canada and Europe, and on the Internet. Co.'s line of ATVs consists of 30 models, including general purpose, sport and four-wheel drive utility models. Co.'s snowmobiles consists of 33 models, ranging from youth models to utility and economy models to performance and competition models. Co. also manufactures V-twin cruiser motorcycles under the Victory® brand consisting of nine models, including the Vegas®, Kingpin®, Hammer and Eight Ball.

Recent Developments: For the quarter ended Mar 31 2008, income from continuing operations increased 52.0% to US$19.1 million from US$12.6 million in the year-earlier quarter. Net income increased 54.0% to US$19.1 million from US$12.4 million in the year-earlier quarter. Revenues were US$388.7 million, up 22.3% from US$317.7 million the year before. Operating income was US$31.2 million versus US$16.0 million in the prior-year quarter, an increase of 94.7%. Direct operating expenses rose 18.9% to US$300.6 million from US$252.8 million in the comparable period the year before. Indirect operating expenses increased 16.3% to US$56.9 million from US$48.9 million in the equivalent prior-year period.

Prospects: Co. is seeing higher sales and earnings per share mainly due to improved operating performance for its parts, garments and accessories (PG&A), side-by-side vehicle and international businesses. Specifically, the improved all terrain vehicles sales reflects strong demand for Co.'s RANGER RZR® side-by-side recreation vehicle and RANGER Crew® six passenger side-by-side utility vehicles. Further, Co.'s PG&A sales are benefiting from increased shipments of PG&A related to each product line, with particularly strong increases in snowmobile and side-by-side vehicle related PG&A. For 2008, Co. is targeting earnings of $3.36 to $3.46 per diluted share, with expected sales growth of 5.0% to 7.0%.

Financial Data
(US$ in Thousands)

	3 Mos	12/31/2007	12/31/2006	12/31/2005	12/31/2004	12/31/2003	12/31/2002	12/31/2001
Earnings Per Share	3.27	3.07	2.58	3.27	2.32	2.46	2.19	1.94
Cash Flow Per Share	5.74	5.96	3.61	3.83	5.82	3.63	4.32	4.12
Tang Book Value Per Share	3.60	4.28	4.01	8.27	7.88	6.81	5.67	5.21
Dividends Per Share	1.400	1.360	1.240	1.120	0.920	0.620	0.560	0.500
Dividend Payout %	42.77	44.30	48.06	34.25	39.66	25.20	25.51	25.77
Income Statement								
Total Revenue	388,684	1,780,009	1,656,518	1,869,819	1,773,206	1,605,869	1,521,282	1,512,042
EBITDA	45,844	247,530	244,716	281,282	265,649	221,584	214,095	199,364
Depn & Amortn	13,546	62,093	71,164	67,936	59,339	54,780	57,527	52,550
Income Before Taxes	29,573	170,336	163,779	208,633	204,199	164,339	154,171	139,563
Income Taxes	10,490	57,738	50,988	64,348	67,386	53,410	50,579	48,149
Net Income	19,083	111,660	106,985	143,278	104,504	110,929	103,592	91,414
Average Shares	34,534	36,324	41,451	43,881	45,035	45,056	47,232	47,134
Balance Sheet								
Current Assets	443,417	447,556	392,961	373,988	465,655	387,716	343,659	305,317
Total Assets	769,202	769,881	778,791	768,956	792,925	671,352	608,646	565,163
Current Liabilities	355,363	388,246	361,420	375,614	405,193	330,478	313,513	308,337
Long-Term Obligations	260,000	200,000	250,000	18,000	18,000	18,008	18,027	18,043
Total Liabilities	624,190	596,899	611,420	399,299	431,193	351,974	331,540	326,380
Stockholders' Equity	145,012	172,982	167,371	369,657	361,732	319,378	277,106	238,783
Shares Outstanding	33,053	34,212	35,455	41,687	42,741	43,362	44,600	45,854
Statistical Record								
Return on Assets %	15.73	14.42	13.82	18.35	14.23	17.33	17.65	17.32
Return on Equity %	73.25	65.61	39.84	39.18	30.60	37.19	40.16	41.22
EBITDA Margin %	11.79	13.91	14.77	15.04	14.98	13.80	14.07	13.19
Net Margin %	4.91	6.27	6.46	7.66	5.89	6.91	6.81	6.05
Asset Turnover	2.46	2.30	2.14	2.39	2.42	2.51	2.59	2.87
Current Ratio	1.25	1.15	1.09	1.00	1.15	1.17	1.10	0.99
Debt to Equity	1.79	1.16	1.49	0.05	0.05	0.06	0.07	0.08
Price Range	57.74-36.45	57.74-42.70	54.56-36.20	73.85-44.43	68.93-40.00	45.40-22.18	38.00-26.94	29.05-18.50
P/E Ratio	17.66-11.15	18.81-13.91	21.15-14.03	22.58-13.59	29.71-17.24	18.45-9.02	17.35-12.30	14.97-9.53
Average Yield %	2.94	2.76	2.74	1.97	1.85	1.85	1.73	2.16

Address: 2100 Highway 55, Medina, MN 55340	**Officers:** Thomas C. Tiller - Chief Executive Officer	**Investor Contact:** 763-513-3477
	Bennett J. Morgan - President, Chief Operating Officer	**No of Institutions:** 259
Telephone: 763-542-0500	**Transfer Agents:**Wells Fargo Bank Minnesota, N.A., South St. Paul, MN	**Shares:** 38,322,680 **% Held:** 96.33
Web Site: www.polarisindustries.com		

PPG INDUSTRIES, INC.

Exchange	Symbol	Price	52Wk Range	Yield	P/E
NYS	PPG	$63.41 (5/29/2008)	82.20-57.50	3.28	14.25

*7 Year Price Score 89.17 *NYSE Composite Index=100 *12 Month Price Score 94.03

Interim Earnings (Per Share)

Qtr.	Mar	Jun	Sep	Dec
2005	0.55	1.34	0.92	0.68
2006	1.11	1.68	0.54	0.94
2007	1.17	1.50	1.15	1.21
2008	0.61	...	...	...

Interim Dividends (Per Share)

Amt	Decl	Ex	Rec	Pay
0.52Q	07/19/2007	08/08/2007	08/10/2007	09/12/2007
0.52Q	10/18/2007	11/07/2007	11/12/2007	12/12/2007
0.52Q	01/17/2008	02/20/2008	02/22/2008	03/12/2008
0.52Q	04/17/2008	05/08/2008	05/12/2008	06/12/2008

Indicated Div: $2.08 (Div. Reinv. Plan)

Valuation Analysis

Forecast EPS $5.45 (05/17/2008)

Market Cap	$10.4 Billion	Book Value	4.4 Billion
Price/Book	2.38	Price/Sales	0.83

Dividend Achiever Status

10 Year Growth Rate	4.37%
Total Years of Dividend Growth	36

Business Summary: Chemicals (MIC: SIC: 2851 NAIC: 325510)

PPG Industries is comprised of five reportable business segments: Performance Coatings, Industrial Coatings, Optical and Specialty Materials, Commodity Chemicals, and Glass. Through these segments, Co. provides: protective and decorative finishes; factory-finished aluminum extrusions and steel and aluminum coils; marine and aircraft equipment; automotive original equipment and other industrial and consumer products; architectural, protective, marine and industrial coatings; Transitions® lenses, sunlenses, optical materials and polarized film; amorphous precipitated silicas; Teslin® synthetic printing sheet; chlor-alkali and derivative products; flat glass; and continuous-strand fiber glass.

Recent Developments: For the quarter ended Mar 31 2008, income from continuing operations decreased 50.6% to US$87.0 million from US$176.0 million in the year-earlier quarter. Net income decreased 48.5% to US$100.0 million from US$194.0 million in the year-earlier quarter. Revenues were US$3.72 billion, up 41.3% from US$2.63 billion the year before. Direct operating expenses rose 44.5% to US$2.42 billion from US$1.68 billion in the comparable period the year before. Indirect operating expenses increased 61.1% to US$1.13 billion from US$704.0 million in the equivalent prior-year period.

Prospects: Looking ahead, Co. expects to continue to experience a difficult North American economy. Nevertheless, Co. noted that it remains on track to achieve its full-year 2008 pretax cost saving targets of $25.0 million to $75.0 million related to its acquisition of SigmaKalon in Jan 2008. In relation to revenue, Co. is seeing opportunities for additional growth of its coatings products due to the customer access provided by SigmaKalon's distribution network and geographic presence. Notably, SigmaKalon is expected to increase Co.'s year-over-year coatings sales by 40.0% in 2008 and to increase the proportion of coatings and specialty products in Co.'s portfolio from 66.0% to 80.0% in two years.

Financial Data

(US$ in Thousands)	3 Mos	12/31/2007	12/31/2006	12/31/2005	12/31/2004	12/31/2003	12/31/2002	12/31/2001
Earnings Per Share	4.45	5.03	4.27	3.49	3.95	2.89	(0.41)	2.29
Cash Flow Per Share	6.93	6.05	6.82	6.28	5.91	6.61	5.16	6.30
Tang Book Value Per Share	N.M.	12.59	7.63	8.46	10.81	7.37	3.48	9.12
Dividends Per Share	2.060	2.040	1.910	1.860	1.790	1.730	1.700	1.680
Dividend Payout %	46.26	40.56	44.73	53.30	45.32	59.86	...	73.36
Income Statement								
Total Revenue	3,720,000	11,206,000	11,037,000	10,201,000	9,513,000	8,756,000	8,067,000	8,169,000
EBITDA	303,000	1,696,000	1,509,000	1,387,000	1,529,000	1,334,000	489,000	1,267,000
Depn & Amortn	141,000	380,000	380,000	372,000	388,000	394,000	398,000	447,000
Income Before Taxes	162,000	1,243,000	1,060,000	947,000	1,063,000	843,000	(28,000)	666,000
Income Taxes	49,000	355,000	278,000	282,000	322,000	293,000	(7,000)	247,000
Net Income	100,000	834,000	711,000	596,000	683,000	494,000	(69,000)	387,000
Average Shares	165,600	165,900	166,500	170,900	173,000	170,900	169,900	168,300
Balance Sheet								
Current Assets	6,949,000	7,136,000	4,592,000	4,019,000	4,054,000	3,537,000	2,945,000	2,703,000
Total Assets	15,899,000	12,629,000	10,021,000	8,681,000	8,932,000	8,424,000	7,863,000	8,452,000
Current Liabilities	4,492,000	4,661,000	2,787,000	2,349,000	2,221,000	2,139,000	1,920,000	1,955,000
Long-Term Obligations	3,639,000	1,201,000	1,155,000	1,169,000	1,184,000	1,339,000	1,699,000	1,699,000
Total Liabilities	11,346,000	8,345,000	6,639,000	5,520,000	5,264,000	5,376,000	5,582,000	5,250,000
Stockholders' Equity	4,374,000	4,151,000	3,234,000	3,053,000	3,572,000	2,911,000	2,150,000	3,080,000
Shares Outstanding	164,096	163,800	164,081	165,277	172,001	170,926	169,442	168,713
Statistical Record								
Return on Assets %	5.62	7.36	7.60	6.77	7.85	6.07	N.M.	4.40
Return on Equity %	18.88	22.59	22.62	17.99	21.01	19.52	N.M.	12.53
EBITDA Margin %	8.15	15.13	13.67	13.60	16.07	15.24	6.06	15.51
Net Margin %	2.69	7.44	6.44	5.84	7.18	5.64	N.M.	4.74
Asset Turnover	0.96	0.99	1.18	1.16	1.09	1.08	0.99	0.93
Current Ratio	1.55	1.53	1.65	1.71	1.83	1.65	1.53	1.38
Debt to Equity	0.83	0.29	0.36	0.38	0.33	0.46	0.79	0.55
Price Range	82.20-57.50	82.20-64.30	69.28-57.02	73.80-55.95	68.55-55.18	64.42-42.64	62.44-41.41	59.54-40.71
P/E Ratio	18.47-12.92	16.34-12.78	16.22-13.35	21.15-16.03	17.35-13.97	22.29-14.75	...	26.00-17.78
Average Yield %	2.89	2.82	2.98	2.88	2.94	3.31	3.24	3.27

Address: One PPG Place, Pittsburgh, PA 15272	Officers: Charles E. Bunch - Chairman, Chief Executive Officer James C. Diggs - Senior Vice President, Secretary, General Counsel **Transfer Agents:** Mellon Investor Services, LLC	Investor Contact: 412-434-3318
Telephone: 412-434-3131		**No of Institutions:** 560
Web Site: www.ppg.com		**Shares:** 136,386,224 % **Held:** 69.93

PRAXAIR, INC.

Exchange	Symbol	Price	52Wk Range	Yield	P/E
NYS	PX	$94.87 (5/29/2008)	95.97-68.09	1.58	25.23

*7 Year Price Score 137.09 *NYSE Composite Index=100 *12 Month Price Score 114.83

Interim Earnings (Per Share)

Qtr.	Mar	Jun	Sep	Dec
2005	0.59	0.63	0.33	0.65
2006	0.68	0.75	0.75	0.82
2007	0.81	0.89	0.94	0.98
2008	0.96	...	...	...

Interim Dividends (Per Share)

Amt	Decl	Ex	Rec	Pay
0.30Q	07/25/2007	09/05/2007	09/07/2007	09/17/2007
0.30Q	10/23/2007	12/05/2007	12/07/2007	12/17/2007
0.375Q	01/23/2008	03/05/2008	03/07/2008	03/17/2008
0.375Q	04/22/2008	06/04/2008	06/06/2008	06/16/2008

Indicated Div: $1.50 (Div. Reinv. Plan)

Valuation Analysis

Forecast EPS	$4.25 (05/16/2008)		
Market Cap	$29.7 Billion	Book Value	5.2 Billion
Price/Book	5.70	Price/Sales	3.01

Dividend Achiever Status

10 Year Growth Rate	18.49%
Total Years of Dividend Growth	15

TRADING VOLUME (thousand shares)

Business Summary: Chemicals (MIC: SIC: 2813 NAIC: 325120)

Praxair is an industrial gas supplier in North and South America, Asia, and Europe. Co.'s primary products include atmospheric gases (oxygen, nitrogen, argon, rare gases) and process gases (carbon dioxide, helium, hydrogen, electronic gases, specialty gases, acetylene). In addition, Co. designs, engineers, and builds equipment that produces industrial gases for internal use and external sale. In addition, Co.'s surface technologies segment, operated through Praxair Surface Technologies, Inc., supplies wear-resistant and high-temperature corrosion-resistant metallic and ceramic coatings and powders. As of Dec 31 2007, Co. served approximately 25 industries.

Recent Developments: For the quarter ended Mar 31 2008, net income increased 15.8% to US$307.0 million from US$265.0 million in the year-earlier quarter. Revenues were US$2.66 billion, up 22.4% from US$2.18 billion the year before. Operating income was US$482.0 million versus US$403.0 million in the prior-year quarter, an increase of 19.6%. Direct operating expenses rose 24.4% to US$1.60 billion from US$1.28 billion in the comparable period the year before. Indirect operating expenses increased 19.6% to US$586.0 million from US$490.0 million in the equivalent prior-year period.

Prospects: For the full year of 2008, Co. is targeting sales growth to range from 13.0% to 16.0% and diluted earnings per share of $4.10 to $4.25, excluding the effect of the first-quarter pension settlement charge, which represents 13.0% to 17.0% growth from its 2007 level. In addition, Co. expects capital expenditures to be about $1.50 billion, supporting an increasing number of contracts for on-site production plants globally, which are expected to come on-stream in the next three years. Meanwhile, for the second quarter of 2008, Co. is projecting diluted earnings per share to range from $1.02 to $1.06, which represents earnings growth of 15.0% to 19.0% above prior year's second quarter level.

Financial Data

(US$ in Thousands)	3 Mos	12/31/2007	12/31/2006	12/31/2005	12/31/2004	12/31/2003	12/31/2002	12/31/2001
Earnings Per Share	3.76	3.62	3.00	2.20	2.10	1.77	1.24	1.31
Cash Flow Per Share	6.48	6.14	5.42	4.56	3.80	3.48	3.07	3.16
Tang Book Value Per Share	9.67	9.64	8.94	7.06	6.08	6.00	4.02	4.00
Dividends Per Share	1.275	1.200	1.000	0.720	0.600	0.458	0.380	0.340
Dividend Payout %	33.91	33.15	33.33	32.73	28.57	25.85	30.65	25.86
Income Statement								
Total Revenue	2,663,000	9,402,000	8,324,000	7,656,000	6,594,000	5,613,000	5,128,000	5,158,000
EBITDA	692,000	2,560,000	2,215,000	1,958,000	1,681,000	1,439,000	1,406,000	1,299,000
Depn & Amortn	210,000	774,000	696,000	665,000	578,000	517,000	483,000	499,000
Income Before Taxes	435,000	1,613,000	1,364,000	1,130,000	948,000	771,000	717,000	576,000
Income Taxes	122,000	419,000	355,000	376,000	232,000	174,000	158,000	135,000
Net Income	307,000	1,177,000	988,000	726,000	697,000	585,000	409,000	430,000
Average Shares	320,409	324,842	329,293	329,685	331,403	330,991	329,490	327,014
Balance Sheet								
Current Assets	2,632,000	2,408,000	2,059,000	2,133,000	1,744,000	1,449,000	1,286,000	1,276,000
Total Assets	14,000,000	13,382,000	11,102,000	10,491,000	9,878,000	8,305,000	7,401,000	7,715,000
Current Liabilities	2,875,000	2,650,000	1,758,000	2,001,000	1,875,000	1,117,000	1,100,000	1,194,000
Long-Term Obligations	3,582,000	3,364,000	2,981,000	2,926,000	2,876,000	2,661,000	2,510,000	2,725,000
Total Liabilities	8,447,000	7,919,000	6,326,000	6,387,000	6,045,000	5,022,000	4,897,000	5,077,000
Stockholders' Equity	5,209,000	5,142,000	4,554,000	3,902,000	3,608,000	3,088,000	2,340,000	2,477,000
Shares Outstanding	313,117	315,488	320,860	322,338	323,620	326,085	324,536	324,285
Statistical Record								
Return on Assets %	9.44	9.61	9.15	7.13	7.65	7.45	5.41	5.56
Return on Equity %	25.13	24.28	23.37	19.33	20.76	21.55	16.98	17.79
EBITDA Margin %	25.99	27.23	26.61	25.57	25.49	25.64	27.42	25.18
Net Margin %	11.53	12.52	11.87	9.48	10.57	10.42	7.98	8.34
Asset Turnover	0.77	0.77	0.77	0.75	0.72	0.71	0.68	0.67
Current Ratio	0.92	0.91	1.17	1.07	0.93	1.30	1.17	1.07
Debt to Equity	0.69	0.65	0.65	0.75	0.80	0.86	1.07	1.10
Price Range	91.75-62.69	91.75-58.85	63.54-50.95	54.08-41.07	45.97-34.70	38.20-25.33	30.30-22.81	27.64-18.65
P/E Ratio	24.40-16.67	25.35-16.26	21.18-16.98	24.58-18.67	21.89-16.52	21.58-14.31	24.43-18.39	21.10-14.24
Average Yield %	1.64	1.65	1.78	1.51	1.52	1.48	1.37	1.44

Address: 39 Old Ridgebury Rd., Danbury, CT 06810-5113	Officers: Stephen F. Angel - Chairman, President, Chief Executive Officer Ricardo S. Malfitano - Executive Vice President **Transfer Agents:** Registrar and Transfer Company, Cranford, NJ	Investor Contact: 203-837-2210
Telephone: 203-837-2000		**No of Institutions:** 808
Web Site: www.praxair.com		**Shares:** 297,699,232 % **Held:** 88.14

PROCTER & GAMBLE CO.

Exchange	Symbol	Price	52Wk Range	Yield	P/E
NYS	PG	$65.47 (5/29/2008)	74.67-61.03	2.44	19.37

*7 Year Price Score 98.39 *NYSE Composite Index=100 ***12 Month Price Score 101.95**

Interim Earnings (Per Share)

Qtr.	Sep	Dec	Mar	Jun
2004-05	0.73	0.74	0.63	0.56
2005-06	0.77	0.72	0.63	0.54
2006-07	0.79	0.84	0.74	0.67
2007-08	0.92	0.98	0.82	...

Interim Dividends (Per Share)

Amt	Decl	Ex	Rec	Pay
0.35Q	07/10/2007	07/18/2007	07/20/2007	08/15/2007
0.35Q	10/09/2007	10/17/2007	10/19/2007	11/15/2007
0.35Q	01/08/2008	01/16/2008	01/18/2008	02/15/2008
0.40Q	04/08/2008	04/16/2008	04/18/2008	05/15/2008

Indicated Div: $1.60 (Div. Reinv. Plan)

Valuation Analysis
Forecast EPS $3.50 (05/17/2008)
Market Cap $199.9 Billion Book Value 69.6 Billion
Price/Book 2.87 Price/Sales 2.46

Dividend Achiever Status
10 Year Growth Rate 11.03%
Total Years of Dividend Growth 54

TRADING VOLUME (thousand shares)

Business Summary: Chemicals (MIC: SIC: 2841 NAIC: 325611)

Procter & Gamble is engaged as a global provider of branded consumer goods products. As of June 30 2007, Co.'s products were sold in more than 180 countries around the world principally through mass merchandisers, grocery stores, membership club stores and drug stores. Co. is organized into three Global Business Units (GBUs): Beauty and Health; Household Care; and Gillette GBU. The business units comprising the GBUs are aggregated into seven reportable segments: Beauty; Health Care; Fabric Care and Home Care; Snacks, Coffee and Pet Care; Baby Care and Family Care; Blades and Razors; and Duracell and Braun.

Recent Developments: For the quarter ended Mar 31 2008, net income increased 7.9% to US$2.71 billion from US$2.51 billion in the year-earlier quarter. Revenues were US$20.46 billion, up 9.5% from US$18.69 billion the year before. Operating income was US$4.11 billion versus US$3.65 billion in the prior-year quarter, an increase of 12.8%. Direct operating expenses rose 10.1% to US$9.97 billion from US$9.06 billion in the comparable period the year before. Indirect operating expenses increased 6.5% to US$6.38 billion from US$5.99 billion in the equivalent prior-year period.

Prospects: For the fiscal year ending June 2008, Co. expects organic volume and organic sales to both grow about 5.0%, with total net sales expected to grow about 9.0% versus the prior fiscal year. Further, Co. projects its operating margins to improve by 20 or more basis points, as overhead productivity improvements, pricing and cost savings programs should more than offset the effects of higher materials and energy costs. Overall, Co. expects earnings per share to range from $3.48 to $3.50 for the fiscal year. Meanwhile, in connection with plans to separate its coffee business and form an independent company, Co. expects to do a spin-off or split-off transaction in the first half of fiscal 2009.

Financial Data
(US$ in Millions)

	9 Mos	6 Mos	3 Mos	06/30/2007	06/30/2006	06/30/2005	06/30/2004	06/30/2003
Earnings Per Share	3.38	3.31	3.17	3.04	2.64	2.66	2.32	1.85
Cash Flow Per Share	4.97	4.98	4.40	4.25	3.72	3.47	3.62	3.35
Tang Book Value Per Share	N.M.	N.M.	N.M.	N.M.	N.M.	N.M.	N.M.	0.42
Dividends Per Share	1.400	1.360	1.320	1.280	1.150	1.030	0.933	0.820
Dividend Payout %	41.39	41.09	41.64	42.11	43.56	38.72	40.19	44.44
Income Statement								
Total Revenue	62,237	41,774	20,199	76,476	68,222	56,741	51,407	43,377
EBITDA	15,908	11,020	5,363	19,144	16,159	13,157	11,712	9,794
Depn & Amortn	2,270	1,503	752	3,130	2,627	1,884	1,733	1,703
Income Before Taxes	12,526	8,769	4,252	14,710	12,413	10,439	9,350	7,530
Income Taxes	3,467	2,420	1,173	4,370	3,729	3,182	2,869	2,344
Net Income	9,059	6,349	3,079	10,340	8,684	7,257	6,481	5,186
Average Shares	3,302	3,342	3,355	3,399	3,286	2,727	2,791	2,803
Balance Sheet								
Current Assets	25,742	26,960	25,182	24,031	24,329	20,329	17,115	15,220
Total Assets	145,405	144,401	141,703	138,014	135,695	61,527	57,048	43,706
Current Liabilities	31,263	31,479	30,874	30,717	19,985	25,039	22,147	12,358
Long-Term Obligations	23,673	23,528	22,172	23,375	35,976	12,887	12,554	11,475
Total Liabilities	75,816	76,158	74,144	71,254	72,787	44,050	39,770	27,520
Stockholders' Equity	69,589	68,243	67,559	66,760	62,908	17,477	17,278	16,186
Shares Outstanding	3,054	3,078	3,106	3,132	3,179	2,473	2,544	2,595
Statistical Record								
Return on Assets %	8.04	7.90	7.69	7.56	8.81	12.24	12.83	12.28
Return on Equity %	16.61	16.66	16.32	15.95	21.61	41.76	38.63	34.70
EBITDA Margin %	25.56	26.38	26.55	25.03	23.69	23.19	22.78	22.58
Net Margin %	14.56	15.20	15.24	13.52	12.73	12.79	12.61	11.96
Asset Turnover	0.58	0.57	0.56	0.56	0.69	0.96	1.02	1.03
Current Ratio	0.82	0.86	0.82	0.78	1.22	0.81	0.77	1.23
Debt to Equity	0.34	0.34	0.33	0.35	0.57	0.74	0.73	0.71
Price Range	74.67-61.03	74.67-61.03	70.51-61.03	66.09-55.60	62.25-52.16	56.73-50.97	55.96-43.35	46.50-37.23
P/E Ratio	22.09-18.06	22.56-18.44	22.24-19.25	21.74-18.29	23.58-19.76	21.33-19.16	24.12-18.69	25.14-20.12
Average Yield %	2.09	2.06	2.07	2.05	2.03	1.90	1.89	1.87

Address: One Procter & Gamble Plaza, Cincinnati, OH 45202	Officers: Alan G. Lafley - Chairman, Chief Executive Officer Clayton C. Daley - Vice-Chairman, Chief	Investor Contact: 800-742-6253
Telephone: 513-983-1100	Financial Officer **Transfer Agents:**	No of Institutions: 1658
Web Site: www.pg.com	The Procter & Gamble Company, Cincinnati, OH	Shares: 1,958,934,400 % Held: 59.06

PROGRESS ENERGY, INC.

Exchange	Symbol	Price	52Wk Range	Yield	P/E
NYS	PGN	$42.35 (5/29/2008)	50.11-41.14	5.81	24.77

*7 Year Price Score 79.17   *NYSE Composite Index=100   *12 Month Price Score 95.06

Interim Earnings (Per Share)

Qtr.	Mar	Jun	Sep	Dec
2005	0.38	(0.01)	1.81	0.62
2006	0.18	(0.19)	1.27	1.02
2007	1.08	(0.75)	1.24	0.40
2008	0.81	...	...	...

Interim Dividends (Per Share)

Amt	Decl	Ex	Rec	Pay
0.61Q	09/21/2007	10/05/2007	10/10/2007	11/01/2007
0.615Q	12/12/2007	01/08/2008	01/10/2008	02/01/2008
0.615Q	03/19/2008	04/08/2008	04/10/2008	05/01/2008
0.615Q	05/14/2008	07/08/2008	07/10/2008	08/01/2008

Indicated Div: $2.46 (Div. Reinv. Plan)

Valuation Analysis

Forecast EPS $3.05 (05/16/2008)

Market Cap	$11.1 Billion	Book Value	8.6 Billion
Price/Book	1.28	Price/Sales	1.25

Dividend Achiever Status

10 Year Growth Rate			2.64%
Total Years of Dividend Growth			19

Business Summary: Electricity (MIC: SIC: 4911 NAIC: 221121)

Progress Energy is a utility holding company. Co.'s wholly owned regulated subsidiaries, Carolina Power & Light Company, and Florida Power Corporation, each a business segment, are primarily engaged in the generation, transmission, distribution and sale of electricity in portions of North Carolina, South Carolina and Florida. As of Dec 31 2007, Co. had more than 21,000 megawatts of regulated electric generation capacity, and served approximately 3.1 million retail electric customers as well as other load-serving entities. Co.'s Corporate and Other segment primarily includes both the operations of Co. and its Progress Energy Service Company, LLC subsidiary.

Recent Developments: For the quarter ended Mar 31 2008, income from continuing operations was unchanged at US$149.0 million compared with the year-earlier quarter. Net income decreased 24.0% to US$209.0 million from US$275.0 million in the year-earlier quarter. Revenues were US$2.07 billion, unchanged from the year before. Operating income was US$365.0 million versus US$351.0 million in the prior-year quarter, an increase of 4.0%. Direct operating expenses declined 0.3% to US$1.37 billion from US$1.38 billion in the comparable period the year before. Indirect operating expenses decreased 4.7% to US$327.0 million from US$343.0 million in the equivalent prior-year period.

Prospects: For 2008, Co. expects lower retail revenues in Florida due to lower than forecasted customer growth. Thus, Co. is pursuing further wholesale contracts that should mitigate, to a certain extent, the effect of lower retail revenues. Meanwhile, Co. remains focused on its investment in carbon-free nuclear power, which should reduce its reliance on more volatile fossil fuels. For example, on Mar 11 2008, Co.'s Progress Energy Florida subsidiary submitted a filing with the Florida Public Service Commission that outlines its need for additional electricity and proposes to meet that need with two nuclear units in Levy County, which are expected to be in service in 2016 and 2017, respectively.

Financial Data
(US$ in Thousands)

	3 Mos	12/31/2007	12/31/2006	12/31/2005	12/31/2004	12/31/2003	12/31/2002	12/31/2001
Earnings Per Share	1.71	1.96	2.28	2.82	3.12	3.28	2.42	2.64
Cash Flow Per Share	6.79	4.89	7.64	5.98	6.62	7.54	7.36	7.06
Tang Book Value Per Share	18.63	18.33	18.09	15.94	14.48	13.78	12.43	10.58
Dividends Per Share	2.445	2.440	2.420	2.360	2.300	2.240	2.180	2.120
Dividend Payout %	143.13	124.49	106.14	83.69	73.72	68.29	90.08	80.30
Income Statement								
Total Revenue	2,066,000	9,153,000	9,570,000	10,108,000	9,772,000	8,743,000	7,945,120	8,461,459
EBITDA	618,000	2,616,000	1,928,000	1,870,000	2,137,000	2,462,000	2,112,404	2,241,745
Depn & Amortn	235,000	1,026,000	637,000	591,000	653,000	1,146,000	1,099,128	1,189,171
Income Before Taxes	237,000	1,036,000	727,000	656,000	851,000	702,000	394,361	389,967
Income Taxes	84,000	334,000	204,000	(45,000)	115,000	(109,000)	(157,808)	(151,643)
Net Income	209,000	504,000	571,000	697,000	759,000	782,000	528,386	541,610
Average Shares	259,000	256,700	250,800	247,000	243,100	237,000	218,166	204,683
Balance Sheet								
Net PPE	16,986,000	16,605,000	15,276,000	16,322,000	16,373,000	16,592,000	12,540,505	11,987,961
Total Assets	26,544,000	26,286,000	25,701,000	27,023,000	25,993,000	26,202,000	21,352,704	20,739,791
Long-Term Obligations	8,901,000	8,976,000	8,835,000	10,446,000	9,521,000	9,934,000	9,747,293	9,483,745
Total Liabilities	17,933,000	17,771,000	17,322,000	18,892,000	18,267,000	18,665,000	14,582,864	14,643,427
Stockholders' Equity	8,611,000	8,515,000	8,379,000	8,131,000	7,726,000	7,537,000	6,769,840	6,096,364
Shares Outstanding	261,000	260,000	256,000	252,000	247,000	246,000	237,992	218,725
Statistical Record								
Return on Assets %	1.68	1.94	2.17	2.63	2.90	3.29	2.51	2.65
Return on Equity %	5.12	5.97	6.92	8.79	9.92	10.93	8.21	9.33
EBITDA Margin %	29.91	28.58	20.15	18.50	21.87	28.16	26.59	26.49
Net Margin %	10.12	5.51	5.97	6.90	7.77	8.94	6.65	6.40
PPE Turnover	0.54	0.57	0.61	0.62	0.59	0.60	0.65	0.73
Asset Turnover	0.34	0.35	0.36	0.38	0.37	0.37	0.38	0.41
Debt to Equity	1.03	1.05	1.05	1.28	1.23	1.32	1.44	1.56
Price Range	52.55-41.32	52.55-43.33	49.39-40.79	45.74-41.03	47.78-40.48	47.38-38.32	52.38-33.58	48.44-39.61
P/E Ratio	30.73-24.16	26.81-22.11	21.66-17.89	16.22-14.55	15.31-12.97	14.45-11.68	21.64-13.88	18.35-15.00
Average Yield %	5.20	5.07	5.48	5.42	5.27	5.29	4.79	4.98

Address: 410 South Wilmington Street, Raleigh, NC 27601-1748	Officers: William D. Johnson - Chairman, President, Chief Executive Officer Peter M. Scott - Executive Vice President, Chief Financial Officer **Transfer Agents:** EquiServe Trust Company, Canton, MA	Investor Contact: 919-546-6111
Telephone: 919-546-6111		No of Institutions: 549
Web Site: www.progress-energy.com		Shares: 161,767,584 % Held: 58.25

PROLOGIS

Exchange	Symbol	Price	52Wk Range	Yield	P/E
NYS	PLD	$62.68 (5/29/2008)	72.42-51.66	3.30	16.67

*7 Year Price Score 117.18 *NYSE Composite Index=100 *12 Month Price Score 104.83

Interim Earnings (Per Share)

Qtr.	Mar	Jun	Sep	Dec
2005	0.29	0.40	0.63	0.43
2006	0.72	0.66	0.65	1.28
2007	0.89	1.50	1.12	0.43
2008	0.73	...	...	...

Interim Dividends (Per Share)

Amt	Decl	Ex	Rec	Pay
0.46Q	08/01/2007	08/14/2007	08/16/2007	08/31/2007
0.46Q	11/01/2007	11/09/2007	11/14/2007	11/30/2007
0.517Q	02/01/2008	02/13/2008	02/15/2008	02/29/2008
0.517Q	05/01/2008	05/13/2008	05/15/2008	05/30/2008

Indicated Div: $2.07

Valuation Analysis
Forecast EPS $3.05 (05/16/2008)

Market Cap	$16.3 Billion	Book Value	7.7 Billion
Price/Book	2.11	Price/Sales	2.37

Dividend Achiever Status

10 Year Growth Rate	5.57%
Total Years of Dividend Growth	13

Business Summary: "Property, Real Estate & Development" (MIC: SIC: 6798 NAIC: 525930)

ProLogis owns, manages and develops industrial distribution facilities. Co.'s business is organized into three segments: property operations, for direct ownership of distribution and retail properties; fund management, for investing management of property funds and the properties; and CDFS business, for development or acquisition of real estate properties. As of Dec 31 2007, Co.'s total portfolio of properties owned, managed and under development, including direct-owned properties and properties owned by property funds and CDFS joint ventures, consisted of 2,773 properties aggregating 510.2 million square feet and serving 4,912 customers in 118 markets in North America, Europe and Asia.

Recent Developments: For the quarter ended Mar 31 2008, income from continuing operations decreased 13.7% to US$195.9 million from US$227.0 million in the year-earlier quarter. Net income decreased 17.4% to US$242.4 million from US$242.4 million in the year-earlier quarter. Revenues were US$1.65 billion, up 72.9% from US$955.6 million the year before. Revenues from property income rose 4.8% to US$268.9 million from US$256.5 million in the corresponding quarter a year earlier.

Prospects: Growth in global trade continues to support Co.'s market fundamentals, which in turn, support the leasing activity in its global development pipeline. Market rental rates are increasing in several of its markets and it is enjoying positive rental rate growth. As a result, Co. expects to continue to see increasing rents in most of its markets and it anticipates absorption of available space to be healthy in 2008. While Co. continues to experience strong demand outside the U.S., it continually assesses its planned development activities and believes it is prudent in this environment to target the lower end of its $4.40 billion to $4.80 billion range for new development starts in 2008.

Financial Data

(US$ in Thousands)	3 Mos	12/31/2007	12/31/2006	12/31/2005	12/31/2004	12/31/2003	12/31/2002	12/31/2001
Earnings Per Share	3.76	3.94	3.32	1.76	1.08	1.16	1.20	0.52
Cash Flow Per Share	4.93	4.77	2.93	2.45	2.63	1.82	2.12	2.01
Tang Book Value Per Share	28.31	27.50	24.11	21.08	14.82	14.35	13.96	12.94
Dividends Per Share	1.898	1.840	1.600	1.480	1.460	1.440	1.420	1.380
Dividend Payout %	50.42	46.70	48.19	84.09	135.19	124.14	118.33	265.38
Income Statement								
Total Revenue	1,652,251	6,204,666	2,463,909	1,868,041	598,139	734,105	675,001	523,125
Depn & Amortn	79,898	314,625	291,976	205,899	180,347	170,861	158,042	148,698
Income Before Taxes	223,254	1,056,038	748,218	344,734	277,104	266,049	277,050	132,869
Income Taxes	27,332	68,899	30,528	26,892	43,562	15,374	28,169	4,725
Net Income	200,359	1,074,340	874,367	396,163	232,795	250,675	248,881	128,144
Average Shares	268,131	267,226	256,852	213,713	191,801	187,222	184,869	175,197
Balance Sheet								
Total Assets	20,629,167	19,724,034	15,903,525	13,114,096	7,097,799	6,369,202	5,923,525	5,603,941
Long-Term Obligations	11,096,922	8,550,930	5,924,090	4,437,826	2,453,959	2,291,201	2,186,072	2,202,465
Total Liabilities	12,816,209	12,208,975	9,452,678	7,567,429	3,929,033	3,270,757	2,994,571	2,882,303
Stockholders' Equity	7,720,246	7,436,398	6,398,579	5,488,023	3,102,493	3,060,668	2,886,487	2,675,999
Shares Outstanding	260,299	257,712	250,912	243,781	185,788	180,182	178,145	175,888
Statistical Record								
Return on Assets %	5.40	6.03	6.03	3.92	3.45	4.08	4.32	2.22
Return on Equity %	14.10	15.53	14.71	9.22	7.53	8.43	8.95	4.57
Net Margin %	12.13	17.32	35.49	21.21	38.92	34.15	36.87	24.50
Price Range	72.42-51.66	72.42-53.19	65.50-47.50	47.14-36.60	43.33-28.39	32.26-23.85	26.00-21.03	23.15-19.70
P/E Ratio	19.26-13.74	18.38-13.50	19.73-14.31	26.78-20.80	40.12-26.29	27.81-20.56	21.67-17.53	44.52-37.88
Average Yield %	3.07	2.87	2.92	3.56	4.21	5.20	5.98	6.47

Address: 4545 Airport Way, Denver, CO 80239	Officers: Jeffrey H. Schwartz - Chairman, Chief Executive Officer Walter C. Rakowich - President, Chief Operating Officer **Transfer Agents:** Equiserve Trust Company N.A.	Investor Contact: 303-576-2622
Telephone: 303-567-5000		No of Institutions: 514
Web Site: www.prologis.com		Shares: 308,413,088 % Held: 109.49

PROTECTIVE LIFE CORP.

Exchange	Symbol	Price	52Wk Range	Yield	P/E
NYS	PL	$42.10 (5/29/2008)	50.03-36.82	2.23	12.87

*7 Year Price Score 86.01   ***NYSE Composite Index=100**   ***12 Month Price Score 102.29**

Interim Earnings (Per Share)

Qtr.	Mar	Jun	Sep	Dec
2005	0.84	0.68	0.98	0.96
2006	1.01	0.94	0.80	1.19
2007	1.27	0.91	1.02	0.85
2008	0.50	...	...	...

Interim Dividends (Per Share)

Amt	Decl	Ex	Rec	Pay
0.225Q	08/07/2007	08/15/2007	08/17/2007	08/31/2007
0.225Q	11/06/2007	11/14/2007	11/16/2007	11/30/2007
0.225Q	02/04/2008	02/13/2008	02/15/2008	03/01/2008
0.235Q	05/06/2008	05/14/2008	05/16/2008	06/02/2008

Indicated Div: $0.94 (Div. Reinv. Plan)

Valuation Analysis

Forecast EPS $3.86 (05/17/2008)

Market Cap	$2.9 Billion	Book Value	2.2 Billion
Price/Book	1.36	Price/Sales	0.99

Dividend Achiever Status

10 Year Growth Rate	8.60%
Total Years of Dividend Growth	18

TRADING VOLUME (thousand shares)

Business Summary: Insurance (MIC: SIC: 6311 NAIC: 524113)

Protective Life is a holding company whose subsidiaries provide financial services through the production, distribution, and administration of insurance and investment products. Co. markets individual life insurance, credit life and disability insurance, guaranteed investment contracts, guaranteed funding agreements, fixed and variable annuities, and extended service contracts throughout the U.S. Also, Co. maintains a separate division focused on the acquisition of insurance policies from other companies. Co.'s operating segments are Life Marketing, Acquisitions, Annuities, Stable Value Products and Asset Protection. As at Dec 31 2007, Co. had insurance in force of $765.18 billion.

Recent Developments: For the quarter ended Mar 31 2008, net income decreased 60.4% to US$35.9 million from US$90.6 million in the year-earlier quarter. Revenues were US$715.6 million, down 9.0% from US$786.5 million the year before. Net premiums earned were US$291.3 million versus US$286.0 million in the prior-year quarter, an increase of 1.9%. Net investment income fell 1.7% to US$408.5 million from US$415.7 million a year ago.

Prospects: Looking ahead, Co. is revising its 2008 guidance for operating income per diluted share to a range of $3.80 to $4.15, excluding any reserve adjustments or unusual or unpredictable benefits or charges that might occur during the year. Notably, Co.'s 2008 projection assumes no substantial changes in credit spreads, interest rates or the slope of the yield curve, attaining its targeted level of sales in its major retail product lines and no material change in the equity markets. Co.'s estimate also assumes lower investment income from participating mortgage loan income and prepayment fees, but is assumed to be replaced by investment income growth from the remaining investment portfolio.

Financial Data
(US$ in Thousands)

	3 Mos	12/31/2007	12/31/2006	12/31/2005	12/31/2004	12/31/2003	12/31/2002	12/31/2001
Earnings Per Share	3.27	4.05	3.94	3.46	3.30	3.07	2.52	1.47
Cash Flow Per Share	11.65	12.12	6.90	13.04	10.60	11.22	12.90	17.02
Tang Book Value Per Share	29.32	33.35	31.62	30.62	30.52	28.33	24.37	19.72
Dividends Per Share	0.900	0.890	0.840	0.760	0.685	0.630	0.590	0.550
Dividend Payout %	27.52	21.98	21.32	21.97	20.76	20.52	23.41	37.41
Income Statement								
Premium Income	291,332	1,126,339	946,122	728,923	698,652	735,877	783,132	618,669
Total Revenue	715,604	3,051,700	2,679,133	2,109,204	1,988,575	1,957,525	1,920,678	1,614,217
Benefits & Claims	494,676	1,893,707	1,637,215	1,253,367	1,130,437	1,151,574	1,162,231	972,624
Income Before Taxes	53,589	436,088	431,908	377,013	385,201	325,412	267,203	209,596
Income Taxes	17,707	146,522	150,347	130,446	134,820	108,362	88,444	68,538
Net Income	35,882	289,566	281,561	246,567	234,580	217,050	177,355	102,943
Average Shares	71,453	71,478	71,390	71,350	71,064	70,644	70,462	69,950
Balance Sheet								
Total Assets	41,749,006	41,786,041	39,795,294	28,966,993	27,211,378	24,573,991	21,953,004	19,718,824
Total Liabilities	39,585,146	39,329,280	37,482,219	26,783,333	25,045,051	22,571,847	20,232,302	18,318,680
Stockholders' Equity	2,163,860	2,456,761	2,313,075	2,183,660	2,166,327	2,002,144	1,720,702	1,400,144
Shares Outstanding	69,829	70,149	69,964	69,694	69,449	68,991	68,675	68,555
Statistical Record								
Return on Assets %	0.57	0.71	0.82	0.88	0.90	0.93	0.85	0.59
Return on Equity %	10.22	12.14	12.52	11.34	11.22	11.66	11.37	8.19
Loss Ratio %	169.80	168.13	173.04	171.95	161.80	156.49	148.41	157.21
Net Margin %	5.01	9.49	10.51	11.69	11.80	11.09	9.23	6.38
Price Range	50.83-36.82	50.83-39.80	50.40-43.04	44.83-37.39	42.92-33.84	34.22-24.71	33.75-27.20	34.51-25.55
P/E Ratio	15.54-11.26	12.55-9.83	12.79-10.92	12.96-10.81	13.01-10.25	11.15-8.05	13.39-10.79	23.48-17.38
Average Yield %	2.09	1.98	1.81	1.83	1.81	2.16	1.93	1.82

Address: 2801 Highway 280 South, Birmingham, AL 35223 Telephone: 205-268-1000 Web Site: www.protective.com	Officers: John D. Johns - Chairman, President, Chief Executive Officer Richard J. Bielen - Vice-Chairman, Chief Financial Officer **Transfer Agents:** Bank of New York, New York, NY	Investor Contact: 205-268-1000 No of Institutions: 274 Shares: 67,753,784 % Held: 82.06

PROVIDENT BANKSHARES CORP

Exchange	Symbol	Price	52Wk Range	Yield	P/E
NMS	PBKS	$9.68 (5/29/2008)	34.07-9.63	4.55	N/A

*7 Year Price Score 60.42 *NYSE Composite Index=100 ***12 Month Price Score 52.91**

Interim Earnings (Per Share)

Qtr.	Mar	Jun	Sep	Dec
2005	0.54	0.55	0.54	0.57
2006	0.55	0.60	0.62	0.35
2007	0.50	0.48	0.50	(0.48)
2008	(0.56)	...	...	...

Interim Dividends (Per Share)

Amt	Decl	Ex	Rec	Pay
0.315Q	07/19/2007	07/26/2007	07/30/2007	08/10/2007
0.32Q	10/18/2007	10/25/2007	10/29/2007	11/09/2007
0.325Q	01/16/2008	01/24/2008	01/28/2008	02/08/2008
0.11Q	04/17/2008	04/24/2008	04/28/2008	05/09/2008

Indicated Div: $0.44

Valuation Analysis

Forecast EPS $0.33 (05/16/2008)
Market Cap $307.2 Million   Book Value 517.5 Million
Price/Book 0.59   Price/Sales 0.76

Dividend Achiever Status

10 Year Growth Rate	13.20%
Total Years of Dividend Growth	16

TRADING VOLUME (thousand shares)

Business Summary: Commercial Banking (MIC: SIC: 6022 NAIC: 522110)

Provident Bankshares is a bank holding company for Provident Bank (the Bank), a Maryland chartered stock commercial bank. The Bank is a regional bank serving Maryland and Virginia, with emphasis on the urban centers serving the Baltimore, Washington, D.C. and Richmond metropolitan areas. The Bank is engaged in the business of acquiring deposits from individuals and businesses and using these deposits to fund loans to individuals and businesses. The Bank also provides related financial services, as well as leases, securities brokerage, investment management and related insurance services. As of Dec 31 2007, Co. had total assets of $6.47 billion and total deposits of $4.18 billion.

Recent Developments: For the quarter ended Mar 31 2008, net loss amounted to US$17.6 million versus net income of US$16.1 million in the year-earlier quarter. Net interest income decreased 8.1% to US$45.0 million from US$48.9 million in the year-earlier quarter. Provision for loan losses was US$3.1 million compared with provision of US$1.1 million in the prior-year quarter, an increase of 196.0%. Non-interest income was US$15.1 million versus US$29.9 million, while non-interest expense declined 6.1% to US$51.4 million.

Prospects: Co. is seeing a decline in its net interest income, as a result of its customers continuing to shift their deposits to higher yielding deposit products, combined with competition on rates paid on deposits. Co. is also experiencing a decline in asset quality, as its non-performing assets increased due to the downturn in the regional housing market. Nevertheless, Co. continues to focus on producing positive results by broadening its presence and customer base in the Virginia and metropolitan Washington markets, and growing commercial business in all markets. Also, Co. expects its 2007 restructuring activities to generate over $20.0 million in cost savings and revenue enhancements in 2008.

Financial Data

(US$ in Thousands)	3 Mos	12/31/2007	12/31/2006	12/31/2005	12/31/2004	12/31/2003	12/31/2002	12/31/2001
Earnings Per Share	(0.07)	1.00	2.12	2.17	1.95	2.05	1.88	1.56
Cash Flow Per Share	2.81	3.10	2.60	2.84	1.64	3.40	3.97	4.12
Tang Book Value Per Share	8.12	9.35	11.41	11.08	10.53	12.86	12.57	11.40
Dividends Per Share	1.270	1.250	1.170	1.090	1.010	0.930	0.850	0.752
Dividend Payout %	...	125.00	55.19	50.23	51.79	45.37	45.21	48.21
Income Statement								
Interest Income	87,775	375,415	366,234	314,802	273,031	240,119	277,046	348,094
Interest Expense	42,786	184,183	162,231	116,092	87,676	91,239	135,522	208,933
Net Interest Income	44,989	191,232	204,003	198,710	185,355	148,880	141,524	139,161
Provision for Losses	3,114	23,365	3,973	5,023	7,534	9,936	9,825	17,940
Non-Interest Income	(15,124)	79,919	113,670	112,509	95,067	88,373	89,180	87,427
Non-Interest Expense	51,431	211,089	214,579	200,737	183,728	158,447	150,861	146,223
Income Before Taxes	(24,680)	36,697	99,121	105,459	89,160	68,870	70,018	62,425
Income Taxes	(7,058)	4,567	29,118	32,509	28,835	17,415	21,713	19,800
Net Income	(17,622)	32,130	70,003	72,950	60,325	51,455	48,305	41,465
Average Shares	31,537	32,195	33,082	33,656	30,971	25,142	25,631	26,662
Balance Sheet								
Net Loans & Leases	4,147,428	4,160,057	3,820,289	3,649,742	3,513,711	2,749,007	2,527,138	2,742,292
Total Assets	6,403,916	6,465,046	6,295,893	6,355,926	6,572,160	5,207,848	4,890,722	4,899,717
Total Deposits	4,370,627	4,179,520	4,140,112	4,124,467	3,782,000	3,079,549	3,187,966	3,356,047
Total Liabilities	5,886,367	5,909,275	5,662,262	5,725,431	5,954,721	4,883,083	4,575,087	4,613,435
Stockholders' Equity	517,549	555,771	633,631	630,495	617,439	324,765	315,635	286,282
Shares Outstanding	31,737	31,621	32,433	32,933	33,102	24,562	24,363	25,111
Statistical Record								
Return on Assets %	N.M.	0.50	1.11	1.13	1.02	1.02	0.99	0.80
Return on Equity %	N.M.	5.40	11.08	11.69	12.77	16.07	16.05	13.78
Net Interest Margin %	51.25	50.94	55.70	63.12	67.89	62.00	51.08	39.98
Efficiency Ratio %	70.79	46.36	44.71	46.98	49.91	48.23	41.19	33.57
Loans to Deposits	0.95	1.00	0.92	0.88	0.93	0.89	0.79	0.82
Price Range	34.99-9.98	35.97-21.14	38.60-34.01	36.37-29.10	37.42-27.13	31.76-22.50	27.65-19.29	25.40-19.62
P/E Ratio	...	35.97-21.14	18.21-16.04	16.76-13.41	19.19-13.91	15.49-10.98	14.71-10.26	16.28-12.58
Average Yield %	4.84	4.05	3.23	3.27	3.20	3.51	3.58	3.35

Address: 114 East Lexington Street, Baltimore, MD 21202 **Telephone:** 410-277-7000 **Web Site:** www.provbank.com	**Officers:** Gary N. Geisel - Chairman, Chief Executive Officer Kevin G. Byrnes - President, Chief Operating Officer **Transfer Agents:** Computershare Shareholder Services, Providence, RI	**Investor Contact:** 410-277-7349 **No of Institutions:** 179 **Shares:** 24,675,620 **% Held:** 74.99

QUESTAR CORP.

Exchange NYS	Symbol STR	Price $63.78 (5/29/2008)	52Wk Range 67.60-46.00	Yield 0.77	P/E 20.84

*7 Year Price Score 147.05 ***NYSE Composite Index=100** ***12 Month Price Score 116.98**

Interim Earnings (Per Share)

Qtr.	Mar	Jun	Sep	Dec
2005	0.55	0.35	0.38	0.59
2006	0.79	0.52	0.54	0.69
2007	0.86	0.64	0.64	0.74
2008	1.05	...	...	...

Interim Dividends (Per Share)

Amt	Decl	Ex	Rec	Pay
0.123Q	08/07/2007	08/15/2007	08/17/2007	09/10/2007
0.123Q	10/23/2007	11/14/2007	11/16/2007	12/10/2007
0.123Q	02/12/2008	02/20/2008	02/22/2008	03/10/2008
0.123Q	05/20/2008	05/28/2008	05/30/2008	06/16/2008

Indicated Div: $0.49 (Div. Reinv. Plan)

Valuation Analysis
Forecast EPS $3.35 (05/17/2008)

Market Cap	$11.1 Billion	Book Value	2.6 Billion
Price/Book	4.33	Price/Sales	3.82

Dividend Achiever Status

10 Year Growth Rate	4.58%
Total Years of Dividend Growth	28

Business Summary: Oil and Gas (MIC: SIC: 1311 NAIC: 211111)

Questar is a natural gas-focused energy company with five major lines of business: gas and oil exploration and production; midstream field services; energy marketing; interstate gas transportation; and retail gas distribution. Co.'s operations are conducted through its Questar Market Resources, Inc., which acquires, explores for, develops and produces natural gas, oil and natural gas liquids, and provides midstream field services including natural gas-gathering and processing services; Questar Pipeline Company, which provides interstate natural gas transportation and storage services; and Questar Gas Company, which provides retail natural gas distribution services in Utah, WY and Idaho.

Recent Developments: For the quarter ended Mar 31 2008, net income increased 23.0% to US$185.8 million from US$151.1 million in the year-earlier quarter. Revenues were US$1.05 billion, up 19.8% from US$872.1 million the year before. Operating income was US$308.6 million versus US$240.3 million in the prior-year quarter, an increase of 28.4%. Direct operating expenses rose 14.5% to US$538.3 million from US$470.1 million in the comparable period the year before. Indirect operating expenses increased 22.6% to US$198.2 million from US$161.7 million in the equivalent prior-year period.

Prospects: For the full year of 2008, Co. now anticipates earnings in the range of $3.25 to $3.40 per diluted share, an increase from its previous range of $3.05 to $3.20 per diluted share. In addition, Co. expects production from its Questar Exploration and Production Co. subsidiary to range from 166.00 billion of cubic feet equivalent (Bcfe) to 169.00 Bcfe, compared with its prior guidance of 160.00 Bcfe to 163.00 Bcfe. Similarly, Co. is projecting well completions at its Pinedale region to be in the range of 70 to 75 wells, versus its previous estimation of 60 to 65 wells, driven by improved drilling performance at Pinedale and additional non-operated drilling activity in the Midcontinent region.

Financial Data
(US$ in Thousands)

	3 Mos	12/31/2007	12/31/2006	12/31/2005	12/31/2004	12/31/2003	12/31/2002	12/31/2001
Earnings Per Share	3.06	2.88	2.54	1.87	1.34	1.03	0.94	0.97
Cash Flow Per Share	6.68	6.63	5.65	4.12	3.46	2.70	2.84	2.30
Tang Book Value Per Share	14.32	14.51	12.43	8.60	8.03	7.06	6.40	6.07
Dividends Per Share	0.490	0.485	0.465	0.445	0.425	0.390	0.362	0.352
Dividend Payout %	16.00	16.84	18.34	23.80	31.84	37.86	38.56	36.34
Income Statement								
Total Revenue	1,045,100	2,726,600	2,835,600	2,724,888	1,901,431	1,463,188	1,200,667	1,439,350
EBITDA	434,700	1,246,000	1,089,300	842,633	587,148	485,609	456,388	405,498
Depn & Amortn	112,600	375,800	316,100	259,734	228,267	203,850	194,369	159,042
Income Before Taxes	296,500	798,000	699,600	513,604	358,881	281,759	262,019	246,456
Income Taxes	110,700	290,600	255,500	187,923	129,580	102,563	91,126	88,270
Net Income	185,800	507,400	444,100	325,681	229,301	173,616	155,596	158,186
Average Shares	176,200	175,900	175,200	174,268	171,444	168,380	165,146	163,316
Balance Sheet								
Net PPE	6,046,400	5,098,600	4,091,400	3,427,542	2,984,660	2,768,529	2,617,798	2,565,098
Total Assets	6,883,100	5,944,200	5,064,700	4,357,073	3,646,658	3,309,055	3,067,850	3,235,711
Long-Term Obligations	1,871,100	1,021,200	1,022,400	983,200	933,195	950,189	1,145,180	997,423
Total Liabilities	4,330,400	3,366,300	2,859,200	2,807,270	2,207,100	2,047,790	1,929,089	2,154,930
Stockholders' Equity	2,552,700	2,577,900	2,205,500	1,549,803	1,439,558	1,261,265	1,138,761	1,080,781
Shares Outstanding	173,288	172,800	171,800	170,639	168,882	166,467	164,107	163,046
Statistical Record								
Return on Assets %	9.12	9.22	9.43	8.14	6.58	5.45	4.94	5.48
Return on Equity %	22.45	21.22	23.65	21.79	16.93	14.47	14.02	15.27
EBITDA Margin %	41.59	45.70	38.42	30.92	30.88	33.19	38.01	28.17
Net Margin %	17.78	18.61	15.66	11.95	12.06	11.87	12.96	10.99
PPE Turnover	0.56	0.59	0.75	0.85	0.66	0.54	0.46	0.64
Asset Turnover	0.49	0.50	0.60	0.68	0.55	0.46	0.38	0.50
Debt to Equity	0.73	0.40	0.46	0.63	0.65	0.75	1.01	0.92
Price Range	57.89-45.65	57.89-38.47	45.01-34.03	44.62-23.41	25.75-17.05	17.68-13.33	14.64-9.70	16.75-9.35
P/E Ratio	18.92-14.92	20.10-13.36	17.72-13.40	23.86-12.52	19.22-12.72	17.16-12.94	15.57-10.32	17.27-9.64
Average Yield %	0.93	0.98	1.17	1.33	2.10	2.49	2.91	2.73

Address: 180 East 100 South Street, P.O. Box 45433, Salt Lake City, UT 84145-0433 Telephone: 801-324-5000 Web Site: www.questar.com	Officers: Keith O. Rattie - Chairman, President, Chief Executive Officer Charles B. Stanley - Executive Vice President, Chief Operating Officer Transfer Agents: Questar Corp., Salt Lake City, UT	Investor Contact: 801-324-5497 No of Institutions: 496 Shares: 151,051,136 % Held: 75.25

RAVEN INDUSTRIES, INC.

Exchange NMS	Symbol RAVN	Price $38.70 (5/29/2008)	52Wk Range 43.21-27.99	Yield 1.34	P/E 23.31

*7 Year Price Score 135.07 ***NYSE Composite Index=100** ***12 Month Price Score 93.61**

TRADING VOLUME (thousand shares)

Interim Earnings (Per Share)

Qtr.	Apr	Jul	Oct	Jan
2005-06	0.39	0.26	0.37	0.29
2006-07	0.41	0.28	0.38	0.32
2007-08	0.47	0.32	0.41	0.33
2008-09	0.60	...	...	...

Interim Dividends (Per Share)

Amt	Decl	Ex	Rec	Pay
0.11Q	08/23/2007	09/21/2007	09/25/2007	10/15/2007
0.11Q	11/19/2007	12/20/2007	12/24/2007	01/15/2008
0.13Q	03/17/2008	03/27/2008	03/31/2008	04/15/2008
0.13Q	05/21/2008	06/23/2008	06/25/2008	07/15/2008

Indicated Div: $0.52 (Div. Reinv. Plan)

Valuation Analysis

Forecast EPS $1.60 (05/16/2008)
Market Cap $697.6 Million   Book Value 124.1 Million
Price/Book 5.62   Price/Sales 2.79

Dividend Achiever Status

10 Year Growth Rate 16.65%
Total Years of Dividend Growth 20

Business Summary: Miscellaneous (MIC: SIC: 3672 NAIC: 334412)

Raven Industries is an industrial manufacturing company that operates through four business segments. The Engineered Films Division produces rugged reinforced plastic sheeting for industrial, construction and agricultural applications. The Electronics Systems Division provides electronic manufacturing services. The Flow Controls Division develops global positioning systems-based control systems, location compensated application control products used for precision farming applications and marine navigation. Aerostar International Inc. sells high altitude aerostats for public and commercial research, military parachutes, and specialty outerwear for security forces.

Recent Developments: For the quarter ended Apr 30 2008, net income increased 27.4% to US$10.9 million from US$8.5 million in the year-earlier quarter. Revenues were US$75.2 million, up 29.4% from US$58.1 million the year before. Operating income was US$16.6 million versus US$12.8 million in the prior-year quarter, an increase of 29.6%. Direct operating expenses rose 30.5% to US$53.2 million from US$40.7 million in the comparable period the year before. Indirect operating expenses increased 18.5% to US$5.4 million from US$4.5 million in the equivalent prior-year period.

Prospects: For the fiscal quarter ending Jul 31 2008, Co. foresees revenues at its Flow Controls division to be lower sequentially but expects the decline to be partially mitigated by higher resource allocation for sales, marketing, and engineering programs. In addition, Co. is projecting a modest increase in sales from its Engineered Films division over its prior fiscal year's levels but anticipates operating income to be challenged by higher resin costs and competitive pricing. Lastly, Co. is forecasting net sales at its Electronic Systems division to be lower compared with its previous fiscal year's level, partially offset by improved revenues of secure communication and aviation electronics.

Financial Data

(US$ in Thousands)	3 Mos	01/31/2008	01/31/2007	01/31/2006	01/31/2005	01/31/2004	01/31/2003	01/31/2002
Earnings Per Share	1.66	1.53	1.39	1.32	0.97	0.75	0.60	0.47
Cash Flow Per Share	1.24	1.50	1.46	1.17	1.04	1.09	0.70	0.99
Tang Book Value Per Share	6.40	6.05	4.97	4.19	3.33	3.26	2.83	2.82
Dividends Per Share	0.460	0.440	0.360	0.280	0.845	0.170	0.140	0.128
Dividend Payout %	27.77	28.76	25.90	21.21	87.11	22.67	23.33	27.42
Income Statement								
Total Revenue	75,166	233,957	217,529	204,528	168,086	142,727	120,903	118,515
EBITDA	18,579	49,568	44,722	42,680	31,831	26,402	21,708	16,839
Depn & Amortn	1,820	7,344	5,885	5,151	3,841	4,616	4,391	3,145
Income Before Taxes	16,759	42,224	38,835	37,494	27,955	21,716	17,254	13,565
Income Taxes	5,877	14,422	13,394	13,232	10,064	7,880	6,069	4,718
Net Income	10,882	27,802	25,441	24,262	17,891	13,836	11,185	8,847
Average Shares	18,153	18,204	18,272	18,314	18,410	18,489	18,695	18,983
Balance Sheet								
Current Assets	114,763	100,869	73,219	71,345	61,592	55,710	49,351	45,308
Total Assets	160,525	147,861	119,764	106,157	88,509	79,508	72,816	67,836
Current Liabilities	28,725	22,108	16,464	20,050	20,950	11,895	13,167	13,810
Long-Term Obligations	...	...	...	9	...	57	151	280
Total Liabilities	36,459	29,586	21,496	21,768	22,427	13,037	14,580	15,804
Stockholders' Equity	124,066	118,275	98,268	84,389	66,082	66,471	58,236	52,032
Shares Outstanding	18,027	18,120	18,039	18,072	17,999	18,041	18,132	18,422
Statistical Record								
Return on Assets %	20.61	20.78	22.52	24.93	21.24	18.17	15.90	13.25
Return on Equity %	26.35	25.68	27.86	32.25	26.92	22.19	20.29	17.69
EBITDA Margin %	24.72	21.19	20.56	20.87	18.94	18.50	17.95	14.21
Net Margin %	14.48	11.88	11.70	11.86	10.64	9.69	9.25	7.46
Asset Turnover	1.72	1.75	1.93	2.10	2.00	1.87	1.72	1.78
Current Ratio	4.00	4.56	4.45	3.56	2.94	4.68	3.75	3.28
Debt to Equity	...	...	...	N.M.	...	N.M.	N.M.	0.01
Price Range	43.21-27.99	43.21-26.59	41.73-25.89	32.75-17.08	26.56-13.34	15.07-7.84	9.00-4.89	5.88-3.02
P/E Ratio	26.03-16.86	28.24-17.38	30.02-18.63	24.81-12.94	27.38-13.75	20.09-10.45	15.00-8.15	12.50-6.43
Average Yield %	1.31	1.26	1.14	1.11	4.60	1.52	2.08	2.99

Address: 205 East 6th Street, P.O. Box 5107, Sioux Falls, SD 57117-5107	Officers: Conrad J. Hoigaard - Chairman Ronald M. Moquist - President, Chief Executive Officer	Investor Contact: 605-336-2750
Telephone: 605-336-2750	Transfer Agents: Wells Fargo Bank, N.A., South St. Paul, MN	No of Institutions: 111
Web Site: www.ravenind.com		Shares: 13,080,430 % Held: 71.40

REALTY INCOME CORP.

Exchange	Symbol	Price	52Wk Range	Yield	P/E
NYS	O	$24.37 (5/29/2008)	30.45-21.48	6.76	22.15

*7 Year Price Score 93.47 *NYSE Composite Index=100 *12 Month Price Score 100.52

Interim Earnings (Per Share)

Qtr.	Mar	Jun	Sep	Dec
2005	0.27	0.28	0.26	0.31
2006	0.27	0.27	0.27	0.29
2007	0.30	0.31	0.28	0.27
2008	0.24	...	...	...

Interim Dividends (Per Share)

Amt	Decl	Ex	Rec	Pay
0.137M	02/12/2008	02/28/2008	03/03/2008	03/17/2008
0.137M	03/18/2008	03/28/2008	04/01/2008	04/15/2008
0.137M	04/22/2008	04/29/2008	05/15/2008	05/15/2008
0.137M	05/13/2008	05/29/2008	06/02/2008	06/16/2008
		Indicated Div: $1.65		

Valuation Analysis

Forecast EPS $1.03 (05/16/2008)

Market Cap	$2.5 Billion	Book Value	1.5 Billion
Price/Book	1.62	Price/Sales	8.01

Dividend Achiever Status

10 Year Growth Rate	5.13%
Total Years of Dividend Growth	13

Business Summary: "Property, Real Estate & Development" (MIC: SIC: 6798 NAIC: 525930)

Realty Income operates as an equity real estate investment trust (REIT), which has in-house acquisition, leasing, legal, retail and real-estate research, portfolio management and capital markets capabilities. In addition, Co.'s wholly-owned REIT subsidiary, Crest Net Lease Inc. is engaged in buying, owning and selling properties, primarily to individual investors. As of Dec 31 2007, Co. owned a portfolio of 2,270 retail properties located in 49 states and with more than 18.5 million square feet of leasable space. Also, as of the date stated above, Co.'s Crest subsidiary had invested $56.2 million in 30 properties, which are classified as held for sale.

Recent Developments: For the quarter ended Mar 31 2008, income from continuing operations decreased 13.7% to US$29.8 million from US$34.5 million in the year-earlier quarter. Net income decreased 18.1% to US$29.8 million from US$36.3 million in the year-earlier quarter. Revenues were US$83.4 million, up 17.0% from US$71.3 million the year before. Revenues from property income rose 18.5% to US$82.0 million from US$69.2 million in the corresponding quarter a year earlier.

Prospects: For the full-year 2008, Co. now expects Funds from Operations (FFO) per share of $1.84 to $1.90, representing annual FFO per share change of approximately -2.6% to 0.5% over 2007 and is also a decrease from its previous guidance of $1.94 to $2.00. Co. noted that this is primarily due to a purposeful reduction of activity in its Crest Net Lease Inc. subsidiary until cap rates stabilize and the economy strengthens. Co.'s FFO outlook also assumes projected net income per share of $0.98 to $1.04 and potential gain on sales of investment properties of $0.05 per share. Co. further expects Crest to contribute $0.01 to $0.02 per share to Co.'s FFO compared with $0.02 to $0.07 per share previously.

Financial Data (US$ in Thousands)	3 Mos	12/31/2007	12/31/2006	12/31/2005	12/31/2004	12/31/2003	12/31/2002	12/31/2001
Earnings Per Share	1.10	1.16	1.11	1.12	1.15	1.08	1.01	0.99
Cash Flow Per Share	3.10	3.18	0.97	1.37	2.27	1.04	1.84	1.54
Tang Book Value Per Share	14.85	15.05	15.47	11.61	11.31	10.69	10.11	8.46
Dividends Per Share	1.601	1.571	1.448	1.353	1.251	1.184	1.154	1.124
Dividend Payout %	146.02	135.39	130.41	120.76	108.80	110.12	113.67	113.51
Income Statement								
Total Revenue	83,423	296,513	240,100	196,676	175,555	156,114	140,980	126,271
Depn & Amortn	24,103	81,049	62,443	48,605	41,779	34,416	31,428	29,426
Net Income	29,761	140,409	110,781	99,119	103,397	86,435	78,667	67,558
Average Shares	100,365	100,333	89,917	80,208	78,598	71,222	67,976	58,562
Balance Sheet								
Total Assets	3,039,464	3,077,352	2,546,508	1,920,988	1,442,315	1,360,257	1,080,230	1,003,708
Long-Term Obligations	1,470,000	1,470,000	920,000	891,700	503,600	506,400	339,700	315,300
Total Liabilities	1,518,177	1,539,260	970,516	931,774	528,580	532,491	357,775	331,915
Stockholders' Equity	1,521,287	1,538,092	1,575,992	989,214	913,735	827,766	722,455	671,793
Shares Outstanding	101,293	101,082	100,746	83,696	79,301	75,818	69,749	65,658
Statistical Record								
Return on Assets %	4.75	4.99	4.96	5.89	7.36	7.08	7.55	6.97
Return on Equity %	8.64	9.02	8.64	10.42	11.84	11.15	11.28	11.38
Net Margin %	35.67	47.35	46.14	50.40	58.90	55.37	55.80	53.50
Price Range	30.45-21.48	30.45-23.47	28.17-21.30	25.68-21.20	26.07-18.13	20.49-16.53	18.46-14.65	14.99-12.22
P/E Ratio	27.68-19.53	26.25-20.23	25.38-19.19	22.93-18.93	22.67-15.76	18.97-15.31	18.28-14.50	15.14-12.34
Average Yield %	6.04	5.70	6.03	5.72	5.76	6.22	6.92	8.11

Address: 600 La Terraza Boulevard, Escondido, CA 92025-1707
Telephone: 760-741-2111
Web Site: www.realtyincome.com

Officers: William E. Clark - Chairman Thomas A. Lewis - Vice-Chairman, Chief Executive Officer
Transfer Agents: The Bank of New York

No of Institutions: 258
Shares: 52,213,732 **% Held:** 48.99

REGENCY CENTERS CORP.

Exchange	Symbol	Price	52Wk Range	Yield	P/E
NYS	REG	$67.02 (5/29/2008)	80.06-54.70	4.33	29.52

*7 Year Price Score 104.92 *NYSE Composite Index=100 *12 Month Price Score 104.96

Interim Earnings (Per Share)

Qtr.	Mar	Jun	Sep	Dec
2005	0.55	0.63	0.41	0.64
2006	0.97	0.47	0.57	0.89
2007	0.75	0.64	0.53	0.73
2008	0.38	...	...	...

Interim Dividends (Per Share)

Amt	Decl	Ex	Rec	Pay
0.66Q	07/31/2007	08/13/2007	08/15/2007	08/29/2007
0.66Q	10/31/2007	11/09/2007	11/14/2007	11/28/2007
0.725Q	02/05/2008	02/15/2008	02/20/2008	03/05/2008
0.725Q	05/06/2008	05/19/2008	05/21/2008	06/04/2008

Indicated Div: $2.90

Valuation Analysis

Forecast EPS $2.78 (05/16/2008)

Market Cap $4.7 Billion	Book Value 1.8 Billion
Price/Book 2.55	Price/Sales 10.11

Dividend Achiever Status

10 Year Growth Rate	4.62%
Total Years of Dividend Growth	13

TRADING VOLUME (thousand shares)

Business Summary: "Property, Real Estate & Development" (MIC: SIC: 6798 NAIC: 525930)

Regency Centers is a real-estate-investment-trust engaged in the ownership, management, leasing, acquisition and development of shopping centers through its operating partnership, Regency Centers, L.P., in which it owned approximately 99.0% of the outstanding operating partnership units as of Dec 31 2007. As of such date, Co. operated and managed a real-estate investment portfolio of 451 shopping centers in 29 states and the District of Columbia, including 232 shopping centers representing 25.7 million square feet of gross leasable area (GLA), owned by consolidated properties, and 219 shopping centers representing 25.4 million square feet of GLA, owned by unconsolidated properties.

Recent Developments: For the quarter ended Mar 31 2008, income from continuing operations decreased 43.5% to US$31.7 million from US$56.2 million in the year-earlier quarter. Net income decreased 44.5% to US$31.6 million from US$57.0 million in the year-earlier quarter. Revenues were US$119.6 million, up 12.4% from US$106.4 million the year before. Revenues from property income rose 11.2% to US$111.2 million from US$100.0 million in the corresponding quarter a year earlier.

Prospects: Looking ahead, Co. intends to continue to grow its portfolio by investing in shopping centers through ground up development of new centers or acquisition of existing centers. Notably, as of Mar. 31 2008, Co. had 45 properties under construction or undergoing major renovations on a combined basis, which when completed, will represent a net investment of $1.10 billion after projected sales of adjacent land and out-parcels. Further, Co. estimates that it will earn an average return on its investment from its existing development projects of 8.3% on a fully allocated basis including direct internal costs and the cost to acquire any residual interests held by minority development partners.

Financial Data

(US$ in Thousands)	3 Mos	12/31/2007	12/31/2006	12/31/2005	12/31/2004	12/31/2003	12/31/2002	12/31/2001
Earnings Per Share	2.27	2.65	2.89	2.23	2.08	2.12	1.84	1.69
Cash Flow Per Share	3.29	3.25	3.19	3.23	2.99	3.84	2.97	3.20
Tang Book Value Per Share	22.16	22.66	22.69	22.12	20.45	19.96	20.34	20.56
Dividends Per Share	2.705	2.640	2.380	2.200	2.120	2.080	2.040	2.000
Dividend Payout %	119.01	99.62	82.35	98.65	101.92	98.11	110.87	118.34
Income Statement								
Total Revenue	119,648	451,508	420,338	394,038	391,948	377,621	380,203	388,550
Depn & Amortn	26,502	93,508	87,413	83,495	81,936	75,023	74,380	67,506
Income Before Taxes	...	164,465	165,727	111,517	135,613	144,146	117,873	137,417
Net Income	31,638	203,651	218,511	162,647	136,327	130,789	110,525	100,664
Average Shares	69,410	69,198	68,432	64,932	61,481	61,242	60,438	59,274
Balance Sheet								
Total Assets	4,195,712	4,143,012	3,671,785	3,616,215	3,243,824	3,098,229	3,061,859	3,109,314
Long-Term Obligations	2,108,500	2,007,975	1,575,386	1,613,942	1,493,090	1,452,777	1,333,524	1,396,721
Total Liabilities	2,277,344	2,194,244	1,734,572	1,739,225	1,610,743	1,562,530	1,419,280	1,478,812
Stockholders' Equity	1,840,345	1,870,386	1,853,317	1,788,825	1,498,717	1,280,978	1,221,720	1,219,051
Shares Outstanding	69,922	69,638	69,017	67,966	62,808	59,907	59,557	57,601
Statistical Record								
Return on Assets %	4.46	5.21	6.00	4.74	4.29	4.25	3.58	3.28
Return on Equity %	9.61	10.94	12.00	9.89	9.78	10.45	9.06	8.24
Net Margin %	26.44	45.10	51.98	41.28	34.78	34.64	29.07	25.91
Price Range	84.96-54.70	92.79-62.22	81.34-59.35	63.11-47.30	55.40-35.11	40.20-30.60	32.40-26.80	27.75-22.94
P/E Ratio	37.43-24.10	35.02-23.48	28.15-20.54	28.30-21.21	26.63-16.88	18.96-14.43	17.61-14.57	16.42-13.57
Average Yield %	3.89	3.50	3.58	4.00	4.79	5.94	6.84	8.02

Address: 121 West Forsyth Street, Suite 200, Jacksonville, FL 32202 **Telephone:** 904-598-7000 **Web Site:** www.regencycenters.com	**Officers:** Martin E. Stein - Chairman, Chief Executive Officer Mary Lou Fiala - President, Chief Operating Officer **Transfer Agents: American Stock** Transfer & Trust Company, New York, NY	**Investor Contact:** 904-598-7000 **No of Institutions:** 260 **Shares:** 78,785,352 **% Held:** 107.03

RENASANT CORP

Exchange	Symbol	Price	52Wk Range	Yield	P/E
NMS	RNST	$23.80 (5/29/2008)	24.79-17.63	2.86	14.88

*7 Year Price Score 78.94   ***NYSE Composite Index=100**   ***12 Month Price Score 105.94**

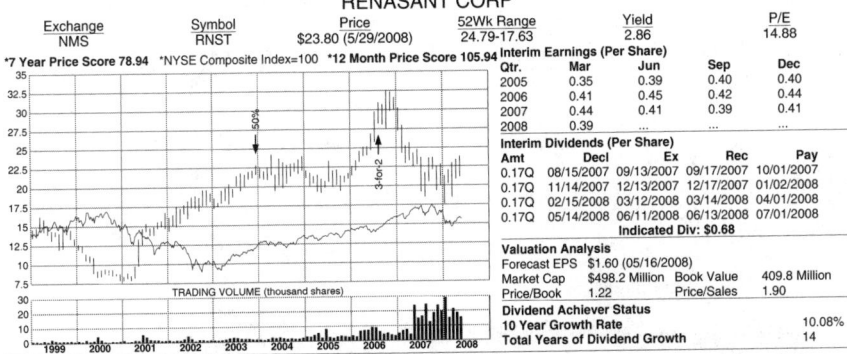

Interim Earnings (Per Share)

Qtr.	Mar	Jun	Sep	Dec
2005	0.35	0.39	0.40	0.40
2006	0.41	0.45	0.42	0.44
2007	0.44	0.41	0.39	0.41
2008	0.39	...	...	...

Interim Dividends (Per Share)

Amt	Decl	Ex	Rec	Pay
0.17Q	08/15/2007	09/13/2007	09/17/2007	10/01/2007
0.17Q	11/14/2007	12/13/2007	12/17/2007	01/02/2008
0.17Q	02/15/2008	03/12/2008	03/14/2008	04/01/2008
0.17Q	05/14/2008	06/11/2008	06/13/2008	07/01/2008
		Indicated Div: $0.68		

Valuation Analysis

Forecast EPS $1.60 (05/16/2008)
Market Cap $498.2 Million   Book Value 409.8 Million
Price/Book 1.22   Price/Sales 1.90

Dividend Achiever Status

10 Year Growth Rate   10.08%
Total Years of Dividend Growth   14

Business Summary: Commercial Banking (MIC: SIC: 6022 NAIC: 522110)

Renasant is a bank holding company. Co. owns and operates Renasant Bank, a Mississippi-chartered bank with operations in Mississippi, Tennessee and Alabama, and Renasant Insurance, Inc., a Mississippi corporation and a wholly-owned subsidiary of Renasant Bank with operations in Mississippi. Renasant Bank is a community bank offering a range of banking and financial services, including checking and savings accounts, business and personal loans, interim construction and residential mortgage loans, student loans, equipment leasing, as well as safe deposit and night depository facilities. As of Dec 31 2007, Co. had total assets of $3.61 billion, and total deposits of $2.55 billion.

Recent Developments: For the quarter ended Mar 31 2008, net income increased 18.9% to US$8.3 million from US$7.0 million in the year-earlier quarter. Net interest income increased 31.4% to US$27.2 million from US$20.7 million in the year-earlier quarter. Provision for loan losses was US$2.6 million versus US$750,000 in the prior-year quarter, an increase of 250.0%. Non-interest income rose 9.3% to US$13.9 million from US$12.7 million, while non-interest expense advanced 19.1% to US$26.8 million.

Prospects: Co. is experiencing an increase in its net interest income, driven by organic loan growth as well as its Jul 2007 acquisition of Capital Bancorp, Inc. Notably, Co. is seeing growth in loans in its Tennessee region. However, Co. also noted declines in loans in its Mississippi and Alabama regions due to an overall slowdown of the regional economies, and expects loan growth in upcoming periods to be relatively modest until improvements in the general economic conditions occur. In addition, Co. does not expect net charge-offs for the remainder of 2008 to decrease from the net charge-offs level of 0.26% annualized as a percentage of average loans incurred during the first quarter of 2008.

Financial Data (US$ in Thousands)	3 Mos	12/31/2007	12/31/2006	12/31/2005	12/31/2004	12/31/2003	12/31/2002	12/31/2001
Earnings Per Share	1.60	1.64	1.71	1.54	1.43	1.46	1.30	1.10
Cash Flow Per Share	2.48	2.32	2.28	3.19	2.01	1.94	2.13	0.43
Tang Book Value Per Share	10.20	9.68	9.94	8.72	9.48	11.20	10.59	9.63
Dividends Per Share	0.670	0.660	0.627	0.580	0.547	0.502	0.462	0.427
Dividend Payout %	41.99	40.24	36.65	37.66	38.32	34.40	35.62	38.71
Income Statement								
Income Before Taxes	11,591	45,170	38,592	33,712	25,259	25,020	24,489	19,696
Income Taxes	3,314	14,069	11,467	9,503	6,816	6,839	6,819	5,109
Net Income	8,277	31,101	27,125	24,209	18,443	18,181	16,370	14,587
Average Shares	21,133	18,989	15,853	15,736	12,955	12,445	12,632	13,215
Balance Sheet								
Total Assets	3,699,276	3,612,287	2,611,356	2,397,702	1,707,545	1,415,214	1,344,512	1,254,727
Total Liabilities	3,289,449	3,213,214	2,358,652	2,162,262	1,528,503	1,277,589	1,211,734	1,131,145
Stockholders' Equity	409,827	399,073	252,704	235,440	179,042	137,625	132,778	123,582
Shares Outstanding	20,930	20,841	15,536	15,434	13,570	12,291	12,543	12,835
Statistical Record								
Return on Assets %	1.00	1.00	1.08	1.18	1.18	1.32	1.26	1.18
Return on Equity %	9.68	9.54	11.11	11.68	11.62	13.45	12.77	11.90
Price Range	25.68-17.63	30.28-18.50	32.55-21.39	23.33-19.17	24.20-19.47	22.83-17.22	19.67-14.33	16.77-7.89
P/E Ratio	16.05-11.02	18.46-11.28	19.04-12.51	15.15-12.45	16.92-13.61	15.63-11.80	15.13-11.02	15.24-7.17
Average Yield %	3.07	2.84	2.33	2.78	2.48	2.50	2.66	3.43

Address: 209 Troy Street, Tupelo, MS 38804-4827
Telephone: 662-680-1001
Web Site: www.renasant.com

Officers: E. Robinson McGraw - Chairman, President, Chief Executive Officer J. Larry Young - Vice-Chairman **Transfer Agents:** Registrar and Transfer Company, Cranford, NJ

No of Institutions: 101
Shares: 7,236,344 **% Held:** 45.66

RLI CORP.

Exchange	Symbol	Price	52Wk Range	Yield	P/E
NYS	RLI	$51.28 (5/29/2008)	60.82-46.93	1.95	7.21

*7 Year Price Score 105.34 *NYSE Composite Index=100   *12 Month Price Score 91.30

TRADING VOLUME (thousand shares)

Interim Earnings (Per Share)

Qtr.	Mar	Jun	Sep	Dec
2005	1.12	1.31	0.96	0.68
2006	0.97	0.89	1.21	2.21
2007	1.32	2.04	2.56	1.39
2008	1.14	...	...	...

Interim Dividends (Per Share)

Amt	Decl	Ex	Rec	Pay
0.22Q	08/23/2007	09/26/2007	09/28/2007	10/15/2007
0.23Q	11/14/2007	12/27/2007	12/31/2007	01/15/2008
0.23Q	02/07/2008	03/27/2008	03/31/2008	04/15/2008
0.25Q	05/01/2008	06/26/2008	06/30/2008	07/15/2008

Indicated Div: $1.00 (Div. Reinv. Plan)

Valuation Analysis

Forecast EPS $4.10 (05/16/2008)
Market Cap $1.1 Billion   Book Value   747.6 Million
Price/Book   1.48   Price/Sales   1.71

Dividend Achiever Status

10 Year Growth Rate   13.73%
Total Years of Dividend Growth   31

Business Summary: Insurance (MIC: SIC: 6331 NAIC: 524126)

RLI is a holding company that underwrites selected property and casualty insurance through its insurance subsidiaries. Co. conducts its operations principally through three insurance companies. RLI Insurance Company, Co.'s principal subsidiary, writes multiple lines insurance on an admitted basis in all 50 states, the District of Columbia and Puerto Rico. Mt. Hawley Insurance Company, a subsidiary of RLI Insurance, writes surplus lines insurance in all 50 states, the District of Columbia, Puerto Rico, the Virgin Islands and Guam. RLI Indemnity Company, a subsidiary of Mt. Hawley, has authority to write multiple lines insurance on an admitted basis in 49 states and the District of Columbia.

Recent Developments: For the quarter ended Mar 31 2008, net income decreased 21.7% to US$25.5 million from US$32.5 million in the year-earlier quarter. Revenues were US$159.0 million, down 1.6% from US$161.6 million the year before. Net premiums earned were US$136.0 million versus US$138.0 million in the prior-year quarter, a decrease of 1.5%. Net investment income rose 1.4% to US$19.3 million from US$19.0 million a year ago.

Prospects: Co.'s near-term outlook appears challenging, reflecting a decline its earnings and revenue. In particular, Co.'s top-line growth is being restrained by a decrease net premium earned as casualty writings continue to decline due to overall softening of rate. Furthermore, Co. noted that the overall condition of the insurance marketplace has remained soft while pricing continued to decline even as coverage terms became less restrictive. Nevertheless, Co. believes that is well positioned to generate underwriting income by focusing on sound underwriting discipline. In the meantime, Co.'s primary focus will continue to be on underwriting profitability as opposed to premium growth.

Financial Data
(US$ in Thousands)

	3 Mos	12/31/2007	12/31/2006	12/31/2005	12/31/2004	12/31/2003	12/31/2002	12/31/2001
Earnings Per Share	7.11	7.30	5.27	4.07	2.80	2.76	1.75	1.55
Cash Flow Per Share	6.81	5.39	6.89	7.78	7.47	7.60	8.12	3.97
Tang Book Value Per Share	33.36	33.77	30.09	26.09	23.60	20.98	17.37	15.36
Dividends Per Share	0.900	0.870	0.750	0.630	0.510	0.400	0.345	0.315
Dividend Payout %	12.66	11.92	14.23	15.48	18.21	14.49	19.71	20.32
Income Statement								
Premium Income	135,965	544,478	530,338	491,307	511,348	463,597	348,065	273,008
Total Revenue	158,964	652,345	632,708	569,302	578,800	519,886	382,153	309,354
Benefits & Claims	69,265	190,868	256,889	251,170	306,131	278,990	203,122	155,876
Income Before Taxes	35,961	254,476	186,893	143,876	100,342	94,278	48,728	41,018
Income Taxes	10,502	78,609	52,254	36,742	27,306	22,987	12,876	10,771
Net Income	25,459	175,867	134,639	107,134	73,036	71,291	35,852	31,047
Average Shares	22,281	24,085	25,571	26,324	26,093	25,846	20,512	20,004
Balance Sheet								
Total Assets	2,609,527	2,626,523	2,771,296	2,735,870	2,468,775	2,134,364	1,719,327	1,390,970
Total Liabilities	1,861,957	1,852,101	2,014,776	2,042,929	1,845,114	1,580,230	1,262,772	1,055,538
Stockholders' Equity	747,570	774,422	756,520	692,941	623,661	554,134	456,555	335,432
Shares Outstanding	21,623	22,155	24,272	25,551	25,315	25,165	24,681	19,825
Statistical Record								
Return on Assets %	6.28	6.52	4.89	4.12	3.16	3.70	2.31	2.32
Return on Equity %	22.22	22.98	18.58	16.27	12.37	14.11	9.05	9.38
Loss Ratio %	50.94	35.06	48.44	51.12	59.87	60.18	58.36	57.10
Net Margin %	16.02	26.96	21.28	18.82	12.62	13.71	9.38	10.04
Price Range	60.82-48.48	60.82-51.00	57.41-45.16	55.68-40.28	43.20-33.55	38.10-25.40	29.60-22.25	23.00-19.40
P/E Ratio	8.55-6.82	8.33-6.99	10.89-8.57	13.68-9.90	15.43-11.98	13.80-9.20	16.91-12.71	14.84-12.52
Average Yield %	1.59	1.52	1.46	1.37	1.34	1.28	1.33	1.50

Address: 9025 N. Lindbergh Drive, Peoria, IL 61615-1499 **Telephone:** 309-692-1000 **Web Site:** www.rlicorp.com	Officers: Gerald D. Stephens - Chairman Jonathan E. Michael - President, Chief Executive Officer **Transfer Agents:** Wells Fargo Shareholder Services, St. Paul, MN	Investor Contact: 309-693-5846 **No of Institutions:** 193 **Shares:** 20,390,200 **% Held:** 88.20

ROBINSON (C.H.) WORLDWIDE, INC.

Exchange	Symbol	Price	52Wk Range	Yield	P/E
NMS	CHRW	$64.73 (5/29/2008)	67.27-45.17	1.36	33.54

*7 Year Price Score 135.60 *NYSE Composite Index=100 *12 Month Price Score 119.40

Interim Earnings (Per Share)

Qtr.	Mar	Jun	Sep	Dec
2005	0.24	0.28	0.31	0.33
2006	0.33	0.38	0.40	0.42
2007	0.42	0.47	0.48	0.49
2008	0.50	...	...	...

Interim Dividends (Per Share)

Amt	Decl	Ex	Rec	Pay
0.18Q	08/16/2007	09/05/2007	09/07/2007	10/01/2007
0.22Q	11/08/2007	12/05/2007	12/07/2007	01/02/2008
0.22Q	02/14/2008	03/05/2008	03/07/2008	04/01/2008
0.22Q	05/15/2008	06/04/2008	06/06/2008	07/01/2008
		Indicated Div: $0.88		

Valuation Analysis

Forecast EPS	$2.16 (05/17/2008)		
Market Cap	$11.0 Billion	Book Value	1.1 Billion
Price/Book	10.24	Price/Sales	1.44

Dividend Achiever Status

10 Year Growth Rate	47.27%
Total Years of Dividend Growth	10

Business Summary: Misc. Transportation Services (MIC: SIC: 4731 NAIC: 488510)

Robinson (C.H.) Worldwide is a global provider of multimodal transportation services and logistics applications, operating through a network of branch offices in North America, Europe, Asia, and South America. Co. is a non-asset based transportation provider that works with approximately 48,000 transportation companies worldwide. In addition to multimodal transportation services, Co. has two other logistics business lines; Sourcing, which is engaged in buying, selling and marketing fresh produce; and Information Services, which consists of its T-Chek Systems, Inc. subsidiary, that provides various management and information services to motor carrier companies and to fuel distributors.

Recent Developments: For the quarter ended Mar 31 2008, net income increased 18.3% to US$86.3 million from US$73.0 million in the year-earlier quarter. Revenues were US$1.99 billion, up 22.6% from US$1.62 billion the year before. Operating income was US$136.1 million versus US$115.2 million in the prior-year quarter, an increase of 18.1%. Direct operating expenses rose 24.6% to US$1.65 billion from US$1.32 billion in the comparable period the year before. Indirect operating expenses increased 11.1% to US$202.0 million from US$181.7 million in the equivalent prior-year period.

Prospects: Co.'s near-term outlook appears to be encouraging. In detail, Co.'s recent top-line improvement is being driven by increases in Transportation, Sourcing and Information Services gross profits. Looking ahead, Co. remains focused on attaining its long-term objective of 15.0% growth for gross profits, income from operations, and earnings per share through internal growth. Additionally, Co. believes that acquisitions that fit its growth requirements should also augment its growth. Meanwhile, Co. anticipates continuing to open new branch offices, which are expected to contribute to its overall long-term growth objective. Accordingly, Co. is planning to open five to ten branches during 2008.

Financial Data

(US$ in Thousands)	3 Mos	12/31/2007	12/31/2006	12/31/2005	12/31/2004	12/31/2003	12/31/2002	12/31/2001
Earnings Per Share	1.93	1.86	1.53	1.16	0.80	0.67	0.56	0.49
Cash Flow Per Share	1.64	1.81	2.01	1.35	0.92	0.65	0.68	0.44
Tang Book Value Per Share	4.68	4.38	3.86	3.11	2.60	2.10	1.59	1.23
Dividends Per Share	0.800	0.760	0.570	0.355	0.255	0.180	0.130	0.105
Dividend Payout %	41.35	40.86	37.25	30.60	32.08	27.07	23.21	21.43
Income Statement								
Total Revenue	1,985,212	7,316,223	6,556,194	5,688,948	4,341,538	3,613,645	3,294,473	3,090,072
EBITDA	146,214	550,880	453,620	344,945	235,028	194,918	171,943	157,509
Depn & Amortn	7,663	27,366	23,932	18,500	11,814	10,992	14,029	19,136
Income Before Taxes	138,551	523,514	429,688	332,753	226,038	186,172	157,914	138,373
Income Taxes	52,233	199,253	162,763	129,395	88,784	72,049	61,589	54,381
Net Income	86,318	324,261	266,925	203,358	137,254	114,123	96,325	83,992
Average Shares	174,028	174,040	174,787	174,698	173,144	172,138	171,514	171,548
Balance Sheet								
Current Assets	1,451,868	1,389,156	1,256,148	1,084,781	845,987	717,329	588,572	503,215
Total Assets	1,873,786	1,811,307	1,631,693	1,395,068	1,080,696	908,149	777,151	683,490
Current Liabilities	782,738	757,619	686,949	612,483	452,819	381,201	343,474	323,528
Total Liabilities	794,848	769,058	687,971	615,031	459,840	391,119	351,321	327,675
Stockholders' Equity	1,078,938	1,042,249	943,722	780,037	620,856	517,030	425,830	355,815
Shares Outstanding	170,668	170,822	172,656	173,029	170,480	170,608	169,012	168,914
Statistical Record								
Return on Assets %	18.93	18.84	17.64	16.43	13.76	13.54	13.19	12.65
Return on Equity %	32.60	32.66	30.97	29.03	24.06	24.21	24.65	25.73
EBITDA Margin %	7.37	7.53	6.92	6.06	5.41	5.39	5.22	5.10
Net Margin %	4.35	4.43	4.07	3.57	3.16	3.16	2.92	2.72
Asset Turnover	4.31	4.25	4.33	4.60	4.35	4.29	4.51	4.65
Current Ratio	1.85	1.83	1.83	1.77	1.87	1.88	1.71	1.56
Price Range	57.85-45.17	56.76-42.89	54.79-36.33	41.48-23.65	28.18-18.62	21.26-13.75	17.52-13.06	15.97-11.79
P/E Ratio	29.97-23.40	30.52-23.06	35.81-23.75	35.76-20.39	35.23-23.28	31.73-20.52	31.28-23.32	32.59-24.06
Average Yield %	1.55	1.50	1.27	1.04	1.18	1.15	1.00	0.74

Address: 8100 Mitchell Road, Eden Prairie, MN 55344	**Officers:** John P. Wiehoff - Chairman, President, Chief Executive Officer James E. Butts - Senior Vice President **Transfer Agents:** Wells Fargo Bank Minnesota, N.A., South St. Paul, MN	**Investor Contact:** 952-937-7847 **No of Institutions:** 405 **Shares:** 140,050,448 **% Held:** N/A
Telephone: 952-937-8500		
Web Site: www.chrobinson.com		

ROHM & HAAS CO.

Exchange	Symbol	Price	52Wk Range	Yield	P/E
NYS	ROH	$54.50 (5/29/2008)	61.27-47.21	3.01	17.58

*7 Year Price Score 97.69 *NYSE Composite Index=100 *12 Month Price Score 104.97

Interim Earnings (Per Share)

Qtr.	Mar	Jun	Sep	Dec
2005	0.70	0.79	0.76	0.60
2006	0.93	0.75	0.85	0.80
2007	0.87	0.74	0.61	0.89
2008	0.87	...	...	...

Interim Dividends (Per Share)

Amt	Decl	Ex	Rec	Pay
0.37Q	07/16/2007	08/08/2007	08/10/2007	09/04/2007
0.37Q	09/28/2007	10/31/2007	11/02/2007	12/01/2007
0.37Q	02/04/2008	02/13/2008	02/15/2008	03/01/2008
0.41Q	05/05/2008	05/14/2008	05/16/2008	06/01/2008

Indicated Div: $1.64 (Div. Reinv. Plan)

Valuation Analysis

Forecast EPS $3.86 (05/16/2008)

Market Cap	$10.7 Billion	Book Value	3.3 Billion
Price/Book	3.25	Price/Sales	1.16

Dividend Achiever Status

10 Year Growth Rate	8.56%
Total Years of Dividend Growth	30

TRADING VOLUME (thousand shares)

Business Summary: Chemicals (MIC: SIC: 2821 NAIC: 325211)

Rohm & Haas is a specialty materials company that operates through seven reportable segments: Electronic Technologies, Display Technologies, Primary Materials, Paint and Coatings Materials, Packaging and Building Materials, Performance Materials Group, and Salt. In addition, Co. serves several market places, including building and construction, electronics, packaging and paper, industrial and other, transportation, household and personal care, water and food. In order to serve these markets, Co. had operations in about 96 manufacturing and 35 research facilities in 27 countries, as of Dec 31 2007.

Recent Developments: For the quarter ended Mar 31 2008, income from continuing operations decreased 9.5% to US$172.0 million from US$190.0 million in the year-earlier quarter. Net income decreased 10.4% to US$172.0 million from US$192.0 million in the year-earlier quarter. Revenues were US$2.51 billion, up 16.1% from US$2.16 billion the year before. Direct operating expenses rose 19.1% to US$1.85 billion from US$1.55 billion in the comparable period the year before. Indirect operating expenses increased 17.6% to US$395.0 million from US$336.0 million in the equivalent prior-year period.

Prospects: On Apr 4 2008, Co. has divested its 40.0% equity interest in UP Chemical Company, a South Korean firm that engages in improved technology used in the production of semiconductor chips. As part of the transaction, Co. received approximately US$114.0 million for its equity interest, reflecting a pre-tax gain of about US$86.0 million. Meanwhile, on Apr 1 2008, Co. has completed its acquisition of FINNDISP, the polymer dispersions division of OY Forcit AB for about US$95.0 million. This acquisition extends Co.'s reach in Nordic Countries and the Commonwealth of Independent States. Separately, Co. expects 2008 sales of about $10.00 billion, reflecting an increase of approximately 15.0% over 2007.

Financial Data

(US$ in Thousands)	3 Mos	12/31/2007	12/31/2006	12/31/2005	12/31/2004	12/31/2003	12/31/2002	12/31/2001
Earnings Per Share	3.10	3.13	3.32	2.85	2.22	1.26	(2.57)	1.79
Cash Flow Per Share	5.09	4.63	3.84	4.27	3.95	4.51	4.41	3.17
Tang Book Value Per Share	0.63	N.M.	4.58	3.14	1.37	0.13	N.M.	N.M.
Dividends Per Share	1.480	1.440	1.280	1.120	0.970	0.860	0.820	0.800
Dividend Payout %	47.71	46.01	38.55	39.30	43.69	68.25	...	44.69
Income Statement								
Total Revenue	2,507,000	8,897,000	8,230,000	7,994,000	7,300,000	6,421,000	5,727,000	5,666,000
EBITDA	397,000	1,451,000	1,570,000	1,453,000	1,319,000	1,014,000	903,000	672,000
Depn & Amortn	122,000	469,000	461,000	481,000	481,000	478,000	457,000	562,000
Income Before Taxes	233,000	880,000	1,042,000	872,000	714,000	415,000	320,000	(64,000)
Income Taxes	56,000	206,000	274,000	224,000	207,000	127,000	102,000	6,000
Net Income	172,000	661,000	735,000	637,000	497,000	280,000	(570,000)	395,000
Average Shares	196,600	211,000	221,200	223,900	224,200	222,400	221,900	220,200
Balance Sheet								
Current Assets	3,816,000	3,527,000	3,411,000	3,205,000	3,247,000	2,527,000	2,543,000	2,421,000
Total Assets	10,549,000	10,208,000	9,553,000	9,727,000	10,095,000	9,445,000	9,706,000	10,350,000
Current Liabilities	1,979,000	1,870,000	1,988,000	1,694,000	1,740,000	1,797,000	1,621,000	1,624,000
Long-Term Obligations	3,230,000	3,139,000	1,688,000	2,074,000	2,563,000	2,468,000	2,872,000	2,720,000
Total Liabilities	7,051,000	6,847,000	5,400,000	5,699,000	6,294,000	6,075,000	6,576,000	6,517,000
Stockholders' Equity	3,284,000	3,146,000	4,031,000	3,917,000	3,697,000	3,357,000	3,119,000	3,815,000
Shares Outstanding	195,846	195,851	218,838	221,962	225,260	222,453	221,131	220,427
Statistical Record								
Return on Assets %	6.41	6.69	7.62	6.43	5.07	2.92	N.M.	3.65
Return on Equity %	17.37	18.42	18.50	16.73	14.05	8.65	N.M.	10.58
EBITDA Margin %	15.84	16.31	19.08	18.18	18.07	15.79	15.77	11.86
Net Margin %	6.86	7.43	8.93	7.97	6.81	4.36	N.M.	6.97
Asset Turnover	0.92	0.90	0.85	0.81	0.75	0.67	0.57	0.52
Current Ratio	1.93	1.89	1.72	1.89	1.87	1.41	1.57	1.49
Debt to Equity	0.98	1.00	0.42	0.53	0.69	0.74	0.92	0.71
Price Range	61.27-47.21	61.27-47.21	53.86-42.77	49.62-39.91	45.17-36.16	42.92-26.67	42.27-30.55	38.27-26.12
P/E Ratio	19.76-15.23	19.58-15.08	16.22-12.88	17.41-14.00	20.35-16.29	34.06-21.17		21.38-14.59
Average Yield %	2.76	2.69	2.61	2.48	2.39	2.53	2.25	2.35

Address: 100 Independence Mall West, Philadelphia, PA 19106-2399 Telephone: 215-592-3000 Web Site: www.rohmhaas.com	Officers: Raj L. Gupta - Chairman, President, Chief Executive Officer Jacques M. Croiseteur - Executive Vice President, Chief Financial Officer Transfer Agents:Computershare Trust Company N.A., Providence, RI	No of Institutions: 408 Shares: 200,514,784 % Held: 81.46

ROPER INDUSTRIES, INC (NEW)

Exchange	Symbol	Price	52Wk Range	Yield	P/E
NYS	ROP	$63.95 (5/29/2008)	70.81-50.05	0.45	22.84

*7 Year Price Score 135.37 *NYSE Composite Index=100 *12 Month Price Score 103.53

Interim Earnings (Per Share)

Qtr.	Mar	Jun	Sep	Dec
2005	0.33	0.41	0.45	0.56
2006	0.42	0.53	0.56	0.62
2007	0.56	0.66	0.70	0.77
2008	0.68	...	...	...

Interim Dividends (Per Share)

Amt	Decl	Ex	Rec	Pay
0.065Q	08/31/2007	10/10/2007	10/12/2007	10/31/2007
0.072Q	11/12/2007	01/09/2008	01/11/2008	01/31/2008
0.072Q	02/18/2008	04/09/2008	04/11/2008	04/25/2008
0.072Q	05/20/2008	07/09/2008	07/11/2008	07/31/2008

Indicated Div: $0.29

Valuation Analysis

Forecast EPS	$3.20 (05/17/2008)		
Market Cap	$5.7 Billion	Book Value	1.9 Billion
Price/Book	3.05	Price/Sales	2.65

Dividend Achiever Status

10 Year Growth Rate	10.31%
Total Years of Dividend Growth	15

Business Summary: Industrial Machinery and Equipment (MIC: SIC: 3823 NAIC: 334513)

Roper Industries is engaged in the designing, manufacturing and distribution of energy systems and controls, scientific and industrial imaging products and software, radio frequency (RF) products and services, and industrial technology products. Co. markets its products and services to a range of markets, including RF applications, water, energy, research/medical and general industry. At Dec 31 2007, Co. operated in four segments: Industrial Technology, Energy Systems and Controls, Scientific and Industrial Imaging, and RF Technology. Co.'s products include fluid properties testing equipment, industrial pumps, digital imaging products and software, and radio frequency identification.

Recent Developments: For the quarter ended Mar 31 2008, net income increased 23.6% to US$63.6 million from US$51.4 million in the year-earlier quarter. Revenues were US$543.0 million, up 13.5% from US$478.4 million the year before. Operating income was US$108.3 million versus US$92.9 million in the prior-year quarter, an increase of 16.6%. Direct operating expenses rose 11.0% to US$266.6 million from US$240.3 million in the comparable period the year before. Indirect operating expenses increased 15.7% to US$168.1 million from US$145.3 million in the equivalent prior-year period.

Prospects: Co.'s near-term outlook appears favorable reflecting growth in net sales and net earnings, aided by sales contributions from its 2007 acquisitions and the 2008 acquisitions of CBORD Group, Inc. and Tech-Pro, Inc. In addition, its acquisition pipeline remains robust and Co. expects to complete additional acquisitions during 2008. Co. is also encouraged by its solid quarter end order backlog, which bodes well for its 2008 second quarter performance. As a result, Co. has increased its diluted earnings per share guidance to $3.13 to $3.21 from $3.10 to $3.20 and expects diluted earnings per share of $0.77 to $0.79 for the second quarter of 2008, excluding the effects of future acquisitions.

Financial Data
(US$ in Thousands)

	3 Mos	12/31/2007	12/31/2006	12/31/2005	12/31/2004	12/31/2003	12/31/2002	10/31/2002
Earnings Per Share	2.80	2.68	2.13	1.74	1.24	0.70	0.01	0.63
Cash Flow Per Share	4.01	3.89	3.02	3.29	2.21	1.13	0.10	1.39
Dividends Per Share	0.268	0.260	0.235	0.212	0.193	0.175	0.165	0.165
Dividend Payout %	9.54	9.70	11.03	12.21	15.52	24.82	1,100.00	26.19
Income Statement								
Total Revenue	542,995	2,102,049	1,700,734	1,453,731	969,764	657,356	83,885	627,030
EBITDA	133,564	529,032	419,717	335,280	203,950	99,052	7,367	129,368
Depn & Amortn	23,521	93,180	82,044	71,319	41,387	16,378	2,620	15,176
Income Before Taxes	97,818	383,657	292,872	220,567	133,716	66,290	1,769	95,686
Income Taxes	34,236	133,624	99,548	67,392	39,864	18,229	529	29,663
Net Income	63,582	250,033	193,324	153,175	93,852	45,239	853	40,053
Average Shares	93,447	93,229	90,880	87,884	75,664	63,984	63,708	63,630
Balance Sheet								
Current Assets	836,157	951,137	627,495	498,207	556,160	381,192	247,565	247,622
Total Assets	3,761,704	3,453,184	2,995,359	2,522,306	2,366,404	1,514,995	824,966	828,973
Current Liabilities	771,996	667,530	587,649	505,625	253,550	161,497	121,344	130,237
Long-Term Obligations	802,848	727,489	726,881	620,958	855,364	630,186	308,684	311,590
Total Liabilities	1,885,936	1,663,378	1,508,520	1,272,518	1,252,318	859,214	443,985	452,961
Stockholders' Equity	1,875,768	1,789,806	1,486,839	1,249,788	1,114,086	655,781	380,981	376,012
Shares Outstanding	89,405	88,773	87,779	85,960	84,832	72,084	62,740	62,726
Statistical Record								
Return on Assets %	7.61	7.75	7.01	6.27	4.82	3.87	0.09	5.03
Return on Equity %	15.32	15.26	14.13	12.96	10.58	8.73	0.21	11.45
EBITDA Margin %	24.60	25.17	24.68	23.06	21.03	15.07	8.78	20.63
Net Margin %	11.71	11.89	11.37	10.54	9.68	6.88	1.02	6.39
Asset Turnover	0.63	0.65	0.62	0.59	0.50	0.56	0.09	0.79
Current Ratio	1.08	1.42	1.07	0.99	2.19	2.36	2.04	1.90
Debt to Equity	0.43	0.41	0.49	0.50	0.77	0.96	0.81	0.83
Price Range	70.81-50.05	70.81-48.61	51.31-38.50	40.51-28.39	31.66-22.64	25.79-13.38	21.57-18.23	25.90-13.68
P/E Ratio	25.29-17.88	26.42-18.14	24.09-18.08	23.28-16.31	25.53-18.25	36.84-19.11	N.M.	41.11-21.71
Average Yield %	0.45	0.44	0.51	0.60	0.71	0.89	0.84	0.80

Address: 6901 Professional Parkway East, Suite 200, Sarasota, FL 34240	Officers: Brian D. Jellison - Chairman, President, Chief Executive Officer John M. Humphrey - Vice President, Chief Financial Officer **Transfer Agents:** Wachovia Bank, N.A., Charlotte, NC	No of Institutions: 401
Telephone: 770-495-5100		Shares: 121,882,040 % Held: 125.53
Web Site: www.roperind.com		

ROSS STORES, INC.

Exchange	Symbol	Price	52Wk Range	Yield	P/E
NMS	ROST	$36.79 (5/29/2008)	36.93-21.48	1.03	19.26

*7 Year Price Score 89.56 ***NYSE Composite Index=100** ***12 Month Price Score 119.05**

Stock price chart (1999–2008) with TRADING VOLUME (thousand shares)

Interim Earnings (Per Share)
Qtr.	Apr	Jul	Oct	Jan
2003-04	0.32	0.35	0.33	0.47
2004-05	0.32	0.22	0.26	0.34
2005-06	0.34	0.29	0.25	0.49
2006-07	0.41	0.32	0.31	0.66
2007-08	0.48	0.37	0.36	0.69

Interim Dividends (Per Share)
Amt	Decl	Ex	Rec	Pay
0.075Q	08/23/2007	09/05/2007	09/07/2007	10/01/2007
0.075Q	11/20/2007	12/10/2007	12/12/2007	01/02/2008
0.095Q	02/07/2008	02/20/2008	02/22/2008	03/31/2008
0.095Q	05/22/2008	06/12/2008	06/16/2008	07/01/2008

Indicated Div: $0.38

Valuation Analysis
Forecast EPS	$2.20 (05/17/2008)		
Market Cap	$4.9 Billion	Book Value	970.6 Million
Price/Book	5.08	Price/Sales	0.82

Dividend Achiever Status
10 Year Growth Rate	20.96%
Total Years of Dividend Growth	13

Business Summary: Retail - Apparel and Accessory Stores (MIC: SIC: 5651 NAIC: 448140)

Ross Stores operates two chains of off-price retail apparel and home accessories stores. As of Feb 2 2008, Co. operated a total of 890 stores, of which 838 are Ross Dress for Less® (Ross) locations in 27 states and Guam and 52 are dd's DISCOUNTS® stores in four states. Both chains target women and men between the ages of 18 and 54. Ross provides apparel, accessories, footwear and home merchandise at savings of 20.0% to 60.0% off department and specialty store regular prices. dd's DISCOUNTS features more moderately-priced assortments of fashion apparel, accessories, footwear and home merchandise at savings of 20.0% to 70.0% off moderate department and discount store regular prices.

Recent Developments: For the year ended Feb 2 2008, net income increased 8.0% to US$261.1 million from US$241.6 million in the prior year. Revenues were US$5.98 billion, up 7.3% from US$5.57 billion the year before. Direct operating expenses rose 7.0% to US$4.62 billion from US$4.32 billion in the comparable period the year before. Indirect operating expenses increased 9.1% to US$931.9 million from US$854.4 million in the equivalent prior-year period.

Prospects: For the fiscal year ending Jan 31 2009, Co. is forecasting approximately $250.0 million in capital requirements to fund expenditures for fixtures and leasehold improvements to open both new Ross and dd's DISCOUNTS stores, the relocation, or upgrade of existing stores, as well as investments in store and merchandising systems, distribution center land, buildings, equipment and systems, and various buying and corporate office expenditures. Going forward, Co. intends to address the challenging conditions for the off-price apparel and home goods market by implementing and improving its existing strategies as well as by strengthening its operations and expanding its merchandise portfolio.

Financial Data
(US$ in Thousands)	02/02/2008	02/03/2007	01/28/2006	01/29/2005	01/31/2004	02/01/2003	02/02/2002	02/03/2001
Earnings Per Share	1.90	1.70	1.36	1.13	1.47	1.26	0.95	0.91
Cash Flow Per Share	2.62	3.58	2.61	2.03	2.08	2.13	1.52	0.85
Tang Book Value Per Share	7.22	6.51	5.80	5.22	5.00	4.15	3.45	2.90
Dividends Per Share	0.300	0.240	0.210	0.170	0.115	0.095	0.085	0.075
Dividend Payout %	15.79	14.12	15.44	15.04	7.82	7.54	8.90	8.24
Income Statement								
Total Revenue	5,975,212	5,570,210	4,944,179	4,239,990	3,920,583	3,531,349	2,986,596	2,709,039
EBITDA	545,819	506,412	439,190	373,578	451,290	396,518	317,210	304,249
Depn & Amortn	120,699	108,135	110,848	94,593	76,739	66,176	62,621	55,063
Income Before Taxes	425,120	398,277	328,342	278,985	374,551	330,342	254,589	249,186
Income Taxes	164,069	156,643	128,710	109,083	146,465	129,164	99,544	97,432
Net Income	261,051	241,634	199,632	169,902	228,102	201,178	155,045	151,754
Average Shares	137,142	141,883	146,532	150,380	155,151	159,492	162,420	166,674
Balance Sheet								
Current Assets	1,398,001	1,514,956	1,228,847	1,122,721	1,120,538	922,420	714,991	631,069
Total Assets	2,371,322	2,358,591	1,938,738	1,735,999	1,657,210	1,361,345	1,082,725	975,047
Current Liabilities	1,010,605	1,083,257	878,983	711,561	711,844	626,684	489,588	434,065
Long-Term Obligations	150,000	150,000	...	50,000	50,000	25,000	...	30,000
Total Liabilities	1,400,673	1,448,761	1,102,566	970,430	901,791	718,157	538,270	507,500
Stockholders' Equity	970,649	909,830	836,172	765,569	755,419	643,188	544,455	467,547
Shares Outstanding	134,096	139,356	144,112	146,717	151,208	154,982	157,920	161,054
Statistical Record								
Return on Assets %	11.07	11.06	10.89	10.04	15.15	16.51	15.11	15.53
Return on Equity %	27.84	27.23	25.00	22.40	32.71	33.97	30.73	31.73
EBITDA Margin %	9.13	9.09	8.88	8.81	11.51	11.23	10.62	11.23
Net Margin %	4.37	4.34	4.04	4.01	5.82	5.70	5.19	5.60
Asset Turnover	2.53	2.55	2.70	2.51	2.60	2.90	2.91	2.77
Current Ratio	1.38	1.40	1.40	1.58	1.57	1.47	1.46	1.45
Debt to Equity	0.15	0.16	...	0.07	0.07	0.04	...	0.06
Price Range	34.86-21.48	33.37-22.80	30.50-22.71	32.85-21.15	28.79-16.48	23.44-16.38	18.16-9.04	12.03-6.38
P/E Ratio	18.35-11.31	19.63-13.41	22.43-16.70	29.07-18.72	19.59-11.21	18.60-13.00	19.12-9.52	13.22-7.01
Average Yield %	1.02	0.85	0.77	0.64	0.51	0.48	0.65	0.87

Address: 8333 Central Ave., Newark, CA 94560-3333	Officers: Norman A. Ferber - Chairman Michael Balmuth - Vice-Chairman, President, Chief Executive Officer Transfer Agents:	No of Institutions: 321
Telephone: 510-505-4400	Bank of New York	Shares: 145,434,784 % Held: 92.51
Web Site: www.rosstores.com		

ROYAL BANCSHARES OF PENNSYLVANIA, INC

Exchange	Symbol	Price	52Wk Range	Yield	P/E
NMS	RBPA A	$10.27 (5/29/2008)	24.00-8.95	5.84	N/A

*7 Year Price Score 61.96 *NYSE Composite Index=100 *12 Month Price Score 72.95

Interim Earnings (Per Share)

Qtr.	Mar	Jun	Sep	Dec
2005	0.32	0.53	0.36	1.16
2006	0.39	0.34	0.48	0.38
2007	0.27	0.32	(0.69)	0.25
2008	0.08	...	...	...

Interim Dividends (Per Share)

Amt	Decl	Ex	Rec	Pay
0.287Q	07/18/2007	07/30/2007	08/01/2007	08/15/2007
0.287Q	10/17/2007	10/29/2007	10/31/2007	11/14/2007
0.15Q	01/18/2008	01/28/2008	01/30/2008	02/13/2008
0.15Q	04/18/2008	04/28/2008	04/30/2008	05/14/2008

Indicated Div: $0.60

Valuation Analysis

Forecast EPS	N/A		
Market Cap	$137.9 Million	Book Value	142.8 Million
Price/Book	0.97	Price/Sales	1.39

Dividend Achiever Status

10 Year Growth Rate	10.41%
Total Years of Dividend Growth	12

Business Summary: Commercial Banking (MIC: SIC: 6022 NAIC: 522110)

Royal Bancshares of Pennsylvania is a two bank holding company. Co.'s principal activities are the ownership and supervising of Royal Bank America and Royal Asian Bank, which engages in a general banking business principally in Montgomery, Chester, Bucks, Philadelphia and Berks counties in Pennsylvania and in Northern and Southern New Jersey and Delaware. Additionally, Co. owns a wholly owned non-bank subsidiary, Royal Investments of Delaware, Inc., which is engaged in investment activities. As of Dec 31 2007, Co. had total assets of $1.28 billion and total deposits of $770.2 million.

Recent Developments: For the quarter ended Mar 31 2008, net income decreased 55.2% to US$1.0 million from US$2.3 million in the year-earlier quarter. Net interest income increased 32.0% to US$9.9 million from US$7.5 million in the year-earlier quarter. Provision for loan losses was US$3.3 million versus US$212,000 in the prior-year quarter, an increase of. Non-interest income fell 49.4% to US$1.3 million from US$2.6 million, while non-interest expense advanced 9.8% to US$6.7 million.

Prospects: Co.'s recent results have been hampered by an increase in provision for loan losses. Notably, as a result of the continued slowdown in the housing market, Co. is experiencing a weakening in the performance of real estate related loans and real estate investments. Nevertheless, Co. is seeing an increase in its net interest margin, primarily as a result of redeploying funds invested in securities into higher yielding loans, and the effects of falling interest rates on deposit and borrowing costs. In particular, Co. allowed higher costing certificates of deposit to mature and replaced those funds with lower cost borrowings from the Federal Home Loan Bank and other institutional sources.

Financial Data
(US$ in Thousands)

	3 Mos	12/31/2007	12/31/2006	12/31/2005	12/31/2004	12/31/2003	12/31/2002	12/31/2001
Earnings Per Share	(0.04)	0.04	1.59	2.37	1.48	1.39	1.29	1.19
Cash Flow Per Share	0.32	0.29	2.43	2.46	1.40	(0.78)	0.95	(0.03)
Tang Book Value Per Share	10.63	11.24	12.39	11.87	10.96	10.53	9.69	9.05
Dividends Per Share	1.013	1.150	1.060	0.957	0.915	0.853	0.802	0.690
Dividend Payout %	...	2,875.00	66.64	40.36	61.66	61.27	62.03	57.84
Income Statement								
Income Before Taxes	1,159	(1,004)	31,583	44,690	27,947	26,522	24,642	21,551
Income Taxes	116	(410)	11,097	12,637	7,914	7,996	7,237	5,797
Net Income	1,043	564	21,568	32,053	20,033	18,526	17,405	15,754
Average Shares	13,364	13,447	13,571	13,536	13,502	13,314	13,474	13,195
Balance Sheet								
Total Assets	1,184,817	1,278,475	1,356,311	1,301,019	1,205,274	1,154,410	1,088,484	930,980
Total Liabilities	1,040,046	1,130,241	1,189,907	1,143,024	1,060,743	1,018,712	966,428	821,894
Stockholders' Equity	142,757	146,367	163,254	155,508	140,876	134,833	121,330	108,449
Shares Outstanding	13,426	13,027	13,180	13,101	12,852	12,804	12,524	11,979
Statistical Record								
Return on Assets %	N.M.	0.04	1.62	2.56	1.69	1.65	1.72	2.02
Return on Equity %	N.M.	0.36	13.53	21.63	14.49	14.46	15.15	14.87
Price Range	24.00-9.24	26.39-11.00	27.25-21.05	25.23-20.55	27.32-19.59	24.41-16.56	19.13-15.29	17.89-10.96
P/E Ratio		..659.75-275.00	17.14-13.24	10.65-8.67	18.46-13.24	17.56-11.91	14.83-11.85	15.03-9.21
Average Yield %	5.65	5.52	4.46	4.31	3.97	4.20	4.64	5.00

Address: 732 Montgomery Avenue, Narberth, PA 19072 Telephone: 610-668-4700 Web Site: www.royalbancshares.com	Officers: Robert R. Tabas - Chairman Joseph P. Campbell - President, Chief Executive Officer Transfer Agents:StockTrans, Inc., Ardmore, PA	Investor Contact: 610-664-5100 No of Institutions: 51 Shares: 1,715,777 % Held: 14.69

RPM INTERNATIONAL INC (DE)

Exchange	Symbol	Price	52Wk Range	Yield	P/E
NYS	RPM	$24.46 (5/29/2008)	24.63-17.92	3.11	14.39

*7 Year Price Score 99.44 ***NYSE Composite Index=100** ***12 Month Price Score 106.93**

Interim Earnings (Per Share)

Qtr.	Aug	Nov	Feb	May
2004-05	0.47	0.08	(0.04)	0.38
2005-06	0.40	0.15	(0.02)	(1.19)
2006-07	0.49	0.42	0.08	0.65
2007-08	0.53	0.43	0.10	...

Interim Dividends (Per Share)

Amt	Decl	Ex	Rec	Pay
0.175Q	07/02/2007	07/11/2007	07/13/2007	07/31/2007
0.19Q	10/04/2007	10/17/2007	10/19/2007	10/31/2007
0.19Q	01/04/2008	01/10/2008	01/14/2008	01/31/2008
0.19Q	04/03/2008	04/10/2008	04/14/2008	04/30/2008

Indicated Div: $0.76 (Div. Reinv. Plan)

Valuation Analysis

Forecast EPS $1.74 (05/16/2008)

Market Cap	$3.0 Billion	Book Value	1.2 Billion
Price/Book	2.43	Price/Sales	0.84

TRADING VOLUME (thousand shares)

Dividend Achiever Status

10 Year Growth Rate	5.36%
Total Years of Dividend Growth	34

Business Summary: Chemicals (MIC: SIC: 2851 NAIC: 325510)

RPM International manufactures, markets and sells chemical product lines, including paints, protective coatings, roofing systems, sealants and adhesives, to the industrial and consumer markets. Co.'s products include those marketed under brand names such as CARBOLINE, DAP, DAY-GLO, DRYVIT, EUCO, FLECTO, ILLBRUCK, RUST-OLEUM, STONHARD, TREMCO and ZINSSER. As of May 31 2007, Co.'s subsidiaries marketed products in 149 countries and territories and operated manufacturing facilities at about 90 locations in the U.S., Argentina, Belgium, Canada, China, Colombia, The Czech Republic, Germany, Italy, Mexico, The Netherlands, New Zealand, Poland, South Africa, the United Arab Emirates and the U.K.

Recent Developments: For the quarter ended Feb 29 2008, net income increased 20.9% to US$12.2 million from US$10.1 million in the year-earlier quarter. Revenues were US$731.8 million, up 7.7% from US$679.5 million the year before. Direct operating expenses rose 5.9% to US$440.5 million from US$416.0 million in the comparable period the year before. Indirect operating expenses increased 10.5% to US$266.2 million from US$241.0 million in the equivalent prior-year period.

Prospects: For the fiscal year ending May 31 2008, Co. is revising its guidance and now anticipates sales growth to be in the range of 8.0% to 10.0%, while earnings are projected to increase by 10.0% to 12.0%. Looking ahead, Co. will closely monitor overall economic conditions while focusing primarily on domestic construction markets. In addition, Co. will continue to attain new business through its brand offerings, new product developments and international expansion in order to offset the weakness in the economy. Meanwhile, Co. expects the Mar 5 2008 acquisition of Prosytec SAS and the Mar 11 2008 acquisition of Increte Systems to be accretive to its earnings within the first year of operations.

Financial Data

(US$ in Thousands)	9 Mos	6 Mos	3 Mos	05/31/2007	05/31/2006	05/31/2005	05/31/2004	05/31/2003
Earnings Per Share	1.70	1.69	1.68	1.64	(0.65)	0.86	1.22	0.30
Cash Flow Per Share	1.91	1.79	1.47	1.71	1.59	1.35	1.32	1.39
Tang Book Value Per Share	0.20	0.27	N.M.	N.M.	N.M.	0.91	0.38	N.M.
Dividends Per Share	0.730	0.715	0.700	0.685	0.630	0.590	0.550	0.515
Dividend Payout %	42.87	42.31	41.67	41.77	...	68.60	45.08	171.67
Income Statement								
Total Revenue	2,567,820	1,836,047	930,339	3,338,764	3,008,338	2,555,735	2,341,572	2,083,549
EBITDA	293,374	247,662	133,745	431,324	(9,369)	261,947	322,638	145,143
Depn & Amortn	62,402	41,775	20,878	76,756	71,763	62,841	76,077	70,578
Income Before Taxes	196,685	181,062	100,149	307,535	(122,475)	163,728	217,616	47,853
Income Taxes	61,412	57,939	31,881	99,246	(46,270)	58,696	75,730	12,526
Net Income	135,273	123,123	68,268	208,289	(76,205)	105,032	141,886	35,327
Average Shares	130,223	130,608	130,026	128,711	116,837	126,364	116,710	115,986
Balance Sheet								
Current Assets	1,678,497	1,510,718	1,546,252	1,570,249	1,369,218	1,271,495	994,617	928,094
Total Assets	3,433,852	3,259,681	3,297,820	3,333,149	2,980,218	2,656,245	2,353,119	2,247,211
Current Liabilities	744,393	738,950	764,676	864,740	713,500	575,339	477,493	427,650
Long-Term Obligations	1,031,740	840,564	921,734	886,416	870,415	837,948	718,929	724,846
Total Liabilities	2,207,022	2,028,580	2,154,457	2,246,279	2,054,277	1,609,736	1,377,827	1,370,203
Stockholders' Equity	1,226,830	1,231,101	1,143,363	1,086,870	925,941	1,046,509	975,292	877,008
Shares Outstanding	121,819	121,782	121,299	120,906	118,743	117,554	116,122	115,496
Statistical Record								
Return on Assets %	6.81	6.90	6.85	6.60	N.M.	4.19	6.15	1.65
Return on Equity %	19.35	19.24	20.33	20.70	N.M.	10.39	15.28	4.07
EBITDA Margin %	11.43	13.49	14.38	12.92	N.M.	10.25	13.78	6.97
Net Margin %	5.27	6.71	7.34	6.24	N.M.	4.11	6.06	1.70
Asset Turnover	1.11	1.12	1.09	1.06	1.07	1.02	1.02	0.97
Current Ratio	2.25	2.04	2.02	1.82	1.92	2.21	2.08	2.17
Debt to Equity	0.84	0.68	0.81	0.82	0.94	0.80	0.74	0.83
Price Range	24.63-17.92	24.63-17.92	24.63-18.57	24.18-17.64	19.46-17.11	19.83-14.02	17.10-12.55	16.06-9.20
P/E Ratio	14.49-10.54	14.57-10.60	14.66-11.05	14.74-10.76	...	23.06-16.30	14.02-10.29	53.53-30.67
Average Yield %	3.33	3.22	3.23	3.23	3.43	3.41	3.73	3.88

Address: 2628 Pearl Road, P.O. Box 777, Medina, OH 44258
Telephone: 330-273-5090
Web Site: www.rpminc.com

Officers: Thomas C. Sullivan - Chairman Frank C. Sullivan - President, Chief Executive Officer
Transfer Agents: National City Bank, Cleveland, OH

No of Institutions: 311
Shares: 105,099,184 **% Held:** 68.28

S & T BANCORP, INC. (INDIANA, PA.)

Exchange	Symbol	Price	52Wk Range	Yield	P/E
NMS	STBA	$32.78 (5/29/2008)	36.22-25.78	3.78	14.13

*7 Year Price Score 79.47 ***NYSE Composite Index=100** ***12 Month Price Score 106.90**

Interim Earnings (Per Share)

Qtr.	Mar	Jun	Sep	Dec
2005	0.51	0.58	0.54	0.55
2006	0.54	0.43	0.57	0.52
2007	0.52	0.56	0.63	0.54
2008	0.60	...	...	...

Interim Dividends (Per Share)

Amt	Decl	Ex	Rec	Pay
0.30Q	06/18/2007	06/27/2007	06/29/2007	07/25/2007
0.30Q	09/17/2007	09/27/2007	10/01/2007	10/25/2007
0.31Q	12/17/2007	12/27/2007	12/31/2007	01/25/2008
0.31Q	03/17/2008	03/28/2008	04/01/2008	04/25/2008

Indicated Div: $1.24

Valuation Analysis

Forecast EPS	$2.40 (05/16/2008)		
Market Cap	$806.9 Million	Book Value	349.1 Million
Price/Book	2.31	Price/Sales	3.20

Dividend Achiever Status

10 Year Growth Rate	8.52%
Total Years of Dividend Growth	18

Business Summary: Commercial Banking (MIC: SIC: 6022 NAIC: 522110)

S&T Bancorp is a bank holding company. Co. has two wholly owned subsidiaries, S&T Bank and 9th Street Holdings Inc. Co. also owns a one-half interest in Commonwealth Trust Credit Life Insurance Co. S&T Bank is a full service bank providing services to its customers through a branch network located in Pennsylvania. S&T Bank's services include accepting time and demand deposit accounts, originating commercial and consumer loans, providing letters of credit, offering discount brokerage services, personal financial planning, credit card services and insurance products. As of Dec 31 2007, Co. had total assets of $3.42 billion and total deposits of $2.62 billion.

Recent Developments: For the quarter ended Mar 31 2008, net income increased 11.7% to US$14.9 million from US$13.3 million in the year-earlier quarter. Net interest income increased 8.3% to US$30.5 million from US$28.2 million in the year-earlier quarter. Provision for loan losses was US$1.3 million versus US$2.2 million in the prior-year quarter, a decrease of 41.3%. Non-interest income fell 6.5% to US$9.5 million from US$10.2 million, while non-interest expense advanced 2.1% to US$18.0 million.

Prospects: On May 13 2008, Co. announced shareholder approval of its previously announced acquisition of IBT Bancorp, Inc. Co. has received all necessary regulatory approvals for completion of the acquisition. As a result, the transaction is expected to be effective in early June 2008, and with this transaction, Co. will have 55 branches and combined assets of over $4.30 billion. Meanwhile, Co.'s results are benefiting from an improvement in its net interest income, led by an increase in average interest-earning assets due to loan growth, as well as an improvement in the net interest margin primarily attributable to the effect of the decline in short-term interest rates.

Financial Data

(US$ in Thousands)	3 Mos	12/31/2007	12/31/2006	12/31/2005	12/31/2004	12/31/2003	12/31/2002	12/31/2001
Earnings Per Share	2.32	2.26	2.06	2.18	2.03	1.94	1.81	1.75
Cash Flow Per Share	2.56	2.58	1.99	1.97	2.34	1.92	1.89	2.85
Tang Book Value Per Share	12.04	11.61	11.20	11.34	11.12	10.48	9.47	11.01
Dividends Per Share	1.217	1.210	1.170	1.130	1.070	1.020	0.970	0.920
Dividend Payout %	52.36	53.54	56.80	51.83	52.71	52.58	53.59	52.57
Income Statement								
Interest Income	50,458	215,605	204,702	172,122	148,638	151,460	151,160	166,702
Interest Expense	19,909	99,167	91,584	59,514	40,890	47,066	56,300	76,713
Net Interest Income	30,549	116,438	113,118	112,608	107,748	104,394	94,860	89,989
Provision for Losses	1,279	5,812	9,380	5,000	4,400	7,300	7,800	5,000
Non-Interest Income	9,510	40,605	40,390	37,568	34,202	36,204	32,680	31,230
Non-Interest Expense	17,955	73,460	69,279	62,646	60,191	60,658	51,766	46,972
Income Before Taxes	20,825	77,771	74,849	82,530	77,359	72,640	67,974	69,247
Income Taxes	5,969	21,627	21,513	24,287	23,001	20,863	19,370	20,062
Net Income	14,856	56,144	53,336	58,243	54,358	51,777	48,604	47,298
Average Shares	24,680	24,888	25,940	26,688	26,799	26,723	26,784	27,051
Balance Sheet								
Net Loans & Leases	2,815,149	2,762,594	2,633,071	2,454,934	2,253,089	2,069,142	1,968,755	1,615,842
Total Assets	3,463,806	3,421,169	3,338,543	3,194,979	2,989,034	2,900,272	2,823,867	2,357,874
Total Deposits	2,605,187	2,621,825	2,565,306	2,418,884	2,176,263	1,962,253	1,926,119	1,611,317
Total Liabilities	3,114,733	3,083,609	2,999,492	2,842,558	2,639,905	2,567,554	2,517,753	2,064,547
Stockholders' Equity	349,073	337,560	339,051	352,421	349,129	332,718	306,114	293,327
Shares Outstanding	24,615	24,551	25,361	26,270	26,600	26,652	26,584	26,646
Statistical Record								
Return on Assets %	1.68	1.66	1.63	1.88	1.84	1.81	1.88	2.03
Return on Equity %	17.01	16.60	15.43	16.60	15.90	16.21	16.22	16.58
Net Interest Margin %	60.54	54.01	55.26	65.42	72.49	68.93	62.75	53.98
Efficiency Ratio %	29.94	28.67	28.27	29.88	32.92	32.32	28.16	23.73
Loans to Deposits	1.08	1.05	1.03	1.01	1.04	1.05	1.02	1.00
Price Range	36.22-25.78	36.22-27.64	37.53-29.84	40.25-33.32	38.40-28.42	31.25-25.05	28.03-23.30	25.30-20.31
P/E Ratio	15.61-11.11	16.03-12.23	18.22-14.49	18.46-15.28	18.92-14.00	16.11-12.91	15.49-12.87	14.46-11.61
Average Yield %	0.97	3.68	3.44	3.06	3.27	3.63	3.80	4.00

Address: 43 South Ninth Street, Indiana, PA 15701 **Telephone:** 724-465-1466 **Web Site:** www.stbank.com	**Officers:** James C. Miller - Chairman Todd D. Brice - President, Chief Executive Officer, Chief Operating Officer **Transfer Agents: American Stock** Transfer & Trust Company, New York, NY	**Investor Contact:** 724-465-1466 **No of Institutions:** 95 **Shares:** 12,608,546 **% Held:** 44.13

SANDY SPRING BANCORP

Exchange	Symbol	Price	52Wk Range	Yield	P/E
NMS	SASR	$26.74 (5/29/2008)	33.47-25.23	3.59	13.30

*7 Year Price Score 68.03   *NYSE Composite Index=100   *12 Month Price Score 94.16

Interim Earnings (Per Share)

Qtr.	Mar	Jun	Sep	Dec
2005	0.53	0.53	0.64	0.54
2006	0.56	0.54	0.55	0.55
2007	0.49	0.51	0.50	0.51
2008	0.50	...	...	...

Interim Dividends (Per Share)

Amt	Decl	Ex	Rec	Pay
0.23Q	08/29/2007	09/06/2007	09/10/2007	09/20/2007
0.23Q	11/15/2007	11/21/2007	11/26/2007	12/06/2007
0.24Q	02/28/2008	03/06/2008	03/10/2008	03/20/2008
0.24Q	05/29/2008	06/05/2008	06/09/2008	06/19/2008
		Indicated Div: $0.96		

Valuation Analysis

Forecast EPS	$2.07 (05/16/2008)		
Market Cap	$437.5 Million	Book Value	319.0 Million
Price/Book	1.37	Price/Sales	1.92

Dividend Achiever Status

10 Year Growth Rate	11.37%
Total Years of Dividend Growth	12

TRADING VOLUME (thousand shares)

Business Summary: Commercial Banking (MIC: SIC: 6021 NAIC: 522110)

Sandy Spring Bancorp is the holding company for Sandy Spring Bank and its principal subsidiaries, Sandy Spring Insurance Corporation, The Equipment Leasing Company, and West Financial Services, Inc. Co. focuses its lending and other services on businesses and consumers in the local market area. Through its subsidiaries, Co. provides a range of leasing, insurance, and investment management services. As of Dec 31 2007, Co. provided a range of commercial banking, retail banking and trust services through 42 community offices in Maryland and Virginia. As of Dec 31 2007, Co. had total assets of $3.04 billion and total deposits of $2.27 billion.

Recent Developments: For the quarter ended Mar 31 2008, net income increased 8.7% to US$8.2 million from US$7.5 million in the year-earlier quarter. Net interest income increased 10.7% to US$26.6 million from US$24.0 million in the year-earlier quarter. Provision for loan losses was US$2.7 million versus US$839,000 in the prior-year quarter, an increase of 217.9%. Non-interest income rose 16.4% to US$12.7 million from US$10.9 million, while non-interest expense advanced 4.6% to US$24.7 million.

Prospects: Co. is seeing improvements in its top- as well as bottom-line performance. In particular, Co.'s net interest income is being driven by the continued growth in the loan portfolio, which has been offset by declining market interest rates that caused loan yields to decline faster than yields on deposits due to its asset sensitive position. At the same time, Co. is experiencing growth in its non-interest income, as a result of higher service charges on deposits driven by increased overdraft fees and an increase in Visa check fees reflecting continued growth in electronic transactions.

Financial Data
(US$ in Thousands)

	3 Mos	12/31/2007	12/31/2006	12/31/2005	12/31/2004	12/31/2003	12/31/2002	12/31/2001
Earnings Per Share	2.01	2.01	2.20	2.24	0.98	2.18	2.08	1.59
Cash Flow Per Share	2.76	2.74	2.91	2.89	1.25	3.41	0.22	0.75
Tang Book Value Per Share	13.77	13.60	14.48	13.21	12.16	12.03	10.81	8.73
Dividends Per Share	0.930	0.920	0.880	0.840	0.780	0.740	0.690	0.607
Dividend Payout %	46.17	45.77	40.00	37.50	79.59	33.94	33.17	38.16
Income Statement								
Interest Income	43,922	180,975	153,443	122,160	109,390	112,467	122,722	127,870
Interest Expense	17,343	76,149	58,687	33,982	34,768	37,432	43,900	61,043
Net Interest Income	26,579	104,826	94,756	88,178	74,622	75,035	78,822	66,827
Provision for Losses	2,667	4,094	2,795	2,600	...	...	2,865	2,470
Non-Interest Income	12,696	44,289	38,895	36,909	30,769	33,736	29,729	21,836
Non-Interest Expense	24,703	99,788	85,096	77,194	92,703	67,226	63,961	54,618
Income Before Taxes	11,905	45,233	45,760	45,293	12,688	41,545	41,725	31,575
Income Taxes	3,700	12,971	12,889	12,195	(1,679)	9,479	11,012	8,429
Net Income	8,205	32,262	32,871	33,098	14,367	32,066	30,713	23,146
Average Shares	16,408	16,087	14,927	14,767	14,709	14,708	14,722	14,558
Balance Sheet								
Net Loans & Leases	2,346,012	2,251,939	1,786,087	1,667,493	1,430,871	1,138,548	1,048,817	983,266
Total Assets	3,160,896	3,043,953	2,610,457	2,459,616	2,309,343	2,333,342	2,307,404	2,081,834
Total Deposits	2,340,568	2,273,868	1,994,223	1,803,210	1,732,501	1,561,830	1,492,212	1,387,459
Total Liabilities	2,841,929	2,728,313	2,372,680	2,241,733	2,114,260	2,139,893	2,128,712	1,931,161
Stockholders' Equity	318,967	315,640	237,777	217,883	195,083	193,449	178,692	150,673
Shares Outstanding	16,361	16,349	14,826	14,793	14,628	14,495	14,536	14,483
Statistical Record								
Return on Assets %	1.08	1.14	1.30	1.39	0.62	1.38	1.40	1.20
Return on Equity %	11.05	11.66	14.43	16.03	7.38	17.23	18.65	16.64
Net Interest Margin %	60.51	57.92	61.75	72.18	68.22	66.72	64.23	52.26
Efficiency Ratio %	43.63	44.30	44.24	48.53	66.14	45.98	41.96	36.48
Loans to Deposits	1.00	0.99	0.90	0.92	0.83	0.73	0.70	0.71
Price Range	35.58-25.49	38.94-26.22	38.82-33.98	38.52-30.61	38.50-31.14	40.25-30.33	35.19-27.90	32.82-15.17
P/E Ratio	17.70-12.68	19.37-13.04	17.65-15.45	17.20-13.67	39.29-31.78	18.46-13.91	16.92-13.41	20.64-9.54
Average Yield %	3.09		2.62	2.44	2.46	2.23	2.18	2.68

Address: 17801 Georgia Avenue, Olney, MD 20832	Officers: Daniel J. Schrider - President Hunter R.	No of Institutions: 99
Telephone: 301-774-6400	Hollar - Chief Executive Officer **Transfer Agents:**	**Shares:** 6,283,913 **% Held:** 37.65
Web Site: www.ssnb.com	American Stock Transfer & Trust Co., New York, NY	

SEACOAST BANKING CORP. OF FLORIDA

Exchange	Symbol	Price	52Wk Range	Yield	P/E
NMS	SBCF	$10.53 (5/29/2008)	23.38-7.67	6.08	23.40

*7 Year Price Score 58.64 ***NYSE Composite Index=100** ***12 Month Price Score 74.43**

Interim Earnings (Per Share)

Qtr.	Mar	Jun	Sep	Dec
2005	0.25	0.33	0.32	0.34
2006	0.34	0.34	0.31	0.30
2007	0.14	0.25	0.01	0.10
2008	0.09	...	...	...

Interim Dividends (Per Share)

Amt	Decl	Ex	Rec	Pay
0.16Q	08/21/2007	09/19/2007	09/21/2007	09/28/2007
0.16Q	11/20/2007	12/18/2007	12/20/2007	01/02/2008
0.16Q	02/19/2008	03/17/2008	03/19/2008	03/31/2008
0.16Q	05/20/2008	06/18/2008	06/20/2008	06/30/2008

Indicated Div: $0.64

Valuation Analysis

Forecast EPS $0.47 (05/16/2008)
Market Cap $201.3 Million Book Value 215.0 Million
Price/Book 0.94 Price/Sales 1.17

Dividend Achiever Status

10 Year Growth Rate 9.09%
Total Years of Dividend Growth 16

Business Summary: Commercial Banking (MIC: SIC: 6022 NAIC: 522110)

Seacoast Banking is a bank holding company. Through First National Bank and Trust Company of the Treasure Coast (the Bank) and its broker-dealer subsidiary, Co. provides a range of deposit accounts and retail banking services, engages in consumer and commercial lending and provides a variety of trust and asset management services, as well as securities and annuity products. The Bank's service area includes Palm Beach, Broward, Martin, St. Lucie, Brevard and Indian River counties, which are located on Florida's southeast coast. The Bank operates 43 banking offices in 14 counties. As of Dec 31 2007, Co. had total assets of $2.42 billion and total deposits of $1.99 billion.

Recent Developments: For the quarter ended Mar 31 2008, net income decreased 36.3% to US$1.8 million from US$2.8 million in the year-earlier quarter. Net interest income decreased 4.1% to US$20.5 million from US$21.4 million in the year-earlier quarter. Provision for loan losses was US$5.5 million versus a credit for loan losses of US$550,000 in the prior-year quarter. Non-interest income rose 462.2% to US$6.2 million from US$1.1 million, while non-interest expense was unchanged at US$18.7 million.

Prospects: Looking ahead, Co. expects higher provision for loan loss and overall loan growth to be in a range of negative 5.0% to 3.0% growth in 2008 due in part to the slowing of residential real estate sales activity in all of its markets and lower demand for commercial loans in the newer metro markets of Orlando, West Palm Beach and Fort Lauderdale. Meanwhile, Co. noted that a second branch in Brevard County and a new office replacing its Rivergate branch in St. Lucie County are under construction and should be completed during the second quarter of 2008. Notably, two existing branches in proximity to new offices planned for 2008 are also expected to close simultaneously with branch openings.

Financial Data (US$ in Thousands)	3 Mos	12/31/2007	12/31/2006	12/31/2005	12/31/2004	12/31/2003	12/31/2002	12/31/2001
Earnings Per Share	0.45	0.51	1.28	1.24	0.95	0.89	0.97	0.90
Cash Flow Per Share	2.01	0.88	1.03	1.46	2.11	7.42	1.56	1.14
Tang Book Value Per Share	8.31	8.26	8.18	7.03	7.00	6.71	6.59	5.90
Dividends Per Share	0.640	0.640	0.610	0.580	0.540	0.460	0.282	...
Dividend Payout %	143.10	125.49	47.66	46.77	56.84	51.69	28.97	...
Income Statement								
Income Before Taxes	2,463	14,163	36,813	32,413	22,999	21,427	24,963	23,456
Income Taxes	700	4,398	12,959	11,654	8,077	7,411	9,677	9,326
Net Income	1,763	9,765	23,854	20,759	14,922	14,016	15,286	14,130
Average Shares	19,046	19,157	18,671	16,749	15,745	15,667	15,350	15,756
Balance Sheet								
Total Assets	2,393,357	2,419,874	2,389,435	2,132,174	1,615,876	1,353,823	1,281,297	1,225,964
Total Liabilities	2,178,404	2,205,493	2,177,010	1,979,454	1,507,664	1,249,739	1,180,550	1,132,445
Stockholders' Equity	214,953	214,381	212,425	152,720	108,212	104,084	100,747	93,519
Shares Outstanding	19,114	19,110	18,974	16,900	15,468	15,503	15,279	15,356
Statistical Record								
Return on Assets %	0.36	0.41	1.06	1.11	1.00	1.06	1.22	1.19
Return on Equity %	4.03	4.58	13.07	15.91	14.02	13.69	15.74	15.90
Price Range	25.36-7.67	25.36-10.28	31.68-23.25	25.62-18.03	23.90-17.35	18.43-14.85	19.64-13.35	14.24-8.16
P/E Ratio	56.36-17.04	49.73-20.16	24.75-18.16	20.66-14.54	25.16-18.26	20.71-16.69	20.24-13.76	15.82-9.07
Average Yield %	3.89	3.25	2.24	2.70	2.63	2.70	1.81	...

Address: 815 Colorado Avenue, Stuart, FL 34994	Officers: Dennis S. Hudson - Chairman, Chief Executive Officer Dale M. Hudson - Vice-Chairman	Investor Contact: 772-288-6085
Telephone: 772-287-4000	Transfer Agents:Continental Stock Transfer and Trust Co	No of Institutions: 95
Web Site: www.seacoastbanking.net		Shares: 8,499,017 % Held: 42.99

SECURITY BANK CORP

Exchange	Symbol	Price	52Wk Range	Yield	P/E
NMS	SBKC	$5.55 (5/29/2008)	20.96-5.50	3.15	N/A

*7 Year Price Score 54.38 *NYSE Composite Index=100 *12 Month Price Score 66.41

Interim Earnings (Per Share)

Qtr.	Mar	Jun	Sep	Dec
2005	0.28	0.32	0.33	0.33
2006	0.35	0.36	0.37	0.25
2007	0.35	0.31	0.03	(0.35)
2008	(1.22)	...	...	...

Interim Dividends (Per Share)

Amt	Decl	Ex	Rec	Pay
0.087Q	...	09/12/2007	09/14/2007	09/28/2007
0.087Q	11/20/2007	12/12/2007	12/14/2007	12/31/2007
0.087Q	02/20/2008	02/28/2008	03/03/2008	03/20/2008
0.044Q	05/20/2008	05/29/2008	06/02/2008	06/20/2008

Indicated Div: $0.17

Valuation Analysis

Forecast EPS	$-1.52 (05/16/2008)		
Market Cap	$128.9 Million	Book Value	309.9 Million
Price/Book	0.42	Price/Sales	0.62

Dividend Achiever Status

10 Year Growth Rate	21.73%
Total Years of Dividend Growth	10

Business Summary: Commercial Banking (MIC: SIC: 6022 NAIC: 522110)

Security Bank is a bank holding company. Through its wholly-owned subsidiaries, Security Bank of Bibb County, Security Bank of Houston County, Security Bank of Jones County, Security Bank of North Metro, Security Bank of North Fulton, and Security Bank of Gwinnett County (collectively known as the Banks), Co. is engaged in providing community banking services. The banks provide a range of retail and commercial banking products and services, as well as investment management and financial planning services through its wholly-owned subsidiary, CFS Wealth Management. As of Dec 31 2007, Co. had total assets of about $2.83 billion and total deposits of approximately $2.30 billion.

Recent Developments: For the quarter ended Mar 31 2008, net loss amounted to US$24.2 million versus net income of US$6.8 million in the year-earlier quarter. Net interest income decreased 35.0% to US$14.8 million from US$22.8 million in the year-earlier quarter. Provision for loan losses was US$42.2 million versus US$1.3 million in the prior-year quarter, an increase of. Non-interest income rose 15.1% to US$5.9 million from US$5.1 million, while non-interest expense advanced 6.4% to US$16.9 million.

Prospects: Co.'s near-term outlook appears to be challenging. In particular, Co.'s earnings are being hurt by an increase in the provision for loan losses related to the substantial increase in its nonperforming assets. In addition, Co.'s net interest income is being hampered by slower growth in its loan portfolio and lower net interest margin as a result of the recent decline in short-term rates. Nevertheless, Co.'s non-interest income growth is being driven by higher level of investment securities sold, partially offset by an increase in the loss on sale of other real estate owned. For 2008, Co. expects its net interest margin to continue to be affected by the level of its nonperforming assets.

Financial Data
(US$ in Thousands)

	3 Mos	12/31/2007	12/31/2006	12/31/2005	12/31/2004	12/31/2003	12/31/2002	12/31/2001
Earnings Per Share	(1.23)	0.34	1.33	1.27	1.08	0.96	0.76	0.65
Cash Flow Per Share	2.44	0.77	2.63	2.12	1.96	4.45	1.99	1.31
Tang Book Value Per Share	7.66	9.20	9.04	6.95	6.66	4.99	5.54	5.16
Dividends Per Share	0.350	0.350	0.300	0.260	0.220	0.200	0.175	0.155
Dividend Payout %	...	102.94	22.56	20.47	20.47	20.83	23.03	24.03
Income Statement								
Interest Income	40,742	192,840	148,082	78,192	53,926	42,895	32,920	33,609
Interest Expense	25,943	102,316	68,647	27,839	14,373	12,912	12,110	16,586
Net Interest Income	14,799	90,524	79,435	50,353	39,553	29,982	20,810	17,022
Provision for Losses	42,199	32,660	4,469	2,833	2,819	2,859	2,603	1,912
Non-Interest Income	5,862	18,981	17,906	16,603	14,833	17,303	13,145	11,147
Non-Interest Expense	16,907	67,073	55,602	38,545	32,129	30,301	22,411	19,371
Income Before Taxes	(38,445)	9,771	37,270	25,495	19,259	13,586	8,331	6,860
Income Taxes	(14,247)	3,184	13,878	9,310	6,940	4,938	3,065	2,518
Net Income	(24,198)	6,588	23,392	16,185	12,319	8,647	5,266	4,342
Average Shares	19,814	19,225	17,564	12,736	11,482	8,993	6,912	6,752
Balance Sheet								
Net Loans & Leases	2,137,567	2,158,220	1,887,643	1,261,533	842,369	699,723	468,921	415,207
Total Assets	2,818,477	2,833,071	2,494,071	1,662,413	1,063,485	911,269	580,762	504,762
Total Deposits	2,309,671	2,298,705	1,970,927	1,291,253	842,558	743,301	440,633	375,065
Total Liabilities	2,508,601	2,526,378	2,187,664	1,483,108	956,814	835,460	523,214	469,984
Stockholders' Equity	309,876	306,693	306,407	179,305	106,671	75,809	39,548	34,777
Shares Outstanding	23,233	18,912	19,166	14,386	11,639	10,048	6,796	6,745
Statistical Record								
Return on Assets %	N.M.	0.25	1.13	1.19	1.24	1.16	0.97	0.95
Return on Equity %	N.M.	2.15	9.63	11.32	13.46	14.99	14.17	13.19
Net Interest Margin %	36.32	46.94	53.64	64.40	73.35	69.90	63.21	50.65
Efficiency Ratio %	36.28	31.67	33.50	40.66	46.73	50.34	48.65	43.28
Loans to Deposits	0.93	0.94	0.96	0.98	1.00	0.94	1.06	1.11
Price Range	21.46-6.26	22.96-9.14	25.55-21.10	25.88-18.06	21.52-14.50	18.00-12.00	12.50-7.34	8.50-6.38
P/E Ratio	...	67.53-26.88	19.21-15.86	20.38-14.22	19.93-13.43	18.74-12.50	16.45-9.65	13.08-9.81
Average Yield %	2.63	2.10	1.30	1.17	1.31	1.31	1.85	2.11

Address: 4219 Forsyth Road, Macon, GA 31210 **Telephone:** 478-722-6200 **Web Site:** www.securitybank.net	**Officers:** Alford C. Bridges - Chairman Edward M. Beckham - Vice-Chairman **Transfer Agents:** Registrar and Transfer Company, Cranford, NJ	**No of Institutions:** 75 **Shares:** 4,323,050 **% Held:** 21.88

SEI INVESTMENTS CO.

Exchange	Symbol	Price	52Wk Range	Yield	P/E
NMS	SEIC	$24.16 (5/29/2008)	33.12-22.89	0.66	19.80

*7 Year Price Score 104.41 ***NYSE Composite Index=100** ***12 Month Price Score 90.99**

Interim Earnings (Per Share)

Qtr.	Mar	Jun	Sep	Dec
2005	0.21	0.22	0.24	0.26
2006	0.27	0.28	0.30	0.31
2007	0.31	0.34	0.37	0.26
2008	0.25	...	...	...

Interim Dividends (Per Share)

Amt	Decl	Ex	Rec	Pay
0.07S	05/23/2007	06/06/2007	06/08/2007	06/21/2007
100%	05/23/2007	06/22/2007	06/11/2007	06/21/2007
0.07S	12/10/2007	01/02/2008	01/04/2008	01/18/2008
0.08S	05/20/2008	06/13/2008	06/17/2008	06/20/2008
		Indicated Div: $0.16		

Valuation Analysis

Forecast EPS	$1.36 (05/16/2008)		
Market Cap	$4.7 Billion	Book Value	761.0 Million
Price/Book	6.12	Price/Sales	3.38

Dividend Achiever Status

10 Year Growth Rate	19.62%
Total Years of Dividend Growth	16

Business Summary: Finance Intermediaries & Services (MIC: SIC: 6211 NAIC: 523120)

SEI Investments is a global provider of investment processing, fund processing, and investment management business outsourcing applications that are designed to help corporations, financial institutions, financial advisors, and affluent families create and manage wealth. Co. operations are divided into six main segments; Private Banks; Investment Advisors; Institutional Investors; Investment Managers; Investments in New Businesses; and LSV Asset Management. At Dec 31 2007, through its subsidiaries and partnerships, Co. administered $426.10 billion in mutual fund and pooled assets, managed $196.80 billion in assets, and operated from more than 20 offices in over a dozen countries.

Recent Developments: For the quarter ended Mar 31 2008, net income decreased 22.8% to US$48.9 million from US$63.4 million in the year-earlier quarter. Revenues were US$333.9 million, up 3.5% from US$322.7 million the year before. Operating income was US$138.5 million versus US$139.2 million in the prior-year quarter, a decrease of 0.5%. Direct operating expenses rose 6.2% to US$45.3 million from US$42.6 million in the comparable period the year before. Indirect operating expenses increased 6.5% to US$150.1 million from US$140.9 million in the equivalent prior-year period.

Prospects: Co. remains encouraged with its outlook as it is seeing improved sales across most of its businesses, further acceptance of its new strategies, continued to operate and expand its Global Wealth Platform, and is progressing in its key investments. Accordingly, Co. believes that the increased opportunities will accelerate growth in its future revenues and profits. Meanwhile, on Apr 7 2008, Co. announced its initial expansion into mainland China through an investment advisory agreement with its client, Yinhua Fund Management Co., Ltd in Beijing, China. Notably, this transaction reflects Co.'s growing global presence and is a key step in its strategy to expand its operations in Asia.

Financial Data

(US$ in Thousands)	3 Mos	12/31/2007	12/31/2006	12/31/2005	12/31/2004	12/31/2003	12/31/2002	12/31/2001
Earnings Per Share	1.22	1.28	1.17	0.92	0.80	0.66	0.63	0.55
Cash Flow Per Share	1.91	1.84	1.75	1.07	0.90	0.85	0.81	0.80
Tang Book Value Per Share	2.28	2.27	1.82	1.55	1.70	1.63	1.27	1.19
Dividends Per Share	0.140	0.070	0.120	0.110	0.145	0.035	0.085	0.045
Dividend Payout %	11.51	5.47	10.30	12.02	18.13	5.30	13.60	8.26
Income Statement								
Total Revenue	333,908	1,369,028	1,175,749	773,007	692,269	636,233	620,819	658,013
EBITDA	90,294	451,385	393,367	314,318	283,426	243,375	243,371	220,123
Depn & Amortn	11,520	37,136	29,147	17,585	16,183	16,788	18,060	19,650
Income Before Taxes	77,807	409,540	358,756	295,209	265,131	224,284	223,048	198,324
Income Taxes	28,861	149,731	121,766	106,865	96,110	81,303	82,528	73,380
Net Income	48,946	259,809	236,990	188,344	169,021	142,981	140,520	124,944
Average Shares	198,211	202,231	203,266	206,276	211,732	216,274	225,606	229,620
Balance Sheet								
Current Assets	701,629	694,934	586,473	305,976	355,679	352,413	261,435	266,142
Total Assets	1,256,095	1,252,365	1,079,705	657,147	615,475	592,629	464,147	460,916
Current Liabilities	230,077	230,367	196,127	167,470	163,569	193,474	134,247	144,343
Long-Term Obligations	39,184	43,971	67,538	9,000	14,389	23,944	33,500	43,055
Total Liabilities	495,105	495,982	449,193	235,459	211,533	228,856	174,140	190,323
Stockholders' Equity	760,990	756,383	630,512	421,688	403,942	363,773	290,007	270,593
Shares Outstanding	192,740	194,375	197,906	197,160	204,350	209,738	218,360	218,360
Statistical Record								
Return on Assets %	20.79	22.28	27.29	29.60	27.90	27.06	30.38	29.87
Return on Equity %	33.99	37.47	45.05	45.62	43.91	43.74	50.13	53.39
EBITDA Margin %	27.04	32.97	33.46	40.66	40.94	38.25	39.20	33.45
Net Margin %	14.66	18.98	20.16	24.37	24.42	22.47	22.63	18.99
Asset Turnover	1.17	1.17	1.35	1.21	1.14	1.20	1.34	1.57
Current Ratio	3.05	3.02	2.99	1.83	2.17	1.82	1.95	1.84
Debt to Equity	0.05	0.06	0.11	0.02	0.04	0.07	0.12	0.16
Price Range	33.12-23.21	33.12-23.34	30.26-18.68	21.05-16.07	21.55-13.70	17.96-11.45	22.88-9.52	25.66-13.95
P/E Ratio	27.15-19.02	25.87-18.23	25.86-15.96	22.88-17.47	26.93-17.13	27.21-17.35	36.31-15.10	46.65-25.36
Average Yield %	0.49	0.24	0.50	0.59	0.87	0.24	0.53	0.23

Address: 1 Freedom Valley Drive, Oaks, PA 19456-1100 **Telephone:** 610-676-1000 **Web Site:** www.seic.com	**Officers:** Alfred P. West - Chairman, Chief Executive Officer Dennis J. McGonigle - Executive Vice President, Chief Financial Officer **Transfer Agents:** American Stock Transfer & Trust Co., New York, NY	**Investor Contact:** 610-676-1000 **No of Institutions:** 369 **Shares:** 112,965,792 **% Held:** 56.15

SHENANDOAH TELECOMMUNICATIONS CO.

Exchange	Symbol	Price	52Wk Range	Yield	P/E
NMS	SHEN	$16.29 (5/29/2008)	25.53-13.51	1.66	19.63

*7 Year Price Score 128.74 *NYSE Composite Index=100   *12 Month Price Score 81.47

TRADING VOLUME (thousand shares)

Interim Earnings (Per Share)

Qtr.	Mar	Jun	Sep	Dec
2005	0.10	0.11	0.14	0.11
2006	0.37	0.12	0.14	0.14
2007	0.17	0.25	0.22	0.16
2008	0.20	...	...	...

Interim Dividends (Per Share)

Amt	Decl	Ex	Rec	Pay
0.09A	10/25/2006	11/13/2006	11/15/2006	12/01/2006
0.16A	10/25/2006	11/13/2006	11/15/2006	12/01/2006
3-for-1	06/18/2007	08/20/2007	08/02/2007	08/17/2007
0.27A	10/23/2007	11/09/2007	11/14/2007	11/30/2007
		Indicated Div: $0.27		

Valuation Analysis

Forecast EPS $0.88 (05/16/2008)

Market Cap	$383.3 Million	Book Value	156.2 Million
Price/Book	2.45	Price/Sales	2.66

Dividend Achiever Status

10 Year Growth Rate		14.18%
Total Years of Dividend Growth		11

Business Summary: Communications (MIC: SIC: 4813 NAIC: 517110)

Shenandoah Telecommunications is a telecommunications holding company that, through its operating subsidiaries, provides both regulated and unregulated telecommunications services to end-user customers and other communications providers in the southeastern U.S. Co.'s subsidiaries provide local exchange telephone services and wireless personal communications services, as well as cable television, video, Internet and data services, long distance, sale of telecommunications equipment, fiber optics facilities, and leased tower facilities. As of Dec 31 2007, Co. had six segments: Wireless Personal Communications Services, Telephone, Converged Services, Mobile, Cable Television and Other.

Recent Developments: For the quarter ended Mar 31 2008, net income increased 17.7% to US$4.8 million from US$4.1 million in the year-earlier quarter. Revenues were US$36.5 million, up 10.4% from US$33.0 million the year before. Operating income was US$8.5 million versus US$7.1 million in the prior-year quarter, an increase of 20.1%. Direct operating expenses rose 10.0% to US$12.5 million from US$11.4 million in the comparable period the year before. Indirect operating expenses increased 6.0% to US$15.4 million from US$14.6 million in the equivalent prior-year period.

Prospects: Co. estimates its 2008 capital expenditures of about $65.0 million, including $28.9 million for 60 additional personal communications service base stations and towers to expand its network coverage and capacity, principally in Pennsylvania, 53 new high speed wireless internet/data access (EVDO) sites to provide EVDO service over more of its network and additional switch capacity to handle the additional growth. Specifically, Co. anticipates bringing on-line the additional 53 EVDO sites by end of 2008, covering further 400,000 potential customers, which should bring EVDO coverage to over 80% of its network's currently covered population.

Financial Data

(US$ in Thousands)	3 Mos	12/31/2007	12/31/2006	12/31/2005	12/31/2004	12/31/2003	12/31/2002	12/31/2001
Earnings Per Share	0.83	0.80	0.77	0.46	0.45	1.41	0.20	0.72
Cash Flow Per Share	1.98	1.87	1.48	1.40	1.50	1.35	1.02	0.74
Tang Book Value Per Share	6.12	5.91	5.26	4.69	4.44	4.44	3.15	3.05
Dividends Per Share	0.270	0.270	0.250	0.153	0.143	0.130	0.123	0.117
Dividend Payout %	32.64	33.75	32.61	33.09	32.09	9.24	61.67	16.13
Income Statement								
Total Revenue	36,487	141,183	169,195	146,391	120,974	105,861	92,957	88,715
EBITDA	15,772	62,845	60,021	42,909	38,470	35,206	13,675	46,820
Depn & Amortn	7,508	29,198	27,290	22,382	19,020	16,631	14,482	11,834
Income Before Taxes	7,931	31,774	30,369	17,451	16,321	15,065	(5,002)	30,859
Income Taxes	3,139	12,971	12,370	6,716	6,078	5,304	(2,109)	9,961
Net Income	4,792	18,803	17,922	10,735	10,243	32,074	4,519	16,372
Average Shares	23,587	23,497	23,331	23,109	22,971	22,824	22,626	22,644
Balance Sheet								
Current Assets	43,302	41,136	30,863	20,801	34,517	40,963	20,494	16,034
Total Assets	223,727	221,524	207,720	204,921	211,247	185,364	164,004	166,797
Current Liabilities	22,750	24,056	21,280	22,741	21,846	15,796	19,900	21,641
Long-Term Obligations	16,574	17,659	21,907	31,392	47,919	39,116	47,561	52,049
Total Liabilities	67,570	70,400	72,531	83,321	97,450	79,156	87,427	92,195
Stockholders' Equity	156,157	151,124	135,189	121,600	113,797	106,208	76,577	74,602
Shares Outstanding	23,530	23,509	23,283	23,061	22,890	22,779	22,656	22,590
Statistical Record								
Return on Assets %	8.94	8.76	8.69	5.16	5.15	18.36	2.73	10.32
Return on Equity %	13.16	13.13	13.96	9.12	9.29	35.09	5.98	23.23
EBITDA Margin %	43.23	44.51	35.47	29.31	31.80	33.26	14.71	52.78
Net Margin %	13.13	13.32	10.59	7.33	8.47	30.30	4.86	18.45
Asset Turnover	0.66	0.66	0.82	0.70	0.61	0.61	0.56	0.56
Current Ratio	1.90	1.71	1.45	0.91	1.58	2.59	1.03	0.74
Debt to Equity	0.11	0.12	0.16	0.26	0.42	0.37	0.62	0.70
Price Range	25.53-13.51	25.53-14.41	16.66-13.42	17.32-8.63	11.41-7.33	9.17-4.54	9.08-5.50	6.82-4.58
P/E Ratio	30.76-16.28	31.91-18.01	21.64-17.42	37.65-18.75	25.36-16.28	6.50-3.22	45.42-27.50	9.47-6.37
Average Yield %	1.43	1.47	1.69	1.26	1.67	1.84	1.57	2.10

Address: 124 South Main Street, Edinburg, VA 22824	Officers: Christopher E. French - President, Chief Executive Officer Earle A. MacKenzie - Executive	No of Institutions: 85
Telephone: 540-984-4141	Vice President, Chief Operating Officer **Transfer**	Shares: 7,898,116 % Held: 33.64
Web Site: www.shentel.com	Agents: The Company	

SHERWIN-WILLIAMS CO.

Exchange	Symbol	Price	52Wk Range	Yield	P/E
NYS	SHW	$56.42 (5/29/2008)	72.99-50.13	2.48	12.51

*7 Year Price Score 111.62 *NYSE Composite Index=100 *12 Month Price Score 94.68

Interim Earnings (Per Share)

Qtr.	Mar	Jun	Sep	Dec
2005	0.58	1.08	1.07	0.55
2006	0.82	1.33	1.30	0.73
2007	0.83	1.52	1.55	0.82
2008	0.64	...	...	...

Interim Dividends (Per Share)

Amt	Decl	Ex	Rec	Pay
0.315Q	07/18/2007	08/22/2007	08/24/2007	09/14/2007
0.315Q	10/19/2007	11/14/2007	11/16/2007	12/07/2007
0.35Q	02/20/2008	02/27/2008	02/29/2008	03/14/2008
0.35Q	04/16/2008	05/14/2008	05/16/2008	06/06/2008

Indicated Div: $1.40 (Div. Reinv. Plan)

Valuation Analysis

Forecast EPS $4.75 (05/16/2008)

Market Cap	$6.7 Billion	Book Value	1.6 Billion
Price/Book	4.15	Price/Sales	0.84

Dividend Achiever Status

10 Year Growth Rate	12.16%
Total Years of Dividend Growth	28

Business Summary: Retail - Hardware (MIC: SIC: 5231 NAIC: 444120)

Sherwin-Williams develops, manufactures, distributes and sell paint, coatings and related products to professional, industrial, commercial and retail customers primarily in North and South America with additional operations in the U.K., Europe, India and China. As of Dec 31 2007, Co.'s reportable operating segments are: Paint Stores Group, which consists of 3,325 company-operated specialty paint stores and seven manufacturing/distribution facilities; Consumer Group, which develops, manufactures and distributes a variety of paint, coatings and related products; and Global Group, which develops, licenses, manufactures, distributes and sells a variety of paint, coatings and related products.

Recent Developments: For the quarter ended Mar 31 2008, net income decreased 30.3% to US$77.9 million from US$111.8 million in the year-earlier quarter. Revenues were US$1.78 billion, up 1.5% from US$1.76 billion the year before. Direct operating expenses rose 3.8% to US$1.00 billion from US$964.8 million in the comparable period the year before. Indirect operating expenses increased 5.5% to US$651.7 million from US$617.7 million in the equivalent prior-year period.

Prospects: Co. will continue to implement price increases and cost reductions across all business segments in the coming months to improve profitability. Hence, for the second quarter of 2008, Co. expects a percentage increase in consolidated net sales in the low single digits over the prior year quarter with diluted net income per share of $1.45 to $1.60. For the full-year 2008, Co. now expects a low single digit percentage increase in consolidated net sales over 2007 and expects diluted net income per share of $4.70 to $4.85. Separately, Co. expects its Paint Stores Group to open around 100 new stores in 2008 while accelerating the closure of redundant store locations from acquisitions.

Financial Data
(US$ in Thousands)

	3 Mos	12/31/2007	12/31/2006	12/31/2005	12/31/2004	12/31/2003	12/31/2002	12/31/2001
Earnings Per Share	4.51	4.70	4.19	3.28	2.72	2.26	0.84	1.68
Cash Flow Per Share	7.52	6.87	6.11	5.24	3.86	3.86	3.72	3.61
Tang Book Value Per Share	0.07	0.92	2.67	3.83	1.90	2.95	3.77	2.59
Dividends Per Share	1.295	1.260	1.000	0.820	0.680	0.620	0.600	0.580
Dividend Payout %	28.69	26.81	23.87	25.00	25.00	27.43	71.43	34.52
Income Statement								
Total Revenue	1,781,682	8,005,292	7,809,759	7,190,661	6,113,789	5,407,764	5,184,788	5,066,005
EBITDA	171,835	1,148,052	1,047,391	849,318	745,785	678,232	653,298	627,174
Depn & Amortn	41,133	163,479	145,917	143,517	125,642	116,564	115,659	148,098
Income Before Taxes	113,029	912,943	834,312	656,215	580,195	522,926	497,164	424,449
Income Taxes	35,083	297,365	258,254	191,601	185,662	190,868	186,463	161,291
Net Income	77,946	615,578	576,058	463,258	393,254	332,058	127,565	263,158
Average Shares	122,096	130,924	137,342	141,078	144,735	147,005	152,435	156,893
Balance Sheet								
Current Assets	2,194,642	2,069,580	2,450,281	1,894,385	1,781,928	1,715,144	1,505,993	1,506,945
Total Assets	5,010,837	4,855,340	4,995,087	4,369,195	4,274,151	3,682,608	3,432,312	3,627,925
Current Liabilities	2,463,947	2,141,385	2,074,815	1,554,371	1,520,137	1,154,170	1,083,496	1,141,353
Long-Term Obligations	293,499	293,454	291,876	486,996	488,239	502,992	506,682	503,517
Total Liabilities	3,391,225	3,069,613	3,002,727	2,638,583	2,626,905	2,223,751	2,090,422	2,140,161
Stockholders' Equity	1,619,612	1,785,727	1,992,360	1,730,612	1,647,246	1,458,857	1,341,890	1,487,764
Shares Outstanding	119,096	122,814	133,565	135,139	140,777	143,406	148,910	153,978
Statistical Record								
Return on Assets %	11.64	12.50	12.30	10.72	9.86	9.33	3.61	7.13
Return on Equity %	32.80	32.59	30.95	27.43	25.25	23.71	9.02	17.78
EBITDA Margin %	9.64	14.34	13.41	11.81	12.20	12.54	12.60	12.38
Net Margin %	4.37	7.69	7.38	6.44	6.43	6.14	2.46	5.19
Asset Turnover	1.61	1.63	1.67	1.66	1.53	1.52	1.47	1.37
Current Ratio	0.89	0.97	1.18	1.22	1.17	1.49	1.39	1.32
Debt to Equity	0.18	0.16	0.15	0.28	0.30	0.34	0.38	0.34
Price Range	72.99-50.13	72.99-57.65	64.61-41.29	48.63-40.75	45.48-33.06	34.74-24.82	33.00-22.06	28.02-20.31
P/E Ratio	16.18-11.12	15.53-12.27	15.42-9.85	14.83-12.42	16.72-12.15	15.37-10.98	39.29-26.26	16.68-12.09
Average Yield %	2.07	1.92	1.92	1.84	1.72	2.12	2.14	2.42

Address: 101 Prospect Avenue, N.W., Cleveland, OH 44115-1075 **Telephone:** 216-566-2000 **Web Site:** www.sherwin.com	**Officers:** Christopher M. Connor - Chairman, Chief Executive Officer John G. Morikis - President, Chief Operating Officer **Transfer Agents:** The Bank of New York, New York, NY	**Investor Contact:** 216-566-2000 **No of Institutions:** 492 **Shares:** 106,009,232 **% Held:** 77.89

SIGMA-ALDRICH CORP.

Exchange	Symbol	Price	52Wk Range	Yield	P/E
NMS	SIAL	$58.40 (5/29/2008)	62.24-41.12	0.89	24.23

*7 Year Price Score 123.36 *NYSE Composite Index=100 *12 Month Price Score 118.00

Interim Earnings (Per Share)

Qtr.	Mar	Jun	Sep	Dec
2005	0.54	0.46	0.47	0.42
2006	0.49	0.52	0.51	0.53
2007	0.56	0.60	0.54	0.64
2008	0.64	...	...	...

Interim Dividends (Per Share)

Amt	Decl	Ex	Rec	Pay
0.115Q	08/14/2007	08/29/2007	08/31/2007	09/14/2007
0.115Q	11/13/2007	11/28/2007	11/30/2007	12/14/2007
0.13Q	02/12/2008	02/27/2008	02/29/2008	03/14/2008
0.13Q	05/06/2008	05/28/2008	05/30/2008	06/13/2008

Indicated Div: $0.52

Valuation Analysis

Forecast EPS	$2.65 (05/16/2008)		
Market Cap	$7.5 Billion	Book Value	1.7 Billion
Price/Book	4.38	Price/Sales	3.57

Dividend Achiever Status

10 Year Growth Rate	13.92%
Total Years of Dividend Growth	26

Business Summary: Chemicals (MIC: SIC: 5169 NAIC: 424690)

Sigma-Aldrich is a Life Science and High Technology company. Co. operates in four business units: Research Essentials, which sells biological buffers, cell culture reagents, biochemicals, chemicals and solvents; Research Specialties, which sells organic chemicals, biochemicals, analytical reagents, chromatography consumables and reference materials; Research Biotech, which supplies immunochemical, molecular biology, cell signaling and neuroscience biochemicals for biotechnology, genomic, and other life science research applications; and Fine Chemicals, which supplies organic chemicals and biochemicals used in development by pharmaceutical, biotechnology, industrial and diagnostic companies.

Recent Developments: For the quarter ended Mar 31 2008, net income increased 12.8% to US$84.5 million from US$74.9 million in the year-earlier quarter. Revenues were US$569.6 million, up 14.9% from US$495.9 million the year before. Direct operating expenses rose 14.9% to US$277.4 million from US$241.5 million in the comparable period the year before. Indirect operating expenses increased 14.2% to US$167.8 million from US$146.9 million in the equivalent prior-year period.

Prospects: For 2008, Co. expects sales to meet its 7.0% organic growth target. Moreover, currency benefits could add another 6.0% to growth if currency exchange rates remain at Mar 31 2008 levels. Hence, based on its sales expectations and modest margin contributions from its supply chain initiative and other process improvements, Co. has raised its estimate for 2008 diluted earnings per share to $2.57 to $2.67, an increase of 9.8% to 14.1% over 2007. Also, Co. may further improve growth in 2008 as it continues to seek to add as much as 3.0% in overall additional annual revenue growth through acquisition of strategically important products, services, platform technologies, businesses and facilities.

Financial Data
(US$ in Thousands)

	3 Mos	12/31/2007	12/31/2006	12/31/2005	12/31/2004	12/31/2003	12/31/2002	12/31/2001
Earnings Per Share	2.41	2.34	2.05	1.88	1.67	1.36	0.89	0.94
Cash Flow Per Share	3.25	3.21	2.49	2.07	2.34	2.19	2.41	1.07
Tang Book Value Per Share	9.00	8.19	7.00	5.71	7.67	6.41	5.45	4.67
Dividends Per Share	0.475	0.460	0.420	0.380	0.340	0.250	0.172	0.166
Dividend Payout %	19.68	19.66	20.49	20.21	20.36	18.45	19.38	17.78
Income Statement								
Total Revenue	569,600	2,038,700	1,797,500	1,666,500	1,409,200	1,298,146	1,206,982	1,179,447
EBITDA	149,700	557,400	493,600	451,500	392,400	352,216	352,302	289,548
Depn & Amortn	25,300	97,800	90,900	90,100	73,400	69,267	66,326	71,373
Income Before Taxes	124,400	437,600	378,700	343,300	311,800	272,823	272,139	201,633
Income Taxes	39,900	126,500	101,900	85,000	78,900	82,393	85,404	60,928
Net Income	84,500	311,100	276,800	258,300	232,900	193,102	130,714	140,705
Average Shares	131,900	133,100	134,900	137,400	139,600	142,252	146,824	150,350
Balance Sheet								
Current Assets	1,379,700	1,282,500	1,112,900	950,200	893,400	815,030	694,887	727,311
Total Assets	2,742,900	2,629,100	2,334,300	2,131,300	1,745,000	1,548,242	1,389,656	1,439,802
Current Liabilities	636,100	635,000	442,600	460,700	230,900	257,378	265,653	397,563
Long-Term Obligations	200,100	207,000	337,900	283,200	177,100	176,259	176,805	177,700
Total Liabilities	1,024,100	1,012,500	923,400	897,900	533,300	548,981	507,482	630,087
Stockholders' Equity	1,718,800	1,616,600	1,410,900	1,233,400	1,211,700	999,261	882,174	809,715
Shares Outstanding	128,900	129,400	132,000	134,400	137,400	138,202	142,506	146,028
Statistical Record								
Return on Assets %	12.15	12.54	12.40	13.33	14.11	13.15	9.24	10.10
Return on Equity %	20.15	20.55	20.94	21.13	21.01	20.53	15.45	16.86
EBITDA Margin %	26.28	27.34	27.46	27.09	27.85	27.13	29.19	24.55
Net Margin %	14.83	15.26	15.40	15.50	16.53	14.88	10.83	11.93
Asset Turnover	0.80	0.82	0.81	0.86	0.85	0.88	0.85	0.85
Current Ratio	2.17	2.02	2.51	2.06	3.87	3.17	2.62	1.83
Debt to Equity	0.12	0.13	0.24	0.23	0.15	0.18	0.20	0.22
Price Range	59.65-41.12	55.87-37.77	39.41-31.54	33.34-27.86	30.67-26.96	28.73-20.59	26.25-19.70	25.61-18.55
P/E Ratio	24.75-17.06	23.88-16.14	19.22-15.38	17.73-14.82	18.37-16.14	21.13-15.14	29.50-22.14	27.24-19.73
Average Yield %	0.98	1.02	1.19	1.24	1.19	0.98	0.73	0.77

Address: 3050 Spruce Street, St. Louis, MO 63103	**Officers:** David R. Harvey - Chairman Jai P. Nagarkatti - President, Chief Executive Officer	**Investor Contact:** 314-286-8004
Telephone: 314-771-5765	**Transfer Agents:** Computershare Investor Services, Chicago, IL	**No of Institutions:** 519
Web Site: www.sigma-aldrich.com		**Shares:** 114,973,824 **% Held:** 74.96

SIMMONS FIRST NATIONAL CORP.

Exchange	Symbol	Price	52Wk Range	Yield	P/E
NMS	SFNC	$30.85 (5/29/2008)	32.08-22.49	2.46	14.83

*7 Year Price Score 87.05   ***NYSE Composite Index=100**   ***12 Month Price Score 114.90**

Interim Earnings (Per Share)

Qtr.	Mar	Jun	Sep	Dec
2005	0.40	0.47	0.50	0.47
2006	0.41	0.51	0.51	0.47
2007	0.46	0.49	0.53	0.44
2008	0.63	...	...	...

Interim Dividends (Per Share)

Amt	Decl	Ex	Rec	Pay
0.18Q	08/31/2007	09/13/2007	09/17/2007	10/01/2007
0.19Q	11/28/2007	12/13/2007	12/17/2007	01/02/2008
0.19Q	02/28/2008	03/13/2008	03/17/2008	04/01/2008
0.19Q	05/29/2008	06/12/2008	06/16/2008	07/01/2008

Indicated Div: $0.76

Valuation Analysis

Forecast EPS	$2.27 (05/16/2008)		
Market Cap	$430.1 Million	Book Value	280.8 Million
Price/Book	1.53	Price/Sales	1.98

Dividend Achiever Status

10 Year Growth Rate	10.31%
Total Years of Dividend Growth	17

Business Summary: Commercial Banking (MIC: SIC: 6021 NAIC: 522110)

Simmons First National is a financial holding company. Co.'s key bank subsidiary is Simmons First National Bank, whose primary market area, with the exception of its nationally provided credit card product, is Central and Western Arkansas. Through its subsidiaries, Co. provides banking services, including consumer (credit card, student and other consumer), real estate (construction, single family residential and other commercial) and commercial loans, checking, savings and time deposits, trust and investment management services, and securities and investment services to individuals and businesses. As of Dec 31 2007, Co. had total assets of $2.69 billion and deposits of $2.18 billion.

Recent Developments: For the quarter ended Mar 31 2008, net income increased 32.8% to US$8.8 million from US$6.6 million in the year-earlier quarter. Net interest income increased 2.5% to US$22.8 million from US$22.2 million in the year-earlier quarter. Provision for loan losses was US$1.5 million versus US$751,000 in the prior-year quarter, an increase of 95.3%. Non-interest income rose 30.9% to US$15.0 million from US$11.5 million, while non-interest expense declined 0.4% to US$23.1 million.

Prospects: Co.'s improved bottom-line results reflect an increase in non-interest income, primarily due to the non-recurring gain from proceeds received on the mandatory partial redemption of its equity interest in Visa, Inc. and Visa U.S.A. In addition, results reflect higher net interest income as a result of a decrease in Co.'s interest expense. However, Co. is experiencing a decline in net interest margin, primarily attributable to significant repricing of earning assets due to declining interest rates, along with its concentrated effort to increase liquidity. Going forward, Co. anticipates further margin compression for the remainder of 2008 due to the continued effect of rate movements.

Financial Data
(US$ in Thousands)

	3 Mos	12/31/2007	12/31/2006	12/31/2005	12/31/2004	12/31/2003	12/31/2002	12/31/2001
Earnings Per Share	2.08	1.92	1.90	1.84	1.65	1.65	1.53	1.16
Cash Flow Per Share	3.32	2.55	2.92	2.57	2.68	3.78	2.26	1.22
Tang Book Value Per Share	15.56	14.97	13.68	12.46	11.76	11.32	11.60	10.59
Dividends Per Share	0.740	0.730	0.680	0.610	0.570	0.525	0.480	0.440
Dividend Payout %	35.50	38.02	35.79	33.15	34.55	31.82	31.27	38.10
Income Statement								
Income Before Taxes	13,187	39,741	39,921	39,465	35,929	34,684	31,775	22,886
Income Taxes	4,371	12,381	12,440	12,503	11,483	10,894	9,697	6,358
Net Income	8,816	27,360	27,481	26,962	24,446	23,790	22,078	16,528
Average Shares	14,069	14,241	14,474	14,687	14,848	14,415	14,376	14,324
Balance Sheet								
Total Assets	2,861,758	2,692,447	2,651,413	2,523,768	2,413,944	2,235,778	1,977,579	2,016,918
Total Liabilities	2,580,969	2,420,041	2,392,397	2,279,683	2,175,722	2,025,783	1,779,974	1,834,555
Stockholders' Equity	280,789	272,406	259,016	244,085	238,222	209,995	197,605	182,363
Shares Outstanding	13,941	13,918	14,196	14,326	14,621	14,101	14,142	14,174
Statistical Record								
Return on Assets %	1.06	1.02	1.06	1.09	1.05	1.13	1.11	0.84
Return on Equity %	10.85	10.30	10.92	11.18	10.88	11.67	11.62	9.29
Price Range	30.40-22.49	31.94-22.49	32.94-25.23	29.56-21.40	30.00-22.80	28.90-17.06	21.30-15.64	18.90-11.13
P/E Ratio	14.62-10.81	16.64-11.71	17.34-13.28	16.07-11.63	18.18-13.82	17.52-10.34	13.92-10.22	16.29-9.59
Average Yield %	2.75	2.65	2.35	2.32	2.16	2.41	2.71	2.94

Address: 501 Main Street, Pine Bluff, AR 71601 Telephone: 870-541-1000 Web Site: www.simmonsfirst.com	Officers: J. Thomas May - Chairman, Chief Executive Officer David Bartlett - President, Chief Operating Officer Transfer Agents: Computershare Investor Services, Chicago, IL	No of Institutions: 80 Shares: 6,609,358 % Held: 46.14

SJW CORP.

Exchange	Symbol	Price	52Wk Range	Yield	P/E
NYS	SJW	$31.90 (5/29/2008)	38.80-28.05	2.02	29.81

*7 Year Price Score 116.29 *NYSE Composite Index=100 *12 Month Price Score 96.07

Interim Earnings (Per Share)

Qtr.	Mar	Jun	Sep	Dec
2005	0.14	0.31	0.50	0.23
2006	0.23	0.35	0.48	1.03
2007	0.11	0.29	0.43	0.20
2008	0.15	...	...	...

Interim Dividends (Per Share)

Amt	Decl	Ex	Rec	Pay
0.151Q	07/26/2007	08/02/2007	08/06/2007	09/01/2007
0.151Q	10/25/2007	11/01/2007	11/05/2007	12/01/2007
0.161Q	01/31/2008	02/07/2008	02/11/2008	03/01/2008
0.161Q	04/30/2008	05/08/2008	05/12/2008	06/01/2008

Indicated Div: $0.65

Valuation Analysis

Forecast EPS 1.29 (05/16/2008)

Market Cap	$586.4 Million	Book Value	238.0 Million
Price/Book	2.46	Price/Sales	2.82

Dividend Achiever Status

10 Year Growth Rate	4.76%
Total Years of Dividend Growth	40

TRADING VOLUME (thousand shares)

Business Summary: Water Utilities (MIC: SIC: 4941 NAIC: 221310)

SJW is a holding company with three subsidiaries: San Jose Water Company, SJWTX, Inc. (doing business as Canyon Lake Water Service Company) and SJW Land Company. San Jose Water Company is a public utility that provides water service to approximately 1.0 million people in an area comprising approximately 138 square miles in the metropolitan San Jose area. SJWTX, Inc. provides service to approximately 36,000 residents in a service area comprising more than 78 square miles in the region between San Antonio and Austin, TX. SJW Land Company operates commercial buildings throughout the states of California, Florida, Connecticut, Texas, Arizona and Tennessee.

Recent Developments: For the quarter ended Mar 31 2008, net income increased 28.1% to US$2.7 million from US$2.1 million in the year-earlier quarter. Revenues were US$41.3 million, up 5.7% from US$39.0 million the year before. Operating income was US$5.8 million versus US$4.4 million in the prior-year quarter, an increase of 30.9%. Indirect operating expenses increased 2.5% to US$35.5 million from US$34.6 million in the equivalent prior-year period.

Prospects: For the full year of 2008, Co. is projecting total capital expenditures to be approximately $49.5 million for its Water Utility Services, excluding capital expenditures financed by customer contributions and advances but including an allocation of approximately $21.0 million to replace this segment's pipes and mains. Specifically, Co.'s capital expenditures consist of normal upgrading and expansion of existing facilities as well as to comply with environmental regulations. Over the next five years, Co.'s Water Utility Services expects to invest approximately $263.3 million in capital expenditures, which includes replacement of pipes and mains as well as maintaining water systems.

Financial Data
(US$ in Thousands)

	3 Mos	12/31/2007	12/31/2006	12/31/2005	12/31/2004	12/31/2003	12/31/2002	12/31/2001
Earnings Per Share	1.07	1.04	2.08	1.18	1.08	1.02	0.78	0.77
Cash Flow Per Share	2.28	2.29	2.44	2.33	2.25	2.30	1.59	1.39
Tang Book Value Per Share	12.95	12.72	12.31	10.55	9.93	8.92	8.11	7.88
Dividends Per Share	0.615	0.605	0.565	0.535	0.510	0.485	0.460	0.429
Dividend Payout %	57.65	58.17	27.16	45.34	47.44	47.55	59.10	55.92
Income Statement								
Total Revenue	41,253	206,601	189,238	180,105	166,911	149,732	145,652	136,083
Depn & Amortn	6,063	22,854	21,299	19,654	18,481	15,225	14,013	13,240
Income Taxes	...	12,549	...	...	...	12,629	9,658	7,391
Net Income	2,718	19,323	38,581	21,840	19,786	18,677	14,232	14,017
Average Shares	18,592	18,552	18,528	18,480	18,394	18,296	18,270	18,270
Balance Sheet								
Net PPE	655,127	645,480	546,811	490,058	462,356	436,353	390,830	367,815
Total Assets	774,311	767,326	705,864	587,709	552,152	511,717	453,223	431,017
Long-Term Obligations	217,186	216,312	163,648	145,281	143,604	139,614	110,000	110,000
Total Liabilities	536,313	530,392	477,682	391,801	367,461	345,349	299,724	281,663
Stockholders' Equity	237,998	236,934	228,182	195,908	184,691	166,368	153,499	149,354
Shares Outstanding	18,382	18,361	18,281	18,270	18,270	18,270	18,270	18,270
Statistical Record								
Return on Assets %	2.65	2.62	5.97	3.83	3.71	...	...	3.41
Return on Equity %	8.53	8.31	18.19	11.48	11.24	...	...	9.55
Net Margin %	6.59	9.35	20.39	12.13	11.85	12.47	9.77	10.30
PPE Turnover	0.33	0.35	0.37	0.38	0.37	...	...	0.39
Asset Turnover	0.28	0.28	0.29	0.32	0.31	...	...	0.33
Debt to Equity	0.91	0.91	0.72	0.74	0.78	0.84	0.72	0.74
Price Range	40.10-28.05	43.00-28.19	39.50-21.56	27.69-16.15	19.45-14.65	14.95-12.57	14.83-12.71	17.75-11.98
P/E Ratio	37.48-26.21	41.35-27.11	18.99-10.37	23.47-13.68	18.01-13.56	14.66-12.32	19.02-16.29	23.05-15.56
Average Yield %	1.87	1.74	2.04	2.43	2.98	3.46	3.42	3.04

Address: 374 West Santa Clara Street, San Jose, CA 95196 Telephone: 408-279-7800 Web Site: www.sjwater.com	Officers: W. Richard Roth - President, Chief Executive Officer Angela Yip - Chief Financial Officer, Treasurer **Transfer Agents:** Boston Equiserve, Boston, MA	No of Institutions: 101 Shares: 9,054,301 % Held: 48.01

SMITH (A.O.) CORP

Exchange	Symbol	Price	52Wk Range	Yield	P/E
NYS	AOS	$35.44 (5/29/2008)	51.15-30.43	2.03	12.10

*7 Year Price Score 93.88 ***NYSE Composite Index=100** ***12 Month Price Score 87.95**

Interim Earnings (Per Share)

Qtr.	Mar	Jun	Sep	Dec
2005	0.48	0.22	0.32	0.53
2006	0.50	0.81	0.55	0.61
2007	0.63	0.87	0.79	0.56
2008	0.72	...	...	...

Interim Dividends (Per Share)

Amt	Decl	Ex	Rec	Pay
0.18Q	07/10/2007	07/27/2007	07/31/2007	08/15/2007
0.18Q	10/09/2007	10/29/2007	10/31/2007	11/15/2007
0.18Q	01/15/2008	01/29/2008	01/31/2008	02/15/2008
0.18Q	04/15/2008	04/28/2008	04/30/2008	05/15/2008

Indicated Div: $0.72 (Div. Reinv. Plan)

Valuation Analysis

Forecast EPS	$2.90 (05/17/2008)		
Market Cap	$1.1 Billion	Book Value	792.4 Million
Price/Book	1.34	Price/Sales	0.46

Dividend Achiever Status

10 Year Growth Rate	4.44%
Total Years of Dividend Growth	15

Business Summary: Electrical (MIC: SIC: 3621 NAIC: 335312)

A. O. Smith is engaged as a manufacturer of water heating equipment and electric motors, serving a range of residential, commercial and industrial end markets principally in the U.S. As of Dec 31 2007, Co. conducted its businesses through two operating segments. In detail, Co.'s Water Products business manufactures and markets a variety of residential gas and electric water heaters, standard and specialty commercial water heating equipment, copper-tube boilers, and water systems tanks. In addition, Co.'s Electrical Products business manufactures and markets a range of hermetic motors, fractional horsepower alternating current and direct current motors.

Recent Developments: For the quarter ended Mar 31 2008, net income increased 12.3% to US$21.9 million from US$19.5 million in the year-earlier quarter. Revenues were US$571.4 million, down 1.0% from US$577.2 million the year before. Direct operating expenses declined 3.4% to US$438.8 million from US$454.4 million in the comparable period the year before. Indirect operating expenses increased 9.1% to US$97.6 million from US$89.5 million in the equivalent prior-year period.

Prospects: Co.'s outlook appears challenging, as the domestic housing market continues to weaken. Furthermore, Co. is beginning to experience the slowdown in the nonresidential market and the decline is likely to be steeper in 2008 than previously projected. In addition, Co. projects raw material costs, particularly steel prices, to remain high for the remainder of 2008. Accordingly, Co. is working to offset these cost increases with productivity and margin enhancement initiatives, which it believes should help mitigate the cost headwinds. In view of that, Co. has lowered its earnings forecast for 2008 to $2.60 to $2.80 per share compared with its previous forecast of $2.70 to $2.90 per share.

Financial Data
(US$ in Thousands)

	3 Mos	12/31/2007	12/31/2006	12/31/2005	12/31/2004	12/31/2003	12/31/2002	12/31/2001
Earnings Per Share	2.93	2.85	2.47	1.54	1.18	1.76	1.86	0.61
Cash Flow Per Share	6.40	6.23	4.24	6.29	2.29	0.87	4.16	2.11
Tang Book Value Per Share	6.45	5.27	3.16	9.52	9.35	9.07	6.95	6.30
Dividends Per Share	0.710	0.700	0.660	0.640	0.620	0.580	0.540	0.520
Dividend Payout %	24.23	24.56	26.72	41.56	52.54	32.95	29.03	85.25
Income Statement								
Total Revenue	571,400	2,312,100	2,161,300	1,689,200	1,653,100	1,530,700	1,469,100	1,151,156
EBITDA	52,000	194,100	190,600	134,500	114,900	143,500	143,291	92,936
Depn & Amortn	16,900	67,500	60,900	52,800	53,900	52,100	50,693	47,076
Income Before Taxes	29,700	99,900	104,800	68,700	47,500	79,000	78,390	22,486
Income Taxes	7,700	11,700	28,600	22,200	12,100	26,800	27,045	7,984
Net Income	21,900	88,200	76,500	46,500	35,400	52,200	51,345	14,502
Average Shares	30,221	30,973	31,003	30,281	29,912	29,710	27,649	23,914
Balance Sheet								
Current Assets	808,700	767,600	760,000	576,000	585,000	547,700	488,251	477,574
Total Assets	1,887,500	1,854,400	1,839,900	1,292,700	1,312,800	1,279,900	1,224,857	1,293,923
Current Liabilities	439,400	472,600	437,300	307,600	245,200	338,600	261,679	255,950
Long-Term Obligations	417,600	379,600	432,100	162,400	272,500	170,100	239,084	390,385
Total Liabilities	1,095,100	1,096,600	1,155,300	679,800	722,200	703,700	713,805	842,045
Stockholders' Equity	792,400	757,800	684,600	612,900	590,600	576,200	511,052	451,878
Shares Outstanding	30,052	30,053	30,684	30,413	29,665	29,246	29,039	23,786
Statistical Record								
Return on Assets %	4.79	4.77	4.88	3.57	2.72	4.17	4.08	1.23
Return on Equity %	12.06	12.23	11.79	7.73	6.05	9.60	10.66	3.22
EBITDA Margin %	9.10	8.39	8.82	7.96	6.95	9.37	9.75	8.07
Net Margin %	3.83	3.81	3.54	2.75	2.14	3.41	3.49	1.26
Asset Turnover	1.22	1.25	1.38	1.30	1.27	1.22	1.17	0.98
Current Ratio	1.84	1.62	1.74	1.87	2.39	1.62	1.87	1.87
Debt to Equity	0.53	0.50	0.63	0.26	0.46	0.30	0.47	0.86
Price Range	51.15-30.43	51.15-32.79	56.66-34.05	37.13-25.13	35.49-23.20	36.50-23.80	32.10-19.15	20.00-14.68
P/E Ratio	17.46-10.39	17.95-11.51	22.94-13.79	24.11-16.32	30.08-19.66	20.74-13.52	17.26-10.30	32.79-24.07
Average Yield %	1.80	1.73	1.55	2.16	2.13	1.91	2.02	2.96

Address: 11270 West Park Place, P.O. Box 245008, Milwaukee, WI 53224-9508 **Telephone:** 414-359-4000 **Web Site:** www.aosmith.com	**Officers:** Paul W. Jones - Chairman, President, Chief Executive Officer Terry M. Murphy - Executive Vice President, Chief Financial Officer **Transfer Agents:** Wells Fargo Bank, N.A., South St. Paul, MN	**Investor Contact:** 414-359-4009 **No of Institutions:** 182 **Shares:** 24,413,344 **% Held:** 73.83

SONOCO PRODUCTS CO.

Exchange	Symbol	Price	52Wk Range	Yield	P/E
NYS	SON	$33.97 (5/29/2008)	44.89-26.46	3.18	19.75

*7 Year Price Score 90.37   *NYSE Composite Index=100   ***12 Month Price Score 99.73**

TRADING VOLUME (thousand shares)

Interim Earnings (Per Share)

Qtr.	Mar	Jun	Sep	Dec
2005	0.37	0.40	0.46	0.38
2006	0.44	0.49	0.60	0.38
2007	0.52	0.41	0.63	0.54
2008	0.13	...	...	...

Interim Dividends (Per Share)

Amt	Decl	Ex	Rec	Pay
0.26Q	07/18/2007	08/15/2007	08/17/2007	09/10/2007
0.26Q	10/16/2007	11/14/2007	11/16/2007	12/10/2007
0.26Q	02/06/2008	02/20/2008	02/22/2008	03/10/2008
0.27Q	04/16/2008	05/14/2008	05/16/2008	06/10/2008

Indicated Div: $1.08 (Div. Reinv. Plan)

Valuation Analysis

Forecast EPS $2.46 (05/16/2008)

Market Cap	$3.4 Billion	Book Value	1.5 Billion
Price/Book	2.33	Price/Sales	0.82

Dividend Achiever Status

10 Year Growth Rate	4.76%
Total Years of Dividend Growth	24

Business Summary: Paper Products (MIC: SIC: 2631 NAIC: 322130)

Sonoco Products manufactures industrial and consumer packaging products and provides packaging services. Co.'s Consumer Packaging segment includes round and shaped rigid packaging; printed flexible packaging; and metal and plastic ends and closures. The Tubes and Cores/Paper segment includes paper and composite paperboard tubes and cores; fiber-based construction tubes and forms; recycled paperboard; linerboard and recovered paper. The Packaging Services segment provides point-of-purchase displays; brand management and supply chain management; while its All Other Sonoco segment offers wooden, metal and composite reels, molded and extruded plastics, and protective packaging.

Recent Developments: For the quarter ended Mar 30 2008, net income decreased 75.0% to US$13.3 million from US$53.1 million in the year-earlier quarter. Revenues were US$1.04 billion, up 8.6% from US$955.7 million the year before. Operating income was US$26.7 million versus US$88.7 million in the prior-year quarter, a decrease of 69.9%. Direct operating expenses rose 10.5% to US$851.6 million from US$770.5 million in the comparable period the year before. Indirect operating expenses increased 65.5% to US$159.7 million from US$96.5 million in the equivalent prior-year period.

Prospects: For the full year of 2008, Co. continues to anticipate base earnings in the range of $2.44 to $2.47 per diluted share. For the second quarter of 2008, Co. now foresees base earnings to range from $0.58 to $0.61 per diluted share. Specifically, both expectations assume no significant change in Co.'s volumes and/or prices due to further changes in overall economic conditions. Meanwhile, Co. is implementing several initiatives to mitigate the weakening economic conditions in North America. For instance, on Apr 11 2008, Co. announced plans to close its small No. 3 specialty paper machine at its Holyoke, MA paper mill, effective June 27 2008, due to softer demand for this specialty paper.

Financial Data

(US$ in Thousands)	3 Mos	12/31/2007	12/31/2006	12/31/2005	12/31/2004	12/31/2003	12/31/2002	12/31/2001
Earnings Per Share	1.72	2.10	1.92	1.61	1.53	1.43	1.39	0.96
Cash Flow Per Share	4.51	4.42	4.82	2.29	2.57	3.43	2.82	3.82
Tang Book Value Per Share	4.81	4.76	4.53	6.16	5.00	6.48	5.26	4.64
Dividends Per Share	1.040	1.020	0.950	0.910	0.870	0.840	0.830	0.800
Dividend Payout %	60.62	48.57	49.48	56.52	56.86	58.74	59.71	83.33
Income Statement								
Total Revenue	1,037,996	4,039,992	3,656,839	3,528,574	3,155,433	2,758,326	2,812,150	2,606,276
EBITDA	72,568	489,223	484,981	437,821	403,333	321,778	410,296	382,772
Depn & Amortn	45,853	181,339	164,863	163,074	163,928	163,234	159,256	158,574
Income Before Taxes	13,487	255,626	274,808	231,126	197,342	108,333	198,493	175,781
Income Taxes	6,449	55,186	93,329	84,174	58,858	37,698	70,614	82,958
Net Income	13,259	214,156	195,081	161,877	151,229	138,949	135,316	91,609
Average Shares	100,702	101,875	101,534	100,418	98,947	97,129	97,178	95,807
Balance Sheet								
Current Assets	1,074,496	1,027,679	942,798	885,500	922,112	755,265	663,267	665,169
Total Assets	3,346,618	3,340,243	2,916,678	2,981,740	3,041,319	2,520,633	2,390,094	2,352,197
Current Liabilities	755,700	758,081	659,832	620,486	639,886	679,594	600,027	460,270
Long-Term Obligations	796,311	804,339	712,089	657,075	813,207	473,220	699,346	885,961
Total Liabilities	1,893,979	1,898,706	1,697,610	1,718,426	1,888,440	1,506,473	1,522,669	1,548,075
Stockholders' Equity	1,452,639	1,441,537	1,219,068	1,263,314	1,152,879	1,014,160	867,425	804,122
Shares Outstanding	99,488	99,431	100,550	99,988	98,793	97,217	96,640	95,713
Statistical Record								
Return on Assets %	5.54	6.85	6.61	5.38	5.42	5.66	5.71	4.01
Return on Equity %	13.07	16.10	15.72	13.40	13.92	14.77	16.19	11.41
EBITDA Margin %	6.99	12.11	13.26	12.41	12.78	11.67	14.59	14.69
Net Margin %	1.28	5.30	5.33	4.59	4.79	5.04	4.81	3.51
Asset Turnover	1.31	1.29	1.24	1.17	1.13	1.12	1.19	1.14
Current Ratio	1.42	1.36	1.43	1.43	1.44	1.11	1.11	1.45
Debt to Equity	0.55	0.56	0.58	0.52	0.71	0.47	0.81	1.10
Price Range	44.89-26.46	44.89-28.51	38.64-29.25	30.48-25.68	29.70-22.86	24.73-19.47	29.70-19.81	26.58-19.69
P/E Ratio	26.10-15.38	21.38-13.58	20.13-15.23	18.93-15.95	19.41-14.94	17.29-13.62	21.37-14.25	27.69-20.51
Average Yield %	2.99	2.77	2.86	3.27	3.39	3.78	3.25	3.36

Address: One North Second Street, Hartsville, SC 29550-3305	Officers: Harris E. DeLoach - Chairman, President, Chief Executive Officer Mancil Jack Sanders -	Investor Contact: 843-383-7524
Telephone: 843-383-7000	Executive Vice President **Transfer Agents:**	No of Institutions: 329
Web Site: www.sonoco.com	The Bank of New York	Shares: 68,684,808 % Held: 61.82

SOUTH FINANCIAL GROUP INC (THE)

Exchange	Symbol	Price	52Wk Range	Yield	P/E
NMS	TSFG	$5.60 (5/29/2008)	24.73-5.60	0.71	N/A

*7 Year Price Score 56.91 ***NYSE Composite Index=100** ***12 Month Price Score 48.48**

Interim Earnings (Per Share)

Qtr.	Mar	Jun	Sep	Dec
2005	0.47	0.38	0.28	(0.22)
2006	0.37	0.39	0.43	0.31
2007	0.27	0.24	0.35	0.13
2008	(2.77)	...	...	...

Interim Dividends (Per Share)

Amt	Decl	Ex	Rec	Pay
0.18Q	08/16/2007	10/11/2007	10/15/2007	11/01/2007
0.19Q	12/14/2007	01/11/2008	01/15/2008	02/01/2008
0.19Q	02/22/2008	04/11/2008	04/15/2008	05/01/2008
0.01Q	05/09/2008	07/11/2008	07/15/2008	08/01/2008

Indicated Div: $0.04

Valuation Analysis

Forecast EPS	$-0.33 (05/17/2008)		
Market Cap	$406.7 Million	Book Value	1.4 Billion
Price/Book	0.30	Price/Sales	0.42

Dividend Achiever Status

10 Year Growth Rate	9.90%
Total Years of Dividend Growth	13

TRADING VOLUME (thousand shares)

Business Summary: Commercial Banking (MIC: SIC: 6022 NAIC: 522110)

The South Financial Group is a financial holding company that operates principally through Carolina First Bank, a South Carolina-chartered commercial bank, which conducts banking operations in South Carolina and North Carolina (as Carolina First Bank), in Florida (as Mercantile Bank), and on the internet (as Bank CaroLine). Co. provides a range of financial services, including deposits, loans, treasury management, merchant processing, full-service brokerage and investments, business and personal insurance, trust, investment management, and financial planning. As at Dec 31 2007, Co. had total assets of approximately $13.88 billion and deposits of $9.79 billion.

Recent Developments: For the quarter ended Mar 31 2008, net loss amounted to US$201.3 million versus net income of US$20.5 million in the year-earlier quarter. Net interest income decreased 1.9% to US$92.7 million from US$94.5 million in the year-earlier quarter. Provision for loan losses was US$73.3 million versus US$9.0 million in the prior-year quarter, an increase of 713.2%. Non-interest income rose 14.6% to US$30.9 million from US$27.0 million, while non-interest expense advanced 229.1% to US$268.2 million.

Prospects: On Mar 11 2008, Co. signed an agreement to purchase assets and assume deposits and other liabilities associated with five retail branch offices in Orlando, FL from BankAtlantic Bancorp. This transaction, which should enable Co. to accelerate its efforts to grow deposits in the Orlando area is expected to close in the later part of the second quarter 2008, pending customary regulatory approval. Moving forward, Co. intends to enhance its deposit mix by working to attract lower-cost transaction accounts through actions such as new transaction account openings, new checking products, and changing incentive plans to place a higher emphasis on lower-cost customer deposit growth.

Financial Data (US$ in Thousands)	3 Mos	12/31/2007	12/31/2006	12/31/2005	12/31/2004	12/31/2003	12/31/2002	12/31/2001
Earnings Per Share	(2.05)	0.99	1.49	0.94	1.80	1.89	1.38	0.98
Cash Flow Per Share	3.03	2.95	1.97	2.97	3.54	3.73	7.14	3.84
Tang Book Value Per Share	12.26	12.04	11.63	10.64	11.08	10.61	8.55	8.76
Dividends Per Share	0.730	0.720	0.680	0.640	0.600	0.560	0.480	0.440
Dividend Payout %	...	72.73	45.64	68.09	33.33	29.63	34.78	44.90
Income Statement								
Interest Income	194,385	880,356	860,200	754,297	542,232	414,128	353,739	382,548
Interest Expense	101,679	497,575	458,829	345,241	175,504	141,537	135,487	197,324
Net Interest Income	92,706	382,781	401,371	409,056	366,728	272,591	218,252	185,224
Provision for Losses	73,292	68,568	32,789	40,592	34,987	20,581	22,266	22,045
Non-Interest Income	30,916	113,311	132,051	55,210	94,767	95,490	59,640	53,827
Non-Interest Expense	268,179	320,848	340,085	328,053	250,244	207,170	162,840	148,504
Income Before Taxes	(217,849)	106,676	160,548	95,621	176,264	140,330	92,786	68,502
Income Taxes	(16,557)	33,400	47,682	25,404	56,657	43,260	28,972	23,571
Net Income	(201,292)	73,276	112,866	69,821	119,117	95,058	59,158	41,892
Average Shares	72,575	74,085	75,543	74,595	66,235	50,328	42,714	42,823
Balance Sheet								
Net Loans & Leases	10,117,352	10,104,860	9,618,760	9,368,799	8,032,141	5,688,537	4,430,954	3,692,176
Total Assets	13,731,720	13,877,684	14,210,516	14,319,285	13,789,814	10,719,401	7,941,010	6,029,442
Total Deposits	9,451,532	9,788,568	9,516,740	9,234,437	7,665,537	6,028,649	4,592,510	3,605,255
Total Liabilities	12,353,399	12,327,276	12,648,484	12,832,378	12,389,211	9,739,532	7,207,799	5,534,245
Stockholders' Equity	1,378,321	1,550,308	1,562,032	1,486,907	1,400,603	979,869	646,799	458,174
Shares Outstanding	72,629	72,455	75,341	74,721	71,252	59,064	47,347	41,228
Statistical Record								
Return on Assets %	N.M.	0.52	0.79	0.50	0.97	1.02	0.85	0.74
Return on Equity %	N.M.	4.71	7.40	4.84	9.98	11.69	10.71	9.04
Net Interest Margin %	47.69	43.48	46.66	54.23	67.63	65.82	61.70	48.42
Efficiency Ratio %	119.03	32.29	34.27	40.53	39.28	40.65	39.39	34.03
Loans to Deposits	1.07	1.03	1.01	1.01	1.05	0.94	0.96	1.02
Price Range	24.73-12.61	27.38-15.57	28.33-25.14	32.53-25.86	32.53-26.00	29.25-19.46	23.46-17.61	19.95-12.25
P/E Ratio	...	27.66-15.73	19.01-16.87	34.61-27.51	18.07-14.44	15.48-10.30	17.00-12.76	20.36-12.50
Average Yield %	3.64	3.16	2.56	2.22	2.06	2.32	2.31	2.71

Address: 102 South Main Street, Greenville, SC 29601 **Telephone:** 864-255-7900 **Web Site:** www.thesouthgroup.com	**Officers:** Mack I. Whittle - Chairman, President, Chief Executive Officer William P. Crawford - Executive Vice President, Secretary, General Counsel **Transfer Agents:** Registrar and Transfer Company, Cranford, NJ	**Investor Contact:** 800-951-2699*54919 **No of Institutions:** 187 **Shares:** 58,649,296 **% Held:** 78.44

SOUTHWEST BANCORP, INC. (OK)

Exchange	Symbol	Price	52Wk Range	Yield	P/E
NMS	OKSB	$17.16 (5/29/2008)	25.00-14.54	2.21	11.36

*7 Year Price Score 81.77 *NYSE Composite Index=100 *12 Month Price Score 92.39

Interim Earnings (Per Share)

Qtr.	Mar	Jun	Sep	Dec
2005	0.43	0.40	0.41	0.31
2006	0.44	0.45	0.46	0.44
2007	0.31	0.47	0.38	0.31
2008	0.36	...	...	...

Interim Dividends (Per Share)

Amt	Decl	Ex	Rec	Pay
0.092Q	08/27/2007	09/13/2007	09/17/2007	10/01/2007
0.092Q	11/19/2007	12/17/2007	12/19/2007	01/02/2008
0.095Q	03/03/2008	03/14/2008	03/18/2008	04/01/2008
0.095Q	05/27/2008	06/13/2008	06/17/2008	07/01/2008
		Indicated Div: $0.38		

Valuation Analysis

Forecast EPS	$1.28 (05/16/2008)
Market Cap	$249.2 Million Book Value 224.2 Million
Price/Book	1.11 Price/Sales 1.28

Dividend Achiever Status

10 Year Growth Rate	13.29%
Total Years of Dividend Growth	13

Business Summary: Commercial Banking (MIC: SIC: 6021 NAIC: 522110)

Southwest Bancorp is the financial holding company for the Stillwater National Bank and Trust Company, SNB Bank of Wichita, Bank of Kansas, Business Consulting Group, Inc., and Healthcare Strategic Support, Inc. Through its subsidiaries, Co. provides commercial and consumer lending, deposit and investment services, and specialized cash management, consulting and other financial services from offices in Oklahoma City, Stillwater, Tulsa, and Chickasha, OK; Austin, Dallas, Houston, San Antonio, and Tilden, TX; and Hutchinson, South Hutchinson, Kansas City and Wichita, KS, and on the internet, through SNB DirectBanker?. As of Dec 31 2007, Co. had total assets of $2.56 billion.

Recent Developments: For the quarter ended Mar 31 2008, net income increased 15.7% to US$5.2 million from US$4.5 million in the year-earlier quarter. Net interest income decreased 4.0% to US$21.8 million from US$22.7 million in the year-earlier quarter. Provision for loan losses was US$2.2 million versus US$1.9 million in the prior-year quarter, an increase of 20.2%. Non-interest income rose 41.1% to US$4.7 million from US$3.3 million, while non-interest expense declined 5.9% to US$15.8 million.

Prospects: Co.'s near-term outlook appears to be challenging. In detail, Co.'s net interest income is being hurt by lower loan yields, which more than offset the favorable effects of increased loan volume. Going forward, Co. anticipates seeing movement toward more conventional unscheduled payoff levels, and currently expects somewhat slower net loan growth for the remainder of 2008. Thus, Co. will continue to focus on growth from existing and additional offices in Oklahoma as well as in potential Texas markets and other states with an emphasis on healthcare and health professionals, businesses, commercial real estate customers as well as strategic expansion of its community banking operations.

Financial Data

(US$ in Thousands)	3 Mos	12/31/2007	12/31/2006	12/31/2005	12/31/2004	12/31/2003	12/31/2002	12/31/2001
Earnings Per Share	1.51	1.46	1.79	1.55	1.48	1.22	1.12	1.00
Cash Flow Per Share	5.51	11.00	15.83	0.19	(9.15)	(8.03)	1.54	1.35
Tang Book Value Per Share	14.66	14.35	13.57	12.16	10.41	9.20	8.35	6.95
Dividends Per Share	0.373	0.370	0.330	0.300	0.280	0.250	0.220	0.160
Dividend Payout %	24.59	25.34	18.44	19.35	18.92	20.49	19.73	16.00
Income Statement								
Interest Income	42,974	177,068	169,760	137,344	104,723	84,079	76,495	90,400
Interest Expense	21,167	84,588	76,922	52,238	32,246	28,611	30,606	48,867
Net Interest Income	21,807	92,480	92,838	85,106	72,477	55,468	45,889	41,533
Provision for Losses	2,236	8,581	11,565	15,785	12,982	8,522	5,443	4,000
Non-Interest Income	4,714	16,550	16,776	17,406	14,085	14,500	12,646	10,741
Non-Interest Expense	15,830	65,474	56,643	51,873	44,412	38,448	33,319	31,165
Income Before Taxes	8,455	34,975	41,406	34,854	29,168	22,998	19,773	17,109
Income Taxes	3,247	13,597	15,409	13,840	10,539	8,106	6,354	5,357
Net Income	5,208	21,378	25,997	21,014	18,629	14,892	13,419	11,752
Average Shares	14,608	14,617	14,492	13,563	12,548	12,159	12,052	11,728
Balance Sheet								
Net Loans & Leases	2,324,020	2,182,248	1,763,897	1,712,068	1,603,931	1,292,988	1,089,224	919,554
Total Assets	2,670,580	2,564,298	2,170,628	2,099,639	1,912,834	1,580,523	1,349,768	1,216,495
Total Deposits	2,094,927	2,058,579	1,765,611	1,657,820	1,500,058	1,204,125	1,021,757	904,796
Total Liabilities	2,446,425	2,346,689	1,973,118	1,929,195	1,786,850	1,470,790	1,253,396	1,131,370
Stockholders' Equity	224,155	217,609	197,510	170,444	125,984	109,935	96,372	85,125
Shares Outstanding	14,524	14,357	14,240	14,021	12,104	11,955	11,546	12,243
Statistical Record								
Return on Assets %	0.90	0.90	1.22	1.05	1.06	1.02	1.05	0.97
Return on Equity %	10.34	10.30	14.13	14.18	15.75	14.44	14.79	14.84
Net Interest Margin %	50.74	52.23	54.69	61.97	69.21	65.97	59.99	45.94
Efficiency Ratio %	33.19	33.82	30.37	33.52	37.38	39.00	37.38	30.81
Loans to Deposits	1.11	1.06	1.00	1.03	1.07	1.07	1.07	1.02
Price Range	27.32-14.54	28.09-16.43	28.41-20.23	24.83-17.11	26.85-16.22	18.90-11.25	13.62-8.80	9.57-5.58
P/E Ratio	18.09-9.63	19.24-11.25	15.87-11.30	16.02-11.04	18.14-10.96	15.49-9.22	12.16-7.86	9.57-5.58
Average Yield %	1.84	1.63	1.35	1.42	1.44	1.75	1.87	2.03

Address: 608 South Main Street, Stillwater, OK 74074	Officers: Robert B. Rodgers - Chairman Rick J. Green - Chief Executive Officer Transfer Agents:	Investor Contact: 405-372-2230
Telephone: 405-372-2230	ComputerShare Investor Services, Chicago, IL	No of Institutions: 112
Web Site: www.oksb.com		Shares: 10,469,978 % Held: 66.78

SOUTHWEST WATER CO.

Exchange	Symbol	Price	52Wk Range	Yield	P/E
NMS	SWWC	$10.53 (5/29/2008)	16.25-10.36	2.28	N/A

*7 Year Price Score 82.72   *NYSE Composite Index=100   *12 Month Price Score 92.18

TRADING VOLUME (thousand shares)

Interim Earnings (Per Share)

Qtr.	Mar	Jun	Sep	Dec
2005	(0.01)	(0.09)	0.14	0.06
2006	0.03	0.08	0.16	0.13
2007	0.03	0.09	0.08	(0.53)
2008	(0.02)	...	...	...

Interim Dividends (Per Share)

Amt	Decl	Ex	Rec	Pay
0.058Q	08/16/2007	09/26/2007	09/28/2007	10/19/2007
0.06Q	12/14/2007	12/26/2007	12/28/2007	01/18/2008
0.06Q	02/28/2008	03/26/2008	03/28/2008	04/18/2008
0.06Q	05/23/2008	06/26/2008	06/30/2008	07/18/2008

Indicated Div: $0.24

Valuation Analysis

Forecast EPS $0.40 (05/16/2008)

Market Cap	$257.6 Million	Book Value 158.1 Million
Price/Book	1.63	Price/Sales 1.17

Dividend Achiever Status

10 Year Growth Rate	9.82%
Total Years of Dividend Growth	12

Business Summary: Water Utilities (MIC: SIC: 4941 NAIC: 221310)

Southwest Water and its subsidiaries provides a range of services including water production, treatment and distribution; wastewater collection and treatment; utility operations and maintenance services; and utility infrastructure construction. Co. owns regulated public utilities and also serves cities, utility districts and private companies under contract. Co.'s businesses are segmented into two operating groups: the Utility Group, which is comprised of its regulated public utilities; and the Services Group, which is comprised of its non-regulated operations. As of Dec 31 2007, Co. served more than 2.0 million customers.

Recent Developments: For the quarter ended Mar 31 2008, loss from continuing operations was US$314,000 compared with income of US$840,000 in the year-earlier quarter. Net loss amounted to US$601,000 versus net income of US$614,000 in the year-earlier quarter. Revenues were US$50.8 million, up 6.0% from US$47.9 million the year before. Operating income was US$1.8 million versus US$3.1 million in the prior-year quarter, a decrease of 41.5%. Direct operating expenses rose 8.6% to US$39.4 million from US$36.3 million in the comparable period the year before. Indirect operating expenses increased 12.6% to US$9.6 million from US$8.5 million in the equivalent prior-year period.

Prospects: Over the long term, Co.'s Utility Group growth strategy focuses on strategically located acquisitions, organic customer growth and managed rate proceedings. In addition, Co.'s Services Group growth strategy will focus on expanding its client base and providing peripheral services, including construction of infrastructure, billing and collection services, meter replacement and laboratory analysis of water and wastewater samples. Notably, Co. expects to expand its presence in a region by pursuing new operations and maintenance contracts with cities, municipalities and private owners of water and wastewater utilities within its geographic presence.

Financial Data
(US$ in Thousands)

	3 Mos	12/31/2007	12/31/2006	12/31/2005	12/31/2004	12/31/2003	12/31/2002	12/31/2001
Earnings Per Share	(0.38)	(0.33)	0.40	0.11	0.23	0.44	0.40	0.42
Cash Flow Per Share	1.08	1.27	1.22	1.18	0.87	0.57	1.55	0.29
Tang Book Value Per Share	5.64	5.72	5.46	4.91	4.15	3.45	4.29	3.85
Dividends Per Share	0.235	0.233	0.215	0.195	0.181	0.161	0.148	0.140
Dividend Payout %	...	...	53.70	177.49	79.37	36.32	37.51	33.15
Income Statement								
Total Revenue	50,763	217,347	224,182	203,181	187,952	172,974	130,800	115,547
EBITDA	5,449	14,487	33,278	30,732	23,299	22,999	19,824	18,854
Depn & Amortn	3,642	11,634	11,037	12,600	11,500	7,549	6,380	6,060
Income Before Taxes	(432)	(4,225)	14,350	11,362	7,098	11,217	9,215	9,755
Income Taxes	(118)	795	5,022	4,061	2,564	4,024	3,213	3,512
Net Income	(601)	(8,046)	9,399	2,399	4,534	7,193	6,002	6,243
Average Shares	24,385	24,101	23,363	21,611	19,413	16,163	15,031	14,738
Balance Sheet								
Net PPE	445,110	417,903	389,625	344,821	302,596	219,519	203,933	171,124
Total Assets	543,948	516,409	491,693	444,725	404,809	296,222	268,744	225,186
Long-Term Obligations	181,869	145,353	128,624	117,603	115,827	73,102	80,985	58,063
Total Liabilities	385,822	357,215	325,166	299,472	278,611	216,555	206,907	170,231
Stockholders' Equity	158,126	159,194	166,527	145,253	126,198	79,667	61,837	54,955
Shares Outstanding	24,467	24,268	23,802	22,185	20,364	16,169	14,310	14,138
Statistical Record								
Return on Assets %	N.M.	N.M.	2.01	0.56	1.29	2.55	2.43	2.96
Return on Equity %	N.M.	N.M.	6.03	1.77	4.39	10.17	10.28	12.06
EBITDA Margin %	10.73	6.67	14.84	15.13	12.40	13.30	15.16	16.32
Net Margin %	(1.18)	(3.70)	4.19	1.18	2.41	4.16	4.59	5.40
PPE Turnover	0.52	0.54	0.61	0.63	0.72	0.82	0.70	0.70
Asset Turnover	0.42	0.43	0.48	0.48	0.53	0.61	0.53	0.55
Debt to Equity	1.15	0.91	0.77	0.81	0.92	0.92	1.31	1.06
Price Range	16.25-10.87	16.25-11.66	19.03-10.85	15.08-9.43	14.07-10.51	11.10-8.22	12.30-8.28	9.74-6.96
P/E Ratio	...	...	47.58-27.13	137.09-85.71	61.17-45.71	25.22-18.68	30.74-20.70	23.20-16.57
Average Yield %	1.86	1.78	1.55	1.62	1.54	1.71	1.51	1.67

Address: One Wilshire Building, 624 South Grand Avenue, Suite 2900, Los Angeles, CA 90017-3782 Telephone: 213-929-1800 Web Site: www.swwc.com	Officers: Mark A. Swatek - Chairman, Chief Executive Officer Anton C. Garnier - Executive Vice-Chairman Transfer Agents: Mellon Investor Services LLC	No of Institutions: 87 Shares: 15,090,262 % Held: 48.57

SOVRAN SELF STORAGE, INC.

Exchange	Symbol	Price	52Wk Range	Yield	P/E
NYS	SSS	$44.33 (5/29/2008)	54.20-35.27	5.68	24.90

*7 Year Price Score 84.42 *NYSE Composite Index=100 *12 Month Price Score 103.62

Interim Earnings (Per Share)

Qtr.	Mar	Jun	Sep	Dec
2005	0.40	0.47	0.52	0.45
2006	0.45	0.50	0.49	0.45
2007	0.44	0.36	0.51	0.50
2008	0.41	...	...	...

Interim Dividends (Per Share)

Amt	Decl	Ex	Rec	Pay
0.62Q	06/07/2007	07/02/2007	07/05/2007	07/20/2007
0.63Q	09/06/2007	10/03/2007	10/05/2007	10/22/2007
0.63Q	12/06/2007	01/03/2008	01/07/2008	01/22/2008
0.63Q	03/13/2008	04/04/2008	04/08/2008	04/22/2008
			Indicated Div: $2.52	

Valuation Analysis

Forecast EPS $1.93 (05/16/2008)

Market Cap	$914.5 Million	Book Value	523.5 Million
Price/Book	1.75	Price/Sales	4.61

Dividend Achiever Status

10 Year Growth Rate	1.72%
Total Years of Dividend Growth	12

TRADING VOLUME (thousand shares)

Business Summary: "Property, Real Estate & Development" (MIC: SIC: 6798 NAIC: 525930)

Sovran Self Storage is a self-administered and self-managed real estate investment trust that acquires, owns and manages self-storage properties throughout the U.S. As of Dec 31 2007, Co. owned and/or managed 358 properties situated in 22 states. Co.'s properties conduct business under the trade name Uncle Bob's Self-Storage®. All of Co.'s assets are owned by, and all its operations are conducted through, Sovran Acquisition Limited Partnership (the Operating Partnership). Co. is a limited partner of the Operating Partnership, and thereby controls the operations of the Operating Partnership, holding a 98.1% ownership interest at Dec 31 2007.

Recent Developments: For the quarter ended Mar 31 2008, net income decreased 6.1% to US$9.0 million from US$9.5 million in the year-earlier quarter. Revenues were US$49.8 million, up 11.7% from US$44.6 million the year before. Revenues from property income rose 11.6% to US$48.3 million from US$43.3 million in the corresponding quarter a year earlier.

Prospects: Co. remains committed on its program of expanding and improving its existing stores, with 17 expansion projects are expected to be placed on line in the second quarter of 2008. Hence, Co. estimates projected cost of these revenue enhancing projects of $40.0 million to $50.0 million in 2008, providing for up to 450,000 square feet of additional space at as many as 40 stores. For full-year 2008, Co. expects conditions in most of its markets to remain relatively stable, and estimates growth in net operating income on a same store basis to be about 3.0% to 3.5%. In addition, Co. expects funds from operations between $3.50 and $3.56 per share, and accretive acquisitions of $50.0 million.

Financial Data
(US$ in Thousands)

	3 Mos	12/31/2007	12/31/2006	12/31/2005	12/31/2004	12/31/2003	12/31/2002	12/31/2001
Earnings Per Share	1.78	1.81	1.89	1.84	1.53	1.46	1.64	1.74
Cash Flow Per Share	3.64	4.06	3.59	3.65	3.54	3.90	3.57	3.35
Tang Book Value Per Share	25.38	24.33	24.67	20.92	20.30	19.11	19.03	20.12
Dividends Per Share	2.500	2.490	2.465	2.430	2.413	2.402	2.370	2.330
Dividend Payout %	140.76	137.57	130.42	132.07	157.68	164.55	144.51	133.91
Income Statement								
Net Income	8,953	39,214	36,610	34,790	32,004	28,423	26,301	24,189
Average Shares	21,664	21,004	18,021	16,633	15,295	13,473	12,945	12,316
Balance Sheet								
Total Assets	1,185,575	1,164,636	1,053,210	784,376	719,573	683,457	652,337	567,838
Total Liabilities	635,700	610,805	495,352	365,037	315,108	285,876	278,755	255,999
Stockholders' Equity	523,534	527,389	530,911	394,085	377,451	368,197	342,774	277,164
Shares Outstanding	20,629	21,676	20,443	17,563	15,972	14,259	12,984	12,354
Statistical Record								
Return on Assets %	3.44	3.54	3.98	4.63	4.55	4.26	4.31	4.34
Return on Equity %	7.31	7.41	7.92	9.02	8.56	8.00	8.49	8.72
Price Range	56.06-35.27	63.32-40.10	59.94-45.78	50.24-38.31	43.53-33.25	37.40-25.62	34.17-27.22	31.44-20.00
P/E Ratio	31.49-19.81	34.98-22.15	31.71-24.22	27.30-20.82	28.45-21.73	25.62-17.55	20.84-16.60	18.07-11.49
Average Yield %	5.50	4.96	4.69	5.44	6.24	7.79	7.82	9.11

Address: 6467 Main Street, Buffalo, NY 14221 Telephone: 716-633-1850 Web Site: www.sovranss.com	Officers: Robert J. Attea - Chairman, Chief Executive Officer Kenneth F. Myszka - President, Chief Operating Officer Transfer Agents: American Stock Transfer & Trust Co., New York, NY	Investor Contact: 716-633-1850 No of Institutions: 149 Shares: 19,014,500 % Held: 90.35

STANLEY WORKS (THE)

Exchange	Symbol	Price	52Wk Range	Yield	P/E
NYS	SWK	$48.91 (5/29/2008)	63.92-44.35	2.54	12.02

*7 Year Price Score 93.17 *NYSE Composite Index=100   *12 Month Price Score 95.08

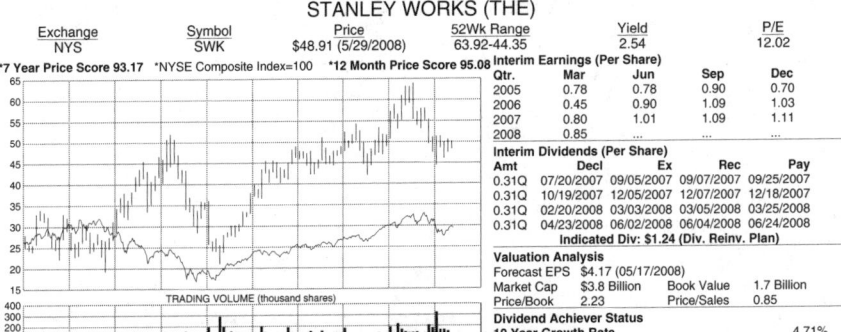

Interim Earnings (Per Share)

Qtr.	Mar	Jun	Sep	Dec
2005	0.78	0.78	0.90	0.70
2006	0.45	0.90	1.09	1.03
2007	0.80	1.01	1.09	1.11
2008	0.85	...	...	...

Interim Dividends (Per Share)

Amt	Decl	Ex	Rec	Pay
0.31Q	07/20/2007	09/05/2007	09/07/2007	09/25/2007
0.31Q	10/19/2007	12/05/2007	12/07/2007	12/18/2007
0.31Q	02/20/2008	03/03/2008	03/05/2008	03/25/2008
0.31Q	04/23/2008	06/02/2008	06/04/2008	06/24/2008

Indicated Div: $1.24 (Div. Reinv. Plan)

Valuation Analysis

Forecast EPS $4.17 (05/17/2008)

Market Cap	$3.8 Billion	Book Value	1.7 Billion
Price/Book	2.23	Price/Sales	0.85

Dividend Achiever Status

10 Year Growth Rate	4.71%
Total Years of Dividend Growth	40

Business Summary: Metal Products (MIC: SIC: 3423 NAIC: 332212)

Stanley Works supplies tools and engineered applications. Co.'s Construction & Do-It-Yourself segment manufactures and markets hand tools, consumer mechanics tools, storage systems, pneumatic tools, fasteners, and electronic leveling and measuring tools. Co.'s Industrial segment manufactures and markets: professional mechanics tools and storage systems; plumbing, heating, air conditioning and roofing tools; hydraulic tools and accessories; assembly tools and systems; and specialty tools. Co.'s Security segment provides access and security applications mainly for retailers, educational, financial and healthcare institutions, as well as commercial, governmental and industrial customers.

Recent Developments: For the quarter ended Mar 29 2008, net income increased 0.6% to US$68.0 million from US$67.6 million in the year-earlier quarter. Revenues were US$1.10 billion, up 3.3% from US$1.06 billion the year before. Direct operating expenses rose 2.3% to US$681.9 million from US$666.8 million in the comparable period the year before. Indirect operating expenses increased 6.2% to US$321.9 million from US$303.1 million in the equivalent prior-year period.

Prospects: For full year 2008, Co. continues to anticipate earnings in the range of $4.20 to $4.40 per diluted share, assuming that markets stabilize in the second half of 2008. However, should weak demand levels continue beyond mid-2008, Co. intends to implement cost reductions initiatives during the second and third quarters of 2008. Separately, on May 15 2008, Co. announced that it has entered into an agreement to acquire Xmark Corporation for a total transaction value of approximately $45.0 million, which should expand the products and services in its security business. Co. expects this transaction, which is projected to close in the second half of 2008, to be accretive to its earnings in 2009.

Financial Data

(US$ in Thousands)	3 Mos	12/29/2007	12/30/2006	12/31/2005	01/01/2005	01/03/2004	12/28/2002	12/29/2001
Earnings Per Share	4.07	4.00	3.46	3.16	4.36	1.27	2.10	1.81
Cash Flow Per Share	7.07	6.63	5.38	4.36	4.54	5.43	3.31	2.59
Tang Book Value Per Share	N.M.	N.M.	N.M.	4.59	3.56	2.65	5.05	7.04
Dividends Per Share	1.230	1.220	1.180	1.140	1.080	1.030	0.990	0.940
Dividend Payout %	30.23	30.50	34.10	36.08	24.77	81.10	47.14	51.93
Income Statement								
Total Revenue	1,096,900	4,483,800	4,018,600	3,285,300	3,043,400	2,678,100	2,593,000	2,624,400
EBITDA	133,900	613,300	488,300	454,700	424,100	219,500	343,700	319,600
Depn & Amortn	40,800	162,200	121,200	96,500	95,000	86,500	71,200	82,900
Income Before Taxes	93,100	451,100	367,100	358,200	329,100	133,000	272,500	236,700
Income Taxes	25,100	114,500	76,400	86,500	88,900	36,300	87,500	78,400
Net Income	68,000	336,600	289,500	269,600	366,900	107,900	185,000	158,300
Average Shares	80,274	84,045	83,704	85,445	84,243	84,839	88,246	87,467
Balance Sheet								
Current Assets	1,899,200	1,768,400	1,638,500	1,825,600	1,371,900	1,200,700	1,190,400	1,141,400
Total Assets	4,954,700	4,779,900	3,935,400	3,545,100	2,850,600	2,423,800	2,418,200	2,055,700
Current Liabilities	1,429,500	1,277,500	1,251,100	875,300	818,800	753,500	680,900	825,500
Long-Term Obligations	1,204,000	1,212,100	679,200	895,300	481,800	534,500	564,300	196,800
Total Liabilities	3,238,100	3,051,400	2,383,400	2,100,200	1,629,300	1,565,200	1,434,400	1,223,400
Stockholders' Equity	1,716,600	1,728,500	1,552,000	1,444,900	1,221,300	858,600	983,800	832,300
Shares Outstanding	78,382	80,378	81,841	83,791	82,407	81,276	86,835	84,658
Statistical Record								
Return on Assets %	7.04	7.75	7.76	8.45	13.95	4.38	8.29	8.06
Return on Equity %	20.58	20.58	19.37	20.28	35.38	11.52	20.43	20.24
EBITDA Margin %	12.21	13.68	12.15	13.84	13.94	8.20	13.25	12.18
Net Margin %	6.20	7.51	7.20	8.21	12.06	4.03	7.13	6.03
Asset Turnover	0.94	1.03	1.08	1.03	1.16	1.09	1.16	1.34
Current Ratio	1.33	1.38	1.31	2.09	1.68	1.59	1.75	1.38
Debt to Equity	0.70	0.70	0.44	0.62	0.39	0.62	0.57	0.24
Price Range	63.92-44.35	63.92-47.46	54.33-41.95	51.17-42.20	48.99-36.50	37.87-21.00	51.98-28.38	46.60-28.50
P/E Ratio	15.71-10.90	15.98-11.87	15.70-12.12	16.19-13.35	11.24-8.37	29.82-16.54	24.75-13.51	25.75-15.75
Average Yield %	2.25	2.17	2.40	2.40	2.53	3.57	2.48	2.46

Address: 1000 Stanley Drive, New Britain, CT 06053

Telephone: 860-225-5111

Web Site: www.stanleyworks.com

Officers: John F. Lundgren - Chairman, Chief Executive Officer James M. Loree - Executive Vice President, Chief Financial Officer **Transfer Agents:** Computershare Investor Services LLC, Chicago, IL

Investor Contact: 860-827-3833

No of Institutions: 380

Shares: 66,589,264 **% Held:** 77.87

STATE AUTO FINANCIAL CORP.

Exchange	Symbol	Price	52Wk Range	Yield	P/E
NMS	STFC	$28.02 (5/29/2008)	32.30-23.79	2.14	15.65

*7 Year Price Score 86.15 *NYSE Composite Index=100 *12 Month Price Score 100.69

TRADING VOLUME (thousand shares)

Interim Earnings (Per Share)

Qtr.	Mar	Jun	Sep	Dec
2005	1.00	0.94	0.41	0.71
2006	0.97	0.10	0.75	1.08
2007	0.74	0.56	0.55	1.00
2008	(0.31)	...	...	...

Interim Dividends (Per Share)

Amt	Decl	Ex	Rec	Pay
0.15Q	08/17/2007	09/12/2007	09/14/2007	09/28/2007
0.15Q	11/09/2007	12/11/2007	12/13/2007	12/28/2007
0.15Q	03/07/2008	03/13/2008	03/17/2008	03/31/2008
0.15Q	05/07/2008	06/12/2008	06/16/2008	06/30/2008

Indicated Div: $0.60 (Div. Reinv. Plan)

Valuation Analysis

Forecast EPS $1.52 (05/16/2008)

Market Cap	$1.1 Billion	Book Value	882.4 Million
Price/Book	1.26	Price/Sales	0.98

Dividend Achiever Status

10 Year Growth Rate	19.39%
Total Years of Dividend Growth	16

Business Summary: Insurance (MIC: SIC: 6331 NAIC: 524126)

State Auto Financial is a property and casualty insurance holding company primarily engaged in writing both personal and business lines of insurance. Co. has three reportable segments: the personal insurance segment, which provides primarily personal auto (standard and nonstandard) and homeowners to the personal insurance market; the business insurance segment, which provides primarily commercial auto, commercial multi-peril, fire and allied lines, other and product liability and workers' compensation insurance to small to medium sized businesses within the commercial insurance market; and the investment operations segment, which provides investment services for Co.'s invested assets.

Recent Developments: For the quarter ended Mar 31 2008, net loss amounted to US$12.5 million versus net income of US$30.8 million in the year-earlier quarter. Revenues were US$301.0 million, up 9.3% from US$275.5 million the year before. Net premiums earned were US$279.2 million versus US$251.9 million in the prior-year quarter, an increase of 10.8%. Net investment income rose 5.2% to US$22.4 million from US$21.3 million a year ago.

Prospects: Going forward, at its personal lines business, Co. plans to utilize its relationship with the Patrons Mutual agency distribution channel to add upgraded product lines and new systems into Connecticut, and intends to continue migrating its CustomFitSM states to the second generation product throughout 2008. Meanwhile, Co.'s business insurance segment is facing rate competition as well as ease of doing business issues. As a result, Co. is enhancing its back office systems, with plans to make bizXpressSM, its web-based quote and issuance system for commercial auto risks, available to agents in most of its states by the end of the second quarter of 2008.

Financial Data
(US$ in Thousands)

	3 Mos	12/31/2007	12/31/2006	12/31/2005	12/31/2004	12/31/2003	12/31/2002	12/31/2001
Earnings Per Share	1.79	2.86	2.90	3.06	2.70	1.58	0.93	0.52
Cash Flow Per Share	5.32	2.97	2.29	5.62	3.69	3.51	3.25	1.64
Tang Book Value Per Share	22.17	23.10	20.35	18.85	16.41	13.71	11.89	10.23
Dividends Per Share	0.550	0.500	0.380	0.270	0.170	0.150	0.135	0.125
Dividend Payout %	30.66	17.48	13.10	8.82	6.30	9.49	14.52	24.04
Income Statement								
Total Revenue	301,000	1,113,400	1,117,400	1,139,500	1,092,400	1,041,696	967,479	623,272
Income Before Taxes	(15,000)	155,300	161,700	172,000	151,600	83,277	37,790	17,976
Income Taxes	(2,500)	36,200	41,300	46,100	41,600	19,655	795	(2,639)
Net Income	(12,500)	119,100	120,400	125,900	110,000	63,622	36,995	20,615
Average Shares	40,300	41,600	41,600	41,100	40,800	40,153	39,743	39,681
Balance Sheet								
Total Assets	2,425,300	2,337,900	2,255,100	2,274,900	2,023,700	1,836,667	1,592,995	1,367,496
Total Liabilities	1,542,900	1,402,400	1,420,900	1,511,400	1,365,500	1,294,376	1,129,226	967,303
Stockholders' Equity	882,400	935,500	834,200	763,500	658,200	542,291	463,769	400,193
Shares Outstanding	39,800	40,500	41,000	40,500	40,100	39,559	39,001	38,937
Statistical Record								
Return on Assets %	3.21	5.19	5.32	5.86	5.68	3.71	2.50	1.82
Return on Equity %	8.67	13.46	15.07	17.71	18.28	12.65	8.56	5.24
Net Margin %	(4.15)	10.70	10.78	11.05	10.07	6.11	3.82	3.31
Price Range	33.97-23.79	34.84-24.42	39.54-28.53	36.69-24.47	30.93-22.68	26.82-15.33	17.19-13.10	17.67-12.50
P/E Ratio	18.98-13.29	12.18-8.54	13.63-9.84	11.99-8.00	11.46-8.40	16.97-9.70	18.48-14.09	33.98-24.04
Average Yield %	1.90	1.65	1.14	0.91	0.62	0.70	0.87	0.81

Address: 518 East Broad Street, Columbus, OH 43215
Telephone: 614-464-5000
Web Site: www.STFC.com

Officers: Robert P. Restrepo - Chairman, President, Chief Executive Officer, Holding/Parent Company Officer Mark A. Blackburn - Executive Vice President, Chief Operating Officer, Holding/Parent Company Officer **Transfer Agents:** National City Bank, Cleveland, OH

Investor Contact: 614-464-5078
No of Institutions: 103
Shares: 11,481,188 **% Held:** 27.07

STATE STREET CORP.

Exchange	Symbol	Price	52Wk Range	Yield	P/E
NYS	STT	$72.28 (5/29/2008)	85.37-59.48	1.27	18.73

*7 Year Price Score 105.83 *NYSE Composite Index=100 *12 Month Price Score 102.64

Interim Earnings (Per Share)

Qtr.	Mar	Jun	Sep	Dec
2005	0.67	0.66	0.43	0.74
2006	0.87	0.68	0.83	0.91
2007	0.93	1.07	0.91	0.54
2008	1.35	...	...	...

Interim Dividends (Per Share)

Amt	Decl	Ex	Rec	Pay
0.22Q	06/21/2007	06/27/2007	06/29/2007	07/16/2007
0.22Q	09/19/2007	09/27/2007	10/01/2007	10/15/2007
0.23Q	12/13/2007	12/28/2007	01/02/2008	01/15/2008
0.23Q	03/20/2008	03/28/2008	04/01/2008	04/15/2008

Indicated Div: $0.92 (Div. Reinv. Plan)

Valuation Analysis

Forecast EPS	$5.17 (05/17/2008)
Market Cap	$28.2 Billion Book Value 10.8 Billion
Price/Book	2.61 Price/Sales 2.26

Dividend Achiever Status

10 Year Dividend Rate	15.14%
Total Years of Dividend Growth	27

Business Summary: Commercial Banking (MIC: SIC: 6022 NAIC: 522110)

State Street is a financial holding company. Through its subsidiaries, including its principal banking subsidiary, State Street Bank and Trust Company, Co. provides a range of products and services for institutional investors worldwide. Co. has two reportable lines of business: Investment Servicing and Investment Management. Co.'s customers include mutual funds and other collective investment funds, corporate and public retirement plans, insurance companies, foundations, endowments and other investment pools, and investment managers. As of Dec 31 2007, Co. had total assets of $142.54 billion and total deposits of $95.79 billion.

Recent Developments: For the quarter ended Mar 31 2008, net income increased 68.8% to US$530.0 million from US$314.0 million in the year-earlier quarter. Net interest income increased 92.3% to US$625.0 million from US$325.0 million in the year-earlier quarter. Non-interest income rose 42.4% to US$1.95 billion from US$1.37 billion, while non-interest expense advanced 46.2% to US$1.77 billion.

Prospects: For the full year of 2008, Co. continues to anticipate an increase in operating earnings per share of between 10.0% and 15.0%, as well as revenue growth in the range of 14.0% to 17.0%, excluding the effects of the fourth-quarter 2007 charge and the effects of integration costs in both 2007 and 2008. Separately, on May 2, 2008, Co. announced that it has entered into a definitive agreement to sell its 50.0% interest in CitiStreet, a benefits servicing business that provides retirement plan recordkeeping and administrative services, to ING Group for about $900.0 million. Co. expects to complete the transaction by the end of the third quarter of 2008, subject to customary closing conditions.

Financial Data
(US$ in Thousands)

	3 Mos	12/31/2007	12/31/2006	12/31/2005	12/31/2004	12/31/2003	12/31/2002	12/31/2001
Earnings Per Share	3.86	3.45	3.29	2.50	2.35	2.15	3.10	1.90
Cash Flow Per Share	3.20	8.15	2.96	7.52	1.24	4.57	3.10	1.44
Tang Book Value Per Share	11.07	12.28	16.35	13.70	12.49	11.65	12.92	11.88
Dividends Per Share	0.900	0.880	0.800	0.720	0.640	0.560	0.480	0.405
Dividend Payout %	23.33	25.51	24.32	28.80	27.23	26.05	15.48	21.32
Income Statement								
Income Before Taxes	803,000	1,903,000	1,771,000	1,432,000	1,192,000	1,112,000	1,555,000	930,000
Income Taxes	273,000	642,000	675,000	487,000	394,000	390,000	540,000	302,000
Net Income	530,000	1,261,000	1,106,000	838,000	798,000	722,000	1,015,000	628,000
Average Shares	393,647	365,488	335,732	334,636	339,605	335,326	327,477	330,492
Balance Sheet								
Total Assets	154,349,000	142,543,000	107,353,000	97,968,000	94,040,000	87,534,000	85,794,000	69,896,000
Total Liabilities	143,543,000	131,244,000	100,101,000	91,601,000	87,881,000	81,787,000	81,007,000	66,051,000
Stockholders' Equity	10,806,000	11,299,000	7,252,000	6,367,000	6,159,000	5,747,000	4,787,000	3,845,000
Shares Outstanding	390,318	386,284	332,438	333,625	333,645	334,474	324,927	323,670
Statistical Record								
Return on Assets %	1.11	1.01	1.08	0.87	0.88	0.83	1.30	0.90
Return on Equity %	16.12	13.59	16.24	13.38	13.37	13.71	23.52	17.67
Price Range	85.37-59.48	82.24-59.48	68.36-54.49	59.29-40.68	56.45-41.07	53.18-31.63	57.59-32.38	62.75-38.66
P/E Ratio	22.12-15.41	23.84-17.24	20.78-16.56	23.72-16.27	24.02-17.48	24.73-14.71	18.58-10.45	33.03-20.35
Average Yield %	1.24	1.26	1.30	1.47	1.33	1.32	1.04	0.80

Address: One Lincoln Street, Boston, MA 02111-2900 Telephone: 617-786-3000 Web Site: www.statestreet.com	Officers: Ronald E. Logue - Chairman, Chief Executive Officer Joseph C. Antonellis - Vice-Chairman Transfer Agents: EquiServe Trust Company, N.A.	Investor Contact: 617-664-3477 No of Institutions: 899 Shares: 342,448,736 % Held: 82.59

STEPAN CO.

Exchange	Symbol	Price	52Wk Range	Yield	P/E
NYS	SCL	$40.12 (5/29/2008)	41.96-27.31	2.09	22.54

*7 Year Price Score 95.49 *NYSE Composite Index=100 *12 Month Price Score 124.64

Interim Earnings (Per Share)

Qtr.	Mar	Jun	Sep	Dec
2005	0.33	0.64	0.43	(0.05)
2006	0.31	0.31	0.61	(0.60)
2007	0.56	0.47	0.31	0.16
2008	0.85	...	...	...

Interim Dividends (Per Share)

Amt	Decl	Ex	Rec	Pay
0.205Q	07/31/2007	08/29/2007	08/31/2007	09/14/2007
0.21Q	10/16/2007	11/28/2007	11/30/2007	12/14/2007
0.21Q	02/12/2008	02/27/2008	02/29/2008	03/14/2008
0.21Q	04/23/2008	05/28/2008	05/30/2008	06/13/2008
		Indicated Div: $0.84		

Valuation Analysis

Forecast EPS	N/A		
Market Cap	$378.0 Million	Book Value	219.2 Million
Price/Book	1.72	Price/Sales	0.27

Dividend Achiever Status

10 Year Growth Rate	4.88%
Total Years of Dividend Growth	40

Business Summary: Chemicals (MIC: SIC: 2841 NAIC: 325611)

Stepan produces specialty and intermediate chemicals. Co. has three segments: surfactants, polymers and specialty products. Surfactants refer to chemical agents that affect the interaction amid two surfaces, providing actions such as detergency, wetting and foaming, dispersing, emulsification, demulsification, viscosity modifications and biocidal disinfectants. Polymers, which include phthalic anhydride, polyols and polyurethane foam systems, are used in plastics, building materials and refrigeration industries. Polymers are also used in coating, adhesive, sealant and elastomer applications. Specialty products include chemicals used in food, flavoring and pharmaceutical applications.

Recent Developments: For the quarter ended Mar 31 2008, net income increased 53.8% to US$8.7 million from US$5.7 million in the year-earlier quarter. Revenues were US$381.5 million, up 21.9% from US$313.0 million the year before. Operating income was US$16.9 million versus US$10.5 million in the prior-year quarter, an increase of 60.3%. Direct operating expenses rose 20.6% to US$335.6 million from US$278.2 million in the comparable period the year before. Indirect operating expenses increased 19.4% to US$29.0 million from US$24.3 million in the equivalent prior-year period.

Prospects: Co.'s results reflect higher global surfactant profitability as it continues to, among others, recapture lost margin on fabric softeners, reduce outsourcing and benefit from its restructuring plans. Within its Polymers business, the decline in phthalic anhydride profitability is mostly offset by volume growth in Co.'s global polyol business. However, Co. remains concerned about the potential effect of a recession and believes that margin loss may result from persistent rising costs in certain areas, such as Europe, albeit the expected strong demand in that region. Thus, Co. will continue its efforts to mitigate these trends, including through increased selling prices as the market allows.

Financial Data

(US$ in Thousands)	3 Mos	12/31/2007	12/31/2006	12/31/2005	12/31/2004	12/31/2003	12/31/2002	12/31/2001
Earnings Per Share	1.78	1.50	0.63	1.35	1.05	0.45	2.05	1.59
Cash Flow Per Share	3.48	5.05	4.25	4.67	4.88	5.13	5.20	5.79
Tang Book Value Per Share	20.62	19.40	16.43	15.07	15.05	14.31	13.98	15.41
Dividends Per Share	0.830	0.825	0.805	0.785	0.772	0.762	0.738	0.708
Dividend Payout %	46.50	55.00	127.78	58.15	73.57	169.44	35.98	44.50
Income Statement								
Total Revenue	381,451	1,329,901	1,172,583	1,078,377	935,816	784,855	748,539	711,517
EBITDA	24,497	70,621	54,658	64,216	61,039	54,758	77,773	73,066
Depn & Amortn	9,353	37,176	38,384	38,769	39,169	41,426	40,117	39,972
Income Before Taxes	12,797	23,715	7,389	17,646	14,633	5,271	30,268	25,926
Income Taxes	4,067	8,687	900	4,170	4,320	360	10,139	9,774
Net Income	8,747	15,118	6,670	13,159	10,324	4,911	20,129	16,152
Average Shares	10,233	10,113	9,284	9,725	9,038	9,086	9,802	10,133
Balance Sheet								
Current Assets	347,240	293,932	268,469	259,248	235,484	204,460	185,112	185,194
Total Assets	625,911	573,185	546,055	516,159	492,776	464,217	439,667	435,488
Current Liabilities	207,456	200,978	180,495	162,904	157,602	132,939	105,017	109,730
Long-Term Obligations	129,123	96,939	107,403	108,945	94,018	92,004	104,304	109,588
Total Liabilities	406,042	366,458	364,518	348,420	323,601	302,150	280,838	275,759
Stockholders' Equity	219,191	206,051	180,786	166,834	168,241	162,067	158,829	159,729
Shares Outstanding	9,422	9,309	9,207	9,040	8,993	8,933	8,880	9,420
Statistical Record								
Return on Assets %	3.05	2.70	1.26	2.61	2.15	1.09	4.60	3.80
Return on Equity %	8.93	7.82	3.84	7.85	6.23	3.06	12.64	10.29
EBITDA Margin %	6.42	5.31	4.66	5.95	6.52	6.98	10.39	10.27
Net Margin %	2.29	1.14	0.57	1.22	1.10	0.63	2.69	2.27
Asset Turnover	2.34	2.38	2.21	2.14	1.95	1.74	1.71	1.67
Current Ratio	1.67	1.46	1.49	1.59	1.49	1.54	1.76	1.69
Debt to Equity	0.59	0.47	0.59	0.65	0.56	0.57	0.66	0.69
Price Range	38.25-25.88	34.90-25.40	33.00-25.05	27.48-20.80	26.15-21.70	26.80-21.55	29.21-23.55	26.38-17.80
P/E Ratio	21.49-14.54	23.27-16.93	52.38-39.76	20.36-15.41	24.90-20.67	59.56-47.89	14.25-11.49	16.59-11.19
Average Yield %	2.67	2.73	2.74	3.26	3.19	3.12	2.77	3.05

Address: Edens & Winnetka Road, Northfield, IL 60093 **Telephone:** 847-446-7500 **Web Site:** www.stepan.com	**Officers:** F. Quinn Stepan - Chairman F. Quinn Stepan - President, Chief Executive Officer **Transfer Agents:** Computershare Investor Services, Chicago, IL	**Investor Contact:** 847-446-7500 **No of Institutions:** 86 **Shares:** 5,308,102 **% Held:** 52.74

STERLING BANCSHARES, INC. (TX)

Exchange	Symbol	Price	52Wk Range	Yield	P/E
NMS	SBIB	$10.24 (5/29/2008)	12.54-8.59	2.15	14.22

*7 Year Price Score 84.97   *NYSE Composite Index=100   *12 Month Price Score 96.19

Interim Earnings (Per Share)

Qtr.	Mar	Jun	Sep	Dec
2005	0.11	0.13	0.13	0.16
2006	0.15	0.17	0.17	0.18
2007	0.17	0.18	0.20	0.18
2008	0.16	...	...	...

Interim Dividends (Per Share)

Amt	Decl	Ex	Rec	Pay
0.052Q	07/30/2007	08/08/2007	08/10/2007	08/24/2007
0.052Q	10/29/2007	11/07/2007	11/09/2007	11/23/2007
0.055Q	01/28/2008	02/06/2008	02/08/2008	02/22/2008
0.055Q	04/29/2008	05/07/2008	05/09/2008	05/23/2008
		Indicated Div: $0.22		

Valuation Analysis

Forecast EPS $0.71 (05/17/2008)
Market Cap $748.7 Million   Book Value   496.4 Million
Price/Book   1.51   Price/Sales   2.28

Dividend Achiever Status

10 Year Growth Rate   12.41%
Total Years of Dividend Growth   14

TRADING VOLUME (thousand shares)

Business Summary: Commercial Banking (MIC: SIC: 6022 NAIC: 522110)

Sterling Bancshares is a bank holding company that provides commercial and retail banking to small- to mid-sized businesses and consumers, mainly in the Houston, Dallas and San Antonio metropolitan areas through its full service banking centers. Co.'s commercial and consumer banking services include demand, savings and time deposits; commercial, real estate and consumer loans; merchant credit card services; letters of credit; and cash and asset management services. Co. also facilitates sales of brokerage, mutual fund, alternative financing and insurance products through third party vendors. As of Dec 31 2007, Co. had total assets of $4.54 billion and total deposits of $3.67 billion.

Recent Developments: For the quarter ended Mar 31 2008, net income decreased 2.6% to US$11.6 million from US$11.9 million in the year-earlier quarter. Net interest income increased 7.6% to US$48.0 million from US$44.6 million in the year-earlier quarter. Provision for loan losses was US$4.2 million versus US$370,000 in the prior-year quarter, an increase of. Non-interest income rose 35.1% to US$10.7 million from US$7.9 million, while non-interest expense advanced 10.5% to US$37.4 million.

Prospects: Co.'s net interest income is being favorably affected by a combination of growth in its loan portfolio and a decline in interest expense due to the utilization of lower cost borrowings. In addition, Co. is seeing higher non-interest income, mainly due to an increase in wealth and asset management fees, driven by its June 2007 acquisition of MBM Advisors, Inc. Also, Co.'s increased other non-interest income is benefiting from growth in lending fees. However, Co.'s net interest margin is being held back by a decline in short-term interest rates that began in late 2007.

Financial Data (US$ in Thousands)	3 Mos	12/31/2007	12/31/2006	12/31/2005	12/31/2004	12/31/2003	12/31/2002	12/31/2001
Earnings Per Share	0.72	0.72	0.66	0.53	0.37	0.73	0.55	0.47
Cash Flow Per Share	0.87	0.97	1.39	0.97	1.92	12.56	(7.27)	(3.59)
Tang Book Value Per Share	4.21	4.04	3.78	3.62	3.68	3.39	2.45	2.18
Dividends Per Share	0.212	0.210	0.187	0.160	0.133	0.120	0.107	0.098
Dividend Payout %	29.60	29.17	28.28	30.38	36.36	16.36	19.51	20.66
Income Statement								
Income Before Taxes	17,173	78,670	67,779	52,172	34,447	42,391	54,812	46,811
Income Taxes	5,564	25,708	21,939	15,950	9,484	14,037	18,139	16,410
Net Income	11,609	52,962	45,840	36,222	24,963	49,110	36,551	30,401
Average Shares	73,405	73,126	69,533	68,641	67,917	66,972	67,134	64,566
Balance Sheet								
Total Assets	4,745,461	4,535,909	4,117,559	3,726,859	3,336,070	3,204,405	3,582,745	2,778,090
Total Liabilities	4,249,091	4,055,650	3,708,274	3,392,387	3,022,898	2,831,809	3,248,344	2,498,989
Stockholders' Equity	496,370	480,259	409,285	334,472	313,172	292,596	249,327	217,369
Shares Outstanding	73,115	73,158	71,000	68,000	67,602	66,963	65,974	65,654
Statistical Record								
Return on Assets %	1.16	1.22	1.17	1.03	0.76	1.45	1.15	1.29
Return on Equity %	11.15	11.91	12.33	11.19	8.22	18.12	15.66	16.15
Price Range	12.54-8.59	13.17-9.79	13.84-10.13	10.77-8.58	10.00-7.95	9.33-7.41	10.20-7.07	10.76-7.22
P/E Ratio	17.42-11.93	18.29-13.60	20.97-15.35	20.33-16.19	27.03-21.48	12.79-10.16	18.55-12.85	22.90-15.37
Average Yield %	1.93	1.82	1.62	1.42	1.49	1.46	1.21	1.17

Address: 2550 North Loop West, Suite 600, Houston, TX 77092
Telephone: 713-466-8300
Web Site: www.banksterling.com

Officers: J. Downey Bridgwater - Chairman, President, Chief Executive Officer Allen D. Brown - Executive Vice President **Transfer Agents:** American Stock Transfer & Trust Company, New York, NY

Investor Contact: 888-577-7242
No of Institutions: 182
Shares: 61,148,376 **% Held:** 76.13

STRYKER CORP.

Exchange	Symbol	Price	52Wk Range	Yield	P/E
NYS	SYK	$63.76 (5/29/2008)	76.48-59.74	0.52	25.00

*7 Year Price Score 114.94 *NYSE Composite Index=100   *12 Month Price Score 97.65

Interim Earnings (Per Share)

Qtr.	Mar	Jun	Sep	Dec
2005	0.42	0.45	0.32	0.45
2006	0.36	0.52	0.46	0.55
2007	0.59	0.65	0.55	0.66
2008	0.70	...	...	...

Interim Dividends (Per Share)

Amt	Decl	Ex	Rec	Pay
0.09a	12/10/2004	12/29/2004	12/31/2004	01/31/2005
0.11a	12/07/2005	12/28/2005	12/30/2005	01/31/2006
0.22a	12/06/2006	12/27/2006	12/29/2006	01/31/2007
0.33a	12/06/2007	12/27/2007	12/31/2007	01/31/2008

Indicated Div: $0.33

Valuation Analysis

Forecast EPS	$2.88 (05/17/2008)		
Market Cap	$26.3 Billion	Book Value	5.9 Billion
Price/Book	4.43	Price/Sales	4.24

Dividend Achiever Status

10 Year Growth Rate	24.29%
Total Years of Dividend Growth	15

TRADING VOLUME (thousand shares)

Business Summary: Medical Instruments & Equipment (MIC: SIC: 3841 NAIC: 339112)

Stryker is a medical technology company with a range of products in orthopaedics and other medical specialties. Co. operates through two reportable business segments: Orthopaedic Implants and MedSurg Equipment. The Orthopaedic Implants segment sells orthopaedic reconstructive (hip, knee and shoulder), trauma, spinal and craniomaxillofacial implant systems; bone cement; and the bone growth factor OP-1. The MedSurg Equipment segment sells surgical equipment; surgical navigation systems; endoscopic, communications and digital imaging systems as well as patient handling and emergency medical equipment.

Recent Developments: For the quarter ended Mar 31 2008, income from continuing operations increased 20.1% to US$290.5 million from US$241.8 million in the year-earlier quarter. Net income increased 19.3% to US$290.5 million from US$243.5 million in the year-earlier quarter. Revenues were US$1.63 billion, up 14.7% from US$1.43 billion the year before. Operating income was US$383.7 million versus US$322.2 million in the prior-year quarter, an increase of 19.1%. Direct operating expenses rose 13.9% to US$500.5 million from US$439.4 million in the comparable period the year before. Indirect operating expenses increased 13.0% to US$750.2 million from US$663.9 million in the equivalent prior-year period.

Prospects: Despite the potential for continued pricing pressure in certain markets, Co. is optimistic with its 2008 outlook regarding the growth rates in orthopaedic procedures and sales growth rates in its orthopaedics products and other medical specialties. Hence, for 2008, Co. is projecting diluted net earnings per share to be approximately $2.88, representing a 22.0% increase over diluted net earnings per share from continuing operations of $2.37 in 2007. The earnings forecast for 2008 also includes a constant currency net sales increase in the range of 11.0% to 13.0% as a result of growth in shipments at Co.'s Orthopaedic Implants and MedSurg Equipment segments.

Financial Data

(US$ in Thousands)

	3 Mos	12/31/2007	12/31/2006	12/31/2005	12/31/2004	12/31/2003	12/31/2002	12/31/2001
Earnings Per Share	2.55	2.44	1.89	1.64	1.14	1.12	0.85	0.66
Cash Flow Per Share	2.59	2.51	2.13	2.14	1.47	1.63	1.28	1.19
Tang Book Value Per Share	11.33	10.83	7.98	5.75	4.44	2.98	1.42	0.65
Dividends Per Share	0.330	0.330	0.220	0.110	0.090	0.070	0.060	0.050
Dividend Payout %	12.93	13.52	11.64	6.71	7.89	6.28	7.06	7.58
Income Statement								
Total Revenue	1,634,400	6,000,500	5,405,600	4,871,500	4,262,300	3,625,300	3,011,600	2,602,300
EBITDA	502,200	1,548,600	1,270,900	1,158,200	874,300	817,700	604,400	509,700
Depn & Amortn	98,200	178,500	167,100	154,900	150,500	142,600	57,400	36,100
Income Before Taxes	404,000	1,370,100	1,103,800	1,003,300	717,000	652,500	506,700	405,700
Income Taxes	113,500	383,400	326,100	328,100	251,300	199,000	161,100	133,900
Net Income	290,500	1,017,400	777,700	675,200	465,700	453,500	345,600	267,000
Average Shares	417,900	417,200	411,800	411,600	410,300	406,800	407,600	406,000
Balance Sheet								
Current Assets	5,063,900	4,904,900	3,534,300	2,870,100	2,142,600	1,397,600	1,151,300	993,100
Total Assets	7,754,100	7,354,000	5,873,800	4,944,100	4,083,800	3,159,100	2,815,500	2,423,600
Current Liabilities	1,149,200	1,333,000	1,351,500	1,248,800	1,113,500	850,500	707,500	533,400
Long-Term Obligations	...	...	...	184,200	700	18,800	491,000	720,900
Total Liabilities	1,821,300	1,975,500	1,682,800	1,692,300	1,331,800	1,004,300	1,317,300	1,367,400
Stockholders' Equity	5,932,800	5,378,500	4,191,000	3,251,800	2,752,000	2,154,800	1,498,200	1,056,200
Shares Outstanding	411,800	411,000	407,900	405,200	402,500	399,400	396,200	393,400
Statistical Record								
Return on Assets %	15.35	15.38	14.38	14.96	12.82	15.18	13.19	11.00
Return on Equity %	20.37	21.26	20.90	22.49	18.93	24.83	27.06	27.94
EBITDA Margin %	30.73	25.81	23.51	23.78	20.51	22.56	20.07	19.59
Net Margin %	17.77	16.96	14.39	13.86	10.93	12.51	11.48	10.26
Asset Turnover	0.90	0.91	1.00	1.08	1.17	1.21	1.15	1.07
Current Ratio	4.41	3.68	2.62	2.30	1.92	1.64	1.63	1.86
Debt to Equity	...	...	...	0.06	N.M.	0.01	0.33	0.68
Price Range	76.48-59.74	76.48-55.12	55.45-40.88	56.10-39.80	57.33-41.75	42.51-30.12	33.62-22.72	30.75-22.06
P/E Ratio	29.99-23.43	31.34-22.59	29.34-21.63	34.21-24.27	50.29-36.62	37.95-26.89	39.55-26.73	46.60-33.42
Average Yield %	0.49	0.49	0.46	0.23	0.19	0.19	0.21	0.19

Address: 2725 Fairfield Road, Kalamazoo, MI 49002 **Telephone:** 269-385-2600 **Web Site:** www.stryker.com	**Officers:** John W. Brown - Chairman Stephen P. MacMillan - President, Chief Executive Officer **Transfer Agents:** National City Bank, Cleveland, OH	**Investor Contact:** 616-385-2600 **No of Institutions:** 902 **Shares:** 261,498,784 **% Held:** 52.44

SUFFOLK BANCORP

Exchange	Symbol	Price	52Wk Range	Yield	P/E
NMS	SUBK	$34.11 (5/29/2008)	35.23-26.08	2.58	13.64

*7 Year Price Score 77.02   ***NYSE Composite Index=100**   ***12 Month Price Score 106.40**

Interim Earnings (Per Share)

Qtr.	Mar	Jun	Sep	Dec
2005	0.48	0.50	0.56	0.56
2006	0.50	0.55	0.60	0.55
2007	0.50	0.53	0.61	0.58
2008	0.79	...	...	...

Interim Dividends (Per Share)

Amt	Decl	Ex	Rec	Pay
0.22Q	08/27/2007	09/12/2007	09/14/2007	10/01/2007
0.22Q	11/26/2007	12/12/2007	12/14/2007	01/02/2008
0.22Q	02/25/2008	03/12/2008	03/14/2008	04/01/2008
0.22Q	05/22/2008	06/11/2008	06/13/2008	07/01/2008
		Indicated Div: $0.88		

Valuation Analysis

Forecast EPS	$2.21 (04/08/2008)
Market Cap	$326.4 Million Book Value 115.5 Million
Price/Book	2.82 Price/Sales 3.16

Dividend Achiever Status

10 Year Growth Rate	10.06%
Total Years of Dividend Growth	18

Business Summary: Commercial Banking (MIC: SIC: 6021 NAIC: 522110)

Suffolk Bancorp is a bank holding company. Through its subsidiary, Suffolk County National Bank (the Bank), Co. provides banking services to its commercial and retail customers in Suffolk County, on Long Island, NY. The Bank provides a line of domestic, retail, and commercial banking services, and trust services. The Bank's primary lending area includes all of Suffolk County, NY, and a limited number of loans or loan-participations in the adjacent markets of Nassau County and New York City. The Bank also serves as an indirect lender to the customers of several automobile dealers. As of Dec 31 2007, Co. had total assets of $1.47 billion and total deposits of $1.14 billion.

Recent Developments: For the quarter ended Mar 31 2008, net income increased 46.8% to US$7.6 million from US$5.1 million in the year-earlier quarter. Net interest income decreased 1.4% to US$15.9 million from US$16.1 million in the year-earlier quarter. Provision for loan losses was US$225,000 versus US$112,000 in the prior-year quarter, an increase of 100.9%. Non-interest income rose 167.8% to US$6.4 million from US$2.4 million, while non-interest expense advanced 0.3% to US$10.4 million.

Prospects: Despite experiencing loan growth, Co. is seeing a decline in its net interest income as interest expense increased slightly due to increased rates paid for Savings, N.O.W. and Money Market deposits, while interest income remained flat as the yield on earning assets declined. Nevertheless, Co. continues to manage its balance sheet to maintain its performance. Notably, Co. is focused on emphasizing on both commercial and personal demand deposits and managing net loan charge-offs. In regards to lending, Co. continues to focus on underwriting to preserve both credit quality and yields in face of competition, with an emphasis on preservation of margins over less profitable growth.

Financial Data
(US$ in Thousands)

	3 Mos	12/31/2007	12/31/2006	12/31/2005	12/31/2004	12/31/2003	12/31/2002	12/31/2001
Earnings Per Share	2.50	2.23	2.20	2.09	1.91	1.92	1.82	1.58
Cash Flow Per Share	2.77	1.97	2.93	3.17	2.74	2.99	2.33	1.39
Tang Book Value Per Share	11.99	11.25	10.52	9.72	9.72	9.07	9.40	9.59
Dividends Per Share	0.880	0.880	0.880	0.790	0.760	0.760	0.660	0.560
Dividend Payout %	35.14	39.46	40.00	37.80	39.79	39.58	36.26	35.44
Income Statement								
Income Before Taxes	11,634	33,790	35,441	35,478	34,305	35,382	35,289	30,920
Income Taxes	4,075	11,662	12,813	13,376	13,430	14,046	14,020	12,235
Net Income	7,559	22,128	22,628	22,102	20,875	21,336	21,269	18,685
Average Shares	9,606	9,915	10,303	10,600	10,913	11,090	11,700	11,839
Balance Sheet								
Total Assets	1,531,463	1,470,581	1,392,649	1,408,283	1,348,218	1,328,757	1,272,717	1,164,947
Total Liabilities	1,415,920	1,361,600	1,284,083	1,306,282	1,242,007	1,228,587	1,163,924	1,068,111
Stockholders' Equity	115,543	108,981	108,566	102,001	106,212	100,170	108,793	96,837
Shares Outstanding	9,568	9,610	10,242	10,406	10,842	10,949	11,489	10,010
Statistical Record								
Return on Assets %	1.67	1.55	1.62	1.60	1.56	1.64	1.75	1.69
Return on Equity %	21.84	20.34	21.49	21.23	20.17	20.42	20.69	20.21
Price Range	35.23-26.08	38.80-26.08	38.75-28.55	37.00-25.99	36.06-29.83	37.33-30.30	36.50-27.00	27.90-15.31
P/E Ratio	14.09-10.43	17.40-11.70	17.61-12.98	17.70-12.44	18.88-15.62	19.44-15.78	20.05-14.84	17.66-9.69
Average Yield %	2.80	2.73	2.65	2.48	2.34	2.29	2.11	2.66

Address: 4 West Second Street,	Officers: Thomas S. Kohlmann - Chairman, President,	Investor Contact: 631-727-5667
Riverhead, NY 11901	Chief Executive Officer J. Gordon Huszagh -	No of Institutions: 74
Telephone: 631-727-5667	Executive Vice President, Chief Financial Officer	Shares: 3,495,426 % Held: 34.84
Web Site: www.scnb.com	Transfer Agents: American Stock Transfer & Trust	
	Co., New York, NY	

SUNTRUST BANKS, INC.

Exchange	Symbol	Price	52Wk Range	Yield	P/E
NYS	STI	$52.96 (5/29/2008)	90.55-50.36	5.82	13.61

*7 Year Price Score 77.47 *NYSE Composite Index=100 ***12 Month Price Score 81.26**

Interim Earnings (Per Share)

Qtr.	Mar	Jun	Sep	Dec
2005	1.36	1.28	1.40	1.43
2006	1.46	1.49	1.47	(1.60)
2007	1.44	1.89	1.18	0.03
2008	0.81	...	...	...

Interim Dividends (Per Share)

Amt	Decl	Ex	Rec	Pay
0.73Q	08/14/2007	08/29/2007	09/01/2007	09/14/2007
0.73Q	11/15/2007	11/28/2007	11/30/2007	12/14/2007
0.77Q	02/12/2008	02/27/2008	02/29/2008	03/14/2008
0.77Q	04/29/2008	05/29/2008	06/02/2008	06/13/2008

Indicated Div: $3.08 (Div. Reinv. Plan)

Valuation Analysis

Forecast EPS $3.45 (05/17/2008)

Market Cap	$18.5 Billion	Book Value	18.4 Billion
Price/Book	1.01	Price/Sales	1.39

Dividend Achiever Status

10 Year Growth Rate	12.18%
Total Years of Dividend Growth	22

Business Summary: Commercial Banking (MIC: SIC: 6021 NAIC: 522110)

SunTrust Banks is a financial services holding company. Through its SunTrust Bank subsidiary, Co. provides deposit, credit, and trust and investment services. Through its other subsidiaries, Co. provides banking, asset management, securities' brokerage, capital market services and credit-related insurance. Co. operates mainly within Florida, Georgia, Maryland, North Carolina, South Carolina, Tennessee, Virginia, and the District of Columbia. Co. conducted its businesses through five segments: Retail, Commercial, Corporate and Investment Banking, Mortgage, and Wealth and Investment Management. As of Dec 31 2007, Co. had total assets of $179.6 billion and total deposits of $117.8 billion.

Recent Developments: For the quarter ended Mar 31 2008, net income decreased 44.3% to US$290.6 million from US$521.3 million in the year-earlier quarter. Net interest income decreased 2.1% to US$1.14 billion from US$1.16 billion in the year-earlier quarter. Provision for loan losses was US$560.0 million versus US$56.4 million in the prior-year quarter, an increase of 892.2%. Non-interest income rose 20.3% to US$1.06 billion from US$878.9 million, while non-interest expense advanced 1.5% to US$1.26 billion.

Prospects: Co. now anticipates savings in 2008 to be about $500.0 million, versus its previous estimate of $150.0 million, given the viability of its ongoing Excellence in Execution Efficiency and Productivity program. For the second quarter of 2008, Co. expects to see continuous margin compressions a result of deposit pricing pressures and deposit mix along with declines in earning asset yields. Should deposit pricing pressures and volumes improve, Co. foresees improvement in margins, despite the continuing potential for increases in nonperforming assets. Meanwhile, Co. believes that the May 1 2008 acquisition of GB&T Bancshares, Inc. should increase its presence in potential Georgia markets.

Financial Data

(US$ in Thousands)	3 Mos	12/31/2007	12/31/2006	12/31/2005	12/31/2004	12/31/2003	12/31/2002	12/31/2001
Earnings Per Share	3.89	4.55	2.82	5.47	5.19	4.73	4.66	4.72
Cash Flow Per Share	(0.62)	10.63	10.82	(13.14)	3.77	14.85	(5.54)	(4.49)
Tang Book Value Per Share	27.38	26.60	26.04	24.67	22.50	28.43	26.56	26.67
Dividends Per Share	...	2.920	2.440	2.200	2.000	1.800	1.720	1.600
Dividend Payout %	...	64.18	86.52	40.22	38.54	38.05	36.91	33.90
Income Statement								
Interest Income	2,258,332	10,035,920	9,792,020	7,731,309	5,218,382	4,768,842	5,135,197	6,279,574
Interest Expense	1,118,465	5,316,376	5,131,555	3,152,343	1,533,227	1,448,539	1,891,488	3,026,974
Net Interest Income	1,139,867	4,719,544	4,660,465	4,578,966	3,685,155	3,320,303	3,243,709	3,252,600
Provision for Losses	560,022	664,922	262,536	176,886	135,537	313,550	469,792	275,165
Non-Interest Income	1,057,502	3,428,684	3,468,372	3,155,044	2,604,446	2,303,001	2,391,675	2,155,823
Non-Interest Expense	1,255,144	5,217,980	4,879,690	4,691,925	3,898,837	3,400,616	3,342,268	3,113,538
Income Before Taxes	382,203	2,249,529	2,986,441	2,866,395	2,257,026	1,909,138	1,823,324	2,019,720
Income Taxes	91,648	615,514	868,970	879,156	684,125	576,841	491,515	650,501
Net Income	290,555	1,634,015	2,117,471	1,987,239	1,572,901	1,332,297	1,331,809	1,375,537
Average Shares	348,072	352,688	362,802	363,454	303,309	281,434	286,052	291,584
Balance Sheet								
Net Loans & Leases	129,145,144	129,888,185	132,199,934	127,222,380	106,956,371	85,342,459	79,985,614	72,411,757
Total Assets	178,986,947	179,573,933	182,161,609	179,712,841	158,869,784	125,393,153	117,322,523	104,740,644
Total Deposits	116,179,280	117,842,650	124,021,629	122,053,178	103,361,251	81,189,519	79,706,628	67,536,422
Total Liabilities	160,555,499	161,521,415	164,348,003	162,825,446	142,882,885	115,661,987	108,553,027	96,381,076
Stockholders' Equity	18,431,448	18,052,518	17,813,606	16,887,395	15,986,899	9,731,166	8,769,496	8,359,568
Shares Outstanding	349,832	348,411	354,902	361,984	360,840	281,923	270,843	283,040
Statistical Record								
Return on Assets %	0.76	0.90	1.17	1.17	1.10	1.10	1.20	1.32
Return on Equity %	7.67	9.11	12.20	12.09	12.20	14.40	15.55	16.57
Net Interest Margin %	50.47	47.03	47.59	59.23	70.62	69.62	63.17	51.80
Efficiency Ratio %	37.85	38.75	36.80	43.10	49.84	48.09	44.40	36.91
Loans to Deposits	1.11	1.10	1.07	1.04	1.03	1.05	1.00	1.07
Price Range	90.61-54.23	90.61-61.09	85.45-70.08	75.73-65.80	76.41-61.80	71.55-51.56	70.00-51.79	71.81-58.10
P/E Ratio	23.29-13.94	19.91-13.43	30.30-24.85	13.84-12.03	14.72-11.91	15.13-10.90	15.02-11.11	15.21-12.31
Average Yield %	1.04	1.04	3.05	3.05	2.90	2.96	2.71	2.48

Address: 303 Peachtree Street, NE, Atlanta, GA 30308	Officers: L. Phillip Humann - Chairman William R. Reed - Vice-Chairman **Transfer Agents:** Sun Trust Bank, Atlanta, GA	Investor Contact: 404-658-4879
Telephone: 404-588-7711		No of Institutions: 630
Web Site: www.suntrust.com		**Shares:** 236,311,248 **% Held:** 62.36

SUPERVALU INC

Exchange	Symbol	Price	52Wk Range	Yield	P/E	
NYS	SVU	$34.74 (5/29/2008)	49.67-26.25	1.96	12.50	

*7 Year Price Score 98.72   ***NYSE Composite Index=100**   ***12 Month Price Score 90.68**

Interim Earnings (Per Share)

Qtr.	Jun	Sep	Nov	Feb
2004-05	1.09	0.57	0.48	0.57
2005-06	0.64	0.24	0.53	0.05
2006-07	0.57	0.61	0.54	0.57
2007-08	0.69	0.69	0.66	0.73

Interim Dividends (Per Share)

Amt	Decl	Ex	Rec	Pay
0.17Q	08/08/2007	08/29/2007	09/03/2007	09/17/2007
0.17Q	10/05/2007	11/29/2007	12/03/2007	12/17/2007
0.17Q	02/06/2008	02/28/2008	03/03/2008	03/17/2008
0.17Q	05/28/2008	05/29/2008	06/02/2008	06/16/2008

Indicated Div: $0.68 (Div. Reinv. Plan)

Valuation Analysis

Forecast EPS $3.10 (05/17/2008)

Market Cap	$7.4 Billion	Book Value	6.0 Billion
Price/Book	1.24	Price/Sales	0.17

Dividend Achiever Status

10 Year Growth Rate	2.77%
Total Years of Dividend Growth	35

Business Summary: Retail - Food & Beverage (MIC: SIC: 5141 NAIC: 424410)

SUPERVALU is a grocery channel that conducts its retail operations throughout the U.S. under three retail food store formats: combination stores (defined as food and pharmacy), food stores and limited assortment food stores. Additionally, Co. provides supply chain services, including wholesale distribution and related logistics support services primarily across the U.S. retail grocery channel. Co. operates in two segments of the grocery industry, Retail food stores and Supply chain services, which includes wholesale distribution services and other support services to retailers. As of Feb 23 2008, Co. conducted its retail operations through 2,474 stores, of which 873 are licensed locations.

Recent Developments: For the year ended Feb 23 2008, net income increased 31.2% to US$593.0 million from US$452.0 million in the prior year. Revenues were US$44.05 billion, up 17.8% from US$37.41 billion the year before. Operating income was US$1.68 billion versus US$1.31 billion in the prior year, an increase of 29.0%. Direct operating expenses rose 16.0% to US$33.94 billion from US$29.27 billion in the comparable period the year before. Indirect operating expenses increased 23.2% to US$8.42 billion from US$6.83 billion in the equivalent prior-year period.

Prospects: For the fiscal year ending Feb 28 2009, Co. continues to anticipate earnings to be in the range of $3.06 to $3.22 per diluted share. Specifically, Co.'s earnings guidance is based on several assumptions, such as projected net sales in the range of $45.00 billion to $45.50 billion. In addition, Co. is forecasting identical store sales growth to range from 1.0% to 2.0%, excluding fuel, while sales attrition in the traditional food distribution business is estimated to be in the range of 2.0% to 4.0%. Lastly, Co. plans to complete 165 major store remodels, and open approximately 15 new traditional supermarkets as well as 55 to 65 limited assortment food stores, including licensed stores.

Financial Data

(US$ in Thousands)	02/23/2008	02/24/2007	02/25/2006	02/26/2005	02/28/2004	02/22/2003	02/23/2002	02/24/2001
Earnings Per Share	2.76	2.32	1.46	2.71	2.07	1.91	1.53	0.62
Cash Flow Per Share	8.23	4.25	4.97	5.88	6.11	4.30	5.93	4.94
Tang Book Value Per Share	N.M.	N.M.	7.37	6.52	4.84	3.24	2.90	1.64
Dividends Per Share	0.670	0.655	0.477	0.603	0.578	0.565	0.555	0.545
Dividend Payout %	24.28	28.23	32.71	22.23	27.90	29.58	36.27	87.90
Income Statement								
Total Revenue	44,048,000	37,406,000	19,863,599	19,543,240	20,209,679	19,160,368	20,908,522	23,194,279
EBITDA	2,650,000	2,146,000	745,836	1,018,685	902,987	866,999	857,227	688,971
Depn & Amortn	966,000	841,000	310,678	303,039	301,589	297,056	340,750	343,779
Income Before Taxes	977,000	747,000	329,148	600,864	454,880	408,004	343,703	154,357
Income Taxes	384,000	295,000	122,979	215,041	174,742	150,962	138,168	72,392
Net Income	593,000	452,000	206,169	385,823	280,138	257,042	205,535	81,965
Average Shares	215,000	196,000	145,699	144,924	135,418	134,877	133,978	132,829
Balance Sheet								
Current Assets	4,147,000	4,460,000	2,168,040	2,126,500	2,037,092	1,647,366	1,604,027	2,091,676
Total Assets	21,062,000	21,702,000	6,038,271	6,278,342	6,152,938	5,896,245	5,824,782	6,407,172
Current Liabilities	4,607,000	4,705,000	1,506,669	1,631,591	1,871,972	1,525,307	1,701,489	2,341,170
Long-Term Obligations	8,502,000	9,192,000	1,405,971	1,578,867	1,633,721	2,019,658	1,875,873	2,008,474
Total Liabilities	15,109,000	16,396,000	3,418,818	3,767,781	3,943,364	3,887,005	3,908,089	4,613,677
Stockholders' Equity	5,953,000	5,306,000	2,619,453	2,510,561	2,209,574	2,009,240	1,916,693	1,793,495
Shares Outstanding	212,000	209,000	136,437	135,478	134,760	133,688	132,889	132,374
Statistical Record								
Return on Assets %	2.78	3.27	3.36	6.22	4.57	4.40	3.37	1.27
Return on Equity %	10.56	11.44	8.06	16.39	13.07	13.13	11.11	4.55
EBITDA Margin %	6.02	5.74	3.75	5.21	4.47	4.52	4.10	2.97
Net Margin %	1.35	1.21	1.04	1.97	1.39	1.34	0.98	0.35
Asset Turnover	2.07	2.70	3.23	3.15	3.30	3.28	3.43	3.61
Current Ratio	0.90	0.95	1.44	1.30	1.09	1.08	0.94	0.89
Debt to Equity	1.43	1.73	0.54	0.63	0.74	1.01	0.98	1.12
Price Range	49.67-26.65	38.95-26.21	35.80-29.85	34.88-25.95	29.43-12.60	30.50-14.32	24.68-12.80	22.50-11.75
P/E Ratio	18.00-9.66	16.79-11.30	24.52-20.45	12.87-9.58	14.22-6.09	15.97-7.50	16.13-8.37	36.29-18.95
Average Yield %	1.69	2.07	1.46	1.99	2.55	2.32	2.91	3.25

Address: 11840 Valley View Road, Eden Prairie, MN 55344	**Officers:** Jeffrey Noddle - Chairman, Chief Executive Officer Michael L. Jackson - President, Chief Operating Officer **Transfer Agents:**	**Investor Contact:** 952-828-4000	
Telephone: 952-828-4000		**No of Institutions:** 433	
Web Site: www.supervalu.com	Wells Fargo Shareowner Services, St. Paul, MN	**Shares:** 212,580,384 **% Held:** 94.33	

SUSQUEHANNA BANCSHARES, INC

Exchange	Symbol	Price	52Wk Range	Yield	P/E
NMS	SUSQ	$19.33 (5/29/2008)	23.77-16.27	5.38	16.66

*7 Year Price Score 66.83 *NYSE Composite Index=100 ***12 Month Price Score 105.04**

Interim Earnings (Per Share)

Qtr.	Mar	Jun	Sep	Dec
2005	0.33	0.40	0.38	0.59
2006	0.38	0.38	0.49	0.41
2007	0.40	0.19	0.38	0.26
2008	0.33	...	...	...

Interim Dividends (Per Share)

Amt	Decl	Ex	Rec	Pay
0.25Q	07/18/2007	07/30/2007	08/01/2007	08/17/2007
0.26Q	09/05/2007	10/30/2007	11/01/2007	11/20/2007
0.26Q	01/16/2008	01/30/2008	02/01/2008	02/20/2008
0.26Q	04/16/2008	04/29/2008	05/01/2008	05/20/2008

Indicated Div: $1.04

Valuation Analysis

Forecast EPS	$1.47 (05/16/2008)		
Market Cap	$1.7 Billion	Book Value	1.7 Billion
Price/Book	0.96	Price/Sales	2.33

Dividend Achiever Status

10 Year Growth Rate	6.33%
Total Years of Dividend Growth	37

TRADING VOLUME (thousand shares)

Business Summary: Commercial Banking (MIC: SIC: 6021 NAIC: 522110)

Susquehanna Bancshares is a financial holding company that provides a range of retail and commercial banking and financial services in the mid-Atlantic region through its subsidiaries. In addition to its commercial bank subsidiaries, which include Susquehanna Patriot Bank, Susquehanna Bank PA, and Susquehanna Bank, Co. operates a trust and investment company, an asset management company that provides investment advisory, asset management, brokerage and retirement planning services, a property and casualty insurance brokerage company, a commercial finance company, and a vehicle leasing company. As of Dec 31 2007, Co. had total assets of $13.08 billion and total deposits of $8.95 billion.

Recent Developments: For the quarter ended Mar 31 2008, net income increased 35.2% to US$28.0 million from US$20.7 million in the year-earlier quarter. Net interest income increased 55.7% to US$98.2 million from US$63.0 million in the year-earlier quarter. Provision for loan losses was US$9.8 million versus US$2.0 million in the prior-year quarter, an increase of 391.9%. Non-interest income rose 25.2% to US$42.9 million from US$34.3 million, while non-interest expense advanced 41.8% to US$92.0 million.

Prospects: For the full year of 2008, Co. is projecting net interest margin to grow by 3.7%, while deposits growth is forecasted to be approximately 1.0%. In addition, Co. is targeting non-interest income growth of approximately 50.0%, while non-interest expense is estimated to increase by approximately 30.0%. Specifically, these expectations include a $300.0 million auto lease securitization scheduled for the third quarter of 2008 instead of the second quarter of 2008. Accordingly, Co. foresees that this securitization to result in a pre-tax gain of $2.5 million. Looking ahead, Co. will continue to explore opportunities to consolidate its banking operations, lower its costs and improve its efficiency.

Financial Data
(US$ in Thousands)

	3 Mos	12/31/2007	12/31/2006	12/31/2005	12/31/2004	12/31/2003	12/31/2002	12/31/2001
Earnings Per Share	1.16	1.23	1.66	1.70	1.60	1.56	1.55	1.41
Cash Flow Per Share	(2.16)	(1.13)	2.10	1.36	1.83	2.50	2.13	1.74
Tang Book Value Per Share	8.47	8.44	11.18	11.23	10.71	12.14	11.96	12.54
Dividends Per Share	1.020	1.010	0.970	0.930	0.890	0.860	0.810	0.770
Dividend Payout %	88.09	82.11	58.43	54.71	55.63	55.13	52.26	54.61
Income Statement								
Income Before Taxes	39,285	...	121,567	112,438	99,546	89,104	89,063	81,337
Income Taxes	11,265	28,670	37,929	32,875	29,366	26,731	27,342	25,621
Net Income	28,020	69,093	83,638	79,563	70,180	62,373	61,721	55,716
Average Shares	85,963	56,366	50,507	46,919	43,872	40,037	39,932	39,593
Balance Sheet								
Total Assets	13,093,107	13,077,994	8,225,134	7,466,007	7,475,073	5,953,107	5,544,647	5,051,092
Total Liabilities	11,359,799	11,348,980	7,288,848	6,685,537	6,723,379	5,405,725	5,010,792	4,557,556
Stockholders' Equity	1,733,308	1,729,014	936,286	780,470	751,694	547,382	533,855	493,536
Shares Outstanding	85,977	85,935	52,080	46,853	46,592	39,861	39,638	39,344
Statistical Record								
Return on Assets %	0.72	0.65	1.07	1.07	1.04	1.08	1.17	1.13
Return on Equity %	5.68	5.18	9.74	10.39	10.78	11.54	12.02	11.77
Price Range	23.77-16.27	27.01-16.47	27.84-22.39	27.24-21.03	26.89-22.44	27.80-20.20	25.97-18.41	22.80-15.75
P/E Ratio	20.49-14.03	21.96-13.39	16.77-13.49	16.02-12.37	16.81-14.03	17.82-12.95	16.75-11.88	16.17-11.17
Average Yield %	5.02	4.68	3.94	3.82	3.58	3.60	3.60	4.00

Address: 26 North Cedar St., Lititz, PA 17543 **Telephone:** 717-626-4721 **Web Site:** www.susquehanna.net	**Officers:** William J. Reuter - Chairman, Chief Executive Officer Eddie L. Dunklebarger - Vice-Chairman, President, Executive Vice President, Chief Operating Officer **Transfer Agents:** The Bank of New York	**Investor Contact:** 717-625-6305 **No of Institutions:** 184 **Shares:** 45,721,444 **% Held:** 81.03

S.Y. BANCORP, INC.

Exchange	Symbol	Price	52Wk Range	Yield	P/E
NMS	SYBT	$24.89 (5/29/2008)	29.31-20.85	2.73	15.08

*7 Year Price Score 87.79   ***NYSE Composite Index=100**   ***12 Month Price Score 102.02**

Interim Earnings (Per Share)

Qtr.	Mar	Jun	Sep	Dec
2005	0.32	0.37	0.39	0.37
2006	0.36	0.40	0.37	0.42
2007	0.39	0.43	0.41	0.44
2008	0.37	...	...	...

Interim Dividends (Per Share)

Amt	Decl	Ex	Rec	Pay
0.16Q	08/22/2007	09/12/2007	09/14/2007	10/01/2007
0.16Q	11/21/2007	12/12/2007	12/14/2007	01/04/2008
0.17Q	02/20/2008	03/13/2008	03/17/2008	04/01/2008
0.17Q	05/21/2008	06/12/2008	06/16/2008	07/01/2008

Indicated Div: $0.68

Valuation Analysis

Forecast EPS $1.63 (05/16/2008)
Market Cap $333.7 Million   Book Value 131.5 Million
Price/Book 2.54   Price/Sales 2.76

Dividend Achiever Status

10 Year Dividend Growth Rate   18.93%
Total Years of Dividend Growth   18

Business Summary: Commercial Banking (MIC: SIC: 6022 NAIC: 522110)

S.Y. Bancorp is a bank holding company with two subsidiaries, Stock Yards Bank & Trust Co. (the Bank) and S.Y. Bancorp Capital Trust I, a statutory business trust with no business operations. At Dec 31 2007, the Bank provided commercial banking services in the Louisville Metropolitan Statistical Area, Indianapolis and Cincinnati via 28 banking offices. In addition to traditional commercial and personal banking activities, the Bank provides trust and investment services, originates and sells single-family residential mortgages, as well as provides securities brokerage services and life insurance products. At Dec 31 2007, Co. had total assets of $1.48 billion and deposits of $1.11 billion.

Recent Developments: For the quarter ended Mar 31 2008, net income decreased 11.7% to US$5.0 million from US$5.7 million in the year-earlier quarter. Net interest income decreased 1.1% to US$13.3 million from US$13.4 million in the year-earlier quarter. Provision for loan losses was US$1.2 million versus US$780,000 in the prior-year quarter, an increase of 57.1%. Non-interest income rose 2.7% to US$7.4 million from US$7.2 million, while non-interest expense advanced 5.0% to US$11.9 million.

Prospects: Co.'s bottom-line results are being negatively affected by a higher provision for loan losses, increasing non- interest expenses arising mainly from its expansion plans, as well as the pressure on its net interest margin. Co. expects the net interest margin issue to persist in the near term, and additional reductions in short-term rates by the Federal Reserve could add further compression. However, offsetting this to some extent, the maturities on certificates of deposit remain short, which is expected to provide Co. an opportunity to reprice these funding sources in the near future. Meanwhile, Co. expects its brokerage volume to continue to be hindered until consumer confidence improves.

Financial Data

(US$ in Thousands)	3 Mos	12/31/2007	12/31/2006	12/31/2005	12/31/2004	12/31/2003	12/31/2002	12/31/2001
Earnings Per Share	1.65	1.67	1.55	1.46	1.27	1.21	1.07	0.93
Cash Flow Per Share	1.52	1.22	2.53	1.98	1.23	3.07	0.96	0.61
Tang Book Value Per Share	9.81	9.73	9.50	8.62	7.92	7.04	6.10	5.12
Dividends Per Share	0.650	0.630	0.573	0.448	0.371	0.290	0.248	0.214
Dividend Payout %	39.51	37.72	36.99	30.72	29.32	24.02	23.11	22.96
Income Statement								
Interest Income	21,878	91,316	86,327	72,343	60,540	60,120	62,924	65,671
Interest Expense	8,617	37,539	32,441	23,108	16,319	17,372	22,344	30,726
Net Interest Income	13,261	53,777	53,886	49,235	44,221	42,748	40,580	34,945
Provision for Losses	1,225	3,525	2,100	225	2,090	2,550	4,500	4,220
Non-Interest Income	7,350	30,246	28,682	27,122	24,676	25,960	22,575	19,263
Non-Interest Expense	11,943	46,531	46,610	44,612	39,093	40,087	35,527	30,306
Income Before Taxes	7,443	33,967	33,858	31,520	27,714	26,071	23,128	19,682
Income Taxes	2,405	9,915	10,962	9,876	8,802	8,362	7,478	6,140
Net Income	5,038	24,052	22,896	21,644	18,912	17,709	15,650	13,542
Average Shares	13,610	14,389	14,741	14,820	14,877	14,673	14,637	14,492
Balance Sheet								
Net Loans & Leases	1,275,816	1,193,259	1,140,786	1,049,280	977,848	877,512	834,402	780,439
Total Assets	1,517,258	1,482,219	1,426,321	1,330,438	1,212,015	1,118,521	1,039,680	937,293
Total Deposits	1,148,008	1,106,707	1,103,242	1,031,357	950,083	881,866	861,087	753,551
Total Liabilities	1,385,711	1,349,195	1,288,877	1,204,641	1,095,368	1,018,107	953,613	865,609
Stockholders' Equity	131,547	133,024	137,444	125,797	116,647	100,414	86,067	71,684
Shares Outstanding	13,405	13,599	14,400	14,506	14,646	14,254	14,104	14,011
Statistical Record								
Return on Assets %	1.59	1.65	1.66	1.70	1.62	1.64	1.58	1.51
Return on Equity %	17.16	17.79	17.40	17.85	17.38	18.99	19.84	20.52
Net Interest Margin %	60.61	58.89	62.42	68.06	73.04	71.10	64.49	53.21
Efficiency Ratio %	40.86	38.28	40.53	44.85	45.88	46.57	41.55	35.68
Loans to Deposits	1.11	1.08	1.03	1.02	1.03	1.00	0.97	1.04
Price Range	29.31-20.85	29.31-21.68	30.03-23.13	24.29-19.97	23.52-18.52	21.81-16.45	20.95-14.95	16.95-9.64
P/E Ratio	17.76-12.64	17.55-12.98	19.37-14.92	16.63-13.68	18.52-14.59	18.02-13.60	19.58-13.97	18.23-10.37
Average Yield %	2.67	2.50	2.16	2.01	1.75	1.58	1.40	1.52

Address: 1040 East Main Street, Louisville, KY 40206 **Telephone:** 502-582-2571 **Web Site:** www.syb.com	Officers: David P. Heintzman - Chairman, President, Chief Executive Officer Kathy C. Thompson - Senior Executive Vice President **Transfer Agents:** Stock Yards Bank & Trust Company	Investor Contact: 502-625-9176 **No of Institutions:** 62 **Shares:** 4,642,146 **% Held:** 32.02

SYNOVUS FINANCIAL CORP.

Exchange	Symbol	Price	52Wk Range	Yield	P/E
NYS	SNV	$11.65 (5/29/2008)	14.52-9.86	5.84	8.44

*7 Year Price Score 79.78 *NYSE Composite Index=100 *12 Month Price Score 98.97

Interim Earnings (Per Share)

Qtr.	Mar	Jun	Sep	Dec
2005	0.37	0.41	0.43	0.44
2006	0.43	0.47	0.47	0.53
2007	0.45	0.49	0.41	0.25
2008	0.24	...	...	...

Interim Dividends (Per Share)

Amt	Decl	Ex	Rec	Pay
0.205Q	09/05/2007	09/18/2007	09/20/2007	10/01/2007
0.00Q	11/30/2007	01/02/2008	12/18/2007	12/31/2007
0.205Q	11/30/2007	12/14/2007	12/18/2007	01/02/2008
0.17Q	03/10/2008	03/18/2008	03/20/2008	04/01/2008

Indicated Div: $0.68 (Div. Reinv. Plan)

Valuation Analysis

Forecast EPS	$0.81 (05/17/2008)		
Market Cap	$3.8 Billion	Book Value	3.5 Billion
Price/Book	1.09	Price/Sales	1.75

Dividend Achiever Status

10 Year Growth Rate	13.47%
Total Years of Dividend Growth	31

TRADING VOLUME (thousand shares)

Business Summary: Commercial Banking (MIC: SIC: 6021 NAIC: 522110)

Synovus Financial, with assets of $33.02 billion as of Dec 31 2007, is a registered bank-holding company. Co. provides integrated financial services including banking, financial management, insurance, mortgage and leasing services via 37 wholly-owned bank subsidiaries in five southeastern states as of Dec 31 2007. Co.'s bank subsidiaries provide commercial banking services, including commercial, financial, agricultural and real estate loans, and retail banking services, including demand and savings deposits; making individual, consumer, installment and mortgage loans; safe deposit; leasing; automated banking; automated fund transfers; Internet based banking; and bank credit card services.

Recent Developments: For the quarter ended Mar 31 2008, income from continuing operations decreased 19.3% to US$81.0 million from US$100.4 million in the year-earlier quarter. Net income decreased 44.8% to US$81.0 million from US$146.8 million in the year-earlier quarter. Net interest income decreased 1.5% to US$278.6 million from US$282.9 million in the year-earlier quarter. Provision for loan losses was US$91.0 million versus US$20.5 million in the prior-year quarter, an increase of 343.8%. Non-interest income rose 60.0% to US$140.0 million from US$87.5 million, while non-interest expense advanced 3.4% to US$201.4 million.

Prospects: Co.'s results are being hampered by lower net interest income along with a decrease in its net interest margin reflecting a decline in its earning asset yields driven mainly by a decrease in loan yields, partially offset by lower effective cost of funds. Looking ahead, Co. anticipates some further net interest margin pressure in the near term as the effect of the recent short-term interest rate decreases implemented by the Federal Reserve Bank is fully realized. Also, Co. believes that the direction of its net interest margin during the rest of 2008 will be significantly influenced by trends in credit costs, deposit pricing competition, and any additional Federal Reserve rate actions.

Financial Data
(US$ in Thousands)

	3 Mos	12/31/2007	12/31/2006	12/31/2005	12/31/2004	12/31/2003	12/31/2002	12/31/2001
Earnings Per Share	1.38	1.60	1.90	1.64	1.41	1.28	1.21	1.05
Cash Flow Per Share	2.26	2.04	2.43	1.99	2.60	2.40	2.43	0.61
Tang Book Value Per Share	9.04	8.77	7.96	6.44	5.75	5.23	5.32	5.75
Dividends Per Share	0.785	0.820	0.780	0.730	0.693	0.660	0.590	0.510
Dividend Payout %	56.69	51.25	41.05	44.51	49.16	51.56	48.76	48.57
Income Statement								
Income Before Taxes	124,642	527,674	973,533	824,022	689,281	611,501	563,880	489,993
Income Taxes	43,648	184,739	356,616	307,576	252,248	222,576	198,533	178,377
Net Income	80,994	526,305	616,917	516,446	437,033	388,925	365,347	311,616
Average Shares	331,719	329,863	324,232	314,815	310,330	304,928	301,197	295,850
Balance Sheet								
Total Assets	33,759,890	33,018,452	31,854,773	27,620,672	25,050,178	21,632,629	19,036,246	16,657,947
Total Liabilities	30,206,316	29,576,862	27,909,414	24,474,370	22,241,605	19,245,752	16,878,294	14,864,363
Stockholders' Equity	3,530,802	3,441,590	3,708,650	2,949,329	2,641,289	2,245,039	2,040,853	1,694,946
Shares Outstanding	330,088	329,867	325,552	312,639	309,974	302,090	300,397	294,673
Statistical Record								
Return on Assets %	1.38	1.62	2.07	1.96	1.87	1.91	2.05	1.97
Return on Equity %	12.45	14.72	18.53	18.48	17.84	18.15	19.56	20.03
Price Range	14.57-9.86	14.60-9.86	13.55-11.27	13.10-11.58	12.65-9.91	12.70-7.57	13.88-7.35	15.07-10.07
P/E Ratio	10.56-7.14	9.13-6.16	7.13-5.93	7.99-7.06	8.97-7.03	9.92-5.91	11.47-6.08	14.35-9.59
Average Yield %	6.32	6.34	6.28	5.94	6.16	6.57	5.50	4.16

Address: 901 Front Avenue, P.O. Box 120, Columbus, GA 31902 **Telephone:** 706-649-2401 **Web Site:** www.synovus.com	**Officers:** Richard E. Anthony - Chairman, Chief Executive Officer Elizabeth R. James - Vice-Chairman, Secretary, Chief People Officer **Transfer Agents:** State Street Bank and Trust Company, Boston, MA	**Investor Contact:** 706-649-5220 **No of Institutions:** 386 **Shares:** 229,214,384 **% Held:** 66.78

SYSCO CORP.

Exchange	Symbol	Price	52Wk Range	Yield	P/E
NYS	SYY	$30.96 (5/29/2008)	35.84-27.48	2.84	17.69

*7 Year Price Score 76.67 ***NYSE Composite Index=100** ***12 Month Price Score 97.90**

TRADING VOLUME (thousand shares)

Interim Earnings (Per Share)

Qtr.	Sep	Dec	Mar	Jun
2004-05	0.35	0.36	0.34	0.43
2005-06	0.33	0.33	0.30	0.41
2006-07	0.30	0.38	0.35	0.49
2007-08	0.43	0.43	0.40	...

Interim Dividends (Per Share)

Amt	Decl	Ex	Rec	Pay
0.19Q	09/19/2007	10/03/2007	10/05/2007	10/26/2007
0.22Q	11/09/2007	01/02/2008	01/04/2008	01/25/2008
0.22Q	02/22/2008	04/02/2008	04/04/2008	04/25/2008
0.22Q	05/14/2008	07/01/2008	07/03/2008	07/25/2008

Indicated Div: $0.88 (Div. Reinv. Plan)

Valuation Analysis

Forecast EPS	$1.79 (05/16/2008)
Market Cap	$18.6 Billion Book Value 3.3 Billion
Price/Book	5.66 Price/Sales 0.50

Dividend Achiever Status

10 Year Growth Rate	17.62%
Total Years of Dividend Growth	31

Business Summary: Retail - Food & Beverage (MIC: SIC: 5141 NAIC: 424410)

Sysco distributes food and related products primarily to the foodservice or 'food-prepared-away-from-home' industry. At June 30 2007, Co. served about 391,000 customers, including restaurants, healthcare and educational facilities, lodging establishments and other foodservice customers. Co.'s Broadline segment distributes a line of food and non-food products to traditional and chain restaurant customers. Co.'s SYGMA segment distributes a line of food and non-food products to chain restaurant customer locations. Co.'s other segments include its specialty produce, custom-cut meat and lodging industry products segments and a company that distributes to internationally located chain restaurants.

Recent Developments: For the quarter ended Mar 29 2008, net income increased 9.0% to US$240.9 million from US$221.0 million in the year-earlier quarter. Revenues were US$9.15 billion, up 6.7% from US$8.57 billion the year before. Operating income was US$417.6 million versus US$384.1 million in the prior-year quarter, an increase of 8.7%. Direct operating expenses rose 6.8% to US$7.41 billion from US$6.94 billion in the comparable period the year before. Indirect operating expenses increased 5.4% to US$1.32 billion from US$1.25 billion in the equivalent prior-year period.

Prospects: For the fourth quarter of the fiscal year ending June 2008, Co. expects fuel costs to be higher versus the prior year by $20.0 million to $25.0 million, based on market prices for diesel and the cost committed to in its existing forward fuel purchase agreements. To mitigate the higher costs, Co. will focus on managing miles driven, improving productivity, and increasing the use of fuel surcharges. Meanwhile, Co.'s estimated capital expenditures for the fiscal year are $550.0 million to $575.0 million, which will used for, among others, its fold-out program; facility, fleet and other equipment replacements and expansions; its National Supply Chain project; and investments in technology.

Financial Data

(US$ in Thousands)	9 Mos	6 Mos	3 Mos	06/30/2007	07/01/2006	07/02/2005	07/03/2004	06/28/2003
Earnings Per Share	1.75	1.70	1.65	1.60	1.36	1.47	1.37	1.18
Cash Flow Per Share	2.40	2.08	2.33	2.28	1.81	1.88	1.82	2.12
Tang Book Value Per Share	2.97	3.03	2.98	2.99	2.67	2.35	2.11	1.68
Dividends Per Share	0.790	0.760	0.740	0.720	0.490	0.580	0.500	0.400
Dividend Payout %	45.04	44.60	44.76	45.00	36.03	39.46	36.50	33.90
Income Statement								
Total Revenue	27,791,906	18,645,349	9,405,844	35,042,075	32,628,438	30,281,914	29,335,403	26,140,337
EBITDA	1,615,696	1,095,680	548,121	2,088,776	1,849,108	1,906,116	1,828,619	1,605,763
Depn & Amortn	275,747	180,640	90,456	362,559	345,062	305,680	283,595	273,142
Income Before Taxes	1,255,919	859,734	431,294	1,621,215	1,394,946	1,525,436	1,475,144	1,260,387
Income Taxes	483,881	328,597	164,305	620,139	548,906	563,979	567,930	482,099
Net Income	772,038	531,137	266,989	1,001,076	855,325	961,457	907,214	778,288
Average Shares	605,773	614,620	617,108	626,366	628,800	653,157	661,919	661,535
Balance Sheet								
Current Assets	4,880,498	4,884,480	5,029,827	4,675,546	4,399,694	4,001,786	3,851,411	3,629,534
Total Assets	9,960,985	9,952,827	10,017,944	9,518,931	8,992,025	8,267,902	7,847,632	6,936,521
Current Liabilities	3,430,197	3,268,683	3,374,745	3,415,089	3,226,403	3,457,570	3,126,634	2,701,129
Long-Term Obligations	2,040,546	2,135,547	1,969,804	1,758,227	1,627,127	956,177	1,231,493	1,249,467
Total Liabilities	6,680,038	6,622,764	6,720,489	6,240,531	5,939,741	5,509,063	5,283,126	4,738,990
Stockholders' Equity	3,280,947	3,330,063	3,297,455	3,278,400	3,052,284	2,758,839	2,564,506	2,197,531
Shares Outstanding	600,086	605,048	608,917	611,840	618,895	628,567	636,535	643,657
Statistical Record								
Return on Assets %	11.12	11.01	10.65	10.85	9.94	11.96	12.07	12.08
Return on Equity %	32.58	32.48	31.97	31.71	29.52	36.22	37.49	36.05
EBITDA Margin %	5.81	5.88	5.83	5.96	5.67	6.29	6.23	6.14
Net Margin %	2.78	2.85	2.84	2.86	2.62	3.18	3.09	2.98
Asset Turnover	3.83	3.80	3.71	3.80	3.79	3.77	3.90	4.06
Current Ratio	1.42	1.49	1.49	1.37	1.36	1.16	1.23	1.34
Debt to Equity	0.62	0.64	0.60	0.54	0.53	0.35	0.48	0.57
Price Range	35.84-27.48	36.72-30.30	36.95-30.30	36.95-26.91	37.20-29.25	38.20-29.89	40.90-28.75	32.34-21.81
P/E Ratio	20.48-15.70	21.60-17.82	22.39-18.36	23.09-16.82	27.35-21.51	25.99-20.33	29.85-20.99	27.41-18.48
Average Yield %	2.46	2.28	2.19	2.17	1.54	1.67	1.41	1.39

Address: 1390 Enclave Parkway, Houston, TX 77077-2099 Telephone: 281-584-1390 Web Site: www.sysco.com	Officers: Richard J. Schnieders - Chairman, Chief Executive Officer Kenneth F. Spitler - President, Chief Operating Officer **Transfer Agents: American Stock** Transfer & Trust Company, New York, NY	Investor Contact: 281-584-1308 No of Institutions: 871 Shares: 531,831,968 % Held: 74.42

T ROWE PRICE GROUP INC.

Exchange	Symbol	Price	52Wk Range	Yield	P/E
NMS	TROW	$59.59 (5/29/2008)	64.70-45.02	1.61	24.52

*7 Year Price Score 136.80 *NYSE Composite Index=100 ***12 Month Price Score 107.84**

TRADING VOLUME (thousand shares)

Interim Earnings (Per Share)

Qtr.	Mar	Jun	Sep	Dec
2005	0.34	0.38	0.42	0.42
2006	0.42	0.49	0.46	0.53
2007	0.51	0.58	0.63	0.68
2008	0.55	...	...	...

Interim Dividends (Per Share)

Amt	Decl	Ex	Rec	Pay
0.17Q	09/06/2007	09/19/2007	09/21/2007	10/05/2007
0.24Q	12/13/2007	12/26/2007	12/28/2007	01/11/2008
0.24Q	02/14/2008	03/12/2008	03/14/2008	03/28/2008
0.24Q	06/05/2008	06/12/2008	06/16/2008	06/27/2008
		Indicated Div: $0.96		

Valuation Analysis

Forecast EPS	$2.47 (05/16/2008)		
Market Cap	$15.5 Billion	Book Value	2.6 Billion
Price/Book	6.00	Price/Sales	6.79

Dividend Achiever Status

10 Year Growth Rate	17.99%
Total Years of Dividend Growth	21

Business Summary: Wealth Management (MIC: SIC: 6282 NAIC: 523930)

T. Rowe Price Group is a financial services holding company that provides investment advisory services to individual and institutional investors in the sponsored T. Rowe Price mutual funds and other investment portfolios. Co. operates its investment advisory business through its subsidiary companies, primarily T. Rowe Price Associates, T. Rowe Price International, and T. Rowe Price Global Investment Services. As of Dec 31 2007, Co. had total assets under management of $400.00 billion, which included $322.00 billion in equity and blended asset investment portfolios and $78.00 billion in fixed income investment portfolios.

Recent Developments: For the quarter ended Mar 31 2008, net income increased 6.0% to US$151.5 million from US$142.9 million in the year-earlier quarter. Revenues were US$559.1 million, up 10.0% from US$508.4 million the year before. Operating income was US$230.1 million versus US$218.9 million in the prior-year quarter, an increase of 5.1%. Indirect operating expenses increased 13.6% to US$329.0 million from US$289.5 million in the equivalent prior-year period.

Prospects: The near term economic outlook appears challenging, reflecting weaker-than-expected economic data, mainly on U.S. employment and retail spending, and the restraining effect of bank capital write-downs on credit availability. However, this risk should be mitigated to some extent by the recent easing of U.S. monetary policy by the Federal Reserve. In the meantime, Co. remains committed to invest in its business in both the U.S. and overseas to service and expand its base of customers and investment offerings and is optimistic that these efforts and an eventual market turnaround will positively affect its future revenues and earnings.

Financial Data
(US$ in Thousands)

	3 Mos	12/31/2007	12/31/2006	12/31/2005	12/31/2004	12/31/2003	12/31/2002	12/31/2001
Earnings Per Share	2.43	2.40	1.90	1.58	1.25	0.89	0.76	0.76
Cash Flow Per Share	2.95	2.86	2.25	2.07	1.46	1.20	1.10	1.18
Tang Book Value Per Share	7.36	7.97	6.63	5.20	3.98	2.65	1.91	1.67
Dividends Per Share	0.820	0.750	0.590	0.485	0.400	0.350	0.325	0.305
Dividend Payout %	33.69	31.25	31.05	30.79	31.87	39.55	42.76	40.13
Income Statement								
Total Revenue	559,100	2,233,100	1,819,300	1,515,815	1,280,349	998,855	925,829	1,027,496
Income Before Taxes	244,400	1,076,800	858,300	679,391	533,783	365,516	309,604	330,589
Income Taxes	92,900	406,200	328,700	248,462	196,523	138,029	115,350	135,078
Net Income	151,500	670,600	529,600	430,929	337,260	227,487	194,254	195,868
Average Shares	273,500	279,200	278,700	273,196	268,270	256,578	255,412	258,090
Balance Sheet								
Total Assets	2,949,400	3,177,300	2,765,300	2,310,546	1,928,825	1,546,577	1,370,433	1,313,115
Total Liabilities	371,100	400,200	338,400	274,444	231,525	217,497	236,593	235,290
Stockholders' Equity	2,578,300	2,777,100	2,426,900	2,036,102	1,697,300	1,329,080	1,133,840	1,077,825
Shares Outstanding	259,575	264,605	264,959	263,356	259,215	249,865	245,297	246,177
Statistical Record								
Return on Assets %	22.94	22.57	20.87	20.33	19.36	15.60	14.48	14.08
Return on Equity %	26.42	25.77	23.73	23.09	22.23	18.47	17.57	18.93
Price Range	64.70-45.02	64.70-44.60	48.31-35.24	37.37-27.41	31.57-22.34	23.70-12.15	21.00-10.73	21.34-12.85
P/E Ratio	26.63-18.53	26.96-18.58	25.43-18.55	23.65-17.35	25.25-17.87	26.63-13.65	27.63-14.11	28.08-16.91
Average Yield %	1.54	1.42	1.43	1.54	1.54	1.94	2.02	1.76

Address: 100 East Pratt Street, Baltimore, MD 21202 Telephone: 410-345-2000 Web Site: www.troweprice.com	Officers: Brian C. Rogers - Chairman, Vice President, Chief Investment Officer Edward C. Bernard - Vice-Chairman, Vice President **Transfer Agents:** Wells Fargo Bank, N.A.	Investor Contact: 410-345-2124 No of Institutions: 631 Shares: 204,131,008 % Held: 68.81

TALBOTS, INC.

Exchange	Symbol	Price	52Wk Range	Yield	P/E
NYS	TLB	$7.49 (5/29/2008)	25.70-6.96	6.94	N/A

*7 Year Price Score 41.85 *NYSE Composite Index=100 *12 Month Price Score 62.35

Interim Earnings (Per Share)

Qtr.	Apr	Jul	Oct	Jan
2003-04	0.51	0.32	0.60	0.38
2004-05	0.58	0.34	0.50	0.28
2005-06	0.63	0.35	0.37	0.37
2006-07	0.51	(0.07)	0.15	0.00
2007-08	0.10	(0.25)	(0.18)	(3.23)

Interim Dividends (Per Share)

Amt	Decl	Ex	Rec	Pay
0.13Q	08/07/2007	08/30/2007	09/04/2007	09/17/2007
0.13Q	10/31/2007	11/29/2007	12/03/2007	12/17/2007
0.13Q	02/28/2008	03/06/2008	03/10/2008	03/24/2008
0.13Q	05/22/2008	05/29/2008	06/02/2008	06/16/2008
		Indicated Div: $0.52		

Valuation Analysis

Forecast EPS	$0.33 (05/16/2008)
Market Cap	$411.4 Million Book Value 454.8 Million
Price/Book	0.90 Price/Sales 0.18

Dividend Achiever Status

10 Year Growth Rate	9.49%
Total Years of Dividend Growth	13

TRADING VOLUME (thousand shares)

Business Summary: Retail - Apparel and Accessory Stores (MIC: SIC: 5621 NAIC: 448120)

Talbots is an international specialty retailer and cataloger of women's, children's, and men's apparel, accessories and shoes sold under the Talbots and J. Jill brand names. Co.'s retail stores segment includes stores in 47 states, the District of Columbia, Canada, and the U.K. under the Talbots and J. Jill brand names. As of Feb 2 2008, Co. operated a total of 1,421 stores with 1,150 stores under the Talbots brand name and 271 stores under the J. Jill brand name. As of Feb 2 2008, Co. operated a total of 862 locations with 595 locations under the Talbots brand name and 267 locations under the J. Jill brand name.

Recent Developments: For the year ended Feb 2 2008, net loss amounted to US$188.8 million versus net income of US$31.6 million in the prior year. Revenues were US$2.29 billion, up 2.6% from US$2.23 billion the year before. Operating loss was US$186.4 million versus an income of US$75.0 million in the prior year. Direct operating expenses rose 5.8% to US$1.55 billion from US$1.47 billion in the comparable period the year before. Indirect operating expenses increased 34.2% to US$921.7 million from US$686.8 million in the equivalent prior-year period.

Prospects: On Apr 1 2008, Co. announced its strategic plan for long-term growth. Components of the plan include adding about 35 new Talbots Womans stores over the next 5 years; higher Accessories segment penetration, while tightening its shoe assortment; clearly differentiating its Collection offering; pursuing Premium Outlet opportunities; and improving J. Jill brand's existing store network through improved merchandise, prospecting to increase customer acquisition and marketing to build greater brand awareness. For fiscal 2008, Co. sees Talbots brand same store sales decreasing 1.0% and the J. Jill brand growing 1.0%, with earnings from continuing operations of $0.47 to $0.52 per diluted share.

Financial Data

(US$ in Thousands)	02/02/2008	02/03/2007	01/28/2006	01/29/2005	01/31/2004	02/01/2003	02/02/2002	02/03/2001
Earnings Per Share	(3.56)	0.59	1.72	1.70	1.81	2.01	2.00	1.80
Cash Flow Per Share	4.26	2.51	4.01	2.83	3.75	3.80	2.60	2.21
Tang Book Value Per Share	2.20	2.76	9.66	8.82	8.91	7.93	7.56	6.90
Dividends Per Share	0.520	0.510	0.470	0.430	0.390	0.350	0.310	0.270
Dividend Payout %	...	86.44	27.33	25.29	21.55	17.41	15.50	15.00
Income Statement								
Total Revenue	2,289,296	2,231,033	1,808,606	1,697,843	1,624,339	1,595,325	1,612,513	1,594,996
EBITDA	(55,600)	196,569	250,692	229,752	237,097	255,180	263,477	237,420
Depn & Amortn	130,792	121,528	98,544	87,637	67,509	59,113	53,461	45,830
Income Before Taxes	(220,957)	50,522	149,042	140,005	167,493	193,214	204,841	187,321
Income Taxes	(32,116)	18,946	55,891	44,639	62,810	72,455	77,840	72,119
Net Income	(188,841)	31,576	93,151	95,366	104,683	120,759	127,001	115,202
Average Shares	53,006	53,485	54,103	56,252	57,901	60,191	63,439	63,995
Balance Sheet								
Current Assets	651,847	692,409	620,661	527,397	496,154	435,898	432,769	506,405
Total Assets	1,502,979	1,748,688	1,146,144	1,062,130	958,392	871,925	831,064	858,596
Current Liabilities	443,044	429,800	244,457	202,638	166,142	147,941	130,292	188,040
Long-Term Obligations	308,337	389,174	100,000	100,000	100,000	100,000	100,000	100,000
Total Liabilities	1,048,200	1,105,377	519,176	473,542	342,266	304,249	263,188	307,825
Stockholders' Equity	454,779	643,311	626,968	588,588	616,126	567,676	567,876	550,771
Shares Outstanding	54,921	53,999	53,359	54,123	56,675	57,505	60,382	63,106
Statistical Record								
Return on Assets %	N.M.	2.15	8.46	9.47	11.47	14.22	15.07	14.60
Return on Equity %	N.M.	4.89	15.37	15.88	17.73	21.33	22.77	23.08
EBITDA Margin %	N.M.	8.81	13.86	13.53	14.60	16.00	16.34	14.89
Net Margin %	N.M.	1.42	5.15	5.62	6.44	7.57	7.88	7.22
Asset Turnover	1.41	1.52	1.64	1.69	1.78	1.88	1.91	2.02
Current Ratio	1.47	1.61	2.54	2.60	2.99	2.95	3.32	2.69
Debt to Equity	0.68	0.60	0.16	0.17	0.16	0.18	0.18	0.18
Price Range	26.18-6.96	30.00-17.38	34.85-24.52	39.81-24.79	38.15-23.02	41.02-22.90	53.75-22.33	53.50-14.13
P/E Ratio	...	50.85-29.46	20.26-14.26	23.42-14.58	21.08-12.72	20.41-11.39	26.88-11.16	29.72-7.85
Average Yield %	2.67	2.12	1.59	1.38	1.28	1.09	0.81	0.83

Address: One Talbots Drive, Hingham, MA 02043-1586 **Telephone:** 781-749-7600 **Web Site:** www.talbots.com	**Officers:** Trudy F. Sullivan - President, Chief Executive Officer Richard T. O'Connell - Executive Vice President, Secretary **Transfer Agents:** Computershare Trust Company, N.A., Providence, RI	**No of Institutions:** 133 **Shares:** 38,363,068 **% Held:** 56.77

TANGER FACTORY OUTLET CENTERS, INC.

Exchange	Symbol	Price	52Wk Range	Yield	P/E
NYS	SKT	$38.22 (5/29/2008)	44.04-33.21	3.98	45.50

*7 Year Price Score 120.60 *NYSE Composite Index=100 *12 Month Price Score 105.10

Interim Earnings (Per Share)

Qtr.	Mar	Jun	Sep	Dec
2005	(0.11)	0.13	0.15	(0.02)
2006	0.44	0.16	0.19	0.24
2007	0.06	0.16	0.22	0.28
2008	0.18	...	...	...

Interim Dividends (Per Share)

Amt	Decl	Ex	Rec	Pay
0.36Q	07/12/2007	07/27/2007	07/31/2007	08/15/2007
0.36Q	10/11/2007	10/29/2007	10/31/2007	11/15/2007
0.36Q	01/10/2008	01/29/2008	01/31/2008	02/15/2008
0.38Q	04/10/2008	04/28/2008	04/30/2008	05/15/2008

Indicated Div: $1.52 (Div. Reinv. Plan)

Valuation Analysis

Forecast EPS $0.81 (05/16/2008)

Market Cap	$1.2 Billion	Book Value	236.3 Million
Price/Book	5.10	Price/Sales	5.18

Dividend Achiever Status

10 Year Growth Rate		2.73%
Total Years of Dividend Growth		14

Business Summary: "Property, Real Estate & Development" (MIC: SIC: 6798 NAIC: 525930)

Tanger Factory Outlet Centers is a fully-integrated, self-administered and self-managed real estate investment trust that focuses on developing, acquiring, owning, operating and managing factory outlet shopping centers in the U.S. As of Dec 31 2007, Co. owned 29 outlet centers, with a total gross leasable area (GLA) of approximately 8.4 million square feet. These factory outlet centers were 98.0% occupied and contained over 1,800 stores, representing approximately 370 store brands. In addition, Co. owned a 50.0% interest in two outlet centers with a GLA of approximately 667,000 square feet.

Recent Developments: For the quarter ended Mar 31 2008, income from continuing operations increased 114.0% to US$7.0 million from US$3.3 million in the year-earlier quarter. Net income increased 112.2% to US$7.0 million from US$3.3 million in the year-earlier quarter. Revenues were US$57.3 million, up 7.9% from US$53.1 million the year before. Revenues from property income rose 8.4% to US$55.9 million from US$51.6 million in the corresponding quarter a year earlier.

Prospects: Co.'s outlook appears constructive. For instance, in addition to the development, construction and leasing of two of its sites in Washington County, south of Pittsburgh, PA and Deer Park (Long Island), NY, Co. noted that it has entered into purchase options on new development sites in Mebane, NC, Port St. Lucie, FL, and Irving, TX. Tenant interest in these new locations appears to be strong and Co. is continuing with its predevelopment work. For 2008, Co. is targeting funds from operations of $2.60 to $2.68 per share, and net income, excluding the effect of any potential gains on the sale of land parcels or any potential sales or acquisitions of properties, of $0.93 to $1.01 per share.

Financial Data

(US$ in Thousands)	3 Mos	12/31/2007	12/31/2006	12/31/2005	12/31/2004	12/31/2003	12/31/2002	12/31/2001
Earnings Per Share	0.84	0.72	1.03	0.16	0.26	0.58	0.54	0.34
Cash Flow Per Share	3.01	3.20	2.89	2.96	3.13	2.23	2.35	2.82
Tang Book Value Per Share	5.11	3.21	3.94	3.84	5.87	6.46	5.00	4.82
Dividends Per Share	1.440	1.420	1.343	1.280	1.245	1.229	1.224	1.219
Dividend Payout %	171.79	197.22	130.34	800.00	478.85	210.04	226.62	363.81
Income Statement								
Total Revenue	57,276	228,765	211,711	202,799	194,553	121,972	113,167	111,068
Depn & Amortn	15,410	63,108	56,514	47,860	50,947	30,852	30,198	29,881
Net Income	6,961	28,576	37,309	5,089	7,046	12,849	11,007	7,112
Average Shares	31,336	31,668	31,081	28,646	27,261	20,566	17,028	15,896
Balance Sheet								
Total Assets	1,073,044	1,060,280	1,040,877	1,000,605	936,378	987,437	477,675	476,272
Long-Term Obligations	727,781	706,345	678,579	663,607	488,007	540,319	345,005	358,195
Total Liabilities	805,764	777,343	727,177	701,025	516,951	562,689	363,410	378,395
Stockholders' Equity	236,261	249,204	274,676	250,214	161,133	167,418	90,635	76,371
Shares Outstanding	31,539	31,329	31,041	30,748	27,443	25,921	18,122	15,859
Statistical Record								
Return on Assets %	3.06	2.72	3.66	0.53	0.73	1.75	2.31	1.48
Return on Equity %	12.80	10.91	14.22	2.47	4.28	9.96	13.18	8.50
Net Margin %	12.15	12.49	17.62	2.51	3.62	10.53	9.73	6.40
Price Range	44.04-33.21	44.04-33.21	40.09-29.48	29.86-21.64	26.48-17.68	21.18-14.43	15.60-10.43	11.66-9.90
P/E Ratio	52.43-39.54	61.17-46.13	38.92-28.62	186.63-135.25	101.87-67.98	36.52-24.87	28.89-19.31	34.28-29.13
Average Yield %	3.70	3.57	3.95	4.94	5.77	7.16	9.02	11.27

Address: 3200 Northline Avenue, Suite 360, Greensboro, NC 27408 **Telephone:** 336-292-3010 **Web Site:** www.tangeroutlet.com	Officers: Stanley K. Tanger - Chairman, Chief Executive Officer Steven B. Tanger - President, Chief Operating Officer **Transfer Agents:** EquiServe Trust Company NA, Providence, RI	**Investor Contact:** 336-292-3010 **No of Institutions:** 179 **Shares:** 37,356,192 **% Held:** 112.77

TARGET CORP

Exchange	Symbol	Price	52Wk Range	Yield	P/E
NYS	TGT	$53.75 (5/29/2008)	70.14-48.08	1.04	16.14

*7 Year Price Score 95.75   *NYSE Composite Index=100   *12 Month Price Score 94.60

Interim Earnings (Per Share)

Qtr.	Apr	Jul	Oct	Jan
2005-06	0.55	0.61	0.49	1.06
2006-07	0.63	0.70	0.59	1.29
2007-08	0.75	0.80	0.56	1.22
2008-09	0.74	...	...	...

Interim Dividends (Per Share)

Amt	Decl	Ex	Rec	Pay
0.14Q	06/14/2007	08/16/2007	08/20/2007	09/10/2007
0.14Q	09/12/2007	11/16/2007	11/20/2007	12/10/2007
0.14Q	01/10/2008	02/15/2008	02/20/2008	03/10/2008
0.14Q	03/13/2008	05/16/2008	05/20/2008	06/10/2008

Indicated Div: $0.56 (Div. Reinv. Plan)

Valuation Analysis

Forecast EPS $3.47 (05/17/2008)

Market Cap	$42.4 Billion	Book Value	14.4 Billion
Price/Book	2.95	Price/Sales	0.66

Dividend Achiever Status

10 Year Growth Rate	12.16%
Total Years of Dividend Growth	36

Business Summary: Retail - General (MIC: SIC: 5331 NAIC: 452990)

Target operates large-format general merchandise discount stores in the U.S., which include Target and SuperTarget stores. Co. also maintains REDcard, its credit card operation and operates Target.com, an online business. Target provides a range of general merchandise and a more limited assortment of food items in its stores. SuperTarget stores provide an array of food items along with general merchandise items. As of Feb 2 2008, Co. owned 1,352 stores, leased 73 stores, and operated 166 owned buildings on leased land (combined)stores for a total of 1,591 locations. Co. also owned 26, leased 5 and operated 1 combined distribution centers for a total of 32 locations.

Recent Developments: For the quarter ended May 3 2008, net income decreased 7.5% to US$602.0 million from US$651.0 million in the year-earlier quarter. Revenues were US$14.80 billion, up 5.4% from US$14.04 billion the year before. Direct operating expenses rose 6.1% to US$10.17 billion from US$9.59 billion in the comparable period the year before. Indirect operating expenses increased 6.7% to US$3.47 billion from US$3.26 billion in the equivalent prior-year period.

Prospects: Co.'s near-term outlook appears to be challenging. For the fiscal year ending Jan 31 2009, Co. continues to anticipate a slight to modest operating margin rate decline in its Retail Segment. In addition, Co. foresees that the effects on profits from average receivables growth will surpass the effects from the projected decline in portfolio yield. Further, Co. estimates effects from recent terms changes should fully offset the effects of slightly lower-than-expected credit card losses. As a result, in its Credit Card segment, Co. expects 60-plus day delinquency rates to remain about 4.0%, and net write-offs as a percentage of average receivables to be in the range of 7.0% to 8.0%.

Financial Data
(US$ in Millions)

	3 Mos	02/02/2008	02/03/2007	01/28/2006	01/29/2005	01/31/2004	02/01/2003	02/02/2002
Earnings Per Share	3.33	3.33	3.21	2.71	3.51	2.01	1.81	1.50
Cash Flow Per Share	5.47	4.89	5.55	5.06	4.24	3.48	1.76	2.22
Tang Book Value Per Share	18.21	18.44	17.94	16.04	14.40	12.14	10.38	8.68
Dividends Per Share	0.540	0.520	0.440	0.360	0.300	0.260	0.240	0.220
Dividend Payout %	16.22	15.62	13.71	13.28	8.55	12.94	13.26	14.67
Income Statement								
Total Revenue	14,802	63,367	59,490	52,620	46,839	48,163	43,917	39,888
EBITDA	1,593	6,931	6,565	5,732	4,860	4,839	4,476	3,759
Depn & Amortn	435	1,659	1,496	1,409	1,259	1,320	1,212	1,079
Income Before Taxes	957	4,625	4,497	3,860	3,031	2,960	2,676	2,216
Income Taxes	355	1,776	1,710	1,452	1,146	1,119	1,022	842
Net Income	602	2,849	2,787	2,408	3,198	1,841	1,654	1,368
Average Shares	809	850	868	889	912	917	914	909
Balance Sheet								
Current Assets	16,759	18,906	14,706	14,405	13,922	12,928	11,935	9,648
Total Assets	42,830	44,560	37,349	34,995	32,293	31,392	28,603	24,154
Current Liabilities	10,959	11,782	11,117	9,588	8,220	8,314	7,523	7,054
Long-Term Obligations	15,130	15,126	8,675	9,119	9,034	10,217	10,186	8,088
Total Liabilities	28,473	29,253	21,716	20,790	19,264	20,327	19,160	16,294
Stockholders' Equity	14,357	15,307	15,633	14,205	13,029	11,065	9,443	7,860
Shares Outstanding	788	818	859	874	890	911	909	905
Statistical Record								
Return on Assets %	6.92	6.98	7.58	7.18	10.07	6.15	6.29	6.29
Return on Equity %	18.67	18.47	18.38	17.73	26.62	18.00	19.17	19.08
EBITDA Margin %	10.76	10.94	11.04	10.89	10.38	10.05	10.19	9.42
Net Margin %	4.07	4.50	4.68	4.58	6.83	3.82	3.77	3.43
Asset Turnover	1.58	1.55	1.62	1.57	1.48	1.61	1.67	1.83
Current Ratio	1.53	1.60	1.32	1.50	1.69	1.55	1.59	1.37
Debt to Equity	1.05	0.99	0.55	0.64	0.69	0.92	1.08	1.03
Price Range	70.14-48.08	70.14-48.08	62.35-45.28	59.98-46.28	52.43-38.59	41.54-26.06	45.72-26.15	44.41-26.68
P/E Ratio	21.06-14.44	21.06-14.44	19.42-14.11	22.13-17.08	14.94-10.99	20.67-12.97	25.26-14.45	29.61-17.79
Average Yield %	0.93	0.86	0.82	0.68	0.68	0.65	0.72	0.60

Address: 1000 Nicollet Mall, Minneapolis, MN 55403 Telephone: 612-304-6073 Web Site: www.target.com	Officers: Robert J. Ulrich - Chairman, Chief Executive Officer Gregg W. Steinhafel - President Transfer Agents:Mellon Investor Services, Jersey City, NJ	Investor Contact: 612-370-6736 No of Institutions: 1052 Shares: 897,739,776 % Held: 85.31

TAUBMAN CENTERS, INC.

Exchange	Symbol	Price	52Wk Range	Yield	P/E
NYS	TCO	$53.88 (5/29/2008)	60.37-43.93	3.08	67.35

*7 Year Price Score 131.17 *NYSE Composite Index=100 *12 Month Price Score 107.98

Interim Earnings (Per Share)

Qtr.	Mar	Jun	Sep	Dec
2005	0.05	(0.09)	(0.18)	1.09
2006	0.10	(0.05)	0.03	0.32
2007	0.19	0.16	0.15	0.40
2008	0.09	...	...	...

Interim Dividends (Per Share)

Amt	Decl	Ex	Rec	Pay
0.375Q	09/06/2007	09/26/2007	09/28/2007	10/22/2007
0.415Q	12/11/2007	12/27/2007	12/31/2007	01/22/2008
0.415Q	02/27/2008	03/27/2008	03/31/2008	04/21/2008
0.415Q	05/29/2008	06/26/2008	06/30/2008	07/21/2008

Indicated Div: $1.66 (Div. Reinv. Plan)

Valuation Analysis

Forecast EPS	$0.82 (05/16/2008)		
Market Cap	$2.8 Billion	Book Value	N/A
Price/Book	N/A	Price/Sales	4.46

Dividend Achiever Status

10 Year Growth Rate	5.01%
Total Years of Dividend Growth	11

Business Summary: "Property, Real Estate & Development" (MIC: SIC: 6798 NAIC: 525930)

Taubman Centers, a real estate investment trust, is the managing general partner of The Taubman Realty Group Ltd. Partnership (the Operating Partnership). The Operating Partnership is an operating subsidiary that engages in the ownership, management, leasing, acquisition, development, and expansion of regional and super-regional retail shopping centers. Co.'s centers are located in metropolitan areas including Atlantic City, Charlotte, Dallas, Denver, Detroit, Los Angeles, Miami, New York City, Orlando, Phoenix, San Francisco, Tampa, and Washington, D.C. As of Dec 31 2007, The Operating Partnership's owned portfolio included 23 urban and suburban shopping centers in 10 states.

Recent Developments: For the quarter ended Mar 31 2008, net income decreased 41.6% to US$8.2 million from US$14.1 million in the year-earlier quarter. Revenues were US$157.4 million, up 8.5% from US$145.0 million the year before. Revenues from property income rose 10.1% to US$89.1 million from US$81.0 million in the corresponding quarter a year earlier.

Prospects: For full-year 2008, Co. is maintaining its guidance on Funds From Operations per diluted share in a range of $3.05 to $3.12. In addition, Co. is projecting net income allocable to common shareholders to be in the range of $0.60 to $0.83 per common share. Also, Co. is forecasting capital spending to be approximately $105.4 million, which includes $24.2 million for new development projects, $79.4 million for existing centers, and $1.8 million for corporate office improvements and equipment. Meanwhile, Co. expects occupancy to be flat to slightly down in the second quarter of 2008 over the prior year and then slightly up for the second half of 2008.

Financial Data
(US$ in Thousands)

	3 Mos	12/31/2007	12/31/2006	12/31/2005	12/31/2004	12/31/2003	12/31/2002	12/31/2001
Earnings Per Share	0.80	0.90	0.40	0.87	(0.10)	0.41	(0.05)	(0.18)
Cash Flow Per Share	4.84	4.87	4.24	3.66	2.68	2.65	2.76	2.39
Tang Book Value Per Share	...	...	1.94	6.12	6.53	6.32	7.17	8.40
Dividends Per Share	1.580	1.540	1.290	1.160	1.095	1.050	1.025	1.005
Dividend Payout %	197.94	171.11	322.50	133.33	...	256.10	...	...
Income Statement								
Property Income	89,145	344,237	325,887	271,941	241,402	212,360	201,197	181,640
Non-Property Income	68,272	282,585	253,397	201,497	190,051	176,123	171,755	159,788
Total Revenue	157,417	626,822	579,284	473,438	431,453	388,483	372,952	341,428
Depn & Amortn	35,335	137,910	137,957	116,857	101,059	95,571	83,598	68,930
Interest Expense	36,982	131,700	128,643	121,612	95,934	84,194	83,667	68,150
Income Before Taxes	14,472	...	...	...	...	...	...	...
Income Taxes	190	...	...	...	...	...	...	...
Net Income	8,205	63,124	45,117	71,735	12,378	37,836	14,426	7,657
Average Shares	53,264	53,622	52,979	50,530	49,021	50,387	51,239	50,500
Balance Sheet								
Total Assets	3,218,729	3,151,307	2,826,622	2,797,580	2,526,067	2,186,970	2,269,707	2,141,439
Long-Term Obligations	...	2,700,980	2,319,538	2,089,948	1,930,439	1,495,777	1,543,693	1,423,241
Total Liabilities	3,213,161	3,119,438	2,688,763	2,442,205	2,167,662	1,768,196	1,798,250	1,618,090
Stockholders' Equity	(41,000)	(15,842)	108,642	326,158	329,188	321,499	374,182	426,074
Shares Outstanding	52,808	52,624	52,931	51,866	48,745	49,936	52,207	50,734
Statistical Record								
Return on Assets %	1.89	2.11	1.60	2.69	0.52	1.70	0.65	0.38
Return on Equity %	190.93	136.04	20.75	21.89	3.79	10.88	3.61	1.67
Net Margin %	5.21	10.07	7.79	15.15	2.87	9.74	3.87	2.24
Price Range	60.37-43.93	63.22-47.07	50.65-35.61	36.04-26.60	30.33-19.30	21.25-15.94	16.99-12.58	15.80-10.75
P/E Ratio	75.46-54.91	70.24-52.30	126.63-89.03	41.43-30.57	...	51.83-38.88	...	...
Average Yield %	3.01	2.82	3.08	3.68	4.46	5.55	6.85	7.71

Address: 200 East Long Lake Rd, Suite 300, P.O. Box 200, Bloomfield Hills, MI 48303-0200
Telephone: 248-258-6800
Web Site: www.taubman.com

Officers: Robert S. Taubman - Chairman, President, Chief Executive Officer Lisa A. Payne - Vice-Chairman, Chief Financial Officer **Transfer Agents:** Mellon Investor Services LLC

Investor Contact: 248-258-7367
No of Institutions: 228
Shares: 58,383,772 **% Held:** 100.90

TCF FINANCIAL CORP.

Exchange	Symbol	Price	52Wk Range	Yield	P/E
NYS	TCB	$16.52 (5/29/2008)	28.98-15.53	6.05	8.98

*7 Year Price Score 67.75   *NYSE Composite Index=100   *12 Month Price Score 81.80

Interim Earnings (Per Share)

Qtr.	Mar	Jun	Sep	Dec
2005	0.47	0.53	0.50	0.50
2006	0.45	0.52	0.51	0.42
2007	0.65	0.49	0.48	0.50
2008	0.38	...	...	...

Interim Dividends (Per Share)

Amt	Decl	Ex	Rec	Pay
0.242Q	07/16/2007	07/25/2007	07/27/2007	08/31/2007
0.242Q	10/15/2007	10/24/2007	10/26/2007	11/30/2007
0.25Q	01/21/2008	01/30/2008	02/01/2008	02/29/2008
0.25Q	04/14/2008	04/30/2008	05/02/2008	05/30/2008

Indicated Div: $1.00 (Div. Reinv. Plan)

Valuation Analysis

Forecast EPS $1.59 (05/17/2008)

Market Cap	$2.1 Billion	Book Value	1.1 Billion
Price/Book	1.85	Price/Sales	1.39

Dividend Achiever Status

10 Year Growth Rate	15.26%
Total Years of Dividend Growth	16

TRADING VOLUME (thousand shares)

Business Summary: Commercial Banking (MIC: SIC: 6021 NAIC: 522110)

TCF Financial is a financial holding company. Co.'s principal subsidiaries are TCF National Bank and TCF National Bank Arizona. Co.'s core businesses include retail banking; commercial banking; small business banking; consumer lending; leasing and equipment finance; and investments and insurance services. As of Dec 31 2007, Co. had 453 retail banking branches, consisting of 194 traditional branches, 244 supermarket branches and 15 campus branches, with 109 branches located in Minnesota, 202 in Illinois, 56 in Michigan, 46 in Colorado, 31 in Wisconsin, five in Indiana and four in Arizona. At such dated, Co. had total assets of $15.98 billion and total deposits of $9.58 billion.

Recent Developments: For the quarter ended Mar 31 2008, net income decreased 42.7% to US$47.4 million from US$82.7 million in the year-earlier quarter. Net interest income increased 5.4% to US$142.8 million from US$135.5 million in the year-earlier quarter. Provision for loan losses was US$30.0 million versus US$4.7 million in the prior-year quarter, an increase of 544.2%. Non-interest income fell 11.2% to US$127.3 million from US$143.3 million, while non-interest expense advanced 2.5% to US$168.3 million.

Prospects: Co. remains focused on its branch expansion as part of its growth strategy for generating new deposit accounts and the related revenue that is associated with the accounts and other products. Accordingly, for the rest of 2008, Co. plans to open eight additional branches, consisting of three traditional branches and five supermarket branches. Further, to enhance deposit growth, Co. intends to relocate four branches to improved locations and facilities, including three traditional branches and one supermarket branch, and to remodel 19 supermarket branches and one campus branch. Also, Co. intends to close and consolidate 12 Colorado supermarket branches into nearby branches by Jul 2008.

Financial Data
(US$ in Thousands)

	3 Mos	12/31/2007	12/31/2006	12/31/2005	12/31/2004	12/31/2003	12/31/2002	12/31/2001
Earnings Per Share	1.84	2.12	1.90	2.00	1.86	1.52	1.58	1.35
Cash Flow Per Share	2.53	2.85	2.80	1.16	3.23	3.10	2.21	0.96
Tang Book Value Per Share	7.74	7.48	6.75	6.04	5.50	5.09	5.15	4.95
Dividends Per Share	0.978	0.970	0.920	0.850	0.750	0.650	0.575	0.500
Dividend Payout %	52.99	45.75	48.42	42.50	40.32	42.62	36.51	37.04
Income Statement								
Income Before Taxes	71,857	372,518	357,108	380,410	384,476	327,783	357,692	329,834
Income Taxes	24,431	105,710	112,165	115,278	129,483	111,905	124,761	122,512
Net Income	47,426	266,808	244,943	265,132	254,993	215,878	232,931	207,322
Average Shares	125,120	125,830	129,225	132,741	137,174	141,540	147,881	153,685
Balance Sheet								
Total Assets	16,370,364	15,977,054	14,669,734	13,365,360	12,340,567	11,319,015	12,202,069	11,358,715
Total Liabilities	15,240,494	14,878,042	13,636,360	12,366,888	11,382,149	10,398,157	11,225,049	10,441,682
Stockholders' Equity	1,129,870	1,099,012	1,033,374	998,472	958,418	920,858	977,020	917,033
Shares Outstanding	126,313	126,602	130,418	133,776	137,186	140,952	147,711	153,863
Statistical Record								
Return on Assets %	1.48	1.74	1.75	2.06	2.15	1.84	1.98	1.84
Return on Equity %	21.06	25.02	24.11	27.10	27.06	22.75	24.60	22.69
Price Range	28.98-15.53	28.98-17.32	28.11-24.48	32.14-24.84	32.53-24.15	26.78-18.52	27.20-17.61	25.35-16.85
P/E Ratio	15.75-8.44	13.67-8.17	14.79-12.88	16.07-12.42	17.49-12.98	17.62-12.19	17.21-11.14	18.78-12.48
Average Yield %	4.21	3.86	3.50	3.50	3.21	2.91	2.43	2.36

Address: 200 Lake Street East, Mail Code EX0-03-A, Wayzata, MN 55391-1693 **Telephone:** 952-745-2760 **Web Site:** www.tcfexpress.com	**Officers:** William A. Cooper - Chairman Gregory J. Pulles - Vice-Chairman, Secretary, General Counsel **Transfer Agents:**EquiServe Trust Company, N.A., Providence, RI	**Investor Contact:** 952-745-2755 **No of Institutions:** 298 **Shares:** 100,194,184 % **Held:** 69.20

TELEFLEX INCORPORATED

Exchange	Symbol	Price	52Wk Range	Yield	P/E
NYS	TFX	$58.69 (5/29/2008)	86.19-47.71	2.32	18.40

*7 Year Price Score 93.22 *NYSE Composite Index=100 *12 Month Price Score 85.65

Interim Earnings (Per Share)

Qtr.	Mar	Jun	Sep	Dec
2005	0.95	0.71	0.82	0.92
2006	0.72	0.90	0.91	0.96
2007	1.12	2.37	(1.45)	1.68
2008	0.58	...	...	...

Interim Dividends (Per Share)

Amt	Decl	Ex	Rec	Pay
0.32Q	07/30/2007	08/13/2007	08/15/2007	09/14/2007
0.32Q	10/23/2007	11/13/2007	11/15/2007	12/14/2007
0.32Q	02/26/2008	03/03/2008	03/05/2008	03/17/2008
0.34Q	05/01/2008	05/13/2008	05/15/2008	06/13/2008

Indicated Div: $1.36 (Div. Reinv. Plan)

Valuation Analysis

Forecast EPS $3.80 (05/16/2008)

Market Cap	$2.3 Billion	Book Value	1.4 Billion
Price/Book	1.71	Price/Sales	1.24

Dividend Achiever Status

10 Year Growth Rate	12.38%
Total Years of Dividend Growth	30

Business Summary: Medical Instruments & Equipment (MIC: SIC: 3841 NAIC: 339112)

Teleflex designs, manufactures and distributes specialty-engineered products. Co. operates its business in three segments: Medical, which designs, manufactures and distributes medical devices primarily used in critical care, surgical applications and cardiac care; Aerospace, which provides engine repair products and services for flight turbine engines and cargo handling systems and equipment for wide body and narrow body aircraft; and Commercial, which designs, manufactures and distributes driver controls and engine and drive assemblies for the marine market, as well as power and fuel systems for truck, rail, automotive and industrial vehicles and rigging products and services.

Recent Developments: For the quarter ended Mar 30 2008, income from continuing operations decreased 32.2% to US$22.9 million from US$33.8 million in the year-earlier quarter. Net income decreased 48.2% to US$22.9 million from US$44.3 million in the year-earlier quarter. Revenues were US$604.5 million, up 37.3% from US$440.3 million the year before. Operating income was US$72.1 million versus US$63.5 million in the prior-year quarter, an increase of 13.6%. Direct operating expenses rose 33.3% to US$371.7 million from US$278.9 million in the comparable period the year before. Indirect operating expenses increased 64.1% to US$160.7 million from US$98.0 million in the equivalent prior-year period.

Prospects: Co. has reiterated its 2008 guidance for earnings from continuing operations of $3.70 to $3.90 per diluted share, excluding special charges of $0.60 to $0.67 per diluted share. Meanwhile, Co. is progressing with the integration of its Oct 2007 acquisition of Arrow International, Inc., which involves the closure of Arrow corporate functions, consolidation of manufacturing, sales, marketing, and distribution functions in North America, Europe and Asia, and correction of regulatory issues, which should be completed by the end of 2008. The continued progress on the integration should allow Co. to accelerate investment in new product research and development going forward.

Financial Data

(US$ in Thousands)	3 Mos	12/31/2007	12/31/2006	12/25/2005	12/26/2004	12/28/2003	12/29/2002	12/30/2001
Earnings Per Share	3.19	3.73	3.49	3.39	0.24	2.73	3.15	2.86
Cash Flow Per Share	6.33	7.21	8.51	8.31	6.35	5.70	5.12	4.87
Tang Book Value Per Share	N.M.	N.M.	17.31	15.79	14.49	19.42	16.61	19.99
Dividends Per Share	1.280	1.245	1.105	0.970	0.860	0.780	0.710	0.660
Dividend Payout %	40.10	33.38	31.66	28.61	358.33	28.57	22.54	23.08
Income Statement								
Total Revenue	604,520	1,934,332	2,646,757	2,514,552	2,485,378	2,282,435	2,076,229	1,905,004
EBITDA	103,014	273,358	367,568	362,772	254,081	282,180	267,605	252,096
Depn & Amortn	30,901	99,616	112,956	114,704	114,595	104,352	95,117	92,401
Income Before Taxes	42,065	109,348	219,027	207,915	102,368	151,491	172,488	159,695
Income Taxes	12,068	122,767	54,140	47,806	14,351	42,388	47,222	47,384
Net Income	22,943	146,484	139,430	138,817	9,517	109,103	125,266	112,311
Average Shares	39,709	39,259	39,988	40,958	40,495	39,942	39,786	39,280
Balance Sheet								
Current Assets	1,024,176	1,009,810	1,139,529	1,168,576	1,148,442	1,006,187	837,895	747,477
Total Assets	4,208,847	4,187,997	2,359,052	2,506,385	2,634,436	2,110,613	1,813,384	1,635,020
Current Liabilities	655,349	690,682	470,775	589,677	535,247	612,671	498,483	495,426
Long-Term Obligations	1,499,111	1,499,130	487,370	505,272	685,912	229,882	240,123	228,180
Total Liabilities	2,815,052	2,816,971	1,127,574	1,346,911	1,459,225	1,048,311	901,103	856,877
Stockholders' Equity	1,356,456	1,328,843	1,189,421	1,142,074	1,109,733	1,062,302	912,281	778,143
Shares Outstanding	39,602	39,451	39,018	40,357	40,424	39,795	39,398	38,932
Statistical Record								
Return on Assets %	3.78	4.47	5.64	5.42	0.40	5.58	7.29	7.42
Return on Equity %	9.75	11.63	11.77	12.36	0.88	11.08	14.86	15.34
EBITDA Margin %	17.04	14.13	13.89	14.43	10.22	12.36	12.89	13.23
Net Margin %	3.80	7.57	5.27	5.52	0.38	4.78	6.03	5.90
Asset Turnover	0.57	0.59	1.07	0.98	1.05	1.17	1.21	1.26
Current Ratio	1.56	1.46	2.42	1.98	2.15	1.64	1.68	1.51
Debt to Equity	1.11	1.13	0.41	0.44	0.62	0.22	0.26	0.29
Price Range	86.19-47.93	86.19-57.25	71.80-50.50	71.80-48.62	54.82-40.72	49.95-34.24	58.57-40.92	50.98-35.71
P/E Ratio	27.02-15.03	23.11-15.35	20.57-14.47	21.18-14.34	228.42-169.67	18.30-12.54	18.59-12.99	17.83-12.49
Average Yield %	1.85	1.74	1.79	1.63	1.82	1.83	1.44	1.49

Address: 155 South Limerick Road, Limerick, PA 19468
Telephone: 610-948-5100
Web Site: www.teleflex.com

Officers: Jeffrey P. Black - Chairman, President, Chief Executive Officer Kevin K. Gordon - Executive Vice President, Chief Financial Officer **Transfer Agents:** American Stock Tranfer & Trust Company, New York, NY

Investor Contact: 610-834-6362
No of Institutions: 304
Shares: 35,102,884 **% Held:** 84.27

TENNANT CO.

Exchange	Symbol	Price	52Wk Range	Yield	P/E
NYS	TNC	$35.53 (5/29/2008)	49.32-31.88	1.46	17.33

*7 Year Price Score 130.11 *NYSE Composite Index=100 *12 Month Price Score 92.25

Interim Earnings (Per Share)

Qtr.	Mar	Jun	Sep	Dec
2005	0.20	0.37	0.34	0.35
2006	0.23	0.48	0.42	0.43
2007	0.31	0.55	0.57	0.66
2008	0.28	...	...	...

Interim Dividends (Per Share)

Amt	Decl	Ex	Rec	Pay
0.12Q	08/15/2007	08/29/2007	08/31/2007	09/17/2007
0.12Q	11/09/2007	11/28/2007	11/30/2007	12/17/2007
0.13Q	02/21/2008	02/27/2008	02/29/2008	03/17/2008
0.13Q	04/29/2008	05/28/2008	05/30/2008	06/16/2008

Indicated Div: $0.52 (Div. Reinv. Plan)

Valuation Analysis

Forecast EPS $2.25 (05/16/2008)

Market Cap	$657.4 Million	Book Value	254.7 Million
Price/Book	2.58	Price/Sales	0.97

Dividend Achiever Status

10 Year Growth Rate		2.92%
Total Years of Dividend Growth		35

Business Summary: Purpose Machinery (MIC: SIC: 3589 NAIC: 333319)

Tennant designs, manufactures and markets cleaning products. Co.'s floor maintenance equipment, outdoor cleaning equipment, coatings and related products are used to clean factories, office buildings, parking lots and streets, airports, hospitals, schools, warehouses and shopping centers, among others. Customers include the building service contract cleaners to whom organizations outsource facilities maintenance, as well as end-user businesses, healthcare facilities, schools and local, state and federal governments who handle facilities maintenance themselves. Co. sells its products through its direct sales and service organization and through a network of authorized distributors worldwide.

Recent Developments: For the quarter ended Mar 31 2008, net income decreased 10.5% to US$5.2 million from US$5.9 million in the year-earlier quarter. Revenues were US$168.6 million, up 8.7% from US$155.1 million the year before. Operating income was US$8.5 million versus US$9.1 million in the prior-year quarter, a decrease of 6.8%. Direct operating expenses rose 8.4% to US$99.0 million from US$91.3 million in the comparable period the year before. Indirect operating expenses increased 11.9% to US$61.1 million from US$54.6 million in the equivalent prior-year period.

Prospects: For full year 2008, Co. has reiterated its guidance for earnings per diluted share of $2.25 to $2.40. The guidance range includes the two acquisitions Co. completed in the first quarter of 2008, which are expected to be neutral to modestly dilutive for the year. At the same time, Co. continues to anticipate organic growth in net sales of 5.0% to 9.0%, fueled by a strong new product pipeline and continued market expansion. Co. also remains on track to realize savings of between $9.0 million and $12.0 million in 2008 from its global low-cost sourcing and lean manufacturing initiatives. Further, Co. continues to target an operating profit margin of 9.5% in the fourth quarter of 2008.

Financial Data
(US$ in Thousands)

	3 Mos	12/31/2007	12/31/2006	12/31/2005	12/31/2004	12/31/2003	12/31/2002	12/31/2001
Earnings Per Share	2.05	2.08	1.57	1.26	0.73	0.78	0.46	0.26
Cash Flow Per Share	2.30	2.13	2.17	2.45	2.03	1.70	1.07	1.88
Tang Book Value Per Share	7.86	11.78	10.60	9.21	8.28	8.22	7.59	7.59
Dividends Per Share	0.489	0.480	0.460	0.440	0.430	...	...	...
Dividend Payout %	23.79	23.08	29.30	34.92	58.90	...	...	...
Income Statement								
Total Revenue	168,600	664,218	598,981	552,908	507,785	453,962	424,183	422,970
EBITDA	13,236	74,810	55,662	46,906	34,019	35,754	31,335	31,916
Depn & Amortn	4,765	18,054	14,321	13,039	12,972	13,879	16,947	18,507
Income Before Taxes	8,296	57,712	43,302	34,994	21,379	22,483	14,898	13,749
Income Taxes	3,061	17,845	13,493	12,058	7,999	8,328	6,633	8,945
Net Income	5,235	39,867	29,809	22,936	13,380	14,155	8,265	4,804
Average Shares	18,844	19,146	18,989	18,210	18,300	18,128	18,096	18,406
Balance Sheet								
Current Assets	249,930	240,724	235,404	211,601	188,631	176,370	162,901	152,387
Total Assets	474,343	382,070	354,250	311,472	285,792	258,873	256,237	246,619
Current Liabilities	98,058	96,673	94,804	88,965	81,853	59,507	70,349	55,648
Long-Term Obligations	89,952	2,470	1,907	1,608	1,029	6,295	5,000	10,000
Total Liabilities	219,636	129,639	124,586	118,370	111,758	93,257	102,092	92,291
Stockholders' Equity	254,707	252,431	229,664	193,102	174,034	165,616	154,145	154,328
Shares Outstanding	18,502	18,499	18,753	18,382	18,006	17,989	17,962	18,072
Statistical Record								
Return on Assets %	9.57	10.83	8.96	7.68	4.90	5.50	3.29	1.88
Return on Equity %	15.96	16.54	14.10	12.49	7.86	8.85	5.36	3.11
EBITDA Margin %	7.85	11.26	9.29	8.48	6.70	7.88	7.39	7.55
Net Margin %	3.10	6.00	4.98	4.15	2.63	3.12	1.95	1.14
Asset Turnover	1.65	1.80	1.80	1.85	1.86	1.76	1.69	1.66
Current Ratio	2.55	2.49	2.48	2.38	2.30	2.96	2.32	2.74
Debt to Equity	0.35	0.01	0.01	0.01	0.01	0.04	0.03	0.06
Price Range	49.32-31.16	49.32-27.84	29.88-21.70	26.00-17.41	22.10-18.41	22.50-14.64	22.00-13.31	24.44-16.45
P/E Ratio	24.06-15.20	23.71-13.38	19.03-13.82	20.63-13.82	30.27-25.22	28.84-18.77	47.83-28.93	93.99-63.27
Average Yield %	0.33	1.27	1.79	2.20	2.15	...	...	...

Address: 701 North Lilac Drive, P.O. Box 1452, Minneapolis, MN 55440 **Telephone:** 763-540-1208 **Web Site:** www.tennantco.com	Officers: H. Chris Killingstad - President, Chief Executive Officer Karel Huijser - Vice President **Transfer Agents:** Wells Fargo Bank, N.A., South St. Paul, MN	Investor Contact: 763-540-1553 **No of Institutions:** 145 **Shares:** 16,322,135 % Held: 85.13

TEPPCO PARTNERS, L.P.

Exchange	Symbol	Price	52Wk Range	Yield	P/E
NYS	TPP	$35.67 (5/29/2008)	45.78-33.22	7.96	18.97

*7 Year Price Score 82.29 *NYSE Composite Index=100 ***12 Month Price Score 92.94**

TRADING VOLUME (thousand shares)

Interim Earnings (Per Share)

Qtr.	Mar	Jun	Sep	Dec
2005	0.55	0.45	0.31	0.42
2006	0.63	0.42	0.39	0.53
2007	1.29	0.44	0.44	0.43
2008	0.57	...	...	...

Interim Dividends (Per Share)

Amt	Decl	Ex	Rec	Pay
0.685Q	07/16/2007	07/27/2007	07/31/2007	08/07/2007
0.695Q	10/12/2007	10/29/2007	10/31/2007	11/07/2007
0.695Q	01/14/2008	01/29/2008	01/31/2008	02/07/2008
0.71Q	04/14/2008	04/28/2008	04/30/2008	05/07/2008

Indicated Div: $2.84

Valuation Analysis

Forecast EPS	$2.02 (05/17/2008)		
Market Cap	$3.4 Billion	Book Value	N/A
Price/Book	N/A	Price/Sales	0.32

Dividend Achiever Status

10 Year Growth Rate	5.86%
Total Years of Dividend Growth	15

Business Summary: Oil and Gas (MIC: SIC: 4922 NAIC: 486210)

TEPPCO Partners is engaged as a common carrier pipeline of refined products and liquefied petroleum gases (LPGs) in the U.S. Co. operates through three business segments: downstream, which includes transportation, marketing and storage of refined products, LPGs and petrochemicals; upstream, which includes gathering, transportation, marketing, and storage of crude oil, and distribution of lubrication oils and specialty chemicals; and midstream, which includes natural gas gathering services, fractionation of natural gas liquids (NGLs) and transportation of NGLs. Texas Eastern Products Pipeline Co., LLC serves as Co.'s general partner and owns a 2.0% general partner interest in Co.

Recent Developments: For the quarter ended Mar 31 2008, net income decreased 53.6% to US$64.1 million from US$138.2 million in the year-earlier quarter. Revenues were US$2.81 billion, up 42.0% from US$1.98 billion the year before. Operating income was US$83.5 million versus US$83.4 million in the prior-year quarter, an increase of 0.1%. Direct operating expenses rose 43.7% to US$2.61 billion from US$1.81 billion in the comparable period the year before. Indirect operating expenses increased 46.1% to US$118.4 million from US$81.0 million in the equivalent prior-year period.

Prospects: Co.'s near-term outlook appears to be constructive. For instance, as part of its strategy to develop a network of refined products distribution facilities along inland waterways in the southeastern U.S., on May 21 2008, Co. announced that it will construct three new refined product terminals along the Tennessee and Cumberland rivers that will supply markets in western Tennessee. The terminals are expected to have 800,000 barrels of storage capacity for gasoline, diesel and biofuels, and provide improved trucking logistics with supply provided by barge transportation. The initiative, which is expected to cost about $75.0 million, is projected to be completed in the first quarter of 2010.

Financial Data

(US$ in Thousands)	3 Mos	12/31/2007	12/31/2006	12/31/2005	12/31/2004	12/31/2003	12/31/2002	12/31/2001
Earnings Per Share	1.88	2.60	1.96	1.71	1.61	1.52	1.79	2.18
Cash Flow Per Share	3.64	3.90	3.71	3.78	4.21	4.00	4.77	4.31
Dividends Per Share	2.760	2.740	2.700	2.675	2.638	2.500	2.350	2.150
Dividend Payout %	147.19	105.38	137.76	156.43	163.82	164.47	131.28	98.62
Income Statement								
Total Revenue	2,808,488	9,658,060	9,607,485	8,618,488	5,958,192	4,255,832	3,242,163	3,556,413
EBITDA	128,195	485,339	375,680	...	...	...	...	...
Depn & Amortn	24,974	106,055	108,252	111,341	112,894	100,728	86,032	45,899
Income Before Taxes	64,958	279,737	183,334	...	...	...	...	...
Income Taxes	819	557	652	...	...	...	...	...
Net Income	64,139	279,180	202,051	162,551	142,381	125,769	117,862	109,131
Average Shares	93,156	89,850	73,657	67,397	62,999	59,765	49,202	39,258
Balance Sheet								
Net PPE	2,252,377	1,793,634	1,642,095	1,960,068	1,703,702	1,619,163	1,587,824	1,180,461
Total Assets	5,603,852	4,750,057	3,922,092	3,680,538	3,197,705	2,940,992	2,770,642	2,065,348
Long-Term Obligations	2,445,495	1,511,083	1,603,287	1,525,021	1,480,226	1,339,650	1,377,692	730,472
Total Liabilities	4,180,545	3,485,430	2,601,762	2,479,168	2,176,257	1,831,671	1,878,800	1,522,167
Shares Outstanding	94,839	89,911	89,804	69,963	62,998	62,998	53,809	40,500
Statistical Record								
Return on Assets %	4.35	6.44	5.32	4.73	4.63	4.40	4.87	5.92
EBITDA Margin %	4.56	5.03	3.91	...	...	...	...	...
Net Margin %	2.28	2.89	2.10	1.89	2.39	2.96	3.64	3.07
PPE Turnover	5.36	5.62	5.33	4.70	3.58	2.65	2.34	3.34
Asset Turnover	2.23	2.23	2.53	2.51	1.94	1.49	1.34	1.93
Price Range	46.15-33.22	46.15-37.40	41.74-35.18	45.29-33.55	42.16-34.79	41.15-27.75	33.00-26.10	35.90-24.75
P/E Ratio	24.55-17.67	17.75-14.38	21.30-17.95	26.49-19.62	26.19-21.61	27.07-18.26	18.44-14.58	16.47-11.35
Average Yield %	6.79	6.53	7.22	6.59	6.73	7.26	7.80	7.32

Address: 2929 Allen Parkway, P.O. Box 2521, Houston, TX 77252-2521 **Telephone:** 713-759-3636 **Web Site:** www.teppco.com	**Officers:** Jerry E. Thompson - President, Chief Executive Officer J. Michael Cockrell - Senior Vice President **Transfer Agents: ChaseMellon** Shareholder Services, L.L.C., Ridgefield Park, NJ	**Investor Contact:** 800-659-0059 **No of Institutions:** 214 **Shares:** 17,875,404 **% Held:** 18.04

3M CO

Exchange	Symbol	Price	52Wk Range	Yield	P/E
NYS	MMM	$77.76 (5/29/2008)	95.85-74.91	2.57	15.19

*7 Year Price Score 88.29   *NYSE Composite Index=100   *12 Month Price Score 95.94

Interim Earnings (Per Share)

Qtr.	Mar	Jun	Sep	Dec
2005	1.03	1.00	1.10	0.99
2006	1.17	1.15	1.18	1.56
2007	1.85	1.25	1.32	1.18
2008	1.38	...	...	...

Interim Dividends (Per Share)

Amt	Decl	Ex	Rec	Pay
0.48Q	08/13/2007	08/22/2007	08/24/2007	09/12/2007
0.48Q	11/12/2007	11/20/2007	11/23/2007	12/12/2007
0.50Q	02/11/2008	02/20/2008	02/22/2008	03/12/2008
0.50Q	05/13/2008	05/21/2008	05/23/2008	06/12/2008

Indicated Div: $2.00 (Div. Reinv. Plan)

Valuation Analysis

Forecast EPS	$5.48 (05/17/2008)		
Market Cap	$54.8 Billion	Book Value	12.4 Billion
Price/Book	4.40	Price/Sales	2.20

Dividend Achiever Status

10 Year Growth Rate	6.12%
Total Years of Dividend Growth	49

TRADING VOLUME (thousand shares)

Business Summary: Medical Instruments & Equipment (MIC: SIC: 3841 NAIC: 339112)

3M is a technology company with a global presence in the following markets: industrial and transportation; health care; display and graphics; consumer and office; safety, security and protection services; and electro and communications. As of Dec 31 2007, Co. had 157 sales offices worldwide, with 9 in the U.S. and 148 internationally. Co.'s products are sold through distribution channels, including directly to users and via wholesalers, retailers, jobbers, distributors and dealers around the world. Co.'s products include: Scotch? brand products, such as Scotch? Magic? Tape, Scotch? Glue Stick and Scotch? Cushioned Mailer, and Post-it? products, such as Post-it? Flags, and Post-it? Note Pads.

Recent Developments: For the quarter ended Mar 31 2008, net income decreased 27.8% to US$988.0 million from US$1.37 billion in the year-earlier quarter. Revenues were US$6.46 billion, up 8.9% from US$5.94 billion the year before. Operating income was US$1.50 billion versus US$2.10 billion in the prior-year quarter, a decrease of 28.6%. Direct operating expenses rose 10.4% to US$3.34 billion from US$3.02 billion in the comparable period the year before. Indirect operating expenses increased 99.8% to US$1.63 billion from US$814.0 million in the equivalent prior-year period.

Prospects: On Apr 1 2008, Co. completed its acquisition of Aearo Technologies Inc., a manufacturer of personal protection and energy absorbing products. This acquisition will enable Co. to expand its occupational health and environmental safety platform by adding hearing protection as well as eyewear and fall protection products to its existing line of respiratory products. Also, at the same date, Co. acquired Les Entreprises Solumed Inc., a Quebec-based developer and marketer of medical products designed to prevent infections in operating rooms and hospitals. Meanwhile, for full-year 2008, Co. continues to expect earnings to increase a minimum of 10.0% over 2007 earnings per share of $4.98.

Financial Data
(US$ in Millions)

	3 Mos	12/31/2007	12/31/2006	12/31/2005	12/31/2004	12/31/2003	12/31/2002	12/31/2001
Earnings Per Share	5.12	5.60	5.06	4.12	3.75	3.02	2.50	1.79
Cash Flow Per Share	6.62	5.95	5.14	5.57	5.47	4.82	3.84	3.90
Tang Book Value Per Share	9.77	8.96	7.04	8.14	9.63	6.62	4.90	6.18
Dividends Per Share	1.940	1.920	1.840	1.680	1.440	1.320	1.240	1.200
Dividend Payout %	37.92	34.29	36.36	40.78	38.40	43.71	49.70	67.04
Income Statement								
Total Revenue	6,463	24,462	22,923	21,167	20,011	18,232	16,332	16,054
EBITDA	1,769	7,265	6,775	5,995	5,577	4,677	4,000	3,362
Depn & Amortn	268	1,072	1,079	986	999	964	954	1,089
Income Before Taxes	1,476	6,115	5,625	4,983	4,555	3,657	3,005	2,186
Income Taxes	470	1,964	1,723	1,694	1,503	1,202	966	702
Net Income	988	4,096	3,851	3,199	2,990	2,403	1,974	1,430
Average Shares	717	732	761	776	796	795	791	799
Balance Sheet								
Current Assets	11,325	9,838	8,946	7,115	8,720	7,720	6,059	6,296
Total Assets	26,769	24,694	21,294	20,513	20,708	17,600	15,329	14,606
Current Liabilities	6,700	5,362	7,323	5,238	6,071	5,082	4,457	4,509
Long-Term Obligations	4,140	4,088	1,112	1,368	798	1,805	2,140	1,520
Total Liabilities	14,334	12,947	11,335	10,413	10,330	9,715	9,336	8,520
Stockholders' Equity	12,435	11,747	9,959	10,100	10,378	7,885	5,993	6,086
Shares Outstanding	704	709	734	754	773	784	780	782
Statistical Record								
Return on Assets %	14.97	17.81	18.42	15.52	15.57	14.60	13.19	9.82
Return on Equity %	32.96	37.74	38.40	31.24	32.65	34.63	32.68	22.67
EBITDA Margin %	27.37	29.70	29.56	28.32	27.87	25.65	24.49	20.94
Net Margin %	15.29	16.74	16.80	15.11	14.94	13.18	12.09	8.91
Asset Turnover	1.01	1.06	1.10	1.03	1.04	1.11	1.09	1.10
Current Ratio	1.69	1.83	1.22	1.36	1.44	1.52	1.36	1.40
Debt to Equity	0.33	0.35	0.11	0.14	0.08	0.23	0.36	0.25
Price Range	95.85-74.91	95.85-73.01	88.13-68.11	86.80-70.07	90.01-74.87	85.25-60.51	65.49-51.85	62.75-43.49
P/E Ratio	18.72-14.63	17.12-13.04	17.42-13.46	21.07-17.01	24.00-19.97	28.23-20.03	26.20-20.74	35.06-24.30
Average Yield %	2.29	2.29	2.39	2.16	1.76	1.92	2.04	2.16

Address: 3M Center, St. Paul, MN 55144-1000
Telephone: 651-733-1110
Web Site: www.3m.com

Officers: George W. Buckley - Chairman, President, Chief Executive Officer Frederick J. Palensky - Executive Vice President, Chief Technology Officer
Transfer Agents: Wells Fargo Shareowner Services, St. Paul, MN

Investor Contact: 651-733-8206
No of Institutions: 1370
Shares: 504,355,712 **% Held:** 66.14

TJX COMPANIES, INC. (NEW)

Exchange	Symbol	Price	52Wk Range	Yield	P/E
NYS	TJX	$32.18 (5/29/2008)	34.45-26.59	1.37	N/A

*7 Year Price Score 99.71 *NYSE Composite Index=100 ***12 Month Price Score 108.92**

Interim Earnings (Per Share)

Qtr.	Apr	Jul	Oct	Jan
2005-06	0.30	0.25	0.36	0.50
2006-07	0.34	0.29	0.48	0.43
2007-08	0.34	0.13	0.54	0.66
2008-09	0.43	...	...	...

Interim Dividends (Per Share)

Amt	Decl	Ex	Rec	Pay
0.09Q	09/11/2007	11/06/2007	11/08/2007	11/29/2007
0.09Q	12/04/2007	02/05/2008	02/07/2008	02/28/2008
0.11Q	04/01/2008	05/06/2008	05/08/2008	05/29/2008
0.11Q	06/03/2008	08/05/2008	08/07/2008	08/28/2008
			Indicated Div: $0.44	

Valuation Analysis

Forecast EPS	$2.23 (05/17/2008)		
Market Cap	$13.7 Billion	Book Value	2.1 Billion
Price/Book	6.39	Price/Sales	N/A

Dividend Achiever Status

10 Year Growth Rate	22.08%
Total Years of Dividend Growth	11

Business Summary: Retail - Apparel and Accessory Stores (MIC: SIC: 5651 NAIC: 448140)

TJX Companies is an off-price retailer of apparel and home fashions. Co.'s T.J. Maxx, Marshalls and A.J. Wright chains in the U.S., its Winners chain in Canada, and its T.K. Maxx chain in Europe sell off-price family apparel and home fashions. Co.'s HomeGoods chain in the U.S. and its HomeSense chain, operated by Winners in Canada, sell off-price home fashions. Co.'s Bob's Stores chain is a branded apparel chain based in the Northeastern U.S. that provides casual, family apparel. As of Jan 26 2008, Co. operated 847 T.J. Maxx stores, 776 Marshalls stores, 191 Winners stores, 226 T.K. Maxx stores, 289 HomeGoods stores, 129 A.J. Wright stores, 71 HomeSense stores, and 34 Bob's Stores.

Recent Developments: For the quarter ended Apr 26 2008, net income increased 19.6% to US$193.8 million from US$162.1 million in the year-earlier quarter. Revenues were US$4.36 billion, up 6.2% from US$4.11 billion the year before. Direct operating expenses rose 6.4% to US$3.32 billion from US$3.12 billion in the comparable period the year before. Indirect operating expenses increased 3.8% to US$757.1 million from US$729.3 million in the equivalent prior-year period.

Prospects: For the fiscal year ending Jan 31 2009, Co. continues to anticipate earnings of $2.11 to $2.16 per share, excluding an expected $0.09 per share benefit from the 53rd week in its fiscal 2009 calendar. Specifically, this range is based upon estimated consolidated comparable store sales growth of 2.0% to 3.0%, of which approximately 0.5 percentage points is due to the effects of foreign currency exchange rates. For the fiscal quarter ended July 2008, Co. is projecting earnings to range from $0.40 to $0.42 per share, based upon estimated consolidated comparable store sales growth of approximately 3.0%, of which approximately 0.5 percentage points is due to the effects of foreign exchange.

Financial Data

(US$ in Thousands)	3 Mos	01/26/2008	01/27/2007	01/28/2006	01/29/2005	01/31/2004	01/25/2003	01/26/2002
Earnings Per Share	...	1.66	1.55	1.41	1.30	1.25	1.08	0.90
Cash Flow Per Share	...	3.08	2.64	2.49	2.22	1.49	1.71	1.66
Tang Book Value Per Share	4.61	4.56	4.65	3.71	3.06	2.74	2.36	2.14
Dividends Per Share	0.360	0.340	0.270	0.225	0.170	0.135	0.113	0.087
Dividend Payout %	...	20.48	17.42	15.96	13.08	10.80	10.42	9.72
Income Statement								
Total Revenue	4,364,125	18,647,126	17,404,637	16,057,935	14,913,483	13,327,938	11,981,207	10,708,998
EBITDA	403,121	1,669,455	1,669,762	1,414,802	1,368,131	1,316,919	1,145,600	1,078,125
Depn & Amortn	111,837	426,766	422,914	405,475	288,438	248,593	207,876	204,081
Income Before Taxes	289,610	1,242,689	1,246,848	1,009,327	1,079,693	1,068,326	937,724	874,044
Income Taxes	95,761	470,939	470,092	318,904	415,549	409,961	359,336	333,647
Net Income	193,849	771,750	738,039	690,423	664,144	658,365	578,388	500,397
Average Shares	450,401	468,046	480,045	491,500	512,649	512,874	537,740	556,267
Balance Sheet								
Current Assets	4,052,239	3,992,294	3,748,813	3,140,127	2,905,120	2,451,748	2,240,540	2,115,926
Total Assets	6,646,702	6,599,934	6,085,700	5,496,305	5,075,473	4,396,767	3,940,489	3,595,743
Current Liabilities	2,822,742	2,760,993	2,382,980	2,251,851	2,204,112	1,690,520	1,566,345	1,315,010
Long-Term Obligations	852,442	853,460	808,027	807,150	598,540	692,321	693,764	702,379
Total Liabilities	4,508,655	4,468,689	3,795,579	3,603,651	3,421,991	2,844,379	2,531,342	2,255,045
Stockholders' Equity	2,138,047	2,131,245	2,290,121	1,892,654	1,653,482	1,552,388	1,409,147	1,340,698
Shares Outstanding	424,701	427,949	453,649	460,967	480,699	499,181	520,515	543,075
Statistical Record								
Return on Assets %	...	12.20	12.78	13.10	14.06	15.54	15.39	15.37
Return on Equity %	...	35.01	35.39	39.05	41.55	43.74	42.18	39.21
EBITDA Margin %	9.24	8.95	9.59	8.81	9.17	9.88	9.56	10.07
Net Margin %	4.44	4.14	4.24	4.30	4.45	4.94	4.83	4.67
Asset Turnover	...	2.95	3.01	3.05	3.16	3.15	3.19	3.29
Current Ratio	1.44	1.45	1.57	1.39	1.32	1.45	1.43	1.61
Debt to Equity	0.40	0.40	0.35	0.43	0.36	0.45	0.49	0.52
Price Range	34.45-26.59	31.87-26.00	30.04-22.23	25.89-20.26	26.35-20.95	23.59-15.93	22.18-16.02	20.31-13.88
P/E Ratio	...	19.20-15.66	19.38-14.34	18.36-14.37	20.27-16.12	18.87-12.74	20.53-14.83	22.56-15.42
Average Yield %	1.22	1.19	1.03	0.97	0.72	0.68	0.57	0.52

Address: 770 Cochituate Road, Framingham, MA 01701 **Telephone:** 508-390-1000 **Web Site:** www.tjx.com	**Officers:** Bernard Cammarata - Chairman Donald G. Campbell - Vice-Chairman **Transfer Agents:** The Bank of New York, New York, NY	**Investor Contact:** 508-390-2323 **No of Institutions:** 621 **Shares:** 463,917,376 **% Held:** 95.15

TOMPKINS FINANCIAL CORP

Exchange	Symbol	Price	52Wk Range	Yield	P/E
ASE	TMP	$45.22 (5/29/2008)	51.15-30.70	2.83	15.70

*7 Year Price Score 83.57 *NYSE Composite Index=100 *12 Month Price Score 118.86

Interim Earnings (Per Share)

Qtr.	Mar	Jun	Sep	Dec
2005	0.64	0.70	0.71	0.73
2006	0.63	0.68	0.68	0.78
2007	0.58	0.65	0.70	0.77
2008	0.77	...	...	...

Interim Dividends (Per Share)

Amt	Decl	Ex	Rec	Pay
0.32Q	07/24/2007	07/31/2007	08/02/2007	08/15/2007
0.32Q	10/24/2007	10/31/2007	11/02/2007	11/15/2007
0.32Q	01/30/2008	02/06/2008	02/08/2008	02/15/2008
0.32Q	04/23/2008	05/01/2008	05/05/2008	05/15/2008
		Indicated Div: $1.28		

Valuation Analysis

Forecast EPS	$3.05 (05/16/2008)		
Market Cap	$433.7 Million	Book Value	209.7 Million
Price/Book	2.07	Price/Sales	2.41

Dividend Achiever Status

10 Year Growth Rate	7.16%
Total Years of Dividend Growth	11

TRADING VOLUME (thousand shares)

Business Summary: Commercial Banking (MIC: SIC: 6022 NAIC: 522110)

Tompkins Financial is a financial holding company. Co. conducts its business through its three wholly-owned banking subsidiaries, Tompkins Trust Company, The Bank of Castile and The Mahopac National Bank, as well as through its insurance subsidiary, Tompkins Insurance Agencies, Inc., and through its financial planning, wealth management and broker-dealer subsidiary, AM&M Financial Services, Inc. Co.'s banking services consist of accepting deposits from the areas served by its banking subsidiaries and using the deposits to originate commercial loans, consumer loans, real estate loans and leases. At Dec 31 2007, Co. had total assets of about $2.36 billion and deposits of about $1.72 billion.

Recent Developments: For the quarter ended Mar 31 2008, net income increased 29.9% to US$7.5 million from US$5.8 million in the year-earlier quarter. Net interest income increased 12.9% to US$19.8 million from US$17.6 million in the year-earlier quarter. Provision for loan losses was US$625,000 versus US$471,000 in the prior-year quarter, an increase of 32.7%. Non-interest income rose 19.8% to US$12.5 million from US$10.4 million, while non-interest expense advanced 6.7% to US$20.4 million.

Prospects: On May 9 2008, Co. announced that it has completed its acquisition of Sleepy Hollow Bancorp, Inc. (Sleepy Hollow), the parent company of Sleepy Hollow Bank, headquartered in Sleepy Hollow, NY, in a cash transaction valued at approximately $30.2 million. Co. also noted that customer accounts and balances have been transferred to Mahopac National Bank, its bank subsidiary that serves the Hudson Valley region. With the addition of the former Sleepy Hollow Bank branches, Mahopac National Bank has expanded its assets to $750.0 million, and increased the number of its locations to 14 branches and one limited-service office serving Westchester, Putnam, and Dutchess Counties.

Financial Data

(US$ in Thousands)	3 Mos	12/31/2007	12/31/2006	12/31/2005	12/31/2004	12/31/2003	12/31/2002	12/31/2001
Earnings Per Share	2.88	2.70	2.78	2.77	2.55	2.41	2.28	1.97
Cash Flow Per Share	4.49	3.87	3.81	3.88	3.63	3.50	2.28	1.97
Tang Book Value Per Share	19.12	17.90	16.73	16.95	17.46	14.60	13.78	11.85
Dividends Per Share	1.260	1.240	1.145	1.066	0.992	0.924	0.872	0.826
Dividend Payout %	43.71	45.93	41.20	38.45	38.82	38.29	38.28	41.98
Income Statement								
Interest Income	33,691	132,441	121,041	106,707	94,673	90,995	93,959	94,158
Interest Expense	13,858	58,412	48,184	31,686	23,327	23,493	28,818	36,175
Net Interest Income	19,833	74,029	72,857	75,021	71,346	67,502	65,141	57,983
Provision for Losses	625	1,529	1,424	2,659	2,860	2,497	2,235	1,606
Non-Interest Income	12,516	44,049	41,091	30,783	27,983	25,255	23,704	19,864
Non-Interest Expense	20,381	78,056	71,910	62,122	58,228	53,857	52,270	46,061
Income Before Taxes	11,343	38,493	40,614	41,023	38,241	36,403	34,340	30,180
Income Taxes	3,802	11,991	12,716	13,207	12,493	12,064	11,292	10,419
Net Income	7,508	26,371	27,767	27,685	25,615	24,205	22,914	19,627
Average Shares	9,696	9,781	9,999	10,000	10,012	10,014	10,053	9,989
Balance Sheet								
Net Loans & Leases	1,440,789	1,425,515	1,311,970	1,257,672	1,159,599	1,057,455	983,642	879,136
Total Assets	2,450,413	2,359,459	2,210,837	2,106,870	1,970,295	1,864,446	1,670,203	1,420,695
Total Deposits	1,840,954	1,720,826	1,709,420	1,683,010	1,560,873	1,411,125	1,340,285	1,087,458
Total Liabilities	2,239,240	2,160,812	2,019,765	1,924,197	1,797,828	1,703,987	1,518,117	1,288,131
Stockholders' Equity	209,688	197,195	189,620	181,221	171,002	158,970	150,597	131,072
Shares Outstanding	9,589	9,544	9,825	9,840	8,931	9,872	9,903	9,872
Statistical Record								
Return on Assets %	1.19	1.15	1.29	1.36	1.33	1.37	1.48	1.44
Return on Equity %	14.00	13.63	14.98	15.72	15.48	15.64	16.27	15.95
Net Interest Margin %	58.87	55.90	60.19	70.31	75.36	74.18	69.33	61.58
Efficiency Ratio %	44.11	44.23	44.35	45.18	47.47	46.33	44.42	40.40
Loans to Deposits	0.78	0.83	0.77	0.75	0.74	0.75	0.73	0.81
Price Range	50.60-30.70	46.42-30.70	50.80-38.10	44.21-35.24	45.45-35.72	42.98-31.03	36.59-27.80	30.77-20.29
P/E Ratio	17.57-10.66	17.19-11.37	18.27-13.71	15.96-12.72	17.82-14.01	17.83-12.88	16.05-12.19	15.62-10.30
Average Yield %	3.16	3.13	2.63	2.67	2.56	2.54	2.66	3.16

Address: P.O. Box 460, Ithaca, NY 14851 **Telephone:** 607-273-3210 **Web Site:** www.tompkinstrustco.com	**Officers:** James J. Byrnes - Chairman James W. Fulmer - Vice-Chairman **Transfer Agents:** American Stock Transfer & Trust Company, New York, NY	**Investor Contact:** 888-503-5753x2319 **No of Institutions:** 84 **Shares:** 3,249,687 **% Held:** 33.44

TOOTSIE ROLL INDUSTRIES INC

Exchange	Symbol	Price	52Wk Range	Yield	P/E
NYS	TR	$25.60 (5/29/2008)	29.95-21.80	1.25	29.43

*7 Year Price Score 68.44 *NYSE Composite Index=100 *12 Month Price Score 100.40

Interim Earnings (Per Share)

Qtr.	Mar	Jun	Sep	Dec
2005	0.21	0.24	0.48	0.43
2006	0.22	0.23	0.51	0.21
2007	0.17	0.18	0.42	0.15
2008	0.12	...	...	...

Interim Dividends (Per Share)

Amt	Decl	Ex	Rec	Pay
0.078Q	12/05/2007	12/13/2007	12/17/2007	01/04/2008
0.078Q	02/26/2008	03/06/2008	03/10/2008	03/31/2008
3%	02/26/2008	03/06/2008	03/10/2008	04/10/2008
0.08Q	06/02/2008	06/16/2008	06/18/2008	07/10/2008

Indicated Div: $0.32

Valuation Analysis

Forecast EPS	$0.82 (05/16/2008)		
Market Cap	$1.4 Billion	Book Value	621.3 Million
Price/Book	2.27	Price/Sales	2.85

Dividend Achiever Status

10 Year Growth Rate	10.73%
Total Years of Dividend Growth	44

TRADING VOLUME (thousand shares)

Business Summary: Food (MIC: SIC: 2064 NAIC: 311340)

Tootsie Roll Industries manufactures and sells confectionery products. The majority of Co.'s products are sold under the registered trademarks Tootsie Roll, Tootsie Roll Pops, Child's Play, Caramel Apple Pops, Charms, Blow-Pop, Blue Razz, Zip-A-Dee Pops, Cella's, Mason Dots, Mason Crows, Junior Mint, Charleston Chew, Sugar Daddy, Sugar Babies, Andes, Fluffy Stuff, Dubble Bubble, Razzles, Cry Baby and Nik-L-Nip. As of Dec 31 2007, Co.'s products were distributed through about 100 candy and grocery brokers and by Co. itself to customers, including wholesale distributors of candy and groceries, supermarkets, and chain grocers, in the U.S. Co.'s key markets are in the U.S., Canada and Mexico.

Recent Developments: For the quarter ended Mar 29 2008, net income decreased 34.2% to US$6.5 million from US$9.8 million in the year-earlier quarter. Revenues were US$91.4 million, down 3.2% from US$94.4 million the year before. Operating income was US$10.5 million versus US$13.2 million in the prior-year quarter, a decrease of 20.4%. Direct operating expenses rose 1.2% to US$60.9 million from US$60.2 million in the comparable period the year before. Indirect operating expenses decreased 4.8% to US$20.1 million from US$21.1 million in the equivalent prior-year period.

Prospects: Co.'s outlook appears challenging, reflecting continued decline in its earnings. Specifically, Co.'s results are being adversely affected by lower sales volumes as well as higher input costs principally relating to major ingredients and packaging materials, freight and distribution as a result of an escalation in energy and fuel costs, and products manufactured in Canada attributable to less favorable foreign exchange rates. In the view of these conditions, Co. is taking several actions including the implementation of selected price increases as well as costs reduction programs with the objective of recovering some of these higher input costs.

Financial Data

(US$ in Thousands)	3 Mos	12/31/2007	12/31/2006	12/31/2005	12/31/2004	12/31/2003	12/31/2002	12/31/2001
Earnings Per Share	0.87	0.91	1.15	1.36	1.09	1.12	1.11	1.12
Cash Flow Per Share	1.44	1.59	0.97	1.45	1.29	1.43	1.19	1.39
Tang Book Value Per Share	6.53	6.73	6.45	6.28	5.15	7.27	6.93	6.69
Dividends Per Share	0.314	0.311	0.302	0.273	0.249	0.249	0.242	0.242
Dividend Payout %	36.10	34.04	26.23	20.14	22.76	22.22	21.71	21.54
Income Statement								
Total Revenue	91,433	497,717	495,990	487,739	420,110	392,656	393,185	423,496
EBITDA	13,317	94,082	112,166	132,556	109,165	107,568	107,798	112,513
Depn & Amortn	4,085	16,380	16,725	16,367	13,565	13,913	12,354	17,926
Income Before Taxes	9,232	77,167	94,715	113,652	94,688	97,947	100,688	100,787
Income Taxes	2,779	25,542	28,796	36,425	30,514	32,933	34,300	35,100
Net Income	6,453	51,625	65,919	77,227	64,174	65,014	66,388	65,687
Average Shares	55,543	56,629	57,495	56,802	58,938	58,283	59,740	58,486
Balance Sheet								
Current Assets	169,754	199,726	190,917	246,596	192,693	243,705	224,948	246,096
Total Assets	795,874	812,725	791,639	813,696	811,753	665,297	646,080	618,676
Current Liabilities	60,174	57,972	62,211	113,656	82,317	62,887	63,096	57,846
Long-Term Obligations	7,500	7,500	7,500	7,500	93,167	7,500	7,500	7,500
Total Liabilities	174,575	174,495	160,958	196,291	241,574	128,716	119,340	110,215
Stockholders' Equity	621,299	638,230	630,681	617,405	570,179	536,581	526,740	508,461
Shares Outstanding	55,000	55,859	56,961	56,434	58,770	57,656	59,067	58,433
Statistical Record								
Return on Assets %	6.05	6.44	8.21	9.50	8.67	9.92	10.50	11.12
Return on Equity %	7.70	8.14	10.56	13.01	11.57	12.23	12.83	13.58
EBITDA Margin %	14.56	18.90	22.61	27.18	25.98	27.39	27.42	26.57
Net Margin %	7.06	10.37	13.29	15.83	15.28	16.56	16.88	15.51
Asset Turnover	0.62	0.62	0.62	0.60	0.57	0.60	0.62	0.72
Current Ratio	2.82	3.45	3.07	2.17	2.34	3.88	3.57	4.25
Debt to Equity	0.01	0.01	0.01	0.01	0.16	0.01	0.01	0.01
Price Range	29.95-21.80	30.81-22.86	31.35-24.84	30.77-26.48	33.42-25.84	31.86-22.86	40.17-24.71	40.34-28.52
P/E Ratio	34.43-25.06	33.86-25.13	27.26-21.60	22.62-19.47	30.66-23.70	28.45-20.41	36.19-22.27	36.02-25.47
Average Yield %	0.31	1.15	1.09	0.97	0.85	0.93	0.76	0.70

Address: 7401 South Cicero Avenue, Chicago, IL 60629 Telephone: 773-838-3400 Web Site: www.tootsie.com	Officers: Melvin J. Gordon - Chairman, Chief Executive Officer Ellen R. Gordon - President, Chief Operating Officer Transfer Agents: Mellon Investor Services	No of Institutions: 148 Shares: 19,081,334 % Held: 34.79

TOTAL SYSTEM SERVICES, INC.

Exchange	Symbol	Price	52Wk Range	Yield	P/E
NYS	TSS	$24.66 (5/29/2008)	33.20-20.23	1.14	20.55

*7 Year Price Score 88.35   *NYSE Composite Index=100   *12 Month Price Score 94.51

Interim Earnings (Per Share)

Qtr.	Mar	Jun	Sep	Dec
2005	0.23	0.26	0.24	0.26
2006	0.26	0.29	0.28	0.44
2007	0.29	0.33	0.35	0.23
2008	0.29	...	...	...

Interim Dividends (Per Share)

Amt	Decl	Ex	Rec	Pay
3.031Q	11/30/2007	12/19/2007	12/17/2007	12/31/2007
0.07Q	11/30/2007	12/19/2007	12/17/2007	01/02/2008
0.07Q	03/10/2008	03/18/2008	03/20/2008	04/01/2008
0.07Q	06/09/2008	06/17/2008	06/19/2008	07/01/2008

Indicated Div: $0.28

Valuation Analysis

Forecast EPS $1.35 (05/16/2008)
Market Cap	$4.9 Billion	Book Value	887.9 Million
Price/Book	5.50	Price/Sales	2.67

Dividend Achiever Status

10 Year Dividend Growth Rate	25.03%
Total Years of Dividend Growth	10

Business Summary: Miscellaneous Business Services (MIC: SIC: 7389 NAIC: 561499)

Total System Services is a provider of electronic payment processing and related services to financial and non-financial institutions. Services include processing consumer, retail, commercial, government services, and debit cards. Co. provides merchant acquiring services to financial institutions and other organizations in the U.S. through its wholly owned subsidiary, TSYS Acquiring Solutions, L.L.C., and in Japan through its majority owned subsidiary, GP Network Corp. Co. also provides optional products and services, such as credit evaluation, fraud detection and prevention, behavior analysis tools, loyalty programs and bonus rewards, to support its core processing services.

Recent Developments: For the quarter ended Mar 31 2008, net income decreased 1.2% to US$56.6 million from US$57.3 million in the year-earlier quarter. Revenues were US$461.7 million, up 7.5% from US$429.6 million the year before. Operating income was US$86.8 million versus US$85.7 million in the prior-year quarter, an increase of 1.3%. Indirect operating expenses increased 9.0% to US$374.9 million from US$343.9 million in the equivalent prior-year period.

Prospects: Looking ahead to 2008, Co. is on track to attain its guidance to grow net income over 2007 in the range of 7.0% to 9.0% to a range of US$254.0 million to US$259.0 million, with basic earnings per share in the range of $1.29 to $1.31. This guidance is based on several assumptions, including estimated 2008 total revenues in the range of $1.93 billion to $1.96 billion, reflecting an increase of between 7.0% and 9.0% compared with $1.81 billion in 2007. In addition, Co. expects to grow its operating income for 2008 in the double digit range of 12.0% to 14.0% to a range of US$396.0 million to US$403.0 million.

Financial Data

(US$ in Thousands)	3 Mos	12/31/2007	12/31/2006	12/31/2005	12/31/2004	12/31/2003	12/31/2002	12/31/2001
Earnings Per Share	1.20	1.20	1.26	0.99	0.76	0.71	0.64	0.53
Cash Flow Per Share	1.87	1.70	1.96	1.21	1.68	1.35	1.00	0.45
Tang Book Value Per Share	1.89	1.67	3.45	2.30	1.97	1.62	1.41	1.31
Dividends Per Share	3.311	3.311	0.270	0.220	0.140	0.077	0.068	0.060
Dividend Payout %	276.74	275.91	21.43	22.22	18.42	10.92	10.55	11.32
Income Statement								
Total Revenue	461,723	1,805,836	1,787,171	1,602,931	1,187,008	1,053,466	955,133	650,408
EBITDA	128,081	506,367	543,208	437,503	310,964	290,037	235,189	210,508
Depn & Amortn	39,229	152,468	184,894	151,214	108,588	98,415	74,504	57,396
Income Before Taxes	88,075	377,691	371,854	291,927	204,291	194,369	163,286	155,793
Income Taxes	33,035	143,668	126,182	103,286	77,210	70,868	57,908	52,891
Net Income	56,614	237,443	249,163	194,520	150,558	140,973	125,805	102,902
Average Shares	197,306	197,165	197,077	197,345	197,236	197,437	197,497	195,604
Balance Sheet								
Current Assets	625,569	586,578	744,716	512,289	448,156	274,363	265,979	206,354
Total Assets	1,522,597	1,479,020	1,634,241	1,410,897	1,281,943	1,001,236	782,868	652,277
Current Liabilities	333,658	273,795	295,787	277,012	277,903	146,971	113,982	102,553
Long-Term Obligations	193,854	256,593	3,625	3,555	4,508	29,748	67	...
Total Liabilities	625,268	625,967	410,652	394,443	413,517	265,263	177,918	149,107
Stockholders' Equity	887,916	844,473	1,217,360	1,012,772	864,612	732,534	602,206	500,812
Shares Outstanding	198,182	197,965	196,912	197,283	196,849	196,815	197,049	194,778
Statistical Record								
Return on Assets %	14.82	15.25	16.36	14.45	13.15	15.80	17.53	16.38
Return on Equity %	21.90	23.03	22.35	20.72	18.80	21.12	22.81	22.62
EBITDA Margin %	27.74	28.04	30.39	27.29	26.20	27.53	24.62	32.37
Net Margin %	12.26	13.15	13.94	12.14	12.68	13.38	13.17	15.82
Asset Turnover	1.15	1.16	1.17	1.19	1.04	1.18	1.33	1.04
Current Ratio	1.87	2.14	2.52	1.85	1.61	1.87	2.33	2.01
Debt to Equity	0.22	0.30	N.M.	N.M.	0.01	0.04	N.M.	...
Price Range	34.33-20.23	34.33-25.50	26.54-18.07	25.38-18.91	31.13-19.70	31.13-13.50	29.00-11.67	35.54-19.25
P/E Ratio	28.61-16.86	28.61-21.25	21.06-14.34	25.64-19.10	40.96-25.92	43.85-19.01	45.31-18.23	67.06-36.32
Average Yield %	11.90	11.14	1.26	0.94	0.60	0.35	0.36	0.24

Address: 1600 First Avenue, Columbus, GA 31901 **Telephone:** 706-649-5220 **Web Site:** www.tsys.com	**Officers:** Philip W. Tomlinson - Chairman, Chief Executive Officer M. Troy Woods - President, Chief Operating Officer **Transfer Agents:** Mellon Investor Services, South Hackensack, NJ	**Investor Contact:** 706-649-5220 **No of Institutions:** 308 **Shares:** 107,249,024 **% Held:** 52.96

TRANSATLANTIC HOLDINGS, INC.

Exchange	Symbol	Price	52Wk Range	Yield	P/E
NYS	TRH	$64.79 (5/29/2008)	75.78-58.84	1.17	8.74

*7 Year Price Score 85.73 *NYSE Composite Index=100 ***12 Month Price Score 98.41**

TRADING VOLUME (thousand shares)

Interim Earnings (Per Share)

Qtr.	Mar	Jun	Sep	Dec
2005	1.35	1.20	(2.19)	0.20
2006	1.54	1.58	1.61	1.73
2007	1.61	1.89	2.12	1.69
2008	1.73	...	...	...

Interim Dividends (Per Share)

Amt	Decl	Ex	Rec	Pay
0.16Q	09/27/2007	11/20/2007	11/23/2007	12/07/2007
0.16Q	11/29/2007	03/05/2008	03/07/2008	03/21/2008
0.16Q	03/25/2008	06/04/2008	06/06/2008	06/20/2008
0.19Q	05/22/2008	09/02/2008	09/04/2008	09/18/2008

Indicated Div: $0.76

Valuation Analysis

Forecast EPS	$7.05 (05/16/2008)		
Market Cap	$4.3 Billion	Book Value	3.4 Billion
Price/Book	1.27	Price/Sales	0.98

Dividend Achiever Status

10 Year Growth Rate	11.28%
Total Years of Dividend Growth	17

Business Summary: Insurance (MIC: SIC: 6331 NAIC: 524126)

Transatlantic Holdings, through its wholly-owned subsidiaries Transatlantic Reinsurance Company, Trans Re Zurich and Putnam Reinsurance Company, provides reinsurance capacity for property and casualty products on a treaty and facultative basis, directly and through brokers, to insurance and reinsurance companies, in both the domestic and international markets. As of Dec 31 2007, Co.'s principal lines of reinsurance included ocean marine and aviation, medical malpractice, auto liability (including non-standard risks), accident and health and surety and credit in the casualty lines, and fire, allied lines, auto physical damage and homeowners multiple peril lines in the property lines.

Recent Developments: For the quarter ended Mar 31 2008, net income increased 7.9% to US$115.7 million from US$107.2 million in the year-earlier quarter. Revenues were US$1.12 billion, up 2.1% from US$1.10 billion the year before. Net premiums earned were US$1.02 billion versus US$965.1 million in the prior-year quarter, an increase of 5.4%. Net investment income rose 0.9% to US$117.2 million from US$116.2 million a year ago.

Prospects: Co. is seeing increased net premiums written in both domestic and international market, primarily reflecting several factors, which include premiums generated by domestic regional offices. Also, Co. is benefiting from increased net investment income due to an increase in fixed maturity income, resulting mostly from investment returns from continued positive operating cash flows. Separately, on Apr 24 2008, Co. announced that it has received regulatory approval to serve the Brazilian reinsurance market as an Admitted Reinsurer, through its representative office in Rio de Janeiro, Brazil. Subsequently, Co. anticipates opportunities to arise from the opening of the Brazilian reinsurance market.

Financial Data
(US$ in Thousands)

	3 Mos	12/31/2007	12/31/2006	12/31/2005	12/31/2004	12/31/2003	12/31/2002	12/31/2001
Earnings Per Share	7.41	7.31	6.46	0.57	3.85	4.60	2.57	0.29
Cash Flow Per Share	16.82	15.53	12.82	9.57	13.73	14.06	9.15	3.71
Tang Book Value Per Share	51.03	50.56	44.80	38.60	39.30	36.24	31.03	28.26
Dividends Per Share	0.615	0.590	0.510	0.440	0.376	0.336	0.314	0.298
Dividend Payout %	8.30	8.07	7.89	77.19	9.77	7.30	12.21	103.33
Income Statement								
Total Revenue	1,119,347	4,381,830	4,049,496	3,768,125	3,990,057	3,452,140	2,615,527	2,030,182
Income Before Taxes	145,219	595,752	539,908	(46,098)	276,212	386,674	188,320	(34,107)
Income Taxes	29,566	108,611	111,756	(84,008)	21,628	83,030	19,002	(52,999)
Net Income	115,653	487,141	428,152	37,910	254,584	303,644	169,318	18,892
Average Shares	66,805	66,654	66,266	66,169	66,189	65,952	65,943	65,920
Balance Sheet								
Total Assets	15,772,029	15,484,327	14,268,464	12,364,676	10,605,292	8,707,758	7,286,525	6,741,303
Total Liabilities	12,391,272	12,135,285	11,310,194	9,820,725	8,018,163	6,331,171	5,255,758	4,895,293
Stockholders' Equity	3,380,757	3,349,042	2,958,270	2,543,951	2,587,129	2,376,587	2,030,767	1,846,010
Shares Outstanding	66,246	66,233	66,037	65,911	65,827	65,585	65,451	65,319
Statistical Record								
Return on Assets %	3.28	3.27	3.22	0.33	2.63	3.80	2.41	0.31
Return on Equity %	15.36	15.45	15.56	1.48	10.23	13.78	8.73	1.02
Net Margin %	10.33	11.12	10.57	1.01	6.38	8.80	6.47	0.93
Price Range	75.78-58.84	75.78-58.84	68.00-53.28	70.94-54.60	73.49-53.80	64.64-49.18	72.80-48.44	73.60-50.54
P/E Ratio	10.23-7.94	10.37-8.05	10.53-8.25	124.46-95.79	19.09-13.97	14.05-10.69	28.33-18.85	253.79-174.29
Average Yield %	0.88	0.85	0.85	0.72	0.59	0.59	0.51	0.48

Address: 80 Pine Street, New York, NY 10005	Officers: Martin J. Sullivan - Chairman Robert Orlich - President, Chief Executive Officer **Transfer Agents:** American Stock Transfer & Trust Company	Investor Contact: 212-770-2040 **No of Institutions:** 191
Telephone: 212-770-2000 **Web Site:** www.transre.com		**Shares:** 63,582,976 **% Held:** 95.60

TRUSTMARK CORP.

Exchange	Symbol	Price	52Wk Range	Yield	P/E
NMS	TRMK	$20.36 (5/29/2008)	30.00-18.99	4.52	10.77

*7 Year Price Score 70.16   *NYSE Composite Index=100   *12 Month Price Score 89.93

Interim Earnings (Per Share)

Qtr.	Mar	Jun	Sep	Dec
2005	0.47	0.39	0.46	0.49
2006	0.52	0.55	0.52	0.49
2007	0.44	0.51	0.51	0.42
2008	0.46	...	...	...

Interim Dividends (Per Share)

Amt	Decl	Ex	Rec	Pay
0.22Q	07/18/2007	08/29/2007	08/31/2007	09/15/2007
0.23Q	10/24/2007	11/28/2007	12/01/2007	12/15/2007
0.23Q	01/22/2008	02/27/2008	03/01/2008	03/15/2008
0.23Q	04/22/2008	05/28/2008	06/01/2008	06/15/2008

Indicated Div: $0.92

Valuation Analysis

Forecast EPS $1.85 (05/16/2008)

Market Cap	$1.2 Billion	Book Value	937.3 Million
Price/Book	1.24	Price/Sales	1.64

Dividend Achiever Status

10 Year Growth Rate	11.77%
Total Years of Dividend Growth	34

Business Summary: Commercial Banking (MIC: SIC: 6021 NAIC: 522110)

Trustmark is a multi-bank holding company. Through its subsidiaries, Co. operates as a financial services organization providing banking and financial services to corporate, institutional and individual customers mainly in Florida, Mississippi, Tennessee and Texas. Co.'s key subsisiary is Trustmark National Bank. Co. operates through four segments: general banking, which provides traditional banking products and services; wealth management, which provides services for accumulating, preserving, and transferring wealth; insurance; and administration, which consists of Co.'s internal operations. As of Dec 31 2007, Co. had total assets of $8.97 billion and deposits of $6.87 billion.

Recent Developments: For the quarter ended Mar 31 2008, net income increased 1.2% to US$26.2 million from US$25.9 million in the year-earlier quarter. Net interest income increased 3.9% to US$74.7 million from US$71.9 million in the year-earlier quarter. Provision for loan losses was US$14.2 million versus US$1.6 million in the prior-year quarter, an increase of 769.0%. Non-interest income rose 27.2% to US$48.5 million from US$38.2 million, while non-interest expense advanced 0.6% to US$69.8 million.

Prospects: Co. remains committed to making investments to support revenue growth and profitability as well as to reallocate resources to areas with additional growth potential. Notably, Co. anticipates opening four new banking centers over the course of 2008 in the Biloxi, Houston, Jackson and Panama City markets. Meanwhile, Co. continues to be engaged in the resolution of credit issues in the Florida Panhandle market. While these actions, including the continued monitoring of the effect of declining real estate values on borrowers, are expected to mitigate the effects of the current credit cycle, Co. believes that weakness in the Florida residential real estate portfolio may persist going forward.

Financial Data

(US$ in Thousands)	3 Mos	12/31/2007	12/31/2006	12/31/2005	12/31/2004	12/31/2003	12/31/2002	12/31/2001
Earnings Per Share	1.89	1.88	2.09	1.81	2.00	2.00	1.94	1.72
Cash Flow Per Share	1.57	1.31	3.13	1.50	2.77	3.39	1.10	3.75
Tang Book Value Per Share	9.77	9.31	8.50	9.27	9.14	8.96	9.25	8.93
Dividends Per Share	0.900	0.890	0.850	0.810	0.770	0.685	0.615	0.555
Dividend Payout %	47.51	47.34	40.67	44.75	38.50	34.25	31.70	32.27
Income Statement								
Interest Income	126,014	543,143	482,746	415,697	364,355	359,388	405,952	477,820
Interest Expense	51,265	242,360	202,175	139,256	88,738	89,558	113,766	209,242
Net Interest Income	74,749	300,783	280,571	276,441	275,617	269,830	292,186	268,578
Provision for Losses	14,243	23,784	(5,938)	19,541	(3,055)	9,771	14,107	13,200
Non-Interest Income	48,516	162,447	155,128	143,107	124,028	157,543	141,870	131,990
Non-Interest Expense	69,826	276,449	260,480	243,276	225,309	236,120	233,841	215,941
Income Before Taxes	39,196	162,997	181,157	156,731	177,391	181,482	186,108	171,427
Income Taxes	13,017	54,402	61,884	53,780	60,682	62,952	64,968	60,146
Net Income	26,179	108,595	119,273	102,951	116,709	118,530	121,140	111,281
Average Shares	57,312	57,786	57,097	56,743	58,273	59,244	62,416	64,876
Balance Sheet								
Net Loans & Leases	7,128,461	7,108,449	6,565,152	5,963,684	5,366,520	4,958,336	4,542,595	4,448,832
Total Assets	9,097,153	8,966,802	8,840,970	8,389,750	8,052,957	7,914,321	7,138,706	7,180,339
Total Deposits	7,344,335	6,869,272	6,976,164	6,282,814	5,450,093	5,089,459	4,686,296	4,613,365
Total Liabilities	8,159,812	8,047,166	7,949,635	7,648,287	7,302,561	7,224,748	6,459,172	6,494,895
Stockholders' Equity	937,341	919,636	891,335	741,463	750,396	689,573	679,534	685,444
Shares Outstanding	57,296	57,272	58,676	55,771	57,858	58,246	60,516	63,705
Statistical Record								
Return on Assets %	1.21	1.22	1.38	1.25	1.46	1.57	1.69	1.58
Return on Equity %	11.86	11.99	14.61	13.80	16.17	17.31	17.75	16.92
Net Interest Margin %	59.32	55.38	58.12	66.50	75.65	75.08	71.98	56.21
Efficiency Ratio %	40.01	39.18	40.84	43.54	46.13	45.68	42.69	35.41
Loans to Deposits	0.97	1.03	0.94	0.95	0.98	0.97	0.97	0.96
Price Range	30.00-18.99	33.32-23.27	33.45-27.65	31.07-24.41	32.42-26.10	29.82-22.74	26.90-20.49	24.70-19.56
P/E Ratio	15.87-10.05	17.72-12.38	16.00-13.23	17.17-13.49	16.21-13.05	14.91-11.37	13.87-10.56	14.36-11.37
Average Yield %	3.55	3.26	2.74	2.87	2.60	2.61	2.53	2.48

Address: 248 East Capitol Street, Jackson, MS 39201 Telephone: 601-208-5111 Web Site: www.trustmark.com	Officers: Richard G. Hickson - Chairman, President, Chief Executive Officer Louis E. Greer - Treasurer, Principal Financial Officer Transfer Agents: Trustmark National Bank, Jackson, MS	Investor Contact: 601-949-6898 No of Institutions: 136 Shares: 23,219,560 % Held: 38.95

UDR INC

Exchange	Symbol	Price	52Wk Range	Yield	P/E
NYS	UDR	$24.91 (5/29/2008)	30.36-19.24	5.30	3.66

*7 Year Price Score 86.37 ***NYSE Composite Index=100** ***12 Month Price Score 106.44**

TRADING VOLUME (thousand shares)

Interim Earnings (Per Share)

Qtr.	Mar	Jun	Sep	Dec
2005	0.08	0.36	0.08	0.50
2006	0.06	0.21	0.42	0.16
2007	0.21	0.01	0.56	0.75
2008	5.48	...	...	...

Interim Dividends (Per Share)

Amt	Decl	Ex	Rec	Pay
0.33Q	07/03/2007	07/11/2007	07/13/2007	07/31/2007
0.33Q	10/03/2007	10/10/2007	10/12/2007	10/31/2007
0.33Q	01/02/2008	01/09/2008	01/11/2008	01/31/2008
0.33Q	04/03/2008	04/09/2008	04/11/2008	04/30/2008

Indicated Div: $1.32

Valuation Analysis

Forecast EPS $-1.33 (05/17/2008)

Market Cap	$3.2 Billion	Book Value	1.6 Billion
Price/Book	2.02	Price/Sales	7.08

Dividend Achiever Status

10 Year Growth Rate		2.70%
Total Years of Dividend Growth		22

Business Summary: "Property, Real Estate & Development" (MIC: SIC: 6798 NAIC: 525930)

UDR is a self-administered real estate investment trust (REIT) that is engaged in the ownership, acquisition, renovation, development and management of apartment communities nationwide. As of Dec 31 2007, Co.'s apartment portfolio included 234 communities located in 30 markets, with a total of 65,867 completed apartment homes. As of such date, Co.'s subsidiaries included two operating partnerships, Heritage Communities L.P., a Delaware limited partnership, and United Dominion Realty L.P., a Delaware limited partnership, and RE3, its subsidiary that focuses on development, land entitlement and short-term hold investments.

Recent Developments: For the quarter ended Mar 31 2008, loss from continuing operations was US$13.3 million compared with a loss of US$13.2 million in the year-earlier quarter. Net income increased to US$725.3 million from US$31.8 million in the year-earlier quarter. Revenues were US$131.1 million, up 3.7% from US$126.4 million the year before. Revenues from property income rose 3.4% to US$125.6 million from US$121.4 million in the corresponding quarter a year earlier.

Prospects: On Mar 3 2008, Co. announced that it has completed the sale of 25,684 apartment homes in 86 communities to DRA Fund VI LLC in a joint venture with Steven D. Bell & Co. for $1.70 billion. Accordingly, Co. will reinvest $500.0 million to $800.0 million of the proceeds into communities that further strengthen its portfolio, primarily in West Coast and DC corridor markets. Co. also expects to use the balance of the proceeds to, among others, reduce its debt. For 2008, Co.'s same-store guidance is unchanged with expected revenue growth of 4.0% to 4.5%. Co. is also estimating funds from operations, excluding potential gains on sales from its RE3 subsidiary, of $1.50 to $1.55 per diluted share.

Financial Data
(US$ in Thousands)

	3 Mos	12/31/2007	12/31/2006	12/31/2005	12/31/2004	12/31/2003	12/31/2002	12/31/2001
Earnings Per Share	6.80	1.53	0.85	1.02	0.56	0.21	0.24	0.27
Cash Flow Per Share	1.82	1.87	1.72	1.82	1.96	2.05	2.14	2.24
Tang Book Value Per Share	10.94	6.28	6.47	6.91	7.43	7.28	6.48	7.10
Dividends Per Share	1.320	1.303	1.238	1.192	1.163	1.133	1.103	1.077
Dividend Payout %	19.41	85.13	145.59	116.91	207.59	539.29	459.38	399.07
Income Statement								
Total Revenue	131,083	500,194	698,058	701,217	606,878	604,435	596,120	623,183
Depn & Amortn	57,683	274,875	252,997	223,418	191,294	172,785	168,584	156,292
Net Income	725,259	221,349	128,605	155,166	97,152	70,404	53,229	61,828
Average Shares	131,665	134,016	133,732	137,013	129,080	115,648	106,952	101,037
Balance Sheet								
Total Assets	5,070,205	4,801,121	4,675,875	4,541,593	4,332,001	3,543,643	3,276,136	3,348,091
Long-Term Obligations	3,179,247	3,502,676	3,338,785	3,159,777	2,879,982	2,132,037	2,057,640	2,064,197
Total Liabilities	3,366,001	3,719,679	3,531,787	3,350,050	3,052,957	2,286,001	2,205,649	2,229,701
Stockholders' Equity	1,596,655	1,019,393	1,055,255	1,107,724	1,195,451	1,163,436	1,001,271	1,042,725
Shares Outstanding	129,360	133,317	135,029	134,012	136,429	127,295	106,605	103,133
Statistical Record								
Return on Assets %	18.64	4.67	2.79	3.50	2.46	2.06	1.61	1.82
Return on Equity %	69.25	21.34	11.89	13.47	8.21	6.50	5.21	5.47
Net Margin %	553.28	44.25	18.42	22.13	16.01	11.65	8.93	9.92
Price Range	31.07-19.24	33.95-19.64	33.66-23.93	25.85-20.64	24.80-17.52	19.37-15.22	16.70-13.95	14.72-10.75
P/E Ratio	4.57-2.83	22.19-12.84	39.60-28.15	25.34-20.24	44.29-31.29	92.24-72.48	69.58-58.13	54.52-39.81
Average Yield %	5.35	4.82	4.33	5.21	5.80	6.53	7.18	8.10

Address: 400 East Cary St., Richmond, VA 23219 **Telephone:** 720-283-6120 **Web Site:** www.udrt.com	Officers: Robert C. Larson - Chairman James D. Klingbeil - Vice-Chairman **Transfer Agents:** ChaseMellon Shareholder Services, LLC, Pittsburgh, PA	No of Institutions: 291 **Shares:** 112,989,824 % Held: N/A

UGI CORP. (NEW)

Exchange	Symbol	Price	52Wk Range	Yield	P/E
NYS	UGI	$26.79 (5/29/2008)	29.30-23.78	2.87	12.70

*7 Year Price Score 105.11 *NYSE Composite Index=100 *12 Month Price Score 102.41

Interim Earnings (Per Share)

Qtr.	Dec	Mar	Jun	Sep
2004-05	0.75	1.12	0.01	(0.09)
2005-06	0.54	0.98	0.18	(0.04)
2006-07	0.58	1.12	0.11	0.09
2007-08	0.74	1.17	...	...

Interim Dividends (Per Share)

Amt	Decl	Ex	Rec	Pay
0.185Q	07/31/2007	09/12/2007	09/15/2007	10/01/2007
0.185Q	11/27/2007	12/12/2007	12/15/2007	01/01/2008
0.185Q	01/29/2008	03/12/2008	03/14/2008	04/01/2008
0.193Q	04/29/2008	06/12/2008	06/16/2008	07/01/2008

Indicated Div: $0.77 (Div. Reinv. Plan)

Valuation Analysis

Forecast EPS $1.95 (05/16/2008)

Market Cap	$2.9 Billion	Book Value	1.6 Billion
Price/Book	1.85	Price/Sales	0.47

Dividend Achiever Status

10 Year Growth Rate	4.25%
Total Years of Dividend Growth	20

Business Summary: Electricity (MIC: SIC: 4932 NAIC: 221210)

UGI is a holding company that distributes and markets energy products and related services via its subsidiaries and joint venture affiliates. Co. is a domestic and international distributor of propane and butane (liquefied petroleum gases); a provider of natural gas and electric service through regulated local distribution utilities; a generator of electricity through its ownership interests in electric generation facilities; a regional marketer of energy commodities; and a provider of heating, air conditioning, refrigeration and electrical services. Co.'s subsidiaries operate in five key segments: AmeriGas Propane, International Propane, Gas Utility, Electric Utility, and Energy Services.

Recent Developments: For the quarter ended Mar 31 2008, net income increased 4.9% to US$126.1 million from US$120.2 million in the year-earlier quarter. Revenues were US$2.36 billion, up 18.0% from US$2.00 billion the year before. Operating income was US$317.4 million versus US$300.5 million in the prior-year quarter, an increase of 5.6%. Direct operating expenses rose 23.1% to US$1.69 billion from US$1.37 billion in the comparable period the year before. Indirect operating expenses increased 7.5% to US$353.5 million from US$328.8 million in the equivalent prior-year period.

Prospects: On Mar 6 2008, Co. announced that its subsidiary, UGI Utilities, Inc., has signed a definitive agreement to acquire the stock of PPL Gas Utilities Corporation, a natural gas utility and retail propane distributor, for approximately $268.0 million plus working capital. Co. expects the acquisition to add to its natural gas and propane distribution businesses in Pennsylvania, including approximately 75,000 natural gas customers and 30,000 propane customers. The transaction is expected to close by Sep 30 2008 and to be accretive to earnings in the first full year of Co.'s ownership. Separately, for the fiscal year ending Sep 2008, Co. continues to expect earnings of $1.95 to $2.05 per share.

Financial Data
(US$ in Thousands)

	6 Mos	3 Mos	09/30/2007	09/30/2006	09/30/2005	09/30/2004	09/30/2003	09/30/2002
Earnings Per Share	2.11	2.06	1.89	1.65	1.77	1.16	1.15	0.90
Cash Flow Per Share	3.70	3.49	4.29	2.65	4.21	2.72	2.95	2.99
Dividends Per Share	...	...	...	0.690	0.650	0.600	...	...
Dividend Payout %	...	...	...	41.82	36.72	51.95	...	...
Income Statement								
Total Revenue	4,126,200	1,764,700	5,476,900	5,221,000	4,888,700	3,784,700	3,026,100	2,213,700
EBITDA	602,900	240,400	745,000	594,400	611,500	426,100	373,000	326,600
Depn & Amortn	90,700	44,900	167,500	147,400	144,700	131,000	103,000	93,500
Income Before Taxes	440,000	159,400	437,900	323,400	336,600	176,000	160,800	124,000
Income Taxes	127,600	48,500	126,700	98,500	119,200	64,400	60,700	46,900
Net Income	206,100	80,000	204,300	176,200	187,500	111,600	98,900	75,500
Average Shares	108,254	108,318	107,941	106,727	105,723	96,682	86,472	83,814
Balance Sheet								
Net PPE	2,475,200	2,419,000	2,397,400	2,214,700	1,802,700	1,781,900	1,336,800	1,271,900
Total Assets	6,127,500	6,068,100	5,502,700	5,080,500	4,571,500	4,235,400	2,781,700	2,614,400
Long-Term Obligations	2,047,700	2,052,500	2,038,800	1,965,000	1,392,500	1,547,300	1,158,500	1,127,000
Total Liabilities	4,323,400	4,451,100	3,988,600	3,841,400	3,367,600	3,222,900	2,077,300	2,001,100
Stockholders' Equity	1,551,100	1,403,300	1,321,900	1,099,600	997,600	834,100	569,800	317,300
Shares Outstanding	106,921	115,152	106,646	105,454	104,849	102,422	85,398	83,103
Statistical Record								
Return on Assets %	3.95	3.89	3.86	3.65	4.26	3.17	3.67	2.92
Return on Equity %	16.00	17.37	16.87	16.80	20.47	15.86	22.30	26.36
EBITDA Margin %	14.61	13.62	13.60	11.38	12.51	11.26	12.33	14.75
Net Margin %	4.99	4.53	3.73	3.37	3.84	2.95	3.27	3.41
PPE Turnover	2.58	2.48	2.38	2.60	2.73	2.42	2.32	1.74
Asset Turnover	1.06	1.01	1.04	1.08	1.11	1.08	1.12	0.86
Debt to Equity	1.32	1.46	1.54	1.79	1.40	1.86	2.03	3.55
Price Range	29.30-23.78	29.30-23.78	29.30-23.78	28.15-20.46	29.74-18.55	18.63-14.47	17.45-11.74	12.22-8.87
P/E Ratio	13.89-11.27	14.22-11.54	15.50-12.58	17.06-12.40	16.80-10.48	16.06-12.47	15.17-10.21	13.57-9.85
Average Yield %	0.70	0.69	...	2.99	2.74	3.69	...	...

| Address: 460 North Gulph Road, King of Prussia, PA 19406
Telephone: 610-337-1000
Web Site: www.ugicorp.com | Officers: Lon R. Greenberg - Chairman, Chief Executive Officer John L. Walsh - President, Chief Operating Officer, Acting Principal Financial Officer
Transfer Agents:Mellon Investor Services LLC | Investor Contact: 610-337-1000
No of Institutions: 265
Shares: 84,022,152 % Held: 72.09 |

UMB FINANCIAL CORP

Exchange	Symbol	Price	52Wk Range	Yield	P/E
NMS	UMBF	$52.43 (5/29/2008)	52.43-35.63	1.26	24.62

*7 Year Price Score 111.46 *NYSE Composite Index=100 *12 Month Price Score 117.85

Interim Earnings (Per Share)

Qtr.	Mar	Jun	Sep	Dec
2005	0.27	0.32	0.38	0.35
2006	0.31	0.35	0.37	0.37
2007	0.41	0.48	0.51	0.37
2008	0.78	...	...	...

Interim Dividends (Per Share)

Amt	Decl	Ex	Rec	Pay
0.14Q	07/24/2007	09/10/2007	09/12/2007	10/01/2007
0.15Q	10/23/2007	12/07/2007	12/11/2007	01/02/2008
0.15Q	01/22/2008	03/07/2008	03/11/2008	04/01/2008
0.165Q	04/22/2008	06/09/2008	06/11/2008	07/01/2008

Indicated Div: $0.66

Valuation Analysis

Forecast EPS $2.52 (05/16/2008)

Market Cap	$2.1 Billion	Book Value	923.8 Million
Price/Book	2.32	Price/Sales	2.99

Dividend Achiever Status

10 Year Growth Rate	5.37%
Total Years of Dividend Growth	16

Business Summary: Commercial Banking (MIC: SIC: 6021 NAIC: 522110)

UMB Financial is a financial holding company. As of Dec 31 2007, Co. owned all of the outstanding stock of four commercial banks, a brokerage company, a community development corporation, a consulting company, a mutual fund servicing company and 14 other subsidiaries. Co.'s four commercial banks are engaged in general commercial banking business entirely in domestic markets. One of the banks is in Missouri, one bank in Kansas, one bank in Colorado, and one bank in Arizona. Co.'s banks offer a full range of banking services to commercial, retail, government and correspondent bank customers. As of Dec 31 2007, Co. has total assets of $9.34 billion and total deposits of $6.55 billion.

Recent Developments: For the quarter ended Mar 31 2008, net income increased 86.8% to US$32.4 million from US$17.3 million in the year-earlier quarter. Net interest income increased 13.0% to US$64.4 million from US$57.0 million in the year-earlier quarter. Provision for loan losses was US$3.0 million versus US$1.5 million in the prior-year quarter, an increase of 100.0%. Non-interest income rose 26.0% to US$85.0 million from US$67.4 million, while non-interest expense advanced 1.1% to US$99.2 million.

Prospects: Co. is encouraged with its recent operating performance reflecting an increase in its revenue and earnings driven primarily by growth in its net interest income attributable mainly to higher volume of average earning assets and increasing net interest margin in a declining interest rate environment. Consequently, Co. believes that its future net interest margin improvements may be more moderate as the earning assets reprice in a lower rate condition. In the meantime, Co. anticipates the economy to remain soft and stronger competition for commercial loans in 2008 and, therefore, expects income growth in its commercial banking and lending segment to be at a measured pace during 2008.

Financial Data
(US$ in Thousands)

	3 Mos	12/31/2007	12/31/2006	12/31/2005	12/31/2004	12/31/2003	12/31/2002	12/31/2001
Earnings Per Share	2.13	1.77	1.40	1.30	0.98	1.35	1.29	1.48
Cash Flow Per Share	5.16	3.15	3.02	2.44	2.69	3.63	2.44	1.91
Tang Book Value Per Share	19.88	18.86	17.41	17.91	17.45	17.26	16.86	15.92
Dividends Per Share	0.580	0.570	0.515	0.455	0.425	0.405	0.400	0.381
Dividend Payout %	27.17	32.20	36.79	35.00	43.15	30.00	31.01	25.83
Income Statement								
Interest Income	103,114	414,413	369,083	271,911	220,402	239,762	294,483	384,839
Interest Expense	38,740	181,729	151,859	83,621	40,350	42,684	76,452	145,139
Net Interest Income	64,374	232,684	217,224	188,290	180,052	197,078	218,031	239,700
Provision for Losses	3,000	9,333	8,734	5,775	5,370	12,005	16,738	14,745
Non-Interest Income	84,989	288,788	254,945	251,873	226,861	245,568	232,206	222,068
Non-Interest Expense	99,226	407,164	381,417	358,069	349,808	354,654	360,949	367,889
Income Before Taxes	47,137	104,975	82,018	76,319	51,735	75,987	72,550	90,934
Income Taxes	14,781	30,762	22,251	20,001	8,896	17,108	15,377	25,704
Net Income	32,356	74,213	59,767	56,318	42,839	58,879	57,173	65,230
Average Shares	40,977	42,006	42,813	43,312	43,487	43,659	44,196	44,291
Balance Sheet								
Net Loans & Leases	4,084,590	3,883,379	3,722,639	3,352,579	2,826,501	2,678,798	2,636,458	2,778,121
Total Assets	8,935,417	9,342,959	8,917,765	8,247,789	7,805,006	7,748,981	8,035,559	8,730,932
Total Deposits	6,536,932	6,550,802	6,308,964	5,920,822	5,383,704	5,635,687	5,846,947	6,375,511
Total Liabilities	8,011,618	8,452,385	8,068,890	7,414,326	6,985,824	6,937,058	7,232,759	7,962,355
Stockholders' Equity	923,799	890,574	848,875	833,463	819,182	811,923	802,800	768,577
Shares Outstanding	40,932	41,327	42,266	42,981	43,282	43,388	43,965	44,402
Statistical Record								
Return on Assets %	1.05	0.81	0.70	0.70	0.55	0.75	0.68	0.79
Return on Equity %	9.99	8.53	7.11	6.82	5.24	7.29	7.28	8.87
Net Interest Margin %	62.43	56.15	58.86	69.25	81.69	82.20	74.04	62.29
Efficiency Ratio %	52.75	57.90	61.12	68.36	78.21	73.07	68.53	60.62
Loans to Deposits	0.62	0.59	0.59	0.57	0.53	0.48	0.45	0.44
Price Range	46.17-35.63	46.17-35.50	37.99-32.05	34.00-26.70	29.14-23.34	25.75-18.13	25.40-18.32	21.72-16.55
P/E Ratio	21.68-16.73	26.08-20.06	27.14-22.89	26.15-20.53	29.73-23.82	19.07-13.43	19.69-14.20	14.68-11.18
Average Yield %	1.45	1.45	1.49	1.52	1.68	1.86	1.91	2.01

Address: 1010 Grand Boulevard, Kansas City, MO 64106 **Telephone:** 816-860-7000 **Web Site:** www.umb.com	**Officers:** J. Mariner Kemper - Chairman, Chief Executive Officer, Region Officer Peter J. Genovese - Vice-Chairman, Region Officer **Transfer Agents:** Computershare Trust Company NA, Canton, MA	**Investor Contact:** 800-892-2434 **No of Institutions:** 153 **Shares:** 27,510,048 **% Held:** 65.14

UNITED BANKSHARES, INC.

Exchange	Symbol	Price	52Wk Range	Yield	P/E
NMS	UBSI	$28.45 (5/29/2008)	34.12-24.23	4.08	13.29

*7 Year Price Score 71.24 ***NYSE Composite Index=100** ***12 Month Price Score 97.54**

Interim Earnings (Per Share)

Qtr.	Mar	Jun	Sep	Dec
2005	0.57	0.57	0.59	0.60
2006	0.58	0.60	0.34	0.60
2007	0.59	0.60	0.60	0.36
2008	0.59	...	...	...

Interim Dividends (Per Share)

Amt	Decl	Ex	Rec	Pay
0.28Q	07/30/2007	09/12/2007	09/14/2007	10/01/2007
0.29Q	11/19/2007	12/12/2007	12/14/2007	01/02/2008
0.29Q	01/28/2008	03/12/2008	03/14/2008	04/01/2008
0.29Q	05/21/2008	06/11/2008	06/13/2008	07/01/2008

Indicated Div: $1.16 (Div. Reinv. Plan)

Valuation Analysis

Forecast EPS	$2.35 (05/16/2008)		
Market Cap	$1.2 Billion	Book Value	771.2 Million
Price/Book	1.60	Price/Sales	2.40

Dividend Achiever Status

10 Year Growth Rate	5.43%
Total Years of Dividend Growth	26

Business Summary: Commercial Banking (MIC: SIC: 6022 NAIC: 522110)

United Bankshares is a bank holding company with total assets of $7.99 billion and total deposits of $5.35 billion as of Dec 31 2007. Co. has two banking subsidiaries operating under the name of United Bank. These subsidiaries engage primarily in community banking. Banking services include the acceptance of deposits; the making and servicing of personal, commercial, floor plan and student loans; and the making of construction and real estate loans. Through United Brokerage Services, Inc., a wholly-owned subsidiary of United Bank (WV), Co. offers a range of investment products as well as financial planning and asset management services to the general public.

Recent Developments: For the quarter ended Mar 31 2008, net income increased 5.3% to US$25.7 million from US$24.4 million in the year-earlier quarter. Net interest income increased 18.3% to US$62.3 million from US$52.7 million in the year-earlier quarter. Provision for loan losses was US$2.1 million versus US$350,000 in the prior-year quarter, an increase of 500.0%. Non-interest income rose 24.8% to US$18.6 million from US$14.9 million, while non-interest expense advanced 31.3% to US$41.4 million.

Prospects: Co.'s near-term outlook appears encouraging, reflecting an increase in tax-equivalent net interest income primarily due to an increase in average earning assets primarily as a result of its Jul 2007 acquisition of Premier Community Bankshares, Inc. However, Co. is experiencing lower net interest margin, as well as lower average yield on earning assets due to the decrease in market interest rates. Looking ahead, Co. remains committed on its efforts to broaden the scope and activity of its trust and brokerage service areas, particularly in the northern Virginia market, to provide additional sources of fee income that complement its traditional banking products and services.

Financial Data
(US$ in Thousands)

	3 Mos	12/31/2007	12/31/2006	12/31/2005	12/31/2004	12/31/2003	12/31/2002	12/31/2001
Earnings Per Share	2.14	2.15	2.13	2.33	2.22	1.85	2.06	1.90
Cash Flow Per Share	1.74	1.94	2.15	2.66	2.17	11.70	(2.28)	(1.38)
Tang Book Value Per Share	10.61	10.39	11.37	11.13	10.80	10.20	10.73	11.80
Dividends Per Share	1.140	1.130	1.090	1.050	1.020	1.000	0.950	0.910
Dividend Payout %	53.19	52.56	51.17	45.06	45.95	54.05	46.12	47.89
Income Statement								
Income Before Taxes	37,430	129,909	130,016	146,674	117,086	112,520	128,333	118,730
Income Taxes	11,734	39,235	40,767	46,265	33,771	33,755	39,400	38,739
Net Income	25,696	90,674	89,249	100,409	97,762	78,765	88,933	79,991
Average Shares	43,418	42,222	41,942	43,024	43,978	42,620	43,113	42,064
Balance Sheet								
Total Assets	7,986,974	7,994,739	6,717,598	6,728,492	6,435,971	6,378,999	5,792,019	5,631,775
Total Liabilities	7,215,821	7,233,540	6,083,506	6,093,287	5,804,464	5,763,808	5,250,480	5,125,246
Stockholders' Equity	771,153	761,199	634,092	635,205	631,507	615,191	541,539	506,529
Shares Outstanding	43,260	43,234	41,058	42,008	43,008	43,689	42,031	42,926
Statistical Record								
Return on Assets %	1.26	1.23	1.33	1.53	1.52	1.29	1.56	1.52
Return on Equity %	13.01	13.00	14.06	15.85	15.64	13.62	16.97	17.07
Price Range	35.21-24.53	39.14-25.84	39.46-34.50	38.48-30.00	39.18-29.35	31.53-26.97	32.01-26.24	28.86-20.19
P/E Ratio	16.45-11.46	18.20-12.02	18.53-16.20	16.52-12.88	17.65-13.22	17.04-14.58	15.54-12.74	15.19-10.63
Average Yield %	3.75	3.48	2.94	3.01	3.11	3.38	3.23	3.65

Address: 300 United Center, 500 Virginia Street East, Charleston, WV 25301 **Telephone:** 304-424-8800 **Web Site:** www.ubsi-wv.com	**Officers:** Richard M. Adams - Chairman, Chief Executive Officer Steven E. Wilson - Executive Vice President, Chief Financial Officer, Treasurer, Secretary **Transfer Agents:**Mellon Investor Services LLC, Ridgefield Park, NJ	**Investor Contact:** 304-424-8704 **No of Institutions:** 170 **Shares:** 23,306,328 **% Held:** 47.92

U.S. BANCORP (DE)

Exchange	Symbol	Price	52Wk Range	Yield	P/E
NYS	USB	$33.28 (5/29/2008)	34.93-28.44	5.11	13.75

*7 Year Price Score 90.86 *NYSE Composite Index=100 *12 Month Price Score 105.55

Interim Earnings (Per Share)

Qtr.	Mar	Jun	Sep	Dec
2005	0.57	0.60	0.62	0.62
2006	0.63	0.66	0.66	0.66
2007	0.63	0.65	0.67	0.49
2008	0.62	...	...	...

Interim Dividends (Per Share)

Amt	Decl	Ex	Rec	Pay
0.40Q	06/19/2007	06/27/2007	06/29/2007	07/16/2007
0.40Q	09/18/2007	09/26/2007	09/28/2007	10/15/2007
0.425Q	12/11/2007	12/27/2007	12/31/2007	01/15/2008
0.425Q	03/18/2008	03/27/2008	03/31/2008	04/15/2008

Indicated Div: $1.70

Valuation Analysis

Forecast EPS $2.55 (05/17/2008)

Market Cap	$57.8 Billion	Book Value	21.6 Billion
Price/Book	2.68	Price/Sales	2.81

Dividend Achiever Status

10 Year Growth Rate	19.33%
Total Years of Dividend Growth	36

Business Summary: Commercial Banking (MIC: SIC: 6021 NAIC: 522110)

U.S. Bancorp is a financial services holding company. Co. is engaged in providing a range of financial services, including lending and depository services through banking offices principally in 24 states at Dec 31 2007. Co. also engages in credit card services, merchant and ATM processing, mortgage banking, insurance, trust and investment management, brokerage, and leasing activities principally in domestic markets. Co. has five reportable operating segments: Wholesale Banking; Consumer Banking; Wealth Management and Securities Services; Payment Services; and Treasury and Corporate Support. As of Dec 31 2007, Co. had total assets of $237.62 billion and total deposits of $131.45 billion.

Recent Developments: For the quarter ended Mar 31 2008, net income decreased 3.5% to US$1.09 billion from US$1.13 billion in the year-earlier quarter. Net interest income increased 9.3% to US$1.80 billion from US$1.65 billion in the year-earlier quarter. Provision for loan losses was US$485.0 million versus US$177.0 million in the prior-year quarter, an increase of 174.0%. Non-interest income rose 18.6% to US$2.04 billion from US$1.72 billion, while non-interest expense advanced 14.2% to US$1.80 billion.

Prospects: On Mar 28 2008, Co. announced that its key bank, U.S. Bank National Association, has agreed to purchase a subsidiary of The Bank of New York Mellon Corp., Mellon 1st Business Bank in California. Through this transaction, Co. will acquire $3.40 billion in assets, $1.10 billion in loans and $2.70 billion in deposits. The acquisition, which should extend Co.'s deposit market position in the Los Angeles area and its middle market customer base, is expected to close by the end of the second quarter of 2008, and to be integrated in the fourth quarter of 2008. Separately, given the existing rate environment and yield curve, Co. expects its net interest margin to remain relatively stable in 2008.

Financial Data

(US$ in Thousands)	3 Mos	12/31/2007	12/31/2006	12/31/2005	12/31/2004	12/31/2003	12/31/2002	12/31/2001
Earnings Per Share	2.42	2.43	2.61	2.42	2.18	1.93	1.71	0.88
Cash Flow Per Share	1.54	1.50	3.05	1.86	2.76	4.51	1.98	1.13
Tang Book Value Per Share	5.42	5.41	5.34	5.62	5.87	5.77	4.93	4.64
Dividends Per Share	1.650	1.625	1.390	1.230	1.020	0.855	0.780	0.750
Dividend Payout %	68.10	66.87	53.26	50.83	46.79	44.30	45.61	85.23
Income Statement								
Income Before Taxes	1,566,000	6,207,000	6,863,000	6,571,000	6,176,400	5,651,400	5,102,700	2,634,200
Income Taxes	476,000	1,883,000	2,112,000	2,082,000	2,009,600	1,941,300	1,776,300	927,700
Net Income	1,090,000	4,324,000	4,751,000	4,489,000	4,166,800	3,732,600	3,289,200	1,706,500
Average Shares	1,749,000	1,758,000	1,804,000	1,857,000	1,912,900	1,936,200	1,926,100	1,939,500
Balance Sheet								
Total Assets	241,781,000	237,615,000	219,232,000	209,465,000	195,104,000	189,286,000	180,027,000	171,390,000
Total Liabilities	220,209,000	216,569,000	198,035,000	189,379,000	175,565,000	170,044,000	161,926,000	154,929,000
Stockholders' Equity	21,572,000	21,046,000	21,197,000	20,086,000	19,539,000	19,242,000	18,101,000	16,461,000
Shares Outstanding	1,738,018	1,727,856	1,764,714	1,814,954	1,857,622	1,922,920	1,916,956	1,951,709
Statistical Record								
Return on Assets %	1.84	1.89	2.22	2.22	2.16	2.02	1.87	1.32
Return on Equity %	20.16	20.47	23.02	22.66	21.43	19.99	19.03	13.60
Price Range	35.03-28.44	36.68-29.26	36.69-29.03	31.32-27.16	31.53-25.13	29.35-18.71	24.10-16.02	25.25-16.57
P/E Ratio	14.48-11.75	15.09-12.04	14.06-11.12	12.94-11.22	14.46-11.53	15.21-9.69	14.09-9.37	28.70-18.83
Average Yield %	5.05	4.85	4.35	4.17	3.60	3.64	3.70	3.48

Address: 800 Nicollet Mall, Minneapolis, MN 55402 Telephone: 651-466-3000 Web Site: www.usbank.com	Officers: Richard K. Davis - Chairman, President, Chief Executive Officer Andrew Cecere - Vice-Chairman, Chief Financial Officer **Transfer Agents:**BNY Mellon Shareowner Services, Pittsburgh, PA	Investor Contact: 612-303-0783 No of Institutions: 1016 Shares: 1,158,903,424 % Held: 61.96

UNITED TECHNOLOGIES CORP.

Exchange	Symbol	Price	52Wk Range	Yield	P/E
NYS	UTX	$70.23 (5/29/2008)	82.07-66.23	1.82	15.71

*7 Year Price Score 114.24 *NYSE Composite Index=100 *12 Month Price Score 100.20

Interim Earnings (Per Share)

Qtr.	Mar	Jun	Sep	Dec
2005	0.64	0.95	0.81	0.63
2006	0.76	1.09	0.99	0.87
2007	0.82	1.16	1.21	1.08
2008	1.03	...	...	...

Interim Dividends (Per Share)

Amt	Decl	Ex	Rec	Pay
0.32Q	06/13/2007	08/15/2007	08/17/2007	09/10/2007
0.32Q	10/10/2007	11/14/2007	11/16/2007	12/10/2007
0.32Q	02/04/2008	02/13/2008	02/15/2008	03/10/2008
0.32Q	04/09/2008	05/14/2008	05/16/2008	06/10/2008

Indicated Div: $1.28 (Div. Reinv. Plan)

Valuation Analysis
Forecast EPS $4.88 (05/17/2008)

Market Cap	$68.3 Billion	Book Value	21.6 Billion
Price/Book	3.17	Price/Sales	1.22

Dividend Achiever Status

10 Year Growth Rate	14.20%
Total Years of Dividend Growth	14

Business Summary: Aviation (MIC: SIC: 3724 NAIC: 336412)

United Technologies has six principal segments: Otis, which is an elevator and escalator manufacturing, installation and service company; Carrier, a manufacturer and distributor of heating, ventilation, and air conditioning and refrigeration systems; UTC Fire & Security, which provides security and fire safety products and services; Pratt & Whitney, which is engaged as a supplier of commercial, general aviation and military aircraft engines; Hamilton Sundstrand, which supplies aerospace and industrial products and aftermarket services; and Sikorsky, which is a manufacturer of military and commercial helicopters and a provider of aftermarket helicopter and aircraft parts and services.

Recent Developments: For the quarter ended Mar 31 2008, net income increased 22.1% to US$1.00 billion from US$819.0 million in the year-earlier quarter. Revenues were US$13.70 billion, up 11.6% from US$12.28 billion the year before. Operating income was US$1.67 billion versus US$1.50 billion in the prior-year quarter, an increase of 11.3%. Direct operating expenses rose 10.9% to US$9.98 billion from US$9.00 billion in the comparable period the year before. Indirect operating expenses increased 15.1% to US$2.05 billion from US$1.78 billion in the equivalent prior-year period.

Prospects: On Mar 2 2008, Co. announced that it has made a proposal to the Board of Directors of Diebold, Incorporated (Diebold), a provider of integrated self-service delivery systems, to acquire all the outstanding shares of Diebold for $40.00 per share in cash, representing a total enterprise value of about $3.00 billion, which was rejected by the Diebold Board of Directors. Despite the initial rejection, this proposal remains outstanding. Moving forward, Co. continues to expect to invest about $2.00 billion in acquisitions for 2008. Meanwhile, for the full-year 2008, Co. expects revenue growth of $59.00 billion with earnings per share in the range of $4.65 to $4.85, or 9.0% to 14.0% over 2007.

Financial Data
(US$ in Millions)

	3 Mos	12/31/2007	12/31/2006	12/31/2005	12/31/2004	12/31/2003	12/31/2002	12/31/2001
Earnings Per Share	4.47	4.27	3.71	3.03	2.76	2.35	2.21	1.92
Cash Flow Per Share	6.04	5.53	4.90	4.37	3.72	3.03	3.02	3.07
Tang Book Value Per Share	1.35	1.50	N.M.	0.91	1.84	2.31	1.46	1.66
Dividends Per Share	1.225	1.170	1.015	0.880	0.700	0.568	0.490	0.450
Dividend Payout %	27.42	27.40	27.36	29.04	25.36	24.20	22.17	23.50
Income Statement								
Total Revenue	13,701	54,759	47,829	42,725	37,445	31,034	28,212	27,897
EBITDA	1,993	8,223	7,131	6,166	5,448	4,644	4,384	4,138
Depn & Amortn	319	1,173	1,033	984	978	799	727	905
Income Before Taxes	1,509	6,384	5,492	4,684	4,107	3,470	3,276	2,807
Income Taxes	430	1,836	1,494	1,253	1,085	941	887	755
Net Income	1,000	4,224	3,732	3,069	2,788	2,361	2,236	1,938
Average Shares	975	988	1,005	1,014	1,010	1,005	1,011	1,010
Balance Sheet								
Current Assets	23,916	22,071	18,844	17,206	15,522	12,364	11,751	11,263
Total Assets	57,053	54,575	47,141	45,925	40,035	34,648	29,090	26,969
Current Liabilities	19,605	17,469	15,208	15,345	12,947	10,295	7,903	8,371
Long-Term Obligations	8,014	8,015	7,037	5,935	4,231	4,257	4,632	4,237
Total Liabilities	34,483	32,308	29,008	28,156	26,027	22,941	20,735	18,600
Stockholders' Equity	21,586	21,355	17,297	16,991	14,008	11,707	8,355	8,369
Shares Outstanding	973	983	955	1,013	1,022	1,028	939	944
Statistical Record								
Return on Assets %	8.32	8.31	8.02	7.14	7.45	7.41	7.98	7.41
Return on Equity %	22.13	21.86	21.77	19.80	21.62	23.54	26.74	24.18
EBITDA Margin %	14.55	15.02	14.91	14.43	14.55	14.96	15.54	14.83
Net Margin %	7.30	7.71	7.80	7.18	7.45	7.61	7.93	6.95
Asset Turnover	1.06	1.08	1.03	0.99	1.00	0.97	1.01	1.07
Current Ratio	1.22	1.26	1.24	1.12	1.20	1.20	1.49	1.35
Debt to Equity	0.37	0.38	0.41	0.35	0.30	0.36	0.55	0.51
Price Range	82.07-64.08	82.07-62.47	66.79-54.47	58.03-48.77	52.76-40.75	47.77-27.07	38.63-24.59	43.60-20.82
P/E Ratio	18.36-14.34	19.22-14.63	18.00-14.68	19.15-16.10	19.12-14.76	20.33-11.52	17.48-11.13	22.71-10.84
Average Yield %	1.68	1.64	1.65	1.70	1.52	1.56	1.50	1.29

Address: One Financial Plaza, Hartford, CT 06103 **Telephone:** 860-728-7000 **Web Site:** www.utc.com	**Officers:** George David - Chairman Louis R. Chenevert - President, Chief Executive Officer, Chief Operating Officer **Transfer Agents:** Computershare Trust Company, N.A., Canton, MA	**No of Institutions:** 1316 **Shares:** 886,846,912 **% Held:** 78.52

UNIVERSAL CORP.

Exchange	Symbol	Price	52Wk Range	Yield	P/E
NYS	UVV	$50.80 (5/29/2008)	67.08-44.48	3.54	13.92

*7 Year Price Score 95.39   ***NYSE Composite Index=100**   ***12 Month Price Score 112.92**

TRADING VOLUME (thousand shares)

Interim Earnings (Per Share)

Qtr.	Jun	Sep	Dec	Mar
2004-05	0.80	0.54	1.08	1.31
2005-06	0.46	1.03	(0.22)	(0.96)
2006-07	(0.23)	0.09	0.79	0.59
2007-08	0.54	1.23	1.56	0.33

Interim Dividends (Per Share)

Amt	Decl	Ex	Rec	Pay
0.44Q	08/07/2007	10/04/2007	10/09/2007	11/12/2007
0.45Q	11/07/2007	01/10/2008	01/14/2008	02/11/2008
0.45Q	02/05/2008	04/10/2008	04/14/2008	05/12/2008
0.45Q	05/22/2008	07/10/2008	07/14/2008	08/11/2008

Indicated Div: $1.80 (Div. Reinv. Plan)

Valuation Analysis

Forecast EPS $4.55 (05/16/2008)

Market Cap	$1.4 Billion	Book Value	1.1 Billion
Price/Book	1.24	Price/Sales	0.64

Dividend Achiever Status

10 Year Growth Rate	5.20%
Total Years of Dividend Growth	37

Business Summary: Tobacco Products (MIC: SIC: 5159 NAIC: 424590)

Universal is engaged in selecting, buying, processing, packing, storing, shipping, and financing leaf tobacco for sale to, or for the account of, manufacturers of consumer tobacco products throughout the world. Through various operating subsidiaries and unconsolidated affiliates located in tobacco-growing countries globally, Co. processes and/or sells flue-cured and burley tobaccos, dark air-cured tobaccos, and oriental tobaccos. Co. also provides other services, such as blending, chemical and physical testing of tobacco, providing inventory management, as well as manufacturing reconstituted sheet tobacco. Co. has three segments: North America, Other Regions and Other Tobacco Operations

Recent Developments: For the year ended Mar 31 2008, income from continuing operations increased 48.4% to US$119.3 million from US$80.4 million a year earlier. Net income increased 168.7% to US$119.2 million from US$44.4 million in the prior year. Revenues were US$2.15 billion, up 6.9% from US$2.01 billion the year before. Operating income was US$191.5 million versus US$163.6 million in the prior year, an increase of 17.1%. Direct operating expenses rose 9.7% to US$1.72 billion from US$1.56 billion in the comparable period the year before. Indirect operating expenses decreased 14.8% to US$238.6 million from US$280.2 million in the equivalent prior-year period.

Prospects: Co.'s near-term outlook appears to be mixed. For the fiscal year ending Mar 31 2009, Co. foresees that flue-cured crops should be sufficient to address future demand, despite available inventory reaching lower levels. However, Co. anticipates no carryover of shipments in its African operations as it is seeing low inventory levels. Further, Co. expects to experience higher costs in most of the major producing areas of the world. Specifically, Co. estimates paying higher price for green tobacco as well as other agricultural products as farmers begin increasing production costs. Lastly, Co. projects that the weakening U.S. dollar will further challenge its operating results going forward.

Financial Data

(US$ in Thousands)	03/31/2008	03/31/2007	03/31/2006	03/31/2005	03/31/2004	06/30/2003	06/30/2002	06/30/2001
Earnings Per Share	3.70	1.13	0.31	3.73	3.94	4.34	4.00	4.08
Cash Flow Per Share	3.31	9.48	2.46	(3.41)	(1.39)	(1.76)	6.41	5.85
Tang Book Value Per Share	29.30	26.47	24.67	26.66	24.57	19.56	17.64	15.77
Dividends Per Share	1.770	1.730	1.690	1.590	1.470	1.400	1.320	1.260
Dividend Payout %	47.84	153.10	545.16	42.63	37.31	32.26	33.00	30.88
Income Statement								
Total Revenue	2,145,822	2,007,272	3,511,332	3,276,057	2,271,152	2,636,776	2,500,078	3,017,579
EBITDA	248,253	226,131	187,755	298,338	246,537	271,758	273,805	305,370
Depn & Amortn	43,240	48,305	68,139	74,133	48,867	53,504	54,987	56,936
Income Before Taxes	180,283	134,877	38,323	165,953	162,638	172,934	170,987	187,395
Income Taxes	63,799	61,126	34,403	68,197	59,329	53,094	59,821	66,336
Net Income	119,156	44,352	7,940	96,013	99,636	110,594	106,662	112,669
Average Shares	32,186	26,051	25,957	25,717	25,277	25,499	26,680	27,645
Balance Sheet								
Current Assets	1,417,060	1,545,365	1,802,598	1,788,808	1,526,669	1,374,997	1,105,037	1,132,646
Total Assets	2,134,112	2,328,822	2,901,341	2,885,324	2,482,773	2,243,074	1,844,415	1,782,373
Current Liabilities	402,326	692,974	937,806	969,761	739,110	824,281	673,431	581,765
Long-Term Obligations	402,942	398,952	762,201	838,687	770,296	614,994	435,592	515,349
Total Liabilities	1,015,299	1,292,267	1,918,671	2,027,691	1,722,940	1,622,796	1,256,420	1,230,244
Stockholders' Equity	1,115,631	1,030,733	964,871	822,388	759,833	620,278	587,995	552,129
Shares Outstanding	27,162	26,948	25,748	25,668	25,446	24,920	26,224	27,184
Statistical Record								
Return on Assets %	5.33	1.70	0.27	3.58	5.60	5.41	5.88	6.38
Return on Equity %	11.07	4.44	0.89	12.14	19.16	18.31	18.71	21.46
EBITDA Margin %	11.57	11.27	5.35	9.11	10.86	10.31	10.95	10.12
Net Margin %	5.55	2.21	0.23	2.93	4.39	4.19	4.27	3.73
Asset Turnover	0.96	0.77	1.21	1.22	1.28	1.29	1.38	1.71
Current Ratio	3.52	2.23	1.92	1.84	2.07	1.67	1.64	1.95
Debt to Equity	0.36	0.39	0.79	1.02	1.01	0.99	0.74	0.93
Price Range	67.08-44.48	61.35-35.02	48.21-36.17	53.01-42.25	52.32-40.78	43.01-31.81	43.05-31.74	41.30-20.63
P/E Ratio	18.13-12.02	54.29-30.99	155.52-116.68	14.21-11.33	13.28-10.35	9.91-7.33	10.76-7.93	10.12-5.06
Average Yield %	3.18	4.12	3.97	3.34	3.27	3.73	3.48	3.91

Address: 1501 North Hamilton Street, Richmond, VA 23230	**Officers:** Allen B. King - Chairman, Chief Executive Officer George C. Freeman - President **Transfer**	**Investor Contact:** 804-359-9311
Telephone: 804-359-9311	**Agents:** Wells Fargo Bank, N.A., St. Paul, MN	**No of Institutions:** 210
Web Site: www.universalcorp.com		**Shares:** 28,034,024 **% Held:** 99.02

UNIVERSAL FOREST PRODUCTS INC.

Exchange	Symbol	Price	52Wk Range	Yield	P/E
NMS	UFPI	$34.05 (5/29/2008)	48.64-26.60	0.35	52.38

*7 Year Price Score 75.47 *NYSE Composite Index=100 ***12 Month Price Score 99.42**

Interim Earnings (Per Share)

Qtr.	Mar	Jun	Sep	Dec
2005	0.49	1.20	1.00	0.84
2006	0.82	1.41	0.91	0.48
2007	0.20	0.86	0.59	(0.56)
2008	(0.24)	...	...	...

Interim Dividends (Per Share)

Amt	Decl	Ex	Rec	Pay
0.055S	10/18/2006	11/29/2006	12/01/2006	12/15/2006
0.055S	05/02/2007	05/30/2007	06/01/2007	06/15/2007
0.06S	10/18/2007	11/28/2007	12/01/2007	12/15/2007
0.06S	04/16/2008	05/28/2008	06/01/2008	06/15/2008
		Indicated Div: $0.12		

Valuation Analysis

Forecast EPS $1.06 (5/16/2008)

Market Cap	$644.9 Million	Book Value	533.0 Million
Price/Book	1.21	Price/Sales	0.26

Dividend Achiever Status

10 Year Growth Rate	5.87%
Total Years of Dividend Growth	14

TRADING VOLUME (thousand shares)

Business Summary: Wood Products (MIC: SIC: 2421 NAIC: 321113)

Universal Forest Products is engaged in the marketing, manufacturing and engineering of wood and wood-alternative products for the do-it-yourself/retail market, structural lumber products for the manufactured housing market, engineered wood components for the site-built construction market, and specialty wood packaging for various markets. In addition, Co. provides framing services for the site-built construction market and various forms for concrete construction. Co.'s principal products include preservative-treated wood, remanufactured lumber, lattice, fence panels, deck components, specialty packaging, engineered trusses, wall panels, and other building products.

Recent Developments: For the quarter ended Mar 29 2008, net loss amounted to US$4.6 million versus net income of US$3.9 million in the year-earlier quarter. Revenues were US$489.5 million, down 10.8% from US$549.0 million the year before. Operating loss was US$4.5 million versus an income of US$10.1 million in the prior-year quarter. Direct operating expenses declined 8.6% to US$434.7 million from US$475.5 million in the comparable period the year before. Indirect operating expenses decreased 6.5% to US$59.4 million from US$63.5 million in the equivalent prior-year period.

Prospects: Co.'s outlook for 2008 appears somewhat mixed. On one hand, Co. noted that consumer spending on home improvement remains weak and expects this market to remain soft throughout the year. Also, Co. is seeing a decline in single-family housing starts. However, Co. is seeing growth in multifamily and non-residential construction. Co. also expects to see growth in its industrial business, and expects to grow its concrete forming business. Moreover, in manufactured housing, Co. believes that the passage of a lending reform package should positively affect this market. For 2008, Co. is targeting net sales of $2.45 billion to $2.55 billion, and net earnings of $22.0 million to $27.0 million.

Financial Data

(US$ in Thousands)	3 Mos	12/29/2007	12/30/2006	12/31/2005	12/25/2004	12/27/2003	12/28/2002	12/29/2001
Earnings Per Share	0.65	1.09	3.62	3.53	2.59	2.18	1.97	1.63
Cash Flow Per Share	5.74	4.58	8.12	3.97	2.79	3.97	0.93	3.96
Tang Book Value Per Share	18.51	19.17	17.72	15.72	12.50	9.71	7.45	6.06
Dividends Per Share	0.115	0.115	0.110	0.105	0.100	0.095	0.090	0.085
Dividend Payout %	17.63	10.55	3.04	2.97	3.86	4.36	4.57	5.21
Income Statement								
Total Revenue	489,512	2,513,178	2,664,572	2,691,522	2,453,281	1,898,830	1,639,899	1,530,353
EBITDA	7,350	101,073	163,267	159,641	128,515	107,563	97,832	90,233
Depn & Amortn	11,881	47,581	39,522	34,796	30,836	27,547	24,639	24,476
Income Before Taxes	(7,752)	38,609	112,135	110,772	83,059	65,792	62,115	54,300
Income Taxes	(3,350)	15,396	38,760	41,050	31,462	24,325	22,983	19,612
Net Income	(4,576)	21,045	70,125	67,373	48,603	40,119	36,637	33,142
Average Shares	18,996	19,362	19,370	19,106	18,771	18,379	18,619	20,377
Balance Sheet								
Current Assets	504,187	500,525	475,135	502,178	406,483	332,313	294,097	234,966
Total Assets	961,442	957,000	913,441	876,920	762,360	684,757	634,794	551,209
Current Liabilities	181,486	162,725	192,222	204,151	183,865	141,878	108,841	110,895
Long-Term Obligations	194,277	205,126	169,417	209,039	185,109	205,049	235,319	154,370
Total Liabilities	428,445	420,332	398,699	445,068	405,591	380,008	371,794	284,347
Stockholders' Equity	532,997	536,668	514,742	431,852	356,769	304,749	263,000	230,862
Shares Outstanding	18,940	18,907	18,858	18,402	18,002	17,813	17,741	17,787
Statistical Record								
Return on Assets %	1.26	2.26	7.86	8.09	6.74	6.10	6.20	6.41
Return on Equity %	2.39	4.01	14.86	16.81	14.73	14.17	14.88	14.24
EBITDA Margin %	1.50	4.02	6.13	5.93	5.24	5.66	5.97	5.90
Net Margin %	N.M.	0.84	2.63	2.50	1.98	2.11	2.23	2.17
Asset Turnover	2.45	2.69	2.98	3.23	3.40	2.89	2.77	2.96
Current Ratio	2.78	3.08	2.47	2.46	2.21	2.34	2.70	2.12
Debt to Equity	0.36	0.38	0.33	0.48	0.52	0.67	0.89	0.67
Price Range	52.62-26.60	54.46-28.22	79.96-43.81	60.40-37.37	43.50-26.69	31.74-15.23	26.86-16.08	23.00-13.00
P/E Ratio	80.95-40.92	49.96-25.89	22.09-12.10	17.11-10.59	16.80-10.31	14.56-6.99	13.63-8.16	14.11-7.98
Average Yield %	0.31	0.28	0.19	0.23	0.31	0.42	0.42	0.48

Address: 2801 East Beltline N.E., Grand Rapids, MI 49525	Officers: William G. Currie - Executive Chairman	No of Institutions: 157
Telephone: 616-364-6161	Michael B. Glenn - President, Chief Executive Officer	Shares: 18,925,932 % Held: 91.53
Web Site: www.ufpi.com	Transfer Agents:American Stock Transfer & Trust Company, New York, NY	

UNIVERSAL HEALTH REALTY INCOME TRUST

Exchange	Symbol	Price	52Wk Range	Yield	P/E
NYS	UHT	$33.78 (5/29/2008)	38.76-29.23	6.93	19.64

*7 Year Price Score 86.20 ***NYSE Composite Index=100** ***12 Month Price Score 101.22**

TRADING VOLUME (thousand shares)

Interim Earnings (Per Share)

Qtr.	Mar	Jun	Sep	Dec
2005	0.64	0.52	0.54	0.44
2006	0.42	0.58	1.32	0.60
2007	0.49	0.67	0.37	0.34
2008	0.35	...	...	...

Interim Dividends (Per Share)

Amt	Decl	Ex	Rec	Pay
0.575Q	09/06/2007	09/13/2007	09/17/2007	09/28/2007
0.58Q	12/03/2007	12/13/2007	12/17/2007	12/31/2007
0.58Q	03/07/2008	03/13/2008	03/17/2008	03/31/2008
0.585Q	06/05/2008	06/12/2008	06/16/2008	06/30/2008

Indicated Div: $2.34 (Div. Reinv. Plan)

Valuation Analysis

Forecast EPS	N/A		
Market Cap	$400.2 Million	Book Value	157.8 Million
Price/Book	2.54	Price/Sales	14.39

Dividend Achiever Status

10 Year Growth Rate	3.04%
Total Years of Dividend Growth	20

Business Summary: "Property, Real Estate & Development" (MIC: SIC: 6798 NAIC: 525930)

Universal Health Realty Income Trust is an organized Maryland real estate investment trust (REIT). As of Dec 31 2007, Co. had 46 real estate investments or commitments located in 14 states in the U.S. consisting of: six hospital facilities including three acute care, one behavioral healthcare, one rehabilitation and one sub-acute; 36 medical office buildings (including three being constructed); and; four preschool and childcare centers. Four of Co.'s hospital facilities are leased to subsidiaries of Universal Health Services, Inc. (UHS). As of Dec 31 2007, UHS owned 6.7% of Co.'s outstanding shares of beneficial interest.

Recent Developments: For the quarter ended Mar 31 2008, income from continuing operations decreased 26.6% to US$4.2 million from US$5.7 million in the year-earlier quarter. Net income decreased 28.4% to US$4.2 million from US$5.8 million in the year-earlier quarter. Revenues were US$7.0 million, unchanged from the year before.

Prospects: Notwithstanding a decrease in net income primarily due to lower revenues and higher interest expense, as well as lower Funds from Operations, Co. is encouraged by the continued improvement of leasing activity at the Canyon Springs Medical Plaza and Centennial Hills Medical Office Building I, which are multi-tenant facilities, as these facilities continue their initial lease-up. In addition, Co. is continuing with the construction on three new medical office buildings located respectively in Palmdale, CA, Las Vegas, NV, and Phoenix, AZ, which are scheduled to be completed and opened during the second quarter of 2008, the fourth quarter of 2008, and the second quarter of 2009, respectively.

Financial Data
(US$ in Thousands)

	3 Mos	12/31/2007	12/31/2006	12/31/2005	12/31/2004	12/31/2003	12/31/2002	12/31/2001
Earnings Per Share	1.72	1.87	2.92	2.15	2.00	2.07	1.84	1.74
Cash Flow Per Share	1.88	1.93	2.10	2.15	2.29	2.48	2.25	2.17
Tang Book Value Per Share	13.32	13.54	13.92	13.20	13.10	12.97	12.73	12.85
Dividends Per Share	2.310	2.300	2.260	2.175	2.000	1.960	1.920	1.875
Dividend Payout %	134.10	122.99	77.40	101.16	100.00	94.69	104.35	107.76
Income Statement								
Total Revenue	6,979	27,960	32,509	33,338	31,777	28,313	28,429	27,574
Depn & Amortn	1,406	5,209	5,757	5,825	5,312	4,536	4,431	4,401
Net Income	4,158	22,191	34,697	25,423	23,671	24,425	21,623	18,349
Average Shares	11,881	11,875	11,866	11,841	11,813	11,779	11,750	10,536
Balance Sheet								
Total Assets	210,857	199,749	194,139	196,889	204,583	194,291	185,117	187,904
Long-Term Obligations	23,892	36,617	26,337	35,548	46,210	...	...	1,446
Total Liabilities	52,976	39,357	29,873	41,137	50,291	42,093	36,255	37,870
Stockholders' Equity	157,795	160,305	164,197	155,450	154,053	152,198	148,862	150,034
Shares Outstanding	11,848	11,841	11,791	11,777	11,755	11,736	11,698	11,678
Statistical Record								
Return on Assets %	10.11	11.27	17.75	12.66	11.84	12.88	11.59	9.88
Return on Equity %	12.73	13.68	21.71	16.43	15.42	16.23	14.47	14.72
Net Margin %	59.58	79.37	106.73	76.26	74.49	86.27	76.06	66.54
Price Range	38.76-29.23	42.05-29.23	40.24-29.72	40.80-27.47	34.50-24.82	30.55-25.30	28.50-22.69	25.70-18.94
P/E Ratio	22.53-16.99	22.49-15.63	13.78-10.18	18.98-12.78	17.25-12.41	14.76-12.22	15.49-12.33	14.77-10.88
Average Yield %	6.71	6.48	6.50	6.56	6.66	7.19	7.59	8.48

Address: Universal Corporate Center, 367 South Gulph Road, King of Prussia, PA 19406-0958
Telephone: 610-265-0688
Web Site: www.uhrit.com

Officers: Alan B. Miller - Chairman, President, Chief Executive Officer Charles F. Boyle - Vice President, Chief Financial Officer **Transfer Agents:** EquiServe Trust Company, N.A., Providence, RI

No of Institutions: 109
Shares: 5,323,916 **% Held:** 42.84

UNIVEST CORP. OF PENNSYLVANIA (SOUDERTON)

Exchange	Symbol	Price	52Wk Range	Yield	P/E
NMS	UVSP	$24.00 (5/29/2008)	28.48-18.21	3.33	11.94

*7 Year Price Score 72.18 *NYSE Composite Index=100 *12 Month Price Score 114.63

TRADING VOLUME (thousand shares)

Interim Earnings (Per Share)

Qtr.	Mar	Jun	Sep	Dec
2005	0.44	0.46	0.51	0.49
2006	0.48	0.46	0.50	0.51
2007	0.48	0.47	0.52	0.51
2008	0.52	...	...	...

Interim Dividends (Per Share)

Amt	Decl	Ex	Rec	Pay
0.20Q	08/17/2007	09/04/2007	09/06/2007	10/01/2007
0.20Q	11/21/2007	12/04/2007	12/06/2007	01/02/2008
0.20Q	02/27/2008	03/10/2008	03/12/2008	04/01/2008
0.20Q	05/28/2008	06/09/2008	06/11/2008	07/01/2008

Indicated Div: $0.80

Valuation Analysis

Forecast EPS	N/A		
Market Cap	$308.2 Million	Book Value	203.3 Million
Price/Book	1.52	Price/Sales	2.15

Dividend Achiever Status

10 Year Growth Rate	15.90%
Total Years of Dividend Growth	17

Business Summary: Commercial Banking (MIC: SIC: 6022 NAIC: 522110)

Univest Corporation of Pennsylvania is a bank holding company. Through its wholly owned subsidiary, Univest National Bank and Trust Co. (the Bank), Co. is engaged in the general commercial banking business and provides a range of banking services and trust services to its customers. The Bank wholly owns Delview, Inc., who through its subsidiaries, Univest Investments, Inc. and Univest Insurance, Inc., provides financial planning, investment management, insurance products and brokerage services. The Bank serves the Montgomery, Bucks and Chester counties of Pennsylvania. As of Dec 31 2007, Co. had total assets of $1.97 billion, and total deposits of $1.53 billion.

Recent Developments: For the quarter ended Mar 31 2008, net income increased 7.6% to US$6.7 million from US$6.2 million in the year-earlier quarter. Net interest income increased 3.1% to US$15.9 million from US$15.4 million in the year-earlier quarter. Provision for loan losses was US$999,000 versus US$624,000 in the prior-year quarter, an increase of 60.1%. Non-interest income rose 10.7% to US$7.7 million from US$6.9 million, while non-interest expense advanced 3.4% to US$13.6 million.

Prospects: Co.'s recent bottom-line performance has been positively affected by increases in its net interest income as well as non-interest income. Specifically, growth in Co.'s net interest income is attributable to higher volumes on lease financings, federal funds sold and other securities, partially offset by a reduction in volume and rates on commercial loans, growth in volume and rates on regular savings deposits as well as decreased volume on certificates of deposit. In addition, Co. is seeing improvement in its non-interest income as a result of the increases in trust fee income, insurance commissions and fee income and life insurance income.

Financial Data

(US$ in Thousands)	3 Mos	12/31/2007	12/31/2006	12/31/2005	12/31/2004	12/31/2003	12/31/2002	12/31/2001
Earnings Per Share	2.01	1.98	1.95	1.91	1.80	1.78	1.61	1.44
Cash Flow Per Share	1.73	2.57	1.46	2.70	2.53	0.44	1.77	1.61
Tang Book Value Per Share	12.16	11.82	10.59	10.02	9.08	7.90	10.41	9.24
Dividends Per Share	0.800	0.800	0.780	0.717	0.667	0.427	0.393	0.350
Dividend Payout %	39.71	40.40	40.00	37.52	37.04	23.97	24.33	24.30
Income Statement								
Interest Income	28,093	116,533	105,166	85,502	74,789	71,965	73,040	79,208
Interest Expense	12,162	54,127	43,651	26,264	18,948	21,150	25,814	34,441
Net Interest Income	15,931	62,406	61,515	59,238	55,841	50,815	47,226	44,767
Provision for Losses	999	2,166	2,215	2,109	1,622	1,000	1,303	763
Non-Interest Income	7,657	26,879	25,417	22,444	22,603	23,480	20,593	17,966
Non-Interest Expense	13,608	52,211	49,958	45,796	44,920	42,023	37,790	35,789
Income Before Taxes	8,981	34,908	34,759	33,777	31,902	31,272	28,726	26,181
Income Taxes	2,260	9,351	9,382	8,910	8,311	8,190	7,620	6,971
Net Income	6,721	25,557	25,377	24,867	23,591	23,082	21,106	19,210
Average Shares	12,854	12,911	13,011	13,008	13,087	12,967	13,068	13,447
Balance Sheet								
Net Loans & Leases	1,344,890	1,342,356	1,340,398	1,236,289	1,161,081	1,049,594	814,860	788,035
Total Assets	2,059,572	1,972,505	1,929,501	1,769,309	1,666,957	1,657,168	1,325,865	1,260,713
Total Deposits	1,616,843	1,532,603	1,488,545	1,366,715	1,270,884	1,270,268	1,043,106	998,137
Total Liabilities	1,856,309	1,773,779	1,744,116	1,596,229	1,506,564	1,511,416	1,192,412	1,139,133
Stockholders' Equity	203,263	198,726	185,385	173,080	160,393	145,752	133,453	121,580
Shares Outstanding	12,843	12,830	13,005	12,947	12,863	12,819	12,824	13,164
Statistical Record								
Return on Assets %	1.30	1.31	1.37	1.45	1.42	1.55	1.63	1.56
Return on Equity %	13.24	13.31	14.16	14.91	15.37	16.53	16.55	16.22
Net Interest Margin %	56.71	53.55	58.49	69.28	74.66	70.61	64.66	56.52
Efficiency Ratio %	38.06	36.41	38.26	42.42	46.12	44.03	40.36	36.83
Loans to Deposits	0.83	0.88	0.90	0.90	0.91	0.83	0.78	0.79
Price Range	26.87-18.21	31.23-18.21	31.41-24.06	31.12-22.57	36.60-25.83	28.30-21.33	21.65-18.72	18.88-11.87
P/E Ratio	13.37-9.06	15.77-9.20	16.11-12.34	16.29-11.82	20.33-14.35	15.90-11.99	13.45-11.63	13.11-8.24
Average Yield %	3.53	3.40	2.85	2.17	2.17	1.85	1.96	2.17

Address: 14 North Main Street, Souderton, PA 18964	Officers: William S. Aichele - Chairman, President, Chief Executive Officer K. Leon Moyer - Senior	No of Institutions: 57
Telephone: 215-721-2400	Executive Vice President **Transfer Agents:**	**Shares:** 3,798,833 % **Held:** 28.61
Web Site: www.univest.net	StockTrans Inc., Ardmore, PA	

VALLEY NATIONAL BANCORP

Exchange	Symbol	Price	52Wk Range	Yield	P/E
NYS	VLY	$17.69 (5/29/2008)	23.52-16.71	4.52	16.53

*7 Year Price Score 72.38   *NYSE Composite Index=100   *12 Month Price Score 95.87

Interim Earnings (Per Share)

Qtr.	Mar	Jun	Sep	Dec
2005	0.32	0.31	0.33	0.34
2006	0.32	0.32	0.34	0.30
2007	0.39	0.31	0.29	0.22
2008	0.25	...	...	...

Interim Dividends (Per Share)

Amt	Decl	Ex	Rec	Pay
0.20Q	11/16/2007	12/05/2007	12/07/2007	01/02/2008
0.20Q	02/29/2008	03/05/2008	03/07/2008	04/01/2008
5%	04/07/2008	05/07/2008	05/09/2008	05/23/2008
0.20Q	05/15/2008	06/04/2008	06/06/2008	07/01/2008

Indicated Div: $0.80 (Div. Reinv. Plan)

Valuation Analysis

Forecast EPS	$1.06 (05/16/2008)	
Market Cap	$2.2 Billion	Book Value 958.8 Million
Price/Book	2.32	Price/Sales 2.83

Dividend Achiever Status

10 Year Growth Rate	6.44%
Total Years of Dividend Growth	16

TRADING VOLUME (thousand shares)

Business Summary: Commercial Banking (MIC: SIC: 6021 NAIC: 522110)

Valley National Bancorp is a bank holding company. Co.'s principal subsidiary, Valley National Bank, provides a range of commercial and retail banking services, including: the acceptance of demand, savings and time deposits; extension of consumer, real estate, Small Business Administration loans and other commercial credits; equipment leasing; and personal and corporate trust, as well as pension and fiduciary services. In addition, Co. owns 100.0% of the voting shares of VNB Capital Trust I, through which it issued trust preferred securities. As of Dec 31 2007, Co. had total assets of $12.75 billion, and total deposits of $8.09 billion.

Recent Developments: For the quarter ended Mar 31 2008, net income decreased 36.1% to US$31.6 million from US$49.4 million in the year-earlier quarter. Net interest income decreased 0.6% to US$95.6 million from US$96.2 million in the year-earlier quarter. Provision for loan losses was US$4.0 million versus US$1.9 million in the prior-year quarter, an increase of 109.4%. Non-interest income fell 46.4% to US$22.0 million from US$41.1 million, while non-interest expense advanced 9.4% to US$70.3 million.

Prospects: On Mar 19 2008, Co. announced an agreement to acquire Greater Community Bancorp, the holding company for Greater Community Bank, for approximately $167.0 million. The purchase should strengthen Co.'s deposit market position in particularly New Jersey counties of Bergen, Passaic and Morris. The transaction, which will be accretive to Co.'s earnings within the first full year of operations, is expected to close late in the third quarter of 2008. Meanwhile, Co. expects its cost of funds to further decline in the second quarter of 2008 as higher cost time deposits mature and reprice at lower rates. Separately, Co. anticipates opening nine additional de novo branches through the rest of 2008.

Financial Data
(US$ in Thousands)

	3 Mos	12/31/2007	12/31/2006	12/31/2005	12/31/2004	12/31/2003	12/31/2002	12/31/2001
Earnings Per Share	1.07	1.21	1.27	1.29	1.28	1.27	1.23	1.03
Cash Flow Per Share	9.77	7.77	1.80	0.92	1.34	1.86	0.91	1.25
Tang Book Value Per Share	6.00	5.92	5.80	5.54	5.51	5.01	5.21	5.30
Dividends Per Share	0.800	0.795	0.775	0.755	0.732	0.697	0.662	0.622
Dividend Payout %	75.08	65.73	61.04	58.68	57.01	54.89	53.76	60.27
Income Statement								
Income Before Taxes	43,331	204,926	203,575	230,227	228,595	233,150	219,296	199,355
Income Taxes	11,748	51,698	39,884	66,778	74,197	79,735	64,680	64,151
Net Income	31,583	153,228	163,691	163,449	154,398	153,415	154,616	135,204
Average Shares	126,021	126,646	129,012	126,588	120,552	120,606	125,531	130,724
Balance Sheet								
Total Assets	12,961,211	12,748,959	12,395,027	12,436,102	10,763,391	9,880,740	9,134,674	8,583,765
Total Liabilities	12,002,439	11,799,899	11,445,437	11,504,192	10,055,793	9,227,951	8,302,936	7,705,390
Stockholders' Equity	958,772	949,060	949,590	931,910	707,598	652,789	631,738	678,375
Shares Outstanding	125,932	125,844	127,181	128,874	120,159	119,856	121,309	128,092
Statistical Record								
Return on Assets %	1.07	1.22	1.32	1.41	1.49	1.61	1.75	1.80
Return on Equity %	14.28	16.14	17.40	19.94	22.64	23.89	23.60	22.10
Price Range	23.70-16.71	23.98-16.89	24.49-20.01	22.89-19.03	23.40-19.87	23.48-17.91	21.60-18.24	19.67-14.58
P/E Ratio	22.15-15.62	19.82-13.96	19.28-15.75	17.74-14.75	18.28-15.52	18.49-14.10	17.56-14.83	19.10-14.15
Average Yield %	3.93	3.69	3.43	3.63	3.39	3.31	3.25	3.68

Address: 1455 Valley Road, Wayne, NJ 07470	Officers: Gerald H. Lipkin - Chairman, President, Chief Executive Officer Stephen P. Davey - Senior	Investor Contact: 973-305-8800
Telephone: 973-305-8800	Vice President **Transfer Agents:**	No of Institutions: 159
Web Site: www.valleynationalbank.com	American Stock Transfer & Trust Company	Shares: 35,138,044 % Held: 27.56

VALSPAR CORP.

Exchange	Symbol	Price	52Wk Range	Yield	P/E
NYS	VAL	$22.29 (5/29/2008)	29.22-18.13	2.51	14.29

*7 Year Price Score 79.53 *NYSE Composite Index=100 *12 Month Price Score 91.65

Interim Earnings (Per Share)

Qtr.	Jan	Apr	Jul	Oct
2004-05	0.11	0.38	0.44	0.50
2005-06	0.22	0.46	0.51	0.51
2006-07	0.18	0.35	0.52	0.45
2007-08	0.21	0.38	...	...

Interim Dividends (Per Share)

Amt	Decl	Ex	Rec	Pay
0.13Q	06/20/2007	06/28/2007	07/02/2007	07/13/2007
0.13Q	08/21/2007	09/27/2007	10/01/2007	10/15/2007
0.14Q	12/12/2007	12/27/2007	12/31/2007	01/14/2008
0.14Q	02/27/2008	03/28/2008	04/01/2008	04/15/2008

Indicated Div: $0.56 (Div. Reinv. Plan)

Valuation Analysis

Forecast EPS	$1.60 (05/17/2008)		
Market Cap	$2.2 Billion	Book Value	1.4 Billion
Price/Book	1.56	Price/Sales	0.66

Dividend Achiever Status

10 Year Growth Rate	11.19%
Total Years of Dividend Growth	29

TRADING VOLUME (thousand shares)

Business Summary: Chemicals (MIC: SIC: 2851 NAIC: 325510)

Valspar is engaged in the business of manufacturing and distributing a portfolio of coatings, paints and related products globally. In addition, Co. manufactures and sells specialty polymers, colorants and gelcoats, as well as sells furniture protection plans. As of Oct 26 2007, Co. conducted its businesses through two operating segments. Co.'s Coatings segment includes a range of decorative and protective coatings for metal, wood, plastic and glass, primarily for sale to original equipment manufacturer customers. Co.'s Paint segment provides a portfolio of interior and exterior paints, stains, primers, varnishes, high performance floor paints and specialty decorative products.

Recent Developments: For the quarter ended Apr 25 2008, net income decreased 1.6% to US$40.8 million from US$41.5 million in the year-earlier quarter. Revenues were US$836.4 million, up 3.5% from US$808.5 million the year before. Operating income was US$77.1 million versus US$78.2 million in the prior-year quarter, a decrease of 1.4%. Direct operating expenses rose 5.4% to US$592.1 million from US$561.6 million in the comparable period the year before. Indirect operating expenses decreased 0.9% to US$167.2 million from US$168.7 million in the equivalent prior-year period.

Prospects: Co.'s near-term outlook appears mixed. Co.'s gross margins are being hurt by higher raw material costs. Conversely, Co.'s recent results are benefiting from solid performances of its packaging, coil and general industrial coatings product lines, which partially offset the weak demand in its architectural and wood product lines, resulting from the decline in the U.S. residential construction and housing markets. Looking ahead, Co. anticipates that demand in U.S. will remain soft during the fiscal year ending Oct 31 2008. In response, Co. intends to focus on reducing costs, gaining new business and investing in its long-term growth opportunities while implementing its pricing initiatives.

Financial Data
(US$ in Thousands)

	6 Mos	3 Mos	10/26/2007	10/27/2006	10/28/2005	10/29/2004	10/31/2003	10/25/2002
Earnings Per Share	1.56	1.53	1.50	1.71	1.42	1.36	1.09	1.17
Cash Flow Per Share	2.61	2.36	1.89	2.82	2.27	2.40	2.44	2.16
Dividends Per Share	0.540	0.530	0.520	0.440	0.400	0.360	0.300	0.280
Dividend Payout %	34.53	34.60	34.67	25.73	28.17	26.57	27.65	23.93
Income Statement								
Total Revenue	1,601,503	765,124	3,249,287	2,978,062	2,713,950	2,440,692	2,247,926	2,126,853
EBITDA	167,530	71,776	393,244	372,354	338,637	330,473	282,939	298,402
Depn & Amortn	39,388	19,429	71,811	68,716	68,395	60,537	55,622	51,143
Income Before Taxes	98,545	36,664	259,771	257,432	225,720	228,537	181,474	198,548
Income Taxes	33,683	12,649	87,656	82,180	78,102	85,701	68,960	78,427
Net Income	64,862	24,015	172,115	175,252	147,618	142,836	112,514	120,121
Average Shares	100,180	100,940	102,617	102,726	104,149	105,418	103,848	102,740
Balance Sheet								
Current Assets	1,098,124	1,049,314	1,029,642	967,123	865,204	802,315	738,831	701,788
Total Assets	3,611,535	3,545,120	3,452,281	3,188,253	2,761,163	2,634,258	2,496,524	2,419,552
Current Liabilities	937,165	923,613	1,029,147	1,195,683	625,631	718,211	531,063	503,895
Long-Term Obligations	807,900	801,695	648,988	350,267	706,415	549,073	749,199	885,819
Total Liabilities	2,143,587	2,121,318	2,034,142	1,929,467	1,700,071	1,633,895	1,627,207	1,682,299
Stockholders' Equity	1,424,778	1,383,546	1,380,797	1,240,063	1,061,092	1,000,363	869,317	737,253
Shares Outstanding	99,438	100,169	100,634	101,904	100,432	102,608	101,461	100,208
Statistical Record								
Return on Assets %	4.94	5.06	5.20	5.91	5.49	5.58	4.50	5.19
Return on Equity %	12.89	12.95	13.17	15.27	14.36	15.32	13.78	17.31
EBITDA Margin %	10.46	9.38	12.10	12.50	12.48	13.54	12.59	14.03
Net Margin %	4.05	3.14	5.30	5.88	5.44	5.85	5.01	5.65
Asset Turnover	0.96	0.97	0.98	1.00	1.01	0.95	0.90	0.92
Current Ratio	1.17	1.14	1.00	0.81	1.38	1.12	1.39	1.39
Debt to Equity	0.57	0.58	0.47	0.28	0.67	0.55	0.86	1.20
Price Range	29.22-18.13	29.22-18.13	29.22-24.57	29.42-21.80	25.38-20.57	25.68-22.43	23.98-18.84	24.95-16.61
P/E Ratio	18.73-11.62	19.10-11.85	19.48-16.38	17.20-12.75	17.87-14.49	18.88-16.50	22.00-17.29	21.33-14.19
Average Yield %	2.19	2.01	1.88	1.68	1.68	1.71	1.37	1.33

Address: 1101 Third Street South,	Officers: William L. Mansfield - Chairman, Chief	No of Institutions: 253
Minneapolis, MN 55415	Executive Officer Gary E. Hendrickson - President,	Shares: 87,866,480 % Held: 77.23
Telephone: 612-332-7371	Chief Operating Officer Transfer Agents:	
Web Site: www.valsparglobal.com	Mellon Investor Services LLC, Jersey City, NJ	

VECTREN CORP

Exchange	Symbol	Price	52Wk Range	Yield	P/E
NYS	VVC	$29.04 (5/29/2008)	30.41-24.96	4.48	16.22

*7 Year Price Score 83.62 *NYSE Composite Index=100 *12 Month Price Score 104.00

Interim Earnings (Per Share)

Qtr.	Mar	Jun	Sep	Dec
2005	0.74	0.18	0.22	0.67
2006	0.76	0.06	0.16	0.46
2007	0.92	0.21	0.22	0.52
2008	0.84	...	...	...

Interim Dividends (Per Share)

Amt	Decl	Ex	Rec	Pay
0.315Q	08/01/2007	08/13/2007	08/15/2007	09/04/2007
0.325Q	10/31/2007	11/13/2007	11/15/2007	12/03/2007
0.325Q	01/30/2008	02/13/2008	02/15/2008	03/03/2008
0.325Q	05/01/2008	05/13/2008	05/15/2008	06/02/2008

Indicated Div: $1.30 (Div. Reinv. Plan)

Valuation Analysis

Forecast EPS	$1.92 (05/16/2008)
Market Cap	$2.2 Billion	Book Value	1.3 Billion
Price/Book	1.75	Price/Sales	0.95

Dividend Achiever Status

10 Year Growth Rate	3.86%
Total Years of Dividend Growth	32

Business Summary: Electricity (MIC: SIC: 4932 NAIC: 221210)

Vectren is an energy holding company. Co.'s wholly owned subsidiary, Vectren Utility Holdings, Inc. (Utility Holdings), serves as the intermediate holding company for three operating public utilities: Indiana Gas Company, Inc., which provides energy delivery services to natural gas customers in central and southern Indiana; Southern Indiana Gas and Electric Co., which provides energy delivery services to electric and gas customers in southwestern Indiana; and the Ohio operations, which provide energy delivery services to natural gas customers in west central Ohio. Utility Holdings also has other assets that provide information technology and related services to the three utilities.

Recent Developments: For the quarter ended Mar 31 2008, net income decreased 8.7% to US$64.0 million from US$70.1 million in the year-earlier quarter. Revenues were US$902.1 million, up 8.2% from US$834.0 million the year before. Operating income was US$108.8 million versus US$95.6 million in the prior-year quarter, an increase of 13.8%. Direct operating expenses rose 9.2% to US$508.0 million from US$465.1 million in the comparable period the year before. Indirect operating expenses increased 4.4% to US$285.3 million from US$273.3 million in the equivalent prior-year period.

Prospects: Co. is projecting consolidated earnings for 2008 to range from $1.75 to $1.95 per share, compared with its December 2007 guidance of $1.85 to $2.05 per share. These expectations are based on normal weather in Co.'s electric business for the rest of 2008, and an assumption of recent lower price volatility throughout 2008 in the wholesale natural gas markets affecting its ProLiance Holdings, LLC joint venture. This estimate also includes projected earnings from the Utility Group of $1.46 to $1.54 per share versus prior estimate $1.35 to $1.45 per share, from the Nonutility Group of $0.31 to $0.42 per share over previous range of $0.52 to $0.62 per share, as well as Corporate and Other.

Financial Data
(US$ in Thousands)

	3 Mos	12/31/2007	12/31/2006	12/31/2005	12/31/2004	12/31/2003	12/31/2002	12/31/2001
Earnings Per Share	1.79	1.87	1.43	1.80	1.42	1.57	1.68	0.95
Cash Flow Per Share	4.88	3.93	4.10	3.55	3.18	2.51	4.32	2.75
Tang Book Value Per Share	13.44	13.05	12.30	12.32	11.70	11.46	9.83	9.68
Dividends Per Share	1.280	1.270	1.230	1.190	1.150	1.110	1.070	1.030
Dividend Payout %	71.60	67.91	86.01	66.11	80.99	70.70	63.69	108.42
Income Statement								
Total Revenue	902,100	2,281,900	2,041,600	2,028,000	1,689,800	1,587,700	1,804,300	2,170,000
EBITDA	173,200	495,800	397,800	416,700	357,200	344,200	341,100	293,700
Depn & Amortn	47,400	184,800	172,300	158,200	140,100	128,700	119,600	123,700
Income Before Taxes	100,500	219,200	139,200	181,000	147,000	149,000	153,400	87,400
Income Taxes	36,500	76,000	30,300	44,100	39,000	37,700	38,900	18,600
Net Income	64,000	143,100	108,800	136,800	107,900	111,200	114,000	63,600
Average Shares	76,500	76,600	76,200	76,100	75,900	70,800	67,900	66,900
Balance Sheet								
Net PPE	2,891,500	2,860,000	2,679,900	2,492,200	2,385,400	2,226,000	1,876,100	1,776,700
Total Assets	4,150,000	4,296,400	4,091,600	3,868,100	3,586,900	3,353,400	2,926,500	2,856,800
Long-Term Obligations	1,329,100	1,245,400	1,208,000	1,198,000	1,016,600	1,072,800	954,200	1,014,000
Total Liabilities	2,884,900	3,062,700	2,917,400	2,724,800	2,492,000	2,281,500	2,056,300	2,007,700
Stockholders' Equity	1,265,100	1,233,700	1,174,200	1,143,300	1,094,800	1,071,700	869,900	848,600
Shares Outstanding	76,400	76,300	76,100	76,000	75,900	75,600	67,900	67,700
Statistical Record								
Return on Assets %	3.39	3.41	2.73	3.67	3.10	3.54	3.94	2.21
Return on Equity %	11.00	11.89	9.39	12.22	9.93	11.45	13.27	8.05
EBITDA Margin %	19.20	21.73	19.48	20.55	21.14	21.68	18.90	13.53
Net Margin %	7.09	6.27	5.33	6.75	6.39	7.00	6.32	2.93
PPE Turnover	0.84	0.82	0.79	0.83	0.73	0.77	0.99	1.26
Asset Turnover	0.58	0.54	0.51	0.54	0.49	0.51	0.62	0.75
Debt to Equity	1.05	1.01	1.03	1.05	0.93	1.00	1.10	1.19
Price Range	30.41-24.96	30.41-24.96	29.25-25.61	29.32-25.39	27.08-22.90	26.00-20.01	25.87-18.69	24.19-19.90
P/E Ratio	16.99-13.94	16.26-13.35	20.45-17.91	16.29-14.11	19.07-16.13	16.56-12.75	15.40-11.13	25.46-20.95
Average Yield %	4.59	4.52	4.52	4.35	4.61	4.81	4.49	4.70

Address: One Vectren Square, Evansville, IN 47708 Telephone: 812-491-4000 Web Site: www.vectren.com	Officers: Niel C. Ellerbrook - Chairman, Chief Executive Officer Carl L. Chapman - President, Chief Operating Officer Transfer Agents: National City Bank, Cleveland, OH	Investor Contact: 800-227-8625 No of Institutions: 260 Shares: 44,986,436 % Held: 55.65

VF CORP.

*7 Year Price Score 112.78 *NYSE Composite Index=100 *12 Month Price Score 97.54

Interim Earnings (Per Share)

Qtr.	Mar	Jun	Sep	Dec
2005	1.07	0.88	1.59	0.89
2006	1.14	0.88	1.75	0.95
2007	1.20	0.72	1.84	1.46
2008	1.33	...	...	...

Interim Dividends (Per Share)

Amt	Decl	Ex	Rec	Pay
0.55Q	07/19/2007	09/06/2007	09/10/2007	09/20/2007
0.58Q	10/18/2007	12/06/2007	12/10/2007	12/20/2007
0.58Q	02/05/2008	03/06/2008	03/10/2008	03/20/2008
0.58Q	04/22/2008	06/06/2008	06/10/2008	06/20/2008
Indicated Div: $2.32 (Div. Reinv. Plan)				

Valuation Analysis

Forecast EPS	$5.94 (05/16/2008)		
Market Cap	$8.4 Billion	Book Value	3.7 Billion
Price/Book	2.30	Price/Sales	1.14

Dividend Achiever Status

10 Year Growth Rate	11.22%
Total Years of Dividend Growth	35

TRADING VOLUME (thousand shares)

Business Summary: Apparel (MIC: SIC: 2329 NAIC: 315228)

VF is an apparel company that is engaged in designing and manufacturing or sourcing from independent contractors a range of apparel and footwear for all ages. As of Dec 31 2007, Co. had five product categories that comprised of Jeanswear, Outdoor, Imagewear, Sportswear and Contemporary Brands. Co.'s products are marketed to consumers shopping in specialty stores, upscale and traditional department stores, national chains and mass merchants. Co.'s brand include: Lee®, Rustler®, Wrangler®, Wrangler Hero®, Timber Creek by Wrangler®, Riders®, JanSport®, The North Face®, Eastpak®, Vans®, Napapijri®, Reef®, Eagle Creek®, Kipling®, Red Kap®, John Varvatos®, and Nautica®.

Recent Developments: For the quarter ended Mar 29 2008, income from continuing operations increased 11.2% to US$149.0 million from US$134.1 million in the year-earlier quarter. Net income increased 7.7% to US$149.0 million from US$138.3 million in the year-earlier quarter. Revenues were US$1.85 billion, up 10.3% from US$1.67 billion the year before. Operating income was US$244.1 million versus US$215.3 million in the prior-year quarter, an increase of 13.4%. Direct operating expenses rose 7.2% to US$1.01 billion from US$945.9 million in the comparable period the year before. Indirect operating expenses increased 14.8% to US$588.1 million from US$512.4 million in the equivalent prior-year period.

Prospects: Looking ahead, Co. expects continued strong revenue growth in the 2008 second quarter, with an anticipated growth of 10.0%. However, Co. estimates a decline in operating margins by 200 basis points from the 11.0% reported over the same period in 2007. In the meantime, Co. expects strong revenue comparisons and a continuation of double-digit earnings per share growth in the second half of 2008, driven by strong profitability in its global businesses, continued growth in its retail revenues and profits as well as the seasonal benefit to revenues from its Outdoor business. For 2008, Co. is maintaining its guidance for revenue growth of 9.0% along with earnings per share increase of 10.0%.

Financial Data
(US$ in Thousands)

	3 Mos	12/29/2007	12/30/2006	12/31/2005	01/01/2005	01/03/2004	01/04/2003	12/29/2001
Earnings Per Share	5.36	5.22	4.72	4.44	4.21	3.61	(1.38)	1.19
Cash Flow Per Share	7.22	7.45	4.45	5.06	6.66	5.06	5.82	6.18
Tang Book Value Per Share	8.30	7.38	12.62	7.77	6.57	8.61	10.91	9.97
Dividends Per Share	2.260	2.230	1.940	1.100	1.050	1.010	0.970	0.930
Dividend Payout %	42.14	42.72	41.10	24.77	24.94	27.98	...	78.15
Income Statement								
Total Revenue	1,846,341	7,219,359	6,215,794	6,502,377	6,054,536	5,207,459	5,083,523	5,518,805
EBITDA	281,198	1,090,028	936,880	949,470	921,773	756,437	735,330	518,289
Depn & Amortn	37,223	121,646	108,377	116,233	140,717	108,019	109,674	168,972
Income Before Taxes	223,472	905,570	777,238	770,813	712,120	598,506	561,728	262,801
Income Taxes	74,440	292,324	242,187	252,278	237,418	200,573	197,300	124,971
Net Income	149,032	591,621	533,516	506,702	474,702	397,933	(154,543)	137,830
Average Shares	111,877	113,348	113,040	114,192	112,730	110,323	112,336	114,764
Balance Sheet								
Current Assets	2,778,483	2,645,129	2,578,010	2,365,376	2,378,568	2,208,531	2,074,540	2,031,420
Total Assets	6,642,143	6,446,685	5,465,693	5,171,071	5,004,278	4,245,552	3,503,151	4,103,016
Current Liabilities	1,238,533	1,134,387	1,014,848	1,152,143	1,372,214	871,857	874,844	813,833
Long-Term Obligations	1,143,620	1,144,810	635,359	647,728	556,639	956,383	602,287	904,035
Total Liabilities	2,990,717	2,869,856	2,200,521	2,339,532	2,464,984	2,264,258	1,808,401	1,944,589
Stockholders' Equity	3,651,426	3,576,829	3,265,172	2,808,213	2,513,241	1,951,307	1,657,848	2,112,796
Shares Outstanding	108,923	109,797	112,184	110,107	111,388	108,170	108,525	109,998
Statistical Record								
Return on Assets %	9.81	9.96	10.06	9.99	10.29	10.30	N.M.	3.27
Return on Equity %	17.50	17.34	17.62	19.10	21.32	22.11	N.M.	6.42
EBITDA Margin %	15.23	15.10	15.07	14.60	15.22	14.53	14.46	9.39
Net Margin %	8.07	8.19	8.58	7.79	7.84	7.64	N.M.	2.50
Asset Turnover	1.20	1.22	1.17	1.28	1.31	1.35	1.32	1.31
Current Ratio	2.24	2.33	2.54	2.05	1.73	2.53	2.37	2.50
Debt to Equity	0.31	0.32	0.19	0.23	0.22	0.49	0.36	0.43
Price Range	95.65-63.79	95.65-68.90	82.60-53.66	61.52-50.85	55.38-42.36	44.05-32.85	45.33-32.09	41.99-28.61
P/E Ratio	17.85-11.90	18.32-13.20	17.50-11.37	13.86-11.45	13.15-10.06	12.20-9.10	...	35.29-24.04
Average Yield %	2.75	2.67	2.92	1.93	2.17	2.64	2.43	2.56

Address: 105 Corporate Center Boulevard, Greensboro, NC 27408	**Officers:** Mackey J. McDonald - Chairman, Chief Executive Officer Eric C. Wiseman - President, Chief Operating Officer **Transfer Agents:** EquiServe Trust Company, Jersey City, NJ	**No of Institutions:** 481
Telephone: 336-424-6000 **Web Site:** www.vfc.com		**Shares:** 91,237,200 **% Held:** 72.21

VORNADO REALTY TRUST

Exchange	Symbol	Price	52Wk Range	Yield	P/E
NYS	VNO	$98.15 (5/29/2008)	121.01-78.74	3.67	20.71

*7 Year Price Score 106.49 *NYSE Composite Index=100 *12 Month Price Score 96.98

Interim Earnings (Per Share)

Qtr.	Mar	Jun	Sep	Dec
2005	1.39	1.25	0.19	0.71
2006	0.91	0.99	0.76	0.69
2007	0.96	0.96	0.74	0.58
2008	2.47	...	...	...

Interim Dividends (Per Share)

Amt	Decl	Ex	Rec	Pay
0.85Q	05/17/2007	08/07/2007	08/09/2007	08/22/2007
0.90Q	07/26/2007	10/10/2007	10/12/2007	10/26/2007
0.90Q	01/16/2008	01/28/2008	01/30/2008	02/20/2008
0.90Q	05/01/2008	05/08/2008	05/12/2008	05/22/2008
		Indicated Div: $3.60		

Valuation Analysis

Forecast EPS	$3.29 (05/16/2008)		
Market Cap	$15.1 Billion	Book Value	6.4 Billion
Price/Book	2.36	Price/Sales	4.74

Dividend Achiever Status

10 Year Growth Rate	9.76%
Total Years of Dividend Growth	14

Business Summary: "Property, Real Estate & Development" (MIC: SIC: 6798 NAIC: 525930)

Vornado Realty Trust is a fully-integrated real estate investment trust. As of Dec 31 2007, Co. owned directly or indirectly all or portions of 111 office properties aggregating about 33.6 million square feet in the New York City metropolitan area and in the Washington, DC and Northern Virginia areas; 177 retail properties in 21 states, Washington, DC and Puerto Rico; nine properties in five states and Washington, DC aggregating about 9.1 million square feet of showroom and office space; a 47.6% interest in Americold Realty Trust; a 32.7% interest in Toys "R" Us, Inc.; 32.8% of the common stock of Alexander's, Inc.; as well as various other interests in other real estate.

Recent Developments: For the quarter ended Mar 31 2008, net income increased 146.9% to US$412.2 million from US$166.9 million in the year-earlier quarter. Revenues were US$652.5 million, up 21.7% from US$536.2 million the year before. Revenues from property income rose 21.9% to US$542.8 million from US$445.4 million in the corresponding quarter a year earlier.

Prospects: Moving forward, Co. plans to achieve its business objective by continuing to execute its operating strategies via investing in properties in select markets such as New York City and Washington, DC, acquiring properties at a discount to replacement cost and where there is a significant potential for higher rents, investing in retail properties in select under-stored locations such as the New York City metropolitan area and developing and redeveloping its existing properties. Meanwhile, on Mar 31 2008, Co. has completed the sale of its 47.6% interest in Americold Realty Trust, its Temperature Controlled Logistics segment for $220.0 million, which resulted in a net gain of $112.6 million.

Financial Data
(US$ in Thousands)

	3 Mos	12/31/2007	12/31/2006	12/31/2005	12/31/2004	12/31/2003	12/31/2002	12/31/2001
Earnings Per Share	4.74	3.23	3.35	3.50	4.35	3.80	1.91	2.47
Cash Flow Per Share	5.45	4.59	5.80	5.70	5.29	4.71	4.72	4.35
Tang Book Value Per Share	36.19	34.58	35.22	31.38	26.95	23.90	21.74	21.22
Dividends Per Share	3.500	3.450	3.790	3.900	3.050	2.910	2.660	2.629
Dividend Payout %	73.85	106.81	113.13	111.43	70.11	76.58	139.27	106.44
Income Statement								
Total Revenue	652,521	3,270,629	2,712,095	2,547,628	1,707,262	1,503,055	1,435,070	985,773
Depn & Amortn	133,691	462,635	389,348	332,978	239,252	210,864	220,692	123,862
Income Before Taxes	131,009	587,502	...	...	...	...	...	...
Income Taxes	(217,329)	10,530	...	...	...	...	...	...
Net Income	412,197	568,906	560,140	539,604	592,917	460,703	232,903	263,738
Average Shares	163,388	158,558	150,411	141,012	133,135	116,651	109,669	92,072
Balance Sheet								
Total Assets	21,486,198	22,478,935	17,954,281	13,637,163	11,580,517	9,518,928	9,018,179	6,777,343
Long-Term Obligations	12,168,503	12,951,812	9,554,798	6,254,883	4,936,633	4,064,385	4,071,320	2,477,173
Total Liabilities	13,709,385	14,866,776	10,675,307	7,117,212	5,619,905	4,520,069	4,353,465	2,727,313
Stockholders' Equity	6,382,140	6,118,399	6,150,770	5,263,510	4,012,741	3,077,573	2,627,356	2,570,372
Shares Outstanding	153,596	153,076	151,093	141,153	127,478	118,247	108,629	99,035
Statistical Record								
Return on Assets %	3.89	2.81	3.55	4.28	5.60	4.97	2.95	4.01
Return on Equity %	12.90	9.27	9.81	11.63	16.68	16.15	8.96	11.35
Net Margin %	63.17	17.39	20.65	21.18	34.73	30.65	16.23	26.75
Price Range	122.55-78.74	135.75-84.52	129.49-85.62	88.64-68.70	76.40-48.09	55.66-33.30	47.10-34.41	41.65-34.56
P/E Ratio	25.85-16.61	42.03-26.17	38.65-25.56	25.33-19.63	17.56-11.06	14.65-8.76	24.66-18.02	16.86-13.99
Average Yield %	3.42	3.08	3.72	4.92	5.04	6.67	6.44	6.89

Address: 888 Seventh Avenue, New York, NY 10019 Telephone: 212-894-7000 Web Site: www.vno.com	Officers: Steven Roth - Chairman, Chief Executive Officer Michael D. Fascitelli - President **Transfer Agents:** American Stock Transfer & Trust Co., New York, NY	No of Institutions: 446 Shares: 141,869,984 % Held: 86.74

VULCAN MATERIALS CO (HOLDING COMPANY)

Exchange	Symbol	Price	52Wk Range	Yield	P/E
NYS	VMC	$76.07 (5/29/2008)	121.53-63.15	2.58	20.34

*7 Year Price Score 106.19 *NYSE Composite Index=100 *12 Month Price Score 86.77

Interim Earnings (Per Share)

Qtr.	Mar	Jun	Sep	Dec
2005	0.52	1.17	1.17	0.87
2006	0.68	1.45	1.39	1.18
2007	0.91	1.45	1.38	0.80
2008	0.13	...	...	...

Interim Dividends (Per Share)

Amt	Decl	Ex	Rec	Pay
0.46Q	11/16/2007	11/21/2007	11/26/2007	12/10/2007
0.49Q	02/08/2008	02/21/2008	02/25/2008	03/10/2008
0.49Q	05/09/2008	05/22/2008	05/27/2008	06/10/2008

Indicated Div: $1.96 (Div. Reinv. Plan)

Valuation Analysis

Forecast EPS $3.52 (05/16/2008)
Market Cap	$8.3 Billion	Book Value	3.7 Billion
Price/Book	2.22	Price/Sales	2.41

Dividend Achiever Status

10 Year Growth Rate	11.37%
Total Years of Dividend Growth	15

Business Summary: Earth & Rock Mining (MIC: SIC: 1422 NAIC: 212312)

Vulcan Materials is a producer of construction aggregates, asphalt and concrete, as well as cement. Co.'s aggregates segment mines, processes, distributes and sells sand, gravel and crushed stone. Its asphalt mix and concrete segment produces and sells asphalt mix, ready-mixed concrete, concrete block, prestressed concrete beams and precast concrete, and sells other building materials; and its cement segment mines, produces and sells Portland cement and masonry cement, imports, grinds, blends and sells cement and slag, and produces and sells calcium products. As of Dec 31 2007, Co. operated 183 crushed stone plants, 51 sand and gravel plants and 16 plants producing other aggregates.

Recent Developments: For the quarter ended Mar 31 2008, income from continuing operations decreased 83.8% to US$14.5 million from US$89.3 million in the year-earlier quarter. Net income decreased 84.3% to US$13.9 million from US$88.9 million in the year-earlier quarter. Revenues were US$817.3 million, up 18.9% from US$687.2 million the year before. Operating income was US$66.8 million versus US$137.1 million in the prior-year quarter, a decrease of 51.3%. Direct operating expenses rose 27.5% to US$662.9 million from US$520.0 million in the comparable period the year before. Indirect operating expenses increased 191.8% to US$87.7 million from US$30.0 million in the equivalent prior-year period.

Prospects: Co.'s outlook for 2008 reflects a prolonged downturn in residential construction, weaker contract awards in other end markets, higher costs for construction inputs and rising energy-related costs. Consequently, Co. expects 2008 aggregates shipments, including contributions from the operations of its Nov 2007 acquisition of Florida Rock Industries Inc., to be flat to up 4.0% versus 2007. However, Co. projects an 8.0% price improvement in spite of relatively lower shipments in higher priced markets. For 2008, Co. expects consolidated earnings from continuing operations of $3.85 to $4.35 per diluted share, including $0.41 earnings gain from the divestiture of its two properties in Apr 2008.

Financial Data

(US$ in Thousands)	3 Mos	12/31/2007	12/31/2006	12/31/2005	12/31/2004	12/31/2003	12/31/2002	12/31/2001
Earnings Per Share	3.74	4.54	4.69	3.73	2.77	1.90	1.66	2.17
Cash Flow Per Share	5.90	7.30	5.94	4.63	5.65	5.10	4.54	5.03
Tang Book Value Per Share	N.M.	N.M.	14.60	15.05	13.77	12.01	11.04	10.02
Dividends Per Share	0.950	0.460	1.480	1.160	1.040	0.980	0.940	0.900
Dividend Payout %	25.37	10.13	31.56	31.10	37.55	51.58	56.63	41.47
Income Statement								
Total Revenue	817,339	3,327,787	3,342,475	2,895,327	2,454,335	2,892,186	2,796,577	3,019,990
EBITDA	64,107	968,477	935,874	709,319	643,898	638,108	576,805	659,098
Depn & Amortn	...	259,382	212,274	208,563	233,651	277,091	267,676	278,209
Income Before Taxes	21,320	667,502	703,461	480,237	375,566	311,425	257,660	324,053
Income Taxes	6,835	204,416	225,963	136,462	114,353	87,971	67,247	101,373
Net Income	13,933	450,910	467,534	388,757	287,385	194,952	169,876	222,680
Average Shares	109,898	99,403	99,777	104,085	103,664	102,710	102,515	102,497
Balance Sheet								
Current Assets	1,159,920	1,157,229	731,379	1,164,722	1,417,959	1,050,242	789,688	729,952
Total Assets	9,060,065	8,936,370	3,424,225	3,588,884	3,665,133	3,636,860	3,448,221	3,398,224
Current Liabilities	2,615,264	2,528,187	493,687	579,014	426,689	542,952	297,709	344,495
Long-Term Obligations	1,529,612	1,529,828	322,064	323,392	604,522	607,654	857,757	906,299
Total Liabilities	5,312,986	5,176,770	1,423,114	1,462,343	1,651,158	1,742,037	1,658,577	1,793,950
Stockholders' Equity	3,747,019	3,759,600	2,001,111	2,126,541	2,013,975	1,802,836	1,696,986	1,604,274
Shares Outstanding	109,441	108,234	94,606	100,326	102,659	101,811	101,557	101,320
Statistical Record								
Return on Assets %	5.93	7.30	13.33	10.72	7.85	5.50	4.96	6.72
Return on Equity %	12.82	15.65	22.65	18.78	15.02	11.14	10.29	14.48
EBITDA Margin %	7.84	29.10	28.00	24.50	26.24	22.06	20.63	21.82
Net Margin %	1.70	13.55	13.99	13.43	11.71	6.74	6.07	7.37
Asset Turnover	0.55	0.54	0.95	0.80	0.67	0.82	0.82	0.91
Current Ratio	0.44	0.46	1.48	2.01	3.32	1.93	2.65	2.12
Debt to Equity	0.41	0.41	0.16	0.15	0.30	0.34	0.51	0.56
Price Range	123.67-63.15	123.67-77.43	93.49-66.97	75.79-52.44	54.95-42.35	48.25-29.06	49.55-32.37	55.10-38.15
P/E Ratio	33.07-16.89	27.24-17.06	19.93-14.28	20.32-14.06	19.84-15.29	25.39-15.29	29.85-19.50	25.39-17.58
Average Yield %	1.03	0.45	1.85	1.84	2.16	2.56	2.23	1.91

Address: 1200 Urban Center Drive, Birmingham, AL 35242-2545	Officers: Donald M. James - Chairman, Chief Executive Officer Daniel F. Sansone - Senior Vice President, Chief Financial Officer, Treasurer	Investor Contact: 205-298-3220
Telephone: 205-298-3000		No of Institutions: 445
Web Site: www.vulcanmaterials.com	Transfer Agents:The Bank of New York Mellon Corporation, Pittsburgh, PA	Transfer Shares: 108,102,288 % Held: 98.86

WAL-MART STORES, INC.

Exchange	Symbol	Price	52Wk Range	Yield	P/E
NYS	WMT	$57.94 (5/29/2008)	58.61-42.27	1.64	18.16

*7 Year Price Score 73.95 *NYSE Composite Index=100 ***12 Month Price Score 117.92**

TRADING VOLUME (thousand shares)

Interim Earnings (Per Share)

Qtr.	Apr	Jul	Oct	Jan
2005-06	0.58	0.67	0.57	0.86
2006-07	0.63	0.50	0.63	0.95
2007-08	0.68	0.72	0.70	1.02
2008-09	0.76	...	...	...

Interim Dividends (Per Share)

Amt	Decl	Ex	Rec	Pay
0.237Q	03/06/2008	12/11/2008	12/15/2008	01/02/2009
0.237Q	03/06/2008	03/12/2008	03/14/2008	04/07/2008
0.237Q	03/06/2008	05/14/2008	05/16/2008	06/02/2008
0.237Q	03/06/2008	08/13/2008	08/15/2008	09/02/2008

Indicated Div: $0.95 (Div. Reinv. Plan)

Valuation Analysis

Forecast EPS	$3.44 (05/17/2008)		
Market Cap	$228.5 Billion	Book Value	63.2 Billion
Price/Book	3.61	Price/Sales	0.59

Dividend Achiever Status

10 Year Growth Rate	20.57%
Total Years of Dividend Growth	32

Business Summary: Retail - General (MIC: SIC: 5331 NAIC: 452990)

Wal-Mart Stores operates in three business segments: Wal-Mart Stores, Sam's Club and International. Co.'s Wal-Mart Stores retail formats include: Supercenters, Discount Stores and Neighbourhood Markets. Co.'s Sam's Club segment consists of membership warehouse clubs, which operate in the U.S., and the segment's online retail format, samsclub.com. As of Jan 31 2008, Co.'s International segment consisted of retail operations in Argentina, Brazil, Canada, China, Costa Rica, El Salvador, Guatemala, Honduras, Japan, Mexico, Nicaragua, Puerto Rico, and the U.K. As of Jan 31 2008, Co. operated 971 discount stores, 2,447 supercenters, 591 Sam's Clubs and 132 Neighborhood Markets in the U.S.

Recent Developments: For the quarter ended Apr 30 2008, net income increased 6.9% to US$3.02 billion from US$2.83 billion in the year-earlier quarter. Revenues were US$95.30 billion, up 10.3% from US$86.41 billion the year before. Operating income was US$5.31 billion versus US$4.85 billion in the prior-year quarter, an increase of 9.5%. Direct operating expenses rose 10.1% to US$71.89 billion from US$65.31 billion in the comparable period the year before. Indirect operating expenses increased 11.4% to US$18.11 billion from US$16.25 billion in the equivalent prior-year period.

Prospects: On June 10 2008, Co. announced that it has agreed to sell its property development subsidiary, Gazeley Limited Group, a developer of distribution warehousing in the UK, India, Mexico as well as mainland Europe and China, to Economic Zones World. Specifically, Co. believes that this transaction should enable it to better focus on its retail operations. Accordingly, Co. expects to complete this transaction to close by the end of July 2008, subject to European regulatory approval and result in a pre-tax gain. Separately, for the fiscal quarter ended Jul 31 2008, Co. is projecting comparable store sales growth in the U.S. to be flat to 2.0% and earnings to range from $0.78 to $0.81 per share.

Financial Data

(US$ in Thousands)	3 Mos	01/31/2008	01/31/2007	01/31/2006	01/31/2005	01/31/2004	01/31/2003	01/31/2002
Earnings Per Share	3.19	3.13	2.71	2.68	2.41	2.07	1.81	1.49
Cash Flow Per Share	5.60	5.01	4.84	4.22	3.52	3.67	2.83	2.30
Tang Book Value Per Share	11.82	12.22	11.57	9.84	9.12	7.83	6.78	5.95
Dividends Per Share	0.897	0.880	0.670	0.600	0.520	0.360	0.300	0.280
Dividend Payout %	28.12	28.12	24.72	22.39	21.58	17.39	16.57	18.79
Income Statement								
Total Revenue	95,303,000	378,799,000	348,650,000	315,654,000	287,989,000	258,681,000	246,525,000	219,812,000
EBITDA	6,938,000	28,313,000	25,956,000	23,247,000	21,496,000	18,877,000	17,076,000	15,367,000
Depn & Amortn	1,628,000	6,317,000	5,459,000	4,717,000	4,405,000	3,852,000	3,432,000	3,290,000
Income Before Taxes	4,814,000	20,198,000	18,968,000	17,358,000	16,105,000	14,193,000	12,719,000	10,751,000
Income Taxes	1,670,000	6,908,000	6,365,000	5,803,000	5,589,000	5,118,000	4,487,000	3,897,000
Net Income	3,022,000	12,731,000	11,284,000	11,231,000	10,267,000	9,054,000	8,039,000	6,671,000
Average Shares	3,967,000	4,072,000	4,168,000	4,188,000	4,266,000	4,372,999	4,445,999	4,480,999
Balance Sheet								
Current Assets	50,295,000	47,585,000	46,588,000	43,824,000	38,491,000	34,421,000	30,483,000	28,246,000
Total Assets	167,483,000	163,514,000	151,193,000	138,187,000	120,223,000	104,912,000	94,685,000	83,451,000
Current Liabilities	61,102,000	58,454,000	51,754,000	48,826,000	42,888,000	37,418,000	32,617,000	27,282,000
Long-Term Obligations	35,963,000	33,402,000	30,735,000	30,171,000	23,669,000	20,099,000	19,608,000	18,732,000
Total Liabilities	104,253,000	98,906,000	89,620,000	85,016,000	70,827,000	61,289,000	55,348,000	48,349,000
Stockholders' Equity	63,230,000	64,608,000	61,573,000	53,171,000	49,396,000	43,623,000	39,337,000	35,102,000
Shares Outstanding	3,943,722	3,973,000	4,131,000	4,165,000	4,234,000	4,310,999	4,394,999	4,452,999
Statistical Record								
Return on Assets %	7.99	8.09	7.80	8.69	9.10	9.07	9.03	8.26
Return on Equity %	20.94	20.18	19.67	21.90	22.01	21.83	21.60	20.08
EBITDA Margin %	7.28	7.47	7.44	7.36	7.46	7.30	6.93	6.99
Net Margin %	3.17	3.36	3.24	3.56	3.57	3.50	3.26	3.03
Asset Turnover	2.40	2.41	2.41	2.44	2.55	2.59	2.77	2.72
Current Ratio	0.82	0.81	0.90	0.90	0.90	0.92	0.93	1.04
Debt to Equity	0.57	0.52	0.50	0.57	0.48	0.46	0.50	0.53
Price Range	58.61-42.27	51.21-42.27	51.75-43.02	53.51-42.49	61.05-51.33	60.08-46.74	63.75-44.60	59.98-44.00
P/E Ratio	18.37-13.25	16.36-13.50	19.10-15.87	19.97-15.85	25.33-21.30	29.02-22.58	35.22-24.64	40.26-29.53
Average Yield %	1.87	1.87	1.43	1.25	1.00	0.66	0.55	0.53

Address: 702 S.W. Eighth Street, Bentonville, AR 72716	**Officers:** S. Robson Walton - Chairman H. Lee Scott - President, Chief Executive Officer **Transfer Agents:** Computershare Trust Company, N.A., Providence, RI	**No of Institutions:** 1422
Telephone: 479-273-4000		**Shares:** 1,715,222,144 **% Held:** 39.10
Web Site: www.wal-mart.com		

WALGREEN CO.

Exchange	Symbol	Price	52Wk Range	Yield	P/E
NYS	WAG	$36.03 (5/29/2008)	47.93-33.01	1.05	17.16

*7 Year Price Score 79.36 *NYSE Composite Index=100 *12 Month Price Score 93.75

Interim Earnings (Per Share)

Qtr.	Nov	Feb	May	Aug
2004-05	0.32	0.48	0.40	0.32
2005-06	0.34	0.51	0.46	0.41
2006-07	0.43	0.65	0.56	0.40
2007-08	0.46	0.69	...	...

Interim Dividends (Per Share)

Amt	Decl	Ex	Rec	Pay
0.095Q	07/11/2007	08/16/2007	08/20/2007	09/12/2007
0.095Q	10/10/2007	11/07/2007	11/12/2007	12/12/2007
0.095Q	01/09/2008	02/14/2008	02/19/2008	03/12/2008
0.095Q	04/09/2008	05/19/2008	05/21/2008	06/12/2008

Indicated Div: $0.38 (Div. Reinv. Plan)

Valuation Analysis

Forecast EPS	$2.21 (05/17/2008)		
Market Cap	$35.7 Billion	Book Value	12.1 Billion
Price/Book	2.96	Price/Sales	0.63

Dividend Achiever Status

10 Year Growth Rate	11.02%
Total Years of Dividend Growth	32

Business Summary: Retail - Miscellaneous (MIC: SIC: 5912 NAIC: 446110)

Walgreen is principally engaged in the retail drugstore business. Co.'s drugstores are engaged in the retail sale of prescription and non-prescription drugs and general merchandise. General merchandise includes, among other things, beauty care, personal care, household items, candy, photofinishing, greeting cards, seasonal items and convenience foods. Co.'s customers can have prescriptions filled at its drugstore counter, as well as through the mail, by telephone and via the Internet. Co. markets products under various trademarks, trade dress and trade names and holds assorted business licenses. As of Aug 31 2007, Co. operated retail stores at 5,997 locations in 48 states and Puerto Rico.

Recent Developments: For the quarter ended Feb 29 2008, net income increased 5.2% to US$685.9 million from US$651.9 million in the year-earlier quarter. Revenues were US$15.39 billion, up 10.5% from US$13.93 billion the year before. Direct operating expenses rose 10.7% to US$10.96 billion from US$9.90 billion in the comparable period the year before. Indirect operating expenses increased 11.0% to US$3.35 billion from US$3.02 billion in the equivalent prior-year period.

Prospects: For the fiscal year ending Sep 2 2008, Co. is anticipating capital expenditures to be in excess of $2.00 billion. In detail, Co. intends to use the capital expenditures for store relocation and expansion activities, with plans of 550 new store openings. Also, expenditures are planned for technology and distribution centers, with a new distribution center in Windsor, CT slated to open in fiscal 2009. Going forward, Co. will continue to expand into new markets and increase presence in existing markets. For instance, Co. is encouraged by the Jan 17 2008 announced acquisition of 20 drugstores in Puerto Rico from Farmacias El Amal, a family-owned chain of 61 drugstores based on the island.

Financial Data

(US$ in Thousands)	6 Mos	3 Mos	08/31/2007	08/31/2006	08/31/2005	08/31/2004	08/31/2003	08/31/2002
Earnings Per Share	2.10	2.07	2.03	1.72	1.52	1.32	1.14	0.99
Cash Flow Per Share	2.51	2.27	2.36	2.41	1.34	1.61	1.46	1.44
Tang Book Value Per Share	11.09	10.51	10.13	10.04	8.77	8.04	7.02	6.08
Dividends Per Share	0.362	0.345	0.328	0.273	0.223	0.182	0.156	0.145
Dividend Payout %	17.23	16.67	16.13	15.84	14.64	13.78	13.65	14.65
Income Statement								
Total Revenue	29,421,500	14,027,900	53,762,000	47,409,000	42,201,600	37,508,200	32,505,400	28,681,000
EBITDA	2,212,900	923,500	3,826,600	3,273,700	2,906,100	2,562,100	2,224,000	1,937,700
Depn & Amortn	396,900	195,700	675,900	572,200	482,100	403,100	346,100	307,300
Income Before Taxes	1,813,900	728,200	3,189,100	2,754,100	2,455,600	2,176,300	1,888,700	1,637,300
Income Taxes	672,500	272,700	1,147,800	1,003,500	896,100	816,100	713,000	618,100
Net Income	1,141,400	455,500	2,041,300	1,750,600	1,559,500	1,360,200	1,175,700	1,019,200
Average Shares	995,000	997,500	1,006,340	1,019,400	1,028,333	1,031,798	1,031,580	1,032,270
Balance Sheet								
Current Assets	10,143,200	10,335,100	9,510,500	9,705,400	8,316,500	7,764,400	6,358,100	5,166,500
Total Assets	20,748,300	20,475,600	19,313,600	17,131,100	14,608,800	13,342,100	11,405,900	9,878,800
Current Liabilities	7,230,500	7,545,400	6,744,300	5,755,300	4,481,000	4,077,900	3,420,500	2,955,200
Total Liabilities	8,685,000	8,985,500	8,209,300	7,015,300	5,719,100	5,114,100	4,210,200	3,648,600
Stockholders' Equity	12,063,300	11,490,100	11,104,300	10,115,800	8,889,700	8,228,000	7,195,700	6,230,200
Shares Outstanding	990,456	991,380	991,141	1,007,862	1,013,512	1,023,292	1,024,908	1,024,908
Statistical Record								
Return on Assets %	10.90	10.73	11.20	11.03	11.16	10.96	11.05	10.89
Return on Equity %	18.50	19.08	19.24	18.42	18.22	17.59	17.51	17.82
EBITDA Margin %	7.52	6.58	7.12	6.91	6.89	6.83	6.84	6.76
Net Margin %	3.88	3.25	3.80	3.69	3.70	3.63	3.62	3.55
Asset Turnover	2.94	2.86	2.95	2.99	3.02	3.02	3.05	3.07
Current Ratio	1.40	1.37	1.41	1.69	1.86	1.90	1.86	1.75
Price Range	47.93-33.01	47.93-36.59	51.48-40.10	49.69-39.80	48.34-35.41	37.74-30.57	35.96-27.35	40.24-30.98
P/E Ratio	22.82-15.72	23.15-17.68	25.36-19.75	28.89-23.14	31.80-23.30	28.59-23.16	31.54-23.99	40.65-31.29
Average Yield %	0.87	0.78	0.73	0.62	0.61	0.53	0.52	0.40

Address: 200 Wilmot Road, Deerfield, IL 60015	**Officers:** Jeffrey A. Rein - Chairman, Chief Executive Officer Gregory D. Wasson - President, Chief Operating Officer **Transfer Agents:** ComputerShare Investor Services, Chicago, IL	**Investor Contact:** 847-914-2972 **No of Institutions:** 1097 **Shares:** 807,335,808 **% Held:** 65.55
Telephone: 847-940-2500		
Web Site: www.walgreens.com		

WASHINGTON FEDERAL INC.

Exchange	Symbol	Price	52Wk Range	Yield	P/E
NMS	WFSL	$22.21 (5/29/2008)	27.09-19.05	3.78	14.24

*7 Year Price Score 84.73 ***NYSE Composite Index=100** ***12 Month Price Score 98.99**

Interim Earnings (Per Share)

Qtr.	Dec	Mar	Jun	Sep
2004-05	0.41	0.47	0.39	0.40
2005-06	0.41	0.42	0.40	0.41
2006-07	0.38	0.38	0.39	0.39
2007-08	0.38	0.40	...	...

Interim Dividends (Per Share)

Amt	Decl	Ex	Rec	Pay
0.21Q	06/25/2007	07/03/2007	07/06/2007	07/20/2007
0.21Q	09/24/2007	10/03/2007	10/05/2007	10/19/2007
0.21Q	12/17/2007	12/26/2007	12/28/2007	01/11/2008
0.21Q	03/24/2008	04/02/2008	04/04/2008	04/18/2008
		Indicated Div: $0.84		

Valuation Analysis

Forecast EPS $1.59 (05/17/2008)

Market Cap	$2.0 Billion	Book Value	1.4 Billion
Price/Book	1.42	Price/Sales	2.83

Dividend Achiever Status

10 Year Growth Rate	6.06%
Total Years of Dividend Growth	24

Business Summary: Other Depository Banking (MIC: SIC: 6035 NAIC: 522120)

Washington Federal is a savings and loan holding company that operates through a savings and loan association subsidiary, Washington Federal Savings. Co. primarily accepts deposits from the general public and invests these funds in first lien mortgages on single-family dwellings, construction loans, land acquisition and development loans, loans on multi-family and other income producing properties, home equity loans and business loans, and in certain U.S. government and agency obligations and other investments permitted by applicable laws and regulations. Co. is also engaged in real estate investment and insurance brokerage activities. At Sep 30 2007, Co. had total assets of $10.29 billion.

Recent Developments: For the quarter ended Mar 31 2008, net income increased 5.9% to US$35.5 million from US$33.5 million in the year-earlier quarter. Net interest income increased 12.9% to US$73.6 million from US$65.2 million in the year-earlier quarter. Provision for loan losses was US$9.5 million versus US$150,000 in the prior-year quarter, an increase of. Non-interest income rose 293.2% to US$12.9 million from US$3.3 million, while non-interest expense advanced 36.1% to US$21.8 million.

Prospects: Looking ahead, Co. believes that its non-performing assets will continue to increase until the housing market begins to recover and that loan losses will also be at a higher level than normal. Nonetheless, with its improving net interest spread and a strong capital position, Co. believes that it will be able to handle the existing market challenges. At the same time, Co. continues to benefit from its completed acquisitions, such as its Feb 2008 acquisition of First Mutual Bancshares, Inc. and its Feb 2007 acquisition of First Federal Banc of the Southwest, Inc. Co. also believes that it will realize additional savings as the full integration of these acquisitions occurs over time.

Financial Data
(US$ in Thousands)

	6 Mos	3 Mos	09/30/2007	09/30/2006	09/30/2005	09/30/2004	09/30/2003	09/30/2002
Earnings Per Share	1.56	1.54	1.54	1.64	1.67	1.51	1.71	1.69
Cash Flow Per Share	1.48	1.69	1.63	1.51	1.65	1.60	1.42	1.61
Tang Book Value Per Share	13.13	14.12	13.85	13.81	13.00	12.26	11.56	10.94
Dividends Per Share	0.835	0.835	0.825	0.805	0.772	0.736	0.701	0.666
Dividend Payout %	53.67	54.22	53.57	49.09	46.22	48.80	40.97	39.39
Income Statement								
Income Before Taxes	106,371	51,437	209,312	218,660	222,308	203,712	224,565	222,354
Income Taxes	37,871	18,389	74,295	75,558	76,419	71,844	79,021	78,400
Net Income	68,500	33,048	135,017	143,102	145,889	131,868	145,544	143,954
Average Shares	87,661	87,614	87,696	87,471	87,478	87,130	84,981	85,333
Balance Sheet								
Total Assets	11,739,249	10,576,641	10,285,417	9,069,020	8,234,450	7,169,205	7,535,975	7,392,441
Total Liabilities	10,363,185	9,234,610	8,967,290	7,806,300	7,047,142	6,049,017	6,480,379	6,431,723
Stockholders' Equity	1,376,064	1,342,031	1,318,127	1,262,720	1,187,308	1,120,188	1,055,596	960,718
Shares Outstanding	87,800	87,475	87,441	87,338	86,933	86,547	86,119	84,572
Statistical Record								
Return on Assets %	1.26	1.37	1.40	1.65	1.89	1.79	1.95	2.00
Return on Equity %	10.20	10.27	10.46	11.68	12.64	12.09	14.44	15.69
Price Range	27.09-19.05	27.09-20.94	27.06-21.63	24.88-21.31	25.08-22.03	23.96-20.24	21.83-15.51	20.59-15.03
P/E Ratio	17.37-12.21	17.59-13.60	17.57-14.05	15.17-12.99	15.02-13.19	15.87-13.40	12.76-9.07	12.19-8.89
Average Yield %	3.52	3.48	3.45	3.46	3.31	3.27	3.74	3.64

Address: 425 Pike Street, Seattle, WA 98101	**Officers:** Guy C. Pinkerton - Chairman Roy M. Whitehead - Vice-Chairman, President, Chief Executive Officer **Transfer Agents:** American Stock Transfer & Trust Company , New York, NY	**Investor Contact:** 206-624-7930
Telephone: 206-624-7930		**No of Institutions:** 216
Web Site: www.washingtonfederal.com		**Shares:** 73,308,912 **% Held:** 77.04

WASHINGTON MUTUAL INC.

Exchange	Symbol	Price	52Wk Range	Yield	P/E
NYS	WM	$9.19 (5/29/2008)	44.41-9.16	0.44	N/A

*7 Year Price Score 50.32 *NYSE Composite Index=100 *12 Month Price Score 47.03

Interim Earnings (Per Share)

Qtr.	Mar	Jun	Sep	Dec
2005	1.01	0.95	0.92	0.84
2006	0.98	0.79	0.77	1.10
2007	0.86	0.92	0.20	(2.11)
2008	(1.40)	...	...	...

Interim Dividends (Per Share)

Amt	Decl	Ex	Rec	Pay
0.56Q	07/18/2007	07/27/2007	07/31/2007	08/15/2007
0.56Q	10/16/2007	10/29/2007	10/31/2007	11/15/2007
0.15Q	01/15/2008	01/29/2008	01/31/2008	02/15/2008
0.01Q	04/15/2008	04/28/2008	04/30/2008	05/15/2008

Indicated Div: $0.04 (Div. Reinv. Plan)

Valuation Analysis

Forecast EPS $-3.23 (05/17/2008)

Market Cap	$8.1 Billion	Book Value	22.4 Billion
Price/Book	0.36	Price/Sales	0.32

Dividend Achiever Status

10 Year Growth Rate	16.72%
Total Years of Dividend Growth	18

TRADING VOLUME (thousand shares)

Business Summary: Other Depository Banking (MIC: SIC: 6035 NAIC: 522120)

Washington Mutual is a thrift holding company providing financial services to consumers and small businesses. Co. has four operating segments for management reporting purposes: the Retail Banking Group, which as of Dec 31 2007, operated a retail bank network of 2,257 stores across 15 states throughout the U.S.; the Card Services Group, which operates a nationwide credit card lending business; the Commercial Group, which conducts a multi-family and commercial real estate lending business in certain markets; as well as the Home Loans Group, which engages in single-family residential real estate lending, servicing and capital markets activities.

Recent Developments: For the quarter ended Mar 31 2008, net loss amounted to US$1.14 billion versus net income of US$784.0 million in the year-earlier quarter. Net interest income increased 4.5% to US$2.18 billion from US$2.08 billion in the year-earlier quarter. Provision for loan losses was US$3.51 billion versus US$234.0 million in the prior-year quarter, an increase of. Non-interest income rose 1.8% to US$1.57 billion from US$1.54 billion, while non-interest expense advanced 2.2% to US$2.15 billion.

Prospects: With the continuing deterioration in the credit markets, in Apr 2008, Co. took steps to align the home lending activities through its retail banking store network and reduce the scale of its home lending operations. Those steps will result in the discontinuation of all home lending conducted through the wholesale channel, the closure of all freestanding home loan centers and sales offices, and the consolidation of certain loan fulfillment centers. These actions are expected to result in the elimination of about 2,600 to 3,000 positions by June 30, 2008. Co. expects to fully realize in 2009 a $550.0 million to $650.0 million reduction in annual noninterest expense through these actions.

Financial Data
(US$ in Thousands)

	3 Mos	12/31/2007	12/31/2006	12/31/2005	12/31/2004	12/31/2003	12/31/2002	12/31/2001
Earnings Per Share	(2.40)	(0.12)	3.64	3.73	3.26	4.21	4.05	3.59
Cash Flow Per Share	12.48	8.91	7.66	1.97	(22.78)	13.84	0.03	(12.68)
Tang Book Value Per Share	6.45	8.33	11.31	10.66	10.21	7.88	9.03	6.29
Dividends Per Share	1.820	2.210	2.060	1.900	1.740	1.400	1.060	0.897
Dividend Payout %	...	...	56.59	50.94	53.37	33.25	26.17	24.98
Income Statement								
Income Before Taxes	(1,994,000)	309,000	4,770,000	5,438,000	3,984,000	6,029,000	6,154,000	4,311,000
Income Taxes	(856,000)	376,000	1,656,000	2,006,000	1,505,000	2,236,000	2,258,000	1,579,000
Net Income	(1,138,000)	(67,000)	3,558,000	3,432,000	2,878,000	3,880,000	3,896,000	3,114,000
Average Shares	856,923	866,183	975,406	919,238	884,050	921,757	960,152	864,700
Balance Sheet								
Total Assets	319,668,000	327,913,000	346,288,000	343,839,000	307,918,000	275,178,000	268,298,000	242,506,000
Total Liabilities	297,219,000	303,329,000	319,319,000	316,223,000	286,692,000	255,436,000	248,164,000	228,341,000
Stockholders' Equity	22,449,000	24,584,000	26,969,000	27,616,000	21,226,000	19,742,000	20,134,000	14,063,000
Shares Outstanding	882,609	869,036	944,478	993,913	874,261	880,985	944,046	873,089
Statistical Record								
Return on Assets %	N.M.	N.M.	1.03	1.05	0.98	1.43	1.53	1.42
Return on Equity %	N.M.	N.M.	13.04	14.05	14.01	19.46	22.79	25.70
Price Range	44.41-9.24	45.56-13.07	46.48-41.47	44.54-36.92	45.28-37.63	46.55-32.98	39.45-28.41	42.69-28.56
P/E Ratio	...	...	12.77-11.39	11.94-9.90	13.89-11.54	11.06-7.83	9.74-7.01	11.89-7.96
Average Yield %	6.16	6.04	4.69	4.63	4.27	3.57	3.00	2.55

Address: 1201 Third Avenue, Seattle, WA 98101	Officers: Kerry K. Killinger - Chairman, Chief Executive Officer Stephen J. Rotella - President, Chief Operating Officer **Transfer Agents:**	Investor Contact: 206-461-3186
Telephone: 206-461-2000		No of Institutions: 673
Web Site: www.wamu.com	Mellon Investor Services, L.L.C., Ridgefield Park, NJ	Shares: 997,987,968 % **Held:** 94.97

WASHINGTON REAL ESTATE INVESTMENT TRUST

Exchange	Symbol	Price	52Wk Range	Yield	P/E
NYS	WRE	$33.95 (5/29/2008)	37.59-26.91	5.10	32.03

*7 Year Price Score 82.60   *NYSE Composite Index=100   ***12 Month Price Score 108.01**

Interim Earnings (Per Share)

Qtr.	Mar	Jun	Sep	Dec
2005	1.01	0.26	0.32	0.26
2006	0.25	0.18	0.23	0.22
2007	0.24	0.18	0.73	0.18
2008	(0.03)	...	...	...

Interim Dividends (Per Share)

Amt	Decl	Ex	Rec	Pay
0.422Q	08/07/2007	09/12/2007	09/14/2007	09/28/2007
0.422Q	11/28/2007	12/12/2007	12/14/2007	12/31/2007
0.422Q	02/21/2008	03/13/2008	03/17/2008	03/31/2008
0.433Q	05/07/2008	06/12/2008	06/16/2008	06/30/2008
		Indicated Div: $1.73 (Div. Reinv. Plan)		

Valuation Analysis

Forecast EPS $0.45 (05/17/2008)

Market Cap	$1.6 Billion	Book Value	465.7 Million
Price/Book	3.41	Price/Sales	6.00

Dividend Achiever Status

10 Year Growth Rate	4.61%
Total Years of Dividend Growth	38

Business Summary: "Property, Real Estate & Development" (MIC: SIC: 6798 NAIC: 525930)

Washington Real Estate Investment Trust is a self-administered, self-managed, equity real estate investment trust. Co.'s business consists of the ownership and development of income-producing real properties in the greater Washington metro region. Co. owns a portfolio of office buildings, medical office buildings, industrial/flex properties, multifamily buildings and retail centers. As of Dec 31 2007, Co. owned a portfolio of 89 properties, consisting of 14 retail centers, 25 office properties, 17 medical office properties, 23 industrial/flex properties, 10 multifamily properties encompassing in the aggregate 12.8 million net rentable square feet, and land for development.

Recent Developments: For the quarter ended Mar 31 2008, loss from continuing operations was US$2.3 million compared with income of US$9.7 million in the year-earlier quarter. Net loss amounted to US$1.5 million versus net income of US$10.7 million in the year-earlier quarter. Revenues were US$70.3 million, up 17.4% from US$59.9 million the year before.

Prospects: Co.'s outlook appears encouraging as it is seeing growth in real estate rental revenue driven by increased economic occupancy in the medical office, office, retail and residential sectors as well as increases in rental rate growth in all sectors. Hence, Co. continues to expect funds from operations per diluted share of $2.11 to $2.21 for 2008. Separately, on Apr 16 2008, Co. entered into an agreement to acquire Lansdowne Medical Office Building, a medical office development under construction in Loudoun County, VA, for $19.5 million. Co. expects the purchase to occur in the first quarter of 2009 and to expand its medical office portfolio with second-year stabilized yield expected at 8.0%.

Financial Data
(US$ in Thousands)

	3 Mos	12/31/2007	12/31/2006	12/31/2005	12/31/2004	12/31/2003	12/31/2002	12/31/2001
Earnings Per Share	1.06	1.34	0.88	1.84	1.09	1.13	1.32	1.38
Cash Flow Per Share	2.31	2.52	1.98	2.08	1.91	1.94	1.80	1.98
Tang Book Value Per Share	9.97	10.42	9.81	9.03	8.71	9.10	8.33	8.33
Dividends Per Share	1.690	1.680	1.640	1.600	1.550	1.470	1.390	1.310
Dividend Payout %	159.73	125.37	186.36	86.96	142.20	130.09	105.30	94.93
Income Statement								
Property Income	70,278	255,655	219,662	190,046	172,067	163,405	152,929	148,424
Non-Property Income	...	...	...	...	327	414	680	...
Total Revenue	70,278	255,655	219,662	190,046	172,394	163,819	153,609	148,424
Depn & Amortn	21,031	73,731	57,103	48,367	41,961	35,755	29,212	26,954
Interest Expense	17,664	61,906	47,846	37,743	34,500	30,040	27,849	27,071
Net Income	(1,488)	61,881	38,661	77,638	45,564	44,887	51,836	52,353
Average Shares	46,623	46,115	43,874	42,203	41,863	39,600	39,281	37,951
Balance Sheet								
Total Assets	1,892,198	1,898,326	1,531,265	1,141,285	1,012,393	927,129	755,997	707,935
Long-Term Obligations	1,170,322	1,131,607	965,328	689,617	493,429	517,182	351,951	359,726
Total Liabilities	1,422,674	1,408,006	1,087,595	759,310	644,755	546,780	428,266	382,717
Stockholders' Equity	465,738	486,544	441,931	380,305	366,009	378,748	326,177	323,607
Shares Outstanding	46,716	46,682	45,042	42,139	42,000	41,607	39,168	38,829
Statistical Record								
Return on Assets %	2.76	3.61	2.89	7.21	4.69	5.33	7.08	7.81
Return on Equity %	11.02	13.33	9.40	20.81	12.20	12.74	15.95	17.98
Net Margin %	(2.12)	24.20	17.60	40.85	26.43	27.40	33.75	35.27
Price Range	39.16-26.91	43.20-29.65	43.30-31.26	33.87-28.15	34.43-25.80	31.04-24.10	30.15-21.96	25.45-21.27
P/E Ratio	36.94-25.39	32.24-22.13	49.20-35.52	18.41-15.30	31.59-23.67	27.47-21.33	22.84-16.64	18.44-15.41
Average Yield %	5.06	4.72	4.39	5.24	5.16	5.33	5.31	5.59

Address: 6110 Executive Boulevard, Suite 800, Rockville, MD 20852-3927 **Telephone:** 301-984-9400 **Web Site:** www.writ.com	**Officers:** George F. McKenzie - President, Chief Executive Officer Laura M. Franklin - Executive Vice President, Corporate Secretary **Transfer Agents:** Computershare Trust Company, N.A., Providence, RI	**No of Institutions:** 217 **Shares:** 29,775,584 **% Held:** 61.05

WASHINGTON TRUST BANCORP, INC.

Exchange	Symbol	Price	52Wk Range	Yield	P/E
NMS	WASH	$24.14 (5/29/2008)	28.61-22.07	3.31	13.49

*7 Year Price Score 79.02 *NYSE Composite Index=100 *12 Month Price Score 100.58

Interim Earnings (Per Share)

Qtr.	Mar	Jun	Sep	Dec
2005	0.40	0.41	0.43	0.45
2006	0.44	0.45	0.48	0.45
2007	0.44	0.46	0.48	0.43
2008	0.43	...	...	...

Interim Dividends (Per Share)

Amt	Decl	Ex	Rec	Pay
0.20Q	06/21/2007	06/28/2007	07/02/2007	07/12/2007
0.20Q	09/20/2007	09/27/2007	10/01/2007	10/11/2007
0.20Q	12/20/2007	12/31/2007	01/03/2008	01/11/2008
0.20Q	03/20/2008	03/27/2008	03/31/2008	04/11/2008
		Indicated Div: $0.80		

Valuation Analysis

Forecast EPS	$1.82 (05/16/2008)		
Market Cap	$322.7 Million	Book Value	191.2 Million
Price/Book	1.69	Price/Sales	1.75

Dividend Achiever Status

10 Year Growth Rate	8.87%
Total Years of Dividend Growth	15

TRADING VOLUME (thousand shares)

Business Summary: Commercial Banking (MIC: SIC: 6022 NAIC: 522110)

Washington Trust Bancorp is a bank holding company. Co. owns all of the outstanding common stock of The Washington Trust Company, a Rhode Island-chartered commercial bank. Through its subsidiaries, Co. provides a range of financial services to individuals and businesses, including commercial and retail lending products, acceptance of demand, savings, money market, time deposits and wealth management services, through its offices in Rhode Island, Massachusetts and southeastern Connecticut. Co. also provides its services through automated teller machines and its Internet website. As of Dec 31 2007, Co. had total assets of $2.54 billion and total deposits of $1.65 billion.

Recent Developments: For the quarter ended Mar 31 2008, net income decreased 2.7% to US$5.8 million from US$6.0 million in the year-earlier quarter. Net interest income increased 1.4% to US$15.1 million from US$14.9 million in the year-earlier quarter. Provision for loan losses was US$450,000 versus US$300,000 in the prior-year quarter, an increase of 50.0%. Non-interest income fell 1.8% to US$11.0 million from US$11.2 million, while non-interest expense was unchanged at US$17.1 million.

Prospects: Co. is experiencing a modest reduction in net income primarily due to a decline in its net interest margin, reflecting the effect of the recent Federal Reserve rate cuts. In addition, Co. is seeing an increase in the loan loss provision charged to earnings, for the most part in response to loan growth. Despite these negative trends, Co. continues to focus on its branch expansion plans. For instance, in Aug 2008, Co. intends to relocate its existing Providence branch to a new facility in the financial district of Providence. Co. also noted that a second branch is planned for Warwick, RI in 2009. The opening of these new branches is subject to approval of state and federal regulators.

Financial Data

(US$ in Thousands)	3 Mos	12/31/2007	12/31/2006	12/31/2005	12/31/2004	12/31/2003	12/31/2002	12/31/2001
Earnings Per Share	1.79	1.75	1.82	1.69	1.54	1.41	1.30	1.07
Cash Flow Per Share	2.23	2.24	2.12	2.19	2.02	2.42	1.60	0.79
Tang Book Value Per Share	9.70	9.33	8.61	7.79	9.64	8.60	7.93	8.15
Dividends Per Share	0.800	0.800	0.760	0.720	0.680	0.760	0.550	0.510
Dividend Payout %	44.57	45.71	41.76	42.60	44.16	53.90	42.31	47.66
Income Statement								
Interest Income	34,926	136,434	131,134	115,693	96,853	86,245	87,339	87,527
Interest Expense	19,850	76,490	69,660	55,037	42,412	37,446	43,057	48,160
Net Interest Income	15,076	59,944	61,474	60,656	54,441	48,799	44,282	39,367
Provision for Losses	450	1,900	1,200	1,200	610	460	400	550
Non-Interest Income	11,044	45,509	42,183	30,946	26,905	26,735	23,258	21,485
Non-Interest Expense	17,142	68,906	65,335	56,393	50,373	47,632	42,990	41,653
Income Before Taxes	8,528	34,647	37,122	34,009	30,363	27,442	24,150	18,649
Income Taxes	2,712	10,847	12,091	10,985	9,534	8,519	7,393	5,541
Net Income	5,816	23,800	25,031	23,024	20,829	18,923	16,757	13,108
Average Shares	13,560	13,604	13,723	13,626	13,542	13,393	12,932	12,202
Balance Sheet								
Net Loans & Leases	1,577,858	1,553,375	1,441,092	1,383,990	1,232,905	945,067	779,639	592,052
Total Assets	2,564,387	2,539,940	2,399,165	2,402,003	2,307,820	1,973,807	1,745,661	1,362,229
Total Deposits	1,635,025	1,646,205	1,677,997	1,639,258	1,457,885	1,206,141	1,110,493	816,876
Total Liabilities	2,373,168	2,353,427	2,226,109	2,243,557	2,155,968	1,835,752	1,616,940	1,264,292
Stockholders' Equity	191,219	186,513	173,056	158,446	151,852	138,055	128,721	97,937
Shares Outstanding	13,368	13,354	13,429	13,361	13,269	13,194	13,042	12,011
Statistical Record								
Return on Assets %	0.98	0.96	1.04	0.98	0.97	1.02	1.08	1.02
Return on Equity %	13.31	13.24	15.10	14.84	14.33	14.19	14.79	14.01
Net Interest Margin %	43.17	43.94	46.88	52.43	56.21	56.58	50.70	44.98
Efficiency Ratio %	37.29	37.87	37.70	38.46	40.70	42.16	38.87	38.21
Loans to Deposits	0.97	0.94	0.86	0.84	0.85	0.78	0.70	0.72
Price Range	28.61-22.07	28.61-23.01	29.34-24.40	30.02-24.12	30.49-23.28	29.19-19.45	23.69-18.00	22.25-13.75
P/E Ratio	15.98-12.33	16.35-13.15	16.12-13.41	17.76-14.27	19.80-15.12	20.70-13.79	18.22-13.85	20.79-12.85
Average Yield %	3.18	3.08	2.84	2.59	2.59	3.22	2.75	2.76

Address: 23 Broad Street, Westerly, RI 02891	Officers: John C. Warren - Chairman, Chief Executive Officer John F. Treanor - President, Chief Operating Officer **Transfer Agents:** American Stock Transfer & Trust Company, New York, NY	No of Institutions: 86
Telephone: 401-348-1200		**Shares:** 4,427,158 **% Held:** 32.18
Web Site: www.washtrust.com		

WEBSTER FINANCIAL CORP (WATERBURY, CONN)

Exchange	Symbol	Price	52Wk Range	Yield	P/E
NYS	WBS	$26.12 (5/29/2008)	45.35-25.15	4.59	16.32

*7 Year Price Score 65.56 *NYSE Composite Index=100 *12 Month Price Score 78.75

Interim Earnings (Per Share)

Qtr.	Mar	Jun	Sep	Dec
2005	0.88	0.85	0.86	0.84
2006	0.82	0.81	0.17	0.67
2007	0.62	0.63	0.64	(0.13)
2008	0.47	...	...	...

Interim Dividends (Per Share)

Amt	Decl	Ex	Rec	Pay
0.30Q	07/24/2007	08/02/2007	08/06/2007	08/20/2007
0.30Q	10/22/2007	11/01/2007	11/05/2007	11/19/2007
0.30Q	01/30/2008	02/11/2008	02/13/2008	02/27/2008
0.30Q	04/22/2008	05/01/2008	05/05/2008	05/19/2008
Indicated Div: $1.20 (Div. Reinv. Plan)				

Valuation Analysis

Forecast EPS	$2.15 (05/17/2008)		
Market Cap	$1.4 Billion	Book Value	1.7 Billion
Price/Book	0.80	Price/Sales	1.17

Dividend Achiever Status

10 Year Growth Rate	11.61%
Total Years of Dividend Growth	15

TRADING VOLUME (thousand shares)

Business Summary: Commercial Banking (MIC: SIC: 6021 NAIC: 522110)

Webster Financial, through its Webster Bank subsidiary and various non-banking financial services subsidiaries, delivers financial services to individuals, families and businesses throughout southern New England and eastern New York State. Co. also offers equipment financing, commercial real estate lending, asset-based lending, and insurance premium financing on a regional or national basis. Also, through Webster Bank, Co. provides commercial banking, retail banking, consumer financing, mortgage banking, trust and investment services through 181 banking offices, 343 automatic teller machines and its internet website As of Dec 31 2007, Co. had total assets of $17.20 billion.

Recent Developments: For the quarter ended Mar 31 2008, income from continuing operations decreased 24.5% to US$26.5 million from US$35.1 million in the year-earlier quarter. Net income decreased 30.5% to US$24.4 million from US$35.0 million in the year-earlier quarter. Net interest income decreased 2.5% to US$124.9 million from US$128.1 million in the year-earlier quarter. Provision for loan losses was US$15.8 million versus US$3.0 million in the prior-year quarter, an increase of 426.7%. Non-interest income rose 1.0% to US$47.8 million from US$47.4 million, while non-interest expense declined 4.2% to US$116.1 million.

Prospects: Co. is seeing a decrease in net interest income as a result of declining short term interest rates and a flattening yield curve, resulting in a decline in net interest margin. Going forward, Co. expects credit conditions to remain challenging possibly through end of 2008 or potentially longer, given the weakening economy. Meanwhile, Co. is focused on completing its OneWebster earnings optimization program launched in Jan 2007, which should have a positive effect on future operating results. The program, which assigns senior officers from each line of business and shared services area to teams dedicated to improve revenues and reduce expenses, will be implemented through 2008 and into 2009.

Financial Data (US$ in Thousands)	3 Mos	12/31/2007	12/31/2006	12/31/2005	12/31/2004	12/31/2003	12/31/2002	12/31/2001
Earnings Per Share	1.60	1.76	2.47	3.43	3.00	3.52	3.16	2.68
Cash Flow Per Share	11.39	5.61	2.95	1.08	7.08	10.93	(1.76)	0.23
Tang Book Value Per Share	18.10	18.46	18.65	17.68	15.85	17.76	16.18	13.97
Dividends Per Share	1.200	1.170	1.060	0.980	0.900	0.820	0.740	0.670
Dividend Payout %	74.86	66.48	42.91	28.57	30.00	23.30	23.42	25.00
Income Statement								
Income Before Taxes	40,792	158,784	193,073	273,156	222,731	243,020	233,977	206,245
Income Taxes	14,303	48,088	59,283	87,301	68,898	79,772	73,965	69,430
Net Income	24,365	96,773	133,790	185,855	153,833	163,248	152,732	133,188
Average Shares	52,297	54,996	54,065	54,236	51,352	46,362	48,392	42,742
Balance Sheet								
Total Assets	17,243,562	17,201,960	17,097,471	17,836,562	17,020,597	14,568,690	13,468,004	11,857,382
Total Liabilities	15,517,269	15,455,751	15,211,031	16,179,759	15,467,046	13,406,218	12,301,714	10,691,338
Stockholders' Equity	1,716,716	1,736,632	1,876,863	1,647,226	1,543,974	1,152,895	1,035,458	1,006,467
Shares Outstanding	52,490	52,475	56,388	53,661	53,628	46,276	45,625	49,149
Statistical Record								
Return on Assets %	0.50	0.56	0.77	1.07	0.97	1.16	1.21	1.15
Return on Equity %	4.73	5.36	7.59	11.65	11.38	14.92	14.96	14.04
Price Range	47.76-26.03	51.13-30.93	49.38-45.36	50.64-43.67	51.65-42.56	46.50-33.93	39.96-30.65	37.06-26.44
P/E Ratio	29.85-16.27	29.05-17.57	19.99-18.36	14.76-12.73	17.22-14.19	13.21-9.64	12.65-9.70	13.83-9.86
Average Yield %	3.14	2.72	2.23	2.11	1.87	2.11	2.09	2.15

Address: Webster Plaza, Waterbury, CT 06702	Officers: James C. Smith - Chairman, Chief Executive Officer Gerald P. Plush - Senior Executive Vice President, Chief Financial Officer Transfer Agents: American Stock Transfer & Trust Co	Investor Contact: 203-578-2318
Telephone: 203-578-2476		No of Institutions: 237
Web Site: www.websteronline.com		Shares: 35,726,976 % Held: 64.51

WEINGARTEN REALTY INVESTORS

Exchange	Symbol	Price	52Wk Range	Yield	P/E
NYS	WRI	$35.15 (5/29/2008)	46.85-28.37	5.97	15.76

*7 Year Price Score 85.92   *NYSE Composite Index=100   *12 Month Price Score 101.99

Interim Earnings (Per Share)

Qtr.	Mar	Jun	Sep	Dec
2005	0.38	0.74	0.65	0.54
2006	0.57	0.95	1.15	0.60
2007	0.53	0.79	0.44	0.67
2008	0.34	...	...	...

Interim Dividends (Per Share)

Amt	Decl	Ex	Rec	Pay
0.495Q	07/27/2007	09/05/2007	09/07/2007	09/14/2007
0.495Q	...	12/05/2007	12/07/2007	12/17/2007
0.525Q	02/26/2008	03/05/2008	03/07/2008	03/17/2008
0.525Q	05/07/2008	06/04/2008	06/06/2008	06/16/2008

Indicated Div: $2.10 (Div. Reinv. Plan)

Valuation Analysis

Forecast EPS	$1.61 (05/16/2008)		
Market Cap	$3.0 Billion	Book Value	1.5 Billion
Price/Book	2.03	Price/Sales	4.84

Dividend Achiever Status

10 Year Growth Rate	5.70%
Total Years of Dividend Growth	19

Business Summary: "Property, Real Estate & Development" (MIC: SIC: 6798 NAIC: 525930)

Weingarten Realty Investors is a real estate investment trust engaged in the management, acquisition and development of real estate, primarily anchored neighborhood, community shopping centers and industrial properties. As of Dec 31 2007, Co. owned or operated under long-term leases, either directly or through its interest in joint ventures or partnerships, 383 developed income-producing properties, including 335 neighborhood and community shopping centers located in Arizona, Arkansas, California, Colorado, Florida, Georgia, Illinois, Kansas, Kentucky, Louisiana, Maine, Missouri, Nevada, New Mexico, North Carolina, Oklahoma, Oregon, Tennessee, Utah, Texas, South Carolina and Washington.

Recent Developments: For the quarter ended Mar 31 2008, income from continuing operations decreased 19.5% to US$28.8 million from US$35.7 million in the year-earlier quarter. Net income decreased 27.2% to US$37.4 million from US$51.4 million in the year-earlier quarter. Revenues were US$155.2 million, up 8.7% from US$142.7 million the year before. Revenues from property income rose 8.4% to US$152.4 million from US$140.7 million in the corresponding quarter a year earlier.

Prospects: Co. is focused on its development pipeline, including 35 properties at various stages of development. Notably, the total investment is projected to be $657.0 million at completion. Also, 15 of Co.'s 35 projects under development should be stabilized by the end of 2009 and these centers are currently 81.0% leased, including tenant-owned square footage. For the remaining 20 projects stabilizing in 2010 and beyond, Co. has committed national or regional anchors for 15 of the projects. Going forward, Co. plans to continue leasing and managing its portfolio as well as investing in development and acquisition opportunities. For 2008, Co. expects funds from operations per share of $3.21 to $3.27.

Financial Data
(US$ in Thousands)

	3 Mos	12/31/2007	12/31/2006	12/31/2005	12/31/2004	12/31/2003	12/31/2002	12/31/2001
Earnings Per Share	2.23	2.44	3.27	2.31	1.54	1.24	1.43	1.23
Cash Flow Per Share	2.76	2.61	2.77	2.25	2.44	2.08	2.16	2.03
Tang Book Value Per Share	17.30	17.29	13.13	12.87	12.30	10.03	11.95	11.92
Dividends Per Share	2.010	1.980	1.860	1.760	1.660	1.560	1.480	1.404
Dividend Payout %	90.08	81.15	56.88	76.19	107.79	125.81	103.26	114.49
Income Statement								
Property Income	152,428	585,702	554,361	534,495	492,036	410,490	359,044	309,457
Non-Property Income	2,732	13,352	7,019	9,550	10,255	8,670	6,366	5,435
Total Revenue	155,160	599,054	561,380	544,045	502,291	419,160	365,410	314,892
Depn & Amortn	43,505	134,676	131,992	128,573	117,053	94,455	79,344	68,316
Interest Expense	35,480	148,829	146,943	130,761	115,506	88,871	65,863	54,473
Income Taxes	747	4,073	1,366	...	...	...	...	...
Net Income	37,394	238,017	305,010	219,653	141,381	116,280	131,867	108,542
Average Shares	84,167	88,893	91,779	93,166	89,511	81,574	80,040	72,553
Balance Sheet								
Total Assets	5,043,685	4,993,343	4,375,540	3,737,741	3,470,318	2,923,794	2,423,889	2,095,747
Long-Term Obligations	3,214,656	3,165,059	2,900,952	2,299,855	2,105,948	1,810,500	1,330,369	1,070,835
Total Liabilities	3,431,521	3,424,635	3,162,079	2,504,097	2,300,428	2,052,427	1,435,493	1,170,789
Stockholders' Equity	1,451,715	1,471,823	1,125,781	1,150,286	1,095,960	821,563	933,413	921,072
Shares Outstanding	83,933	85,146	85,765	89,403	89,066	81,888	78,114	77,280
Statistical Record								
Return on Assets %	4.67	5.08	7.52	6.09	4.41	4.35	5.84	5.80
Return on Equity %	15.99	18.33	26.80	19.56	14.71	13.25	14.22	14.00
Net Margin %	24.10	39.73	54.33	40.37	28.15	27.74	36.09	34.47
Price Range	49.00-28.37	52.16-31.44	47.83-37.10	40.50-33.49	40.90-27.55	30.70-23.80	25.76-20.57	22.40-17.80
P/E Ratio	21.97-12.72	21.38-12.89	14.63-11.35	17.53-14.50	26.56-17.89	24.76-19.19	18.01-14.38	18.21-14.48
Average Yield %	5.17	4.61	4.50	4.73	5.03	5.59	6.26	6.99

Address: 2600 Citadel Plaza Drive, P.O. Box 924133, Houston, TX 77292-4133 **Telephone:** 713-866-6000 **Web Site:** www.weingarten.com	**Officers:** Stanford Alexander - Chairman Martin Debrovner - Vice-Chairman **Transfer Agents:** Mellon Investor Services, LLC, Ridgefield Park, NJ	**Investor Contact:** 713-866-6050 **No of Institutions:** 316 **Shares:** 58,804,200 **% Held:** 60.96

WELLS FARGO & CO. (NEW)

Exchange	Symbol	Price	52Wk Range	Yield	P/E
NYS	WFC	$27.98 (5/29/2008)	37.47-25.48	4.43	12.11

*7 Year Price Score 86.58   *NYSE Composite Index=100   *12 Month Price Score 92.43

Interim Earnings (Per Share)

Qtr.	Mar	Jun	Sep	Dec
2005	0.54	0.56	0.58	0.57
2006	0.59	0.61	0.64	0.64
2007	0.66	0.67	0.68	0.37
2008	0.60	...	...	...

Interim Dividends (Per Share)

Amt	Decl	Ex	Rec	Pay
0.31Q	07/24/2007	08/08/2007	08/10/2007	09/01/2007
0.31Q	10/23/2007	11/07/2007	11/09/2007	12/01/2007
0.31Q	01/22/2008	02/06/2008	02/08/2008	03/01/2008
0.31Q	04/29/2008	05/07/2008	05/09/2008	06/01/2008

Indicated Div: $1.24 (Div. Reinv. Plan)

Valuation Analysis

Forecast EPS	$2.35 (05/17/2008)		
Market Cap	$92.4 Billion	Book Value	48.2 Billion
Price/Book	1.92	Price/Sales	1.69

Dividend Achiever Status

10 Year Growth Rate	14.39%
Total Years of Dividend Growth	20

TRADING VOLUME (thousand shares)

Business Summary: Commercial Banking (MIC: SIC: 6021 NAIC: 522110)

Wells Fargo is a financial holding company that provides retail, commercial and corporate banking services through banking stores in 23 states. Co. also provides other financial services through subsidiaries engaged in various businesses, mainly: wholesale banking, mortgage banking, consumer finance, equipment leasing, agricultural finance, commercial finance, securities brokerage and investment banking, insurance agency and brokerage services, computer and data processing services, trust services, investment advisory services, mortgage-backed securities servicing and venture capital investment. As of Dec 31 2007, Co. had assets of $575.44 billion and deposits of $344.46 billion.

Recent Developments: For the quarter ended Mar 31 2008, net income decreased 10.9% to US$2.00 billion from US$2.24 billion in the year-earlier quarter. Net interest income increased 15.0% to US$5.76 billion from US$5.01 billion in the year-earlier quarter. Provision for loan losses was US$2.03 billion versus US$715.0 million in the prior-year quarter, an increase of 183.6%. Non-interest income rose 8.4% to US$4.80 billion from US$4.43 billion, while non-interest expense declined 1.2% to US$5.46 billion.

Prospects: Co. is focused on its cross-selling strategy and increasing product offerings, while producing firm credit policies for underwriting new business and monitoring and reviewing its loan portfolio. Notably, Co. expects majority of its adjustable-rate mortgages resetting in 2008 to be at or below their current rate starting in the second quarter. Meanwhile, Co.'s Wells Fargo Bank, N.A. subsidiary recently announced an agreement to acquire the account relationships of Citibank, N.A.'s customer households in six northern Nevada and two California Sierra Foothills communities, which will close in third quarter 2008. Co. expects the deal to further strengthen its deposit market in northern Nevada.

Financial Data (US$ in Thousands)	3 Mos	12/31/2007	12/31/2006	12/31/2005	12/31/2004	12/31/2003	12/31/2002	12/31/2001
Earnings Per Share	2.31	2.38	2.49	2.25	2.04	1.83	1.58	0.98
Cash Flow Per Share	0.90	2.71	9.53	(2.77)	5.92	9.28	(4.11)	(3.28)
Tang Book Value Per Share	5.47	4.98	4.70	4.93	5.43	4.78	4.45	3.01
Dividends Per Share	1.210	1.180	1.080	1.000	0.930	0.750	0.550	0.500
Dividend Payout %	52.32	49.58	43.37	44.44	45.48	41.10	34.81	50.76
Income Statement								
Income Before Taxes	3,073,000	11,627,000	12,745,000	11,548,000	10,769,000	9,477,000	8,854,000	5,479,000
Income Taxes	1,074,000	3,570,000	4,263,000	3,877,000	3,755,000	3,275,000	3,144,000	2,056,000
Net Income	1,999,000	8,057,000	8,482,000	7,671,000	7,014,000	6,202,000	5,434,000	3,423,000
Average Shares	3,317,900	3,382,800	3,410,100	3,411,000	3,426,800	3,395,000	3,436,000	3,453,800
Balance Sheet								
Total Assets	595,221,000	575,442,000	481,996,000	481,741,000	427,849,000	387,798,000	349,259,000	307,569,000
Total Liabilities	547,062,000	527,814,000	436,120,000	441,081,000	389,983,000	353,329,000	279,040,903	280,355,000
Stockholders' Equity	48,159,000	47,628,000	45,876,000	40,660,000	37,866,000	34,469,000	30,358,000	27,214,000
Shares Outstanding	3,302,351	3,297,102	3,377,150	3,355,166	3,389,183	3,396,219	3,371,813	3,390,990
Statistical Record								
Return on Assets %	1.44	1.52	1.76	1.69	1.72	1.68	1.65	1.18
Return on Equity %	16.52	17.23	19.60	19.54	19.34	19.13	18.88	12.75
Price Range	37.47-25.48	37.47-29.49	36.81-30.52	32.17-28.89	31.63-27.40	29.47-22.07	26.61-21.32	26.97-19.43
P/E Ratio	16.22-11.03	15.74-12.39	14.78-12.26	14.30-12.84	15.50-13.43	16.10-12.06	16.84-13.49	27.52-19.82
Average Yield %	3.63	3.40	3.17	3.30	3.18	2.97	2.26	2.17

Address: 420 Montgomery Street, San Francisco, CA 94163 **Telephone:** 866-249-3302 **Web Site:** www.wellsfargo.com	**Officers:** Richard M. Kovacevich - Chairman John G. Stumpf - President, Chief Executive Officer **Transfer Agents:** Wells Fargo Shareowner Services	**Investor Contact:** 415-396-0523 **No of Institutions:** 1345 **Shares:** 2,672,955,392 **% Held:** 72.63

WESBANCO, INC.

Exchange	Symbol	Price	52Wk Range	Yield	P/E
NMS	WSBC	$22.23 (5/29/2008)	31.53-18.18	5.04	11.82

*7 Year Price Score 70.64   *NYSE Composite Index=100   *12 Month Price Score 96.58

Interim Earnings (Per Share)

Qtr.	Mar	Jun	Sep	Dec
2005	0.48	0.50	0.44	0.48
2006	0.25	0.52	0.53	0.49
2007	0.56	0.59	0.47	0.47
2008	0.36	...	...	...

Interim Dividends (Per Share)

Amt	Decl	Ex	Rec	Pay
0.275Q	08/23/2007	09/05/2007	09/07/2007	10/01/2007
0.275Q	11/21/2007	12/05/2007	12/07/2007	01/02/2008
0.28Q	02/29/2008	03/12/2008	03/14/2008	04/01/2008
0.28Q	05/21/2008	06/11/2008	06/13/2008	07/01/2008

Indicated Div: $1.12 (Div. Reinv. Plan)

Valuation Analysis

Forecast EPS	$1.72 (05/17/2008)		
Market Cap	$590.1 Million	Book Value	587.9 Million
Price/Book	1.00	Price/Sales	1.92

Dividend Achiever Status

10 Year Growth Rate	3.49%
Total Years of Dividend Growth	22

TRADING VOLUME (thousand shares)

Business Summary: Commercial Banking (MIC: SIC: 6021 NAIC: 522110)

WesBanco is a bank holding company. Through its subsidiaries, Co. provides financial services including retail banking, corporate banking, personal and corporate trust services, brokerage services, mortgage banking and insurance through two reportable segments, community banking and trust and investment services. As of Dec 31 2007, Co. operated two commercial banks, WesBanco Bank, Inc. and Oak Hill Banks through 115 offices, one loan production office and 152 ATM machines located in West Virginia, Ohio, and Western Pennsylvania. Co. also serves as investment adviser to mutual funds under the name "WesMark Funds". As of Dec 31 2007, Co. had total assets of $5.38 billion.

Recent Developments: For the quarter ended Mar 31 2008, net income decreased 20.5% to US$9.5 million from US$11.9 million in the year-earlier quarter. Net interest income increased 28.7% to US$38.6 million from US$30.0 million in the year-earlier quarter. Provision for loan losses was US$5.4 million versus US$1.5 million in the prior-year quarter, an increase of 271.6%. Non-interest income rose 14.1% to US$15.1 million from US$13.2 million, while non-interest expense advanced 38.4% to US$36.5 million.

Prospects: Co. is seeing an increase in net interest income primarily due to a higher average balance sheet from the acquisition of Oak Hill Financial, Inc. in Nov 2007 although net interest margin decreased. Also, Co's provision for loan losses increased reflecting economic conditions adversely affecting its market areas. Looking ahead, Co. intends to merge Oak Hill Banks into WesBanco Bank in the second quarter of 2008 and convert the data processing systems to improve efficiency and standardize products and delivery systems. Co. will continue to integrate the Oak Hill operations into WesBanco in 2008 and expects to realize cost savings from the acquisition in the second half of 2008.

Financial Data

(US$ in Thousands)	3 Mos	12/31/2007	12/31/2006	12/31/2005	12/31/2004	12/31/2003	12/31/2002	12/31/2001
Earnings Per Share	1.88	2.09	1.79	1.90	1.90	1.80	1.70	1.60
Cash Flow Per Share	2.54	2.75	3.37	2.00	2.38	2.77	2.32	2.02
Tang Book Value Per Share	11.81	11.44	12.64	12.19	13.74	13.20	13.02	14.46
Dividends Per Share	1.105	1.100	1.060	1.040	1.000	0.960	0.935	0.920
Dividend Payout %	58.67	52.63	59.22	54.74	52.63	53.33	55.00	57.50
Income Statement								
Income Before Taxes	11,754	52,690	48,298	54,479	47,158	44,812	45,446	41,284
Income Taxes	2,251	8,021	9,263	11,722	8,976	8,682	10,620	12,282
Net Income	9,503	44,669	39,035	42,757	38,182	36,130	34,826	29,002
Average Shares	26,556	21,392	21,816	22,528	20,083	20,056	20,459	18,123
Balance Sheet								
Total Assets	5,302,784	5,384,326	4,098,143	4,422,115	4,011,399	3,445,006	3,297,231	2,474,454
Total Liabilities	4,714,835	4,804,007	3,681,268	4,006,885	3,641,218	3,126,570	2,972,060	2,216,253
Stockholders' Equity	587,949	580,319	416,875	415,230	370,181	318,436	325,171	258,201
Shares Outstanding	26,547	26,547	21,496	21,955	20,837	19,741	20,461	17,854
Statistical Record								
Return on Assets %	0.90	0.94	0.92	1.01	1.02	1.07	1.21	1.21
Return on Equity %	8.44	8.96	9.38	10.89	11.06	11.23	11.94	11.23
Price Range	31.84-18.18	34.10-20.16	34.00-28.10	32.39-24.87	32.75-25.88	28.74-21.99	25.86-19.42	26.10-17.69
P/E Ratio	16.94-9.67	16.32-9.65	18.99-15.70	17.05-13.09	17.24-13.62	15.97-12.22	15.21-11.42	16.31-11.05
Average Yield %	4.29	3.95	3.44	3.57	3.44	3.85	4.02	4.23

Address: 1 Bank Plaza, Wheeling, WV 26003	Officers: James C. Gardill - Chairman John D. Kidd - Vice-Chairman Transfer Agents:	Investor Contact: 304-234-9000
Telephone: 304-234-9000	WesBanco, Inc. c/o Computershare Investor Services, LLC	No of Institutions: 108
Web Site: www.wesbanco.com		Shares: 12,267,708 % Held: 55.84

WESCO FINANCIAL CORP.

Exchange	Symbol	Price	52Wk Range	Yield	P/E
ASE	WSC	$423.26 (5/29/2008)	440.00-377.00	0.36	N/A

*7 Year Price Score 85.38 *NYSE Composite Index=100 *12 Month Price Score 107.52

Interim Earnings (Per Share)

Qtr.	Mar	Jun	Sep	Dec
2005	2.59	2.69	2.51	33.58
2006	3.29	3.33	3.31	3.00
2007	3.17	3.90	3.43	(89.67)
2008	2.91	...	...	...

Interim Dividends (Per Share)

Amt	Decl	Ex	Rec	Pay
0.375Q	07/19/2007	07/31/2007	08/02/2007	09/06/2007
0.375Q	09/06/2007	10/30/2007	11/01/2007	12/06/2007
0.385Q	01/17/2008	02/05/2008	02/07/2008	03/06/2008
0.385Q	03/20/2008	05/06/2008	05/08/2008	06/05/2008

Indicated Div: $1.54

Valuation Analysis

Forecast EPS	N/A		
Market Cap	$3.0 Billion	Book Value	2.5 Billion
Price/Book	1.20	Price/Sales	4.72

Dividend Achiever Status

10 Year Growth Rate	3.15%
Total Years of Dividend Growth	36

Business Summary: General Construction Supplies & Services (MIC: SIC: 7359 NAIC: 532310)

Wesco Financial operates three principal businesses: Co.'s insurance segment, which consists of the operations of Wesco-Financial Insurance Company that engages in the property and casualty insurance business, and The Kansas Bankers Surety Company that provides specialized insurance coverages for banks; Co.'s furniture rental segment, which consists of CORT Business Services Corporation that provides rental furniture, accessories and related services; and Co.'s industrial segment, which buys stainless steel, low carbon sheet and strip steel, coated metals, spring steel, brass, phosphor bronze, aluminum and other metals, cuts these metals to order, and sells them.

Recent Developments: For the quarter ended Mar 31 2008, net income decreased 8.3% to US$20.7 million from US$22.6 million in the year-earlier quarter. Revenues were US$160.2 million, up 6.3% from US$150.7 million the year before. Direct operating expenses rose 26.0% to US$59.5 million from US$47.2 million in the comparable period the year before. Indirect operating expenses increased 3.8% to US$72.7 million from US$70.1 million in the equivalent prior-year period.

Prospects: Co. is seeing a decrease in consolidated earnings primarily due to an increase in operating expenses incurred by the furniture rental business from its initiative to target its rental relocation services at corporate clients and a slight softening in underwriting and investment income of the insurance businesses. Furniture sales revenue also declined due primarily to the continued softening of the housing market and higher energy prices. On the brighter side, Co. believes that the expansion of its relocation services as its CORT Business Services Corporation subsidiary shifts its marketing towards targeting corporate relocation departments will result in profitable long-term revenue growth.

Financial Data
(US$ in Thousands)

	3 Mos	12/31/2007	12/31/2006	12/31/2005	12/31/2004	12/31/2003	12/31/2002	12/31/2001
Earnings Per Share	(79.47)	15.33	12.93	41.37	6.66	10.49	7.40	7.38
Cash Flow Per Share	14.97	11.57	18.61	14.24	17.29	17.28	26.47	23.11
Tang Book Value Per Share	314.72	318.58	299.69	275.83	259.89	254.44	237.64	231.46
Dividends Per Share	1.510	1.500	1.460	1.420	1.380	1.340	1.300	1.260
Dividend Payout %	...	9.78	11.29	3.43	20.72	12.77	17.57	17.07
Income Statement								
Total Revenue	160,196	630,924	605,727	888,290	509,313	614,317	575,677	561,079
EBITDA	27,941	202,441	178,998	474,691	104,708	152,370	132,831	146,892
Depn & Amortn	...	41,515	41,732	38,887	36,473	44,114	51,914	65,564
Income Before Taxes	27,941	160,926	137,266	435,804	68,235	108,256	80,917	81,328
Income Taxes	7,224	51,765	45,233	141,225	20,808	34,852	28,199	28,792
Net Income	20,717	109,161	92,033	294,579	47,427	74,711	52,718	52,536
Average Shares	7,119	7,119	7,119	7,119	7,119	7,119	7,119	7,119
Balance Sheet								
Current Assets	509,385	606,234	1,317,737	1,248,100	1,207,170	1,112,630	417,237	164,655
Total Assets	3,150,134	3,113,009	2,970,305	2,728,511	2,571,535	2,538,395	2,406,975	2,319,693
Current Liabilities	326,892	396,892	403,657	343,202	323,506	296,172	272,086	262,459
Long-Term Obligations	44,800	37,200	38,200	42,300	29,225	12,679	32,481	33,649
Total Liabilities	640,860	578,150	569,967	498,079	454,592	460,205	448,813	407,296
Stockholders' Equity	2,509,274	2,534,859	2,400,338	2,230,432	2,116,943	2,078,190	1,958,162	1,912,397
Shares Outstanding	7,119	7,119	7,119	7,119	7,119	7,119	7,119	7,119
Statistical Record								
Return on Assets %	3.51	3.59	3.23	11.12	1.85	3.02	2.23	2.20
Return on Equity %	4.35	4.42	3.97	13.55	2.25	3.70	2.72	2.70
EBITDA Margin %	17.44	32.09	29.55	53.44	20.56	24.80	23.07	26.18
Net Margin %	12.93	17.30	15.19	33.16	9.31	12.16	9.16	9.36
Asset Turnover	0.21	0.21	0.21	0.34	0.20	0.25	0.24	0.23
Current Ratio	1.56	1.53	3.26	3.64	3.73	3.76	1.53	0.63
Debt to Equity	0.02	0.01	0.02	0.02	0.01	0.01	0.02	0.02
Price Range	462.00-377.00	499.75-378.00	495.25-362.00	405.00-337.14	429.75-323.00	370.01-286.00	334.00-298.00	347.90-273.00
P/E Ratio	...	32.60-24.66	38.30-28.00	9.79-8.15	64.53-49.85	35.27-27.26	45.14-40.27	47.14-36.99
Average Yield %	0.37	0.35	0.35	0.39	0.37	0.42	0.42	0.41

Address: 301 East Colorado Boulevard, Suite 300, Pasadena, CA 91101-1901 **Telephone:** 626-585-6700 **Web Site:** www.wescofinancial.com	Officers: Charles T. Munger - Chairman, President, Chief Executive Officer Jeffrey L. Jacobson - Vice President, Chief Financial Officer **Transfer Agents:** Mellon Investor Services	No of Institutions: 115 **Shares:** 6,510,395 % **Held:** 90.16

WEST COAST BANCORP (OR) (NEW)

Exchange	Symbol	Price	52Wk Range	Yield	P/E
NMS	WCBO	$11.55 (5/29/2008)	31.85-11.06	4.68	16.99

*7 Year Price Score 76.65   *NYSE Composite Index=100   *12 Month Price Score 61.71

TRADING VOLUME (thousand shares)

Interim Earnings (Per Share)

Qtr.	Mar	Jun	Sep	Dec
2005	0.29	0.40	0.44	0.42
2006	0.44	0.45	0.49	0.48
2007	0.49	0.50	0.52	(0.46)
2008	0.13	...	...	...

Interim Dividends (Per Share)

Amt	Decl	Ex	Rec	Pay
0.12Q	06/19/2007	07/09/2007	07/11/2007	07/31/2007
0.135Q	09/25/2007	10/09/2007	10/11/2007	10/31/2007
0.135Q	12/11/2007	01/09/2008	01/11/2008	01/31/2008
0.135Q	03/25/2008	04/09/2008	04/11/2008	04/30/2008

Indicated Div: $0.54

Valuation Analysis

Forecast EPS	$0.90 (05/16/2008)		
Market Cap	$179.9 Million	Book Value	207.9 Million
Price/Book	0.87	Price/Sales	0.85

Dividend Achiever Status

10 Year Growth Rate	15.70%
Total Years of Dividend Growth	11

Business Summary: Commercial Banking (MIC: SIC: 6022 NAIC: 522110)

West Coast Bancorp is a financial holding company that operates through its full-service, commercial bank subsidiary West Coast Bank. At Dec 31 2007, Co. had facilities in 41 cities and towns in western Oregon and southwestern Washington, operating a total of 59 full-service and four limited-service branches. In addition, Co. operates a mortgage loan office in Bend, OR as well as a mortgage loan office and Small Business Administration lending office in Vancouver, WA. Co. also owns West Coast Trust Company, Inc., an Oregon trust company that provides agency, fiduciary and other related trust services. At Dec 31 2007, Co. had total assets of $2.65 billion and total deposits of $2.09 billion.

Recent Developments: For the quarter ended Mar 31 2008, net income decreased 74.6% to US$2.0 million from US$7.9 million in the year-earlier quarter. Net interest income decreased 15.4% to US$23.6 million from US$27.9 million in the year-earlier quarter. Provision for loan losses was US$8.7 million versus US$2.8 million in the prior-year quarter, an increase of 211.6%. Non-interest income rose 27.1% to US$10.2 million from US$8.0 million, while non-interest expense advanced 5.6% to US$22.2 million.

Prospects: Co.'s top- and bottom-line results are being adversely affected by a decline in net interest margin, mainly due to the effect of the interest reversals on loans in the two-step loan portfolio, lower value and balances of non-interest bearing demand deposits, and higher cost of carrying nonperforming assets. Nevertheless, Co. is seeing higher non-interest income primarily due to solid growth in deposits service charges and payment systems revenue. Meanwhile, Co. expects real estate construction loan balances to contract in 2008. Hence, Co. anticipates a slight overall asset growth and total loan balances may be lower at the end of 2008 compared with year end 2007.

Financial Data
(US$ in Thousands)

	3 Mos	12/31/2007	12/31/2006	12/31/2005	12/31/2004	12/31/2003	12/31/2002	12/31/2001
Earnings Per Share	0.68	1.05	1.86	1.55	1.42	1.26	1.13	0.90
Cash Flow Per Share	3.11	3.80	1.76	2.07	2.27	2.45	1.76	1.11
Tang Book Value Per Share	12.42	12.43	11.92	10.68	9.91	9.23	8.62	7.94
Dividends Per Share	0.510	0.495	0.435	0.383	0.347	0.318	0.295	0.268
Dividend Payout %	74.51	47.14	23.39	24.68	24.47	25.20	26.11	29.72
Income Statement								
Income Before Taxes	2,842	23,963	44,570	34,851	31,705	29,135	27,193	21,455
Income Taxes	842	7,121	15,310	11,011	9,697	9,338	8,990	6,695
Net Income	2,000	16,842	29,260	23,840	22,008	19,797	18,203	14,760
Average Shares	15,589	16,045	15,730	15,344	15,526	15,674	16,069	16,452
Balance Sheet								
Total Assets	2,620,894	2,646,614	2,465,372	1,997,138	1,790,919	1,662,882	1,532,327	1,435,701
Total Liabilities	2,412,957	2,438,373	2,264,490	1,840,015	1,643,065	1,522,829	1,398,940	1,306,911
Stockholders' Equity	207,937	208,241	200,882	157,123	147,854	140,053	133,387	128,790
Shares Outstanding	15,580	15,592	15,585	14,691	14,872	15,075	15,325	16,025
Statistical Record								
Return on Assets %	0.43	0.66	1.31	1.26	1.27	1.24	1.23	1.06
Return on Equity %	5.23	8.23	16.35	15.63	15.25	14.48	13.89	11.81
Price Range	32.49-11.06	34.44-18.50	35.52-25.81	27.87-20.43	27.11-19.43	22.05-14.18	17.15-13.02	14.25-9.19
P/E Ratio	47.78-16.26	32.80-17.62	19.10-13.88	17.98-13.18	19.09-13.68	17.50-11.25	15.18-11.52	15.83-10.21
Average Yield %	2.08	1.72	1.47	1.56	1.57	1.76	1.96	2.20

Address: 5335 Meadows Road, Suite 201, Lake Oswego, OR 97035	Officers: Lloyd D. Ankeny - Chairman Robert D. Sznewajs - President, Chief Executive Officer	No of Institutions: 98
Telephone: 503-684-0884	**Transfer Agents:** Wells Fargo Shareowner Services, Saint Paul, MN	**Shares:** 8,592,999 **% Held:** 54.53
Web Site: www.wcb.com		

WEST PHARMACEUTICAL SERVICES, INC.

Exchange	Symbol	Price	52Wk Range	Yield	P/E
NYS	WST	$47.68 (5/29/2008)	51.95-36.12	1.17	23.37

*7 Year Price Score 128.75 *NYSE Composite Index=100 *12 Month Price Score 110.23

Interim Earnings (Per Share)

Qtr.	Mar	Jun	Sep	Dec
2005	0.42	0.40	0.24	0.35
2006	0.55	0.62	0.39	0.45
2007	0.77	0.73	0.36	0.20
2008	0.76	...	...	...

Interim Dividends (Per Share)

Amt	Decl	Ex	Rec	Pay
0.14Q	09/20/2007	10/22/2007	10/24/2007	11/07/2007
0.14Q	12/14/2007	01/18/2008	01/23/2008	02/06/2008
0.14Q	02/27/2008	04/21/2008	04/23/2008	05/07/2008
0.14Q	05/07/2008	07/21/2008	07/23/2008	08/06/2008

Indicated Div: $0.56 (Div. Reinv. Plan)

Valuation Analysis

Forecast EPS $2.48 (05/16/2008)

Market Cap	$1.5 Billion	Book Value	510.0 Million
Price/Book	3.02	Price/Sales	1.50

Dividend Achiever Status

10 Year Growth Rate	6.40%
Total Years of Dividend Growth	15

Business Summary: Rubber Products (MIC: SIC: 3069 NAIC: 326299)

West Pharmaceutical Services manufactures components and systems for injectable drug delivery and plastic packaging and delivery system components for the healthcare, personal care and consumer products markets. Co.'s Pharmaceutical Systems segment designs, manufactures and sells a range of elastomer, metal and plastic components used in parenteral drug delivery for the branded pharmaceutical, generic and biopharmaceutical industries. Co.'s Tech Group segment provides custom contract-manufacturing applications utilizing plastic injection molding and manual and automated assembly processes targeted to the healthcare and consumer products industries.

Recent Developments: For the quarter ended Mar 31 2008, net income decreased 1.1% to US$26.2 million from US$26.5 million in the year-earlier quarter. Revenues were US$270.7 million, up 5.1% from US$257.6 million the year before. Operating income was US$38.1 million versus US$39.6 million in the prior-year quarter, a decrease of 3.8%. Direct operating expenses rose 5.6% to US$187.2 million from US$177.2 million in the comparable period the year before. Indirect operating expenses increased 11.3% to US$45.4 million from US$40.8 million in the equivalent prior-year period.

Prospects: Co. will introduce several products in 2008, including silicone oil-free prefillable syringes and a passive safety needle system, which are expected to add new sources of revenue growth beginning in two or three years. For the full-year 2008, at revised exchange rates, Co. now expects consolidated sales of $1.08 billion with Pharmaceutical Systems revenue of $830.0 million to $840.0 million and Tech Group revenue (includes $15.0 million of inter-company sales) of $260.0 million to $270.0 million. In addition, Co. expects net income of $80.3 million to $85.5 million and diluted earnings per share of $2.33 to $2.47. Co. also expects consolidated gross profit margin of 29.5%.

Financial Data (US$ in Thousands)	3 Mos	12/31/2007	12/31/2006	12/31/2005	12/31/2004	12/31/2003	12/31/2002	12/31/2001
Earnings Per Share	2.04	2.05	2.00	1.40	0.63	1.10	0.64	(0.18)
Cash Flow Per Share	3.68	3.95	4.33	2.75	2.70	2.38	1.58	1.08
Tang Book Value Per Share	10.83	9.97	7.46	5.49	8.38	7.15	5.42	5.03
Dividends Per Share	0.540	0.530	0.490	0.450	0.425	0.405	0.385	0.365
Dividend Payout %	26.44	25.85	24.50	32.14	67.46	36.99	60.16	...
Income Statement								
Total Revenue	270,700	1,020,100	913,300	699,700	541,600	490,700	419,700	396,900
EBITDA	52,800	151,500	147,800	114,800	81,500	87,500	59,700	73,300
Depn & Amortn	14,700	56,600	52,700	42,600	33,300	33,000	33,000	32,000
Income Before Taxes	35,000	86,400	84,500	60,200	41,200	47,000	17,200	27,800
Income Taxes	8,500	17,200	24,600	17,300	11,100	16,700	4,100	8,600
Net Income	26,200	70,700	67,100	45,600	19,400	31,900	18,400	(5,200)
Average Shares	36,100	36,200	33,600	32,525	30,842	29,092	28,868	28,696
Balance Sheet								
Current Assets	419,800	412,300	281,700	237,200	226,500	216,700	161,300	158,500
Total Assets	1,210,800	1,185,600	918,200	823,600	658,700	623,600	536,800	511,300
Current Liabilities	155,700	182,900	156,900	124,800	116,500	118,900	87,700	75,300
Long-Term Obligations	417,000	394,600	235,800	280,700	150,800	167,000	159,200	184,300
Total Liabilities	695,800	694,700	498,900	486,000	357,600	366,000	335,300	334,500
Stockholders' Equity	510,000	485,300	414,500	333,500	301,100	257,600	201,500	176,800
Shares Outstanding	32,329	32,200	32,900	31,772	30,709	29,264	28,960	28,688
Statistical Record								
Return on Assets %	6.05	6.72	7.70	6.15	3.02	5.50	3.51	N.M.
Return on Equity %	14.46	15.71	17.94	14.37	6.93	13.90	9.73	N.M.
EBITDA Margin %	19.50	14.85	16.18	16.41	15.05	17.83	14.22	18.47
Net Margin %	9.68	6.93	7.35	6.52	3.58	6.50	4.38	N.M.
Asset Turnover	0.89	0.97	1.05	0.94	0.84	0.85	0.80	0.74
Current Ratio	2.70	2.25	1.80	1.90	1.94	1.82	1.84	2.10
Debt to Equity	0.82	0.81	0.57	0.84	0.50	0.65	0.79	1.04
Price Range	51.95-36.12	52.14-36.12	52.13-25.30	29.83-23.10	25.03-16.55	17.80-8.50	16.05-8.28	14.03-11.45
P/E Ratio	25.47-17.71	25.43-17.62	26.07-12.65	21.31-16.50	39.73-26.26	16.18-7.73	25.07-12.93	...
Average Yield %	1.25	1.19	1.31	1.70	2.13	3.06	3.01	2.86

Address: 101 Gordon Drive, P.O. Box 645, Lionville, PA 19341-0645 Telephone: 610-594-2900 Web Site: www.westpharma.com	Officers: Donald E. Morel - Chairman, Chief Executive Officer Steven A. Ellers - President, Chief Operating Officer Transfer Agents: American Stock Transfer and Trust Company, New York, NY	Investor Contact: 610-594-3345 No of Institutions: 205 Shares: 35,953,704 % Held: 103.82

WESTAMERICA BANCORPORATION

Exchange	Symbol	Price	52Wk Range	Yield	P/E
NMS	WABC	$55.43 (5/29/2008)	60.21-39.53	2.53	17.71

*7 Year Price Score 78.94 *NYSE Composite Index=100 *12 Month Price Score 120.02

Interim Earnings (Per Share)

Qtr.	Mar	Jun	Sep	Dec
2005	0.70	0.84	0.89	0.85
2006	0.81	0.77	0.77	0.77
2007	0.76	0.74	0.74	0.74
2008	0.92	...	...	...

Interim Dividends (Per Share)

Amt	Decl	Ex	Rec	Pay
0.34Q	07/26/2007	08/02/2007	08/06/2007	08/17/2007
0.34Q	10/25/2007	11/01/2007	11/05/2007	11/16/2007
0.34Q	01/24/2008	01/31/2008	02/04/2008	02/15/2008
0.35Q	04/24/2008	05/01/2008	05/05/2008	05/16/2008

Indicated Div: $1.40 (Div. Reinv. Plan)

Valuation Analysis

Forecast EPS $3.10 (05/17/2008)

Market Cap	$1.6 Billion	Book Value	399.1 Million
Price/Book	4.00	Price/Sales	5.42

Dividend Achiever Status

10 Year Growth Rate	14.22%
Total Years of Dividend Growth	18

Business Summary: Commercial Banking (MIC: SIC: 6021 NAIC: 522110)

Westamerica Bancorporation is a bank holding company. Co. provides a range of banking services to individual and corporate customers in Northern and Central California through its subsidiary bank, Westamerica Bank. The principal communities served are located in Northern and Central California, from Mendocino, Lake and Nevada Counties in the North to Kern County in the South. In addition, Co. owned 100.0% of the capital stock of Community Banker Services Corporation at Dec 31 2007, a company engaged in providing Co. and its subsidiaries data processing services and other support functions. As of Dec 31 2007, Co. had total assets of $4.56 billion and total deposits of $3.26 billion.

Recent Developments: For the quarter ended Mar 31 2008, net income increased 13.6% to US$26.8 million from US$23.6 million in the year-earlier quarter. Net interest income increased 3.2% to US$42.6 million from US$41.3 million in the year-earlier quarter. Provision for loan losses was US$600,000 versus US$75,000 in the prior-year quarter, an increase of 700.0%. Non-interest income rose 26.8% to US$19.4 million from US$15.3 million, while non-interest expense declined 6.5% to US$23.1 million.

Prospects: Co.'s near-term outlook appears encouraging. In particular, Co. is experiencing an increase in net interest income, due to lower rates paid on interest-bearing liabilities and average balances of such liabilities, partially offset by lesser average earning assets and yields on loans. In addition, Co. is seeing an improvement in net interest margin as rates paid on interest-bearing liabilities declined faster than yields on earning assets. Similarly, Co. is benefiting from a decline in non-interest expense, attributable primarily to the reversal of an accrual for Visa related litigation. Lastly, Co.'s non-interest income is being driven by securities gains on sale of Visa common stock.

Financial Data

(US$ in Thousands)	3 Mos	12/31/2007	12/31/2006	12/31/2005	12/31/2004	12/31/2003	12/31/2002	12/31/2001
Earnings Per Share	3.13	2.98	3.11	3.27	2.93	2.85	2.55	2.36
Cash Flow Per Share	3.82	3.64	3.46	3.70	3.56	3.51	2.69	2.80
Tang Book Value Per Share	9.03	8.77	9.18	8.74	11.33	10.54	10.22	9.19
Dividends Per Share	1.360	1.360	1.300	1.220	1.100	1.000	0.900	0.820
Dividend Payout %	43.42	45.64	41.80	37.31	37.54	35.09	35.29	34.75
Income Statement								
Income Before Taxes	38,288	120,467	134,425	147,932	132,363	134,209	128,079	124,573
Income Taxes	11,510	30,691	35,619	40,491	37,145	39,146	40,941	40,294
Net Income	26,778	89,776	98,806	107,441	95,218	95,063	87,138	84,279
Average Shares	29,210	30,165	31,739	32,897	32,461	33,369	34,225	35,748
Balance Sheet								
Total Assets	4,342,302	4,558,959	4,769,335	5,149,209	4,737,268	4,576,385	4,224,867	3,927,967
Total Liabilities	3,943,193	4,164,356	4,345,100	4,722,495	4,378,659	4,236,014	3,883,368	3,613,608
Stockholders' Equity	399,109	394,603	424,235	426,714	358,609	340,371	341,499	314,359
Shares Outstanding	28,772	29,018	30,547	31,882	31,640	32,287	33,411	34,220
Statistical Record								
Return on Assets %	2.04	1.92	1.99	2.17	2.04	2.16	2.14	2.12
Return on Equity %	22.65	21.93	23.22	27.36	27.17	27.88	26.57	25.85
Price Range	54.77-39.53	53.01-40.25	55.10-46.14	58.31-48.16	61.05-47.58	53.28-38.70	45.67-35.57	42.00-32.55
P/E Ratio	17.50-12.63	17.79-13.51	17.72-14.84	17.83-14.73	20.84-16.24	18.69-13.58	17.91-13.95	17.80-13.79
Average Yield %	2.90	2.88	2.57	2.31	2.10	2.26	2.19	2.16

Address: 1108 Fifth Avenue, San Rafael, CA 94901
Telephone: 707-863-8000
Web Site: www.westamerica.com

Officers: David L. Payne - Chairman, President, Chief Executive Officer John A. Thorson - Senior Vice President, Chief Financial Officer **Transfer Agents:** Computershare Investor Services LLC

No of Institutions: 176
Shares: 23,165,596 **% Held:** 75.91

WGL HOLDINGS, INC.

Exchange	Symbol	Price	52Wk Range	Yield	P/E
NYS	WGL	$35.27 (5/29/2008)	35.50-29.94	4.03	13.72

*7 Year Price Score 86.84   *NYSE Composite Index=100   *12 Month Price Score 105.09

Interim Earnings (Per Share)

Qtr.	Dec	Mar	Jun	Sep
2004-05	0.88	1.63	(0.17)	(0.24)
2005-06	0.91	1.16	(0.04)	(0.24)
2006-07	0.92	1.29	0.26	(0.27)
2007-08	0.95	1.63	...	...

Interim Dividends (Per Share)

Amt	Decl	Ex	Rec	Pay
0.343Q	06/28/2007	07/06/2007	07/10/2007	08/01/2007
0.343Q	09/26/2007	10/05/2007	10/10/2007	11/01/2007
0.343Q	12/14/2007	01/08/2008	01/10/2008	02/01/2008
0.355Q	03/06/2008	04/08/2008	04/10/2008	05/01/2008

Indicated Div: $1.42 (Div. Reinv. Plan)

Valuation Analysis

Forecast EPS $2.40 (05/17/2008)

Market Cap	$1.7 Billion	Book Value	1.1 Billion
Price/Book	1.62	Price/Sales	0.68

Dividend Achiever Status

10 Year Growth Rate	1.47%
Total Years of Dividend Growth	31

Business Summary: Gas Utilities (MIC: SIC: 4924 NAIC: 221210)

WGL Holdings is a holding company. Through its subsidiaries, Co. sells and delivers natural gas, and provides energy-related products and services to customers in Washington, D.C., and the surrounding metropolitan areas in Maryland and Virginia. Co.'s subsidiary, Washington Gas, is engaged in the delivery and sale of natural gas that is predominantly regulated by state regulatory commissions. Through wholly owned subsidiaries of Washington Gas Resources, Co. also offers energy-related products and services that are closely related to its core business. Co. has three operating segments: regulated utility; retail energy marketing; and commercial heating, ventilating and air conditioning.

Recent Developments: For the quarter ended Mar 31 2008, net income increased 27.9% to US$81.0 million from US$63.4 million in the year-earlier quarter. Revenues were US$1.02 billion, down 8.9% from US$1.12 billion the year before. Operating income was US$145.0 million versus US$115.9 million in the prior-year quarter, an increase of 25.1%. Direct operating expenses declined 13.3% to US$838.9 million from US$967.2 million in the comparable period the year before. Indirect operating expenses decreased 1.9% to US$36.1 million from US$36.8 million in the equivalent prior-year period.

Prospects: For the fiscal year ending Sep 2008, Co. believes that a supportive regulatory framework, the expansion of its asset optimization program, customer growth and favorable unregulated margins will continue to drive earnings growth. Hence, Co. expects earnings of $2.34 to $2.44 per share for fiscal 2008, including projected fiscal 2008 earnings from its regulated utility segment of $2.07 to $2.13 per share and from its unregulated business segments of $0.27 to $0.31 per share. Separately, Co. recently announced a five-year average annual growth target of 6.0% to 8.0% and plans to focus on generating stable revenue growth, investing in infrastructure and growing its unregulated business.

Financial Data

(US$ in Thousands)	6 Mos	3 Mos	09/30/2007	09/30/2006	09/30/2005	09/30/2004	09/30/2003	09/30/2002
Earnings Per Share	2.57	2.23	2.19	1.79	2.11	1.98	2.30	0.80
Cash Flow Per Share	3.59	3.43	4.34	1.76	4.78	4.97	2.96	4.23
Tang Book Value Per Share	21.80	20.48	19.89	18.86	18.36	17.54	16.83	15.78
Dividends Per Share	1.370	1.365	1.360	1.340	1.315	1.290	1.275	1.265
Dividend Payout %	53.37	61.21	62.10	74.86	62.32	65.15	55.43	158.13
Income Statement								
Total Revenue	1,771,663	751,626	2,646,008	2,637,883	2,186,302	2,089,603	2,064,248	1,569,969
EBITDA	284,833	115,328	320,161	300,258	...	...	...	...
Depn & Amortn	49,401	25,135	93,256	95,947	93,730	95,348	88,375	77,021
Income Before Taxes	210,742	77,456	178,037	156,007	...	...	...	...
Income Taxes	145,883	57,502	70,137	61,313	102,096	97,182	106,642	64,755
Net Income	128,235	47,197	107,900	87,578	104,813	97,957	113,662	40,441
Average Shares	49,781	49,645	49,377	48,905	49,008	48,847	48,756	48,563
Balance Sheet								
Net PPE	2,168,726	2,161,612	2,150,441	2,067,895	1,969,683	1,915,551	1,874,923	1,606,843
Total Assets	3,224,773	3,458,888	3,046,361	2,791,406	2,600,600	2,504,908	2,436,052	2,113,664
Long-Term Obligations	597,432	593,513	616,419	576,139	584,150	590,164	636,650	667,951
Total Liabilities	2,118,228	2,417,460	2,037,421	1,841,426	1,678,435	1,623,311	1,589,661	1,319,088
Stockholders' Equity	1,078,372	1,013,255	1,008,940	949,980	922,165	881,597	846,391	794,576
Shares Outstanding	49,466	49,464	49,316	48,878	48,704	48,652	48,611	48,564
Statistical Record								
Return on Assets %	4.08	3.33	3.70	3.25	4.11	3.95	5.00	1.93
Return on Equity %	12.22	11.15	11.02	9.36	11.62	11.31	13.85	5.02
EBITDA Margin %	16.08	15.34	12.10	11.38	...	...	...	...
Net Margin %	7.24	6.28	4.08	3.32	4.79	4.69	5.51	2.58
PPE Turnover	1.20	1.25	1.25	1.31	1.13	1.10	1.19	1.00
Asset Turnover	0.82	0.81	0.91	0.98	0.86	0.84	0.91	0.75
Debt to Equity	0.55	0.59	0.61	0.61	0.63	0.67	0.75	0.84
Price Range	35.46-29.94	35.46-29.94	35.46-29.94	32.31-27.38	34.52-27.80	30.28-26.27	28.64-22.38	29.45-20.16
P/E Ratio	13.80-11.65	15.90-13.43	16.19-13.67	18.05-15.30	16.36-13.18	15.29-13.27	12.45-9.73	36.81-25.20
Average Yield %	4.15	4.16	4.17	4.47	4.20	4.58	4.97	4.82

Address: 101 Constitution Avenue, N.W., Washington, DC 20080	**Officers:** James H. DeGraffenreidt - Chairman, Chief Executive Officer Terry D. McCallister - President, Chief Operating Officer **Transfer Agents:** BNY Mellon Shareowner Services, Pittsburgh, PA	**No of Institutions:** 260
Telephone: 703-750-2000		**Shares:** 42,277,012 **% Held:** 72.15
Web Site: www.wglholdings.com		

WHITNEY HOLDING CORP.

Exchange	Symbol	Price	52Wk Range	Yield	P/E
NMS	WTNY	$22.68 (5/29/2008)	31.34-21.48	5.47	10.75

*7 Year Price Score 74.71 ***NYSE Composite Index=100** ***12 Month Price Score 94.13**

Interim Earnings (Per Share)

Qtr.	Mar	Jun	Sep	Dec
2005	0.47	0.46	0.14	0.56
2006	0.57	0.60	0.53	0.51
2007	0.55	0.51	0.71	0.45
2008	0.45	...	...	...

Interim Dividends (Per Share)

Amt	Decl	Ex	Rec	Pay
0.29Q	08/22/2007	09/12/2007	09/14/2007	10/01/2007
0.29Q	11/28/2007	12/12/2007	12/14/2007	01/02/2008
0.31Q	02/27/2008	03/12/2008	03/14/2008	04/01/2008
0.31Q	05/28/2008	06/12/2008	06/16/2008	07/01/2008

Indicated Div: $1.24 (Div. Reinv. Plan)

Valuation Analysis

Forecast EPS $1.69 (05/16/2008)

Market Cap	$1.5 Billion	Book Value	1.2 Billion
Price/Book	1.20	Price/Sales	1.86

Dividend Achiever Status

10 Year Growth Rate	8.93%
Total Years of Dividend Growth	14

TRADING VOLUME (thousand shares)

Business Summary: Commercial Banking (MIC: SIC: 6021 NAIC: 522110)

Whitney Holding is a bank holding company. Through its subsidiary, Whitney National Bank, Co. is engaged in community banking and serves a market area that covers the five-state Gulf Coast region stretching from Houston, TX, across southern Louisiana and the coastal region of Mississippi, to central and south Alabama, the western panhandle of Florida, and to the Tampa Bay city area of Florida. In addition, Co. owns Whitney Community Development Corp., which provides financial support to corporations or projects that promote community welfare in areas with mainly low or moderate incomes. As of Dec 31 2007, Co. had total assets of $11.03 billion and deposits of $8.58 billion.

Recent Developments: For the quarter ended Mar 31 2008, net income decreased 19.3% to US$29.9 million from US$37.0 million in the year-earlier quarter. Net interest income decreased 1.1% to US$113.5 million from US$114.8 million in the year-earlier quarter. Provision for loan losses was US$14.0 million versus a credit for loan losses of US$2.0 million in the prior-year quarter. Non-interest income rose 18.4% to US$28.5 million from US$24.0 million, while non-interest expense declined 2.9% to US$83.9 million.

Prospects: Co.'s near-term outlook appears challenging, reflecting a decrease in net interest income coupled with lower net interest margin. Specifically, Co. is experiencing lower overall yield on earning assets primarily due to the steep reduction in benchmark rates for the large variable-rate segment of its loan portfolio. Going forward, Co. is continuing to manage its deposit and loan rates to mitigate the effect of the rate environment on its net interest income. Additionally, Co. continues to develop action plans to drive down expenses and realign corporate investments, as part of a strategic initiative to improve its efficiency ratio.

Financial Data
(US$ in Thousands)

	3 Mos	12/31/2007	12/31/2006	12/31/2005	12/31/2004	12/31/2003	12/31/2002	12/31/2001
Earnings Per Share	2.11	2.23	2.20	1.63	1.57	1.63	1.59	1.27
Cash Flow Per Share	3.15	3.16	3.17	1.83	2.44	2.44	2.51	2.08
Tang Book Value Per Share	13.51	13.37	12.10	11.54	12.31	12.32	11.69	10.32
Dividends Per Share	1.180	1.160	1.080	0.983	0.893	0.820	0.740	0.684
Dividend Payout %	55.81	52.02	49.09	60.33	57.02	50.41	46.64	54.04
Income Statement								
Income Before Taxes	44,092	225,364	213,809	145,356	140,335	144,641	141,967	112,401
Income Taxes	14,237	74,310	69,164	43,007	43,198	46,099	46,644	36,581
Net Income	29,855	151,054	144,645	102,349	97,137	98,542	95,323	75,820
Average Shares	65,841	67,858	65,853	62,953	62,083	60,594	60,182	59,754
Balance Sheet								
Total Assets	10,781,912	11,027,264	10,185,880	10,109,006	8,222,624	7,754,982	7,097,881	7,243,650
Total Liabilities	9,567,487	9,798,528	9,072,918	9,147,963	7,317,859	6,914,669	6,297,398	6,525,762
Stockholders' Equity	1,214,425	1,228,736	1,112,962	961,043	904,765	840,313	800,483	717,888
Shares Outstanding	64,264	65,825	65,930	63,340	62,101	60,671	60,101	59,500
Statistical Record								
Return on Assets %	1.34	1.42	1.43	1.12	1.21	1.33	1.33	1.12
Return on Equity %	11.90	12.90	13.95	10.97	11.10	12.01	12.56	11.31
Price Range	31.77-21.48	33.10-22.74	37.06-28.06	33.44-24.65	30.79-26.63	27.33-21.08	25.68-18.65	21.71-16.00
P/E Ratio	15.06-10.18	14.84-10.20	16.85-12.75	20.52-15.12	19.61-16.96	16.76-12.93	16.15-11.73	17.09-12.60
Average Yield %	4.36	4.03	3.15	3.28	3.16	3.55	3.39	3.68

Address: 228 St. Charles Avenue, New Orleans, LA 70130	Officers: John C. Hope - Chairman, Chief Executive Officer, Chief Operating Officer R. King Milling -	Investor Contact: 504-299-5208
Telephone: 504-586-7272	Vice-Chairman **Transfer Agents: American Stock**	**No of Institutions:** 198
Web Site: www.whitneybank.com	Transfer & Trust Company, New York, NY	**Shares:** 39,461,404 **% Held:** 53.67

WILEY (JOHN) & SONS INC.

Exchange	Symbol	Price	52Wk Range	Yield	P/E
NYS	JW A	$46.44 (5/29/2008)	49.35-35.98	0.95	20.73

*7 Year Price Score 102.12 *NYSE Composite Index=100 *12 Month Price Score 108.12

Interim Earnings (Per Share)

Qtr.	Jul	Oct	Jan	Apr
2004-05	0.32	0.42	0.53	0.08
2005-06	0.46	0.45	0.69	0.26
2006-07	0.38	0.52	0.57	0.24
2007-08	0.68	0.65	0.67	...

Interim Dividends (Per Share)

Amt	Decl	Ex	Rec	Pay
0.11Q	06/21/2007	07/02/2007	07/05/2007	07/16/2007
0.11Q	09/20/2007	09/28/2007	10/02/2007	10/15/2007
0.11Q	12/13/2007	12/24/2007	12/27/2007	01/15/2008
0.11Q	03/12/2008	03/28/2008	04/01/2008	04/15/2008
		Indicated Div: $0.44		

Valuation Analysis

Forecast EPS	$2.03 (05/16/2008)		
Market Cap	$2.7 Billion	Book Value	632.7 Million
Price/Book	4.28	Price/Sales	1.66

Dividend Achiever Status

10 Year Growth Rate	14.73%
Total Years of Dividend Growth	14

TRADING VOLUME (thousand shares)

Business Summary: Non-Media Publishing (MIC: SIC: 2731 NAIC: 511130)

Wiley (John) & Sons is a global publisher of print and electronic products via three core businesses: the Professional/Trade business which produces professional and consumer books and subscription products; the Scientific, Technical and Medical business which produces scientific, technical and medical journals, encyclopedias, books and online products; and the Higher Education business which publishes textbooks and educational materials, including integrated online teaching and learning resources, for undergraduate and graduate students, teachers and lifelong learners. In addition, Co. maintains publishing, marketing and distribution centers in the U.S., Canada, Europe, Asia and Australia.

Recent Developments: For the quarter ended Jan 31 2008, net income increased 19.7% to US$40.0 million from US$33.4 million in the year-earlier quarter. Revenues were US$429.3 million, up 44.7% from US$296.7 million the year before. Operating income was US$68.0 million versus US$50.7 million in the prior-year quarter, an increase of 34.2%. Direct operating expenses rose 48.5% to US$139.7 million from US$94.0 million in the comparable period the year before. Indirect operating expenses increased 45.8% to US$221.6 million from US$152.0 million in the equivalent prior-year period.

Prospects: On June 4 2008, Wiley-Blackwell, the scientific, technical, medical and scholarly publishing business of Co., announced a new agreement to publish the Asian Journal of Control on behalf of the Chinese Automatic Control Society (CACS) and the Asian Control Association (ACA). Separately, on June 3 2008, Co. announced that it has acquired a list of higher education mathematics and statistics titles from Key College Publishing, the higher education division of California-based Key Curriculum Press. Co. anticipates that the acquisition will provide strong opportunities for targeted growth and expansion of its mathematics list both in the United States and globally.

Financial Data
(US$ in Thousands)

	9 Mos	6 Mos	3 Mos	04/30/2007	04/30/2006	04/30/2005	04/30/2004	04/30/2003
Earnings Per Share	2.24	2.14	2.01	1.71	1.85	1.35	1.41	1.38
Cash Flow Per Share	5.09	2.77	3.37	3.87	4.18	4.01	3.43	2.75
Dividends Per Share	0.430	0.420	0.410	0.400	0.360	0.300	0.260	0.200
Dividend Payout %	19.20	19.63	20.40	23.39	19.46	22.22	18.44	14.49
Income Statement								
Total Revenue	1,240,769	811,608	388,562	1,234,936	1,044,185	974,048	922,962	853,971
EBITDA	265,368	166,974	75,023	215,292	199,333	232,121	211,412	193,106
Depn & Amortn	85,865	56,601	27,761	49,602	45,529	89,235	81,143	72,583
Income Before Taxes	126,907	74,791	29,773	139,502	143,844	135,663	125,110	112,559
Income Taxes	8,364	(3,768)	(10,396)	39,883	33,516	51,822	36,270	25,284
Net Income	118,543	78,559	40,169	99,619	110,328	83,841	88,840	87,275
Average Shares	59,280	59,147	59,086	58,287	59,792	62,093	63,226	63,086
Balance Sheet								
Current Assets	619,100	444,111	473,364	405,437	326,308	338,918	324,006	283,844
Total Assets	2,766,996	2,614,998	2,616,645	2,531,115	1,026,009	1,032,569	1,014,582	955,972
Current Liabilities	712,089	482,209	498,329	598,883	362,109	341,311	306,365	323,265
Long-Term Obligations	988,106	1,067,355	1,104,905	977,721	160,496	196,214	200,000	200,000
Total Liabilities	2,134,280	1,962,983	2,029,369	2,001,607	624,169	635,995	599,518	611,968
Stockholders' Equity	632,716	652,015	587,276	529,508	401,840	396,574	415,064	344,004
Shares Outstanding	58,366	58,434	58,027	57,552	57,145	59,331	61,694	61,630
Statistical Record								
Return on Assets %	6.95	6.96	6.50	5.60	10.72	8.19	8.99	9.42
Return on Equity %	23.40	22.71	23.17	21.39	27.64	20.66	23.34	28.12
EBITDA Margin %	21.39	20.57	19.31	17.43	19.09	23.83	22.91	22.61
Net Margin %	9.55	9.68	10.34	8.07	10.57	8.61	9.63	10.22
Asset Turnover	0.85	0.83	0.75	0.69	1.01	0.95	0.93	0.92
Current Ratio	0.87	0.92	0.95	0.68	0.90	0.99	1.06	0.88
Debt to Equity	1.56	1.64	1.88	1.85	0.40	0.49	0.48	0.58
Price Range	49.35-35.98	49.35-35.12	49.35-31.86	41.00-31.86	44.90-35.73	36.91-29.27	31.58-24.07	27.30-19.61
P/E Ratio	22.03-16.06	23.06-16.41	24.55-15.85	23.98-18.63	24.27-19.31	27.34-21.68	22.40-17.07	19.78-14.21
Average Yield %	1.03	1.02	1.05	1.11	0.91	0.90	0.97	0.87

Address: 111 River Street, Hoboken, NJ 07030-5774 Telephone: 201-748-6000 Web Site: www.wiley.com	Officers: Peter Booth Wiley - Chairman William J. Pesce - President, Chief Executive Officer **Transfer Agents:** Registrar and Transfer Company, Cranford, NJ	No of Institutions: 228 Shares: 44,022,624 % Held: 81.01

WILMINGTON TRUST CORP. (DE)

Exchange	Symbol	Price	52Wk Range	Yield	P/E
NYS	WL	$33.03 (5/29/2008)	43.11-28.18	4.18	12.56

*7 Year Price Score 78.32 *NYSE Composite Index=100 *12 Month Price Score 93.00

Interim Earnings (Per Share)

Qtr.	Mar	Jun	Sep	Dec
2005	0.59	0.59	0.65	0.70
2006	0.64	0.67	0.07	0.68
2007	0.62	0.70	0.67	0.65
2008	0.62	...	...	...

Interim Dividends (Per Share)

Amt	Decl	Ex	Rec	Pay
0.335Q	07/19/2007	07/30/2007	08/01/2007	08/15/2007
0.335Q	10/19/2007	10/30/2007	11/01/2007	11/15/2007
0.335Q	01/17/2008	01/30/2008	02/01/2008	02/15/2008
0.345Q	04/18/2008	04/29/2008	05/01/2008	05/15/2008
	Indicated Div: $1.38 (Div. Reinv. Plan)			

Valuation Analysis

Forecast EPS	$2.40 (05/16/2008)		
Market Cap	$2.2 Billion	Book Value	1.1 Billion
Price/Book	1.94	Price/Sales	2.02

Dividend Achiever Status

10 Year Growth Rate	6.47%
Total Years of Dividend Growth	26

Business Summary: Commercial Banking (MIC: SIC: 6022 NAIC: 522110)

Wilmington Trust is a financial holding company. Co.'s Regional Banking business is engaged in lending, deposit-taking, and other banking activities in Delaware, Maryland, New Jersey, and Pennsylvania. Co.'s Wealth Advisory Services' activities encompass a range of financial planning, investment management, fiduciary, and family office services for individuals and families. Co.'s Corporate Client Services business provides a variety of trustee, agency, and administrative services in jurisdictions in the U.S., the Caribbean, and Europe with legal, tax, and creditor protections, while its affiliate Money Managers segment comprises of Cramer Rosenthal McGlynn and Roxbury Capital Management.

Recent Developments: For the quarter ended Mar 31 2008, net income decreased 3.7% to US$41.4 million from US$43.0 million in the year-earlier quarter. Net interest income decreased 4.3% to US$86.9 million from US$90.8 million in the year-earlier quarter. Provision for loan losses was US$10.0 million versus US$3.6 million in the prior-year quarter, an increase of 177.8%. Non-interest income rose 12.5% to US$102.8 million from US$91.4 million, while non-interest expense advanced 4.6% to US$115.5 million.

Prospects: On Apr 30 2008, Co.'s Wilmington Trust FSB subsidiary has completed the acquisition of AST Capital Co. Accordingly, Co. expects the transaction to strengthen its position in the retirement plan services business and to provide more prospects for growth, while further strengthen its sources of revenues. Additionally, Co. anticipates the acquisition to add about $27.0 million of revenue (annualized) and be non-dilutive to its earnings in 2008. Meanwhile, Co. believes that the expansion of its Corporate Client Services (CCS) business in Europe with the Formation of Wilmington Trust SP Services (Amsterdam) BV should help continue CCS' momentum while further support its sources of revenue.

Financial Data (US$ in Thousands)	3 Mos	12/31/2007	12/31/2006	12/31/2005	12/31/2004	12/31/2003	12/31/2002	12/31/2001
Earnings Per Share	2.63	2.64	2.06	2.52	2.09	2.02	2.01	1.90
Cash Flow Per Share	3.56	3.28	3.94	3.10	2.97	2.99	2.66	4.14
Tang Book Value Per Share	11.50	11.21	10.70	9.26	7.78	8.08	7.31	7.25
Dividends Per Share	1.340	1.320	1.245	1.185	1.125	1.065	1.005	0.945
Dividend Payout %	50.91	50.00	60.44	47.02	53.83	52.72	50.00	49.74
Income Statement								
Income Before Taxes	64,200	282,600	216,300	266,900	221,500	207,700	206,784	190,049
Income Taxes	22,700	99,700	72,700	93,600	78,700	72,200	73,002	66,009
Net Income	41,400	182,000	143,800	173,000	141,900	134,400	133,157	125,170
Average Shares	67,338	68,851	69,707	68,570	67,755	66,536	66,301	65,942
Balance Sheet								
Total Assets	11,703,700	11,485,700	11,157,000	10,228,100	9,510,200	8,820,200	8,131,275	7,518,462
Total Liabilities	10,560,000	10,365,300	10,097,700	9,214,900	8,604,800	8,019,200	7,390,001	6,835,932
Stockholders' Equity	1,143,500	1,120,300	1,059,300	1,013,000	905,300	800,800	741,269	682,530
Shares Outstanding	67,294	67,086	68,459	67,903	67,405	66,063	65,627	65,400
Statistical Record								
Return on Assets %	1.59	1.61	1.34	1.75	1.54	1.59	1.70	1.69
Return on Equity %	16.10	16.70	13.88	18.04	16.59	17.43	18.70	19.64
Price Range	43.11-28.18	44.54-33.16	45.32-39.37	40.69-33.01	38.30-33.95	36.21-26.35	34.58-25.30	33.42-25.65
P/E Ratio	16.39-10.71	16.87-12.56	22.00-19.11	16.15-13.10	18.33-16.24	17.93-13.04	17.20-12.59	17.59-13.50
Average Yield %	3.59	3.30	2.90	3.26	3.11	3.47	3.22	3.14

Address: Rodney Square North, 1100 North Market Street, Wilmington, DE 19890-0001	Officers: Ted T. Cecala - Chairman, Chief Executive Officer Robert V. A. Harra - President, Chief Operating Officer Transfer Agents:	Investor Contact: 302-651-8069
Telephone: 302-651-1000 Web Site: www.wilmingtontrust.com	Wells Fargo Shareowner Services, St. Paul, MN	No of Institutions: 274 Shares: 45,421,668 % Held: 61.13

WOLVERINE WORLD WIDE, INC.

Exchange	Symbol	Price	52Wk Range	Yield	P/E
NYS	WWW	$28.87 (5/29/2008)	30.76-20.21	1.52	16.31

*7 Year Price Score 109.58 *NYSE Composite Index=100* ***12 Month Price Score 110.17**

Interim Earnings (Per Share)

Qtr.	Mar	Jun	Aug	Dec
2006	0.34	0.25	0.46	0.42
2007	0.39	0.28	0.54	0.49
2008	0.46	...	...	...

Interim Dividends (Per Share)

Amt	Decl	Ex	Rec	Pay
0.09Q	07/13/2007	09/27/2007	10/01/2007	11/01/2007
0.09Q	12/19/2007	12/28/2007	01/02/2008	02/01/2008
0.11Q	02/12/2008	03/28/2008	04/01/2008	05/01/2008
0.11Q	04/18/2008	06/27/2008	07/01/2008	08/01/2008

Indicated Div: $0.44

Valuation Analysis
Forecast EPS $1.90 (05/17/2008)

Market Cap	$1.4 Billion	Book Value 455.4 Million
Price/Book	3.15	Price/Sales 1.19

TRADING VOLUME (thousand shares)

Dividend Achiever Status

10 Year Growth Rate	20.10%
Total Years of Dividend Growth	14

Business Summary: Leather and Leather Products (MIC: SIC: 3149 NAIC: 316219)

Wolverine World Wide is a designer, manufacturer and marketer of a line of casual shoes, rugged outdoor and work footwear. Co.'s products are marketed worldwide under several brand names including Bates®, Cat® Footwear, Harley-Davidson® Footwear, Hush Puppies®, HyTest®, Merrell®, Patagonia® Footwear, Sebago® and Wolverine®. At Dec 29 2007, Co.'s footwear was distributed domestically through 90 Company-owned retail stores and to various accounts such as department stores, footwear chains, catalogs, specialty retailers, mass merchants and Internet retailers. Co.'s products are marketed worldwide in nearly 200 countries through Company-owned wholesale operations, licensees and distributors.

Recent Developments: For the quarter ended Mar 22 2008, net income increased 6.3% to US$23.7 million from US$22.3 million in the year-earlier quarter. Revenues were US$288.2 million, up 2.6% from US$281.1 million the year before. Operating income was US$36.3 million versus US$32.7 million in the prior-year quarter, an increase of 11.0%. Direct operating expenses declined 0.2% to US$166.7 million from US$167.1 million in the comparable period the year before. Indirect operating expenses increased 4.9% to US$85.3 million from US$81.3 million in the equivalent prior-year period.

Prospects: Co.'s revenue growth is primarily led by its Outdoor group and its international business. In addition, Co.'s results are benefiting from gross margin expansion, along with robust order backlog at the end of the first quarter of 2008. Accordingly, for full-year 2008, Co. is increasing its earnings per share estimate from its previous estimate of $1.80 to $1.88 to its new range of $1.83 to $1.90, which is consistent with its stated long-term objective of delivering double-digit earnings per share growth, while investing in growth initiatives for the future. Further, Co. continues to expect revenue to range from $1.23 billion to $1.26 billion.

Financial Data

(US$ in Thousands)	3 Mos	12/29/2007	12/30/2006	12/31/2005	01/01/2005	01/03/2004	12/28/2002	12/29/2001
Earnings Per Share	1.77	1.70	1.47	1.27	1.09	0.85	0.77	0.71
Cash Flow Per Share	2.26	2.35	1.98	2.14	1.86	1.71	1.47	0.87
Tang Book Value Per Share	8.19	8.40	8.24	7.45	7.16	6.56	5.59	5.76
Dividends Per Share	0.360	0.360	0.300	0.260	0.195	0.147	0.090	0.107
Dividend Payout %	20.29	21.18	20.41	20.47	17.89	17.32	11.74	14.95
Income Statement								
Total Revenue	288,238	1,198,972	1,141,887	1,060,999	991,909	888,926	827,106	720,066
EBITDA	40,328	161,362	142,914	131,287	116,141	93,095	88,514	86,168
Depn & Amortn	4,626	22,791	20,622	20,040	19,071	17,947	16,860	17,621
Income Before Taxes	35,639	138,571	122,292	111,247	97,070	75,148	71,654	68,547
Income Taxes	11,938	45,685	38,645	36,780	30,879	23,262	23,599	23,307
Net Income	23,701	92,886	83,647	74,467	65,938	51,716	47,912	45,240
Average Shares	51,493	54,487	56,931	58,675	60,474	61,081	62,689	63,673
Balance Sheet								
Current Assets	483,102	445,641	485,313	420,748	430,855	386,636	363,345	374,802
Total Assets	678,173	638,378	671,092	626,580	639,571	578,881	531,994	543,678
Current Liabilities	126,335	122,632	120,915	104,037	110,251	85,766	80,177	74,521
Long-Term Obligations	60,066	...	10,741	21,439	32,169	43,903	57,885	75,818
Total Liabilities	222,820	159,599	166,533	164,259	180,714	148,473	162,754	169,526
Stockholders' Equity	455,353	478,779	504,559	462,321	458,291	430,094	369,097	374,152
Shares Outstanding	49,681	51,234	55,462	56,129	57,898	59,179	59,955	62,333
Statistical Record								
Return on Assets %	14.03	14.23	12.93	11.80	10.85	9.16	8.93	8.74
Return on Equity %	19.91	18.94	17.35	16.22	14.89	12.73	12.93	12.75
EBITDA Margin %	13.99	13.46	12.52	12.37	11.71	10.47	10.70	11.97
Net Margin %	8.22	7.75	7.33	7.02	6.65	5.82	5.79	6.28
Asset Turnover	1.79	1.84	1.76	1.68	1.63	1.57	1.54	1.39
Current Ratio	3.82	3.63	4.01	4.04	3.91	4.51	4.53	5.03
Debt to Equity	0.13	...	0.02	0.05	0.07	0.10	0.16	0.20
Price Range	30.34-20.21	30.77-23.72	29.39-20.44	25.25-19.50	21.48-13.57	14.19-9.59	12.83-8.60	12.80-8.37
P/E Ratio	17.14-11.42	18.10-13.95	19.99-13.90	19.88-15.35	19.71-12.45	16.69-11.29	16.66-11.17	18.03-11.79
Average Yield %	1.35	1.31	1.21	1.19	1.14	1.19	0.84	1.00

Address: 9341 Courtland Drive,	Officers: Timothy J. O'Donovan - Chairman, Chief	Investor Contact: 616-866-5589
Rockford, MI 49351	Executive Officer Blake W. Krueger - President, Chief	No of Institutions: 233
Telephone: 616-866-5500	Executive Officer **Transfer Agents:**	Shares: 49,805,392 % Held: 77.66
Web Site:www.wolverineworldwide.com	Computershare Investor Services, Chicago, IL	

WRIGLEY (WILLIAM) JR. CO.

Exchange	Symbol	Price	52Wk Range	Yield	P/E
NYS	WWY	$77.00 (5/29/2008)	77.71-54.29	1.74	32.63

*7 Year Price Score 101.63 *NYSE Composite Index=100 *12 Month Price Score 120.13

Interim Earnings (Per Share)

Qtr.	Mar	Jun	Sep	Dec
2005	0.46	0.58	0.46	0.34
2006	0.32	0.51	0.53	0.46
2007	0.52	0.61	0.59	0.56
2008	0.61	...	...	...

Interim Dividends (Per Share)

Amt	Decl	Ex	Rec	Pay
0.29Q	08/15/2007	10/11/2007	10/15/2007	11/01/2007
0.29Q	10/24/2007	01/11/2008	01/15/2008	02/01/2008
0.335Q	02/01/2008	04/11/2008	04/15/2008	05/01/2008
0.335Q	05/13/2008	07/11/2008	07/15/2008	08/01/2008

Indicated Div: $1.34 (Div. Reinv. Plan)

Valuation Analysis

Forecast EPS	$2.52 (05/16/2008)		
Market Cap	$20.9 Billion	Book Value	2.7 Billion
Price/Book	7.61	Price/Sales	3.76

Dividend Achiever Status

10 Year Growth Rate	11.77%
Total Years of Dividend Growth	27

TRADING VOLUME (thousand shares)

Business Summary: Food (MIC: SIC: 2067 NAIC: 311340)

William Wrigley Jr. is engaged as a manufacturer and marketer of chewing gum and other confectionery products, both in the U.S. and abroad. Co. markets chewing gum and other confectionery products primarily through distributors, wholesalers, corporate chains and cooperative buying groups. As of Dec 31 2007, Co.'s brands were sold in more than 180 countries and territories, under various brand names which include, among others, Doublemint®, Orbit®, Wrigley's Spearmint®, Winterfresh®, Airwaves®, Cool Air®, Excel®, Freedent®, Juicy Fruit®, Hubba Bubba®, Solano®, Altoids®, Wrigley's 5®, Life Savers® and P.K.®.

Recent Developments: For the quarter ended Mar 31 2008, net income increased 18.1% to US$168.6 million from US$142.7 million in the year-earlier quarter. Revenues were US$1.45 billion, up 15.7% from US$1.25 billion the year before. Operating income was US$269.6 million versus US$210.2 million in the prior-year quarter, an increase of 28.2%. Direct operating expenses rose 13.3% to US$681.0 million from US$601.0 million in the comparable period the year before. Indirect operating expenses increased 13.1% to US$501.0 million from US$442.8 million in the equivalent prior-year period.

Prospects: On Apr 28 2008, Co. announced that it had reached an agreement with Mars, Incorporated, a confectionery and consumer goods company, under which Mars will acquire 100.0% of the outstanding stock of Co. and has agreed to pay $80 per each share of Co.'s Common Stock and Class B Common Stock in a transaction valued at approximately $23.00 billion. As a result of this transaction, Co. will become a private company. The proposed transaction is expected to be completed within six months to a year, subject to customary closing conditions, including stockholder approval and certain governmental regulatory clearances.

Financial Data
(US$ in Thousands)

	3 Mos	12/31/2007	12/31/2006	12/31/2005	12/31/2004	12/31/2003	12/31/2002	12/31/2001
Earnings Per Share	2.36	2.28	1.90	1.83	1.75	1.58	1.42	1.29
Cash Flow Per Share	3.90	3.65	2.60	2.70	2.57	2.30	1.33	1.39
Tang Book Value Per Share	3.05	3.31	2.98	2.55	7.00	6.48	5.41	4.54
Dividends Per Share	1.160	1.126	1.112	1.075	0.925	0.865	0.805	0.745
Dividend Payout %	49.08	49.39	58.53	58.68	52.80	54.61	56.53	57.84
Income Statement								
Total Revenue	1,451,550	5,389,100	4,686,011	4,159,306	3,648,592	3,069,088	2,746,318	2,429,646
EBITDA	320,487	1,215,945	1,030,980	961,593	862,347	771,581	668,989	595,692
Depn & Amortn	57,326	217,778	200,113	175,285	141,851	120,040	85,568	68,325
Income Before Taxes	247,940	932,163	769,047	754,660	720,496	651,541	583,421	527,366
Income Taxes	79,341	300,158	239,670	237,408	227,542	205,647	181,896	164,380
Net Income	168,599	632,005	529,377	517,252	492,954	445,894	401,525	362,986
Average Shares	275,489	277,413	278,399	282,283	281,841	281,203	281,431	281,686
Balance Sheet								
Current Assets	1,702,778	1,549,778	1,481,227	1,306,094	1,505,910	1,290,591	1,006,292	913,843
Total Assets	5,399,972	5,231,512	4,661,598	4,460,201	3,166,703	2,520,410	2,108,296	1,765,648
Current Liabilities	1,331,741	1,101,120	1,027,129	980,811	717,970	464,794	386,087	332,324
Long-Term Obligations	1,000,000	1,000,000	1,000,000	1,000,000	...	...	...	...
Total Liabilities	2,650,615	2,414,032	2,273,506	2,245,779	988,019	699,589	585,720	489,451
Stockholders' Equity	2,749,357	2,817,480	2,388,092	2,214,422	2,178,684	1,820,821	1,522,576	1,276,197
Shares Outstanding	271,717	275,375	276,907	278,512	280,963	281,075	281,320	281,187
Statistical Record								
Return on Assets %	12.61	12.78	11.61	13.56	17.29	19.27	20.73	21.73
Return on Equity %	25.65	24.28	23.00	23.55	24.58	26.67	28.69	30.13
EBITDA Margin %	22.08	22.56	22.00	23.12	23.64	25.14	24.36	24.52
Net Margin %	11.62	11.73	11.30	12.44	13.51	14.53	14.62	14.94
Asset Turnover	1.07	1.09	1.03	1.09	1.28	1.33	1.42	1.45
Current Ratio	1.28	1.41	1.44	1.33	2.10	2.78	2.61	2.75
Debt to Equity	0.36	0.35	0.42	0.45	...	...	...	...
Price Range	68.44-50.84	68.44-48.89	53.23-43.16	53.98-47.13	51.74-40.98	43.12-37.98	43.30-33.04	39.27-32.16
P/E Ratio	29.00-21.54	30.02-21.44	28.02-22.72	29.50-25.75	29.57-23.42	27.29-24.04	30.49-23.26	30.44-24.93
Average Yield %	1.96	1.96	2.34	2.10	2.01	2.10	2.03	2.08

Address: 410 North Michigan Avenue, Chicago, IL 60611	Officers: William Wrigley - Chairman William D. Perez - President, Chief Executive Officer **Transfer Agents:** Computershare Trust Company, N.A., Providence, RI	Investor Contact: 180-087-40474
Telephone: 312-644-2121		**No of Institutions:** 629
Web Site: www.wrigley.com		**Shares:** 185,656,224 **% Held:** 70.68

Mergent's Dividend Achievers Order Form

SUBSCRIPTIONS AND SINGLE ISSUES

SUBSCRIPTIONS: (1 year, 4 issues)

☐ New order   ☐ Renewal

U.S.	☐ Individual: $199	☐ Institutional: $220
Canada/Mexico	☐ Individual: $199	☐ Institutional: $260
All Others	☐ Individual: $223	☐ Institutional: $294

Call 888-378-2537 or see mailing instructions below.

MULTIPLE COPY SUBSCRIPTIONS *DISCOUNT*:

• Save 25% on subscriptions when you order 10 to 100 copies.

• Save more than 40% when you order 100 copies or more.

Call special sales representative Sandy Quade at 1-203-643-8066 to order.

SINGLE ISSUES:

Order single issues from Mergent's popular handbooks
(Customer will receive lastest version of selection below)

☐ Dividend Achievers: $50

☐ Handbook of Nasdaq Stocks: $99

☐ Handbook of Common Stocks: $109

Call 888-378-2537 or see mailing instructions below.

Copy or detach and send to:

John Wiley & Sons, Journals Dept, 5th Floor
989 Market Street, San Francisco, CA 94103-1741

Order Form can be faxed to: **888-481-2665**

Total Amount: $_____
(No sales tax for U.S. subscriptions. Canadian residents, add GST for subscription orders.)

☐ Payment enclosed (U.S. check or money order only. All payments must be in U.S. dollars.)

☐ VISA ☐ MC ☐ Amex # _____ Exp. Date_____

Card Holder Name _____ Card Issue #_____

Signature _____ Day Phone _____

☐ Bill Me (U.S. institutional orders only. Purchase order required.)

Purchase order # _____

Federal Tax ID13559302   GST 89102 8052

Name _____

Address_____

Phone _____ E-mail _____

wiley.com